THE OXFORD HANDBOOK OF
POLITICAL ECONOMY

THE OXFORD HANDBOOKS OF POLITICAL SCIENCE

General Editor: Robert E. Goodin

The *Oxford Handbooks of Political Science* is a ten-volume set of reference books offering authoritative and engaging critical overviews of all the main branches of political science.

The series as a whole is under the General Editorship of Robert E. Goodin, with each volume being edited by a distinguished international group of specialists in their respective fields:

POLITICAL THEORY
John S. Dryzek, Bonnie Honig & Anne Phillips

POLITICAL INSTITUTIONS
R. A. W. Rhodes, Sarah A. Binder & Bert A. Rockman

POLITICAL BEHAVIOR
Russell J. Dalton & Hans-Dieter Klingemann

COMPARATIVE POLITICS
Carles Boix & Susan C. Stokes

LAW & POLITICS
Keith E. Whittington, R. Daniel Kelemen & Gregory A. Caldeira

PUBLIC POLICY
Michael Moran, Martin Rein & Robert E. Goodin

POLITICAL ECONOMY
Barry R. Weingast & Donald A. Wittman

INTERNATIONAL RELATIONS
Christian Reus-Smit & Duncan Snidal

CONTEXTUAL POLITICAL ANALYSIS
Robert E. Goodin & Charles Tilly

POLITICAL METHODOLOGY
Janet M. Box-Steffensmeier, Henry E. Brady & David Collier

This series aspires to shape the discipline, not just to report on it. Like the Goodin–Klingemann *New Handbook of Political Science* upon which the series builds, each of these volumes will combine critical commentaries on where the field has been together with positive suggestions as to where it ought to be heading.

THE OXFORD HANDBOOK OF

POLITICAL ECONOMY

Edited by

BARRY R. WEINGAST
and
DONALD A. WITTMAN

OXFORD
UNIVERSITY PRESS

OXFORD
UNIVERSITY PRESS

Great Clarendon Street, Oxford OX2 6DP
Oxford University Press is a department of the University of Oxford.
It furthers the University's objective of excellence in research, scholarship,
and education by publishing worldwide in

Oxford New York

Auckland Cape Town Dar es Salaam Hong Kong Karachi
Kuala Lumpur Madrid Melbourne Mexico City Nairobi
New Delhi Shanghai Taipei Toronto

With offices in

Argentina Austria Brazil Chile Czech Republic France Greece
Guatemala Hungary Italy Japan Poland Portugal Singapore
South Korea Switzerland Thailand Turkey Ukraine Vietnam

Oxford is a registered trade mark of Oxford University Press
in the UK and in certain other countries

Published in the United States
by Oxford University Press Inc., New York

© the several contributors 2006

The moral rights of the authors have been asserted
Database right Oxford University Press (maker)

First published 2006

First published in paperback 2008

All rights reserved. No part of this publication may be reproduced,
stored in a retrieval system, or transmitted, in any form or by any means,
without the prior permission in writing of Oxford University Press,
or as expressly permitted by law, or under terms agreed with the appropriate
reprographics rights organization. Enquiries concerning reproduction
outside the scope of the above should be sent to the Rights Department,
Oxford University Press, at the address above

You must not circulate this book in any other binding or cover
and you must impose the same condition on any acquirer

British Library Cataloguing in Publication Data

Data available

Library of Congress Cataloging in Publication Data

Data available

Typeset by SPI Publisher Services, Pondicherry, India
Printed in Great Britain
on acid-free paper by
Ashford Colour Press, Gosport, Hampshire
ISBN 978–0–19–927222-8 (Hbk.)   978–0–19–954847-7 (Pbk.)
5 7 9 10 8 6 4

Dedicated to my parents, Barbara and Edward Weingast
B.W.

Dedicated to Noah, Emily, and Joshua
D.W.

Contents

About the Contributors   xiii

PART I INTRODUCTION

1. The Reach of Political Economy   3
   BARRY R. WEINGAST & DONALD A. WITTMAN

PART II VOTERS, CANDIDATES, AND PRESSURE GROUPS

2. Voters, Candidates, and Parties   29
   STEPHEN ANSOLABEHERE

3. Rational Voters and Political Advertising   50
   ANDREA PRAT

4. Candidate Objectives and Electoral Equilibrium   64
   JOHN DUGGAN

5. Political Income Redistribution   84
   JOHN LONDREGAN

6. The Impact of Electoral Laws on Political Parties   102
   BERNARD GROFMAN

PART III LEGISLATIVE BODIES

7. Legislatures and Parliaments in Comparative Context   121
   MICHAEL LAVER

8. The Organization of Democratic Legislatures   141
   GARY W. COX

9. Coalition Government   162
   DANIEL DIERMEIER

10. Does Bicameralism Matter?   180
    MICHAEL CUTRONE & NOLAN MCCARTY

PART IV INTERACTION OF THE LEGISLATURE, PRESIDENT, BUREAUCRACY, AND THE COURTS

11. The New Separation-of-Powers Approach to American Politics   199
    RUI J. P. DE FIGUEIREDO, JR., TONJA JACOBI
    & BARRY R. WEINGAST

12. Pivots   223
    KEITH KREHBIEL

13. The Political Economy of the US Presidency   241
    CHARLES M. CAMERON

14. Politics, Delegation, and Bureaucracy   256
    JOHN D. HUBER & CHARLES R. SHIPAN

15. The Judiciary and the Role of Law   273
    MATHEW D. MCCUBBINS & DANIEL B. RODRIGUEZ

PART V CONSTITUTIONAL THEORY

16. Constitutionalism   289
    RUSSELL HARDIN

17. Self-Enforcing Democracy   312
    ADAM PRZEWORSKI

18. Constitutions as Expressive Documents   329
    GEOFFREY BRENNAN & ALAN HAMLIN

19. The Protection of Liberty, Property, and Equality   342
    RICHARD A. EPSTEIN

20. Federalism   357
    JONATHAN A. RODDEN

PART VI SOCIAL CHOICE

21. Social Choice — 373
    HERVÉ MOULIN

22. A Tool Kit for Voting Theory — 390
    DONALD G. SAARI

23. Interpersonal Comparisons of Well-Being — 408
    CHARLES BLACKORBY & WALTER BOSSERT

24. Fair Division — 425
    STEVEN J. BRAMS

PART VII PUBLIC FINANCE AND PUBLIC ECONOMICS

25. Structure and Coherence in the Political Economy of Public Finance — 441
    STANLEY L. WINER & WALTER HETTICH

26. Political Economy of Fiscal Institutions — 464
    JÜRGEN VON HAGEN

27. Voting and Efficient Public Good Mechanisms — 479
    JOHN LEDYARD

28. Fiscal Competition — 502
    DAVID E. WILDASIN

PART VIII POLITICS AND MACROECONOMICS

29. The Non-Politics of Monetary Policy — 523
    SUSANNE LOHMANN

30. Political-Economic Cycles — 545
    ROBERT J. FRANZESE, JR., & KAREN LONG JUSKO

31. Voting and the Macroeconomy — 565
    DOUGLAS A. HIBBS, JR.

32. The Political Economy of Exchange Rates — 587
    J. LAWRENCE BROZ & JEFFRY A. FRIEDEN

PART IX DEMOCRACY AND CAPITALISM

33. Capitalism and Democracy — 601
    TORBEN IVERSEN

34. Inequality — 624
    EDWARD L. GLAESER

35. Comparative Perspectives on the Role of the State in the Economy — 642
    ANNE WREN

36. Democratization: Post-Communist Implications — 656
    ANNA GRZYMALA-BUSSE & PAULINE JONES LUONG

PART X HISTORICAL AND COMPARATIVE DEVELOPMENT AND NON-DEMOCRATIC REGIMES

37. Paths of Economic and Political Development — 673
    DARON ACEMOGLU & JAMES A. ROBINSON

38. Authoritarian Government — 693
    STEPHEN HABER

39. The Role of the State in Development — 708
    ROBERT H. BATES

40. Electoral Systems and Economic Policy — 723
    TORSTEN PERSSON & GUIDO TABELLINI

41. Economic Geography — 739
    ANTHONY J. VENABLES

PART XI INTERNATIONAL POLITICAL ECONOMY

42. International Political Economy: A Maturing Interdiscipline — 757
    DAVID A. LAKE

43. National Borders and the Size of Nations — 778
    ENRICO SPOLAORE

44. European Integration — 799
    BARRY EICHENGREEN

45. Trade, Immigration, and Cross-Border Investment   814
   RONALD ROGOWSKI

PART XII INTERNATIONAL RELATIONS AND CONFLICT

46. Central Issues in the Study of International Conflict   831
   BRUCE BUENO DE MESQUITA

47. Ethnic Mobilization and Ethnic Violence   852
   JAMES D. FEARON

48. Democracy, Peace, and War   869
   DAN REITER & ALLAN C. STAM

49. Anarchy   881
   STERGIOS SKAPERDAS

PART XIII METHODOLOGICAL ISSUES

50. Economic Methods in Positive Political Theory   899
   DAVID AUSTEN-SMITH

51. Laboratory Experiments   915
   THOMAS R. PALFREY

52. The Tool Kit of Economic Sociology   937
   RICHARD SWEDBERG

53. The Evolutionary Basis of Collective Action   951
   SAMUEL BOWLES & HERBERT GINTIS

PART XIV OLD AND NEW

54. Questions about a Paradox   971
   KENNETH J. ARROW

55. Politics and Scientific Enquiry: Retrospective on a Half-century   980
   JAMES M. BUCHANAN

56. The Future of Analytical Politics 996
    MELVIN J. HINICH

57. What is Missing from Political Economy 1003
    DOUGLASS C. NORTH

58. Modeling Party Competition in General Elections 1010
    JOHN E. ROEMER

59. Old Questions and New Answers about Institutions:
    The Riker Objection Revisited 1031
    KENNETH A. SHEPSLE

Author Index 1050
Subject Index 1066

About the Contributors

Daron Acemoglu is Charles Kindleberger Professor of Applied Economics at the Department of Economics at MIT; he is also winner of the 2005 John Bates Clark Medal.

Stephen Ansolabehere is Elting R. Morison Professor of Political Science at MIT.

Kenneth J. Arrow is Joan Kennedy Professor of Economics Emeritus and Professor of Operations Research Emeritus at Stanford University. He was awarded the Nobel Prize in 1972.

David Austen-Smith is Earl Dean Howard Distinguished Professor of Political Economy at Northwestern University.

Robert H. Bates is Eaton Professor of Science of Government, Harvard University.

Charles Blackorby is a Professor of Economics at the University of Warwick.

Walter Bossert is Professor of Economics and CIREQ Research Fellow at the University of Montreal.

Samuel Bowles is Research Professor and Director of the Behavioral Sciences Program at the Santa Fe Institute and Professor of Economics at the University of Siena.

Steven J. Brams is Professor of Politics at New York University.

Geoffrey Brennan is Professor in the Social and Political Theory group at the Australian National University, and holds a regular visiting position jointly in the Philosophy Department at UNC–Chapel Hill and the Political Science Department, Duke University.

J. Lawrence Broz is Associate Professor of Political Science at the University of California, San Diego.

James M. Buchanan is Distinguished Professor Emeritus of Economics at George Mason University and Distinguished Professor Emeritus of Economics and Philosophy at Virginia Polytechnic Institute and State University. He was awarded the Nobel Prize in Economics in 1986.

Bruce Bueno de Mesquita is Silver Professor of Politics at New York University and Senior Fellow at the Hoover Institution, Stanford University.

Charles M. Cameron is Professor of Politics and Public Affairs at Princeton University and Visiting Professor of Law at New York University School of Law.

Gary W. Cox is Distinguished Professor of Political Science at the University of California, San Diego.

Michael Cutrone is a doctoral student in the Department of Politics at Princeton University.

Rui J. P. de Figueiredo, Jr., is an Associate Professor at the Haas School of Business and Department of Political Science at the University of California at Berkeley.

Daniel Diermeier is the IBM Professor of Regulation and Competitive Practice, Kellogg School of Management, MEDS Department, and Professor of Political Science, Weinberg College of Arts and Sciences, Northwestern University.

John Duggan is Professor of Political Science and Economics and is Director of the W. Allen Wallis Institute of Political Economy at the University of Rochester.

Barry Eichengreen is George C. Pardee and Helen N. Pardee Professor of Economics and Political Science at the University of California, Berkeley.

Richard A. Epstein is James Parker Hall Distinguished Service Professor of Law at University of Chicago.

James D. Fearon is Geballe Professor in the School of Humanities and Sciences and Professor, Department of Political Science, Stanford University.

Robert J. Franzese, Jr., is Associate Professor of Political Science at the University of Michigan.

Jeffry Frieden is Professor of Government at Harvard University.

Herbert Gintis is External Faculty, Santa Fe Institute, and Professor, Central European University.

Edward L. Glaeser is the Fred and Eleanor Glimp Professor of Economics at Harvard University.

Bernard Grofman is Professor of Political Science and Adjunct Professor of Economics at the University of California, Irvine.

Anna Grzymala-Busse is Associate Professor of Political Science at the University of Michigan.

Stephen Haber is Peter and Helen Bing Senior Fellow at the Hoover Institution, and A. A. and Jeanne Welch Milligan Professor in the School of Humanities and Sciences at Stanford University.

Jürgen von Hagen is Professor of Economics at the University of Bonn, research fellow at the Center for Economic Policy Research (London), and a fellow of the German Academy of Natural Scientists Leopoldina.

Alan Hamlin is Professor of Political Theory at the University of Manchester.

Russell Hardin is Professor of Politics at New York University.

Walter Hettich is Professor of Economics at California State University, Fullerton.

Douglas A. Hibbs, Jr., is Professor Emeritus of Economics and Senior Research Fellow at the CEFOS Institute at Gothenburg University, Sweden.

Melvin J. Hinich is Research Professor at the Applied Research Laboratories of the University of Texas at Austin and Professor of Government and Economics.

John D. Huber is Professor of Political Science at Columbia University.

Torben Iversen is Harold Hitchings Burbank Professor of Political Economy at Harvard University.

Tonja Jacobi is Assistant Professor at Northwestern University School of Law.

Pauline Jones Luong is an Associate Professor in the Department of Political Science at Brown University.

Keith Krehbiel is the Edward B. Rust Professor of Political Science at Stanford University's Graduate School of Business.

David A. Lake is Professor of Political Science at the University of California, San Diego.

Michael Laver is Professor of Political Science at New York University.

John Ledyard is the Allen and Lenabelle Davis Professor of Economics and Social Sciences at the California Institute of Technology.

Susanne Lohmann is Professor of Political Science and Public Policy and Director of the Center for Governance at UCLA.

John Londregan is Professor of Politics and International Affairs at Princeton University's Woodrow Wilson School.

Karen Long Jusko is a graduate student in the Department of Political Science at the University of Michigan.

Nolan McCarty is Associate Dean and Professor of Politics and Public Affairs at the Woodrow Wilson School at Princeton University.

Mathew D. McCubbins is a Chancellor's Associates Chair in Political Science at UC San Diego.

Hervé Moulin is the George A. Peterkin Professor of Economic Theory at Rice University.

Douglass C. North is Professor of Economics at Washington University, St Louis, and a Senior Fellow at the Hoover Institution, Stanford University. He was awarded the Nobel Prize in 1993.

Thomas R. Palfrey is Professor of Politics and Economics at Princeton University.

Torsten Persson is Director of the Institute for International Economic Studies at Stockholm University, and Centennial Professor at the London School of Economics.

Andrea Prat is Professor of Economics at the London School of Economics.

Adam Przeworski is Carroll and Milton Petrie Professor of Politics at New York University.

Dan Reiter is Professor of Political Science at Emory University.

James A. Robinson is Professor of Government at Harvard University.

Jonathan A. Rodden is Ford Career Development Associate Professor of Political Science at MIT.

Daniel B. Rodriguez is Warren Distinguished Professor of Law and former Dean at the University of San Diego School of Law.

John E. Roemer is Elizabeth S. and A. Varick Stout Professor of Political Science and Economics at Yale University.

Ronald Rogowski is Professor of Political Science and interim Vice-Provost of International Studies at UCLA.

Donald G. Saari is a Distinguished Professor of Mathematics and of Economics, and Director of the Institute for Mathematical Behavioral Sciences at the University of California, Irvine.

Kenneth A. Shepsle is George Markham Professor of Government and Associate of the Institute for Quantitative Social Science at Harvard University.

Charles R. Shipan is the J. Ira and Nicki Harris Professor of Social Science in the Department of Political Science at the University of Michigan.

Stergios Skaperdas is Professor of Economics at the University of California, Irvine.

Enrico Spolaore is Professor of Economics at Tufts University.

Allan C. Stam is Daniel Webster Professor of Government at Dartmouth College.

Richard Swedberg is Professor of Sociology at Cornell University.

Guido Tabellini is Professor of Economics at Bocconi University, where he is also President of the Innocenzo Gasparini Institute of Economic Research.

Anthony J. Venables is Professor of International Economics at the London School of Economics.

Barry R. Weingast is Senior Fellow, Hoover Institution, and the Ward C. Krebs Family Professor, Department of Political Science, Stanford University.

David E. Wildasin is Endowed Professor of Public Finance in the Martin School of Public Policy and Administration, and Professor, Department of Economics, University of Kentucky.

Stanley L. Winer is Canada Research Chair Professor in Public Policy at the School of Public Policy and the Department of Economics, Carleton University.

Donald A. Wittman is Professor of Economics at the University of California, Santa Cruz.

Anne Wren is an Assistant Professor of Political Science, Stanford University.

PART I
INTRODUCTION

CHAPTER 1

THE REACH OF POLITICAL ECONOMY

BARRY R. WEINGAST
DONALD A. WITTMAN

OVER its long lifetime, the phrase "political economy" has had many different meanings. For Adam Smith, political economy was the science of managing a nation's resources so as to generate wealth. For Marx, it was how the ownership of the means of production influenced historical processes. For much of the twentieth century, the phrase political economy has had contradictory meanings. Sometimes it was viewed as an area of study (the interrelationship between economics and politics) while at other times it was viewed as a methodological approach. Even the methodological approach was divided into two parts—the economic approach (often called public choice) emphasizing individual rationality and the sociological approach where the level of analysis tended to be institutional.

In this *Handbook*, we view political economy as a grand (if imperfect) synthesis of these various strands. In our view, political economy is the methodology of economics applied to the analysis of political behavior and institutions. As such, it is not a single, unified approach, but a family of approaches. Because institutions are no longer ignored, but instead are often the subject matter of the investigation, this approach incorporates many of the issues of concern to political sociologists. Because political behavior and institutions are themselves a subject of study, politics also becomes the subject of political economy. All of this is tied together by a set of methodologies, typically associated with economics, but now part and parcel of political science itself.[1] The unit of analysis is typically the individual. The individual is motivated to achieve goals (usually preference maximization but in evolutionary games, maximization of surviving offspring), the theory is based in mathematics (often game theoretic), and the empirics either use sophisticated statistical techniques or involve experiments where money is used as a motivating force in the experiment (see Palfrey, this volume).

The purpose of this Introduction is to illustrate the intellectual excitement in political economy by covering some important elements on the scholarly frontier. As such, it neither provides an outline of the volume nor a summary of the major topics and results. In this chapter, we discuss a set of approaches and issues that have spawned interesting results and that are likely to spur considerable research in the next decade.

We divide our essay into five sections. In Section 1, we discuss research on endogenous institutions. The research agenda on institutions follows a natural progression. The first step is to determine how institutions affect behavior. Indeed, this step seems a necessary condition for a theory of endogenous institutions. Having built up a large literature on the effects of institutions, students of political economy have begun to treat institutions as endogenous (thereby incorporating some of the subject matter of sociology and anthropology). We focus our attention on legislative institutions because this is where much of the work has been done. The success of institutional analysis of legislatures is not surprising, as scholars have collected a large body of data and evidence (both quantitative and qualitative) on legislatures. For example, votes have been recorded with party affiliations and other attributes noted. These large data sets allow hypotheses to be tested and theory to be refined. Because the rules of the US Congress are internal to Congress, voting procedures, the type of committees, and committee assignments are all endogenous. So legislatures are fertile ground for exploring institutional choice.

One of the technically most challenging but at the same time one of the most exciting areas of research in political economy concerns the revelation and aggregation of information, the subject of Section 2. This work is exciting because many of the results contradict earlier beliefs based on decision-theoretic models and because this research answers many puzzles. Here, our focus is on voters, particularly voters who are uninformed in one way or another, but are nevertheless rational. Since this research area is still in its infancy, we expect much more to be done in the ensuing years.

Section 3 is devoted to evolutionary models of human and political behavior. Political economy is now at the confluence of two related paradigms: utility maximization and evolutionary fitness. Both employ survival arguments in the context of competitive forces—for example candidates need to win elections to survive. And both employ the concept of equilibrium. These two concepts of survival and equilibrium distinguish political economy from other approaches to political behavior. However, these two approaches at times provide contradictory insights. As we will

---

[1] See Austen-Smith, this volume.

show, some kinds of irrational behavior may improve evolutionary fitness. So at the same time that political economy is pushing the envelope of hyper-rationality (as illustrated in Section 2), it is also trying to incorporate elements of emotions and irrationality (Section 3). Furthermore, while political economy has traditionally been based on self-regarding behavior, a considerable body of research in evolutionary politics tries to explain other-regarding behavior, such as altruism and vengeance.

Scientific knowledge depends to a great extent on the interplay between empirical knowledge and theoretical development. Not surprisingly, our most comprehensive knowledge is about the advanced industrial democracies in general and legislatures in particular, where the great number of observations (of votes, party affiliation, etc.) allow for an extensive testing of hypotheses and considerable refinement of theory.[2] Our *Handbook of Political Economy* reflects this emphasis.

Nevertheless, over time, there has been a spread of knowledge from the core areas of research. This spread has occurred for several reasons. First, the same behavioral relations that we observe within democracies may occur across political systems once we account for the divergent institutional constraints on the actors. For example, authoritarians may not face elections, but they too need political support to remain in power (see Bueno de Mesquita, this volume). Second, more information is being collected so that cross-country comparisons can now be done.[3] Finally, the political phenomena in non-democratic countries raise a host of questions typically ignored in democratic countries that demand answers: why is there ethnic conflict? When is democracy a stable political system? What if any is the relationship between democracy and capitalism? And why are so many nations underdeveloped?[4]

In Section 4, we consider the spread of political economy to new areas of research. Here the empirical and theoretical answers are the least certain, but perhaps the most interesting because of their novelty. We use, as our illustrative example, work on the size and wealth of nations. A motivating reason for choosing the size of nations as our prime example of the spread of political economy is that rational choice models have often been (unfairly) accused of dealing with "epiphenomena" such as voting rather

---

[2] This disproportionate focus of political economy research has arisen for several reasons. First, the political economy tools were first developed studying democratic countries and are therefore more easily adapted to other democratic countries than to non-democratic ones. Second, close observation and data are more easily obtained in democratic countries so that theories applying to them have been honed the most. Third, the institutional tools of political economy are more readily applied to the more highly developed institutions of the advanced industrial democracies, in contrast to the less stable and less institutionalized politics in the developing world.

[3] Indeed, another defining characteristic of the political economy approach is the use of large data sets that enable econometric comparisons across a variety of countries, where the varieties are captured by different independent variables. For examples of cross-country comparisons, see Persson and Tabellini (this volume) and Glaeser (this volume). The econometric approach is in stark contrast to the older comparative politics literature, which compared two or three countries at a time.

[4] For *Handbook* surveys of these fields see, respectively: Fearon (this volume), Przeworski (this volume), Iverson (this volume), and both Acemoglu and Robinson (this volume) and Bates (this volume).

than with "deeper and more substantive" issues. The size and wealth of nations clearly passes the gravitas test.

1 Endogenous Institutions: The Structure of Congress

Institutions can be studied at three different levels. First, the most basic and common level takes institutions as given and studies their effects. Second, the first method can be used as a form of comparative institutional analysis to study the implications of different forms of institutions. Third, the deepest level of institutional analysis is to take the institutions themselves as endogenous; and to explain how and why institutions are structured in particular ways, and why some types of institutions survive but not others. The third approach is both the newest and the least explored of the three approaches to institutions and is therefore likely to be a major frontier in the coming years.

To illustrate the differences in the three approaches to institutions, we focus on legislatures, where scholars have made significant progress on institutional choice. We begin our discussion with models that take legislative institutions as given and study their effects. In a relatively 'institution-free' legislature with majority rule voting in one dimension, legislative choice will be the preference of the median legislator. By adding institutional features to this simple spatial model of legislative choice, scholars have studied the implications of a variety of institutional details. For example, several scholars have studied the effect of *committee* gatekeeping authority (Denzau and MacKay 1983; Shepsle and Weingast 1981) or *party* gatekeeping authority (Cox and McCubbins 2005) on legislative choice. The idea is that committees (during the mid-twentieth century) or parties (during the late twentieth century and early twenty-first century) held the power to keep issues within their jurisdiction from coming up for a vote. In contrast to the median voter model, the gatekeeping models show that some non-median status quos can be sustained: the gatekeeper will keep the gates closed for any status quo that she prefers to the median's ideal. This research agenda has produced a wealth of knowledge about how legislative institutions affect both legislative policy choices and policy decisions by the other branches. For example, Laver and Shepsle (1996; see Laver, this volume) show how parliamentary institutions affect policy choice; Krehbiel (1998, this volume) demonstrates the effects of internal congressional rules (notably, the filibuster) for policy-making, including how policy-making changes with various types of electoral change; Ferejohn and Shipan (1990; see Huber and Shipan, this volume) show how potential threats of legislation affect bureaucratic decision-making even without any legislation passing; and Marks (1988; see McCubbins and Rodriguez, this volume) demonstrates the close relationship between legislative preferences and judicial decisions that interpret the meaning of statutes.

The second type of institutional analysis utilizes the above methodology to make comparative statements about different institutions. For example, pivotal politics models show the differences in behavior between a unicameral majoritarian system, a bicameral system where each chamber uses majority rule, and a bicameral system in which one chamber employs a filibuster rule allowing a minority of legislators to prevent the passage of legislation. The first institution always results in the median legislature's ideal policy. The second institution creates a gridlock range of possible policy choices—the set of points between the ideal policies of the median in each chamber. Any status quo policy in this set is an equilibrium in that there does not exist a majority in each chamber that can overturn it. The third institution extends the set of status quo points that cannot be overturned even further: the possibility of a filibuster means that only policies commanding 60 per cent in one chamber and a majority in the other can overturn a policy, so more status quo policies are stable. For a further discussion of these issues see Krehbiel (this volume) and Cutrone and McCarty (this volume).

Third, a much smaller set of papers studies the structure of the legislature itself and treats its institutions as endogenous.[5] Four different approaches have been used to explain legislative structure: (1) legislator preferences, (2) committees as commitment devices, (3) parties as transactions cost reducers, and (4) committees as information providers.[6] We will now discuss each in turn.

1.1 Legislator Preferences

The simplest of the approaches bases legislative choice on legislator preferences and relies on the "majoritarian postulate," which holds that legislative policy and procedural choices are made by majorities (Krehbiel 1991). In the context of one-dimensional models of policy choice, the preference-based approach has the following implications (Krehbiel 1993). First, policy choice corresponds to that of the median legislator. Second, suppose that legislators join one of two parties, and, further, that those to the right of the median largely join one party while those to the left of the median largely join the other party.

Suppose that the status quo is to the right of the median and the proposed legislation seeks to move policy left toward the median voter's ideal. The "cutting line" divides the set of voters into those favoring the status quo and those favoring the proposal. In this context, the cutting line is that policy halfway between the status quo and the proposed alternative (assuming that legislator utility functions are symmetric). Since the status quo is to the right of the median, so too will be the cutting line. The proposal makes every legislator to the right of the cutting line worse off, so they vote against the policy; while every legislator to the left of the cutting line is better off under the proposal and will vote for it.

---

[5] Weingast 2002 surveys this mode of analysis in different contexts. Shepsle (this volume) provides a variant on these themes.

[6] Laver (this volume) covers some of these issues; see also the summary in Shepsle and Weingast 1995.

Given the assumption of how legislators choose parties, nearly all legislators from the left party vote for the proposal; while most of those of the right party vote against it. Indeed, if the status quo is not too far to the right relative to the distribution of legislature preferences, then most of the members of the right party will vote against the change. In other words, voting on this legislature will exhibit polarization by party even though the party exerts no pressure on its members to vote one way or another.

A lesson of this model is that polarized party voting can emerge as the combined result of legislative preferences and sorting into parties without being a function of any legislative institutions that advantage parties or that constrain member behavior.

Although this approach rationalizes only minimalist legislative institutions, it provides an important baseline from which to judge other models. While most approaches rely on legislator preferences to some degree, we term this approach a preference-based approach because it relies solely on legislative preferences and the median voter model to explain political phenomena, such as polarized party voting.

1.2 Committees as Commitment Devices

The second approach is exemplified by Weingast and Marshall's (1988) "Industrial organization of Congress." This approach built on previous theoretical and empirical work. Going back to Buchanan and Tullock (1962), many models of legislative choice emphasized logrolling and vote-trading. By logrolling and trading votes, members and the districts they represented were better off. Logrolling can thus be seen as a legislative institution parallel to market institutions in the economic sphere.

Empirically, the substantive literature on Congress emphasized the central importance of committees, which were seen to dominate the policy-making process. That literature emphasized committee specialization and self-selection onto committees by members most interested in the committee jurisdiction (Fenno 1966, 1973; Shepsle 1978). Clearly, this form of committee organization suited members' electoral goals (Mayhew 1974). So committee organization was seen as reflecting the preferences of the legislators and their constituents. In this view, the key to understanding legislative organization was legislative exchange.

Weingast and Marshall sought an explanation of congressional organization that accounted for the fundamental features then found in the substantive literature. They based their approach on two observations: first, the legislature faced many different issues that cannot be combined into a single dimension: agriculture is not commensurate with civil rights, banking, or defense. Second, vote-trading had significant enforcement problems as a means of legislative exchange. For example, suppose that one group of legislators seeks to build dams and bridges, another group seeks regulatory control of some market, and that neither group alone comprises a majority. The two groups could, per logrolling, agree to support one another's legislation. But this raises a problem: once their dams and bridges are built, what stops those receiving them from joining those locked out of the original trade to renege on the deal by passing new legislation ending the regulation? Because of the possibility of reneging, some logrolls will fail *ex ante* as legislators fear their deals will ultimately fail.[7]

Enforcement problems imply that direct exchange of votes is not likely to provide a durable means of legislative exchange. Instead, Weingast and Marshall argued that legislators were likely to institutionalize their exchanges in the form of a legislative committee system (LCS) that granted legislators greater powers over policies within the committee's jurisdiction. They showed that, in the context of a mechanism to grant rights to committee seats in combination with self-selection onto committees, the LCS made members with different preferences better off.

Consider the problem of reneging noted above. Self-selection onto committees with gatekeeping power prevents this type of reneging. Suppose the group favoring dams and bridges seek to renege on their original deal and introduce legislation to undo the regulation. This legislation now goes to the committee with jurisdiction. Populated by those who favor maintaining the regulation, committee members prevent the legislation from coming before the legislature. This preserves both the status quo and the original legislative exchange.

This approach also addresses an important question raised by the majoritarian postulate. This postulate questions why a majority would ever vote to reduce or restrict its own powers in the future. In the context of a single dimension of legislative choice, it is hard to understand why the median (and hence a majority) would vote to restrict itself. In the context of multiple dimensions, however, no median exists. The exchange postulate underlying the LCS provides an answer to the question: a majority votes to restrict itself on a series of different policy issues simultaneously. Although this restricts the majority's actions on each dimension, if each member is assigned to a committee of higher value than the average, this exchange makes each better off (see also Calvert 1995).

In this model, committee organization solves the problem of legislative exchange. Given pervasive enforcement problems of direct exchange of votes, legislators instead choose to organize the legislature in such a way as to institutionalize a pattern of exchange that furthers the goals of all.

1.3 Legislative Parties as Solutions to Collective Dilemmas

The third approach uses legislative parties to explain legislative organization and behavior. In this view, parties are more than just a collection of people choosing the same party label. Cox and McCubbins (1993), for example, argue that legislators face a series of collective action problems that political parties can resolve. For example individual legislators have trouble passing their own legislation; and without coordinating, legislator activity fails to add up to enough to help each get

---

[7] A second enforcement problem is that exchange of votes over time creates additional opportunities for reneging, especially as bills evolve.

re-elected. In particular, all legislators face a common-pool problem in which they have incentives to shift costs onto each other. Parties overcome these problems by enforced coordination.[8]

In the face of various coordination and related problems, Cox and McCubbins argue that members have an incentive to use parties to coordinate the behavior of their members for several ends: to produce legislation more attractive to their members; to develop a national reputation or brand name; and, in combination, to use these tools to help re-elect their members (see also Wittman 1989, 1995).Committees in this view are a tool of the majority party used to further party goals; namely, to propose legislation benefiting party members and to prevent legislation that would make party majorities worse off. The majority party's delegation to each committee, rather than being composed of those most interested in the policy as in the Weingast and Marshall approach, were representative of the party. This particularly holds for gatekeeping committees, such as the budget committee where the members do not self-select. Tests of the representatives of committees tend to support the party view (see, e.g. Cox and McCubbins 1993). Also consistent with this view was the striking partisan aspect of congressional voting, particularly since 1980.

However, this party-centric approach has not been without its critics. Krehbiel (1993) presented a major challenge to this perspective by asking, 'where's the party?' Relying on the preference-based approach noted above, he showed that many of the findings of the party-centric perspective were consistent with the majoritarian perspective. We have already noted how polarized party voting, rather than being a product of the party organization of the legislature, can result from simple preferences in combination with legislator sorting into parties. Another aspect is the representativeness of committees. As noted, the party perspective emphasizes that each party's delegation to a committee is representative of the party; but if both parties do this, then the overall committee will be representative of the chamber, also consistent with the majoritarian perspective.

The debate about parties has spurred a remarkable empirical literature. See for example, Cox and McCubbins (2005), Krehbiel (this volume), and Groseclose and Snyder (2001). We do not have time in our introduction to cover this literature, but we do want to emphasize that the research in endogenous legislative institutions is empirical, as well.

1.4 Information Explanations for Structure

The final approach to legislative organization, associated with Gilligan and Krehbiel (1989) and Krehbiel (1991), emphasizes that legislators are uncertain about the impact of their choices on actual outcomes. Legislators therefore have an incentive to organize the legislature to reflect the task of gaining expertise and information that

---

[8] See also Cox (this volume) who shows how legislative parties arise endogenously as a means to resolve the problem of potential overuse of plenary time.

reduces this uncertainty. In this world, committees are bodies of legislative experts in the policies of their jurisdiction. Committee expertise allows committee members to reduce the uncertainty between legislation and actual outcomes.

This perspective has significant implications for legislative organization, including the choice of rules governing consideration of legislation on the floor. For example, because expertise requires costly investment, legislators will undertake this costly investment only if the system somehow compensates them for this. Krehbiel argues that restrictive rules that bias legislative choice in favor of committees are the answer. Although restrictive rules prevent legislators from choosing policy associated with the median voter *ex post*, legislators are better off *ex ante* because committee expertise allows committees to reduce the uncertainty associated with the difference between legislation and policy outcomes.

1.5 Concluding Thoughts

The debate about legislative institutions has been lively, and no consensus has yet emerged on the determinants of legislative organization. We cannot yet say whether one perspective will ultimately triumph (as Gilligan and Krehbiel 1995 suggest) or whether a synthesis of perspectives is likely to emerge (as Shepsle and Weingast 1995 suggest).

From a broader perspective, the study of legislative institutions provides a template for how research on institutions is likely to proceed in the future. The first stage is to see how a particular institution affects behavior; next, similar but somewhat different institutions are compared; then in the final stage, institutions are treated as being endogenous. If the history of research on endogenous legislative institutions is any guide, there will be disagreement on which institutions are endogenous to other institutions. These controversies, in turn, help shape our understanding of institutions and provide a deeper understanding of organizations.

2 REVELATION AND AGGREGATION OF INFORMATION: VOTING

In this section, we consider the revelation and aggregation of information. This is a game-theoretic, as opposed to a decision-theoretic, approach to information. An exciting aspect of this research is that it often turns the standard theoretic wisdom on its head. We illustrate by looking at voting behavior.[9]

Traditional democratic theory argues that, for democracy to work, voters should inform themselves about the candidates and the issues. Moreover, voters should be unbiased and rely on unbiased sources of information. Practice in all working

---

[9] Ansolabehere (this volume) reviews the broad topic of voting behavior.

democracies differs greatly from this ideal. Voters appear to be notoriously uninformed (and, indeed, have little incentive to become informed). Some voters base their choice of candidate solely on party label, while other voters rely on biased sources of information, including information provided by pressure groups.

Does this apparent lack of information imply that democracy will fall far from its ideal? Possibly not, if the lack of information is more apparent than real. In the following pages, we show how voters can make logical inferences so that their behavior is similar to perfectly informed voters.

We start with an easy example to illustrate how information revelation arises. A number of articles study the endogenous timing of elections in parliamentary systems.[10] Because it has access to information, the ruling party is able to forecast future economic performance and other events that are likely to impact on voters' welfare. This information is not likely to be available to the voters. The party in power has an incentive to call an election when it is at the height of its popularity.

However, this decision-theoretic analysis does not consider the voter response to an early election call. Voters can infer from an early election call that the ruling party expects to do worse in the future. Voters can therefore infer that there is likely to be bad news in the future.[11] The ruling government realizes that voters will act this way. As a result, governments are less likely to call early elections than they would otherwise be, and when they do, voters will take this information into account and be less positively inclined towards the government. Smith (2003, 2004) provides empirical evidence in support of this argument. Polls taken after the announcement of an early election show a decline from polls taken before the announcement. Incorporating the voters' response made obsolete much of the earlier research on endogenous timing of elections that did not consider the possibility that voters could make inferences.

Let us now consider another area where earlier research assumed mechanical, uninformed voters, but more recent research assumes uninformed but rational voters, often with starkly differing results. Starting with Ben Zion and Eytan (1974) and continuing on into the recent past (see Baron 1994; Grossman and Helpman 1996), an extensive literature has assumed that the more money a candidate spends on advertising, the more votes the candidate receives from uninformed voters. Sources of money tend to come from interests on the extremes of the political distribution. To get contributions that pay for such advertising, candidates move their policies away from the median voter toward a pressure group's most preferred position.

Let us look at the Grossman and Helpman model in greater detail.[12] Grossman and Helpman assume the following: voters, candidates, and pressure groups are arrayed along a one-dimensional issue space. Each voter has a most preferred position with a concave utility function over policy; this means that voters are risk averse.[13] There are

---

[10] See for example, Cargill and Hutchison 1991 and the long list of citations found in Smith 2003, n. 6.
[11] Here, we ignore other reasons for calling an early election, in particular the desire of the ruling party in a coalition government to strengthen its hand.
[12] For heuristic purposes, we simplify their model.
[13] Risk aversion means that voters prefer a sure thing over a lottery having the same expected value as the sure thing.

two types of voters: informed voters who know the positions of the candidates and uninformed voters who have no knowledge of the candidates' or pressure group's positions. Informed voters vote for the candidate closest to the voter's most preferred position. Uninformed voters respond only to political advertising—the more money spent on advertising by one of the candidates, the greater the percentage of uninformed voters voting for the candidate.

Each candidate wants to maximize the percentage of votes that he or she receives. There is one pressure group (say, on the extreme right). The pressure group is willing to donate money to one of the candidates if the candidate moves right from the median voter.

The election proceeds as follows:

1. The pressure group makes a one-time take-it-or-leave-it offer to one of the candidates. If the candidate agrees to move right of the median informed voter, then the pressure group provides funds to the candidate for political advertising. If the agreement is accepted, it is binding on both sides.
2. The candidate receiving the offer decides whether to accept or reject it.
   If the candidate accepts the offer, then the other candidate knows the position of the candidate accepting the offer. The other candidate will then choose a position between the candidate and the median informed voter to capture as many informed voters as possible.
   If the candidate rejects the offer, then the pressure group is out of the picture. Per the standard Downsian (1957) model, both candidates will then choose to be at the median of the informed voters.
3. The positions of the candidates are then made public to the *informed* voters. The candidate who received the donation then advertises.
4. The voters choose.

Given the set-up of the model, it is not hard to see that the candidate will be willing to move right from the median of the informed voters as long as the advertising from the campaign funds sufficiently increases the number of uninformed voters to compensate for the loss of informed voters caused by the movement to the right and away from the median informed voter.

The model seems to imply that pressure groups are likely to undermine the political process. But is it rational for uninformed voters to act in the way postulated? Let us consider the model more carefully.

In the above model, the candidates, pressure group, and informed voters are all rational, but not the uninformed voters. As already mentioned, uninformed voters vote mechanically. But being uninformed does not mean being irrational. Suppose instead that the uninformed do not vote mechanically but can make logical inferences. We consider two variants with different characterizations of uninformed voter behavior.

First, let us continue to assume that the uninformed voters know neither the positions of the candidates nor the position of the pressure group (the pressure group being equally likely to be on the left or the right). Campaign advertising is, by its very nature, public so that an ordinary person can infer which candidate received the most contributions by observing which candidate has the most political advertising. The uninformed voters can simply watch television and passively observe the candidate who has the most advertisements. Given the logic of the model, the uninformed can infer that the candidate doing the advertising is further away from the median informed voter than the candidate not doing the advertising.

Given our assumption that the uninformed voter does not even know whether the pressure group is on the left or the right, the uninformed voter faces a greater risk from the candidate who is doing the advertising. Both candidates will on average be at the median informed voter's most preferred position, but the candidate receiving the campaign funds will be more extreme. Thus the risk-averse uninformed voter should vote for the candidate not doing the advertising! The rational voter does not act like the mechanical voter in this case. Of course, if this behavior characterizes uninformed voters, then the candidate will not accept campaign donations from the pressure group in the first place.

Now suppose that the uninformed know something. For example, they may know that the National Rifle Association supports one of the candidates, and as a consequence these voters can infer that the candidate receiving the funds is closer than the median informed voter is to the position of the NRA. More generally, the uninformed voter may know whether the pressure group is on the right. If the uninformed voter also knows where he or she stands relative to the median voter, the uninformed voter to the left of the median voter can infer that he or she should vote for the other candidate, while those uninformed voters to the right will be inclined to vote for the candidate receiving funds from the right-wing pressure group.

Consider two cases: if uninformed voters tend to be to the right of the median informed voter, then the candidate may accept funds from the right-wing pressure group and even advertise this to be the case. This occurs when the candidate gets sufficiently more votes from the uninformed voters on the right than she loses from the uninformed voters on the left to make up for the reduced vote share from informed voters. Alternatively, if there are more uninformed voters to the left of the median informed voter, the candidate would lose if she accepted the deal from the pressure group. Hence she would not do so in the first place.

In this version of the model, pressure group contributions help the uninformed voters. If the mass of uninformed voters is to the right of the median of the informed voters (and hence, the overall median is to the right of the median of the informed voters), then one candidate will accept the funds and the effect of campaign donations will be to move the candidate to the right from the median of the informed voters. On the other hand, if more uninformed voters lie to the left of the median, neither candidate will accept funds from a pressure group on the right.[14] In short, pressure groups aid the political process, rather than undermine it!

We have just modeled the case where some voters are uninformed about the candidates' positions. Another possibility is that voters are informed about the candidates'

---

[14] The exact result requires more technical specification and can be found in Wittman 2005*a*.

positions but not about their relative quality. Again, the voters are rational and the pressure group has private information (in this case, about the relative quality of the candidates). A number of recent papers consider this case but employ differing subsidiary assumptions: advertising has content (see Coate 2004; Wittman forthcoming); advertising has no content, but expenditures on advertising signal information (Prat 2002, this volume); pressure groups make the offers (Coate, Prat), candidates make the offers; there is one pressure group, there are multiple pressure groups; the candidates are only interested in winning, and the candidates have policy goals. These various modeling efforts do not all come to the same positive conclusion as the previous paragraph. In general, the results depend on whether the value of the revealed information is outweighed by the loss from inferior candidate positions when the candidates compete for pressure group funds. In turn, this balance depends to a great degree on the number of pressure groups and whether it is the candidates or the pressure groups that make the offer. All these various modeling efforts take into account that information valuable to uniformed voters is revealed by the pressure group's donation or endorsement and all of them assume rationality of the voters. This is the key methodological advance—how voters can incorporate information that others might want to distort or hide (see Prat, this volume).

We have shown how uninformed voters can make inferences from behavior and thereby become more informed. Because all of this is embedded in a game, all other players take this behavior and information into account when they make their decisions; and of course the uninformed take the other players' strategies into account when they make their own inferences.[15]

The final example for this section considers aggregation of information in the context of voting. Suppose a set of voters face a decision about how much money to spend. To gain intuition, we begin with an exceedingly simple example. Suppose that there are five voters with identical preferences: three have unbiased estimates of the correct action to take, while two are fully informed. The voters know whether they are informed or not. The uninformed know that there are informed voters, but not how many. Suppose further that the correct action is to spend $7 million and that, with equal probability, the uninformed players receive a signal that it should be 5, 7, or 9 million dollars. Assuming that the voters cannot communicate with each other, how likely is it that the majority rule decision is not 7? The answer is zero if the voters are rational: all the uninformed voters will rationally abstain. By doing so, they know that only informed voters will participate and that these informed voters will make the correct decision.

This example illustrates two important but related issues. First, the more informed people will choose to vote (here, at least, the argument does not go against conventional wisdom). Second, the potential voter asks: given that he will be pivotal, should

---

[15] There are other ways in which voters can be informed despite an apparent lack of information. Parties create brand names so that party labels are in fact informative about a candidate's position (Cox and McCubbins 1993, 2005). Relying on biased information can be rational for voters who have strong priors in favor of one of the parties (Calvert 1985). And, uninformed voters can learn from polls of informed voters (McKelvey and Ordeshook 1986).

he vote, and if he votes, how should he vote. In other words, the decision to vote and how to vote does not just depend on whether the person will be pivotal, but also on the preferences and information structure of all of the voters. Our understanding of the problem is no longer in terms of decision theory but of game theory.

To illustrate this idea in terms of a more complicated, but more realistic model, assume that there are three voters (or three groups of voters), labeled V, V_i, and V_u; and two states of the world, labeled 1 and 2. Assume that voter V votes for candidate D regardless of the state of the world. The second voter is independent but informed and will be labeled V_i. This voter knows the state of the world and votes for D when the state of the world is 1 and votes for R when the state of the world is 2: given V_i's preferences, D makes a better president if the state of the world is 1 while R makes a better president if the state of the world is 2. The third voter, V_u, is also independent (with the same preference structure as V_i), but is uninformed. However, V_u knows the preferences and information sets of the other two voters.

How should V_u vote if the probability of state 1 (where D is V_u's preferred candidate) is more likely than the probability of state 2? The decision-theoretic model, where V_u's vote is based on the mostly likely state of the world (state 1), suggests that V_u vote for D. But the game-theoretic pivot model argues that V_u should vote for R. The reasoning is as follows. If the state of the world is 1, then both voter V and voter V_i vote for D, and D will win regardless of V_u's vote. When the state of the world is 2, then the other two voters will split their vote and V_u will be pivotal. Under such circumstances, V_u should vote for R since she prefers R to D in state 2. So V_u always votes for R.[16] Behaving in this way allows the informed voter, V_i, whose preferences are similar to V_u's, to be pivotal in all circumstances. This behavior results in better outcomes for V_u than those suggested by the decision-theoretic perspective. Because the latter tells V_u always to vote for D, V_u votes for D even in the state 2 when she prefers R.

These two examples show that uninformed voters can make inferences about how to behave that make them better off, even when they remain ignorant of critical aspects of the election. Now this particular example requires V_u to know a lot about the other voters, but the conceptual apparatus can be incorporated into other models where the information requirements are not so high. To get back to our earlier discussion of pressure groups where some voters are uninformed about the candidates' positions, Wittman (2005) shows that the uninformed voters to the right (left) of the median voter should always employ the following rule of thumb: vote for (against) the candidate endorsed by the right-wing pressure group.[17] Sometimes this could result in some of the uninformed voters on the right voting for the wrong candidate, and at other times this could result in some of the uninformed voters on the left voting for the wrong candidate. However, even if all the mistaken votes for one candidate were reversed this would not change the outcome. So fully rational but uninformed voters consider the effect of their behavior when pivotal even if their likelihood of being

---

[16] For a more extended discussion see Fedderson and Pesendorfer 1996, 1999.
[17] The actual model employs additional assumptions that assure that certain pathologies do not arise.

pivotal is small. Indeed, in this example, by their rule of thumb, the uninformed make the informed median over all voters the pivot.

To summarize: democratic theory has long held that ignorant voters harm the operation of democracy. The force of this section is to demonstrate that uninformed voters and uninformed actors more generally can make inferences based on the behavior of others, the structure of their strategic situation, and signals received from other actors. These inferences make uninformed voters better off than predicted by decision-theoretic models; and they improve the workings of democracy more than predicted by traditional democratic theory.[18] We believe that in the next decade the aggregation and revelation of information will continue to be a very important mode of research and that it will continue to overturn received wisdom (see Moulin, this volume; and Ledyard, this volume; for further examples).

3 Evolutionary Models of Human and Political Behavior

Both economics and evolutionary models of human behavior employ the concepts of survival and equilibrium (Alchian 1950). Nonetheless, the implications of economic and biological models at times conflict. Although people who are capable of achieving their goals because of either their physical or mental prowess are more likely to survive and produce offspring, it is not clear that fitness would accrue to those who maximized utility and were happier. Furthermore, at times evolutionary fitness may be gained by being less rational; for example, the emotional may serve as a useful commitment device (see Hirshleifer 2001).

Humans are pre-eminently social animals. Political structures are one kind of social structure, and such structures need to be compatible for better or worse with the biology of human behavior. Are people naturally xenophobic, vengeful, or generally limited in their capacity for empathy? One can generate all kinds of hypotheses about human behavior. But economics and/or evolutionary biology demand that the hypothesized behavior survives in a competitive equilibrium. The principle of survival in equilibrium imposes discipline on modeling efforts because not all hypotheses satisfy this criterion.

Models of pure self-regarding preferences have generated considerable insight into the political process—as this *Handbook* attests—yet such an assumption is not requisite for rational behavior. People may be other regarding in that they care about their children or feel altruistic or vengeful towards others.[19] How other-regarding

---

[18] See Ansolabehere (this volume) who makes this point.
[19] The phrase "other regarding" gets around the problem that altruistic behavior may make the person feel good and therefore altruism could be termed selfish behavior.

behavior survives in equilibrium is a major research question that still has not been fully answered.

Let us start with an easy question. Why are human parents altruistic to their children? Infants and small children need care in order to survive. Parental altruism helps to ensure the genetic transmission. But genetic relatedness rapidly approaches zero as the population increases in size. So this simple explanation for altruism falters when we want to extend it to the population as a whole.

A significant number of researchers seek to understand the role of vengeance. The phenomenon of suicide bombers inspires some of this interest—being a suicide bomber hardly appears to improve genetic fitness. Further interest in vengeance is inspired by experiments demonstrating that the standard income-maximizing model does not work well in certain situations. For example, consider the ultimatum game in which person A is given a certain amount of money (say ten dollars); A then offers a share of this money to B; B then either rejects or accepts the offer. If B rejects the offer, neither gets any of the money and the game is over. A theory that is based on humans being purely self-regarding predicts that A should offer B a trivial amount, say one cent. Because one cent is better than nothing, B is better off accepting the offer than rejecting it. Experiments consistently reveal that B subjects often reject low offers even though this hurts them financially. Further, experiments also reveal that A subjects often offer significant amounts to B to forestall such a rejection.[20]

This vengeful behavior by B is contrary to income maximization. Thus, the key intellectual puzzle to resolve is how vengeful behavior can be evolutionarily stable.

Scholars provide two types of answers. One is that a reputation for vengeful behavior may enhance fitness because others may avoid provoking revenge by avoiding doing harm to the vengeful person in the first place. Following this intuition, some evolutionary models show that, under certain circumstances, two types of people, vengeful and non-vengeful, can survive in equilibrium (Friedman and Singh 2005).[21]

Here we will concentrate on the second approach—the co-evolution of memes (social constructs) and genes—because that is more relevant to our understanding of collective choice and social cooperation. Humans are more social than their ancestors, and many argue that this sociability evolved along with the social institutions that made such sociability result in greater reproductive success. Consider the following thought experiment. If chimpanzees had language (which in itself enhances sociability) and could do calculus, would chimpanzee society look like human society if they were able to observe our customs? The co-evolution argument says no. Shame, guilt, the ability to be empathetic or vengeful, and certain conceptual possibilities that make us human would all be much more circumscribed in chimpanzees, which themselves

---

[20] The explanation for the rejection is that the person dividing the money has not been "fair." For a further discussion of fairness in experiments and the implications for political behavior see Palfrey (this volume).

[21] To get this result, Friedman and Singh develop a new equilibrium concept—evolutionary perfect Bayesian equilibrium. Their paper, as is the case for much of the research on the evolutionary stability of vengeance, employs sophisticated mathematical modeling. This illustrates another theme of our chapter—that political economy, unlike other intellectual approaches to political science, emphasizes logical rigor, which often requires considerable mathematics.

show more of these qualities than marsupials. Without pro-social emotions, all humans (rather than just a few) might be sociopaths, and human society as we know it might not exist despite the institutions of contract, government law enforcement, and reputation.[22]

Groups that overcome prisoner's dilemmas (and other social dilemmas) are likely to be more productive in gathering food and more successful in warfare against other groups. In turn, this leads to greater reproductive success. The central question for evolutionary models is how, if at all, evolutionary pressure keeps individual shirking in check. It seems, for example, that a person who is slightly less brave in battle is more likely to survive and have children than his braver compatriots. Bravery at once increases the risk for the brave while making it more likely that the less brave survive. If bravery/cowardice is genetic, how is a downward spiral of cowardice prevented?

The answer proceeds along the following lines: if the individuals are punished for shirking (in this case, being cowardly), this will keep them in line. But, because engaging in punishment is costly (possibly resulting in the would-be punisher's death), who will do the punishing? The evolutionary approach suggests that punishment, a kind of vengeance, will be a successful strategy for the punisher if he gains even a mild fitness advantage (status, more females, etc.). This is because, in equilibrium, the cost to the punisher is relatively small since punishment does not have to be meted out very often. Punishment need not be carried out frequently to be effective. It is the threat that is important. To the degree that shirkers by being punished (possibly by being banished from the tribe) become less fit, the need to engage in punishment decreases even more as there are fewer shirkers. And given that those who punish are more aligned with the interests of the society and therefore may be more likely to survive, there may be enough potential punishers so that the need for any individual to bear the costs of punishment is reduced still further (which of course means that the benefits received will also be reduced). If altruism and vengeance are gene based rather than meme based, there may have been a co-evolution of memes and genes. Over the eons, human society may have encouraged pro-social genetically based emotions.[23]

The force of this argument is that pro-social emotions bypass the cognitive optimizing process that is at the core of rational economic man. This cognitive difference implies that at times we should observe profound differences between the evolutionary model and the economic model. Under certain circumstances, seemingly irrational behavior, such as vengeance or shame, may be evolutionarily stable even if it runs counter to utility maximization. Moreover the relatively slow genetic evolution in comparison with meme evolution (especially in the last 100 years) yields a further

---

[22] For further discussion along these lines see Bowles and Gintis, this volume; Friedman and Singh 2000; Boyd et al. 2003; Gintis et al. 2005.

[23] This just gives the flavor of the argument. Once again, it is worthwhile to emphasize that the research summarized here employs very carefully specified models. The challenge for researchers in the field is to characterize a situation where vengeance survives, but does not become so intense that it undermines social relations. At the same time, the researcher must account for the possibility that non-vengeful types may want to mimic vengeful types. Finally, the researcher must mix the memes and genes so that they are in a stable equilibrium.

conclusion: it is quite possible that some of the pro-social emotions whose genetic basis evolved over the last 100,000 or more years are maladapted to the modern world.

At present the evolutionary study of genes and memes has produced very tentative results. Human behavior is part mammalian (possibly even reptilian), part primate, and part hominid. Although some have argued that much of human psychology developed in the savannah, it is not clear what part of human psychology developed then or earlier or, to a lesser degree, later. Also, we have only a rudimentary picture of human life in the savannah so evolutionary models of this period are very speculative. Furthermore, it is not clear whether the transmission of behavior is through memes or genes. On the other side of the coin, there appears to be much room for further research, and we believe that in the coming decade there will be many advances.[24]

4 Pushing the Envelope of Investigation

As political economy has matured, it has begun to tackle a wider range of topics. This work includes a series of larger questions, such as the origins of dictatorship and democracy. In this section, we consider one of these frontier topics—the size of nations.

Much of history reflects the expansion and contraction of nations. The conquests of Alexander the Great, the rise and decline of the Roman Empire, the aggressive expansions of Napoleon and Hitler, and the dissolution of the USSR are just a few examples. At the other end of the spectrum, many tiny countries, such as Singapore and Andorra, have survived a considerable length of time.

For over two millennia, historians and philosophers have asked why some nations have expanded, why others have contracted, and what is the optimal size of a polity (Plato, for example, said that the optimal size was 5,040 families). In this section, we discuss the political economy contribution to this area. In the process, we show how research in political economy builds upon earlier foundations.

The political economy approach to the size of nations starts with the basic Downsian characterization of voter preferences. In this case, voter or citizen preferences can be placed along a line (or a circle). This line or circle is then divided into n parts (not necessarily equal), each part representing a country. Each country chooses a policy position, X_j, which might be the median or mean of the citizens' preferences. A citizen's utility for her nation's policy is assumed to be decreasing in distance from her own preferred position, x (e.g. $-|x - X_j|$ or $-(x - X_j)^2$). Individuals at the

---

[24] Another group of social scientists employ a different strategy for generalizing about human behavior from the standard model of rationality, by drawing on cognitive science and psychology (e.g. North 2005). Space constraints prevent an adequate treatment.

boundary of two countries can choose in which country to reside (see Spoloare, this volume; Alesina and Spoloare 2003, for a more complete coverage.).[25]

Each citizen would like to have his or her country's policy as closely aligned as possible to her preferred policy. If policy were the only factor, all countries would be composed of only one citizen. But other factors run counter to such extreme decentralization. The most important are economies of scale in production and military power. When barriers to free trade exist between countries, a more populous country achieves greater economies of scale through its larger domestic market. A larger population also allows for greater military power, which may make war against smaller and weaker states more profitable because of the higher probability of success. At the same time greater military power makes predation by other states less profitable to these other states and therefore less likely (see Skaperdas, this volume).

These insights can readily be converted into a comparative statics analysis. When barriers to free trade are reduced (so that economies of scale can be achieved within a small country as long as it has sufficient international sales) and the returns to warfare are decreased, the number of countries will increase and the average country size will decrease. The returns to warfare depend greatly on the nature of the victim country's wealth. If the wealth is in oil, the predating county can expropriate most of the wealth; when the wealth is in human capital, the predating country can expropriate very little. In the latter case, the benefits to predation are reduced, the threat of war is less credible, and the benefits of being a large country are diminished.

In a simple model where wealth is distributed evenly among the citizens, those citizens at the periphery of the country will be most dissatisfied with their country's policy. They are therefore the most likely citizens to exit and join the adjacent country. Because of economies of scale in production and military power, this "migration" is costly to those citizens left behind. In order to forestall such migration, countries might institute a non-linear transfer scheme that grants citizens on the periphery greater resources. Le Breton and Weber (2001) make this argument and point to a number of cases, such as Quebec in Canada and some of the border states of India, where the center grants special rights to the peripheral states. This extension of the basic model affords a nice illustration of how political economy often grows. Instead of two competing models, the basic model is expanded so that we have a more general theory.

In the basic model, all of the countries have the same characteristics; and, when population is uniformly distributed on the line or circle, all countries are of the same size. Extensions of the basic model allow countries to have different characteristics. Nations are characterized as a nexus of public goods. A wise public policy choice may significantly increase the overall wealth of the citizenry. Successful countries create conditions for high productivity in the economic sphere by enforcing property rights and providing social overhead capital, while at the same time minimizing political costs by creating a system of rules that reduce influence costs and allow for

---

[25] Of course, individuals might not be free to migrate. See Friedman 1977 for an explanation for the Iron Curtain and the promotion of linguistic boundaries.

diverse preferences. Countries also need an effective military apparatus to protect their wealth from predation by other countries. Success in these endeavors may lead to immigration and geographical expansion, while failure to meet these goals may lead to extensive emigration or break-up of a country (see Wittman 2000).

Bolton and Roland (1997) consider another modification of the model. Until now we have assumed that the citizens are similar in all respects except for their preference for public policy, which has been given exogenously. Suppose instead that individuals differ in productivity and income, which determines their preference for redistributive public policy. Suppose further that there are two sections of the country and that each section votes by majority rule. Then two sections of a country may separate because of significant productivity differences. All of this is reflective of Tiebout's (1956) argument that jurisdictions specialize to reflect the preferences and wealth of their constituents.[26]

To summarize, political economy is making use of its basic tools to investigate an ever deepening set of questions. Ultimately, fewer institutions are treated as being exogenously determined and more institutions, including the nation state, are treated as variables to be explained. In this way, anthropology and history become part of political economy.

We conclude this section on pushing the envelope with a final observation. As the topics in this *Handbook* illustrate, the bulk of political economy research has focused on institutions and behavior within advanced industrial democracies. In these settings, the formal institutions of courts, legislatures, executives, bureaucracy, and elections can all be taken as given. Hundreds, if not thousands of papers have been written on these topics. Not surprisingly, the most progress has been made in these areas.

In contrast, political economy work that studies phenomena in countries outside of the advanced industrial democracies has made far less progress. Nevertheless, there are a number of exciting developments. We briefly mention a few areas of nascent research (posed as questions) that are likely to blossom in the future and that we cover in the *Handbook*:

- What do authoritarians maximize and why do they make the decisions they do? In past, many scholars assumed that they maximize their share of rents (e.g. North 1981, ch. 3; Olson 2001). Yet this approach remains inadequate because it takes as given that the authoritarian remains in power, something deeply problematic (as Tullock 1987 observed). Bueno de Mesquita et al. (2003; see Bueno de Mesquita, this volume, for a summary) provide a new approach arguing that authoritarians maximize their likelihood of staying in power. Haber (this volume) provides a program for future research on this topic.
- Why does democracy survive in some countries but not others? Przeworski (this volume) argues against some common answers and suggests that per capita wealth is an important reason.

---

[26] For an extensive discussion of the Tiebout hypothesis, see Wildasin (this volume). For ethnic causes of division, see Fearon (this volume).

- And while we are on the subject of democracy, what is the relationship between democracy and capitalism? Iverson (this volume) surveys various political economy models that try to answer this question.
- Why do so many countries remain poor? And why did a handful of countries in the eighteenth and nineteenth centuries manage to rise well above the rest of the world? Here too we have important new political economy models that seek to answer these questions (see, for example Acemoglu and Robinson, this volume; and Bates, this volume).
- What are the sources and circumstances of ethnic coalitions and violence? Fearon (this volume) provides an overview of the political economy approach and an agenda for future research.

In short, the extension of political economy methods beyond the advanced industrial nations is rapidly developing, and this *Handbook* provides overviews that can serve as building blocks for further research.

5 THE INTELLECTUAL ARMS RACE

Although we have characterized political economy as a set of agreed-upon methodological approaches, the set is quite large; different models and empirical studies frequently come to quite opposing conclusions. Scholarly works tend to play off each other so that there is an ever-increasing level of sophistication. Thus, while we have characterized political economy as a synthesis of fields, the synthesis will nonetheless provide sparks and an exciting research agenda for decades to come.

REFERENCES

ALCHIAN, A. 1950. Uncertainty, evolution, and economic theory. *Journal of Political Economy*, 58: 211–21.
ALESINA, A., and SPOLAORE, E. 2003. *The Size of Nations*. Cambridge, Mass.: MIT Press.
BARON, D. P. 1994. Electoral competition with informed and uninformed voters. *American Political Science Review*, 88: 33–47.
BEN-ZION, U., and EYTAN, Z. 1974. On money, votes and policy in a democratic society. *Public Choice*, 17: 1–10.
BOLTON, P., and ROLAND, G. 1997. The breakup of nations: a political economy analysis. *Quarterly Journal of Economics*, 112: 1057–89.
BOYD, R., GINTIS, H., BOWLES, S., and RICHERSON, P. J. 2003. Evolution of altruistic punishment. *Proceedings of the National Academy of Sciences*, 100: 3531–5.
BUCHANAN, J., and TULLOCK, G. 1962. *Calculus of Consent*. Ann Arbor: University of Michigan Press.

Bueno de Mesquita, B., Smith, A., Siverson, R. M., and Morrow, J. D. 2003. *The Logic of Political Survival.* Cambridge, Mass.: MIT Press.

Calvert, R. L. 1985. The value of biased information: a rational choice model of political advice. *Journal of Politics,* 47: 530–55.

—— 1995. Rational actors, equilibrium, and social institutions. In *Explaining Social Institutions,* ed. J. Knight and I. Sened. Ann Arbor: University of Michigan Press.

Cargill, T. F. and Hutchison, M. 1991. Political business cycles with endogenous election timing: evidence from Japan. *Review of Economics and Statistics,* 73: 733–9.

Coate, S. 2004. Pareto-improving campaign finance policy. *American Economic Review,* 94: 628–5.

Cox, G. W., and McCubbins, M. D. 1993. *Legislative Leviathan.* Berkeley: University of California Press.

—— —— 2005. Setting the agenda. Manuscript, Dept. of Political Science, UCSD.

Denzau, A. T., and Mackay, R. J. 1983. Gatekeeping and monopoly power of committees: an analysis of sincere and sophisticated behavior. *American Journal of Political Science,* 27: 740–61.

Downs, A. 1957. *An Economic Theory of Democracy.* New York: Harper and Row.

Feddersen, T., and Pesendorfer, W. 1996. The swing voter's curse. *American Economic Review,* 86: 408–24.

—— —— 1999. Abstentions in elections with asymmetric information and diverse preferences. *American Political Science Review,* 69: 381–98.

Fenno, R. F. 1966. *Power of the Purse.* Boston: Little, Brown.

—— 1973. *Congressmen in Committees.* Boston: Little, Brown.

Ferejohn, J., and Shipan, C. 1990. Congressional influence on bureaucracy. *Journal of Law, Economics, and Organization,* 6: 1–20.

Friedman, Daniel, and Singh, N. 2000. Negative reciprocity: the coevolution of memes and genes. *Evolution and Human Behavior,* 25: 155–73.

—— —— 2005. Equilibrium vengeance. Working paper, University of California, Santa Cruz.

Friedman, David 1977. A theory of the size and shape of nations. *Journal of Political Economy,* 85: 59–77.

Gilligan, T., and Krehbiel, K. 1989. Asymmetric information and legislative rules with a heterogeneous committee. *American Journal of Political Science,* 33: 459–90.

—— —— 1995. The gains from exchange hypothesis of legislative organization. In *Positive Theories of Congressional Institutions,* ed. K. A. Shepsle and B. R. Weingast. Ann Arbor: University of Michigan Press.

Gintis, H., Bowles, S., Boyd, R., and Fehr, E. 2005. *Moral Sentiments and Material Interests: On the Foundations of Cooperation in Economic Life.* Cambridge, Mass.: MIT Press.

Groseclose, T., and Snyder, J. 2001. Estimating party influence on congressional roll call voting: regression coefficients vs. classification success. *American Political Science Review,* 95: 689–98.

Grossman, G. M., and Helpman, E. 1996. Electoral competition and special interest politics. *Review of Economic Studies,* 63: 265–86.

Hirshleifer, J. 2001. On the emotions as guarantors of threats and promises. In J. Hirshleifer, *The Dark Side of the Force.* Cambridge: Cambridge University Press.

Krehbiel, K. 1991. *Information and Legislative Organization.* Ann Arbor: University of Michigan Press.

—— 1993. Where's the party? *British Journal of Political Science,* 23: 235–66.

—— 1998. *Pivotal Politics.* Chicago: University of Chicago Press.

―― and SHEPSLE, K. A. 1996. *Making and Breaking Governments: Cabinets and Legislatures in Parliamentary Democracies*. Cambridge: Cambridge University Press.
LE BRETON, M., and WEBER, S. 2003. The art of making everybody happy: how to prevent a secession. *IMF Staff Papers*, 50: 403–35.
MCKELVEY, R., and ORDESHOOK, P. 1986. Information, electoral equilibria, and the democratic ideal. *Journal of Politics*, 48: 909–37.
MARKS, B. A. 1988. A model of judicial influence on congressional policymaking: *Grove City College v. Bell*. Working Paper 88–7, Hoover Institution, Stanford University.
MAYHEW, D. 1974. *Congress: The Electoral Connection*. New Haven, Conn.: Yale University Press.
NORTH, D. C. 1981. *Structure and Change in Economic History*. New York: Cambridge University Press.
―― 2005. *Understanding the Process of Economic Change*. Princeton, NJ: Princeton University Press.
OLSON, M. 2001. *Power and Prosperity: Outgrowing Communist and Capitalist Dictatorships*. New York: Basic Books.
PRAT, A. 2002. Campaign advertising and voter welfare. *Review of Economic Studies*, 69: 997–1017.
SHEPSLE, K. A. 1978. *Giant Jigsaw Puzzle*. Chicago: University of Chicago Press.
―― and WEINGAST, B. R. 1981. Structure-induced equilibrium and legislative choice. *Public Choice*, 37: 503–19.
―― ―― 1995. Introduction. In *Positive Theories of Congressional Institutions*, ed. K. A. Shepsle and B. R. Weingast. Ann Arbor: University of Michigan Press.
SMITH, A. 2003. Election timing in majoritarian parliaments. *British Journal of Political Science*, 33: 397–418.
―― 2004. *Election Timing*. Cambridge: Cambridge University Press.
TIEBOUT, C. 1956. The pure theory of local expenditures. *Journal of Political Economy*, 64: 16–24.
TULLOCK, G. 1987. *Autocracy*. Hingham, Mass.: Kluwer Academic.
WEINGAST, B. R. 2002. Rational choice institutionalism. In *Political Science: State of the Discipline*, ed. I. Katznelson and H. Milnor. New York: Norton.
―― and MARSHALL, W. J. 1988. The industrial organization of Congress: why legislatures, like firms, are not organized as markets. *Journal of Political Economy*, 96: 132–63.
WITTMAN, D. 1989. Why democracies produce efficient results. *Journal of Political Economy*, 97: 1395–424.
―― 1995. *The Myth of Democratic Failure*. Chicago: University of Chicago Press.
―― 2000. The wealth and size of nations. *Journal of Conflict Resolution*, 44: 885–95.
―― 2005. Pressure groups and political advertising: how uninformed voters can use strategic rules of thumb. Working paper, Dept. of Economics, University of California, Santa Cruz.
―― forthcoming. Candidate quality, pressure group endorsements, and the nature of political advertising. *European Journal of Political Economy*.

PART II

VOTERS, CANDIDATES, AND PRESSURE GROUPS

PART II

VOTERS, CANDIDATES, AND PRESSURE GROUPS

CHAPTER 2

VOTERS, CANDIDATES, AND PARTIES

STEPHEN ANSOLABEHERE

FIFTY years ago, Anthony Downs's *An Economic Theory of Democracy* laid the foundations for what has become the modern political economy theory of elections. Downs presents a simple model of the motivations of voters, candidates, and parties. He begins where classical democratic theory begins—with the assumption that people seek their self-interest in politics. In a society where individuals rationally pursue their self-interest, who wins in democratic elections and what policies will government follow?

Voters, in Downs's treatment, are concerned about the policies that the government will implement. Policy choices involve trade-offs which can be represented as a single dimension, such as more or less restrictive money supply, or more or less government spending. Each voter has spatial preferences over the issue, characterized by a policy that the individual most prefers, deviations from which lead to less good outcomes for that voter.

For their part, politicians seek to win office, and parties, which are treated as teams of politicians, seek to win control of the government. Electoral politics consists of the policy promises that candidates and parties offer to implement if elected. Voters choose the candidate closest to their ideal policy.

From this model come a set of predictions about the behavior of voters, candidates, and parties that have organized contemporary political economy and political science more broadly. The core prediction holds that competition for office will lead candidates and parties to represent the public policies that most strongly appeal to the median voter.

The spatial theory of voting has proven extremely successful. Any issue that can be characterized as involving conflicting beliefs or preferences among voters may be viewed through the lens of the spatial model. As a result, the framework has been widely used to describe the general ideological clash between political parties or social classes and the politics of social issues, such as abortion and race relations.[1]

The analytical simplicity of the approach has paved the way for wide application to the operation of governments. Legislatures, courts, and administrative agencies make collective decisions under majority rule and super-majority rule, and executives also have a "vote" in the making of laws, such as the power to make proposals in parliaments and veto power in the USA. The logic behind the median voter result emerges throughout the extensive literature that characterizes the politics of group decision-making along a spatial or ideological dimension. Indeed, theorists often characterize an electorate or committee with just the ideal policy of the median voter.[2]

The political economy approach has also revolutionized the methodology of political science. At the time *An Economic Theory of Democracy* was written, political science was dominated by behavioralism, which draws heavily on social psychology. Strong correlations, such as between partisan identification and voter preference or between education and political participation, are often taken as basic, behavioral relationships. But the application of economic reasoning and of game theory to politics changed the way scholars think about the basic correlations in aggregate electoral and survey data. The behavior we observe, such as election results and the policies parties pursue, reflects the equilibrium among competing candidates and voters, as well as basic behavioral or structural relationships. Although the psychology of the spatial model is quite spare, it offers a powerful approach to the study of political strategy and the forces that shape collective decision-making.

The wide adoption of the economic methodology to the study of elections, however, should not lead us to believe that the spatial framework provides a complete or even consistent characterization of electoral politics. The theory is, in many respects, a work in progress, and its development has proceeded in response to critiques of the consistency of the theory and empirical failings of its predictions. Four lines of criticism have been particularly important, and I will organize my discussion around these.

First, the assumption that individuals maximize their self-interest in politics immediately leads to two paradoxes—rational non-participation and rational ignorance. If an individual did not vote, the results of a national election would differ imperceptibly. The marginal benefits to voting and of becoming informed so as to

---

[1] Page and Shapiro 1992 offer a critical examination of the spatial model applied to survey data in the United States. Russell Dalton 2002 provides an extensive analysis of public opinion, voting, and representation in advanced industrial economies.

[2] See, for example, Krehbiel 1998. The models analyzed there represent the committees and the entire legislature with just the median (or other pivotal player) of those bodies.

make the correct decision, therefore, must be extremely small, much smaller than the inconvenience of voting and of learning about public affairs.

Second, the spatial characterization of preferences does not capture many aspects of the electoral decision that are of paramount importance. Voters value performance as much as policy. On many questions people do not disagree about policy. Rather, they want the government to produce better outcomes, regardless of the policy. Indeed, the abilities of politicians to lead and to govern may be more important than the policies promised.

Third, the central prediction of the spatial theory, the median voter theorem, does not hold. Candidates and parties generally do not converge on the median voter's ideal policy. This problem has been perhaps the most fruitful for the development of a more robust economic theory of elections.

Fourth, people are assumed to be fully informed about the candidates and issues of the day, yet nearly a century of public opinion research has shown the striking lack of information about public affairs and electoral choices. Voters may want to find the best possible candidate or party, but they are only rational to the extent to which they understand the choices. How do voters steer through the maze of claims and counter-claims in contemporary campaigns? And, at the end of the campaign, are voters sufficiently informed to cast a vote consistent with their own interests or beliefs about what is right?

In the pages that follow, I will discuss the response to each of these four problems. While I will organize the discussion around the problems themselves, one overarching theme deserves emphasis. In thinking about these puzzles and problems, the contemporary economic theory of democracy has moved away from the individualism embodied in traditional democratic theory, such as that of John Locke and James Madison, and has moved much closer to sociology and psychology.

The assumption of narrow self-interest or maximizing *private* benefits, such as income, has slowly leached out of the economic theory of democracy. In its place, contemporary theorists assign voters generic spatial preferences and put aside the question of why people vote. Voters have beliefs about what is best for them or society and they act accordingly. Involvement in politics has become a "consumption" benefit, rather than a pecuniary one.

Political economists have also come to recognize that individuals do not act alone in the political sphere. Groups, especially political parties, structure the choices in elections. Party identification and party labels, social psychologists have long told us, provide the information for vote choice.[3] Parties also determine how we assess performance of the government and how candidates are selected to run for office, and they even determine what is left and right in politics.

The challenge facing contemporary political economists is to understand the implications of moving away from an individualistic and narrowly self-interested model of the voter. Why are parties essential to democracy? Why do people perceive politics in terms of ideology? Such questions, of course, lie at the heart of political science

---

[3] This is spelled out most clearly in Campbell et al. 1960.

generally. Emerging to the response to these four problems, then, is a more comprehensive theory of politics.

1 MODELING PERFORMANCE AND POLICY

An early critique of the spatial model came from social psychologist Donald Stokes (1963). Stokes argued that ideological issues matter relatively little to people compared to assessments of the attributes of the candidates or the performance of the incumbent administration. All voters may want more economic growth or more spending on local projects. They may want lower crime and traffic safety. All may desire international peace, democracy, and national unity. All other things being equal, voters may want someone whom they know and trust, who is honest, or who is more competent in the administration of government. These are examples of what Stokes termed valence issues—matters on which voters agree on the general objective on which they judge, not the candidates' promises or policies but their personal attributes or performance in office.

Evidence of such factors abounds in empirical research on elections and the economy and on the psychology of voting. Voters reward incumbent presidents for good times and punish them for bad times.[4] Another sort of valence advantage is a politician's personal vote. Incumbent politicians in the United States have significant personal votes derived from the things they have done for constituents, their higher levels of name recognition, and simply the selection process.[5] Also, the governing party in a parliamentary system may expect to have an electoral advantage in the general election. The sitting prime minister calls elections, and elections are called strategically so that the circumstances of the election are most favorable to the sitting government.[6]

Valence issues are easily incorporated into the simple spatial model. For simplicity of exposition, I will assume that the valence term captures the competence of the candidate or party, which in turn translates into better economic performance. A candidate's competence is a fixed attribute; it is not something the candidate can maximize or alter during a campaign. A positive valence means that this candidate has better than average competence in governing. Voters judge candidates not only on the basis of their policy promises, but also on the basis of their competence. If the candidates promise identical policies, then all voters will choose the candidate with the higher valence term. The differential between candidates' valence attributes is termed their valence advantage (or deficit).

---

[4] See Hibbs (this volume) for an extensive discussion.
[5] See Levitt and Wolfram 1997 and Ansolabehere and Snyder 2002 for evidence on the extent of personal voting and incumbency advantages. Cain, Ferejohn, and Fiorina 1987 offer an extensive examination of the sources of the personal vote in the United States and United Kingdom. Jacobson 1997 documents that differential candidate experience matters in elections.
[6] Baron 1998 develops a general model of parliamentary governments.

The addition of the valence term alters voter decision-making and the logic of spatial competition. Specifically, some voters will choose a more competent candidate, even if the other candidate is ideologically closer to those voters' ideal points. A simple formulation helps make clear exactly how this more complicated model works. Let z be the ideal point of a voter along a spatial dimension Z. Suppose that there are two candidates, A and B. Let candidate A's and candidate B's positions along Z be the points a and b, respectively. Let v be the net valence difference between candidates. The net utility that voter z receives from candidate A versus candidate B is: $\Delta U = v - (z - a)^2 + (z - b)^2$. The voter chooses A if ΔU is bigger than 0 and she chooses B if ΔU is less than 0.

Introducing the valence issue immediately affects the electoral outcome. As with the simple spatial calculus, one can determine the voter who is indifferent between the parties and characterize that voter's ideal policy. That voter's ideal policy is referred to as a "cut-point" along the dimension Z. Voters with ideal policies to the left of the cut-point vote for party A and those with ideal policies to the right of the cut-point vote for party B. The cut-point is the value of z such that $\Delta U = 0$. Specifically, if the candidates are diverged:

$$c = [(a + b)/2] + [v/(2(a - b))].$$

The cut-point determines the share of votes won by the candidates. The percentage of the vote won by the left candidate is the percentage of the electorate with ideal points to the left of c.

Several empirical implications immediately follow.

First, the median voter is pivotal only in the special case where v equals 0. When voters ignore valence issues, the cut-point equals the midpoint between the candidates' positions. However, when voters value valence issues, the cut-point is no longer the midpoint but shifts to the left or right depending on which candidate enjoys the valence advantage. And, when the candidates are converged, all voters choose the advantaged candidate.

Second, the cut-point need not lie between the two candidates. If the valence advantage is large relative to the difference between the candidates, then the ideal point of the voter who is indifferent between the candidates may lie outside the interval between the two candidates' positions. Empirical researchers commonly assume that the voter who is indifferent between the candidates lies between the candidates. Typically, the midpoint is used to measure the cut-point. For example, analyses of surveys such as the National Election Study usually take as given that the voter indifferent between the candidates lies toward the "center" (Brady and Sniderman 1985; Rabinowitz and MacDonald 1989). Also, studies of elections and roll call voting use the midpoint between the candidates as measures of the ideal point of the indifferent voter (Platt, Poole, and Rosenthal 1992). This assumption is acceptable if voters ignore valence issues. However, when valence issues or candidate attributes take on importance, such as incumbency advantages or economic performance, this assumption is no longer valid. To estimate the position of the indifferent voter one must measure the valence issues as well as the parties' ideological positions.

Third, the electoral effect of a candidate's personal vote, especially the incumbency advantage, ought to depend on the ideological positions of the candidates. In analysis of legislative elections, the personal vote is the valence advantage that a candidate enjoys because he or she has the attributes sought by the constituency. Once in office, the things a politician does, such as constituent service, might add to that personal vote. The formula for the cut-point suggests that the positions of the candidates or parties should affect the magnitude of a candidate's personal vote. Suppose for instance that candidates are drawn from the same pool of talent over time and that all candidates run under their parties' ideological labels, but that the distance between the parties changes over time. When the parties are far apart, changes in the personal vote and incumbency advantage will alter a candidate's vote share only a small amount. However, when the parties are close together the personal vote will have a much larger affect on election results. The effect of incumbency on votes, then, ought to depend on the positions of the candidates and parties.

Fourth, the cut-point analysis suggests a particular specification for the analysis of aggregate election results: regress vote shares on the midpoint between the parties and indicators of performance divided by the distance between the parties. This simple insight has gone unnoticed in the extensive literatures on national, legislative, and state elections.

The literature on economic voting and election forecasts is a case in point. An extensive literature uses economic indicators such as income growth or unemployment to predict elections. The coefficients from a regression are used to construct an equation from which one may forecast the vote shares of the parties under the circumstances that may hold in a future election (see for example Fair 1996). Such data analyses do not include ideology; hence, voters either do not value ideology or ideology independently affects the vote. The cut-point analysis implies that the latter is definitely untrue. Changes in economic performance are captured by the valence term v. Changes in v affect the cut-point, but the magnitude of the effect depends on the distance between the parties, i.e. $a - b$. When the parties are quite distinct, the effect of a change in the economy on the vote will be muted. But, when the parties are nearly converged, slight changes in economic performance will have substantial effects on the vote. The specification that emerges from the cut-point analysis is that the presidential vote won by the incumbent party should be regressed on estimates of the midpoint between the candidates and the economic indicators divided by the distance between the presidential candidates in a given election. The positions of the candidates can be derived from survey data.

It is worth noting that the comparative statics for the cut-point do not mean that ideology "matters" more or less in the psychology of individual voters. The utility function of the voter does not change. Rather, the positioning of the candidates affects on what basis voters can distinguish the candidates. Analyses of survey results do not measure the actual structure of voter preferences but revealed preferences, given the positions of the candidates. I direct this comment primarily at those using survey data to "test" the spatial theory. A number of odd results in the literature, such as directional voting (Rabinowitz and MacDonald 1989) or asymmetries in spatial perceptions (Brady and Sniderman 1985), may result from the assumed positions of the candidates in survey research analyses or the assumption that the indifferent voter is the one midway between the candidates.

Stokes's assertion that valence issues matter, thus, seems correct and correctable. Inclusion of a valence term can capture assessments of candidate competence, integrity, and performance. This simple generalization of voter preferences, however, surely changes the incentives facing candidates and parties, and, therefore, what positions candidates ought to take in equilibrium. The question of candidate positioning represents an even more significant empirical challenge to the spatial theory of elections, and one to which I now turn.

2 WHY DO CANDIDATES DIVERGE?

The median voter theorem is perhaps the single most important theoretical result in modern political science. It is simple and elegant; it is widely applied to the study of elections and government; and, by most accounts, it is false.

In a two-candidate election or two-party system, the simple spatial model predicts that the competing candidates will promise the same policy—that preferred most by the median voter. The settings most likely to approximate the assumptions of this theory are the US Congress and presidency and the UK Parliament. Extensive studies of British and American elections find that the parties in fact take divergent positions, and neither party represents the median voter's ideal policy.[7]

Political economists take the median voter theorem the same way many biologists view the Hardy–Weinberg Law. The strong empirical prediction is almost surely wrong and, as a result, one of the basic assumptions is incorrect. The challenge is to find the factor or factors that explain divergence.

Many explanations have been offered—including primary elections, incumbency advantages, political parties, uncertainty and risk aversion, interest group contributions, candidates' personal preferences, election laws, and potential third parties. I will discuss four of these explanations here.

[7] An important literature in political science examines the policy positions of the parties and their candidates in the US House of Representatives. One line examines the roll call votes of candidates who have served in the House and run against each other, as happens when one candidate beats an incumbent (Fiorina 1974; Ansolabehere, Snyder, and Stewart 2001). The second line examines surveys of candidates for office (Erikson and Wright 1997; Ansolabehere, Snyder, and Stewart 2001). While both face sample selection problems, they show very similar patterns. There is a large gap between the average Democratic candidate and the average Republican candidate overall, and the candidates competing with each other within a given district almost always take different positions, with the Democrat on the left and the Republican on the right.

Valence issues. Valence issues yield a median voter result with divergence. When one candidate or party expects to have a valence advantage the candidates will stake out divergent positions along the policy dimension. Ansolabehere and Snyder (2000) and Wittman (2005) provide general conditions under which equilibria will exist and the characteristics of equilibria. In the simplest case, two candidates seek to win office (rather than vote maximization); one has a fixed advantage that all voters consume; and voters' utilities are as described in the previous section. The candidate with the valence advantage locates at the median voter and wins with certainty. The other candidate can locate anywhere. If voters have random utilities and candidates maximize the probability of winning, the advantaged candidate will locate at the median and the disadvantaged candidate will locate some distance away from the median in order to maximize his chance of winning. If the disadvantaged candidate is too close to the advantaged candidate voters will only be able to distinguish the candidates on the basis of the valence advantage and the advantaged candidate will have very high probability of winning. If the disadvantaged candidate locates very far from the median, he will attract few votes.

Contestation. Competition in the spatial model is limited to position-taking by a fixed number of candidates (two). The possibility of entry changes the logic, and leads to divergence. If entry is possible, a third party or candidate may wish to contest the election. Suppose the two parties are located at the median, as predicted by the simple theory. If the third party locates at a position a small distance from the median, the third party will win the largest share of the votes. Suppose the third party locates slightly to the left of the median. That party will win all votes to the left of that position—nearly half of the electorate—while the two incumbent parties will split the vote to the right. As a result the third party would win, and clearly has an incentive to enter.

Palfrey (1984) shows that the possibility of entry leads to an equilibrium between the two parties in which neither is at the median and the third party has no incentive to enter. His argument requires a refinement of the Nash equilibrium, as one must consider subgame perfect strategies. One equilibrium is for the incumbent parties to locate at the fortieth percentile and sixtieth percentile points. They will split the vote evenly. A third party has no incentive to enter on the right or on the left, as doing so will only make the party furthest away a certain winner, and the third party has no chance of winning. Neither party will want to move toward the middle. Doing so will prompt a third party to form slightly to the outside of that party. The third party would then win the most votes. By taking symmetric positions about the median, the two incumbent parties can therefore effectively box out entrants and will retain a fifty–fifty chance of winning.

The calculus of entry will differ with alternative electoral institutions. In a proportional representation system, for instance, a third party would be guaranteed some representation if it entered. It may then become part of a coalition government. Cox (1996) considers a wide range of electoral institutions and the effects that they have on the number of parties or candidates that will contest. Electoral institutions, Cox argues, determine the number of candidates and the positions they will take. Only the plurality rule single-member district systems create an incentive for two-party or two-candidate elections.

Candidate preferences. The resolution to the paradoxes of rationality, I have suggested, is to treat voting as consumption. People like to vote, and they are motivated to choose the candidate who is in their judgement the best alternative rather than to maximize the returns to voting. It is reasonable to project the same motivations to politicians. Wittman (1983) shows that if candidates have policy preferences and seek office to get their preferences implemented, then competing candidates will offer divergent positions. See also Besley and Coate's (1997) citizen-candidate model.

The labor market for politicians may sustain the expression of candidate preferences in electoral competition. The labor market for politics is hierarchical—those in higher positions typically started their political careers in local offices, such as school committees. Local posts are usually part-time or volunteer jobs. The appeal of such posts is the ability to make a difference in the community, rather than the pay. Those who get involved in local government, then, are motivated at first by ideological or "consumption" benefits, rather than by the value of office.

At higher levels of government most elected officials (federal and state legislators and statewide officers) are attorneys and businessmen. They are not compensated well in most democracies compared with their professional opportunities. In order to sustain such a pool of high-quality candidates, it may be the case that these politicians need non-monetary compensation in order to stay involved in politics. Voters may be willing to tolerate some extremism in order to get more professional people in office.

One objection to this account is that since anyone can run, a citizen near the median will run for office and win. A centrist has a clear incentive to enter the political arena if the sitting politician is an extremist: the centrist will surely win. Even if the median voter does not run, successive elections will choose candidates increasingly close to the median. So the median is the limit to a sequence of elections.

Ideological candidates may be sustained through the candidate selection process. In most democracies candidates are selected through party organizations or legislative caucuses. Those organizations may wish to select candidates consistent with a particular ideology. For example, unions in the United Kingdom have considerable influence on the nomination of candidates for Parliament under the Labour Party label. In the United States, primary elections tend to screen candidates. Primary electorates are drawn from the liberal and conservative segments of the ideological spectrum, and moderates have a very difficult time emerging from this process (Aldrich 1980). Those doing the nominating may not wish to trade off ideology for winning, especially if the circumstances of a given election favor the opposing party.

Political parties' platform choices. Downs assumed that political parties are teams— groups of individuals working for a common goal. The individual's utilities within a party are the same and the same as the party's. Most of the subsequent research has maintained this assumption. Cox (1996), for example, uses interchangeably parties and candidates.

Politicians within a party do not have identical interests. If one assumes that candidates simply seek to win their own seat, each politician will want the party's platform to be identical to the preference of the median voter in his district. Those in far-left seats want the party to move to the left so as to guarantee a win in their districts; those in center-left seats want to pull the party toward the middle in order to secure their seats.

Collective decision-making within parties in which there are conflicting interests leads to predictions of policy divergence. Snyder (1994) and Snyder and Ting (2002) present models of elections in which parties must first make collective decisions to choose a platform under which all must run. In equilibrium, the parties offer distinct platforms. Those on the left of the left party and the right of the right party keep their parties from converging.

Party platform choice, contestation, candidate selection, and valence issues have emerged as elements of a richer political economy theory of elections. Each of these elements is sufficient to explain the empirical regularity of policy divergence between candidates or parties. But each captures somewhat different electoral forces. A model with valence issues, for example, predicts that the advantaged candidate will take a centrist policy position, while the logic of party platform choice predicts that neither party takes a convergent policy position. None of these models, however, yields the sharp prediction against which data can be compared. As a result, the median voter theorem remains an important baseline against which we compare behavior.

3 Twin Paradoxes

More troubling than the failure of the median voter theorem, the political economy theory of elections leads immediately to two paradoxes of rationality. *An Economic Theory of Democracy*—and liberalism generally—posits that individuals seek their own self-interest. However, a theory of democracy based on narrow self-interest, such as income maximization, leads immediately to two predictions: rational non-participation and rational ignorance. Citizens should not take the time to vote or expend the considerable effort to stay abreast of public affairs. In order to have meaningful elections people must vote and understand the choices they face in order to even have meaningful elections. As such, the theory apparently implies that democracy will fail.

The argument goes as follows. Self-interested citizens, the theory prescribes, make electoral choices and take actions, such as voting or reading about politics, to maximize the expected benefits of a given action net the cost of those activities. A utility-maximizing citizen will choose a level of political activity, such that the marginal expected benefit of the activity equals the marginal cost. This is the familiar formulation of utility maximization from consumer theory in microeconomics.

Utility maximization in the electoral setting, though, leads to the conclusion that people should vote very infrequently. The marginal expected benefit consists of two components—the benefit received if one's favored candidate wins less the benefit lost if the opposition wins and the marginal effect of voting on the election outcomes. Marginal expected benefits approach zero if there is no difference between the candidates or if one's vote has an imperceptible effect on the election outcome. If the median voter theorem holds, then the candidates do not differentiate and there is no differential benefit to voting. Even if the candidates take distinct positions, the marginal effect on the outcome is about nil if the electorate is sufficiently large.

This logic implies that only those individuals whose votes make the difference between winning and losing will vote. Ledyard (1984) proves that the Nash equilibrium of a participation game is for voters to use a mixed strategy in which the probability of voting is approximately zero for most voters, and slightly higher from those near the median in a spatial model.

Downs further observes that this logic implies that an individual will not devote much effort to learning about the electoral choices. It is not an optimizing strategy to devote considerable time and effort to learning the details of the policy choices presented by competing candidates and parties. It is rational to be politically ignorant.

Compounding this logic further is the incentive to free ride, as described in Mancur Olson's *Logic of Collective Action*. If ideologically similar people are going to vote or learn about politics or participate in similar ways, why should I? Utility maximization implies that individuals will give only small amounts of money to political campaigns and will spend little time attending political meetings or engaging in other forms of political action.

These two paradoxes are deeply troubling. They raise a fundamental question about the power of the theory to explain vote choice, as well as turnout. Once the individual is in the voting booth, what does the theory really predict about how the individual will behave? If the action taken is to vote and to vote for a specific candidate or party, the marginal expected utility of voting for a given candidate is still exceedingly small. If voters have random utility functions, as is commonly conjectured by empirical researchers working in this tradition, then the random component surely dwarfs the marginal expected utility calculations of voting for one candidate or another. It is hard, then, to entertain the notion that citizens are maximizing utility when they vote.

One response to this logic is to reject the theory. Donald Green and Ian Shapiro express this view most sharply in *The Pathologies of Rational Choice*. Reviewing the empirical literature they argue that the basic empirical predictions regarding turnout and competition suggest that the economic theory of democracy ought to be rejected on empirical grounds. They are most troubled by the implications of the theory for participation. Rational non-participation ought to be common, except in very close or uncertain elections. However, closeness does not lead to much higher turnout, and in very uncompetitive races people still vote at high rates—around 50 per cent in US national elections and higher in other countries.

The paradoxes of rationality, however, apply broadly to democratic theory, not just to economic reasoning. These problems are common sense, and have been considered in one form or another by those working in all of the main intellectual traditions of political science. Judge Learned Hand (1952, 93), for instance, considered these two paradoxes in reflecting on his own behavior in his essay "Democracy: its presumptions and realities" delivered to the Federal Bar Association more than two decades before Downs published his treatise. Hand wrote:

> My vote is one of the most unimportant acts of my life; if I were to acquaint myself with the matters on which it ought really to depend, if I were to try to get a judgment on which I was willing to risk affairs of even the smallest moment, I should be doing nothing else, and that seems a fatuous conclusion to a fatuous undertaking. Because, if all were done, for what after all does my single voice count among so many? Surely I can play my part better in the society where I chance to be, if I stick to my last, and leave governing to those who have the temerity to accept the job.

I first came across reference to this essay not in a critique of the spatial model or political economy, but in the classic book *Voting*, written by Bernard Berleson, Paul Lazarsfeld, and William McPhee—three of the leading sociologists of the behavioral revolution. They had no answer for Hand's observation, except to describe "political man" as somewhere between narrowly self-interested and purely other regarding. That has become the received answer for Learned Hand's observation among sociologists and pluralist thinkers in political science, but it is not an explanation. Discarding the political economy approach because it does not explain participation seems fatuous—no social science model as yet truly explains participation. For his part, Learned Hand took this paradox of democracy to be a failing of the traditional theories of democracy.

It is not, then, a failure of the political economy approach in particular, but a failure of social sciences generally that we do not yet have a coherent theory for why individuals seeking their own needs will become informed, will vote, and, given that they do vote, will vote in ways consistent with their interests and beliefs.

A second response to the paradoxes of rational ignorance and non-participation is to take on the matter directly, beginning with the assumption that people are self-interested. Generally speaking, the most promising approaches move away from calculations of citizens' personal returns or narrow self-interest, and introduce either the consumption value of voting or mechanisms for coordinating individuals to participate, especially groups.

Perhaps the first attempt to resolve the paradox of non-participation was that of William Riker and Peter Ordeshook (1968). They add to the basic mathematical formulation introduced by Downs a constant term that captures a citizen's sense of duty to vote. Individuals with sufficiently high duty will vote, and those with a low sense of duty will not.

The introduction of citizen duty represents a fundamental shift in the logic away from the view that people pursue their narrow self-interest, such as the maximization of income. Citizen duty does the trick. It generates a prediction of positive turnout, but it is not theoretically satisfying. The assumption offers little guidance for understanding who will vote and who will not vote, or who will devote themselves to learning about the issues and candidates and who will not. Citizen duty becomes the new black box.

In addition, the citizen duty term does not address the issue of what people will do once in the voting booth. In Riker and Ordeshook's formulation, those who vote are the citizens for whom their sense of duty is of sufficiently high value to offset the cost of voting. However, if we still maintain that voters maximize their expected benefits, the marginal benefit of voting for one candidate over another remains infinitesimal. Voters, then, are nearly tossing coins in the polling booth.

A further refinement on the consumption motivation is "expressive voting." This argument holds that people who care more about the outcome in the sense of having a greater utility differential in their assessments of the candidates will be more likely to vote.[8] This depends on the shapes of utility functions, but some simple implications may be derived. One simple implication is that individuals who are indifferent between the candidates (lying between the candidates on a spatial dimension) will be less likely to vote. There is some empirical support for this claim as self-described moderates and political independents do vote less than ideological extremists and strong partisans (see Rosenstone and Hansen 1993, 273).

Most contemporary political economy theorizing tacitly embraces this assumption. Formal models of elections explicitly or implicitly assume that voters merely choose the ideologically closer candidate or party. If voters care only about the ideological distance function once in the voting booth then either the loss function is the motivation for behavior or the reason for voting is independent of one's political preferences. It does not matter to the individual voter in such analyses that the action taken has only an infinitesimal affect on the expected utility. Voters, then, do not optimize expected utility; they merely consume based on the proximity of the choices.

Another way out of the paradox of non-participation is to embed individuals within social groups. A particularly promising example is the work of Coate and Conlin (2002). They build on John Harsanyi's notion of rule utilitarianism and develop the notion of group rule utilitarianism. The argument goes roughly as follows. Suppose that we all have the same preferences (to pass a certain measure), but that because of rational non-voting the measure would not pass. A rule utilitarian solution holds that we would all be better off if everyone voted than if no one voted, so the group has an incentive to create a mechanism which induces all to vote.[9]

Coate and Conlin extend this argument to the situation where there are conflicting interests or preferences at stake in an election. Individuals belong to social groups and those groups are the foundation for political competition. For example, in a vote over property taxes in a local community, there are property owners and renters. Among

---

[8] For an exposition of this idea, see Schuessler 2000.
[9] One may take this reasoning further. If the group can exert this degree of coordination, then surely it would arrive at the rule of requiring just one of the members to vote. If just one person voted the measure would pass. That member would bear the same cost of voting as when all people voted, but no one else would bear the cost of voting. Hence, group utility would be higher than if all people voted.

the members of a group the costs of voting vary. The way to maximize group utility, then, is to coordinate the members of the group such that those with high costs know that they don't have to vote and those with low costs know that they do. The actual level of voting within each group will depend on the size of the groups, the benefit from the outcome, and the distribution of costs within each group.

The answer to the paradoxes of rational ignorance and rational non-participation, then, lies in rethinking the individual's calculus. Maximizing remuneration from voting is a dead end. The two promising avenues for further enquiry are to assume that the utility derived from electoral participation and electoral choice is strictly "consumption" or to assume that there exist mechanisms for coordinating groups of individuals to political action.

The consumption approach is most widely adopted today in models of electoral competition and vote choice. The formal literature on political economy takes as given that people vote and that competition is waged over a spatial dimension, perhaps also with a valence component. This assumption allows theorists to derive a wide range of predictions about economic and social policy-making, but it ultimately restricts the political economy of elections to the analysis of vote choice, but not participation. For many applications that may be adequate, but there is considerable evidence that participation is not entirely separate from preference.

Mechanisms for coordination, such as churches, unions, political parties, and other social organizations, present a more promising avenue of future enquiry. The interesting questions from this approach are why people develop group identities and how vote coordination occurs. While Coate and Conlin model group behavior as a form of rule utilitarianism, it may be possible to treat social groups as serving individual interest. Currently, the best explanation for why people form and join organizations is that offered by Mancur Olson—political organizations are a byproduct of other social and economic activities. And membership in such groups is thought to depend on the ability of the organization to devise selective benefits for those who join. In essence, groups exist not for political ends but for private benefits and income maximization. It remains to be seen whether a model with endogenous group formation by income-maximizing individuals can sustain positive levels of political action and turnout.

The overall response to the paradoxes of rationality, though, has been to assume that voters are not motivated only by self-interest. Although subtle, this shift in interpretation is profound. It certainly takes the teeth out of the paradoxes of rationality. Something is also lost. The modern political economy of elections presents a fundamentally different idea about people's motivations. This notion reduces elections to differences of opinion, rather than differences of interests. The economic theory of democracy and liberal democratic theory more generally began with the notion that people pursue their self-interest. With self-interest as a starting point the paradoxes of rationality still seem inescapable. The paradoxes of rationality, then, amount to impossibility theorems. It is impossible for individual self-interest to drive mass politics. Instead, mass politics is determined by citizens' beliefs about what is morally right or collectively best.

4 Learning and Communication

Non-participation presents a conundrum because the logic leads to a prediction that is evidently false. About half of the American voting age population turns out for national elections even when the election is not close.

Rational ignorance has a somewhat different flavor. The logic leads to an apparently correct prediction: most people don't know much about politics and public policies, even policies that affect them directly. Indeed, the first public opinion researchers in the United States concluded that the public comes nowhere near the view of the ideal citizen assumed in most theorizing about democracy. However, if this is true, then democracy seems like something of an impossibility.

There are, in fact, two conundrums. First, if people know little, then their vote choices may be virtually random. As a result, elections may have little meaning and not be good mechanisms for controlling politicians and the government. Second, voters may be fooled. If people are not attentive, they may not know enough to judge the veracity of campaign advertising and may be swayed easily by false promises. Again, the electorate may choose politicians who will not serve as good agents.

It should be noted that the informedness of the electorate represents another notion of rationality and rational choice. Democratic theories begin with the notion that people are informed about the policies their government has implemented and about the state of the world. That information is assumed to be correct. People do not act out of irrational or incorrect beliefs about the world that they have been fooled into holding. Such a statement is a normative conjecture. Hence, V. O. Key begins his book *The Responsible Electorate* with the simple assertion that "voters are not fools." This is a hotly contested assertion, especially because of the enormous survey research literature showing that people don't know many basic facts about government or the candidates.

Yet, somehow people are able to form opinions and make autonomous decisions, and it is generally thought that public policy drives public opinion. Individual-level, in-depth studies of voter learning find that people are not readily deceived. Experiments involving campaign advertising that I conducted with Shanto Iyengar in 1994 show that voters are most responsive to messages that touch on issues of highest concern to them, such as the economy, that voters on the whole have strong and (on average) correct prior beliefs about the ideological positions of candidates, and that voters do not change their opinions in response to messages on which candidates do not have credible positions. Indeed, this sort of finding is well established in survey research dating back to the 1940s. Political communications generally reinforce individuals' predispositions rather than converting them to new ways of thinking.

Studies of aggregate public opinion, most notably Robert Erikson, Michael MacKuen, and James Stimson, *The Macro Polity*, and Ben Page and Robert Shapiro, *The Rational Public*, show that policy is responsive to public opinion. These studies document that over a forty-year period aggregate public opinion is not highly volatile, as one would expect if people randomly answered questions, and that, on issues where public sentiment has changed dramatically, such as race relations, public sentiment generally leads public policy changes. Politicians do not, then, promise what people want to hear and do whatever they, the politicians, want. Politicians and government policy respond to the electorate.

The puzzle is why and how do voters gain the information they need? One possibility is that people become informed because they have high consumption value to politics and devote considerable effort to learning the issues—voters are political junkies. But, in truth, they are not. Individuals generally score poorly on political knowledge measures, but, in aggregate or on average, public opinion reflects and responds to the basic facts about public problems, such as the state of the economy or war.

The answer, both social psychologists and political economists agree, is that a few simple facts about candidates carry a great deal of information. Perhaps the most important pieces of information are the incumbency of a candidate or party and political party labels. Nearly all people know which party controls the presidency in the USA and they have a sense of whether times are good or bad. These two pieces of information are all that are necessary to reach a judgement as to whether to reward the incumbent party.

As far as ideology is concerned, political party labels contain nearly all of the relevant information. Analyses of the American National Election Study show that people perceive the Democratic and Republican parties to be approximately located at the median of the Democratic voters and the median of Republican voters (e.g. Brady and Sniderman 1985; Page and Shapiro 1992). And the public opinion data are consistent with the extensive literature on the partisanship of representatives in the US Congress. Analysis of roll call voting data documents that the parties consist of two pools of ideologically distinct candidates. While there is some degree of responsiveness of candidates to voters' preferences, that is slight compared to the importance of party in representatives' decision-making (Ansolabehere, Snyder, and Stewart 2001). A rational voter can readily infer how a politician will vote on most matters simply from the party label.

Other sorts of seemingly vacuous news can be extremely informative. For example, Richard McKelvey and Peter Ordeshook study the effects of polls and endorsements on people's judgements about the ideological positions of competing candidates. In a series of experiments and theoretical analyses they show that news about which candidate leads in the polls can reveal to uninformed voters the knowledge held by informed voters. Moreover, McKelvey and Ordeshook (1985, 1986) argue that democracy does not require a very high density of informed people in order to produce election results that resemble those of an election in which all people are fully informed. Endorsements from groups can also have the same effect. For further discussion of information aggregation and signaling in elections, see Thomas Palfrey's chapter in this volume.

The upshot of this line of reasoning is that an individual's rational ignorance may not be a problem for democracy after all. The low levels of information that have long concerned public opinion researchers are offset by the properties of information aggregation across large numbers of people.

Polls and endorsements convey information from other citizens. A third form of information comes from the candidates and parties themselves in the form of television ads, direct mailings, speeches, door-to-door canvassing, and the like. Candidates and parties and those who fund them bear the cost of gathering, distilling, and disseminating information. How effective are campaign advertisements and expenditures, and why?

Two research traditions show starkly different results. Studies of aggregate election data find weak effects of campaign spending on election outcomes, such as vote shares and probabilities of winning (e.g. Jacobson 1980). Particularly puzzling, there is a negative correlation between House incumbents' campaign expenditures and vote shares. The methodological problem lies in untangling the simultaneous relationship between spending and election chances. Donors may be more likely to give to a "winner," just as the funds that they give to a candidate are used to affect the chances of winning.

Experimental studies of the campaign communications often find very large effects of exposure to campaign advertisements on voter turnout and voter intentions. Shanto Iyengar and I (1996) found in a laboratory study involving approximately 3,000 subjects that exposure to a single advertisement on average increased individuals' intentions to vote for the candidate featured in the ad by 7 percentage points. Alan Gerber and Donald Green have performed a set of field experiments of the effectiveness of get-out-to-vote activities involving tens of thousands of people. They find significant, and sometimes quite large, effects of canvassing, phone banks, and direct mail. They estimate that it costs about $40 to persuade the marginal voter to turn out. [10]

Why do voters believe campaign appeals, such as mailings and television ads? They don't, it turns out, believe everything they hear. Consider, for example, position-taking. Viewers of televised advertisements respond most favorably to candidate positions when those positions are consistent with the ideologies of the party and were on important issues. For example, when Democrats advertised that they were tough on crime they received less of an increase in vote support than the Republicans did. It was hard for candidates to change much what voters thought to be important and what positions voters thought the candidates represented.[11]

Is this rational behavior on the part of voters? Why might voters be able to sort through the facts this way? I think that voters, though they are not very good at probability calculations, do reason in ways that are captured by Bayesian and classical inference models. If people have strong beliefs about what the parties represent, then it is hard for individual candidates to deviate from those positions. In learning models, voters are most responsive to biased information that comes from a source they believe and gives information contrary to what one would expect that source to state (see Calvert 1985).

---

[10] They report a number of experiments in different papers. For estimates of the causal effects and costs per vote of direct voter contact see Gerber and Green 2000.

[11] Ansolabehere and Iyengar 1994.

More puzzling is the value of advertising that consists of little more than the candidate's name. Billboards and handbills often just state the candidate's name and office, and not always party and incumbency. A candidate's name seems to be a fairly minimal sort of information, except perhaps where race or ethnicity is clearly at stake. Gary Jacobson (1997) finds that the incumbency advantage is due, in part, to the higher name recognition of office-holders. Jacobson argues that knowledge of a candidate's name indicates that the candidate is willing to spend the effort to appeal to and represent voters.

Alan Gerber suggests a further dimension to and a potential problem with this reasoning. Candidates and parties must raise campaign funds to pay for political communications. If donations come from interest groups in exchange for political favors, then the fact that a candidate advertises his or her name or issue positions ought to signal to voters that the candidate has made a large number of side deals with special interests. In that case, the candidate whose name you see may be a less good representative than the alternative.[12] Hence, it is unclear whether rational voters should infer that the candidate whose name they recognize or whose positions they have learned from advertising will be a better representative. Formal analyses by Alan Gerber, Steve Coate, and others argue that voters must trade off the uncertainty associated with an unknown against the utility loss from interest group contributions. Hence, campaign financing is thought to be a necessary evil: voters must accept some interest group influence in order to get the information that they would not collect on their own. Rational ignorance, then, is costly.

An alternative argument implies that campaign contributions may serve to aggregate the information of other citizens, just as polls and surveys do. Most campaign contributions come not from interest groups, but from other citizens.[13] James Snyder and I have argued elsewhere that citizens' donations reflect a "consumption motivation," not unlike that assumed in much of the literature on electoral competition and participation (see Ansolabehere, de Figueiredo, and Snyder 2003). A well-financed candidate, then, is one who appeals to his or her natural party base and is of sufficiently high quality that the activists within the party are willing to donate to his or her campaign. If campaign fundraising mainly reflects a participation in the form of giving by others, then rational voters may be able to infer a candidate's quality from name recognition or levels of spending.

Which of these arguments is true is ultimately an empirical question. However, they reflect two different versions of the political economy approach to elections. The line of reasoning presented by Gerber, Prat, and others reflects a view that political action is motivated by private benefit and narrow self-interest. The line of reasoning beginning with Jacobson ultimately rests on the notion that participation—either in the form of giving or voting—is driven by "consumption motivations." While the consumption argument may have less sharp predictions about voter learning, the

---

[12] Examples of this line of reasoning are Gerber 1999 and Prat 2001.
[13] For a general discussion of the politics of campaign finance see Sorauf 1992.

narrow self-interest view leads us back, ultimately, to the paradox of rational non-participation of voters.

5 CONCLUSION

The economic theory of democracy has transformed political science and economics. It has introduced a methodology for theorizing about political strategy, laid out the logic of electoral competition, and distilled the implications for what government does and how well democratic government represents the public.

The theory is not without problems. The implications of the rational pursuit of self-interest in politics lead to results that are paradoxical (rational non-voting), pessimistically true (rational ignorance), or empirically falsified (the median voter theorem).

As contemporary political economy theorists have grappled with these difficulties, a somewhat different economic theory of democracy has emerged, one rooted not in narrow self-interest but in individuals' beliefs and ideologies. Ideology might be rooted in self-interest, but it need not be. Voters' preferences might as readily reflect what they believe to be morally right or socially best.[14] People vote and vote the way they do as a form of "consumption."

This shift in thinking came about in reaction to the paradoxes of rational non-participation and rational ignorance, but it has opened an entirely new vista for enquiry. Where do people's beliefs come from and what sustains voting on the basis of belief and ideology in politics? These questions have long been the purview of social psychology. However, in the quest for a coherent economic theory of democracy, political economists have increasingly pushed into understanding social organization, social groups, and the flow of information in mass societies. And our understanding of such social institutions and behavior is in its infancy.

Even still, the political economy of democracy remains closely tied to the simple model of Hotelling and Downs. The one-dimensional spatial model is the basic tool of political economy and political science, and the median voter theorem has become a convenient baseline case or null hypothesis. It is a handy interpretative guide to politics in established democracies. Deviation from the median voter theorem indicates that at least one of the simple spatial theory's assumptions no longer holds. But theorists are no longer stymied by such criticisms. The addition of valence issues, candidate preferences, electoral institutions, interest groups, and political parties to

---

[14] There is extensive evidence in the social psychology literature on economic voting that suggests voters' preferences indeed reflect their beliefs about what is socially just or in the collective interest, rather than their own personal interest. Kinder and Kiewiet 1981 offer the seminal study of this question in the area of economic voting.

the simple spatial framework has yielded a rich set of models and predictions and a more general and powerful economic theory of democracy.

References

ALDRICH, J. 1980. *Before the Convention*. Chicago: University of Chicago Press.
ANSOLABEHERE, S., DE FIGUEREIDO, J., and SNYDER, J. M., JR. 2003. Why is there so little money in US elections? *Journal of Economic Perspectives*, 17: 105–30.
—— and IYENGAR, S. 1994. Riding the wave and issue ownership: the importance of issues in political advertising and news. *Public Opinion Quarterly*, 58: 335–57.
—— —— 1996. *Going Negative*. New York: Free Press.
—— and SNYDER, J. M., JR. 2000. Valence politics. *Public Choice*, 103: 327–36.
—— —— 2002. The incumbency advantage in US elections: an analysis of state and federal offices, 1942–2000. *Election Law Journal*, 1: 315–38.
—— —— and STEWART, C. H., III. 2001. Candidate positions in US House elections. *American Journal of Political Science*, 45: 136–59.
BARON, D. 1999. Comparative dynamics of parliamentary government. *American Political Science Review*, 92: 593–609.
BERLESON, B., LAZARSFELD, P., and McPHEE, W. 1954. *Voting*. Chicago: University of Chicago Press.
BESLEY, T., and COATE, S. 1997. An economic model of representative democracy. *Quarterly Journal of Economics*, 112: 85–114.
BRADY, H., and SNIDERMAN, P. 1985. Attitude attribution: a group basis for political reasoning. *American Political Science Review*, 79: 1061–978.
CAIN, B., FEREJOHN, J., and FIORINA, M. 1987. *The Personal Vote*. Cambridge, Mass.: Harvard University Press.
CALVERT, R. 1985. The value of biased information: a rational choice model of political advice. *Journal of Politics*, 47: 530–55.
CAMPBELL, A., CONVERSE, P., MILLER, W., and STOKES, D. 1960. *The American Voter*. Chicago: University of Chicago Press.
COATE, S., and CONLIN, M. 2002. Voter turnout: theory and evidence from Texas liquor referenda. NBER Working Paper No. W8720. Available at: http://ssrn.com/abstract=297346.
COX, G. 1996. *Making Votes Count*. New York: Cambridge University Press.
DALTON, R. J. 2002. *Citizen Politics: Public Opinion and Political Parties in Advanced Industrial Democracies*, 3rd edn. New York: Chatham House.
DOWNS, A. 1957. *An Economic Theory of Democracy*. New York: Harper and Row.
ERIKSON, R. S., MACKUEN, M. B., and STIMSON, J. 2002. *The Macro Polity*. New York: Cambridge University Press.
—— and WRIGHT, G., JR. 1997. Voters, candidates, and issues in congressional elections. In *Congress Reconsidered*, ed. L. C. Dodd and B. I. Oppenheimer, 6th edn. Washington, DC: Congressional Quarterly Press.
FAIR, R. 1996. Econometrics and presidential elections. *Journal of Economic Perspectives*, 10: 89–102.
FIORINA, M. 1974. *Representatives, Roll-Calls, and Constituencies*. Lexington, Mass.: Lexington.
GERBER, A. 1999. Rational voters, candidate spending, and incomplete information. Working paper, Department of Political Science, Yale University.

_____ and GREEN, D. 2000. The effects of canvassing, telephone calls, and direct mail on voter turnout: a field experiment. *American Political Science Review*, 94: 653–63.
GREEN, D., and SHAPIRO, I. 1994. *Pathologies of Rational Choice*. New Haven, Conn.: Yale University Press.
HAND, L. 1952. Democracy: its presumptions and realities. In *The Spirit of Liberty: Papers and Addresses*. New York: Knopf.
JACOBSON, G. 1980. *Money in Congressional Elections*. New Haven, Conn.: Yale University Press.
_____ 1997. *The Politics of Congressional Elections*, 4th edn. New York: Addison-Wesley.
KEY, V. O. 1965. *The Responsible Electorate*. New York: Vintage.
KINDER, D., and KIEWIET, R. 1981. Sociotropic politics: the american case. *British Journal of Political Science*, 11: 129–61.
KREHBIEL, K. 1998. *Pivotal Politics: A Theory of U.S. Lawmaking*. Chicago: University of Chicago Press.
LEDYARD, J. 1984. The pure theory of two-candidate elections. *Public Choice*, 44: 7–41.
LEVITT, S. D., and WOLFRAM, C. D. 1997. Decomposing the sources of incumbency advantage in the US House. *Legislative Studies Quarterly*, 22: 45–60.
MCKELVEY, R., and ORDESHOOK, P. 1985. Sequential elections with limited information. *American Journal of Political Science*, 29: 480–512.
_____ _____ 1986. Information, electoral quilibria, and the democratic ideal. *Journal of Politics*, 48: 909–37.
OLSON, M. 1961. *The Logic of Collective Action*. Cambridge, Mass.: Harvard University Press.
PAGE, B., and SHAPIRO, R. 1992. *The Rational Public*. Chicago: University of Chicago Press.
PALFREY, T. R. 1984. Spatial equilibrium with entry. *Review of Economic Studies*, 51: 139–56.
PLATT, G., POOLE, K., and ROSENTHAL, H. 1992. Directional and Euclidean theories of voting behavior: a legislative comparison. *Legislative Studies Quarterly*, 17: 561–72.
PRAT, A. 2001. Campaign advertising and voter welfare. Working paper, London School of Economics.
RABINOWITZ, G., and MACDONALD, S. E. 1989. A directional theory of issue voting. *American Political Science Review*, 83: 93–121.
RIKER, W., and ORDESHOOK, P. 1968. A theory of the calculus of voting. *American Political Science Review*, 62: 28–42.
ROSENSTONE, S., and HANSEN, J. M. 1993. *Participation, Mobilization, and American Democracy*. New York: Macmillan.
SCHUESSLER, A. 2000. *The Logic of Expressive Choice*. Princeton, NJ: Princeton University Press.
SNYDER, J. M., JR. 1994. Safe seats, marginal seats, and party platforms: the logic of party platform differentiation. *Economics and Politics*, 6: 201–13.
_____ and TING, M. 2002. An informational rational for political parties. *American Journal of Political Science*, 46: 90–110.
SORAUF, F. J. 1992. *Inside Campaign Finance*. New Haven, Conn.: Yale University Press.
STOKES, D. 1963. Spatial models of party competition. *American pointical Science Review*, 57: 368–77.
WITTMAN, D. 1983. Candidate motivation: a synthesis. *American Political Science Review*, 142–57.
_____ 2005. Valence characteristics, costly policy and the median-crossing property: a diagrammatic exposition. *Public Choice*, 124: 365–82.

CHAPTER 3

RATIONAL VOTERS AND POLITICAL ADVERTISING

ANDREA PRAT

1 INTRODUCTION

Most political scholars agree that organized groups play a key role in modern democracy. One aspect of special interest politics that has caught the attention of both academic researchers and the public at large, especially in the USA, is campaign contributions. Candidates to various federal and state offices receive monetary donations from various corporations and pressure groups.[1]

What do candidates do with the money they receive from lobbies? In Western democracies, politicians appear to use contributions not mainly to increase their personal wealth but rather to finance their electoral campaigns. While electoral spending includes canvassing, the production of printed material, and organizational costs, it is television advertising that gets the lion's share of US campaign spending (Ansolabehere and Iyengar 1996).

Given this observation, it becomes clear that any theory of special interest politics must explain what political advertising does. Most existing models assume an ad hoc influence function, which maps campaign expenditure into vote share (Grossman

---

* I am grateful to Scott Ashworth and Steve Coate for providing useful comments.

[1] For a discussion of campaign finance in the USA, see Levitt 1995. In other countries, the situation is heterogeneous because of the presence of limits on campaign spending (which are discussed below). See Kaid and Holtz-Bacha 1995 for an overview of electoral campaigning in various Western democracies.

and Helpman 2001, ch. 10). The more a candidate spends (perhaps in relation to the expenditure of his opponents), the higher the share of voters who vote for him. The problem of modeling the influence function as a black box is twofold. First, results depend on the functional form we choose, but it is unclear what the most plausible form is. Second, we cannot perform welfare analysis. Unless we know what advertising does to voter utility, we cannot evaluate the relative merit of alternative regulatory regimes.

The lack of microfoundation for political advertising is a serious drawback because it prevents us from making policy recommendations. There is no consensus on how campaign finance should be regulated. Different countries have chosen radically different ways. The USA imposes some limits on contributions but leaves the expenditure side unregulated. Some European countries impose draconian limits on both contributions and expenditures, and may provide more or less generous public funding.[2] The need to build a microfounded model of campaign finance has been recognized for some time (e.g. Morton and Cameron 1992). However, it is only recently that theorists have moved in that direction. The present contribution will offer a critical review of the existing literature.

Microfounded models of campaign finance begin with the assumption that voters are rational: they are not systematically fooled by advertising.[3] However, voters may have limited information about the characteristics of candidates and the political platforms they support. Candidates may use advertising to provide voters with positive information about themselves and negative information about their opponents. There are two possible approaches to informative advertising, depending on how information transmission is modeled.

First, one may assume that advertising conveys no direct information (Potters, Sloof, and van Winden 1997; Prat 2002a, 2002b).[4] Still, it can provide information indirectly. The fact that advertising is intrinsically expensive (time on television and space on newspapers are scarce goods) means that advertising is a way to burn money publicly. The willingness and/or the ability to destroy a large amount of resources may constitute a credible signal of some otherwise non-verifiable information. For instance, in a model of repeated purchases, a new seller may burn money in order to signal to potential buyers that he has a high-quality product and that he believes that buyers will buy more of it after they experience its quality (a seller with a low-quality product would not be willing to spend the same amount on advertising because he knows that sellers will only buy from him once).

---

[2] The US Supreme Court ruled that campaign advertising constitutes political speech and cannot be in any way limited (*Buckley* v. *Valeo*, 1976). This sets the USA apart from other Western democracies, in which campaign advertising enjoys no such strong constitutional protection. For instance, in 1998 the European Court of Human Rights ruled (*Bowman* v. *UK*) that limits on campaign spending do not necessarily violate the right to freedom of expression as long as they are not unreasonably low.

[3] A microfoundation of campaign finance need not have rational voters. However, it is natural to begin by examining the case that is closer to the standard Bayesian paradigm. In the conclusion, we discuss the possibility of developing a model that incorporates cognitive biases.

[4] This approach is inspired by models of advertising used in industrial organizations, such as Kihlstrom and Riordan 1984 and Milgrom and Roberts 1986.

Second, one may assume that advertising provides information directly (Ashworth 2006; Bailey 2004; Coate 2004a, 2004b; Schultz 2003; Wittman 2004). Advertising conveys to viewers some verifiable information that would not be available otherwise. Then, providing positive information to viewers will generate a positive response.[5]

It is not clear which of the two approaches is the more realistic. In the case of political advertising, often ads convey verifiable information on the political record of the candidate or his opponents. However, it is also true that some commercials are extremely expensive but appear to contain little new information. Indeed, Ansolabehere and Iyengar (1996) use an experimental setting to show that political advertising is effective even when, by design, it contains no direct information.

The present contribution will pursue both approaches and compare their results. We use a simple model in which voters are fully rational but they are uninformed about some non-policy characteristics of candidates (valence). Specifically, with a certain probability voters observe quality directly, otherwise they are uninformed. Lobbies can make campaign contributions, which candidates can spend on advertising. We use a service-induced model of campaign finance. Candidates can make policy promises to lobbies (we briefly discuss a version with position-induced contributions).

Under both approaches to advertising, there exists a similar political equilibrium in which high-quality candidates (but not the low-quality ones) receive funds from interest groups in exchange for policies that hurt the median voter and benefit lobbies. The campaign contributions are then spent on political advertising which voters observe. If advertising is directly informative, voters learn the quality of the candidate directly. If advertising is not directly informative, voters infer that the candidate must be high quality because in equilibrium lobbies only contribute to high-quality candidates. Lobbies do not give money to low-quality candidates not out of a direct concern for quality but because they know the money will be wasted if voters find out that the candidate is actually bad.

Thus, equilibrium behavior is qualitatively similar under both approaches. Welfare implications are similar in one respect: prohibiting campaign contributions may be optimal because the informational benefit that they bring can be lower than the equilibrium policy cost they impose. As we shall see in more detail, in equilibrium good candidates may need to promise large numbers of favors in order to secure an amount of contributions that is sufficient to differentiate themselves from bad candidates. But the welfare analysis differs in one important aspect: a role for public funding of the kind used in some European countries exists only if advertising is directly informative. If advertising is non-directly informative, then public financing cannot convey to voters any information, and it is purely wasteful.

---

[5] Austen-Smith 1987 provides the first model in which political advertising is assumed to convey direct information, even though the information transmission mechanism is represented in reduced form.

The plan of the present contribution is as follows. The next two sections consider, respectively, non-directly informative advertising and directly informative advertising. Section 4 discusses how a microfounded model of campaign finance can be used to reinterpret the available empirical evidence. Section 5 concludes with a discussion of the main lessons and possible future research.

2 Non-directly Informative Advertising

The main points of this contribution can be made in a straightforward model (a minimalist version of the one used in Prat 2002a). By keeping the formalization as simple as possible, we can use the same basic set-up to explore the two possible approaches to advertising. We now focus on non-directly informative advertising, leaving informative advertising for the next section.

There are four players: a voter, a lobby, and two candidates. There are two possible policies: $p = 0$ and $p = 1$. The voter gets utility $-p$ from policy, while the lobby gets utility hp from policy, where $h > 0$. Thus, $p = 0$ is the voter-preferred policy and $p = 1$ is the lobby-preferred policy.[6] The candidates do not care about policy: they only derive utility from being elected.

The two candidates, 1 and 2, simultaneously announce the policies that they are going to implement if elected: $p_1 \in \{0, 1\}$ and $p_2 \in \{0, 1\}$. Candidates are characterized not only by the policy stance they assume but also by some innate quality (often referred to as valence in political economy) which does not relate to policy but nevertheless affects voter utility. We assume that the quality of candidate 2 is given, while the first candidate can be good or bad. Formally, the quality of candidate 1 is given by $\theta \in \{b, g\}$, which is a random variable (the two realizations are equally likely). Quality is known to the candidates and to the lobby but not necessarily to the voter. With a certain exogenous probability $\sigma \in (0, 1)$, the voter discovers the value of θ, otherwise she does not know it. Thus, the parameter σ measures the precision of voter information.

The voter's payoff depends on quality as well as policy. The voter's utility is

$$u = \begin{cases} -p_1 + k & \text{if 1 is elected and } \theta = g \\ -p_1 - k & \text{if 1 is elected and } \theta = b \\ -p_2 & \text{if 2 is elected} \end{cases}$$

---

[6] For simplicity, assume that the lobby represents the interests of non-voters, such as foreign entities. Below, we argue that the main results would not change even if the lobby represented a minority of voters.

where k is a positive parameter that denotes the importance of valence in the eyes of the voter.

Finally, we have to describe the interaction between the lobby and the candidates. The existing papers assume that contributions are either *service induced* or *position induced*. In the service-induced case, the candidate enters a binding agreement with the lobby: in exchange for a campaign contribution, he commits to take a certain policy position. In the position-induced case, such agreements are impossible: first candidates select their policy positions, then lobbies make donations. In equilibrium, one expects candidates to choose positions that are close to the lobbies' interests in order to attract larger donations.

In this model, we use a service-induced model (we discuss a position-induced variant briefly at the end of this section). Before the electoral campaign starts, the lobby can offer any positive sum m to candidate 1.[7] If the candidate accepts the offer, he commits to announcing and implementing policy $p_1 = 1$. The candidate can use campaign contributions only to finance advertising (not to enrich himself). Furthermore, he has no personal wealth. Thus, the amount of campaign advertising equals the amount of the contribution.[8]

The lobby's payoff depends on the policy that is implemented and the size of the campaign contribution that is made. Let $e \in \{1, 2\}$ be the identity of the election winner. If the offer is accepted, the lobby's utility is $hp_e - m$. If the offer is rejected, the lobby receives hp_e. The candidates maximize the probability of being elected. Neither the lobby nor the candidates care about quality in a direct way.[9]

The timing of the game is as follows:

1. The lobby and the two candidates observe quality θ. The lobby makes an offer m to candidate 1.
2. Candidate 1 accepts or rejects the offer.
3. The two candidates simultaneously announce their policies: p_1 and p_2. If candidate 1 has accepted the offer, he must announce $p = 1$. Otherwise, he is free to announce any policy.
4. The voter observes the campaign contribution m and the two policies p_1 and p_2. With probability σ, he also observes θ. The voter votes for 1 or 2.

As candidate 2 cannot receive money from the lobby, he will always select the voter's preferred policy: $p_2 = 0$. From now on, we only focus on the other three players: the voter, the lobby, and candidate 1. Still, this is a complex signaling game with several equilibria. For instance, there are pooling equilibria in which the voter believes that campaign spending is uninformative and, therefore, the candidate never

---

[7] The assumption that only one candidate has uncertain quality and only that candidate can receive money is made for analytical convenience. See Prat 2002a for a general analysis.

[8] Another assumption that is worth spelling out is that the voter observes the policy position selected by candidate 1. At the end of the section, we briefly discuss unobservable policy.

[9] The separating equilibrium discussed below holds a fortiori if the lobby has the same preference of voters over candidate quality, while it may not exist if they have opposite preferences (Potters, Sloof, and van Winden 1997).

accepts a deal from the lobby. We focus on the simplest equilibrium in which campaign spending plays a role:

Proposition 1: *If quality is sufficiently important ($k \geq 1$), the game has a perfect Bayesian equilibrium in which:*

1. *If candidate 1 is bad ($\theta = b$), the lobby offers no money to the candidate. If he is good ($\theta = g$), the lobby offers campaign contribution*

$$m = \bar{m} \equiv h(1 - \sigma).$$

2. *If the voter does not observe the quality θ directly, she forms the following belief*

$$\tilde{\theta} = \begin{cases} b & \text{if } m < \bar{m} \\ g & \text{if } m \geq \bar{m} \end{cases}$$

If she observes θ directly, let $\tilde{\theta} = \theta$.
3. *Candidate 1 accepts an offer from the lobby if and only if $m \geq \bar{m}$. If the candidate rejects the offer, he chooses policy $p_1 = 0$.*
4. *The voter votes for 1 if and only if*

$$p_1 + \tilde{\theta} \geq 0.$$

The key to understanding this equilibrium is the campaign spending threshold

$$\bar{m} \equiv h(1 - \sigma).$$

If the voter observes that candidate 1 has received at least $\bar{m}$, she must infer that the candidate's quality is high, because the lobby would not be willing to spend that much money on a bad candidate. This is not because the lobby cares about the candidate's quality intrinsically, but rather because the lobby knows that with probability σ a bad candidate is discovered and loses the election. If the lobby strikes a deal with a bad candidate, the lobby's expected policy payoff is $h(1 - \sigma)$. By burning an amount of money equal to $\bar{m}$, the lobby supplies a credible signal that the candidate is good. Given the voter's belief, a good candidate who is offered $\bar{m}$ will be elected for sure if he accepts. Therefore, he does accept. A bad candidate receives no campaign contribution: voters learn his quality and he loses the election even if he chooses $p_1 = 0$. There is nothing a bad candidate can do to improve his situation because the lobby is not willing to contribute $\bar{m}$ to his campaign.

This equilibrium exists only if the valence dimension is sufficiently important with respect to the policy dimension: $k \geq 1$. If $k < 1$, the voter will never elect candidate 1 if he chooses $p = 1$ even if his innate quality is high.

What are the welfare implications of this simple model? The voter behaves rationally: she bases her decision on advertising because the policy cost of making a favor to the lobby (equal to 1) is lower than the benefit of having a good candidate rather than a bad one (k). So, within the same equilibrium, the informational benefit of advertising cannot be smaller than its policy cost. However, this need not be true across equilibria, and there is scope for campaign regulation that improves the voter utility. For instance, in this case a ban on contributions may be optimal.

To see this, compute the voter's expected payoff in the equilibrium above. With probability $\frac{1}{2}$, candidate 1 is good, and the voter receives utility $k - 1$. With probability $\frac{1}{2}$, the candidate is bad, and the voter elects candidate 2 and receives 0. The expected payoff is thus

$$U_c = \frac{1}{2}(k-1).$$

Suppose instead that campaign contributions are prohibited and focus on the pooling equilibrium in which the two candidates select the voter's preferred policy ($p_1 = p_2 = 0$) and the quality of candidate 1 is revealed only if there is direct information, which happens with probability σ. The expected utility is

$$U_{NC} = \frac{1}{2}\sigma k.$$

Assume that $\sigma < \frac{1}{2}$ and $k > 1$. We now see that:

Proposition 2: *Prohibiting campaign contributions increases the voter's expected payoff if and only if the quality dimension is not too important:*

$$k < \frac{1}{1-\sigma}.$$

The intuition behind the result is simple. In an equilibrium with political contributions, all good candidates sell out to the lobby. A candidate who receives no campaign money is perceived as a bad candidate and loses the election. Campaign finance brings the electorate an informational benefit (the voter always knows the quality of candidate 1) and a policy cost (all the good candidates choose the policy preferred by the lobby). If quality does not play an extremely important role in the voter's utility, the policy cost is higher than the informational benefit: the voter would be better off if contributions were prohibited.

This welfare result takes into account the utility of voters only, not that of the lobby. Note however that the result does not depend on h, the intensity of the lobby's preference. We can thus let h tend to zero, without affecting the result above. But if h is small enough and we take a utilitarian approach, the lobby's payoff becomes negligible, and Proposition 2 is still valid as stated.

The main findings of this simple model are robust to several extensions. One can examine the effect of having multiple lobbies or multiple candidates who can receive contributions, heterogeneous voters, or a richer policy space and/or signal space (Prat 2002a, 2002b).

One may also relax the assumption that voters are able to observe the policy favors that candidates promise to lobbies. In this simple two-policy setting, there would still be an equilibrium similar to the one in proposition 1. However, in a richer policy space (e.g. a line), good candidates may choose a policy that is even more skewed towards the lobby's interest (Prat 2002a).

Sloof (1999) shows that a full disclosure policy is beneficial to voters. If voters do not fully observe the deals between lobbies and candidates, it is useful to require that candidates disclose the origin of the campaign contributions they receive. In an equilibrium with disclosure, candidates who receive money from extreme lobbies are believed to have chosen extreme policies and are shunned by voters. This provides candidates with an incentive to make deals with moderate lobbies only.

Finally, one may believe that the position-induced model is more realistic than the service-induced model used here. In this particular setting, this would make no difference. To see this, keep the current set-up but assume that lobbies and candidates cannot make deals. First, candidate 1 chooses policy p; then, the lobby makes a contribution m. It is immediately clear that there exists a separating equilibrium analogous to Proposition 1, in which all good candidates select the lobby's preferred policy and receive an amount of contribution that the lobby would not be willing to give to a bad candidate. The welfare implications do not change either.

However, the finding that a position-induced model and a service-induced model produce the same results is unlikely to carry over to other settings. Coate (2004b) considers a position-induced campaign finance model in which voters are uncertain over the candidates' ideological position.[10] In turn, candidates are chosen by parties. In equilibrium, the presence of campaign contributions makes parties choose more moderate candidates. A cap on donations hurts the median voter.

3 INFORMATIVE ADVERTISING

In the previous section, advertising was just money burning and could not convey information directly. Even so, we showed that it can provide indirect information in equilibrium. We now consider the possibility that advertising provides direct information.[11] As we shall see, the main results obtained in the previous section still hold, with one important exception.

Suppose that the model is as in the previous section except that now the advertising technology is different. By spending an amount a, candidate 1 can inform all voters about his quality θ. As before, the candidate does not have personal wealth, and must rely on campaign contributions from the lobby. As it makes little sense for the lobby to make a campaign contribution which is different from zero or a, we restrict attention to $m \in \{0, a\}$.[12]

Essentially, the game follows the timing used in the previous section. First, the lobby decides whether or not to offer a to the candidate. If the candidate is offered a, he accepts or rejects the lobby's offer. If he accepts, he announces $p_1 = 1$ and spends the money on advertising to reveal his quality θ to the voter. If he rejects, he

[10] Coate 2004b uses directly informative advertising. See also Vanberg 2004.
[11] Among the existing models of informative campaign advertising, the present analysis is closest to Ashworth 2006 and Coate 2004a. Like those two papers, it includes an exchange of favors between politicians and lobbies and it reaches similar results on campaign finance regulation. However, being an extremely simplified version, it misses several other insights. For instance, in contrast to the two papers cited above, the present chapter assumes that political favors are observed by voters.
[12] We assume that the voter does not observe the amount of campaign contribution m directly.

chooses $p_1 = 0$. With probability σ the voter observes the quality directly. The voter also observes the policy announcements of the two candidates and she chooses the winner.

In the previous section, the voter formed a potentially complex belief function, which mapped every advertising level into a posterior distribution on candidate 1's quality. Now, beliefs are simpler because advertising provides hard information. Still, the voter must form a belief for the case in which she observes no advertising, which we denote with $\hat{\theta}_0$ (in this sense, indirect information transmission play a role even when advertising is directly informative).

We can show the following:

Proposition 3: *If advertising is not too expensive ($a \leq h$) and quality is sufficiently important ($k \geq 1$), there exists a perfect Bayesian equilibrium in which:*

1. *The lobby offers amount a to candidate 1 if and only if his quality is high ($\theta = g$).*
2. *If the voter does not observe the quality θ directly, she believes that candidate 1 is bad ($\hat{\theta}_0 = b$).*
3. *Candidate 1 accepts an offer of a.*
4. *The voter votes for 1 if and only if*

$$-p_1 + \tilde{\theta} \geq 0,$$

where $\tilde{\theta} = \hat{\theta}_0$ if there is no advertising, and $\tilde{\theta} = \theta$ if there is advertising.

This separating equilibrium mirrors the equilibrium with money burning described in Proposition 1. A good candidate receives an amount a from the lobby and uses it to reveal his quality to the electorate, while a bad candidate receives no money because it would be of no use revealing his quality. If the voter observes no advertising, she correctly infers that candidate 1 must be bad.

For such an equilibrium to exist, two conditions must be met. First, the candidate must be willing to accept the lobby's contribution, which is true only if the voter prefers a good candidate with the wrong policy to a bad candidate with the voter-preferred policy. This holds if the voter puts sufficient weight on innate quality ($k \geq 1$). Second, the lobby must have sufficient incentive to contribute a. Given the first condition, the lobby knows that a good candidate who advertises is elected for sure. Therefore, the lobby is willing to contribute a if the monetary cost is lower than the policy benefit ($a \leq h$).

The equilibrium with informative advertising is similar to the one with uninformative advertising which we identified in the previous section. The only difference is that the contribution level is exogenously given by a, rather than endogenously determined by the voter's belief. It is not a surprise that we obtain a welfare result identical to the one we had with non-directly informative advertising, namely:

Proposition 4: *Prohibiting campaign contributions increases the voter's expected payoff if and only if the quality dimension is not too important:*

$$k < \frac{1}{1 - \sigma}.$$

If quality matters but not too much ($k \in (1, \frac{1}{1-\sigma})$), the presence of campaign contributions generates a policy cost that is higher than the informational benefit it brings.

However, the two approaches to advertising lead to diametrically opposed conclusions with regard to public financing of electoral campaigns. Suppose candidate 1 is provided with an amount s of money which is paid for by the voter. This amount must be spent on advertising. Clearly, the presence of s makes no difference if advertising is non-directly informative. The voter knows that candidate 1 receives a given amount of public funding and she just discounts it. If instead advertising is informative, things change. If public funding is sufficient to cover the advertising cost ($s \geq a$), the candidate has no reason to make a deal with the lobby. Information about the candidate's quality is revealed at no policy cost. As long as the amount of advertising needed is not too high ($a \leq 1$), the voter prefers an equilibrium in which the candidate's quality is revealed through public funding to the equilibrium in Proposition 4. We summarize this reasoning as follows:

Proposition 5: *Public funding for electoral campaigns is inefficient if advertising is non-directly informative and can be efficient if advertising is directly informative.*

Another important insight of the direct information approach relates to the incumbency advantage. In Ashworth (2006), voters expect the incumbent to have a higher quality than the challenger (perhaps because the incumbent has undergone prior selection). Lobbies realize that, everything else equal, the incumbent is more likely to be elected and they are willing to contribute more to the incumbent's campaign. To secure the amount necessary to reveal his quality, the incumbent needs to promise lobbies fewer favors than the challenger. A challenger of a given quality is thus at a disadvantage vis-à-vis an incumbent of the same quality. This finding can explain the strong incumbency advantage observed in the USA. It also implies that the size of the advantage would be reduced by the introduction of public financing.[13]

4 IDENTIFICATION OF THE EXPENDITURE FUNCTION

Several empirical papers (surveyed in Levitt 1995) have sought to estimate the expenditure function, that is, the relationship between the amount of money that a candidate spends and his vote share. It was soon recognized that the raw relationship is misleading because the amount of money a candidate gets may be related to his

---

[13] The incumbency effect has not been studied with non-directly informative advertising. If voters observe advertising spending perfectly, one would expect no advantage for a priori favorite candidates: money burning is equally effective at all levels. However, the incumbency effect identified by Ashworth 2003 could be present if spending is not perfectly observable (as in Hertzendorf's 1993 model of commercial advertising).

quality, which in turn is linked to the vote share through other channels. Authors like Levitt (1994) have devised ingenious ways to control for unobserved heterogeneity.

We will now argue that, even if we were able to control for candidate quality perfectly, we would still face an identification problem. In a model with rational voters, the expenditure function is not a primitive. Rather, it is a complex equilibrium phenomenon that takes into account the behavior of lobbies and candidates.

This point is developed in detail in Prat (2002b), but the core argument can be sketched informally. In a separating equilibrium of a model with rational voters, there exists a positive association between these three variables: (i) the amount that a candidate spends on his campaign; (ii) the quality of that candidate; and (iii) the amount of policy favors that the candidate promises to lobbies. Of these variables, only (ii) is exogenous. Moreover, in equilibrium the vote share that a candidate receives is positively associated with (i) and (ii), and negatively associated with (iii).

Let us use our model to reinterpret the existing empirical work. The authors cited above regress vote share on (i), trying to control for (ii). However, they disregard (iii). The relationship they observe is not, as they claim, the effect on electoral outcome of an extra dollar of campaign spending (Levitt 1994). Rather, they estimate the effect on electoral outcome of an extra dollar of campaign spending net of the political cost of persuading lobbies to donate the extra dollar.

Most available estimates of the coefficient of expenditure function are very low. Some are not significantly different from zero. These estimates have been used to infer that campaign spending has little effect on electoral outcome and to make policy recommendations. For instance, Levitt (1994) argues that there is no role for public financing because spending is useless.

The same estimates have a different interpretation in a model with rational voters. A coefficient close to zero indicates that the informational benefit of advertising is offset by the political cost of raising money from lobbies. The lobbies appropriate all the informational surplus (defined as the difference in utility for the median voter between having a low-quality politician and a high-quality one) in the form of policies geared toward lobbies. This means that in equilibrium the voter faces a depressing choice between electing low-quality candidates with good policy or high-quality candidates with policy that is so bad that it makes them as valuable as a low-quality candidate with good policy. As Prat (2002b) proves, in this case prohibiting campaign contributions must be beneficial to the median voter.

On the other hand, those estimates do not imply that public financing is necessarily useless. The informational benefit of advertising may be high. If advertising provides direct information, Proposition 5 suggests a role for public financing.

Obviously, more research is needed, both theoretical and empirical. However, it is clear that campaign finance is a complex equilibrium phenomenon and that the empirical estimation strategy should follow a more structural approach in order to disentangle the various forces at play and to arrive at estimates that can be used for policy purposes. Stratmann (2003) takes a step in that direction: he exploits variations in campaign finance regulation and advertising cost across US states to differentiate between the informational effect and the political cost of campaign spending.

One promising avenue for future empirical work relates to the role of candidates' personal wealth. A rich candidate, such as Ross Perot or Jon Corzine, can fund his electoral campaign directly. Potentially, this could help distinguish between the two approaches to advertising. If advertising is not directly informative, lobbies' money certifies the quality of a candidate. It is not obvious that this role can be replicated by personal wealth. Instead, if advertising is directly informative, the origin of the funds used to pay for advertising is inconsequential.[14]

5 Discussion

We have considered a simple model of campaign finance in which voters are rational but uncertain about the quality of political candidates. In equilibrium, political advertising can provide voters with useful information, either through direct transmission or via costly signaling. The counterpart of this informational benefit is the political cost of raising campaign contributions to pay for advertising.

Despite its simplicity, the model yields several policy-relevant implications:

1. Even though voters are rational, there is scope for restricting contributions. Prohibiting contributions eliminates both the informational benefit derived from advertising and the policy cost generated by deals between lobbies and candidates. As we showed, the net effect may be positive or negative. Empirical work should attempt to estimate both components of this trade-off.
2. There may be a role for public financing of electoral campaigns, but only if advertising is directly informative.
3. A full disclosure policy is beneficial to voters. Candidates should be required to publicize the origin of the campaign contributions they receive.
4. A model of campaign finance with rational voters may explain the strong incumbency advantage observed in the USA.
5. Empirical work faces an identification problem. In a microfounded model of campaign finance, the expenditure function (the relation between candidate's expenditure and candidate's vote share) is not a primitive of the model but rather an equilibrium phenomenon.

Public opinion perceives campaign finance as a negative feature of modern democracy. Political scholars should offer a coherent conceptual framework to analyze the validity of this perception and to evaluate possible forms of regulation. The present contribution has argued that such a conceptual framework must be microfounded starting from primitive assumptions on voters' preferences and information.

All the existing papers on microfounded campaign finance assume that voters are rational, in the sense that they cannot be systematically fooled. One may object that

---

[14] Gerber 1998 uses challenger wealth as an instrumental variable in the estimation of campaign spending effectiveness.

this is an unrealistic requirement, especially in a sphere of decision-making, such as voting, which is characterized by both free riding and complexity. Agreeing with such an objection does not imply going back to the "black box." A microfounded model of campaign finance need not include full Bayesian rationality. On the contrary, it would be interesting to develop a model of campaign finance starting from non-standard assumptions on the way voters make decisions. Such model could incorporate some of the cognitive biases that are by now well documented in the psychological literature. A non-Bayesian microfounded model of campaign finance would still be amenable to welfare analysis, and may provide insights that are not available with rational voters.

References

Ansolabehere, S., and Iyengar, S. 1996. *Going Negative: How Political Advertisements Shrink and Polarize the Electorate.* New York: Free Press.

Ashworth, S. 2006. Campaign finance and voter welfare with entrenched incumbents. *American Political Science Review*, 100: 41–53.

Austen-Smith, D. 1987. Interest groups, campaign contributions, and probabilistic voting. *Public Choice*, 54: 123–39.

Bailey, M. 2004. Can representation be fair when campaign contributions come mostly from business? An exploration in multiple dimensions. Working paper, Georgetown University.

Coate, S. 2004a. Pareto improving campaign finance policy. *American Economic Review*, 94: 625–55.

——2004b. Political competition with campaign contributions and informative advertising. *Journal of the European Economic Association*, 2: 772–804.

Gerber, A. 1998. Estimating the effect of campaign spending on Senate election outcomes using instrumental variables. *American Political Science Review*, 92: 401–11.

Grossman, G. M., and Helpman, E. 2001. *Special Interest Politics.* Cambridge, Mass.: MIT Press.

Hertzendorf, M. N. 1993. I'm not a high-quality firm but I play one on TV. *RAND Journal of Economics*, 24: 236–47.

Kaid, L. L., and Holtz-Bacha, C. 1995. *Political Advertising in Western Democracies: Parties and Candidates on Television.* Beverly Hills, Calif.: Sage.

Kihlstrom, R. E., and Riordan, M. H. 1984. Advertising as a signal. *Journal of Political Economy*, 92: 427–50.

Levitt, S. D. 1994. Using repeat challengers to estimate the effect of campaign spending on election outcomes in the US House. *Journal of Political Economy*, 102: 777–98.

——1995. Policy watch: congressional campaign finance reform. *Journal of Economic Perspectives*, 9: 183–94.

Milgrom, P., and Roberts, J. 1986. Price and advertising signals of product quality. *Journal of Political Economy*, 94: 796–821.

Morton, R., and Cameron, C. 1992. Elections and the theory of campaign contributions: a survey and critical analysis. *Economics and Politics*, 4: 79–108.

POTTERS, J., SLOOF, R., and VAN WINDEN, F. 1997. Campaign expenditures, contributions and direct endorsements: the strategic use of information and money to influence voter behavior. *European Journal of Political Economy*, 13: 1–31.

PRAT, A. 2002a. Campaign advertising and voter welfare. *Review of Economic Studies*, 69: 997–1017.

—— 2002b. Campaign spending with office-seeking politicians, rational voters, and multiple lobbies. *Journal of Economic Theory*, 103: 162–89.

SCHULTZ, C. 2003. Strategic campaigns and redistributive politics. Working paper, Copenhagen University.

SLOOF, R. 1999. Campaign contributions and the desirability of full disclosure laws. *Economics and Politics*, 11: 83–107.

STRATMANN, T. 2003. Tainted money? Contribution limits and the effectiveness of campaign spending. Working paper, George Mason University.

VANBERG, C. 2004. The implications of funding asymmetries in a model of electoral competition with informative advertising and rational voting. Working paper, Cornell University.

WITTMAN, D. 2004. Candidate quality, pressure group endorsements, and the nature of political advertising. Working paper, University of California, Santa Cruz; forthcoming in *European Journal of Political Economy*.

CHAPTER 4

CANDIDATE OBJECTIVES AND ELECTORAL EQUILIBRIUM

JOHN DUGGAN

1 INTRODUCTION

ELECTIONS, as the institution through which citizens choose their political agents, are at the core of representative democracy, and it is therefore appropriate that they occupy a central position in the study of democratic politics. The formal analysis of elections traces back to the work of Hotelling (1929) and Downs (1957), who apply mathematical methods to understand the outcomes of elections. This work, and the literature stemming from it, has focused mainly on the positional aspects of electoral campaigns, where we conceptualize candidates as adopting positions in a "space" of possible policies prior to an election. In this chapter, I maintain that focus by considering the main results for the canonical model of elections, in which candidates adopt policy platforms simultaneously and the winner is committed to the platform on which he or she ran. These models abstract from much of the structural detail of elections, including primary elections, campaign finance and advertising, the role of interest groups, etc. Nevertheless, in order to achieve a deep understanding of elections in their full complexity, it seems we must address the equilibrium effects of position-taking by candidates in elections.

* I thank David Epstein, Mark Fey, Cesar Martinelli, and Martin Osborne for helpful feedback.

In this chapter, I cover known foundational results on spatial models of elections, taking up issues of equilibrium existence, the distance (or lack thereof) between the equilibrium policy positions of the candidates, and the characterization of equilibria in terms of their social welfare properties. The chapter is structured primarily according to assumptions on voting behavior. I first consider results for the case in which candidates can precisely predict the behavior of voters, who are modeled in a deterministic fashion. I refer to this as the "Downsian model." I then consider two models of probabilistic voting, where voting behavior cannot be precisely predicted by the candidates and is modeled as a random variable. Within each section, I consider the most common objective functions used to model the electoral incentives of different types of candidates, including candidates who seek only to win the election, candidates who seek to maximize their share of the vote, and candidates who seek the best policy outcome from the election.

Of several themes in the chapter, most prominent is the difficulty in obtaining existence of equilibrium, especially when the policy space is multidimensional. As a point of reference for the existence issue, early articles by Debreu (1952), Fan (1952), and Glicksberg (1952) give useful sufficient conditions for existence of equilibrium in the games we analyze.[1] Their existence result, which we will refer to as the "DFG theorem," first assumes each player's set of strategies is a subset of $\Re^n$ that is non-empty, compact (so it is described by a well-defined boundary in $\Re^n$), and convex (so a player may move from one strategy toward any other with no constraints). These regularity assumptions are easily satisfied in most models. Second, and key to our analysis, DFG assumes that the objective function of each player is:

- jointly continuous in the strategies of all players (so small changes in the strategies of the players lead to small changes in payoffs)
- quasi-concave in that player's own strategy, given any strategies for the other players (so any move toward a better strategy increases a player's payoff).

These continuity and convexity conditions are typically violated in electoral models. We will see that in some cases existence of equilibrium can be obtained despite this obstacle, but in many cases it cannot.

The well-known median voter theorem establishes that there is a unique equilibrium in the unidimensional Downsian model, and in it both candidates locate at the median of the voters' ideal policies. When the policy space is multidimensional, however, equilibria typically do not exist in the Downsian model. Probabilistic voting smooths the objective functions of the candidates and is commonly thought to mitigate the existence problem. We will give reasonable (if somewhat restrictive) conditions under which this is true for vote-motivated candidates, but, due to non-convexities in other models, probabilistic voting can actually introduce non-existence of equilibrium, even in one dimension.

---

[1] Nash 1950 proves existence of mixed strategy equilibrium for finite games. Since our games involve convex (and therefore infinite) policy spaces, his result does not apply here.

2 The Electoral Framework

We will focus on the spatial model of politics, as elaborated by Davis, Hinich, and Ordeshook (1970), Ordeshook (1986), and Austen-Smith and Banks (1999). Here, we assume that the policy space X is a subset of Euclidean space of some finite dimension, d. Thus, a policy is a vector $x = (x_1, \ldots, x_d)$, where x_k may denote the amount of spending on some project or a position on some issue, suitably quantified. We assume that X is non-empty, compact, and convex. We consider an election with just two political candidates, A and B (sometimes interpreted as parties), and we analyze an abstract model of campaigns: we assume that the candidates simultaneously announce policy positions x_A and x_B in the space X, and we assume that the winning candidate is committed to his or her campaign promise. Following these announcements, a finite, odd number n of voters, denoted $i = 1, 2, \ldots, n$, cast their ballots $b_i \in \{1, 0\}$, where $b_i = 1$ denotes a vote for candidate A and $b_i = 0$ denotes a vote for B, the winner being the candidate with the most votes. We do not allow abstention by voters.

To describe the various objectives attributed to candidates in the literature, let $U_A(x_A, x_B, b_1, \ldots, b_n)$ denote candidate A's utility when the candidates take positions x_A and x_B and the vector of ballots is $(b_1, \ldots, b_n)$. Define the notation $U_B(x_A, x_B, b_1, \ldots, b_n)$ similarly. The first main approach to modeling candidate objectives is to view the candidates as primarily concerned with their electoral prospects. Accordingly, our first objective function dictates that a candidate cares only about whether he or she garners a majority of votes. In other words, only the sign, rather than the magnitude, of the margin of victory matters.

Win motivation. The candidates receive utility equal to one from winning, zero otherwise, so that

$$U_A(x_A, x_B, b_1, \ldots, b_n) = \begin{cases} 1 & \text{if } \sum_i b_i > \frac{n}{2} \\ 0 & \text{if } \sum_i b_i < \frac{n}{2}, \end{cases}$$

with candidate B's utility equal to one minus the above quantity.

The second objective function also captures the idea that candidates care primarily about electoral success, but now measured in the number of votes for the candidate.

Vote motivation. The candidates' utilities take the simple linear form

$$U_A(x_A, x_B, b_1, \ldots, b_n) = \sum_i b_i,$$

with candidate B's utility being $n - \sum_i b_i$.[2]

By the term *office motivation*, we refer to the situation in which either both candidates are win motivated or both are vote motivated. The second main approach to

---

[2] Note that, since we rule out abstention by voters, vote motivation is equivalent by a positive affine transformation to plurality motivation: the margin of victory for candidate A, for example, is just $(2 \sum b_i) - n$.

modeling candidate objectives is to assume that candidates care only about the policy outcome of the election.

Policy motivation. Assume the candidates have policy preferences represented by strictly concave, differentiable utility functions u_A and u_B. In words, the graphs of these utility functions are smooth and "dome shaped." Under these assumptions, each candidate has an *ideal policy*, which yields a strictly higher utility than all other policies, and we denote these as $\tilde{x}_A$ and $\tilde{x}_B$. We assume these ideal policies are distinct, so that $\tilde{x}_A \neq \tilde{x}_B$. Then candidate A's utility from policy positions x_A and x_B and ballots $(b_1, \ldots, b_n)$ is

$$U_A(x_A, x_B, b_1, \ldots, b_n) = \begin{cases} u_A(x_A) & \text{if } \sum_i b_i > \frac{n}{2} \\ u_A(x_B) & \text{if } \sum_i b_i < \frac{n}{2}, \end{cases}$$

and likewise for candidate B.

To model voting behavior, let $P_i(x_A, x_B)$ denote the probability that voter i votes for candidate A, i.e. casts ballot $b_i = 1$, given policy platforms x_A and x_B. The probability of a vote for candidate B is then $1 - P_i(x_A, x_B)$. This representation of voting behavior allows for voters to vote in a deterministic fashion or, perhaps reflecting a lack of information on the candidates' parts, in a probabilistic way. Finally, let $P(x_A, x_B)$ denote the probability that candidate A wins the election, given the individual vote probabilities. Of course, B's probability of winning is one minus this amount. We assume that candidates are expected utility maximizers, so that candidate A seeks to maximize $E[U_A(x_A, x_B, b_1, \ldots, b_n)]$, where the expectation is taken over vectors of ballots $(b_1, \ldots, b_n)$ with respect to the distribution induced by the $P_i(x_A, x_B)$ probabilities, and likewise for candidate B. If we "integrate out" the vector of ballots, we may write expected utilities as functions $EU_A(x_A, x_B)$ and $EU_B(x_A, x_B)$ of the candidates' policy positions alone.

Given these expected utilities, we may subject the electoral model to an equilibrium analysis to illuminate the locational incentives of the candidates. We say a pair (x_A^*, x_B^*) of policy platforms is an *equilibrium* if neither candidate can gain by unilaterally deviating, i.e. we have

$$EU_A(y, x_B^*) \leq EU_A(x_A^*, x_B^*) \quad \text{and} \quad EU_B(x_A^*, y) \leq EU_B(x_A^*, x_B^*)$$

for all policies y.

3 THE DOWNSIAN MODEL

We now specify voting behavior, following Downs (1957) and others, by assuming that voters vote in an essentially deterministic fashion as a function of the candidates' platforms: each voter simply votes for the candidate who offers the best political platform, voting in a random way (by flipping a fair coin) only when indifferent.

Downsian model. We assume that each voter i has preferences over policies represented by a utility function u_i satisfying strict concavity and differentiability (the same conditions imposed on candidate utilities under policy motivation). Under these assumptions, voter i has a unique *ideal policy*, denoted $\tilde{x}_i$, which yields a strictly higher utility than any other policy. A common special case is quadratic utility, in which a voter cares only about the distance of a policy from his or her ideal policy, e.g. $u_i(x) = -||x - \tilde{x}_i||^2$ for all x (where $||\cdot||$ is the usual Euclidean norm). In this case, the voters' indifference curves take the form of concentric circles centered at the ideal policy. For convenience, we assume that the ideal policies of the voters are distinct. We assume a voter votes for the candidate with the preferred policy position, randomizing only in case of indifference, i.e.

$$P_i(x_A, x_B) = \begin{cases} 1 & \text{if } u_i(x_A) > u_i(x_B) \\ 0 & \text{if } u_i(x_A) < u_i(x_B) \\ \frac{1}{2} & \text{else.} \end{cases}$$

This assumption may be interpreted as "sincere" voting. Assuming voting is costless, it is consistent with elimination of weakly dominated voting strategies in the voting game.

3.1 Office Motivation

In the Downsian model, win motivation takes the following simple form:

$$EU_A(x_A, x_B) = \begin{cases} 1 & \text{if } \#\{i \mid u_i(x_A) > u_i(x_B)\} > \#\{i \mid u_i(x_B) > u_i(x_A)\} \\ 0 & \text{if } \#\{i \mid u_i(x_B) > u_i(x_A)\} > \#\{i \mid u_i(x_A) > u_i(x_B)\} \\ \frac{1}{2} & \text{else,} \end{cases}$$

and likewise for candidate B, while the alternative of vote motivation is

$$EU_A(x_A, x_B) = \#\{i \mid u_i(x_A) > u_i(x_B)\} + \frac{1}{2}\#\{i \mid u_i(x_A) = u_i(x_B)\},$$

and likewise for B. The distinction between these two formalizations of office motivation is actually irrelevant for the equilibrium analysis under deterministic voting, and we state our results in terms of office motivation generally.

It is easy to see that both objectives are marked by discontinuities and non-convexities, so that both of the conditions needed for the DFG theorem are violated. For example, Figure 4.1 depicts the indifference curves of three voters through a policy x, along with their ideal policies. If candidate B, say, locates at the policy x, then candidate A obtains a majority of votes by locating in any of the three shaded "leaves." The candidate's utility under win motivation from locating at x' is zero, and it is one at x''. Now consider A's utility when moving from x' directly to x'': when the candidate enters the shaded leaf, the utility jumps up discontinuously to

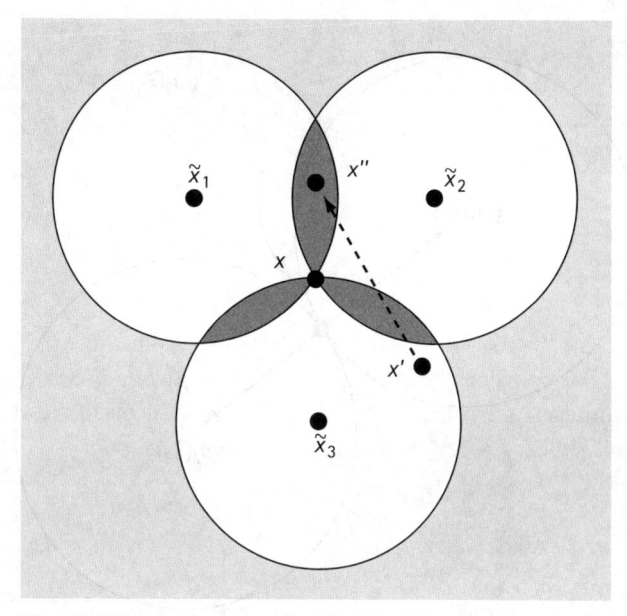

Fig. 4.1 Discontinuity and non-convexity

one (violating continuity); it then jumps back down to zero and then back up to one (violating quasi-concavity) before reaching x''. Similar observations hold for vote motivation.

The formal equilibrium analysis of the model relies on the concept of the "gradient" of a voter's utility function, the vector

$$\nabla u_i(x) = \left(\frac{\partial u_i}{\partial x_1}(x), \ldots, \frac{\partial u_i}{\partial x_d}(x)\right)$$

pointing in the direction of steepest ascent of the voter's utility at a policy x. A direct implication of Plott's (1967) social choice analysis of majority voting is that there is at most one equilibrium, and that this equilibrium (if it exists) is characterized by two conditions: both candidates locate at the ideal policy of some voter, and the gradients of the voters at that policy must be paired in such a way that, for every voter whose gradient points in one direction from the ideal policy, there is exactly one voter whose gradient points in the opposite direction. The latter condition is referred to as "radial symmetry" and is depicted in Figure 4.2, where voter 1's gradient is diametrically opposed to voter 2's.

Theorem 1: (Plott): *In the Downsian model, assume office motivation. There is at most one equilibrium. The platform pair (x_A^*, x_B^*) is an equilibrium if and only if (i) there is a voter k such that the candidates locate at k's ideal policy, i.e. $x_A^* = x_B^* = \tilde{x}_k$, and (ii) radial symmetry holds at $\tilde{x}_k$, i.e. each voter $i \neq k$ can be associated with a voter $j \neq k$ (in a 1–1 way) so that $\nabla u_j(\tilde{x})$ points in the direction opposite $\nabla u_i(\tilde{x})$.*

The most common application of the Downsian model is the unidimensional model, where policies represent positions on a single salient issue. In this case,

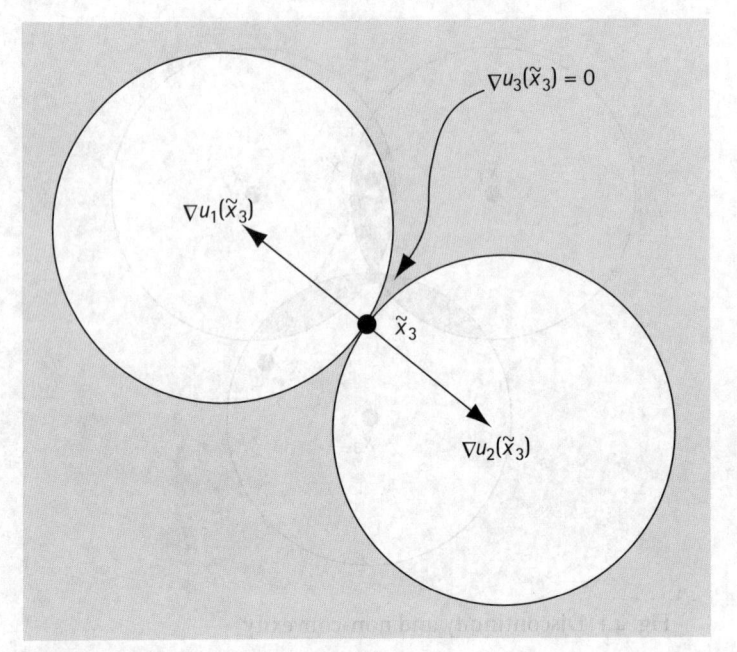

Fig. 4.2 Radial symmetry in equilibrium

Theorem 1 implies that there is a unique equilibrium, and in equilibrium the candidates both locate at the median ideal policy. Known as the "median voter theorem," this connection was made by Hotelling (1929) in his model of spatial competition and by Downs (1957) in his classic analysis of elections.

Corollary 1: (Hotelling; Downs): *In the Downsian model, assume X is unidimensional and office motivation. There is a unique equilibrium, and in equilibrium the candidates locate at the median ideal policy.*

When the policy space is multidimensional, the necessary condition of radial symmetry becomes extremely restrictive—so restrictive that it will be violated for almost all specifications of voter preferences, with the implication that equilibria will almost never exist. And if there were an equilibrium, as in Figure 4.2, then arbitrarily small perturbations of voter preferences could break radial symmetry, implying that existence is a "razor's edge" phenomenon.

3.2 Policy Motivation

The objective function representing policy motivation takes the form

$$EU_A(x_A, x_B) = \begin{cases} u_A(x_A) & \text{if } \#\{i \mid u_i(x_A) > u_i(x_B)\} > \#\{i \mid u_i(x_B) > u_i(x_A)\} \\ u_A(x_B) & \text{if } \#\{i \mid u_i(x_B) > u_i(x_A)\} > \#\{i \mid u_i(x_A) > u_i(x_B)\} \\ \frac{u_A(x_A) + u_A(x_B)}{2} & \text{else} \end{cases}$$

in the Downsian model. The above objective function also suffers from discontinuities and non-convexities, but it differs fundamentally from the office motivation in other ways. Nevertheless, Roemer (1994) proves a median voter theorem for policy motivation, and Wittman (1977) and Calvert (1985) prove related results for multidimensional policy spaces and Euclidean preferences that yield the median voter result in the special case of one dimension. As with office motivation, there is a unique equilibrium, and in equilibrium both candidates locate at the median ideal policy.

Theorem 2: (Wittman; Calvert; Roemer): *In the Downsian model, assume X is unidimensional and policy motivation. If $\tilde{x}_A < \tilde{x}_k < \tilde{x}_B$, then there is a unique equilibrium (x_A^*, x_B^*). In equilibrium, the candidates locate at the median ideal policy: $x_A^* = x_B^* = \tilde{x}_k$.*

Theorem 2 leaves open the question of whether equilibria exist when the policy space is multidimensional. Duggan and Fey (2005a) give the example depicted in Figure 4.3, where there is no equilibrium under win motivation, yet it is an equilibrium under policy motivation for the candidates to locate at voter 3's ideal policy: as the candidates' indifference curves suggest, neither can move to a position that beats $\tilde{x}_3$ in a majority vote (the shaded area in the figure) and is preferable to $\tilde{x}_3$. Furthermore, this equilibrium is robust to small perturbations in the preferences of voters and candidates, suggesting more positive results on equilibrium existence under policy motivation.

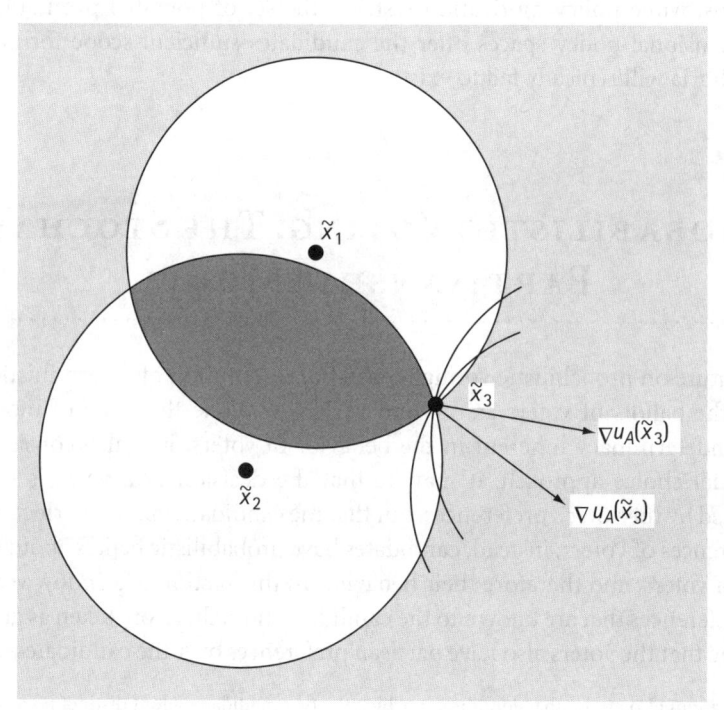

Fig. 4.3 Equilibrium with policy motivation but not win motivation

The next result shows that the kind of positive result depicted in Figure 4.3 is, unfortunately, limited to the two-dimensional case. The result, due to Duggan and Fey (2005a), gives a strong necessary condition on equilibria at which the candidates' gradients do not point in the same direction, as they do not in Figure 4.3. The first part of the condition is that the candidates must locate at the same position.[3] The second part, like radial symmetry from Theorem 1, requires that the gradients of certain voters be diametrically opposed, though now the restriction applies only to voters whose gradients do not lie on the plane spanned by the gradients of the candidates.

Theorem 3: (Duggan and Fey): *In the Downsian model, assume policy motivation. (i) If (x_A^*, x_B^*) is an equilibrium such that neither candidate locates at his or her ideal policy, then the candidates' positions are identical: $x_A^* = x_B^* = x^*$. (ii) And if the candidates' gradients at x^* do not point in the same direction, then x^* is the ideal point of some voter k, i.e. $x^* = \tilde{x}_k$; and each voter $i \neq k$ whose gradient does not lie on the plane spanned by the candidates' gradients can be associated with a voter $j \neq k$ (in a 1–1 way) so that $\nabla u_j(x^*)$ points in the direction opposite $\nabla u_i(x^*)$.*

The implications of this theorem are sharpest when the policy space has at least three dimensions: then the plane spanned by the candidates' gradients is lower dimensional, and there will typically be at least one voter whose gradient does not lie on this plane; and this voter must be exactly opposed by another. We conclude that equilibria will almost never exist, and when there is an equilibrium, it is razor's edge. Thus, while policy motivation restricts the set of potential profitable moves, multidimensional policy spaces offer the candidates sufficient scope for deviations that equilibria will typically fail to exist.

4 Probabilistic Voting: The Stochastic Partisanship Model

The literature on probabilistic voting relaxes the assumption of deterministic voting, viewing the ballots of voters as random variables. While this class of models may capture indeterminacy inherent in the behavior of voters, it is also consistent with the rational choice approach: it may be that the decision of a voter is ultimately determined by the voter's preferences, but that the candidates do not perfectly observe the preferences of voters; instead, candidates have probabilistic beliefs about the preferences of voters, and therefore their behavior. In this section, we endow voters with policy preferences that are known to the candidates (and therefore taken as given), but we assume that the voters also have partisan preferences over the candidates unrelated

---

[3] Roemer 2001 also argues that equilibria in which the two candidates adopt distinct policy positions almost never exist.

to their policy positions. The intensities of these partisan preferences are unknown to the candidates.

Stochastic partisanship model. Assume that each voter i has a strictly concave, differentiable utility function u_i, as in the deterministic voting model, but now assume a "utility bias" β_i in favor of candidate B.[4] We incorporate these biases into our model of voting behavior by assuming that i votes for A if and only if the utility of candidate A's platform exceeds that of B's platform by at least β_i. That is, i votes for A if and only if $u_i(x_A) \geq u_i(x_B) + \beta_i$, i.e. $\beta_i \leq u_i(x_A) - u_i(x_B)$. We assume that the profile $(\beta_1, \ldots, \beta_n)$ of biases is a random variable from the candidates' perspective, and we assume that each β_i is distributed (not necessarily independently) according to the distribution F_i. We assume that each F_i is continuous and strictly increasing on an interval that includes all possible utility differences $u_i(x) - u_i(y)$, as x and y range over all of X,[5] so that the probability that voter i votes for candidate A given platforms x_A and x_B is $F_i(u_i(x_A) - u_i(x_B))$. We do not assume biases are identically distributed, but we impose a weak symmetry assumption. Letting f_i denote the density of F_i, we assume for simplicity that the likelihood that a voter is unbiased is the same for all voters: $f_i(0) = f_j(0)$ for all voters i and j. A convenient special case is that in which the F_i are uniform with identical supports. We refer to this as the *uniform partisanship model.*

We first consider equilibrium existence and characterization under the assumption of vote-motivated candidates, and we then examine the results for win motivation.

4.1 Vote Motivation

In the probabilistic voting framework, vote motivation is formalized as

$$EU_A(x_A, x_B) = \sum_i P_i(x_A, x_B),$$

with $EU_B(x_A, x_B)$ equal to n minus the above quantity. Because F_i and u_i are assumed continuous, it follows that candidate A's utility, $\sum_i F_i(u_i(x_A) - u_i(x_B))$ is continuous, and likewise for B. Furthermore, as we will see, the linear form of the candidates' utilities in terms of individual vote probabilities invites a simple sufficient condition under which quasi-concavity, the second condition of the DFG theorem, holds.

Denote the unique maximizer of the sum of voter utilities by

$$\overline{x} = \arg\max_{x \in X} \sum_i u_i(x).$$

---

[4] In case β_i is negative, we can think of this as a bias for candidate A. We maintain the terminology with candidate B as the point of reference.

[5] An implication is that, given any two platforms for the candidates, there is some chance (perhaps very small) that the voter's bias outweighs any policy considerations.

This policy is often referred to as the "utilitarian optimum," suggesting welfare connotations that are difficult to justify.[6] We use the somewhat more neutral term *utilitarian point*. When voter utilities are quadratic, it is well known that the utilitarian point is equal to the mean of the voters' ideal policies.

Our first result establishes that, in equilibrium, the candidates must take the same policy position. This policy is exactly the utilitarian point, implying that the candidates must adopt the same central position in the policy space in equilibrium, regardless of the dimensionality of the policy space. Versions of this result have appeared in several places, notably in the work of Hinich (1977, 1978) and Lindbeck and Weibull (1987, 1993).[7] The general statement here is due to Banks and Duggan (2005). When voter utilities are quadratic, an implication is Hinich's "mean voter" theorem.

Theorem 4: (Hinich; Lindbeck and Weibull; Banks and Duggan): *In the stochastic partisanship model, assume vote motivation. If (x_A^*, x_B^*) is an interior equilibrium, then both candidates locate at the utilitarian point: $x_A^* = x_B^* = \overline{x}$.*

Since the objective functions of the candidates are continuous, existence of equilibrium follows from the DFG theorem if quasi-concavity holds. The sufficient condition we give is fulfilled, for example, if the bias terms of the voters are distributed uniformly or closely enough to uniform. Thus, in contrast to Theorem 1, which implies the generic non-existence of equilibria in multiple dimensions under deterministic voting, Theorem 5 offers reasonable (if somewhat restrictive) conditions that guarantee an equilibrium under probabilistic voting. Hinich, Ledyard, and Ordeshook (1972, 1973) give similar sufficient conditions in a model that allows for abstention by voters, and Lindbeck and Weibull (1993) make similar observations. By Theorem 4, if there is an equilibrium, then it is unique, and both candidates locate at the utilitarian point.[8]

Theorem 5: (Hinich, Ledyard, and Ordeshook; Lindbeck and Weibull): *In the stochastic partisanship model, assume vote motivation, and assume the following for each voter i:*

- *$F_i(u_i(x))$ is concave in x*
- *$F_i(-u_i(x))$ is convex in x.*

There exists an equilibrium.

Theorems 4 and 5 taken together may suggest a puzzling discrepancy between the Downsian and stochastic partisanship models. Consider the possibility of modifying the Downsian model by introducing a "small" amount of bias, i.e. define distributions

---

[6] Note that an individual's vote probability P_i and a distribution F_i pin down a unique utility function u_i in the stochastic partisanship model. Our symmetry requirement that $f_i(0) = f_j(0)$ then allows us to compare voter utilities, but there is no special normative basis for this.

[7] Ledyard 1984 derives a similar result from a model of costly and strategic voting.

[8] Our results for vote motivation in the stochastic partisanship model have immediate consequences for a closely related model in which voter partisanship enters into voting behavior in a multiplicative way. Banks and Duggan 2005 show that, by a simple transformation, Theorems 4 and 5 have corresponding statements in the multiplicative model, capturing results of Coughlin and Nitzan 1981 for the special case of the binary Luce model.

F_i that pile probability mass near zero. By Theorem 4, the equilibria of the stochastic partisanship model so defined must be at the utilitarian point, and it may therefore appear that the equilibrium moves from the median ideal policy in the Downsian model to the utilitarian point in the presence of the slightest noise in voting behavior. Or, to use Hinich's (1977) terminology, it may appear that the median is an "artifact."

In fact, however, Theorem 4 only gives a necessary condition for equilibria in the stochastic partisanship model: it says that *if* there is an equilibrium, then both candidates must locate at the utilitarian point, leaving the possibility that there is no equilibrium. Banks and Duggan (2005) and Laussel and Le Breton (2002) show that this is necessarily the case: when voting behavior is close to deterministic in the stochastic partisanship model, there is *no* equilibrium in pure strategies.[9] Thus, the introduction of probabilistic voting into the Downsian model can actually create equilibrium existence problems, even in the unidimensional model, where the median voter theorem holds.

4.2 Win Motivation

In the probabilistic voting framework, win motivation is formalized as

$$EU_A(x_A, x_B) = P(x_A, x_B),$$

with candidate B's utility equal to one minus the above quantity. Because the candidates' probability of winning is the probability of a particular event (receiving more votes than the opponent) with respect to a binomial probability distribution, this objective function lacks the nice linear form of vote motivation.

As under vote motivation, the objective functions of the candidates are continuous. Quasi-concavity is more difficult to maintain under win motivation, but there is nevertheless a close connection between the equilibria generated by the two objective functions. Our first result, due to Duggan (2000a), establishes that there is only one possible equilibrium under win motivation: the utilitarian point, familiar from the analysis of vote motivation. Thus, again, equilibrium incentives drive the candidates to take identical positions at a central point in the policy space.

Theorem 6: (Duggan): *In the stochastic partisanship model, assume win motivation, and assume the following for each voter i:*

- $F_i(0) = 1/2$
- $F_i(u_i(x))$ *is concave in* x
- $F_i(-u_i(x))$ *is convex in* x.

If (x_A^*, x_B^*) *is an interior equilibrium, then both candidates locate at the utilitarian point:* $x_A^* = x_B^* = \overline{x}$.

---

[9] This overturns Theorem 2 of Hinich 1978. See Banks and Duggan 2005 for an extended discussion.

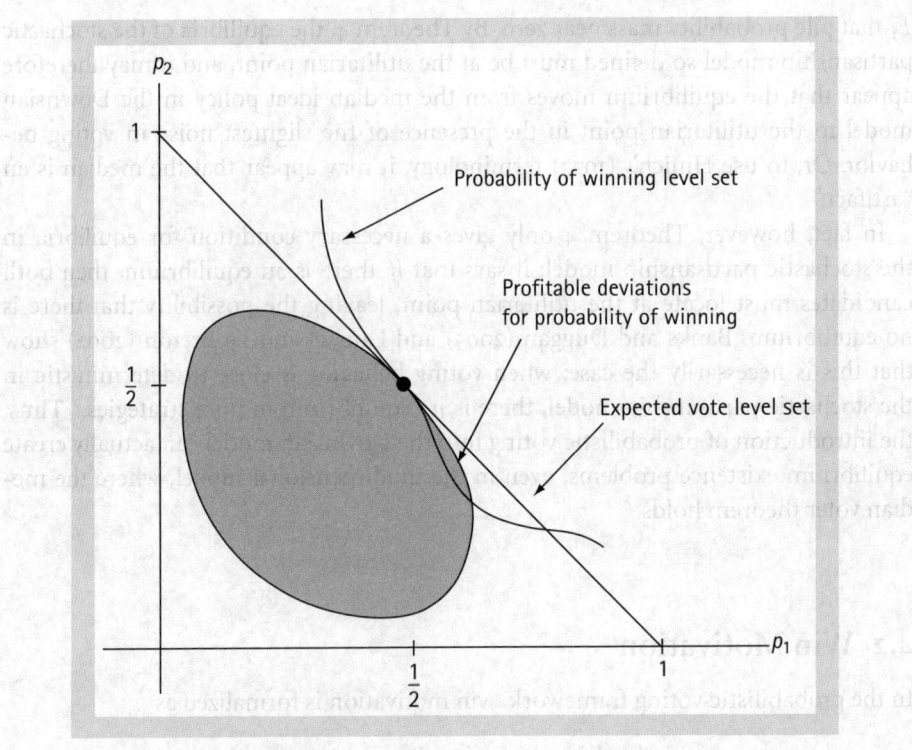

Fig. 4.4 Difficulty with win motivation

Of the assumptions in Theorem 6, the first is a form of symmetry, saying that neither candidate is *ex ante* advantaged. The second and third conditions are those used in Theorem 5 to ensure the existence of an equilibrium under vote motivation. Here, those conditions serve a related purpose, which is depicted graphically in Figure 4.4 for the case of two voters. Fixing candidate B's policy at the utilitarian point, $x_B = \bar{x}$, a choice of x_A will determine a vector

$$(P_1(x_A, \bar{x}), P_2(x_A, \bar{x}), \ldots, P_n(x_A, \bar{x}))$$

of individual vote probabilities for candidate A. Varying x_A within the policy space X, this generates the set of probability vectors "achievable" by candidate A, the shaded area in Figure 4.4. Note that, by the first assumption of Theorem 6, candidate A wins with probability one-half if the candidate chooses $x_A = \bar{x}$, and so the vector $(1/2, 1/2)$ lies in this set. The second and third assumptions imply that the set of achievable probability vectors is convex.

A consequence of Theorem 6 is that, in order to obtain a full understanding of equilibria under win motivation, we need only understand the conditions under which it is indeed an equilibrium for the candidates to locate at the utilitarian point. Clearly, under the conditions of Theorem 5, locating at the utilitarian point is an equilibrium under vote motivation: this is apparent in Figure 4.4, as the tangency at probability vector $(1/2, 1/2)$ shows that there is no other achievable vector of probabilities lying on a higher level set for expected vote. In contrast, the probability-of-winning objective is not linear in vote probabilities, and its convexity properties are generally poor. This is illustrated figuratively in Figure 4.4 by the "dip" in the probability-of-winning level set, which creates the possibility for a deviation by candidate A that is profitable under win motivation.

The next result gives a simple condition in terms of the second derivatives of voters' utility functions that rules out the problem illustrated in Figure 4.4. Assuming, for simplicity, that individual bias terms are uniformly distributed, it is sufficient that the Hessian matrix of at least one voter's utility function is negative definite at the utilitarian point. Since we maintain the assumption that utilities are concave, the Hessian is already negative semi-definite, so the added restriction of negative definiteness seems hardly objectionable.[10] The result is stated in the context of the uniform partisanship model in Duggan (2000a), whereas Patty (2005) provides an extension to a more general model of voting and to multiple candidates.

Theorem 7: (Duggan; Patty): *In the uniform partisanship model, assume win motivation. If the Hessian matrix of u_i at $\overline{x}$ is negative definite for some voter i, then $(\overline{x}, \overline{x})$ is a local equilibrium.*

Note that the result does not deliver the existence of a (global) equilibrium, but only a "local" equilibrium, which is immune to small deviations by one of the candidates. Thus, it leaves the possibility that one candidate could increase his or her probability of winning by positioning far from the utilitarian point.

5 Probabilistic Voting: The Stochastic Preference Model

The second main approach to modeling probabilistic voting focuses only on policy considerations (dropping partisanship) and allows for the possibility that the candidates do not perfectly observe the policy preferences of voters.

Stochastic preference model. Assume each voter i has a strictly concave, differentiable utility function $u_i(\cdot, \theta_i)$, where θ_i is a preference parameter lying in a Euclidean space Θ. We assume that the vector $(\theta_1, \ldots, \theta_n)$ of parameters is a random variable from the candidates' perspective, and we assume that each θ_i is distributed according to a distribution function G_i. We do not assume that these random variables are independent, but we assume that the distribution of preferences is sufficiently "dispersed" for each voter, in the following sense: for every voter i and all distinct policies

---

[10] Duggan 2000a gives an example showing that the added restriction of negative definiteness is needed for Theorem 7: the assumption of strict concavity alone is not enough for the result. See Aranson, Hinich, and Ordeshook 1974 for earlier results on the equivalence of vote and win motivation.

x and y, we have

$$\Pr(\{\theta_i \mid u_i(z, \theta_i) > u_i(y, \theta_i) > u_i(x, \theta_i)\}) > 0,$$

where z is the midpoint between x and y, and we also have

$$\Pr(\{\theta_i \mid u_i(x, \theta_i) = u_i(y, \theta_i)\}) = 0.$$

Given parameter θ_i, our assumptions imply that voter i has a unique ideal policy, and we let H_i denote the distribution of voter i's ideal policy. In the case of a unidimensional policy space, for example, $H_i(x)$ is the probability that i's ideal policy is less than or equal to x, and by our dispersion assumption it is continuous and strictly increasing. It is common to identify θ_i with voter i's ideal policy and to assume that $u_i(\cdot, \theta_i)$ is quadratic, and our dispersion condition is then satisfied under the uncontroversial assumption that the distribution of ideal policies is continuous with full support. When all voters appear *ex ante* identical to the candidates, we drop the i index on u and G, and we assume without loss of generality that there is a single voter. We refer to this as the *representative voter stochastic preference model*.

Paralleling the previous section, we first consider the objective of vote motivation, and we then consider win motivation, both objectives defined as above. We end with the analysis of policy motivation, which has been considered primarily in the context of the stochastic preference model.

5.1 Vote Motivation

An immediate technical difference between the stochastic preference and stochastic partisanship models is that we now lose full continuity of the candidates' expected votes, as discontinuities appear along the "diagonal," where $x_A = x_B$. To see this, consider the representative voter stochastic preference model in the context of a unidimensional policy space. Fix x_B to the right of the median of G, and let x_A approach x_B from the left. Then candidate A's expected utility converges to $G(x_B) > 1/2$, but at $x_A = x_B$, A's expected utility is $1/2$. The only value of x_B where such a discontinuity does not occur is at the median of G. Thus, the stochastic preference model generally exhibits discontinuities when one candidate "crosses over" the other.

Despite the presence of these discontinuities, there is a unique equilibrium when the policy space is unidimensional, and it is easily characterized. Let H_a be the distribution defined by $H_a(x) = \frac{1}{n} \sum_i H_i(x)$, and let x_a be the unique median of this average distribution. The next result, which is proved in Duggan (2005), establishes that in equilibrium the candidates must locate at the median x_a of the average distribution. Thus, we are back to a "median-like" result, but now the equilibrium is at the median of the average distribution.

Theorem 8: (Duggan): *In the stochastic preference model, assume X is unidimensional and vote motivation. There is a unique equilibrium (x_A^*, x_B^*). In equilibrium, both candidates locate at the median of the average distribution: $x_A^* = x_B^* = x_a$.*

When the policy space is multidimensional, the task of equilibrium characterization is more difficult, and we simplify matters by specializing to the representative voter stochastic preference model. We say a policy x is a *generalized median in all directions* if, compared to every other policy y, the voter is more likely to prefer x to y than the converse: for every policy y, we have

$$\Pr(\{\theta \mid u(y, \theta) > u(x, \theta)\}) \leq \frac{1}{2}.$$

By strict concavity and our dispersion condition, if there is a generalized median in all directions, then there is exactly one, which we denote x_γ. In the quadratic version of the model, x_γ is equivalent to a median in all directions, in the usual sense.[11] When the policy space is multidimensional, such a policy exists, for example, if G has a radially symmetric density function, such as the normal distribution. This can be weakened, but existence of a median in all directions is quite restrictive when the policy space has dimension at least two.

The next result provides a characterization of equilibria in the multidimensional stochastic preference model: in equilibrium, the candidates must locate at the generalized median in all directions. Under our maintained assumptions, a generalized median in all directions is essentially an "estimated median," as in Calvert (1985), so the next result is close to a result contained in that paper.

Theorem 9: (Calvert): *In the representative voter stochastic preference model, assume vote motivation. There is an equilibrium (x_A^*, x_B^*) if and only if there is a generalized median in all directions. In this case, the equilibrium is unique, and the candidates locate at the generalized median: $x_A^* = x_B^* = x_\gamma$.*

As we have seen before, strategic incentives drive the candidates to take identical positions in equilibrium, but the implication for equilibrium existence in multidimensional policy spaces is negative, as existence of a generalized median in all directions is extremely restrictive.

5.2 Win Motivation

Under win motivation in the stochastic preference model, we again have discontinuities along the diagonal. Despite this, there is a unique equilibrium when the policy space is unidimensional, as with vote motivation, but now the characterization is changed. Let H_μ denote the distribution of the median ideal policy, i.e. $H_\mu(x)$ is the probability that the median voter's ideal policy is less than or equal to x. By our dispersion assumption, H_μ is strictly increasing and has a unique median, denoted x_μ. The next result, due to Calvert (1985), establishes that in equilibrium the candidates must locate at the same policy, the median of x_μ. Thus, in the unidimensional version

---

[11] That is, every hyperplane through x_γ divides the space in half: the probability that the representative voter's ideal policy is to one side of the hyperplane is equal to one half.

of the stochastic preference model, we are back to a median-like result, but now the equilibrium is at the median of the distribution of medians.

Theorem 10: (Calvert): *In the stochastic preference model, assume X is unidimensional and win motivation. There is a unique equilibrium (x_A^*, x_B^*). In equilibrium, the candidates locate at the median of the distribution of median ideal policies: $x_A^* = x_B^* = x_\mu$.*

For multidimensional policy spaces, the equilibrium result in Theorem 9 for the representative voter model carries over directly, as in this model the objectives of vote motivation and win motivation coincide, and we have the same negative conclusion regarding existence of equilibria in multiple dimensions.

5.3 Policy Motivation

In the probabilistic voting framework, policy motivation is formalized as

$$EU_A(x_A, x_B) = P(x_A, x_B)u_A(x_A) + (1 - P(x_A, x_B))u_A(x_B),$$

and likewise for candidate B. We maintain the focus of our analysis on the stochastic preference model, except for our first result, which gives an easy necessary condition for equilibria that holds for both probabilistic voting models. The result, which is proved by Wittman (1983, 1990),[12] Hansson and Stuart (1984), Calvert (1985), and Roemer (1994), shows that the candidates can never locate at identical positions in equilibrium.

Theorem 11: (Wittman; Hansson and Stuart; Calvert; Roemer): *In the stochastic partisanship or stochastic preference models, assume policy motivation. If (x_A^*, x_B^*) is an equilibrium, then the candidates do not locate at the same policy position: $x_A^* \neq x_B^*$.*

Theorem 11 leaves open the question of whether an equilibrium exists in the first place. Under our maintained assumptions, measure-theoretic arguments can be used to show that each voter i's probability $P_i(x_A, x_B)$ is continuous in the positions of the candidates whenever x_A and x_B are distinct, and as discontinuities no longer occur when one candidate crosses over another, the candidates' objective functions under policy motivation are continuous. Thus, one of the main conditions in the DFG theorem is fulfilled. But the candidates' objective functions may not be quasi-concave, making equilibrium existence a non-trivial issue. In the quadratic stochastic preference model with a unidimensional policy space and uniform distribution G, the candidates' objective functions are strictly concave. This allows us to apply the DFG theorem to obtain existence, a simple observation noted by Duggan and Fey (2005b). If we depart from uniform G, then, perhaps surprisingly, equilibria can fail to exist due to convexity problems. Duggan and Fey (2005b) show that this failure can

---

[12] Wittman's 1983, 1990 model is slightly different from the one here, as he assumes a hybrid of vote and policy motivation.

occur even in highly structured settings—with quadratic utilities and a symmetric, single-peaked density for the distribution of voter ideal policies.[13]

6 CONCLUSION

Of many themes throughout this chapter, the most prominent has been the difficulty in ensuring existence of equilibria. This is especially true for the Downsian model when the policy space is multidimensional. Probabilistic voting models eliminate some of the discontinuities of the Downsian model, and in the context of vote-motivated candidates in the stochastic partisanship model, we have reasonable (if somewhat restrictive) sufficient conditions for equilibrium existence in multiple dimensions. These conditions ensure that the candidates' objective functions are quasiconcave, as required by DFG, but existence remains an issue under win or policy motivation or in the stochastic preference model.

One approach to solving the existence problem, initially explored by Kramer (1978), is to analyze mixed strategy equilibria, which capture the idea that a candidate's policy position cannot be precisely predicted by his or her opponent at the time campaign platforms are chosen. Duggan and Jackson (2005) show that mixed strategy equilibria exist in the stochastic preference model generally and in the Downsian model as well if we treat voters as players (so that indifferent voters may randomize arbitrarily between the candidates).

A second approach to the existence issue, taken by Roemer (2001; see also this volume), is to modify the objectives of the candidates to demand more of a deviation to be profitable. Roemer endows parties (rather than individual candidates) with multiple objectives of office and policy motivation, as well as an interest in "publicity," whereby a party seeks to announce policy platforms consonant with its general stance, regardless of whether these platforms win. Roemer shows that, if we assume a deviation must satisfy all three of these objectives to be profitable, then an equilibrium exists in some two-dimensional environments.

A third approach, referred to as "citizen-candidate" models, is pursued by Osborne and Slivinski (1996) and Besley and Coate (1997). They model candidates as policy motivated and assume candidates cannot commit to campaign promises, removing all positional aspects from the electoral model. Instead, the strategic variable is whether to run in the election, and equilibria are guaranteed to exist. A related modeling approach, referred to as "electoral accountability," views elections as repeated over time and takes up informational aspects of elections. Work in this vein, such as Ferejohn (1986), Banks and Sundaram (1993, 1998), Duggan (2000b), and Banks and

---

[13] Hansson and Stuart 1984 claim that an equilibrium exists if each candidate's probability of winning is concave in the candidate's own position, but their claim rests on the incorrect assumption that the candidates' objective functions are then concave. Thus, the question of general sufficient conditions for existence is open.

Duggan (2006), again abstracts away from campaigns. Politicians do make meaningful choices while in office, however, as candidates must consider the information (about preferences or abilities) their choices convey to voters. Equilibria of a simple (stationary) form can often be shown to exist quite generally in these models.

REFERENCES

ARANSON, P., HINICH, M., and ORDESHOOK, P. 1974. Election goals and strategies: equivalent and non-equivalent candidate objectives. *American Political Science Review*, 68: 135–52.

AUSTEN-SMITH, D., and BANKS, J. 1999. *Positive Political Theory*, i: *Collective Preference*. Ann Arbor: University of Michigan Press.

—— —— 2005. *Positive Political Theory*, ii: *Strategy and Structure*. Ann Arbor: University of Michigan Press.

BANKS, J., and DUGGAN, J. 2005. Probabilistic voting in the spatial model of elections: the theory of office-motivated candidates. In *Social Choice and Strategic Decisions: Essays in Honor of Jeffrey S. Banks*, ed. D. Austen-Smith and J. Duggan. New York: Springer-Verlag.

—— —— 2006. A dynamic model of democratic elections in multidimensional policy spaces. Mimeo.

—— and SUNDARAM, R. 1993. Moral hazard and adverse selection in a model of repeated elections. In *Political Economy: Institutions, Information, Competition and Representation*, ed. W. Barnett et al. New York: Cambridge University Press.

—— —— 1998. Optimal retention in agency problems. *Journal of Economic Theory*, 82: 293–323.

BESLEY, T., and COATE, S. 1997. An economic model of representative democracy. *Quarterly Journal of Economics*, 112: 85–114.

CALVERT, R. 1985. Robustness of the multidimensional voting model: candidate motivations, uncertainty, and convergence. *American Journal of Political Science*, 29: 69–95.

COUGHLIN, P., and NITZAN, S. 1981. Electoral outcomes with probabilistic voting and Nash social welfare maxima. *Journal of Public Economics*, 15: 113–21.

DEBREU, G. 1952. Existence of a social equilibrium. *Proceedings of the National Academy of Sciences*, 38: 886–93.

DOWNS, A. 1957. *An Economic Theory of Democracy*. New York: Harper and Row.

DUGGAN, J. 2000a. Equilibrium equivalence under expected plurality and probability of winning maximization. Mimeo.

—— 2000b. Repeated elections with asymmetric information. *Economics and Politics*, 12: 109–36.

—— 2006. A note on uniqueness of electoral equilibrium when the median voter is unobserved. *Economics Letters*.

—— and FEY, M. 2005a. Electoral competition with policy-motivated candidates. *Games and Economic Behavior*, 51: 490–522.

—— —— 2005b. Indeterminacy in elections with policy-motivated candidates and a single issue dimension. Mimeo.

—— and JACKSON, M. 2005. Mixed strategy equilibrium and deep covering in multidimensional electoral competition. Mimeo.

FAN, K. 1952. Fixed-point and minimax theorems in locally convex linear spaces. *Proceedings of the National Academy of Sciences*, 38: 121–6.

FEREJOHN, J. 1986. Incumbent performance and electoral control. *Public Choice*, 50: 5–25.
GLICKSBERG, I. 1952. A further generalization of the Kakutani fixed point theorem, with application to Nash equilibrium. *Proceedings of the American Mathematical Society*, 3: 170–4.
HANSSON, I., and STUART, C. 1984. Voting competitions with interested politicians: platforms do not converge to the preferences of the median voter. *Public Choice*, 44: 431–41.
HINICH, M. 1977. Equilibrium in spatial voting: the median voter result is an artifact. *Journal of Economic Theory*, 16: 208–19.
——1978. The mean versus the median in spatial voting games. In *Game Theory and Political Science*, ed. P. Ordeshook. New York: NYU Press.
——LEDYARD, J., and ORDESHOOK, P. 1972. Nonvoting and the existence of equilibrium under majority rule. *Journal of Economic Theory*, 4: 144–53.
——————1973. A theory of electoral equilibrium: a spatial analysis based on the theory of games. *Journal of Politics*, 35: 154–93.
HOTELLING, H. 1929. Stability in competition. *Economic Journal*, 39: 41–57.
KRAMER, G. 1978. Existence of electoral equilibrium. In *Game Theory and Political Science*, ed. P. Ordeshook. New York: NYU Press.
LAUSSEL, D., and LE BRETON, M. 2002. Unidimensional Downsian politics: median, utilitarian, or what else? *Economics Letters*, 76: 351–6.
LEDYARD, J. 1984. The pure theory of large two-candidate elections. *Public Choice*, 44: 7–41.
LINDBECK, A., and WEIBULL, J. 1987. Balanced-budget redistribution as the outcome of political competition. *Public Choice*, 52: 273–97.
————1993. A model of political equilibrium in a representative democracy. *Journal of Public Economics*, 51: 195–209.
NASH, J. 1950. Equilibrium points in N-person games. *Proceedings of the National Academy of Sciences*, 36: 48–9.
ORDESHOOK, P. 1986. *Game Theory and Political Theory*. New York: Cambridge University Press.
OSBORNE, M., and SLIVINSKI, A. 1996. A model of political competition with citizen-candidates. *Quarterly Journal of Economics*, 111: 65–96.
PATTY, J. 2005. Local equilibrium equivalence in probabilistic voting models. *Games and Economic Behavior*, 51: 523–36.
PLOTT, C. 1967. A notion of equilibrium and its possibility under majority rule. *American Economic Review*, 57: 787–806.
ROEMER, J. 1994. A theory of policy differentiation in single issue electoral politics. *Social Choice and Welfare*, 11: 355–80.
——2001. *Political Competition: Theory and Applications*. Cambridge, Mass.: Harvard University Press.
WITTMAN, D. 1977. Candidates with policy preferences: a dynamic model. *Journal of Economic Theory*, 14: 180–9.
——1983. Candidate motivation: a synthesis of alternative theories. *American Political Science Review*, 77: 142–57.
——1990. Spatial strategies when candidates have policy preferences. In *Advances in the Spatial Theory of Voting*, ed. J. Enelow and M. Hinich. New York: Cambridge University Press.

CHAPTER 5

POLITICAL INCOME REDISTRIBUTION

JOHN LONDREGAN

1 INTRODUCTION

DOUGLASS NORTH has characterized government as possessing a monopoly on the legitimate use of force. This makes the government the primary custodian of property rights, while at the same time leaving it uniquely suited to seize and dispose of individuals' resources. While some resources at the disposition of the government are allocated to the provision of non-excludable "public" goods (lighthouses are a classic if somewhat prosaic example), or to partially excludable goods (transportation networks are subject to congestion, but during off-peak hours they have aspects of public goods), an important element of public policy involves the redistribution of private consumption goods. It is to the last-mentioned class of activity, the political redistribution of income, that this chapter is devoted. I shall take a positive rather than a normative approach to the subject that seeks to explain why we observe the redistributive policies that we do, rather than taking up the related problem of what policies of redistribution should be implemented.

Income redistribution is often associated with action on the part of government, while it is customary to think of policies that preserve the distribution of income arising from the workings of markets and other non-governmental productive activities as being passive ones. Yet any allocation of income requires the active enforcement of property rights by the government, so-called "laissez-faire" policies

* I am grateful to seminar audience at the Juan March Institute for useful comments.

rely on government action every bit as much as actively redistributive policies. The distribution of income is always political.

In some cases we have governments that are not generally accountable for their actions. In these environments redistribution often amounts to *kleptocracy*, with a dictator, ruling clique, or royal family as the primary recipients of redistribution. Olson (1993) recognized that even in these cases, the kleptocrat may increase the harvest of loot if he can credibly commit to not steal everything.

When government policy is accountable to the general public matters become much more complicated,[1] and it is to income redistribution within a framework of democratic institutions that this chapter is devoted. One important set of analyses not covered here are focused on legislative bargaining, Baron and Ferjohn (1989) being a notable example. Those models focus on the features of legislative organization, and use the division of a prize as a paradigm for legislative decision-making. Because the subject of legislative organization is taken up in detail in other chapters in this volume, I do not concentrate on that important set of models here. Likewise, I do not focus on models of lobbyists, such as Grossman and Helpman (1994), even though the goal of many lobbyists is to influence the political redistribution of income, as such models are also the subject of another chapter in this volume.

This overview begins in Section 2 with a simpler but widely used class of models in which the menu of redistributive options is artificially restricted by limiting taxes and transfers to schemes that make post-tax income a deterministic and non-decreasing function of pre-tax income. Because the functional form relating post-tax to pre-tax incomes lends itself to extensions on other dimensions, for example to modeling public goods provision when individuals can choose to relocate to other jurisdictions, models of this class have become building blocks of the literature on redistributive politics. Attention then turns to competitive models that allow for much greater flexibility in the choice of redistribution schemes, with Section 3 focusing on models that emphasize the potential instability of redistributive politics, while Section 4 considers models with built-in sources of stability. In Section 5 attention turns to several models of redistributive politics that try to explain the choice of redistributive instruments when more efficient alternatives are available. A final section concludes.

2 Competition over Restricted Income Tax Schedules

If we restrict our attention to redistributive schemes that involve a constant lump-sum payment to everyone, coupled with a linear (Meltzer and Richard 1981), or quadratic (Roemer 1999), tax scheme, then political competition can lead to

---

[1] Of course, on normative grounds virtually everyone will prefer this complexity to the crass simplicity of a kleptocratic regime.

progressive tax schemes in which those with high incomes subsidize those with lower incomes.

In a classic paper Meltzer and Richard (1981) set forth a simple model of income redistribution that captures the essential trade-off between equality and output maximization that is intrinsic to redistributive schemes. In this model government policy consists of a tax rate t levied on all income, and a lump-sum egalitarian transfer r. An individual with a pre-tax income of y pays ty in taxes, and receives a transfer of r, resulting in a post-transfer income of c:

$$c = y(1 - t) + r \qquad (1)$$

Individuals are each endowed with one unit of labor, which they can divide between work and leisure. While they get no direct utility out of work, individuals do enjoy leisure activity, and they enjoy goods consumption.[2] Individuals differ in their workplace productivity, denoted by x. If an individual with productivity level x devotes a fraction n of her time to work, her pre-tax income will be given by x per unit of time spent working:

$$y = nx \qquad (2)$$

In this framework, the government devotes all of tax revenues to financing the lump-sum transfer r, so each person's transfer is simply their equal share of tax revenues. Individuals recognize that they are small relative to the size of society, and so they treat the lump sum they receive as not depending on their own personal work effort.[3] Thus, all individuals with the same level of productivity have the same preferences concerning taxes and transfers, while the level of transfers, r, is fully determined by the tax rate t.

Meltzer and Richard show that in their set-up, an individual's most preferred tax rate depends on her productivity level, and that this preferred rate tends to fall with an individual's own labor market productivity.[4] However, individuals do take the incentive effects of taxation on the labor supply of others into account when evaluating potential tax rates.

Meltzer and Richard argue that in equilibrium competition among political entrepreneurs will lead to a government that implements the preferred tax policy of the voter with the median productivity level $\dot{x}$. If the distribution of productivity levels is skewed rightward (so that the median voter has a below-average income) the result will be a positive level of redistributive taxation that stops short of full equalization of incomes. Taxation stops short of full equalization because the median

---

[2] Technically, Meltzer and Richard assume that individuals' preferences can be represented by a quasi-concave utility function over consumption and leisure time which is increasing in both its arguments.

[3] In Meltzer and Richard's model individuals are part of a continuum, and each person's contribution to tax revenues is effectively zero, so the impact of each person's labor supply decision on the average transfer is literally negligible.

[4] Strictly, if $t^*(x)$ denotes the preferred tax rate of each individual with productivity level x, then t^* is a non-increasing function of x.

voter recognizes the disincentive effects of a high tax rate. As tax rates rise toward 1 individuals shift away from work and into leisure.

A crucial consideration hinges on whether the median voter works. Among tax rates that dissuade the median voter from work, she will prefer the rate that maximizes the size of the per capita transfer. Above that rate work effort falls off so rapidly that even though people pay a higher tax rate on their remaining work hours, it is not enough to offset the decreased amount of work, and total revenues decline. In this case, the Meltzer and Richard outcome is quite similar to the notion of a "stationary bandit" (Olson 1993), namely a government that seeks to maximize the resources it extracts from the economy, and which sets a tax rate below full confiscation only because to take everything would suffocate individuals' incentives to produce. However, among voters whose preferred tax rates are below that which would remove them from the labor force, there is an additional impact of an increased tax rate, in that it reduces their pre-tax incomes. So the preferred tax rate is a decreasing function of a worker's productivity: if the median voter works in equilibrium, then the median tax rate will be lower than the revenue-maximizing level.

This model represented a significant innovation over earlier models. It did not follow Marx (1867) in predicting that, "false consciousness" aside, people would choose to expropriate fully those with more wealth. Neither did it rely on the assumption of a poorly informed electorate, about which I will have more to say later in this chapter. Meltzer and Richard showed that partial income redistribution could be the result of decisions by fully informed voters. The authors were interested in an empirical regularity known as "Wagner's Law" which held that as incomes rise so does the "taste" for redistributive policies. Meltzer and Richard's analysis directs attention instead to the degree of income inequality, as measured by the distance between the economy-wide mean income and the income of the median voter, suggesting that periods of rapid economic growth, which Kuznets (1955) predicted would be characterized by increased inequality, would be accompanied by higher rates of taxation when voting rights are universal.

Of course, the Meltzer and Richard framework begs a number of questions. Notably there is the restriction to a linear income tax scheme. One response to this is offered by Roemer (1999) (see his article in this volume) who allows tax and transfer schemes that are quadratic functions of individuals' pre-tax incomes, though this added complexity (and realism) comes at the price of not allowing for production.

Restricted tax schemes have become standard building blocks from which more complex models of income redistribution are confected. Analysts interested in the distributive impact of some other feature of the political system such as the potential for migration, which is discussed in detail in the chapter by David Wildasin in this volume, have frequently appended a more sophisticated model for political decision-making to a version of Meltzer and Richard's linear tax scheme.

An interesting case in point is Austen-Smith (2000), who generalizes the Meltzer–Richard model to encompass heterogeneous types of economic activity, and who compares the effects of different electoral systems on the level of redistribution. Austen-Smith's model generates the prediction that proportional representation militates in favor of a more equal distribution of income than simple majority rule,[5] a prediction that seems to be borne out empirically (see for example Persson and Tabellini 2000).

3 COMPETITION OVER UNRESTRICTED TRANSFER SCHEMES

The analysis of income redistribution in this context has an interesting parallel in the literature on industrial organization. Bertrand (1883) noted that competition among a finite number of identical sellers possesses a fundamental tendency toward instability: given any prevailing price each seller can capture all of the market by infinitesimally undercutting her competitors' prices. Subsequent analyses by Sraffa (1926), Hotelling (1929), and de Palma et al. (1985) identified conditions under which infinitesimal price reductions result in only infinitesimal changes in market shares, conferring a degree of stability on market outcomes.

One important family of models of income redistribution, which will be examined in this section, possesses an instability similar to that highlighted by Bertrand (1883); in these models redistributive schemes are highly vulnerable to being undercut by competing alternatives that offer infinitesimal improvements to a voting majority.

Models in which decision are made by majority vote without restrictions on the potential allocation of transfers[6] generically fail to possess equilibria for reasons discussed in McKelvey (1976). Working within the framework of cooperative game theory, Aumann and Kurz (1977a) show that this indeterminacy is removed if individuals can destroy their endowments rather than allow them to be distributed to others.

In Aumann and Kurz's model,[7] agents are distributed along a continuum, there is no production, and redistribution is costless, save that each individual can, if she chooses to, destroy her own endowment before redistribution takes place. Total endowments are finite; utility functions (the function for type t individuals is denoted u_t) satisfy some fairly standard regularity conditions.[8] The equilibrium budget must balance. Individuals' ability to destroy their output constrains the benefits that a majority coalition can vote for itself. In equilibrium an individual's allocation will be larger the greater her initial endowment, and the less risk averse she is. The intuition here is that groups of agents engage in brinksmanship, threatening to disrupt

---

[5] The mechanics of his model hinge crucially on his assumptions about the objectives of the political parties.

[6] With no productive activities and a continuously divisible stock of a single resource this amounts to N voters selecting a point on an $N - 1$ dimensional simplex.

[7] This model is discussed in Aumann and Kutz 1977a and fully elaborated in Aumann and Kurz 1977b.

[8] Each agent's utility function is increasing, concave, continuously differentiable, and uniformly bounded.

coalitions and, in particular, to destroy their own output if they are treated badly in the allocation of consumption. In such an environment, risk aversion is a liability, limiting the set of threats that are credible, while intensifying one's sensitivity to the threats of others.

Weingast (1979) takes the specter of uncertainty about equilibrium allocations as his point of departure. He considers an N-person legislature (with N an odd number to preclude ties) considering N projects, each of which confers a benefit of b to a different district, while it entails a cost c, which must be evenly shared across all N districts. Each agent wants to maximize the well-being of her own district. Individuals are torn between their desire to maximize their benefits as a part of the winning coalition, by restricting its membership as much as possible, and their fear of being excluded from the winning coalition. If more projects are funded, the cost of providing them goes up, but the probability that a randomly chosen legislator is excluded from the benefits goes down.

If all coalitions of size M are equally likely, a legislator's probability of having her project funded, and receiving a benefit of b, will be $\frac{M}{N}$, while the cost per district of funding M projects is $\frac{M}{N}c$, which she must pay whether her project is chosen or not. Her *ex ante* expected payoff if the winning coalition is of size M is the difference between the expected payoff and the certain cost, namely:

$$\frac{M}{N}(b-c) \tag{3}$$

Provided $b > c$, so that the projects' benefits exceed their costs, the value of M which maximizes a legislator's *ex ante* expected payoff is $M = N$, which entails a universal coalition. On the other hand, if a legislator knows she will belong to the winning coalition her *ex post* payoff will be:

$$b - \frac{M}{N}c \tag{4}$$

In this case, the legislator will want to make M as small as possible, subject to the coalition still being able to impose its will. With N odd and strict majority rule, the value for M that achieves this is $M = \frac{N+1}{2}$, a bare majority. [9]

What if the agents in Weingast's model had the ability to destroy their output, as in the Aumann and Kurz model discussed previously? In this case, the costs of the projects undertaken by the winning coalition would have to be paid for entirely by the winners, as the losers would destroy their output. Thus, the per capita benefits for the winning coalition would be $b - c$ regardless of the coalition's size, eliminating the temptation identified in equation (4) to exclude members from the winning coalition.[10] Weingast's conclusion that legislators would prefer a universalistic coalition is

---

[9] Riker referred to such alliances among the smallest possible decisive group as "Minimum Winning Coalitions."

[10] Of course, these results are sensitive to the "all or nothing" nature of the projects, and the linearity of costs.

further strengthened if we transplant into his model the assumption of Aumann and Kurz that one can destroy one's output.

Another model that allows freedom in choosing the form of the tax schedule is presented by Snyder and Kramer (1988). These authors allow for considerable flexibility in the shape of the tax schedule, but they posit a very simple model for production. In exchange for this simplicity they obtain some remarkably strong results about tax rates. They show that any non-linear tax schedule, where the net tax to an individual depends on her market income y: $t(y)$, can be dominated by a linear one, and that steeper tax schedules can result in less equalizing redistribution than those that rise more gently (depending on the level of lump-sum taxes or subsidies). Given an additional condition on the elasticity of labor demand in the underground economy, Snyder and Kramer show that the equilibrium tax policy will be equivalent to a linear one. While this result is remarkable, it hinges crucially on unconventional assumptions about the labor market.

While electoral competition is often modeled in terms of two candidates competing in a majoritarian system, elections frequently involve non-majoritarian electoral rules, and multiple candidates. Meyerson (1993) shows that electoral rules have a profound impact on the sorts of offers candidates will make. He develops a common framework for comparing various electoral configurations. Candidates compete by offering redistributive benefits that are uncorrelated with the campaign promises of other candidates. Imagine the candidates handed out lottery tickets which could be redeemed if they were elected, while the voters care only about their transfer, so that each voter ranks the candidates in the order of the size of the transfer each has offered.

Myerson considers a stylized setting with a very large number of voters[11] each of whom casts a "sincere" vote that reflects his actual preference ranking, and a fixed amount of money that the winning candidate can distribute if she is victorious. A key feature of Myerson's model is that the "lottery tickets" handed out randomly by candidates cannot be shown to anyone else. Thus, Myerson's framework precludes candidates targeting specific groups, and it rules out their making offers contingent on the offer a voter has from the candidate's competitors. This assumption makes the model tractable, but at a significant cost in terms of realism.

Meyerson obtains analytical results for systems involving a "single non-transferable vote," which includes the "simple plurality" rule widely used in the United States, as well as for "Borda Counts," "negative plurality voting," and for multiple non-cumulative votes. He also presents simulation results for "approval voting."

A sense of how the electoral system affects the transfers politicians offer is conveyed by Meyerson's analysis of distributive politics under a simple plurality rule, and under negative approval voting.

The simple plurality rule is probably the system most familiar to the reader: each voter casts a ballot for one candidate, and the candidate receiving the most votes is elected. Under negative approval voting, each voter casts one "negative ballot," and the candidate receiving the fewest negative ballots is elected. With only two

---

[11] His voters are modeled as a continuum.

candidates, the two systems are effectively identical: a vote for "candidate A" under simple plurality rule has the same effect as a negative vote for "candidate B" under negative approval voting.

With either voting system, the equilibrium for a two-candidate election will not involve the candidates making matching offers to each voter. Why not? Suppose that one candidate was foolish enough to do so: offering an equal amount to each voter. His opponent could then exclude a small set of voters from benefits while she used the savings to slightly outbid him for the remaining voters, thereby winning the election. In equilibrium each candidate will make a range of unequal offers. In the case of a two-candidate election with either simple plurality rule or negative approval voting, each candidate's offers will be uniformly distributed on the interval [0, 2], with some voters getting nothing, while the most highly bribed receive as much as twice the average offer. If the other candidate is using a uniform distribution for offers, then the increased probability of outbidding the other candidate for a given voter that results from a small increase in the offer to that voter is just offset by the increased cost. When both candidates employ this strategy we are in equilibrium as neither has an incentive to change her behavior. If we normalize the mean transfer to equal 1, then the standard deviation of the distribution of transfers offered by each candidate under either simple plurality rule or negative approval voting will equal $\frac{1}{\sqrt{3}}$, or about 0.58.

Now suppose that instead of two candidates competing in an election, there are three. In this setting the simple plurality rule and negative approval voting no longer coincide. First let's see what happens with the simple plurality rule. The uniform distribution on the interval [0, 2] over offers is no longer going to be a symmetric equilibrium. If the other two candidates used such a distribution, then the third contender could promise two and a half times the mean offer of 1 to 40 per cent of the voters, and nothing to the remainder, and expect to receive 40 per cent of the vote, thereby defeating each of his opponents who would divide the remaining votes evenly between themselves. This pressure to make unequal offers carries over to the equilibrium, as barely a third of the electorate is needed to prevail. In the symmetric equilibrium each candidate makes generous offers to a minority of voters while making much smaller offers to a majority of the electorate. Relative to the mean offer of 1, candidates' offer distributions will be skewed[12] with a minimum offer of 0, a maximum of 3, and a standard deviation of approximately 0.89. With the simple plurality rule in elections with three or more contenders, candidates need friends more than they fear enemies—with sincere voting, a candidate who is everyone's second choice receives no votes under a simple plurality rule.

With negative approval voting in a three-candidate election, the incentives run in the opposite direction. Suppose that two of the candidates offered a uniform distribution (on the interval [0, 2]) of payments to voters. The third candidate could win the election by offering a more equal distribution! For example, by offering everyone the

---

[12] In the symmetric equilibrium the probability density function $f(x)$ for each candidate's offers will be $f(x) = \frac{1}{2\sqrt{3}} x^{-\frac{1}{2}}$ for x on the interval [0, 3], and zero otherwise.

average transfer, the third candidate would incur negative votes only from the 25 per cent of voters who received offers above one-half from both of the other candidates, whereas the other candidates would evenly divide the remaining negative votes, each getting 37.5 per cent. Of course, equal offers is not an equilibrium, even with three candidates, but the offer distribution that does emerge in the symmetric equilibrium[13] includes a maximum offer of only $\frac{3}{2}$ times the average, a minimum offer of 0 and a standard deviation of only 0.45, about half the value for the equilibrium offers under simple majority rule. With more than two contenders under negative approval voting candidates are more concerned about not making enemies than they are with cultivating loyal friends—a candidate who is the next to last choice of every voter receives no negative votes!

Myerson shows that among the array of electoral systems he considers, simple plurality rule, with its intense rewards for cultivating a plurality of supporters, and its mild penalties for making enemies, leads to particularly unequal allocations of campaign promises.

4 Redistribution Targeted to Heterogeneous Groups

We now turn to models in which voters have allegiances to politicians or political parties that cannot be fully unmade during the course of a single election cycle. Several of these models[14] share a common structure. So to simplify the exposition, I will present their common ideas in the context of the Dixit and Londregan (1996) model, showing which parts of the structure need to be modified to lead to each of the other models.

Voters in these models care about consumption, and they have attachments to parties. The parties make balanced budget promises about the amount of redistribution they will offer. While the parties are not acquainted with the voters and their preferences on an individual level, they can treat different groups of voters differently, and they observe the distribution of party attachments for each group. These groups reflect the accuracy of politicians' information about the voters. Poorly informed politicians may only be able to apply a fairly coarse partition of the electorate: men and women, blue-collar and white-collar workers, renters and retirees, and so forth. More astute politicians (and those better supplied with accurate information) may be able to make much finer distinctions, for example treating beer-drinking Catholic steel workers' union members in Pittsburgh differently from teetotaling Protestant

---

[13] In the symmetric equilibrium the probability density function $f(x)$ for each candidate's offers will be $f(x) = \frac{1}{\sqrt{9-6x}}$ for x on the interval $[0, \frac{3}{2})$, and zero otherwise.

[14] These are developed in Coughlin 1986; Lindbeck and Weibull 1987; Dixit and Londregan 1995, 1996, 1998, 2000.

steel workers' union members from Youngstown. However fine the information partition available to the parties, they recognize that the groups retain some heterogeneity: even among the beer-drinking Catholic steel workers' union members of Pittsburgh one will find a few Republicans. Of course, the distribution of preferences will differ across groups.

Each party must promise to treat all members of a given group in the same way, but they can treat different groups of voters differently.[15] The parties try to maximize their vote shares.[16] The key feature to this family of models is that voters make a trade-off between their partisan attachment and the attractiveness of the transfers that are on offer.

To formalize this, index groups by $g \in \{1, \ldots, G\}$. Suppose the value to a member of group g of privately consuming c_g is $U_g(c_g)$. There are two parties, labeled L and R. Suppose that party L offers every individual in group g an after-tax-and-transfer consumption level of c_{gL}, while party R offers c_{gR}. A member of group g with a partisan attachment to party R measured by X (with higher values of X indicating greater levels of partisan attachment) will vote for party L if the difference between the utility of consuming party L's offered income transfer $U_g(c_{gL})$, and the utility of consuming party R's offered income transfer $U_g(c_{gR})$ exceeds her partisan attachment to party R:

$$U_g(c_{gL}) - U_g(c_{gR}) > X \tag{5}$$

while she will give her vote to party R if the inequality is reversed.

Here, to keep things simple, everyone in the group has the same pre-transfer earnings power, and the same post-transfer consumption. However, each group member has her own degree of attachment, X, to party R. Define $X_g(c_{gL}, c_{gR})$ as the attachment to party R that leaves a group g voter indifferent between voting for L and voting for R. Of course, this depends on c_{gL} and c_{gR}. Holding the offer from party R constant, an increase in c_{gL} will increase X_g, while a more generous offer from party R, corresponding to a larger value for c_{gR} will lead to a reduction in X_g.

If we let the function $\Phi_g(X)$ tell us what fraction of group g have an attachment to party R of X or less, while N_g is the number of individuals in group g, then party L will receive $N_g \Phi_g(X_g)$ votes from members of group g, while party R receives the other $N_g[1 - \Phi_g(X_g)]$ votes.[17] If we add up the votes $N_g \Phi_g(X_g(c_{gL}, c_{gR}))$, from each group, we have the total vote for party L:

$$V_L(\{c_{gL}, c_{gR}\}_{g=1}^{G}) = \sum_{g=1}^{G} N_g \Phi_g(X_g(c_{gL}, c_{gR})) \tag{6}$$

---

[15] At this point it is useful to note that there is a strong similarity between models in which politicians are uncertain about the type of an individual, as in Coughlin, and models in which they confront a heterogeneous group of individuals who must all be treated equally, as in the Cox and McCubbins, and Dixit and Londregan models. In *ex ante* terms, making an offer to N individuals each of whom has a 40% chance of accepting it is very similar to making the same offer to a group, 40% of whom will accept it.

[16] Though Lindbeck and Weibull 1987 and Dixit and Londregan 1998 consider variants of the model in which the parties seek instead to maximize their probability of election.

[17] All voters are assumed to vote for their most preferred party rather than abstain.

Since everyone votes, the objective for a vote-maximizing party L is to make V_L as large as possible, while party R maximizes its vote by making V_L as small as it can.

While every party would like to audition for the role of Santa Claus, offering high consumption levels to all voters, they face the grim reality of a budget constraint. The transfers made to all groups must sum up to the total resource endowment of the government, B. In several models, this is zero, so that every transfer to one group of voters entails a transfer from other voters. If we let T_{gp} denote the net per capita transfer to group g offered by party p, then the cost of the party p promise to group g is simply $N_g T_{gp}$, the per capita transfer times the number of members in the group; notice that this number could be negative if group g is taxed to finance transfers to other groups. The budget constraint requires that when we add up the costs of the party p platform across groups, the total cost does not exceed B:

$$\sum_{g=1}^{G} N_g T_{gp} \leq B \text{ where } p \in \{L, R\} \tag{7}$$

In a vote-maximizing equilibrium, party L chooses the consumption levels it offers to voters, $\{c_{gL}\}_{g=1}^{G}$, in order to maximize its total vote (6) subject to satisfying the budget constraint (7), taking the offers of party R; $\{c_{gR}\}_{g=1}^{G}$ as given, while party R chooses its consumption offers; $\{c_{gR}\}_{g=1}^{G}$ to minimize the party L vote (6) subject to the budget constraint (7) on its own transfer offers, and taking the offers of party L; $\{c_{gL}\}_{g=1}^{G}$, as given.

This framework subsumes several important variants[18] as special cases. One of these is Coughlin (1986), who assumes a particular functional form for the distribution of preferences that leaves the median member of every group indifferent between the parties but allows some groups to be more responsive to redistributive offers than are others. This is a stylized setting with no deadweight losses due to taxes and transfers, and full symmetry between the parties. Under these circumstances he finds that the parties will make identical offers to each group, with the most responsive groups gleaning the highest transfers.

Lindbeck and Weibull (1987) substantially generalize Coughlin's formulation to encompass a much wider and more interesting set of circumstances. In particular, they generalize the utility function, and the model for politicians' uncertainty about voter's leanings, allowing for the possibility that groups exhibit electoral biases. However, they continue to assume that the parties are the same in terms of their abilities to transfer resources.[19] Lindbeck and Weibull generalize Coughlin's prediction that both parties will make identical transfer offers to every group.

Lindbeck and Weibull go on to consider the impact of voter apathy (so that indifferent voters do not bother to cast ballots), which shifts the balance in favor of groups

---

[18] For example the models of Coughlin 1986 and Lindbeck and Weibull 1987, and Dixit and Londregan 1995.

[19] In one formulation of their model they do experiment with deadweight losses from taxation, which they refer to as "administrative costs," but these are taken to be quadratic, and to be the same no matter which party is levying the tax.

of voters with relatively many members at the point of indifference between voting or not voting, as opposed to favoring groups with relatively many voters indifferent between the two parties. Lindbeck and Weibull also consider the possibility that parties seek to maximize the probability of winning, as opposed to trying to maximize their plurality. In this case parties' attention is shifted toward voters who tend to be partisans of the more popular party.

One of the most striking behavioral implications of the Lindbeck and Weibull model is their claim that, absent voter apathy, redistributive politics will tend to favor "swing voters" with relatively moderate preferences. To obtain this implication, Lindbeck and Weibull make a set of assumptions almost as strong as Coughlin's, and their result hinges on assumptions about differences in the marginal responsiveness of different groups to offers of income redistribution. If relatively moderate voters are assumed to be relatively responsive to transfers, then they will fare relatively well.

In a closely related model[20] Dixit and Londregan (1996) point out that the actual size of groups is largely irrelevant to the transfer they receive. What matters is the relative payoff in votes per dollar that a party receives when it makes a transfer to the group. This helps to explain why relatively small groups, such as US alfalfa farmers, can receive large per capita subsidies at the expense of large groups, for which the subsidies impose small per capita costs. This is what we would expect if the beneficiaries, for example the alfalfa farmers, included relatively many "swing voters" prepared to change their votes on the basis of the transfers they receive, while groups paying the taxes to finance the transfers contain a relatively small proportion of swing voters. This provides a potential explanation for small groups benefiting at the expense of large ones that relies neither on imperfect information nor on the costs of collective action.

Note that Lindbeck and Weibull are both from Sweden, where subsequent empirical analysis of local transfer schemes supports the hypothesis that communities with relatively many swing voters receive relatively favorable treatment in redistributive politics (Johansson 2003). In contrast, Ansolabehere and Snyder (2003) find that in state-level politics in the USA, it is the counties that are the most stalwart supporters of the party in power that receive the most favorable treatment in redistributive politics. So it is perhaps not surprising that Cox and McCubbins (1986), two students of US politics, construct a model in which core supporters of each political party are more responsive to offers of redistributive benefits.

Unlike Coughlin and Lindbeck and Weibull, Cox and McCubbins identify core supporters as more reliably responsive to offers of redistributive benefits.[21] Dixit and Londregan (1996) show that one can obtain very similar results to those of Cox and McCubbins within the framework presented here if one assumes that the parties differ in their efficiency at making transfers. If core supporters are easier to reach

---

[20] In this version of the model party L seeks to maximize its vote share, given by (6) subject to the budget constraint in equation (7), with no "leaky bucket" problems, while party R seeks to minimize the party L vote subject to its own budget constraint.

[21] The Cox and McCubbins model takes equation (6) as primitive, rather than deriving it from an individual-level model of voter behavior.

with transfers this will increase the "payoff" in votes per dollar of making transfers to them. Of course, this has to be weighed against core groups' loyalties, which may make it unnecessary to offer them bribes. In the context of urban machine politics in the nineteenth-century USA the assumption that the parties' efficiency at making transfers differed across groups and parties seems to fit well, and it is perhaps not surprising that the urban political machines of that era tended to cultivate groups of core supporters. In the context of twenty-first-century politics in Scandinavia with a large government bureaucracy that is relatively insulated from direct partisan control we might expect the parties to be about equally efficient at making transfers, leading to the focus of tactical redistribution on swing voters observed by Johansson (2003).

With the exception of the Cox and McCubbins model, which takes the voting probability functions as given rather than explicitly tracing them back to voters' preferences, all of the models considered thus far in this section share the feature that voters have attachments to parties that are additively separable from consumption. Yet one of the most important objects of political conflict in the contemporary world is the redistribution of income itself. The assumption that political preferences and preferences over private consumption are separable is untenable when the parties' main ideological programs are focused on the distribution of incomes.

Dixit and Londregan (1998) address this concern by constructing a model that encompasses both "tactical redistribution" aimed at appealing to voters by offering them higher levels of private consumption, and "programmatic" redistribution, in which the parties' ideological programs prescribe different levels of income inequality and inefficiency. In this model, the overall shape of the income distribution has aspects of a public good, but it is a public good about which voters harbor disagreements.

In Dixit and Londregan (1998) the budget constraint is augmented to encompass the deadweight losses of taxation by making these a quadratic function of the difference between initial allocations and actual consumption; thus redistribution is accompanied by inevitable inefficiencies.

Rather than simply seeking to maximize votes, the parties in Dixit and Londregan (1998) care about winning and they care about policy. Policy preferences in this model are weighted averages of two archetypes: an extreme leftist social welfare function that cares only about inequality, and an extreme rightist social welfare function that cares only about avoiding the inefficiencies imposed by taxation.

Taking these one at a time, the archetypal leftist social welfare function seeks to minimize the variation of incomes. That is to say, it seeks to make the distance of each person's consumption from average small, with large deviations from the average being treated as disproportionately more serious. Dixit and Londregan capture this idea using the sample variance of incomes, e.g. the average squared distance of incomes from the sample mean consumption level of $\bar{c}$. Given that consumption for each member of group g is c_g, and that group g has N_g members, the average squared deviation is given by $-S_0^L(\{c_g\}_{g=1}^G)$ where:

$$S_0^L(\{c_g\}_{g=1}^G) = -\Sigma_{g=1}^G N_g(c_g - \bar{c})^2 \tag{8}$$

Notice that the archetypal social welfare function for the left, $S_0^L(\{c_g\}_{g=1}^G)$, which is largest when the variance of consumption levels is smallest, depends on the consumption level of each group.

Now let's turn to the archetypal social welfare function for the right. This welfare function cares only about minimizing the inefficiencies implied by taxation and transfers. These are modeled as increasing with the square of the gap between an individual's actual consumption level, c, and her endowment, y, yielding a loss of $-(y-c)^2$. As all members of the same group g have the same endowment, y_g, and the same consumption level, c_g, the contribution of the N_g members of group g to the deadweight losses is $N_g(c_g - y_g)^2$. When we add up these deadweight losses for all the groups we have the archetypal rightist social welfare function $S_0^R(\{c_g, y_g\}_{g=1}^G)$:

$$S_0^R(\{c_g, y_g\}_{g=1}^G) = -\Sigma_{g=1}^G N_g(c_g - y_g)^2 \qquad (9)$$

Political parties (and individuals) in the Dixit and Londregan (1998) model care about *both* inefficiencies and inequality, but those on the right place more weight on inefficiencies, while their counterparts on the left place greater weight on inequality.

Voters also differ in the relative weights they place on both sets of considerations. A type χ voter in group g will side with the party whose promised redistributive scheme offers the highest value for:

$$a_g c_g + (1-\chi) S_0^L(\{c_g\}_{g=1}^G) + \chi S_0^R(\{c_g, y_g\}_{g=1}^G) \qquad (10)$$

Notice that in this framework[22] there is no longer a primitive preference for one party or the other. Instead voters care about the transfer they receive, the level of taxes, and the amount of inequality implied by each party's proposed policies. However, voters with higher values of χ will, all else equal, be more sympathetic to the goals of party R, while lower values for χ predispose voters towards party L. There is a similarity between χ, the relative weight placed on the rightist welfare function, and X, the partisan attachment to party R that was central to several of the models discussed previously.

The parties choose redistributive schemes subject to the budget constraint in order to maximize a payoff that depends on the value to them of being elected, and on their preferences over the promised policy platform, which itself balances the goals of efficiency and equality. All else equal, the party on the left will give more weight to equality while the party on the right will place more emphasis on efficiency when committing to taxes and transfers. More "power-hungry" parties will be less willing to sacrifice votes in order to adopt ideologically pure platforms, and so they will more aggressively favor blocks of swing voters.

---

[22] As in several of the other models considered in this chapter, groups differ in their willingness to sacrifice their most preferred distribution of income for greater private consumption benefits. Higher values for a correspond to groups that are less concerned about the overall distribution of resources, as compared with the level of their own personal consumption.

In the equilibrium that emerges from this framework each party offers a linear tax rate τ on income,[23] with the party placing relatively more weight on equality setting a higher tax rate, and then, depending on parties' degree of power hunger, the resulting revenues are divided between redistribution from the well off to the poor and lump-sum payments to groups of swing voters. Qualitatively, the tendency for tactical redistribution to favor "swing voters" survives even when the focus of programmatic differences between the parties is the very distribution of income itself.

5 Imperfect Information and Redistribution

Another approach to modeling redistribution is to assume that voters are not equally well informed. Notably, Olson (1965) looked at asymmetries among voters. He contended that small, well-organized groups with high per capita stakes would tend to be better informed (and otherwise more effective in the political struggle for resources) than their larger, poorly organized counterparts with low per capita stakes. Part of this heuristic argument is formalized by Lohmann (1998), who shows that in the context of a model with quadratic preferences, politicians will rationally tilt policy in favor of better-informed blocks of voters, be they large or small. This is because the better-informed voters are more responsive to offers of transfers (and threats of taxes) than are their less well-informed fellow citizens. Add a story about why small groups with high per capita stakes are better informed and this leads to Olsen's prediction. Coate and Morris (1995) also model redistribution using a framework in which information asymmetries have an important effect on redistributive outcomes.

A completely different approach to imperfect information is provided by Piketty (1995). His interest is in the persistence of individuals' political orientations as their economic interests change. He offers an interesting potential explanation for this: in the context of a model akin to that of Meltzer and Richard (1981), individuals' preferences for redistribution are sensitive to their beliefs about the incentive effects of taxation. In Piketty's model, infinitely lived dynasties of individuals form beliefs about the relative importance of effort and luck (parameterized by a parameter that measures the impact of effort) on economic outcomes. The greater the importance of effort, the higher the deadweight losses from taxation, and the lower an individual's preferred tax rate—even when individuals care about the level of inequality. Piketty notes that under plausible assumptions, dynasties with a greater belief in the importance of effort will tend to be wealthier, while those that believe in luck will

[23] While the linear functional form depends on the details of the utility function, it is perhaps surprising that this redistributive model which allows parties to select G distinct tax rates results in a linear tax rate on income (albeit one that is supplemented by lump-sum taxes and transfers), thus obtaining endogenously as a result of the model the sort of tax rate which parties are exogenously constrained to use in many of the models discussed in Section 2.

tend to be poorer, though as long as there is at least some luck involved in economic outcomes there will be a mixture of dynasties among both the well off and the impoverished.[24] Moreover, dynasties will adapt, partially, to new information, so that the newly poor shift their views leftward, but will remain to the right of their chronically poor neighbors in the income distribution, and likewise, the *nouveaux riches* will be to the right of their parents, but to the left of "old money" dynasties that have remained well off for generations. The qualitative predictions of the Piketty model are consistent with some stylized facts from polling data comparing economically mobile individuals with people whose incomes have remained stable, and with some cross-national evidence. By recognizing the importance of imperfect information on the part of voters about the structure of the economic system Piketty has opened up a very promising, and as yet under-exploited, avenue for future research.

6 CONCLUSION

I do not pretend that the preceding pages constitute anything like an exhaustive review of the literature on the political redistribution of income. Instead, they are intended to introduce some of the salient issues, and to inspire or provoke scholars to contribute to our advancing knowledge about this central topic.

As the reader has seen, the literature on political income redistribution has taken several directions, depending on the particular interests of researchers. One strand of the literature imposes restrictions on the set of tax schedules that can be imposed. Keeping the redistributive component of the model simple facilitates the incorporation of other considerations into tractable models, an approach that has been taken with respect to locational models, in which citizens can simultaneously vote with their hands (by casting ballots in local elections) and with their feet (by relocating to districts with policies they prefer).[25] This approach has also been applied to the analysis of non-majoritarian electoral systems.

Another segment of the literature has examined the the fundamental instability of pure redistributive politics, in which almost any allocation is subject to "poaching" by political entrepreneurs, and by those who are badly treated by the status quo allocation. Building on these models, scholars have integrated redistributive politics with other, not necessarily orthogonal, considerations of party loyalty and programmatic ideological policies on the part of candidates and parties. Another direction taken in response to the "chaos" of pure redistributive politics has been to seek stability in the form of institutions, such as those that promote universal coalitions in legislatures.

---

[24] To keep his model simple Piketty resorts to some technical slight of hand to prevent his agents from experimenting to learn more about the importance of effort. Work by Rothschild 1974; McLennan 1984; Easley and Kiefer 1988; and Aghion et al. 1991 indicates that even when such experimentation takes place there are circumstances in which even infinitely lived agents will not choose to learn fully the characteristics of their economic environment.

[25] See the chapter in this volume by David Wildasin for a discussion of this family of models.

Yet another family of models focused on political income redistribution has looked at the importance of asymmetric information in shaping the distributive policies of governments. While the literature has almost universally adapted the hypothesis that agents know the structure of the model, relaxing this assumption to allow asymmetric information about the structure of the economy, opens an exciting frontier for further research.

Along all fronts, the literature discussed here has been cumulative, with scholars building on existing results developed by others. This has facilitated rapid progress over the past thirty years, and holds out the promise of much more to come during the next thirty.

REFERENCES

AGHION, P., BOLTON, P., HARRIS, C., and JULIEN, P. 1991. Optimal learning by experimentation. *Review of Economic Studies*, 58: 621–54.

ANSOLABEHERE, S., and SNYDER, J. M. 2003. Party control of state government and the distribution of public expenditures. MIT Dept. of Economics Working Paper No. 03–38.

AUMANN, R. J., and KURZ, M. 1977a. Power and taxes. *Econometrica*, 45: 1137–61.

—— 1977b. Power and taxes in a multi-commodity economy. *Israel Journal of Mathematics*, 27: 185–234.

AUSTEN-SMITH, D. 2000. Redistributing income under proportional representation. *Journal of Political Economy*, 108: 1235–69.

BARON, D., and FEREJOHN, J. 1989. Bargaining in legislatures. *American Political Science Review*, 83: 1181–206.

BERTRAND, J. 1883. Théorie mathématique de la richesse sociale. *Journal de savats*, 67: 499–508.

BUCHANAN, J., and TULLOCK, G. 1962. *The Calculus of Consent: Logical Foundations for Constitutional Democracy*. Ann Arbor: University of Michigan Press.

COASTE, S., and MORRIS, S. 1995. On the form of transfers to special interests. *Journal of Political Economy*, 103: 1210–35.

COUGHLIN, P. 1986. Elections and income redistribution. *Public Choice*, 50: 27–91.

COX, G. D., and MCCUBBINS, M. D. 1986. Electoral politics as a redistributive game. *Journal of Politics*, 48: 370–89.

DE PALMA, A., GINSBURGH, V., PAPAGEORGIOU, Y., and THISSE, J.-F. 1985. The principle of minimum differentiation holds under sufficient heterogeneity. *Econometrica*, 53: 767–82.

DIXIT, A., and LONDREGAN, J. B. 1995. Redistributive politics and economic efficiency. *American Journal of Political Science*, 89: 856–66.

—— —— 1996. The determinants of success of special interests in redistributive politics. *Journal of Politics*, 58: 1132–55.

—— —— 1998. Ideology, tactics, and efficiency in redistributive politics. *Quarterly Journal of Economics*, 113: 497–529.

—— —— 2000. Political power and the credibility of government debt. *Journal of Economic Theory*, 94: 80–105.

EASLEY, D., and KIEFER, N. 1988. Controlling a stochasitic process with unknown parameters. *Econometrica*, 56: 1045–64.

GROSSMAN, G., and HELPMAN, E. 1994. Protection for sale. *American Political Science Review*, 84: 833–50.

HOTELLING, H. 1929. Stability in competition. *Economic Journal*, 39: 41–57.
JOHANSSON, E. 2003. Intergovernmental grants as a tactical instrument: empirical evidence from Swedish municipalities. *Journal of Public Economics*, 87: 883–915.
KUZNETS, S. 1955. Economic growth and income inequality. *American Economic Review*, 45: 1–28.
LINDBECK, A., and WEIBULL, J. 1987. Balanced budget redistribution as the outcome of political competition. *Public Choice*, 52: 273–97.
LOHMANN, S. 1998. An information rationale for the power of special interests. *American Political Science Review*, 92: 809–27.
MCKELVEY, R. 1976. Intransitivities in multidimensional voting models and some implications for agenda control. *Journal of Economic Theory*, 12: 472–82.
MCLENNAN, A. 1984. Price dispersion and incomplete learning in the long run. *Journal of Economic Dynamics and Control*, 7: 331–47.
MARX, K. 1867. *Das Kapital und seine international Wirkung*. Hamburg: O. Meissner.
MELTZER, A. H., and RICHARD, S. F. 1981. A rational theory of the size of government. *Journal of Political Economy*, 89: 914–27.
MEYERSON, R. D. 1993. Incentives to cultivate favored minorities under alternative electoral systems. *American Political Science Review*, 87: 856–69.
OLSON, M. 1965. *The Logic of Collective Action*. Cambridge, Mass.: Harvard University Press.
——1993. Dictatorship, democracy, and development. *American Political Science Review*, 96: 567–76.
PERSSON, T., ROLAND, G., and TABELLINI, G. 2000. Comparative politics and public finance. *Journal of Political Economy*, 108: 1121–61.
PIKETTY, T. 1995. Social mobility and redistributive politics. *Quarterly Journal of Economics*, 110: 551–84.
ROEMER, J. 1999. The democratic political economy of progressive income taxation. *Econometrica*, 67: 1–19.
ROTHSCHILD, M. 1974. A two-armed bandit theory of market pricing. *Journal of Economic Theory*, 9: 185–202.
SNYDER, J. M., and KRAMER, G. H. 1988. Fairness, self-interest, and the politics of the progressive income tax. *Journal of Public Economics*, 36: 197–230.
SRAFFA, P. 1926. The laws of returns under competitive conditions. *Econometric Journal*, 36: 535–50.
WEINGAST, B. R. 1979. A rational choice perspective on congressional norms. *American Journal of Political Science*, 23: 245–62.

CHAPTER 6

THE IMPACT OF ELECTORAL LAWS ON POLITICAL PARTIES

BERNARD GROFMAN

To understand electoral system effects we must understand both the *formal properties* of electoral rules (including the prosaic fact that the maximum number of parties elected in a constituency is capped by the number of seats that are up for election) and the (short-run and long-run) *incentives for voters, candidates, and parties* created by those rules. While the formal properties of electoral rules determine how "inputs," i.e. completed ballots, will be converted into electoral outcomes, it is the structure of electoral incentives that helps determine both what options will actually be available to the voters on the ballot and how voters will decide among those options. In particular, when there is *strategic voting* such that voters do not always support the candidate/party they most prefer if they do not believe that this candidate/party has a realistic chance to be elected, then the nature of the relationship between underlying voter preferences, electoral rules, and electoral outcomes may be significantly affected. Electoral incentives—in conjunction with beliefs about likely outcomes under different scenarios—affect not just voter choice but also *how many* parties or candidates we can expect and also *which* candidates/parties might choose to run.[1] Electoral incentives affect as well how those candidates/parties will position themselves, and how they can be expected to behave if elected to office.

---

[1] Voters often are prohibited from expressing their support for alternatives that are not on the ballot, and even if allowed a write-in ballot, write-in votes are unlikely to be efficacious.

Electoral incentives cannot be expected to operate "instantaneously," however. Rather, even if institutions remain essentially unchanged, it will take time until voters, candidates, and parties come to understand how a given set of institutions, embedded as they are within a particular political context, will affect outcomes. Moreover, the structure of electoral incentives involves a complex interplay between the incentives for voters and those for candidates and parties. Ideally, we seek to endogenize all relevant factors in a model of dynamic equilibrium—which requires a game-theoretic perspective.[2]

The formal study of the properties of voting rules has a long history, dating at least as far back as Condorcet (1785). For example, consider the *Condorcet criterion*, which is the requirement that a voting rule always choose the *majority winner*, aka the *Condorcet winner*, i.e. that candidate, if any, who can defeat each and every one of the other alternatives in paired contest. If such a candidate exists, among voting rules that pick a single winner, a classic social choice question is 'Which rules satisfy the *Condorcet criterion*?' Major contributions to the axiomatic underpinnings of electoral rules have been made by economists such as Black (1958) and Arrow (1962), and recent work by economists, mathematicians, and others has built on those foundations.

In political science, the publication of Douglas Rae's seminal dissertation *The Political Consequences of Electoral Laws* (Rae 1967; 2nd edn. 1971) marks the beginning of the present empirical and theoretical renaissance in electoral studies, of which works such as Duverger (1955), Eckstein (1963), and Grumm (1958) were harbingers. Subsequent to Rae's work, a vast empirical and statistical modeling literature on electoral systems and their effects has grown up (much of it summarized in works such as Lijphart 1992, 1999; Taagepera and Shugart 1989), while important recent work has dealt with electoral system adoptions and changes (Boix 1999; Grofman and Lijphart 2002; Colomer 2004).[3]

In one short chapter it is impossible to review the wide range of contributions to what is now an established sub-field, with a journal of its own, *Electoral Studies*, since the areas that were once the central concerns of researchers—fairness of results in terms of the relationships between votes and seats, incentives for party proliferation, and issues of cabinet stability—now constitute only a small and diminishing proportion of work in the sub-field. Also, the definition of the sub-field has widened to consider electoral laws more broadly and not just rules for converting votes into seats, e.g. rules affecting suffrage, ballot format, candidate eligibility, campaign finance regulation, legal constraints on political advertising, calendaring overlaps between presidential and legislative campaigns, etc.

Here, to keep our task manageable we (*a*) focus on empirical research rather than on the axiomatic (and hence implicitly normative) underpinnings of different voting rules, or on formal modeling results that look at incentive considerations in a purely

---

[2] Gary Cox (1997) is an exemplar of this research style. For example he has looked at how voter preferences and the levels of expected support for the various available alternatives condition to what extent and in what ways we might expect *strategic voting by* individual voters (or voting blocs).

[3] For many purposes it is useful to take electoral rules as given, but it is also as well to recognize that parties seek electoral rules that advantage them.

theoretical fashion; (*b*) we confine ourselves to comparisons of only a limited number of polar electoral system types, with a focus on the list form of proportional election methods, on the one hand, and plurality elections, on the other—two of the most important voting methods both from a theoretical standpoint and in terms of the frequency of their use in the world's major democracies (see e.g. Reynolds and Reilly 1997); and (*c*) we report results for only one of the four main concerns of the field (parties, voters, governance, and policy outputs) by looking at electoral system effects on only the first of these, parties. In particular, we examine electoral system effects on the number of parties, disproportionality of partisan representation, the degree of dispersion of party ideological locations, the strength of internal party discipline, etc.

1 DEFINITIONS

Before we can turn to a discussion of electoral system theory and the search for empirical regularities, it is necessary to begin with some basic definitions.

As noted earlier, list PR and plurality methods are two of the most important methods in common use.

Under *plurality*, in a district where there are m places to be filled, every voter has m votes and the m candidates with the highest votes are declared elected. We refer to m as *district magnitude*. When $m = 1$, commonly called *a single-member district*, and we use plurality, we have the form of elections that in Britain and other English-speaking nations are referred to as *first past the post*. When $m > 1$, we have what is commonly called a *multimember district*. In multimember districts that also use plurality, we have what is called *plurality bloc voting*. Under the most basic form of proportional representation, involving choice among a ranked list of candidates from a set of political parties in districts where $m > 1$, commonly known as party *list PR*, voters have just one vote to cast (for a political party), and the parties are then entitled to elect a number of candidates proportional to the party's share of the votes cast. Under pure party list voting, if a party vote share entitles it to elect, say k, representatives from a given m seat district, then the top k names on the party's pre-designated list will be the ones chosen to represent that party.

It is common to view electoral systems along a continuum from *majoritarian* to *proportional*. List PR and plurality methods may be used to exemplify the poles of this continuum.

One standard way to define the proportionality continuum is to take an a priori approach in which proportionality is defined in terms of *the threshold of exclusion*, the *maximum* support that can be attained by a party while still failing to win even one seat in a district (Loosemore and Hanby 1971). Defining the low proportionality end of this continuum are plurality and majoritarian systems where the threshold of exclusion is 1/2. In a given district of size m, the party which captures a plurality of the votes in that district gains all m seats; thus, the threshold of exclusion for that district is 1/2 since a majority party *ipso facto* must have a plurality of the votes. Defining the high-proportionality end of the continuum are systems involving proportional representation in nationwide districts, where the threshold of exclusion is roughly $1/S$, where S is the size of the legislature.[4] In between are multimember districts using proportional representation in districts of size less than S. For example, in a district that elects nine members, the threshold of exclusion would be roughly 10 per cent+ under most proportional voting rules because, no matter how votes were divided among the remaining parties, any party with 10 per cent+ share of the vote cannot be denied representation (at least one of nine seats) in that district.[5]

However, as Rein Taagepera (personal communication, 4 June 2004) observes: "The same electoral rules can lead to vastly different disproportionality, even in the same country and even in consecutive elections," so a purely theoretically derived index of disproportionality such as the threshold of exclusion may be misleading. To deal with this problem, scholars commonly calculate empirical indices of disproportionality over several different elections held under a given set of electoral rules. For *partisan elections*, i.e. elections involving competition where all or most politically viable candidates run on a party label, the two most common measures of overall proportionality are the *Loosemore–Hanby Index of Distortion* (Loosemore and Hanby 1971):

$$D = 1/2 \; \Sigma |v_i - s_i|,$$

with v_i the vote share of the ith party and s_i the seat share of that same party;[6] and the *Gallagher Index* (Gallagher 1991):

$$Gh = [1/2 \Sigma (v_i - s_i)^2]^{0.5}.$$

For two-party competition, another approach to measuring disproportionality empirically is in terms of what is called the swing ratio. Tufte (1973) proposed that, in two-party legislative competition, a party can expect to be receive a share of seats such that

$$\log s/(1-s) = k \log v/(1-v) + \varepsilon,$$

In this equation, k is an estimate of the *swing ratio*. The closer k is to 1, the closer we are to a purely proportional system. The swing ratio has been empirically estimated to be around 1.7 for recent elections to the US House of Representatives. In the long-term democracies, it is very close to one for elections under PR.

---

[4] The extreme case of plurality bloc voting, when $m = S$, is called an *at-large election*.

[5] Another approach to defining the theoretical proportionality continuum puts so-called *semi-proportional systems* such as cumulative voting and limited voting in between plurality and strictly proportional methods. In *cumulative voting*, each voter has multiple votes to cast and can split his vote among several candidates or cumulate it on a single candidate. Under *limited voting*, each voter has k votes to cast, where k is less than district magnitude m. The closer k is to m, the less proportional is the method.

[6] The usual citation to this index is Loosemore and Hanby 1971 but the same idea is found in other contexts in earlier work (see Taagepera and Grofman 2003).

Now we turn to an examination of hypotheses and evidence about the effects of electoral systems on parties and candidates.

2 Effects of Electoral Systems on Parties and Candidates

2.1 Impact on Number of Candidates/Parties who Compete/Win

Duverger (1955) hypothesized that single-member district plurality will tend to generate two-party competition at the level of individual districts, and Duverger also proposed that PR systems would generate multiparty competition. We can synthesize these two results in terms of our earlier discussion by proposing that the lower the threshold of exclusion, the greater the number of parties we can expect to compete in a given district. The key reason we expect such a result is that when parties (and their candidates) are instrumental in seeking office in order to win (and not just, say, to "send a message"), then only parties that have some reasonable prospect of achieving electoral success should enter political competition. Plurality systems have the highest threshold of exclusion of any electoral system, while among PR systems, the higher the district magnitude, the lower the threshold of exclusion (or of representation), and thus the easier it is for parties to achieve representation with only relatively limited electoral support. Thus, for any electoral rule (with the exception of plurality bloc voting), expectations of possible electoral success should increase with district magnitude, and thus more parties should be expected to compete at the district level.

However, if there are numerous small parties or independent candidacies (some of them even "joke" candidacies), and many of those seeking office receive very few votes, simply counting up the number of parties contesting for office can be almost meaningless. Indeed, while we can simply count the number of parties with officeholders represented in a district (or in the entire legislature), even this number can be misleading for some purposes, since it does not take into account the relative sizes of the parties. Clearly a legislature with five parties of roughly the same size can have very different political alliances and distribution of real political power from a parliament with two parties whose combined seat share is 95 per cent and three minuscule parties.

Laakso and Taagepera (1979) addressed this problem by proposing what in political science is known as *the Laakso–Taagepera Index of the Effective Number of Parties*, defined as

$$1/(\Sigma\ v_i^2), \text{ for vote share}$$

and

$$1/(\Sigma\ s_i^2), \text{ for seat share.}$$

When we calculate *effective number of parties* we take into account the relative sizes of the parties, so that small parties are heavily discounted.[7] Much of the literature on electoral systems effects uses the effective number of parties rather than the number of parties, per se. However, we should not interpret the term "effective" literally. The Laakso–Taagepera index is simply a useful way to provide a single number to summarize a range of values (i.e. party vote shares or party seat shares).[8]

Empirical work supports the theoretical expectations that both the (effective) number of parties competing for office and the (effective) number of parties represented in parliament increases monotonically with m (see e.g. Taagepera and Shugart 1989; Lijphart 1992). Cox (1997) provides a game-theoretic argument that the number of viable parties who compete in a constituency will be bounded by $m + 1$. Taagepera and Shugart (1989) provide empirical evidence to show that, in general, the average *effective* number of parties elected to office in a constituency is roughly the square root of m, and thus increases (but not in a linear fashion) with m. Their argument is a statistical one about bounded variables and the principle of insufficient information. In a nutshell, since the number of parties elected from a district of magnitude m must be between 1 and m, they take the *geometric mean* of these bounds as their best a priori estimate of the (effective) number of parties represented in a given constituency of size m.

In more recent work Taagepera and Shugart (1993) have examined how to move from the number of parties expected to compete at the district level to predictions about how many (effective) parties we can expect to find at the national level. They model outcomes as a statistical function of the mean value of m and of the size of the legislature.

While district magnitude, m, is the most studied variable in terms of its impact on the number of parties competing for and winning office in a given district, and its importance is undoubted, there certainly are other features of electoral laws (conceived broadly) that also have important impacts on party proliferation. For example, in systems where there are separate presidential elections, the nature of the linkage between presidential and legislative elections can significantly affect the number of political parties. Summarizing past empirical work, Geddes (2003, 208) observes: "Where presidential and legislative elections occur at the same time ... two-party systems tend to emerge" even if legislative elections are held under PR.[9]

---

[7] For example, if there were four parties, one with 40%, one with 30%, one with 20%, and one with 10% of the vote, the effective number of parties at the electoral level would be 3.33.

[8] Also, the Laakso–Taagepera Index fails to take into account the pivotal power of parties. An alternative approach (not yet found in the electoral systems literature) is first to calculate a *power score* such as the *Banzhaf Index* or the *Shapley Shubik value* (Brams 1975), and then calculate the effective number of parties based on a normalization of each party's power score shares that sums to one.

[9] However, we would also expect that presidential systems without run-offs that use single-member districts for their legislative elections would exhibit the lowest levels of party fragmentation of any of the presidential systems. In my view, the USA falls into this latter category. While the US Constitution provides for a run-off that is resolved (under special voting provisions) by the US House of Representatives if no candidate receives a majority of votes in the Electoral College, the winner-take-all Electoral College vote allocation provisions of forty-eight of the fifty states make the likelihood of such a resolution of a presidential contest unlikely.

The essential idea behind this result is that competition for the single office of president generates pressure for parties to coalesce behind a presidential candidate who has a chance of winning. But if they do that, they begin to lose their separate identities; while, on the other hand, parties that are not associated with a viable presidential candidate come to be seen as irrelevant and lose support. It is easier for parties to resist such pressures for coalescing when elections for different offices occur on different schedules, since parties that have no hope of winning presidential office can, nonetheless, hope to continue to do well in legislative and municipal elections.

However, the generalization given above must be qualified by the observation that, in presidential systems which use PR for legislative elections, "[p]residential run-offs encourage the formation of small parties" (Geddes 2003, 208).[10] This effect is expected to be strongest when a victory on the first round is scored only if a candidate receives an absolute majority of the votes cast. When there are run-offs, "rather than forming pre-election coalitions, small parties enter the first round in order to establish their bargaining power as coalition partners for the second round."[11] Thus, for presidential systems with legislative elections held under PR, "party fragmentation tends to be greater in countries with presidential run-offs" than in countries where simple plurality determines the presidential winner (Geddes 2003, 208).[12]

Another electoral system feature that substantially affects the degree of party fragmentation is the set of rules governing ballot access. Many non-democratic nations have stringent legal restrictions on competition, or in practice make it impossible for other parties to compete successfully with the ruling party. But even in some democratic nations with genuine political competition, such as the USA we can find a fairly drastic form of cartelized politics, in which existing major parties seek to restrict the domain of competition to bar further entrants by raising substantial legal barriers to new parties (or independents) qualifying for a listing on the ballot.

2.2 Effect on Proportionality of Party Representation

Based on the formal (mechanical) properties of electoral systems, using some straightforward algebra, we would expect that, *ceteris paribus*, the closer the threshold of exclusion of the electoral rule is to zero, the more disproportional will be the results of elections under that rule. In other words, the more proportional the electoral rule, the more proportional the expected results. Thus, under a system where the threshold of exclusion was $1/S$, if S is large, we might expect very little disproportionality

---

[10] Duverger hypothesized that there are strong incentives for party proliferation in two-stage run-off systems in which only candidates who received some specified level of support in the first round are allowed to compete in the second and final round.

[11] See further discussion of run-off rules later in the text.

[12] In general, for systems using PR for legislative elections, Jones 1995 argues that, while district magnitude is the most important single determinant of party fragmentation in parliamentary systems, its effects are overshadowed in presidential systems by the presence or absence of run-offs and by the nature of the election calendar.

between votes and seats. In contrast, if we had two-party plurality competition, the theoretically worst case would give us a disproportionality of nearly one-half;[13] while disproportionality under plurality could even approach one as the number of parties increases.

But we also expect that, the closer the threshold of exclusion is to zero, the more parties there are that will contest the election, since the incentives are for smaller parties to contest if there is a chance they might be successful.[14] The existence of both a mechanical and an incentive effect means that differences in disproportionality as we increase district magnitude are not as large as we might first think based on the purely mechanical effects of district magnitude. The reason is that PR systems with high district magnitude tend to be contested by more parties than PR systems with a lower district magnitude and, even with a highly proportional system, some of these parties will still not achieve representation. Thus, the incentive effect of district magnitude, which acts to increase disproportionality by increasing the number of parties, operates in an opposite direction to the mechanical effect of district magnitude in reducing disproportionality.[15] Moreover, there are many other complicating factors, such as spillover effects in which parties with little chance in a given constituency nonetheless run candidates there in order to enhance their stature as national parties, or to assist candidates of the party running for other offices in the same or an overlapping constituency by motivating party supporters to participate in the election. Nonetheless, empirically, there is a strong relationship in which high district magnitude is associated with low disproportionality.

2.3 Effect on Biases in Favor of the Larger Parties and Against the Smallest Parties in the Translations of Votes into Seats

If district magnitude is large, and there are no special threshold rules that exclude parties that receive less than some given percentage of the vote from being eligible for seats in the parliament, list PR and other forms of proportional representation tend to treat large parties and smaller parties relatively symmetrically in translating vote shares into seat shares.

In plurality-based competition in single-member districts there can be strong biases in favor of the largest party. For example, for multiparty competition under single-member district plurality in Great Britain, in the 2005 election, we saw the plurality vote-getting party, Labour, win a clear majority of the seats despite having

---

[13] Since only one seat is to be filled, for two-party competition, the Loosemore–Hanby Index would be about one-half when one party received just barely more than half the vote, and the other barely less than half the vote.

[14] Recall that the threshold of exclusion is a theoretical construct. Often parties will be able to elect a representative with a much lower share of the vote.

[15] In other words, there is reciprocal causality between number of parties and disproportionality. Taagepera and Shugart (1989) were apparently the first to call attention to the phenomenon of the countervailing incentive effects of increased district magnitude on disproportionality.

barely more votes nationwide than its two major rivals (36 per cent). Similarly, for the past decades we have seen a substantial bias against the smallest party in Great Britain, the Liberal (later Liberal Democrat) Party, in its ability to translate vote share into seat share.[16] And, in plurality systems, biases against third parties can be self-reinforcing in that, as Duverger hypothesized, they can generate strategic voting among potential supporters toward a larger party with a better chance of winning the election in order to avoid "wasting one's vote".[17]

2.4 Incentives for Non-convergence of Party Platforms and for the Formation of "Extremist" Parties

From Duverger (1955), as noted above, we anticipate that single-seat plurality elections will tend to generate two-party competition (at least at the constituency level). From Downs (1957) we anticipate that, if we have two parties in a plurality-based system, and if there is one principal dimension of political competition, each party will locate at the preferences of the overall median voter. But, as noted earlier, Taagepera and Grofman (1985) have found that, empirically, the effective number of parties winning representation is approximately $I + 1$, where I is the number of issue dimensions. Thus, in a two-party competition we should see only a single issue dimension. But combining the theoretical insights of Downs and Duverger and the empirical findings about dimensionality, theory leads us to expect—at least under the assumptions specified above—that the politics of the candidates who run for legislative office in plurality systems will be centrist.

However, when we look at real-world elections under plurality, while we find the kinds of centripetal pressures that Downs (1957) models, we also find strong countervailing centrifugal effects. Among the most important of these countervailing forces are the role of political activists in pushing for policies closer to their liking, the nature of the party nomination process (with party primaries tending to reinforce divergence from the overall voter median because of the restricted enrollment in the party primary electorate with disproportionate participation by hard-core supporters of the party, and the tendency to select candidates who reflect the views of those voters), the existence of geographically based differences in party support and political attitudes, and the presence of policy-motivated goals of elected politicians.[18]

Even in plurality systems with predominantly two-party competition at the national level, such as the USA, we do not find two major parties that look completely like Lewis Carroll's Tweedledum and Tweedledee. Indeed, I have argued that the

---

[16] Another form of electoral system bias is *partisan bias*, i.e. a *party-specific* asymmetry in the translation of votes into seats, such that, for identical vote share, different parties will receive different seat shares (Grofman 1983). Bias occurs because some parties are more "efficient" in turning their votes into seats than other parties. For example, in two-party competition in a legislature, one party may win its seats with an average of 70% of the vote, while the other party may win its seats with an average of only 55% of the vote. Partisan biases may arise "naturally" as a result of the partisan distribution of votes across territory, and/or they may be manipulated.

[17] We return to this topic later.   [18] See esp. Wittman 1973, 1977, 1983, 1990.

Downsian convergence result gets it quite wrong. In plurality elections, rather than being the rule, full convergence should rather be thought of as a bizarre exception (Grofman 2004). In a nutshell, the argument is that the Downsian convergence result rests on more than a dozen specific assumptions, and that changing almost any one of these assumptions makes the convergence result go away (cf. Adams, Merrill, and Grofman 2005). Based on their empirical work, Merrill and Grofman (1999) suggest that plurality politics is apt to generate what they call "moderate divergence."

Moreover, the Downsian convergence result for two-candidate plurality elections is what is expected to happen within a *single* constituency. However, even if, within any single constituency, the candidates of every party are offering identical platforms, if local candidates have "wiggle room" to move their positions closer to the views of the median voter in their constituency, then the platforms espoused by the candidates of a given party need not be identical across constituencies. If (*a*) there is considerable variation in the location of the median voter across constituencies (as was the case for much of US history, with the South being more conservative than the rest of the nation, at least on issues having to do with social values), and (*b*) if, when we have otherwise identical candidates of opposite parties in a given constituency, the voters in that constituency use their proximity to the *national* party positions as a cue to decide among them, we can get national divergence of parties even though, locally, parties are more convergent. This is arguably the situation which was characteristic of the USA in the 1980s, in which constituencies (predominantly urban ones) where the median voter is a liberal tended to elect Democrats, and constituencies where the median voter is a conservative (especially constituencies in the South) tended to elect Republicans. Thus, national divergence of party positions can occur even when, locally, we have substantial (or even complete) convergence.[19]

In contrast, when we turn to look at incentives for ideological spread in PR systems, it is easy to see that PR systems offer the opportunity for relatively small groups of like-minded voters to elect a candidate of choice. In particular, ideologically fringe groups have an incentive to compete (as might other types of minorities, e.g. ethnic-based parties) because they have a real chance to win some representation, especially when district magnitude is high. Consequently, theory leads us to expect not just more parties but also a wider *range* of (ideological and other) points of view represented in the legislature under list PR than under plurality (Cox 1990, 1997). And this is confirmed by the empirical data. Of course, there may still be incentive effects, such that voters will choose not to support parties that have no chance to be part of a governing coalition even if those parties might win representation in a proportional voting system. Still, incentive effects to shift away from parties that have little chance of being part of a governing coalition will be weaker in situations under PR where voters might realistically expect their first-choice party to at least win some representation than in situations under plurality where a vote for

---

[19] More recently, it can be argued that we have (perceived) policy divergence of Democratic and Republican candidates in the USA even at the local level, because "wiggle room" has been largely eliminated in favor of Steinian propositions of the form "A Republican is a conservative is a Republican," and "A Democrat is a liberal is a Democrat."

a minor party is truly wasted except as a protest vote or in terms of a belief that support for the party this election is a means of building toward the party's future success.

2.5 Effect on Degree of "Localist" Perspectives of Representatives

Electoral system scholars have tried to understand the links between election system type and the extent to which parliamentarians exhibit a localistic orientation. But degree of proportionality is not the only useful way to distinguish among electoral systems. There are other features across which voting rules can be compared which give us categorization schemes that can also be used for predictive purposes. For example, one such typology considers the nature of the ballot, with the key distinction being between ballots that only require voters to mark one or more x's, on the one hand, and those that require voters to supply a partial or complete ranking of alternatives, on the other. This distinction cuts across the PR–plurality distinction. While list PR only requires x's from the voter, another form of proportional representation, the *single transferable vote*, requires voters to list their rankings among alternatives.[20] Another useful categorization scheme is based on the degree to which voters vote only for individual candidates or only choose among parties, with *non-partisan elections*, where party labels are barred, anchoring one pole, and *pure list PR elections*, where voters cast a single vote and must accept the party list ranking of candidates, anchoring the other pole. List PR and STV do not fall on the same point on this continuum either.[21]

Carey and Shugart (1995) hypothesize that the probability that legislators are more likely to pursue localistic concerns, such as pursuing "pork-barrel" projects for their constituencies is greater, the greater the electoral incentives they have to cultivate a *personal vote*, i.e. a vote based on the service record or personal traits of an individual candidate, as distinct from support for that candidate based on the general policies of the party which nominates him. Carey and Shugart (1995) propose to rank electoral systems in terms of the incentives for cultivation of personal votes by looking at the values of four variables: (Each of these distinctions allows us to specify hypotheses about electoral systems, some of which are discussed below.) (*a*) the extent to which party leaders can determine which candidates are nominated, (*b*) the degree to which

---

[20] The *single transferable vote*, also know by its abbreviation STV and as the *Hare* system, requires that voters must rank order their preferences for candidates. If there are m seats to be filled and n voters then winning candidates much receive a *Droop quota* of votes (the greatest integer bound of the quotient $n/(m + 1)$). If no candidate receives a Droop quota of first preference votes, the candidate with the fewest first preference votes is eliminated and, for those ballots where she was first choice, votes are reallocated to the next candidate on the voter's list. This process continues until exactly m candidates have received a Droop quota, or until the pool of eligibles is down to as many candidates as there are seats remaining to be filled.

[21] Each of these distinctions allows us to specify hypotheses about electoral systems, some of which are discussed below.

any given candidate's electoral fate rides on the votes received by others of his *own* party, (c) in party list systems, the extent to which party leaders control the exact placement of candidates on the party list and thus, by placing favored candidates near the top of the list, can make it more likely that they will be elected, and (d) district magnitude, m.[22]

From the Carey and Shugart perspective, list PR methods with large district magnitudes anchor one end of the party-centric continuum, with the lowest expected levels of localism, while the system used in Japan during much of the post-Second World War period, the single non-transferable vote (SNTV) with small magnitude constituencies, represents the other end of the continuum.[23] Plurality-based single-member district systems are intermediate, but toward the localistic end of the continuum. They tend to be characterized by what Wattenberg (1992) called "candidate-centered politics," i.e. politics where the personal characteristics of the local candidates matter as much as or more than the national party platform in affecting voter choices, and where elections tend to be decided by voter preferences on issues that are local to the constituency as much as or more than over national issues.

2.6 Impact on Within-party Ideological Homogeneity

As suggested earlier, we may think of candidates as being tethered by a rubber band to the ideology espoused by the parties whose label they run on. How elastic that rubber band is (i.e. how far it will stretch and thus how much wiggle room the candidacy has to deviate from the party position) varies with a number of different factors.

One important factor seems to be the degree of party control over the party nomination process. If central party organizations can deny dissidents the right to campaign under the party label, they can preserve (to the extent that they wish to) the party's ideological purity.

Another important factor is the control central party leaders have over the career path of party members. If advancement within party ranks is largely or entirely centrally controlled, then, *ceteris paribus*, we would expect that deviation from the party line could better be kept in check.[24] In the extreme, as in some party systems in the former Soviet Union, we may have a party authorized to expel members, including sitting legislators, more or less at the discretion of party leaders, and a rule that legislators elected on a given party's label who are no longer in that party may no longer serve in the legislature. Under such rules, party leaders can control party dissidents quite thoroughly.

---

[22] They treat each of these variables as dichotomous (e.g. distinguishing only between $m = 1$ and $m > 1$) and weigh the first three factors equally to arrive at a composite index.

[23] SNTV allows voters one vote, in a district in which there are m seats to be filled. Thus, the threshold of exclusion for SNTV is $1/(m + 1)$. See Grofman et al. 1999.

[24] See discussion in Katz 1980, 8–9.

Ceteris paribus, in a pure party list PR system, voters in the general election have no effect on party orderings in determining which of the party's candidates will be selected, and in most such systems, the party leaders completely control the order in which candidates are located on the party list. We expect that such systems will exhibit greater party cohesion (as signaled by the unwillingness of party members to cast legislative votes that diverge from the national party position) than single-member district plurality systems where the nomination process is localized. The argument is simply that when the national party controls your re-election chances there are considerable costs to not doing what party leaders want.[25]

Another factor is how political geography and the nature of the districting process affect the nature of district homogeneity. If we have districts that differ greatly in their voters' ideological characteristics, there will be incentives for parties to allow variation in candidate platforms at the local level in order to increase the party's chances of winning seats. Thus, the nature of the districting process is relevant. The more alike in ideological characteristics are the constituencies being constructed, the easier it is for parties to enforce ideological unity on their candidates. Of course, since, under list PR, it is like-minded voters who aggregate to form the party constituency, list PR systems might be expected to lend themselves to more homogeneous parties than plurality systems and, relatedly, we might expect that, *ceteris paribus*, countries with high district magnitude would be the ones most likely to have ideologically cohesive parties.

Because we expect high district magnitude to yield more ideologically homogeneous parties we should also expect that, *ceteris paribus*, party candidates will be closer to the mean party supporter of that party in countries with high district magnitudes than in countries with low district magnitudes, because in the former set of countries we should expect highly differentiated party systems with large numbers of parties where both voters and candidates with policy preferences can readily find a party close to their own issue position.[26]

2.7 Impact on Incentives for Party Factionalism

The nature of the electoral system used for general elections potentially affects the internal homogeneity of political parties. One important consideration is whether or not the electoral rules allow for/require that candidates of the same party compete with each other for votes as well as with candidates of the other parties. Some electoral rules, perhaps most notably the *single non-transferable vote (SNTV)*, with m seats to be filled, but with each voter having only one vote, set up a situation in which party

---

[25] However, this is not to say that you cannot have strong parties even under plurality. For example, Great Britain has managed to do this by only partly decentralizing the nomination process; in that nation's contemporary politics often, when it comes to nominations, the national party proposes, while the local party only disposes.

[26] For some relevant (but inconclusive) empirical results bearing on this issue see Holmberg 1999, esp. table 5.5, p. 104; Wessels 1999, esp. figure 7.4, p. 156.

members are potentially in competition with one another. This encourages party factionalism, as organized factions within the party support candidates with factional ties against those of other factions within the party. Thus, we expect that countries using SNTV will be likely to have factionalized parties. This expectation is confirmed for Japan during the post-Second World War period when SNTV was used for its lower national chamber (Reed 1990; see chapters on Japan in Grofman et al. 1999). However, SNTV's incentives for factionalism can be overcome if the party leadership is strong enough—as apparently was true in Taiwan which also used SNTV, for the long-time ruling party (see chapters on Taiwan in Grofman et al. 1999).

3 CONCLUSIONS

The remarks above give some feel for what is known/theorized about electoral systems effects in one important domain, consequences for parties and candidates. But, as noted earlier, effects on parties are only one of four large-scale topics that have been important in electoral system research, and despite the sub-field's remarkable expansion and development over the past several decades, there remain a number of challenges for future research on electoral system impacts:

1. More work is needed on the linkages between electoral system effects and public policy outcomes.
2. We need to understand better the interaction between electoral system effects and institutional features such as federalism and presidentialism.[27]
3. We need to better understand how the "minutiae" of electoral rules (including the rules of the nominating process and subtle differences in implementation among largely identical voting rules) help determine electoral system consequences.[28]

And last, but not least,

4. We need to answer better the question: "How much do electoral systems matter, as compared to factors such as social heterogeneity, political culture, political history, or other institutional practices?" (cf. Norris 2004, 5–6, and the discussion of electoral systems as embedded institutions in Bowler and Grofman 2000).

---

[27] For example, both Persson and Tabellini 2003 and Jones 1995 have argued that some effects of electoral systems may be totally different when the electoral rules are part of a presidential system from when they are part of parliamentary systems.

[28] For example, in the empirical work on turnout across nations, the effects of electoral systems, per se, on turnout do not appear nearly as large in their impact as factors such as whether voter registration is automatic, the availability of weekend voting or other extensions of time to cast a ballot, and, perhaps most importantly, the imposition of compulsory voting (Jackman 1987).

References

ADAMS, J., MERRILL, S., III, and GROFMAN, B. 2005. *A Unified Theory of Party Competition: A Cross-national Analysis Integrating Spatial and Behavioral Factors*. Cambridge: Cambridge University Press.

ARROW, K. J. 1962. *Social Choice and Individual Values*. New York: John Wiley and Sons; originally published 1951.

BALINSKI, M. L., and YOUNG, H. P. 1982. *Fair Representation: Meeting the Idea of One Man, One Vote*. New Haven, Conn.: Yale University Press.

BLACK, D. 1958. *The Theory of Committees and Elections*. Cambridge: Cambridge University Press.

BOIX, C. 1999. Setting the rules of the game: the choice of electoral systems in advanced democracies. *American Political Science Review*, 93: 609–24.

BOWLER, S., and GROFMAN, B. (eds.). 2000. *Elections in Australia, Ireland and Malta under the Single Transferable Vote*. Ann Arbor: University of Michigan Press.

BRAMS, S. 1945. *Game Theory and Politics*. New York: Simon and Schuster.

CAMPAGNA, J., and GROFMAN, B. 1990. Party control and partisan bias in 1980s congressional redistricting. *Journal of Politics*, 52: 1242–57.

CAREY, J. M., and SHUGART, M. 1995. Incentives to cultivate a personal vote: a rank ordering of electoral formulas. *Electoral Studies*, 14: 417–40.

COLOMER, J. (ed.). 2004. *Handbook of Electoral System Design*. New York: Palgrave.

CONDORCET, MARQUIS DE 1785. *Essai sur l'application de l'analyse à la probabilité des decisions rendues à la pluralité des voix*. Paris: De l'Imprimeur Royal.

COX, G. 1990. Centripetal and centrifugal incentives in electoral systems. *American Journal of Political Science*, 34: 903–35.

―― 1997. *Making Votes Count: Strategic Coordination in the World's Electoral Systems*. New York: Cambridge University Press.

DOWNS, A. 1957. *An Economic Theory of Democracy*. New York: Harper and Row.

DUVERGER, M. 1955. *Political Parties*. New York: Wiley.

ECKSTEIN, H. 1963. Impact of electoral systems on representative government. Pp. 247–54 in *Comparative Politics*, ed. H. Eckstein and D. Apter. New York: Macmillan.

ESAIASSON, P. 1999. Not all politics is local: the geographical dimension of policy representation. Pp. 110–36 in *Policy Representation in Western Democracies*, ed. R. Pierce, J. Thomassen, R. Herra, S. Holmberg, P. Esaiasson, and B. Wessels. New York: Oxford University Press.

GALLAGHER, M. 1991. Proportionality, disproportionality and electoral systems. *Electoral Studies*, 10: 33–51.

GEDDES, B. 2003. *Paradigms and Sand Castles: Theory Building and Research Design in Comparative Politics*. Ann Arbor: University of Michigan Press.

GROFMAN, B. 1983. Measures of bias and proportionality in seats–votes relationships. *Political Methodology*, 9: 295–327.

―― 2004. Downs and two-party convergence. *Annual Review of Political Science* (ed. N. Polsby), 7: 25–46.

―― and LIJPHART, A. (eds.). 2002. *The Evolution of Electoral and Party Systems in the Nordic Nations*. New York: Agathon Press.

―― and REYNOLDS, A. 2001. Electoral systems and the art of constitutional engineering: an inventory of the main findings. Pp. 125–63 in *Rules and Reason: Perspectives on Constitutional Political Economy*, ed. R. Mudambi, P. Navarra, and G. Sobbrio. New York: Cambridge University Press.

—— LEE, S.-C., WINCKLER, E., and WOODALL, B. (eds.). 1999. *Elections in Japan, Korea and Taiwan under the Single Non-transferable Vote: The Comparative Study of an Embedded Institution*. Ann Arbor: University of Michigan Press.

GRUMM, J. G. 1958. Theories of electoral systems. *Midwest Journal of Political Science*, 2: 357–76.

HOLMBERG, S. 1999. Collective policy congruence compared. Pp. 87–109 in *Policy Representation in Western Democracies*, ed. R. Pierce, J. Thomassen, R. Herra, S. Holmberg, P. Esaiasson, and B. Wessels. New York: Oxford University Press.

JACKMAN, R. W. 1987. Political institutions and voter turnout in the industrial democracies. *American Political Science Review*, 81: 405–24.

JONES, M. 1995. *Electoral Laws and the Survival of Presidential Democracies*. Notre Dame, Ind.: University of Notre Dame Press.

KATZ, R. 1980. *A Theory of Parties and Electoral Systems*. Baltimore: Johns Hopkins University Press.

LAAKSO, M., and TAAGEPERA, R. 1979. Effective number of parties: a measure with application to west Europe. *Comparative Political Studies*, 12: 3–27.

LIJPHART, A. 1984. *Democracies: Patterns of Majoritarian and Consensus Government in Twenty-One Countries*. New Haven, Conn.: Yale University Press.

—— 1992. *Parliamentary versus Presidential Government*. Oxford: Oxford University Press.

—— 1999. *Patterns of Democracy*. New Haven, Conn.: Yale University Press.

—— and GIBBERD, R. W. 1977. Thresholds and payoffs in list systems of proportional representation. *European Journal of Political Research*, 5: 219–44.

LOOSEMORE, J., and HANBY, V. J. 1971. The theoretical limits of maximum distortion: some analytic expressions for electoral systems. *British Journal of Political Science*, 1: 467–77.

MERRILL, S., and GROFMAN, B. 1999. *A Unified Theory of Voting*. New York: Cambridge University Press.

NORRIS, P. 2004. *Electoral Rules and Political Behavior*. New York: Cambridge University Press.

PERSSON, T., and TABELLINI, G. 2003. *The Economic Effects of Constitutions*. Cambridge, Mass: MIT Press.

RAE, D. 1967. *Political Consequences of Electoral Laws*. New Haven, Conn.: Yale University Press (2nd edn. 1971).

REED, S. R. 1990. Structure and behavior: extending Duverger's Law to the Japanese case. *British Journal of Political Science*, 20: 335–56.

REYNOLDS, A., and REILLY, B. 1997. *The International IDEA Handbook of Electoral Systems Design*. Stockholm: International IDEA.

SHUGART, M., and WATTENBERG, M. 2001. *Mixed-Member Electoral Systems: The Best of Both Worlds?* New York: Oxford University Press.

TAAGEPERA, R. 1998a. Effective magnitude and effective threshold. *Electoral Studies*, 17: 393–404.

—— 1998b. Nationwide inclusion and exclusion thresholds of representation. *Electoral Studies*, 17: 405–17.

—— and GROFMAN, B. 1985. Rethinking Duverger's Law: predicting the effective number of parties in plurality and PR systems—parties minus issues equals one. *European Journal of Political Research*, 13: 341–52.

—— 2003. Mapping the indices of seats–votes disproportionality and inter-election volatility. *Party Politics*, 9: 659–77.

—— and SHUGART, M. 1989. *Seats and Votes: The Effects and Determinants of Electoral Systems*. New Haven, Conn.: Yale University Press.

TAAGEPERA, R. 1993. Predicting the number of parties: a quantitative model of Duverger mechanical effect. *American Political Science Review*, 87: 455–64.

TUFTE, E. R. 1973. The relationship between seats and votes in two-party systems. *American Political Science Review*, 67: 540–7.

WATTENBERG, M. 1992. *The Rise of Candidate-Centered Politics: Presidential Elections of the 1980s*. Cambridge, Mass: Harvard University Press.

WESSELS, B. 1999. System characteristics matter: empirical evidence from ten representation studies. Pp. 137–61 in *Policy Representation in Western Democracies*, ed. R. Pierce, J. Thomassen, R. Herra, S. Holmberg, P. Esaiasson, and B. Wessels. New York: Oxford University Press.

WITTMAN, D. 1973. Parties as utility maximizers. *American Political Science Review*, 18: 490–8.

—— 1977. Candidates with policy preferences: a dynamic model. *Journal of Economic Theory*, 14: 180–9.

—— 1983. Candidate motivation: a synthesis of alternative theories. *American Political Science Review*, 77: 142–57.

—— 1990. Spatial strategies when candidates have policy preferences. Pp. 66–98 in *Advances in the Spatial Theory of Voting*, ed. J. M. Enelow. New York: Cambridge University Press.

PART III

LEGISLATIVE BODIES

CHAPTER 7

LEGISLATURES AND PARLIAMENTS IN COMPARATIVE CONTEXT

MICHAEL LAVER

1 Legislatures or Parliaments in Comparative Context?

THE words "legislature" and "parliament" are often used interchangeably. The distinction between them, however, can be used to structure the analysis of legislatures and/or parliaments in a comparative context. Legislatures legislate; they pass laws. The notion of a "legislature" is thus located firmly in the classical view of a *separation of powers between legislature, executive, and judiciary*. This distinguishes law-making both from the business of government and from the interpretation, adjudication, and enforcement of any laws that are made. A "parliament," on the other hand, does legislate but in contemporary politics is also something much more than a legislature. In the constitutional structure of "parliamentary government" that characterizes most European states, as well as "European-style" modern democracies such as Australia, Canada, and New Zealand, *the executive is constitutionally responsible to the legislature*.

The matter of whether or not the executive is responsible to the law-making body lies at the heart of my distinction between a "legislature" and a "parliament." Parliamentary elections are in essence about choosing governments, not law-makers. This in turn creates distinctive incentives for elected politicians, who must remain loyal to political parties if they want to get into government, while heads of government often have discretion over the strategic timing of parliamentary elections. Under a separation-of-powers regime, legislative elections have no effect on the identity of the government, although they have an impact on what the government is able to do. This affects the incentive structure of politicians, whose loyalty to political parties, for example, becomes more of an open question.

Thus I use the distinction between legislatures and parliaments, a distinction between two very different types of politics, to structure the discussions that follow. I begin in the next section by looking at parliamentary politics, before moving on to look at legislative politics in separation-of-powers regimes. I conclude by revisiting this distinction in the context of the different types of empirical technique we can use to measure the policy positions of elected politicians.

2 Legislatures and "Parliamentary" Government

In a parliamentary system, the executive both derives from, and is constitutionally responsible to, the legislature—typically its lower house.[1] The government remains in office as long as it retains the "confidence" of the legislature. The most important political job for the "legislature" in a parliamentary government system is thus not legislating at all, but making and breaking governments. The reverse side of this constitutional coin is that the legislature typically cannot dissolve itself, but can typically be dissolved, directly or indirectly, by the executive.[2]

2.1 Parliamentary Confidence and the Executive

The twin procedural peaks of parliamentary government are two types of vote in the legislature—the confidence/no confidence vote and the investiture vote. The former is the more fundamental. A government that loses a legislative vote of no confidence is constitutionally deemed dismissed, if it does not resign voluntarily in anticipation of this catastrophic event. If such a provision is not in the constitution, then the country concerned does not have a parliamentary government system. Faced with an actual or threatened motion of no confidence, governments often attempt to regain the political initiative by proposing their own parliamentary

---

[1] The politics of legislative bicameralism, a widely cited analysis of which can be found in Tsebelis and Money 1997, is covered elsewhere in this *Handbook*—see Cutrone and McCarty, this volume.
[2] Gallagher, Laver, and Mair 2006 summarize the mutual powers of legislature and executive to terminate each other in European parliamentary democracies.

motion of confidence, which typically takes procedural precedence. Failing to win a confidence vote has the same constitutional effect on the government as losing a no confidence vote.[3]

The actual legislative defeat and subsequent fall of a government on a no confidence vote is in practice very rare in parliamentary democracies, just as an actual checkmate is very rare in a chess game played between grandmasters. What is important is that parliament does have its big constitutional stick and that the government knows this. Facing defeat on an actual or potential parliamentary confidence vote, governments usually find they can cut their losses by resigning in anticipation. Furthermore, governments in parliamentary democracies typically have the strategic procedural option of converting a parliamentary motion on any substantive matter, however trivial, into a formal motion of confidence in the government, creating a situation in which the very future of the government is constitutionally bound to the fate of the matter under consideration by parliament. This goes well beyond the mere threat to resign if the government loses the vote on the substantive issue in question.

The relationship between legislature and executive in a parliamentary government system is thus strategically rich and complex. On the face of things, parliaments may seem to have far-reaching powers to make and break governments. The other side of the coin is that governments have far-reaching powers to say to the legislature: "You may oppose us on this particular issue but, if you don't let us have our way, you can go find yourself a whole new government. This is no idle threat; we've chained ourselves to the mast on this motion and thrown away the key—if it goes down we go down with it." Once the confidence procedure has been triggered, unless the issue at stake is so important that some legislative majority really would prefer a whole new government to conceding, the executive is in a strong position to get its own way in the face of legislative opposition. John Huber (1996) produced an incisive and widely cited analysis of the politics of this particular process in France (see also Diermeier and Feddersen 1998).

The fundamental need for the government to be able to win parliamentary confidence votes is often tested constitutionally using a formal parliamentary investiture vote at the point of government formation. Not all parliamentary government systems require formal investiture votes, although those that do have been shown to have governments that are, on average, longer lived (Warwick 1994) and less likely to be minority governments (Strom 1990). Effectively, however, the rules of parliamentary government mean that any incoming government is immediately exposed to an implicit motion of no confidence. Anticipating this, there is no point in a government forming in the first place if it cannot subsequently win confidence motions in the legislature. This is why it is the parliamentary no confidence procedure, not the parliamentary investiture vote, that defines parliamentary government.

---

[3] The vote seeking parliamentary approval for government's annual budget usually has the same constitutional status as a confidence vote.

2.2 Parliamentary Government, Elections, and Endogenous Election Timing

Despite the fact that parliaments are not as powerful in parliamentary government systems as might seem on naive readings of the relevant constitutions, the constitutional power of parliaments to make and break governments has a fundamental impact on practical politics. Because the constitutional source of the government is indeed parliament, parliamentary elections at the national level are more about "electing" governments than they are about choosing a set of representatives to deliberate and vote on legislation. Thus the prominent politicians campaigning in parliamentary elections are typically party leaders. Many of these people present themselves to voters as candidates for the position of prime minister (chief executive). Crucially, *if citizens want to change their government in a parliamentary government system then they do this by voting in parliamentary elections*. Everything else about legislative politics in parliamentary government systems is ultimately an embellishment of this simple constitutional fact.

There is once more a reverse side to this coin. In most parliamentary government systems, while the government is formally responsible to parliament, parliament itself can be dissolved, and parliamentary elections triggered, at the initiative of government. Indeed only very rarely can parliament dissolve itself. This is no minor technical matter since it raises the crucial possibility of the strategic timing of parliamentary elections—something of great benefit to the head of government. Political scientists have analyzed the strategic incentives facing governments when considering the timing of parliamentary elections in terms of both *manipulation* (governments massage the economy to create "political business cycles" that favor them at election time) or more opportunistic *surfing* (governments time elections to catch favorable economic waves over which they have little control).[4] Indeed, choosing the best time to hold the next parliamentary election, although this would never be admitted in public, is one of the most important political jobs for any prime minister. In an era of widespread and reasonably accurate public opinion polling, this puts the head of government in a privileged position vis-à-vis parliament and indeed all other politicians. While all other politicians must work with the actual parliament in place at any given time, the PM in most parliamentary government systems has the luxury of deciding whether she or he wants to work with the current parliament, or with the parliament likely to result if the present one were to be dissolved and new parliamentary elections held (Lupia and Strom 1995; Diermeier and Stevenson 1999).

The endless stream of opinion poll results and other estimates of likely election outcomes, combined with endogenous election timing, feed directly into the balance of power between legislature and executive, in a process that would merit significant further study. When the legislative opposition is rampant at the polls and the government fears an election, for example, it is much less attractive for the government

---

[4] Smith 2004 and Kayser 2005 provide overviews of this work; see also Alesina, Cohen, and Roubini 1997.

to turn individual legislative proposals into issues of confidence and thereby to dare parliament to use its nuclear option of voting no confidence. In contrast, when the government is riding high in the polls and the parliamentary opposition fears an election, then the government's legislative business managers can adopt a "make my day" approach, staking the future of the administration on (quite possibly more extreme) legislative proposals. If we ask ourselves why sitting governments with safe legislative majorities might respond to negative public opinion poll feedback when they are years away from the next scheduled election—and this is one of the great mysteries of politics—then one answer might be found, within parliamentary government systems with endogenous election timing, in the way in which bad poll results for government parties make it procedurally more difficult for the executive to bully the legislature.

2.3 Government Setting of the Parliamentary Agenda

A consequence of these rules, combined with the tight party discipline to which we shortly turn, is a strong tendency in parliamentary government systems for the executive to have a vicelike grip on the legislative agenda. Nowhere in the earthly world are legislators free to debate whatever they feel like debating when they get out of bed on any given day, so legislative agenda-setting is always important (Romer and Rosenthal 1978; Cox and McCubbins 2005). In parliamentary government systems, however, there is a strong tendency for the source of nearly all parliamentary business to be the government itself—to a large extent, parliament is a place for debating, amending, and passing government legislation. This is not found in any constitution, but emerges from rules and conventions governing the flow of parliamentary business and is underpinned by the fact that the government must have the votes to control parliament and its affairs.

Apart from the important constitutional obligation for the government to have its annual budget passed by the legislature, the decision to initiate particular pieces of legislative business is normally at the discretion of government. If some issue is likely to place the government in difficulty, for example, delays can mysteriously arise in drafting the necessary legislation, difficult technical issues can mean that the relevant bill never sees the light of day. A government with a secure parliamentary majority, furthermore, can use legislative standing orders to accelerate, decelerate, and guillotine the passage of particular legislative proposals and *in extremis* can ram measures through parliament very fast indeed—even in the space of a single day. The bottom line is that, in most parliamentary government systems, there is little chance of a detailed proposal having extensive legislative deliberation, much less being passed into law, against the wishes of the government. Furthermore, the government is not a unitary actor and does not draft legislation at the cabinet table. Rather, division of labor and responsibility between cabinet ministers means that most draft legislation originates in a particular government department, under the jurisdiction of a particular cabinet minister. The division of ministerial responsibility into policy jurisdictions is reviewed empirically in Laver and Shepsle (1994), and forms the basis of a theoretical model in Laver and Shepsle (1996). What gets debated in the legislature is thus the outcome of a two-stage agenda-setting process, whereby a designated department under a particular cabinet minister first presents draft legislation for approval by cabinet. What emerges from this process as government policy then sets the legislative agenda.

2.4 Legislative Parties and Party Discipline

It is difficult to proceed further with our discussion of the politics of modern parliaments without talking about *political parties*. Although parties are often not mentioned in the constitutions establishing parliamentary government systems, it is clear that these would likely be very chaotic indeed in the absence of coherent parliamentary parties. Whatever constitutions might say, furthermore, most members of most modern parliaments are indeed members of political parties. The benefits to a legislator of party membership range from the electoral benefits of the party label, to practical benefits in the legislature that can range from office and research facilities to speaking privileges in debates, to rights to propose motions, to benefits that arise from the fact that, in most parliamentary government systems, parliamentary parties are the de facto gatekeepers to high political office (Blondel and Cotta 1996). This latter point is crucial, since it means that parliaments are to a large extent the recruiting grounds for membership of the government. The career track of many politicians in parliamentary government systems involves a "promotion" from the legislature to the executive. Party leaders in parliamentary government systems thus have control over the very highest political rewards, notably coveted positions in the executive.

In this sense parliamentary parties are "political clubs" that are autonomous political systems in their own right. The leaders of these parties are (or are potentially) able to take control of the key political payoffs and offer these to members of their club, excluding all others. Club membership involves abiding by club rules on pain of expulsion, and these include rules on how members will behave in the legislature. The result is a highly incentive compatible system with two interacting pieces. First, party leaders are able to offer rewards to loyal party members, in the form of access to a share of executive perquisites over which party leaders maintain very firm control; these are very highly valued by members. Second, party leaders rely on the loyalty of disciplined party members to maintain control of the executive—or to mount a credible challenge for such control. Without being able to rely on the deployment of a disciplined bloc of votes in parliament, party leaders cannot credibly bargain with other party leaders over the making and breaking of governments. Neither can party leaders in government maintain their control of the executive, since such control requires firm control over voting in parliament, in order to win crucial votes of confidence and enact the government's legislative program. The result is the endogenous emergence of disciplined behavior by party legislators.[5] In practical

[5] For a set of discussions of party discipline in parliamentary government systems, see Bowler, Farrell, and Katz 1999.

terms legislative party discipline boils down to parliamentarians accepting that they will vote the way their party hierarchy tells them to vote, even when they disagree with this, on pain of banishment from a party that offers them considerable rewards, to face the subsequent miseries of life in the political wilderness.

The very concept of party discipline, so central to the understanding of legislative politics in parliamentary government systems, sensitizes us to the need for an analysis of the relationship between intra-party and inter-party politics. This is a significantly under-researched area; scholars too often take the easy way out with an assumption that parliamentary parties, because they do usually behave in such a disciplined way, can be modeled as "unitary actors." But such discipline, as we have seen, is endogenous. Indeed it is useful to reserve the notion of "party discipline" *only* for the endogenous emergence of coordinated behavior by party legislators as a result of internal party politics.

A striking example of this could be seen when Margaret Thatcher, arguably one of postwar Europe's most powerful prime ministers, was ignominiously bundled out of her seemingly invincible positions as head of the British government and leader of the majority party in Westminster as a result of the internal politics of her party. It was the constitution of the Conservative Party, not the (unwritten) constitution of the United Kingdom of Great Britain and Northern Ireland, that governed the changing of the British prime minister. And this is by no means an isolated example.

The net point is that politics in parliamentary government systems is to a large extent party politics, both within and between parties, while party politics in practice transcends the constitutional distinction between legislature and executive. When a government party makes a policy decision, therefore, it can be effectively impossible to determine whether this is a decision of the party in government, the party in parliament, or indeed the wider party organization in the country as a whole. In practice it is likely to be a complex interaction between all three. For this reason alone, it is not productive in a parliamentary government system to analyze legislative politics outside of its wider political context.

2.5 Legislative and Executive Coalitions

If parliamentarians behaved as uncoordinated individuals, then making and breaking governments in parliamentary government systems would be chaotic, since the set of parliamentarians expected to vote for the government on a putative confidence motion would likely be ever changing. Any political shock or voting cycle could cause the government to be defeated in a heartbeat. Structure is brought to this process by the fact that members of political parties operate in a coordinated way *in both the legislative and the executive spheres*. As we have seen, this structure allows a party or coalition of parties controlling the executive to extend this control to the legislature. The distinction between two quite different coalitions is crucial in this context.

- One is the *government coalition* per se. This is the set of politicians who are actually members of the government, who may belong to one or more political parties. This set is typically defined as those holding cabinet portfolios, although this definition could be considerably extended—to "junior" ministers and other senior political patronage appointments. The number of political appointments needed to control the entire government machine in a parliamentary government system is actually quite large, and this is significant when it comes to government formation (Laver and Shepsle 2000).
- The other is the *parliamentary support coalition* for the government. This is the (quite possibly ever-changing) set of parliamentarians expected to vote for the government on any putative government motion, including a confidence/no confidence motion, that might be called at a particular moment in time. Members of a government's parliamentary support coalition may or may not belong to the same political parties as members of the executive coalition per se. A particular motion may attract the support of parliamentarians who would actually vote to defeat the government in a vote of no confidence, for example. Or, as happened with the Likud government in Israel in March 2005, defections from legislative members of a government party may be compensated by legislative support for from parties "outside" the government coalition.

It is important not to elide this important distinction. Countries with parliamentary government regimes are *not* governed by their parliaments, but by executive coalitions supported by parliament. There is "baseline" parliamentary support for a government in the event of a no confidence motion, which measures the extent to which, everything considered, legislators prefer the incumbent regime to some credible alternative. But it is constitutionally possible that, on individual votes, there may be shifting parliamentary majorities. And, unless the government decides to attach a motion of confidence to one of these, it is quite possible for it to lose a series of legislative votes without threat to its continued existence.

Legislative Politics and "Minority" Governments

The distinction between government coalitions and their parliamentary support coalitions is clarified when we consider the phenomenon, common in parliamentary government systems, of "minority" governments. When no single party commands a parliamentary majority, any government must nonetheless rely on a majority legislative support coalition in order to win votes of confidence. This is true whether the government comprises politicians from one party or several. When the government party or parties do not themselves control a parliamentary majority, there is a "minority" government. Minority governments have been of increasing interest to political scientists following work by Strom (1990). Constitutionally, a minority government can remain in office as long as there are enough parliamentarians, not belonging to the parties in government, who nonetheless support the government in confidence votes.[6]

[6] "Support" is taken to include abstentions that, had they been votes against the government, would have caused it to be defeated.

If parliamentarians were concerned only with getting into government, then minority governments would be hard to explain. A majority of legislators, coming from parties not in the government, would simply vote the government out, install themselves in office, and enjoy the "smell of the leather," to steal a phrase from Irish politics. The conventional answer from theorists of government formation is that the existence of minority governments is evidence that legislators also care about policy, and that minority governments can survive when the legislative opposition is divided over policy (Strom 1990; Laver and Shepsle 1996; Laver and Schofield 1998). Opposition parliamentarians do not vote the government out, in this account, because they cannot agree on the policy program to be promoted by any credible alternative.

Legislative Politics and Single-party Majority Governments

Another important reason to pay attention to the distinction between the government coalition and its parliamentary support coalitions can be found when we analyze the politics of single-party majority governments in parliamentary democracies. In these cases, members of the government coalition all belong to one party and this party controls a legislative majority. Such cases are rarely analyzed, by either theorists or empirical researchers, perhaps because they are mistakenly assumed to be theoretically trivial. But this is to treat parties as unitary actors and ignore the crucial role of parliamentary party discipline in binding together executive and legislative politics. Even when there is a single-party majority government, however, the constitutional requirement that the government must maintain the confidence of the legislature remains in full force. This means that the government is only secure if its legislative support coalition—all members of which belong to the same political party but all of whom remain individual decision-making agents whose autonomy is deeply enshrined in most constitutions—remains loyal. In short the government is secure only as long as the discipline of the parliamentary party supporting it remains effective. And this in turn means that the most important practical politics between elections in parliamentary government systems takes place *inside the majority legislative party*. Thus single-party majority governments are no different from explicit coalitions in needing to maintain a parliamentary majority who deem themselves better off than under the alternatives.

This matter is largely ignored by theorists of party competition, who tend to devote themselves to analyzing politics between, rather than politics within, political parties. But, as any student of British politics under Margaret Thatcher or Tony Blair would testify, there was a lot of legislative politics between elections, despite the commanding parliamentary majorities enjoyed by the one-party governments led by both. Thatcher, as we have seen, was humiliatingly dethroned from her position as prime minister as a result of such politics. Blair (successfully) walked a very high wire within the Labour Party when he was leader of a party enjoying a huge parliamentary majority, following his commitment to British participation in the US-led military invasion of Iraq. In each case, intense politicking among legislators was the result of the fact that these prime ministers led majority parties that were deeply divided on key issues. These issues were felt so intensely that factions of legislators within the governing party credibly appeared willing to split the party, and to damage if not destroy "their own" government rather than meekly follow the party line and vote in the legislature against their sincere preferences. Ignoring this when analyzing legislative party politics under single-party executives misses the whole point of what was going on. But only a theoretical account that makes a clear distinction between the government and its parliamentary support coalition, and furthermore treats parliamentary parties as endogenous coalitions of legislators, is in a position to get to analytical grips with such high politics.

The Parliamentary Opposition

Treating parliamentary parties as endogenous coalitions of parliamentarians is intellectually liberating, not just because it gives us an interesting way to analyze the self-evidently important politics of single-party majority governments, but also because it gives us analytical leverage on the legislative role of opposition parties in parliamentary democracies. Faced with a government controlling a legislative majority by virtue of the discipline of its parliamentary parties, legislators who oppose the government cannot themselves muster the votes to beat it on anything. But this by no means implies they might as well go off on an extended holiday, sipping mixed drinks and daydreaming of a better tomorrow. Opposition politicians have plenty of interesting work to do back at the legislature, since the way to defeat the government in such situations is to split open its legislative support coalition. This may mean splitting a coalition of different parties, or splitting a single government party, by finding and opening up the internal fission lines that always exist within a set of politicians who do not share identical preferences. This type of legislative maneuvering was discussed by Riker (1986) as the political "art" he called "heresthetics." Unfortunately, heresthetics is difficult to analyze in a systematic way, although it has been revisited in another context by Epstein and Shvetsova (2002), who see it as the matter of how to "snatch victory out of the jaws of defeat".

3 Legislatures and "Presidential" Government

Even in US-style presidential systems, in which the separation of powers between legislature and executive is usually considered to be clear-cut, legislative politics does not unfold independently of the behavior of the executive. (See Cameron 2000; Krehbiel 1999.) That is, the political bottom line in almost any system of government—whatever the constitutional separation of powers—is that legislatures need executives if they are going to be able to do what they are likely to want to do, not least to fund the costs of their legislative initiatives. And executives need legislatures, not least because even the government has to act in accordance with the law, while almost all constitutions demand legislative approval, in some shape or form, of the executive's annual budget. Thus, while the president of the United States of America cannot be dismissed by Congress—except in extraordinary circumstances arising from successful impeachment—neither can he or she ignore Congress.

Thinking more generally about the role of legislatures in presidential government regimes, we have to remember that the "model generator" for much of the vast body of work on this subject—the United States Congress—is located in a constitutional framework that in comparative terms generates a relatively weak presidency. Thus (no doubt to the regret of many past presidents) the US president has no power to dismiss either house of Congress, has very limited power over the congressional agenda, and very limited power to issue presidential decrees that override laws passed by the legislature. However, Congress cannot get rid of the president and can only indirectly influence the behavior of the executive.[7]

When considering the wide range of intellectually influential theoretical work on the US legislature, therefore, we must be alert to the possibility that the model generator is itself *sui generis*. Nonetheless it is precisely the relative weakness of the US president, manifested in the clear-cut separation of powers between executive and legislature, that has created such a fertile modeling environment.

3.1 Legislative Parties

One dramatic difference between parliamentary government and separation-of-powers regimes has to do with the role of legislative parties. As we have seen, in parliamentary government systems, the incentives for legislators to join highly disciplined parties are considerable. Parties provide the entire career structure for any aspiring politician, from the first baby steps in politics to the most powerful offices in the land. At the same time, the fact that party leaders are current or aspiring key members of the executive means that they have strong incentives to deploy the rewards and punishments that bring about the legislative party discipline that makes control of the executive possible. In a parliamentary government system, the puzzle is why legislative party discipline would ever fail. In contrast, in legislative systems such as in the USA, the puzzle is why party discipline ever succeeds. Decoupling legislature and executive puts legislative parties in a completely different strategic context. Most strikingly, keeping the executive in power does not require disciplined legislative parties, and legislative and executive career structures are to a large extent also decoupled. No doubt congressional ranks include many aspiring US presidents, but key executive appointments are almost never "promotions" from Congress, which has its own quite distinct career structure, manifested in the committee system. Party

---

[7] For a comparative overview of executive–legislative relations in "presidential" regimes, which ranks the USA at the bottom end of a scale of presidential power, see Samuels and Shugart 2003.

hierarchs in the executive thus do not have the futures of ambitious members of Congress in their pockets.

Political scientists interested in US politics have offered two types of solution to the puzzle of party discipline. The first analyzes electoral incentives for legislators, arising from the value of a party label. The second analyzes strategic incentives within the legislature that may reward members of a cartel of legislators who behave in a coordinated fashion.

Electoral Incentives

Arguments about electoral incentives for party cohesion in Congress typically describe parties as "brands" used by voters to infer information about candidates. Actual or aspiring politicians join political parties so as to signal credible policy positions to voters, in order to increase their chances of election. A widely cited recent formulation and analysis of the argument that parties provide informative brand labels, building on arguments made by scholars such as Cox and McCubbins (1993), can be found in Snyder and Ting (2002), with recent interesting extensions by Levy (2004). This argument about the endogenous rationale for political parties has also developed from work by Osborne and Slivinski (1996), as well as Besley and Coate (1997), on "party-free" electoral competition between "citizen-candidates."

One of the characterizing assumptions of this approach is that voters make inferences about candidates' policy preferences only by observing their party membership, treating this as a costly signal and ignoring as cheap talk everything that candidates might actually say about their own policy preferences. Candidates in these models have underlying policy preferences and thus prefer to join parties comprising likeminded colleagues. Despite occasional references to "party discipline," this approach offers no explicit model of intra-party politics—save for the assumption that the party policy platform is chosen by either a dictatorial leader or simple majority voting by party members (Snyder and Ting 2002, 102). Legislators are also assumed to be able to join, and to remain within, any party they choose. The main lesson we draw from this work in the legislative context is that electoral incentives may make party labels valuable commodities. If a party's decision-making regime can credibly threaten to withdraw the party label from legislators who fail to abide by party decisions about legislative behavior, then this makes such decisions easier to enforce. However, the very strong "incumbency effect" in US electoral politics, whereby incumbent legislators are very difficult indeed to unseat when facing re-election, gives individual legislators a personal power base that is likely to undermine this potential source of party cohesion.

Legislative Incentives

A second set of incentives for legislators to join political parties derives from the range of payoffs in the legislative game that accrue to politicians who belong to larger rather than smaller cartels of legislators.[8] For Cox and McCubbins, the main legislative resource that can be captured by a majority coalition of legislators is agenda control. Agenda power is achieved by controlling the allocation between legislators of agenda-setting offices, such as committee chairs. On this argument, the power to make these allocations is delegated by party members to the party hierarchy, which can use such rewards to enhance party discipline, which in turn feeds back to enhance the value of the party label in the electoral game.

This analysis contrasts with an alternative influential argument, put forward by Krehbiel (1993, 1998). According to Krehbiel, what looks like party-coordinated legislative behavior arises because US legislators choose which party to affiliate to on the basis of their intrinsic policy preferences—in effect joining a party of like-minded individuals and then independently choosing to behave in the same way as party colleagues on the floor of the House, without any need for "discipline" to be imposed by their party's internal decision-making regime.

Despite the stark theoretical distinction between these analyses of party-structured legislative roll calls, distinguishing them empirically is difficult because both may be observationally equivalent. It may be that legislators are voting the same way because they like the same policies, or because they are responding to the same non-policy incentive structure put in place by the party's internal regime. Snyder and Groseclose (2000) present an innovative empirical analysis that sets out to distinguish these effects by making a distinction between two types of roll call. On one hand there are "lop-sided" roll calls. Snyder and Groseclose assume, first, that legislators will treat these as a foregone conclusion and, second, that party leaders will see them as offering no rationale for the "costly" deployment of party discipline.[9] On the other hand there are "close" roll calls, for which coordinated legislator behavior makes the difference between winning and losing. Snyder and Groseclose find strong evidence that the "party effect" is much higher for close than for lop-sided roll calls. They infer from this that US parties can and do influence the behavior of their legislative members when this makes a real difference, and do not attempt to do so when it does not.

While this body of work is ingenious empirically, its theoretical underpinnings do not really deal with the obvious endogeneity of the anticipated "closeness" and "lop-sidedness" of roll calls, especially in a two-party context. In a nutshell in the US system, if a roll call is expected to be lop-sided, this amounts to an expectation that party discipline will not be applied—but how is this expectation formed? Thus a party effect may be capable of being *measured* but, as Snyder and Groseclose freely admit, we do not come much closer to *explaining* it. Thus the main lessons from this work concern the incentives for legislators to form cartels that enable them better to fulfill their objectives within the institutional structure of Congress, and the possibility that members of those cartels will delegate to party hierarchs the right to allocate key political resources captured by the party.

---

[8] A recent comprehensive overview can be found in Cox and McCubbins 2005.
[9] Recall that imposing party discipline need not be seen as costly for party leaders under parliamentary government.

Overall, however, and taking everything into account, there can be no doubt that analyses of legislative behavior in parliamentary government and separation-of-powers systems must differ radically, given the very different incentives for party-coordinated behavior by legislators. We have no a priori reason to suppose that party politics will be in any way similar under the two quite different constitutional regimes.

3.2 Divided Government/*Cohabitation*

When the chief executive is not constitutionally responsible to the legislature, an important aspect of legislative politics is the potential for "divided government" (see Fiorina 1996) and "gridlock" (see Binder 2003). When the executive and different houses of the legislature are chosen in different ways and/or at different stages of the political cycle, periodic fluctuations in levels of political support, and the differential representation of political constituencies by different electoral rules and districting regimes, mean that the houses will differ in their partisan composition. Similarly induced partisan differences between executive and legislature, seen as "divided government" in the USA and *cohabitation* in France, generate an obvious potential for conflict. While divided government in this sense is typically seen as a feature of US-style presidential government, there is a clear sense in which minority government in a parliamentary government system is analogous to this. In each case there is an executive coalition that faces a majority legislative coalition under different partisan control, in a constitutional environment where co-decision is required on at least some important issues. See Elgie (2001) for an exploration of divided partisan control in different parliamentary systems.

In the USA, however, the much weaker incentives for legislative party discipline mean that all governments are to some extent divided ones. Even when the executive and both houses of the legislature are controlled by the same party, it is by no means a foregone conclusion that the executive will be able to have all the legislation it desires passed as a matter of routine. The constitutional separation of powers is manifested in the absence of a legislative vote of no confidence in the executive and the inability of the executive to make some legislative proposal a matter of confidence in the government. The executive thus does not have the same big procedural stick to wield over the legislature.

The lack of rigid party discipline and the independent electoral power bases of individual legislators (enhanced by a strong incumbency effect) combine to underpin a strong de facto separation of powers between legislature and executive. The net effect is that the executive is always forced to accommodate itself to a congressional politics that can be analyzed as an independent system in its own right. Threats by members of the "government" party in the USA to vote against "government" legislation are credible and can be used to extract significant concessions from an unwilling executive. Conversely, even when there is divided government in the USA, this does not mean that the executive will be defeated at every turn, since an executive coalition dominated by one party can buy off members of a majority legislative coalition dominated by the other. Thus the lack of rigid party discipline in Congress cuts both ways for the president. On one hand, the president cannot even rely on unconditional support from members of his or her own party. On the other hand the president can realistically seek support from members of the legislative "opposition." (Indeed it has in the past been common for a Republican president such as Eisenhower and Nixon to reach out to Southern Democrats to form the so-called "conservative coalition.")

3.3 Legislative Committees as Sources of Structure

The lack of incentives for strong party discipline in the US Congress creates a potential for political instability. In addition, when the set of issues under consideration is multidimensional, the potential for instability is magnified (see McKelvey and Schofield 1986, 1987). Nevertheless, the actual politics we observe is much more stable than all of this might imply. The potential misfit between theoretical expectations of chaos and empirical observations of relative order and stability has been resolved within the profession for the US legislature by a burgeoning "new institutionalist" literature that has focused on the ways in which particular congressional institutions structure politics so as to induce relatively orderly behavior.

This approach to the analysis of legislative politics unpacks the logic of a set of axioms derived from stylized descriptions of key aspects of the way in which the US Congress does its business. Topics that have been extensively analyzed within this research tradition include, among others: ways in which the legislative committee system interacts with the plenary legislature; logrolling between groups of legislators who trade votes across a portfolio of issues; agenda-setting and the impact of different types of amendment rule; and the politics of constitutionally enshrined vetoes over legislation.

There is no space here to review this substantial literature (for which, see Shepsle and Weingast 1995), but perhaps the most internationally "portable" and influential intuition that can be derived from this was generated by Shepsle's early work on ways in which the congressional committee system can bring about "structure-induced equilibrium". The logic of this argument is straightforward but powerful. This is that legislation is processed, not in an unconstrained rough and tumble on the floor of either house, but via a specialized committee system that in effect breaks down a multidimensional legislative program into a set of unidimensional legislative proposals. Each committee has jurisdiction over a single key dimension of policy; intra-committee politics can move a proposal under its jurisdiction along this policy dimension, but cannot directly change policy proposals under the jurisdiction of other committees. This strong structure in the congressional decision-making process is argued to induce equilibrium outcomes that would otherwise be unattainable, while intra-committee politics is further structured by the agenda-setting powers of the committee chairs.

The portability of this intuition became evident with its application to the role of cabinet ministers in parliamentary government systems, where each minister has jurisdiction over a particular policy portfolio (Laver and Shepsle 1996). Just as is the case in separation-of-powers regimes, public policy is not set on the floor of the legislature. The role of cabinet ministers as agenda-setters within their own policy jurisdiction thus induces equilibrium outcomes that could not otherwise be achieved. Indeed, re-importing the same argument back into Congress, we find a case for seeing congressional committee chairs as fulfilling at least some of the roles, in the US system, that are fulfilled by cabinet ministers under parliamentary government.

4 MEASURING THE POLICY POSITIONS OF LEGISLATORS

By way of a conclusion, we can revisit some of the main features of legislative politics under different constitutional regimes by considering the important empirical matter of how we might measure the preferred policy positions of members of a given legislature. While it might superficially seem obvious that surveys of legislators themselves would be the best way to do this, such surveys are fraught with problems. First, they cannot be retrospective; thus time series of past legislator positions are impossible to construct in this way. Second, decoding the information behind the survey response of highly sophisticated and instrumental politicians is likely very problematic. Third, respondent fatigue means that response rates in such surveys are very low, resulting in a huge potential selection bias that can be hard both to detect and to correct. Fourth, many legislative parties (in Europe at least) now screen such surveys, instructing members to respond only to those that are approved by the party leadership. Those seeking extended time series of legislator policy positions that can be retrieved retrospectively and collected using instruments that do not pollute their own data, therefore, have tended to rely on two main sources of information—legislative voting records and political texts.

As far as the US Congress is concerned, the primary source of information on the policy positions of legislators has become the systematic analysis of roll call voting data, with a remarkable recent coordination among scholars on using the NOMINATE procedures, both static and dynamic, devised by Poole and Rosenthal (1997). Essentially, this approach *assumes* a spatial model of party competition in which differences between the policy positions of legislators can be represented as Euclidean distances. Conditional on these assumptions, the spatial policy positions of legislators are retrieved by analyzing roll call voting records, essentially treating a pair of legislators with more similar voting records as being closer to each other than are a pair of legislators with less similar records.

Given this set-up, Poole and Rosenthal (1997, 22) give themselves the job of retrieving "the locations of 11,000 legislators and 70,000 roll calls from the 11,000,000 recorded individual decisions of Congresses stretching from 1789 to 1985." This is no mean feat, and the promise of generating extended time series of the estimated policy positions of every individual US legislator has made the Poole and Rosenthal approach extremely attractive to many other legislative scholars.

What is particularly striking in an environment in which levels of party discipline, as we have seen, are relatively low, is that this approach allows us to plot what is happening inside legislative parties, and thereby to investigate the structure of intra-party coalitions and factions. Indeed this is actually the main thing that the NOMINATE technique does allow us to plot. If there are two opposing parties with rigid discipline in the sense that all party X legislators always voted in the same way as each other and in the opposite way to all legislators from party Y, then NOMINATE will simply tell us the two parties and their legislators are different, which we already know, and add no metric information to this. But, as we have seen in the USA, party lines are not rigidly drawn and all legislators from the same party do not always vote in the same way. This allows us to use variations in legislators' roll call voting behavior to map their policy positions in a common space that describes policy differences both within and between parties.

This highlights the fundamental problem that arises if we want to export techniques of congressional roll call analysis to political systems in which there are very high levels of legislative party discipline. In a multiparty system where party discipline is close to 100 per cent, roll call analysis might conceivably allow us to retrieve the positions of *parties*, rather than individual *legislators*—since legislators would be revealing their party membership in their voting record, rather than their ideal policy positions. However, since multiparty systems also beget coalition cabinets, and since members of such cabinets are bound together by constitutional rules of collective cabinet responsibility, it is likely that all parties in the executive coalitions will vote in the same way, despite having different policy positions. It is also possible that all members of a diverse opposition to the government will vote in the same way, and against the government. High levels of party discipline combine with the parliamentary government system, therefore, to undermine quite fundamentally the potential of roll call analysis to give us useful information about the policy positions of either individual legislators or, indeed, legislative parties.

One European setting to which NOMINATE has successfully been exported, however, is the European Parliament, where the absence of an executive sustained in office by the legislature, and consequently loose discipline among European party groups, allow roll call analysis to yield fruitful results (Hix 2001, 2004).

The main alternative data source from which we might hope to retrieve long retrospective time series of legislator policy positions is political text. The longstanding Comparative Manifestos Project (CMP) has hand-coded party manifestos to generate time series of the *electoral* policy positions of *parties* that span the postwar era for most parties in most democratic states (Budge et al. 2001). The comprehensive coverage of this data-set has made it a popular choice with researchers, including sophisticated spatial modelers, despite the fact that each text is coded once and once only by a human coder, so that no policy position generated comes with any estimate whatsoever of associated error. Thus, when looking at "movement" in some time series generated from CMP data, or when inspecting the cross-sectional difference between the positions of two parties, it is impossible to distinguish measurement error from "real" underlying change in the policy positions under investigation. Such problems, however, may soon be overcome by computerized text analysis. For example, Laver, Benoit, and Garry (2003) proposed a language-blind computerized technique for political text analysis that reliably retrieves valid party policy positions, and also reports associated standard errors. Giannetti and Laver (2005) recently extended the application of this technique to the analysis of speeches in the Italian legislature, retrieving estimated policy positions for individual Italian legislators. Sooner rather than later, therefore, systematic research programs using computerized text analysis will provide alternative sources of information about the policy positions of individual legislators, and will be applied retrospectively for as far back as political texts are available.

Putting all of this together, therefore, whether we are talking about theory or about measurement, the constitutional setting that distinguishes legislatures from parliaments, and that distinguishes separation-of-powers from parliamentary government regimes, makes a big difference to how we analyze political interaction between elected public representatives. And the biggest key to that distinction has to do with the different strategic incentives conditioning membership of legislative parties.

REFERENCES

ALESINA, A., COHEN, G., and ROUBINI, N. 1997. *Political Cycles and Macroeconomy*. Cambridge, Mass.: MIT Press.

BAGEHOT, W. 1963. *The English Constitution*. London: Fontana.

BESLEY, T. J., and COATE, S. 1997. An economic model of representative democracy. *Quarterly Journal of Economics*, 112: 85–114.

BINDER, S. 2003. *Stalemate: Causes and Consequences of Legislative Gridlock*. Washington, DC: Brookings Institution Press.

BLONDEL, J., and COTTA, M. (eds.). 1996. *Party and Government: An Inquiry into the Relationship between Governments and Supporting Parties in Liberal Democracies*. London: Macmillan.

BOWLER, S., FARRELL, D., and KATZ, R. (eds.). 1999. *Party Discipline and Parliamentary Government*. Columbus: Ohio State University Press.

BUDGE, I., KLINGEMANN, H.-D., VOLKENS, A., BARA, J., and TANNENBAUM, C., with FORDING, R., HEARL, D., KIM, H. M., MCDONALD, M., and MENDES, S. 2001. *Mapping Policy Preferences: Parties, Electors and Governments: 1945–1998: Estimates for Parties, Electors and Governments 1945–1998*. Oxford: Oxford University Press.

CAMERON, C. C. 2000. *Veto Bargaining: The Politics of Negative Power*. New York: Cambridge University Press.

COX, G., and MCCUBBINS, M. 1993. *Legislative Leviathan*. Berkeley: University of California Press.

—— —— 2005. *Setting the Agenda: Responsible Party Government in the US House of Representatives*. Cambridge: Cambridge University Press.

DIERMEIER, D., and FEDDERSEN, T. 1998. Cohesion in legislatures and the vote of confidence procedure. *American Political Science Review*, 92: 611–21.

____ and STEVENSON, R. 1999. Cabinet survival and competing risks. *American Journal of Political Science*, 43: 1051–68.

ELGIE, R. 2001. *Divided Government in Comparative Perspective*. Oxford: Oxford University Press.

EPSTEIN, L., and SHVETSOVA, O. 2002. Heresthetical maneuvering on the U.S. Supreme Court. *Journal of Theoretical Politics*, 14: 93–122.

FIORINA, M. 1996. *Divided Government*, 2nd edn. Boston: Allyn and Bacon.

GALLAGHER, M., LAVER, M., and MAIR, P. 2006. *Representative Government in Modern Europe*, 4th edn. New York: McGraw-Hill.

GIANNETTI, D., and LAVER, M. 2005. Policy positions and jobs in the government. *European Journal of Political Research*, 44: 91–120.

HIX, S. 2001. Legislative behaviour and party competition in the European Parliament: an application of Nominate to the EU. *Journal of Common Market Studies*, 39: 663–88.

____ 2004. *The Political System of the European Union*, 2nd edn. Houndmills: Palgrave.

HUBER, J. 1996. *Rationalizing Parliament: Legislative Institutions and Party Politics in France*. Cambridge: Cambridge University Press.

KATZ, R. S. 1996. The United States: divided government and divided parties. Pp. 202–24 in *Party and Government: An Inquiry into the Relationship between Governments and Supporting Parties in Liberal Democracies*, ed. J. Blondel and M. Cotta. London: Macmillan.

KAYSER, M. A. 2005. Who surfs, who manipulates? The determinants of opportunistic election timing and electorally motivated economic intervention. *American Political Science Review*, 99: 17–27.

KREHBIEL, K. 1993. Where's the party? *British Journal of Political Science*, 23: 235–66.

____ 1998. *Pivotal Politics: A Theory of U.S. Lawmaking*. Chicago: University of Chicago Press.

____ 1999. The party effect from A to Z and beyond. *Journal of Politics*, 61: 832–40.

LAVER, M., BENOIT, K., and GARRY, J. 2003. Estimating the policy positions of political actors using words as data. *American Political Science Review* 97: 311–31.

____ and SCHOFIELD, N. 1998. *Multiparty Government: The Politics of Coalition in Europe*. Ann Arbor: University of Michigan Press.

____ and SHEPSLE, K. (eds.). 1994. *Cabinet Ministers and Parliamentary Government*. Cambridge: Cambridge University Press.

____ ____ 1996. *Making and Breaking Governments: Cabinets and Legislatures in Parliamentary Democracies*. Cambridge: Cambridge University Press.

____ ____ 2000. *Ministrables* and government formation: munchkins, players and big beasts of the jungle. *Journal of Theoretical Politics*, 12: 113–24.

LEVY, G. 2004. A model of political parties. *Journal of Economic Theory*, 115: 250–77.

LUPIA, A., and STROM, K. 1995. Coalition termination and the strategic timing of parliamentary elections. *American Political Science Review*, 89: 648–65.

MCCARTY, N., POOLE, K. T., and ROSENTHAL, H. 2001. The hunt for party discipline in Congress. *American Political Science Review*, 95: 673–87.

MCKELVEY, R. D., and SCHOFIELD, N. 1986. Structural instability of the core. *Journal of Mathematical Economics*, 15: 179–98.

____ ____ 1987. Generalized symmetry conditions at a core point. *Econometrica*, 55: 923–33.

OSBORNE, M. J., and SLIVINSKI, A. 1996. A model of political competition with citizen-candidates. *Quarterly Journal of Economics*, 111: 65–96.

POOLE, K., and ROSENTHAL, H. 1997. *Congress: A Political-Economic History of Roll Call Voting*. New York: Oxford University Press.

RIKER, W. H. 1986. *The Art of Political Manipulation*. New Haven, Conn.: Yale University Press.

ROMER, T., and ROSENTHAL, H. 1978. Political resource allocation, controlled agendas and the status quo. *Public Choice*, 33: 27–43.

SAMUELS, D. J., and SHUGART, M. S. 2003. Presidentialism, elections and representation. *Journal of Theoretical Politics*, 15: 33–60.

SHEPSLE, K., and WEINGAST, B. (eds.). 1995. *Positive Theories of Congressional Institutions*. Ann Arbor: University of Michigan Press.

SMITH, A. 2004. *Election Timing*. Cambridge: Cambridge University Press.

SNYDER, J. M., JR., and GROSECLOSE, T. 2000. Estimating party influence on roll call voting: regression coefficients versus classification success. *American Political Science Review*, 95: 689–98.

—— and TING, M. M. 2002. An informational rationale for political parties. *American Journal of Political Science*, 46: 90–110.

STROM, K. 1990. *Minority Government and Majority Rule*. Cambridge: Cambridge University Press.

TSEBELIS, G., and MONEY, J. 1997. *Bicameralism*. Cambridge: Cambridge University Press.

WARWICK, P. 1994. *Government Survival in Parliamentary Democracies*. Cambridge: Cambridge University Press.

CHAPTER 8

THE ORGANIZATION OF DEMOCRATIC LEGISLATURES

GARY W. COX

1 INTRODUCTION

WHY are legislatures organized as they are? If one could use a time machine to drive steadily backward in the history of the world's longest-lived democratic assemblies, one would find fewer and simpler rules the further back one went. Extrapolating from these trends, one would eventually arrive at what I call the legislative state of nature—briefly, an assembly in which all business is conducted in the plenary session (no committees) and members' ability to talk and make motions is largely unrestricted and unregulated. In this chapter, I argue that certain universal features of modern democratic assemblies—namely specialized agenda-setting offices and parties—arise as a response to the scarcity of plenary time in the legislative state of nature.

The root problem is this: in the legislative state of nature, it is far easier to delay legislation in the plenary session (e.g. by filibustering, introducing endless amendments, and the like) than to accelerate it. Yet, each bill must be considered and voted on in the plenary session, before it can be enacted. Hence, a plenary bottleneck emerges.

To get anything done, members must regulate access to plenary time. The purpose of this chapter is to explore the range of legislative institutions used to regulate

* I thank the editors for their helpful suggestions.

plenary time and their consequences. The necessity of regulating plenary time leads, I argue, to the universal creation of offices endowed with special agenda-setting powers. Thus, while legislators are everywhere equal in voting power, they are everywhere unequal in agenda-setting power.

The existence of powerful agenda-setting offices (e.g. cabinet ministers, committee chairs) raises two further questions, on which the bulk of the chapter focuses. First, who gets the offices? Here I argue that the lure of office promotes the formation of legislative parties and coalitions. Indeed, parties dominate the pursuit of intra-legislative office even more completely than they dominate the pursuit of office in general elections. Second, how do different structures of agenda power affect legislative processes and outputs? Here I note that much recent theorizing about legislatures begins by postulating a particular structure of agenda-setting powers and then derives conclusions about an array of legislative outcomes, such as legislative productivity, gridlock, overspending, and the direction of policy change. I review literature in this vein, stressing differences between veto power and proposal power (the first risking gridlock, the second external costs); and between centralized and decentralized agenda power (again entailing a trade-off between gridlock and external costs).

2 PLENARY TIME

In order to introduce the legislative state of nature, it helps first to discuss plenary time. Although the details of legislative procedure differ widely across the world's democratic legislatures, one generalization holds universally: important bills can only pass pursuant to motions formally stated and voted upon in the plenary session. This legal requirement gives rise to the typical format of a legislative journal, which reads as a sequence of motions and votes on those motions, one after the other.

The necessity of acting pursuant to formally stated motions means that every bill must consume at least some plenary time, if it is to have a chance at enactment. Thus, plenary time is the sine qua non of legislation. Yet, there are only twenty-four hours in a day and, hence, plenary time is also in limited supply.

In principle, one could get around the necessity of transacting bills in the plenary by delegating law-making authority—either to committees (e.g. *leggine*), or to chief executives (e.g. decree authority), or to bureaucratic agencies (e.g. rule-making authority), or to subsidiary legislatures (e.g. Stormont).[1] In practice, however, democratic legislatures retain an important core of legislative authority that is inalienable, in the sense that the plenary retains (and cannot forswear) the ability to rescind any delegations it may choose to make.

[1] In Italy, *leggine* (little laws) can be passed directly by committees, without consideration in the plenary session. On executive decree authority, see Carey and Shugart 1998. On delegated rule-making authority in bureaucracies, see Huber and Shipan 2002. On the Stormont assembly, see Green 1979.

3 THE LEGISLATIVE STATE OF NATURE

Because plenary time is essential to passing legislation and because the plenary cannot get around this simply by abdicating, the management of plenary time has been the crucial battleground of most of the biggest fights over legislative procedure across the democratic world. In order to set the stage for a discussion of these fights over procedure—and where they lead—consider the following legislative "state of nature:" (1) bills can only pass pursuant to formal motions and votes in the plenary session; (2) motions pass if a majority of members vote for them;[2] (3) the plenary session faces a hard budget constraint on time;[3] and (4) access to plenary time is egalitarian and unregulated. By *egalitarian* I mean that every member has an equal probability of being recognized to make a motion at any stage of the legislative process. By *unregulated* I mean that, once a motion has been made to pass a bill, then (*a*) all who wish may speak; and (*b*) there are no limits on debate.

What is life in the legislative state of nature like? As soon as the aggregate demand for bills, hence plenary time, rises above a minimum threshold, a plenary bottleneck emerges. All bills must go through the plenary bottleneck in order to be enacted but only a subset can do so, leading to a coordination or bargaining problem to decide which subset it will be.

Several features of the plenary bottleneck are worth pointing out. First, in the legislative state of nature, each member's power to delay or block legislation greatly exceeds his or her power to push legislation through to passage. On the one hand, any member can block any bill, simply by talking indefinitely (ignoring personal fatigue). On the other hand, no member or coalition of members can force an end to others' filibusters. Thus, at least when the budget constraint on plenary time begins to bind, each member has a natural bargaining strategy—delay until one's demands are met. Another way to put it is that *the de facto decision rule in a state-of-nature legislature is closer to unanimity than to majority rule.*

Second, the existence of the plenary bottleneck, when combined with the practical necessity of securing unanimous consent to traverse it and the inalienability of the plenary's sovereignty over its core areas of legislative competence, means that gains from trade—either in bills or in labor—are unlikely to be realized. An ordinary logroll—we'll vote later for your motion to pass your bill if you vote now for ours—is problematic in the legislative state of nature, as the promise can be broken (Weingast and Marshall 1988). An agreement to trade labor—we'll specialize in this subject matter and reveal our findings if you reciprocate in another area—is also problematic, as neither side can be sure that any bills it reports to the plenary session, better informed though they may be, will actually be passed as reported (Gilligan and Krehbiel 1990; Krehbiel 1991).

---

[2] In fact, motions typically pass if a majority of voting members vote for them and the total number voting exceeds a minimum known as the quorum. I shall ignore this refinement.

[3] No plenary could meet more than twenty-four hours per day, for example.

Third, if members wish to use plenary time for purposes other than legislating—e.g. to publicize their positions to their constituents—then the plenary bottleneck becomes even more difficult to traverse. Each member must forbear tapping into the common pool of plenary time, in order to conserve enough to pass a legislative program. Yet, each member has both motive and opportunity to consume plenary time in pursuit of local publicity. The result, as in analogous problems, is overexploitation of the common-pool resource (Cox 1987, ch. 6).

Note that the primary problems of the state-of-nature assembly are coordination games (navigating the plenary bottleneck), trust games (arranging logrolls), and common-pool games (stemming from equal access to plenary time)—not cycling. Cycling does not arise, even as a theoretical problem, because the state-of-nature decision rule approximates unanimity rule.

4 Legislative Organization: Diminishing Delay but Creating Inequality

In this section, I view legislative organization as designed—either intentionally or via evolutionary adaptation—to solve the problems that arise in the legislative state of nature. Of the four conditions characterizing the state of nature, I shall take the first (that bills can pass only pursuant to formally stated motions in the plenary session) and second (majority rule) as defining features of a democratic legislature. The third condition, that the plenary faces a hard budget constraint on time, is an exogenous constraint.

Given these stipulations, we have the following theoretical conjecture:

Busy legislatures are inegalitarian. All busy legislatures will evolve rules that create inequalities in members' access to plenary time and diminish ordinary members' ability to delay.

By a "busy" legislature, I mean one in which the marginal cost of plenary time—defined as the sum of the marginal opportunity costs borne by all the legislators, when the session is extended by an additional day—is high. Put more colloquially, a legislature is busy, to the extent that its members are champing at the bit to get back to other activities (campaigning, private law practice, etc.) by the end of the session.[4] The claim is that either a process of global optimization by a single coalition at a particular time, or a sequence of myopic and partial optimizations by differing

[4] From this perspective, even legislatures that sit for relatively brief periods during the year, such as the Japanese Diet, can be considered "busy."

coalitions at different times, will lead to unequal proposal rights and a reduced default power of delay (in busy legislatures).

Before considering why this prediction might follow, note that it does jibe with what we observe. Looked at analytically, the rules of any given legislature can be read as setting up the following structures: (1) an array of legislative (and sometimes executive) *offices*, endowed with *special agenda-setting powers* and other *resources* (examples below); (2) an array of motions, specifying the available actions in the giant chess game of parliamentary maneuvering; and (3) a set of procedures for voting on offices and motions. In the state of nature, there are neither offices nor motions that curb members' power to delay. Yet, all busy real-world legislatures—I am thinking here of national assemblies—exhibit both offices and methods of curbing delay.

4.1 What Are the Offices and Their Endowments?

Offices endowed with special agenda-setting powers and other resources fall into two main categories: executive and legislative. The main types of executive office are presidents/premiers, senior (cabinet) ministers, and junior ministers, while legislative offices include presiding officers, members of directing boards, committee chairs, and committee members.

By "special agenda-setting powers," or agenda power for short, I refer to any *special* ability to determine which bills are considered on the floor and under what procedures (cf. Cox and McCubbins 2005). Because any member in the US House can participate in an attempt to discharge a bill, I would not count "the ability to participate in a discharge attempt" as an "agenda power." Such an ability is not special; it is general. In contrast, only members of the Rules Committee can participate in fashioning special rules;[5] and only chairs can delay bills merely by not scheduling them—to mention two proper examples of agenda power. Looking beyond the USA, several Latin American presidents exercise special agenda-setting powers, such as those entailed in the urgency procedure in Brazil (Figueiredo and Limongi 1999; Amorim Neto, Cox, and McCubbins 2003) and Chile (Siavelis 2002). Conference committees in various systems often exercise special agenda-setting powers, e.g. when they can make take-it-or-leave-it offers to the two legislative chambers (Tsebelis and Money 1997). Directing boards (e.g. the Rules Committee in the US House, the College of Leaders in Brazil's *Câmara*, the presidium in the Polish *Sejm*) exercise various special powers to determine which bills, in what order, and under what terms of debate, will be considered on the floor (Döring 1995; Figueiredo and Limongi 1999). Many other examples exist but those given suffice to illustrate the concept.

In addition to special agenda-setting powers, offices may also be endowed with other resources, the prime example being staff. So far as I know, there is no comparative survey of legislative staff resources across the world's legislatures.

---

[5] A "special rule" is a resolution reported by the Rules Committee that regulates the consideration of a bill or resolution.

4.2 Why Do Offices Rise and Defaults Sink?

Why do the agenda powers of office-holders rise and the delaying powers of ordinary (i.e. non-office-holding) members fall in busy legislatures? Why is voting power everywhere equal, while agenda power is everywhere unequal?

In the cases I know best, a central storyline runs as follows. At some point, the plenary time constraint binds when important and controversial issues are at stake. Motivated by the desire to enact legislation on these pressing issues, a majority of members are willing to reduce ordinary members' powers of delay and enhance office-holders' special powers to expedite business. Eventually, the equilibrium reached is distinctly inegalitarian: there are office-holders with privileged access to the plenary agenda, who drive the important legislation; and there are non-office-holders with default access to the plenary agenda, who seek legislative accomplishment chiefly through alliance with office-holders (or by becoming office-holders themselves) and who exercise some residual but reduced power of delay.[6]

One case that fits the general storyline just sketched is the nineteenth-century UK House of Commons, in the crucial decades during which modern parliamentary norms of governance were established (Cox 1987, 1993; Dion 1997). Another is the late nineteenth-century US House of Representatives, when Reed's rules were brought in (Binder 1997; Dion 1997; Cox and McCubbins 2005). A third case is the transition from the Fourth to the Fifth Republic in France, when the package vote and a revamped confidence procedure were introduced (Huber 1996).

In all these stories, delay is curbed *and* special proposal powers are created. Is this just a coincidence or should we have expected it?

If we imagine a group seeking to pass controversial legislation in the state of nature, logically there are only two options they might explore (if some form of compromise with the opposition is rejected). One option is to endow some of the group's members with special abilities to make proposals (e.g. raise their recognition probabilities, necessarily lowering other members'). If, however, ordinary members' abilities to delay remain undisturbed, the de facto unanimity rule obtaining in the state of nature will render the improved proposal powers created by the group largely useless. Another option is to curb the ability of individuals to delay, by inventing something like the previous question motion (which ends debate and brings the matter at hand to a vote). Absent the creation of special proposal powers, such a reform would move the legislature from unanimity rule toward pure majority rule. However, the fundamental problems besetting the legislative process—the plenary bottleneck, reneging, lack of specialization, overuse of the common pool of time—can all appear under pure majority rule, too.[7]

Thus, in order to address the problems that plague legislation in the state of nature, it is necessary *both* to curb delay *and* to create special proposal powers. The default

---

[6] This is not to say that ordinary members are reduced everywhere to nonentities. The office-holders may be more powerful but how much more powerful is a variable.

[7] Another theoretical problem arises when the decision rule is majority rather than unanimity: cycling. See e.g. Andrews 2002; Aldrich 1995; Laver and Shepsle 1996.

powers wielded by ordinary members must fall, while the special powers wielded by office-holders must rise.[8]

5 Legislative Organization: Parties

If the typical democratic legislature possesses an array of offices endowed with special agenda-setting powers, then the question naturally arises as to which members will secure which offices. This is where political parties come in. Parties have "co-evolved" with electoral democracy, in the sense that they have both influenced the rules by which elective offices can be won and have in turn been influenced by those rules. Parties have also "co-evolved" with intra-legislative elections, such as investiture votes, votes to install committee members, votes to choose Speakers, and so on (Carroll, Cox, and Pachón 2004a). Indeed, one might say that modern democratic legislatures and modern democratic political parties are unthinkable without one another.

5.1 Parties Are the Only Viable Route to High Office

The role of parties is particularly clear when one focuses on how offices are allocated among legislators. The general rule is:

Parties (and factions) are the only viable route to high office, in virtually all democratic legislatures.

The exceptions to this rule appear even rarer than are the exceptions to the analogous rule in the electoral arena.

To clarify the point, note first that the presence of organized political groups—often called "fractions" in the literature—is explicitly recognized in the rules of procedure in most democratic assemblies of the world.[9] Typically, these groups correspond closely to the parties and alliances that have competed in elections, although in some cases (e.g. Italy and Spain) "mixed groups" of deputies can also form.

---

[8] Another route to solving the problems of the state-of-nature legislature would be purely extra-parliamentary: if one could establish sufficient control over nominations and elections, so that one could command a majority of legislators to do one's bidding, then one need only curb delay. Offices are not necessary because by hypothesis one can dictate one's followers' actions using extra-parliamentary carrots and sticks. Such complete dominance of electoral payoffs is, however, confined to authoritarian regimes.

[9] Even when the standing orders do not explicitly mention fractions—as in the USA—they still exist (the two parties' caucuses) and still are essential to the process by which intra-legislative elections are conducted. In the US House, for example, the majority party leadership decides the allocation of committee seats and chairs between the two parties and informs the minority party of its decision. Each party then, through internal procedures, produces a slate of nominations stipulating which of its members will occupy each committee position allocated to it. These two slates are then combined into a single omnibus resolution that is voted up or down (no amendments allowed) on the floor of the House.

Having made this initial point, note next that there are two main ways in which legislative offices are allocated. First, some offices are allocated directly to party fractions. For example, fraction heads automatically qualify for a seat on the directing boards in Austria, Belgium, France, and Germany (Somogyvári 1994, 165). Committee seats too are often allocated directly to fractions, with each fraction then determining which of their members get the fraction's allotted posts (Shaw 1979; Carroll, Cox, and Pachón 2004a).[10] Second, some offices are allocated by an electoral process within the legislature. For example, Speakers are often directly elected by the assembly, committee chairs are often elected by the relevant committee, slates of nominees for cabinet portfolios are sometimes approved in investiture votes, and so forth.

Regardless of whether posts are directly allocated to fractions or fractions compete for them in intra-legislative elections, it is extremely difficult for the analog of write-in candidates or independents to make any headway in the competition for offices. A member's nomination by a party group is essential. Even in systems, such as Russia, with large numbers of independents, party groups still quickly become the only viable route to intra-legislative office (cf. Remington and Smith 1995; Remington 1998).

If any single legislator could form a viable party group at any time, then the necessity of a party nomination would be less constraining. However, two widespread features of intra-legislative office allocations erect clear barriers to entry. First, would-be fractions must typically prove that they have some minimum number of members, before they can be officially recognized. This threshold, expressed as a percentage of the total number of members in the assembly, varies from country to country: Austria (2.7 per cent), Belgium (1.4 per cent), Chile (7.5 per cent), France (5.2 per cent), Germany (5 per cent), Italy (3.2 per cent), Spain (4.3 per cent).[11] Second, the fractions that succeed in getting into government typically get a larger-than-proportional share of key offices (Carroll, Cox, and Pachón 2004a). In the case of committee chairs, for example, the governing coalition's percentage exceeded its seat percentage by 45.3 points in Australia, 31.3 in Belgium, 27.0 in Chile, 38.0 in Luxembourg, and 12.3 in the Netherlands—to cite some figures from 2003.[12]

5.2 Party-rule Symbiosis

Not only are legislative parties the only viable route to legislative office, but they often set up (or at least influence) the rules of the intra-legislative electoral game. Making *legislative* rules can be compared to making *electoral* rules. In both cases, scholars typically assume that parties seek rules that will help them win and that different rules favor different parties. Given these assumptions, the successful parties in a polity should support the rules and the rules should in turn help those parties. Although

---

[10] Relatedly, staff allocations are often made directly to fractions (with individual members then dependent on their fractions for certain kinds of staff support).

[11] See Somogyvári 1994, 165; and the rules posted on the parliamentary websites for Chile (www.camara.cl) and Spain (www.congreso.es).

[12] Author's calculations from information provided on the official websites of each assembly.

the literature does not use this term, a convenient analogy is that parties and rules are symbionts.

Within the legislative arena, one finds a strong correlation between the effective number of parties in a system and the proportionality of the rules used to allocate intra-legislative (e.g. committee) and executive (e.g. cabinet) posts (Carroll, Cox, and Pachón 2004a). This is consistent with either rules affecting the number of parties, parties rewriting the rules, or both, per the metaphor of symbiosis.

6 THE TYPES OF AGENDA POWER

I have stressed that legislatures are, in good part, electoral arenas that elect an array of offices endowed with special agenda powers. In this section, I consider what those agenda powers are and how they are structured. Agenda powers can be classified in various ways. Here, I focus on the ability to *prevent* proposals from being considered in the plenary session, or *ensure* that they are considered. Much of the literature focuses instead on "downstream" agenda power, such as the ability to control the terms of debate or the nature of amendments on the floor (e.g. Dion and Huber 1996 for the USA; Rasch 2000 for the European parliaments).

6.1 Positive Versus Negative Agenda Power

One way to categorize agenda power is in terms of whether it is negative or positive. Negative agenda powers allow their wielders to delay or, in the extreme, veto the placement of bills on the plenary agenda. For example, the US House Rules Committee has at times had the right to refuse to report a special rule for a bill, thereby preventing its appearance on the floor. Positive agenda powers allow their wielders to hasten or, in the extreme, ensure the placement of bills on the plenary agenda. For example, the US House Rules Committee can report a special rule which, if adopted by the House, transfers a given bill off the calendars and onto the floor for consideration.

Distributing veto powers to more legislators implies a smaller (no larger) set of bills that all veto players can agree on, leading to frustration of various sorts and eventually to gridlock. Distributing proposal powers to more legislators implies a larger (no smaller) set of bills that the floor *must* decide upon, leading to external costs of various sorts and possibly to cycling (McKelvey 1976; Schofield 1978). There is thus a trade-off between increasing veto power and increasing proposal power.[13] Formal and informal models of legislative parties differ in whether they depict parties as controlling the agenda via the allocation of proposal rights (positive agenda power) or

---

[13] Such a trade-off was noted long ago, in connection with the question of how large a majority (bare, 3/5, 2/3, etc.) would be optimal, by Buchanan and Tullock (1962).

veto rights (negative agenda power); they hence implicitly or explicitly posit different resolutions of the positive/negative trade-off.

Two examples of theories in which proposal rights are the key resource allocated by parties to their members are Laver and Shepsle's (1996) model of ministerial government and Diermeier and Feddersen's (1998) model of the vote of confidence. In a common interpretation of Laver and Shepsle's model, multiparty coalition governments allocate ministerial portfolios to their various member parties, with each minister then possessing both positive and negative agenda power in his or her respective jurisdiction. Thus, each minister can make proposals directly to the assembly, without needing cabinet clearance. In Diermeier and Feddersen's model (which builds on the seminal work of Baron and Ferejohn 1989), coalitions of legislators allocate increased "recognition probabilities" to their members, thereby increasing their ability to make proposals. Once recognized, a given member of a coalition again needs no pre-clearance for his or her proposals.

An alternative view of coalitions is that they allocate negative agenda power, or veto rights, among their members. Tsebelis (2002) takes this view of parliamentary coalitions, viewing each member party as possessing a general veto over the entire range of issues the coalition must face. Similarly, Cox and McCubbins (2002) view majority parties primarily as allocating veto (or delaying) power to various offices held by their senior partners, such as committee chairs and Speakers.

6.2 General Versus Jurisdiction-specific Agenda Power

Some offices—such as presiding officers and directing boards—exercise general control over the flow of bills to the plenary. Other offices—such as permanent or conference committees—exercise control over the flow of bills only within specialized or even bill-specific jurisdictions. There is a trade-off between these sorts of agenda power, too. For example, if the directing board is given the right to block any bill from reaching the floor, then necessarily no policy committee can be given jurisdiction-specific proposal power. In the US case, committees that do have the right to put their bills directly on the floor are called "privileged," while those whose handiwork must pass muster with the Rules Committee or Speaker to gain access to the floor are "non-privileged."

6.3 Early Versus Late Agenda Power

Some offices have early influence over bills; others have late influence. For example, non-privileged committees in the US House have mostly negative agenda power and they exert it early in the legislative process. In contrast, conference committees have both negative and positive agenda power and they exert it late in the legislative process.

In general, assemblies that allocate a lot of early negative agenda power are analogous to filtration systems: bills must pass through several filters (veto gates) before they can reach the floor. In contrast, assemblies that allocate a lot of late positive agenda power are analogous to rapid response teams: whatever else has happened previously in the legislative process, the last-mover is given a chance to make a final, take-it-or-leave-it offer. Models of this sort include Weingast (1992), analyzing the power of committees in the US House; Heller (2001), analyzing the power of governments in European parliaments; and Krehbiel and Meirowitz (2002), analyzing the power of the minority party in the US House.

6.4 Decentralized Versus Centralized Agenda Power

A final distinction is between centralized and decentralized agenda power. Are both positive and negative agenda powers for all jurisdictions concentrated in a single officer's or body's hands? Are jurisdiction-specific vetoes and proposal rights delegated to a variety of committees (as in the committee government model familiar in US studies; cf. Cox and McCubbins 1993 for a review) or ministers (Laver and Shepsle 1996)?

7 THE CONSEQUENCES OF NEGATIVE AGENDA POWER

Many models in legislative studies posit a set of players with varying combinations of veto and proposal power; and then derive conclusions about legislative output, given the postulated distribution of agenda power. In this section, I consider studies in which the main assumptions are about which actors possess vetoes. There are three main legislative outputs on which such studies focus: the sheer volume of bills enacted by the assembly; reactions to gridlock; and the rate at which posited agenda setters are defeated.

7.1 Gridlock and the Volume of Legislation

Cox and McCubbins (2001) focus on the trade-off between making political systems more resolute (able to stick with decisions once made) and making them more decisive (able to make decisions to begin with). They define the "effective" number of vetoes in a system as a function of the number of institutional veto points and the diversity of preferences of the agents controlling those veto points, noting that "changing policy becomes increasingly costly as the number of parties to a negotiation [veto players], or as the diversity of their preferences, increases" (p. 27).

Tsebelis (2002) also stresses that both the ability and the desire to veto must be considered. He argues in particular that, the more veto players there are, and the more divergent their preferences are, the fewer bills (i.e. changes to the status quo) they will be able to agree upon—hence the lower will be the number of bills produced by the assembly.

There are various empirical studies that use this basic "veto player" logic to explain varying legislative outputs. To cite just three examples: Tsebelis (1995, 2002) focuses on law production in European parliaments; Alt and Lowry (1994) focus on how divided government in the American states affects the rapidity with which those states respond to fiscal crises; and Heller (1997) considers how bicameralism affects fiscal deficits in a variety of European states.

7.2 Reactions to Gridlock

What happens when veto players with diverse preferences can agree on no (or few) changes to the status quo, yet each believes that some changes are crucial? Several scholars have noted that this is a recipe for frustration, with several possible outlets for that frustration. For example, when policy committees' bills were blocked by the Rules Committee in the US House during the "textbook Congress" era, the policy committees attempted to end run Rules in a variety of ways: Calendar Wednesday, allowing discharge of special rules, the twenty-one-day rule, and so forth (cf. Cox and McCubbins 2005, ch. 4).

It is not just bi- or multilateral vetoes that produce frustration. The opposition in any assembly will, if the government controls the agenda, typically be shut out of the legislative process, in the sense that its bills will not be advanced, its issues will receive short shrift, and so on. Thus, oppositions worldwide seek ways to "go public," to appeal to the electorate. As Maltzman and Sigelman (1996, 822) argue regarding the US House, the majority party firmly controls the agenda, hence "minority party leaders routinely seek to use publicity to advance an alternative agenda."[14]

What specific techniques are used to "go public?" There are many. Some are embedded in the legislative process—bones tossed to the opposition by the government. In this category would be question time in many parliamentary systems, one- and five-minute morning speeches in the US House (Maltzman and Sigelman 1996), and time reserved for opposition motions in many assemblies. Other techniques of "going public" are extra-legislative. Included here are press conferences, demonstrations on the steps of the assembly, rallies, marches, and the like (Evans 2001; Thompson 1986; Cook 1989). For the most part, these various techniques of "going public" are tools wielded by the intra-legislative losers. The winners are too busy legislating.

---

[14] Similar points have been made previously by Jones 1970 and Cook 1989, again in the US context.

7.3 Roll Rates

The most direct implication of any model positing that a specific body has a veto is that this body should never lose, in the particular sense of having an unwanted policy change forced upon them. Note that veto players can be *disappointed*: they can want to change the status quo but be unable to do so. In contrast, they should never be *rolled*: that is, they should never want to preserve the status quo but be unable to do so, as this gives the lie to the assumption that they are a veto player. Cox and McCubbins make the distinction between a roll and a disappointment central to both their theoretical and empirical analysis of legislatures. Thus, rather than examine the number of actions taken (e.g. bills passed), they examine the roll rates of posited veto players.

In particular, they investigate the rates at which governing parties in a variety of systems observably oppose, yet fail to stop, bills. Tsebelis (2002), formalizing traditional views, pictures coalition governments in parliamentary systems as composed of parties each of which wields a veto over placing bills on the plenary agenda. In broad conformity with this notion, Cox, Masuyama, and McCubbins (2001) find that the roll rates for parties in several *majority* governments in parliamentary systems are generally below 5 per cent. Some Latin American presidents also choose to form parliamentary-style *majority* support coalitions and, when they choose this route in Brazil, the result is similar to that in parliamentary systems, with governing parties' roll rates generally below 5 per cent (Amorim Neto, Cox, and McCubbins 2004). In the USA, the "governing party"—the majority party in either the US House (Cox and McCubbins 2002) or the US Senate (Campbell, Cox, and McCubbins 2002)—has a roll rate well below 5 per cent from the 1890s to the present. The only cases in which governing parties are rolled at high rates occur when *minority* governments, under either parliamentary or presidential conditions, form (and then only when those minority governments did not have a majority support coalition). This occurred, for example, in Denmark under minority government during the 1970s and 1980s (Damgaard and Svenson 1989) and in Brazil under the minority government of Collor (Amorim Neto, Cox, and McCubbins 2003). Thus, as an empirical matter, there is some support for the thesis that, when majority governments form, they distribute vetoes among their pivotal components.

8 THE CONSEQUENCES OF POSITIVE AGENDA POWER

The previous section discussed veto players. The more and more diverse are the veto players, the smaller the volume of bills that can be enacted; and the greater is the incentive to "end run" the veto of one or more players. Even when there is only one veto player, those disagreeing with the ensuing vetoes still have incentives to "go public" or otherwise get around the veto player blocking advancement of their interests. Finally, true veto players should never be rolled, although they can be disappointed.

In this section, rather than focus on vetoes and the problem of gridlock with which they are associated, I consider proposal power and the external costs that such power entails. Thus, I examine the other side of the trade-off noted above between gridlock and external costs (cf. Buchanan and Tullock 1962).

8.1 Decentralization of Positive Agenda Power and Overspending

A convenient starting point is a model in which several distinct committees (e.g. Weingast and Marshall 1988) or ministries (Laver and Shepsle 1996) have positive agenda control in their respective jurisdictions. Thus, each can ensure floor consideration of any bill it chooses. Given this assumption, each committee or ministry can impose external costs on other members of the governing coalition. In particular, spending will be greater than it would be, were all bills forced to pass a consequential central screening by an agent internalizing the broader interests of the governing coalition.

In comparative studies, the model of decentralized positive agenda power has appeared in examinations of fiscal policy. For example, in an examination of developed democracies, Bawn and Rosenbluth (2004) find systematically greater spending in multiparty governing coalitions than in single-party governments (and argue that spending ministers do not as fully internalize the reputational costs imposed on their coalition partners by their expenditures, when those partners are in other parties). (See Inman and Ingberman 1988; Poterba and von Hagen 1999; and Persson, Roland, and Tabellini 2003 for similar analyses.)

In US studies, the model of decentralized agenda power is commonly known under the rubric of "committee government" (cf. Cox and McCubbins 1993, chs. 1–3). In the pure form of this model, each congressional committee could veto bills without fear of being overturned by the chamber; and could secure a hearing on the floor for any bill it favored. The hypothesized results of this decentralization of power included overspending, as each committee pushed programs sought by powerful special interests relevant to its particular jurisdiction (cf. Weingast and Marshall 1988).

8.2 Counterbalancing Positive Agenda Power

Another vein in the literature accepts that external costs would arise, were positive agenda power decentralized, but then argues that legislators anticipate and take steps to ameliorate this problem. The argument is thus similar to those reviewed above, in which agents do not meekly accept the consequences of veto power but seek ways to avoid such consequences.

One argument in which agents seek to counterbalance the anticipated effects of positive agenda power runs as follows. Suppose that the majority party in the US House is able to grant positive agenda power to, or withhold it from, committees. Those to which such grants are made, known as "privileged" committees in the US literature, expose the party to greater risks of external costs. Simply put, these committees may put legislation on the floor that will displease large segments of, or even roll, the majority. Two methods of mitigating this risk are to stack the committee with additional majority party members; and to demand a higher standard of party loyalty from those placed on privileged committees. Cox and McCubbins (1993) provide evidence that both these methods are employed in the US House.

A second argument in which agents counterbalance the effects of positive agenda power has to do with partners in coalition governments. Several recent studies have pointed to different possible mechanisms by which partners in coalition governments can monitor each other: by the appointment of junior ministers of different party from their seniors (Thies 2001); by the appointment of committee chairs of different party from their corresponding ministers (Hagevi 2000, 238; Carroll, Cox, and Pachón 2004*b*); or more generally by the necessity of pushing ministerial bills through the legislative process in the assembly (Martin and Vanberg 2004).

9 THE CONSEQUENCES OF CENTRALIZED AGENDA POWER

Thus far, I have separately considered the consequences of negative and positive agenda power. What if a given agent possesses both positive and negative agenda power across all jurisdictions? The best-known formal models illustrating the consequences of such power are McKelvey (1976), for the case of multidimensional choice spaces, and Romer and Rosenthal (1978, 1979), for the case of unidimensional choice spaces. Both models show that the agenda-setting agent has considerable influence over the ultimate policy choice made by the assembly, especially when the reversionary policy is "bad." That is, the more distasteful the policy outcome absent further legislative action will be, the wider the range of proposals that the agenda-setter can offer that the assembly will accept.

Consider three prominent illustrations of how "bad" reversions can arise, thus enhancing the agenda-setter's influence. First, on a single dimension of fiscal policy, the reversion may be *zero* spending. Since zero spending, or the utter abolition of the program in question, is usually far from the favored outcome of the bulk of legislators, a monopoly agenda-setter can find lots of alternatives that are favored by a majority (cf. Romer and Rosenthal 1978, 1979). Second, even if the reversion considered dimension by dimension is not extreme, the agenda-setter may be able to find a combination of issues on which the reversion is relatively more extreme, again widening the set of feasible alternatives that she can propose. McKelvey (1976) entertained the further possibility that the agenda-setter might be able strategically to worsen the reversionary policy, in opening legislative gambits, before offering a final bill. Third, even if the reversionary policy is not *ideologically* extreme, it may simply be dysfunctional. Londregan (2000) shows how agenda-setters can exploit low-valence reversionary policies to move policy ideologically in their favor, even when facing entrenched veto players with opposed ideological preferences.

In the work just reviewed, centralized agenda control is valuable essentially because it allows the agenda-setter to resolve a coordination game (namely which of the many policies jointly preferable to the reversion shall we choose?) promptly and on terms of its own choosing. Empirical studies of centralized agenda power resonate to some extent with this central insight. I consider two such studies in particular.

9.1 Policy Directions

Suppose that agent X has the power to block or propose any bill and is considering a sequence of single-issue bills. The further left (right) is X's ideal point along the conventional left–right political spectrum, the larger will be the proportion of bills that X proposes which move policy leftward (rightward). This prediction, which follows from a simple adaptation of the setter model (Cox and McCubbins 2005), catches only part of the agenda-setter's advantage (her ability to dictate the direction of policy change, rather than her ability to leverage a "bad" reversion). However, it has the advantage of being testable (because the direction in which a given bill proposes to move policy is easily determined, when there is a recorded vote on final passage of that bill).

Cox and McCubbins (2005) test such a model in the context of the US House of Representatives, assuming that the agenda-setter corresponds to the majority party's median. They find that the model accurately predicts policy directions in the House, whereas competing models based on other assumptions about who sets the agenda (e.g. the floor median) do not.

9.2 Omnibus Bills

Döring (1995) and Henning (1995) also consider a model in which the government is a monopoly supplier of legislation. The government can choose either to produce simple bills, whose passage will not require the use of agenda power, or to produce more complex and conflictual bills, whose passage will be facilitated by agenda power. They argue that increasing the government's agenda power lowers the "price" of the more complex and conflictual bills, while leaving the price of simple/non-conflictual bills unchanged. Accordingly, a government will increase its "purchase" of complex/conflictual bills when its agenda power increases, assuming that complex/conflictual bills are normal goods (in the economist's sense). Since

(1) complex/conflictual bills always require more time to process, even when the government has strong agenda powers, and (2) the government faces a hard time constraint, any increase in the percent of complex bills will necessarily mean a lower volume of legislation overall. Thus, all told, one expects fewer but more complex/conflictual bills when the government's agenda power is greater. Döring (1995c) provides some cross-national evidence for part of this story in a study of west European legislatures.

10 THE CHOICE OF AGENDA POWER

Thus far, I have reviewed research that analyzes the consequences of a given structure of agenda power. Another line of research has begun to emerge, in which the distribution of agenda power is itself an endogenous choice. Formal theoretical works of this sort include several based on the seminal Baron and Ferejohn (1989) model. For example, Muthoo and Shepsle (2004) consider the optimal allocation of recognition probabilities between generations of legislators; while Diermeier and Feddersen (1998) and Baron (1998) allow a restricted choice of recognition probabilities in forming a government. Another line of argument is that associated with the theory of conditional party government in the USA, which posits that members of the majority party will be more willing to delegate agenda powers to their central leaders, when the majority is more homogeneous internally and more polarized from the minority (Aldrich and Rohde 2000). Relatedly, Cox and McCubbins (2005) argue that the majority party will adjust the mix of positive and negative agenda powers it delegates, in favor of the former, when it becomes more internally homogeneous. Empirical studies of changing structures of agenda power are many and beyond the scope of this review (for the US case, see e.g. Binder 1997; Dion 1997; Cox and McCubbins 2005).

11 CONCLUSION

Democratic legislatures can pass bills only pursuant to motions formally stated and adopted in their plenary sessions. Plenary time is thus the sine qua non of legislation.

In the legislative state of nature, access to plenary time is egalitarian and unregulated. This leads to difficulties in accruing gains from trade, either in bills or in legislative labor; and to common-pool problems in the use of plenary time.

Because the problems that arise in the legislative state of nature are severe, at least when the legislature is busy, no current democratic legislature exists in such a state. While voting power remains equal everywhere, special power to propose to the plenary and to block proposals to the plenary has been delegated to various offices, such as presiding officers, members of directing boards, and members and chairs of permanent and conference committees.

The existence of offices endowed with special agenda-setting powers has in turn profoundly affected the character and functioning of legislatures. First, legislative parties have emerged as the only viable routes to the high offices in the gift of the legislature; and have been actively involved in choosing and adapting the rules regulating accession to such offices. Second, different structures of delegated agenda powers have led to different legislative processes and outputs. While fleshing that spare statement out remains a central task of comparative legislative studies, one can note what is perhaps the most fundamental distinction: that between positive and negative agenda power. Delegating negative agenda power—the power to delay or prevent bills from reaching the plenary session—can lead to veto politics, gridlock, and the costs of inaction. Delegating positive agenda power—the power to hasten or ensure bills' reaching the plenary session—can lead to overspending and other (external) costs of action. Both kinds of problem can sometimes be ameliorated by political parties (as they can control access to high offices, hence impose fiduciary standards on their occupants; see Wittman 1995, ch. 6; Cox and McCubbins 1993, 2005).

It is important to note the difference between the perspective on legislatures offered here, in which endogenously created offices are key to securing control of the agenda, and the perspective offered by the theory of responsible party government, in which the emphasis is on discipline producing cohesion, with cohesive voting then conferring control of the agenda. It is true that control over the agenda could in principle be secured purely through control of a majority of votes in the assembly, without the need of special offices occupied by party leaders. However, there is no democratic legislature in which governing parties rely solely on their own internal discipline, in order to control the legislative agenda. It is only when the control of leaders over their followers exceeds that usually found in democracies that parties might be able to dispense with the institutional mechanisms emphasized here.

REFERENCES

ALDRICH, J. H. 1995. *Why Parties?* Chicago: University of Chicago Press.
—— and ROHDE, D. W. 2000. The consequences of party organization in the House: the role of the majority and minority parties in conditional party government. In *Polarized Politics: Congress and the President in a Partisan Era*, ed. J. Bond and R. Fleisher. Washington, DC: CQ Press.
ALT, J., and LOWRY, R. 1994. Divided government, fiscal institutions and budget deficits: evidence from the states. *American Political Science Review*, 88: 811–28.
AMORIM NETO, O., COX, G. W., and D. MCCUBBINS, M. 2003. Agenda power in Brazil's Câmara dos Deputados, 1989 to 1998. *World Politics*, 55: 550–78.
ANDREWS, J. 2002. *When Majorities Fail: The Russian Legislature, 1990–1993*. Cambridge: Cambridge University Press.

BARON, D. 1998. Comparative dynamics of parliamentary governments. *American Political Science Review*, 92: 593–603.

——— and FEREJOHN, J. 1989. Bargaining in legislatures. *American Political Science Review*, 83: 1181–206.

BAWN, K., and ROSENBLUTH, F. 2004. Short versus long coalitions: how electoral agency shapes the political logic of costs and benefits. Unpublished manuscript, UCLA and Yale University.

BINDER, S. A. 1997. *Minority Rights, Majority Rule: Partisanship and the Development of Congress*. Cambridge: Cambridge University Press.

BUCHANAN, J. M., and TULLOCK, G. 1962. *The Calculus of Consent: Logical Foundations of Constitutional Democracy*. Ann Arbor: University of Michigan Press.

CAMPBELL, A., COX, G. W., and MCCUBBINS, M. D. 2002. Agenda power in the Senate, 1877 to 1986. In *Party, Process, and Political Change in Congress: New Perspectives on the History of Congress*, ed. D. W. Brady and M. D. McCubbins. Palo Alto, Calif.: Stanford University Press.

CAREY, J., and SHUGART, M. (eds.). 1998. *Executive Decree Authority*. Cambridge: Cambridge University Press.

CARROLL, R., COX, G. W., and PACHÓN, M. 2004a. How parties create electoral democracy, chapter 2. Prepared for presentation at the 2004 meetings of the American Political Science Association, Chicago, 1–4, Sept.

——— ——— ——— 2004b. Shadowing ministers. Unpublished manuscript, University of California, San Diego.

COOK, T. E. 1989. *Making Laws and Making News: Media Strategies in the U.S. House of Representatives*. Washington, DC: Brookings Institution Press.

COX, G. W. 1987. *The Efficient Secret*. Cambridge: Cambridge University Press.

——— 1993. The development of collective responsibility in the U.K. *Parliamentary History*, 13: 32–47.

——— and MCCUBBINS M. D. 1993. *Legislative Leviathan*. Berkeley: University of California Press.

——— ——— 2001. The institutional determinants of economic policy outcomes. Pp. 21–63 in *Presidents, Parliaments and Policy*, ed. M. D. McCubbins and S. Haggard. New York: Cambridge University Press.

——— ——— 2002. Agenda power in the House of Representatives. In *Party, Process, and Political Change in Congress: New Perspectives on the History of Congress*, ed. D. W. Brady and M. D. McCubbins. Palo Alto, Calif.: Stanford University Press.

——— ——— 2005. *Setting the Agenda: Responsible Party Government in the U.S. House of Representatives*. Cambridge: Cambridge Universtity Press.

——— MASUYAMA, M., and MCCUBBINS, M. D. 2000. Agenda power in the Japanese House of Representatives. *Japanese Journal of Political Science*, 1: 1–22.

DAMGAARD, E., and SVENSON, P. 1989. Who governs? Parties and policies in Denmark. *European Journal of Political Research*, 17: 731–45.

DIERMEIER, D., and FEDDERSEN, T. 1998. Cohesion in legislatures and the vote of confidence procedure. *American Political Science Review*, 92: 611–22.

DION, D. 1997. *Turning the Legislative Thumbscrew: Minority Rights and Procedural Change in Legislative Politics*. Ann Arbor: University of Michigan Press.

——— and HUBER, J. 1996. Procedural choice and the House Committee on Rules. *Journal of Politics*, 58: 25–53.

DÖRING, H. 1995. Time as a scarce resource: government control of the agenda. In *Parliaments and Majority Rule in Western Europe*, ed. H. Döring. Frankfurt: Campus Verlag.

EVANS, C. L. 2001. Committees, leaders and message politics. In *Congress Reconsidered*, ed. L. Dodd and B. Oppenheimer, 7th edn. Washington, DC: CQ Press.

FIGUEIREDO, A. C., and LIMONGI, F. 1999. *Executivo e legislativo na nova ordem constitucional*. Rio de Janeiro: Editora FGV.

GILLIGAN, T., and KREHBIEL, K. 1990. Organization of informative committees by a rational legislature. *American Journal of Political Science*, 34: 531–64.

GREEN, A. 1979. *Devolution and Public Finance: Stormont from 1921 to 1972*. Glasgow: Centre for the Study of Public Policy, University of Strathclyde.

GROSECLOSE, T., and MCCARTY, N. 2000. The politics of blame: bargaining before an audience. *American Journal of Political Science*, 45: 100–19.

HAGEVI, M. 2000. Nordic light on committee assignments. In *Beyond Westminster and Congress: The Nordic Experience*, ed. P. Esaiasson and K. Heidar. Columbus: Ohio State University Press.

HELLER, W. B. 1997. Bicameralism and budget deficits: the effect of parliamentary structure on government spending. *Legislative Studies Quarterly*, 22: 485–516.

—— 2001. Making policy stick: why the government gets what it wants in multiparty parliaments. *American Journal of Political Science*, 45: 780–98.

HENNING, C. H. 1995. A formal model of law production by government as a natural monopoly. In *Parliaments and Majority Rule in Western Europe*, ed. H. Döring. Frankfurt: Campus Verlag.

HUBER, J. 1996. *Rationalizing Parliament: Legislative Institutions and Party Politics in France*. Cambridge: Cambridge University Press.

—— and SHIPAN, C. 2002. *Deliberate Discretion?* Cambridge: Cambridge University Press.

INMAN, R., and INGBERMAN, D. 1988. The political economy of fiscal policy. In *Public Economics: A Reader*, ed. P. G. Hare. Oxford: Basil Blackwell.

JONES, C. 1970. *The Minority Party in Congress*. Boston: Little, Brown.

KREHBIEL, K. 1991. *Information and Legislative Organization*. Ann Arbor: University of Michigan Press.

—— and MEIROWITZ, A. 2002. Power and the motion to recommit. *Legislative Studies Quarterly*, 27: 191–218.

LAVER, M., and SHEPSLE, K. 1996. *Making and Breaking Governments: Cabinets and Legislatures in Parliamentary Democracies*. New York: Cambridge University Press.

LONDREGAN, J. 2000. *Legislative Institutions and Ideology in Chile*. Cambridge: Cambridge University Press.

MCKELVEY, R. 1976. Intransitivities in multidimensional voting models and some implications for agenda control. *Journal of Economic Theory*, 12: 472–82.

MALTZMAN, F., and SIGELMAN, L. 1996. The politics of talk: unconstrained floor time in the U.S. House of Representatives. *Journal of Politics*, 58: 819–30.

MARTIN, L. W., and VANBERG, G. 2004. Policing the bargain: coalition government and parliamentary scrutiny. *American Journal of Political Science*, 48: 13–27.

MUTHOO, A., and SHEPSLE, K. A. 2004. Agenda-setting power in organizations with overlapping generations of players. Unpublished manuscript, Harvard University.

PERSSON, T., ROLAND, G., and TABELLINI, G. 2003. How do electoral rules shape party structures, government coalitions, and economic policies? Unpublished manuscript, University of Stockholm.

POTERBA, J., and VON HAGEN, J. (eds.). 1999. *Fiscal Institutions and Fiscal Performance*. Chicago: University of Chicago Press.

RASCH, B. E. 2000. Parliamentary floor voting procedures and agenda setting in Europe. *Legislative Studies Quarterly*, 25: 3–23.

REMINGTON, T. F. 1998. Political conflict and institutional design: paths of party development in Russia. In *Party Politics in Post-Communist Russia*, ed. J. Lowenhardt. London: Frank Cass.

―― and S. SMITH, S. 1995. The development of parliamentary parties in Russia. *Legislative Studies Quarterly*, 20: 457–89.
ROMER, T., and ROSENTHAL, H. 1978. Political resource allocation, controlled agendas, and the status quo. *Public Choice*, 33: 27–44.
―――― 1979. Bureaucrats versus voters: on the political economy of resource allocation by direct democracy. *Quarterly Journal of Economics*, 93: 563–87.
SCHOFIELD, N. 1978. Intransitivities of simple dynamic games. *Review of Economic Studies*, 45: 575–94.
SHAW, M. 1979. Conclusions. In *Committees in Legislatures*, ed. J. D. Lees and M. Shaw. Oxford: Martin Robertson.
SIAVELIS, P. 2002. Exaggerated presidentialism and moderate presidents: executive–legislative relations in Chile. In *Legislative Politics in Latin America*, ed. S. Morgenstern and B. Nacif. Cambridge: Cambridge University Press.
SOMOGYVÁRI, I. 1994. Legal institutions in standing orders of the parliaments of advanced democracies. In *The Emergence of East Central European Parliaments*, ed. A. Ágh. Budapest: Hungarian Centre of Democracy Studies.
THIES, M. 2001. Keeping tabs on one's partners: the logic of delegation in coalition governments. *American Journal of Political Science*, 45: 580–98.
THOMPSON, J. A. 1986. Bringing home the bacon: the politics of pork barrel in the North Carolina legislature. *Legislative Studies Quarterly*, 11: 91–108.
TSEBELIS, G. 1995. Veto players and law production in parliamentary democracies. In *Parliaments and Majority Rule in Western Europe*, ed. H. Döring. New York: St Martin's Press.
―― 2002. *Veto Players*. Princeton, NJ: Princeton University Press.
―― and MONEY, J. 1997. *Bicameralism*. New York: Cambridge University Press.
WEINGAST, B. 1992. Fighting fire with fire: amending activity and institutional change in the post-reform Congress. In *The Postreform Congress*, ed. R. H. Davidson. New York: St Martin's Press.
―― and MARSHALL, W. 1988. The industrial organization of Congress. *Journal of Political Economy*, 96: 132–63.
WITTMAN, D. 1995. *The Myth of Democratic Failure*. Chicago: University of Chicago Press.

CHAPTER 9

COALITION GOVERNMENT

DANIEL DIERMEIER

1 Introduction: A Shift in Perspective

THE year 1990 marked a turning point in the study of governmental coalitions. Laver and Schofield (1990) published a comprehensive and detailed review of the field up to the late 1980s. In addition, a significant set of new papers broke with the established research traditions. First, Baron (1989) published the initial applications of non-*cooperative* game theory (the "Baron–Ferejohn" model) to the study of governmental coalitions (Baron and Ferejohn 1989). Second, Laver and Shepsle (1990) used structure-induced equilibrium models to study the formation and stability of cabinets. Third, Strom (1990) presented a comprehensive account of minority governments and coalitional stability.[1]

These papers had one important element in common: all focused on the role of institutions in the study of governmental coalitions. The *New Institutionalism* had arrived in the study of coalition government. The point of this new approach was not that political institutions had been overlooked as a potentially important object of study. Political institutions—such as party systems, electoral rules, or constitutional features—have always played an important role in the study of coalition government. Rather, the claim was *methodological*: to have explanatory content and empirical accuracy, formal models of politics must incorporate institutional details.[2] This shift in perspective has had important consequences for the praxis and progress of coalition research in the last fifteen years.

---

[1] Laver (this volume) covers many of these issues in greater detail.
[2] See Diermeier (1997) and Diermeier and Krehbiel (2003) for a detailed discussion of the methodological aspects of institutionalism.

It is the distinctive characteristic of parliamentary democracies that the executive derives its mandate from and is politically responsible to the legislature. This has two consequences. First, unless one party wins a majority of seats, a rare case in electoral systems under proportional representation, the government is not determined by an election alone, but is the result of an elaborate bargaining process among the parties represented in the parliament. Second, parliamentary governments may lose the confidence of the parliament at any time, which leads to their immediate termination. Thus, historically, two questions have dominated the study of coalition government. Which governments will form? And how long will they last? Institutionalism has fundamentally changed the way researchers are conceptualizing and answering these questions.

This chapter is designed as follows. I first discuss important empirical work that motivated the institutionalist shift in the study of government coalitions. In the next two sections I discuss the most widely used institutionalist approaches: Laver and Shepsle's structure-induced equilibrium approach and the sequential bargaining model used by Baron and others. I then discuss two alternative approaches (demand bargaining and efficient bargaining) to model coalition formation that try to overcome some of the technical difficulties of older approaches. In the next two sections I discuss the consequences of the institutionalist perspective for empirical work. First, I review the area of cabinet stability, one of the most active areas in coalition research. In the penultimate section I discuss recent work that relies on structural estimation as its methodology to study coalition government empirically. A conclusion contains a summary and discusses some open questions.

2 The Arrival of Institutionalism

Institutionalism is difficult to define. It should not be identified with the analysis of institutions. Rather it is a methodological approach. The common element to all versions of institutionalism is a rejection of the social choice research program of finding institution-free properties (as illustrated by McKelvey 1986). Beyond that, institutionalism consists of rather different research programs that stem from different methodological approaches.

In the context of the study of government coalition the institutionalist approach implies a re-evaluation of existing theoretical traditions. Consider Axelrod's (1972) theory of proto-coalitions as an example.[3] In his model, ideologically connected proto-coalitions expand stepwise by adding new parties until they reach political

---

[3] Axelrod's theory of proto-coalitions is not the only example of an "institution-free" approach to government coalitions. Other examples include cooperative bargaining theory (e.g. the Shapley value, bargaining set) or social choice theoretic approaches (e.g. the core, the uncovered set). For a technically very sophisticated example of recent work in this area see e.g. Schofield, Sened, and Nixon 1998. Their model combines social choice-based, institution-free models of cabinet formation with Nash equilibria at the electoral level.

viability. The important point here is *how* the explanation works. Note that Axelrod's account only relies on the number of parties, their seat share, and their ideological position. From the perspective of the theory, other aspects of the cabinet formation process are *irrelevant*, e.g. who can propose governments, how long the process can last. Some disregard of existing structure, of course, is the essence of formal modeling. The question is whether such a stripped-down model of government formation explains the empirical phenomena. To rephrase the famous quote by Einstein: models should be as simple as possible, but not simpler.

The answer to this question is, of course, empirical. Are there phenomena that cannot be explained with an institution-free approach? Before the institutional shift in the early 1990s much of the empirical study of government coalitions was focused on one issue: the question of government formation. That is, suppose we know the number of parties, their seat shares, and (in some models) their ideological position, which governments would form?[4] The success of this research program was mixed. Although it consisted of a fruitful interplay of theoretical and empirical work, all told, institution-free models failed to predict which governments would form.

Two roots in the literature helped introduce institutionalist models into the study of government coalitions. The first root was empirical. Specifically, two independent empirical traditions played a critical role: Kaare Strøm's work on minority cabinets and Browne et al.'s study of cabinet stability. The second root was theoretical and consistent in the development of institutionalist models of cabinet formation (Laver and Shepsle 1990; Baron 1989).

Strøm's work (1985, 1990) was important in various respects. First, it focused on a puzzling, but prevalent, case of coalition governments: minority governments, i.e. cabinets where the parties that occupy portfolios together do not control a majority of seats in the legislature. As Strøm pointed out, their existence is neither rare (roughly a third of all coalition governments are of the minority type), nor does it constitute a crisis phenomenon. Denmark, for example, is almost always governed by minority governments, but hardly qualifies as a polity in crisis. Moreover, many of the minority governments are surprisingly stable.

The existence of minority governments constituted an embarrassment for existing theories of coalition formation. Why don't the opposition parties that constitute a chamber majority simply replace the incumbent minority government by a new cabinet that includes them?

The influence of Strøm's work, however, went beyond the mere recognition of minority governments. It had important methodological consequences for the study of coalition governments in general. First, it refocused the government formation question from "which government will form?" to "which type of government will form?"[5] That is, what are the factors that lead some countries regularly to choose minority cabinets (e.g. Denmark), while others (e.g. Germany) almost always choose minimum winning coalitions, while yet others (e.g. Italy) frequently choose

---

[4] See e.g. Laver and Schofield 1990 for a detailed overview of this literature.

[5] See, however, Martin and Stevenson 2001 for a recent, institutional, empirical study of coalition formation that tried to answer the first question.

super-majority governments. Second, it gave an account of minority governments using institutionalist explanations such as the existence of a strong committee system.[6]

The second empirical tradition was the study of cabinet stability pioneered by Browne, Srendreis, and Gleiber (1984, 1986, 1988). Browne et al. viewed cabinet survival as determined by "critical events," exogenous random shocks that destabilize an existing government. These random shocks are assumed to follow a Poisson process which implies a constant hazard rate for cabinet terminations.[7] Strom's (1985, 1988) approach, on the other hand, was institutional. Here the goal was to identify a robust set of covariates that influence mean cabinet duration. Since government type—i.e. whether the cabinet had majority or minority status—was one of the proposed independent variables, Strom's approach thus integrated his work on cabinet stability and minority governments.

In 1990 King et al. presented a "unified" model of cabinet dissolutions that combined the attribute approach proposed by Strom (1985, 1988) and the events approach introduced by Browne, Srendreis, and Gleiber (1986, 1988). Following this insight, a whole list of papers, especially by Paul Warwick, pointed out that the unified model is but a special case of a whole class of survival models (Warwick 1992a, 1992b, 1992c, 1994; Warwick and Easton 1992; Diermeier and Stevenson 1999, 2000).

While this literature provided rich new empirical regularities, an equally compelling theoretical framework was lacking. Competing candidates for such a framework, however, were being developed independently using different versions of game theory as their models of coalition formation: the Laver–Shepsle model and Baron's sequential bargaining models.

3 STRUCTURE-INDUCED EQUILIBRIUM: THE LAVER–SHEPSLE MODEL

In his seminal paper Shepsle (1979) formally introduced institutional structure as a committee system. The key idea was to assume additional constraints in the spatial decision-making environments. Specifically, Shepsle assumed that each legislator is assigned to exactly one issue. This assignment can be interpreted as a committee system in the context of the US Congress. Intuitively, a committee has exclusive jurisdiction on a given issue. Using a result by Kramer (1972), it can easily be shown that structure-induced equilibria exist for every committee assignment.[8] The basic idea is to have the committees vote sequentially on each issue separately. Since each issue corresponds to a single-dimensional policy space, the median voter theorem guarantees that a core exists on that dimension. The final outcome then is the composite of the sequence of committee decisions. The key methodological idea of

---

[6] See Diermeier and Merlo 2000 for a critical discussion of Strom's theory of minority cabinets.
[7] For a detailed discussion of the cabinet termination literature see Laver 2003. Laver also discusses alternative conceptualization of the lifespan of governments, such as party turnover (e.g. Mershon 1996).
[8] For a thorough formal analysis see e.g. Austen-Smith and Banks 2005.

SIE theory thus consists in transforming a social choice problem in which the core does not exist (multidimensional choice spaces) into a more structured problem in which the core (as the issue-by-issue core) does exist. Formally, issue-by-issue voting corresponds to an agenda restriction, since in later states of the process decisions on earlier dimensions cannot be revisited. What made this particular agenda restriction plausible is that it corresponded well to features of real legislative decision-making such as a committee system.

Laver and Shepsle (1990) apply this methodology to the study of cabinets. In the context of coalitional government, however, the key decision-makers are not committees and individual legislators, but cabinets and parties. Laver and Shepsle thus interpret the issue assignments from Shepsle (1979) as cabinet portfolios assigned to parties. Holders of portfolios can unilaterally determine the policy choice on that dimension.

Going beyond the original SIE analysis, Laver and Shepsle then ask under what circumstances such portfolio assignments are in the majority core of a voting game on cabinet assignments. Consider the example in Figure 9.1.[9] In this example there are three parties A, B, and C with their ideological positions along two policy dimensions represented by small circles. Each combination of letters represents a possible coalition government. Suppose that every two-party coalition represents a majority, while each single-party government is a minority government. The idea of their model is that it takes a government (modeled as an allocation of portfolios) to beat a government. Government BA, for example, is stable because there is no alternative government in its win set even though there are policies strictly preferred to the policy implemented by BA. But according to Laver and Shepsle's model these policies do not constitute *credible* alternatives to BA since they cannot be implemented by any government. As in the case of congressional committee systems discussed above, the Laver–Shepsle results therefore depend on an agenda restriction. The twin assumption is that in a parliamentary system policies are decided in cabinets, not by the legislature *and that each minister effectively can exercise dictatorial control over his respective portfolio dimension.*

Laver and Shepsle show not only that portfolio assignments can be stable, but that the stable assignments may be of the minority type. Finally, by perturbing the key parameters of the equilibrium governments, Laver and Shepsle also hint at an explanation for cabinet stability.[10]

With one model, so it seems, Laver and Shepsle succeeded in addressing all the major empirical themes discussed above. Moreover, their methodology also promised to shed some new light on the old question of which specific cabinet would form. The appeal of the Laver–Shepsle model is that it maintains the basic features of spatial, institution-free models, but seems to add just enough structure to account for the new empirical challenges.

[9] Adapted from Laver and Shepsle 1990, 875.
[10] See Laver and Shepsle 1994, 1996 for rich analyses of various institutional features of government formation and termination using their framework. Laver and Shepsle 1998 model cabinet stability using random perturbations.

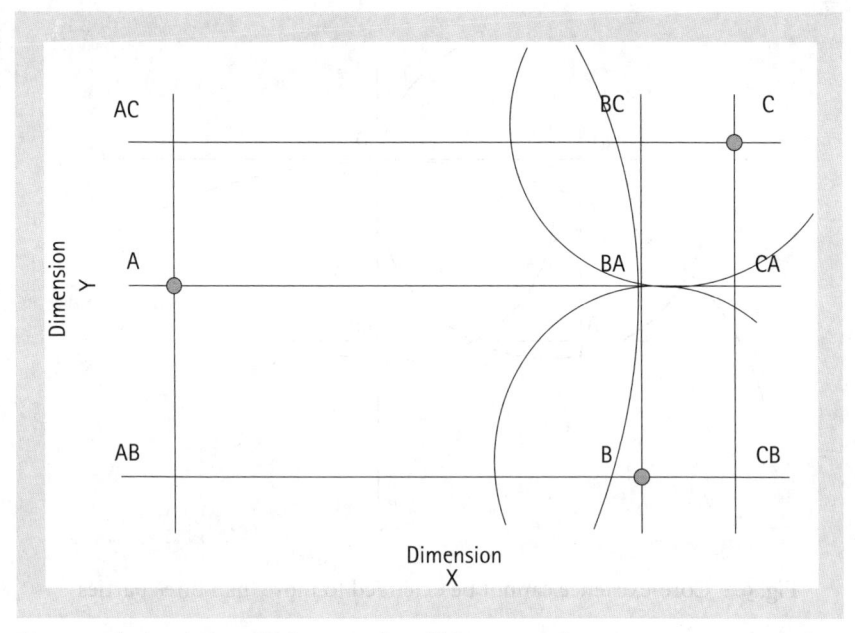

Fig. 9.1 Ideal points and win-sets of credible proposals

As in the case of Shepsle's model for the US Congress, the explanatory power of the Laver–Shepsle model depends on the empirical plausibility of its key assumption about cabinet decision-making. The results, for example, do not go through in a model where ruling parties bargain over policies in cabinets.[11] But there is a more serious, methodological problem with the model. This problem has nothing to do with the plausibility of any of the assumptions, but with the solution concept used by Laver and Shepsle.

This problem, ironically, was pointed out by Austen-Smith and Banks (1990) in a paper in the same issue of the *American Political Science Review* where the Laver–Shepsle article was published. Austen-Smith and Banks show that except in the very special case of three parties, two dimensions, and Euclidean ("circular") preferences, structure-induced equilibria in the portfolio assignment game may not exist. Figure 9.2 (adapted from figure 5 in Austen-Smith and Banks 1990) demonstrates this point. In this example there is one large party, D, with 49 per cent of the vote share and three smaller parties with a vote share of 17 per cent each. Note that parties D and C each prefer cabinet D to cabinets A, B, and AB, while parties A, B, C, which jointly constitute a majority, prefer B to D. Finally, A and D prefer D over C. Therefore, the core of cabinet assignment problem is empty.

The methodological problems uncovered by Austen-Smith and Banks consist in the insight that core existence in the Laver–Shepsle model cannot be guaranteed. Note that in cases of an empty core the Laver–Shepsle theory has no empirical content; it does not predict anything. Put differently, the agenda restrictions considered by Laver

---

[11] See the next two sections for such models.

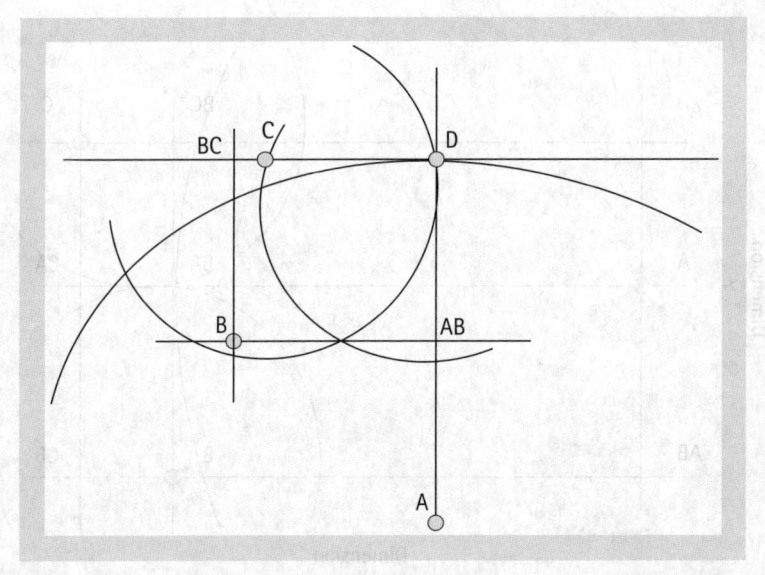

Fig. 9.2 Core-existence cannot be extended to more than three parties

and Shepsle are not sufficient to avoid the well-known core non-existence problems (Plott 1967).

Elsewhere (e.g. Diermeier 1997; Diermeier and Krehbiel 2003) I have argued that the root cause of these problems lies in the use of the core as a solution concept while non-cooperative game theory (with Nash equilibrium as its solution concept) does not suffer similar problems. One could, for example, reformulate the Laver–Shepsle framework as a non-cooperative bargaining model among party leaders. The theoretical literature on coalition government, however, has not taken this path. Rather, a whole variety of alternative frameworks, all based on non-cooperative game theory, have been proposed over the last fifteen years. It is to those applications of non-cooperative game theory that we turn next.

4 Sequential Bargaining: The Baron–Ferejohn Model

The Baron–Ferejohn ("BF") model of legislative bargaining (Baron and Ferejohn 1989) is one of the most widely used formal frameworks in the study of legislative politics. One of the first direct applications of the model to a specific problem in political science was the problem of government formation (e.g. Baron 1989, 1991).

In all variants of the BF model, a proposer is selected according to a known rule. He then proposes a policy or an allocation of benefits to a group of voters. According to a given voting rule, the proposal is either accepted or rejected. If the proposal is accepted, the game ends and all actors receive payoffs as specified by the accepted proposal. Otherwise, another proposer is selected, etc.[12] The process continues until a proposal is accepted or the game ends.

Consider a simple version of the model where there are three political parties with no party having a majority of the votes in the legislature. The BF model predicts that the party with proposal power will propose a minimal winning coalition consisting of him- or herself and one other member, leaving the third party with a zero payoff. The proposing party will give a proposed coalition partner just the amount necessary to secure an acceptance. This amount (or continuation value) equals the coalition partner's expected payoff if the proposal is rejected and the bargaining continues. Proposals are thus always accepted in the first round. Note that the proposing party maximizes its payoff by choosing as a coalition partner one of the parties with the lowest continuation value. The division of spoils will in general be highly unequal, especially if the parties are very impatient.

Consider a simple, two-period, example of the model where three parties divide $1. If the money is not divided after two periods, each party receives nothing. Suppose further that each party has an equal amount of seats and that in each period the probability that any given party is chosen as the proposer is proportional to seat share, i.e. each party is selected with probability 1/3. In the last period each recognized proposer will propose to keep the entire $1 and allocate nothing to the other two parties. This proposal will be accepted by the other parties.[13] Now consider each party's voting decision in period one. If the proposal is rejected, each party again has a probability of 1/3 of being selected as proposer in the second period. But as we just showed, in that case the proposer will get the entire $1. Therefore, the expected payoff from rejecting a proposal is 1/3 for each party. This expected payoff is also called the "continuation value." Call it D_i for each party I (here $D_i = 1/3$ for each i). Now consider the incentives of a proposer in period one. By the same argument as above[14] each proposer will make a proposal that allocates $1 $-$ D_i (here $2/3) to himself, D_i to one other party (his "coalition partner"), and nothing to the remaining party. This proposal will be accepted.[15]

---

[12] A variant of this set-up allows (nested) amendments to a proposal before it is voted on. This is the case of an open amendment rule (Baron and Ferejohn 1989).

[13] Why would the non-proposing parties vote for a proposal where they receive nothing? The idea is the following. Since the model assumes that all parties' relevant motivations are fully captured by their monetary rewards, parties would accept any ε-amount for sure. But then the proposer can make this ε as small as he wishes. The technical reason is that a proposal that allocates everything to the proposer is the only subgame perfect Nash equilibrium in the second period. From the proposer's point of view offering ε more than $0 cannot be optimal since he can always offer less than ε. From the other parties' points of view accepting $0 with probability one is optimal (they are indifferent), but voting to accept with any probability less than one cannot be optimal, since in that case the proposer would be better off offering some small ε which the parties would accept for sure.

[14] See also the previous footnote.

[15] In their general model, Baron and Ferejohn show that an analogous argument also holds if the game is of potentially infinite duration. That is, parties are selected to propose until agreement is reached. To ensure equilibrium existence future payoffs need to be discounted. The more they are discounted, i.e. the more impatient the parties, the higher the payoff to the proposer. In subsequent years Baron systematically applied the model to various aspects of government formation such as different

Compared to the Laver–Shepsle model, the Baron–Ferejohn model has many methodological advantages. Because of the use of non-cooperative game theory, equilibrium existence is assured even in environments (e.g. dividing a fixed benefit under majority rule) where the core is empty.[16]

These features make the model very suitable for institutional analysis.

However, compared to the Laver–Shepsle model, the Baron–Ferejohn model is much more difficult to work with, especially if one leaves the purely distributive ("divide-the-dollar") environment and includes policy preferences. In that case only the simplest environment of three symmetric parties with Euclidean preferences is reasonably manageable.[17] Also, the model is only about coalition formation, not stability.

Therefore, even though the Baron–Ferejohn model does not have the same methodological challenges as the Laver–Shepsle model, its applicability in the study of coalition government is constrained by its technical difficulties. These shortcomings have limited its use in explaining, for instance, minority government formation or cabinet stability.[18]

5 Alternative Frameworks: Demand Bargaining and Efficient Negotiations

The methodological shortcomings of the Laver–Shepsle framework and the technical challenges of using the Baron–Ferejohn model in an environment with policy preferences have led to a search for alternative bargaining models over coalition governments. Two candidates have received the most interest: demand bargaining and efficient negotiations.

---

voting and proposal rules (Baron 1989), parties with spatial preferences (Baron 1993), and multistage decision-making (Baron 1996). See Baron 1993 for a detailed overview.

[16] The curious reader may ask why the Baron–Ferejohn model does not face the same methodological issues as the Laver–Shepsle model. Suppose parties would vote over selection probabilities. Don't we face similar non-existence problems as discussed in the Laver–Shepsle model? Such a question confuses two different methodologies. Laver and Shepsle use the core as their solution concept. *If* we use the core, non-existence problems reappear at the level of institutional choice. But if we use Nash equilibrium, then the collective choice over selection probabilities again needs to be modeled as a non-cooperative game and this game generally will have a Nash equilibrium. For a more detailed discussion of this subtle point see Diermeier 1997; Diermeier and Krehbiel 2003. For a model of voting over proposal rights see Diermeier and Vlaicu 2005.

[17] See Austen-Smith and Banks 2005 and Banks and Duggan 2000, 2003, for a thorough analysis of the Baron–Ferejohn model. In the general case of convex preferences we also have to worry about multiple equilibria. See also Eraslan and Merlo 2002.

[18] See, however, Baron 1998 who proposed a model based on Diermeier and Feddersen 1998 where minority governments could be stable, but would not be chosen in equilibrium. See also Kalandrakis 2004.

The demand bargaining approach in the study of coalition government is due to Morelli (1999). In Morelli's approach agents do not make sequential *offers* (as in the Baron–Ferejohn model), but make sequential *demands*, i.e. compensations for their participation in a given coalition. Specifically, the head of state chooses the first mover. After that, agents make sequential demands until every member has made a demand or until a majority coalition forms. If no acceptable coalition emerges after all players have made a demand, a new first demander is randomly selected; all the previous demands are void, and the game proceeds until a compatible set of demands is made by a majority coalition. The order of play is randomly determined from among those who have not yet made a demand, with proportional recognition probabilities.[19]

To see the difference from the Baron–Ferejohn model consider the three-party example as above. Morelli (1999, proposition 1) shows that in this case the distribution of benefits is ($1/2, $1/2) among some two-party coalition. In contrast to the Baron–Ferejohn model there is *no* proposer premium. Intuitively, each party has the same bargaining power in the demand bargaining game and that is reflected in the equilibrium outcome.

An alternative approach was proposed by Merlo (1997) based on the work of Merlo and Wilson (1995). As in the original Baron–Ferejohn model and in Morelli's model, a set of players bargain over a perfectly divisible payoff by being recognized and then making offers. If the offer is accepted by all parties, the government forms; if not, bargaining continues. However, there are two key differences. First, all players need to agree to a proposed distribution. Second, the value of the prize changes over time. Merlo interprets this change as shifting common expectations about the lifespan of the chosen coalition caused, for example, by shifting economic indicators (e.g. Warwick 1994). Merlo and Wilson (1995, 1998) show that this game has a unique stationary subgame perfect equilibrium.[20] Second, the equilibrium of the bargaining game satisfies the so-called *separation principle*: any equilibrium payoff vector must be Pareto efficient, and the set of states where parties agree must be independent of the proposer's identity. A very rough intuition for the result is that because all members of the coalition need to agree to an allocation, the coalition behaves *as if* it desired to maximize the joint payoff. With changing payoffs this implies that for some states the parties would be better off to delay agreement to wait for a better draw. Therefore, bargaining delays can occur in equilibrium.[21] In contrast to earlier accounts (e.g. Strom 1988) that had interpreted long formation times as evidence of a crisis, Merlo and Wilson showed that delays may be optimal from the point of view of the bargaining parties. By not agreeing immediately (and thus forgoing a higher

---

[19] Earlier models of demand bargaining used an exogenous order of play. See e.g. Selten 1992; Winter 1994a, 1994b.

[20] Both unanimity *and* randomly changing payoffs are important for both the uniqueness result and the efficiency property (Binmore 1986; Eraslan and Merlo 2002). Majority rule, for example, leads to multiple equilibria and inefficiency. Parties agree "too early" to ensure that they will be included in the final deal.

[21] For an empirical studies of the cabinet formation processes see Diermeier and van Roozendaal 1998; Diermeier and Merlo 2000; Martin and Vanberg 2003.

immediate payoff) parties could wait for political-economic circumstances associated with a higher expected government duration.

One of the appealing features of both the Morelli and Merlo and Wilson approaches is their close connections to the data. Morelli's approach, for example, is motivated by the so-called *Gamson's Law* which states that cabinet portfolios among the members of the ruling coalition should be allocated in proportion to their (normalized) seat share (Gamson 1961).[22] Models based on Baron and Ferejohn (1989) cannot account for this regularity since they imply a proposer premium regardless of the distribution of seats. Morelli's model, however, does imply Gamson's Law if proposer selection is done proportionally to seat share.[23]

Merlo and Wilson's (1998) model also implies portfolio distributions close to Gamson's Law provided the negotiating parties have low discount factors—i.e. if they are very patient. If parties are impatient, however, proposers are able to capture higher payoffs.[24]

A different variant of efficient bargaining third was recently proposed by Baron and Diermeier (2001). Their model focuses on an environment where parties bargain not only over distributive benefits, but also over (multidimensional) policy. The model proceeds as follows. A proposer party ("formateur") is selected proportionally to seat share. That party then selects a "proto-coalition" (Axelrod 1970), i.e. a list of parties that agree to negotiate under unanimity rule. If the proposed coalitional agreement fails to win a majority in the chamber, a caretaker government implements an exogenously given status quo policy. Bargaining within a proto-coalition is efficient and leads to a unique policy outcome for each proto-coalition.[25] The intuition is that during proto-coalitions parties can make side payments to each other using the distributive benefits. This ensures that no matter how the bargaining process is structured, the parties must agree on the same efficient policy.[26]

In contrast to previous bargaining models, the policy location *does not* depend on the details of the bargaining process such as recognition probabilities or discount factors. It *only* depends on the ideal points of the members of the proto-coalition. This allows Baron and Diermeier to embed their coalition formation model into a more complicated, full equilibrium, model that includes an election state under proportional representation[27] as well as analysis of policy dynamics across legislative periods.

[22] See also Browne and Franklin 1973; Browne and Fendreis 1980; Schofield and Laver 1985; Laver and Schofield 1990.
[23] Diermeier and Merlo 2004 provide evidence that formateurs (i.e. proposers) are indeed selected proportionally.
[24] The Morelli and Merlo–Wilson approach has led to an empirical re-evaluation of the data underlying Gamson's Law. The key question is whether the data show a proposer premium. See Warwick and Druckman 2001; Ansolohabere et al. 2003; Frechette, Kagel, and Morelli 2004.
[25] For an empirical test of the Baron–Diermeier model and other coalition models see Carrubba and Volden 2000.
[26] If preferences are assumed to be quadratic, that policy is the centroid of the parties' ideal policy locations.
[27] See Austen-Smith and Banks 1988 for an electoral model under proportional representation that uses a simplified version of sequential bargaining.

6 NON-COOPERATIVE BARGAINING: THE QUESTION OF CABINET STABILITY

After having tackled the problem of government formation, non-cooperative models were then applied to the issue of cabinet stability. A first connection was established by Lupia and Strom (1995) who proposed a game-theoretic model of cabinet termination by re-evaluating the key notion of "critical events" (Browne, Frendreis, and Gleiber 1984, 1986, 1988). Lupia and Strom suggested that external events should be interpreted as the input of a coalition bargaining process, representing each party's outside option if the current government falls. Whether a cabinet terminates depends on the attractiveness of this outside option compared to each party's payoff from the current government.

This interpretation of the impact of random events marks a potentially important shift in the study of cabinet terminations. Cabinets are interpreted as equilibria of an underlying bargaining process that must be sustained over time as the political environment and thus the distribution of bargaining power among governing parties changes.

The long-term impact of the Lupia–Strom model was mainly conceptual. The actual bargaining model is too simplistic to capture dynamics of coalition bargaining.[28] Their approach demonstrated that what is needed is a multistage bargaining approach with an explicitly modeled stochastic process to capture the changing political environment that may lead to critical events.

A first step in this direction is the Diermeier–Merlo model (Diermeier and Merlo 2000). As in Lupia and Strom, Diermeier and Merlo conceptualize coalition governments as sustained equilibria in an underlying bargaining game. Bargaining is assumed to be efficient proto-coalition bargaining, similar to Baron and Diermeier (2001), but is now embedded in a multistage bargaining game with random shocks both to electoral prospects and to the parties' reservation values. Such shocks may lead to the termination of government before the end of the game. In that case, a new cabinet would take office. Cabinets may avoid termination by redistributing ("reshuffle") distributive benefits among the incumbent parties in response to external events.

Government formation consists of two steps. First, a formateur is selected proportional to seat share. Then that formateur chooses a proto-coalition which is assumed to bargain efficiently. Any proto-coalition agreement needs to be approved by a chamber majority.

Diermeier and Merlo are particularly interested in the study of minority government. They identify a government with an allocation of cabinet portfolios: a party that supports a minority government on critical votes but does not hold any portfolios is not part of the government, but is only part of the supporting coalition. Government policy is negotiated in the cabinet subject to majority approval

---

[28] See Diermeier and Stevenson 2000; Diermeier and Merlo 2000.

in parliament. This assumption is justified by the observation that in parliamentary democracies ministries, not independent agencies, implement government policies. Any policy bargain that involves parties without a seat at the cabinet table therefore would lack credibility.[29] The inability to bargain credibly over policy with parties outside the cabinet is a key feature of the model that is then used to study minority cabinets and cabinet stability. Governments also have control over perks (e.g. seats on public boards) that can be distributed to any party in the legislature. These are the keys to maintaining support for a minority government.

The first important result in the Diermeier-Merlo model is that both minority and super-majority cabinets can occur as equilibrium phenomena. Moreover, minority and surplus coalitions are not rare exceptions, but may form for all parameter values. The traditional literature had viewed minority and surplus governments as an exception that needed to be explained (e.g. Strom 1990). The Diermeier–Merlo model, however, suggests exactly the opposite: in a single-period model, minimal winning coalitions would *never* form. The underlying reason is that formateurs can choose from many viable coalition governments. They will thus choose the government that yields the highest payoff. In the case of risk-averse preferences this implies that if the formateur party ever benefits from policy compromise, it is even better to include all other parties into the bargain rather than just one. This case corresponds to a super-majority government. If policy compromise is too expensive for the formateur, a minority government results.

So, why do we observe minimal winning coalitions?[30] Surprisingly, minimal winning coalitions only occur because of dynamic considerations. The key insight relies on the importance of bargaining inefficiency for cabinet termination. Diermeier and Merlo show that as long as bargaining is efficient, governing parties will have an incentive to reshuffle distributive benefits in response to external shocks rather than taking the risk of being left out of the ensuing new government. If efficient bargaining is not possible, however, as in the case of bargaining between the minority government and the parties in its supporting coalition, governments may fall. It follows that during initial cabinet formation formateurs need to anticipate the possible costs of early termination and reshuffles. Diermeier and Merlo show that for some parameter values minimal winning cabinets are the best deal. On the one hand, they avoid early termination; on the other hand, renegotiations occur only with one party, not with two. For other parameter values surplus or minority coalitions are optimal. So all observed cabinet types can be recovered as equilibrium phenomena.

One important consequence of the Diermeier and Merlo framework is that formateurs anticipate the benefits and costs from maintaining a given cabinet over time. Both costs and benefits depend on the cabinet type. So, depending on the parameters, formateurs will choose different cabinet types, including some minority cabinets that are likely to terminate early. The stability and the relative occurrence of different types of governments are thus *jointly determined in equilibrium*. As we will see in the next

---

[29] A similar argument was made by Laver and Shepsle 1990.
[30] They make up about half of all observed coalitions.

section, this insight has important consequences for the empirical study of coalition government.

7 THE NON-COOPERATIVE APPROACH: CONSEQUENCES FOR EMPIRICAL RESEARCH

Once we model the formation and stability of governments as equilibrium phenomena the methodological foundations for empirical studies of coalitions need to be reconsidered. To see the problem it is useful to revisit existing empirical studies of cabinet stability. From Strom (1985) to Diermeier and Stevenson (1999), all studies had been regression models, i.e. a suitably defined stochastic process with sets of covariates that influence termination probabilities. Since Strom (1985), all these models have contained institutional characteristics, both of the polity (e.g. constitutional features) and of cabinet (e.g. its majority status). The main lesson, however, from an approach that models cabinets as equilibria is that expectations about cabinet duration influence the choice of initial cabinets; they are jointly selected in equilibrium. Empirically, this implies that we cannot treat cabinet-specific features as proper independent variables in a regression model. Rather, we are facing a selection problem.

A series of recent papers (Merlo 1997; Diermeier, Eraslan, and Merlo 2003a, 2003b) has tried to resolve these problems by using a structural estimation approach. The approach consists in specifying a bargaining model of government formation, estimating the model's parameters, assessing the ability of the model to account for key features of the data, and then using the estimated structural model to conduct (counterfactual) experiments of comparative institutional analysis.

The first example is Merlo (1997) who uses the Merlo–Wilson framework to conduct a structural estimation of government formation and cabinet stability in Italy. Diermeier, Eraslan, and Merlo (2003a, 2003b) propose a model of proto-coalition bargaining similar to Baron and Diermeier (2001) and Diermeier and Merlo (2000) to study the effect of constitutional characteristics on cabinet formation and duration.

An instructive example is the analysis of governmental bicameralism (Diermeier, Eraslan, and Merlo 2003b).[31] In countries with governmental bicameralism (e.g. Italy), both chambers need to approve a new government, but a vote in either chamber terminates the government. This may suggest that removing governmental bicameralism would significantly improve the average duration of governments. Diermeier, Eraslan, and Merlo show that this intuition is flawed. Using data from Belgium they find that eliminating bicameralism does not affect government durability, but does have a significant effect on the composition of governments leading to smaller coalitions. Surplus governments are virtually eliminated, but are being

---

[31] See Cultrone and McCarty, this volume.

replaced not by minimal winning governments, but by minority governments. These surprising results are due to an equilibrium replacement effect. Removing bicameralism does indeed affect the relative durability of possible coalitions of different type, but this then affects which cabinets are selected in equilibrium. That is, for each coalition type (minimal winning, minority, etc.) expected duration may increase, but under unicameralism formateurs may now select minority coalitions when (under bicameralism) they would have selected coalitions with majority status. In the Belgian case these two effects cancel each other out resulting in no change in average government durability, but a sharp increase in the proportion of minority governments.

8 Conclusion

The last fifteen years have seen a fundamental transformation in the study of coalition government. Institutionalist approaches increasingly dominate empirical and theoretical research programs. Moreover, paralleling the development in other areas of formal political science, non-cooperative game theory has become the most widely used methodology. On the theoretical dimension, this approach has led to models that integrate government formation and government termination. These are promising developments, even though the existing models can only be considered first steps. For example, both the Lupia–Strom model and Diermeier–Merlo are restricted to the three-party case.

On the one hand, this approach marks a promising shift in the study of coalition government. In particular, the specification of explicit models of inter-party bargaining is likely to focus attention on the role of institutional features of the bargaining environment in determining cabinet formation and stability. On the other hand, the bargaining approach creates various challenging methodological problems. First, Diermeier and Stevenson (2000) showed that testing the Lupia–Strom model requires careful specifications of the stochastic model that precludes the usage of "off-the-shelf" event study methods. Second, Merlo (1997) pointed out that changing expectations about government duration (due to external events such as the release of macroeconomic data) may lead party leaders to delay the formation of a government. Hence, governments that actually form should be viewed as the result of strategic selection by the members of the proto-coalition. Third, Diermeier and Merlo (2000) and Diermeier, Eraslan, and Merlo (2003a, 2003b) have shown that expectations about government duration may also influence which governments are chosen in the first place. Together, these results imply that government type, formation time, and government duration are all simultaneously determined in equilibrium. That is, taking the concept of governments-as-equilibria seriously may require a radical departure from existing empirical approaches that rely on regression-based reduced form specifications. A shift to structural models offers one promising, but technically challenging, new direction.

REFERENCES

ANSOLABEHERE, S., SNYDER, J. M. J., STRAUSS, A. B., and TING, M. M. 2003. Voting weights and voter advantages in the formation of coalition governments. Mimeo.

AUSTEN-SMITH, D., and BANKS, J. S. 1988. Elections, coalitions and legislative outcomes. *American Political Science Review*, 82: 405–22.

—— 1990. Stable governments and the allocation of policy portfolios. *American Political Science Review*, 84: 891–906.

—— 2005. *Positive Political Theory*, ii: *Strategies and Structures*. Ann Arbor: University of Michigan Press.

AXELROD, R. 1970. *Conflict of Interest*. Chicago: Markham.

—— 1972. Where the votes come from: an analysis of electoral coalitions. *American Political Science Review*, 66: 11–20.

BANKS, J. S., and DUGGAN, J. 2000. A bargaining model of collective choice. *American Political Science Review*, 94: 73–88.

—— 2003. A bargaining model of legislative policy-making. Mimeo.

BARON, D. P. 1989. A noncooperative theory of legislative coalitions. *American Journal of Political Science*, 33: 1048–84.

—— 1991. A spatial theory of government formation in parliamentary systems. *American Political Science Review*, 85: 137–65.

—— 1993. Government formation and endogenous parties. *American Political Science Review*, 87: 34–47.

—— 1996. A dynamic theory of collective goods programs. *American Political Science Review*, 90: 316–30.

—— 1998. Comparative dynamics of parliamentary governments. *American Political Science Review*, 92: 593–609.

—— and DIERMEIER, D. 2001. Elections, governments, and parliaments in proportional representation systems. *Quarterly Journal of Economics*, 116: 933–67.

—— and FEREJOHN, J. A. 1989. Bargaining in legislatures. *American Political Science Review*, 83: 1181–206.

BINMORE, K. 1986. Bargaining and coalitions. In *Game-Theoretic Models of Bargaining*, ed. A. Roth. Cambridge: Cambridge University Press.

BROWNE, E. C., and FRANKLIN, M. 1973. Aspects of coalition payoffs in European parliamentary democracies. *American Political Science Review*, 67: 453–69.

—— and FRENDREIS, J. P. 1980. Allocating coalition payoffs by conventional norm: assessment of the evidence for cabinet coalition situations. *American Journal of Political Science*, 24: 753–68.

—— and GLEIBER, D. W. 1984. An "events" approach to the problem of cabinet stability. *Comparative Political Studies*, 17: 167–97.

—— 1986. The process of cabinet dissolution: an exponential model of duration and stability in western democracies. *American Journal of Political Science*, 30: 628–50.

—— 1988. Contending models of cabinet stability: a rejoinder. *American Political Science Review*, 82: 923–30.

CARRUBBA, C. J., and VOLDEN, C. 2000. Coalitional politics and logrolling in legislative institutions. *American Journal of Political Science*, 44: 261–77.

DIERMEIER, D. 1997. Explanatory concepts in positive political theory. Mimeo, Graduate School of Business, Stanford University.

—— ERASLAN, H. K. K., and MERLO, A. 2003a. A structural model of government formation. *Econometrica*, 71: 27–70.

DIERMEIER, D. 2003b. Bicameralism and government formation. Mimeo.
─── and KREHBIEL, K. 2003. Institutionalism as a methodology. *Journal of Theoretical Politics*, 15: 123–44.
─── and MERLO, A. 2000. Government turnover in parliamentary democracies. *Journal of Economic Theory*, 94: 46–79.
─── 2004. An empirical investigation of coalitional bargaining procedures. *Journal of Public Economics*, 88: 783–97.
─── and STEVENSON, R. 1999. Cabinet survival and competing risks. *American Journal of Political Science*, 43: 1051–98.
─── 2000. Cabinet terminations and critical events. *American Political Science Review*, 94: 627–40
─── and VAN ROOZENDAAL, P. 1998. The duration of cabinet formation processes in western multi-party democracies. *British Journal of Political Science*, 28: 609–26.
─── and VLAICU, R. 2005. Voting to propose. Mimeo, Northwestern University.
ERASLAN, H., and MERLO, A. 2002. Majority rule in a stochastic model of bargaining. *Journal of Economic Theory*, 103: 31–48.
FRÉCHETTE, G. R., KAGEL, J. H., and MORELLI, M. 2004. Behavioral identification in coalitional bargaining: an experimental analysis of demand bargaining and alternating offers. Mimeo.
GAMSON, W. A. 1961, A theory of coalition formation. *American Sociological Review*, 26: 373–82.
KALANDRAKIS, T. 2004. Genericity of minority government: the role of policy and office. Mimeo.
KING, G., ALT, J., BURNS, N., and LAVER, M. 1990. A unified model of cabinet dissolution in parliamentary democracies. *American Journal of Political Science*, 34: 846–71.
KRAMER, G. 1972. Sophisticated voting over multidimensional choice spaces. *Journal of Mathematical Sociology*, 2: 165–80.
LAVER, M. 2003. Government termination. *Annual Review of Political Science*, 6: 23–40.
─── and SCHOFIELD, N. 1990. *Multiparty Government*. Oxford: Oxford University Press.
─── and SHEPSLE, K. A. 1990. Coalitions and cabinet government. *American Political Science Review*, 84: 873–90.
─── ─── (eds.). 1994. *Cabinet Ministers and Parliamentary Government*. Cambridge: Cambridge University Press.
─── ─── 1996. *Making and Breaking Governments: Cabinets and Legislatures in Parliamentary Democracies*. Cambridge: Cambridge University Press.
─── ─── 1998. Events, equilibria and government survival. *American Journal of Political Science*, 42: 28–54.
LUPIA, A., and STROM, K. 1995. Coalition termination and the strategic timing of parliamentary elections. *American Political Science Review*, 89: 648–69.
MCKELVEY, R. D. 1976. Intransitivities in multidimensional voting models and some implications for agenda control. *Journal of Economic Theory*, 12: 472–82.
─── 1986. Covering, dominance, and institution-free properties of social choice. *American Journal of Political Science*, 30: 283–314.
MARTIN, L. W., and STEVENSON, R. T. 2001. Government formation in parliamentary democracies. *American Journal of Political Science*, 45: 33–50.
─── and VANBER, G. 2003. Wasting time? The impact of ideology and size on delay in coalition formation. *British Journal of Political Science*, 33: 323–32.
MERLO, A. 1997. Bargaining over governments in a stochastic environment. *Journal of Political Economy*, 105: 101–31.
─── and WILSON, C. 1995. A stochastic model of sequential bargaining with complete information. *Econometrica*, 63: 371–99.

—— 1998. Efficient delays in a stochastic model of bargaining. *Economic Theory*, 11: 39–55.
MERSHON, C. 1996. The costs of coalition: coalition theories and Italian governments. *American Political Science Review*, 90: 534–54.
MORELLI, M. 1999. Demand competition and policy compromise in legislative bargaining. *American Political Science Review*, 93: 809–20.
PLOTT, C. 1967. A notion of equilibrium and its possibility under majority rule. *American Economic Review*, 57: 787–806.
SCHOFIELD, N. J., and LAVER, M. 1985, Bargaining theory and portfolio pay-offs in European coalition governments. *British Journal of Political Science*, 15: 143–64.
—— SENED, I., and NIXON, D. 1998. Nash equilibria in multiparty competition with "stochastic" voters. *Annals of Operations Research*, 84: 3–27.
SELTEN, R. 1992. A demand commitment model of coalition bargaining. In *Rational Interaction Essays in Honor of John Harsanyi*, ed. R. Selten. Berlin: Springer Verlag.
SHEPSLE, K. A. 1979. Institutional arrangements and equilibrium in multidimensional voting models. *American Journal of Political Science*, 23: 27–60.
STROM, K. 1985. Party goals and government performance in parliamentary democracies. *American Political Science Review*, 79: 738–54.
—— 1988. Contending models of cabinet stability. *American Political Science Review*, 82: 923–30.
—— 1990. *Minority Government and Majority Rule*. Cambridge: Cambridge University Press.
WARWICK, P. 1992*a*. Ideological diversity and government survival in western European parliamentary democracies. *Comparative Political Studies*, 25: 332–61.
—— 1992*b*. Rising hazards: an underlying dynamic of parliamentary government. *American Journal of Political Science*, 36: 857–76.
—— 1992*c*. Economic trends and government survival in west European parliamentary democracies. *American Political Science Review*, 86: 875–87.
—— 1994. *Government Survival in Parliamentary Democracies*. Cambridge: Cambridge University Press.
—— and DRUCKMAN, J. N. 2001. Portfolio salience and the proportionality of payoffs in coalition governments. *British Journal of Political Science*, 31: 627–49.
—— and EASTON, S. T. 1992. The cabinet stability controversy: new perspectives on a classic problem. *American Journal of Political Science*, 36: 122–46.
WINTER, E. 1994*a*. The demand commitment bargaining: a snowball in cooperation. *Economic Theory*, 4: 255–73.
—— 1994*b*. Non-cooperative bargaining in natural monopolies. *Journal of Economic Theory*, 64: 202–20.

CHAPTER 10

DOES BICAMERALISM MATTER?

MICHAEL CUTRONE
NOLAN McCARTY

1 INTRODUCTION

PERHAPS the most conspicuous variation in the form of modern legislatures concerns the practice of granting legislative authority to two separate chambers with distinct memberships. While the majority of national governments empower but a single chamber, at least a third of national legislatures practice some form of bicameralism, as do forty-nine of the fifty American state governments.[1] Bicameralism is also at the center of many contemporary debates about the design of institutions in new democracies. For example, many proposals for the post-Hussein constitution of Iraq have identified bicameralism as an important ingredient in building a stable democracy in a nation beset with strong religious and ethnic cleavages.[2]

Scholars have made a number of arguments to explain the emergence of bicameral legislatures. One of the most common arguments for the emergence of bicameralism in Britain and its American colonies is that it helped to preserve "mixed

---

[1] Tsebelis and Money 1997, 15, define bicameral legislatures as "those whose deliberations involve two distinct assemblies." This definition, however, masks considerable variation in the roles of each chamber in policy-making. We define bicameralism more narrowly, as the requirement of concurrent majority support from distinct assemblies for new legislation.

[2] These proposals and the positions of different Iraqi groups are discussed in Public International Law and Policy Group 2003.

governments," ensuring that upper-class elements of society were protected (Wood 1969; Tsebelis and Money 1997). In such settings, bicameralism allowed the upper chamber, dominated by aristocrats, to have a veto on policy. More generally, an explicit role of some bicameral systems has been the protection of some minority which is over-represented in the upper chamber.

A second rationale for bicameralism is the preservation of federalism. The United States, Germany, and other federal systems use a bicameral system in order to ensure the representation of the interests of individual states and provinces, as well as the population of the country. Under "federal bicameralism," the lower house is typically apportioned on the basis of population, while the upper house is divided amongst the regional units. Some countries, such as the United States, provide equal representation for the states regardless of their population or geographic size, while others, like the Federal Republic of Germany, unequally apportion the upper chamber by providing additional representation to the larger units.

Despite its prominence, the role of bicameralism in contemporary legislatures has not received the scholarly attention that other legislative institutions have. In this chapter, we review and analyze many of the arguments made on behalf of bicameralism using the tools of modern legislative analysis—the spatial model, multilateral bargaining theory, and a game of incomplete information.[3] This analytical approach allows us to distinguish the effects of bicameralism from those of other institutional features that are often packaged with it, such as super-majoritarian requirements, differing terms of office, and malapportionment.

2 Spatial Models of Policy-making

The spatial model of policy-making has become the workhorse model in the study of legislative institutions. Its stark parsimony makes tractable the analysis of a number of institutional arrangements. Such models have proven quite useful in studying the consequences of bicameralism and other multi-institutional policy-making settings (i.e. Tsebelis and Money 1997; Ferejohn and Shipan 1990).

Before we draw out the implications for bicameralism, consider a baseline unicameral model. Assume that a unicameral legislature has an odd number of members, n, with ideal points, x_i, arrayed along a single ideological dimension represented by the real line. We index the ideal points from left to right so that x_1 is the leftmost member and x_n is the rightmost member. The legislature seeks to pass legislation to change a policy with a status quo q, which is also represented by a point on the spectrum. We assume that each legislator has single-peaked, symmetric preferences so that member i weakly prefers y to z if and only if $|y - x_i| \leq |z - x_i|$, (that is, if and only if y is

---

[3] We will not review the arguments about the role of bicameralism in the formation and duration of parliamentary cabinets (Druckman and Thies 2002; Diermeier, Eraslan, and Merlo 2003).

closer to i's ideal point). The standard prediction, based on Black's (1958) theorem, is that the outcome of this type of chamber would lie at the ideal point of the median legislator x_m where $m = \frac{n+1}{2}$. Any other policy outcomes could be defeated by some other policy proposal in a pairwise majority vote. This outcome is independent of the status quo location, q.

Krehbiel (1998) and Brady and Volden (1997) have extended the insights of the simple spatial model into multi-institutional settings. Krehbiel's formulation, dubbed "Pivotal Politics," is based on the interaction of "pivotal" legislators. A legislator is pivotal if her support is necessary for the passage of new legislation given the institutional structure of the policy-making process and the distribution of preferences.

Krehbiel's model can easily be modified to accommodate bicameralism and concurrent majorities. To do so, consider a basic spatial model with two legislative chambers of sizes n_1 and n_2, both odd. Under concurrent majoritarianism, any revision to the status quo must receive majority support in both chambers. Let $m_1 = \frac{n_1+1}{2}$ and $m_2 = \frac{n_2+1}{2}$ be the medians in the two chambers. It is easily seen that if m_1 prefers the status quo q to some proposal y, a majority of chamber 1 will also prefer q to y. Thus, m_1's support is necessary or "pivotal" to the passage of any revision to q. Similarly, m_2 is pivotal in chamber 2.

Since m_1 and m_2 must agree to any policy change, the model predicts that any status quo between m_1 and m_2 (more formally, any q within the interval $[\min\{x_{m_1}, x_{m_2}\}, \max\{x_{m_1}, x_{m_2}\}]$) cannot be legislated upon. Any attempt to revise q would be vetoed by one of the chamber medians—thus Krehbiel refers to the aforementioned interval as the "gridlock interval."

However, when the status quo is outside this "gridlock interval," the two chambers will prefer to enact new legislation. Clearly, the new legislation will lie in the gridlock interval, because otherwise some other policy proposal will be strictly preferred by some concurrent majority. The pivotal politics model does not give specific point predictions about which policies will be adopted when q is outside the gridlock interval. Such predictions will depend on specific protocols for inter-branch bargaining such as differential rights of initiation and procedures for the reconciliation of differences such as the conference committee.[4]

While quite simplistic, this model demonstrates two of the arguments which are forwarded in support of bicameral systems. The first is that bicameralism may lead to more stable policies. When the medians of the two chambers diverge (so that the gridlock interval is a non-empty set), a set of policies will be stable in the presence of small electoral shocks which shift the chamber medians. An argument for stability is included in *The Federalist Papers*. Riker (1992) also espouses this stability argument as a rationale for bicameral institutions. Also apparent from this illustration is that bicameralism requires compromise agreements between the majorities of each chamber. Policy outcomes will lie in the interval between the two chamber medians. This compromise effect lies at the heart of arguments about the presence of bicameralism in federal and consociational democracies (Lijphart 1984).

---

[4] See Tsebelis and Money 1997 for models of inter-chamber reconciliation procedures.

Although theoretically compelling, the stability and compromise rationales depend on a degree of preference divergence across branches. Without a systematic difference between x_{m_1} and x_{m_2}, few compromises between the chambers are likely to be stable. Thus, if stability and compromise were the constitutional designer's objective, one would expect to see bicameralism operate in conjunction with rules that create divergent preferences between the chambers, such as different electoral rules for each chamber. In many cases, the electoral bases and procedures differ dramatically across chambers as in the USA or Germany. However, many systems have chambers with "congruent" preferences (Lijphart 1984), such as those which prevail in the American state legislatures, especially following the decision of *Baker v. Carr* which eliminated many malapportioned upper chambers. Even allowing for idiosyncratic differences in chamber medians, unicameralism and congruent bicameralism should produce nearly identical results. While short-term policies would fluctuate based on the preferences of these two medians, long-run policies would locate at the expected median—the same outcome which occurs in a unicameral legislature.[5]

One objection to this purely preference-based model of bicameralism is that it ignores the role that political parties might play in the policy-making process (e.g. Cox and McCubbins 2003; Chiou and Rothenberg 2003). When studying the unicameral case, Cox and McCubbins suggest a model of partisan gatekeeping that produces a unicameral gridlock interval between the ideal point of the median member of the majority party and the chamber median. Therefore, if we let x_{ji} be the ideal point of the median member of the majority party of chamber i, the gridlock interval within chamber i is $[\min\{x_{j_i}, x_{m_i}\}, \max\{x_{j_i}, x_{m_i}\}]$. When considering the bicameral case, policy change requires that q not fall in either gridlock interval, and the bicameral gridlock interval is simply the union of both chamber intervals and the non-partisan gridlock interval or $[\min\{x_{j_1}, x_{j_2}, x_{m_1}, x_{m_2}\}, \max\{x_{j_1}, x_{j_2}, x_{m_1}, x_{m_2}\}]$. Clearly, this partisan gridlock interval will be largest when the majority party member of one chamber lies to the right of the median while the majority party of other lies to the left. Generally, this will occur when the different parties control the different chambers.

The spatial model can also incorporate a number of features that are often associated with bicameralism, such as super-majority requirements for one of the chambers. Now assume that chamber 2 requires $k > \frac{n_2+1}{2}$ votes to pass new legislation. This requirement now makes members k and $n_2 - k$ pivotal for changes to the status quo. Therefore, the gridlock interval for this chamber is $[\min\{x_{m_1}, x_{n_2-k}\}, \max\{x_{m_1}, x_k\}]$. It is easy to see that super-majoritarianism increases the size of the gridlock interval. However, in cases where the two chambers are reasonably congruent, super-majoritarianism will cause m_1 no longer to be pivotal, making one chamber, in some sense, redundant. Perhaps more importantly, this analysis shows that the key features of bicameralism, stability and compromise, can be obtained by unicameral

---

[5] An implication of this perspective is that, once the Supreme Court invalidated malapportionment in *Baker v. Carr*, policy in previously malapportioned states should have become less stable.

legislatures with suitably chosen super-majority procedures. The spatial model provides no rationale for choosing one institution over the other.

A number of scholars have recently studied the empirical effects of bicameralism based on the predictions of the spatial model. Binder (1999, 2003) finds that the differences in chamber preferences are negatively correlated with her measure of legislative production in the post-Second World War period.[6] Chiou and Rothenberg (2003) also test several gridlock models fully incorporating bicameralism and partisan effects. Although they find no evidence of effects attributable solely to bicameralism, party cohesion and strong presidential leadership of the party have implications for legislative gridlock. Looking at the state level, Rogers (2003) investigates the effects on legislative productivity of moving from a bicameral legislature to a unicameral one, and vice versa. Unfortunately, he is able to examine only four cases and finds mixed evidence across the cases. While theoretical arguments state that bicameralism reduces legislative productivity with respect to that under a unicameral system, none of the cases provided unequivocal support of this proposition. Further, two of the four cases actually had greater amounts of legislation being produced under a bicameral legislature than under unicameralism. Thus, the question of the importance of inter-chamber differences in US policy-making remains somewhat contested.

2.1 Spatial Models of Malapportionment

Given that our review of spatial models suggests that bicameralism matters when the chambers are apportioned differently, the obvious question is: under what circumstances would malapportionment be a reasonable constitutional design? In a recent paper, Crémer and Palfrey (1999) provide an answer. They consider a model where the citizens of various jurisdictions must decide on a level of centralization and representation at a constitutional phase, taking into full account what policy outcomes will result in the policy choice phase once the constitutional choices are set.[7] In their model, district elections are conducted and the outcomes of these elections generate both a district policy and an input into a national policy. Appealing to the median voter theorem, Crémer and Palfrey assume that the policy (both its local component and its national input) produced in each of these elections is the ideal policy of the district's median voter.

---

[6] There are a number of methodological issues related to Binder's finding. In her 1999 paper, she measures "bicameral differences" using chamber medians using W-NOMINATE scores (Poole and Rosenthal 1997). However, these scores are not generally comparable across chambers. Her measure correlates only weakly with those derived from related measures that facilitate inter-chamber comparisons. In her 2003 book, Binder introduces a new measure of bicameral differences based on differences in chamber support on conference committee reports. However, since bicameral majorities on conference committee reports are often a necessary condition for the passage of significant legislation, there is a potentially large endogeneity problem.

[7] In a precursor, Crémer and Palfrey 1996 study preferences for centralization under representation by population, but do not consider a mixed representation system.

The choices of centralization and representation determine how these local electoral outcomes map into policy outputs. Centralization is modeled as variation in the extent to which policy outcomes may differ across jurisdictions. With complete centralization, the policy outcome in all jurisdictions is a national policy formed by a weighted average of all of the district outcomes. In a completely decentralized system, each jurisdiction sets its own policy according to its electoral median. In the intermediate case, or a federal system, policy is a weighted average of the national and local policies. The degree of centralization is the weight placed on the national policy.

In choosing the form of representation, citizens choose the weights that the national policy places on the outcome of each district election. In the case of *population representation*, the weights are proportional to district population. In *unit representation*, each district receives the same weight, regardless of population.

An important assumption is that each voter is uncertain about the policy preferences of other voters and therefore the ultimate policy outcome (both its local and its national components). Formally, each voter knows her own ideal point and the jurisdiction in which she lives. She also knows that the vector of district medians $\{m_1, \ldots, m_n\}$ is drawn from a normal distribution with a mean of 0 and a variance of V. The ideal points of voters within district i are centered on m_i with a variance of 1. An important implication of this set-up is that (in expectation) each voter is closer to the median of her district than she is to the overall median.

Voters are assumed to be risk averse.[8] Thus, the primary benefit of centralization is that it reduces variation in policy outcomes. Since the national policy is based on a larger "sample" of medians, this is a consequence of the law of large numbers.[9] Of course, the cost of centralization is that it may move policy away from that preferred by the voter. Therefore, the voters' preferences over representation are derived from their desire to control the policy effects of centralization.

Within this basic set-up, Crémer and Palfrey derive the induced preferences of voters across the domains of centralization and representation. Their primary findings are as follows:

- Voters with extreme policy preferences (relative to the expected median of the centralized polity) prefer completely decentralized policy-making. The greater opportunity to get the policy they want from their district outweighs any variance reduction afforded by centralization.
- Moderate voters (those close to the expected median) are unanimously opposed to population representation for any level of centralization. This is because the unit rule is the choice mechanism that minimizes the variation in centralized policy. The intuition behind this result is best expressed in terms of estimation theory. We can think of the weighted average of district medians that forms

---

[8] Voters are assumed to have quadratic preferences so that their expected utility decomposes into losses associated with the difference between their ideal point and the expected policy outcome and losses associated with the variance of the policy outcome.

[9] It is assumed that voters may not move to jurisdictions with preferred policies to take advantage of the inter-jurisdictional variation. However, even if voters were imperfectly mobile (meaning, they could move at a cost) they would prefer some reduction in the variation in policy outcomes.

national policy as an estimate of the overall median. Since the district medians are normally distributed with identical variances, the least variance estimator is the one that weighs all observations (district medians) identically. The unit rule accomplishes this.[10]

- Given a high level of centralization, extreme voters from large districts will prefer population representation. This increases the voting weight of their district in the centralized legislature. Since voters are closer to their own district medians (in expectation), this reduces the policy loss of decentralization.
- Given a low level of centralization, moderate voters (even some from small districts) will prefer population representation because this reduces the influence of extreme small districts on the centralized policy. In this case, such voters are willing to trade some of the variance reduction afforded by the unit rule to increase the likelihood of a moderate policy.
- Under the unit rule, preferences over centralization do not depend on district population. However, if representation is a mixture of rules, large district voters prefer more centralization than those from small districts.

Given these results about induced preferences, Crémer and Palfrey examine voting equilibria in the constitutional stage. If a majority rule equilibrium exists,[11] they show that it involves representation based solely on the unit principle. However, if the level of centralization is fixed and representation is voted on separately, the "conditional" voting equilibrium generates representation which is a mix between the population and unit principles. The rationale is that if centralization is fixed, extreme voters from large districts and moderate voters from small districts will vote in favor of positive levels of population representation.

The Crémer–Palfrey model provides a reasonable microfoundation for endogenously malapportioned legislatures. However, it falls short of a rationale for bicameralism because it "black boxes" the legislative institutions that make centralized policy. Thus, it is plausible that a malapportioned unicameral legislature could provide the representational foundation for greater centralization just as well as two chambers based on different representational principles.

3 MULTIDIMENSIONAL SPATIAL MODELS

While an extensive literature exists on unidimensional models, much less is known when the policy issues are multidimensional in nature. Some authors have stressed the role of bicameralism in ameliorating the intransitivity of majority rule (McKelvey

---

[10] This result would be different if the medians were heteroskedastic and the variance depended on district size. If the variance of the medians was declining in population, the minimum variation policy might be obtained via population representation.

[11] In this context, a majority rule equilibrium is a combination of centralization and representation for which no other combination is preferred by a majority.

1976; Schofield 1978). These authors have focused on the question of whether or not it can produce a core[12] or reduce the size of the uncovered set[13] in the absence of a core in a unicameral legislature. Cox and McKelvey (1984) demonstrate that the necessary condition for the existence of a core in a multicameral legislature is the incongruence of the median preferences across chambers. In a unidimensional setting, the core will exist and will be the interval connecting the medians of the two chambers—the same as the gridlock interval we extracted from the *Pivotal Politics* model. Hammond and Miller (1987), extending this line of analysis, deduced the necessary conditions for the core in two dimensions. Tsebelis (1993) proves the generic non-existence of the core when the policy space is larger than two dimensions. Because the conditions required for bicameralism to generate a core are so demanding, Tsebelis focuses on the weaker solution concept of the uncovered set. Unlike the bicameral core, the bicameral uncovered set is guaranteed to exist. He shows that the bicameral uncovered set is always at least as big as the unicameral uncovered set.

4 Bicameralism and Distributive Politics

Given bicameralism's historical rationale as an institution to provide benefits for specified classes and groups, a natural question to ask is whether bicameralism is an effective way of engineering particular distributive outcomes.

A number of distributive implications for bicameralism and related institutional arrangements can be derived from the legislative "divide-the-dollar" bargaining games pioneered by Baron and Ferejohn (1989). Before discussing specific models addressing bicameralism, we review their basic framework.

Assume that a legislature with N (an odd number) members must allocate one unit of resources (i.e. a dollar). Baron and Ferejohn consider bargaining protocol with a random recognition rule under which at the beginning of each period one of the players is selected to make a proposal. Let p_i be the probability that legislator i is selected to make the proposal, and we assume that this probability of recognition is constant over time. We will focus on the "closed rule" version of the model where the proposer makes a take-it-or-leave-it offer for the current legislative session. The proposer in each period makes an offer $(x_1, x_2, \ldots, x_N)$ such that x_i is the share for player i. We require $\sum_{i=1}^{N} x_i \leq 1$. If a simple majority, $n = \frac{N+1}{2}$, vote for the proposal it passes, the benefits are allocated, and the game ends. If this proposal is rejected, a new

---

[12] The core is the set of alternatives that cannot be defeated by some other alternative given the voting rule.
[13] The uncovered set is based on the covering relation: some alternative y "covers" x if y defeats x according to the voting rule and if the set of points that defeat y is strictly smaller than the set of points that defeat x. The uncovered set is the set of points not covered by some other alternative.

proposer is chosen at the beginning of the next session. All players discount payoffs secured in future sessions by a factor d.

This game has lots of subgame perfect equilibria. In fact, for sufficiently large N and d, any division of the dollar can be supported as a subgame perfect Nash equilibrium. Thus, Baron and Ferejohn and subsequent authors generally limit their analyses to stationary equilibria. A stationary equilibrium to this game is one in which:

1. A proposer proposes the same division every time she is recognized regardless of the history of the game.
2. Members vote only on the basis of the current proposal and expectations about future proposals. Because of assumption 1, future proposals will have the same distribution of outcomes in each period.

Let $v_i(h_t)$ be the expected utility for player i for the bargaining subgame beginning in time t given some history of play, h_t. This is known as legislator i's *continuation value*. Given the assumption of stationarity, continuation values are independent of the history of play so that $v_i(h_t) = v_i$ for all h_t, including the initial node h_0. Therefore, the continuation value of each player is exactly the expected utility of the game. Finally, we will focus only on equilibria in which voters do not choose weakly dominated strategies in the voting stage—a voter, therefore, will accept any proposal that provides at least as much as the discounted continuation value. This implies that any voter who receives a share $x_i \geq \delta v_i$ will vote in favor of the proposal while any voter receiving less than δv_i will vote against.[14] Thus, the proposer will maximize her share by allocating δv_i to the n members with the lowest continuation values.

As a benchmark for comparison with the models that we discuss below, consider the case where all members have the same recognition probability so that $p_i = \frac{1}{N}$ for all i. In this case, the unique expected payoffs from the stationary subgame perfect equilibrium are $v_i = \frac{1}{N}$. Thus, the dollar is split evenly in expectation.[15]

4.1 Concurrent and Super-majoritarianism

McCarty (2000a) considers an extension of the Baron–Ferejohn model to study the distributional effects of concurrent majorities and a number of other features associated with bicameralism. He assumes that there are two chambers, 1 and 2, with sizes $m_1 + m_2 = N$. A proposal must receive at least k_i in chambers $i = \{1, 2\}$ to pass. In each period, a proposer is selected at random where each member of chamber i is selected with probability p_i. Thus, the proposal probabilities are constant within chambers, but may vary across chambers. This may reflect constitutional provisions that give certain chambers an advantage in initiating certain types of legislation.

---

[14] The requirement that legislators vote in favor of the proposal when indifferent is a requirement of subgame perfection in this model.
[15] In reality, the split will be uneven with the proposer gaining the most and a minority receiving nothing.

McCarty derives the ratio of the expected payoffs for a member of chamber 1 to a member of chamber 2, $r_{12} = \frac{v_1}{v_2}$, as a function of the passage thresholds of each chamber k_i, the chamber sizes m_i, and the chamber-specific time discount factor d_i. His model predicts that:

$$r_{12} = \frac{p_1\left(1 - \delta_2 \frac{k_2}{m_2}\right)}{p_2\left(1 - \delta_1 \frac{k_1}{m_1}\right)}.$$

From this equation, a number of implications about bicameralism can be derived. For our purposes, the most important is that the size of the chamber, m_i, does not have an effect independent of the chamber's majority requirement k_i. If $\frac{k_1}{m_1} = \frac{k_2}{m_2}$ (as would be the case if both chambers were majoritarian), the relative payoffs depend only on the allocation of proposal power and the discount factors. If both chambers are co-equal in their ability to initiate legislation and discount the future equally, the requirement of concurrent majorities has no distributive implications.

The main implication of this analysis is that the fact that upper chambers are generally smaller does not make them more powerful. This prediction stands in direct contrast to "power indices," such as those of Shapley and Shubik (1954). Such indices are based on the assumption that all winning coalitions are equally likely, therefore members of the smaller chamber are more likely to be included. In the McCarty model, legislative proposers choose majorities in each chamber to minimize the total costs. Thus, competition to be included in the majority coalition for the chamber eliminates any small chamber advantage.

While McCarty's model predicts that concurrent majoritarianism does not have distributive consequences, a chamber's use of super-majority requirements, such as the US Senate's cloture provision, benefits its members as it ensures that a greater proportion of that chamber will be included in any winning coalition. In this sense, the model's results are very similar to those of Diermeier and Myerson (1999), who argue that, in a bicameral system, each chamber would like to introduce at least as many internal veto points as the other chamber. This reduces competition within the chamber thereby increasing the returns to its members. On the other hand, it is not so clear that this would happen since members of one chamber represent the same constituents as the other chamber. It is also consistent with the argument we derived from the pivotal politics model that super-majoritarianism is more consequential than concurrent majorities.

Secondly, note that the relative payoffs of chamber 1 to chamber 2 are increasing in p_1 and decreasing in p_2. Thus, constitutional procedures that give different chambers differential rights to initiate legislation have distributional consequences. In expectation, the chamber which possesses the right to introduce legislation will receive a larger benefit than the chamber which lacks initiation rights.

Finally, consider the implications of time discounting. *Ceteris paribus*, the chamber whose members have the highest discount factors gets more of the benefits. Since one would naturally assume a correlation between the discount factor and term length, a chamber whose members are elected for longer terms should get more of the dollar.

A limitation of McCarty's model is that it implicitly assumes that legislators represent disjoint constituencies whereas in actual bicameral systems voters are typically represented on both levels. Ansolabehere, Snyder, and Ting (2003) (which we discuss in more detail in a later section) develop a distributive model of bicameralism which incorporates dual representation. Consistent with McCarty, they find that, absent malapportionment or super-majoritarianism, per capita benefits are equal for all voters.

4.2 Bicameral Pork

Sequential choice models can also be used to make predictions about the extent to which bicameral legislatures will be more or less fiscally prudent than unicameral legislatures. In this section, we extend the models of Baron (1991) and McCarty (2000b) to determine which system is most likely to pass legislation whose total costs exceed total benefits.

Using exactly the same framework as the previous section, we assume that the bicameral legislature is considering a set of possible spending proposals with varying levels of aggregate benefit B and total cost T. Following the same closed rule described in the previous section, a proposer is selected in each period to propose an allocation of B under closed rule. If the proposal passes, the benefits are allocated according to the proposal and each legislator pays the same per capita tax, $t \equiv \frac{T}{N}$. If the proposal fails, no benefits are allocated, discounting occurs with a common factor d, and a new proposer is selected in the next period.

As a benchmark for comparison, consider a unicameral legislature requiring $k_1 + k_2$ of N votes. This is simply a fusion of the two chambers and their voting rules. A direct application of Baron shows that any project such that

$$\frac{B}{T} \geq \frac{(1-\delta)(k_1 + k_2)}{N - \delta(k_1 + k_2)}$$

will be enacted in a unicameral chamber. Note that this critical benefit–cost ratio is less than 1 since $N > k_1 + k_2$. Thus, the unicameral legislature enacts many inefficient programs where $B < T$.

Now we consider whether bicameralism increases or decreases the tendency to enact inefficient projects. Using derivations similar to those found in McCarty, we can compute the critical benefit–cost ratio for a bicameral legislature. It turns out that the threshold is exactly the same as that for the unicameral case. Thus, if both chambers have the same recognition probabilities and voting rules, there is no difference between bicameralism and unicameralism when it comes to the pork barrel. This contradicts the predictions of Heller (1997) which are derived from a multidimensional spatial model. This sketch of a bicameral pork-barrel game suggests that, as we saw in the purely distributive game, any effect of bicameralism must depend on voting rules that vary across chambers, asymmetric recognition probabilities, or as we discuss in the next section, malapportionment.

4.3 Malapportionment

Distributive legislative models also speak directly to the effects of malapportionment. As we discussed above, the unique stationary subgame perfect equilibrium of the Baron–Ferejohn model predicts that if all legislators have the same proposal power, their *ex ante* payoffs will be identical. Since legislative payoffs are equal, the per capita payoffs to constituents will be much higher in districts with fewer voters. Thus, malapportionment will lead to skewed distributions of benefits.

While the malapportionment result from the Baron–Ferejohn model is somewhat mechanical, a recent model of Ansolabehere, Snyder, and Ting (2003) produces a richer set of implications of malapportionment. In their basic model:

- The lower chamber (House) represents districts with equal population and the upper chamber (Senate) represents states containing different numbers of districts. Each district has one representative as does each state.
- Public expenditures are allocated to the district level and legislators are responsive to their median voters. Thus, House members seek to maximize the benefits going to thier district while a senator is assumed to maximize the benefits going to the median district in her state.[16]
- Both chambers vote by majority rule with all proposals emanating from the House.

Each period begins with a House member selected at random to propose a division of the dollar which is voted on by the House and Senate. If the proposal obtains majority support in both chambers, it passes and the game ends. If not, the game moves to the next period and a new proposer is selected from the House.

The authors show that in all symmetric,[17] stationary, subgame perfect Nash equilibria the expected payoffs to all House members are identical, regardless of the size of their state. Since all districts are equal population, per capita benefit levels are constant despite malapportionment in the Senate.

However, if the game is modified so that senators may make proposals, there is a small state advantage attributable to malapportioned proposal rights.

---

[16] Since senators do not make proposals in the simplest version of their model, we need not worry about how they would allocate money within their own states.

[17] Symmetry here implies that all house members from states of the same size are treated symmetrically. The authors indicate that other payoff distributions are sustainable when this assumption is dropped.

5 INFORMATIONAL EXPLANATIONS

Another potential argument for bicameralism is that it may promote more informed legislative decision-making. Since passage is required by multiple chambers, a "two-heads are better than one" logic suggests that bicameralism should lead to better legislative decisions. Rogers (2001) attempts to formalize this logic to provide an informational rationale for bicameralism. In his model, the reconciliation of inter-chamber differences through a "conference" committee allows for the aggregation of information that is dispersed across chambers.[18] Since it allows the dispersed information to be aggregated, a bicameral process is less likely to produce the wrong decision than a unicameral process. In fact, information is better aggregated when the chambers have congruent preferences. Thus, Rogers presents his model as an argument for congruent bicameralism.

While suggestive, Rogers's model is restrictive, and it is unclear how well it would generalize. Each chamber is modeled as a unitary actor with an exogenously given level of information about the desirability of its policy choices. It is not clear why the dispersal of information across chambers should be so much greater than within chambers. Indeed, it is not clear why consolidating the two chambers into a single unicameral chamber does not aggregate information at least as well as the bicameral procedures.

A more general analysis of the role of bicameralism in aggregating information can be grounded in models of voting under incomplete information and common values—the so-called "Condorcet jury problem." These models seem to suggest a much more circumscribed informational benefit of bicameralism.

Consider n legislators who must decide whether to choose policy 0 or policy 1. They all have a common preference for choosing the correct policy. They each get an independent signal about which policy is the common preference. We assume that each player's signal is correct with probability π.[19] This model predicts that the probability of making a correct decision under majority rule is an increasing function of both committee size n and signal quality π.

We can compare these results to bicameralism by dividing the n legislators into two chambers. We assume that each chamber votes via majority rule. Now the probability of making a correct decision depends on which policy is enacted when the chambers disagree. However, if the disagreement policy turns out to be incorrect, bicameralism would perform far worse due to the requirement that both chambers reach the correct decision. Thus, the probability of a bicameral correct decision is much lower than that for unicameralism since each chamber is smaller and thus more likely to produce the

---

[18] A conference committee composed of members appointed from each chamber to negotiate inter-chamber differences is a common way of ensuring that bills pass each chamber in an identical form. Typically, a conference committee produces a final bill or report which is voted up or down in each chamber.

[19] Allowing the signal quality to vary across individuals is unlikely to change our analysis so long as signal quality does not vary systematically across chambers in the bicameral case.

wrong decision. If the disagreement policy is the correct one, bicameralism would do better since it requires two majorities to overturn the disagreement policy. Thus, superiority of bicameralism would depend entirely on which outcome is designated as the default. Of course, if they had this information *ex ante*, they wouldn't need to vote!

Another problem for bicameralism is that it will never be the *ex post* best decision rule. Under unicameral majority rule, all legislators would agree *ex post* that it is best to implement the majority's preference. However, under bicameralism, all legislators would like to reverse any decision that disagreed with the majority of all votes cast.[20]

While the arguments based on the Condorcet jury models suggest that the requirement of concurrent majorities is unlikely to aggregate information better than simple majority rule, bicameralism may still affect the incentives of legislators to acquire information and develop legislative expertise. If information conveys a legislative advantage, bicameralism might induce inter-chamber competition in information acquisition. On the other hand, if information is a public good, bicameralism might induce more free riding. Rogers (1998) develops a game-theoretic model of the decision of each chamber to become informed about the consequences of pending legislation. His model predicts that the chamber with the lower information costs generally obtains a first mover advantage as the second chamber free rides off its information. However, again it is not clear why the free-riding incentives across chambers would exceed those within chambers. The same competition to obtain agenda control by acquiring superior information would presumably exist within a unicameral legislature.

6 CONCLUSIONS

In this chapter, we have considered a number of theoretical arguments in favor of bicameralism as an organizing principal for modern legislatures. Regardless of the theoretical framework or the collective action problem to be solved, we find that both the positive and normative arguments in favor of bicameralism tend to be weak and underdeveloped. Most of the effects of bicameralism are due primarily to quite distinct institutional choices, such as malapportionment and super-majoritarianism, which correlate empirically with bicameralism. There seems to be no logical reason why the benefits of these institutions—like the protection of minority rights and the

---

[20] A critical objection to this analysis is that the legislators were non-strategic. In the bicameral context, strategic legislators should condition their vote based on their beliefs in states of the world where they would provide the tie-breaking vote in their chamber given their expectations of the outcome in the other body. In a fully strategic model, Austen-Smith and Banks (1996) show that, for a given legislature, priors, and signal quality, there is an optimal q-rule which fully aggregates all information and makes the optimal decision given this information. Thus, a unicameral legislature using the optimal voting rule would do at least as well as any bicameral arrangement.

preservation of federalism—could not be obtained by a suitably engineered unicameral legislature or through vigorous judicial review.

One might respond to our analysis by suggesting that while the benefits of bicameralism are low, so are the costs. This may well be the case for the largely symbolic upper chambers of advanced democracies. However, the costs could be quite large in developing democracies if a misplaced faith in the virtues of bicameralism precludes more effective protections for political minorities.

References

ANSOLABEHERE, S., SNYDER, J., and TING, M. 2003. Bargaining in bicameral legislatures: when and why does malapportionment matter? *American Political Science Review*, 97: 471–81.

AUSTEN-SMITH, D., and BANKS, J. S. 1996. Information aggregation, rationality, and the Condorcet jury theorem. *American Political Science Review*, 90: 34–45.

BARON, D. P. 1991. Majoritarian incentives, pork barrel programs, and procedural control. *American Journal of Political Science*, 35: 57–90.

—— and FEREJOHN, J. A. 1989. Bargaining in legislatures. *American Political Science Review*, 83: 1181–206.

BINDER, S. A. 1999. The dynamics of legislative gridlock, 1947–1996. *American Political Science Review*, 93: 519–33.

—— 2003. *Stalemate*. Washington, DC: Brookings Institution Press.

BLACK, D. 1958. *The Theory of Committees and Elections*. Cambridge: Cambridge University Press.

BRADY, D. W., and VOLDEN, C. 1997. *Revolving Gridlock: Politics and Policy from Carter to Clinton*. Boulder, Colo.: Westview Press.

CHIOU, F.-Y., and ROTHENBERG, L. 2003. When pivotal politics meets party politics. *American Journal of Political Science*, 47: 503–22.

COX, G. W., and MCCUBBINS, M. 2003. *Legislative Leviathan Revisited*. Unpublished book manuscript.

—— and MCKELVEY, R. 1984. A ham sandwich theory for general measures. *Social Choice and Welfare*, 1: 75–83.

CRÉMER, J., and PALFREY, T. R. 1996. In or out? Centralization by majority vote. *European Economic Review*, 40: 43–60.

—— —— 1999. Political confederation. *American Political Science Review*, 93: 69–83.

DIERMEIER, D., ERASLAN, H., and MERLO, A. 2003. Bicameralism and government formation. Working paper, Dept. of Economics, University of Pennsylvania.

—— and MYERSON, R. 1999. Bicameralism and its consequences for legislative organization. *American Economic Review*, 89: 1182–96.

DRUCKMAN, J. N., and THIES, M. F. 2002. The importance of concurrence: the impact of bicameralism on government formation and duration. *American Journal of Political Science*, 46: 760–71.

FEREJOHN, J., and SHIPAN, C. 1990. Congressional influence on the bureaucracy. *Journal of Law, Economics, and Organization*, 6: 1–20.

HAMMOND, T. H., and MILLER, G. J. 1987. The core of the constitution. *American Political Science Review*, 81: 1155–74.

Heller, W. B. 1997. Bicameralism and budget deficits: the effect of parliamentary structure on government spending. *Legislative Studies Quarterly*, 12: 485–516.

Krehbiel, K. 1998. *Pivotal Politics: A Theory of U.S. Lawmaking*. Chicago: University of Chicago Press.

Lijphart, A. 1984. *Democracies: Patterns of Majoritarian and Consensus Government in Twenty-One Democracies*. New Haven, Conn.: Yale University Press.

McCarty, N. 2000a. Proposal rights, veto rights, and political bargaining. *American Journal of Political Science*, 44: 506–22.

—— 2000b. Presidential pork: executive politics and distributive politics. *American Political Science Review*, 94: 117–29.

McKelvey, R. 1976. Intransitivities in multidimensional voting models and some implications for agenda control. *Journal of Economic Theory*, 12: 472–82.

Poole, K. T., and Rosenthal, H. 1997. *Congress: A Political-Economic Theory of Roll Call Voting*. New York: Oxford University Press.

Public International Law and Policy Group 2003. *Establishing a Stable Democratic Constitutional Structure in Iraq: Some Basic Considerations*. Century Foundation. Available at: www.pilpg.org/areas/peacebuilding/simulations/iraq.

Riker, W. 1992. The justification of bicameralism. *International Political Science Review*, 12: 101–16.

Rogers, J. 1998. Bicameral sequence: theory and state legislative evidence. *American Journal of Political Science*, 42: 1025–60.

—— 2001. An informational rationale for congruent bicameralism. *Journal of Theoretical Politics*, 13: 123–51.

—— 2003. The impact of bicameralism on legislative production. *Legislative Studies Quarterly*, 28: 509–28.

Schofield, N. 1978. Instability of simple dynamic games. *Review of Economic Studies*, 45: 575–94.

Shapley, L., and Shubik, M. 1954. A method for evaluating the distribution of power in a committee system. *American Political Science Review*, 48: 787–92.

Tsebelis, G. 1993. The core, the uncovered set, and conference committees in bicameral legislatures. Unpublished manuscript, University of California, Los Angeles.

—— and Money, J. 1997. *Bicameralism*. New York: Cambridge University Press.

Wood, G. 1969. *The Creation of the American Republic, 1776–1787*. New York: Norton.

PART IV

INTERACTION OF THE LEGISLATURE, PRESIDENT, BUREAUCRACY, AND THE COURTS

CHAPTER 11

THE NEW SEPARATION-OF-POWERS APPROACH TO AMERICAN POLITICS

RUI J. P. DE FIGUEIREDO, JR.
TONJA JACOBI
BARRY R. WEINGAST

1 INTRODUCTION

AMERICAN politics is undergoing a quiet revolution. The study of American politics has long been organized by sub-fields—Congress, the presidency, the courts, and the bureaucracy. The advantage of this approach is that it allowed political scientists to gain expertise on a relevant portion of American politics and to create the scientific study of each institution. The liabilities of this approach are equally

* The authors thank Charles Cameron, Gary Cox, William Howell, Kenneth Shepsle, and Donald Wittman for helpful comments.

clear: it has created somewhat of a silo approach to American politics in which discoveries and knowledge in one sub-field or silo tended to have little impact on the others.

Since 1990, a new approach to studying American politics has emerged based on rational choice methods that we call the "new separation-of-powers approach." Often more implicitly than explicitly, the traditional approach to American politics emphasized separation of powers as the independence of the branches. In contrast to the traditional approach, the new one explicitly studies the interaction of the institutions, incorporating a broader range of actors and embedding them in models of strategic interaction. The results are dramatic. Scholars demonstrate that we cannot fully understand the behavior of one institution without understanding it *in the context* of the others.

Although traditional scholars always recognized the effect of one institution on another, they had no way to provide a systematic characterization of these interactions, many of which were instead characterized as caveats on the more general operation of the primary institution. In contrast, the new approach sees the constraints posed by other institutions as the foundational issue that defines the context, and thus the nature, of an institution's power to act.

The purpose of this chapter is to exposit the logic of the new approach and then to draw its implications for American politics.[1] Although still in its early stages, the new separation-of-powers approach has enhanced both theoretical and empirical analyses. Essentially, it allows scholars at once to study interlinked phenomena occurring in multiple institutions, which had previously not been systematically considered.

The new approach embeds institutional actors in the political environments that impose systematic constraints on them. For example, rather than seeing the president as largely unconstrained, due to her broad powers, the new approach formalizes the effect of the president's need to account for congressional authority and preferences. This move is important because it implies that the characteristics and behavior of *outside* actors are as important as those of actors inside an institution in explaining variations in the behavior of the institution under study.

Moreover, the new approach demonstrates that these constraints can best be understood in a strategic context: to further their own goals, actors in each branch must anticipate the reactions of actors in the other branches. Although students of American politics have always known this, the new models provide the game-theoretic technology for studying how this occurs. For example, the judiciary is not seen in isolation, even for judges with lifetime tenure. In the case of judicial determination of the meaning of a statute, judges will take the likely congressional responses into account. Because being overturned by Congress is costly, judges have an incentive to act strategically in their decisions so as not to be overturned; and this requires making decisions more favorable to Congress.

[1] The other chapters in this section survey the new literature as it applies to the presidency (Cameron), bicameralism (Cutrone and McCarty), the bureaucracy (Huber and Shipan), and the courts (McCubbins).

Another potential for the approach involves its implications for empirical analysis. The two biggest problems that hinder students of American political institutions are: too few degrees of freedom and confounds to causality—including selection bias, spuriousness, and simultaneous causality. As we show below, the new approach has the potential to address both of these problems.

Lack of sufficient variation is a fundamental problem in the study of many American political institutions. Consider the case of the presidency: the United States has had only forty-four presidents. This creates a "degrees of freedom problem:" the number of relevant variables affecting presidential choice vastly exceeds the number of cases, making it difficult to make inferences about presidential behavior. The approach provides an elegant solution to this problem in two ways. First, it increases the number of cases by reconceptualizing the independent variable; many presidents face variations in their environment, such as the partisan composition of the Congress. Thus, the unit of analysis becomes not just a presidency, but a president–Congress combination. Second, by incorporating other institutions, it allows scholars to study interactions that happen over and over—in the case of the president these include appointments, budgets, and vetoes.

More generally, the new separation-of-powers approach has helped authors unpack causality. This is particularly difficult for students of political institutions, since causality tends to flow both to and from the institution and other variables. In most cases, to identify the unique causal effects of a particular variable under study, the solution is to look for other information, outside the phenomenon being studied. The embrace of separation-of-powers models allows students to do this by introducing *structure*—the constraints that institutions put on public officials in making policy—and *strategy*—the way in which the actors involved condition their behavior on that structure as well as other players' actions or, importantly, potential actions. The introduction of structure imposes *constraints*, which in turn help identify causal effects.

The ability to understand causality has resulted in repeated demonstrations that appearances in American institutional politics can be deceiving. Studying an institution in isolation tends to make it appear more important and central to decision-making than studying it within the separation-of-powers system. The reason is that, when studying one institution in isolation, it is often easy to miss how behavior in that institution anticipates reactions from another (Weingast and Moran 1983).

For example, many observe the bureaucracy make choices without any systematic political input from elected officials, and infer that the bureaucracy therefore chooses the policy it wanted without much influence by elected officials. These scholars rely on an internalist bureaucratic logic that focuses on the organization itself to explain bureaucratic choices (e.g. Derthick and Quirk 1985; Wilson 1980). The separation-of-powers approach, in contrast, embeds the bureaucracy in a political context and argues that bureaucracies face a complex incentive system. Bureaucratic officials understand these incentives and, anticipating the likely reaction of interest groups and political officials, make policy choices.

This chapter proceeds as follows. The next three sections discuss the new separation of powers as it applies to the presidency, the courts, and the bureaucracy. Our conclusions follow after a penultimate, synthetic section.

2 THE PRESIDENCY

As noted above, the traditional approach to the presidency tends to study the president in isolation. In a literal sense, this claim is false. Every case study of the president contains major actors and institutions outside the president: the president constantly struggles not only with other institutions—Congress, the courts, and the bureaucracy—but also others—interest groups, the media, and foreign countries. Per the degrees of freedom problem, studying cases implies too many relevant independent variables, far larger than the number of cases. Similarly, studying divergent cases makes it harder to infer the systematic effect of particular institutions on the presidency. Indeed, because the characteristics of the other institutions and the environment exhibit so much variation, the lack of a method of accounting for these differences has obscured systematic influences.

The new separation-of-powers approach to the presidency resolves this problem by explicitly embedding the study of the president in a spatial model that allows us to study systematically her interaction with other institutions, typically in the context of something the president does again and again. This approach mitigates the degrees of freedom problem by studying multiple instances of the same category of behavior.

Consider the literature on budgets. Historically, the literature on budgeting differs from other literatures on the presidency in that the interaction of Congress and the president has always been central (e.g. Fisher 1975; Wildavsky 1964).

The advantage of the new separation-of-powers approach is that spatial models and other techniques provide a method of accounting for differences in the other institutions and the environment so that more systematic inferences can be made. For example, consider Kiewiet and McCubbins's asymmetric veto model (1988). They demonstrate a remarkable asymmetry in the presidential veto threat that had previously not been understood as a major principle of presidential power in budgeting: the veto threat works only when the president wants a budget that is less than that wanted by the median in Congress.

To see the logic of this conclusion, consider the following spatial model for a particular budget problem (Figure 11.1). The line represents the range of budgets, from 0 on the left to very large budget on the right.

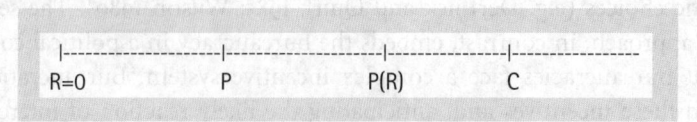

```
|--------------------|--------------------|--------------------|--------------------
R=0                  P                    P(R)                 C
```

Fig. 11.1 The effect of the presidential veto on budgeting: the president prefers a lower budget than Congress

```
|----------------|--------------------|--------------------------------------|
R=0              C                    P                                    P(R)
```

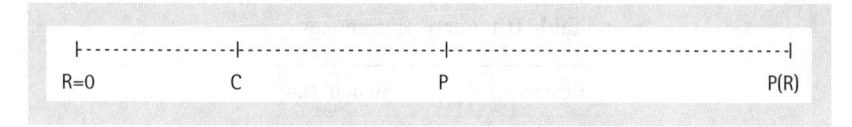

Fig. 11.2 The effect of the presidential veto on budgeting: the president prefers a higher budget than Congress

R is the reversion policy that goes into effect if Congress and the president cannot agree on a budget.[2] P is the president's ideal policy and C is the ideal policy of Congress (presumably that of the median member of Congress). P(R) represents that policy to which the president is exactly indifferent with the reversion point, implying that the president prefers all policies in between P and P(R) to either P or P(R).

If Congress proposes a budget at its ideal policy of C, the president will veto it. C is outside of the set of budgets (R, P(R)) that the president prefers to R, so she is better off with a veto that yields R = 0 than with C. Because Congress wants a significantly higher budget than the president, the best it can do is propose P(R), which the president will accept. As seen from the figure, the president's veto threat is effective and forces Congress to adjust what it proposes. Moreover, because Congress can anticipate the policies that the president will accept or veto, no veto occurs. Despite the absence of an observable veto or even an explicit threat by the president, the veto constrains congressional decision-making: they are forced to pass the budget P(R) instead of their preferred C.[3]

Now suppose that the relative preferences of Congress and the president are reversed, where the president wants a significantly higher budget than the Congress, as illustrated in Figure 11.2.

In this situation, the president's threat to veto a budget that she feels is too small is not credible. Suppose Congress passes its ideal budget, C. The president may threaten to veto the budget if Congress fails to pass a budget that is higher than C, but this threat is vacuous. If the president vetoes C, she winds up with R, which is significantly worse than C. Hence the president will accept C.

McCubbins (1990) provides a variant on this logic to explain an odd feature of the Ronald Reagan presidency. Reagan sought to transform the relationship of the government and the economy by "getting the government off the back of the American people." As part of this effort, he sought a dramatic reduction in the budget for domestic programs. In collaboration with his director of the Office of Management and Budget, David Stockman, Reagan's proposed budget cuts in 1981 were legendary and helped solidify his reputation as cutting the government. Despite appearances, domestic spending increased dramatically under Reagan after 1981. Surely Reagan did not intend this result, so how did it happen?

---

[2] For simplicity, we will ignore the veto override provisions; per Cameron 1996 and Krehbiel 1998, these are easy to add, but just complicate the point.
[3] This formulation assumes that Congress has full information about the president's preferences. Cameron (this volume; 1996) shows how to relax the model to allow uncertainty about the president's preferences. This model derives from that of Romer and Rosenthal 1978.

Table 11.1 Party preferences

Democrats	Republicans
D, r	d, R
D, R	D, R
Q	Q
d, r	d, r
d, R	D, r

McCubbins provides a persuasive interpretation that rests on a variant of the above and the observation that Reagan faced divided government: although Reagan was a strong president and had the support of a Republican majority in the Senate, the Democrats retained control of the House. Both parties therefore held a veto over policy-making.

With respect to policy content, Democrats wanted higher domestic spending and lower defense spending, while Reagan and the Republicans wanted the reverse: lower domestic and higher defense spending. When faced with a trade-off, both parties would settle for increasing both policies rather than retaining the status quo.

Table 11.1 represents the preferences for both Republicans and Democrats. Domestic programs are represented by the letter d; defense programs by r. A capital letter indicates an increase in the program while a lower-case letter indicates a decrease. Q is the status quo. Democrats prefer first (D, r); next (D, R); then the status quo, Q; next (d, r), and last (d, R). Republicans' preferences are similar, *mutatis mutandis*.

Because the two houses of Congress were divided, Congress could not act as one and present the president with a fait accompli budget. Instead, Democrats in the House had to compromise with Republicans in the Senate to produce legislation for the president to sign.

McCubbins argues that this implies the only equilibrium outcome from Congress is that both programs are increased. To see this, consider the preferences in Table 11.1. As is readily apparent, the only outcome that both Democrats and Republicans prefer to the status quo is (D, R), increasing both programs. This is the only budget that can pass both houses of Congress. As to President Reagan, he could threaten to veto such a budget unless Congress passed one that lowers domestic spending while increasing defense spending, but the veto threat is not credible. Because the Democrats in the House prefer the status quo (Q) to lowering domestic and increasing defense spending (d, R), they were better off passing (D, R) and letting Reagan veto it than giving in to Reagan. Despite threats to veto increases in both, Reagan would not do so because of a variant of the above logic. Because he prefers increases in both (D, R) to the status quo (Q), Reagan's veto threat is not credible. Reagan's rhetoric about cutting domestic spending aside, he regularly signed budgets increasing domestic spending.

As a second illustration of the separation-of-powers approach, we consider recent models of appointments (Gely and Spiller 1992; Binder and Maltzman 2002; Cameron, Cover, and Segal et al. 1990; Chang 2003; Jacobi 2005; Moraski and Shipan 1999; Nokken and Sala 2000; Snyder and Weingast 2000). Traditional models of the presidency tended to consider appointments the purview of the president despite the fact that formal rules which give the power to nominate to the president also explicitly require the "advice and consent" of the Senate. The reason is that, in general, few nominations are rejected, seeming to imply a norm of congressional deference so that the president typically gets her way. Indeed, many have claimed that because senatorial consideration of appointments is often perfunctory, the Senate exerts little influence or power over them. This view implies that the president is unconstrained in her appointments and will therefore choose the nominee that best furthers her goals.

The new separation-of-powers models of the appointment process yields a different interpretation, focusing on both the presidential nomination and the Senate approval of appointments. The most obvious implication is that, because the Senate has a veto, the president is forced to take senatorial preferences into account. Per the observational equivalence, an alternative explanation for the observation that the Senate rarely rejects a nominee is that the president has taken the possibility of rejection into account and never puts forth a nomination that will be rejected. Because rejection is highly embarrassing and can make the president seem weak, the president will seek to avoid rejection, and this forces her to take into account senatorial preferences. Indeed, presidents often vet candidates with the committee prior to announcing a nomination.

Consider a simple model of appointments to a regulatory body or multimember court, such as the Supreme Court (Snyder and Weingast 2000). The president and the Senate have differing preferences over policy. Appealing to a standard bargaining framework, we assume that policy arises in a two-step process. First, elected officials bargain to produce a target policy; second, they implement the policy through a regulatory board who choose policy by voting. In the first stage, elected officials produce some form of compromise over policy; if not split the difference, at least something for both sides. For simplicity, assume that the relevant policy concerns a regulatory agency whose policy choice we designate R.

Figure 11.3 illustrates this compromise by assuming a president on the left and a Senate on the right. Their compromise regulatory policy is R, perhaps biased toward the president, but a compromise nonetheless.

To implement their target policy, elected officials must appoint the regulatory board so that the median board member's preferences correspond to R. We illustrate this in Figure 11.4 for a five-member board with members whose ideal policies are located at 1, 2, M, 4, and 5. When the median's ideal is located at the elected officials' compromise policy of R, the board implements the elected officials' compromise policy.

The importance of this model is that it affords comparative static results predicting the effects on regulatory appointments and policy after an election that changes the

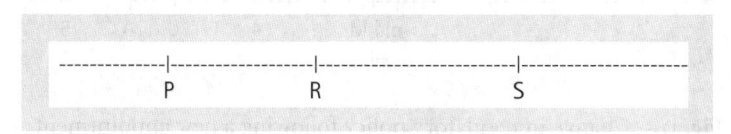

```
--------------|------------------|------------------------|---------------------
              P                  R                        S
```

Fig. 11.3 President–Senate bargaining over policy

```
----------|--------|----------------|------------|--------|------------|----------------
    1        2              M=R           4          C           5
```

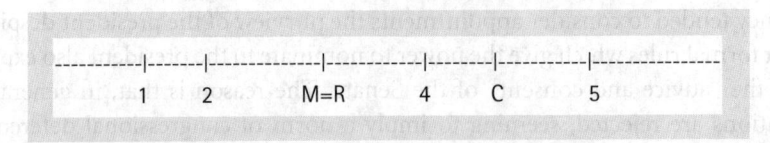

Fig. 11.4 Regulatory board implementing regulatory policy, R

identity and policy preferences of the elected officials. Suppose, for example, that the new president is on the right, replacing the old one on the left. The new president and Senate bargain to form a new compromise between their ideal points, say in between board members 4 and 5 at policy C.

Most independent regulatory agency board members serve for a fixed term rather than at the pleasure of the president, and can only be removed under circumstances of gross misconduct. Thus, a president–Senate combination that wants to move policy to C cannot do so by firing members from the current board. Instead, they must wait until current members resign, die, or complete their term.

This model makes predictions about how every appointment will affect the median—move to the right, stationary, or to the left. Suppose that board member 4 is the first to leave the board. No matter what a nominee's preferences are, the president cannot move the median to the right: the three leftmost board members are fixed, implying that so too is the median. If, instead, member 2's term is up, then the elected officials can move policy from the current median to the ideal of member 4 by appointing a new board member to the right of 4. This is illustrated in Figure 11.5

If elected officials appoint a new member at A to the right of 4, then 4 becomes the new median board member, and regulatory policy will move from the old policy, R, to the new policy 4. Elected officials can move policy to their target policy of C when they have the opportunity to replace one of the now three leftmost members—members 1, old M, or 4—with someone to the right of C. In general, after three appointments on a five-member board, a president–Senate combination can move the median anywhere. This implies that after three appointments, the model predicts that the president and Senate have reached their target policy so that further appointments need not be used to move the median.

Snyder and Weingast apply this model to the National Labor Relations Board (NLRB), a major agency making labor regulatory policy. They test this model's predictions by examining every regulatory appointment from 1950 through 1988, a total of forty-three appointments. Given some assumptions about presidential–Senate preferences, the model yields a prediction about how a new appointment will move the median—to the left, none, or to the right.

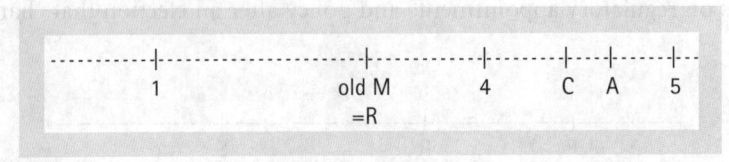

```
-----------|-----------------------|-------------|--------|---|------|---
           1                         old M          4       C   A     5
                                      =R
```

Fig. 11.5 Change in regulatory policy following a new appointment

Table 11.2 Regulatory appointments to the NLRB

Predicted sign of change	Actual sign of change			Total
	−	0	+	
−	6	3	1	10
0	3	12	3	18
+	0	6	9	15
Total	9	21	13	43

Source: Snyder and Weingast 2000, table 2.

Table 11.2 summarizes the results. As can be seen, most appointees are as predicted: when the predicted sign change of the median is negative (a move to the right), 60 per cent of the actual appointees move the median to the left; when the predicted sign is 0, two-thirds are as predicted; and when the predicted sign is positive, 60 per cent are as predicted. Moreover, using a nested-regression framework, they test this model against both the null model and the presidential dominance hypothesis (predicting that only the president's preferences matter). The separation-of-powers model outperforms *both* the presidential dominance and null models.

In short, the model shows the importance of the interaction of the president and Senate with respect to appointments. Both branches matter, and the president must take the Senate's preferences into account when making nominations, lest she risk failure.

2.1 Conclusions

The new separation-of-powers approach provides powerful new insights into presidential behavior. The use of spatial models and other techniques affords an accounting system that allows us to keep track of different parameters in the political environment, in turn, allowing us to say how presidential behavior varies with the political environment. The models of veto behavior, budgets, and appointments all show the systematic influence of Congress on the president. To further her goals, the president must anticipate the interaction with Congress.

3 THE COURTS

As with the other branches, the courts operate within, and constitute part of, the political system: the policy positions of Congress, the president, and the bureaucracy constrain judges in their policy-making role. The new separation-of-powers analysis shows how the formal constraints that operate on the judiciary force it to consider the likely responses of the other institutional players to its decisions. For instance, being overturned by Congress is institutionally costly to the courts, as overrides make the courts appear weak, lower their legitimacy, and waste judicial resources. As such, we expect courts to make their decisions in a way that avoids congressional override. Understanding the powers and preferences of the elected branches provides central information in predicting judicial action.

This is not a unidirectional effect: the courts also constrain the other players in separation-of-powers games. Because judicial action shapes policy outcomes, Congress, the president, and agencies will anticipate court decisions, and the potential for judicial review will be taken into account during the law-making process. Just as courts prefer not to be overruled by Congress, Congress generally prefers not to have its legislation struck down or altered by the courts. If Congress cannot force the judiciary to adhere to its own policy preferences, then its members must take judicial preferences into account when they write legislation. Consequently, the position of the judiciary shapes the behavior of Congress, the president, and bureaucratic agencies. These two effects together show how judicial interactions with the other branches of government shape the application of law and limit the power of Congress and the executive.

The new separation-of-powers analysis treats judicial decisions not as one-shot cases determined by their idiosyncratic characteristics, but as repeated iterations of interactions between the branches. Whether a court reviews the constitutionality of legislation, the interpretation of a statute, or an administrative decision, judicial action is always subject to the responses of other political bodies. This interaction offers a means of predicting judicial decision-making behavior, and accounting for its variation. Central to this analysis is the recognition that judicial action takes place within the context of a political environment that will react to, and anticipate, judicial action.

Judicial literature has long recognized that the judiciary is subject to responses from the elected branches (e.g. Dahl 1957; McCloskey 1960; Rosenburg 1991). In particular, traditional legal literature emphasized judicial vulnerability to the elected branches of government, through their control of Federal Court jurisdiction, the threat of impeachment, and control over budget and appointments. However, prior to the new separation-of-powers literature, these formal constraints were never modeled in terms of their effect on judicial decision-making. Rather, judicial scholarship on how judges make decisions was framed by a debate between traditional legal scholars, who emphasized the role of judicial character in the voluntary exercise of self-restraint (e.g. Bickel 1986; Fuller 1978), and political science's attitudinalists, who empirically established that judicial decisions were strongly correlated with individual characteristics of judges, such as the party of the appointing president (e.g. Segal and Spaeth 1993).

This debate was informative about what determines judicial preferences, but it told us little of what constraints operated on the judiciary, given those preferences. In particular, it gave little consideration to the position of the other institutional players in determining the outcome of cases. Figure 11.6 illustrates this point, in stylized form.

```
|---+---------------+---------------+-------------------+---|
    C               L               P                   J
```

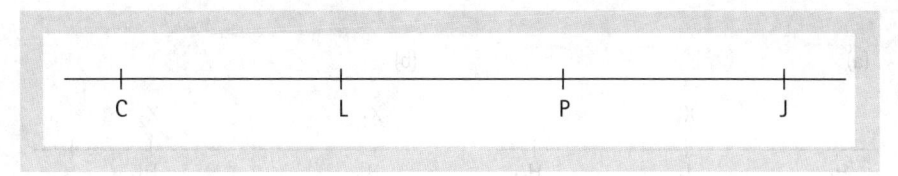

Fig. 11.6 Institutional preferences

The line represents a range of possible policy choices and judicial outcomes. C, P, and J represent the locations of the ideal policies for Congress, the president, and the court, respectively.

According to the attitudinalists, cases will be decided at J, the point that represents the preferences of the judiciary. According to traditional legal scholarship, judges will do their best to make determinations at point L, the exogenously determined "best" legal outcome, regardless of its relationship to J. For the attitudinalists, the other players, Congress (C) and the president (P), are relevant only in terms of the correlation that can be anticipated between P (and to some extent the Senate) and J, due to the appointment power; whereas for the traditional legal scholars, P and C may be somewhat informative as to the limits of public acceptability, which informs judicial legitimacy, but not in a formally predictable way.

Although new separation-of-powers models provide an approach to the appointment process that determines the position of J (as we discussed in the previous section), most such models of the courts begin with a variant of the attitudinalist model: that judges have a consistent set of goals based on ideology, political preferences, and broader values. The new separation-of-powers approach poses new questions, particularly: taking the position of J as given, how will judges decide issues? And how will those decisions be affected by the positions of the other institutional players?

The first step in answering these questions is to set aside the idea that the judiciary is the unconstrained last mover, or the last mover who is constrained only by internal norms. Although legislative overrides occur infrequently, the ubiquitous possibility of congressional override of judicial statutory interpretation shapes judicial behavior. This point was first formally analyzed by Marks, who ascertained when Congress will be unable to change judicial alterations of legislative policy, even if the majority of legislators do not support the judicial alteration. Marks (1988) showed that both committees in Congress and bicameralism expand the range of stable equilibria the judiciary can institute.[4]

Figures 11.7a and 11.7b illustrate Marks's insight. H_M is the median House voter, H_C is the median House committee member. J_1 in Figure 11.7a and J_2 in Figure 11.7b are two examples of possible court positions. Marks showed how a court's ability to determine policy hinges on the positions of H_M and H_C. The distance between the preferences of the House median and the House committee median prevents any agreement being able to be reached to overturn any judicial ruling within that

---

[4] In keeping with the models of his era, Marks relied on a model of committee agenda power. The same form of results can be obtained using a more recent model of party agenda power (see Aldrich 1995 or Cox and McCubbins 2005).

(a)

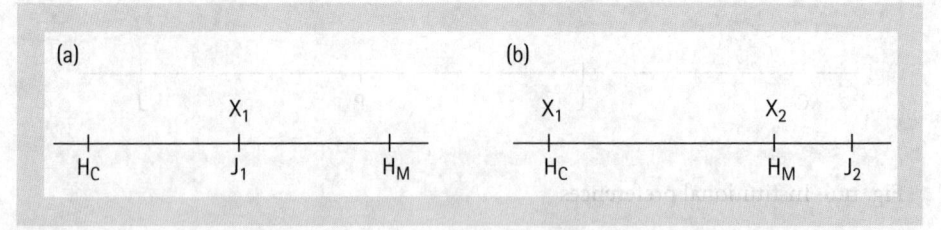

$H_C \quad J_1 \quad X_1 \quad H_M$

(b)

$H_C \quad X_1 \quad H_M \quad X_2 \quad J_2$

Fig. 11.7 The effect of congressional committees on judicial decision-making

range. For example, in Figure 11.7a, a court at J_1 could effectively entrench a policy X_1; because the Committee and the House have opposing preferences, they cannot agree how to change this ruling. The addition of bicameralism expands the range in which courts can impose their policy preferences: Marks showed that the judiciary can act free from fear of being overturned in the range of the maximum distance between not only H_M and H_C, but also the Senate equivalents, S_M and S_C.

Marks assumed that judicial decision-making was exogenous to legislative structure, and so assumed judges did not act in a sophisticated fashion. Thus he considered that only judicial rulings that occurred within the legislative core, such as X_1 in Figure 11.7a, could have a lasting effect.[5] However, it follows from his analysis that a sophisticated court positioned outside the equilibrium range, such as J_2, would shift its ruling from its ideal point, J_2, which would be overruled, to the closest stable equilibrium, in this case X_2.

Not only is this simple model informative about the constraints that operate on judicial decision-making, but it also explains one aspect of congressional behavior, in particular why we should not expect to see frequent congressional override of judicial decisions. While many have concluded that the infrequency of congressional override suggests that this institutional mechanism is ineffective, new separation-of-powers models suggest the opposite. Because the threat of congressional override is powerful and credible, it does not need to be exercised (Spiller and Tiller 1996). As with the observational equivalence of the presidential veto, the lack of congressional overrides is consistent with a very powerful threat of these overrides and a very weak one. We do not expect to see these threats exercised: they are operative by their mere potential.

3.1 Further Insights

When the new approach was first applied to the judiciary, some scholars saw it as conflicting with the attitudinalist school. Attitudinalists believe that judges achieve their desired outcomes through sincerely voting their unconstrained policy preferences, whereas new separation-of-powers scholars argue that those preferences are exercised in the context of institutional constraints, and so judges strategically incorporate the preferences of other relevant political actors (Segal 1997; Maltzman, Spriggs,

---

[5] In Figure 11.7b, Marks predicted the equilibrium would revert to X_1 at H_C, because the court would decide at J_2, and be overridden.

and Wahlbeck 1999). However, the new approach provides the logical conclusion of the attitudinalist insight: if there are any costs to the institutional repercussions of pursuing unsustainable outcomes, such as being overturned by Congress, it would be irrational for judges to pursue their preferences without accounting for the limits of their policy-making capacity. Judges are unlikely to be so shortsighted in pursuing their preferences.

Capturing the limits on the judical pursuit of their policy preferences allows the new approach to improve on the explanatory power of the attitudinal model, as well as to provide new theoretical insights in a number of different areas affecting the judiciary's relations with the other branches. Scholars have shown how the president and the Senate can each shape the ideological make-up of courts through strategic use of the appointment power. Moraski and Shipan examined when the Senate's advice and consent role will be determinative: its power depends on the Senate's position relative to the president and the existing court median. Only when the Senate is the moderate player does it have a direct influence on the confirmation process (1999, 1077). Jacobi modeled the effect of senatorial courtesy on nominations, and how confirmation outcomes depend on the configuration of preferences among the president, the Senate median, and the home state senator. When the objecting home state senator is the moderate player, the president can strategically draw the equilibrium outcome closer to her preferences (2005, 209). Segal, Cameron, and Cover showed that senatorial support for judicial nominees depends on the relative position of their constituency and the nominee. When both a senator and the nominee are to the left or right of the median constituent, the senator is more likely to vote for the nominee (1992, 111). New separation-of-powers analysis has illustrated how and when the ideology of judicial nominees will vary with the ideology of other institutional players.

Similarly, judicial agenda-setting literature has benefited greatly from the new separation-of-powers analysis. This literature documents how judges partially circumvent their institutional inability to initiate their own agendas. For example, judges exercise *certiorari* voting strategically (e.g. Caldelra, Wright, and Zorn 1999), considering both probable outcomes in deciding whether to grant *certiorari* (Boucher and Segal 1995) and which cases will most influence lower courts, so as to maximize the proportion of total decisions favorable to their policy preferences (Schubert 1962). Epstein, Segal, and Victor (2002) showed that Supreme Court judges consider both the internal level of heterogeneity of the court, as well as the position of the court median relative to Congress, when deciding between accepting constitutional or statutory interpretation cases.

Appointments and agenda-setting are just two areas that have benefited from the new approach to traditional questions about judicial behavior, by looking beyond the judiciary itself. Judges anticipate potential opposition to their decisions, and if that opposition can be credibly exercised, they can be expected to adjust their actions to avoid negative consequences. Consequently, the positions of other institutional actors constitute constraints on judicial decision-making. Incorporating these factors allows for comparative statics, such that we can predict changes in judicial behavior, for example movements resulting from a change in the political administration. At the same time, potential judicial action can constrain other actors: as long as courts can impose costs on Congress, the president, or administrative agencies, those actors can be expected to adjust their decisions to avoid such costs. The new separation-of-powers analysis provides a variety of mechanisms for formalizing and predicting when these constraints will be active. As such, it both incorporates an understanding of the judiciary into broader political analysis, and provides important tools and insights to judicial specialists.

4 THE BUREAUCRACY

As with the study of Congress, the presidency, and the courts, the study of bureaucracy also began with relatively limited consideration given to other institutions. Beginning in the late 1970s, however, this started to change, as rational choice theorists (and, to a limited extent, empiricists) began to recognize that there was much greater ability to study their phenomena of interest by incorporating the other branches into their analyses (Huber and Shipan, this volume, review this literature in detail).

4.1 Setting the Table

Prior to the 1970s, the study of bureaucracy was largely confined to historical, normative, and behavioral analyses. With respect to the first, the dominant theory focused on the independence of bureaucrats from other actors in the separation-of-powers system, effectively legitimizing and systemizing the "silo"-based approach (e.g. Bernstein 1955; Mills 1956).[6]

As Moe (1984, 1990) points out, the normative questions were the domain of another stream of literature: public administration. This literature was primarily interested in how agencies could and *should* be organized. This focus on internal organization meant that external organization—how agencies fit in a complex system of separation of powers—was largely subordinated.

Finally, the behavioral theory of organization, exemplified by the psycho-sociological approach of March and Simon (1958; see also Simon 1947; Selznick 1948) also focused primarily on internal organization—how tasks are divided within an organization, what such specialization means for organizational effectiveness in the context of the human cognitive limitations, and what types of pathologies might result.

Following on the pioneering work of Niskanen (1971), by the 1980s scholars began to model the interaction between bureau and other institutional actors in a more fully

---

[6] The so-called "capture" hypothesis was further developed in the 1970s by the Chicago School of economists who argued that agencies often served economic interests who supported regulation as a barrier to entry (Stigler 1971; Peltzman 1976).

strategic setting. One of the most important of these was the work that responded to the widely held claim that agencies were unresponsive to Congress and the president. Employing the tools and principles of the new economics of organizations, such as agency theory and transaction cost economics, these scholars began the process of both broadening the explanatory power of models of bureaucratic behavior and using models to help identify causality and sort out apparently observationally equivalent hypotheses.

4.2 Congressional and Presidential Dominance

For those working on more explicitly modeling the interaction between Congress and the bureaucracy, the initial focus was on the variety of instruments that legislators could avail themselves of to control the bureaucracy; and relatedly, the patterns of use of these instruments we would expect to see under various hypotheses of bureaucratic decision-making.

Weingast and Moran (1983), for example, studied the strategic interaction between an agency (in this case the Federal Trade Commission) and an oversight committee in Congress. They emphasized the varied and effective instruments—budgets, oversight, authority, and structure—which could be used by Congress to turn bureaucratic policy-making toward their will. One important move they made was to point out that *evaluating* bureaucratic behavior was very difficult when only looking at an agency by itself. Addressing the question of who controls whom, they pointed out that lack of oversight could *either* mean that agencies were unfettered *or* that threats were so effective that the need to exercise such disciplining mechanisms was minimal. In other words, one could not observe the use of punitive measures and draw conclusions about the nature of control.

McCubbins and Schwartz (1984) made a similar contribution by further emphasizing the importance of an *equilibrium theory* of agency control. They pointed out that in addition to "police patrol" oversight, Congress could also use "fire alarm" oversight. In other words, to monitor agencies, they could rely on "exception reporting," eschewing active vigilance in favor of particularized, ad hoc intervention in response to complaints by interest groups or constituents. Such an information-gathering structure, they argued, would be much more efficient than monitoring all agencies, all of the time.

At the same time, other scholars were shifting the focus from the dyad of Congress–bureaucracy to a different dyadic relationship—between president and bureaucracy. Indeed, the primary criticism of the Congress-centric approach (referred to as "Congressional Dominance") was that it ignored the president (Moe 1987; Wilson 1989). Perhaps the best example of an attempt to steer scholars away from Congress and toward the president is the work by Moe (1985). Moe argued that the president's power to appoint, combined with senatorial deference, means that when considering "control" of the bureaucracy, the president is the primary principal. In his study of the

National Labor Relations Board (NLRB), Moe argued that one could not understand the agency's policy-making without understanding this institutional feature.[7]

The insights of the 1980s were a step forward as they shifted from an internal to external, strategic focus. The criticisms that each of the schools made of each other presaged the emergence of a more recent vein of scholarship which explicitly considered the interaction of *multiple* institutional actors and therefore brought the "new separation-of-powers" approach in earnest to bureaucracy studies.

4.3 Agency Discretion in a Separation-of-powers Context

In a number of contexts, scholars have continued to focus on how each of the institutional players interacts to explain bureaucratic behavior. To illustrate this development, we focus on perhaps the primary example that integrates *all* institutional actors—bureaucracy, presidents, Congress, and the courts: the literature on how much discretion agencies are granted to make policy.

This literature focuses on two related issues: first, the degree of ambiguity or specificity of policy that Congress and the president jointly pass, which the courts often review; and second, the degree to which the structure and process created by legislation and judicial decisions constrain or expand agency discretion.

Connecting legal and historical studies of the Administrative Procedure Act of 1946 (Shapiro 1982; Bonfield 1986; Davis 1978), and the insight concerning the usefulness of *ex ante* control mechanism from McCubbins and Schwartz (1984), McCubbins, Noll, and Weingast (1987, 1989) argued that agency discretion was in part determined by the procedures dictated by Congress that agency policy-making must follow. These procedures create a set of requirements—including rules of notice, standing, information gathering, and judicial review—for agency rule-making. By introducing strict limits on discretion, administrative procedures ensure that outcomes will be closer to an elected official's ideal than if the agency had an unlimited range of options. But the mechanism only works if there is *ex post* enforcement of the rules. Thus, McCubbins, Noll, and Weingast argue that the courts were crucial in making this an effective control mechanism. If the courts ruled consistently with the intent of Congress, then the bureau would have strong incentives to follow their intent. On the other hand, by implication, if the courts were not aligned with the legislature, such mechanisms would provide the bureau with more latitude to implement policy.

More recently, the work on grants of discretion and administrative procedures has been extended in two ways. First, the range of actors included has been expanded. Second, these extended models have allowed scholars to conduct more detailed empirical analysis. For example, Epstein and O'Halloran (1994, 1996, 1999) address the

---

[7] Indeed, developing Moe's argument further, a series of studies (Keech and Morris 1997; Grier 1987; Havrilesky 1995; and Chappell, McGregor, and Vermilyea 2005) develop both theoretical models and empirical evidence to demonstrate the influence of presidential appointments on agency behavior. Notably, Moe's work presaged the later work (above) of Snyder and Weingast 2000 which then extended the analysis of the NLRB to consider agency, president, *and* Senate.

fundamental question that earlier scholars who examined "runaway bureaucracy" were concerned with: "Can the virtues of separate powers intended by the Founders be maintained alongside significant delegation to the executive [by the legislature]?" Epstein and O'Halloran include four important sets of actors in the politics of agency rule-making: Congress, its committees, the president, and agencies. They observe that, when passing legislation, congresspersons on the floor must make two choices: first, who should they obtain information from—a potentially biased committee or a potentially biased executive agency? And second, how much discretion should they provide to an agency if the agency is allowed to make policy?[8] They show that these trade-offs will depend on *political alignment*: the key will be who they can more rely on to act as if they had the Congress's interests in mind. Further, the degree of constraint imposed on agencies, when they are delegated policy implementation, will depend on how aligned the president and agencies are with the Congress: a closely aligned agency can be expected to use its information to implement policies which would be close to those that Congress would prefer; otherwise, it will be highly constrained through the use of strict rules, procedures, and very specific legislation.

Prior to Epstein and O'Halloran's work, scholars had primarily considered the question of legislative delegation in a dyadic form: Congress either delegating to a committee or delegating to an agency. Expanding the set of actors to consider all of these players simultaneously allows one to see that committee and agency are partial *substitutes*. Indeed, Epstein and O'Halloran's model indicates why the study of dyadic delegation relationships is inappropriately specified: because the legislature has choices and will delegate selectively based on its own strategic considerations, the policies and form of delegation observed will necessarily be a *selected* sample of the full set of possible delegatory choices. This means that what we observe in practice will not be understood without correcting for such sample selection.

By including a broader range of actors, Epstein and O'Halloran's approach allows them to *identify* the selection mechanism in order more precisely to consider empirical relationships. Indeed, this is precisely how the new separation-of-powers analysis informs their empirical work. They employ a data-set of federal statutes to measure the degree to which administrative procedures constrain grants of authority to agencies. They find, among other things, that, when the executive branch, including the president and bureaucracy, are closer in their policy preferences to the Congress, Congress will at once be more willing to delegate *and* will provide less constraining rule-making procedures when they do delegate to a bureau.

The literature on discretion and administrative procedures has been expanded by the work of Huber and Shipan (Huber and Shipan 2002; see also Huber, Shipan, and Pfahler 2001). Like Epstein and O'Halloran, they point out the importance of understanding variation in administrative discretion—either through the specificity

---

[8] This emphasis on the tension between the need to *control* agencies and the need to exploit the *expertise* held within agencies is the central concern of much of the literature on delegation to bureaucracies. Banks 1989, Banks and Weingast 1992, Kiewiet and McCubbins 1991, Bawn 1995, Gailmard 2002, Lupia and McCubbins 1994, and de Figueiredo, Spiller, and Urbiztondo 1999 are all examples of contributions to this discussion.

of substantive policy instructions or through the degree of procedural limitations—by examining the roles of various actors in a separation-of-powers system. Following Epstein and O'Halloran's logic, they argue that "statutory control" of agency authority will be tighter when there is misalignment between institutional actors—divided government. Their contribution is to extend this finding to examine the interaction between divided government and other factors: divided control of the legislature itself; legislative capacity and substitute mechanisms for control.

As with Epstein and O'Halloran, Huber and Shipan's work provides an example of the leverage obtained by incorporating the separation-of-powers approach to explain the American bureaucracy. Theoretically, they broaden the range of variables that can be identified to have an effect. Indeed, they demonstrate that two aspects of separation of powers—divided control between legislative and executive functions and bicameral legislatures—are critical to understanding when and how constraints on delegation to agencies will occur.

Further, as with Epstein and O'Halloran, they are able to employ the constraints in the system to inform empirical analysis. They show that the specificity of legislation is increasing in institutional misalignment and that these effects are even greater in the presence of intra-institutional divisions. This result is only possible because they expand the normal delegation question from simply a legislature to a bureau, to a more nuanced view including elected executives (presidents or governors) and multiple houses of the legislature.[9]

4.4 Conclusion

Like many judges, civil servants, and appointees that work within government, agencies are not elected. Indeed, they are enabled, broadly, by legislation that is passed by Congress and approved by the president; their budgets are determined by the same institutions; heads of agencies are often appointed by consent between legislators and the president; and their decisions are often subject to judicial review. This means, almost by definition, that understanding government agencies requires incorporation of politics and processes that occur in institutions of government outside the bureaucracy.

5 A Synthetic Application

To this point we have focused on behavior within particular institutions, emphasizing that explanations of most institutional behavior in American politics require students to look *outside* the institution of interest. More generally, analysts may also be interested not only in the behavior of any single institution, but additionally in the outcomes of the interaction of a range of actors.

---

[9] Recent extensions to this work include de Figueiredo (2002, 2003; Vanden Bergh and de Figueiredo 2003; de Figueiredo and Vanden Bergh 2004).

```
(a)
                    X₁
    ──┼─────┼─────┼─────┼─────┼─────────────┼──
      A     Q    C(H)   J₁    C             H

(b)
                         X₂
    ──┼─────┼─────┼─────┼─────┼──┼──────────┼──
      A     Q    C(H)  J(H)   C  J₂         H
```

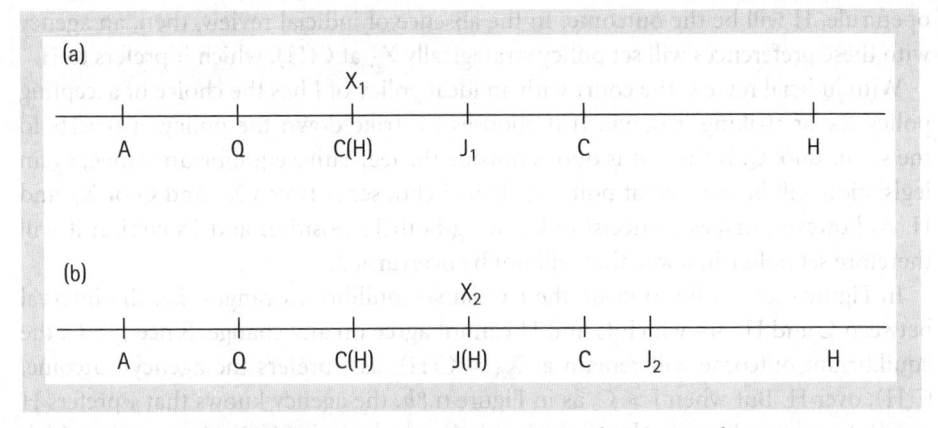

Fig. 11.8 The effect of judicial review on administrative decision-making

This type of analysis, which looks to institutional interaction not to explain one institution but rather to understand the more complete political system, is probably most telling when the dependent variable is policy outcomes. As an illustration of the power of this approach, we discuss Ferejohn and Shipan's (1989, 1990) study of telecommunications policy, which examines the interaction of Congress, the courts, and an administrative agency.

Ferejohn and Shipan's model shows why legislative monitoring of agency actions will often fail to force an agency to change policy. Once Congress has delegated power to an agency, the agency can often exploit its first mover advantage, and make a decision that will not have the support of a majority of the legislature, but nonetheless neither Congress nor the president can alter the agency decision. Because the agency has the power of making the first move, it can choose a position in the gridlock region that elected officials will not be able to overturn, just as in Marks's model of judicial decision-making.[10] But Ferejohn and Shipan also showed that the overall effect of judicial review of administrative decisions is to move policy outcomes back toward the preferences of the congressional median. This effect is illustrated in Figure 11.8a and 11.8b.

A is the position of the Agency, C is the position of the Committee median, and H is the position of the House median. As is common in spatial models, the model assumes that each of these actors prefers policies closer to their position than further away from their position, regardless of the direction of policy. Using this assumption, C(H) is the point to the left of C that is equally distant from C as H is; thus, C(H) is a point at which C is indifferent between it and H.

A's policy discretion allows it to set policy anywhere between C(H) and H, knowing that political officials cannot overturn any decision in this range. When A < C(H), if A sets policy at its own ideal point, new legislation will be enacted, and under an

---

[10] For the purposes of this section, it doesn't matter if the gridlock region is generated involving a mix of veto pivot, filibuster pivot, and the president (à la Krehbiel 1998), the majority party median and floor median in Congress (à la Cox and McCubbins 2005), or the floor median and the committee median (à la Ferejohn and Shipan 1989 or Marks 1988).

open rule, H will be the outcome. In the absence of judicial review, then, an agency with these preferences will set policy strategically X_A at C(H), which it prefers to H.

With judicial review, the court with an ideal policy of J has the choice of accepting policy X_A or striking it down. If it chooses to strike down the policy, it reverts to the status quo, Q. If the status quo is outside the legislative equilibrium range, again legislation will be enacted at point H. Thus J chooses between X_A and Q or X_A and H. A, however, makes its decision knowing both J's position and J's choice; it will therefore set policy in a way that will not be overturned.

In Figure 11.8a, Q lies outside the legislative equilibrium range—i.e. the interval between C and H—in which C and H cannot agree on any change. Since J < C, the equilibrium outcome will remain at X_A = C(H), as J prefers the agency outcome, C(H), over H. But when J > C, as in Figure 11.8b, the agency knows that J prefers H to C(H), and so will strike down any legislation to the left of J(H), the point at which J is indifferent to H. So in Figure 11.8b, the equilibrium outcome is for the agency to choose J(H).

Ferejohn and Shipan show that in every possible permutation, judicial review either has no effect or draws the equilibrium outcome away from A and toward C. This study illustrates how the potential for judicial review influences the interactions between agencies and Congress.

This model also showed how judicial review can draw the policy outcome back towards congressional preferences by mitigating the influence of the presidential veto. The president can veto congressional amendments of agency action, so in effect the president can choose between supporting congressional action and allowing the decision to revert to the agency's decision. This constrains Congress's choice of actions, which in turn broadens the agency's discretionary range. The threat of the judiciary overriding an agency's action has the effect of reducing the agency's range of discretion, and so drawing the equilibrium policy outcome back toward the congressional median. Thus Ferejohn and Shipan showed how judicial action shapes congressional–bureaucratic relations and congressional–presidential relations.

6 CONCLUSIONS

This chapter has surveyed a series of works emphasizing the new separation-of-powers approach to American politics. American politics specialists have always understood the importance of interaction among the branches of government, but until recently, they have not had the technology to study this interaction systematically. Rational choice methods, including game theory and spatial models, provide a means of studying this interaction directly. In an important sense, it provides a method of accounting for how differences in one branch affect behavior in another.

An important lesson of the approach is that behavior in each branch is deeply strategic—actors understand that their decisions are part of a complex decision-making process. To further their goals, decision-makers must anticipate reactions by the other branches. This applies to Congress anticipating both a potential presidential veto and judicial statutory interpretation for the president with respect to Senate confirmation of her appointments; for agencies anticipating either coherence or conflict between branches and making policy accordingly; and for the courts with respect to congressional overturning of their statutory and administrative decisions.

Another lesson is the importance of the sequence of decision-making. Actors that move first can often forestall the action of those downstream. Agencies have a range of discretion based on the gridlock region created by the differences between the views in Congress and those of the president. Similarly, Howell (2003) shows how, by carefully choosing the ideological location of the policy in the executive order, the president can assure a more favorable outcome in the subsequent legislative game.

In a real sense, this approach portends a revolution in the study of American politics. It demonstrates that studying the major institutions in isolation is problematic, implying that the study of American politics is moving toward a more synthetic approach. The separation of powers no longer means that each branch acts separately, but rather in a strategic and interactive environment.

Of course, the theory is just developing. Indeed, the inclusion of broader and more sequentially dependent strategies in the new approach has also led, not surprisingly, to a "rollback" in the richness of the interactions between the actors. Models focusing on a single institution explore a wide range of issues and subtleties, including cooperation and conflict with various degrees of incomplete information, hierarchies, and agency relationships. Because the separation-of-powers models require by definition a broader set of players, they have tended to remain with a few exceptions primarily in the realm of so-called complete information spatial models. In other words, increasing richness in the institutional dimension has been perhaps necessarily accompanied by less richness in another. That said, having established a necessary base in more stark theories of institutional interaction, scholars have already fruitfully begun the process of bringing more strategic and informational richness into the study of the American separation-of-powers system (see Chang, de Figueiredo, and Weingast 2001 for a discussion of recent applications in the area of bureaucracy). We expect considerable growth over the coming years.

References

ALDRICH, J. H. 1995. *Why Parties? The Origin and Transformation of Party Politics in America.* Chicago: University of Chicago Press.

BANKS, J. 1989. Agency budgets, cost information and auditing. *American Journal of Political Science*, 33: 670–99.

—— and WEINGAST, B. R. 1992. The political control of bureaucracies under asymmetric information. *American Journal of Political Science*, 36: 509–24.

BAWN, K. 1995. Political control versus expertise: congressional choices about administrative procedures. *American Political Science Review*, 89: 62–73.

BERNSTEIN, M. H. 1955. *Regulating Business by Independent Commission.* Princeton, NJ: Princeton University Press.
BICKEL, A. M. 1986. *The Least Dangerous Branch: The Supreme Court at the Bar of Politics*, 2nd edn. New Haven, Conn.: Yale University Press.
BINDER, S., and MALTZMAN, F. 2002. Senatorial delay in confirming federal judges, 1947–1998. *American Journal of Political Science*, 46: 190–9.
BONFIELD, A. E. 1986. *State Administrative Rule Making.* Boston: Little, Brown.
BOUCHER, R. L., and SEGAL, J. A. 1995. Supreme Court justices as strategic decision makers: aggressive grants and defensive dsenials on the Vinson Court. *Journals of Politics*, 47: 824–37.
CALDEIRA, G. A., WRIGHT J. R., and ZORN, C. J. W. 1999. Sophisticated voting and gate-keeping in the Supreme Court. *Journal of Law, Economics and Organization*, 15: 549–72.
CAMERON, C. 1996. *Veto Bargaining.* New York: Cambridge University Press.
CAMERON, C., COVER, A., and SEGAL, J. 1990. Senate voting on Supreme Court nominees: a neoinstitutional model. *American Political Science Review*, 84: 525–34.
CANES-WRONE, B. 2003. Bureaucratic decisions and the composition of the lower courts. *American Journal of Political Science*, 47: 205–14.
CHANG, K. 2003. *Appointing Central Bankers.* New York: Cambridge University Press.
―― DE FIGUEIREDO, R. J. P., JR., and WEINGAST, B. R. 2001. Rational choice theories of bureaucratic control and performance. In *The Elgar Companion on Public Choice* ed., W. F. Shughart III and L. Razzolini. New York: Edward Elgar.
CHAPPELL, H. W., JR., MCGREGOR, R. R., and VERMILYEA, T. 2005. *Committee Decisions on Monetary Policy: Evidence from Historical Records of the Federal Open Market Committee.* Cambridge, Mass.: MIT Press
COX, G. W., and MCCUBBINS, M. D., 2005. *Setting the Agenda: Responsible Party Government in the U.S. House of Representatives.* Cambridge: Cambridge University Press.
DAHL, R. A. 1957. Decision-making in a democracy: the Supreme Court as a national policymaker. *Journal of Public Law*, 6: 279–95.
DAVIS, K. C. 1978. *Administrative Law Treatise*, vol. i. San Diego, Calif.: Davis KC.
DE FIGUEIREDO, R. J. P., JR. 2002. Electoral competition, political uncertainty and policy insulation. *American Political Science Review*, 96: 321–33.
―― 2003. Endogenous budget institutions and political insulation: why states adopt the item veto. *Journal of Public Economics*, 87: 2677–701.
―― SPILLER, P. T., and URBIZTONDO, S. 1999. An informational perspective on administrative procedures. *Journal of Law, Economics and Organization*, 15: 283–305.
―― and VANDEN BERGH, R. G. 2004 The political economy of state-level administrative procedure acts. *Journal of Law and Economics*, 47: 569–88.
DERTHICK, M., and QUIRK, P. J. 1985. *The Politics of Deregulation.* Washington, DC: Brookings Institution.
EPSTEIN, D., and O'HALLORAN, S. 1994. Administrative procedures, information, and agency discretion. *American Journal of Political Science*, 38: 697–722.
―― ―― 1996. Divided government and the design of administrative procedures: a formal model and empirical test. *Journal of Politics*, 58: 373–97.
―― ―― 1999. *Delegating Powers: A Transaction Cost Politics Approach to Policy Making under Separate Powers.* New York: Cambridge University Press.
EPSTEIN, L., SEGAL, J., and VICTOR, J. N. 2002. Dynamic agenda-setting on the United States Supreme Court: an empirical assessment. *Harvard Journal on Legislation*, 39: 395–433.
FEREJOHN, J. A., and SHIPAN, C. R. 1989. Congressional influence on administrative agencies: a case study of telecommunications policy. In *Congress Reconsidered*, ed. L. C. Dodd and B. I. Oppenheimer, 4th edn. Washington, DC: Congressional Quarterly Press.

_____ 1990. Congressional influence on bureaucracy. *Journal of Law, Economics and Organization*, 6: 1–21.
FISHER, L. 1975. *Presidential Spending Power*. Princeton, NJ: Princeton University Press.
FULLER, L. 1978. Forms and limits of adjudication. *Harvard Law Review*, 92: 353–403.
GAILMARD, S. 2002. Agency expertise, subversion and bureaucratic discretion. *Journal of Law, Economics and Organization*, 18: 536–55.
GELY, R., and SPILLER, P. T. 1992. The political economy of Supreme Court constitutional decisions: the case of Roosevelt's Court-packing plan. *International Review of Law and Economics*, 12: 45–67.
GRIER, K. 1987. Presidential elections and Federal Reserve policy: an empirical test. *Southern Economic Journal*, 54: 475–86.
HAVRILESKY, T. 1995. *The Pressures on American Monetary Policy*, 2nd edn. Dordrecht: Kluwer.
HOWELL, W. 2003. *Power without Persuasion: The Politics of Direct Presidential Action*. Princeton, NJ: Princeton University Press.
HUBER, J. D., and SHIPAN, C. R. 2002. *Deliberate Discretion: The Institutional Origins of Bureaucratic Autonomy in Modern Democracies*. New York: Cambridge University Press.
_____ and PFAHLER, M. 2001. Legislatures and statutory control of the bureaucracy. *American Journal of Political Science*, 45: 330–45.
JACOBI, T. 2005. The senatorial courtesy game: explaining the norm of informal vetoes in "advice and consent" nominations. *Legislative Studies Quarterly*, Vol. XXX, May: 193, 218.
KEECH, W. R., and MORRIS, I. L. 1997. Appointments, presidential power, and the Federal Reserve. *Journal of Macroeconomics*, 19: 253–67.
KIEWIET, D. R., and McCUBBINS, M. 1988. Presidential Influence on congressional appropriation decisions. *American Journal of Political Science*, 32: 713–36.
_____ 1991. *The Logic of Delegation: Congressional Parties and the Appropriations Process*. Chicago: University of Chicago Press.
KREHBIEL, K. 1998. *Pivotal Politics*. Chicago: University of Chicago Press.
LUPIA, A. D., and McCUBBINS, M. D. 1994. Designing bureaucratic accountability. *Law and Contemporary Problems*, 57: 91–126.
McCARTY, N. 2004. The appointments dilemma. *American Journal of Political Science*, 48: 413–28.
McCLOSKEY, R. G. 1960. *The American Supreme Court*. Chicago: University of Chicago Press.
McCUBBINS, M. D. 1990. Party governance and U.S. budget deficits: divided government and fiscal stalemate. In *Politics and Economics in the Eighties*, ed. A. Alesina and G. Carliner. Chicago: University of Chicago Press.
_____ NOLL, R., and WEINGAST, B. R. 1987. Administrative procedures as instruments of political control. *Journal of Law, Economics and Organization*, 3: 243–77.
_____ 1989. Structure and process, politics and policy: administrative arrangements and the political control of agencies. *Virginia Law Review*, 75: 431–82.
_____ and SCHWARTZ, T. 1984. Congressional oversight overlooked: police patrols vs. fire alarms. *American Journal of Political Science Review*, 28: 165–79.
MALTZMAN, F., SPRIGGS, J. F., II, and WAHLBECK, P. J. 1999. Strategy and judicial choice: new institutionalist approaches to supreme court decision-making. In *Supreme Court Decision-Making: New Institutionalist Approaches*, ed. C. W. Clayton and H. Gillman. Chicago: University of Chicago Press.
MARCH, J. G., and SIMON, H. 1958. *Organizations*. New York: Wiley.
MARKS, B. A. 1998. A model of judicial influence on congressional policy-making: Grove City College v. Bell. Unpublished Hoover working paper manuscript, Stanford, Calf.
MILLS, C. W. 1956. *The Power Elite*. Oxford: Oxford University Press.

Moe, T. M. 1984. The new economics of organizations. *American Journal of Political Science*, 28: 739–77.
—— 1985. The control and feedback in economic regulation: the case of the NLRB. *American Political Science Review*, 79: 1094–116.
Moe, T. M. 1987. Interests, institutions, and positive theory: the politics of the NLRB. *Studies in American Political Development*, 2: 236–99.
—— 1990. The politics of structural choice: towards a theory of public bureaucracy. In *Organization Theory: From Chester Barnard to the Present and Beyond*, ed. O. E. Williamson. Berkeley: University of California Press.
Moraski, B., and Shipan, C. 1999. The politics of Supreme Court nominations: a theory of institutional constraints and choices. *American Journal of Political Science*, 43: 1069–95.
Niskanen, W. 1971. *Bureaucracy and Representative Government*. Chicago: Aldine Press.
Nokken, T. P., and Sala, B. J. 2000. Confirmation dynamics: presidential appointments to independent agencies, 1953–1988. *Journal of Theoretical Politics*, 12: 91–112.
Peltzman, S. 1976. Toward a more general theory of regulation. *Journal of Law and Economics*, 19: 211–40.
Romer, T., and Rosenthal, H. 1978. Political resource allocation, controlled agendas, and the status quo. *Public Choice*, 33: 27–43.
Rosenberg, G. N. 1991. *The Hollow Hope: Can Courts Bring about Social Change?* Chicago: University of Chicago Press.
Schubert, G. 1962. Policy without law: an extension of the certiorari game. *Stanford Law Review*, 14: 284–327.
Segal, J. A. 1997. Separation of powers games in the positive theory of Congress and the courts. *American Political Science Review*, 91: 28–44.
—— and Spaeth, H. J. 1993. *The Supreme Court and the Attitudinal Model*. New York: Cambridge University Press.
—— Cameron, C., and Cover, A. 1992. A spatial model of roll-call voting: services, constituents, president, and interest groups and Supreme Court confirmations. *American Journal of Political Science*, 36: 96–121.
Selznick, P. 1948. Foundations of the theory of organization. *American Sociological Review*, 13: 25–35.
Shapiro, M. 1982. *Who Guards the Guardians?* Athens: University of Georgia Press.
Simon, H. A. 1947. *Administrative Behavior*. New York: Macmillan.
Snyder, S. K., and Weingast, B. R. 2000. The American system of shared powers: the president, Congress, and the NLRB. *Journal of Law, Economics and Organization*, 16: 269–305.
Spiller, P., and Tiller, E. 1996. Invitations to override: congressional reversals of Supreme Court decisions. *International Review of Law and Economics*, 16: 503–21.
Stigler, G. 1971. The theory of economic regulation. *Bell Journal of Economics*, 2: 3–21.
Vanden Bergh, R. G., and de Figueiredo, R. J. P., Jr. 2003. Political uncertainty and administrative procedures. In *Uncertainty in American Politics*, ed. B. Burden. Cambridge: Cambridge University Press.
Weingast, B. R., and Moran, M. J. 1983. Bureaucratic discretion or congressional control: regulatory policymaking by the FTC. *Journal of Political Economy*, 91: 765–800.
Wildavsky, A. 1964. *Politics of the Budgetary Process*. Boston: Little, Brown.
Wilson, J. Q. 1980. *The Politics of Regulation*. New York: Basic Books.
—— 1989. *Bureaucracy: What Government Agencies Do and Why They Do It*. New York: Basic Books.

CHAPTER 12

PIVOTS

KEITH KREHBIEL

INSTITUTIONAL analysis of political behavior is increasingly common in political economy and political science. In its most complete form, such analysis begins with a blend of substantive knowledge, good instincts, or possibly just lucky guesses, about which constitutional, legal, or organizational features politicians regard as constraining their behavior. Constraints are then characterized in a game form, an equilibrium concept is specified, the game is solved, predictions are derived, and tests are conducted. *Comparative institutional analysis* is a logical extension in which a common political setting—such as a legislature—is studied by juxtaposing and testing the predictions of two or more institutional theories.

Pivot theories are increasingly common in such research. Their key characteristics can be classified as exogenous (assumed) or endogenous (derived). Exogenous features include preferences, players, policy space, and a *status quo point*: a policy that remains in effect if no other policy displaces it in the course of decision-making. Endogenous features include statements of equilibrium behavior, characterization of stable outcomes, and identification of a corresponding *gridlock interval*: a set of potential status quo points where in the status quo policy does not change in equilibrium even though a majority of voters prefers change. Once solved, pivot theories earn their adjective by focusing on *pivot points* (or simply *pivots*): the preferences and identities of a subset of players who, in equilibrium and for some status quo point(s), are crucial in the outcome.[1]

This chapter has two objectives: to provide an accessible overview of pivot theories, and to develop and illustrate a new form of comparative institutional analysis as a means for discriminating between such theories. Although in principle the substantive focus could be on any collective choice organization, in practice more

---

* Discussions with Nolan McCarty and Jon Woon and comments from Brian Crisp, Ken Shepsle, Barry Weingast, and Donald Wittman are gratefully acknowledged.

[1] Increasingly precise notions of *crucial* are given below.

pivot theories have been developed to study US national decision-making than other types of decision-making. Consequently, the substantive motivation and empirical application center on US politics.

1 A Baseline: Median Voter Theory

The simplest pivot theory is undoubtedly the well-known median voter theory (Black 1958).[2] In the present context, the median voter model has several noteworthy charcteristics that make it a useful baseline against which to compare alternative models. First, because the final collective choice in this model is always the policy corresponding with the most preferred policy (or ideal point) of the median voter, the status quo has no effect on outcomes. Second, the median voter is always pivotal: that is, he is not only a member of all winning coalitions but also a necessary and sufficient member of all minimum winning coalitions. Third, gridlock never occurs: that is, new policies are passed whenever there exists a majority favoring such passage. Finally, although the median voter can be seen as a pivot theory, it should be viewed as a special case inasmuch as none of these results hold once institutional details are added to the framework.

2 Super-majority Pivots: The Pivotal Politics Theory

The pivotal politics model as introduced (Krehbiel 1996) and elaborated (Brady and Volden 1998; Krehbiel 1998; Wawro and Schickler 2004) embraces US national law-making as its substantive focus.[3] Previously, a rich tradition of scholarship had addressed the consequences, or perhaps lack thereof, associated with the increasingly regular pattern in US politics of split party control in the executive and legislative branches. The conventional wisdom was that the ostensibly increasing tendency for policy stalemate—*gridlock* in the vernacular of the 1980s and 1990s—was predominantly attributable to divided government. For example, when a Republican president confronted a Democratic Congress, as was common in the post-Second World War period, it seemed only natural that Democrats would dig in their heels to impede, if not deny, enactment of the president's agenda. In contrast, when party control is unified across branches of government, Congress is supportive rather than resistant to presidential initiatives, so major policy change can occur. Or, so it was said.

[2] The standard model assumes a unidimensional choice space, single-peaked preferences, an odd number of voters, simple-majority voting, and an open amendment procedure. These assumptions will likewise hold for other pivot theories to be considered.
[3] See also Mo 2001 and Nacif 2003 for applications in Korea and Mexico, respectively.

Conventional wisdom is meant to be challenged, and few if any scholars of the US political system have amassed a more impressive set of challenges to received wisdom than David Mayhew. In his 1991 tour de force *Divided We Govern*, Mayhew executed a novel, laborious, and deeply insightful research design to address the question: does it matter much whether the government is divided or unified? In terms of passing major legislation (coded subjectively but convincingly), the answer was an emphatic "no." Governing regimes in US politics invariably need to exert substantial effort to overcome various obstacles to policy-making, but, as an empirical matter, this is true in unified as well as divided government. Moreover, when the natural propensity for gridlock is overcome, the winning coalitions credited for such achievements are almost invariably larger than minimum majority in size and thus bipartisan in composition.

In this context, two stylized facts served as the impetus for the development of the pivotal politics theory of law-making. First, why is gridlock common and seemingly independent of party control? Second, why, when gridlock ceases to exist, are winning coalitions large and bipartisan? The answer offered by pivotal politics theory fits in a nutshell with room to spare: super-majoritarianism. Its concrete manifestations and analytic characterizations are somewhat more intricate but, nevertheless, can be made transparent to anyone with a basic grasp of spatial voting models.

Borrowing from median voter theory, the pivotal politics model postulates that, for any given issue the government may consider, a single, primary dimension is sufficient for representing decision-makers' essential conflicting interests. Formally, each player (legislators in a unicameral law-making body plus a president) has symmetric, single-peaked preferences over a unidimensional policy space, $x \in R$. These assumptions on preferences have been common, beginning with the median voter theory and extending through the important movement of "new institutionalism" pioneered by Shepsle (1979) and his colleagues (e.g. Denzau and Mackay 1983; Shepsle and Weingast 1987). Also common has been the assumption that, on any given dimension, there exists an exogenous status quo point, q, which represents the policy outcome in the event that the players of the game fail to come to an agreement on the new policy, x.

The pivotal politics theory deviates from its predecessors in its specification of voting rules. A noteworthy feature of the US Senate is its conferral, first by precedent and eventually codified in its standing rules, of the right of any of its individuals to engage in "extended debate," i.e. to filibuster. Depending upon the period of history studied, such rights effectively raised the voting threshold for law-making activity from a simple majority standard of $(n + 1)/2$ to a super-majority standard of 3/5 or 2/3. (For present purposes, we will confine attention to the contemporary case of 3/5 cloture.) Furthermore, the pivotal politics theory puts the president into the law-making equation in a similarly super-majoritarian way. In this instance, the justification lies in the US Constitution. The president's signature is a sufficient condition for policy change on any legislation Congress passes, but, in the absence of the president's signature, legislation either fails or requires a veto override by two-third majorities in the legislative body.

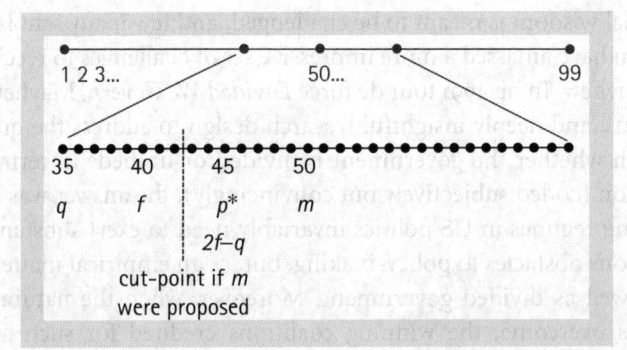

```
    •————————————•————————————•
    1 2 3...           50...            99

    •••••••••••|•••••••••••••••••••
    35    40    45    50
    q     f    p*    m
              |
              2f−q
         cut-point if m
         were proposed
```

Fig. 12.1 Cloture super-majoritarianism makes f pivotal

Whereas prior spatial models relied upon constraints on amendment activity to obtain results different from those of median voter theory,[4] the incorporation of super-majoritarian voting rules in pivotal politics theory is consequential even in the absence of such constraints. Figure 12.1 illustrates the central intuition, which is generalized and illustrated more completely in Figure 12.2. Suppose there are ninety-nine legislators distributed uniformly over the interval [1, 99]. Suppose also that the collective choice the last time government considered the issue in question was $q = 35$. Clearly, a majority coalition exists that would like to move the policy to the point $x = 50$, the median voter's ideal point. If this were attempted, however, every legislator whose ideal point lies to the left of 42.5 (the midpoint between 35 and 50) has an incentive not to let the policy proceed to a vote. Armed with the right to filibuster the bill, these legislators have a credible threat. The only way to proceed is to invoke cloture, which, according to contemporary Senate rules, requires a 3/5 vote. The question from the perspective of the proponents of a rightward shift in policy becomes: by how much can the proposed bill exceed the status quo and yet persuade the pivotal voter on cloture to cast his vote in favor of closing debate?

The identity of the filibuster pivot f is determined by the cloture rule. Specifically, the filibuster pivot in this 99-person scenario is the 40th voter from the left and whose ideal point equals 40.[5] If he votes to invoke cloture, the filibuster is terminated by a vote of 60–39 > 3/5. If he votes against the cloture motion, however, the filibuster persists by a vote of 59–40 < 3/5. Given this fact, and a somewhat more subtle fact that the filibuster pivot—so defined—has interests congruent with the thirty-nine legislators to his left in this scenario, the optimal proposal strategy of any bill proponent is 45.

---

[4] For example, Romer and Rosenthal 1978 characterized an agenda setter as a first-stage player who crafts a proposal for an electorate that is restricted to accepting or rejecting the single proposal (and where rejection is tacit acceptance of an exogenous status quo). This is, in effect, the denial of amendment rights to the second-stage players, i.e. a closed rule. Shepsle and Weingast 1987 impose similar constraints in the legislative context, but subsequent to open-rule consideration on the floor.

[5] A common error is to designate the 40th voter in the US Senate as the filibuster pivot because, with N = 100, a 60–40 vote invokes cloture. However, then the Senate's filibuster pivot is actually the 41st voter (the 60th from the right), because hers is the last, and thus pivotal, vote needed for the cloture motion to carry. I use N = 99 in the example only because it simplifies matters to have a unique median of 50.

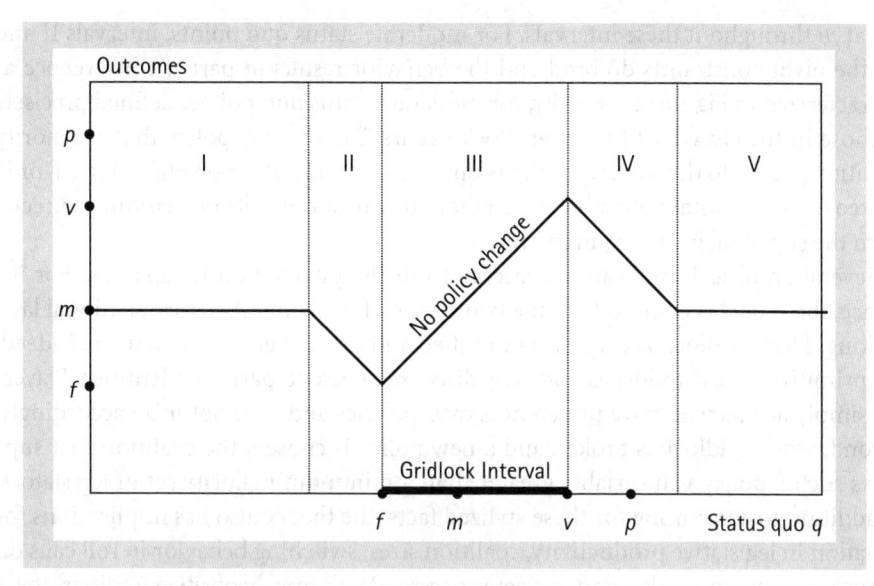

Fig. 12.2 Equilibrium in the pivotal politics theory

It is merely an analytic convenience that the proposer is the median voter. Any right-of-median voter would make the same proposal because he or she faces the same optimization problem: to make the filibuster pivot indifferent between the optimal proposal p^* and the status quo q. Any proposal less than 45 is not optimal for such proposers because it fails to extract all available rents. Any proposal more than 45 is not optimal for such proposers because it triggers a successful filibuster and leaves the undesirable status quo point in effect. Only with $x = 45$ is there no alternative proposal that can both beat a filibuster and gain a majority. Therefore, the equilibrium proposal in such cases is, in general, $2f - q$.

From the opposite end of the spectrum—that is, a status quo point that lies on the upper end of the spectrum—the president and the veto pivot (the 66th legislator in this scenario) are the constraints against which bill proponents optimize. Dispensing with an example, suffice it to say the equilibrium proposal is $2v - q$.[6]

With only a couple of qualifications, these two examples of pivotal voters serve effectively as building blocks for the complete statement of equilibrium in the pivotal politics game. Figure 12.2 graphs all possible equilibrium outcomes (vertical axis) as a function of variable status quo points and fixed ideal points (horizontal axis). As many as five types of behavior occur in the model, defined in terms of the extremity of the status quo relative to pivotal legislators' ideal points. For status quo points in the most extreme intervals, I and V, the super-majoritarian constraint does not bind proposal-making, and the median voter outcome results. Therefore, the graph is

---

[6] This example assumes that the president's ideal point p is greater than 66. Substitute p for v otherwise. Formally, the game is multistage, finite, and complete information in structure. As an analytic convenience, it suffices to focus on the behavior of at most four players: the median voter, a president, a 2/3 veto pivotal voter on the president's side of the median, and a 3/5 filibuster pivot on the side of the median opposite the president (see Krehbiel 1996)

flat at m throughout these intervals. For moderate status quo points, intervals II and IV, the pivot constraints do bind and the behavior results in partial convergence as characterized in Figure 12.1. Finally, for moderate status quo points, defined precisely as those in the closed set $[f, v]$, gridlock occurs. That is, any policy that a majority coalition prefers to the status quo elicits opposition of one of the pivotal voters, f or v. Moreover, the pivotal voters have a credible threat of opposition stemming directly from the super-majority requirement.

Several empirical implications emerge from the pivotal politics analysis. For instance, the model accommodates the two stylized facts about American national law-making. First, gridlock is common in unified and divided government alike. Indeed, the primitives of the model exclude any direct reference to partisan identities. Players are simply agents who have preferences over policies and who optimize accordingly. Second, when gridlock is broken and a new policy is chosen, the coalition that supports such a policy is invariably greater than a minimum majority set of legislators. In addition to accounting for these stylized facts, the theory also has implications for variation in legislative productivity, coalition sizes, switching behavior in roll calls on cloture and veto overrides, and budget processes. With mostly positive findings, these predictions are explored extensively in Krehbiel (1998) and Brady and Volden (1998).

However, the pivotal politics theory is also subject to widespread criticism, with two sins of omission drawing the most attention. First, the theory strays from the new institutionalism tradition of legislative modeling based on assumptions about restrictive amendment procedures and agenda-setting by preference outliers. Second, the theory is deafeningly silent about political parties.

3 PARTY PIVOTS: THE PROCEDURAL CARTEL THEORY

Attributed to John Dingell, the former and formidable chairman of the House Committee on Energy and Commerce, a favorite quotation of congressional scholars is: "You take substance and give me procedure, and I'll screw you every time." In this vein, it is not surprising that students of legislative behavior are sensitive to the many ways in which institutional features can give rise to outcome-consequential strategic behavior. Nor is it surprising that procedural control and partisan motivations regularly go hand in hand. So, for example, in an industrious research agenda spanning more than a decade, Gary Cox and Matthew McCubbins have been at the forefront of efforts to advance the thesis that, through procedures, the majority party is the dominant entity in legislative politics, both in the USA and abroad. The foundational model on which the thesis is built is called *procedural cartel theory* which—while presented as a much different substantive model of law-making from median voter or pivotal politics theory—nevertheless satisfies the defining analytical features of pivot theories.

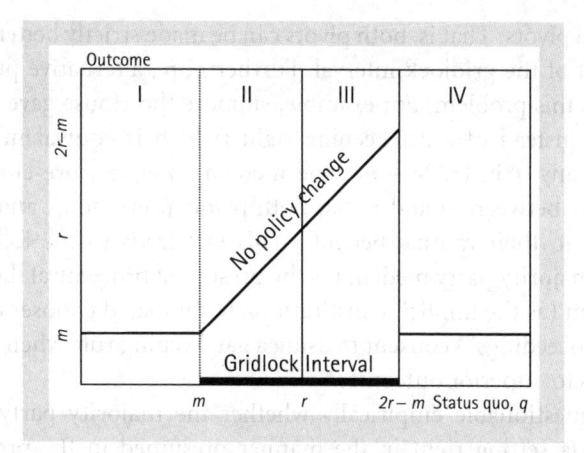

Fig. 12.3 Equilibrium in the procedural cartel theory

Consider analytics first. The core model in Cox and McCubbins's (2005) *Setting the Agenda* is clearly recognizable as the gatekeeping model of Denzau and Mackay (1983). Much as the pivotal politics theory is reducible to four players and four stages, the Denzau–Mackay/Cox–McCubbins theory is reducible to two players and two stages. In stage one, an agenda-setter denoted by r—e.g. the Republicans' median voter—has "unconditional agenda power," by which the authors mean the ability to block any and all attempts to change the exogenous status quo. In stage two, if and only if a stage-one bill is proposed, the full legislature selects the median voter's ideal point under an open rule. The gatekeeping assumption has an immediate implication: a necessary condition for policy change is that a *majority of the majority party* prefers the legislature's median voter's ideal point to the status quo. Conversely, gridlock prevails whenever this condition is not met.

Figure 12.3 illustrates the equilibrium of the gatekeeping model in parallel fashion with the pivotal politics diagram in Figure 12.2. Clearly, the majority party median, r, resembles the pivotal voters f and v in pivotal politics theory. His consent, like that of the veto or filibuster pivot, is a necessary and sufficient condition for policy change.

Although the party cartel theory satisfies the generic features of pivot theories, several distinctions between it and the earlier pivotal politics model are subjects of ongoing debate in the field.

First, the procedural pivot (i.e. majority party gatekeeper) in the cartel model is *not* in general indifferent between the final policy (the legislative median) and the status quo, as is often the case for pivots in the pivotal-politics model. This observation follows from the fact that the majority party median r is not a constraint against which other players optimize but rather plays the role of dictatorial obstructionist whenever the status quo lies within $|r - m|$ units of his ideal point, r.

Second, like the pivotal politics theory, the procedural cartel theory also provides an account for gridlock. However, within the cartel theory's relatively large range of status quo points that cannot be changed in equilibrium—namely, those in $(m, 2r - m)$—half of these policies $(r, 2r - m)$ are not Pareto optimal with respect to the two potential pivots. That is, both pivots can be made strictly better off by policies in the other half of the gridlock interval. Furthermore, alternative procedures exist that can address this problem. For example, suppose the House gave the committee an *ex post* veto instead of a gatekeeping right (which is equivalent to an *ex ante* veto). Then for any q in $(r, 2r - m)$, the median voter can pre-empt the veto by selecting a policy between m and r that both pivots prefer to q, and such a policy will be adopted to their mutual benefit.[7] This fact leads to the following puzzle: why would the majority party median (as the presumed procedural dictator) and the legislative median (as the implicit constitutionally stipulated chooser of "the rules of [the House's] proceedings") consent to using a gatekeeping rule when other available rules lead to Pareto-superior outcomes?[8]

Third, it is questionable empirically whether the majority party in fact has a monopoly agenda setting right in the manner presumed in the procedural cartel theory. If *codified* procedures are consulted, the assumption of an institutionalized majority party gatekeeping right is difficult to defend. Under Rule XV of the House, for example, a simple majority of the House can discharge legislation from obstructionists or so-called gatekeepers. In the Senate, the roughly comparable procedural mechanism is for an individual to propose a non-germane amendment to legislation before the body.

Finally, the designated gridlock interval in the party cartel theory is distinctively lopsided relative to the legislative median. Gridlock favors the majority party at the expense not only of the minority party but also the chamber median voter. Yet, the theory predicts that in *all* observable instances of successful law-making, the outcome is the *legislative* median, not the *majority party* median. For policies to be non-centrist, therefore, depends crucially upon a historical path in which erstwhile median outcomes somehow become stuck away from the center and within the current-period gridlock interval. This inescapable historical endogeneity of the status quo is a critical concern below.

4 COMPARATIVE EMPIRICAL ANALYSIS

A recent and instructive instance of comparative institutional analyis focuses on two of the three pivot models reviewed above. In order to test the procedural cartel and median voter models "head to head," Cox and McCubbins (2005, ch. 3) advocate empirical analysis of *roll rates*. A party is said to be rolled when a majority of its members vote against a measure, a majority of the opposite party's members vote for a measure, and the measure is enacted.[9] The rate at which a party is rolled, therefore,

---

[7] The optimal such proposal is $b = 2r - q$. This is an instance of the Romer–Rosenthal model (1978).
[8] Crombez, Krehbiel, and Groseclose 2006 generalize this argument.
[9] In principle, enactment is not a necessary condition for a roll to occur. In practice, however, the authors confine their attention to votes on final passage. They defend this choice on grounds that such votes uniquely and clearly represent binary choices between the exogenous status quo and the proposal

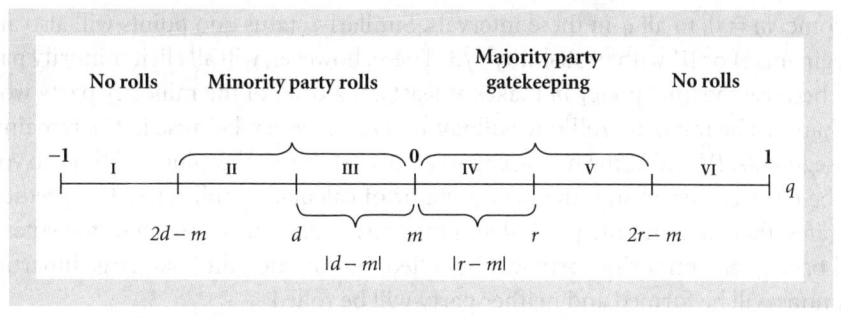

![Figure showing number line from -1 to 1 with segments I-VI, labeled "No rolls", "Minority party rolls", "Majority party gatekeeping", "No rolls" across the top, and markers at 2d−m, d, m, r, 2r−m with brackets |d−m| and |r−m|]

Fig. 12.4 Roll rate dependence on the distribution of the status quo

is defined as the proportion of final-passage roll calls on which these conditions are met. A party with a low roll rate is presumed to have agenda power, while, conversely, a party that is rolled often is said to be weak.

An immediate implication of the procedural cartel model is that a rational gatekeeper, in this case the majority party, is *never* rolled. Consequently its roll rate should be constant and zero. The minority party is expected to be rolled regularly because it has no presumed gatekeeping rights. In contrast, the median voter model, which Cox and McCubbins call the "floor agenda model," implies that roll rates for each party will be a function of the distance between that party's median voter and the legislature's median voter. Cox and McCubbins then attempt to explain variation in roll rates via regression analysis. Let r and d respectively denote the majority and minority party medians, respectively. They estimate regressions of the form:

$$\text{Minority roll rate} = \alpha + \beta|d - m| + \varepsilon. \tag{1}$$

$$\text{Majority roll rate} = \alpha + \gamma|r - m| + \varepsilon. \tag{2}$$

The logic of the test is illustrated in Figure 12.4. Assume that at any given law-making opportunity, legislators' ideal points are spread out over a finite interval, say $[-1, 1]$. For ease of illustration, suppose the median of the minority party is $d = -1/3$, the chamber median is $m = 0$, and the majority party median is $r = 1/3$. Reflection points[10] of the two parties therefore lie at $-2/3$ and $2/3$, and the policy space is conveniently partitioned into six segments, I–VI.

Clearly, predicting roll rates under the cartel theory (or any given pivot model) requires assumptions about the *distribution of status quo points*. In the simplest case, suppose q is distributed uniformly over $[-1, 1]$. Then status quo points will arise in segments I or VI with probability $1/6 + 1/6 = 1/3$. None of these status quo points elicit rolls, because majorities of both parties prefer the cartel-theoretic equilibrium

---

as possibly amended. Accordingly, such votes are regarded as more appropriate grounds for inference than would be, say, procedural votes, frivolous amendments, etc.

[10] A reflection point of, say, a party median p with respect to the chamber median m, denoted $R(p, m)$, is the point whose distance from p equals that between p and m but that lies on the non-m side of p. With distance-based (Euclidean) preferences, $R(p, m) = 2p - m$. By construction the pivotal player with ideal point p is indifferent between m and its reflection point about p, i.e. $R(p, m)$.

outcome, $m = 0$, to all q in these intervals. Similarly, status quo points will also arise in segments II or III with probability 1/3. These, however, will all elicit minority party rolls because the final policy m makes at least a majority of the minority party worse off than q. The minority roll rate will *not* be 1/3, however, because in the remaining two segments, IV and V, the majority party will exercise gatekeeping and thus no votes will be observed or go into the denominator of calculating roll rates. The predicted roll rates, then, are: minority = 1/2 and majority = 0. That is, on half of the votes on final passage the minority party will be rolled, but on the other half large bipartisan coalitions will be formed and neither party will be rolled.

With this example—and its corresponding assumption of a fixed, uniform, exogenous distribution of status quo points—it is easy to see how an expansion of the distance between the minority median and chamber median $|d - m|$ increases the minority party roll rate and, therefore, rationalizes the prediction in equation (1) that $\beta > 0$. It is likewise easy to see that a change in the extremity of the majority party median $|r - m|$ affects the majority party's incidence of gatekeeping but not its constant-zero roll rate; therefore, the prediction in equation (2) is that $\gamma = 0$. But finally, it should also be abundantly clear that the distribution of status quo points is absolutely essential to deriving these predictions. If the distribution were, for example, asymmetric rather than symmetric, variable over time, or normal rather than uniform, knowledge about what the theory predicts declines precipitously.

A few miscellaneous points have a bearing on comparative institutional analysis using roll rate data. First, under the median voter theory, both β and γ should be positive. Second, the pivotal politics theory does not make predictions in the regression framework with these variables because party medians play no role in that theory. Third, cartel theory also implies that the constant terms, a, in the equations should not be significantly different from zero. Finally, the empirical plausibility of the assumption of fixed, exogenous, constant, and uniformly distributed status quo points for each Congress is questionable. Among the many objections that might be raised, the main cause for concern here is that this framework, in effect, defies history. That is, no matter what laws the Congress at time t enacts, the succeeding Congress at time $t + 1$ is presumed to begin with a new history-independent distribution of status quo points.[11]

Two of Cox and McCubbins's findings comport with the stated expectations for the cartel agenda model. The estimate of β is positive and significant. The estimate of γ is positive and insignificant. However, both constant terms are *negative* and significantly different from zero, and the pseudo-R^2 measures are low (.037 and .052).[12] Overall, the hypothesized preference variables fail to account for much variation in roll rates, and the degree of discrimination between the two theories is not sharp. As a probable cause for this the lack of discrimination in the tests, we next revisit the issue of how status quo points are generated.

[11] Cox and McCubbins do not necessarily assume uniformly distributed status quo points, but their analysis does not address the history-independence problem.
[12] See, for example, Cox and McCubbins 2005, table 5.2, and the surrounding text.

5 Endogenous Status Quo Points

The limitations of prior comparative institutional analyses underscore the need for an explicit status-quo-generating framework. Such an approach not only can place institutional models on equal footing but also may obtain sharper and more discriminating predictions than prior approaches. The framework described below integrates four components:

- actual data on legislators' preferences,
- a presumption that a well-specified pivot theory is in effect (namely, median voter, pivotal politics, or procedural cartel),
- a generally applicable stochastic model that relies on the focal theory to generate endogenously the distribution of status quo points for the next Congress,
- actual data on roll rates, that is, the proportion of roll calls on which a party is on the losing side of a winning coalition.

The method performs calculations and evaluates data Congress by Congress. Its distinctive feature is that when any given Congress commences, the distribution of status quo points it addresses is *not* arbitrary, atheoretical, or exogenously imposed as is customary in most prior tests. Rather, each Congress inherits its unique distribution of status quo points from the stochastically shocked equilibrium outcomes of the previous Congress. Given an endogenously derived distribution of status quo points along with preference measures of relevant medians and pivots, expected roll rates compatible with the focal theory are calculated.[13] These expected roll rates are then compared with actual roll rates using a minimum sum-of-squared-errors criterion. Finally, different theories are compared in terms of their ability to account for roll rates. More precisely and formally, the procedure is as follows.

1. Postulate a model of stochastic status quo points as a function of prior equilibrium policies, namely, $q_t = x^*_{t-1} + \varepsilon$ where q_t is the status quo at time t, x^*_{t-1} is an equilibrium policy from the prior period, and ε is a random variable distributed uniformly or normally with mean = 0 and variance to be specified (and adjusted for robustness checks).
2. Begin with a neutral policy seed x^*_0 centered on the historic average of chamber preferences, and apply the status quo model to generate a distribution of status quo points for period 1.
3. Incorporate real-world data (DW-NOMINATE scores[14]) to identify pivot points for each congress in the time series. For roll rate analysis, record the majority and minority party medians as well.
4. For each theory under consideration, indexed $j \in \{M, C, P\}$ for median voter, procedural cartel, and pivotal politics, respectively, and for each Congress t in the time series,

---

[13] The calculations parallel those discussed above and illustrated in Figure 12.4.
[14] Under the assumptions identified in Poole and Rosenthal (2000) these data are comparable over time.

Table 12.1 Average observed roll rates, 80th–99th Congresses

	Majority	Minority
House	0.02	0.26
Senate	0.04	0.20

(a) Use the theory to calculate equilibrium outcomes $x_j^*(q_t)$ for each bin or interval in the policy space for which q_t has non-zero mass.[15]

(b) Calculate the corresponding predicted proportions of minority party rolls $\hat{y}_{t,j}$ and majority party rolls $\hat{z}_{t,j}$.

(c) Reapply the model of stochastic status quo points to x_t^* to derive q_{t+1}.

5. Conduct comparative institutional analysis by assessing the relative abilities of theories to predict actual party rolls. Specifically, define the *sum of squared roll rate errors* (SSRE) for theory j as:

$$SSRE_j = \sum_{t=80}^{N} \left[(y_t - \hat{y}_{t,j})^2 + (z_t - \hat{z}_{t,j})^2 \right],$$

where y_t and z_t are the actual observed minority and majority party roll rates.[16]

6 Findings

Findings are summarized in three tables and a figure. Table 12.1 reports minority and majority roll rates for both houses in the Congress. As noted elsewhere (Groseclose and Snyder 2003; Cox and McCubbins 2005), proportions of minority rolls exceed majority rolls by a large margin, and this asymmetry seems to support the procedural cartel theory over the median voter and pivotal politics theories. Such inferences are questionable, however, in the absence of a baseline model that clarifies expectations. Consider two such models: *symmetric bipartisanship* and *majority party dominance*. In the first instance, assume that each party rolls the other exactly one-half of the time. In the second instance, assume that the majority party always rolls the minority party. Table 12.2 reports computations of the sum of squared roll

---

[15] To simplify calculations significantly, we move from a continuous choice space to a fine-grained discrete choice space by partitioning the preference and policy space into narrow bins. Specifically, for measures of preferences such as DW-NOMINATE ratings in $[-1, 1]$, a bin width of .05 produces a 41-bin partition (centered on 0, i.e. the center bin is $(-.025, .025)$) in which all ideal points lie, pivots can be identified, roll rate predictions can be derived, etc.

[16] The procedure is implemented in a MATLAB program written by Jon Woon. Code and documentation are available upon request.

Table 12.2 Sum of squared roll rate errors of baseline models

	Symmetric bipartisanship $\hat{y} = \hat{z} = .5$	Majority dominance $\hat{y} = 0; \hat{z} = .1$
House	7.85	14.40
Senate	6.50	13.36

rate errors in actual data relative to these polar baseline models. The result is the opposite of that suggested in Table 12.1. In the House and Senate alike, the symmetric-bipartisanship baseline fits the data much better than the majority-party dominance baseline, with the latter generating approximately twice as much the error as the former.

Tables 12.1 and 12.2 are both somewhat misleading, however, for approximately opposite reasons. Table 12.1 fails to specify baseline expectations and thereby gives rise to inferences that overstate asymmetry. Table 12.2 is based on baseline expectations that are either perfectly symmetric or completely asymmetric and then aggregates data in a way that masks underlying asymmetry. So, although the symmetric-bipartisan baseline more closely approximates the data overall, the majority party dominance baseline provides better account for cross party differences in roll rates.

The more important aim of the present analysis, however, concerns the three theoretically derived sets of expectations embedded in the endogenous status quo procedure. The results are mixed, but some interesting, stark, and heretofore undiscovered patterns emerge. Table 12.3 subdivides the findings along several dimensions: House versus Senate, uniform versus binomial-normal distributions of the shock parameter, median versus cartel versus pivot theories, and finally, the theories' sum of squared roll rate errors for the minority party, the majority party, and both parties combined. Likewise, Figure 12.5 summarizes these data graphically.[17]

Perhaps the most striking finding is the imbalanced performance of the procedural cartel theory. For majority party rolls, it is invariably the best of the three models (columns 4–6). The reason is transparent: the cartel theory predicts no majority

---

[17] The horizontal axes in Figure 12.5 are denominated by the numbers of bins into which an equilibrium outcome at time t can be shocked to generate a status quo at time $t+1$. For example, a maximum range of 41 means that the equilibrium policy in the current period could be moved as far as 20 bins to the left or 20 bins to the right as the status quo for the next period, which is approximately half the range of legislators' DW-NOMINATE ratings. Notice, however, that in the binomial approximations of the normal distribution, while the range in this scenario is the same as in the case of the uniform distribution, the variance will be considerably smaller because of the unimodality. Consequently, for any point x on the horizontal axis of the left-hand-side figures, the actual variance is greater than the corresponding point x on the right-hand-side figures.

Table 12.3 Comparative analysis of three models using the endogenous status quo method

			Minority Rolls			Majority Rolls			Combined		
Chamber	Dist.	Var.	(1) Median	(2) Cartel	(3) Pivot	(4) Median	(5) Cartel	(6) Pivot	(7) Median	(8) Cartel	(9) Pivot
House	Uniform	L	2.95 1	10.97 3	4.37 2	4.97 2	0.01 1	5.26 3	7.91 1	10.98 3	9.63 2
House	Uniform	M	1.91 1	6.75 3	1.91 2	4.10 3	0.01 1	3.57 2	6.01 2	6.76 3	5.49 2
House	Uniform	H	0.92 2	2.84 3	0.66 1	2.25 3	0.01 1	1.67 2	3.16 3	2.85 2	2.33 2
House	Normal	L	4.97 1	13.82 3	8.24 2	5.60 2	0.01 1	7.24 3	10.57 1	13.83 2	15.48 3
House	Normal	M	4.42 1	13.03 3	6.86 2	5.35 2	0.01 1	6.31 3	9.77 1	13.04 2	13.17 3
House	Normal	H	4.05 1	12.45 3	5.92 2	5.22 2	0.01 1	5.84 3	9.27 1	12.47 3	11.76 2
Senate	Uniform	L	2.63 1	10.40 3	5.27 2	3.55 3	0.12 1	2.24 2	6.18 1	10.53 3	7.51 2
Senate	Uniform	M	2.09 1	6.41 3	2.47 2	2.84 3	0.12 1	1.76 2	4.93 2	6.54 3	4.24 2
Senate	Uniform	H	1.25 2	2.91 3	1.19 1	1.38 3	0.12 1	0.70 2	2.63 2	3.03 3	1.89 1
Senate	Normal	L	4.11 1	12.85 3	10.54 2	3.92 3	0.12 1	1.14 2	3.14 1	12.97 3	11.68 2
Senate	Normal	M	3.56 1	12.09 3	8.55 2	3.62 3	0.12 1	1.44 2	3.44 1	12.21 3	9.99 2
Senate	Normal	H	3.29 1	11.56 3	7.30 2	3.53 3	0.12 1	1.66 2	3.66 1	11.68 3	8.96 2

Note: House data are from 80th–105th Congresses (Cox and McCubbins 2005); Senate data are from 80th–99th Congresses (Cox and McCubbins 2002). Normal distributions are approximated by binomials. Range is measured in number of bin units (see n. 17): L = 21, M = 41, H = 61. Pairs of cell entries are the sum of squared roll rate errors and the rank order of performance across the three models within the chamber-distribution-variance combination.

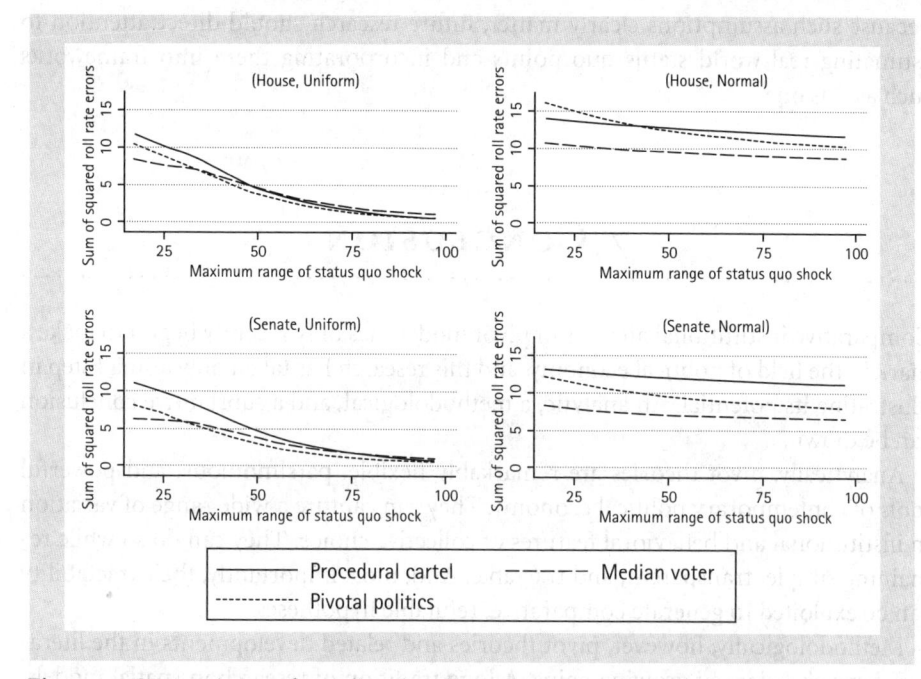

Fig. 12.5 Comparison of predicted roll rate errors using endogenous-status-quo method

party rolls, and few such rolls occur. Meanwhile, the median voter and pivotal politics theories systematically over-predict such rolls.[18]

But while the cartel theory is uniformly successful in predicting majority party roll rates, it is uniformly abysmal in predicting those for the minority party. Without exception, it predicts far more minority party rolls than in fact occur. Indeed, *all* of the errors summarized in column 2 are due to over-prediction and these are considerably greater than any other theory's errors in columns 1–6. Consequently, when roll types are combined and the overall predictive accuracy of the theories is compared in columns 7–9, the cartel theory is the poorest performer.

For most assumptions about the distribution of the status quo shock term, the median voter theory performs best of the three models. This is always the case under the assumption of approximately normally distributed shocks. The pivotal politics theory, in contrast, generates the fewest errors under the assumption of high variance of uniformly distributed shocks.

The mixed nature of the findings—and especially their clear dependence on the assumptions about the error term of the status quo shock—has two implications. First, the findings underscore the importance of employing an explicit framework that can accommodate a wide range of assumptions about the status quo. Second,

[18] When the House data in the first six rows of Table 12.3 are partitioned into Congresses in which a given theory over- versus under-predicts, the pivot and the median voter theories *never* predict fewer majority party rolls than occur. It is likewise rare in the Senate.

because such assumptions clearly matter, future research should direct attention to estimating real-world status quo points and incorporating them into frameworks such as this one.

7 Conclusion

Comparative institutional analysis of pivot models has only recently begun to make a mark in the field of political economy, and this research has taken only a small step in illustrating its potential. An analytic, a methodological, and a substantive conclusion can be drawn.

Analytically, pivot theories are remarkably flexible, parsimonious, and powerful tools of contemporary political economy. They can capture a wide range of variation in institutional and behavioral features of collective choice. They can do so while remaining simple, transparent, and tractable. And, most importantly, their tractability can be exploited to generate comparative, refutable hypotheses.

Methodologically, however, pivot theories and related developments in the literature have experienced growing pains. A long tradition of research in spatial models, in legislative studies and elsewhere, has drawn substantial analytic leverage from the concept of an exogenous status quo point, which, within a well-specified game form in which voters have well-defined preferences, leaves one such decision-maker pivotal in equilibrium. With a rich assortment of such theories at our disposal, attention has increasingly turned to empirical analysis that seeks to discriminate between models that identify different pivots depending upon which institutional features the models encapsulate. Such analyses are more subtle and delicate than is often acknowledged because of an important difference between the status quo as an analytic construct and the status quo as an empirical phenomenon. Analytically, the status quo is exogenous, pure and simple. Empirically, however, the status quo is typically an outcome from a previous process of collective choice in the same institutional setting to which the theory is intended to apply. Consequently, improvements in empirical tests of pivot theories seem crucially dependent upon more careful attention to theory-consistent distributions of status quo points. This study has demonstrated a new method that is uniquely responsive to this concern.

Substantively, the combination of analytic explicitness and a methodological approach that accounts for status quo endogeneity seems quite important. Previous studies tend not to be explicit about assumptions about the status quo and come to conclusions of two types: either strong claims about the superiority of partisan theories (e.g. Cox and McCubbins 2002, 2005; Campbell, Cox, and McCubbins 2002; Chiou and Rothenberg 2002), or exasperation about the inability to discriminate between competing theories (Krehbiel, Meirowitz, and Woon, 2004). This study reaches much different conclusions from the first type and somewhat sharper conclusions than the second. The cartel theory clearly provides the best account for the paucity of majority party rolls, which it should: the distances between its majority party gatekeeping assumption, its no-majority-roll prediction, and the *ex ante* known paucity of such rolls are razor-thin. On the other hand, the party cartel theory is clearly inadequate in predicting minority party rolls once status quo distributions are endogenized. Meanwhile, the pivotal politics theory exhibits a higher mean and lower variance in performance than the cartel theory. Yet, it is not the pivotal politics model but rather the original and simplest pivot model—Black's median voter theory—that performs best in most circumstances.

References

BLACK, D. 1958. *The Theory of Committees and Elections*. London: Cambridge University Press.
BRADY, D., and VOLDEN, C. 1998. *Revolving Gridlock*. New York: Westview Press.
CAMPBELL, A., COX, G., and MCCUBBINS, M. 2002. Agenda power in the U.S. Senate, 1877–1986. In *Party, Process, and Political Change in Congress*, ed. D. Brady and M. McCubbins. Stanford, Calif.: Stanford University Press.
CHIOU, F. Y., and ROTHENBERG, L. 2003. When pivotal politics meets partisan politics. *American Journal of Political Science*, 47: 503–22.
COX, G., and MCCUBBINS, M. 2002. Agenda power in the U.S. House of Representatives, 1877–1986. In *Party, Process, and Political Change in Congress*, ed. D. Brady and M. McCubbins. Stanford, Calif.: Stanford University Press.
—— —— 2005. *Setting the Agenda*. Cambridge: Cambridge University Press.
CROMBEZ, C., KREHBIEL, K., and GROSECLOSE, T. 2006. Gatekeeping. *Journal of Politics*, 68.
DENZAU, A., and MACKAY, R. 1983. Gatekeeping and monopoly power of committees: an analysis of sincere and sophisticated behavior. *American Journal of Political Science*, 27: 740–61.
GROSECLOSE, T., and SNYDER, J. M., JR. 2003. Interpreting the coefficient of party influence: comment on Krehbiel. *Political Analysis*, 11: 104–7.
KREHBIEL, K. 1996. Institutional and partisan sources of gridlock: a theory of divided and unified government. *Journal of Theoretical Politics*, 8: 7–40.
—— 1998. *Pivotal Politics: A Theory of US Lawmaking*. Chicago: University of Chicago Press.
—— MEIROWITZ, A., and WOON, J. 2005. Testing theories of legislatures. In *Essays in Honor of Jeffrey S. Banks*, ed. J. Duggan and D. Austen-Smith. Berlin: Springer-Verlag.
—— SHEPSLE, K., and WEINGAST, B. 1987. Why are congressional committees powerful? *American Political Science Review*, 81: 929–45.
MAYHEW, D. R. 1991. *Divided We Govern*. New Haven, Conn.: Yale University Press.
MO, J. 2001. Political culture and legislative gridlock: politics of economic reform in precrisis Korea. *Comparative Political Studies*, 34: 467–92.
NACIF, B. 2003. Policy making under divided government in Mexico. Working Paper #305, Kellogg Institute, University of Notre Dame.
POOLE, K. T., and ROSENTHAL, H. 2000. *Congress: A Political-Economic History of Roll Call Voting*. Oxford: Oxford University Press.
ROMER, T., and ROSENTHAL, H. 1978. Political resource allocation, controlled agendas, and the status quo. *Public Choice*, 33: 27–43.

SHEPSLE, K. A. 1979. Institutional arrangements and equilibrium in multidimensional voting models. *American Journal of Political Science*, 23: 27–59.
—— and WEINGAST, B. R. 1987. The institutional foundations of committee power. *American Political Science Review*, 81: 85–104.
WAWRO, G. J., and SHICKLER, E. 2004. Where's the pivot? Obstruction and lawmaking in the pre-cloture senate. *American Journal of Political Science*, 48: 758–74.

CHAPTER 13

THE POLITICAL ECONOMY OF THE US PRESIDENCY

CHARLES M. CAMERON

By virtue of the extraordinary economic and military might of the United States, the American president is the most powerful elected official in the world. Not surprisingly, the American president is also the most intensively studied of all political executives. Nonetheless, a distinctly *political economic* understanding of the presidency is a recent undertaking. Despite this novelty, progress has been rapid and continues apace.

As the political economy approach has developed, several features distinguish it from the earlier legalistic, biographical, historical, and behavioral schools of presidential analysis. First, the political economy approach consciously suppresses the details of presidents' individual personalities in favor of an admittedly simplistic but highly tractable psychology. Typically, analysts assume that straightforward goals, such as advancing policy objectives or securing re-election, motivate presidents. In adopting this view, the new approach to the presidency emulates modern work on Congress, the bureaucracy, and the judiciary.

Second, the political economy approach self-consciously embeds the president in the American separation-of-powers (SOP) system.[1] The SOP system, hardwired into American government by the Constitution, compels the president to interact repeatedly with Congress and, to a lesser degree, the federal courts. And, from the time of the New Deal, the SOP system also compels the president to interact with huge

---

[1] De Figueiredo, Jacobi, and Weingast (this volume) survey the emerging literature on the new separation-of-powers approach as applied to the major American national institutions.

standing bureaucracies filled with a *mélange* of civil servants and political appointees. Accordingly, the political economy approach emphasizes presidential interaction with the other branches of government. This emphasis on cross-branch interaction distinguishes the political economic approach from traditional, White House-centric approaches.

Third, the political economy approach is relentlessly strategic. The SOP system obliges the president to anticipate how others will respond to his actions. Not surprisingly, then, non-cooperative game theory is the lingua franca of the new approach.

Fourth, the new work focuses on concrete actions—e.g. making veto threats or actually vetoing bills, selecting nominees for the Supreme Court or independent regulatory agencies, issuing executive orders, crafting a presidential program, "going public" to direct mass attention to particular issues—rather than amorphous entities like "presidential decision-making," "presidential power," or "crisis management."

This hard-nosed emphasis on how presidents actually govern leads naturally to the fifth and sixth attributes of the political economy approach: its emphasis on presidential activism rather than passivity, and its drive to combine theoretical rigor with rich empirical tests. The former distinguishes the political economy approach from much of the work inspired by Richard Neustadt's *Presidential Power*, which emphasized how little presidents can do ("presidential power is the power to persuade"). The political economy approach recovers a puissant presidency, albeit one ever constrained by the separation-of-powers system.

Finally, the emphasis on the tools of governance neatly finesses the "small *n* problem" that hamstrung presidential studies. The political economy approach shifts the unit of analysis from individual presidents to episodes of governance—from a handful of people to a multitude of vetoes, executive orders, nominations, speeches, presidential program items, and so on. As a result data are no longer scarce; they are abundant. Somewhat surprisingly, then, the new work on the presidency has assumed a distinguished position in the "empirical implications of theoretical models" (EITM) movement in political science, an effort to combine formal models with systematic data.

This chapter is organized as follows. In the following section I briefly review how the American constitutional and political order shapes presidents' incentive structure and defines the available tools of governance. This background material is critical because the political economy approach emphasizes how presidents use specific governance tools within the confines of the separation-of-powers system. I then examine the intellectual roots of the political economy approach and provide an overview of significant developments. Somewhat provocatively, I claim that scholars have identified three causal mechanisms at work in presidential governance. The three causal mechanisms are veto power, proposal power, and strategic pre-action. The first two are somewhat self-explanatory but explained carefully below. In strategic pre-action, the president initiates action by unilaterally altering a state variable, whose value then shapes his own or others' subsequent behavior in a game typically involving veto or proposal power. I then review specific works, organized around the three causal mechanisms. The new work has considerable normative import, conceivably altering how one evaluates American politics. I gesture in this normative direction, but conclude by pointing to under-exploited research opportunities and new frontiers for analysis.

1 Constitutional and Electoral Foundations

In contrast to parliamentary systems, the American separation-of-powers system prohibits legislative parties from selecting the chief executive. Similarly, the US Constitution explicitly prohibits congressmen from serving simultaneously in the executive. The president cannot introduce legislation in Congress, nor can cabinet ministers or agency officials. The president's government does not fall if Congress modifies the president's "budget" (simply a set of suggestions to Congress, with no direct constitutional authority) or disregards his avowed legislative priorities, no matter how important. Thus, cabinet government cannot exist in the United States; top officials have no sense of collective responsibility to a legislative party; the policy preferences of the president routinely differ from that of the majority party in one or both chambers of the legislature ("divided party government" occurs about 40 per cent of the time); and there is little sense in which the president himself is an agent of a legislative principal or, needless to say, vice versa. Instead, the mass electorate selects the president, using a baroque voting system (the Electoral College) reflecting the population size of states. An elected president then serves for a fixed four-year term (subject to impeachment) whose timing is uncoupled from political crises or major events of the day. And, the president may be re-elected at most once (post-1951).[2] Consequently, the president's "principal," if he may be said to have one at all, is a geographically based coalition in the mass public. Even this coalition may exert a reduced pull in a second term.

Understanding the consequences of this peculiar constitutional design has long constituted the core of US presidential studies (Ford 1898; Wilson 1908; Corwin 1948; Neustadt 1960; Edwards 1989). In this system, presidential governance involves (1) using a small number of constitutionally protected powers (e.g. nominating Supreme Court justices and ambassadors, exercising a qualified veto over legislation, negotiating treaties), (2) utilizing additional statutorily granted or judicially protected powers (e.g. executive orders), and (3) innovating around various constitutionally or statutorily ambiguous powers (e.g. war-making as commander-in-chief, "prerogative" powers supposedly inherent in the idea of a chief executive). It also involves (4)

[2] Serving two and one-half terms is possible, if a vice-president succeeds to a president's uncompleted term.

setting agency policy in the vast federal bureaucracy, within the bounds of delegated statutory authority and judicial oversight, using decentralized appointments and centralized administrative review, (5) leveraging the president's direct relationship with the mass electorate into legislative influence, via public exhortations ("going public"), and (6) crafting for Congress a comprehensive "federal budget" (a mammoth set of explicit recommendations) and a "legislative program" (specific bills drafted and proffered to Congress), exploiting the superior resources and information of the federal bureaucracy and presidential advisers. Tasks auxiliary to presidential governance include selecting personal staff, defining their jobs, organizing them bureaucratically, and directing their efforts.

2 Development of the Political Economy Approach

The political economy approach to the presidency emerged in the mid to late 1980s as scholars influenced by the rational choice revolution in congressional studies puzzled over the role of the executive in this peculiar constitutional order. Methodologically, the pioneering studies wove together concepts from organization economics, agency theory, and transactions cost economics to form heuristic frameworks for interpreting case studies or structuring quantitative analysis (Moe 1985, 1989; Miller 1993). Particularly influential were Moe's "structure" and "centralization" hypotheses: presidents have incentives to construct administrative agencies responsive to their desires, and to centralize many of their own tasks, such as crafting a legislative program. Also influential was his "politicization" hypothesis: presidents have incentives to control the bureaucracy by appointing loyal, if inexpert, lieutenants.[3] Moe's creative syntheses have continued to inspire empirical studies of centralization (Rudalevige 2003) and the politics of agency design (Lewis 2003).

More recent studies construct explicitly game-theoretic models of presidential governance, often with an eye to empirical application. Broadly speaking, the contemporary game-theoretic approach has produced substantial insights about three tools of governance: (1) the presidential veto (Matthews 1989; McCarty 1997; Cameron 2000; Groseclose and McCarty 2001), (2) executive orders (Howell 2003), and (3) presidential rhetoric (Canes-Wrone 2006). In addition, some progress has been made analyzing the use of three others: (1) presidential nominations, especially to the US Supreme Court (Moraski and Shipan 1999), but also to executive agencies (McCarty 2004) and independent regulatory agencies (Snyder and Weingast 2000), (2) presidential budgets (Kiewiet and McCubbins 1989; Kiewiet and Krehbiel 2002), and

---

[3] Within this tradition, considerable empirical effort went into parsing the degree of presidential versus legislative influence over bureaucratic policy; references may be found in Hammond and Knott 1996 (*inter alia*).

(3) the presidential program (Cameron 2005). Studies on budgeting were discussed in de Figueiredo, Jacobi, and Weingast's introductory chapter; I discuss the others below.

3 Causal Mechanisms and Presidential Governance

The political economy approach identifies a small number of causal mechanisms at work in presidential governance, especially *veto power*, *proposal power*, and (for want of a better phrase) *strategic pre-action*. I will describe each shortly, illustrating by reference to specific models. However, a critical feature of all three is that their operation depends crucially—but predictably—on the *strategic context*. Depending on the model, the strategic context includes the policy preferences of the president and Congress, the alignment of the president's policy preferences with those of voters, the ideological character of pre-existing policies (the location of the 'status quo'), the strength of the president's co-partisans in Congress, the extent of ideological polarization in Congress, and the alignment of civil servants' policy preferences with those of the president. The operation of the three causal mechanisms also depends on available "technology," such as the capability of the president to reach mass audiences with messages and information.

Veto power. Political economy analyses of the veto typically employ variants of Romer and Rosenthal's celebrated monopoly agenda-setter model (1978).[4] (See Krehbiel's discussion of "pivotal politics" in this volume.) In the basic model, a proposer (Congress) makes a take-it-or-leave-it offer (a bill) to a chooser (the president). If the president vetoes the bill, a status quo policy remains in effect.

Figure 13.1 illustrates how the course of veto bargaining depends crucially on the strategic context, which in this case is the policy preferences of the president and Congress and the location of the status quo. In the figure, both Congress and president have single-peaked preferences over policies (bills). The most preferred policy for the president is denoted p, that of Congress c, and the location of the status quo q. For ease of exposition, the president's utility function is scaled so that the value of the status quo is zero. Note that there is a point, $p(q)$, located on the opposite side of the president's utility function from q, that affords the president the same utility as q. Clearly, the president will (weakly or strongly) prefer any bill in the interval $[q, p(q)]$ to q and prefer q to any bill outside this interval. Therefore the president will veto any bill outside this interval in order to preserve q. And, equally clearly, Congress should pass the bill in the interval $[q, p(q)]$ it most prefers to q, as the president will accept this bill in preference to the status quo.

---
[4] As exceptions, McCarty 2000*a* and 2000*b* investigate an executive veto within a Baron–Ferejohn legislative bargaining game.

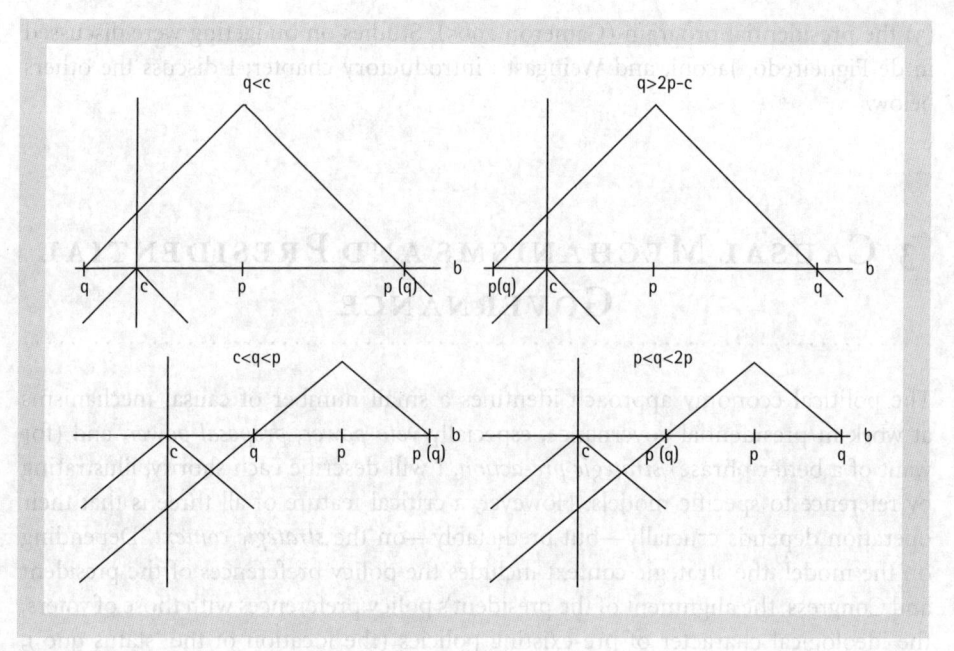

Fig. 13.1 Policy-making and the presidential veto

In the upper left-hand panel, the status quo is located to the left of c. In this configuration, Congress's most preferred policy c lies within the interval $[q, p(q)]$, so Congress can enact a bill at c, and the president will accept the bill. Thus, the president may be said to be "accommodating" (Matthews 1989) in this strategic context. In the lower left-hand panel, the status quo is located in the interval between the two players' ideal points. The policy in $[q, p(q)]$ most preferred by Congress is simply q itself. In other words, in this strategic context there is no policy that Congress prefers to the status quo that the president will not veto—the president is "recalcitrant." The only possible outcome is q (presumably, under these circumstances Congress would not enact a bill). In the lower right-hand panel, the status quo is located to the right of the president's ideal point p. In this configuration, the element of $[p(q), q]$ most preferred by Congress is $p(q)$. So Congress enacts a bill located at $p(q)$, which the president will accept—in this strategic context the president is "compromising," because he will accept a compromise bill. In the upper right-hand panel, q is so far to the right of p that $p(q) < c$. In this configuration, Congress can again enact its ideal policy c, which the president will accept—once again, the president is accommodating. Note that as p moves closer to c, the president will be accommodating for most status quos.

As this exposition suggests, the ability to pass a take-it-or-leave-it bill confers a strong advantage on Congress. This is a fundamental fact about take-it-or-leave-it bargaining, and a foundational issue in the American separation-of-powers system. A recurrent challenge for the president is to find devices that undercut or offset Congress's inherent advantage. Many of the models discussed below indicate how presidents can do so, for example by building a reputation as a policy extremist or skillfully employing veto threats. Of course, the president does not have it all his own way: the blame game model discussed below shows how the presence of attentive publics wary of extremist presidents can actually strengthen Congress's hand.

The basic model offers insights about veto power, but very little about actual vetoes since none occur in equilibrium. Six variants on the basic model have proven useful in understanding the details of actual veto bargaining.[5] The first variant adds some uncertainty about presidential preferences. In this variant, vetoes occur when Congress mistakenly places a bill outside the interval the president will accept. This will occur with much frequency only when the president and Congress have disparate preferences, e.g. during divided party government. Otherwise, Congress's ideal point almost always lies in the interval. The second variant adds a veto override player, whose identity may be somewhat uncertain. This variant is useful for understanding override politics, including failed override attempts. The third variant retains uncertainty about presidential preferences and additionally allows Congress to modify and re-pass a bill after a veto.

This model of "sequential veto bargaining" has considerable strategic complexity, because Congress uptakes its beliefs about the president's preferences during the course of bargaining and adjusts its subsequent offers accordingly. In turn, the president has an incentive to veto an initial bill in order to extract later concessions. But holding out for a better bill can be risky since a breakdown in bargaining will saddle the president with an unattractive status quo. Cameron 2000 shows that many of the most consequential laws of the postwar era were shaped through sequential veto bargaining in a fashion consistent with the model. The fifth variant, "blame game vetoes," adds an electorate which is somewhat uncertain about the president's policy preferences. In this case, a hostile Congress may present the president with "veto bait," a bill whose veto will confirm the public's adverse impressions of the president. This model makes the interesting prediction that vetoes will decrease the president's popularity, a prediction which receives support in Groseclose and McCarty (2001).

A final variant of great empirical relevance allows the president to issue a cheap-talk veto threat before Congress presents him with a bill. I discuss this variant below as it hinges on strategic pre-action. Finally, it is important to note that Ferejohn and Shipan (1990), Krehbiel (1998), and Brady and Volden (1998) all embed the presidential veto in larger models of policy-making in separation-of-powers systems, as discussed in de Figueiredo, Jacobi, and Weingast's introductory chapter.

Proposal power. Presidents can sometimes turn the tables, and present Congress with take-it-or-leave-it offers. Examples include nominations, treaties, and reorganization plans. Again, variants of the Romer–Rosenthal model are useful for studying these governance tools, where a strong advantage accrues to the president.[6] To illustrate I consider two models. The first concerns nominations, the second the president's legislative program.

---

[5] Readers interested in the presidential veto may wish to consult Cameron and McCarty 2004, which provides more details on the indicated variants as well as several others.

[6] As an alternative, Conley 2001 examines a simple legislative bargaining model in which an "electoral mandate" may advantage the president, conferring a kind of proposal power. She examines systematic data on presidential mandate claiming, and uses the model to interpret many episodes of political history.

Moraski and Shipan's model of Supreme Court nominations examines presidential proposal power in a setting of great intrinsic interest (1999). In addition, many of the issues raised there recur in Snyder and Weingast's interesting model of appointments to independent regulatory commissions (2000). In the nominations model, the players are Supreme Court justices, the president, and the median voter in the Senate. All players are purely policy motivated, so the goal of the president is to alter the Supreme Court's policy choices by reconfiguring the membership of the court. Justices are treated exactly as if they were legislators in a standard one-dimensional setting, so Supreme Court decisions correspond to the ideal point of the median justice. In a court with a single vacancy there are eight justices. Arraying the ideal points of the justices from left to right, denote the ideal points of the two middle justices, justices 4 and 5, as j_4 and j_5. It will be seen that a successful nomination can move the median to a point in the interval $[j_4, j_5]$ but no further. (Of course, in a polarized court this interval can be quite large.) The model treats the nomination as a one-shot game, with the implicit status quo being policies set at the midpoint between j_4 and j_5. Thus, the effective choice facing the Senate is between the new median created by the addition of the president's nominee to the court, and the midpoint between the two middle justices on an eight-judge court. Moraski and Shipan make the (strong) auxiliary assumption that if the president is indifferent over a range of confirmable nominees who all produce the same median on the court, the president picks one at or as close as possible to his own ideal point. Given this assumption, the model makes strong predictions about how the ideology of the president's nominee will change with the location of the president's ideal point, that of the median senator, and j_4 and j_5. (Thus, these four ideal points constitute the strategic context in the model.)

As one would expect from the one-shot veto model, in some configurations the president can successfully offer a nominee at the president's ideal point. These configurations correspond to the accommodating regime in the veto model. In other configurations, the president will offer a nominee whose ideology the Senate finds utility equivalent to the midpoint between justices 4 and 5 (this is analogous to the compromising regime in the veto model). Finally, in some configurations the president can do no better than offer the effective status quo (these configurations correspond to the recalcitrant regime in the veto model). Broadly speaking, the president has a strong inherent advantage: in many configurations the Senate will confirm the president's most preferred nominee or one who moves the court's median a considerable distance toward the president's ideal policy.

Testing the model requires a determination of which strategic configuration governed each nomination, because the model predicts different nominee locations across the three regimes. Not surprisingly, accurately measuring the location of ideal points on a common scale becomes critical. Moraski and Shipan claim considerable empirical support for the model, although Bailey and Chang (2001), who test the model with arguably better data on the location of the players' ideal points, contest the claim. In both cases, however, the number of cases considered is quite small (less than two dozen). Thus, one may say the jury is still out on the model's detailed predictions. But the model surely casts light on the strategic issues facing a policy-minded president who wishes to alter the composition of the Supreme Court or (by extension) regulatory commissions.

Cameron (2005) presents another model in which presidential proposal power looms large. In this simple formal model of the president's legislative program, crafting well-formulated bills is costly of time and effort. But the president can utilize the vast resources of the executive establishment to craft bills at little cost to himself. This creates an opportunity for him. By drafting a well-formulated bill in the executive branch and presenting it to Congress gratis, the president can save Congress much of the cost of legislating. The president can use this opportunity to "pull" the content of enactments in his preferred direction. More specifically, consider a status quo outside the gridlock region (see Krehbiel's chapter in this volume) that presents Congress with a target worth the cost of legislating. As indicated in the discussion of the veto model, Congress will craft a bill located either at its ideal point or at a point that president finds utility-equivalent to the status quo (that is, assuming the benefit of legislating outweighs the cost). By crafting a "free" bill at a point he prefers to this bill, the president can present Congress with the choice between a "status quo" composed of the president's "free" bill and the costly bill Congress would draft on its own.

This burden-sharing model of the legislative program turns the traditional approach to the presidential program on its head. The traditional approach suggests that somehow the president forces Congress to adopt his legislative proposals. In the burden-sharing model, the president anticipates congressional activism and moves to shape or steer it by offering Congress bills broadly similar to what Congress would have written anyway, but "bent" somewhat to the president's advantage.

This extremely simple model makes some clear empirical predictions. For example, presidential legislative activism should surge when the gridlock region is small and social movements active. Under those circumstances, congressional activism is both practical and attractive; hence, the president has an incentive to proffer many bills in order to shape congressional activism. Using time series data on the size of the gridlock region and on social movement activism, Cameron finds that presidential legislative activism surges and slumps in the predicted fashion.

Strategic pre-action. In some circumstances, the president can take an irreversible action that alters the value of a state variable affecting the subsequent strategic interaction between the president and other actors.[7] Models of this kind often have rich and tractable comparative statics, facilitating systematic empirical work. Three examples illustrate the basic idea: the politics of executive orders, the strategy of going public, and the use of veto threats.

Using an executive order, the president can unilaterally modify a status quo policy (the state variable), at least within certain legal limits. Congress can then respond legislatively—but Congress's bill must survive a presidential veto and possibly a filibuster. In addition, congressional committees with gatekeeping power may not wish to release bills to the floor, if they prefer the president's policy to that the floor

---

[7] Models of this kind have a conceptual, and in some cases mathematical, resemblance to certain models of firm strategy in industrial organization (see e.g. Fudenberg and Tirole 1984)

will enact. By carefully choosing the ideological location of the policy in the executive order, the president can assure a more favorable outcome in the subsequent legislative game. Howell (2003) extensively analyzes the strategy of executive orders, developing game-theoretic models and testing them against systematic data, with success. [8]

The president can "go public" on an issue, raising its saliency (the state variable) to the public (Kernell 1993; Cohen 1997). Congress then legislates on the issue. To understand the strategy of going public, consider the following simple model, inspired by Canes-Wrone (2001). If the median voter in Congress writes and passes a bill (a point on the line) he receives a benefit proportional to the proximity of the bill's content to his ideal policy. But he suffers an electoral loss whose magnitude depends, first, on the distance between the policy and the desires of his constituents and, second, on the public saliency of the issue.[9] More specifically, if the issue's saliency is low, the congressman suffers little electoral loss from a policy distant from his constituents' wishes; if its saliency is large, the electoral loss is considerable.

It is easy to see that if the electoral loss displays increasing differences in policy distance and saliency (as is plausible), Congress will shift the location of a bill away from its preferred policy and toward that of constituents as saliency increases. This creates a strategic opportunity for the president: going public increases the issue's saliency thereby altering the content of Congress's bill. However, going public will serve the president's interest only if he prefers Congress's policy choice when saliency is high to its choice when saliency is low—that is, when the president favors popular policies. Canes-Wrone 2004 explores the strategy of going public in depth using models with this flavor, and tests their predictions against multiple data-sets, with success.

Matthews's pioneering model of veto threats provides a third example of strategic pre-action. The state variable is Congress's beliefs about the president's policy preferences. In the first period, the president manipulates those beliefs using a cheap-talk veto threat. In the second period, Congress and president play a standard veto game, as outlined above.

The logic of the veto threat model is rather subtle. Suppose Congress is uncertain whether the president's preferences make him accommodating, compromising, or recalcitrant. If Congress believes too firmly that the president is accommodating and offers a bill at its ideal point when in fact the president is actually compromising, it will trigger a veto that could have been avoided by a less aggressive but nonetheless Pareto improving bill. In addition, there is a range of accommodating presidents who prefer Congress's ideal policy over a more distant bill aimed at a compromiser.[10] So there is the possibility for mutually advantageous communication between president and Congress. On the other hand, this communication cannot be perfect. For example, if the president is actually a compromiser, Congress would exploit perfect information about the president's preferences to offer a bill at $p(q)$,

---

[8] Policy-making by executive agencies, analyzed in Ferejohn and Shipan 1990, has strong similarities to the politics of executive orders.

[9] The congressman's preferred policy may differ from that of his constituents because of the influence of special interest groups, or because Congress is disproportionately composed of extremist ideologues who gained public office despite the disparity in their views from that of their constituents.

[10] If $c = 0$ and $q > 0$, then for these types $p < 0$, since Congress will then offer a bill at 0 rather than something higher.

leaving the president no better off than with the status quo. Moreover, there is a range of accommodating presidents who benefit from a bill oriented toward compromising presidents rather than accommodating ones.[11] These types of president would like Congress to believe them more extreme than they actually are.

Matthews shows that there exists an equilibrium in which the president begins play by employing one of two somewhat ambiguous messages.[12] In equilibrium, the president's first message has the meaning "I will accept your ideal point." Upon receipt of this message (corresponding to no veto threat), Congress offers a bill at its ideal point, which the president accepts. The second message (the veto threat message) has the equilibrium meaning, "I may not accept your ideal point." Upon receipt of this message, Congress offers a compromise bill shaded toward the president, which he may or may not veto. Cameron 2000 tests the model empirically, using data on veto threats in the postwar era. He finds that presidents almost never veto bills absent threats; threats almost always lead to congressional concessions; and the larger the concession, the more likely the president is to accept the bill. Matthews's model predicts exactly these patterns.

4 NORMATIVE IMPLICATIONS OF PRESIDENTIAL GOVERNANCE

Because the new game-theoretic models of presidential governance make crisp predictions based on explicit causal mechanisms, they sometimes raise normative issues in a particularly clear fashion. For example, models of veto bargaining typically imply that final policies lie between the ideal points of president and Congress. In a period in which most voters are ideologically moderate relative to extreme politicians (Fiorina, Abrams, and Pope 2004), this property of veto bargaining can be seen as normatively attractive.

A second example concerns pork-barrel politics. It is often claimed that presidents have an incentive to veto Congress's pork-barrel bills. McCarty (2000a) examines this claim in a formal model of pork-barrel legislation, the Baron–Ferejohn model (see the chapter by Diermeier in this volume). He finds that presidents have an incentive to veto allocations of pork that disadvantage the president's co-partisans in Congress—but little incentive to do so if the allocation favors his co-partisans. Thus, the presidential veto need not dramatically reduce overall levels of pork, only who receives it. McCarty's findings call into question a favorite bromide of presidential scholars.

Perhaps the most interesting example concerns mass opinion and presidential governance. A long-standing question among presidential scholars is: do the president's public appeals or high-visibility actions facilitate democratic outcomes? Or are they

---

[11] For example, if $c = 0$ and $q = 1$, a president with $p = \frac{1}{2}$ would prefer Congress believe $p = 3/4$, as it would then offer a bill at $3/4$.

[12] As is typical in cheap-talk models, there is another equilibrium in which messages do not convey information.

merely cynical pandering to an ill-informed electorate (Jacobs and Shapiro 2000)? Canes-Wrone, Herron, and Shotts (2001) address this question in an explicit way, using a model in which presidents may have an incentive to take actions that are popular in the short term but possibly harmful to public welfare over a longer horizon. (Obvious examples are manipulating monetary and fiscal policy, as in models of the political-business cycle.) They note that pandering carries a risk to the president, since later events may expose the president's cynical manipulations in disastrous fashion. Given this risk, Canes-Wrone et al. argue that pandering requires rather special conditions, i.e. a marginally popular president (relative to a challenger) facing a proximate election. Otherwise, the risks tend to outweigh the benefits. The model suggests distinctive patterns in the popularity of presidential policies—for example, the likelihood the president chooses a popular policy—should be unrelated to his personal popularity when elections are distant (since under those circumstances his primary incentive is to "get it right" rather than pander). Canes-Wrone and Kenneth Shotts test many of these predictions using budgetary and public opinion data (Canes-Wrone 2004). They find some evidence of pandering late in the first term of moderately popular incumbent presidents. Canes-Wrone 2004 discusses alternative institutional designs that might mitigate this tendency (e.g. limiting presidents to a single term), but is careful to note that every obvious alternative has substantial costs as well as benefits.[13]

5 RESEARCH OPPORTUNITIES

The political economic approach to the presidency is still in its infancy. Research opportunities abound.

Most obvious are extensions of existing work. For example, further analysis of presidential proposal power, including nominations and treaties, is clearly warranted. Formalizing Moe's structure, centralization and politicization hypotheses would sharpen our understanding of the causal mechanisms at work, and supply firmer foundations for empirical work. Politicization is seriously understudied, in particular. More work on the theoretical foundations of the presidential program would be a useful advance, as would further work on models of the president's budgetary recommendations.[14]

Beyond these extensions lie new areas for research. A tractable topic of great appeal is the president's use of favors and patronage in pursuit of legislative objectives.[15]

---

[13] Chappell and Keach 1983 consider the welfare consequences of moving to a single six-year term, in the context of a political-business cycle model.

[14] Larocca 2004 presents an informational model of lobbying, potentially applicable to presidential lobbying of Congress.

[15] Kelley 1969 pioneered the rational choice analysis of this subject, which certainly could be treated in detail with modern tools (note Snyder 1991). Appropriate data are known to exist in the presidential libraries. Brady and Volden 1998 and Krehbiel 1998 present suggestive empirical evidence on vote switchers.

This topic is vastly under-studied relative to its importance. More speculative is the development of "presidential personnel economics," taking off from analytical work in organization and personnel economics in the private sector (see e.g. Lazear 1995). This work would analyze the analytics of staffing and organizing the White House and presidential agencies. This is an area in which traditional scholars have compiled impressive data but have not laid much in the way of theoretical foundations. Finally, applying the political economy approach to specific policy arenas, such as presidential governance of national security, is a potentially worthwhile endeavor.

With a wider variety of explicit, empirically powerful models in hand, analysts could study complementarities across the instruments of governance: for example, how a centralization strategy, legislative program, presidential budget, public rhetoric, executive orders, and administrative appointments hang together in a sensible way, in a given strategic context. In other words, scholars could study *integrated presidential strategy*. In my opinion, a well-developed theory of integrated presidential strategy would be a landmark achievement in presidential studies. It could revolutionize our understanding of specific presidencies and revise our overall evaluation of the institution itself. I suspect we will see efforts of this kind within a decade.

6 CONCLUSION

The political economy approach shifts the analytic focus from the personality or psychology of individual *presidents* to the institutional character of the *presidency*. Despite its novelty, this approach has already advanced our substantive understanding of presidential governance, particularly vetoes, executive orders, public rhetoric, nomination politics, the presidential program, and budgetary politics. It has also stimulated creative thinking about, and valuable empirical work on, the design of executive agencies and the centralization of executive functions. The deep insight driving the political economic approach is that presidential governance in a separation-of-powers system involves a few, relatively simple causal mechanisms whose operation depends predictably on the strategic context. This insight is surely portable to the study of chief executives in other countries.

REFERENCES

BAILEY, M., and CHANG, K. 2001. Comparing presidents, senators, and justices: interinstitutional preference estimation. *Journal of Law, Economics, and Organization*, 17: 477–506.

BRADY, D. W., and VOLDEN, C. 1998. *Revolving Gridlock: Politics and Policy from Carter to Clinton*. Boulder, Colo.: Westview Press.

CAMERON, C. 2000. *Veto Bargaining: Presidents and the Politics of Negative Power*. New York: Cambridge University Press.

Cameron, C. 2005. A primer on the president's program. Working paper, Woodrow Wilson School, Princeton University.

—— and McCarty, N. 2004. Models of vetoes and veto bargaining. *Annual Review of Political Science*, 7: 409–35.

Canes-Wrone, B. 2001. A theory of presidents' public agenda-setting. *Journal of Theoretical Politics*, 13: 183–208.

—— 2006. *Who Leads Whom? Presidents, Policy Making, and the Mass Public.* Chicago: University of Chicago Press.

—— Herron, M. C., and Shotts, K.W. 2001. Leadership and pandering: a theory of executive policy making. *American Journal of Political Science*, 45: 532–50.

Chappell, H. W., and Keech, W. R. 1983. Welfare consequences of the six-year presidential term evaluating in the context of a model of the U.S. economy. *American Political Science Review*, 77: 75–91.

Cohen, J. E. 1997. *Presidential Responsiveness and Public Policy-Making: The Public and the Policies That Presidents Choose.* Ann Arbor: University of Michigan Press.

Conley, P. H. 2001. *Presidential Mandates: How Elections Shape the National Agenda.* Chicago: University of Chicago Press.

Corwin, E. S. 1948. *President, Office and Powers, 1787–1948.* New York: New York University Press.

Edwards, G. C. 1989. *At the Margins: Presidential Leadership of Congress.* New Haven, Conn.: Yale University Press.

Ferejohn, J., and Shipan, C. 1990. Congressional influence on the bureaucracy. *Journal of Law, Economics, and Organization*, 6 (Special Issue): 1–20.

Ford, H. J. 1898. *The Rise and Growth of American Politics.* New York: Macmillan.

Fiorina, M., Abrams, S., and Pope, J. 2004. *Culture War? The Myth of a Polarized America.* New York: Longman Press.

Fudenberg, D., and Tirole, J. 1984. The fat-cat effect, the puppy-dog ploy, and the lean and hungry look. *American Economic Review: Papers and Proceedings*, 74: 361–6.

Groseclose, T., and McCarty, N. 2001. The politics of blame: bargaining before an audience. *American Journal of Political Science*, 45: 100–19.

Hammond, T. H., and Knott, J. H. 1996. Who controls the bureaucracy? Presidential power, congressional dominance, legal constraints, and bureaucratic autonomy in a model of multi-institutional policy-making. *Journal of Law, Economics, and Organization*, 12: 119–66.

Howell, W. 2003. *Power without Persuasion: A Theory of Unilateral Action.* Princeton, NJ: Princeton University Press.

Jacobs, L. R., and Shapiro, R. Y. 2000. *Politicians Don't Pander: Political Manipulation and the Loss of Democratic Responsiveness.* Chicago: University of Chicago Press.

Kelley, S. 1969. Patronage and presidential legislative leadership. Pp. 268–77 in *The Presidency*, ed. A. Wildavsky. Boston: Little, Brown.

Kernell, S. 1993. *Going Public: New Strategies of Presidential Leadership.* Washington, DC: CQ Press.

Kiewiet, R., and Krehbiel, K. 2002. Here's the president, where's the party? U.S. appropriations on discretionary domestic spending, 1950–1999. *Leviathan*, 30: 115–37.

—— and McCubbins, M. D. 1988. Presidential influence on congressional appropriations decisions. *American Journal of Political Science*, 32: 713–36.

Krehbiel, K. 1998. *Pivotal Politics: A Theory of U.S. Lawmaking.* Chicago: University of Chicago Press.

Larocca, R. 2004. Strategic diversion in political communication. *Journal of Politics*, 66: 469–91.

Lazear, E. P. 1995. *Personnel Economics.* Cambridge, Mass.: MIT Press.

LEWIS, D. 2003. *Presidents and the Politics of Agency Design: Political Insulation in the United States Government Bureaucracy 1946–1997*. Stanford, Calif.: Stanford University Press.

MATTHEWS, S. A. 1989. Veto threats: rhetoric in a bargaining game. *Quarterly Journal of Economics*, 103: 347–69.

McCARTY, N. 1997. Presidential reputation and the veto. *Economics and Politics*, 9: 1–26.

—— 2000a. Presidential pork: executive veto power and distributive politics. *American Political Science Review*, 94: 117–29.

—— 2000b. Proposal rights, veto rights, and political bargaining. *American Journal of Political Science*, 44: 506–22.

—— and POOLE, K. 1995. Veto power and legislation: an empirical analysis of executive and legislative bargaining from 1961 to 1986. *Journal of Law, Economics, and Organization*, 11: 282–312.

MILLER, G. 1993. Formal theory and the presidency. Pp. 289–336 in *Researching the Presidency: Vital Questions, New Approaches*, ed. G. Edwards, III, J. H. Kessel, and B. Rockman. Pittsburgh, Pa.: University of Pittsburgh Press.

MOE, T. 1985. The Politicized Presidency. Pp. 235–72 in *The New Direction in American Politics*, ed. J. Chubb and P. Peterson. Washington, DC: Brookings Institution.

—— 1989. The politics of bureaucratic structure. Pp. 235–72 in *Can the Government Govern?* ed. J. Chubb and P. Peterson. Washington, DC: Brookings Institution.

MORASKI, B., and SHIPAN, C. R. 1999. The politics of Supreme Court nominations: a theory of institutional constraints and choices. *American Journal of Political Science*, 43: 1069–95.

NEUSTADT, R. 1960. *Presidential Power*. New York: Macmillan.

ROMER, T., and ROSENTHAL, H. 1978. Political resource allocation, controlled agendas, and the status quo. *Public Choice*, 33: 27–44.

RUDALEVIGE, A. 2002. *Managing the President's Program: Presidential Leadership and Legislative Policy Formulation*. Princeton, NJ: Princeton University Press.

SHUGART, M. S., and CAREY, J. M. 1992. *Presidents and Assemblies: Constitutional Design and Electoral Dynamics*. Cambridge: Cambridge University Press.

SNYDER, J. 1991. On buying legislatures. *Economics and Politics*, 3: 93–109.

SNYDER, S., and WEINGAST, B. R. 2000. The American system of shared powers: the president, Congress, and the NLRB. *Journal of Law, Economics, and Organization*. 16: 269–305.

WILSON, W. 1908. *Constitutional Government in the United States*. New York: Columbia University Press.

CHAPTER 14

POLITICS, DELEGATION, AND BUREAUCRACY

JOHN D. HUBER
CHARLES R. SHIPAN

MODERN democratic government cannot function without bureaucracy. Given the vast array of policy issues that come before government, the complexity of these issues, and the resources needed to address them, elected politicians have no choice but to delegate at least some responsibility over these issues to bureaucracies. Of course, once politicians delegate, they also face a potential loss of control over the issues that they have delegated. This tension between the necessity of delegation and the potential problems associated with delegation underlines the fundamentally political nature of bureaucracy. Government bureaucracies are surrounded, and affected, by other political actors, including legislators and courts, presidents and governors, prime ministers and cabinet ministers, and interest groups, all of whom attempt to manage this tension. Any analysis of bureaucracies, therefore, needs to view them through the lens of political analysis.

Prior to the 1980s, a dominant theme in the literature on bureaucracy emphasized the "administrative state." The complexity of policy issues and the rapid expansion of government involvement into new policy areas made it very difficult for politicians to make important policy decisions. By contrast, the increasing professionalism and specialization of bureaucracy equipped bureaucrats with the expertise and experience needed to make these decisions. Consequently, the argument went, bureaucrats run

---

* We are grateful to Mike Ting for helpful comments and to Eduardo Leoni for research assistance.

the show, while politicians essentially have no choice but to sit on the sidelines and watch.

In the early 1980s, scholars began strongly to challenge the administrative dominance perspective. In particular, researchers began to examine the design of rules for bureaucratic decision-making and political oversight of bureaucracy (e.g. McCubbins, Noll, and Weingast 1987, 1989; Moe 1989). With the correct institutions governing agency decision-making, some argued, politicians ensure that bureaucratic actors pursue the goals of politicians. Although researchers disagreed about whether this in fact was true, and, more generally, about which elements of structure and process were central to understanding bureaucratic behavior, these arguments have set the agenda for much research on bureaucracy in the last twenty years. A large number of formal models of delegation have explored the instruments that politicians use to delegate to bureaucrats. These models, which have spawned a rich empirical literature, typically focus on two types of delegation instruments: *ex ante* instruments, which allow politicians to establish the level of discretion bureaucrats have when making policy, and *ex post* instruments, which allow politicians or other political actors to monitor or audit bureaucrats after agents take action.

This chapter reviews some of these recent models and associated empirical research. We begin by describing the four core theoretical arguments that consistently emerge from these models about the circumstances under which politicians should be expected to grant either more or less discretion to bureaucrats. After reviewing these arguments, we describe empirical tests that focus on patterns of delegation strategies. We argue that considerable support is accumulating for these arguments, and that we can therefore use the models on which they are based to make inferences about the circumstances under which administrative dominance is most likely. We conclude by reviewing recent theoretical models that provide insights into the circumstances under which the logic of these theoretical arguments breaks down. By considering questions of theoretical robustness, we are able to describe areas that are ripe for additional theorizing and empirical research.

1 Core Arguments about Delegation Strategies

In this section we sketch the four most prominent arguments that have emerged from efforts to model delegation. Two standard assumptions underlie these arguments. First, politicians and bureaucrats often want to achieve different objectives. This is not always true, of course; but when it is not, delegation presents few problems, since politicians can trust bureaucrats to act in their interests. Second, there is asymmetric information about how to achieve policy goals, with bureaucrats typically having more expertise than politicians. The challenge for politicians is how to draw on this

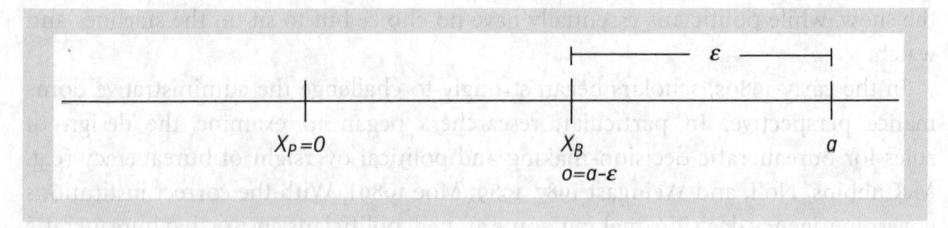

Fig. 14.1 Politicians, bureaucrats, and policy uncertainty

expertise given that bureaucrats want to put it to ends that differ from those desired by politicians.

Many models use a simple, unidimensional spatial framework to implement these two assumptions. A typical model will have a single Politician with ideal point at x_P, and a single Bureaucrat with ideal point at x_B, as illustrated in Figure 14.1. The level of policy conflict between them is simply the distance between x_P and x_B. As this distance grows, the Politician becomes increasingly worried that delegating more authority to the Bureaucrat will lead to a policy outcome that the Politician does not like. In the examples that follow, we assume $x_P = 0 < x_B$ and that both players have quadratic preferences.

The Bureaucrat's informational advantage is often introduced into delegation models by assuming uncertainty about the outcome that will occur if a particular policy is adopted. A common way to model this asymmetry is to assume that after some policy action, a, is taken, the outcome from this policy is $o = a - \varepsilon$. The random variable ε is typically drawn from some well-behaved distribution with finite support, for instance, a uniform distribution. If $\varepsilon \in [-E, E]$, then E is a parameter that measures policy uncertainty. As E gets larger, so too does uncertainty about the outcome that will result from adopting a particular policy a. Both players might know the distribution from which ε is drawn, but the Bureaucrat has more information. Models typically make the information asymmetry as stark as possible by assuming that the Bureaucrat knows the exact value of ε, whereas the Politician knows only the distribution from which ε is drawn. If, for example, the Bureaucrat knows ε and is allowed to implement any policy choice he wants, he can choose a policy a that will produce an outcome equal to his ideal point, as shown in Figure 14.1.

Scholars use the framework described above to explore the strategies that politicians can use to encourage bureaucrats to adopt policies that serve the interests of politicians. The models tell us how different forms of delegation yield different outcomes. One central thrust of the literature is to use these results to understand the factors that influence *how much* authority politicians should delegate to bureaucrats. Politicians can use legal instruments, such as legislative statutes or regulations, to determine the range of policies that bureaucrats can adopt or the types of actions they can take in making policy decisions.

Epstein and O'Halloran (1994) developed a modeling technology that allows one to make explicit the amount of discretion that politicians delegate to bureaucrats. In models of this type, the Politician specifies an interval, such as $[\underline{x}, \overline{x}]$, from which the

```
|——— ε=1 ———|                    |——— ε=1 ———|
|————|——————|——————|——————|——————————————|
o|z,ε=1    xp    z=½          xB              a|y,ε=1
                 a|z,ε=0 or 1  a|y,ε=0
                 o|z,ε=0
```

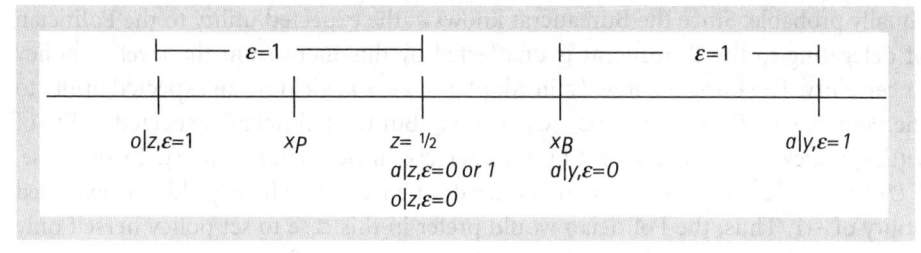

Fig. 14.2 The decision to delegate in spatial models

Bureaucrat must choose his policy action. The lowest discretion law occurs, for example, when $\underline{x} = \overline{x}$—in other words, when the Politician tells the Bureaucrat precisely what to do. As the interval $[\underline{x}, \overline{x}]$ expands, the Bureaucrat has more discretion in the policy space from which to choose his action.

To illustrate the logic of the central results in the literature, we consider a simple example of the type of delegation model originally developed by Epstein and O'Halloran. In this example, the Politician can chose one of two delegation strategies. She can give the Bureaucrat no discretion, instead instructing him to implement some specific policy, z (e.g. $\underline{x} = \overline{x} = z$). Or she adopt some law, y, that gives complete discretion to the Bureaucrat to adopt any policy he wishes (e.g. y is such that $\underline{x} = -\infty$ and $\overline{x} = \infty$). The example also puts the simplest possible structure on policy uncertainty: $\varepsilon \in \{0, 1\}$ and each ε occurs with probability of one-half.

When will the Politician prefer to delegate substantial authority to the Bureaucrat, and when will she prefer to grant minimal discretion? Suppose the Politician delegates policy-making to a Bureaucrat by adopting $y = [-\infty, \infty]$. As shown in Figure 14.2, the Bureaucrat will take action $a = x_B + \varepsilon$, ensuring an outcome at x_B and yielding the Politician an expected utility of $EU_P(y = [-\infty, \infty]) = -x_B^2$. The Politician will compare the utility she receives from a policy at the Bureaucrat's ideal point with the expected utility she receives from her optimal low discretion statute, z. The expected utility of z is $EU_P(z) = -\frac{1}{2}z^2 - \frac{1}{2}(z-1)^2$, which is maximized when $z = \frac{1}{2}$. As illustrated in Figure 14.2, this yields an outcome at $\frac{1}{2}$ if $\varepsilon = 0$, and an outcome at $-\frac{1}{2}$ if $\varepsilon = 1$. Consequently, the expected utility to the Politician of adopting her optimal z is $-\frac{1}{4}$, and the Politician prefers $z = \frac{1}{2}$ to $y = [-\infty, \infty]$ whenever $x_B > \frac{1}{2}$.

The example illustrates the fundamental tension that bureaucrats' policy expertise can create for politicians. A politician can allow substantial discretion to bureaucrats, but only at the risk that bureaucrats will use their policy expertise against the politician. But if a politician tries to counter this risk by writing a low-discretion statute, the policy expertise of the bureaucrat is wasted, potentially making both politicians and bureaucrats worse off than they could have been. In Figure 14.2, for example, if $z = \frac{1}{2}$, then whenever $\varepsilon = 1$, the outcome is $o = -\frac{1}{2}$. Both the Politician and the Bureaucrat would have preferred $z = 1$, yielding an outcome at x_P.

Given this tension, what factors lead Politicians to delegate more versus less discretion to bureaucrats? One central theme in the literature concerns the effect of *policy uncertainty*. Suppose that there was a higher level of uncertainty than in the previous example. It may be the case, for instance, that $\varepsilon \in \{0, 2\}$, with each ε

equally probable. Since the Bureaucrat knows ε, the expected utility to the Politician of delegating to the Bureaucrat is unaffected by this increase in the level of policy uncertainty. The Bureaucrat will still adopt $a = x_B + \varepsilon$, yielding an expected utility to the Politician of $EU_P(y = [-\infty, \infty]) = -x_B^2$. But the Politician's expected utility of setting policy herself is lowered by the increase in policy uncertainty. In this case, $EU_P(z) = -\frac{1}{2}z^2 - \frac{1}{2}(z-2)^2$ is maximized when $z = 1$, which yields an expected utility of -1. Thus, the Politician would prefer in this case to set policy herself only when $x_B > 1$. A core argument that consistently emerges from models of delegation is that as politicians' *policy uncertainty* increases relative to that of the bureaucracy, it becomes more attractive for the politicians to delegate more policy-making authority to the bureaucrats (e.g. Epstein and O'Halloran 1994, 1999; Bawn 1995).

The level of policy conflict between the Politician and Bureaucrat is also one of the central variables that influences the type of delegation strategy politicians adopt. The core argument about policy conflict, called the *ally principle*, is that all else equal, as the policy preferences of politicians and bureaucrats converge, politicians will delegate more discretion to bureaucrats. Return to the example where $\varepsilon \in \{0, 1\}$. If $x_B \leq \frac{1}{2}$, the Politician can delegate substantial discretion. She need not fear that in so doing she will invite the Bureaucrat to use his expertise against the Politician because the Bureaucrat's interests are more or less aligned with the Politician's. By contrast, if $x_B > \frac{1}{2}$, the Politician must worry that the Bureaucrat will use his expertise against the Politician. The Politician responds to this concern by limiting discretion (and adopting $z = \frac{1}{2}$). Bureaucratic discretion will therefore be largest when the bureaucrat is an ally of the politician.

Politicians influence bureaucratic behavior not only by using the *ex ante* strategies (i.e. actions that are taken before bureaucrats actually implement policies) to limit bureaucratic discretion described above. Following bureaucratic policy actions, politicians—and other political actors, such as courts or auditing agencies—can monitor bureaucratic behavior and attempt to influence their policy-making activities. Because of this second opportunity to influence agency actions, *ex ante* limits on discretion and *ex post* monitoring are often viewed as substitutes. Models generally show that politicians are more likely to prefer low discretion statutes when the monitoring environment is sufficiently weak. When the Politician can rely on *ex post* monitoring, she will have less incentive to pay the cost of writing a low discretion statute, as she'd prefer to rely instead on less costly *ex post* mechanisms. This *substitution effect* frequently recurs in the theoretical literature (e.g. Bawn 1997; Epstein and O'Halloran 1994; Gailmard 2002; Huber and Shipan 2002; Huber and McCarty 2004; Bendor and Meirowitz 2004).

The models discussed thus far have assumed a single politician whose preferences are stable during the play of the game. But a central distinguishing feature of delegating to bureaucrats, as opposed to delegating to employees, is that there typically is substantial uncertainty about the preferences of future politicians, since politicians are often replaced by others who have different policy goals. *Political uncertainty*, then, is uncertainty about the future preferences of politicians, and this variable is central to early theorizing about delegation by Moe (1989), Shepsle (1992), and Horn (1995). More recently, de Figueiredo (2002) explicitly models the effects of political uncertainty on discretion. In his model, politicians have an opportunity to "lock in" policy by limiting bureaucratic autonomy. The model suggests that politicians are most likely to do so when they feel it is unlikely they will control the political process in the future. This allows current politicians to tie the hands of future politicians by constraining bureaucratic autonomy.

2 Empirical Tests of the Four Arguments

After the publication of the early "structure and process" articles in the 1980s, considerable empirical research focused on whether *ex ante* efforts to restrict bureaucratic behavior actually allow effective congressional control over the bureaucracy in the USA.[1] Unfortunately, this empirical literature is highly inconclusive, with some studies finding evidence of such effectiveness (e.g. Bawn 1997; Potoski 1999; Balla and Wright 2001; Potoski and Woods 2001), while others find either mixed support or no support at all (e.g. Hamilton and Schroeder 1994; Balla 1998; Spence 1999; Nixon, Howard, and DeWitt 2002). As we have argued previously (Huber and Shipan 2000, 2002), this lack of conclusiveness is not surprising given the elusiveness of pinning down the quality of control over bureaucracy. In our view, no one has yet been able to solve the very difficult problem of assessing empirical relationships between the preferences of bureaucrats and politicians on the one hand and policy outcomes on the other. Even if accurate measurement were possible, since all theoretical models indicate "control" will never be perfect, one would be left with the difficult task of imposing subjective judgements as to whether particular outcomes indicate sufficient control.

The four theoretical arguments described above, which emerge from a variety of related formal models, have highlighted an alternative pathway for empirical research. The models provide predictions about where final policy outcomes will be located vis-à-vis the preferences of bureaucrats and politicians. But they also provide predictions about the circumstances under which particular delegation strategies—such as more versus less discretion in legislation—should be adopted. Since these strategies are typically easier to observe than are outcomes, the predictions about delegation strategies are easier to test. And if empirical tests support the four arguments from the models, we can have confidence that the models are on the right track, and thus that the model's implications for understanding delegation *outcomes* are worth taking seriously. So how have policy uncertainty, the ally principle, substitution effects, and political uncertainty fared in empirical tests?

One strategy for measuring the amount of discretion politicians give to bureaucrats is to look at the design of bureaucratic agencies. Volden's (2002b) study of welfare boards in state governments provides one of the most impressive sets of empirical

---

[1] Howell and Lewis 2002 and Lewis 2003 provide evidence that presidents successfully use such tools to influence agencies.

tests. Using a variety of dependent variables, including whether the legislature has delegated authority to a welfare board, whether powers are delegated to a policy board or an advisory board, and whether delegation is to independent agencies or those controlled by the executive, he finds robust support for the effects of policy uncertainty: when legislatures face more policy uncertainty in the form of greater demographic changes, they are more likely to delegate authority to agencies and to establish welfare boards. At the same time, he finds mixed support for the ally principle. Like many others, he begins by positing that policy conflict between legislator and bureaucrat will be highest during divided government (i.e. when the governor is of a different party from the legislature), but he finds that in actuality the effects of conflict are more subtle than that. When preferences are aligned, legislatures will delegate to welfare boards and give the government appointment powers. When preferences are *not* aligned, however, they are still willing to delegate; but they limit these grants of delegation by placing checks on the appointment powers of governors.

Wood and Bohte (2004) also focus on the design of administrative agencies. Drawing on the laws that established 141 US administrative agencies, they examine and code a number of design attributes, including the autonomy of leaders, the authority to engage in rule-making, budgetary autonomy, and the existing of reporting requirements. Their analysis provides substantial support for the ally principle, with features that foster independence more common when there are high levels of conflict (as measured by vetoes and overrides) between the legislative and executive branches.

Other tests have focused not on the design of agencies, but on the nature of legislation itself. Epstein and O'Halloran's (1999) book-length treatment of delegation and the use of procedural means to control discretion is seminal. They measure discretion in legislation by coding the nature of procedural provisions in all key regulatory laws passed in the post-Second World War US Congress, identifying, for example, whether agencies are subject to time or spending limits and whether agencies are required to either report to or consult with the legislature about policy decisions and actions. Consistent with the ally principle, they find that preference conflict, measured by divided government, leads to legislation that places greater constraints on agencies. And consistent with the idea of policy uncertainty, they find that Congress delegates the most discretion to agencies in situations that are more informationally demanding.[2]

Huber and Shipan (2002) also focus on discretion levels in legislation. Their study differs from Epstein and O'Halloran in two significant respects. First, their study is broadly comparative, focusing on how variation in the institutional context in which politicians find themselves influences delegation strategies. To this end, they examine differences in delegation processes *on the same issue* across political systems. They therefore cannot test the uncertainty principle because issue type is held constant. Second, based on an analysis of labor laws across parliamentary democracies and health laws across the US states, they argue that the primary way politicians influence discretion is not by the inclusion of procedural details in legislation, but rather by specifying in more or less detail the substantive policies bureaucrats must implement. They find strong support for the ally principle, with divided government leading

---

[2] Potoski 1999 finds similar effects in US states.

to less discretion in the states and coalition or minority government leading to less discretion in parliamentary systems. But they find that the degree to which coalition status or divided government diminishes discretion depends on other variables. Low discretion laws require legislative resources, and thus the ally principle is not robust to situations of low legislative professionalism in the American states, or to high levels of cabinet turnover in parliamentary democracies. And the ally principle depends on there being a clearly identifiable "politician." In the American states, when only one chamber of the legislature is against the governor, while the other supports him or her, the legislature is less able to use legislative details to limit discretion than in cases where there is unified opposition to the governor across the two chambers.

Franchino also finds support for the uncertainty and policy conflict arguments in his studies of delegation in the European Union. He finds that the Council of Ministers delegates more authority to a supranational bureaucracy, the European Commission, in specialized and technical policy areas, as measured by the existence of detailed rules within the laws themselves, the creation of "action programmes," and the use of specialized committees to write the law. He also finds that as conflict between member states increases in the Council, discretion for implementation typically declines (e.g. Franchino 2004, n.d.; see also 2001).

An impressive degree of support, then, is building for the ally principle and policy uncertainty. Scholars have also begun to test for, and find evidence of, substitution effects. For over two decades now, researchers have examined the extent to which *ex post* mechanisms cause bureaucrats to anticipate potential reprisals from legislatures and to modify their actions accordingly (e.g. Weingast and Moran 1983; Wood and Waterman 1991; Olson 1999; Shipan 2004). More recently, scholars have begun to examine the link between *ex ante* and *ex post* strategies (e.g. Aberbach 1990). If little oversight occurs, is this because bureaucrats anticipate what politicians desire, and thus need not be monitored directly, or because bureaucrats have substantial autonomy to do what they want? Bawn (1997) finds evidence of this substitution effect at the level of individual member of Congress: those members who sit on relevant oversight committees are least likely to seek *ex ante* limits on discretion.[3] Looking across systems, Huber and Shipan (2002) find evidence of the substitution effect. In the American states, they find that the presence of a legislative veto over agency actions allows state legislatures to write less detailed statutes. And across parliamentary democracies, they show that countries write less detailed labor laws when the legal system is structured to protect the politicians' interests as *ex post* and when corporatist bargaining arrangements give politicians an *ex post* check on labor policy.

Finally, several studies have begun to examine the effects of political uncertainty (i.e. uncertainty about the identity of future politicians). The Wood and Bohte (2004) study discussed earlier, for example, finds strong evidence that Congress is much more likely to limit agency discretion when political uncertainty is high (e.g. conflict exists within the enacting coalition and levels of electoral turnover are high). At the state level, Volden (2002*b*) finds that legislatures are far more likely to establish policy boards, which are insulated from political winds, if the dominant party in

---

[3] See, however, Balla 2000.

the legislature is in decline.[4] In the cross-national context, Gilardi (2002) examines a range of policy areas and finds that agencies are likely to be most independent when political uncertainty is high. And Huber (2000) reports that politicians in parliamentary systems adopt global budgets for health care departments, thereby limiting discretion, when cabinet turnover is high.[5]

3 IMPLICATIONS OF THE FORMAL AND EMPIRICAL WORK ON THE FOUR ARGUMENTS

As the preceding section illustrates, empirical support is beginning to accumulate for the four arguments about delegation described above. Bureaucrats are granted more discretion when there is policy conflict between politicians and bureaucrats, when policy uncertainty is high, when *ex post* opportunities to influence bureaucratic behavior are limited, and when politicians have more certainty that they will retain power into the future. But these tests focus on patterns of delegation strategies, rather than on the substantive outcomes of political-bureaucratic interactions. If we take the results of the empirical tests to suggest that the models are on the right track, what are the more general lessons about the outcomes of delegation processes?

At the most basic level, one implication of these empirical tests is that some nontrivial level of political control over bureaucrats must exist. It is interesting to observe that these tests to date do not have clear measures of bureaucratic preferences. Instead, the typical approach is to assume that there exists a privileged political actor who exercises non-trivial control over bureaucrats. In studies of Congress, this political actor is the president, and empirical measures of preference conflict between the "Politician" (Congress) and the "Bureaucrat" (president who controls agencies) are usually captured by the presence or absence of divided government. In studies of the US states, divided government is also used, and in parliamentary democracies, scholars have focused on division across parties during coalition and minority government. With these proxies for preference conflict, we find substantial support for the ally principle. If in fact the president (or governor or cabinet minister) is not exercising influence over bureaucracy, it is very difficult to imagine why this support would exist in the data. To our knowledge, there is no competing theory that assumes the absence of political control and that yields the same prediction that legislators should give less discretion to agencies during periods of divided (or coalition) government.

Second, these results about divided and coalition government also remind us that "bureaucratic politics" is often simply one more arena where standard distributive battles among politicians are waged. Legislators who craft new legislation or design

---

[4] De Figueiredo 2003 also provides evidence about the effects of political uncertainty on policy insulation in US state legislatures.
[5] See also Bernhard 2002 on the political factors that lead to central bank independence.

new agencies are not simply worried about how they might motivate recalcitrant bureaucrats. They are also worried about how they can use legislation and agency design to control rival politicians. Delegation, then, is often as much about using bureaucracy to control the actions of other politicians as it is about figuring out strategies to counter administrative dominance. This perspective on bureaucracy is not something one finds in the models themselves, but rather in the results from empirical tests of insights from the models.

Third, these models and empirical tests caution us about making inferences about administrative dominance by simply observing the strategies of politicians. If politicians exercise little *ex post* oversight, is this because they cannot influence bureaucrats? If legislators write vague statutes that give bureaucrats wide scope to fill in the policy details, does this mean that bureaucrats are likely to use their discretion to work against the interests of politicians? The fact that the data support the four arguments suggests a clear "no" to both questions. Politicians are likely to give substantial discretion to bureaucrats precisely in those situations where it is in the interest of politicians to do so, such as when the bureaucrat is an ally, or when the legislative majority can rely on effective *ex post* mechanisms—such as friendly judges—to help ensure desirable policy outcomes even in the presence of considerable bureaucratic discretion.

The fact remains, however, that with existing models and empirical techniques, we do not know how much control over bureaucrats exists. Indeed, the models underline that such control is quite difficult to achieve. In the stark model presented above, for instance, when policy uncertainty is low ($\bar{x} \in \{0, 1\}$), the Politician delegates authority to the Bureaucrat only if policy conflict is relatively low ($x_B \leq \frac{1}{2}$). As policy uncertainty increases, the Bureaucrat's policy expertise becomes more valuable to the Politician, and thus the Politician delegates authority even if policy conflict is larger ($x_B \leq 1$). The model therefore underlines the simple fact that the ability of bureaucrats to usurp the policy-making role of politicians increases as their relative expertise increases.

Since empirical tests support the models with these policy uncertainty assumptions, one clear implication is that administrative dominance is most likely when technical complexity is high. This, of course, has been central to the study of delegation since at least the work of Max Weber. But the more general models go beyond this simple insight to help identify more precisely the conditions under which the ability of politicians to use delegation strategies to control bureaucrats is most limited. Consider models that combine *ex ante* and *ex post* strategies and assume that the politicians must pay a cost to adopt legislation that limits discretion. The models show that the ability of politicians to influence bureaucratic behavior is substantially limited only when several specific conditions exist:

(a) Politicians and bureaucrats disagree about which outcome to pursue (such as should exist during divided or coalition government);
(b) Politicians must lack the capacity to pay the cost of writing detailed statutes that limit discretion (such as in systems with unprofessionalized legislatures);

(c) Politicians must not be able to rely on *ex post* mechanisms (such as auditing or courts) to ensure desirable bureaucratic actions.

Only when these three conditions are simultaneously met can we infer that statutes granting large discretion to bureaucrats are essentially abdicating policy-making authority to them.

4 THEORETICAL ROBUSTNESS: HOW FRAGILE ARE THE ARGUMENTS?

The four arguments—policy uncertainty, the ally principle, substitution effects, and political uncertainty—are robust in two senses. First, they have emerged from a number of different types of models, albeit models that make similar assumptions about policy uncertainty. Second, empirical research is beginning to build support for them. Recent theoretical research, however, has begun to reveal circumstances under which the theoretical predictions falter. What are these circumstances, and what are the implications of these models for future studies of bureaucracy?

As noted above, the models of delegation to bureaucrats that generate the four arguments typically assume that bureaucrats have more expertise than politicians. But what if politicians try to redress this imbalance by investing in information themselves? Gailmard (2002) examines this question, and his model has implications for theoretical arguments about preference divergence and delegation. For reasons similar to those discussed in conjunction with the stark model above, his model illustrates that as the preferences of a Bureaucrat diverge from a Politician's, the value of policy expertise to the Politician increases. But this fact, Gailmard observes, should create incentives for the Politician to invest more in information when these preferences diverge. Since the Politician's policy expertise increases with preference divergence, the Politician has less need to grant the Bureaucrat discretion. Thus, with endogenous specialization by the Politician, discretion can decrease with policy conflict because policy uncertainty can also decrease.

Bendor and Meirowitz (2004) take a different approach to fleshing out the origins of information asymmetries. Like Gailmard, they focus on endogenous investment in expertise, but unlike Gailmard, they focus on incentives for bureaucrats to become informed. In one variant that they analyze, a Bureaucrat cannot precommit to becoming informed about ε, but rather must pay a cost to do so *after* the discretion level is announced. In this model, the ally principal can fail. If the Politician does not delegate, the Bureaucrat's expected utility is that associated with the Politician's uninformed policy choice. Since this is a better outcome for an allied Bureaucrat than for one with divergent preferences, the Bureaucrat with divergent preferences has more incentive to pay the cost of specialization. The Politician, recognizing this incentive to specialize, is more likely to delegate to a non-ally bureaucrat under certain levels of policy uncertainty. Both the Gailmard and the Bendor–Meirowitz model suggest, then, that the ally principle may depend a great deal on the assumption of some exogenous source of information asymmetry. If one tries to make this asymmetry endogenous, then the ally principle can be turned on its head, with more discretion going to bureaucrats who are further from the politician's ideal point.

The standard models from which the ally principle emerges also assume that bureaucrats are very good at what they do (i.e. that they have high "capacity")—bureaucrats not only know ε, they can execute whatever policy action they wish. But even if individuals at the top of a bureaucratic hierarchy know which policy consequences will result from adopting a particular policy, they may be unable to execute this policy. Huber and McCarty (2004) explore delegation when bureaucratic capacity is low. Their model distinguishes between policy uncertainty, as described above, and bureaucratic capacity, which is the Bureaucrat's ability to execute his intended action. A Bureaucrat with low capacity has less ability to take the action he intends, even if he knows ε. Low capacity therefore makes it more difficult for the Bureaucrat to comply with a statute—the Bureaucrat may try to comply, but his lack of capacity may push the action he intends out of compliance. Consequently, a low-capacity Bureaucrat with preferences that diverge from the Politician's is less likely to make policy concessions toward the Politician's ideal point because the impact of such efforts on policy compliance is relatively low. In this situation, the Politician must give more discretion to the "enemy" Bureaucrat. This extra discretion induces the "enemy" Bureaucrat to forgo attempting to implement his most preferred policy, and instead to make policy concessions toward the Politician's ideal point. Consequently, the ally Bureaucrat, who pays a much lower policy cost of his unreliable attempts at policy compliance, receives less discretion than the "enemy" Bureaucrat.

The ally principle stems from models where a single Politician delegates to a single Bureaucrat. In many political systems, however, the distribution of agenda power for, say, setting discretion levels is divided among several politicians. If the multiple politicians are making collective decisions by majority rule in a single chamber, then the existence of multiple politicians may not be much of an issue. One could simply assume that the "politician" who seeks an ally in the bureaucracy is the median legislator, or some other pivotal politician. But often institutional separation of powers will create multiple pivotal politicians. In such cases, how does one think about an ally principle?

Studies of this question focus primarily on presidential systems. These studies assume legislatures propose and presidents veto, and typically explore the extent to which discretion levels—which are proposed by the legislature, not the president—are influenced by the extent to which the bureaucracy is an ally of the legislature. Volden (2002a), for example, develops a model where an executive can veto legislation that sets discretion levels. His model suggests that when the executive and legislature have divergent preferences, the ally principle will hold for some configurations of status quos and ideal points, but will fail for others. If the status quo is extreme relative to the preferences of the legislature and executive agent, for instance, then as the ideal points of the legislature and agent diverge, with the agent moving closer to the status quo, more discretion must be given to the agent in order to induce the agent to change the status quo. Similar results are found in Bendor and Meirowitz (2004) and Huber and Shipan (2002).

McCarty (2004) examines the multi-principal issue through the lens of the appointment processes. The politicians who grant discretion, McCarty notes, are often different from those who control appointments, with non-trivial consequences for strategic behavior. In his model, a President, who has the power to appoint a Bureaucrat, is constrained by the Legislature, which grants policy-making discretion to this Bureaucrat by providing budgetary resources to change the policy. If the President appoints a Bureaucrat who is too close to the President's ideal point, then the Legislature, whose preferences diverge from the President, will write laws that limit discretion. Given the Bureaucrat's expertise, both the President and the Legislature can be made better off if the President appoints a Bureaucrat who is between the President's and the Legislature's ideal point rather than at the President's ideal point. To this end, the President must be able to commit to not changing the Bureaucrat's ideal point after the Legislature establishes the discretion level. Constitutional or statutory provisions that limit the power of the President to remove bureaucrats from office are one obvious source of such precommitment.

Ting (2001) examines the possibility that a different sort of commitment problem can be overcome in a repeated-play setting. His model describes why we might expect *ex ante* and *ex post* strategies to be complements rather than substitutes. In Ting's model, the Politician establishes a budget, which determines bureaucratic discretion by constraining the types of policy that the Bureaucrat can implement. After the Bureaucrat implements a policy, the Politician can invest resources in *ex post* monitoring. Without repeated play, the Politician's auditing strategy is independent of the outcome she observes because she cannot *precommit* to conditioning intensity of audits on this outcome. If the game is repeated, with a new ε drawn in each period, the Politician can indirectly condition auditing on outcomes by conditioning future budget levels (which influence audit strategies) on outcomes. This can only occur, however, if the Politician and Bureaucrat have sufficiently similar preferences. In such cases, *ex ante* discretion and *ex post* monitoring are not substitutes, but complements. Larger budgets provide greater discretion, and since without precommitment politicians cannot condition monitoring on observing outcomes, they will increase discretion (i.e. budgets) only when they can increase monitoring.

5 Conclusion

Considerable energy has been devoted to developing models of the strategies that politicians use to shape bureaucratic behavior. Central to these models are two assumptions: first, bureaucrats, left to their own devices, will pursue outcomes that are not necessarily in the interest of politicians, and second, bureaucrats have more policy expertise than politicians. From these two assumptions, four theoretical arguments consistently emerge regarding delegation strategies. First, as *policy uncertainty* increases, politicians can achieve better outcomes by giving more discretion to bureaucrats. Second, as the policy preferences of politicians and bureaucrats converge, politicians can achieve better outcomes by giving more discretion to bureaucrats. Third, as *ex post* mechanisms to achieve policy goals become more effective, politicians should give bureaucrats more discretion. And fourth, greater political uncertainty provides current politicians with the incentive to shield bureaucratic actions from future political influence.

Empirical research, much of it on the US Congress or the US states, has begun to build support for these arguments. We can therefore have some confidence that the predictions from these models—not simply about delegation strategies, but also about delegation outcomes—are on the right track. This has allowed us to understand the strategies that politicians can use to create incentives for bureaucrats to act on behalf of politicians, and also to understand the circumstances under which exercising effective control over bureaucrats is most difficult.

As impressive as the research has been at bringing politics and political institutions into the study of bureaucracy, many questions remain unanswered. First, as we noted, the ally principle and the uncertainty principle are foundations for the study of delegation, but recent formal models suggest that both principles are fragile. The models, for example, identify specific conditions that lead to the failure of the ally principle, conditions related to endogenous specialization, low bureaucratic capacity, or separation of powers with extreme status quos. Yet most empirical work focuses on straightforward tests of the two principles, without taking into account the factors that models suggest could lead to their failure. By taking seriously some of the nuances in recent theoretical models, future empirical research could shed new light on the extent to which these two simple but pervasive principles shape delegation processes. One clear domain for testing models where bureaucrats are uninformed or of low capacity is in developing democracies. In any event, these most recent models require empirical scholars to consider carefully the precise circumstances under which it is appropriate to test the four arguments that have largely dominated the literature.

Second, courts represent one of the central yet neglected ways in which politicians can influence policy outcomes and agency actions. Empirical work (e.g. Spriggs 1996; Hanssen 2000; Howard and Nixon 2002; Canes-Wrone 2003) has examined how judges influence bureaucratic actions, or how legal structures influence *ex ante* delegation strategies (e.g. Huber and Shipan 2002). And spatial models have begun to examine similar issues (e.g. Shipan 2000). Yet given the relevance of the legislative–judicial–bureaucratic relationship to political science and to administrative law (e.g. Shapiro 2002), this is clearly an area that is ripe for further research.

Finally, studies of delegation—particularly formal models—typically rest on the premise that politicians adopt strategies that lead to the best obtainable policy choice by a bureaucrat in some current policy space. But the choices politicians make in delegating today can have ramifications long into the future. As Lewis (2004) points out, for example, a politicized bureaucracy, where politicians can make numerous bureaucratic appointments, might allow politicians to ensure the presence of their allies in the bureaucracy. This benefit, however, could be accompanied by a non-trivial cost, which is that it will be more difficult to attract quality personnel to work in the non-politicized parts of bureaucracies. Similarly, scholars have noted that basic features of bureaucratic organization, such as the existence of meritocratic recruitment, influence corruption levels (Rauch and Evans 2000) or economic growth (Evans and Rauch 1999).

It is clear, then, that there exists considerable variation in such institutions *within* bureaucracies—that is, in the politicization of appointments, pay levels of bureaucrats, rules for hiring and promotion, and so on. But little attention has been paid to explaining the sources or consequences of this variation. Thus, linking studies of the politics of delegation to studies of structures internal to bureaucracies, which have been chiefly the domain of sociology (but see Whitford 2002), represents one of the most important avenues for future research on bureaucracy.

REFERENCES

ABERBACH, J. D. 1990. *Keeping a Watchful Eye*. Washington, DC: Brookings Institution.
BALLA, S. J. 1998. Administrative procedures and political control of the bureaucracy. *American Political Science Review*, 92: 663–74.
—— 2000. Legislative organization and congressional review of agency regulations. *Journal of Law, Economics, and Organization*, 16: 424–48.
—— and WRIGHT, J. R. 2001. Interest groups, advisory committees, and congressional control of bureaucracy. *American Journal of Political Science*, 45: 799–812.
BAWN, K. 1995. Political control versus expertise: congressional choices about administrative procedures. *American Political Science Review*, 89: 62–73.
—— 1997. Choosing strategies to control the bureaucracy: statutory constraints, oversight, and the committee system. *Journal of Law, Economics, and Organization*, 13: 101–26.
BENDOR, J. and MEIROWITZ, A. 2004. Spatial models of delegation. *American Political Science Review*, 98: 293–310.
BERNHARD, W. 2002. *Banking on Reform*. Ann Arbor: University of Michigan Press.
CANES-WRONE, B. 2003. Bureaucratic decisions and the composition of the lower courts. *American Journal of Political Science*, 47: 205–14.
DE FIGUEIREDO, R. J. P., JR. 2002. Electoral competition, political uncertainty, and policy insulation. *American Political Science Review*, 96: 321–33.
—— 2003. Budget institutions and political insulation: why states adopt the item veto. *Journal of Public Economics*, 87: 2677–701.
EPSTEIN, D., and O'HALLORAN, S. 1994. Administrative procedures, information, and agency discretion. *American Journal of Political Science*, 38: 697–722.
—— —— 1999. *Delegating Powers*. New York: Cambridge University Press.
EVANS, P., and RAUCH, J. 1999. Bureaucracy and growth: a cross-national analysis of the effects of "Weberian" state structures on economic growth. *American Sociological Review*, 64: 748–65.
FEREJOHN, J., and SHIPAN, C. 1990. Congressional influence on bureaucracy. *Journal of Law, Economics, and Organization*, 6: 1–20.

FRANCHINO, F. 2001. Delegation and constraints in the national execution of the EC policies: a longitudinal and qualitative analysis. *West European Politics*, 24: 169–92.

——— 2004. Delegating powers in the European Community. *British Journal of Political Science*, 34: 269–93.

——— n.d. The powers of the Union: who does what and why in the European Union. Manuscript, University College London.

GAILMARD, S. 2002. Expertise, subversion, and bureaucratic discretion. *Journal of Law, Economics, and Organization*, 18: 536–55.

GILADI, F. 2002. Policy credibility and delegation to independent regulatory agencies: a comparative empirical analysis. *Journal of European Public Policy*, 9: 873–93.

HAMILTON, J. T., and SCHROEDER, C. H. 1994. Strategic regulators and the choice of rulemaking procedures: the selection of formal vs. informal rules in regulating hazardous waste. *Law and Contemporary Problems*, 57: 111–60.

HANSSEN, F. A. 2000. Independent courts and administrative agencies: an empirical analysis of the states. *Journal of Law, Economics, and Organization*, 16: 534–71.

HORN, M. J. 1995. *The Political Economy of Public Administration.* New York: Cambridge University Press.

HOWARD, R. M., and NIXON, D. C. 2002. Regional court influence over bureaucratic policy-making: courts, ideological preferences, and the Internal Revenue Service. *Political Research Quarterly*, 55: 907–22.

HOWELL, W. G., and LEWIS, D. E. 2002. Agencies by presidential design. *Journal of Politics*, 64: 1095–114.

HUBER, J. D. 2000. Delegation to civil servants in parliamentary democracies. *European Journal of Political Research*, 37: 397–413.

——— and MCCARTY, N. 2004. Bureaucratic capacity, delegation and political reform. *American Political Science Review*, 98: 481–94.

——— and SHIPAN, C. R. 2000. The costs of control: legislators, agencies, and transaction costs. *Legislative Studies Quarterly*, 25: 25–52.

——— ——— 2002. *Deliberate Discretion: The Institutional Foundations of Bureaucratic Autonomy.* New York: Cambridge University Press.

LEWIS, D. E. 2003. *Presidents and the Politics of Agency Design.* Stanford, Calif.: Stanford University Press.

——— 2004. Presidents and the politicization of the institutional presidency. Working paper, Princeton University.

MCCARTY, N. 2004. The appointments dilemma. *American Journal of Political Science*, 48: 413–28.

MCCUBBINS, M. D., NOLL, R. G., and WEINGAST, B. R. 1987. Administrative procedures as instruments of political control. *Journal of Law, Economics, and Organization*, 3: 243–77.

——— ——— ——— 1989. Structure and process, politics and policy: administrative arrangements and the political control of agencies. *Virginia Law Review*, 75: 431–82.

MOE, T. M. 1989. The politics of bureaucratic structure. In *Can the Government Govern?* ed. J. E. Chubb and P. E. Peterson. Washington, DC: Brookings Institution.

NIXON, D. C., HOWARD, R. M., and DEWITT, J. R. 2002. With friends like these: rule-making comment submissions to the Securities and Exchange Commission. *Journal of Public Administration Research and Theory*, 12: 59–76.

OLSON, M. K. 1999. Agency rulemaking, political influences, regulation and industry compliance. *Journal of Law, Economics, and Organization*, 15: 573–601.

POTOSKI, M. 1999. Managing uncertainty through bureaucratic design: administrative procedures and state air pollution control agencies. *Journal of Public Administration Research and Theory*, 9: 623–39.

POTOSKI, M., and WOODS, N. 2001. Designing state clean air agencies: administrative procedures and bureaucratic autonomy. *Journal of Public Administration Research and Theory*, 11: 203–22.

RAUCH, J., and EVANS, P. 2000. Bureaucratic structure and bureaucratic performance in less developed countries. *Journal of Public Economics*, 74: 49–71.

SHAPIRO, M. 2002. Judicial delegation doctrines: the US, Britain, and France. *West European Politics*, 25: 173–99.

SHEPSLE, K. A. 1992. Bureaucratic drift, coalitional drift, and time inconsistency: a comment on Macey. *Journal of Law, Economics, and Organization*, 8: 111–18.

SHIPAN, C. R. 2000. The legislative design of judicial review: a formal analysis. *Journal of Theoretical Politics*, 12: 269–304.

—— 2004. Regulatory regimes, agency actions, and the conditional nature of political influence. *American Political Science Review*, 93: 467–80.

SPENCE, D. B. 1999. Managing delegation ex ante: using law to steer administrative agencies. *Journal of Legal Studies*, 28: 413–59.

SPRIGGS, J. F. 1996. The Supreme Court and federal administrative agencies: a resource-based theory and analysis of judicial impact. *American Journal of Political Science*, 40: 1122–51.

TING, M. M. 2001. The "power of the purse" and its implications for bureaucratic policy-making. *Public Choice*, 106: 243–74.

VOLDEN, C. 2002*a*. A formal model of the politics of delegation in a separation of powers system. *American Journal of Political Science*, 46: 111–33.

—— 2002*b*. Delegating power to bureaucracies: evidence from the states. *Journal of Law, Economics, and Organization*, 18: 187–220.

WEINGAST, B. R., and MORAN, M. J. 1983. Bureaucratic discretion or congressional control: regulatory policy-making by the FTC. *Journal of Political Economy*, 91: 765–800.

WHITFORD, A. B. 2002. Decentralization and political control of the bureaucracy. *Journal of Theoretical Politics*, 14: 167–93.

WOOD, B. D., and BOHTE, J. 2004. Political transaction costs and the politics of administrative design. *Journal of Politics*, 66: 176–202.

—— and WATERMAN, R. W. 1991. The dynamics of political control of the bureaucracy. *American Political Science Review*, 85: 801–28.

CHAPTER 15

THE JUDICIARY AND THE ROLE OF LAW

MATHEW D. McCUBBINS

DANIEL B. RODRIGUEZ

1 INTRODUCTION

POSITIVE Political Theory (PPT) affords a fresh perspective on how we understand the courts and judicial behavior. Traditional legal analysis of law and politics makes two critical assumptions: first, it studies the courts in isolation; second, it interprets judges as acting last in the policy-making process; that is, at the end of a series of steps by Congress, the president, or the bureaucracy that conclude with a judicial determination. From this perspective, judges appear to be unconstrained by external forces. The only source of constraint is the rule of law itself, manifested in precedent, *stare decisis*, and control by judges higher up the chain of command. Hence, the traditional view assumes the law, courts, and judicial behavior are the only factors relevant for explaining what judges do and how they decide cases.

Although traditional scholars always knew that other political actors were important, they saw episodes of political influence as isolated rather than systematic. It is a commonplace in the literature on early American constitutional law, for example, to note that political factors underlay the Supreme Court's decision in *Marbury* v. *Madison* (1803) and, perhaps even more explicitly, in the controversy over President Franklin D. Roosevelt's court-packing scheme of the 1930s. However, these stories are powerfully resonant in traditional constitutional law discourse *precisely because* they are viewed as exceptional, as representing those rare instances in which rule of law values were trumped by political (read: sinister) forces.

The PPT approach to studying law denies both of these assumptions. Instead, this approach embeds the courts in a political system where judges are constrained in their decision-making; and second, it shows that, except for constitutional cases, the court does not act last but acts in the middle of a highly interactive process. With respect to administrative law or statutory interpretation cases, for example, Congress can always overturn a judicial ruling. This implies that, if judges believe it is costly to be overturned, they will act strategically so as to avoid being overturned. In short, the political process *constrains* the types of decisions judges can make.

Because judges act in the middle of a political process and are *not* the endpoint, they must act strategically to get what they want. That is, judges must anticipate how other political actors will react and must take these reactions into account.

This chapter proceeds as follows: in the second section, we discuss the implications of our approach for issues in statutory interpretation. The third section discusses the relationship between political and legal controls of bureaucracy. The fourth section draws the implications for judicial independence within the larger separation-of-powers system.

2 Statutory Interpretation

Legal scholars view statutory interpretation as a process by which courts discern the meaning of ambiguous legislative language through various approaches and techniques (Eskridge, Frickey, and Garrett 2001). The principal disagreement in the large literature on interpretation is whether and in what circumstances courts ought to use extrinsic aids beyond the legislative text, such as legislative history and interpretative canons, to reconstruct the meaning of statutes where this meaning is in dispute (McCubbins and Rodriguez 2006). Ordinarily, this normative debate is divorced from positive theories of legislation or of the interpretative process.

By contrast, positive political theory has contributed uniquely to these debates by articulating a theory of court–Congress relations and statutory interpretation. Armed with this positive theory, scholars can more fruitfully assess the political dimensions of interpretation and, as well, the impact of one or another prescription on the dynamics of legislative politics and judicial performance. One fundamental insight of positive political theory is that courts act strategically when they interpret statutes (Ferejohn and Weingast 1992*a*). In particular, courts are constrained in their interpretative choices by the possibility that Congress will overturn their decisions.

Consider the spatial model shown in Figure 15.1, where J is the judge's most preferred position, P the president's, and C Congress's (we assume, for simplicity, that C represents the median voter within that body): For the purposes of this model, we assume that Congress and the president have acted to produce a law. A dispute over the law's meaning has ended up before a court and the judge must interpret

```
----------x------------x------x------x----------
          J            P      L      C
```

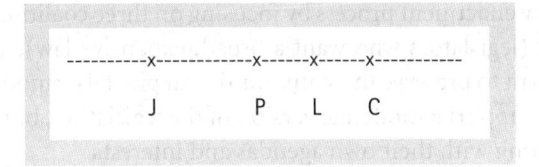

Fig. 15.1 Political constraints on interpretation

the statute in order to determine what the legislation means. After the court makes its decision, Congress and the president have an opportunity to pass legislation overturning the judicial decision. Critically, the court knows when it interprets the statute that Congress and the president can react by overturning its decision.

Suppose that the court acts in accordance with its own preferences and tries to impose policy J. Insofar as J is to the left of both of their preferences, Congress and the president will react. Because each prefers a range of policies to J, they will pass legislation overturning the court's decision; this legislation will reflect a compromise between their most preferred points of P and C respectively. We call this compromise legislation L.

If, on the other hand, the court interprets the statute to implement policy P, then this policy is an equilibrium. That is, since there is no policy that the president prefers to P, no legislation can pass to overturn the court's decision. By acting strategically, the court has not only forestalled a legislative overturning of its decision, but it has obtained a better final policy outcome—P—than if it had originally decided the case at its ideal J—which would have yielded policy outcome L.

As Brian Marks (1988) and other scholars following in the PPT tradition have explained,[1] the difficulty in passing new legislation implies that courts may implement a policy inconsistent with legislative preferences; that is, the courts may reinterpret legislation away from its original intention in a manner that the president and Congress cannot overcome. Because Congress and the president disagree about policy, the courts can choose any interpretation in between P and C without fear of having their decision overruled (McNollgast 1994, 1992; Eskridge and Ferejohn 1992; Gely and Spiller 1992).

A significant positive conclusion for the debate over statutory interpretation follows from this analysis: statutory interpretations may well depart from the original preferences of the enacting Congress and the president, but, because of the "industrial organization of Congress" and the ability of key legislators to entrench their preferences through rules and institutions, the current legislature may be unable to overturn interpretations that pry the statute loose from its original meaning.

McNollgast (1994, 1992) and Rodriguez and Weingast (2006a, 2003) provide a PPT framework for understanding the determination of statutory interpretation decisions. Their approach reveals the mechanisms by which courts strategically use pieces of legislative history in order to reconstruct the original statutory bargain among pivotal legislators and thereby to expand the scope of the statute. First, they

---

[1] See Eskridge and Ferejohn 1992 for a survey of the literature.

model the statutory enactment process by focusing on three coalitions of legislators—ardent supporters (legislators who want a broad, expansive law), ardent opponents (legislators who want to preserve the status quo), and pivotal or moderates (legislators who are willing to support a moderate version of the legislation, but not an expansive one)—each operating with their own agendas and interests.

Because their support is necessary to produce legislation, pivotal legislators influence the outcome of the final legislation in significant ways. Their compromise version of the legislation differs from the ardent supporters' original proposal in ways that make it more palatable to the moderates.

Nonetheless, ardent supporters remain committed to a more expansive policy and often undertake efforts to move policy in a more progressive direction *ex post*. One way to do this is to insert into the legislative record the sort of legislative "history" that supports an expansionist reading. The advantage of this strategy arises when courts are interested in proffering an expansionist policy, as many were in the late 1960s and early 1970s. Such courts will grasp onto these strategically motivated statements and use them to justify their expansionist readings. As a consequence, these judicial determinations replace the legislative bargain, which represents the calculated efforts of pivotal moderate legislators, with a version of the legislation supported by ardent supporters and sympathetic courts.

Rodriguez and Weingast (2003) have described this process through an extended analysis of the passage of the watershed Civil Rights Act of 1964 and its subsequent interpretation by liberal federal courts of the 1970s and 1980s. In 1964, supporters of a strong civil rights bill lacked sufficient support in Congress to convert their vision into national law. Despite their success in clearing the significant hurdles in the House of Representatives, civil rights proponents faced the powerful threat of the Southern filibuster in the Senate and thereby the same fate that had befallen one hundred years' worth of civil rights legislation.

The solution to this impasse, as Rodriguez and Weingast explain, lay in the willingness of pivotal moderates within the Republican Party and its congressional leadership to consider supporting a carefully drafted legislative compromise. Once in the hands of the courts, however, judges unraveled the bargain struck by the coalitions of ardent supporters and moderates. Courts rewrote the statute by substituting more expansionist interpretations for moderate language and structure. Moreover, even where these interpretations departed from the preferences of the members of Congress serving at the time these decisions were rendered, the institutional impediments described above made it extremely difficult for Congress to correct these "mistaken" interpretations. As Eskridge (1991) demonstrates, Congress was unable to overturn the judicial rulings to restore the original bargain.[2] Thus, the political dynamics of legislative policy-making, as well the dynamics of court–Congress relations, reinforces the PPT insight that strategic legislators influence the

---

[2] Indeed, Eskridge 1991 further argues that the conservative Burger Court made these expansionary readings to forestall even stronger new civil rights legislation from the more liberal Congresses of the 1970s.

scope and direction of public policy through their attentiveness to the processes of statutory interpretation.[3]

The previous discussion shows how courts interact with the political branches and affect policy. Clearly, justices can alter policy. But because their (non-constitutional) decisions can be overturned by Congress, courts must act strategically to further their goals. If, for example, courts begin to take an activist role, then they can—for a time at least—expand the meaning of recently passed legislation. This activism has a critical feedback effect, however, in that expansionist courts in effect tell the moderates in Congress that the compromises necessary to get them to sign on to legislation are precarious; the court may well replace these compromises with an expansive reading. Expansionary judicial behavior therefore forces the moderates to choose between the status quo and the stronger bill, even when their moderate compromise has been crafted in Congress. In many cases, they will choose the status quo. This analysis suggests that judicial activism/expansionary readings make new progressive legislation *less* likely (Rodriguez and Weingast 2003, 2006a). There is a trade-off; therefore, courts must consider their effect not only on the reading of existing statutes, but on the process of producing new statutes.

A final conclusion is normative: If one of the goals of statutory interpretation is to help create fidelity to the legislative process defined by the Constitution, then the courts should refrain from expansionary readings. The better approach to interpreting statutes is one in which courts use available techniques to respect the will of Congress, as expressed by the compromise between the ardent supporters and the moderates. This approach is more consistent with constitutional values, with the avowed intent of the communicator, and with the cause of legislative supremacy and progressive law-making (Boudreau, McCubbins, and Rodriguez 2005; McCubbins and Rodriguez 2006).

3 LEGAL CONTROL OF THE BUREAUCRACY

Courts play a significant role in controlling the bureaucracy. They do so through three principal mechanisms: (1) administrative procedure, (2) constitutional review of agency decision-making, and (3) administrative law through the so-called "hard look" review. The traditional view of legal scholars is that courts' primary function with regard to the bureaucracy and policy process is keeping agencies away from politics and safeguarding norms of procedural fairness and administrative reasonableness in the face of ubiquitous political pressure and influence (Merrill 1997; Stewart 1975). PPT scholars have revisited this assumption and have developed a vein of scholarship

---

[3] See also Rodriguez 1992 who discusses how legislators can affect statutory interpretation process through *ex ante* mechanisms.

that emphasizes the ways in which courts *reinforce* strategies of political control through their various judicial doctrines and techniques.[4]

Administrative procedural review is the most typical way by which courts supervise the bureaucratic process. This review includes enforcing the procedural rules established by statute and administrative regulation and also through judicially created procedural guidelines. Through the creation and enforcement of administrative procedures, the courts also play a role in the political control of the bureaucracy (Spiller 1996; Ferejohn and Shipan 1990). For *ex post* controls, such as fire alarms, to succeed as a tool for controlling the bureaucracy, they must be credible (Lupia and McCubbins 1998). The creation of credible fire alarms involves establishing appropriate procedures for managing the collection and dissemination of information about an agency's activities (McNollgast 1987, 1989).

3.1 Implications of the Administrative Procedure Act

The US Administrative Procedure Act of 1946 (APA), as interpreted by the courts, establishes several provisions facilitating political control of agency decision-making: First, an agency cannot announce a new policy without providing notice of a change. Second, agencies must solicit comments allowing interested parties to state their views. These notice and comment provisions ensure that the agency discovers the relevant political interests and the political costs and benefits associated with various actions.[5] Third, agencies must allow interested parties to participate in the decision-making process to the extent specified in the organic statute creating the agency (McCubbins and Page 1986). If hearings are held, interested parties may present evidence and cross-examine witnesses, and rules against *ex parte* communications protect against the possibility of secret deals between agencies and constituent groups. Because participation in the administrative process is costly, it allows leaders to gauge the level of involvement of interested parties (Noll 1971). Fourth, agencies must provide a rational link between the evidence received from interested parties and the final agency policy decision. Fifth, agencies must make a record of the final vote of each member in the proceeding available for review. The entire decision-making process provides political leaders with numerous opportunities to respond when an agency seeks to move in a direction which diverges from leaders' preferences. Many countries have adopted measures similar to the American APA to achieve political control of the bureaucracy (Spiller 1996).[6]

[4] For a survey of this literature, see Rodriguez 1994, 91–105.
[5] Although not all groups with political interests at stake will participate in the notice and comment process, failure to participate signals that these non-participating actors are less likely to become a significant electoral force in the future.
[6] In addition to ensuring agency compliance with the APA, courts apply procedural rules embodied in the organic statutes creating and regulating the agencies and also in procedural regulations adopted by the agencies themselves. These rules reflect the same legislative interests manifest in the APA, in that they facilitate legislative control, while also subserving other critical values such as procedural fairness, regularity, and regulatory efficacy (Edley 1990). The PPT approach to administrative procedures does

What these various forms of procedural rules have in common is that they have profound political implications. As noted, fire alarms need to be credible to work. This means that congressional constituents must have access to agency proceedings and information. It also means that agencies cannot plot in secrecy, against either Congress or its constituents. Moreover, these procedures also facilitate Congress's *ex post* enforcement mechanisms. Congress cannot know all about what every agency does. Yet, when their attention is needed, these procedures ensure that all politically relevant information is available to them. These procedures reveal: who are the relevant parties, what are the interests, what they want, and how much do they care about it. The procedures also reveal the various policy options. Of course, if Congress had to focus on all this information for each agency, they would fail. But the ability to bring their attention to any given agency if necessary grants agencies *ex ante* incentives to avoid being put in the "*ex post*" hot seat by serving congressional interests in the first place.

Critically, these structural and procedural constraints have their effect only if courts enforce them. One key piece of evidence that courts can be expected to enforce these constraints and thereby facilitate legislative interests is that legislatures typically delegate enforcement of administrative procedures to courts (McNollgast 1987). The reasons for this delegation are not difficult to fathom: Reliable judicial enforcement increases the likelihood that the agency's choice will mirror political preferences without the need for political oversight (McCubbins and Schwartz 1984).

While the discussion thus far has focused on administrative procedure and the courts' role in supervising the bureaucracy through procedural review, courts have available to them two other important mechanisms of control. First, courts may invalidate agency action on the grounds that such action violates the US Constitution. Constitutional review is a draconian device that, when implemented, constricts the actions of both the agencies and the legislature. Despite well-known instances of the courts' use of procedural due process to restrain agencies and Congress, the due process "revolution" portended by administrative law scholars of the 1970s and 1980s never came to pass; rather, courts have only seldom invoked the trump of procedural due process, instead relying on other techniques of control to supervise the bureaucracy (Rodriguez and Weingast 2006*b*). PPT provides a compelling explanation for this strategy: Courts are more likely to control agencies in order to carry out legislative preferences and interests than to implement trans-statutory values through constitutional rules. Non-constitutional review strikes a balance, from the perspective of the courts, between the political imperatives of bureaucratic control and the values underlying procedural fairness as implemented by the courts.

Second, courts may invalidate agency action on the grounds that such action is "arbitrary" or "capricious" or, in the case of formal agency proceedings, is unsupported by the evidence taken as a whole. Since at least the early 1970s, the courts have been employing these standards to give agency decisions a so-called "hard

---

not draw a bright line distinction between these twin functions of procedural rules. They can be viewed profitably as serving both political interests and broad "procedural justice" goals.

look;" and this mechanism of review has been described by scholars as enforcing a requirement that agency decisions be substantively "reasonable" (Shapiro 1988). The courts' sensitivity to the political dimensions of judicial control can be seen in the ways in which they practice this "hard look" review. PPT scholars have explained how hard look review in administrative law is, by contrast to the traditional view among legal scholars, politically sophisticated.[7]

3.2 The *Chevron* Decision

To suggest how the courts are embedded within the political system and use their jurisprudential decisions to further political goals, we discuss the *Chevron* puzzle, first articulated by Cohen and Spitzer (1994). In *Chevron v. Natural Resources Defense Council* (1984), the Supreme Court ruled that courts were to defer to agency interpretations of the statutes they administer unless Congress had directly spoken to the issue and the agency interpretation contradicted Congress's expressed wish or unless the agency's decision was "unreasonable." The puzzle is why the Supreme Court should announce a doctrine that seemed to limit the courts' role in agency decision-making.

Cohen and Spitzer's resolution of the puzzle concerns the political configuration across American national institutions that held at the time of *Chevron*, namely, Congress, the presidency, the judiciary, and the bureaucracy. By the mid-1980s, President Ronald Reagan was in command of the presidency and had peopled the bureaucracy with a wide range of conservatives whose views contrasted with the more progressive views in Congress and the bureaucracy throughout the late 1960s and 1970s. Republicans had also recaptured the Senate in 1980 and held it in the next congressional election, making this institution considerably more conservative than in previous years. By 1984, the Supreme Court also had a conservative cast. The lower courts, however, remained largely appointees of the Democrats and therefore more liberal.

Though Reagan officials throughout the bureaucracy began cutting back on regulation, many lower courts prevented this change in approach. The issues in *Chevron* were a case in point: The DC Circuit overturned an Environmental Protection Agency decision, which would have permitted the use of a market-like mechanism for the control of air pollution. In overruling the lower court's decision and announcing a rule that would instruct courts to defer to agencies' interpretative judgements, the Supreme Court furthered the Republicans' agenda, thus allowing Reagan officials in the bureaucracy to alter a wide range of public policies. The limitation imposed on courts is rational, in this argument, because it helped the Supreme Court limit the lower courts' ability to forestall conservative-motivated policy change.

The main conclusion reached by the PPT approach to studying the political and legal controls of the bureaucracy is that these two dimensions of control are both

---

[7] See, e.g., McNollgast 1989, 1987. While this seminal work focused on the role of *ex ante* procedural rules and structures, more recent work focuses on the role of the courts. See, e.g., Rodriguez and Weingast 2006*b*.

ubiquitous and mutually reinforcing. These insights stand in sharp contrast to the traditional depiction of agencies as neutral embodiments of expertise—a view captured well by the Progressives' saying that "there is no Republican or Democratic way to pave a street" and the depiction of courts as using constitutional and administrative law to rescue apolitical agencies from the baleful influence of Congress and the president. The more accurate picture, as this modern PPT literature reveals, is of the bureaucracy and the judiciary embedded in the dynamic political system. Political and legal controls, therefore, are two sides of the same coin.

4 JUDICIAL INDEPENDENCE

> The judiciary, ... may truly be said to have neither FORCE nor WILL, but merely judgment; and must ultimately depend upon the aid of the executive arm even for the efficacy of its judgments.
>
> (Hamilton, *Federalist 78*; emphasis in original)

What does it mean for a judiciary to be "independent?" What are the conditions required for judicial independence to exist? Scholars have long grappled with the meaning of judicial independence, offering a wide range of definitions and approaches to this concept. Understanding judicial independence is especially problematic because "judicial" may have many possible meanings; it may refer to either individual judges, a particular court, or the entire court system in a given country (Russell 2001; Ferejohn 1999). Equally problematic is the term "independence," a relative term which can only be understood by analyzing the judicial entity in relation to its independence from some other entity, such as other political branches or undue external influences. As a result of these definitional challenges, scholars have developed two main approaches for defining and analyzing judicial independence.

The first approach examines how certain institutions and institutional rules allow judges to exercise independence. For some scholars, such as Landes and Posner (1975), judicial independence springs from the separation-of-powers concept mandated in the US Constitution which allows the Supreme Court in adjudicating cases to stand apart from the "intrusiveness of the political process" (p. 875). For other scholars, institutional rules define judicial independence. Segal and Spaeth (2002) and Segal (1997), leading proponents of the attitudinal approach, declare that Supreme Court justices vote their sincere preferences due to the "rules and structures of the U.S. political system." Other scholars advocating an institutional approach focus on specific rules which facilitate independence. For these scholars, judicial independence is defined either directly or indirectly by life tenure (Burbank and Friedman 2002; Landes and Posner 1975; Domingo 2000), by lengthy tenure (Burbank and Friedman 2002; Magaloni 2003; Moreno, Crisp, and Shugart 2003), by a judicial appointment process involving more than one branch of the government (Moreno, Crisp, and

Shugart 2003), by the judiciary's control over its own budget and administration (Russell 2001; Domingo 2000), or by discipline and removal of judges (Abraham 2002). Scholars advocating an institutional approach to judicial independence focus on either one particular institutional rule or a combination of rules which vary the degree of judicial independence (see Epstein, Knight, and Shvetsova 2002).

Under the second approach to judicial independence, scholars disregard these various institutional rules,[8] which vary among countries, and instead focus on the ability of individual judges to exercise discretion in deciding particular cases. Ferejohn (1999), the leading advocate of this approach, defines judicial independence in the American legal system as "independent judges within a dependent judiciary" (p. 381). For Ferejohn, judges are "independent" if they are free to make decisions without fear of consequence. At the same time, Ferejohn, like Hamilton, recognized that the federal judiciary is "institutionally dependent on Congress and the president, for jurisdiction, rules, and execution of judicial orders" (p. 353). Despite the Founding Fathers' recognition of this important connection between the courts and other branches of government, most legal and political scholars have focused on the institutional approach to judicial independence.

The New Institutionalist and PPT literatures define judicial independence as an outcome that emerges from strategic interactions among the judiciary, the legislature, and the executive. Indeed, using a model of the strategic analysis of the judiciary with the separation-of-powers system, McNollgast (2006) argues that judicial independence is not the automatic result of constitutional or statutory provisions that establish life tenure for judges, nor is judicial independence limited by checks and balances or legal traditions. *Rather, judicial independence waxes and wanes with changes in the political composition of our three branches of government.* The logic of this claim can be seen using Figure 15.1 above. The key observation is that the room for judicial independence—the ability to make judicial determinations that are not overturned by the political branches—is in part a function of the distance between P and C: any judicial ruling in this region is a policy equilibrium since no legislation can pass to overturn it; that is, any proposal that makes the president better off makes Congress worse off, and vice versa.

This logic implies that, during periods of divided government, the space between P and C is large. Therefore one chamber of the legislature or the executive branch is likely to protect judicial independence by vetoing (or threatening to veto) legislative actions that would overturn court decisions or, more aggressively, threaten the judiciary. By contrast, McNollgast's (1995) approach implies that unified control of government weakens judicial independence, as the legislature and executive can more easily coordinate on governmental changes that may undermine the judiciary's independence. Of course when there is not divided government, appointments to the judiciary make the preferences of the judiciary close to those of P and C.

---

[8] Although not offering a concrete alternative approach, Stephenson 2001 and Cameron 2002 reject defining judicial independence in terms of institutional rules. Cameron 2002 asserts that "explicit structural protections" may be only "parchment barriers to an aggressive executive or legislature unconstrained by voters who value judicial independence" (p. 139).

The foundation of these conclusions stem from what we call the courts' Hamiltonian dilemma—Alexander Hamilton's observation in *Federalist 78* that courts, by themselves, cannot implement their own orders or opinions. Although it is difficult for Congress and the president to overturn a court decision with which they disagree,[9] it is much more difficult to get political officials to implement judicial decisions that they oppose. In the PPT framework, judicial decisions are merely one form of policy. And, as with other policies requiring enforcement and implementation, for judicial orders and opinions to have an effect, they must obtain compliance from those to whom the orders and opinions are directed, including lower courts, executive agencies, commissions, state and local governments, and their agencies, corporations, and individuals. In this way, the limits on judicial independence are the direct results of the relative impoverishment of judicial power and of the legislature and executive's ability to take advantage of the judiciary's relative weakness.[10]

Several conclusions follow from this insight. To begin with, the Supreme Court, due to imperfect information and limited resources for hearing appeals, cannot enforce perfect adherence to its judicial doctrines by its agents. By this view, doctrine is not what the court believes is the best policy to pursue for its own sake, but rather is an instrument to gain compliance from various agents. In areas where potential case numbers are huge relative to the court's ability to review cases, the court must set a lax standard—as in *Brown*'s ambiguous message to school districts to desegregate with "all deliberate speed." In areas where the cases are relatively few and the policies are ones that the judiciary values highly, such as abortion, the court can set a tight standard. In this sense, doctrine is, at least in part, the strategic creation by the higher courts in their efforts to ensure a degree of judicial compliance.

A consequence of the courts' Hamiltonian dilemma is that political actors can take advantage of this situation by exacerbating the court's scarcity, influencing judicial doctrines by expanding the number and reach of executive agencies, commissions, lower courts, and so on. By forcing the court to decide more cases, or by restricting its ability to review cases, political officials indirectly affect doctrine by forcing the Supreme Court to widen or narrow the range of acceptable decisions. In this way, elected officials create and use structure and process to influence judicial policy in much the same way that they use administrative structure and process to influence agency policy-making (McNollgast 1987, 1989).

McNollgast (1995) demonstrated how a united set of political branches opposing a Supreme Court could force it to alter its doctrine in their favor by expanding the lower judiciary and forcing the court to face many more potentially non-complying lower courts. Lower court expansion exacerbates the Supreme Court's compliance problem, forcing it to expand the range of acceptable decisions—that is, in the direction favored by political officials. Political officials, then, indirectly affect the

---

[9] On congressional overturns of court decisions, see Eskridge 1991 and Spiller and Tiller 1996.
[10] As an illustration of the many enforcement difficulties that the judiciary faces, note how overseeing compliance with school desegregation decrees, especially in the face of hostile school boards, is a lifetime ambition for a court, one which necessarily precludes addressing other matters and one for which compliance notoriously fades into the shadows once the spotlight no longer shines on the issue.

agenda for the judiciary's choice of doctrine by causing the court to shift its focus in policy-making; courts are forced to leave some areas unattended, while using their scarce resources to affect doctrine in other areas. The main result is that the more closely aligned and coordinated are the political branches, the more likely they are to agree on policy outcomes, which then reduces the number of issues on which the court can exercise meaningful independent discretion.

5 Conclusion

The emerging PPT literature on the judiciary and the role of law stresses the political nature of legal decision-making and the dynamic relationship among the legislative, executive, and judicial branches. It also reinforces the wisdom of public law scholars working within the tradition of Shapiro, Melnick, and others, who have stressed the unavoidable and intentional role of courts in the policy process (see Rubin 2005 for a useful recent account of this view). Yet, as a relatively new vein of scholarship in the PPT tradition, there are many questions that require systematic attention. For example, what is the precise relationship between political mechanisms of control and legal doctrine? Despite the centrality of politically attentive judicial decision-making, is there still something separate from ordinary politics that we can view as "the rule of law?" How are the processes of judicial decision-making affected by the structure and organizational design of the state and federal judiciary? These, and other pressing questions, rightly occupy the attention of scholars working within the PPT tradition.

References

ABRAHAM, H. 2002. The pillars and politics of judicial independence in the United States. In *Judicial Independence at the Crossroads: An Interdisciplinary Approach*, ed. S. Burbank and B. Friedman. Thousand Oaks, Calif.: Sage.

BOUDREAU, C., MCCUBBINS, M., and RODRIGUEZ, D. 2005. Statutory interpretation and the intentional(ist) stance. *Loyola of Los Angeles Law Review*, 38: 2131–46.

BURBANK, S., and FRIEDMAN, B. 2002. Reconsidering judicial independence. In *Judicial Independence at the Crossroads: An Interdisciplinary Approach*, ed. S. Burbank and B. Friedman. Thousand Oaks, Calif.: Sage.

CAMERON, C. 2002. Judicial independence: how can you tell it when you see it? And, who cares. In *Judicial Independence at the Crossroads: An Interdisciplinary Approach*, ed. S. Burbank and B. Friedman. Thousand Oaks, Calif.: Sage.

COHEN, L., and SPITZER, M. 1994. Solving the *Chevron* puzzle. *Law and Contemporary Problems*, 57: 65–110.

DOMINGO, P. 2000. Judicial independence: the politics of the Supreme Court in Mexico. *Journal of Latin American Studies*, 32: 705–35.

EDLEY, C. 1990. *Administrative Law*. New Haven, Conn.: Yale University Press.

EPSTEIN, L., KNIGHT, J., and SHVETSOVA, O. 2002. Selecting selection systems. In *Judicial Independence at the Crossroads: An Interdisciplinary Approach*, ed. S. Burbank and B. Friedman. Thousand Oaks, Calif.: Sage.

ESKRIDGE, W. 1991. Reneging on history? Playing the Court/Congress/president civil rights game. *California Law Review*, 79: 613–84.

—— and FEREJOHN, J. 1992. The Article I, Section 7 game. *Georgetown Law Journal*, 80: 523–64.

—— FRICKEY, P., and GARRETT, E. 2001. *Cases and Materials on Legislation: Statutes and the Creation of Public Policy*, 3rd edn. St Paul, Minn.: West Group.

FEREJOHN, J. 1999. Independent judges, dependent judiciary: explaining judicial independence. *Southern California Law Review*, 72: 353–84.

—— and SHIPAN, C. 1990. Congressional influence on bureaucracy. *Journal of Law, Economics and Organization*, 6: 1–20.

—— and WEINGAST, B. 1992a. Limitation of statutes: strategic statutory interpretation. *Georgetown Law Journal*, 80: 565–82.

—— —— 1992b. A positive theory of statutory interpretation. *International Review of Law and Economics*, 12: 263–79.

GELY, R., and SPILLER, P. 1992. Congressional control or judicial independence: the determinants of U.S. Supreme Court labor-relations decisions, 1949–1988. *Rand Journal of Economics*, 23: 463 ff.

LANDES, W., and POSNER, R. The independent judiciary in an interest-group perspective. *Journal of Law, Economics and Organization*, 18: 875–901.

LUPIA, A., and MCCUBBINS. M. 1994. Designing bureaucratic accountability. *Law and Contemporary Problems*, Winter/Spring: 91–126.

MCCUBBINS, M., and PAGE, T. 1986. The congressional foundations of agency performance. *Public Choice*, 51: 173–90.

—— and RODRIGUEZ, D. 2006. What statutes mean. Manuscript.

—— and SCHWARTZ, T. 1984. Congressional oversight overlooked: police patrols versus fire alarms. *American Journal of Political Science*, 2: 165–79.

MCNOLLGAST. 1987. Administrative procedures as instruments of political control. *Journal of Law, Economics, and Organization*, 3: 243–77.

—— 1989. Structure and process, politics and policy: administrative arrangements and the political control of agencies. *Virginia Law Review*, 75: 431–82.

—— 1992. Positive canons: the role of legislative bargains in statutory interpretation. *Georgetown Law Journal*, 80: 705–42.

—— 1994. Legislative intent: the use of positive political theory in statutory interpretation. *Law and Contemporary Problems*, Winter/Spring: 3–37.

—— 1995. Politics and the courts: a positive theory of judicial doctrine and the rule of law. *Southern California Law Review*, 68: 1631–83.

—— 2006. Conditions for judicial independence. *Journal of Contemporary Legal Issues*, 15.

MAGALONI, B. 2003. Authoritarianism, democracy, and the Supreme Court: horizontal exchange and the rule of law in Mexico. In *Democratic Accountability in Latin America*, ed. S. Mainwairing and C. Wenia. Oxford: Oxford University Press.

MARKS, B. 1988. A model of judicial influence on congressional policy-making: *Grove City College v. Bell*. Hoover Institution Working Papers in Political Science No. P-88-7.

MORENO, E., CRISP, B., and SHUGART, M. 2003. The accountability deficit in Latin America. In *Democratic Accountability in Latin America*, ed. S. Mainwairing and C. Wenia. Oxford University Press.

NOLL, R. 1971. The behavior of regulatory agencies. *Review of Social Economy*, 29: 15–19.

RODRIGUEZ, D. 1992. Statutory interpretation and political advantage. *International Review of Law and Economics*, 12: 217–31.

────── 1994. The positive political dimensions of regulatory reform. *Washington University Law Quarterly*, 72: 1–150.

────── and WEINGAST, B. 2003. The positive political theory of legislative history: new perspectives on the 1964 Civil Rights Act and interpretation. *University of Pennsylvania Law Review*, 151: 1417–542.

────── ────── 2006a. The paradox of expansionist statutory interpretations. *Northwestern University Law Review*, 101.

────── ────── 2006b. Is administrative law inevitable? Manuscript.

RUBIN, E. 2005. *Beyond Camelot*. Princeton, NJ: Princeton University Press.

RUSSELL, P. 2001. Toward a general theory of judicial independence. In *Judicial Independence in the Age of Democracy: Critical Perspective from Around the World*, ed. P. Russell and D. O'Brien. Charlottesville: University Press of Virginia.

SEGAL, J. 1997. Separation of powers games in the positive theory of congress and the courts. *American Political Science Review*, 91: 28–44.

────── and SPAETH, H. 2002. *The Supreme Court and the Attitudinal Model Revisted*. New York: Cambridge University Press.

SHAPIRO, M. 1988. *Who Guards the Guardians?* Athens: University of Georgia Press.

SPILLER, P. 1996. A positive political theory of regulatory instruments: contracts, administrative law or regulatory specificity. *Southern California Law Review*, 69: 477–514.

────── and TILLER, E. 1996. Invitations to override: congressional reversals of supreme court decisions. *International Review of Law and Economics*, 16: 503–21.

STEPHENSON, M. 2001. Where the devil turns... the political foundations of independent judicial review. Paper presented at the American Political Science Association Annual Meeting, San Francisco.

STEWART, R. 1975. The reformation of American administrative law. *Harvard Law Review*, 88: 1667–813.

PART V
CONSTITUTIONAL THEORY

CHAPTER 16

CONSTITUTIONALISM

RUSSELL HARDIN

THERE are two contrary schools of constitutional theory. These ground constitutions in contracts, as in the long-standing contractarian tradition in political philosophy, or in convention or coordination. The former theories are almost all at the normative level; the latter are inherently explanatory or causal theories as well as, often, normative. I will canvass these two theoretical approaches and then I will turn to discussion of what constitutions do. In modern contexts, virtually all constitutions are ostensibly designed to secure democratic government. Arguably, the greatest failing of every such constitution is its seeming incapacity to make institutional sense of democracy. There is no clearly correct institutional structure for making democratic decisions; sensibly different systems will produce different results. This is, however, a failure of democratic theory and practice, and a failure of collective human capacities when acting in very large groups. Arguably the most important aspect of constitutionalism for modern nations, especially those that have had histories of autocracy, is in placing limits on the power of government. In the view of many, this is the central point of constitutionalism: limited government.

Much of contemporary work on constitutionalism takes up prior debates and brings them into contemporary analytical frameworks, such as game theory, bargaining theory, theories of commitment, and so forth. Most of it is comparative and grounded very solidly in real-world examples. Some of it has been stimulated by recent constitutional changes in newly democratizing nations, such as those of eastern Europe, in redemocratizing nations, such as many in Latin America, and in South Africa with the enfranchisement of blacks after the end of apartheid. And some of it is now being stimulated by efforts to understand suprastate constitutions, especially that of the European Union.

---

* I wish to thank the editors for extremely careful readings and criticisms of an earlier draft.

In general, it is absurd to assess the normative qualities of a constitution from its content alone. The whole point of a constitution is to organize politics and society in particular ways. For example, modern constitutions typically organize a state apparatus, provide for representative democracy, define certain rights for citizens, and sometimes provide for some degree of distributive justice (often through so-called economic and social rights, as distinct from the historical political rights of civil liberties). Hence, constitutions are inherently consequentialist devices. To judge a constitution normatively requires attention to its actual consequences. Since the consequences of a particular constitution are likely to depend to some extent on the nature of the society it is to govern, what would count as a good constitution for one society might be a disastrous constitution for another society. Purely abstract discussion of constitutions and constitutionalism is therefore pointless and misdirected. Constitutionalism without social science is an arid intellectual pastime.[1] For many theoretical enterprises, looking to specific examples is a necessary part of making sure the theory is polished and adequate. In the discussion of constitutionalism, looking at specific examples forces us to recognize that the theory is not unitary, but is fractured and contingent on circumstances.

Crossing or underlying all of these discussions is a background methodological and intentional theory: political economy (see Brennan and Hamlin 1995). The political economy approach to politics and institutions is based on economic motivations, somehow defined. Thomas Hobbes says that if mere consent to living in justice were sufficient, we would need no government "at all, because there would be peace without subjection" (1651/1994, ch. 17, 86/107). This claim is wrong for the reason that undercuts others of Hobbes's arguments; we would still need coordination on many purposes and we would need collective actions in many contexts in which spontaneous provision, even by those who consent to live in justice, would be unlikely. But Hobbes's dismissal of the likelihood that people can be universally motivated by commitment to justice is compelling. That dismissal and his arguments for the kinds of motivations that people actually have make him an early political economist.

Against the assumptions of political economy, some moves in contemporary political philosophy depend on attributing very strong motivations of fairness or public-spiritedness to citizens. For example, Brian Barry supposes that if people have the right motivations, contractualism (as discussed below) will work. But there is no good reason to suppose that a population can be re-educated into having powerful motivations of—in Barry's hope—fairness rather than self-seeking. Constitutional political economy seems bound to deal with cases in which interests often enough trump, so that what we need are safeguards against each other. John Rawls supposes that once we establish a just regime, that regime will educate future generations to be just. Institutions "must be not only just but framed so as to encourage the virtue of justice" (1971, 261; 1999, 231). He also says that once we have just institutions, the initial condition of self-interest no longer applies and citizens and legislators have a

---

[1] Rawls shares this view (see 1971/1999, section 42), as do most libertarians, as well as, of course, all political economists, including Hume and Smith.

duty to support such institutions (1971, 334; 1999, 293–4). To design a constitutional order on the assumption that such motivations will generally trump self-interest, family interest, and narrow group interests of various kinds runs against experience and against James Madison's (1788/2001b, 268–9) and David Hume's (1742/1985) view that we should design the institutions themselves to be proof against abuse by office-holders. Madison and Hume see liberalism as inherently grounded in distrust of political office-holders, not in supposing that these leaders will generally work for the public interest. Madison's constitution is the pre-eminent constitutional response to liberal distrust (on liberal distrust, see further Hardin 2002).

The central claim that grounds constitutionalism in political economy is that, in general, it is to our *mutual advantage* to preserve social order because it is the interest of *each of us* that it be preserved. There may, of course, be collective action problems in preserving it, so that its serving mutual advantage does not guarantee its survival. Indeed, mutual advantage can have more than one implication in cases of unequal coordination and very commonly in cases of multiple possible coordinations that are all more or less equally attractive, at least when viewed *ex ante*.

I will briefly discuss the two main schools of constitutional theorizing before turning to what constitutions can do for us. Then I focus on the two main problems of modern constitutional democracy: the nature of representative democracy and the problem of placing enforceable limits on government.

1 CONTRACTARIAN THEORIES

The metaphorical claim that government is established by contract is one of the mainstays of traditional political theory. Against the metaphor, there are several objections to the claim that a constitution is analogous to an ordinary contract in any useful sense. These objections include the following. Contracts are typically enforceable by a third party (usually the state); constitutions are not. Contracts typically govern a fairly limited quid pro quo between the parties; it is hard even to define who might be the parties engaged in such an exchange when a constitution is drawn up. The exchanges governed by a contract typically get completed and the contracts cease to govern further; constitutions typically govern into the distant and unforeseeable future and they have no project for "completion" in sight—they are never to be "fulfilled." Contracts require genuine agreement to make them binding; constitutions require merely acquiescence to make them work. Contracts govern exchanges, which have the strategic structure of a prisoner's dilemma; constitutions govern coordination of a population on a particular form of government and therefore have the strategic structure of coordination games. Finally, note that, if a constitution is a contract, then we must make a contract on what contract will mean. That may not be a logical impossibility, but it is an oddly circular idea. Under our coordination constitution, we can make a law of contracts to govern many of our future interactions and, indeed, to enable many of them.

Let us spell out one of these points a bit further. In a two-person prisoner's dilemma, there is an outcome that would be best for one player and worst for the other player. In a coordination game, the best outcome for each player is also the best or near-best for the other player. It is implausible that the major groups involved in adopting the US or any other constitution could face an outcome that was best for one very important group and worst for another, as in a prisoner's dilemma.

The two most important groups in the US case were arguably the financial and shipping interests of the northeastern cities and the plantation interests of the southern states. Alexander Hamilton and other financiers could not have supposed they would be best off when Thomas Jefferson and other agrarians were worst off. Any regime that did not enable them to cooperate in managing the export of southern crops and the import or manufacturing of farm implements would have harmed both groups. Any regime that enabled them to cooperate more efficiently in doing these things benefited both groups. The central issue of the Constitution was to eliminate trade barriers between the thirteen states and to regularize tariffs with other nations. That was the issue that brought these two groups into the design and adoption of the Constitution as a mutually beneficial arrangement. They faced a relatively straightforward coordination problem (Hardin 1999, ch. 3).

Contractarian theorists typically ignore all of these issues and use the metaphor of contract to ground a claim that citizens are somehow obligated to defer to government by their consent, as the parties to a real contract would be obligated. Traditional contractarian theorists do acknowledge one deep problem for their theories. Contractual obligation without actual personal agreement seems like nonsense, especially given that it is prior agreement that is supposed to make a contractarian order binding. Yet it is hard to ground any claim that future generations agree to an extant contractarian order (unless migration from one nation to another is easy). Moreover, Hume (1748/1985) compellingly dismisses even the claim that there could ever have been a genuine agreement on political order in any modern society. He also argues that actual citizens do not believe their own legal or political obligations depend on their having agreed to their social order.

Hume's arguments and facts are so devastating to the idea of the social contract that one must wonder why it continues to be in discussion at all. Rawls essentially agrees with Hume's central conclusion. He says that, because citizens have not genuinely contracted for or agreed to any political obligation, they cannot have such obligations (1971, 113–14; 1999, 97–8). Yet he still perversely classifies his theory as part of the contractarian tradition (1971, 32–3; 1999, 28–30).[2] There seems to be a sense that contractarianism is morally superior to utilitarianism, and Rawls poses his theory this way. This is a deeply odd view. A utilitarian acts on behalf of others. Those who enter contracts typically are concerned with their own benefits and do not care about the benefits to their partners in trade. The former is other regarding; the latter is

---

[2] Jean Hampton (1980) argues correctly that Rawls's theory is not contractarian.

self-seeking. It is a saving grace of contemporary claims for contractarianism that they are not about contracts. Unfortunately, they are rather about rationalist agreement on what are the right principles to follow.

A huge part of the discussion of contractarian theories addresses how we are to understand the idea of contractual obligation when there cannot be an actual contract or agreement by the relevant parties (in this case, the citizens). The nearest thing we ever have to actual contracts is votes on the adoption or amendment of a constitution. But these votes typically require only some kind of majority, ranging from simple to super-majority. Unanimity is an impossible condition for a working constitution or amendment in a real society. But unanimity is required for a legal contract to be binding. Hence, in a sense that is contrary to any plausible sense of "contractarian," contractarian constitutions must be imposed on a significant fraction of the populace.

Traditional, straight contractarianism appears to be on the wane. Few people argue for it in principle, although many scholars continue to present contractarian arguments from John Locke (1690/1988), Hobbes (1651/1994), and others from the distant past. In part such contractarianism has simply been rejected, as by coordination theorists. In part it has been displaced by contractualist argument. Despite the growing flood of work on it (the most important are Barry 1995; Scanlon 1982, 1998), the latter program is not yet well defined. Traditional contractarianism is relatively well defined and therefore its deep flaws are clear. It is a peculiar but perhaps false advantage of the contractualist program that it is ill defined. Its vagueness means that debate over it will often thrive, even debate over what the program is.

Contractualism is supposed to resolve or sidestep the problem of fitting some degree of moral obligation to a regime to which one has not actually agreed. Thomas Scanlon's original definition is: "An act is wrong if its performance under the circumstances would be disallowed by any system of rules for the general regulation of behaviour which no one could reasonably reject as a basis for informed, unforced general agreement" (Scanlon 1982, 110). A further statement is often taken as definitive, although it is peculiar: "On this view what is fundamental to morality is the desire for reasonable agreement, not the pursuit of mutual advantage" (p. 115 n.). Why is it this desire that is fundamental rather than achieving moral action or outcomes? I will ignore the concern with this desire because it trivializes our concern. Scanlon (1998) himself has primarily been interested in applying the contractualist idea to moral theory. The most extensive and articulate defense of the idea of reasonable agreement in political theory is probably that of Brian Barry (1995, 3), who says, "I continue to believe in the possibility of putting forward a universally valid case in favour of liberal egalitarian principles."

Unfortunately, Scanlon's criterion of reasonableness is somewhat tortured and ill defined. Its use has become unmoored from his original defense of it. As first presented, the term supposedly attested to the claim that moral theory is analogous to mathematics (Scanlon 1982, 104–5). Mathematicians know mathematical truths; moral theorists can similarly know moral truths. We do not know either of these by observation but only through some inner faculty of reasoning. That the analogy is not apt is suggested by the fact that there is no terminological analog of "reasonableness" in mathematics. Every mathematician knows that the square root of 2 is not a rational number (that is, a number that can be expressed as a fraction in the form of whole integers in both the numerator and the denominator). No one would say further that this claim is reasonable. It just is true mathematically. If you say this is false, mathematicians will say you are a crackpot or an ignoramus, not that you are unreasonable. One wonders what are the analogs of axioms and theorems in moral theory.

The claim that morality is analogous to mathematics is a perverse variant of intuitionism in ethics.[3] Intuitionists believe they can intuit whether, say, a particular action is right or wrong. Unfortunately, they do not agree with each other. If disagreement were similarly pervasive in mathematics, there would not be mathematics departments in great universities.

If all of us reject some principle, presumably no one would disagree with the conclusion that we should collectively reject applications of that principle in practice and, furthermore, that it is reasonable for us to do so, whatever "reasonable" might mean in this vernacular claim. Scanlon's principle must, however, be stronger than this. If you think you are reasonable to reject some principle that the rest of us support, what can we say to you? We might be quasi-Kantian and suppose that we can deduce the true principle here and we can therefore say to you that you are simply wrong. That would surely violate the element of agreement that Scanlon and other contractualists want. They do not suppose that agreement on certain principles is incumbent on any and every one as a matter of moral or transcendental logic. They mean agreement to be genuine, which is to say they mean that there must be a possibility of disagreement.

Rawls, on the contrary, sometimes seems to intend a quasi-Kantian principle of rationalist agreement. He assumes that any single representative person behind his veil of ignorance would reach the principles of his system of justice (1971, 139; 1999, 120). It is hard to imagine how that could be true unless those principles are somehow definitively correct in the sense that they are rationally deducible. One who does not agree with the deduction of his rules of justice has evidently failed to understand. There is rationally no possibility of disagreement. To my knowledge there is no major, serious constitutional theorist who has such a rationalist view of the design of constitutions. Because Rawls's purpose eventually is to design the institutions of justice for a society, one might suppose that he intends his theory to produce a constitution. Although he grants that the design of institutions would have to deal with social constraints, thus making its content contingent, he nevertheless seems to think that the content of these institutions, and hence of his constitution, must be fully determinate once his theory and the relevant social contingencies are taken fully into account.[4] If so, he holds a very strange—rationalist—position in the world of constitutional theory. No working constitutional lawyer could take that position seriously. General determinacy in constitutional theory is an implausible goal.

---

[3] Although Scanlon (1982, 109) defends it against a particular sense of intuitionism.
[4] For his views on determinacy, see Hardin 2002, ch. 7.

Note that in the coordination theories discussed below, you could well disagree with some rule we have adopted, even think it an unreasonable rule, and yet you could still think it reasonable for yourself to abide by the rule. For example (a recently painful example for many Americans), the US Constitution establishes an indirect device for electing presidents. The device is to count votes at the state level and then to count peculiarly weighted scores for the individual states at the level of the Electoral College, which finally chooses the president if a majority of its members agrees on a particular candidate. On three occasions (nearly 6 per cent of all presidential elections), the Electoral College has elected the candidate who got the second-largest number of citizens' votes, and the candidate with the highest number of such votes lost. Most recently, this was the result in the presidential election of 2000, in which Al Gore had a clear plurality of the national vote but lost the election to George Bush in the Electoral College—with a bit of help from Bush's friends on the Supreme Court.

Many US citizens as well as many non-citizen observers think that the result of the election of 2000 was in some moral sense wrong or was a violation of democracy. But no citizen seems to have thought it right to oppose the result by taking action that would have made Gore the president. Indeed, one can imagine that a poll would show that Americans overwhelmingly agreed that the constitutional rule on election of the president should be followed even though they might also have agreed that the system was perverse and should be changed. It would take a relatively strained effort to argue that that rule could in some sense meet the contractualist criterion. But it is easy to show why the rule arose originally and why it continues to prevail despite the possibility of a constitutional amendment to block what many people think was a travesty of democracy on the two most recent occasions when the apparent loser in the national election became president.[5]

Hence, you might morally or even merely self-interestedly reject a constitutional rule or principle. And you might readily be able to think your rejection reasonable in any sense that the contractualist would want. But still you would most likely conclude that it would be unreasonable for anyone in the system to act, in a particular election, against the application of the rule. That rule has the great force of a convention that can be altered only through the actions of large numbers in concert. The only powerful defense of it in a specific application of it, such as in 2000, is that *it is the rule* and that the rule is a convention that is not readily changeable even though presumably no one drafting a constitution today would include such a perverse institution as

---

[5] The first election that gave the presidency to the loser of the popular vote in a two-party split was that of Rutherford B. Hayes in 1876. But in that instance, there was a corrupt deal to distort the process. Such corruption is, of course, a travesty of democracy, but that is not an issue in the judgement of the American constitutional rules for election of presidents. The availability of the Electoral College let the deal take the form it did, but one can imagine that the deal would have been made no matter what the system had been. The second case was the election of Benjamin Harrison in 1888. In that election, Grover Cleveland received more votes but Harrison nevertheless won in the Electoral College. The 1824 election left four candidates without a clear winner in the Electoral College, and selection passed to the House of Representatives. In 1800 an ambiguity in the system forced the final decision into the House.

the Electoral College.[6] This defense does not make the rule morally *right*, it only makes the rule *govern*. In this instance, the argument from convention trumps any argument from simple rightness or agreement unless the argument from agreement simply takes over the argument from convention. It would be unreasonable to reject a powerful convention in any specific application of it. This can, of course, be true even though it would be reasonable to change the convention before its next application.

The chief difficulty with the contractualist program for those who are not its advocates is that there is no definition of reasonableness and no clear account of how others can judge reasonableness in general even if we might suppose that the vernacular term fits some obvious cases (for which we have no need of constitutional or moral theory). The term reasonable has unfortunately been left as a residual notion that is not defined by the contractualists. Scanlon's definition is vacuously circular. We "desire to be able to justify [our] actions to others on grounds they could not reasonably reject." A footnote supposedly clarifies this: "Reasonably, that is, given the desire to find principles which others similarly motivated could not reasonably reject" (Scanlon 1982, 116 and 116 n.). The historical dodges of the fact that supposedly contractarian obligations that were never literally agreed to were somehow hypothetically or tacitly agreed seem much more compelling than this murky move to ground normative claims in their "reasonableness."

Advocates of the contractualist program seem to think they can spot reasonableness when they see it. Hence, what they give us are examples of reasonableness or unreasonableness rather than elaborations of principles for assessing reasonableness. For example, Barry believes "that it would be widely acknowledged as a sign of an unjust arrangement that those who do badly under it could reasonably reject it" (Barry 1995, 7). But Rawls's difference principle might leave us with a society in which the worst-off class do badly relative to many others. This would be true if great productivity were motivated by substantial rewards to the most productive members of the society, so that they are very well off in comparison to the worst-off groups. In that case, the worst off might suffer far worse misery if they did not suffer such inequality. It would be hard to argue—at least to a Rawlsian—that making the worst-off citizens substantially better off is unjust. If Rawls's theory of justice is reasonable, then even gross inequality might be seen as reasonable. We must look at the whole picture of the society if we are to understand and to judge its justice and reasonableness.

Part of the rationale of the difference principle is causal. There is, at least possibly, a causal trade-off between efficiency of production and equality of rewards. Rawls openly supposes that the causal chain is from greater equality to lesser production, so that some inequality is required if the worst off are not to be abjectly miserable. If this were not thought to be true, there would be no reason to have such a complicated theory as Rawls presents, because pure equality would be a credible theory. At some

---

[6] The College was designed to block pure democracy by using a forum of political elites to make the final choice of who would be president. But presumably, the architects of the College did not intend such undemocratic results as those of 1888 and 2000.

points, however, Barry very nearly equates reasonableness and equality.[7] Once this move is made, there is little more needed to establish a theory of distributive justice merely by definition. It might still be very difficult to design institutions that would achieve extensive equality (Hume 1751/1975, section 3, part 2, 193–4).

2 COORDINATION THEORIES

Before Hume there were three main theories of social order. These are based on theological views, contractarian agreement or consent, and draconian coercion by the state. Hume dismissively rejects all three. The theological views are simply false or at least beyond demonstration (1748/1985). Locke and others propose contractarian consent as an alternative justification for the state and an alternative ground for obligation to the state, but as noted above, Hume demolishes the claim for consent. Hobbes's argument from draconian force seems empirically wrong for many very orderly societies and Hume rejects it almost entirely, although he shares many social scientific views with Hobbes. Having demolished all of the then acceptable accounts of obedience to the state, Hume therefore has to propose a dramatically different, fourth vision.

In essence his theory is a dual-convention theory. Government derives its power (not its right) to rule by convention and the populace acquiesces in that rule by its own convention. Once empowered by these two conventions, the government has the capacity to do many things, including ancillary things unrelated to the purpose of maintaining social order. This dual-convention argument is compelling for most stable governments in our time. Moreover, for democratic governments the dual-convention theory virtually demands constitutional limits on the power of government to interfere in democratic processes. The earlier theories could make as good sense without constitutional provisions and the absolutist versions of the theological and draconian power visions virtually deny any role for a limiting constitution.

For both of the conventions in the dual-convention theory of government, acquiescence is the compelling fact. Hume argues, by example, that ten million British citizens simply acquiesced in the succession of William and Mary to the English throne, all by act of "the majority of seven hundred" in the English and Scottish parliaments (Hume 1748/1985, 472–3). Acquiescence is Hume's term (p. 469). We acquiesce because it would be very difficult to organize what would de facto have to be a collective action to topple a going convention or to organize a new one. While we can readily just happen into a convention, such as the conventions of driving on the left or right, we cannot so readily alter one once it is established. You might detest the convention we have and you might even discover that apparently most of us detest it.

---

[7] For example, Barry (1995, 7) says, "The criterion of reasonable acceptability of principles gives some substance to the idea of fundamental equality while at the same time flowing from it."

But you may not be able to mobilize the opposition that would be necessary to change it. The foolishness of the Electoral College has seemed perverse to many Americans ever since its first anomalous result in 1888. In the interim, a couple of elections came close to faltering in that system. And finally the election of 2000 was very nearly a destabilizing event that could have been very harmful if a national crisis had arisen during the period in which the result could have been in limbo. Yet there has been no substantial effort to change it.[8]

On this account, a constitution does not commit us in the way that a contract does (Hardin 1989). It merely raises the costs of doing things some other way through its creation of a coordination convention that is itself an obstacle to recoordination.[9] More often than not our interests are better served by acquiescing in the rules of that constitution than by attempting to change it. This is true not because we will be coerced to abide by those rules if we attempt not to but because it will be in our interest simply to acquiesce. The forms of commitment that are important for constitutional and even for conventional social choice in many forms are those that derive from the difficulties of collective action to recoordinate on new rules. These are not simply problems of internal psychological motivation and they are not problems of sanctions that will be brought to bear. They are inherent in the social structure of the conventions themselves, a structure that often exacts costs from anyone who runs against the conventions more or less automatically without anyone or any institution having to take action against a rule breaker.

Establishing a constitution is itself a massive act of coordination that, if it is stable for a while, creates a convention that depends for its maintenance on its self-generating incentives and expectations. Given that it is a mystery how contracting could work to motivate us to abide by a constitution to which we have contracted, we should be glad that the problem we face is such that we have no need of a contract or its troublesome lack of enforcement devices. Moreover, the acquiescence that a successful constitution produces cannot meaningfully be called agreement. Some citizens might prefer extant constitutional arrangements to any plausible alternative, but for those who do not, their obedience to the constitutional order has more the quality of surrender than of glad acceptance. Indeed, if our constitution is solidly ensconced, surrender or acquiescence gives us the best we can get, given that almost everyone else is abiding by it—even if almost all of them are merely acquiescing or surrendering in abiding by it.

Hobbes is commonly invoked as one of the founders of the contractarian tradition in political thought. Ironically, he is even more clearly a founder of the coordination theory of government. He presents an argument from contract but finally dismisses it as having no likely historical precedent.[10] He then goes on to defend the powers

[8] It would be hard to change because the rule seemingly gives power to small states, which together could block any amendment.

[9] The costs of changing constitutions and conventions may outweigh any benefit from the change. But a great advantage of democratic constitutions is that they reduce the costs of switching leaders.

[10] "There is scarce a commonwealth in the world whose beginnings can in conscience be justified" (Hobbes 1651/1994, "Review," 392/492), because they were generally established by conquest or usurpation, not by contract or agreement.

of a ruler—or, we might prefer to say, a state or a government—on the grounds that not abiding by the rule of a state would wreak havoc in our lives. Hence, for our own good, which is to say for our mutual advantage, we should abide by the laws of our state. This is an argument that carries even for a government that usurps the powers of an extant government. Once the usurper government is well established and is able to maintain order, it should then be obeyed.

The difference between Hobbes the contract theorist and Hobbes the power theorist is the difference between a political philosopher and a social scientist. His arguments from contract are about an imaginary and maybe even an ideal or desirable world. That world is a cute story, not a basis for philosophical argument. His arguments from power and coordination are about the actual worlds that he inhabited and that we inhabit. Although there are many discussions in his works on politics that have normative overtones, his most coherent and extensive discussions are arguments from political sociology. As already noted, constitutional content must be contingent on the conditions of the society that the constitution is to govern (see further Dahl 1996). This is in the nature of coordination and convention. If a particular rule does not coordinate our actions, it cannot become one of the conventions of our constitutional regime.

3 Caveats and Clarifications

It should be clear that the issue here is *establishing* government. It is the strategic structure of that choice or problem that we wish to understand. This is not the same as understanding the problems that government, once established, will resolve (as in Weingast 1997, 248). The latter can be coordination, exchange (prisoner's dilemma), collective actions (n-prisoner's dilemma), and fundamental conflict problems, all of which might be handled by a relatively strong established government, unless, for example, the conflicts are too deep for resolution. Contract theories suppose that *this problem*—establishing a constitution for a form of government—is one of exchange and bargaining between groups with varied interests. If a constitution is to work in its early years, it must, however, successfully coordinate its populace on acquiescence to the new government that it establishes.

The nature or content of debates over the design of a constitution may not fit the strategic structure of the problem of constitutional design. Much that is said at a constitutional convention is apt to be blather and the fraction of time given over to blather might far outweigh the time spent on central issues. Successful or failed coordination on a constitution and government is the core problem.

Some of the easiest resolutions for the new government under the US Constitution of 1787–8 were among the hardest of the problems under the weak prior government of the Articles of Confederation. Coordinating on a central government with even modest powers implied a nearly instant resolution of such problems as certain common-pool resource issues, tariff regulation, trade between the states, and military conflict between the states. Before the new constitutional order these had been conflictual problems, with free riding, cheating, and the threat of instability. Pennsylvania and Virginia succeeded in having a joint trade policy, but other states went their own ways. Having a central government with sole jurisdiction over these issues turned them into, roughly, coordination problems, because on collective issues the central government must legislate for all one way or the other. No state could impose a tariff on trade with other states or with foreign countries. The possibility of free riding on the resolution of a typical common-pool resource issue was virtually eliminated because under central government the choices were reduced to the binary pair: provide the resource to all and tax all, or provide it to none and tax none.

The thesis of coordination is a causal thesis, not a definition of what a constitution is. A constitution can include anything people might want. But if it is filled with perversities, it is likely to fail to coordinate us. Even if it looks like a model constitution (suppose its text is adopted whole from another, long successful constitution), it may fail to coordinate *us*. For example, the people of Rwanda are arguably so deeply divided that no constitution could gain wide support from both Hutu and Tutsi ethnic groups (for a full account see Hardin 1999, ch. 7). Most constitutions have failed fairly soon after their adoption (France may have set the record for failures in the decade or more after the Revolution). If a particular constitution in a particular society fails to coordinate, we would say that it is a failed constitution, not that it was not a constitution after all. It is wrong to say that a constitution is a coordination device as though by definition. But the reverse is true: a successful constitution must have been a successful coordination device.

Suppose that a particular constitution is apparently the result of a bargain. If that constitution is to work in establishing social order, it must coordinate us on acquiescence to our new government. This is likely to be a critical problem in the early years before the government has acquired the power to enforce its mandate. Hence, what makes the constitution work is that it coordinates us on social order and is virtually self-enforcing. Hobbes supposes that most regimes in the world were established by acquisition or conquest, which is to say that someone usurped the power already in place or some outside body that already had substantial power came in and established an order. He sees and states the problem of establishing power if we attempt to create a sovereign by contract. Even though we the citizens might entirely agree that we want our government to have requisite power to maintain order and to do various other things, we cannot turn our power over to a newly ensconced regime. Hobbes rightly says, "no man can transferre his power in a naturall manner" (Hobbes 1642/1983, 2.5.11, p. 90; see further, Hardin 1991, 168–71). Hence, the contractarian foundation crumbles before its state is empowered.

Hobbes's (1651/1994, ch. 20) account of government by acquisition or conquest suggests an important fact about a constitutionally created regime. Once it is in place and working to achieve order it can then be seized by some group and its powers put to use in continuing an order that is far less beneficial to many who were much better served by the prior regime. This is possible simply because social order at that point is the result of popular acquiescence to the regime rather than of genuine approval or support of it. Acquiescence might be readier once a government gains great power to block opposition. To get initial coordination on a constitution and its regime, however, is likely to require a fairly broad degree of support. But it does not require continuing support to maintain a regime that once has power and control of the mechanisms of office.

The core issue in constitutionalism is how a government under a constitution is empowered (especially initially). Once it is, it can maintain social order and it can resolve prisoner's dilemma and other interactions, including other coordination problems. Trivially, for example, it can establish orderly traffic laws. Constitutionalism is a two-stage problem. At the first stage temporally, we coordinate on a constitution and its form of government. At the second stage, that government then enables us to maintain order and to resolve various ordinary problems, many of which are between individuals or small groups of individuals rather than, like the constitution, at the whole-society level.

Finally note that in the law, contracts have been pushed in two directions against the simple, classical model implicit in the discussion here. First, many issues have been taken out of the realm of binding contractual agreement no matter what we agree to. For example, your apartment lease might say you cannot have house pets but the law may say you can, and the contract for the lease is not binding even though you might sign it. Second, many issues in especially complex deals cannot be easily adjudicated by courts, so that relevant contracts are not enforceable by legal authorities but must be self-enforcing (Williamson 1985). They may, for example, be enforced by the incentives we have to maintain good relations or good reputations. In this respect, contracts have become more like constitutions. One could say that the meaning of contract has changed or that we have displaced it with other devices. A defender of the social contract tradition could, falsely, say that finally we have developed a conception of contract that fits what the tradition has really been about.

4 WHAT CONSTITUTIONS DO

To achieve justice and social order we must design institutions or norms to bring about just resolutions. Hence, justice is inherently a two-stage concern. It will bring about mutual advantage but the actions we take within the justice system will not each by itself necessarily bring about mutual advantage. It is the whole scheme of justice that is mutually advantageous, not its adjudications in specific cases.

We might object and say that the system ought to be corrected and overridden when it does not produce the more mutually advantageous outcome in a particular case. Rawls (1955) demolishes such views in his argument that we create an institution, whose design determines the roles of individuals within it, and these roles determine behavior. In the stage of institutional design, we should do our best to make the institution achieve results that are mutually advantageous overall. Our institution of justice depends on this two-stage argument: in one stage, role-holders follow the rules of their roles as defined by the institution, and at the other stage the institution achieves welfare.

This is, of course, the structure of constitutional government. The constitution stipulates institutions of government; those institutions make and implement policies. In a constitutional government we cannot simply decide at every turn what would be the best thing to do, even the mutually advantageously best thing to do, and then do it. We must do what can be accomplished within and by the constitutionally established institutions. It is common for citizens to miss this principle and to suppose we can do whatever they think best in this case right now. That would de facto eliminate the institutional devices that we have designed to accomplish our mutual-advantage goals. Acting as many citizens want would serve us very badly and would finally make government unlimited.

Successful constitutions coordinate us at a minimum on social order without need for Hobbes's draconian enforcement. But in some contexts such coordination may be infeasible. For example, in a society that is too violently split, coordination of major groups behind a single regime may not be possible, so that any intended constitutional order breaks down. A constitution cannot motivate people who are grievously hostile to its provisions (Hardin 1999, ch. 7). A constitution is like democracy in the account of Robert Dahl (1957, 132–3), who says, "In a sense, what we ordinarily describe as democratic 'politics' is merely the chaff. It is the surface manifestation, representing superficial conflicts. [These] disputes over policy alternatives are nearly always disputes over a set of alternatives that have already been winnowed down to those within the broad area of basic agreement." Constitutional democracy can manage the chaff of political conflict but it cannot manage really deep conflict between large groups that are hostile adversaries.[11]

Violently opposed groups are likely to want to seize the reins of government to serve themselves, as in Rwanda. This already happens in ordinary, more or less successfully working constitutional democracies such as the United States and the United Kingdom. The 2000 election in the United States cannot possibly be seen as giving a mandate to the government of George Bush, but even his strong supporters must grant that he treated his accession to office as giving him opportunity to undo much of the welfare and tax structures of the past and to put in their place structures to serve the wealthiest members of the society and to end environmental and other regulations that have undercut business profits. His margin of victory in the election had little or no effect on what he was able to do. What mattered was seizing control of the government.

[11] This is roughly Tocqueville's (1945/1835, 1840: i. 260) view as well: "When a community actually has a mixed government—that is to say, when it is equally divided between adverse principles—it must either experience a revolution or fall into anarchy." We should qualify Dahl's claim with the note that "the broad area of basic agreement" need only be an area in which the politically effective groups are in agreement (Hardin 1999, ch. 7)

5 Representative Democracy

The central problem of representative democracy is related to the central problem in a theory of distributive justice. What results is the product of the actions of large numbers of people. We cannot suppose that considerations of the goodness or rightness of those results drive the individuals whose actions taken collectively produce the results. For example, in distributive justice, what we have to distribute is the result of the contributions of all. If we stipulate that the distribution must be egalitarian, we thereby separate the incentive for individual productivity from the reward or share of the production that goes to the individual. This fact makes the social product a vast instance of a collective action problem with likely millions of free riders and poverty for all. If, however, we allow rewards to stimulate production, we wreck any chance for equality in the final distribution of what is produced. We could imagine a two-stage allocation. First, we reward people for their own productivity and we subtract the sum of all these rewards from the total production. What is left is for egalitarian distribution. Rawls's theory of justice essentially resolves the problem of the likely conflict between efficiency of production and equity in distribution by allowing inequalities that raise the level of the fund left over for egalitarian distribution.

In the workings of representative democracy, we similarly can imagine that the best result of democratic procedures would be essentially equal participation by all in the determination of who is to govern for the next period. Unfortunately, this is again a collective action problem. From my own personal incentives, I have no reason to participate in elections beyond the extent to which my participation affects my own interests or the interests of any groups whose welfare I might wish to support.

From the very beginnings of its use, there has been debate on what representative democracy means and how it can work. In a society of large scale, direct democracy is not possible and some form of representative democracy is the best that we can do. Already at the time of its constitution, with only three million inhabitants, the USA was far too large, both geographically and numerically, for direct democracy.

Almost all of the debate around the adoption of the US Constitution supposes that representatives are to represent their own communities. (The revolutionary war against England was prompted by the lack of representation of the colonies in the British Parliament.) Indeed, the major divide between Federalists and Anti-Federalists was over the question whether communities and various kinds of groups could be adequately represented if the communities exceeded relatively small sizes. Under a law of 1776, the colony of Massachusetts provided one representative for a community of 120 citizens plus an additional representative for each additional 100 citizens (Wood 1969, 186). With such representation, the national legislature would be huge and unworkable. In England this problem was addressed with the claim that many people received virtual representation, because all delegates to Parliament represented the entire nation, as especially argued by Algernon Sidney (1698/1990, section 44, 565) and Edmund Burke (1774/1969, 72–4). When the American colonists complained that they were taxed without any representation in the English government, Thomas Whateley replied that they were virtually represented, which was as good as any Englishman in the mother country got (for much of the debate see Beer 1993, 164–8; Hardin 1999, 178–81; Reid 1989, 50–62; Wood 1969, 173–81).

The problems of scale that riddled Federalist and Anti-Federalist debates have since been analyzed by political economists including Joseph Schumpeter (1942/1950) and Anthony Downs (1957). Their chief conclusions, which are very well known, are that citizens commonly lack incentive to vote in elections and that, even if they do vote, they lack even more the incentive to learn enough about candidates and issues to vote intelligently in their own interests (for a range of views, see Hibbing and Theiss-Morse 2002; Wittman 1995; and several contributions to Lupia, McCubbins, and Popkin 2000). Institutionally, we can reduce the costs and tedium of voting by increasing the number of polling places, making absentee voting easy, and so forth. But we still cannot readily get voters to learn what they need to know. Indeed, this problem may be getting harder as the economic issues that once clearly separated liberal from conservative parties cease to be the dominant concern in elections. These problems have helped to spur changes in the electoral and therefore in the governmental process. Two of these have been analyzed as audience democracy and corporate democracy. To date, there are no institutional innovations in the works to deal with these problems.

Audience democracy is the term of Bernard Manin (1997). He argues that the nature of campaigning has changed in ways that reward performance on the stage more than stances on issues. The playwright Arthur Miller (2001) notes that successful politicians today tend to master performing before the camera and that, in fact, we the voters value them in part for their success in their acting. After a long lifetime in the theater, and some experience in the very different world of film, Miller's comments add great force to Manin's argument. He analyzes changes in performance style from Franklin Roosevelt to George W. Bush. Unfortunately, given the great difficulty of imparting any useful information to large numbers of voters, performance may be the best ticket many politicians have. Indeed, a great performer can be politically shallow and still triumph. Short of making politics intrinsically so interesting that potential voters actively want to read about it, there is no institutional reform that seems likely to overcome the impact of a good performance—other than putting an end to campaigning.

Contemporary government in the United States and many other nations can be characterized as "corporate democracy" in the following sense (Hardin 2004). Adolph Berle and Gardner Means (1932, 119–25 and *passim*) note that the rise of the corporate form of organization of private firms breaks the link between ownership and management, thus opening the possibility of conflict of interest between owners and professional managers. Among the legal forms that property in the corporate form might take as a result of such separation is analogous to what we have seen in many corporations historically, including many in recent years during the extraordinary stock bubble of the 1990s. This form creates "a new set of relationships, giving to the groups in control powers which are absolute and not limited by any implied obligation with respect to their use." Seven decades before Enron, Berle and Means (pp. 354–5) argue that through their absolute control of a corporation the managers "can operate it in their own interests, and can divert a portion of the [corporation's income and assets] to their own uses." We therefore face the potential for "corporate plundering."

In a variant of this argument, John C. Calhoun says, "The advantages of possessing the control of the powers of the government, and thereby of its honors and emoluments, are, of themselves, exclusive of all other considerations, ample to divide ... a community into two great hostile parties" (Calhoun 1853/1992, 16). The political class can be parasitic on the society that they ostensibly serve and that has the power of election over them. The supposedly powerful citizenry with its power of election over officials does not have the power to refuse to elect all of them; it can only turn out the occasional overtly bad apple. In the United States, it seldom has the temerity to overcome incumbents' advantage.[12]

Alternatively, Berle and Means (1932, 352) suppose that the corporate form might develop into what would now be called a socially conscious institution. They quote Walter Rathenau's 1918 view that the private "enterprise becomes transformed into an institution which resembles the state in character." The reverse seems to have happened. The state has been transformed to resemble loosely controlled corporations. Elected officials act as "professional" managers on behalf of the citizenry who "own" the nation. The officials are co-owners along with the citizens, but their rewards from management often far transcend anything they can gain as their share of the general good produced by their contributions to government, just as the corporate managers of Tyco, WorldCom, and Enron gained far more from looting these firms than from the genuine increase in value of the stock they owned.

6 LIMITS ON GOVERNMENT

For Hobbes the argument for coordination on a sovereign ruler is not an argument for a constitution or a constitutional order in any sense that these terms normally connote. A typical reason for having a constitution is to place limits on government. Indeed, "constitutional government" is commonly taken to mean limited government. Hobbes wants no limits on government sovereignty, in part because he cannot imagine how those limits could be imposed without opening up the possibility of overriding the government more generally. That would mean that the government is not sovereign.

---

[12] Consider the 2002 congressional elections in the United States. Only four incumbents in the House of Representatives (which has 435 members, all of whom are elected at two-year intervals) lost to non-incumbent challengers (a few incumbents lost to other incumbents because their districts were changed to reflect demographic changes). Overall, 90% of all candidates won by margins of more than 10% of the votes cast. When districts are redrawn by a state government after each decennial census (as for the 2002 election), they are often gerrymandered to ensure election of the candidates in the state's dominant party. For data, see Richie 2002.

Hume (1739–40/1978, book 3) resolves such issues in social order with the introduction of the idea of conventions that are de facto self-regulating or endogenously self-enforcing (see further Hardin 1982, ch. 10–14; 1999, chs. 1 and 3).[13] Understanding this possibility resolves some of Hobbes's problems. With the power of conventions to block actions of many kinds, government can be limited in many respects even while it can be powerful in those arenas in which its power would be beneficial to the populace.

Among the early advocates of limited government are Locke (1690/1988), Sidney (1698/1990), Hume, Adam Smith (1776/1976), Wilhelm von Humboldt (1854/1969), and Mill (1859/1977). Locke and Sidney argue against the theocratic theory of Robert Filmer (1680/1949), who advocates, with Hobbes, absolute power for the sovereign, although Filmer wants only monarchs as sovereigns and not bodies of aristocrats as Hobbes would allow. Hume and Smith especially argue against mercantilist economic policies that protect native industries against imports. In an argument against using government to achieve "perfect" equality, Hume (1751/1975, section 3, part 2, 193) also contends that this would empower government far too grievously. This is, of course, partially a straw-man argument because no one other than perhaps Gerrard Winstanley (1652/1973) and the Levelers of seventeenth century England seriously advocates perfect equality. Most theorists who argue for egalitarianism generally mean only to bring about substantially greater equality of distribution than typical wealthy societies achieve, as in the noteworthy cases of Rawls (1971/1999) with his difference principle and Barry (1995). The workings of Rawls's difference principle turn on social possibilities, so that it is conceivable that it would allow very substantial inequalities.

Hume's task therefore is largely to show that government officials can be constrained to act for the general good. Why? In part because they act on general principles that do not directly affect their own interests. The consequences of today's breach of equity are remote and cannot counterbalance any immediate advantage of better behavior (Hume 1739–40/1978, 3.2.7, p. 535). When we consider actions in the distant future, all their minute distinctions vanish, and we give preference to the greater good (p. 536). The trick is to change our circumstances to make us observe the laws of justice as our nearest interest. We appoint magistrates who have no interest in any act of injustice but an immediate interest in every execution of justice (p. 537).

This last claim is perhaps too optimistic. Insofar as our magistrates have no interest in the injustices committed by others, we can generally expect them not to have a bias in favor of injustice. Indeed, through sympathy we can expect them to have at least a slight bias in favor of justice in any matter that does not concern themselves. All we need to do to constrain them from acting unjustly therefore is to block any actions that they might take on their own behalf or on behalf of their relatives and friends. We can do this to some degree by having different offices overseeing each other. This is not merely the separation of powers, which is typically intended to block

---

[13] See further Przeworski's discussion of self-enforcing democracy, this volume.

institutions from acting on some institutional agenda rather than to block individual office-holders from acting in their own personal interest against the public interest. It is rather more nearly Madison's (1788/2001b, 268) device of having ambition counter ambition, person to person. Montesquieu argues for separation of powers. Hume and Madison propose the monitoring of all by all, which is Hume's device for a small society regulated by norms (or conventions), so that such a society might not need constitutionally devised institutions of government.[14]

It is not clear that the Hume–Madison device works. It has more in common with competitors in a market than with Montesquieu's hiving off some duties to one agency and other duties to other agencies. I block your action because I think it is wrong, but I do so because I have a slight leaning toward the public interest through the influence of my concern for mutual advantage, which includes my own advantage as a likely minor part. My action against you is apt to be costless to me and it might even be rewarded by other office-holders or even by the citizens who, if they have no direct interest in the matter at issue, also have a slight leaning for the mutual advantage. I therefore have a motive from interest to block your illegitimate self-interested action.

Before too optimistically accepting the Hume–Madison device, recall the nature of corporate democracy as discussed above. As Calhoun argues, it is not merely the individual elected official but the class of them that is problematic. Government may be limited in many ways, but it can still be used by office-holders and some of the more powerful interests to make government their special benefactor while it carries out its other tasks.

7 CONCLUDING REMARKS

To argue that a particular constitutional system is "necessary" or "right" is very hard, because there is commonly evidence that other possibilities are attractive, plausibly even superior in principle. Caesar (1787/1987), writing during the debates over the adoption of the US Constitution, put the case clearly: "Ingenious men will give every plausible, and, it may be, pretty substantial reasons, for the adoption of two plans of Government, which shall be fundamentally different in their construction, and not less so in their operation; yet both, if honestly administered, might operate with safety and advantage." Caesar's conclusion is a defining principle in the

---

[14] Hume supposes that, although our present interest may blind us with respect to our own actions, it does not with respect to the actions of others, so we can judge the latter from sympathy with the general effect of those actions (Hume 1739–40/1978, 3.2.8, p. 545) or, as we might prefer to say, out of concern for the mutual advantage. Most members of our small community therefore can be expected to sanction misbehavior that affects the interests of others. Government itself has more of the character of a small society than does the whole society that it governs. (This would have been far more true in Hume's and Madison's day than it is today, with our enormous government agencies whose total populations exceed the national populations of their day.)

coordination theory of constitutionalism. There may be no best constitution, although there may be many that are comparably good and far more others that would be bad.[15]

Still it may be clear that to change from a system which we already have in place to some in-principle more attractive alternative would be very difficult and plausibly too costly to justify the change. The more pervasive, articulated, and important the system is, the more likely this will be true. Swedes could change their convention of driving on the left to driving on the right at modest cost, as they did in 1967 (Hardin 1988, 51–3); they could not change their system of jurisprudence or the remnants of their Judaeo-Christian moral system at low enough cost to justify serious thought to select superior systems. To this day, the people of the state of Louisiana, formerly part of colonial France, live under a legal system that is based on the Napoleonic Code, while the US federal system and the systems of the other forty-nine states are based on the British common law.

The only thing that might make an extant system right is that it is extant. We could not expect to design an ideal or even a much better system because we could not be sure how it would work in the longer run. As Madison (1787/2001a, 183) writes in *Federalist 37*, "All new laws, though penned with the greatest technical skill, and passed on the fullest and most mature deliberation, are considered as more or less obscure and equivocal, until their meaning be liquidated and ascertained by a series of particular discussions and adjudications." Hence, rationalist theories of morality and government are inherently irrelevant to our lives. At the margins, however, we might be able to revise our constitutional system by drawing on the experience of others.

Conventions do not have a normative valence per se. Some are beneficial and some are harmful. Both beneficial and harmful conventions can be self-reinforcing even when their only backing is sensibly motivated individual actions. If we could easily redesign government, law, norms, practices, and so forth, we might immediately choose to do so in many cases. The very strong Chinese convention of foot-binding was horrendously harmful, and it was deliberately changed (Mackie 1996). The still surviving convention of female genital mutilation is similarly horrendously brutal and it is being eradicated in some parts of Africa. In the light of such harmful norms, we must grant in general that it is possible to contest whether some pervasive convention costs us more than it harms us; but successful major constitutional change is rare.

We face the fundamental problem that we need government to enable us to accomplish many things and to protect us from each other but that giving government the power to do all of this means giving it the power to do many other, often harmful things as well. We depend on constitutional cleverness to design institutions that accomplish the former and block the latter. The cleverest person in this task

---

[15] John Locke's 1669 "constitutions" for Carolina included, as their last substantive clause, the silly, naive proviso that it "shall be and remain the sacred and unalterable form and rule of government of Carolina forever" (Locke 1669/1993, 232).

historically was probably Madison. But Americans have long since lived past the institutions he helped design and the present government under his constitution would be unrecognizable to him. These changes have happened while a few hundred million Americans essentially acquiesced.

REFERENCES

BARRY, B. 1995. *Justice as Impartiality*. Oxford: Oxford University Press.
BEER, S. H. 1993. *To Make a Nation: The Rediscovery of American Federalism*. Cambridge, Mass.: Harvard University Press.
BERLE, A. A., and MEANS, G. C. 1932. *The Modern Corporation and Private Property*. New York: Macmillan.
BRENNAN, G., and HAMLIN, A. 1995. Constitutional political economy: the political philosophy of *Homo economicus? Journal of Political Philosophy*, 3: 280–303.
BURKE, E. 1774/1969. Speech to the electors of Bristol (1774). Pp. 68–75 in Burke, *Speeches and Letters on American Affairs*. London: Everyman.
CAESAR, no. 2. 1787/1987. Pp. 60–1 in *The Founders' Constitution*, ed. P. Kurland and R. Lerner, 5 vols., vol. i. Chicago: University of Chicago Press.
CALHOUN, J. C. 1853/1992. A Disquisition on Government. Pp. 5–78 in *Union and Liberty: The Political Philosophy of John C. Calhoun*, ed. R. M. Lence. Indianapolis, Ind.: Liberty Fund.
DAHL, R. A. 1957. *A Preface to Democratic Theory*. Chicago: University of Chicago Press.
——1996. Thinking about democratic constitutions: conclusions from democratic experience. Pp. 175–206 in *NOMOS 38: Political Order*, ed. I. Shapiro and R. Hardin. New York: New York University Press.
DOWNS, A. 1957. *An Economic Theory of Democracy*. New York: Harper.
FILMER, R. 1680/1949. *Patriarcha: A Defence of the Natural Power of Kings against the Unnatural Liberty of the People*. Pp. 49–126 in *Patriarcha and Other Political Works of Sir Robert Filmer*, ed. P. Laslett. Oxford: Oxford University Press.
HAMPTON, J. 1980. Contracts and choices: does Rawls have a social contract theory? *Journal of Philosophy*, 77: 315–38.
HARDIN, R. 1982. *Collective Action*. Baltimore: Johns Hopkins University Press for Resources for the Future.
——1988. *Morality within the Limits of Reason* Chicago: University of Chicago Press.
——1989. Why a constitution? Pp. 100–20 in *The Federalist Papers and the New Institutionalism*, ed. B. Grofman and D. Wittman. New York: Agathon Press.
——1991. Hobbesian political order. *Political Theory*, 19: 156–80.
——1999. *Liberalism, Constitutionalism, and Democracy*. Oxford: Oxford University Press.
——2002. Liberal distrust. *European Review*, 10: 73–89.
——2003. *Indeterminacy and Society*. Princeton, NJ: Princeton University Press.
——2004. Transition to corporate democracy? Pp. 175–97 in *Building a Trustworthy State in Post-Socialist Transition*, ed. J. Kornai and S. Rose-Ackerman. New York: Palgrave Macmillan.
HIBBING, J. R., and THEISS-MORSE, E. 2002. *Stealth Democracy: Americans' Beliefs about How Government Should Work*. Cambridge: Cambridge University Press.

HOBBES, T. 1642/1983. *De Cive*, ed. H. Warrender; originally published in Latin. Oxford: Oxford University Press.

—— 1651/1994. *Leviathan*, ed. E. Curley. Indianapolis: Hackett. (Page citations are to the original edition/this edition.)

HUMBOLDT, W. VON. 1854/1969. *The Limits of State Action*, ed. J. W. Burrow. Cambridge: Cambridge University Press; repr. Liberty Press, 1993.

HUME, D. 1739–40/1978. *A Treatise of Human Nature*, ed. L. A. Selby-Bigge and P. H. Nidditch, 2nd edn. Oxford: Oxford University Press.

—— 1742/1985. Of the independency of Parliament. Pp. 42–6 in *David Hume: Essays Moral, Political, and Literary*, ed. E. F. Miller. Indianapolis, Ind.: Liberty Classics.

—— 1748/1985. Of the original contract. Pp. 465–87 in *David Hume: Essays Moral, Political, and Literary*, ed. E. F. Miller. Indianapolis, Ind.: Liberty Classics.

—— 1751/1975. *An Enquiry Concerning the Principles of Morals*. Pp. 167–323 in Hume, *Enquiries*, ed. L. A. Selby-Bigge and P. H. Nidditch, 3rd edn. Oxford: Oxford University Press.

LOCKE, J. 1669/1993. The fundamental constitutions of Carolina. Pp. 210–32 in *Political Writings of John Locke*, ed. D. Wootton. New York: Mentor.

—— 1690/1988. *Two Treatises of Government*. Cambridge: Cambridge University Press.

LUPIA, A., MCCUBBINS, M., D. and POPKIN, S. L. (eds.) 2000. *Elements of Reason: Cognition, Choice, and the Bounds of Rationality*. Cambridge: Cambridge University Press.

MACKIE, G. 1996. Ending foot-binding and infibulation: a convention account. *American Sociological Review*, 61: 999–1017.

MADISON, J. 1787/2001a. *Federalist 37*. Pp. 179–85 in A. Hamilton, J. Jay, and J. Madison, *The Federalist*, ed. G. W. Carey and J. McClellan. Indianapolis, Ind.: Liberty Fund.

—— 1788/2001b. *Federalist 51*. Pp. 267–72 in A. Hamilton, J. Jay, and J. Madison, *The Federalist*, ed. G. W. Carey and J. McClellan. Indianapolis, Ind.: Liberty Fund.

MANIN, B. 1997. *The Principles of Representative Government*. Cambridge: Cambridge University Press.

MILL, J. S. 1859/1977. *On Liberty*. Pp. 213–310 in *Collected Works of John Stuart Mill*, ed. J. M. Robson, vol. xviii. Toronto: University of Toronto Press.

MILLER, A. 2001. *On Politics and the Art of Acting*. New York: Viking.

RAWLS, J. 1955. Two concepts of rules. *Philosophical Review*, 64: 3–32.

—— 1971/1999. *A Theory of Justice*. Cambridge, Mass.: Harvard University Press.

REID, J. P. 1989. *The Concept of Representation in the Age of the American Revolution*. Chicago: University of Chicago Press.

RICHIE, R. 2002. Fair elections update: election 2002 and the case for reform. Washington, DC: Center for Voting and Democracy.

SCANLON, T. M. 1982. Contractualism and utilitarianism. Pp. 103–28 in *Utilitarianism and Beyond*, ed. A. Sen and B. Williams. Cambridge: Cambridge University Press.

—— 1998. *What We Owe to Each Other*. Cambridge, Mass.: Harvard University Press.

SCHUMPETER, J. A. 1942/1950. *Capitalism, Socialism and Democracy*, 3rd edn. New York: Harper.

SIDNEY, A. 1698/1990. *Discourses Concerning Government*, ed. T. G. West. Indianapolis, Ind.: Liberty Classics.

SMITH, A. 1776/1976. *An Inquiry into the Nature and Causes of the Wealth of Nations*, ed. R. H. Campbell, A. S. Skinner, and W. B. Todd. Oxford: Oxford University Press; repr. Liberty Press, 1979.

TOCQUEVILLE, A. DE. 1945/1835, 1840. *Democracy in America*, 2 vols. New York: Knopf.

WEINGAST, B. R. 1997. The political foundations of democracy and the rule of law. *American Political Science Review*, 91: 245–63.

WILLIAMSON, O. E. 1985. *The Economic Institutions of Capitalism: Firms, Markets, Relational Contracting*. New York: Free Press.
WINSTANLEY, G. 1652/1973. *The Law of Freedom in a Platform or, True Magistracy Restored*, ed. R. W. Kenny. New York: Schocken.
WITTMAN, D. A. 1995. *The Myth of Democratic Failure: Why Political Institutions Are Efficient*. Chicago: University of Chicago Press.
WOOD, G. S. 1969. *The Creation of the American Republic, 1776–1787*. Chapel Hill: North Carolina University Press; repr. Norton, 1972.

CHAPTER 17

SELF-ENFORCING DEMOCRACY

ADAM PRZEWORSKI

1 INTRODUCTION

DEMOCRACY endures only if it self-enforcing. It is not a contract because there are no third parties to enforce it. To survive, democracy must be an equilibrium at least for those political forces which can overthrow it: given that others respect democracy, each must prefer it over the feasible alternatives.

Without getting mired in definitional discussions, here is how democracy works (for a fuller account, see Przeworski 1991, ch. 1):

1. Interests or values are in conflict. If they were not, if interests were harmonious or values were unanimously shared, anyone's decisions would be accepted by all, so that anyone could be a benevolent dictator.
2. The authorization to rule is derived from elections.
3. Elections designate "winners" and "losers." This designation is an instruction to the participants as to what they should and should not do. Democracy is an equilibrium when winners and losers obey the instructions inherent in their designations.
4. Democracy functions under a system of rules. Some rules, notably those that map the results of elections on the designations of winners and losers, say the majority rule, are "constitutive" in these sense of Searle (1995), that is, they enable behaviors that would not be possible without them. But most rules emerge in equilibrium: they are but descriptions of equilibrium strategies. Most importantly, I argue below, under democracy governments are moderate not because they are constrained by exogenous, constitutional, rules but because they must anticipate sanctions were their actions more extreme.

My purpose is to examine conditions under which such a system would last. I begin by summarizing early nineteenth-century views according to which democracy could not last because it was a mortal threat to property. Then I summarize two models motivated by the possibility that if the degree of income redistribution is insufficient for the poor or excessive for the wealthy, they may turn against democracy. These models imply that democracy survives in countries with high per capita incomes, which is consistent with the observed facts. Finally, I discuss interpretations and extensions, raising some issues that remain open.

2 Democracy and Distribution

During the first half of the nineteenth century almost no one thought that democracy could last.[1] Conservatives agreed with socialists that democracy, specifically universal suffrage, must threaten property. Already James Madison (*Federalist 10*) observed that "democracies have ever been spectacles of turbulence and contention; have ever been found incompatible with personal security or the rights of property." The Scottish philosopher James Mackintosh predicted in 1818 that if the "laborious classes" gain franchise, "a permanent animosity between opinion and property must be the consequence" (cited in Collini, Winch, and Burrow 1983, 98). Thomas Macaulay in his speech on the Chartists in 1842 (1900, 263) pictured universal suffrage as "the end of property and thus of all civilization." Eight years later, Karl Marx expressed the same conviction that private property and universal suffrage are incompatible (1952/1851, 62). According to his analysis, democracy inevitably "unchains the class struggle:" The poor use democracy to expropriate the riches; the rich are threatened and subvert democracy, by "abdicating" political power to the permanently organized armed forces. The combination of democracy and capitalism is thus an inherently unstable form of organization of society, "only the political form of revolution of bourgeois society and not its conservative form of life" (1934/1852, 18), "only a spasmodic, exceptional state of things ... impossible as the normal form of society" (1971, 198).

Modern intuitions point the same way. Take the median voter model (Meltzer and Richard 1981): each individual is characterized by an endowment of labor or capital and all individuals can be ranked from the poorest to the richest. Individuals vote on the rate of tax to be imposed on incomes generated by supplying these endowments to production. The revenues generated by this tax are either equally distributed to all individuals or spent to provide equally valued public goods, so that the tax rate uniquely determines the extent of redistribution.[2] Once the tax rate is decided,

[1] The only exception I could find was James Mill, who challenged the opponents "to produce an instance, so much as one instance, from the first page of history to the last, of the people of any country showing hostility to the general laws of property, or manifesting a desire for its subversion" (cited in Collini, Winch, and Burrow 1983, 104).

[2] I will refer to redistribution schemes in which tax rates do not depend on income and transfers are uniform as linear redistribution schemes.

individuals maximize utility by deciding in a decentralized way how much of their endowments to supply. The median voter theorem asserts that there exists a unique majority rule equilibrium, this equilibrium is the choice of the voter with the median preference, and the voter with the median preference is the one with median income. And when the distribution of incomes is right skewed, that is, if the median income is lower than the mean, as it is in all countries for which data exist, majority rule equilibrium is associated with a high degree of equality of post-fisc (tax and transfer) incomes, tempered only by the deadweight losses of redistribution.[3]

Moreover, these intuitions are widely shared by mass publics, at least in the new democracies. The first connotation of "democracy" among most survey respondents in Latin America and eastern Europe is "social and economic equality:" in Chile, 59 per cent of respondents expected that democracy would attenuate social inequalities (Alaminos 1991), while in eastern Europe the proportion associating democracy with social equality ranged from 61 per cent in Czechoslovakia to 88 per cent in Bulgaria (Bruszt and Simon 1991). People do expect that democracy will breed social and economic equality.

Yet democracy did survive in many countries for extended periods of time. In some it continues to survive since the nineteenth century. And while income distribution became somewhat more equal in some democratic countries, redistribution was quite limited.[4]

2.1 Some Facts

The probability that a democracy survives rises steeply in per capita income. Between 1950 and 1999, the probability that a democracy would die during any year in countries with per capita income under $1,000 (1985 PPP dollars) was 0.0845, so that one in twelve died. In countries with incomes between $1,001 and $3,000, this probability was 0.0362, or one in twenty-eight. Between $3,001 and $6,055, this probability was 0.0163, one in sixty-one. And no democracy ever fell in a country with per capita income higher than that of Argentina in 1975, $6,055. This is a startling fact, given that throughout history about seventy democracies collapsed in poorer countries, while thirty-seven democracies spent over 1,000 years in more developed countries and not one died. These patterns are portrayed in Figure 17.1, which shows a loess smooth of transitions to democracy as a function of per capita income (the vertical bars are local 95 per cent confidence intervals).

Income is not a proxy for something else. Benhabib and Przeworski (2006) ran a series of regressions in which the survival of democracy was conditioned on per capita

---

[3] This is not true in models that assume that the political weight of the rich increases in income inequality. See Bénabou 1997, 2001.

[4] These assertion may appear contradictory. Yet it seems that the main reason for equalization was that wars and major economic crises destroyed large fortunes and they could not be accumulated again because of progressive income tax. For long-term dynamics of income distribution, see Piketty 2003 on France, Piketty and Saez 2003 on the United States, Saez and Veall 2003 on Canada, Banerjee and Piketty 2003 on India, Dell 2003 on Germany, and Atkinson 2002 on the United Kingdom.

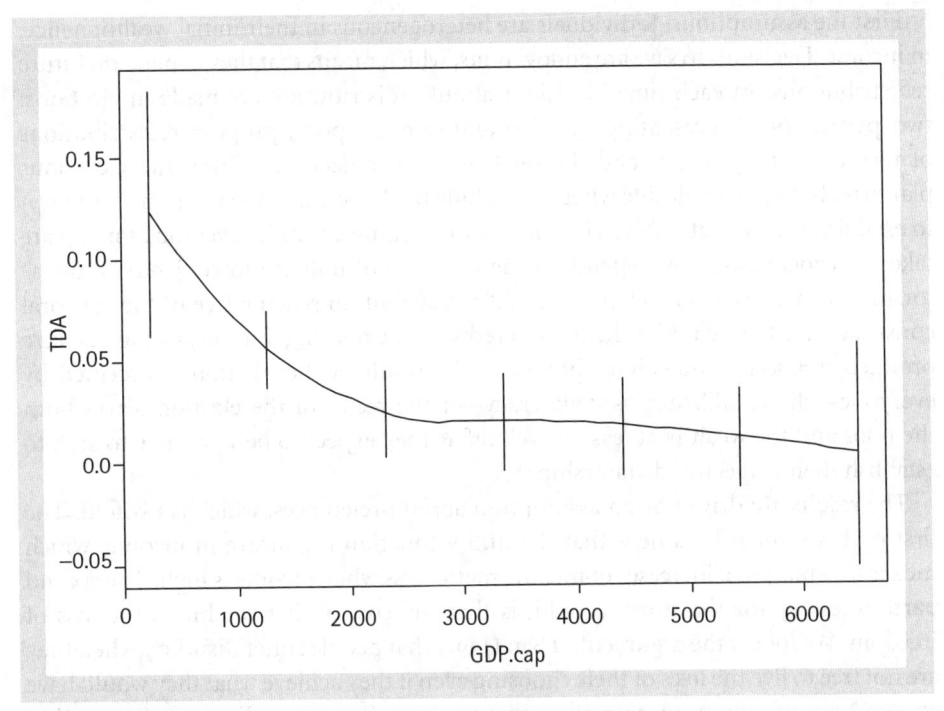

Fig. 17.1 Transitions to dictatorship by per capita income

income and several variables that are adduced in the literature as rival hypotheses: education (Lipset 1960, 38–40), complexity of social structure (Coser 1956), ethno-linguistic divisions (Mill 1991, 230), and political participation (Lamounier 1979). We found that while education, complexity, and ethno-linguistic divisions did matter in the presence of income, none replaces the crucial role of income in determining the stability of democracy.

3 MODELS AND RESULTS

Why would income matter for the stability of democracy, independently of everything else?[5] Here is the answer given by Benhabib and Przeworski (2006) and in a different version by Przeworski (2005).[6]

---

[5] The same is not true about dictatorships. Przeworski and Limongi 1997, Przeworski et al. 2000, Acemoglou et al. 2004, as well as Gleditsch and Choung 2004, agree that survival of dictatorships is independent of income, although Boix and Stokes (2003) claim that its probability declines in income. If democracies are more frequent in wealthier countries, it is only because they survive in such countries whenever a dictatorship falls for whatever reasons.

[6] The two models differ in that the former is fully dynamic, while the latter is static, that is, income and the rates of redistribution are taken as constant. The latter model, however, allows an extension to electoral equilibria in which parties do not converge to the same platform, which is necessary to derive some results discussed below.

First the assumptions. Individuals are heterogeneous in their initial wealth; hence, in income. Decisions to save are endogenous, which means that they depend on future redistributions. At each time, decisions about redistribution are made in elections: two parties, one representing the rich and one the poor, propose redistributions of income, voting occurs, and the median voter is decisive.[7] Given the victorious platform, both parties decide whether to abide by the result of the election or attempt to establish their dictatorship. The chances of winning a conflict over dictatorship are taken as exogenous: they depend on the relations of military force. Under a dictatorship, each party would choose its best redistribution scheme free of the electoral constraint: for the rich this scheme is to redistribute nothing; for the poor to equalize productive assets as quickly as possible. The result of the election is accepted by everyone—the equilibrium is democracy—if the result of the election leaves both the poor and the wealthy at least as well off as they expect to be were they to seek to establish their respective dictatorships.

The results are driven by an assumption about preferences, which is twofold. The first part is standard, namely, that the utility function is concave in income, which means that marginal increases of income matter less when income is high. The second part, necessary for the story to hold, is that the cost of dictatorship is the loss of freedom. We follow the argument of Sen (1991) that people suffer disutility when they are not free to live the lives of their choosing even if they achieve what they would have chosen.[8] Specifically, even if we allow that the losers in the conflict over dictatorship may suffer more, we also allow that everyone may dislike dictatorship to some extent (see below). Importantly, this preference against dictatorship (or for democracy) is independent of income: as Dasgupta (1993, 47) put it, the view that the poor do not care about freedoms associated with democracy "is a piece of insolence that only those who don't suffer from their lack seem to entertain" (see also Sen 1994).

These assumptions imply that when a country is poor either the electoral winner or loser may opt for dictatorship, while when a country is wealthy, the winner pushes the loser to indifference, but not further. Since the marginal utility of income declines in income, while the dislike of dictatorship (or the value of democracy) is independent of income, at a sufficiently high income the additional gain that would accrue from being able to dictate redistribution becomes too small to overcome the loss of freedom. As Lipset (1960, 51) put it, "If there is enough wealth in the country so that it does make too much difference whether some redistribution takes place, it is easier to accept the idea that it does not matter greatly which side is in power. But if loss of office means serious losses for major groups, they will seek to retain office by any means available."[9] Figure 17.2 portrays this pattern.

---

[7] Benhabib and Przeworski 2006 show that even though each party offers a plan for the infinite future, so that party competition occurs in infinite number of dimensions, no majority coalition of poor and wealthy can leave both better off than the decision of the median voter. Moreover, given a linear redistribution scheme, the identity of the median voter does not change over time. Hence, the same median voter is decisive at each time with regard to the entire path of future redistribution.

[8] On the value of choice and its relation to democracy, see Przeworski 2003.

[9] For a general game-theoretic approach to the dependence of social conflict and cooperation on wealth, based on the non-homotheticity of preferences, see Benhabib and Rustichini 1996.

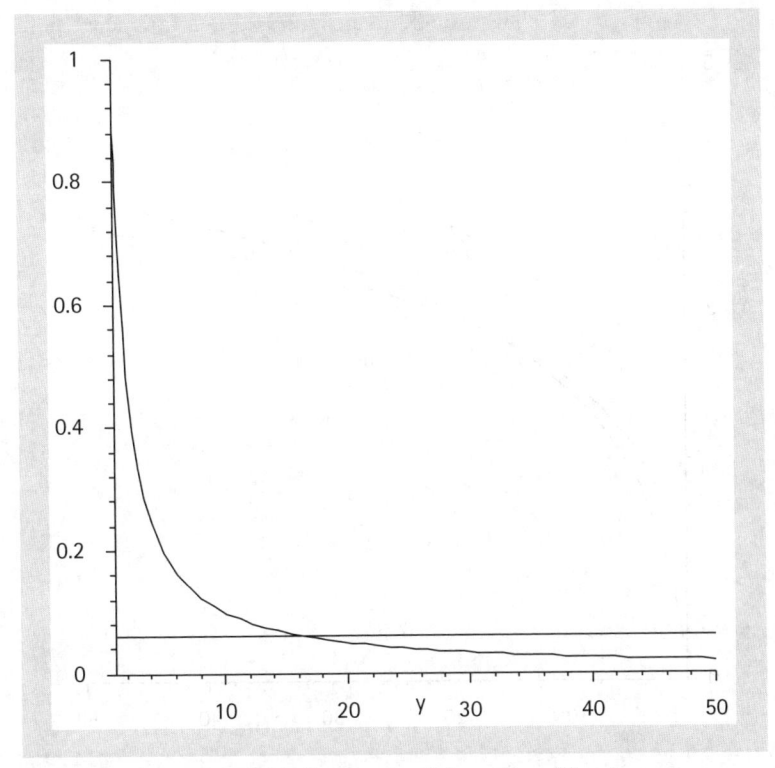

Fig. 17.2 Marginal utility of income and the value of freedom

In Figure 17.3 the solid line represents the value of democracy, the dotted line is the value of income accruing to the dictator, while the dashed line is the value of dictatorship to the dictator, that is, the value that combines higher income and the dislike of dictatorship, all these values as functions of per capita income. As we see, the values of the two regimes cross at some income level: democracy becomes more valuable. And although their crossing points are different, the same is true for the rich and the poor.

Hence, democracies survive in wealthy countries. When the country is sufficiently wealthy, the potential increase in income that would result from establishing a dictatorship is not worth the sacrifice of freedom. Some redistribution occurs but its extent is acceptable for both the poor and the rich.

Both models conclude that conditional on the initial income distribution and the capacity of the poor and the wealthy to overthrow democracy, each country has a threshold of income (or capital stock) above which democracy survives. This threshold is lower when the distribution of initial endowments is more equal and when the revolutionary prowess of these groups is lower. In the extreme, if income distribution is sufficiently egalitarian or if military forces are balanced, democracy survives even in poor countries. Yet in poor unequal countries there exist no redistribution schemes that would be accepted by both the poor and the wealthy. Hence, democracy cannot survive. As endowments increase, redistribution schemes that satisfy both the poor

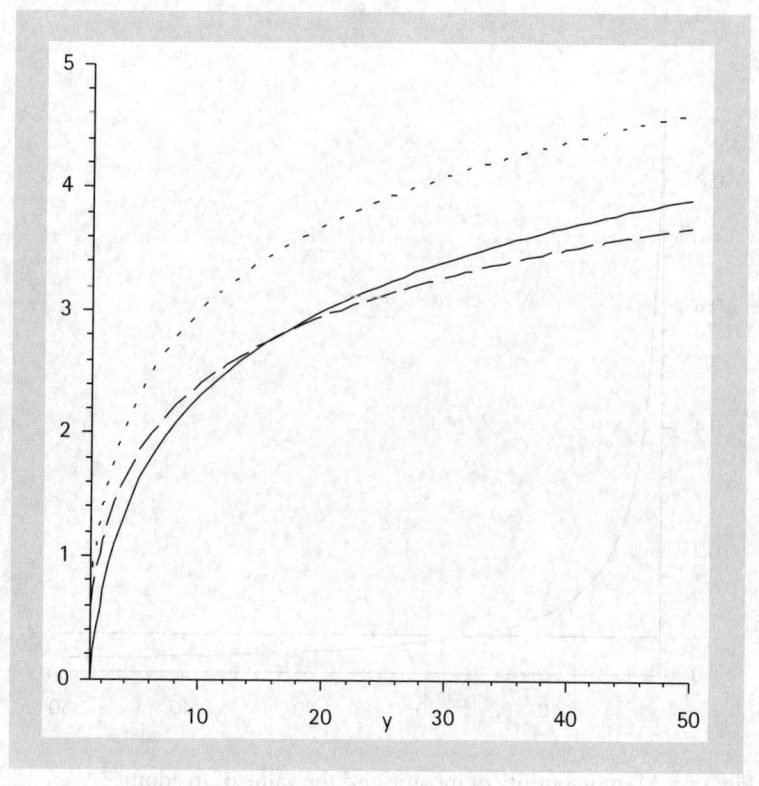

Fig. 17.3 Values of dictatorship and democracy

and the wealthy emerge. Moreover, as income grows, the wealthy tolerate more and the poor less redistribution, so that the set of feasible redistributions becomes larger. Since the median voter prefers one such scheme to the dictatorship of either group, the outcome of electoral competition is obeyed by everyone and democracy survives.

4 INTERPRETATIONS

4.1 Development and Democracy

Democracy always survives when a society is sufficiently wealthy. Each society, characterized by income distribution and the relations of military power, has an income threshold above which democracy survives.

This result sheds light on the role of economic crises in threatening democracy. What matters is not the rate of growth per se but the impact of economic crises on per capita income. Each country has some threshold of income above which democracy survives. Economic crises matter if they result in income declining from above to below this threshold but not when they occur at income levels below or well above this threshold. In Trinidad and Tobago, per capita income fell by 34 per cent between 1981 and 1990 but the 1990 income was still $7,769 and democracy survived. In New Zealand, income fell by 9.7 per cent between 1974 and 1978, but the 1978 income was $10,035. Yet in Venezuela, which enjoyed democracy for forty-one years, per capita income declined by 25 per cent from 1978 to 1999, when it reached $6,172. Hence, this decline may be responsible for the emergence of anti-democratic forces in that country.

In countries with intermediate income levels, it is possible that one party obeys only if it wins while the other party obeys unconditionally.[10] Results of elections are then obeyed only when they turn out in a particular way. One should thus expect that there are countries in which the same party repeatedly wins elections and both the winners and the losers obey the electoral decisions, but in which the winners would not accept the verdict of the polls had it turned differently.[11]

Democracy can survive in poor countries but only under special conditions, namely, when the distribution of income is very egalitarian or when neither the rich nor the poor have the capacity to overthrow it. Hence, democracies should be rare in poor countries. When one side has overwhelming military power, it turns against democracy. But even when military power is more balanced, democracy survives in poor countries only if the expected redistribution reflects the balance of military force. If democracy is to survive in poor countries, political power must correspond to military strength. Note that this was the ancient justification of majority rule. According to Bryce (1921, 25–6; italics supplied), Herodotus used the concept of democracy "in its old and strict sense, as denoting a government in which the will of the majority of qualified citizens rules, ... *so that physical force of the citizens coincides (broadly speaking) with their voting power.*" Condorcet (1986/1785, 11) as well, while interpreting voting in modern times as a reading of reason, observed that in the ancient, brutal times, "authority had to be placed where the force was."

4.2 Income Distribution and Income Redistribution

Democracy survives only if redistribution of income remains within bounds that make it sufficient for the poor and not excessive for the rich. In poor unequal countries there is no redistribution scheme that satisfies simultaneously these two constraints. These bounds open up as per capita income increases, so that in sufficiently wealthy countries democracy survives when redistribution is quite extensive and when it is quite limited. In poor countries in which democracy endures, the tax rate tracks the constraint of rebellion by either the poor or the wealthy, while in wealthy ones it is constrained only by electoral considerations.

Note that several poor democracies that have a highly unequal income distribution redistribute almost nothing. While systematic data seem impossible to obtain, poor

---

[10] This result is based on an electoral model in which, for any reason, parties do not converge to the same platform, so that it matters which party wins. See Przeworski 2005.
[11] This is the "Botswana" case of Przeworski et al. 2000.

democracies appear to redistribute much less than wealthy ones: the average percentage of taxes in GDP is 9.3 in democracies with per capita income below $1,000, 15.3 in democracies with income between $1,000 and $3,000, 19.8 between $3,000 and $6,000, and 28.0 above $6,000. The explanation must be that the threat of rebellion by the rich is tight in poor countries.[12]

4.3 Electoral Chances and the Design of Institutions

Przeworski (1991) argued that democracy is sustained when the losers in a particular round of the electoral competition have sufficient chances to win in the future to make it attractive for them to wait rather than to rebel against the current electoral defeat.[13] The argument was that when the value of electoral victory is greater than the expected value of dictatorship which, in turn, is greater than the value of electoral defeat, then political actors will accept a temporary electoral defeat if they have reasonable prospects to win in the future. In light of the model presented here, such prospects are neither sufficient nor necessary for democracy to survive. In poor countries, they may be insufficient, since even those groups that have a good chance to win may want to monopolize power and use it without having to face electoral constraints. Above some sufficiently high income level, in turn, losers accept an electoral defeat even when they have no chance to win in the future, simply because even permanent losers have too much at stake to risk turning against democracy. Political forces are "deradicalized" because they are "bourgeoisified."

Hence, the model implies that while democracy survives in wealthy countries under a wide variety of electoral institutions, poorer countries must get their institutions right. Specifically, institutional choice matters for those countries in which democracy can survive under some but not under all distributions of electoral chances.

4.4 Constitutions

By "constitutions," I mean only those rules that are difficult to change, because they are protected by super-majorities or by some other devices. Note that in some countries, such as contemporary Hungary, constitutional rules can be changed by a simple majority, while in other countries, such as Germany, some clauses of the constitution cannot be changed at all.

Constitutions are neither sufficient nor necessary for democracy to survive. Constitutions are not sufficient because agreeing to rules does not imply that results of their application will be respected. We have seen that under some conditions, parties obey electoral verdicts only as long as they turn out in a particular way. Hence, the

---

[12] A rival hypothesis is that poor societies are less unequal, so that there is less room for redistribution. Yet, with all the caveats about data quality, Przeworski et al. (2000, table 2.15) show that the average Gini coefficients are almost identical is societies with per capita income less than $1,000 and with income above $6,000.

[13] This argument and the subsequent discussion assume again that parties do not converge to the same platforms in the electoral equilibrium, so that results of elections matter.

contractarian theorem—"if parties agree to some rules, they will obey them" or "if they do not intend to obey them, parties will not agree to the rules" (Buchanan and Tullock 1962; Calvert 1994)[14]—is false. If one party knows that it will be better off complying with the democratic verdict if it wins but not when it loses while the other party prefers democracy unconditionally, parties will agree to some rules knowing full well that they may be broken. Under such conditions, a democracy will be established but it will not be self-enforcing.

To see that constitutions are not necessary, note that above some income threshold democracy survives even though the rules of redistribution are chosen by each incumbent. Hence, democratic government is moderate not because of some exogenous rules but for endogenous reasons: either because of the rebellion or the electoral constraint, whichever bites first. In equilibrium a democratic government obeys some rules that limit redistribution, but the rules that are self-enforcing are those that satisfy either constraint.

The same is true of other rules over which incumbents may exercise discretion, say electoral laws. The incumbent may be better off changing the electoral system in its favor. But if such a change would cause the opposition to rebel and if the incumbent prefers status quo democracy to a struggle over dictatorship, then the incumbent will desist from tampering with the electoral system.

Hence, the rules that regulate the functioning of a democratic system need not be immutable or even hard to change. When a society is sufficiently wealthy, the incumbents in their own interest moderate their distributional zeal and tolerate fair electoral chances. Democratic governments are moderate because they face a threat of rebellion. Democratic rules must be thought of as endogenous (Calvert 1994, 1995).

Theories which see institutions as endogenous face a generic puzzle: if rules are nothing but descriptions of equilibrium strategies, why enshrine them in written documents? In some cities there are laws prohibiting pedestrians from crossing at a red light, while other cities leave it to the discretion of the individuals. Endogenous theories of institutions imply that people motivated by their personal security would behave the same way regardless whether or not such laws are written. After all, the United Kingdom does not have a written constitution and yet the British political system appears to be no less rule bound than, say, the United States. An answer to this puzzle offered by Hardin (2003) is that constitutions coordinate, that is, they pick one equilibrium from among several possible. To continue with the example, rules must indicate whether pedestrians should stop at red or green lights: both rules are self-enforcing but each facilitates different coordination. Weingast (1997) is correct in claiming that the constitution is a useful device to coordinate actions of electoral losers when the government engages in excessive redistribution or excessive manipulation of future electoral chances.

---

[14] According to Calvert (1994, 33), "Should players explicitly agree on a particular equilibrium of the underlying game as an institution, and then in some sense end their communication about institutional design, they will have the proper incentives to adhere to the agreement since it is an equilibrium.... Any agreement reached is then automatically enforced (since it is self-enforcing), as required for a bargaining problem."

Thus, laws do play a role in constituting democratic equilibria. Calvert (1994) goes too far when he claims that institutions are just descriptions of equilibria in pre-existing situations.[15] For democracies to exist, political parties must know at least how to interpret the results of voting; that is, they must be able to read any share of votes (or seats) as a "victory" or "defeat." This rule plays a twofold role: (1) A democratic equilibrium may exist under this rule but need not under other rules. For example, an equilibrium may exist when the rule is that a party is the winner if it receives a majority of votes but not if the rule were that it obtains one-third. (2) Given one rule, a different party may be "the winner" than given some other rule under which a democratic equilibrium also exists. Hence, the particular rule both enables a democratic equilibrium and picks one among several equilibria possible. Conversely, even if the rules are endogenous, it is always a particular law that political forces obey. As Kornhauser (1999, 21) puts it, "The legal structure identifies which of many equilibria the players will in fact adopt. The enactment of a law results in the institution of a new equilibrium."

5 OPEN ISSUES

5.1 Democracy in Ethnically Divided Societies

Consider countries in which some positive probability of winning future elections is necessary and sufficient to induce the current losers to wait for their turn. One would think that this possibility is closed in societies in which a single ethnic group constitutes a majority of the population. If all members of this group always vote together, as Rabushka and Shepsle (1972) or Horowitz (1985) would expect, minorities have a zero probability of winning, now and in the future. Hence, if they can mobilize any military power, they rebel.[16]

Yet even when we consider as democracies only those countries in which there was an alternation in office, democracies appear to be more, rather than less, stable in societies in which one ethnic group constitutes a majority. While cross-national measures of ethnicity are notoriously controversial (Alesina et al. 2003; Fearon 2003), Figure 17.4 shows a loess plot of the probability of democracy dying (TDA) in countries with per capita income lower than $6,055 as a function of the relative size of the largest ethnic group (ETHNIC), as given by a widely used Soviet source, *Atlas Narodov Mira* (1964).

[15] In Calvert's story, the institution that induces the cooperative equilibrium is the "director." This equilibrium would not have occurred in the original situation he describes without the institution of the "director." Hence, it is not an equilibrium of the underlying situation.

[16] One should not conclude that minorities would necessarily rebel in such situations: a unified majority ethnic group may be sufficiently powerful militarily to intimidate its opponents. Hence, one possibility is that elections continue to occur, the same party always wins, and the losers obey the results: this has been true of Botswana, discussed above.

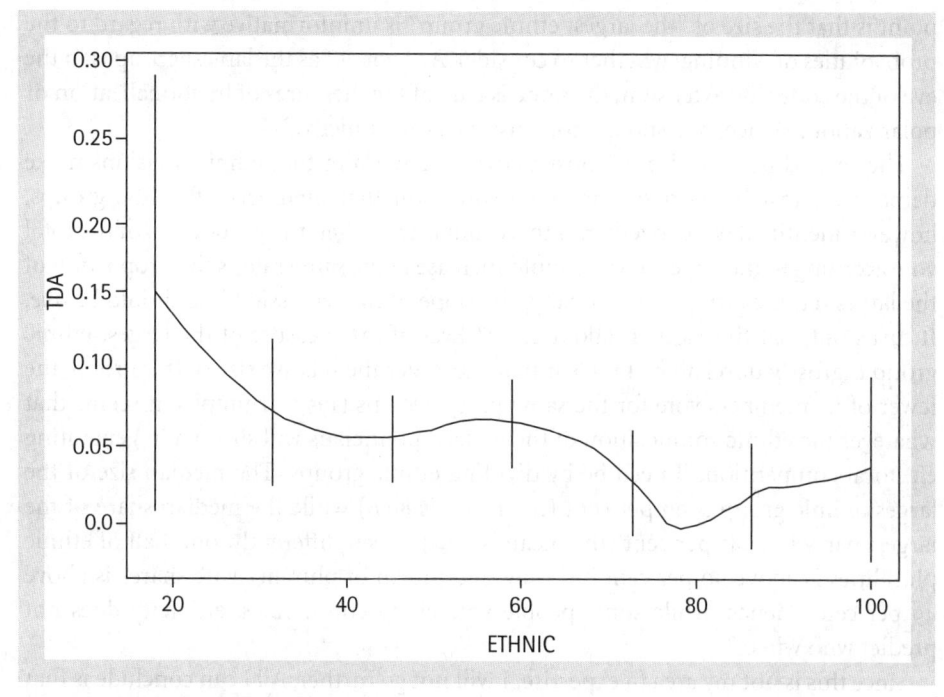

Fig. 17.4 Transitions to dictatorship as a function of the size of largest ethnic group

Contrary to prevailing theories, the probability democracy would die falls as the relative size of the largest ethnic group increases. Why would it be so? One possibility is that widely used unidimensional measures of ethnicity are simply misleading. Following Chandra and Humphreys (2002), assume that ethnic identities are two dimensional. Since to make my point I need to generate just a single example, suppose that the distribution of "primordial" groups is as follows:[17]

	1	2	Total
A	25	35	60
B	30	10	40
Total	55	45	100

Now suppose, in the spirit of the citizen-candidate model (Osborne and Silivinsky 1996; Besley and Coate 1998), that anyone can present him- or herself as a candidate at some cost and that voters maximize expected utility. The winner distributes some spoils, say government jobs, and the total number of jobs to be distributed is a concave function of the share of the votes won. Under these assumptions, there is a unique electoral equilibrium, in which party 1 forms and wins with 55 per cent of the vote. (By concavity, each member of the group $A1$ is more likely to get a job as a member of a smaller winning coalition, so that $A1$'s prefer to vote 1 than A.) The

---

[17] "Primordialism" is out of fashion and these days everyone is a "constructivist." But most "constructivists" are just "primordialists" one step removed: they invariably assume that identities are made out of something taken as primitives, the "identity repertoire" (Laitin 1998).

point is that the size of "the largest ethnic group" is uninformative with regard to the probabilities of winning: whether to consider A, 1, or $A2$ as the largest group is in the eye of the coder. By extension, the same is true of the measures of fractionalization or polarization. Hence, one should not trust data on ethnicity.[18]

The second point is more "constructivist." The claim that ethnic divisions make democracy unstable is based on the assumption that members of ethnic groups, however identified, vote together. If this claim is true, then the proportion of the total vote accruing to the largest party should increase at the same rate as the proportion of the largest ethnic group in the society: the slope of the regression line should be *one*. It turns out that this slope is about *zero*.[19] Even if the measure of the largest ethnic group is grossly unreliable, it is clear that the larger the relative size of this group, the fewer of its members vote for the same party. Downs (1957) triumphs: it seems that whatever the ethnic composition of the society, politicians will succeed in generating electoral competition, if need be by dividing ethnic groups. The median size of the largest ethnic group is 90 per cent (the mean is 80.6) while the median share of the largest party is 42.45 per cent (the mean is 41.45). Seen differently, one-half of ethnic pluralities is above 90 per cent but only one-fourth of plurality vote shares is above 49 per cent. Hence, while some people vote along ethnic lines, ethnicity does not predict who wins.[20]

Since this is not my area of expertise, I will not go further. All I can conclude is that the relation between ethnic divisions and the viability of democracy remains obscure.

5.2 Culture and Democracy

In a democratic equilibrium, the protagonists obey the verdicts of the polls and limit their actions to those enabled by law. They participate in a competition that is regulated by rules and they obey the results; they are law abiding; they act so as to perpetuate democracy. Moreover, neither the winners nor the losers engage each time in the calculations imputed to them in the model. Democracy, in a well-worn phrase, is "the only game in town." All this is just a description of the equilibrium, "equilibrium culture."

There is nothing wrong with such descriptions, but only as long as they are not infused with causal interpretations: it is one thing to describe the equilibrium actions and beliefs as a "culture" and another to claim that this culture is what generates the equilibrium.[21] Yet it is just a small step to transform these observable actions into

---

[18] Alesina et al.'s (2003) discussion of endogeneity of ethnic divisions misses the point: the issue is not whether ethnic identities change over time but whether such identities can be politically activated in different ways. Fearon 2003 delves deeper into multilayered structures of ethnicity, but he still does not admit multidimensional traits.

[19] Data for the vote share of the largest party are from IDEA. Linear regression generates $\beta = 0.0306$, with $s.e. = 0.0234$. Non-parametric smoothing shows no departures from linearity.

[20] For a study seeking to explain why members of particular ethnic groups vote for the ethnic parties see Chandra 2004.

[21] This ambiguity is most apparent in Weingast's (1997) attempt to reconcile different explanations of democratic stability.

motivations, to say that democracy lasts because individuals are motivated by a sense of duty to accept outcomes of competition in which they participate, because they respect the normativity of the law, because they cherish democracy, because their behavior is driven by habit. If a democratic equilibrium is sustained by a strategic pursuit of self-interest, then in equilibrium the political actors are law abiding. But this does not mean that the equilibrium is supported by the motivation to obey the law. In equilibrium people learn to behave out of habit, just as we learn to stop at a crossroads on seeing a red light. Only if something happens that disturbs the habit—the Algerian war in France, the Aldo Moro affair in Italy—may political forces actually calculate. Hence, in developed countries, democracy is taken for granted. But this does not imply that it is not based on a calculation.

Situations induced by interests and those generated by culture look the same. Hence, observing equilibria is not sufficient to identify the mechanism which generates them. But any plausible cultural story would have to account for the relation between the stability of democracy and income.

To understand how culture might enter into the construction of the equilibria analyzed here, we need to return to the utility function underlying the model. The explanation of why democracy survives in wealthy societies offered by Benhabib and Przeworski (2005) is that decreasing marginal returns to income are overwhelmed by a dislike of dictatorship when income is high. It turns out that, while some assumption about dislike of dictatorship is necessary to generate such a result, the same result can be obtained by assumptions that carry different interpretations. Let μ^s be the loss of utility experienced by the dictator and μ^u the loss experienced by people dominated under dictatorship. Compare the following assumptions:

1. $\mu^s = \mu^u = \mu > 0$
2. $\mu^u > \mu^s = 0$
3. $\mu^u > \mu^s > 0$.

The first assumption says that everyone is characterized by the same preference against dictatorship (or, again, for democracy), regardless of whether they would end up dictating or being dictated to. We could then think of μ as a parameter characterizing a particular culture, the value it attaches to democracy. The income threshold above which democracy survives would then be a function of this parameter, as well as of income distribution and the military prowess of the different groups.

Yet cultural interpretations fare poorly when they are implemented empirically. Following the seminal study of Almond and Verba (1965), asking people questions about their preferences for systems of government became a routine activity all around the world. Answers to such questions are interpreted as harbingers of democratic stability and are often read nervously: Brazil, for example, seemed to verge on the brink in 1991 since only 39 per cent of the respondents thought that democracy is always the best system of government, as contrasted with, say, Chile, where in 1990 76 per cent did. Almond and Verba, Inglehart (1990), and Granato, Inglehart, and Leblang (1996) attempted to show that answers to such questions can predict whether democracy survives or falls. But while surveys of "democratic attitudes" are conducted repeatedly in old and new democracies and while pages of academic journals are filled with percentages of Americans, Spaniards, Chileans, Poles, or Kazakhs saying that they like or do not like democracy (for a taste, see *Journal of Democracy*, 12, 2001), there is not a shred of evidence that these answers have anything to do with the actual survival of democracy.

The second assumption says only that no one likes to be oppressed by a dictatorship. This is the way this preference is formulated in Przeworski (2005), where it is motivated by the fear of physical insecurity. Hence, this is not an assumption about culture: it says that political actors fear losing a conflict over dictatorship because they are afraid to be imprisoned or killed. Under this assumption democracy prevails in wealthy countries because the eventual gain of income is not worth risking physical security.

Finally, the third is introduced just for completeness, since it is a combination of the former two.

To conclude, if we take the first assumption, culture may enter into an explanation in a subtle way, but thus far there is no empirical evidence that it does.[22]

REFERENCES

ACEMOGLOU, D., JOHNSON, S., ROBINSON, J. A., and YARED, P. 2004. Income and democracy. Manuscript, Department of Economics, MIT.

ALAMINOS, A. 1991. *Chile: transición political y sociedad*. Madrid: Centro de Investigaciones Sociológicas.

ALESINA, A., DEVLEESCHAUWER, A., EASTERLY, W., KURAT, S., and WACZIARG, R. 2003. Fractionalization. *Journal of Economic Growth*, 8: 155–94.

ALMOND, G. A., and VERBA, S. 1965. *The Civic Culture: Political Attitudes and Democracy in Five Nations*. Boston: Little, Brown.

ATKINSON, A. B. 2002. Top incomes in the United Kingdom over the twentieth century. Unpublished manuscript.

BANERJEE, A., and PIKETTY, T. 2003. Top Indian incomes, 1922-2000. Unpublished manuscript.

BÉNABOU, R. 1997. Inequality and growth. *NBER Macroeconomics Annual 1997*, 11–74.

—— 2000. Unequal societies: income distribution and the social contract. *American Economic Review*, 90: 96–129.

BENHABIB, J., and PRZEWORSKI, A. 2005. The political economy of redistribution under democracy. *Economic Theory*, in press.

—— and RUSTICHINI, A. 1996. Social conflict and growth. *Journal of Economic Growth*, 1: 125–42.

BESLEY, T., and COATE, S. 1998. Sources of inefficiency in a representative democracy: a dynamic analysis. *American Economic Review*, 88: 139–56.

BOIX, C., and STOKES, S. C. 2003. Endogenous democratization. *World Politics*, 55: 517–49.

---

[22] For an analysis of cultural interpretations of democratic stability, see Przeworski, Cheibub, and Limongi 1998.

BRUSZT, L., and SIMON, J. 1991. Political culture, political and economical orientations in central and eastern Europe during the transition to democracy. Manuscript, Erasmus Foundation for Democracy, Budapest.

BRYCE, J. 1921. *Modern Democracies*. London: n-p.

BUCHANAN, J., and TULLOCK, G. 1962. *The Calculus of Consent: Logical Foundations of Constitutional Democracy*. Ann Arbor: University of Michigan Press.

CALVERT, R. 1994. Rational actors, equilibrium, and social institutions. In *Explaining Social Institutions*, ed. J. Knight and I. Sened. Ann Arbor: University of Michigan Press.

—— 1995. The rational choice theory of social institutions: cooperation, coordination, and communication. Pp. 216–68 in *Modern Political Economy*, ed. J. S. Banks and E. A. Hanushek. New York: Cambridge University Press.

CHANDRA, K. 2004. *Why Ethnic Parties Succeed: Patronage and Ethnic Counts in India*. New York: Cambridge University Press.

—— and HUMPHREYS, M. 2002. Incorporating constructivist propositions into theories of democracy. Unpublished manuscript.

COLLINI, S., WINCH, D., and BURROW, J. 1983. *That Noble Science of Politics*. Cambridge: Cambridge University Press.

CONDORCET, MARQUIS DE 1986/1785. Essai sur l'application de l'analyse à la probabilité des décisions rendues à la pluralité des voix. Pp. 9–176 in *Sur les élections et autres textes*, ed. Olivier de Bernon. Paris: Fayard.

COSER, L. 1956. *The Functions of Social Conflict*. Glencoe, Ill: Free Press.

DASGUPTA, P. 1993. *An Inquiry into Well-Being and Destitution*. Oxford: Oxford University Press.

DELL, F. 2003. Top incomes in Germany over the twentieth century: 1891–1995. Unpublished manuscript.

DOWNS, A. 1957. *An Economic Theory of Democracy*. New York: Harper and Row.

FEARON, J. D. 2003. Ethnic and cultural diversity by country. *Journal of Economic Growth*, 8: 195–222.

GLEDITSCH, K. S., and CHOUNG, J. L. 2004. Autocratic transitions and democratization. Manuscript, Department of Political Science, University of California, San Diego.

GRANATO, J., INGLEHART, R., and LEBLANG, D. 1996. Cultural values, stable democracy, and development: a reply. *American Journal of Political Science*, 40: 680–96.

HARDIN, R. 1989. Why a constitution? Pp. 100–20 in *The Federalist Papers and the New Institutionalism*, ed. B. Grofman and D. Witman. New York: Agathon Press.

—— 2003. *Liberalism, Constitutionalism, and Democracy*. New York: Oxford University Press.

HOROWITZ, D. 1985. *Ethnic Groups in Conflict*. Berkeley: University of California Press.

INGLEHART, R. 1990. *Culture Shift in Advanced Industrial Society*. Princeton, NJ: Princeton University Press.

KORNHAUSER, L. A. 1999. The normativity of law. *American Law and Economics Review*, 1 (1/2): 3–25.

LAITIN, D. 1998. *Identity in Formation*. Ithaca, NY: Cornell University Press.

LAMOUNIER, B. 1979. Notes on the study of re-democratization. Latin American Working Paper No. 58, Wilson Center, Washington, DC.

LIPSET, S. M. 1960. *Political Man: The Social Bases of Politics*. Garden City, NJ: Doubleday.

MACAULAY, T. B. 1900. *Complete Writings*, vol. xvii. Boston: Houghton-Mifflin.

MADISON, J. 1982/1788. *The Federalist Papers by Alexander Hamilton, James Madison and John Jay*, ed. G. Wills. New York: Bantam.

MARX, K. 1934/1852. *The Eighteenth Brumaire of Louis Bonaparte*. Moscow: Progress.
──── 1952/1851. *Class Struggles in France, 1848 to 1850*. Moscow: Progress.
──── 1971. *Writings on the Paris Commune*, ed. H. Draper. New York: International.
MELTZER, A. H., and RICHARDS, S. F. 1981. A rational theory of the size of government. *Journal of Political Economy*, 89: 914–27.
MILL, J. S. 1991/1857. *Representations on Representative Government*. Buffalo, NY: Prometheus.
OSBORNE, M. J., and SLIVINSKY, A. 1996. A model of political competition with citizen-candidates. *Quarterly Journal of Economics*, 111: 65–96.
PIKETTY, T. 2003. Income inequality in France, 1901–1998. *Journal of Political Economy*, 111: 1004–42.
──── and SAEZ, E. 2003. Income inequality in the United States, 1913–1998. *Quarterly Journal of Economics*, 118: 1–39.
PRZEWORSKI, A. 1991. *Democracy and the Market: Political and Economic Reforms in Eastern Europe and Latin America*. New York: Cambridge University Press.
──── 2003. Freedom to choose and democracy. *Economics and Philosophy*, 19: 265–80.
──── 2005. Democracy as an equilibrium. *Public Choice*, 123: 253–73.
──── CHEIBUB, J. A., and LIMONGI, F. 1998. Culture and democracy. Pp. 125–46 in *World Culture Report*. Paris: UNESCO.
──── and LIMONGI, F. 1997. Modernization: theories and facts. *World Politics*, 4a: 253–73.
──── ALVAREZ, M, E., CHEIBUB, J. A., and LIMONGI, F. 2000. *Democracy and Development*. New York: Cambridge University Press.
RABUSHKA, A., and SHEPSLE, K. 1972. *Politics in Plural Societies*. Columbus, Oh.: Charles E. Merrill.
ROEMER, J. E. 2001. *Political Competition*. Cambridge, Mass.: Harvard University Press.
SAEZ, E., and VEALL, M. R. 2003. The evolution of high incomes in Canada, 1920-2000. Working Paper 9607, National Bureau of Economic Research.
SEARLE, J. R. 1995. *The Construction of Social Reality*. New York: Free Press.
SEN, A. 1991. Welfare, preference and freedom. *Journal of Econometrics*, 50: 15–29.
──── 1994. Freedom and needs. *New Republic*, 10 Jan.
WEINGAST, B. R. 1997. Political foundations of democracy and the rule of law. *American Political Science Review*, 91: 245–63.

CHAPTER 18

CONSTITUTIONS AS EXPRESSIVE DOCUMENTS

GEOFFREY BRENNAN

ALAN HAMLIN

1 INTRODUCTION

Two aspects of our title require clarification. One is the idea of a constitution; the other the notion of expressiveness. In each case, we shall try to clarify the concept by appeal to a contrast. In the case of a constitution, the contrast will be between a constitution as a legal document and the more general idea of a constitution as the rules of the sociopolitical game envisaged in the academic tradition known as Constitutional Political Economy (CPE) and associated with the work of James Buchanan and others (among whom we number ourselves). This contrast occupies Section 2.

In Section 3, we attempt to clarify the notion of expressive activity, following earlier work on expressive voting. The relevant contrast here is with activity that is instrumental, in the sense that it is designed to bring about some further outcome—some outcome, that is, other than the expressing of an attitude, opinion, or view on the matter in hand. The expressive case, by contrast, is that where the expression just *is* the end, in and of itself. Our most basic points are: first, if voting and other political behavior is expressive in nature, this will carry implications at the constitutional level; and second, that constitutions themselves may be seen, at least in part, in expressive rather than instrumental terms.

We continue the argument in support of the relevance of expressiveness in the constitutional setting in Section 4, where we address the issue of how expressiveness operates in the setting of electoral politics, and also provide examples of the expressive dimension in existing constitutional documents.

The two distinctions we have invoked provide us with a simple two-by-two matrix of logical possibilities. In Section 5, we lay out that matrix explicitly, and use it to explore the role of expressive elements in constitutions. Our conclusion here is that, though we might regret the intrusion of expressive elements and considerations in written constitutions, we should also be alert to the role of the expressive in the definition and enforcement of constitutions in their more general sense. Indeed, written constitutions may serve to channel the expressive element in relatively innocuous directions.

2 Constitutional Documents and Rules of the Game

Within the CPE tradition, a central piece of the analytic scheme is the distinction between the in-period and constitutional levels of decision-making.[1] The standard analogy is between deciding on the rules of a game (the constitutional level) and plays of the game within those rules (the in-period level). The distinction serves a function that is somewhat similar to that of John Rawls's veil of ignorance—but whereas Rawls's device is a thought experiment designed to inform our understanding of justice, Buchanan envisages the distinction between in-period and constitutional levels in behavioral terms. Disagreements about the appropriate rules of the socio-political-economic game are argued to be easier to resolve than disagreements within the game, precisely because agents are, in the former setting, less fully informed about their own particular positions and interests. Clashes of interest that would be unresolvable at the in-period level may be resolved by the application of rules that themselves secure unanimous agreement at the constitutional level. (See Buchanan's chapter in this volume.)

So, for example, individuals who may turn out to be natural competitors in the in-period marketplace might well agree, at the constitutional level, on the general property rights structure that would be best for the operation of the market order. Equally, individuals with very different in-period political objectives may nevertheless agree on the basic rules of the democratic political process. Agreement at the constitutional level grounds the rules of the game which then generate in-period outcomes.

To a significant extent, Buchanan's picture of political disagreement and the role of the constitutional move reflect his view that interests play the predominant role in motivating behavior at all levels within the political process, just as they do within

---

[1] See, for example, Buchanan and Tullock 1962; Brennan and Buchanan 1985; Buchanan 1990.

markets. This view is shared by most public choice scholars and other economists interested in political institutions.

We have argued against this view elsewhere,[2] and shall sketch some of the relevant arguments below. The essential point in the present context is the implication that, if our critique of instrumental self-interested voting at the in-period level is right, then the force of the constitutional/in-period distinction is weakened. Constitutional and in-period political decisions are basically alike in that both are heavily influenced by expressive considerations.

For the moment, however, we want to focus on the distinction between a constitutional document and the rules of the game in the CPE sense. It should be clear that there is no necessary connection between the rules of the game as envisaged by Buchanan, and any written document that is dignified by the name of constitution. Such written documents may or may not fully specify the general rules of the sociopolitical-economic game. Perhaps some such rules are embodied in other non-constitutional documents—ordinary laws and statutes, for example. Perhaps they are not written anywhere, but depend rather on institutional habits, conventions, and norms. More formally, a general constitution is defined by its content: it just is the rules of the game, however they are signified or embodied. In this sense the constitution literally constitutes the society as a society. By contrast a constitutional document is any document that bears that name. A constitutional document may seek to describe and codify the underlying constitution of a society, but it may be more or less successful in these aims, and it may also include other material of a different character.

There are a number of aspects to the distinction between these two senses of constitution that are worth noting—differences in terms of: enforcement processes; intended audience; processes of enactment; and processes by which the constitution (under whichever interpretation) may be reformed. We will briefly consider these in turn.

To the extent that they actually operate as constitutions, constitutional documents are normally intended to be interpreted and enforced through explicit legal procedures—procedures that involve specific legal institutions, and conceivably ones explicitly dedicated to that purpose (e.g. constitutional courts).[3] The constitutional document has automatic standing in that setting. By contrast, the rules of the socio-political-economic game may be enforced in any number of ways, depending on the precise form the rules in question take. In a simple coordination game, for example, like that involving which side of the road to drive on, the emergent rule may be essentially self-enforcing—that is, enforced by the self-interest of individuals operating under appropriate information regarding the convention (see Hardin's contribution to this volume). Other rules may emerge as social norms and be enforced by social esteem and disesteem. Or perhaps the esteem and disesteem may attach not so much to the observance of the norm itself as to acts of punishment: if it is common knowledge that punishing a violator of some prevailing norm is itself a source of esteem,

---

[2] Brennan and Lomasky 1993; Brennan and Hamlin 1998, 2000; see also Schuessler 2000.
[3] Of course many constitutions fail to operate. Such failure can take many forms.

then I might be induced to comply with the norm even if I care nothing for any disesteem I might incur from violating.[4] Often legal stipulations simply give expression to and support prevailing norms—a point made forcefully by Ellickson (2001).

A constitutional document is usually adopted or ratified by a process that involves discussion and, ultimately, some form of explicit endorsement. It has an intended audience—or several such. By virtue of its enforcement procedures, it is addressed to the courts—to the persons who will interpret and enforce it. But because of the (normal) requirement of popular endorsement—perhaps via a plebiscite—its intended audience also includes the voters whose support is sought.

In principle, the rules of the game have only the audience of players: the rules must seem appropriate to those who are subject to them. But that appropriateness may just be a matter of common practice—of habit, or imitation. Conceivably, none of the persons who abide by the rules need be aware that they are doing so, provided only that they do abide by them. Perhaps some rules fall into the Hayekian category of "tacit knowledge:" one can learn to observe such rules only by observation and imitation. The rules of "bel canto" singing are arguably of this kind. Perhaps some politically relevant rules are also of this type.

A constitutional document normally lays down processes by which it may itself be altered. Sometimes those processes are especially restrictive, reflecting the high legal status that the constitutional document enjoys. Sometimes, more general constitutional provisions are just a matter of ordinary law. So, for example, although the UK is renowned for having an unwritten constitution, because it lacks documents that enjoy full constitutional status, many aspects of the rules of the political game are specified in ordinary legislation. Sometimes, elements of the constitution are laid down in historical documents—Magna Carta, say—which are such that the very idea of amending them is either meaningless or at least deeply implausible. In all such cases, elements of the wider constitution may be written down somewhere, but their status is more like that of a convention, in the sense that reform cannot be secured merely by stipulation.

There is a good deal more that might be said about the possible differences between constitutional documents and more general constitutions. However, it should be conceded that in the CPE tradition it is typically assumed that a written constitution can embody the constitutional rules, and indeed should do so. That is the conceived function of constitutional documents, and to the extent that such documents do not specify the rules of the game that is seen to represent a "failure." Equally, the inclusion of material other than the specification of the rules of the game is likely to be seen as at best "cheap talk" and at worst a hostage to fortune in providing the basis for later interpretation of the "spirit" of the constitution.[5]

We think this CPE view is excessively narrow. As a matter of fact, many constitutional documents embody a good deal more than the constitutional rules—and many a good deal less. Whether these facts are to be lamented is a matter we shall take up below.

---

[4] For more detailed discussion of the roles of esteem and disesteem see Brennan and Pettit 2004.
[5] For a constitutional study undertaken in that spirit, see Brennan and Casas Pardo 1991.

3 Expressive and Instrumental Considerations

The second distinction we seek to put into play is that between expressive and instrumental activity. This distinction may be relevant in many settings, including the context of the rational account of voting behavior, and our account takes off from that case. Specifically, our claim is that voting behavior in large-scale electoral contexts characteristic of Western democracies is properly understood more in expressive than in instrumental terms, and that this carries implications for the understanding of constitutions.

The point of departure for this claim is the observation that in large-scale popular elections the individual voter cannot reasonably expect to determine the electoral outcome. The probability that the outcome will be decided by exactly one vote is vanishingly small. Yet only in that case is it true that all those on the winning side were causally efficacious in bringing about the outcome. In all other cases, no individual's vote has any effect on the outcome: that outcome would be the same whether I voted or not and whichever way I happened to vote, if I did. Even if policy is influenced by vote shares—rather than just who wins—it is deeply implausible that a single vote will have any noticeable impact on policy. In short, an individual's vote is inconsequential.

Some commentators within the rational actor school of politics have considered that this fact shows that it is irrational to vote—and that, therefore, those who actually participate in democratic elections are irrational in at least this regard. Voting would, on this view, only become rational if the level of turnout fell to the point where the probability of being decisive became significant. But suppose we both hold to the presumption that individuals are rational, and accept that turnout levels are high enough to imply that no individual voter can reasonably expect to be decisive. Then we must explain voting behavior (both the fact of voting, and the way in which the vote is cast) in terms that identify a motivation for individual action other than that of bringing about a particular electoral outcome.

The simplest and most natural explanation of voter behavior in large-scale elections under the rationality assumption is that voters desire to express an attitude or opinion with respect to one candidate, party, or policy relative to others. Voters act not to bring about an intended electoral outcome (action we term "instrumental") but simply to express a view or an evaluative judgement over the options (action we term "expressive"). In that sense, they are acting in the same sort of way that they act when they cheer at a football match, or when they express an opinion in the course of dinner party conversation.

Expressive desires or preferences are similar to instrumental desires or preferences in many ways, but they differ from their instrumental cousins in one key respect—their satisfaction can be achieved without necessarily involving particular further consequences. Thus, I can satisfy my expressive desire to voice my opinion that Z should happen, without believing that doing so will actually bring Z about, and, indeed, without any expectation that Z will happen. It is, in this case, the simple expression of the opinion that matters.

One might object that if voting is a private act, it is not clear how it can be given an expressive interpretation. After all, we usually express opinions in public, when others are able to hear us. We would offer two types of response to this objection. First, even if we accept that voting behavior is private, we note that you can be your own audience, and that using the opportunity provided by voting to articulate and reinforce your own self-image can be an important aspect of building identity and self-esteem. To see oneself as the sort of person who votes Republican, or indeed as someone who just votes, may be an important part of one's identity. Such essentially private expressions can also reinforce group memberships—identifying yourself (to yourself) as a member of a specific group or class. Even the example of cheering at a football game carries over—we certainly recognize the phenomenon of fans cheering for their team even when watching the game alone on TV.

The second line of response questions the private nature of voting. Of course, the actual act of voting may be private, but voting is also the topic of considerable debate. While it would certainly be possible for an individual to separate voting from the talk of voting (and there is some evidence that some people do so dissemble), surely the most obvious and psychologically plausible way to proceed is to suit the voting action to the expressive wish; so that if you wish to say, in public, that you voted for X, the obvious action is to vote for X, particularly given that voting in any other way will in any case be inconsequential.

Though expressive activity can be swept up under a general ascription of rationality, it should not be assumed that the substantive content of the attitudes or opinions expressed is necessarily the same as the interests or preferences that would be revealed if the actor reasonably expected to be decisive. There is no a priori reason to think that expressive views and instrumental preferences will be identical, or even strongly positively correlated. The critical question in the expressive case is: what will I cheer for? The critical question in the instrumental case is: what will be best for me all things considered? Of course it is very unlikely that the answers to these questions will always be different—but there are good reasons to think that in at least some relevant cases expressive opinion and instrumental interests will come apart.

A key aspect of expressive behavior is that the individual will be free to express support for a candidate or policy without reference to the cost that would be associated with that candidate or policy actually winning. Imagine that I believe policy X to be "good" in itself, but that the adoption of policy X would carry costs to me that would outweigh the benefits. I would not choose X if I were decisive but, faced with a large-scale vote for or against X, I would be happy to express my support for X given that, in this context, the instrumental balancing of costs and benefits is virtually irrelevant. Equally, individuals may vote to articulate their identity—in ideological, ethnic, religious, or other terms. Or because they find one or other of the candidates especially attractive in some sense that they find salient. In each case, the basic point is that the expressive benefit is not counterbalanced by consideration of the costs that would be associated with a particular overall outcome of the election. On this view, individuals will vote in line with their interests (that is, their all-things-considered interests taking account of all benefits and costs) only when those interests connect fully and directly with the relevant expressive factor.

Within the rational actor tradition, the "veil of insignificance" characteristic of the voting context (the phrase is originally Hartmut Kliemt's) has been used to explain why voters will typically be rationally ignorant about the political options open to them. However, the issue goes beyond mere rational ignorance. Even a fully informed voter—perhaps *especially* a fully informed voter—would have negligible reason to vote for the candidate who, if elected, would yield the voter the highest personal payoff. That is what being "insignificant" means.

If this is right, then the propensity of rational choice political theorists to extrapolate directly from market behavior founded on all-things-considered interests to electoral behavior is based on a mistake. Further, an account of democratic political process grounded on interest-based voting is likely not only to misrepresent political behavior but also to misdiagnose the particular problems to which democratic politics is prone and against which constitutional provisions have to guard.

Three final points: first, it is important to distinguish the expressive idea from a range of other ideas associated with individual motivation. The expressive idea is importantly distinct from, for example, the ideas of altruism or moral motivation. This point is subtle, because it may be that, in particular cases, expressive behavior tends to be more altruistic or more moral than behavior that is undertaken on the basis of all-things-considered interests. But, there is nothing in the expressive idea itself that makes this true of necessity—expressive behavior in other cases may be cruel or malign rather than benevolent. The core of the expressive idea lies in the structure of expressing an opinion without reference to the consequences, rather than the particular content of the opinion expressed.

Second, it is important not to confuse the point that certain individual behavior is inconsequential and hence expressive with the point that the aggregate of all such behavior does carry consequences. Clearly, whatever motivates voters, the electoral outcome is determined by the aggregation of all votes. The issue is not whether voting in aggregate has consequences: it is rather whether those consequences necessarily explain how individuals vote—whether the connection between consequences and individual action is the same here as in contexts where each individual gets what she individually chooses.

Third and relatedly, we should be careful to distinguish the content of an expression from the fact that it *is* an expression. In particular, the content may be consequentialist, even though the expression itself remains "expressive." So for example, if A writes a letter to the editor of the local paper expressing the view that a particular policy is a bad one in consequential terms, the norm that A expresses is consequentialist, but the letter-writing remains an expressive activity. In the same way, if A votes (cheers) for policies that satisfy consequentialist norms, that fact does not make A's voting itself an instrumental act.

4 THE CONSTITUTIONAL RELEVANCE OF EXPRESSIVE BEHAVIOUR

The second part of our claim is that expressive political behavior carries implications for the understanding of constitutions. We advance this claim in each of two senses. First, the recognition of expressive behavior within electoral politics will carry implications for the design and evaluation of constitutions. This was a major theme of Brennan and Hamlin (2000). The second sense applies the expressive idea to the constitutional process itself and was the subject of Brennan and Hamlin (2002)—where we argued that the shift to the constitutional level does not do the work normally claimed of it in the CPE tradition once appropriate account is taken of the expressive nature of mass political behavior. There are two parts to this argument. First, as argued above, the over-concentration on an instrumental analysis of politics has caused a misdiagnosis of a central problem of democratic politics. Under an interest-based view of voting the central problem is identified as the principal–agent problem, so that the essential role of a constitution is to structure the relationship between voters and their political agents so as to ensure maximum responsiveness to voters' interests. By contrast, the recognition of the expressive dimension of politics shifts attention to the problem of utilizing institutional design to identify the real interests of voters given that their expressive voting behavior may not reveal them.

Second, if this is so at the level of in-period politics it will be no less so at the constitutional level of choice. This is most obvious where a draft constitution is subject to ratification by popular vote. In a popular ratification process, not only is the individual voter almost certain to be insignificant, there is also the fact that the draft constitution is likely to include a range of elements that will induce voters to engage expressively. Ideas of nationality, identity, justice, democracy, and other "basic values" that might be articulated in the constitution are likely to excite expressive reactions that are not necessarily or directly related to the all-things-considered interests of the individual. And knowing this, those who are responsible for drafting the constitution will face clear incentives to design the constitution in a way that will encourage the voters to cheer, regardless of whether this design will best serve the interests of the voters.

Even where the constitution is not subject to a formal ratification by popular vote, there are likely to be other mechanisms at work, through the process of political representation, or via the popular media, which exert an essentially expressive pressure on the content and form of the constitution.

Written constitutions, we argue, are often best seen as symbolic and expressive statements of the political mindset of the time and place. Of course, this is not to deny that written constitutions may include statements that bear directly on the rules of political process. But there remains an issue of how such statements are to be interpreted. The CPE tradition has identified the constitutional specification of rules as the outcome of self-interest, operating in the distinctive setting where no one knows which "self" one will turn out to be. But constitutional statements about rules are, we think, more plausibly understood as the result of expressive preferences over such rules.

The claim that written constitutions are to be understood as largely symbolic and expressive will hardly be controversial in many circles. The preambles and opening sections of most written constitutions are almost exclusively concerned with what we would term expressive issues—issue of identification, morality, justice, and so on. We will illustrate the point by reference to just two current constitutions; but there is no shortage of such examples. The constitution of the Republic of Ireland (1937) opens:

In the Name of the Most Holy Trinity, from Whom is all authority and to Whom, as our final end, all actions both of men and States must be referred,
We, the people of Éire,
Humbly acknowledging all our obligations to our Divine Lord, Jesus Christ, Who sustained our fathers through centuries of trial,
Gratefully remembering their heroic and unremitting struggle to regain the rightful independence of our Nation,
And seeking to promote the common good, with due observance of Prudence, Justice and Charity, so that the dignity and freedom of the individual may be assured, true social order attained, the unity of our country restored, and concord established with other nations,
Do hereby adopt, enact, and give to ourselves this Constitution.

The Irish constitution thereby establishes a political context that is explicitly religious and historical, that invokes past "trials" and "struggles," and that commits to seeing "the unity of our country restored."

The constitution of Poland (1997) opens:

Having regard for the existence and future of our Homeland,
Which recovered, in 1989, the possibility of a sovereign and democratic determination of its fate,
We, the Polish Nation—all citizens of the Republic,
Both those who believe in God as the source of truth, justice, good and beauty,
As well as those not sharing such faith but respecting those universal values as arising from other sources,
Equal in rights and obligations towards the common good—Poland,
Beholden to our ancestors for their labours, their struggle for independence achieved at great sacrifice, for our culture rooted in the Christian heritage of the Nation and in universal human values,
Recalling the best traditions of the First and the Second Republic,
Obliged to bequeath to future generations all that is valuable from our over one thousand years' heritage,
Bound in community with our compatriots dispersed throughout the world,
Aware of the need for cooperation with all countries for the good of the Human Family,
Mindful of the bitter experiences of the times when fundamental freedoms and human rights were violated in our Homeland,

> Desiring to guarantee the rights of the citizens for all time, and to ensure diligence and efficiency in the work of public bodies,
> Recognizing our responsibility before God or our own consciences,
> Hereby establish this Constitution of the Republic of Poland as the basic law for the State, based on respect for freedom and justice, cooperation between the public powers, social dialogue as well as on the principle of subsidiarity in the strengthening the powers of citizens and their communities.

Here, the Polish constitution identifies a re-emergent national identity, linked to earlier republics and to the Christian tradition.

These examples may be supplemented by reference to recent attempts to write a new preamble for the Australian constitution as discussed by McKenna (2004). The people appointed (and self-appointed) to this task have been mainly poets/authors, rather than constitutional lawyers. What at first caused McKenna surprise—as a political scientist—was the "moving, highly personal, even intimate" quality of these contending preambles. McKenna's initial response was skeptical:

> While I admired [a particular draft] preamble as a piece of creative writing, my training in political science had me wondering how the High Court might find his attempt to emulate the Book of Genesis useful in interpreting the constitution. (2004, 29)

Yet McKenna's more reflective judgement is different—"I came to see their fanciful nature as positive" (p. 29). We would suggest that this change of view marks a shift from the instrumental to the expressive perspective. What is most striking to us is McKenna's view that the fact that "Since its inception in 1901, the federal constitution has not figured greatly in explaining our identity or character" speaks to a certain kind of failure. Here is McKenna's perspective:

> We are a nation forged through remembering the human sacrifice and horror of war, a people whose most profound political instincts lie outside the words of our constitution. While we live under a written constitution, the values and principles of our democracy remain largely unwritten—truths embodied in the practice of daily life—truths we have yet to distil. If Australians can be said to have a constitution in any real sense it is an imaginary constitution. One comprised of scraps of myth and wishful thinking that bears little relation to the text of the document itself... Finding the right words to express the uniqueness of this land and the depth of our relationship with it could serve to promote a sense of popular ownership of the constitution. If the constitution touches ordinary Australians, if it speaks to the living and not to the dead, then the people are more likely to vote for it. (p. 32)

For McKenna, then, a reasonable claim on a written constitution is that it should express the common identity of the citizenry, and the source of the citizen's attachment to the nation. McKenna is surely not alone when he looks to the constitution to deliver an expression of national unity, or when he assesses the extant constitution in those terms. And this suggests that a written constitution that operates as an expressive document is not necessarily a mark of failure, so much as a recognition that a written constitution may do more (and less) than lay out the rules of the political/social/economic game.

5 Instrumental and Expressive Constitutions

We now return to our initial pair of distinctions—between the expressive and the instrumental, on the one hand; and between the written and the general rules of the game, on the other. These distinctions cross-cut in the manner illustrated in Figure 18.1, and identify four possible scenarios. We now wish to explore this matrix a little more fully.

The previous section focused on expressive considerations in the context of written constitutions, and so may be placed in box 2 in Matrix A, this in contrast to the more usual focus within the CPE tradition which clearly lies in box 1. But another aspect of much CPE analysis is that it tends to ignore the distinction between the written constitution and the more general rules of the game. And this is understandable in the instrumental setting. That is, we see no great issues at stake in the contrast between box 1 and box 3 in our matrix. As long as we retain the instrumental perspective, the precise nature of the constitution—written or unwritten, constructed or emergent, formal or informal—may not matter much. What matters behaviorally is that there are rules and that these rules are recognized by the players. Of course, within Buchanan's normative scheme, the constitutional rules must be seen as "agreed" among the citizenry in some sense. But agreement does not imply a particular form of constitution, and so the main thrust of our point remains. The source of a particular rule, and exactly how it is documented, or otherwise identified, does not seem to bear on either our acceptance of the rule, or our behavior under the rule.

Once we admit the relevance of the expressive perspective, however, additional considerations come into play. For example, in drawing out the contrast between box 2 and box 4 in our matrix, the distinction between constitutional rules that are explicitly constructed and those that emerge by more implicit or tacit processes seems quite significant. As we have already argued, the explicit process leading to a written constitution (or constitutional amendment) is likely to be subject to considerable expressive pressures precisely because of the nature of the involvement of individual

Type of "constitution"	Account of electoral preference	
	Instrumental	Expressive
Written constitution	1	2
Rules of the game	3	4

Fig. 18.1 Matrix A: four possibilities

citizens in that process. But in the case of emergent constitutional rules, the involvement of individual citizens is at a different level. Rather than the constitution being a matter for voting (and therefore the expression of views), rules emerge as the byproducts of the cumulative actions of many individuals where each action is motivated by reference to some end other than the setting of a constitutional rule. Thus, the individual actions that contribute to the formation of the emergent rule can be expected to reflect the all-things-considered interests of the individuals concerned rather than the issues that will cause them to cheer. Note that both written and emergent rules derive from the individual actions of a large number of individuals— it is the nature and motivation underlying individual actions that differs, not the number of people involved.[6]

This distinction between emergent rules (deriving ultimately from interested actions) and explicitly constructed and collectively endorsed rules (deriving from expressive actions) provides not just an example of how cells 2 and 4 in Matrix A may differ, but also an interesting observation in its own right. However one must be careful when considering what the observation shows. One interpretation would be that emergent rules are more likely to serve the interests of the population than are constructed rules, so that constitutions that evolve are generally to be preferred to those that are designed. Indeed one might go so far as to claim support for a Burkean/Oakeshottian position in relation to evolved institutions.[7] While we recognize this interpretation, we think that it goes a step too far. We would prefer to emphasize the different roles that are played by constructed and emergent rules/institutions, and thereby recognize the value of constitutions of both kinds. As we have seen, a written constitution provides an excellent opportunity for expressing ideas of identity and culture that may play a very positive role in reinforcing society's view of itself, in shaping the political climate, and in supporting the perceived legitimacy of the prevailing order.

A written constitution may also provide a useful codification of political procedures. But there is some danger, we believe, in asking a written constitution to perform the function of fully defining the rules of the sociopolitical-economic game (rather than codifying rules that have already emerged). This danger derives from the expressive nature of the constitution-making process. There is a clear risk that constructed rules will have more to do with rhetorical appeal than with practical efficacy, more to do with symbols than with reality, more to do with their ability to raise a cheer than with their ability to serve interests. On the other hand, these very same features seem likely to establish an enthusiasm for and loyalty to the prevailing constitutional order that purely evolved rules may lack.

---

[6] In Brennan and Hamlin 2002 we sketch an alternative resolution that reserves constitution setting powers to a small constitutional convention that is insulated as far as possible from the pressures of the people, while still being representative of their interests. See also Crampton and Farrant 2004; Mueller 1996.

[7] We explore aspects of conservatism more explicitly in Brennan and Hamlin 2004, where we identify a bias in favour of the status quo as a central analytic component of conservatism, while acknowledging that skepticism and a distrust of constructivism are also conservative themes.

If our general position here is correct, it should be possible to exploit the strengths of both written and unwritten elements of the constitutional order. The issue is not so much whether it is best to have a constitution in written or unwritten form, but rather how to manage the mix in the most appropriate way.

REFERENCES

BRENNAN, G., and BUCHANAN, J. M. 1985. *The Reason of Rules*. Cambridge: Cambridge University Press.
—— and CASAS PARDO, J. 1991. A reading of the Spanish constitution. *Constitutional Political Economy*, 2: 53–79.
—— and HAMLIN, A. 1995. Constitutional political economy: the political philosophy of *Homo economicus*? *Journal of Political Philosophy*, 3: 280–303.
—— —— 1998. Expressive voting and electoral equilibrium. *Public Choice*, 95: 149–75.
—— —— 2000. *Democratic Devices and Desires*. Cambridge: Cambridge University Press.
—— —— 2002. Expressive constitutionalism. *Constitutional Political Economy*, 13: 299–311.
—— —— 2004. Analytic conservatism. *British Journal of Political Science*, 34: 675–91.
—— and LOMASKY, L. 1993. *Democracy and Decision*. Cambridge: Cambridge University Press.
—— and PETTIT, P. 2004. *The Economy of Esteem*. Oxford: Oxford University Press.
BUCHANAN, J. M. 1990. The domain of constitutional economics. *Constitutional Political Economy*, 1: 1–18.
—— and TULLOCK, G. 1962. *The Calculus of Consent*. Ann Arbor: University of Michigan Press.
CRAMPTON, E., and FARRANT, A. 2004. Expressive and instrumental voting: the Scylla and Charybdis of constitutional political economy. *Constitutional Political Economy*, 15: 77–88.
ELLICKSON, R. C. 2001. The market for social norms. *American Law and Economics Review*, 3: 1–49.
MCKENNA, M. 2004. The poetics of place: land, constitution and republic. *Dialogue*, 23: 27–33.
MUELLER, D. 1996. *Constitutional Democracy*. Oxford: Oxford University Press.
SCHUESSLER, A. 2000. *A Logic of Expressive Choice*. Princeton, NJ: Princeton University Press.

CHAPTER 19

THE PROTECTION OF LIBERTY, PROPERTY, AND EQUALITY

RICHARD A. EPSTEIN

In his *Second Treatise on Government*, John Locke argued that the purpose of government was to protect the "lives, liberties and estates" of the people over whom it exercised political control (Locke 1690, 66 §123). Stated in the broadest terms, constitutional theory has been a tug of war between the claims of liberty and property on the one side, and rival claims made in the name of the public interest on the other. The division is deep, as some writers (Blackstone 1979; Claeys 2003; Epstein 2003; Sellers 1994) stress property protection, and others (Wood 1969; Novak 1996) a broad conception of public interest. This tension holds fast whether we speak about property, contract, or equal protection of the laws. In an ideal constitution, the overall social objective is one that allows for state intervention when it produces some net social benefit, without leaving any individuals worse off than they were before the state acted. That condition is most easily satisfied when state powers are directed to national security, to the control of private violence and fraud, to the regulation of monopoly, and to the provision of the needed infrastructure on which these activities can take place. The implicit corollary is that legislative interference with competitive markets should be prohibited even when done in the name of health and safety.

Striking that ideal balance between markets and regulation depends on having the right substantive provisions in a constitution. A socialist constitution that guarantees all persons state supplies of food, clothing, shelter, and housing will degenerate because the state guarantees will make it impossible for the rules of supply and demand to determine the quantity and price of ordinary goods. The United States Constitution, for all its imperfections, rightly starts from the opposite pole. Its implicit assumption is that government powers are limited and enumerated in large measure to forestall the deadly operation of faction, or the political competition over resources that results in social losses. Its major subtext is to sanction public intervention only where it promises to be a source of net social gain. Obtaining these results through purely democratic processes is highly improbable because of the perverse way in which self-interested political factions can undermine the overall advancement of the public good. Hence the use of judicial review as a check on majoritarian political processes. To be sure, the United States Constitution was drafted long before any explicit development of public choice theory (see Buchanan and Tullock 1962), but the central lessons of public choice theory do much to explain the basic structures of the US constitutional order. It is convenient to think of the Constitution as a master agreement that allows the political branches to supply public goods while discouraging the rent-seeking and factions that rip societies apart.

The achievement of this overarching goal depends not only on the proper objects of protection—liberty and property, chiefly—but also on the second non-textual element of constitutional law: choosing the correct standard of judicial review for any federal or state statute, regulation, or order that is challenged as violating one of these guarantees. In theory, we might expect some uniform standard of review to govern all challenges regardless of the clause under which it is made. But from its very outset, the Supreme Court has operated loosely, if erratically, under three different standards of review when considering legislation with different origins, which in modern times have been conceptualized as follows. The first standard of *strict scrutiny* holds that a statute passes constitutional muster only if the limitation it poses on a protected constitutional interest is justified with reference to some compelling state end, and achieved by the means that are precisely calibrated to that purpose, so that they are neither overly broad nor under-inclusive. At the other extreme, government actions under a *rational basis* standard pass constitutional muster so long as a rational person would think that some justification for the regulation could be advanced in light of the history and tradition of the United States, even for laws the court finds foolish or offensive. That is, find one reason to support the statute, and the court will overlook the full range of objections raised against it. The standard of *intermediate scrutiny* occupies the middle ground, and requires that the state use reasonable means to achieve a substantial social end. These verbal formulations are of course elusive, but the bottom line is that the higher the standard of review, the more likely it is that the statute will be struck down, either on its face or as applied to the particular case. Until very recently, the implicit rule of thumb was "strict in form but fatal in fact," while the rational basis test was tantamount to "proper in form, then valid in effect." Only with intermediate scrutiny, which in practice lies closer to strict scrutiny, was there any real uncertainty as to which way a constitutional challenge would come out. In all cases, the court engages in some type of "balancing" between the protected private right and the offsetting government interest. Sometimes the balance is decided on a case-by-case basis, and sometimes by category. As the number and complexity of the cases increase, the number of feasible permutations rapidly grows as well.

Unfortunately, the Constitution is silent on the question of how to choose that all-important standard of review. Today, with an implicit nod to public choice theory, the basic judicial approach rests on three elements. First, when the court has some confidence in the legislative or administrative processes, it is likely to defer to their judgements. Second, when the court thinks that certain classes of claimants, namely those individuals who are found in "discrete and insular" minorities, are unable to protect their interests within the political process, then these persons will receive greater protection than others whose access to that process is regarded as sufficient to defend their interests (see *Carolene Products Co.* v. *United States* 1938, 152 n. 4). Third, those constitutional rights that are regarded as essential to maintaining an open and democratic political process will in general receive greater protection than those which are not. Now, what remains to be determined is how this framework applies to various substantive areas. The appropriate line of division is as follows. We first look at areas involving political issues, which contain large pockets of "preferred freedoms" (e.g. speech) or "suspect classifications" (e.g. race) that attract higher standards of review. We then look to the economic and property interests that, subject to some key exceptions, are subject to lower, often rational basis review. A central defect of modern law is that it uses a lower standard of review in dealing with economic liberties and property rights, notwithstanding the omnipresent dangers of faction discussed above. Accordingly, this chapter will trace the pattern of judicial review as it applies first to political, social, and moral issues, and then move on to the parallel discussions for matters of economic liberty and private property. Its central theme is not that the standard of review is too high in the former cases, but that it is too low in the latter, noting the anomalies that arise along the way.

1 POLITICAL, SOCIAL, AND MORAL ISSUES

Freedom of speech. The court has offered strong protection of freedom of speech, especially on controversial political issues. The initial struggle over this principle was tested by various political protest movements that were subject to criminal prosecution for being a grave threat to public order and safety, by inciting violence in the form of riots or civil disobedience. One such successful prosecution in the aftermath of the First World War gave rise to Justice Holmes's stirring dissent in *Abrams* v. *United States* (1919, 624). The Court upheld a twenty-year prison term for Russian anarchist leafleteers. Holmes insisted that the state show a clear and imminent danger of harm before punishing speech, a position that became American law during the Vietnam conflict in *Brandenburg* v. *Ohio* (1969). Rules on conspiracy and aiding and abetting the commission of specific offenses involving treason, violence, and fraud fall securely within the scope of the police power; the abstract (i.e. unrelated to a call for immediate action that threatens the life or property of others) and public advocacy of some unpopular or alien cause does not, because the fear of government suppression of dissent is too great. The simple insight here is that protest is inconvenient to political elites but informative to the citizenry in the formation of public opinion and their participation in elections and public affairs. The kinds of actions that can be proscribed under the police power as crimes are all actions that would be considered torts when directed against private individuals. There is good reason why social welfare is advanced when the state can halt or punish activities that produce often catastrophic net social losses. But ordinary individuals cannot squelch criticism against their own conduct precisely because it allows other individuals to form better estimates of their overall performance, which in turn will allow reputable individuals to advance at the expense of their more dubious rivals. The same logic applies to public affairs where honest and accurate criticism improves performance in the public sector where direct competition is hard to come by.

The police power also received a narrow reading in New York Times v. Sullivan (1964), arising out of civil rights protests in the South. Here the court provided ample constitutional protection against defamation suits brought against individuals who criticize public officials. These critics may only be sued for statements uttered with "actual malice," which covers only statements known to be false or those made with reckless disregard of their truth, as proved by clear and convincing evidence. That protection is surely warranted with respect to true statements of fact and broad statement of opinions, but New York Times is in fact difficult to justify to the extent that it allows for the destruction of reputations without recourse (Epstein 1986). The appropriate question to ask is whether the gains from free speech are offset by the greater reluctance of able people to enter the political arena knowing that they have no redress for hurtful false statements made without actual malice. There is some reason to think that the New York Times actual malice standard is too protective of speech.

Recently, the Supreme Court, however, took the wrong turn when it sanctioned extensive government regulation of political speech that is neither false nor defamatory. Thus, in dealing with the regulation of political campaigns, the court in McConnell v. Federal Election Commission (2003) held that the private interest in the funding of speech undertaken by others is weaker than direct participation in political discourse, while the danger of the corruption of the electoral process, real or apparent, by moneyed interests justified extensive congressional regulation of campaign expenditures. The perceived risk (which was at best weakly documented) led to a judicial relaxation of the traditional strict scrutiny standard normally applicable to political speech, even for legislation that systematically favors incumbents and is subject to evasion by issue-oriented groups who operate independent of political parties. As a matter of efficiency, there is no reason to favor contributions of labor over those of capital, which this law does. The theory of public choice suggests that the court confused interest group politics with public-regarding legislation.

Strong First Amendment protections of "expression" also extend to literary and artistic forms that go beyond printed materials and broadcasts to include painting, dancing, theater, movies, and the like, whether political or not. The court believes that censorship or suppression of these activities impoverishes the common culture even for speech that some regard as indecent or offensive. Even obscene speech, spurred on by the rise of cable broadcasting, receives more protection today with the liberalization of community norms. It is only when the state interest involves the protection of minor children from forced participation in pornographic acts that the balance tips to the other side. As Justice Scalia noted in his pointed *McConnell* dissent, today the marketplace of ideas appears to be more open to defamers, pornographers, or flag burners than to organized participants in the political process.

The Supreme court has also ruled that the First Amendment protection covers "commercial" speech leading to the sale of products, as opposed to the expression of political opinions by business entities (*Virginia Board of Pharmacy* v. *Virginia Consumer Council* 1976). But even with ordinary advertisements, the court itself has proved sharply divided in the level of protection offered. The ability to obtain information about various commodities has been defended as essential for the operation of the general economic and social system, especially with advertisements for legal services. Yet generally state regulation is permissible (in contrast with political speech) in order to block false and misleading advertising claims to ordinary consumers. The controlling belief is that factual statements about truth and falsity can be found with products but not in politics. But that distinction is hard to maintain when false political speech is directed to specific, factual matters such as who voted for or against specific legislation. Likewise, the antitrust laws and non-discriminatory taxes may be applied to speechlike activities so long as they are not singled out for special burdens. Stated simply, the law has become highly complex because of different forms of protected speech on the one side and the wide range of potential justifications for its limitation on the other. The judicial suspicion of big business and concentrated wealth accounts for the disparities in the level of protection afforded different forms of speech.

Equal protection of the laws. The same tough attitude that has applied to speech has carried over to laws that classify individuals on the grounds of race, where the weapon of choice has been the equal protection clause. Thus, *Brown* v. *Board of Education* (1954) overruled the infamous "separate but equal" decision in *Plessy* v. *Ferguson* (1896). The court in *Brown* invalidated the long-standing practice of segregated schools and other facilities, even though the historical evidence that the Fourteenth Amendment was intended to bar segregation was mixed and controversial. The vulnerability of black citizens to a white-dominated political process led the court to reject decisively the standard police power justification that segregation maintained civil order and ensured the purity of the races. Over a decade later, in *Loving* v. *Virginia* (1967), the court struck down an anti-miscegenation law that had been defended on similar grounds. In contrast, in *Grutter* v. *Bollinger* (2003), the court upheld Michigan's affirmative action program, showing deference to state officials even under a (softened) strict scrutiny standard because diversity in state education counted as a compelling state interest that justified a departure from the color-blind rule in *Brown*.

The equal protection clause has also been applied, but under an intermediate scrutiny standard, to invalidate a wide range of distinctions between men and women, including sex-based rules that deal with the ability to serve as administrators of estates or receive dependent military or social security benefits (*Reed v. Reed* 1971). But efforts to attack economic classifications have generally foundered because the court does not see in these regulations the risk of political domination and oppression that has been found in more sensitive classifications.

Consistent with the basic effort to prevent rent extraction, there is much to applaud judicial intervention to protect discrete and isolated minorities. But there is no reason to withhold that same kind of scrutiny from other forms of regulation that often have blatant protectionist motives. There is no a priori reason why ordinary businesses, both large and small, cannot come out on the losing end of political struggles. Thus a deferential Supreme Court went astray when it rejected an equal protection challenge to a statutory ban on plastic milk containers at the behest of paper manufacturers (*Minnesota v. Clover Leaf Creamery Co.* 1981). The statute looked like naked protectionism thinly disguised by an appeal to environmental justifications whose weakness was belied by the widespread use of plastic containers everywhere else.

2 Constitutional Protection of Contract and Property

The relaxed attitude of the Supreme Court to equal protection challenges to economic regulation comes at the end of a long history of judicial action on the topic. Before the New Deal revolution of 1937, the court gave less protection to social and political rights, and greater protection to contractual rights, economic liberties, and private property. Today the protections have flipped. What explains the demotion of economic interests, and the difference between various classes of rights?

Contracts clause. The court's foray into economic rights before the Civil War invoked the contracts clause to limit state action. The court quickly and sensibly held that the clause limited the state's ability to discharge individuals from indebtedness incurred before the passage of law that delayed the creditors' right to collect on indebtedness, or to discharge a debt under an insolvency or bankruptcy law that was passed subsequent to the creation of the debt. But the Supreme court refused to recognize any individual right to protect a contractual entitlement against an insolvency statute that was passed before the formation of a contract, which was then created with reference to the statutory form. The earlier position exhibited hostility to the *retroactive* limitation of contract rights but not to their *prospective* limitation (Epstein 1984). That split held roughly until the Great Depression when the Supreme

Court upheld certain mortgage moratoria statutes intended to supply comprehensive debtor relief against immediate foreclosure (*Home Building & Loan Ass'n* v. *Blaisdell* 1934). At that point, the court invoked larger police power justifications for social stability to sustain some, but not all, of these statutes. Since then, the protection for vested rights under individual contracts has ebbed and flowed, but there is today no per se prohibition against the retroactive undoing of contractual protections for completed transactions. In *Usery* v. *Turner Elkhorn Mining Co.* (1976), the court upheld a retroactive imposition of liability on coal mining firms whose workers suffered from black lung disease, even in the absence of any liability at the time of the exposure. But in *Eastern Enterprises* v. *Apfel* (1998), a sharply divided court struck down a compensation scheme that reached deeper into the past, and imposed more substantial liabilities.

The distinction between *Turner* and *Apfel* is tenuous at best. Much may be said for a simple rule that would ban all retroactive imposition of liability, and which would comport with elementary notions of individual fairness. Economically, that rule would stabilize expectations and reduce the level of political intrigue that arises in an effort to redo the past by making it more difficult for one interest group to shift costs to another. Nor does opening up closed transactions advance the health and safety of workers by improving working conditions. Accordingly, any question of compensation for injured workers or other individuals should be a matter of general public support, as with the special fund for the victims of 9/11, whose validity has been affirmed. But there was not sufficient political clout to attract contributions for general revenues, either here, or in the much larger current dispute about compensation for the victims of asbestos-related diseases, for whom a political solution has yet to be worked out.

Economic liberties. The scope of state power was radically changed by the passage of the Civil War amendments to the Constitution. On its face, the privileges or immunities clause reads as though it limits the power of the state to pass prospective regulation that limits the rights of citizens. ("No state shall make or enforce any law which shall abridge the privileges or immunities of Citizens of the United States.") An important antebellum decision, *Corfield* v. *Coryell* (1823), held that Article IV § 2 ("The Citizens of Each state shall be entitled to all Privileges and Immunities of Citizens of the several States") meant that a state which conferred the right to contract on its own citizens had to recognize an equal right in the citizen of another state. In and of itself, that clause created a *non-discrimination* rule that did not protect any prospective entitlement to enter into contracts. But the parallel language in the Fourteenth Amendment reads as though it creates a right to contract for "citizens," but not for all "persons," with its flat prohibition against certain forms of state action. Nonetheless, in the epic *Slaughterhouse Cases* (1872), a sharply divided court effectively read this clause out of the Constitution by holding that only the rights that individuals held as United States citizens, such as the right to cross state boundary lines or to petition the United States government, were covered by the clause.

Once the natural line of development was blocked, the defenders of economic liberties turned to "liberty of contract" under the due process clause to gain their revenge (*Allgeyer* v. *Louisiana* 1897). That clause was broader than the privileges and immunities clause because it was not limited to citizens, but applied to all persons, including aliens. Yet this broad reading of the due process clause had to overcome two objections: first, that the scope of "liberty" only embraced the ability to move about without hindrance; second, that due process referred only to procedural rights such as notice and fair hearing. The rejections of both limitations were a self-conscious effort to undo the initial error in *Slaughterhouse*. But under either clause, the police power limited freedom of contract, but not for "labor" or, as we would say, "anti-competitive" restrictions on contractual freedom, which fell outside the health and safety provision of the police power. Accordingly, this interpretation struck down federal and state statutes that required private employers to bargain with union representatives as improper interferences with liberty of contract (*Adair* v. *United States* 1908; *Coppage* v. *Kansas* 1914), or which prevented employers with more than five employees from hiring more than 20 per cent aliens (*Truax* v. *Raich* 1915). The most famous and controversial decision of the period, *Lochner* v. *New York* (1905), held that a statute prohibiting some bakers from working more than ten hours per day could not be justified on grounds of health. *Lochner* has been widely but mistakenly condemned as an improper interference with legislative power. Sunstein (1987) has suggested that the decision showed an undefended preference for common law baselines that were wrongly thought to be "prepolitical" in nature. But *Lochner* committed no such vice, for its functional justification was that competition worked in the long-term interests of employers and employees alike, and that courts must guard against the factional intrigue that distorts the smooth operation of markets at both the federal and state level. Strauss (2003) rejects Sunstein's argument, only to urge that *Lochner* was wrong because of its inordinate affection for contractual freedom. But here too the evidence suggests otherwise. *Lochner* never challenged the power of the state to suppress conspiracy, bribery, or extortion, all of which have negative social consequences. Nor did the court strike down the legislative abolition of the laissez-faire defense of assumption of risk or the state creation of workers' compensation schemes. The court also upheld the antitrust laws against claims that liberty of contract protected cartel formation (see *United States* v. *Addyston Pipe & Steel Co.* 1899). *Lochner*'s real sin was to repudiate the progressive movement's fervent belief that differences in wealth between employer and employee made fair contracting impossible. But this canonical progressive position involves the elementary confusion between market power, which is dangerous, and firm size, which is not. To its credit, *Lochner* represents a view that high levels of judicial scrutiny are needed to combat legislative abuses—the very attitude that proves so influential in many First Amendment cases.

To this day, there is no real evidence of any economic dislocation attributable to *Lochner*'s view that, absent monopoly, the terms of private contract should be left to the parties and not to the minimum wage, labor, or anti-discrimination law. So *Lochner* was an efficient decision that was repudiated by the New Deal conviction that the choice between monopoly and competition was one for legislative choice, not constitutional structure. The overwhelming weight of legal opinion is, alas, contrary to *Lochner*. In part the dominant position rests on the deep suspicion of systematic exploitation in labor markets, and in part on the superior expertise of legislative bodies over courts. Needless to say, the risk of faction is always downplayed in these evaluations. A return to the earlier legal regime would require an enormous revamping of current legal arrangements, and the force of time makes that change most unlikely no matter how justifiable as a matter of first principle.

Contracts affected with the public interest. Similar to freedom of contract is the ancient doctrine allowing the state to impose controls on that subset of contracts described as "affected with the public interest." In its early English form, that doctrine allowed the state to regulate the rates of those firms with legal or natural monopolies. Thus, in *Allnut* v. *Inglis* (1810), the King's Bench held that the sole customs tax-exempt warehouse, which was licensed to store goods intended for export, could charge only reasonable rates for its services. The fear was that if left unregulated it would raise rates effectively to nullify the customs exemption, a clear efficiency explanation. As incorporated into American constitutional law in *Munn* v. *Illinois* (1876), the court upheld the rate regulation for the grain elevators with their "virtual monopoly" over storage facilities. But in *Smyth* v. *Ames* (1898), the court backed off *Munn* and held that any rate restrictions must not be confiscatory, because they had to allow railroads, and by implication other natural monopolies, to recover their costs and make a reasonable profit. Thereafter, the court allowed the states to choose whether to treat the "rate base" as only that invested capital that was used or usable within the business, or to allow returns on all capital invested, regardless of its wisdom. To this day, there is no clear consensus on the best form to regulate monopoly, but no powerful constitutional constraint on the form of regulation chosen so long as "the bottom line" allowed the firm to avoid confiscation by making a reasonable rate of return on the business (*Duquesne Light Co.* v. *Barasch* 1989).

The court repudiated the traditional view of contracts affected with the public interest in *Nebbia* v. New York (1934), where the state was allowed to set rates to prop up local cartels. More concretely, New York was allowed to set *minimum* rates for milk in an intensely competitive environment. A weak nod to a traditional health justification was not supported by any evidence that low prices led to health hazards that ordinary inspection programs could not control. As with the labor cases, the court accepted the even-handed wisdom of democratic processes would work within the state. The demise of the "affected with the public interest" doctrine reflected the same New Deal-type unhappiness that surrounded *Lochner*. Even before the watershed events of 1937, there were clear cracks in the classical literal framework.

The earlier doctrine afforded constitutional protection to competitive structures, but, as with labor regulation after 1937, the New Deal Court treated the choice between competition and monopoly as wholly within the legislative purview, notwithstanding the standard economic demonstration of the superior welfare effects of competition. The contrary position (held by a tiny minority, including this author) is that this economic rationale is sufficiently powerful that a permanent, i.e. constitutional, prohibition against the state formation of cartels makes good sense as a way to stabilize entitlements and foster a market economy. Such a doctrine is indeed used to this very day with the dormant commerce clause, which, absent any contrary command of Congress (which rarely comes), makes sure that no state imposes anti-competitive restrictions on the goods and services from other states. Indeed, shortly after *Nebbia*, the court struck down taxes on out-of-state dairy products that threatened to undermine competitive federalism. The efficiency gains from competition were well understood as between states, but not between firms (*Baldwin v. G.A.F. Seelig, Inc.* 1935). And it has maintained that position consistently; for example, by striking down systems of uniform taxation that supply rebates only to in-state dairy producers (*West Lynn Creamery, Inc. v. Healy* 1994).

Takings. The rate-making cases, with their explicit concern with confiscation, segue neatly into the general discussion of the takings clause, which today applies to both the federal government and the states. The basic distinction under this law is between physical and regulatory takings (Michelman 1967; Epstein 1985). Is there an economic explanation for the different treatment? The former involves situations where the state challenges the exclusive possession that an owner can make of his property. It arises not only by ordering an owner to vacate all or part of his property, today or in the future, but also by requiring the owner to allow others to use that property jointly with him, even in some limited capacity, such as installing a small cable box on a landlord's property (*Loretto v. Teleprompter* 1982). Regulatory takings, on the other hand, encompass those situations where the state allows the owner to remain in possession of his property but restricts his power to use or dispose of it. Examples of regulatory takings include height and set back restrictions or a zoning rule that prohibits commercial development.

This distinction is subject to serious objections. First, the line in some cases is not all that clear: a rent control statute that allows a tenant to remain in possession of leased property looks as though it denies the landlord exclusive protection of property, but nonetheless it is still treated as a regulatory taking (*Yee v. Escondido* 1992). Second, the rationale for this distinction is unclear. The court has defended its view on the ground that the distinction is historically rooted, and that physical takings are easy to identify and few in number, which makes the high standard of review administrable. But a zoning ordinance that reduces the value of a valuable plot of land by 80 per cent or more is far more potent than and may be every bit as selective as the small physical intrusion in *Loretto*. Most importantly, the forces of faction are every bit as powerful with regulation as they are with cases of direct occupation.

Notwithstanding the weaknesses of its underlying analytical framework, this physical/regulatory distinction plays a vital role in setting the standard of judicial review in takings cases. Physical takings are virtually per se compensable for the fair market value of the property taken. The entire action therefore turns on *whether* the property may be taken, and if so, *how much* compensation ought to be provided in these instances. On the former question, everyone concedes that land may be condemned for roads and public buildings and parks. The standard rationale for this power is that it allows the state to overcome the holdout power of individuals by requiring the taking, but prevents expropriation (and the negative impact it would have on investment) by offering them just compensation for their losses. In addition, however, the court has deferred to the ostensible expertise and impartiality of the legislature by holding that any "conceivable" public purpose satisfies the "public use" requirement of the takings clause (*Hawaiian Housing Auth.* v. *Midkiff*, 1984). Thus property could be transferred from one party to another to break up a local monopoly or on tenuous findings of blight control. The thunderbolt in this area, however, was *Kelo v. City of New London* (2005) where a five-to-four majority of the Supreme Court upheld condemnation of private homes for economic development, which in turn provoked a firestorm of public protest and federal and state efforts to curb that limitless holding. The insecurity of property rights has increased political intrigue, and the use of restricted formulas for compensation has resulted in inefficient takings that have moved property from higher to lower valued uses. On these matters, some state courts, angered by high-handed local tactics, have taken a more restrictive view of public use under the analogous provisions of their own constitutions.

Once the public use hurdle is overcome, compensation is owed when the state occupies all or part of a parcel of property. The theoretical ideal suggests that the compensation offered should leave the property owner indifferent between his former holdings and the state compensation package. The legal rules advance that goal in part by concentrating on the value of the property lost, and not that which is retained. In addition, most courts properly make adjustments for any gains or losses in the value of retained lands as a function of the taking, so that increased value from access to a highway will reduce compensation, while any impediment to retained land will increase it. But in calculating compensation, the legal rules that focus on the fair market value of the "property taken" will in practice fall far below this standard. The rules do not allow for any compensation of the owner's subjective value because of distinctive uses or attachments to property. That restriction is defensible perhaps on the ground that subjective value is hard to measure. But even so, a small fixed bonus of, say, 5 or 10 per cent is administrable, and offers a serviceable proxy for these hard to measure elements of value. Less defensible than the subjective value rule are the exclusions of any costs of defending against the taking, doing appraisals, moving, and destroying good will. The upshot, however, is that the lax standards on public use and just compensation lead to too much taking activity. It has been sometimes suggested that individuals who are unhappy with these rules could purchase "takings insurance," but the risk that the state would selectively condemn such insured lands makes it highly unlikely that any insurer would offer it, knowing that local political processes could target insured lands for government occupation or regulation.

The second half of the takings issue involves regulatory takings, where the key question is whether any compensation is owed at all for "mere" use restrictions. Here, as noted, the lower standard of review means that many cases of value lost through regulation are treated as non-compensable. In *Pennsylvania Coal Co.* v. *Mahon* (1923), Justice Holmes famously held that a government was required to pay compensation when it required a mine owner to conduct his operations so as not to remove the support for the land and structures of the surface owner. The obvious defense of *Mahon*'s result was that the miner had purchased the so-called support estate from the surface owner, to whom he had to return it without compensation. But instead of relying on that unexceptionable ground, Justice Holmes invalidated the regulation because it went "too far," and thus plunged regulatory takings into deep confusion from which they have never escaped. Normally, the "how far" is relevant to determine the amount of compensation owed—the more that is taken the more that must be paid. But here this manifest matter of degree was used to determine the yes/no decision of whether any compensation was owed at all. Three years later, in *Euclid* v. *Ambler Realty* (1926), the court held that a zoning ordinance that limited the owner of a sixty-eight-acre contiguous commercial site to only residential uses did not go too far because the zoned property had lost only 75 per cent of its previous value, even though the proposed commercial use posed no threat of a nuisance to adjacent land. Justice Sutherland did not realize that this private loss also counts as a social loss, and he did not calculate whether the social gains from the regulation exceeded that local loss. Requiring local officials to buy the right to limit development use would have helped answer the question of comparative evaluation because it would increase the likelihood that regulations would be imposed only when the community received benefits greater than its costs. But so long as some viable use was left no compensation was owed for the development rights that were taken. *Euclid* also gave the police power a broad construction by treating (with covert racial overtones) the desire to stop the construction of multi-unit dwellings as a legitimate public end. In essence, the zoning law set up a system of veto rights, which could (as happened in *Euclid*) be sold back to the owner in exchange for some other political concession. Once again it was the judicial faith in public planning that led the court to disregard the risks of faction, and the exclusionary effects that zoning laws could have on outsiders to the local community.

Euclid set the course by giving a narrow definition of takings coupled with a broad account of the police power. The modern formulation of the takings doctrine dates from *Penn Central Transp. Co.* v. *New York* (1978), where the court upheld New York's designation, without compensation, of the Penn Central building as a landmark, which prevented the owner from using or selling the air rights over the structure. These air rights are an ordinary property interest under state law, and the statute singled out one landowner in a downtown area filled with tall buildings. In upholding the statute, the court rejected the use of any fixed formula that stressed the disproportionate impact of this regulation on a few selected sites. It opted instead for an "ad hoc" balancing test. Under this test, the "economic impact of the regulation on the claimant and, particularly, the extent to which the regulation has interfered with distinct investment-backed expectations are, of course, relevant considerations. So, too, is the character of the governmental action" (*Penn Central* v. *New York* 1978, 124).

This shadowy formula, however, gives no hint of what is meant by "investment-backed" expectations, nor did it require the state to show any strong health or safety interest. The upshot was that so long as the existing use of the current facility was viable, then the loss of development rights was not compensable. The subtext of Justice Brennan's influential decision is that the legislature could take into account the non-market values of preservation. But once again he ignored an alternative approach more consistent with public choice principles. Treat the preservation restrictions as a public use, but require the city to pay for the site value losses incurred by the owner.

In *Lucas v. South Carolina Coastal Commission* (1992), the state prohibited any new construction at all, so the safety valve available in *Penn Central* did not apply. In response to the draconian restriction, the court cut back somewhat on its *Penn Central* formula by holding that any land use regulation that permitted no "viable economic use" of vacant land constituted a regulatory taking unless those restrictions were needed to prevent the occurrence of a common law nuisance, which could not be established in the case of the construction of an ordinary beach house. South Carolina quickly amended its statute to allow development after tortuous processes, and to this day no one quite knows how many obstacles may be thrown in the path of development before the delays and conditions trigger compensation for the value of land immobilized through regulation. Since *Lucas*, it seems clear the court has looked favorably on moratoria delays ostensibly for planning purposes, and it appears that multiple delays, especially if done by different agencies, each start the clock running anew, so that "temporary" takings of twenty years have passed constitutional muster, even though a sounder solution would require that the state, after a short planning interlude, compensate annually for the lost use value of the property. (See *Tahoe-Sierra Preservation Council, Inc. v. Tahoe Regional Planning Agency* 2002). In addition, today's set of permissible environmental and slow-growth purposes goes far beyond the prevention of common law nuisance. Thus, in *Tahoe-Sierra*, the run-off of plant life from previous undeveloped land introduced ugly green algae into the pure blue waters of Lake Tahoe. In allowing the planning authority to block new construction, the court allowed concrete driveways of little value to remain in place. Yet insisting that the incumbents pay to prevent newcomers from building as earlier arrivals had done would have forced the incumbents to consider the future costs of their own prior actions. By ignoring these incentives, the *Tahoe* decision gave undue weight to the expertise of local land use planning operations, without taking into account their powerful local biases. Outside developers in some instances provide counterweight to these insider pressures, but their influence is predictably lower when the only new construction is on isolated plots of land which are too small to support developer coalitions. Only the super-rich make it through—by building mansions on large plots of lake-front property. It further gave the perverse incentive in other areas to build even if construction is not the most efficient use of the land to avoid later delays.

3 CONCLUSION

The current state of constitutional law places different types of liberty and property interests in different categories, and thus subjects them to different levels of review. In general, this fragmentation leads to a loss of coherence in constitutional law, which creates odd boundary problems (e.g. is an anti-sign ordinance a speech or a property issue?). These problems are better solved by uniform rules with one objective: to slow down those government maneuvers that shift wealth across factions, thereby reducing public choice problems, while allowing those projects to go forward that create social improvements that are shared, typically pro rata, by all individuals in question, thereby enhancing efficiency. That objective can only be achieved by applying something akin to intermediate scrutiny to all forms of regulation regardless of their content. That review should test for disparate impact and allow only a relatively narrow set of police power justifications. Many have objected to this view on the grounds that courts are at least as fallible as legislatures, but without their democratic legitimacy. Yet oddly enough, it is difficult to identify *any* beneficial legislation that the court struck down under these earlier views, unless one thinks that minimum wage laws and collective bargaining improve overall social welfare. But for those who accept the dominance of competitive markets in spheres in which they can operate, the unity of liberty, property, and equality that forms the core of the Lockean heritage may be implemented in a constitutional system that allows the state to overcome coordination and holdout problems without opening the door to rent dissipation through the unlovely squabbles that all too often dominate the current political scene. The frequent judicial disregard of the insights of public choice theory has done much to squander away a worthy constitutional tradition.

REFERENCES

BLACKSTONE, W. 1979. *Commentaries on the Law of England*, 4 vols. Chicago: University of Chicago Press (orig. pub. 1765–9).
BUCHANAN, J., and TULLOCK, G. 1962. *The Calculus of Consent*. Ann Arbor: University of Michigan Press.
CLAEYS, E. R. 2003. Takings, regulations, and natural property rights. *Cornell Law Review*, 88: 1549–671.
EPSTEIN, R. A. 1984. Toward a revitalization of the contract clause. *University of Chicago Law Review*, 51: 703–51.
—— 1985. *Takings: Private Property and the Power of Eminent Domain*. Cambridge, Mass.: Harvard University Press.
—— 1986. Was *New York Times* v. *Sullivan* wrong? *University of Chicago Law Review*, 53: 782–818.
—— 2003. The "necessary" history of property and liberty. *Chapman Law Review*, 6: 1–29.
FREUND, E. 1904. *The Police Power*. Chicago: Callaghan.
LOCKE, J. 1980. *Second Treatise of Government*, ed. C. B. Macpherson. Indianapolis, Ind.: Hackett (orig. pub. 1690).
MICHELMAN, F. I. 1967. Property, utility and fairness: comments on the ethical foundations of "just compensation" law. *Harvard Law Review*, 80: 1165–258.
NOVAK, W. J. 1996. *The People's Welfare: Law and Regulation in Nineteenth-Century America*. Chapel Hill: University of North Carolina Press.
SELLERS, M. N. S. 1994. *American Republicanism: Roman Ideology in the United States Constitution*. New York: New York University Press.
STRAUSS, D. A. 2003. Why was *Lochner* wrong? *University of Chicago Law Review*, 69: 373–86.
SUNSTEIN, C. R. 1987. *Lochner*'s legacy. *Columbia Law Review*, 87: 873–919.
WOOD, G. 1969. *The Creation of the American Republic, 1776–1787*. Chapel Hill: University of North Carolina Press.

List of Cases

Abrams v. United States, 250 US 616 (1919).
Adair v. United States, 208 US 161 (1908).
Allgeyer v. Louisiana, 1645 US 578 (1897).
Allnut v. Inglis, 104 English Reports 206 (KB 1810).
Baldwin v. G.A.F. Seelig, Inc., 294 US 511 (1935).
Brandenburg v. Ohio, 395 US 444 (1969).
Brown v. Board of Education, 347 US 483 (1954).
Carolene Products Co. v. United States, 304 US 144 (1938).
Coppage v. Kansas, 236 US 1 (1914).
Corfield v. Coryell, 6 Fed. Cases 546 (CCED Pa. 1823).
Duquesne Light Co. v. Barasch, 488 US 299 (1989).
Eastern Enterprises v. Apfel, 524 US 498 (1998).
Euclid v. Ambler Realty, 272 US 265 (1926).
Grutter v. Bollinger, 123 S. Ct. 2325 (2003).
Hawaiian Housing Auth. v. Midkiff, 467 US 229 (1984).
Home Building & Loan Ass'n v. Blaisdell, 290 US 398 (1934).
Kelo v. City of New London, 125 S. Ct 2655 (2005).
Lochner v. New York, 198 US 45 (1905).
Loretto v. Teleprompter Manhattan CATV, 458 US 419 (1982).
Loving v. Virginia, 388 US 1 (1967).
Lucas v. South Carolina Coastal Commission, 505 US 1003 (1992).
McConnell v. Federal Election Commission, 124 S. Ct. 619 (2003).
Minnesota v. Clover Leaf Creamery Co., 449 US 456 (1981).
Munn v. Illinois, 94 US 113 (1876).
Nebbia v. New York, 291 US 502 (1934).
New York Times v. Sullivan, 376 US 254 (1964).
Penn Central Transp. Co. v. New York, 438 US 105 (1978).
Pennsylvania Coal Co. v. Mahon, 260 US 393 (1923).
Plessy v. Ferguson, 163 US 537 (1896).
Reed v. Reed, 404 US 71 (1971).
Slaughterhouse Cases, 83 US 36 (1872).
Smyth v. Ames, 1690 US 466 (1898).
Tahoe-Sierra Preservation Council, Inc. v. Tahoe Regional Planning Agency, 535 US 302 (2002).
Truax v. Raich, 239 US 33 (1915).
United States v. Addyston Pipe & Steel Co., 175 US 211 (1899).
Usery v. Turner Elkhorn Mining Co., 428 US 1 (1976).
Virginia Board of Pharmacy v. Virginia Consumer Council, 425 US 748 (1976).
West Lynn Creamery, Inc. v. Healy, 512 US 186 (1994).
Yee v. Escondido, 503 US 519 (1992).

CHAPTER 20

FEDERALISM

JONATHAN A. RODDEN

At least since Montesquieu, theorists of federalism have viewed it as a solution to a basic challenge—how to extend effective government beyond the confines of the city-state. For Rousseau, good government was not possible in countries with large populations or vast territories without some form of federalism. James Madison saw federalism as a way to provide collective goods covering a large territory without sacrificing local accountability. More recently, political scientists see federalism as a path to peace and democracy in divided societies, while welfare economists see it as a way to enhance the efficiency and accountability of government, and public choice theorists see it as a way of protecting liberty and curbing government's natural tendency toward excess.

While each of these perspectives has produced testable positive arguments, the abstract advantages of decentralized, federal systems over more centralized alternatives often take center stage. The purpose of this chapter is to review the positive political economy literature that has arisen in response to the disjuncture between such classic normative theories and the practice of federalism around the world. The normative tradition made blunt assumptions about the malevolence or benevolence of public officials and attempted to design optimal federations, drawing on the notion that federalism implies a rigid and clean separation of the spheres of sovereignty allocated to central and lower-level governments while paying little attention to institutions and modes of preference aggregation. This approach led to the establishment of some useful normative benchmarks, but was not well suited as the foundation for empirical work. The new political economy literature draws more directly on political science by assuming that public officials are motivated by electoral goals. As a result, it places much greater emphasis on political incentive structures like parties, legislative organization, and electoral rules. Thus the new literature leads to more refined empirical predictions in which the effects of federalism—for instance upon fiscal behavior or accountability—are contingent upon other political, institutional, or demographic factors. Moreover, the prevailing view of federalism as a clean division of sovereignty between higher- and lower-level governments is giving way to a notion that authority over taxation, expenditures, borrowing, and policy decisions is inherently murky, contested, and frequently renegotiated between governments, with federal constitutions analogized to the "incomplete contracts" of industrial organization theory.

The first section of the chapter introduces the classical approach to the study of federalism. The second section reviews the influential normative approaches in economics in the 1970s and 1980s and some of the empirical literatures they spawned. The third section reviews the newer positive political economy literature and the resulting empirical work as complements to the normative approach, highlighting crucial questions of institutional design—fiscal discipline, accountability, macroeconomic and political stability—in contexts as diverse as the European Union, Brazil, and Iraq. Because this literature has largely ignored the endogeneity of institutions, the fourth section counsels caution in drawing policy implications from the new literature as it stands, and goes on to preview a nascent literature that attempts to explain cross-national variations in forms of federalism as well as diachronic evolution within countries.

1 THE CLASSICAL NORMATIVE ROOTS OF THE MODERN POLITICAL ECONOMY LITERATURE

Montesquieu and Rousseau argued that citizens are more likely to get what they want from government if it encompasses a small, relatively homogeneous area rather than a vast territory. Yet small units are vulnerable to attack, while large jurisdictions can, if properly structured, avoid internal warfare and pool resources to repel attacks by outsiders. Alexander Hamilton emphasized additional advantages of large size—above all free trade—and modern public economics has added a few more, including advantages in tax collection, inter-regional risk-sharing, common currencies, and scale economies in the production of public goods.

The goal of federalism—to achieve simultaneously the advantages of small and large governmental units—boils down to a vexing dilemma of institutional design. While Alexander Hamilton ruminated that a fragmented federation cannot provide collective goods or fight effectively against centralized despots, Thomas Jefferson feared a center that would accumulate too much power and run roughshod over the rights of the constituent units. Herein lies the central tension of much scholarship on federalism among political scientists since *The Federalist*: federations have a natural tendency to become either too centralized—perhaps even despotic—or so decentralized and weak that they devolve into internal war or fall prey to external enemies.

Thus the task facing institutional designers is the creation of a central government that is simultaneously strong and limited: strong enough to achieve the desired collective goods, but weak enough to preserve a robust sense of local autonomy. This was the central project in William Riker's (1964) classic work on federalism and the political science literature that followed. It is also the central challenge of institutional design in federations ranging from the European Union to Brazil and India.

Political scientists take federalism as a necessity in large, diverse societies, and have been preoccupied with finding the right balance between centripetal and centrifugal forces, searching for institutional, cultural, and political circumstances that allow for stable federalism and the avoidance of oppression or war in diverse societies (e.g. Bednar 2001; de Figueiredo and Weingast 2005). Recently, Russia's precarious balance between despotism and dismemberment has taken center stage (Treisman 1999; Filippov, Ordeshook, and Shvetsova 2004).

However, many of the world's federations are plagued with neither centralized dictatorship nor armed insurrection, but rather with bad policies, poor fiscal management, and in some cases persistent economic crisis. Policy-makers in Brazil and Argentina, for example, are less concerned with interstate military conflict than with inter-provincial trade wars and distributive battles over revenues and debt burdens.

The classical approaches in economics provided general prescriptions for a more efficient federal system to alleviate the problems of poor fiscal management and bad policies, but assumed away problems of politics, incentives, and stability. This division of labor between classical public finance, which concentrated on optimal tax collection and the optimal provision of public goods, and classical political science, which concentrated on the problems of centrifugal versus centripetal forces, has, until recently, allowed some important questions to fall between the cracks separating the disciplines.

2 BENEVOLENT DESPOTS, LOCAL COMPETITION, AND LEVIATHANS

Let us examine more closely the influential first generation of economic theories that generated such optimism about decentralization and federalism. Some of the basic insights of public finance theory suggest that federalism should have beneficial, even if unintended consequences for efficiency, accountability, and governance. Above all, decentralized federalism is thought to align the incentives of political officials with citizen welfare by improving information and increasing competition. First, the most basic observation is that in any political entity larger than a city-state, local governments will have better information than distant central governments about local conditions and preferences. The welfare economics literature, which takes its name from Wallace Oates's 1972 book *Fiscal Federalism*,[1] flows naturally from the

---

[1] Oates was preceded by Musgrave 1959.

classics of political philosophy that emphasize the advantages of small jurisdictions. It assumes that political leaders are benevolent despots who maximize the welfare of their constituents, and prescribes decentralization according to the principle that "the provision of public services should be located at the lowest level of government encompassing, in a spatial sense, the relevant benefits and costs" (Oates 1999, 5). Once the "assignment problem" is solved and appropriate tasks are devolved to local governments, "the hope is that state and local governments, being closer to the people, will be more responsive to the particular preferences of their constituencies and will be able to find new and better ways to provide... services" (Oates 1999, 1).

Second, a vast literature on "competitive federalism" examines the supposition that, under decentralization, governments must compete for mobile citizens and firms, who sort themselves into the jurisdictions that best reflect their preferences for bundles of governmental goods and policies. The first generation of theory analogized decentralized governments to the private market and celebrated the efficiency gains associated with the promotion of competition among decentralized providers of public goods. Much research has been inspired by the work of Charles Tiebout (1956), according to whose simple market analogy, intergovernmental competition allows citizen landowners to sort into communities that offer their desired levels of taxes and bundles of goods, thus allowing citizens a powerful preference revelation mechanism beyond voting and lobbying.[2]

In contrast to the above, the "Leviathan" theory (Hayek 1939; Brennan and Buchanan 1980) takes a less generous view of governments. Under centralization, Leviathan has monopoly power over the tax base and will extract as much as possible given the constraint that people can withhold their labor if taxed too much. In contrast, under decentralization, politicians and bureaucrats must compete with one another over mobile sources of revenue, preventing them from lining their pockets and resulting in smaller and less wasteful government. This notion has been revisited by Weingast (1995) and Persson and Tabellini (2000), who view capital mobility under federalism as a way for government to commit not to over-tax capital or over-regulate the economy.

As pointed out by Winer's essay in this volume, the social planner model has not been a good starting point for empirical work. For instance, the actual vertical structure of tax authority in much of the world does not resemble the textbook solutions to the "tax assignment problem" in fiscal federalism theory, and intergovernmental grant programs are not limited to conditional, open-ended matching grants aimed at internalizing externalities (e.g. Inman 1988). Though preferences are difficult to measure and the causal mechanism difficult to identify, empirical implications of the Tiebout model are more amenable to testing (e.g. Brueckner 1982; Gramlich and Rubinfeld 1982). Even more empirically tractable is the simple version of the Leviathan hypothesis, which has received mixed support in US and comparative studies (e.g. Marlow 1988; Zax 1989; Oates 1985).

[2] For more detailed reviews of this literature see the contributions of Winer and Wildasin to this volume.

3 POSITIVE POLITICAL ECONOMY: RETHINKING INSTITUTIONS AND POLITICS

The classic economics literature yielded some testable positive claims, most of which linked federalism and decentralization to broad improvements in efficiency, giving the literature a strong normative flavor that found its way into policy debates. As decentralization and federalism spread around the world along with democratization in the 1990s, these claims seemed increasingly anachronistic in the face of subnational debt accumulation and bailouts among large federations and evidence of corruption and inefficiency associated with decentralization programs. Furthermore, cross-national empirical studies linked federalism with macroeconomic distress (Wibbels 2000; Treisman 2000b) and corruption (Treisman 2000a).

Though these experiences by no means constituted natural experiments for evaluating classical economic theories of federalism, they engendered a decade of scholarship aimed at rethinking federalism. It was not difficult to identify politics as the missing component in the prevailing literature. Leaving behind benevolent dictators and malevolent rent-seekers, the new literature takes more seriously the role of preference aggregation through voting and lobbying. Some of the recent contributions rely on the median voter framework, some on probabilistic voting models, and others on the citizen-candidate framework. Most derive insights from assumptions that politicians are primarily interested in maintaining and enhancing their political careers, through either re-election or movement to more desirable offices.

Thus political incentives—ranging from electoral rules to legislative organization and party structures—take center stage in the new literature, which draws on theoretical traditions developed to address legislative bargaining and principal–agent problems, and borrows liberally from concepts in industrial organization theory. A key theme is that like multilayered firms, federations will not function effectively unless incentives are properly structured. Returning to the classic theme of *The Federalist*, the central challenge is how to structure incentives so that local politicians have strong incentives to collect information and serve their constituents, while minimizing incentives and opportunities to exploit common-pool problems and undermine the provision of national collective goods.

Three themes stand out in this new literature—the nature of political representation, the structure of intergovernmental fiscal systems, and the organization of political parties.

3.1 Representation

While the classic economics literature minimized the role of other institutions, political scientists have emphasized the role of such institutions as independent courts, legislatures, and requirements of super-majorities for constitutional changes. In most federations, provinces and their representatives are involved as veto players in the national legislative process, usually through an upper chamber that represents the units, and the logic of population-based representation is supplanted or complemented by the logic of territorial representation.

In the positive political economy literature, theorists and empirical researchers have picked up on the range of variation in modes of political representation and begun to explore its implications. One prominent strand of research attempts to improve upon the welfare economics literature by modeling central government decisions—especially concerning the distribution of intergovernmental grants—as bargains struck among self-interested, re-election-seeking politicians attempting to form winning legislative coalitions rather than reflections on collective goods and the internalization of externalities. Inman and Rubinfeld (1997) review how central government finance of local public goods might yield a different distributive pattern if the legislature features an open agenda rule (Baron and Ferejohn 1989) than if it operates under a norm of universalism (Weingast and Marshall 1988). In the former case, 50 per cent plus one of the jurisdictions receives funding, while in the latter case, all states receive the high demander's preferred allocation.

Drawing on the citizen-candidate model of electoral democracy, Besley and Coate (2003) contrast distributive politics under "minimum winning coalition" and what they call "cooperative" legislatures. In the former case, inefficiencies are created by misallocations of resources and uncertainty about who will be in the winning coalition. In the case of a cooperative legislature, inefficiencies emerge because voters strategically delegate by electing representatives with high demands for public spending. They also provide a new perspective on Oates's classic normative questions about the costs and benefits of fiscal centralization. If spillovers are high and localities prefer similar expenditures, a centralized system can produce good outcomes, but as spillovers decrease and localities are more heterogeneous, centralization becomes less attractive. In related work, Lockwood (2002) presents an extensive form bargaining game among legislators seeking projects in which spillovers affect the legislative outcome and, again, the case for decentralization.

Dixit and Londregan (1998) consider the interaction of redistributive decisions made at the federal and state levels in federations, demonstrating different outcomes from those that would be achieved in a unitary system. Persson and Tabellini (1996) consider a model that contrasts decisions about social insurance that would be made by the same population under unitary-style majority rule versus federal-style bargaining among territorial representatives. If autarky is the threat point, bargaining yields less social insurance because relatively rich regions have more bargaining power. Majority rule voting yields more social insurance because it allows for the formation of coalitions of poor voters across state boundaries.

Work by political scientists has explored the possibility that in contrast to majority rule, territorial bargaining and super-majority rules often allow groups making up a minority of the population, but with a strong attachment to the status quo (e.g. provincially owned banks in Brazil and Argentina, slavery in the antebellum United States), to undermine reform efforts that would be favored by a majority (Rodden

2006; Riker 1964). Moreover, empirical work shows the extent to which the overrepresentation of small states, most often in the upper legislative chamber, distorts the allocation of resources in their favor (Gibson, Calvo, and Falleti 2004; Lee 1998; Rodden 2002).

3.2 Intergovernmental Fiscal Structures[3]

Drawing from the normative tradition, economists and political scientists alike have been keen to view federalism as a form of "dual sovereignty," whereby the federal government and states are sovereign over their own spheres of authority, and citizens can hold each separately responsible within their respective spheres (see Brennan and Buchanan 1980; Riker 1964). Yet case studies and systematic attempts at crossnational data collection reveal that in most policy areas, at least two or three layers of government are jointly involved in funding, regulating, and implementing policies in federal and unitary systems alike. Rather than enhancing accountability and protecting liberty by neatly dividing sovereignty vertically, federalism can create a situation in which sovereignty is unclear and contested. To borrow from the vocabulary of industrial organization theory, federal constitutional contracts governing the assignment of taxes and expenditure responsibilities are incomplete—they are open to ongoing renegotiation and invite a variety of opportunistic behaviors.

When the ultimate locus of fiscal sovereignty is unclear, provinces can attempt to externalize their fiscal burdens onto one another. Rodden (2006) argues that when the center is heavily involved in financing and regulating local governments, it cannot commit not to bail them out in the event of debt-servicing crises, which under some conditions creates poor incentives for fiscal discipline *ex ante*. In a related literature, Careaga and Weingast (2002) present a simple model in which governments that raise their own revenue have incentives to provide market-enhancing public goods, while governments that rely heavily on revenue-sharing from the central government are more likely to use resources on patronage and rent-seeking. An important reason to choose public goods is that they will ultimately foster growth and push out the budget constraint, but this incentive is lost when these additional revenues flow to the common national pool rather than the local government. Weingast (2004) mobilizes case studies suggesting that periods of rapid economic development in federations featured self-financing subnational entities. Finally, returning to the Leviathan model, Stein (1999) and Rodden (2003) find that the relationship between decentralization and the size of government depends upon the balance between local taxation and intergovernmental grants.

3.3 Political Parties

The recent focus on institutional incentives and variations among types of federalism and decentralization has ushered in a return to the central variable in William Riker's

[3] For a further discussion of fiscal institutions, see von Hagen (this volume).

work on federalism—the organization of political parties. Riker (1964) asserted that the key requirement for a "balanced" federal system is the maintenance of a decentralized party system, where candidates for central government offices rely on provincial and local party organizations for nominations and campaign activities. Using some Latin American case studies, Garman, Haggard, and Willis (2001) assert that there is a correlation between limitations on the powers of the central government and decentralization of the party system.

Moreover, recent studies emphasize the organization of political parties when trying to answer current questions about the stability and effectiveness of federations. While Riker was concerned with identifying institutions that would combat centripetal forces in federations like the United States, Filippov, Ordeshook, and Shvetsova (2004) seek to explain what can keep centrifugal forces in check in federations like Russia. The answer, they argue, lies in the creation of integrated national political parties in which subnational politicians must rely on their central government co-partisans in order to achieve electoral success. Returning to the question of fiscal discipline discussed above, Tommasi, Jones, and Sanguinetti (2000) and Rodden (2006) suggest that an integrated party system can also reduce the incentives of provincial governments to create negative externalities for the federation as a whole, and can help federations renegotiate faulty intergovernmental fiscal contracts.

4 THE NEXT HURDLE: ENDOGENOUS INSTITUTIONS

The central message in the new positive political economy literature is one that has been repeated perhaps to the point of banality in political science—institutions matter. Whether federalism in practice looks anything like federalism as envisioned in welfare economics or public choice theory depends on a host of other incentive structures. Yet for anyone asserting that federal institutions play a causal role in explaining outcomes—say democratic stability, macroeconomic success, or income inequality—a nagging problem is the knowledge that institutions themselves are responses to underlying social, cultural, or demographic factors. Thus the emerging political economy literature must deal more seriously with problems of endogeneity and selection.

Empirically, one can attempt to find instruments for federalism or apply matching techniques (see Diaz-Cayeros 2004), but the new political economy literature reviewed above no longer asserts a simple causal role for federalism per se. Its effects are now thought to depend on more specific aspects of federal design, including representative institutions, intergovernmental fiscal systems, and parties. The remainder of this chapter highlights some contributions to, and sizes up the problems and prospects for, the nascent endogenous federalism literature, focusing on the same three themes as above.

4.1 Representation

First, consider the endogeneity of representation schemes. Why do some countries end up with firm constitutional protections for states, like territorial upper chambers and super-majority requirements? Why are small territorial units over-represented in some countries and not in others? These questions direct attention to bargaining games that take place at key moments of institutional design or reform, and invite a broad historical approach that compares events as seemingly diverse as Philadelphia in 1787, the recent EU Constitutional Convention, and high-level intergovernmental meetings about constitutional reform in Argentina or Canada.

The simplest story is that at the time of the initial federal bargain, small states—or states dominated by ethnic or linguistic groups that are minorities in the federation as a whole—will only sign on if they receive credible institutional protections against exploitation by large or ethnic majority states. Another possibility—not yet formalized in the literature but consistent with casual empiricism—is that at moments of constitutional design, the wealthy elite favor a strong upper chamber that over-represents rural, conservative areas, creating a buffer against the demands of urban labor.

Crémer and Palfrey (1999) present a model in which choices over the level of centralization, and between population- and territory-based forms of representation, are made by strategic actors who anticipate the policy consequences of their choices. In addition to conflicts between voters in small and large states (under centralization, voters from large states choose population-based representation, while voters from small states prefer unit representation), they model conflicts between moderates and extremists on a single left–right dimension, and consider interactions between the two axes of conflict. One of the key results is the proposition that since centralization mitigates policy risk, moderates prefer more centralization than extremists.

4.2 Intergovernmental Fiscal Arrangements

Income distribution is at the heart of another new endogenous federalism literature that attempts to explain cross-national differences and within-country shifts in the locus of tax power. A key argument in the new political economy literature is that the distribution of taxing and spending powers has important implications for the performance of federations, yet little is known about the determinates of tax centralization. For Boix (2003), instituting federalism with a decentralized locus of decision-making over taxation and redistribution is a technique for holding countries together in the face of uneven inter-regional income distribution. Decentralized taxation reassures rich regions that their wealth will not be expropriated by poor regions. In the same spirit, Bolton and Roland (1997) present a model in which decisions about the relative (de)centralization of tax-transfer decisions is driven by strategic actors who understand that shifting to a different locus of decision-making shifts the location of the median voter in the income spectrum, and hence the overall level of redistribution. For instance, the median voter in a relatively poor state with a highly skewed income distribution would not favor union with a wealthier state if its income distribution is sufficiently even that equilibrium redistribution would be lower in the new federation.

Future research might fruitfully combine the median voter logic with an economic geography approach recognizing that industrialization is often accompanied by agglomeration economies and pronounced income differences between the industrializing center and the poorer, largely agricultural periphery. In most decentralized fiscal systems the median jurisdiction is much poorer than the mean, implying that the majority of states want centralized taxation and distribution while the few wealthy states want to maintain decentralization. Thus in the long run, decentralized taxation with a weak center may be difficult to sustain as a political equilibrium when wealth is highly concentrated in one or two jurisdictions.

Once tax centralization has been achieved, this logic explains why it is often so stable. While the Italian north and wealthy German states like Baden-Württemberg and Bavaria are demanding tax decentralization, they are clearly outnumbered by jurisdictions—home to a majority of the population—that benefit from the status quo redistributive tax-transfer system. However, even if the wealthy regions with preferences for decentralized taxation are outnumbered, they may be able to limit centralization if they are in a position to make credible secession threats, as in Belgium and Spain—the two European countries that have made the boldest recent moves toward increased subnational tax autonomy.

All of these stories about the distribution of income and preferences are based on very simple theoretical frameworks that assume one (redistributive) dimension and rely on the median voter. The same is true of a new literature that views the assignment of responsibilities in a federation as emerging naturally from the underlying distribution of preferences over public goods (e.g. Crémer and Palfrey 2002; Panizza 1999). Politicians' preferences are identical to those of their voters, and agency problems and careerist politicians are not yet part of the picture. Nor are the roles of potentially cross-cutting ethnic and linguistic cleavages. The empirical record of such simple median voter models is sketchy. Above all, future theory work should consider the possibility that players in constitutional choice games do not simply reflect the preferences of their constituents. For instance, O'Neill (2003) argues that in Latin America, decentralization is an attractive strategy for central government politicians not when it satisfies voters' preferences on any issue dimension, but when support in future subnational elections appears to be more secure than in national elections, often because of investments in local patronage networks.

Moreover, perhaps the most vexing challenge in this literature is to identify the direction of causality (Beramendi 2003). On the one hand, income inequality might shape the form that federalism takes when institutions are designed, or create pressures that stabilize or unravel existing arrangements. On the other hand, if federal institutions are sufficiently stable and resistant to reform, federal institutions shape long-term inequality. For instance, a decentralized tax system might prevent redistribution if it fosters tax competition and allows the wealthy to cluster in homogeneous jurisdictions or, according to a large literature summarized in Obinger, Leibfried, and

Castles (2005), status quo bias may have caused welfare states to expand more slowly in post-war OECD federations than among their unitary neighbors.

4.3 Political Parties

Unfortunately, political scientists are no closer to resolving an endogeneity problem related to the organization of political parties, even though the question has been on the agenda since the 1950s. Riker (1964) insisted that the decentralization of political parties drives administrative and fiscal decentralization, and more recently, Garman, Haggard, and Willis (2001) concur. Yet Chhibber and Kollman (2004) argue that administrative centralization drives party centralization. It is difficult to judge the direction of causality since within countries, centralization in the party and the fiscal systems often takes place simultaneously. Diaz-Cayeros (forthcoming) argues that in Mexico, elites interested in creating a nationwide common market and an integrated system of taxation found it difficult to commit not to expropriate the resources and patronage that sustained rural elites. A hegemonic party, the Institutional Revolutionary Party (PRI), emerged as a commitment device that promised rural elites a guaranteed flow of resources in the future. In this story, neither tax centralization nor party centralization caused the other, but both emerged as part of a pact among self-interested elites. The relationship between geography and the nationalization (or fragmentation) of economies and party systems remains one of the most intriguing and wide-open research areas in comparative political economy.

5 CONCLUSION

There has always been a peculiar relationship between positive and normative approaches to federalism in economics and political science. *The Federalist* had a normative agenda: propaganda to support a constitutional proposal that the authors viewed as quite flawed. In order to make their normative case in favor of a second-best solution, however, they undertook serious positive analysis—in terms of both abstract deductive theory and inductive analyses of previous experience with federalism around the world. Their assumptions—above all that "men are not angels"—and their approach—what they called "a science of politics"—produced a set of writings that became the foundation for the modern positive political economy literature in spite of its thinly veiled normative agenda.

The welfare economics approach assumes that men are indeed angels and asks how such angels would set up a federation, but then moves rather awkwardly to the examination of positive empirical hypotheses. A prominent strand of public choice theory does not attempt to veil its conservative normative agenda, assuming that men are devils, seeking to design federations that will constrain them. The political science literature often comes from a normative starting point that federalism is beneficial or—in large or divided societies—simply necessary, and seeks to establish conditions under which it is stable. Yet the most celebrated contribution to this literature, William Riker's 1964 book, after charting a rigorously and dispassionately positive course, was shaped by the American civil rights movement and ended with the rather jarring conclusion that American federalism was primarily about institutionalizing racism.

The new wave of "positive" literature that reintroduces politics and institutions still has strong normative content. It has moved beyond simple questions about whether federalism is good or bad, but much of the literature is still motivated by a normative question about the conditions under which federalism and other forms of multitiered government work well or fail. This is certainly appropriate, given the importance of questions related to federal design for peace, political stability, and economic well-being around the world. The new literature shows that federalism can have a wide variety of effects, depending upon its design and the institutions and social structures with which it is combined. Above all, the new literature is beginning to establish trade-offs. Federalism might be viewed as working well or badly in a particular society depending on one's normative perspective. For instance, a highly decentralized system of taxation might create good incentives for local fiscal discipline and warm the hearts of fiscal conservatives, yet it may seem to progressives like a scheme to preserve inequality and marginalize the poor. Likewise, institutions that facilitate stability or fiscal discipline might undermine accountability.

Ideally, some of the emerging trade-offs would help guide institutional designers in Brussels, Brasilia, or Baghdad. But better answers are needed to a more basic, purely positive set of questions—how is it that federations come to be structured the way they are? Can institutions be tweaked and outcomes changed, or are they epiphenomenal? Such debates often take on a frustrating theological tone of predestination versus free will, but as always, the largest and most difficult questions are the most pressing. Hopefully the next generation of research on federalism will not shy away from them.

References

Baron, D., and Ferejohn, J. 1989. Bargaining in legislatures. *American Political Science Review*, 83: 1181–206.

Bednar, J. 2001. Shirking and stability in federal systems. Unpublished paper, University of Michigan.

Beramendi, P. 2003. *Decentralization and Income Inequality*. Madrid: Centro de Estudios Avanzados en Ciencias Sociales, Instituto Juan March.

Besley, T., and Coate, S. 2003. Centralized versus decentralized provision of local public goods: a political economy approach. *Journal of Public Economics*, 87: 2611–37.

Boix, C. 2003. *Democracy and Redistribution*. Cambridge: Cambridge University Press.

BOLTON, P., and ROLAND, G. 1997. The breakup of nations: a political economy analysis. *Quarterly Journal of Economics*, 112: 1057–90.
BRENNNAN, G., and BUCHANAN, J. 1980. *The Power to Tax: Analytical Foundations of a Fiscal Constitution*. New York: Cambridge University Press.
BRUECKNER, J. 1982. A test for allocative efficiency in the local public sector. *Journal of Public Economics*, 19: 311–31.
CAREAGA, M., and WEINGAST, B. R. 2002. Fiscal federalism, good governance, and economic growth in Mexico. Pp. 399–435 in *In Search of Prosperity: Analytic Narratives on Economic Growth*, ed. D. Rodrik. Princeton, NJ: Princeton University Press.
CHHIBBER, P., and KOLLMAN, K. 2004. *The Formation of National Party Systems: Federalism and Party Competition in Britain, Canada, India, and the United States*. Princeton, NJ: Princeton University Press.
CRÉMER, J., and PALFREY, T. 1999. Political confederation. *American Political Science Review*, 93: 69–82.
────── 2002. Federal mandates by popular demand. *Journal of Political Economy*, 108: 905–27.
DE FIGUEIREDO, R., and WEINGAST, B. 2005. Self-enforcing federalism. *Journal of Law, Economics, and Organization*, 21: 103–35.
DIAZ-CAYEROS, A. 2004. The centralization of fiscal authority: an empirical investigation of Popitz's Law. Paper presented at the University of Chicago Comparative Politics Workshop.
────── forthcoming. *Overawing the States*. Cambridge: Cambridge University Press.
DIXIT, A., and LONDREGAN, J. 1998. Fiscal federalism and redistributive politics. *Journal of Public Economics*, 68: 153–80.
FILIPPOV, M., ORDESHOOK, P., and SHVETSOVA, O. 2004. *Designing Federalism: A Theory of Self-Sustainable Federal Institutions*. Cambridge: Cambridge University Press.
GARMAN, C., HAGGARD, S., and WILLIS, E. 2001. Fiscal decentralization: a political theory with Latin American cases. *World Politics*, 53: 205–36.
GIBSON, E., CALVO, E., and FALLETI, T. 2004. Reallocative federalism: territorial overrepresentation and public spending in the western hemisphere. Pp. 173–96 in *Federalism: Latin America in Comparative Perspective*, ed. E. Gibson. Baltimore: Johns Hopkins University Press.
GRAMLICH, E., and RUBINFELD, D. 1982. Micro estimates of public spending demand functions and tests of the Tiebout and median-voter hypotheses. *Journal of Political Economy*, 90: 536–60.
HAYEK, F. VON 1939. The economic conditions of interstate federalism. *New Commonwealth Quarterly*, 5: 131–49; repr. in F. von Hayek, *Individualism and Economic Order*. Chicago: University of Chicago Press, 1948.
INMAN, R. 1988. Federal assistance and local services in the United States: the evolution of a new federalist fiscal order. Pp. 33–74 in *Fiscal Federalism: Quantitative Studies*, ed. H. Rosen. Chicago: University of Chicago Press.
────── and RUBINFELD, D. 1996. Designing tax policy in federalist economies: an overview. *Journal of Public Economics*, 60: 307–34.
────── 1997. The political economy of federalism. Pp. 73–105 in *Perspectives on Public Choice: A Handbook*, ed. D. Mueller. Cambridge: Cambridge University Press.
LEE, F. 1998. Representation and public policy: the consequences of Senate apportionment for the distribution of federal funds. *Journal of Politics*, 60: 34–62.
LOCKWOOD, B. 2002. Distributive politics and the benefits of decentralisation. *Review of Economic Studies*, 69: 313–38.
MARLOW, M. 1988. Fiscal decentralization and government size. *Public Choice*, 56: 259–70.

MUSGRAVE, R. 1959. *The Theory of Public Finance: A Study in Public Economy*. New York: McGraw-Hill.
OATES, W. 1972. *Fiscal Federalism*. New York: Harcourt Brace Jovanovich.
──── 1985. Searching for Leviathan: an empirical study. *American Economic Review*, 75: 748–57.
──── 1999. An essay on fiscal federalism. *Journal of Economic Literature*, 37: 1120–49.
OBINGER, H., LEIBFRIED, S., and CASTLES, F. G. (eds.) 2005. *Federalism and the Welfare State: New World and European Experiences*. Cambridge: Cambridge University Press.
O'NEILL, K. 2003. Decentralization as an electoral strategy. *Comparative Political Studies*, 36: 1068–91.
PANIZZA, U. 1999. On the determinants of fiscal centralization: theory and evidence. *Journal of Public Economics*, 74: 97–139.
PERSSON, T., and TABELLINI, G. 1996. Federal fiscal constitutions: risk sharing and redistribution. *Journal of Political Economy*, 104: 979–1009.
──── ──── 2000. *Political Economics*. Cambridge, Mass.: MIT Press.
RIKER, W. 1964. *Federalism: Origins, Operation, and Significance*. Boston: Little, Brown.
RODDEN, J. 2002. Strength in numbers? Representation and redistribution in the Eropean Union. *Eropean Union Politics*, 3: 151–75.
──── 2003. Reviving Leviathan: fiscal federalism and the growth of government. *International Organization*, 57: 695–729.
──── 2006. *Hamilton's Paradox: The Promise and Peril of Fiscal Federalism*. Cambridge: Cambridge University Press.
STEIN, E. 1999. Fiscal decentralization and government size in Latin America. *Journal of Applied Economics*, 2: 257–91.
TIEBOUT, C. 1956. A pure theory of local government expenditures. *Journal of Political Economy*, 64: 416–24.
TOMMASI, M., JONES, M., and SANGUINETTI, P. 2000. Politics, institutions, and fiscal performance in a federal system: an analysis of the Argentine provinces. *Journal of Development Economics*, 61: 305–33.
TREISMAN, D. 1999. *After the Deluge: Regional Crises and Political Consolidation in Russia*. Ann Arbor: University of Michigan Press.
──── 2000a. The causes of corruption: a cross-national study. *Journal of Public Economics*, 76: 299–457.
──── 2000b. Decentralization and inflation: commitment, collective action, or continuity? *American Political Science Review*, 94: 837–58.
WEINGAST, B. 1995. The economic role of political institutions: market-preserving federalism and economic development. *Journal of Law, Economics, and Organization*, 11: 1–31.
──── 2004. The performance and stability of federalism: an institutional perspective. Pp. 149–74 in *Handbook of the New Institutional Economics*, ed. C. Menard and M. Shirley. Dordrecht: Kluwer Academic Press.
──── and MARSHALL, W. 1988. The industrial organization of Congress. *Journal of Political Economy*, 96: 132–63.
WIBBELS, E. 2000. Federalism and the politics of macroeconomic policy and performance. *American Journal of Political Science*, 44: 687–702.
ZAX, J. S. 1989. Is there a Leviathan in your neighborhood? *American Economic Review*, 79: 560–7.

PART VI
SOCIAL CHOICE

CHAPTER 21

SOCIAL CHOICE

HERVÉ MOULIN

1 INTRODUCTION

SOCIAL choice is part and parcel of the formal and axiomatic revolution that took over economic analysis and, to a lesser degree, political and other social sciences in the middle of the twentieth century. In the shadow of game theory and of the theory of general equilibrium, social choice theory focuses on the normative foundations of political and economic institutions.

Understanding the depth of Arrow's celebrated impossibility theorem was its sole agenda until the beginning of the 1970s, a line of research that has all but died out in the last three decades. Saari (this volume) offers a refreshing viewpoint on a whole range of impossibility results. The current research retains the social engineering spirit of Arrow's aggregation of preferences, while reaching out to a much broader set of resource allocation problems. A good example of this enlarged vision is "fair division" (Brams, this volume): developed by mathematicians such as Steinhaus in the 1940s and 1950s, then by economists like Foley, Kolm, and Varian in the 1960s and 1970s, it is now a mainstream subject within the field of social choice.

In economics the social engineering approach is called "mechanism design." It inspires a large body of research in microeconomic theory, addressing mostly positive (descriptive, predictive) issues, e.g. the influence of auction design on the seller's revenue. The social choice component of mechanism design specializes in the normative aspects of mechanism design, and has evolved into a broad theory of distributive justice.

This brief overview concentrates on the interface between traditional notions of *endstate* justice such as welfarism (Blackorby and Bossert, this volume) and the more modern theme of strategic implementation, bringing the full methodological benefit

* I am very grateful to the editors for critical comments on an earlier draft.

of game theory to the discussion of *procedural* justice. I propose a simple explanation for the overwhelming success of this cross-fertilization.

Section 2 outlines a general model of mechanism design. Section 3 defines the classical notions of procedural and endstate justice in the context of that model, and Section 4 argues that a single-minded concern for only one mode of justice is untenable. Section 5 submits that the property of strategy-proofness captures the attractive mechanisms for which the two interpretations of justice coincide. Section 6 surveys the extensive research of the last three decades identifying strategy-proof mechanisms in a variety of microeconomic problems.

2 THE MICROECONOMIC APPROACH TO DISTRIBUTIVE JUSTICE

When political or economic resources are distributed, the two criteria by which a selfish *Homo economicus* evaluates the process are his rights and his welfare. When voting, I wish to maximize the extent to which my vote could influence the final outcome, and I also wish that the candidate finally elected be one whom I like better than other names on the ballot. Most of the normative discussion of allocation mechanisms thus revolves around two main questions. With what rights are individual agents endowed, what influence can they have on the final allocation, by what free, unconstrained actions? To what degree does the actual distribution of resources, the outcome, or *endstate*, fulfill the individual values and aspirations of the agents, what level of *welfare* does it allow them to reach?

The conceptual dichotomy between rights and welfare has deep roots in political philosophy: a good example is Berlin's richly nuanced distinction (Berlin 1969) between negative freedom (the extent of my rights), and positive freedom (the freedom of choosing my own goals and aspirations, and my ability to fulfill them). In a microeconomic formulation the former is captured by a description of the legal moves/messages each participant is allowed to make/send (e.g. the set of admissible ballots in an election). The latter is the choice of my own measure of welfare (my preferences) and my ability to reach a high level of welfare.

Ignoring several subtle aspects of the interaction between individual rights and welfare (on which more, three paragraphs below), many canonical models of resource allocation are described as a 4-tuple $(N, X, \mathcal{R}, G)$ where:

- the "society" is the set $N = \{1, 2, \ldots n\}$ of concerned agents, with generic element i, $i \in N$.
- the set X describes all feasible states of the world, or endstates; in particular X embodies the set of resources and technological constraints.

- the set $\mathcal{R}$ contains all possible "welfare functions." Such a function takes into account all relevant components of an individual welfare, such as preferences, values, aspirations, but also tastes and needs, endowments of talents and skills, disabilities, etc. One possible representation of individual welfare is as a utility function, associating to each possible endstate (each element of X) a numerical measure of welfare. Here we adopt the more general "ordinal" description of welfare as a preference ordering of X: each element R of $\mathcal{R}$ is a binary relation comparing pairs of endstates (deciding which of any two endstates gives the higher welfare level), but refraining from associating a cardinal measure to each endstate. Thus $\mathcal{R}$ is the set of all possible welfare orderings R. The advantages of the ordinal approach over the cardinal one are well known (see for instance Mas-Colell, Whinstone, and Green 1990).
- the game form G describing individual rights, and their interaction. It consists of a set M_i of actions among which agent i freely chooses one element m_i, and a mapping f from $M_1 \times \ldots \times M_n$ into X, specifying which endstate z results for each profile $(m_1, \ldots, m_n)$ of individual actions. The notation m_i reminds us that the action often consists of sending a message. When this message is a report of agent i's preference ordering R_i, we speak of a *direct game form*.

The model $(N, X, \mathcal{R}, G)$ encompasses many familiar examples. Voting is the simplest one. The set of voters is N, and X is an arbitrary finite set of candidates. Preferences over X are only restricted by the standard rationality postulates of transitivity and completeness (see Mas-Colell, Whinston, and Green 1990). In plurality voting, each voter writes the name of a single candidate on his ballot, thus the set of actions—in this case messages—available to voter i is the set of candidates, that is $M_i = X$. The candidate with the largest number of votes is elected, which defines unambiguously (except for the tie-breaking rule) the mapping of G from profiles of ballots into X. More complicated voting rules such as the Borda Count require a much larger set of actions M_i; here each voter reports his entire preference ordering of X, therefore $M_i = \mathcal{R}$. Multistage voting rules (such as voting by successive eliminations) give rise to even bigger and more complex action spaces, because the participants are involved in a multiperiod strategic game.

The Divide and Choose mechanism is another simple illustration of our general model. The set X describes all possible divisions of a given "cake" between two agents, $N = \{1, 2\}$. The preference ordering R_i compares all shares of the cake from the point of view of agent i. Besides the postulates of transitivity and completeness, further restrictions may apply, for instance it is natural to assume that a larger piece of cake is always desirable. The agent with the role of Divider, say agent 1, must choose a division of the cake in two pieces, therefore $M_1 = X$. The Chooser, on the other hand, can only pick one of the two pieces cut by the Divider, therefore M_2 specifies which piece is chosen from every possible division left by the Divider.

It should be clear from the above examples that the model $(N, X, \mathcal{R}, G)$ encompasses a huge variety of applications from market mechanisms to political processes and everything in between. However, the model rests on a handful of heroic assumptions worth repeating. The three basic components, welfare ($\mathcal{R}$), rights (M_i), and the set of endstates (X), are three clearly defined and separate entities whose interaction is limited to two aspects. First, the endstate z only depends on the profile of actions m via the mapping f, namely the game form. Second, the final welfare level only depends upon the endstate z, and not directly upon the individual actions.

Conspicuously absent from the model are two important elements of the interaction of rights and welfare. First, the fact that the nature and extent of my rights affect my welfare: which game I play, and what role I have in it matters to me. Formally the *whole set* M_i influences R, not just my particular action m_i. Second, I bear some responsibility in shaping my own welfare because I am free to choose my values and goals.

The former point inspires the literature on freedom of choice, where the central question is to extend an ordinary welfare relation comparing single outcomes, to another welfare relation comparing choice sets (subsets of outcomes) (see Bossert, Pattanaik, and Xu 1994; Dutta and Sen 1996; Laslier et al. 1998; Pattanaik and Xu 1998, 2000a, 2000b; Sugden 1998). The latter point explains the paradox of adaptive preferences: agents who adapt their expectations to their lot enjoy a higher welfare than those who do not, and this responsibility should be accounted for when we define fair endstates. One solution is to introduce additional variables in the microeconomic formulation, so as to differentiate between those characteristics for which an agent is responsible, and those for which she is not: Roemer and Fleurbaey initiated this fruitful line of research (Bossert 1995; Fleurbaey 1995a, 1995b; Roemer 1993, 1996, 2000; Sen 1991).

Another simplifying assumption of the general model is the identification of the game form G with an allocation of rights. Since Gardenfors (1981), this is an approach endorsed by many authors (e.g. Gaertner, Pattanaik, and Suzumura 1992). The more traditional approach insists that a right confers on an individual the ability to fix some features of the final outcome; that the two approaches are not identical is discussed in particular by Deb, Pattanaik, and Razzolini (1997).

3 Endstate Justice versus Procedural Justice

These shortcomings notwithstanding, the logical separation of welfare and rights has considerable advantages. By separating ends—the distribution of welfare—from means—the set of actions and the game form G—we can contrast and combine two familiar one-sided interpretations of justice: on the one hand endstate justice (e.g. classical utilitarianism), on the other hand procedural justice, rooted in the liberal tradition.

Endstate justice: fair outcome. Endstate justice is a judgment on the profile $(R_1, \ldots, R_n)$ of individual characteristics and the state of the world z, deciding whether this particular endstate is equitable at this particular profile. The equity criteria bear on the individual welfare levels, as well as on the endstate.

The most popular criterion is an index of collective utility, aggregating cardinal measures of individual welfare (Blackorby and Bossert, this volume). An alternative route eschews cardinal measures of welfare and relies only on the profile of ordinal preference orderings, together with some physical characteristics of the endstate. A very influential instance of this ordinal interpretation of endstate justice is the test of "No Envy." We are dividing a given bundle of resources (a "cake") among participants endowed with identical property rights over the resources, and different preferences over the various shares of resources. Everyone cares only about the share she receives. We say that a particular division of the cake is "envy free" if no participant prefers the share of someone else to her own share. For instance, the outcome of the Divide and Choose procedure is envy free if the Divider prudently cuts two pieces of equal value (to him). For very general division problems, a systematic way to obtain an envy free and Pareto optimal allocation is to endow each participant with an equal share of the resources and compute a competitive equilibrium from these egalitarian property rights. See Moulin and Thomson 1997 for a review of the No Envy test and of competing ordinal interpretations of endstate justice in microeconomic fair division problems.

In some important problems of fair division, individual characteristics capture the pattern of responsibilities in the production of a joint surplus or cost. A typical example involves a scholar delivering lectures in several different cities: the question is to divide fairly her total travel cost between her successive hosts. We know the cost of her entire trip, as well as the (presumably lower) cost of all trips in which she would have visited only a subset of the original cities. The celebrated formula known as the "Shapley value" proposes to compute the cost share of each city as follows: order the cities arbitrarily and compute the incremental cost share of a given city (the cost of adding this city to the set of cities preceding it in the given order); then take the average of these incremental shares over all orderings, each with equal probability. The normative properties of the Shapley value, and of several extensions and variants, are the subject of much axiomatic research (see Moulin 2002; Moulin and Sprumont 2005; Sprumont 1998; Thomson 2003).

The normative statement of endstate justice is oblivious to any particular procedure we may use to implement a particular endstate. The information about individual characteristics relevant to the computation of a just endstate is private to each participant, and must be somehow retrieved from these agents. As discussed in the following sections, this elicitation process is not straightforward, because rational selfish agents cannot be expected to report their private information truthfully, if they can improve their welfare by not doing so. This is the familiar "incentive compatibility" issue: because crucial information is dispersed, the process of gathering it to determine a just endstate is a strategic game G, exactly as in the previous section. This game must be carefully designed to allow proper discovery of the necessary information. Yet in the context of endstate justice, neither the design of G, nor the behavior of its players has any normative content. The judgement of justice is entirely *ex post*, oblivious to the means by which the endstate is reached.

Procedural justice: fair play. Procedural justice is a judgement on the game form G itself, independent of the way the game is subsequently played by the agents, and of the particular endstate that results. The normative discussion is limited to the rules of the game (the procedure); no outcome (endstate) can be called unfair if the rules have been scrupulously observed while the game was played, just as a fair lottery cannot produce an unfair outcome. This time the judgement of justice is entirely *ex ante*; it bears only on the means regardless of the ends.

Consider Divide and Choose. If we deem this procedure fair to divide a certain cake among two given agents, then it does not matter if the Divider plays the game well or not. If she has some idea about the preferences of the Chooser, she may be able to obtain a share worth more than one half (to her), provided her expectation of the chooser's behavior is correct; if she is wrong and ends up with a share worth less than one half, she can only blame herself, not the procedure.

Naturally, a fair procedure may yield an unfair endstate, and a fair endstate may result from an unfair procedure.

Examples of the former include provision of a public good by voluntary subscription, where a single agent often ends up bearing the entire cost of the good (see Ledyard, this volume). Indeed, if Ann likes the good enough that she is willing to pay the full price of the public good, every other agent will gladly get a free ride and this is a Nash equlibrium configuration. Another instance is when fair competition results in a blatantly unfair endstate. The canonical example is the celebrated "gloves market" with 101 owners of a right glove and 100 owners of a left glove. Assume a pair of gloves is worth $1 but a single glove is worthless. If the price of a right glove is positive, there is excess supply of these gloves; a price of zero for the right gloves is the only way to balance demand and supply. Then the owners of a left glove each get one right glove so that the competitive equilibrium gives all the surplus to the left glove owners.

Examples of the latter include the choice of the "just" candidate by a benevolent dictator; or the envy-free division of the cake between two agents by the Divide and Choose game form. In this asymmetric game form, the Divider cuts the pie in two shares among which the Chooser picks the one she prefers. In this game both agents can guarantee that their share is at least as valuable (to them) as the other share: the Divider can cut to shares of equal value to him.

Endstate justice and procedural justice pursue similar goals. They look for "solutions" to simple problems of resource allocations and justify these solutions by a suitable set of axioms (normative requirements). Under procedural justice this solution is a distribution of rights, a game form; under endstate justice it is a social choice function, associating an outcome deemed *just* to every profile of individual characteristics.

4 The Complementarity of Endstate and Procedural Justice

We develop the commonplace "means matter as well as ends" in the context of the general model of Section 2.

Procedural justice is not concerned with the strategic properties of the procedure. Whether or not the game has a zero, many, or single equilibrium outcome does not matter. Even irrational actions by the agents are of no concern: my negative freedom includes the privilege of being unpredictable (Berlin 1969). A serious objection to this position comes from the familiar concept of efficiency, also known as Pareto optimality. An outcome z (endstate) is Pareto optimal (efficient) if there exists no other feasible outcome which is weakly preferred to z by all agents, and strictly preferred to z by at least one agent. This is the only rationality test of the endstate that is common to all doctrines of the social order derived from methodological individualism.

In our model, the requirement of efficiency means that upon playing the game G, an efficient outcome should result. This forces our attention to the strategic properties of G. In particular,

- suppose that the game G has no equilibrium for some profile of individual characteristics. This precludes rational behavior by the participants: anything can happen, including inefficiencies. A typical example is majority voting when the majority relation has a cycle. Where we stop in the cycle may be a matter of pure luck, or of who is able to control the agenda of the relevant committee. The cycles of the majority relation encompass large subsets of inefficient outcomes so there is the very real possibility of an inefficient endstate. This point is emphatically demonstrated by McKelvey's theorem (McKelvey 1976) in the spatial voting context.
- symmetrically, suppose our game G has a large set of equilibrium outcomes, then the selection of a particular endstate is a difficult coordination problem. If the coordination fails, inefficiency is to be expected. The standard example is the division of a surplus by means of the Nash demand game. Each player independently requests a share of a dollar. If the demands are compatible, they are satisfied; otherwise everyone goes home empty handed. Any division of the dollar between the players is a legitimate (and efficient) equilibrium of the game. However, the definition of the game does not help the participants to coordinate their demands on a particular division of the dollar. If they choose their demands independently, chances are they will not be compatible, resulting in an inefficient endstate.

To meet the compelling requirement of endstate efficiency, the game form must have a unique equilibrium outcome (or at least a small set of such outcomes), moreover this outcome must pass the test of Pareto optimality.

A good example where these demanding properties are met is the exchange and distribution of private goods in a competitive environment: many agents with convex preferences each with a "small" initial endowment relative to the market size. The set of (efficient) competitive allocations is then small and coincides with the set of equilibrium outcomes under a variety of strategic scenarios, both cooperative (core stability) and non-cooperative (market bidding games) (see e.g. Mas-Colell, Whinston, and Green 1990).

On the other hand, many procedures commonly used to allocate certain scarce resources display either a unique but inefficient equilibrium outcome, or a large or empty set of such equilibria.

Examples of the former include the exploitation of common property resources under free access (Hardin 1968), and the provision of public goods by voluntary subscription, the classic exposition of which is by Olson (1965) (see also Ledyard, this volume).

Examples of the latter include voting by a qualified majority: the quota is the relative size of the majority required to pass a motion. With a small quota of 51 per cent, we only require simple majority and cycles are likely to appear: in this case there is no equilibrium when coalitions of agents can easily coordinate their actions. If the quota is large, say 90 per cent, then the equilibrium set is likely to be large: there are many outcomes z that cannot be defeated by any other outcome z' because this would require that 90 per cent of the voters prefer z' to z. (See Nakamura 1979.)

We can speak of private ownership as the *natural* system of rights when the issue is to produce and exchange private goods, because the resulting trading game has all the desirable strategic features, namely a small set of efficient equilibrium outcomes. But for many important resource allocation problems, no *natural* system of rights, no canonical game form stands out to our attention. Examples include:

- the quota (size of the qualified majority) we should require to amend the constitution;
- how we should regulate access to common property exhaustible resources, so as to avoid the tragedy of the commons;
- how we should produce and trade under decreasing marginal costs, as is the case for "natural monopolies;"
- how we should share costs under widespread externalities.

The point is that any reasonable answer to these questions must take into account the endstate consequences of the procedure, which procedural justice alone is deliberately ignoring.

We turn to the central objections to "pure" endstate justice and return to the implementation problem alluded to in Section 3. As some of the individual characteristics included in R_i are privately known only to the concerned agent (and perhaps to some of her fellow citizens), the mechanism designer relies on a game form to elicit these private characteristics, either directly by asking each agent to simply report this piece of information, or indirectly by designing a game form of which the equilibrium outcome (or outcomes) is (are) just in the endstate sense. Such a game form, whether direct or indirect, "implements" the social choice function recommended by endstate justice.

If endstate justice is the only motivation of our benevolent dictator, the choice of the game form G is "value free" and we can take an opportunistic attitude toward the resolution of the implementation problem. Any mechanism with the correct equilibrium outcomes (as specified by the social choice function) is legitimate, even if this involves one or more of the following features:

- endowing agents with unequal rights (a non-anonymous game form), even though the social choice function to be implemented is anonymous and treats equal agents equally;
- using coercive threats to extract private information from the agents and/or to influence their strategic choices; metaphorically speaking, burning the agents' feet to make them reveal their characteristics under duress;
- using more subtle, yet no less objectionable, twists to force the agents to reveal mutually their private information, as in the mechanisms introduced by Maskin (1985) amounting to a sophisticated version of "unanimity at gunpoint:" the agents must unanimously agree in their report about the entire profile of characteristics, lest the dictator enforces an endstate very bad for everyone;
- changing the game form frequently, as dictated by circumstantial information, for instance about the statistical distribution of individual characteristics.

These features run contrary to the simple and pervasive intuition that agents do care about their rights and about the decision process. In the case of the implementation problem, this means that the benevolent dictator should not be allowed to extract the private information held by individual agents in any way she pleases. She should not bully them into revealing information without giving them some real influence on the process itself. Not to place any limits on the procedures that can be used affords her too much power. Means matter as well as ends.

5 Endstate Justice cum Procedural Justice

Granted that means matter as well as ends, what is the next logical step? How can we combine endstate and procedural justice in the general model of Section 2?

In this section we define formally the concepts of strategy-proofness and group strategy-proofness. We submit that they provide a general answer to the above question. We postpone until the next section the discussion of examples showing these two concepts at work.

Assume from now on that R_i represents a preference ordering over X, and varies within the domain $\mathcal{R}$, known to the mechanism designer, who however is not aware of the actual preferences of real agents. Choosing a single outcome in X for every profile R of individual preferences determines a mapping φ from the set of actual preference profiles $\mathcal{R}^N$ into X, and provides an exhaustive interpretation of endstate justice. On the other hand this mapping can be interpreted as a *direct* game form, namely one where an action by agent i is simply to report his preference ordering, so that the only strategic move available to an agent is to *misreport* his preferences. In most cases, we should expect the agents strategically to misreport. Think of plurality voting when my favorite candidate is a sure loser, but my second choice is in a close race to win: the rational use of my ballot is then to support my second choice, instead of *truthfully* casting my vote for my first choice. Now if the strategic equilibrium of the direct game form does not, in general, consist of reporting one's true preferences, there is no common ground to compare the mapping φ qua social choice function, and qua game form (no matter what criterion of procedural justice we apply to the game form).

This is why we are particularly interested in those game forms where all agents always want to *tell the truth*, namely report their true preference ordering, irrespective of the reports (truthful or not) sent by other agents. Formally the mapping φ from $\mathcal{R}^N$ into X has the property that for all profiles $R = (R_1, \ldots, R_n)$ reporting one's true preferences is for every participant a "best response" strategy to the strategic choices of the other participants.

The strategy "report truthfully any preferences" is then a dominant strategy, and implements our social choice function in a simple and robust way, irrespective of the degree of dispersion of the information on private characteristics. Knowing what the other agents' preferences are, and/or what they will report, is worthless to any single participant (we provide examples in the next section).

The convenience of the direct game form and the robustness of the dominant strategy equilibrium as a rationality scenario are two positive properties making implementation very credible. But the appeal of a strategy-proof social choice function runs deeper. As the game form and social choice functions are the same formal object, the same tests of equity apply to both. For instance a property like anonymity—equal treatment of equal reports—of the mapping φ is at the same time a statement of endstate justice and of procedural justice. In Rawls's terminology, we have a situation of "perfect procedural justice," where the means are justified precisely to the extent that the ends are. Endstate and procedural justice coincide.

Next we observe that an even more demanding property than strategy-proofness is required to pass the most thorough tests of strategic determinism and predictability. *Group strategy-proofness* states that it is never profitable for any subgroup or coalition of agents jointly to misreport their preferences.

Thus not only is the knowledge of other agents' actions worthless to me, even the opportunity to coordinate my strategy with that of other agents is useless. Under group strategy-proofness the prediction that the participants will report their preferences truthfully is robust against both non-cooperative and cooperative moves. It is oblivious not only to the dispersion of information mentioned earlier, but also to the possibility that some players may enter binding agreements.

The advantages of (group) strategy-proof social choice functions are so clear that the search for such social choice functions in a variety of contexts has been active and multifarious.

Note that group strategy-proof social choice functions always exist. Two obvious—and equally repugnant—instances are the *imposed* social choice functions, always choosing the same endstate irrespective of the profile of messages, and the *dictatorial* social choice functions, choosing for all profiles an endstate that maximizes the preferences of a certain agent—the dictator—fixed once and for all (and if the dictator is indifferent between several endstates, choosing one that suits best the preferences of the second person in line, and so on). The imposed social choice functions ignore efficiency entirely, and the dictatorial ones violate even the mildest requirements of endstate/procedural justice.

The interesting and difficult question is how far can a social choice function go toward efficiency and fairness while preserving the (group) strategy-proofness property? The question is mathematically difficult and still widely open in many contexts. Yet recent research provides a large number of partial answers from which much may be learned.

6 Strategy-proof Allocation Mechanisms

Two excellent surveys on the material of this section are Barberà (2001) and Sprumont (1995). For the literature review below, the following taxonomy of results on strategy-proofness will be useful:

- *positive results*: strategy-proofness is compatible with both equity and efficiency. Examples include voting with single-peaked preferences, house barter, matching, and fair division under single-peaked preferences;
- *negative results*: strategy-proofness imposes a loss of efficiency and/or equity so severe as to force us to drop one or the other requirements altogether. Examples include voting between three or more alternatives where strategy-proofness is only compatible with imposed or dictatorial social choice functions, trading of multiple private goods, and production under decreasing marginal costs;
- *"neutral" results*: strategy-proofness is not compatible with full efficiency; yet we can find equitable group strategy-proof social choice functions for which the efficiency loss is not too severe. Examples include public decisions with monetary compensations under quasi-linear utilities, house assignment with lotteries, and cost- and surplus-sharing under increasing marginal cost.

The concept of strategy-proofness was invented in the early 1970s, and the first two decades of the literature are dominated by two seminal negative results.

In the voting problem with unrestricted domain of preferences, the Gibbard–Satterthwaite theorem (Gibbard 1973) conveys the striking result that a strategy-proof rule among three or more candidate/outcomes must be dictatorial. This result is technically equivalent to Arrow's theorem, hence establishes a direct link between the problems of aggregating and of truthfully revealing individual preferences.

In the problem of exchanging private commodities, a conjecture by Hurwicz in 1972 (and only recently proven in full generality, see Schummer 1997; Serizawa 2002) states a similarly disheartening message: a strategy-proof exchange mechanism in which agents trade voluntarily cannot be efficient.

Yet even in the basic problems of voting and exchange, the situation is not as negative as these benchmark results suggest.

When candidates can be arranged along a one-dimensional line and preferences of the voters are single peaked, majority voting is (group) strategy-proof, efficient, and fair. This result goes back to Black's 1948 observation that the *median* peak is the non-manipulable Condorcet winner: it does not pay for a voter whose peak is to the left of the median to report a peak even more to the left, because the median will be unaffected; if this voter reports a peak to the right of his true peak, the only time this move affects the median is when it shifts the median to the right, hence further away from the true peak. The entire family of group strategy-proof voting rules in the one-dimensional model is well understood: all such rules are derived from the median rule by adding a number of *fixed* ballots (Moulin 1980). Extending this result to the popular "spatial voting" model, where candidates live in a Euclidean vector space and preferences are separable in each coordinate, yields a handful of positive or neutral results (Barberà, Gu, and Stacchetti 1993; Barberà, Jackson, and Neme 1997; Barberà, Massó, and Neme 1997; Barberà, Massó, and Serizawa 1998; Peters, van den Stel, and Storcken 1993a, 1993b).

The one-dimensional problem of fairly dividing a single commodity under single-peaked preferences without free disposal yields similarly a rich family of (group) strategy-proof social choice functions, interpretable as rationing methods. If the general family is complex (Barberà, Jackson, and Neme 1997; Moulin 1999b), the uniform rationing method stands out as its unique member that is also fair (Sprumont 1991). This positive result proves helpful in the more general and as yet uncompleted search for (group) strategy-proof methods in the classic Arrow–Debreu economy with multiple commodities (Barberà and Jackson 1995).

By far the most important family of strategy-proof social choice functions uncovered at the outset of the literature is the versatile class of Vickrey–Clarke–Groves mechanisms (hereafter VCG). The prototype of these mechanisms is the familiar *second price auction* due to Vickrey. Buyers bid for the object and the highest bidder wins the object but pays only the second highest price. Because of this feature, the simple strategy of bidding one's true valuation of the object (reservation price) is "dominant:" it is the best reply to any profile of bids by other participants. Bidding below my true valuation will not change the price I pay if I win, and will only make it less likely that I win the object. Bidding above my true valuation is consequential only if I win the object at a price higher than my true valuation. Contrast this with the more common *first price auction*, where the winner pays his own bid: surely he will submit a bid lower than his reservation price, since the latter bid eliminates the possibility of making any profit.

The classic exposition of the VCG mechanism is Green and Laffont (1979). These versatile mechanisms can be used in *any* resource allocation problem where individual preferences are quasi-linear with respect to a numeraire good (the same for every agent). The corresponding social choice functions associate to every preference profile a feasible allocation and a profile of monetary transfers. Strategy-proofness holds if the transfers are chosen in such a way that the net charge to any individual agent equals the marginal social worth of her own message, plus an arbitrary term independent of her message. This yields a partial answer to the free rider problem in the provision of a public good (see Ledyard, this volume), as well as a general compensation method for public decision-making. The appeal of the VCG mechanisms (or social choice functions) is limited, severely in some contexts, for two reasons: they are inefficient, and they are manipulable by coalitions, i.e. strategy-proof but not group strategy-proof.

VCG mechanisms are particularly well suited to assign indivisible objects when monetary transfers are feasible, as in an auction. Indeed they originate in Vickrey's 1961 observation that the second price auction is strategy-proof on the buyer side. They play a growing role in the design of auctions to assign multiple objects (Ausubel and Milgrom 2002; Bikhchandani and Ostroy 2002; Bikhchandani et al. 2002; Pápai 2003). Other recent applications include cost-sharing (Moulin and Shenker 2001) and the scheduling of jobs (Mitra, 2001, 2002; Suijs 1996).

An early observation in Shapley and Scarf (1974) shows that the barter of indivisible goods, without monetary transfers, leads to a unique core stable allocation when each agent is only interested in consuming one object. This unique outcome obtains by the simple "top trading cycle" algorithm, and defines a group strategy-proof mechanism (Ma 1994). Substantial generalizations of this positive result (Ehlers, Klaus, and Pápai 2002; Pápai 2000, 2001; Svensson 1999) throw much light on the rich structure of the set of group strategy-proof mechanisms for assigning indivisble goods in the absence of initial property rights (distribution as opposed to exchange).

Bilateral matching is a natural generalization of the assignment problem (without money), where each agent seeks a match on the other side of the market, and everyone has preferences over potential mates. The celebrated Gale–Shapley algorithm provides an elegant and eminently practical resolution of the matching problem, also a group strategy-proof mechanism from the point of view of one side of the market. Concrete applications of the algorithm keep emerging, from the assignment of students to schools, of tenants to housing units, to the exchange of kidneys for transplant (Roth and Sotomayor 1990; Sönmez 1996).

Much new ground has been broken in the models of cooperative productions where a group of users "share" a given technology in the sense that they all contribute some input and receive a share of the output. Two well-known examples are the provision of a public good and the exploitation of a "commons," namely, a technology producing a private good under increasing marginal costs. Unrestricted access to the technology leads to severe inefficiencies due to the free rider problem in the former model, and to the tragedy of the commons in the latter.

The most interesting characterization results combine (group) strategy-proofness with normative requirements of fairness, in particular the fundamental *horizontal equity* (often called *anonymity*), requiring that equal messages yield equal allocations. An anonymous group strategy-proof game form always produces an "envy-free" allocation (Moulin 1993). The nature of the results (positive, negative, or neutral) depends much on the nature of the good produced by the shared technology. In the provision of a pure public good problem we have negative or at best neutral results: for instance, strategy-proofness is not compatible with the natural *stand-alone lower bound*, computed as the welfare level of an agent who pays the full cost of the public good (Saijo 1991; Serizawa 1999). On the other hand, the production of a private good yields strikingly positive results: the serial cost-sharing method emerges as uniquely fair, (group) strategy-proof, and not too inefficient (Moulin and Shenker 1992; Shenker 1995). This method can also be adapted to the provision of an excludable public good—a non-rival private good (Deb and Razzolini 1999; Moulin 1994; Olszewski 2004). A general characterization of (group) strategy-proof social choice functions that does not use simplifying requirements of fairness may not be too far from our reach (Leroux 2004; Moulin 1999*a*).

7 Concluding Comments

Group strategy-proofness is a tractable requirement in a number of specialized allocation problems: majority voting with single-peaked preferences, uniform rationing of a single commodity, assignment of indivisble goods and matching, serial cost-sharing of a private or excludable public good with increasing marginal cost. Yet the initial negative results continue to place tight limits on the flexibility that the strategy-proofness property allows to the mechanism designer. In many cases we must settle for a less demanding equilibrium concept, hence a less plausible prediction of implementation, in order to secure an efficient and endstate-just outcome. The question is now to strike a compromise between two conflicting objectives:

- we want a simple mechanism, with natural message spaces, easily understandable rules, and a fair distribution of rights (as required by procedural justice).
- we want a mechanism implementing the desired social choice function in a manner as strategically robust as possible (as required by endstate justice).

The precise nature of this trade-off is still far from clear at this point of a research effort that started nearly three decades ago. For recent surveys of the implementation problem, the reader may consult Moore (1992) and Jackson (2001).

References

Ausubel, L. M., and Milgrom, P. R. 2002. Ascending auctions with package bidding. *Frontiers of Theoretical Economics*, 1: 1–42.

Barberà, S. 2001. An introduction to strategy-proof social choice functions. *Social Choice and Welfare*, 18: 619–53.

———Gul, F., and Stacchetti, E. 1993. Generalized median voter schemes and committees. *Journal of Economic Theory*, 61: 262–89.

———and Jackson, M. 1995. Strategy-proof exchange. *Econometrica*, 63: 51–87.

——— ———and Neme, A. 1997a. Strategy-proof allotment rules. *Games and Economic Behavior*, 18: 1–21.

———Massó, J., and Neme, A. 1997b. Voting under constraints. *Journal of Economic Theory*, 76: 298–321.

———and Serizawa, S. 1998. Strategy-proof voting on compact ranges. *Games and Economic Behavior*, 25: 272–91.

———Sonnenschein, H., and Zhou, L. 1991. Voting by committees. *Econometrica*, 59: 595–609.

Berlin, I. 1969. *Four Essays on Liberty*. Oxford: Oxford University Press.

Bikhchandani, S., and Ostroy, J. M. 2002. The package assignment model. *Journal of Economic Theory*, 107: 377–406.

———deVries, S., Schummer, J., and Vohra, R. V. 2002. Linear programming and Vickrey auctions. In *Mathematics of the Internet: E-Auction and Markets*, ed. B. Dietrica and R. V. Vohra. The IMA Volumes in Mathematics and its Applications 127. New York: Springer-Verlag.

Bossert, W. 1995. Redistribution mechanisms based on individual characteristics. *Mathematical Social Sciences*, 29: 1–17.

———Pattanaik, P. K., and Xu, Y. 1994. Ranking opportunity sets: an axiomatic approach. *Journal of Economic Theory*, 63: 326–45.

Deb, R., Pattanaik, K., and Razzolini, L. 1997. Game forms, rights, and the efficiency of social outcomes. *Journal of Economic Theory*, 72: 74–95.

———and Razzolini, L. 1999. Auction-like mechanisms for pricing excludable public goods. *Journal of Economic Theory*, 88: 340–68.

Dutta, B., and Sen, A. 1996. Ranking opportunity sets and Arrow impossibility theorem: correspondence results. *Journal of Economic Theory*, 71: 90–101.

Ehlers, L., Klaus, B., and Pápai, S. 2002. Strategy-proofness and population-monotonicity for house allocation problems. *Journal of Mathematical Economics*, 38: 329–39.

Fleurbaey, M. 1995a. Equal opportunity or equal social outcome? *Economics and Philosophy*, 11: 25–55.

———1995b. Three solutions for the compensation problem. *Journal of Economic Theory*, 66: 505–21.

Gaertner, W., Pattanaik, P. K., and Suzumura, K. 1992. Individual rights revisited. *Economica*, 59: 161–77.

Gärdenfors, P. 1981. Rights, games and social choice. *Noûs*, 15: 341–56.

Gibbard, A. 1973. Manipulation of voting schemes: a general result. *Econometrica*, 41: 587–601.

Green, J., and Laffont, J. J. 1979. *Incentives in Public Decision Making*. Amsterdam: North-Holland.

Hardin, G. 1968. The tragedy of the commons. *Science*, 162: 1243–8.

Jackson, M. O. 2001. A crash course in implementation theory. *Social Choice and Welfare*, 18: 655–708.

LASLIER, J. F., FLEURBAY, M., GRAVEL, N., and TRANNOY, A. (eds.). 1998. *Freedom in Economics*. London: Routledge.

LEROUX, J. 2004. Pooling private technologies: improving upon autarky. Mimeo, Rice University.

MA, J. 1994. Strategy-proofness and the strict core in a market with indivisibilities. *International Journal of Game Theory*, 23: 75–83.

MCKELVEY, R. D. 1976. Intransitivities in multi-dimensional voting models and some implications for agenda control. *Journal of Economic Theory*, 12: 472–82.

MAS-COLELL, A., WHINSTON, A., and GREEN, J. 1990. *Microeconomic Theory*. Oxford: Oxford University Press.

MASKIN, E. 1985. The theory of implementation in Nash equilibrium: a survey. In *Social Goals and Social Organization*, ed. L. Hurwicz, D. Schemeidler, and H. Sonnenschein. Cambridge: Cambridge University Press.

MITRA, M. 2001. Mechanism design in queueing problems. *Economic Theory*, 17: 277–305.

——2002. Achieving the first best in sequencing problems. *Review of Economic Design*, 7: 75–91.

MOORE, J. 1992. Implementation, contracts, and renegotiation in environments with complete information. In *Advances in Economic Theory*, ed. J. J. Laffort. Cambridge: Cambridge University Press.

MOULIN, H. 1980. On strategy-proofness and single peakedness. *Public Choice*, 35: 437–55.

——1993. On the fair and coalition strategyproof allocation of private goods. In *Frontiers of Game Theory*, ed. K. Binmore, A. Kirman, and P. Tani. Cambridge, Mass.: MIT University Press.

——1994. Serial cost sharing of excludable public goods. *Review of Economic Studies*, 61: 305–25.

——1999a. Incremental cost sharing: characterization by group strategyproofness. *Social Choice and Welfare*, 16: 279–320.

——1999b. Rationing a commodity along fixed paths. *Journal of Economic Theory*, 84: 41–72.

——2002. Axiomatic cost and surplus-sharing. In *The Handbook of Social Choice and Welfare*, ed. K. Arrow, A. Sen, and K. Suzumura. Amsterdam: North-Holland.

——and SHENKER, S. 1992. Serial cost sharing. *Econometrica*, 50: 1009–39.

———— 2001. Strategyproof sharing of submodular costs: budget balance versus efficiency. *Economic Theory*, 18: 511–33.

——and SPRUMONT, Y. 2005. On demand responsiveness in additive cost sharing. *Journal of Economic Theory*, 125: 1–35.

——and THOMSON, W. 1997. Axiomatic analysis of resource allocation problems. In *Social Choice Reexamined*, ed. K. Arrow, A. Sen, and K. Suzumura. IEA Conference 116. London: Macmillan.

NAKAMURA, K. 1979. The vetoers in a simple game with ordinal preferences. *International Journal of Game Theory*, 8: 55–61.

OLSON, M. 1965. *The Logic of Collective Action*. Cambridge, Mass.: Harvard University Press.

OLSZEWSKI, W. 2004. Coalition strategy-proof mechanisms for provision of excludable public goods. *Games and Economic Behavior*, 46: 88–114.

PÁPAI, S. 2000. Strategyproof assignment by hierarchical exchange. *Econometrica*, 68: 1403–33.

——2001. Strategyproof single unit award rules. *Social Choice and Welfare*, 18: 785–98.

——2003. Groves sealed bid auctions of heterogeneous objects with fair prices. *Social Choice and Welfare*, 20: 371–85.

PATTANAIK, P. K., and XU, Y. 1998. On preference and freedom. *Theory and Decision*, 44: 173–98.

—— —— 2000a. On ranking opportunity sets in economic environments. *Journal of Economic Theory*, 93: 48–71.

—— —— 2000b. On diversity and freedom of choice. *Mathematical Social Sciences*, 40: 123–30.

PETERS, H., VAN DER STEL, H., and STORCKEN, T. 1993a. Range convexity, continuity, and strategy-proofness of voting schemes. *Methods and Models of Operations Research*, 38: 213–29.

—— —— —— 1993b. Generalized median solutions, strategy-proofness and strictly convex norms. *Methods and Models of Operations Research*, 38: 19–53.

ROEMER, J. E. 1993. A pragmatic theory of responsibility for the egalitarian planner. *Philosophy and Public Affairs*, 22: 146–66.

—— 1996. *Theories of Distributive Justice*. Cambridge, Mass.: Harvard University Press.

—— 2000. *Equality of Opportunity*. Cambridge, Mass.: Harvard University Press.

ROTH, A., and SOTOMAYOR, M. 1990. *Two-Sided Matching: A Study in Game-Theoretic Modeling and Analysis*. London: Cambridge University Press.

SAIJO, T. 1991. Incentive compatibility and individual rationality in public good economies. *Journal of Economic Theory*, 55: 203–12.

SCHUMMER, J. 1997. Strategy-proofness versus efficiency on restricted domains of exchange economies. *Social Choice and Welfare*, 14: 47–56.

SEN, A. K. 1991. Welfare, preference and freedom. *Journal of Econometrics*, 50: 15–29.

SERIZAWA, S. 1999. Strategy-proof and symmetric social choice functions for public good economies. *Econometrica*, 67: 121–45.

—— 2002. Inefficiency of strategy-proof rules for pure exchange economies. *Journal of Economic Theory*, 106: 219–41.

SHAPLEY, L., and SCARF, H. 1974. On cores and indivisibility. *Journal of Mathematical Economics*, 1: 23–8.

SHENKER, S. 1995. Making greed work in networks: a game theoretic analysis of switch service disciplines. *Transactions on Networking*, 3: 819–31.

SÖNMEZ, T. 1996. Strategy-proofness in many-to-one matching problems. *Economic Design*, 1: 365–80.

SPRUMONT, Y. 1991. The division problem with single-peaked preferences: a characterization of the uniform allocation rule. *Econometrica*, 59: 509–19.

—— 1995. Strategy-proof collective choice in economic and political environments. *Canadian Journal of Economics*, 28: 68–107.

—— 1998. Ordinal cost sharing. *Journal of Economic Theory*, 81: 126–62.

SUGDEN, R. 1998. The metric opportunity. *Economics and Philosophy*, 14: 307–37.

SUIJS, J. 1996. On incentive compatibility and budget balancedness in public decision making. *Economic Design*, 2: 193–209.

SVENSSON, L. 1999. Strategy-proof allocation of indivisible goods. *Social Choice and Welfare*, 16: 557–67.

THOMSON, W. 2003. Axiomatic and game-theoretic analysis of bankruptcy and taxation problems: a survey. *Mathematical Social Sciences*, 45: 249–98.

CHAPTER 22

A TOOL KIT FOR VOTING THEORY

DONALD G. SAARI

1 INTRODUCTION

FOR someone outside of social choice, this area may seem to be discouragingly consumed with voting paradoxes and/or the impossible such as Arrow's and Sen's theorems. Just thumbing through journals reveals negative results stating that what we might want to do cannot be done, and all of this is described in a technical language that even a mathematician would find difficult to parse. But in recent years, positive conclusions have been found and negative assertions put to rest or placed in perspective. In this chapter I describe some results that could be useful tools to analyze actual elections. An outline follows:

1. During any close election we might wonder whether the outcome would have changed had a different election rule been used. But the difficulty and time required to compute outcomes often limit us to checking only a couple of methods. There now exist ways to quickly find all outcomes for most of the voting methods that have ever been considered for actual use. This includes "positional methods" where weights are assigned to candidates according to their position on a ballot, as well as approval voting.
2. To adopt a voting rule, we want to identify all of its properties. Using terms associated with the axiomatic approach, we want to know "what we are getting." How can this be done? After a cautionary warning about the axiomatic method, two approaches are described.
3. The voting literature is filled with commentary about strategic behavior and other disturbing anomalies such as where a winning candidate loses because

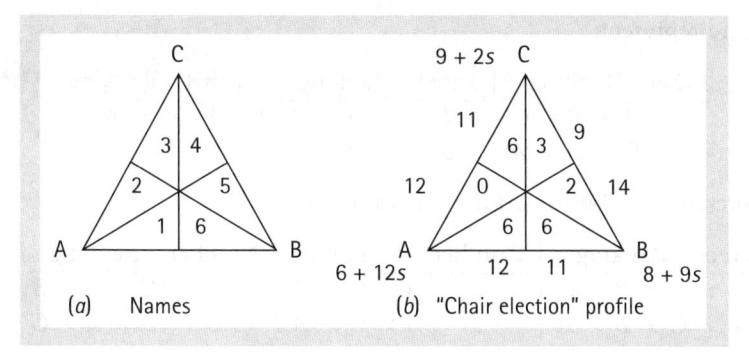

Fig. 22.1 Profile representation and tallies

she receives *more* support. The pragmatic question is to find simple ways to analyze specific rules to understand whether and when such problems can occur. I indicate how to do this.

4. Do Arrow's and Sen's theorems, partially responsible for two Nobel prizes, really mean what we have believed for several decades? I indicate why this is not the case.

As my emphasis is to show how to use these results to analyze and understand daily concerns, theoretical support and specific details about the approaches are left to the references.

2 REPRESENTING PROFILES

A profile lists the number of voters who have each ranking of the candidates. But when computing election outcomes, moving up and down the list to see who is ranked above whom is tedious. To avoid this problem, I developed a geometric approach (Saari 1994, 2001a) to describe profiles and compute election outcomes. (See Nurmi's 2003 use of my methods to analyze elections.) The approach uses an equilateral triangle (Figure 22.1) where the vertices represent candidates {Ann, Barb, Connie} (denoted by A, B, and C). The first step is to assign a ranking to each point in the triangle. Using a "closer is better" sense, let points closer to the A than the B vertex represent "A preferred to B" denoted by $A \succ B$. Because the vertical line connecting the midpoint of the A–B edge with the C vertex identifies all points equidistant from the A and B vertices, it represents the tied $A \sim B$ ranking. Points to the left of this vertical line represent $A \succ B$, while those to the right represent $B \succ A$.

Similarly, the three interior lines connecting vertices with the midpoint of the opposite side represent the three binary indifferences. They divided the triangle into six smaller triangles or *ranking regions*: each region represents the strict transitive three-candidate ranking determined by its proximity to each vertex. In Figure 22.1a, for instance, points in region "3" are closest to the C vertex, next closest to the A, and furthest from B: they define the $C \succ A \succ B$ ranking. The numbers in

Figure 22.1a represent:

Label	Ranking	Label	Ranking	Label	Ranking
1	$A \succ B \succ C$	2	$A \succ C \succ B$	3	$C \succ A \succ B$
4	$C \succ B \succ A$	5	$B \succ C \succ A$	6	$B \succ A \succ C$

(1)

To represent a profile for {Ann, Barb, Connie}:

Number	Ranking	Number	Ranking	Number	Ranking
6	$A \succ B \succ C$	0	$A \succ C \succ B$	6	$C \succ A \succ B$
3	$C \succ B \succ A$	2	$B \succ C \succ A$	6	$B \succ A \succ C$

(2)

to elect a departmental chair, place the number of voters with each ranking in the appropriate ranking region: this equation 2 "Chair" profile is in Figure 22.1b.

As described in Saari (2001), the geometric representation sorts profile entries in a manner that simplifies tallying elections; e.g. as all voters preferring $A \succ B$ are to the left of the vertical line, their sum $6 + 0 + 6 = 12$ is A's tally in the $\{A, B\}$ election. This number, with B's $3 + 2 + 6 = 11$ tally from the right of the line, is listed under the edge. All pairwise outcomes are similarly computed with the outcomes listed near the appropriate triangle edge. According to these votes, Ann is the *Condorcet winner*—she beats all others in pairwise majority votes.

Our standard voting system, where a voter votes for his favorite candidate and the candidate with the most votes wins, is called the *plurality vote*. But rather than voting just for one candidate, we might give 9, 7, 0 points, respectively, to a voter's top-, second-, and third-ranked candidate. This is called a "positional election:" it is where the weights $w_1 \geq w_2 \geq w_3 = 0$ are assigned, respectively, to a voter's top, second, and bottom "positioned" (ranked) candidates and the societal ranking is determined by the sum of points each candidate receives. Without loss of generality, scale all weights by dividing by w_1 to obtain $(1, s, 0)$. So with the earlier 9, 7, 0 points assignment, the rescaling assigns 1, $s = \frac{7}{9}$, 0 points to a voter's top-, second-, and third-ranked candidate. To use weights that play a major role in what follows, the *Borda Count* is where 2, 1, 0 points are assigned to the candidates, so its scaled weights are $(1, \frac{1}{2}, 0)$. The *antiplurality* vote, 1, 1, 0 (called this because by voting for two, you are effectively voting against someone), already is in scaled form.

To compute tallies, notice that Ann's outcome is [number of voters with A top-ranked]+ s [number of voters with A second ranked]. In Figure 22.1b, the first bracket's value is A's plurality outcome, or the sum of numbers in regions with A as a vertex: $6 + 0 = 6$. The second bracket—the number of voters with A second ranked—involves the two triangles one step removed from where A is top ranked—the adjacent regions that both contain 6. Thus A's positional tally is $[6 + 0] + s[6 + 6] = 6 + 12s$. All positional tallies are similarly computed and listed by the appropriate Figure 22.1b vertex. Readers unfamiliar with this process should experiment by computing election outcomes for other profiles.

According to Figure 22.1b the plurality ($s = 0$) ranking is $C \succ B \succ A$ with a 9:8:6 tally, so Connie, rather than Condorcet winner Ann, wins. But as the antiplurality system ($s = 1$) has the opposite outcome of $A \succ B \succ C$ with a 18:17:11 tally, Condorcet winner Ann wins with some of the positional methods. Later I show the reader how to construct this Chair profile and many others.

3 PROCEDURE LINE AND HULLS

The above approach simplifies computing tallies but it does not display the different outcomes. The next geometric approach that I developed (Saari 1994, which has been used by Nurmi 2003, Tabarrok 2001, Tabarrok and Spector 1999 to analyze elections) rectifies this deficiency. To explain, re-express the (6, 8, 9) plurality outcome (in the A, B, C order) of the Chair example as $(\frac{6}{23}, \frac{8}{23}, \frac{9}{23})$ describing each candidate's fraction of the vote: call this the *normalized election tally*. As x, y, z represent, respectively, the fraction of the vote received by Ann, Barb, and Connie, we have:

$$x, y, z \geq 0, \quad x + y + z = 1. \tag{3}$$

When the points in equation 3 are graphed on an x, y, z coordinate system, the region connects the point on each positive axis that is one unit from the origin. As a quick drawing will prove, the figure is an equilateral triangle (Figure 22.2a): points in this triangle identify normalized tallies. For instance, the A-vertex corresponds to $x = 1$ where A receives all of the vote. The triangle's midpoint, where all lines cross, represents a *complete tie* with $x = y = z = \frac{1}{3}$, which means that each candidate receives a third of the vote. The midpoint on the right-side leg, where $x = 0, y = z = \frac{1}{2}$, represents a $B \sim C \succ A$ election outcome.

Procedure line. To find all possible positional election outcomes for a profile, plot the normalized plurality and antiplurality outcomes and connect them with a straight line (Saari 1994). To illustrate, the normalized plurality and antiplurality outcomes of the Chair election $(\frac{6}{23}, \frac{8}{23}, \frac{9}{23})$ and $(\frac{18}{46}, \frac{17}{46}, \frac{11}{46})$ are plotted in Figure 22.2a. (In an equilateral triangle with leg length 2 where (u, v) represents the coordinates, the $(1, 0, 0), (0, 1, 0), (0, 0, 1)$ unanimity election outcomes are plotted in the figure as

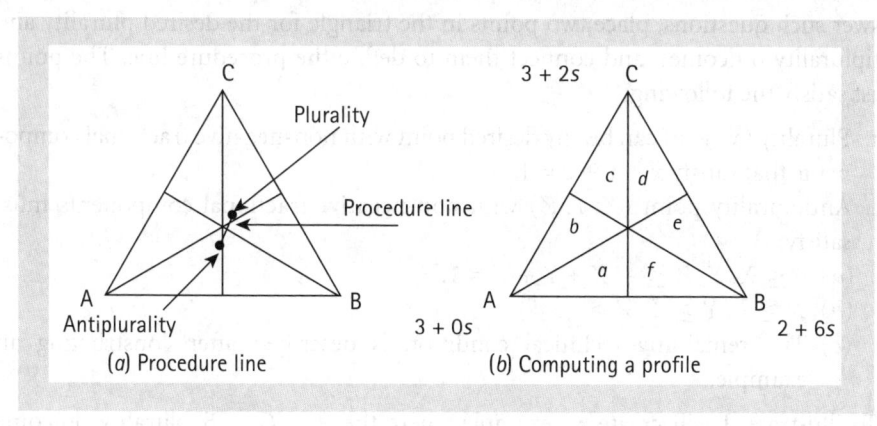

Fig. 22.2 Procedure lines

the (u, v) points $(0, 0)$, $(2, 0)$, $(1, \sqrt{3})$. In general, plot the election point (x, y, z) according to:

$$u = 2y + z, \quad v = \sqrt{3}z;$$

e.g. the Chair plurality point is at $u = 2 \approx \frac{8}{23} + \frac{9}{23} = 1\frac{2}{23} \approx 1.0870$, while $v = \frac{9}{23} \times \sqrt{3} \approx 0.6777$.) The importance of the line connecting the plurality and antiplurality points, the *procedure line*, is that each point represents some positional procedure's normalized election tally, and all positional outcomes are represented on this line. To explain, notice that the values listed by the vertices in Figure 22.1b, which specify all possible positional outcomes, define a linear equation (i.e. the exponent on s is one). Thus the set of outcomes define a line: this is the procedure line.

All sorts of information comes from the positioning of this procedure line; e.g. in Figure 22.2a, each candidate from the Chair election can "win" with an appropriate positional method. As examples, Ann wins with the antiplurality method ($s = 1$), Barb with the earlier defined Borda Count ($s = \frac{1}{2}$), and Connie with the plurality vote ($s = 0$). This ambiguity raises an issue: who is the true "choice of the voters?" The fact the procedure line crosses seven regions (three are line segments and four are open triangles) means that this profile defines the *seven different positional election rankings*:

$$C \succ B \succ A, C \sim B \succ A, B \succ C \succ A, B \succ A \sim C,$$
$$B \succ A \succ C, A \sim B \succ C, A \succ B \succ C.$$

Most of the procedure line is in regions where Barb wins, which means that most positional methods elect B; e.g. we can argue that B is the appropriate choice. Beyond cataloguing all positional outcomes allowed by a profile, Tabarrok (2001; Tabarrok and Spector 1999) uses the procedure line and hull (that is needed with more than three candidates: Saari 2001a) to extract comparisons about elections and the "true winner."

Creating profiles and profile lines. Can we construct profiles to illustrate particular behaviors; e.g. is there a profile with the plurality $A \sim C \succ B$ and antiplurality $B \succ C \succ A$ outcomes? If so, what happens with the other positional outcomes? To answer such questions, place two points in the triangle for the desired plurality and antiplurality outcomes, and connect them to define the procedure line. The points must satisfy the following:

1. Plurality (x, y, z) can be any desired point with non-negative fractional components that satisfy $x + y + z = 1$.
2. Antiplurality point (X, Y, Z) with non-negative fractional components must satisfy:
   (a) $0 \leq X, Y, Z \leq \frac{1}{2}$, $X + Y + Z = 1$.
   (b) $X \geq \frac{x}{2}, Y \geq \frac{y}{2}, Z \geq \frac{z}{2}$.
   (c) The remaining technical condition is described after constructing an example.

To illustrate, I will create an example where the $A \sim C \succ B$ plurality outcome is accompanied by the antiplurality $B \succ C \succ A$. Let $(x, y, z) = (\frac{3}{8}, \frac{2}{8}, \frac{3}{8})$ define the desired $A \sim C \succ B$ plurality ranking. (So, A and C each receive $\frac{3}{8}$ of the vote, B receives $\frac{2}{8}$.) These normalized plurality tallies require the normalized antiplurality tallies to satisfy $\frac{3}{16} \leq X \leq \frac{1}{2}, \frac{1}{8} \leq Y \leq \frac{1}{2}, \frac{3}{16} \leq Z \leq \frac{1}{2}$. To have the $B \succ C \succ A$ antiplurality outcome, let $X = \frac{3}{16}, Z = \frac{5}{16}, Y = \frac{8}{16}$. By plotting the (x, y, z) and (X, Y, Z) point to create the procedure line, it follows that any supporting profile allows the six election rankings $A \sim C \succ B, C \succ A \succ B, C \succ A \sim B, C \succ B \succ A, C \sim B \succ A, B \succ C \succ A$.

To construct a supporting profile, convert (x, y, z) and (X, Y, Z) to integer values where the integer antiplurality outcomes sum to twice the plurality outcomes. (This is because with the plurality and antiplurality votes, each voter casts, respectively, one and two points.) With our example, multiply the plurality outcome by its common denominator of eight to get $(3, 2, 3)$, and the $(\frac{3}{16}, \frac{8}{16}, \frac{5}{16})$ outcome by its common denominator of 16 to obtain the desired $(3, 8, 5)$. (This approach always works if the common denominator for the normalized antiplurality tally is twice that of the normalized plurality tally.)

Now notice from Figure 22.1b that the s-coefficient for each candidate is the difference between her plurality and antiplurality tallies. So a profile satisfying our example defines the A, B, and C positional outcomes of $3 + s(3 - 3)$, $2 + s(8 - 2)$, and $3 + s(5 - 3)$. These values are listed next to the appropriate Figure 22.2b vertex. Compute the a through f integer values in Figure 22.2b as above; e.g. Ann's tally of $3 + 0s = [a + b] + s[f + c]$. Ann has no "second-place votes," so $c = f = 0$. As Barb's plurality vote is $2 = (e + f)$ and $f = 0$, we have that $e = 2$. Similarly, $d = 3$. It remains to divide Ann's $a + b = 3$ first-place votes to satisfy the s-coefficients for Barb and Connie: the only choice is $a = 3$. Thus, the eight-voter supporting profile for the example has three voters preferring $A \succ B \succ C$, two preferring $B \succ C \succ A$, and three preferring $C \succ B \succ A$.

The missing technical condition is that a candidate's s-coefficient cannot exceed the sum of the other two candidates' plurality votes; e.g. as the s-coefficient comes from the other candidates' first-place votes, there must be enough of them.

This approach makes it easy to construct profiles to exhibit all sorts of interesting behavior. In practical terms, just draw a line in the triangle. Almost any line suffices: if the endpoints are close to the center, the above conditions will be satisfied. Often just the positioning of the procedure line suffices to discover conclusions; e.g. in this manner we now know the following. I leave the proofs to the reader; they just involve drawing an appropriate line in an equilateral triangle:

- For any ranking, there is a profile where all normalized positional outcomes agree and yield the selected ranking. (Select the normalized plurality and antiplurality points to be the same; the procedure line becomes a point where all normalized tallies agree.)
- Select any ranking for the plurality and for the antiplurality outcomes. There exists a profile with these outcomes. In fact, select any two different positional methods and any two ranking: there exists a profile so that the first rule's outcome is the first ranking while the second rule's outcome is the second ranking.

- For any number from {1, 2, ..., 7}, there exists a profile with precisely that number of different positional outcomes.

Approval voting. To show how to compute outcomes for other rules, I illustrate the approach with approval voting (AV). AV, analyzed and promoted by Brams and Fishburn (1983), is where a voter votes "approval" for as many candidates as desired. So a voter with $A \succ B \succ C$ preferences could vote for Ann, or for Ann and Barbara. While a vote for all three is admissible, Brams and Fishburn cogently argue that such a vote is not rational because, by not distinguishing among the candidates, the voter's ballot has no effect.

Obviously, if voters vote in different ways, the AV outcome can change. Indeed, Ann from the Chair election could receive *thirteen* different AV election tallies ranging from 6 to 18 votes! A quick way to determine all values a candidate can receive is to recognize that the range is defined by her plurality (vote for one) and antiplurality (vote for two) tallies. As there are 13 different AV tallies for Ann, 10 for Barb, and 3 for Connie, the Chair profile admits $13 \times 10 \times 3 = 390$ different AV election tallies! (It is easy to create scenarios that support each outcome.)

Plotting 390 points is not appealing, so to identify all AV outcomes plot the eight extreme tallies constructed from the plurality (6, 8, 9) and antiplurality (18, 17, 11) by interchanging values from each list. This selection represents where a candidate receives only first-place votes (plurality tally) or all possible second-place votes (antiplurality tally). As the eight extreme tallies are:

$$(6, 8, 9) \quad (18, 8, 9) \quad (6, 17, 9) \quad (6, 8, 11)$$
$$(18, 17, 11) \quad (6, 17, 11) \quad (18, 8, 11) \quad (18, 17, 9), \tag{4}$$

plot (Figure 22.3) the eight normalized tallies:

$$\left(\tfrac{6}{23}, \tfrac{8}{23}, \tfrac{9}{23}\right) \left(\tfrac{18}{35}, \tfrac{8}{35}, \tfrac{9}{35}\right) \left(\tfrac{6}{32}, \tfrac{17}{32}, \tfrac{9}{32}\right) \left(\tfrac{6}{25}, \tfrac{8}{25}, \tfrac{11}{25}\right)$$
$$\left(\tfrac{18}{46}, \tfrac{17}{46}, \tfrac{11}{46}\right) \left(\tfrac{6}{34}, \tfrac{17}{34}, \tfrac{11}{34}\right) \left(\tfrac{18}{37}, \tfrac{8}{37}, \tfrac{11}{37}\right) \left(\tfrac{18}{44}, \tfrac{17}{44}, \tfrac{9}{44}\right) \tag{5}$$

Connect all points with straight lines: the enclosed region contains all 390 tallies that are (essentially) equally spaced in this region. While "only" 390 points in this Figure 22.3 AV hull are AV election tallies, because they are closely packed into a small region, it is reasonable to view all points in this distorted rectangle as admissible AV tallies.

The Figure 22.3 graph identifies several conclusions: a partial sample follows. (For more AV properties, see Saari 1994, 2001a; Saari and van Newenhizen 1988.)

1. If the reader finds it disturbing that the Chair profile allows seven different positional outcomes, the reader will be more disturbed by Figure 22.3 showing that *any ranking can be a sincere AV outcome* for this profile! This is because the AV hull meets all six short-line segments (representing a tie between candidates), the center point (complete tie), and all six open regions (strict election outcomes). This indeterminate phenomenon is not a peculiarity of the Chair election example: multiple outcomes are to be expected. Indeed, even an unanimity profile allows different election rankings.

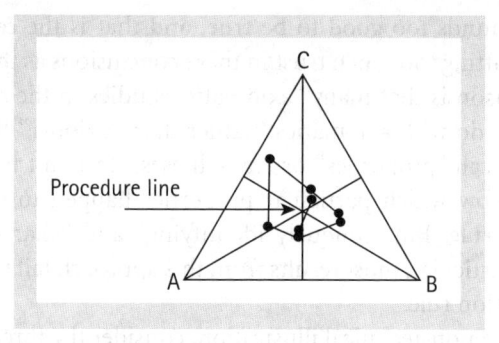

Fig. 22.3 Approval Voting hull

2. For any profile, every positional election ranking is a sincere AV election outcome. This is because two of the plotted points are the procedure line's endpoints. Consequently, for any profile, the procedure line *always* is in the AV hull.
3. As Figure 22.3 demonstrates, most points in the AV hull (e.g. most AV tallies) elect the Condorcet loser Connie! This geometry, then, shows how easy it is for AV to elect the Condorcet loser.

With so many AV outcomes, we must wonder which ones are likely to occur. Valued help in answering this question comes from extending Brams and Fishburn's commentary that a voter must distinguish among candidates, rather than voting for all, to avoid losing any say in who is elected. Similarly, in an election closely contested between a voter's two top choices, the rational voter should vote for only one candidate: otherwise the voter has no say in which candidate is elected. To illustrate with the 1992 US presidential elections, voters preferring "Clinton ≻ Bush ≻ Perot," or "Bush ≻ Clinton ≻ Perot" would vote only for their top-ranked candidate: by voting for two, their vote would not influence the Clinton–Bush outcome and, from a pragmatic perspective, it would be equivalent to not voting. Similarly, because the Perot voters wanted their candidate to come close to one of the major candidates, they probably would vote only for Perot. Thus the only voters with any rational motivation to vote for two candidates are those with Perot second ranked. If enough did so, we would have had President Perot. (See Tabarrok 2001 for supporting data.) An unfortunate but natural consequence is that in closely contested elections, AV reduces to the plurality vote—the procedure it was designed to replace—or worse.

4 Dictionaries, Paradoxes, and Properties

In selecting election rules, we should be guided by their properties. This suggests using the "axiomatic representations" of voting rules. After all, as papers using this method occasionally argue, this approach tells us "what we are getting."

This approach sounds too good to be true, and that is the case. My cautionary advice is to avoid putting too much trust in these conclusions as they can be seriously misleading. The reason is that many "axiomatic" studies in the social sciences have little, if anything, to do with axiomatics. Rather than "axioms," they are using what we mathematicians call "properties" or "hypotheses." In blunt terms, most of these conclusions only show which particular properties happen to identify uniquely a particular decision rule. But "uniquely identifying" and "characterizing" are very different traits: in particular, most results from this approach fail to characterize what you get from a decision rule.

To illustrate with a non-technical illustration, consider the three traits (1) Finnish-American heritage, (2) born in a particular year in the Upper Peninsula of Michigan, and (3) does research in social choice and the Newtonian N-body problem. While these traits uniquely identify me, they do not characterize me. Knowing just this, you do not know "what you are getting." Similarly the traditional "axiomatic studies" often identify properties that, by emphasizing special settings, uniquely identify an election rule. But unless these properties can be used to derive all properties of the rule, then instead of being "axioms," they are just special properties the rule happens to satisfy.

If the axiomatic approach does not accomplish what we want, how do we find all properties of a voting rule? In addressing this question, I was influenced by the research of Nurmi, Brams, and Fishburn. In particular, Fishburn (1981) published an intriguing paradox (that is, a counterintuitive outcome) where the sincere plurality election outcome is $A \succ B \succ C \succ D$, but if D drops out, the sincere election outcome for the same voters—nobody changes preferences!—becomes the *reversed* $C \succ B \succ A$. Fishburn's reversal example is more than an amusing curiosity: it illustrates a peculiar and unexpected property of the plurality vote.

The ranking "paradoxes" in the literature must be taken seriously because they identify properties of election rules. Similarly, "paradoxes that cannot occur" identify a rule's positive properties. To illustrate with the Borda Count (where 2, 1, 0 points are assigned, respectively, to a voter's top-, second-, and bottom-ranked candidate), this rule does not allow the list

$$(B \succ C \succ A, A \succ B, A \succ C, B \succ C)$$

to ever happen. This and other lists of Borda rankings that cannot occur define the important property that the Borda Count never ranks the Condorcet loser (the candidate that loses to all candidates in pairwise elections) above the Condorcet winner. Does this property extend to any other positional method? (No.)

To find all ranking properties of election procedures, we could find all possible lists of election rankings that could ever occur. To illustrate with Fishburn's example, rather than just the plurality $(A \succ B \succ C \succ D, C \succ B \succ A)$ listing, we want to know what happens with all subsets of candidates. Can we have, for instance, a plurality listing

$$(A \succ B \succ C \succ D, C \succ B \succ A, D \succ B \succ A, D \succ C \succ A, D \succ C \succ B,$$
$$A \succ B, B \succ C, C \succ D, D \succ A, A \succ C, B \succ D)$$

where the plurality ranking reverses if any candidate is dropped, but the pairwise outcomes are cyclic? As there are many profiles with precisely this property, this listing defines another property of the plurality vote.

By modifying notions from "chaotic dynamics" (the intrepid reader can check Saari 1995), I was able to find everything that could ever happen for any number of candidates, any number of voters, and all combinations of positional voting methods (Saari 1989, 1990). To explain the discouraging results with, say, candidates $\{A, B, C, D, E\}$, rank them in any desired manner; e.g. $A \succ B \sim C \succ D \sim E$. For each way to drop a candidate, rerank the remaining four in any desired manner; e.g. dropping E, select $D \succ C \succ B \succ A$, dropping D choose $E \succ A \succ B \sim C$... Next, dropping two candidates creates ten three-candidate subsets: rank each in any desired manner. Finally, rank each pair in any desired manner. For any listing designed in this almost random fashion, there is a profile so that for each subset of candidates, the sincere plurality election outcome is the selected ranking. This conclusion, which holds for any number of candidates, is a discouraging commentary on our standard election method: it means that with the plurality vote "anything can happen."

Beyond the plurality vote, select a positional method for each subset of candidates; e.g. maybe the "vote for three" scheme for five-candidate sets, "vote for two" for four-candidate subsets, and a $(7, 6, 0)$ method for all triplets. The same assertion holds: *for almost all* choices of positional methods, anything can happen. This "almost all" modifier provides hope by suggesting that by carefully selecting voting methods, we might provide consistency among election outcomes. This is the case. It turns out that there are certain special combinations of positional methods that prohibit some ranking lists from ever occurring, so they impose some consistency among the election rankings as candidates are added or dropped. But the choices can be complicated. As an illustration, if four candidate elections are tallied by assigning 3, 1, 0, 0 points, respectively, to a top-, second-, third-, and bottom-ranked candidate, then the four-candidate outcome never bottom-ranks a candidate who wins all three-candidate plurality contests. Rather than describing these complicated results, let me cut to the chase by identifying the unique method with the ultimate consistency.

With n-candidates, the Borda Count assigns a candidate the same number of points as there are lower-ranked candidates on the ballot. So for five candidates, the Borda Count assigns 4, 3, 2, 1, 0 points, respectively, to a top-, second-, third-, fourth-, and bottom-ranked candidate. A main result is that the *maximum consistency in election rankings is attained only by using the Borda Count with all subsets of candidates*. More precisely, any ranking list coming from the Borda Count *also arises with any other combination of voting rules!* But if a non-Borda method is assigned to any subset of candidates, the system generates ranking outcomes that never occur with the Borda method. Moreover, the differences in kinds and numbers of unexpected election outcomes (paradoxes) are mind boggling. To illustrate with seven candidates, it would be impressive if, for instance, the number of plurality ranking lists is three times that of the Borda Count: this multiple would measure the increased inconsistency of the plurality vote. This assertion, however, is far too modest: the plurality vote generates more than 10^{50} more lists than the Borda Count! This number, a 1 followed by fifty zeros, is so large that even if a million of the world's fastest computers started counting at the "Big Bang" they would not be even 1 per cent of the way to this number. The situation becomes worse with eight candidates.

Only the Borda Count provides maximal consistency among election rankings and avoids, by far, the most "paradoxes." To develop some intuition about the source of the Borda Count consistency, consider a voter with preferences $A \succ B \succ C$. In the three pairwise elections, this voter votes as follows:

$$
\begin{array}{c|ccc}
\text{Pair} & A & B & C \\
\hline
\{A, B\} & 1 & 0 & - \\
\{A, C\} & 1 & - & 0 \\
\{B, C\} & - & 1 & 0 \\
\hline
\text{Total} & 2 & 1 & 0
\end{array}
\tag{6}
$$

The bottom "Total" line agrees with the number of points assigned by the Borda Count to candidates for this $A \succ B \succ C$ ranking. (This phenomenon holds for any number of candidates.) In other words, the Borda Count is the natural extension of the pairwise vote because its tally for any candidate equals the sum of votes the candidate would have received in all pairwise comparisons.

5 The "Will of the Voters"

A basic problem remains: how do we determine the "will of the voters?" Maybe, for instance, a "paradox" avoided by the Borda Count best reflects what the voters want. But to know what the voters want, we must concentrate on what they say they want—we must examine the information coming from the profiles. Although obvious, I did not entertain this approach until I recognized that our traditional approach of finding properties of voting rules failed to provide the desired insight. The reason for this failing is that the traditional approach emphasizes partially processed information about the voter preferences rather than preferences. Also, there are too many properties to allow a careful study; e.g. it is impossible in any number of lifetimes to examine the 10^{50} ways the plurality vote differs from *each* list of Borda rankings.

A full description of how to analyze preferences to determine the "will of the voters" is in Saari (1999, 2000, 2001a), so only basic notions are described here. The idea is to find "configurations of preferences" where it is arguable that the outcome should be a complete tie: if a voting rule does not deliver a complete tie, then it may introduce a bias favoring certain candidates. I conjectured that all possible voting differences (for positional, pairwise, and methods based on them) could be explained in this manner. This conjecture turned out to be correct. I indicate what happens for three candidates. (The result holds for any number of candidates (Saari 2000), but a more readable book version is being prepared.)

In selecting these configurations, certain properties must be observed.

1. The configuration must make it arguable that the outcome should be a complete tie.
2. While the outcomes of certain decision rules should be a complete tie, others should not be tied so that we can distinguish among voting rules.
3. Enough configuration of preferences should be found so that all profiles can be analyzed. (But no other configurations as this would become redundant information.)

Surprisingly, for three candidates, only two different configurations of preferences are needed to analyze all possible three-candidate election outcomes. After describing both configurations, I use them to derive some examples and explain some theoretical results in the literature. Details and supporting arguments are left to the references Saari (1999, 2000, 2001a).

Neutral reversal requirement (NRR). Imagine the advantages if your spouse's political views are completely opposite of yours: on a sunny day neither of you needs to vote as your votes would cancel. This is NRR. For example, with the two-voter profile $(A \succ B \succ C, C \succ B \succ A)$, the pairwise majority votes always are tied: a pairwise ranking in $A \succ B \succ C$ is reversed in $C \succ B \succ A$. But with positional methods captured by $(1, s, 0)$, we have the tally:

Ranking	A	B	C
$A \succ B \succ C$	1	s	0
$C \succ B \succ A$	0	s	1
Total	1	$2s$	1

(7)

So, a complete tie vote occurs if and only if $2s = 1$, or with the Borda Count. All other positional methods introduce a bias; e.g. using $s < \frac{1}{2}$ causes a $A \sim C \succ B$ outcome biased against B. Conversely, using $s > \frac{1}{2}$ causes $B \succ A \sim C$ biased in favor of B. The surprising fact (Saari 1999, 2001a) is that *all possible differences among three-candidate positional election outcomes are caused by these NRR reversal components!* Below I use this fact to create profiles.

Neutral Condorcet requirement (NCR). The next set of three-candidate requirements is based on the *Condorcet triplet*. The two sets are

$$A \succ B \succ C, \quad B \succ C \succ A, \quad C \succ A \succ B$$

and

$$A \succ C \succ B, \quad C \succ B \succ A, \quad B \succ A \succ C$$

where a top-ranked candidate is dropped to bottom place in the next ranking. Because each candidate is in first, second, and third place with a Condorcet triplet, it is reasonable to argue that the outcome should be a complete tie: it is for positional outcomes where each candidate's tally is $w_1 + w_2 + w_3$ or $1 + s$.

The pairwise majority vote *refuses* to honor NCR by delivering the $A \succ B$, $B \succ C$, $C \succ A$ cycle for the first Condorcet triplet: each outcome has a 2:1 vote. The reason

(a) NCR and pairwise votes   (b) NRR and positional outcomes

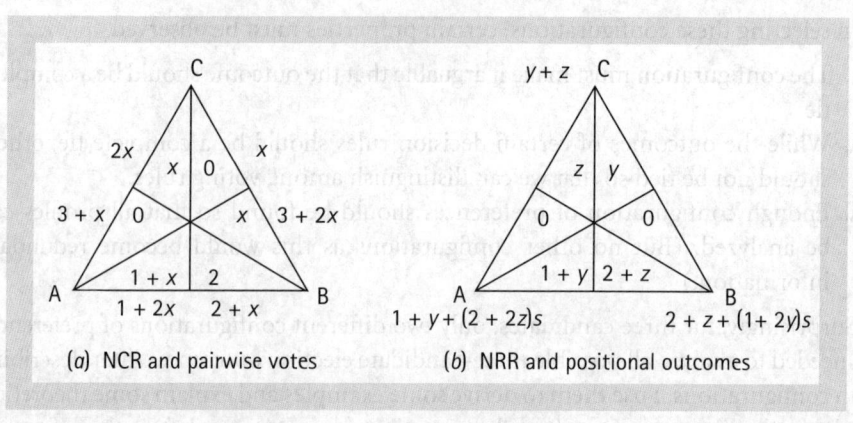

Fig. 22.4 Constructing examples

for this bias is that by myopically concentrating on how a pair fares in each ranking, the pairwise vote misses the broader symmetry supporting a complete tie. Surprisingly (Saari 1999, 2001a), *all possible differences between the Borda Count and pairwise outcomes, and all possible differences among methods based on pairwise outcomes, are caused by profile components given by the Condorcet triplets.*

Constructing examples. Surprisingly, the two-century-old topic of comparing voting procedures reduces to the simple observation whether a profile has components in the NRR and NCR directions. Readers interested in exploring this approach for three candidates should check Saari (1999, 2001a); see Saari (2000) for $n \geq 3$ candidates. To illustrate, I show how to construct examples that do anything that can arise.

Start with the profile where one voter prefers $A \succ B \succ C$ and two prefer $B \succ A \succ C$. This profile has the positional outcomes A, B, C of, respectively, $1 + 2s, 2 + s, 0$. Thus for $s < 1$, the outcome is $B \succ A \succ C$. The pairwise votes are compatible with $B \succ A$, $B \succ C$, $A \succ C$ outcomes that crown Barb as the Condorcet winner. With this profile, most standard methods agree giving the same $B \succ A \succ C$ outcome.

To distort this profile to create the Chair profile, first change the Condorcet winner from B to A without affecting any positional ranking. According to NCR, this requires adding x units of the Condorcet triplet, $A \succ B \succ C, B \succ C \succ A, C \succ A \succ B$, that favors A over B. Adding this configuration, depicted by the x values in Figure 22.4a, has no effect on the positional rankings (each candidate receives the same $x + xs$ bonus points). Figure 22.4a shows that the pairwise tallies are:

$A : B$ with $1 + 2x : 2 + x$, $A : C$ with $3 + x : 2x$, $B : C$ with $3 + 2x : x$.

Thus A is the Condorcet winner with an x value satisfying

$$1 + 2x > 2 + x, \quad 3 + x > 2x,$$

or $x = 2$. These new terms affect the pairwise outcomes but not the positional or Borda outcomes.

Next, add "configurations of preferences" to alter the positional outcomes but not the Borda and pairwise outcomes. According to the above, we must add NRR reversal terms. To make C the plurality winner, add (see Figure 22.4b) y units of $(A \succ B \succ C, C \succ B \succ A)$ and z units of $(C \succ A \succ B, B \succ A \succ C)$. According to Figure 22.4b, the plurality ($s = 0$) tallies for A: B: C are $1 + y : 2 + z : y + z$. So the $C \succ B \succ A$ plurality ranking occurs with y and z values satisfying:

$$y + z > 2 + z > 1 + y.$$

One solution has $y = z = 3$; along with the above $x = 2$, they create the Chair profile. Only the Borda Count satisfies both NRR and NCR, so only this rule is immune to these perturbations: the Borda ranking remains $B \succ A \succ C$. Notice that we could have selected any ranking for the plurality method and created a supporting profile.

Some consequences. Several consequences follow from this construction including the historical debate whether the Condorcet or Borda winner better reflects the voters' beliefs. As indicated above, *all possible differences in the Borda and Condorcet winners are caused by Condorcet terms!* (This statement holds for any number of candidates.) Consequently, this two-century debate reduces to determining the appropriate outcome for the Condorcet triplet. Namely, if you support the Condorcet winner, then you must explain why the Condorcet triplet outcome should not be a tie. As I have never heard a convincing argument, I must support the Borda winner. This comparison of Borda and Condorcet winners is illustrated with the construction of the Chair election example where the bias introduced by Condorcet triplet changes the Condorcet winner from B to A.

As another example, there are many papers that analyze whether a procedure must elect the Condorcet winner. To understand the results, notice from NRR that any non-Borda positional procedure, or rules using these positional procedures, cannot satisfy this condition because their outcomes are changed by adding profile portions with no effect on pairwise outcomes. (This comment is illustrated by the construction of the Chair example.) Because the Condorcet winner can be altered by using Condorcet triplets (or Condorcet n-tuples for $n \geq 3$ candidates), only those procedures based on pairwise outcomes can possibly satisfy this condition.

6 Strategic and Other Behavior

The important Gibbard–Satterthwaite theorem (Gibbard 1973; Satterthwaite 1975) shows that with three or more candidates, all "reasonable" election methods (e.g. where each candidate can be elected and we exclude dictatorial rule) allow settings where it is to the advantage of some voter to vote "strategically" rather than sincerely. By doing so, the voter ensures a personally better election outcome. But we know this; for instance, had more Nader voters voted strategically for Gore in Florida, we would have President Gore instead of President Bush. Beyond strategic voting, there are many other peculiarities; e.g. Fishburn and Brams (1983) showed that with a plurality run-off system, situations occur where a voter obtains a personally better election outcome by *not voting*. Other fascinating examples and problems have been discovered; e.g. with the plurality run-off, a winning candidate could lose by receiving more votes. One of the better references describing these difficulties is Nurmi (2003).

In Saari (1994), I constructed an argument to explain all of these behaviors and to determine whether a specific procedure experiences any of these problems, when this can occur, and how to cause the changed outcome. While it answered the questions, it was technical. So, recently I developed a simpler equivalent approach (Saari 2003). While the explanation is in Saari (2003), let me illustrate the ideas with {Anni, Lillian, Katri} denoted by A, L, and K. If a profile (say, the sincere profile) elects Anni, but an altered form of this profile (say, strategic behavior, or someone not voting, or more voters now supporting Anni, or ...) elects Katri, then in some sense the changed profile moved over the tied Katri–Anni region. Thus, the approach emphasizes tied outcomes as follows:

1. For a given rule, find all scenarios with a nearly tied outcome in some election.
2. Determine how the final outcome changes by breaking the tie in different ways.
3. Determine who could vote differently to break the tie and benefit from the new conclusion.

To illustrate, consider a positional election run-off election with the $L \succ A \succ K$ outcome so A and L advance to the run-off where L beats A to win. Now suppose A and K are nearly tied; e.g. the election outcome is nearly $L \succ A \sim K$. If a change allows K to edge ahead of A, the run-off is between L and K. If K beats L in the run-off, then any way that alters the Anni–Katri near-tie alters the final outcome. Profiles with this behavior exist; we know this from the above "dictionary approach" describing all lists of election rankings. This discussion shows that many profiles define the positional outcome

$$(L \succ A \sim K, L \succ A, K \succ L, K \succ A)$$

where a slight change in the profile, one way or another, breaks the positional tie and retains the pairwise outcomes. To benefit by such actions a voter must prefer $K \succ L$. But to vote strategically for Katri over Anni, he must sincerely prefer $A \succ K$. Consequently, the only voter in this scenario that could alter the outcome has $A \succ K \succ L$ preferences and strategically votes either $K \succ A \succ L$ or $K \succ L \succ A$ to force the Lillian and Katri run-off rather than Anni and Lillian. To create illustrating profiles, use the method in the previous section.

If a voter fails to vote and the outcome changes in his favor, he would have voted for Anni over Katri: he prefers $A \succ K$. For the Katri outcome, rather than Lillian, to be personally better, he prefers $K \succ L$. Hence, only an $A \succ K \succ L$ voter could benefit by not voting. In this simple manner, all of these voting anomalies can be understood and analyzed.

7 ARROW AND SEN

The seminal Arrow's (1951) and Sen's (1970a) theorems have rightfully played a major role in shaping the direction of social choice over the last half-century: both show that assumptions we assume are innocuous, are not. The general interpretation is that these theorems mean that "no decision rule is fair." But this is not the case: both Arrow's and Sen's theorems admit surprisingly benign interpretations that make it possible to find ways to sidestep their conclusions. While the details are described in Saari (2001b), it is worth developing some intuition to understand at least Arrow's result. Related arguments explain Sen's result, which claims there can be serious conflicts between individual rights and unanimity, and I refer the interested reader to Saari (2001b). I also suggest Saari and Petron (2006) to see a surprising interpretation that, rather than an infringement on individual rights, Sen's result could represent a dysfunctional society.

Treat Arrow's theorem as describing the inputs (voters' preferences), outputs (election ranking), and election rule. For inputs, assume that each voter has a complete, transitive ranking of the alternatives with no restrictions. For outputs, assume that the societal ranking is transitive. For the election rules, assume (a *unanimity over a pair* condition) that when everyone has the same ranking of a particular pair, that ranking is the societal outcome: this is called the Pareto condition. After all, if everyone prefers Alice to Carol, we should rebel against a Carol $\succ$ Alice societal ranking.

To motivate the last condition, suppose a prize committee announces their Alice $\succ$ Beth $\succ$ Carol ranking with Alice as the winner. Imagine the reaction from Beth's supporters if they discover that if more committee members had a better opinion of Carol, Beth would have won! What does Carol have to do with the {Alice, Beth} ranking? So *binary independence* (or independence of irrelevant alternatives) asserts that a pair's societal ranking depends strictly on what the voters think of this particular pair: all other information is irrelevant.

While seemingly innocuous, Arrow proved that with three or more alternatives, the only decision rule satisfying these conditions is a dictator! An explanation why this occurs and how to sidestep the conclusion is in Saari (2001b). Here I offer a new intuitive explanation. But first, let me offer an example that builds on experiences all academics have shared with those ballots asking us to vote for one candidate from each school of an university. To simplify the numbers, suppose that three deans are to select a student judiciary committee, where, for obvious reasons, each dean must vote for one of the two candidates from each school. Let the candidates be:

Sciences	Engineering	Arts
Alice	Connie	Elaine
Barb	Diane	Florence

(8)

Suppose by a 2:1 vote, the elected committee is {Alice, Connie, Elaine}. To determine whether this outcome is appropriate, consider all possible voter preferences. Four have one voter preferring one set of candidates, another preferring the opposite committee, and the third voter breaks the tie with his {Alice, Connie, Elaine} choice: it is difficult to argue against the outcome here. The last possibility has the voter preferences {Alice, Connie, Florence}, {Alice, Diane, Elaine}, and {Barb, Connie, Elaine}. But even here the outcome is supported by 2 : 1 votes.

To introduce doubt, suppose the last possibility is the actual vote and it captures the voters' intent to include at least one candidate from the top and bottom lines; maybe these lines are distinguished by race and the deans wanted a mixed-race committee:

	Sciences	Engineering	Arts
Black	Alice	Connie	Elaine
White	Barb	Diane	Florence

(9)

If so, then even though each voter voted consistently with this objective, the outcome violated their intent. This undesired choice is no surprise because the pairwise vote, and any binary independence rule, only examines a particular pair. It cannot, and does not, reflect intended relationships among the pairs. It is unrealistic to expect a voting rule that satisfies binary independence to do this extra duty.

Now alter the example with a name change involving the binary rankings of A, B, C. Namely replace Alice with $A \succ B$, Barb with $B \succ A$, Connie with $B \succ C$, Diane with $C \succ B$, Elaine with $C \succ A$, and Florence with $A \succ C$. With this name change, the "mixed-race rankings" become *transitive rankings*, while the "single race committees" are cyclic rankings. Moreover, the voter rankings {Alice, Connie, Florence}, {Alice, Diane, Elaine}, and {Barb, Connie, Elaine} become the Condorcet triplet $\{A \succ B \succ C, B \succ C \succ A, C \succ A \succ B\}$. Because the two examples differ only by a name change, any comment about the dean selection problem applies to voting over pairs. In particular, because binary independence strips any mixed-race intended relationship from the first problem, *Arrow's theorem occurs because binary independence strips away the intended "transitivity" relationship!* (This is made precise in Saari 2001b.)

By recognizing that binary independence strips away the intended transitivity relationship from preferences, we can rectify the problem: find ways to reintroduce the transitivity information. By doing so, positive assertions are forthcoming; e.g. the Borda Count replaces Arrow's dictator. Incidentally, a similar explanation holds for Sen's theorem.

8 Conclusion

The message of this chapter is that the beautiful results in voting theory and social choice can add an important dimension to our understanding of the strengths and weaknesses of decision rules. While a technical understanding is helpful, it is not necessary. Even developing a basic intuition, which I tried to provide, can eliminate misinterpretations and help us address more subtle election properties.

REFERENCES

Arrow, K. 1951. *Social Choice and Individual Values*. New York: Wiley (2nd edn. 1963).
Brams, S., and Fishburn, P. 1983. *Approval Voting*. Boston: Birkhauser.
Fishburn, P. 1981. Inverted orders for monotone scoring rules. *Discrete Applied Mathematics*, 3: 27–36.
—— and Brams, S. 1983. Paradoxes of preferential voting. *Mathematics Magazine*, 56: 207–14.
Gibbard, A. 1973. Manipulation of voting schemes: a general result. *Econometrica*, 41: 587–601.
Nurmi, H. 2003. *Voting Procedures under Uncertainty*. New York: Springer-Verlag.
Saari, D. G. 1989. A dictionary for voting paradoxes. *Journal of Economic Theory*, 48: 443–75.
—— 1990. The Borda Dictionary. *Social Choice and Welfare*, 7: 279–317.
—— 1994. *Basic Geometry of Voting*. New York: Springer-Verlag.
—— 1995. A chaotic exploration of aggregation paradoxes. *SIAM Review*, 37: 37–52.
—— 1999. Explaining all three-alternative voting outcomes. *Journal of Economic Theory*, 87: 313–35.
—— 2000. Mathematical structure of voting paradoxes. *Economic Theory*, 15: 1–101.
—— 2001a. *Chaotic Elections! A Mathematician Looks at Voting*. Providence, RI: American Mathematical Society.
—— 2001b. *Decisions and Elections: Explaining the Unexpected*. New York: Cambridge University Press.
—— 2003. Disturbing aspects of voting theory. *Economic Theory*, 22: 529–56.
—— and Petron, A. 2006. Negative externalities and Sen's liberalism theorem. *Economic Theory*.
—— and van Newenhizen, J. 1988. Is Approval Voting an "unmitigated evil?" *Public Choice*, 59: 133–47.
Satterthwaite, M. 1975. Strategyproofness and Arrow's conditions. *Journal of Economic Theory*, 10: 187–217.
Sen, A. 1970a. The impossibility of a Paretian liberal. *Journal of Political Economy*, 78: 152–7.
—— 1970b. *Collective Choice and Individual Welfare*. San Francisco: Holden Day.
Tabarrok, A. 2001, Fundamentals of voting theory illustrated with the 1992 election, or could Perot have won in 1992? *Public Choice*, 106: 275–97.
—— and Spector, L. 1999. Would the Borda Count have avoided the civil war? *Journal of Theoretical Politics*, 11: 261–88.

CHAPTER 23

INTERPERSONAL COMPARISONS OF WELL-BEING

CHARLES BLACKORBY
WALTER BOSSERT

1 INTRODUCTION

THIS chapter provides a brief survey of the use of interpersonal comparisons in social evaluation. We focus on principles for social evaluation that are welfarist (Sen 1979): principles that use information about individual well-being to rank alternatives, disregarding all other information. Utility functions are indicators of individual well-being and we use the terms utility and well-being synonymously. Sentient non-human animals have experiences and it is possible to take account of their interests in social evaluation. We focus on human beings in this chapter and refer the interested reader to Blackorby and Donaldson (1992) for a discussion of the ethics of animal exploitation.

We begin with the idea that a society has a number of options from which to choose those that are "best" in some sense. This requires that the society be able to rank the options according to their social goodness. We call these options alternatives; an alternative is a complete description of everything that matters to society. Of course, each individual member of this society can also rank these alternatives in terms of

---

* We thank Barry Weingast and Donald Wittman for comments and suggestions. Financial support through a grant from the Social Sciences and Humanities Research Council of Canada is gratefully acknowledged.

their goodness for herself or himself; in fact, we assume that each individual has a utility function that is an indicator of his or her well-being experienced in the alternatives. A list of utility functions, one function for each individual, is called a utility profile. The social ranking is to be determined by a social evaluation functional. A social evaluation functional associates a social ordering of the alternatives with every utility profile in its domain. Welfarism obtains if and only if there exists a social evaluation ordering of vectors of individual utilities that can be used, together with the information about well-being in a profile, to rank the alternatives.

Welfarist principles regard values such as individual liberty and autonomy as instrumental: valuable because of their contribution to well-being. Because of this, it is important to employ a comprehensive notion of well-being such as that of Griffin (1986). Individuals who are autonomous and fully informed may have self-regarding preferences that accord with their well-being, but we do not assume that they do. If they do, the individual utility functions are representations of these preferences.

Welfarism rests mainly on the view that any two alternatives in which everyone is equally well off are equally good, a condition that is called Pareto indifference. The Pareto indifference axiom is implied by a condition proposed by Goodin (1991). Goodin suggests that if one alternative is declared socially better than another, then the former should be better than the latter for at least one member of society. This is a fundamental property of a principle for social evaluation and we consider it a strong argument in favor of welfarism. Without this requirement, we run the risk of recommending social changes that are empty gestures, benefiting no one and, perhaps, harming some or all.

Because Pareto indifference applies separately to each utility profile, we need a way to require a principle for social evaluation to behave consistently across different profiles. Such a condition is provided by the axiom binary independence of irrelevant alternatives. We say that two utility profiles coincide on an alternative x if each individual's utility of x is the same in both profiles. The independence axiom requires that if two profiles coincide on an alternative x and on an alternative y, then the social ranking of x and y must be the same for both profiles.

The most commonly employed domain of a social evaluation functional consists of all logically possible utility profiles. On this unlimited domain, a social evaluation functional satisfies Pareto indifference and binary independence of irrelevant alternatives if and only if it is welfarist.

Arrow's (1951) fundamental theorem states that there do not exist satisfactory welfarist principles if the only information that can be used in social evaluation is ordinally measurable and interpersonally non-comparable utility information. Sen (1970) shows that the conclusion of Arrow's theorem remains true if Arrow's ordinal interpretation of individual utility is replaced by a cardinal interpretation and no interpersonal comparisons of well-being are permitted. Taking these results as our starting point, we illustrate how the Arrow–Sen impossibility can be avoided if various forms of interpersonal utility comparisons are possible.

Information invariance conditions require that the social evaluation principle respect the informational environment regarding the measurability and interpersonal comparability of well-being. The term measurability refers to the informational contents of individual utility functions and, therefore, is concerned with intrapersonal comparisons of well-being only. In contrast, interpersonal comparability specifies the kind of comparisons that can be made across different individuals.

Two types of measurability assumptions are employed—ordinal measurability and cardinal measurability. If utilities are ordinally measurable, the only information that can be used is information regarding the ranking of the alternatives with respect to their goodness for an individual. Thus, if a utility function is used as a representation of an individual goodness ranking, any utility function that preserves the ranking of alternatives can be used without changing the available information. Because any increasing transformation of a utility function represents the same ranking as the original function, it follows that statements such as "individual i is better off in alternative x than in alternative y" are meaningful because they are preserved by all increasing transformations of i's utility function. In the case of ordinal measurability, an individual utility function is unique up to increasing transformations—all increasing transformations (and only those) preserve the informational contents of the utility function. Ordinal measurability does not permit us to perform intrapersonal comparisons of utility differences. This is guaranteed by cardinal measurability. A cardinal utility function is unique up to increasing affine transformation, that is, transformations whose graphs are positively sloped straight lines. In that case, it follows that statements such as "individual i's difference in well-being between alternatives x and y is greater than the difference in i's well-being between z and w" are meaningful because they are preserved by all admissible transformations in this informational environment.

Measurability assumptions are silent regarding the interpersonal comparability of utilities. To specify what types of comparisons can be carried out across individuals, these assumptions have to be combined with interpersonal comparability requirements. The assumptions we consider in this chapter are ordinal and cardinal non-comparability and, in addition, ordinal and cardinal full comparability. Ordinal and cardinal non-comparability are informational environments that do not allow for any interpersonal comparability. They allow admissible transformations to be independent across individuals and, thus, the only meaningful statements are the intrapersonal comparisons permitted by the corresponding measurability assumption. Ordinal and cardinal full comparability impose restrictions on admissible transformations across individuals. In particular, if utilities are ordinally measurable and interpersonally fully comparable, the only transformations that can be applied are increasing transformations that are common for all individuals. Thus, interpersonal comparisons of utility levels such as "individual i is better off in x than individual j in y" are possible because all these comparisons are preserved if the same transformation is applied to all utilities. In the case of cardinal full comparability, only increasing affine transformations that are the same for all individuals can be applied and, as a consequence, not only utility levels but also utility differences are interpersonally comparable. This is the case because statements such as "the difference between individual i's utility in alternative x and j's utility in y is greater than the difference between k's utility in z and ℓ's utility in w" are preserved if any common increasing affine transformation is applied to all individuals' utilities.

As is standard in the literature, we express information assumptions by specifying the transformations that can be applied to utility profiles without changing their informational contents. If two utility vectors $u = (u_1, \ldots, u_n)$ and $v = (v_1, \ldots, v_n)$ are subjected to a vector of admissible transformations under a given informational environment, information invariance with respect to that environment demands that the social ranking of the transformed vectors is the same as that of u and v.

We review some of the most important characterization results for welfarist social evaluation principles. Due to space limitations, we cannot provide an exhaustive survey but we attempt to mention the most relevant references for further reading. For the same reason, we do not provide any proofs but refer the interested reader to the original contributions or more extensive surveys.

Section 2 introduces our basic notation along with a formal definition of social evaluation functionals. In addition, we present the welfarism theorem which shows that welfarism is a consequence of three fundamental axioms. Because welfarism permits us to work with a single ordering of utility vectors (called a social evaluation ordering), this ordering is employed instead of the social evaluation functional in the remainder of the chapter. In Section 3, we formulate some basic axioms for social evaluation orderings and define the orderings that are of particular importance in this chapter. Information invariance properties are introduced in Section 4, and Section 5 contains an overview of some important results. Section 6 concludes the chapter with a discussion of possible extensions and applications of our model in choice problems.

2 Welfarist Social Evaluation

Consider a society of at least two individuals. There is a set of at least three alternatives and a principle for social evaluation is supposed to rank these alternatives on the basis of the utilities of the members of this society. Individual i's well-being is represented by a utility function U_i that assigns a level of utility (well-being) to each of the alternatives. Thus, $U_i(x)$ is i's well-being in alternative x. Suppose there are n individuals. A utility profile is a vector $U = (U_1, \ldots, U_n)$ of individual utility functions, one for each individual i.

A social evaluation functional assigns a social ranking of alternatives to each profile of utility functions in its domain. Thus, the social ranking depends on the utility profile. The domain of the social evaluation functional is the set of all profiles for which the functional is supposed to generate a social ordering. Although we will impose an unlimited-domain assumption requiring that the social evaluation functional produces a social ranking for any logically possible profile, we note that, in some applications, it may make sense to restrict this domain. For example, in economic environments where the alternatives are allocations of commodity bundles, it is common to restrict the individual utilities by assuming, for instance, that consuming more of all goods is always better than consuming less.

We assume that a social ranking is an ordering—a reflexive, transitive, and complete social goodness relation. A social evaluation functional is welfarist if and only if there exists a social evaluation ordering (referred to as a social welfare ordering by Gevers 1979) on the set of all possible utility vectors such that, for any profile $U = (U_1, \ldots, U_n)$ and for any two alternatives x and y, x is socially at least as good as y for the profile U if and only if the utility vector $u = (u_1, \ldots, u_n) = (U_1(x), \ldots, U_n(x)) = U(x)$ is at least as good as the utility vector $v = (v_1, \ldots, v_n) = (U_1(y), \ldots, U_n(y)) = U(y)$ according to the social evaluation ordering. Welfarism is a consequence of three axioms: unlimited domain, Pareto indifference, and binary independence of irrelevant alternatives. We now provide formal definitions of these axioms.

Unlimited domain requires the social evaluation functional to produce a social ordering for every logically possible utility profile. That is, no individual utility function and no combination of such functions is excluded as a possible way of assigning individual well-being to the alternatives.

Unlimited domain: The social evaluation functional generates a social ordering for every logically possible utility profile.

Pareto indifference demands that if, according to a utility profile U, the individual utilities for two alternatives x and y are the same, then x and y must be equally good according to the social ranking generated by U.

Pareto indifference: For all alternatives x and y and for all profiles U, if $U(x) = U(y)$, then x and y are equally good for the profile U.

Binary independence of irrelevant alternatives is a consistency condition that imposes restrictions across different profiles. If the utilities for two alternatives x and y are the same in two profiles U and V, then the social rankings of x and y resulting from the two profiles should be the same.

Binary independence of irrelevant alternatives: For all alternatives x and y and for all profiles U and V, if $U(x) = V(x)$ and $U(y) = V(y)$, then the ranking of x and y for the profile U is the same as the ranking of x and y for the profile V.

For a social evaluation functional that satisfies unlimited domain, Pareto indifference and binary independence of irrelevant alternatives together are equivalent to welfarism. This result, which is implicit in d'Aspremont and Gevers (1977) and explicit in Hammond (1979), is referred to as the welfarism theorem. It requires our maintained assumption that there are at least three alternatives.

Theorem 1: *Suppose a social evaluation functional satisfies unlimited domain. The social evaluation functional satisfies Pareto indifference and binary independence of irrelevant alternatives if and only if there exists a social evaluation ordering of all utility vectors such that, for all alternatives x and y and for all profiles U, x is at least* as good as y for the profile U if and only if the utility vector U(x) is at least as good as the utility vector U(y) according to the social evaluation ordering.

This result is quite remarkable. It states that, given the welfarism axioms, a single ordering of utility vectors is sufficient to establish the social ranking for any profile. Note that the social evaluation ordering does not depend on the profile under consideration—the same ordering must be used for any profile. Thus, the only information required to rank two alternatives x and y for a profile U consists of the two utility vectors U(x) and U(y); knowledge of any other features of the individual utility functions is not needed.

Blackorby, Bossert, and Donaldson (2005a) prove a generalized version of the welfarism theorem where multiple profiles of individual and social non-welfare information are permitted.

3 Axioms and Examples

We now formulate some basic axioms regarding the social evaluation ordering of utility vectors. The first of these is anonymity. It ensures that the social evaluation ordering treats individuals impartially, paying no attention to their identities: if we relabel the utilities in a utility vector u, the resulting vector is as good as u. Such a relabeling is called a permutation of a utility vector. A permutation of $u = (u_1, \ldots, u_n)$ is a utility vector $v = (v_1, \ldots, v_n)$ such that each index i in u is matched to exactly one index j in v such that $u_i = v_j$. For example, (u_2, u_1, u_3) is a permutation of (u_1, u_2, u_3). Anonymity requires that any permutation of a utility vector u is as good as u itself. This is a strengthening of Arrow's (1951) condition that prevents the existence of a dictator.

> *Anonymity*: For all utility vectors u and v, if v is a permutation of u, then u and v are equally good.

As an example, consider the utility vectors $u = (1, 0, -3)$ and $v = (0, -3, 1)$. v is a permutation of u because $v_1 = u_2$, $v_2 = u_3$, and $v_3 = u_1$. Thus, anonymity requires the two vectors to be equally good.

Pareto principles impose monotonicity properties on the social evaluation ordering. They require that the social evaluation ordering respond positively to increases in utility. The weak Pareto principle requires an increase in everyone's utility to be regarded as a social improvement.

> *Weak Pareto*: For all utility vectors u and v, if $u_i > v_i$ for all i, then u is better than v.

For example, weak Pareto requires that the utility vector $u = (1, -2, 4)$ is better than $v = (-1, -3, 0)$ because everyone is better off in u than in v. In conjunction with anonymity, weak Pareto also implies that if everyone is better off in a permutation of a utility vector u than in v, then u is better than v even if u and v cannot be compared according to the weak Pareto principle alone. For example, let $u = (-2, 1, 4)$ and $v = (-1, -3, 0)$. Weak Pareto alone is silent about the ranking of u and v. However, anonymity implies that u and $(1, -2, 4)$ are equally good and, as mentioned earlier, $(1, -2, 4)$ is better than v by weak Pareto. By transitivity, u must be better than v. (See also Suppes 1966 for a discussion.)

The strong Pareto requirement extends weak Pareto to cases in which no one's utility decreases and at least one individual's well-being increases.

Strong Pareto: For all utility vectors u and v, if $u_i \geq v_i$ for all i with at least one strict inequality, then u is better than v.

To illustrate the difference between strong Pareto and weak Pareto, consider the two utility vectors $u = (2, -2, 0)$ and $v = (2, -3, 0)$. Strong Pareto requires that u is better than v but weak Pareto does not.

Continuity is a condition that prevents the goodness relation from exhibiting "large" changes in response to "small" changes in the utility distribution.

Continuity: For all utility vectors u and v and for all sequences of utility vectors $\langle u^j \rangle_{j=1, 2,...}$ where $u^j = (u^j_1, \ldots, u^j_n)$ for all j,

(a) if the sequence $\langle u^j \rangle_{j=1, 2,...}$ approaches v and u^j is at least as good as u for all j, then v is at least as good as u;
(b) if the sequence $\langle u^j \rangle_{j=1, 2,...}$ approaches v and u is at least as good as u^j for all j, then u is at least as good as v.

To illustrate the continuity axiom, consider the following example. Let $u = (1, -1, -1)$ and $v = (0, 0, 0)$. Suppose that a sequence of utility vectors $\langle u^j \rangle_{j=1, 2,...}$ is given by $u^j = (0, 0, 1/j)$ for all j and that u is at least as good as u^j for all j. Because the sequence $\langle u^j \rangle_{j=1, 2,...}$ approaches v, continuity requires that u is at least as good as v.

The next axiom is an equity requirement; see d'Aspremont and Gevers (1977) and Deschamps and Gevers (1978). It is called minimal equity and, loosely speaking, it requires that the social ordering does not always favor inequality. More precisely, the axiom requires the following. Consider two utility vectors u and v such that the utilities of all but two individuals i and j are the same in u and in v and the utilities of i and j are closer together in u than in v in the sense that $v_j > u_j > u_i > v_i$; that is, in moving from v to u, the better-off individual j loses and the worse-off individual i gains, without reversing their relative ranks. The pair given by $u = (3, 4, 7)$ and $v = (3, 2, 12)$ is an example for such a situation. Individual 1 has the same utility in both, individual 2 is worse off than individual 3 in both vectors, individual 2 gains and individual 3 loses when moving from v to u. An extremely equality-averse ordering would always declare v better than u in these circumstances, and the minimal equity axiom requires that this is not the case: there must be at least one pair of utility vectors u and v with these properties such that u is at least as good as v.

Minimal equity: There exist utility vectors u and v and individuals i and j such that $v_j > u_j > u_i > v_i$, $u_k = v_k$ for all other individuals k and u is at least as good as v.

Finally, we introduce a separability property. This independence condition limits the influence of the well-being of unconcerned individuals on the social ordering. Suppose that a social change affects only the utilities of the members of a population subgroup. Independence of the utilities of unconcerned individuals requires the social assessment of the change to be independent of the utility levels of people outside the sub-group.

Independence of the utilities of unconcerned individuals: For all utility vectors u, v, $\bar{u}$ and $\bar{v}$ and for all sub-groups of individuals, if $u_i = \bar{u}_i$ and $v_i = \bar{v}_i$ for all individuals i in this sub-group, and $u_j = v_j$ and $\bar{u}_j = \bar{v}_j$ for all individuals j not in this sub-group, then u is at least as good as v if and only of $\bar{u}$ is at least as good as $\bar{v}$.

In this definition, the individuals not in the sub-group are the unconcerned—they have the same utilities in u and v and in $\bar{u}$ and $\bar{v}$. Independence of the utilities of unconcerned individuals requires the ranking of u and v to depend on the utilities of the concerned individuals, those in the sub-group, only. The corresponding separability axiom for social evaluation functionals can be found in d'Aspremont and Gevers (1977) where it is called separability with respect to unconcerned individuals. D'Aspremont and Gevers's separability axiom is called elimination of (the influence of) indifferent individuals in Maskin (1978) and in Roberts (1980b). In the case of two individuals, the independence axiom is implied by the strong Pareto principle. Therefore it is usually applied to societies with at least three individuals.

To illustrate this independence condition, consider the utility vectors $u = (2, -1, 0)$, $v = (1, 0, 0)$, $\bar{u} = (2, -1, 5)$, and $\bar{v} = (1, 0, 5)$. Individual 3 is unconcerned when considering the ranking of u and v because her or his utility is the same in both situations. The same is true for $\bar{u}$ and $\bar{v}$—again, individual 3's utility is the same in both. The concerned individuals—individuals 1 and 2—have the same utilities in u and in $\bar{u}$, and in v and in $\bar{v}$. Thus, the ranking of u and v should be the same as the ranking of $\bar{u}$ and $\bar{v}$: the utility level of the unconcerned individual 3 should not influence the social ranking.

We conclude this section with some examples of social evaluation orderings, restricting attention to those characterized in this chapter.

The strongly dictatorial social evaluation orderings pay attention to the utility of a single individual only. That is, a social evaluation ordering is strongly dictatorial if and only if there exists an individual k such that, for all utility vectors u and v, u is at least as good as v if and only if individual k's utility in u is greater than or equal to k's utility in v. For example, suppose we have a strong dictatorship with individual 2 as dictator. Then the utility vector $u = (-5, 2, -1)$ is better than the utility vector $v = (1, 1, 5)$ because $u_2 = 2$ is greater than $v_2 = 1$. Strong dictatorships satisfy weak Pareto, continuity, minimal equity, and independence of the utilities of unconcerned individuals. Anonymity and strong Pareto are violated.

A strong positional dictatorship assigns dictatorial power to a position in the society rather than to a named individual. A social evaluation ordering is a strong positional dictatorship if and only if there exists a position k such that, for all utility vectors u and v, u is at least as good as v if and only if the utility of the kth-best-off individual in u is greater than or equal to the utility of the kth-best-off individual in v. An important special case is the maximin ordering which is obtained for $k = n$, that is, the social ranking is determined by the utility of the worst off. If $k = 1$, the maximax ordering, which pays attention to the best off only, results. Note that strong positional dictatorships are not strong dictatorships because the kth-best-off individual in one utility vector is not necessarily the same as the kth-best-off individual in another. For example, consider the maximin ordering (the strong positional dictatorship where $k = n$) and the utility vectors $u = (2, 1, 3)$ and $v = (0, 1, 4)$. According to maximin, u is better than v because the worst-off individual in u (individual 2) has a higher utility than the worst-off individual in v (individual 1). Strong positional dictatorships satisfy anonymity, weak Pareto, and continuity. They violate strong Pareto and independence of the utilities of unconcerned individuals. All strong positional dictatorships except maximax satisfy minimal equity.

Utilitarianism ranks any two utility vectors by comparing their sums of utilities. Thus, according to utilitarianism, for all utility vectors u and v, u is at least as good as v if and only if the sum of the utilities in u is greater than or equal to the sum of the utilities in v. For example, according to utilitarianism, the utility vectors $u = (1, -1, 0)$ and $(0, 0, 0)$ are equally good because they have the same total utility. Utilitarianism satisfies all of the axioms introduced earlier in this section.

A social evaluation ordering is a weakly utilitarian ordering if and only if it respects the betterness relation of utilitarianism. That is, for all utility vectors u and v, if total utility in u is greater than total utility in v, then u is better than v. Weak utilitarianism is a class of orderings rather than a single ordering because the ranking of two utility vectors with the same total utility is not specified. For example, if $u = (2, -1, 0)$ and $v = (3, 0, -3)$, any weakly utilitarian ordering must declare u better than v because total utility in u is higher. On the other hand, the ranking of $u = (1, -1, 0)$ and $v = (0, 0, 0)$ is not determined: unlike utilitarianism, weak utilitarianism does not require the two vectors to be equally good.

Leximin is a modified version of maximin in which utility vector u is better than utility vector v if the worst-off individual in u is better off than the worst-off individual in v. If these individuals are equally well off, the utilities of the next-worse-off individuals are used to determine the social ranking, and the procedure continues until either there is a strict ranking or the two utility vectors are permutations of each other, in which case they are declared equally good. For example, according to leximin, the utility vector $u = (2, 1, -3)$ is better than the vector $v = (-3, 1, 0)$. This is the case because the worst-off individuals (individual 3 in u, individual 1 in v) are equally well off and the second-worst-off individual in u (individual 2) is better off than the second-worst-off individual in v (individual 3). Leximin satisfies all of our axioms except continuity.

4 INFORMATION INVARIANCE

Information invariance conditions restrict the information regarding the measurability and interpersonal comparability of individual utilities that can be used in social evaluation. As mentioned in the introduction, allowing for interpersonal comparisons of well-being is a promising way out of the negative conclusion of Arrow's theorem which we will discuss shortly. The most common way to represent informational environments is to define the set of invariance transformations that can be applied to utility vectors without changing their informational contents. Information invariance with respect to the information assumption represented by the set of admissible transformations then requires that the ranking of any two utility vectors is the same as the ranking of the transformed vectors. This approach was developed in contributions such as d'Aspremont and Gevers (1977), Roberts (1980a, 1980b), and Sen (1974) and we follow it in this chapter. We present the information invariance assumptions that are used in the remainder of the chapter and refer the reader to Blackorby and Donaldson (1982), Blackorby, Donaldson, and Weymark (1984), Bossert and Weymark (2004), d'Aspremont (1985), d'Aspremont and Gevers (1977, 2002), DeMeyer and Plott (1971), Dixit (1980), Gevers (1979), Roberts (1980b), and Sen (1970, 1974, 1977, 1986), for example, for more extensive discussions.

If the only information that can be used is ordinal utility information without interpersonal comparability, we obtain Arrow's (1951) informational environment that requires information invariance with respect to ordinal non-comparability. The set of admissible transformations consists of all vectors of independent increasing transformations.

Information invariance with respect to ordinal non-comparability: For all utility vectors u and v and for all increasing functions $\Phi_1, \ldots, \Phi_n$, u is at least as good as v if and only if $(\Phi_1(u_1), \ldots, \Phi_n(u_n))$ is at least as good as $(\Phi_1(v_1), \ldots, \Phi_n(v_n))$.

Ordinal non-comparability implies that intrapersonal comparisons of utility levels are possible. This is the case because an inequality such as $u_i \geq v_i$ is preserved whenever an increasing transformation is applied to all utility values of individual i: we have $u_i \geq v_i$ if and only if $\Phi_i(u_i) \geq \Phi_i(v_i)$ for all increasing functions Φ_i. Interpersonal comparisons of utility levels are not possible in this informational environment. For example, suppose that $u_i = 1$ and $v_j = 0$. Clearly, $u_i > v_j$. However, under ordinal non-comparability, this inequality does not permit us to say that individual i is better off in utility vector u than individual j in v because the inequality is not preserved by all vectors of admissible transformations. Letting $\Phi_i(u_i) = u_i$ and $\Phi_j(v_j) = v_j + 2$, it follows that $\Phi_i(u_i) = 1 < 2 = \Phi_j(v_j)$ and the inequality is reversed. Of the social evaluation orderings defined in the previous section, only strong dictatorships satisfy information invariance with respect to ordinal non-comparability.

If utilities are cardinally measurable and no requirements regarding the interpersonal comparison of utilities are imposed, we obtain the information assumption cardinal non-comparability.

Information invariance with respect to cardinal non-comparability: For all utility vectors u and v, for all positive constants $a_1, \ldots, a_n$ and for all constants $b_1, \ldots, b_n$, u is at least as good as v if and only if $(a_1 u_1 + b_1, \ldots, a_n u_n + b_n)$ is at least as good as $(a_1 v_1 + b_1, \ldots, a_n v_n + b_n)$.

Information invariance with respect to ordinal non-comparability and information invariance with respect to cardinal non-comparability are equivalent (see Sen 1970 and, for a diagrammatic illustration, Blackorby, Donaldson, and Weymark 1984). Intuitively, this is the case because, for any two utility vectors u and v and for any vector of increasing transformations, the values of the transformations can be replicated by the values of a vector of increasing affine transformations because a straight line is determined by two points on that line. As an immediate consequence of this equivalence, it follows that, among the social evaluation orderings of the previous section, strong dictatorships are the only ones satisfying information invariance with respect to cardinal non-comparability.

If utility levels are comparable both intrapersonally and interpersonally but no further information is available, we obtain ordinal full comparability. In that case, only common increasing transformations can be applied to the utilities without changing the information relevant for social evaluation.

Information invariance with respect to ordinal full comparability: For all utility vectors u and v and for all increasing functions Φ_0, u is at least as good as v if and only if $(\Phi_0(u_1), \ldots, \Phi_0(u_n))$ is at least as good as $(\Phi_0(v_1), \ldots, \Phi_0(v_n))$.

Ordinal full comparability implies that utility levels can be compared interpersonally. The inequality $u_i \geq v_j$ is preserved even for different individuals i and j if a common transformation Φ_0 is applied to all utility values: we have $u_i \geq v_j$ if and only if $\Phi_0(u_i) \geq \Phi_0(v_i)$ for all increasing functions Φ_0. Comparisons of utility differences are not possible in this informational environment, either intrapersonally or interpersonally. For example, suppose that $u_i = 2$, $v_i = 0$, $w_i = 3$, and $t_i = 2$. We have $u_i - v_i = 2 > 1 = w_i - t_i$. However, this inequality is not preserved if an arbitrary increasing transformation is applied to the individual utilities. Letting $\Phi_i(u_i) = u_i^3$, it follows that $\Phi_i(u_i) - \Phi_i(v_i) = 8 < 19 = \Phi_i(w_i) - \Phi_i(t_i)$ and the inequality is reversed. Information invariance with respect to ordinal full comparability is satisfied by the strongly dictatorial social evaluation orderings, the strong positional dictatorships, and leximin. Utilitarianism does not satisfy this invariance property.

If utilities are cardinally measurable and fully interpersonally comparable, both utility levels and utility differences can be compared interpersonally. In this case, the only admissible transformations are increasing affine transformations which are identical across individuals.

Information invariance with respect to cardinal full comparability: For all utility vectors u and v, for all positive constants a_0 and for all constants b_0, u is at least as good as v if and only if $(a_0 u_1 + b_0, \ldots, a_0 u_n + b_0)$ is at least as good as $(a_0 v_1 + b_0, \ldots, a_0 v_n + b_0)$.

Utility levels and utility differences can be compared because inequalities both of the form $u_i \geq v_j$ and of the form $u_i - v_j \geq w_k - t_\ell$ are preserved if a common increasing affine transformation is applied to all utilities. This information invariance axiom is satisfied by the strong dictatorships, the strong positional dictatorships, utilitarianism, and leximin.

5 IMPOSSIBILITIES AND CHARACTERIZATIONS

In the absence of interpersonal comparisons of well-being, there do not exist satisfactory social evaluation principles. A variant of Arrow's (1951) theorem (see also Blau 1957) formulated for social evaluation orderings states that only strong dictatorships satisfy weak Pareto, continuity, and information invariance with respect to ordinal non-comparability.

Theorem 2: *A social evaluation ordering satisfies weak Pareto, continuity, and information invariance with respect to ordinal non-comparability if and only if it is a strong dictatorship.*

Sen (1970) proves that replacing information invariance with respect to ordinal non-comparability by information invariance with respect to cardinal non-comparability does not provide an escape from the negative conclusion of Arrow's theorem. This observation is an immediate consequence of the equivalence of the two information invariance conditions mentioned in the previous section. Thus, we obtain the following result.

Theorem 3: *A social evaluation ordering satisfies weak Pareto, continuity, and information invariance with respect to cardinal non-comparability if and only if it is a strong dictatorship.*

Clearly, strongly dictatorial principles are not anonymous and, therefore, if this impartiality requirement is added to the list of axioms in Theorem 2 or in Theorem 3, an impossibility results. Continuity is not required in this impossibility theorem.

Theorem 4: *There exists no social evaluation ordering satisfying anonymity, weak Pareto, and information invariance with respect to ordinal or cardinal non-comparability.*

The impossibility result of Theorem 4 remains true if anonymity is weakened to the requirement that rules out the existence of a dictator (see Arrow 1951).

The conclusion we draw from Theorem 4 is that interpersonal comparisons of utility must be permitted to obtain reasonable principles for social evaluation. One possibility is to replace information invariance with respect to ordinal or cardinal non-comparability by information invariance with respect to ordinal full comparability. If anonymity, weak Pareto, and continuity are added, we obtain a characterization of the class of strong positional dictatorships.

Theorem 5: *A social evaluation ordering satisfies anonymity, weak Pareto, continuity, and information invariance with respect to ordinal full comparability if and only if it is a strong positional dictatorship.*

We now discuss some axiomatizations of the utilitarian and leximin principles. In addition to having an information invariance assumption as one of the axioms, another common feature of the remaining results is that they all employ the separability condition independence of the utilities of unconcerned individuals. For that reason, they all require the assumption that there are at least three individuals; for two individuals, the axiom has no additional power given that the strong Pareto principle is also imposed.

Deschamps and Gevers (1978) examine the class of social evaluation orderings satisfying information invariance with respect to cardinal full comparability. If this axiom is added to anonymity, strong Pareto, minimal equity, and independence of the utilities of unconcerned individuals, only weakly utilitarian orderings and leximin remain as possibilities.

Theorem 6: *Suppose there are at least three individuals. If a social evaluation ordering satisfies anonymity, strong Pareto, minimal equity, independence of the utilities of unconcerned individuals, and information invariance with respect to cardinal full comparability, then it is weakly utilitarian or leximin.*

Some remarks regarding the role played by the various axioms in the theorem statement are in order. Anonymity and strong Pareto ensure that the principle is impartial and responds positively to increases in individual utilities. The independence condition plays an important role because it brings out the separability property that is shared by utilitarianism and leximin. Although other principles (such as generalized utilitarianism which uses the sum of transformed utilities instead of the sum of utilities; see, for instance, Blackorby, Bossert, and Donaldson 2002) satisfy this property, they are ruled out by information invariance with respect to cardinal full comparability. This assumption ensures that, in addition to utility levels, utility differences are interpersonally comparable and the linearity of (weak) utilitarianism guarantees that these principles satisfy the requirement whereas other generalized utilitarian orderings do not. Minimal equity is required merely to rule out the extremely equality-averse leximax ordering. Leximax proceeds analogously to leximin but it starts by comparing the utilities of the best off and works its way down to the worst off in case of ties.

Theorem 6 is not an if-and-only-if result because not all weakly utilitarian orderings satisfy all axioms: the axioms also place restrictions on how a weakly utilitarian ordering ranks utility vectors which have the same sum. However, it shows that there do not exist many orderings other than utilitarianism and leximin satisfying the axioms of the theorem statement. The following two theorems illustrate how utilitarianism or leximin can be obtained by modifying one or another of the axioms.

We begin with utilitarianism, which has received a considerable amount of attention in the literature on social choice. The following theorem is due to Maskin (1978; see also Deschamps and Gevers 1978). It is obtained by replacing minimal equity with continuity in Theorem 6.

> **Theorem 7:** *Suppose there are at least three individuals. A social evaluation ordering satisfies anonymity, strong Pareto, continuity, independence of the utilities of unconcerned individuals, and information invariance with respect to cardinal full comparability if and only if it is utilitarian.*

Theorem 7 illustrates the power of the continuity axiom. Leximin clearly is not continuous and neither is leximax. Consequently, neither of these principles survives if this property is added. Because minimal equity is required in Theorem 6 only to exclude leximax, it is no longer needed in Theorem 7 because this principle is already ruled out by continuity. Continuity also forces equal goodness according to utilitarianism to be respected if the corresponding betterness relation is respected and, therefore, utilitarianism rather than the weakly utilitarian rules are obtained.

D'Aspremont and Gevers (1977) provide an alternative characterization of utilitarianism that does not require the independence axiom (see also Blackwell and Girshick 1954; Milnor 1954; and Roberts 1980*b*).

A characterization of the leximin ordering due to d'Aspremont and Gevers (1977) replaces information invariance with respect to cardinal full comparability by information invariance with respect to ordinal full comparability in Theorem 6.

> **Theorem 8:** *Suppose there are at least three individuals. A social evaluation ordering satisfies anonymity, strong Pareto, minimal equity, independence of the utilities of unconcerned individuals, and information invariance with respect to ordinal full comparability if and only if it is leximin.*

Clearly, ordinal full comparability rules out all weakly utilitarian principles (including utilitarianism itself) and, as a consequence, Theorem 8 follows immediately from Theorem 6.

Hammond (1976) provides an alternative characterization of leximin. Because it does not employ an information invariance condition, we do not state it here.

6 Concluding Remarks

This chapter provides a brief introduction to welfarist social choice theory. It is argued that the most promising route of escape from the negative conclusion of Arrow's theorem is to consider informational environments that allow for interpersonal comparisons of well-being.

We focus on establishing a social ranking of alternatives in this chapter. Because actual decision problems typically are choice problems, it is natural to ask what to do about constraints facing a society, such as those resulting from resource limitations. The approach to constrained social choice implicitly followed in this chapter is that of constrained optimization. We propose to select, for each choice problem identified by a feasible set of alternatives, a best element according to the social objective represented by the social ordering. If the suitability of a social objective on ethical grounds is independent of the constraints (a position we advocate), our approach which does not model constraints explicitly does not involve any loss of generality.

The model discussed in this chapter can be generalized in various ways. Two of the most important extensions involve considerations of uncertainty and the possibility of population change. Due to space constraints, we cannot present them in detail and provide brief summaries instead, accompanied by some suggestions for further reading.

Welfarist social evaluation under uncertainty is discussed, for example, in Blackorby, Bossert, and Donaldson (2002, 2003), Blackorby, Donaldson, and Weymark (1999, 2006), Harsanyi (1955, 1977), Mongin (1994), and Weymark (1991, 1993, 1994, 1995). While most contributions (such as those of Harsanyi) focus on the ranking of probability distributions, an attractive alternative is to fix the probabilities of the possible states that may occur and represent the social choice situation under uncertainty by considering prospects—vectors of alternatives, one for each possible state that may materialize. This model is a natural generalization of the one considered here. Instead of actual (*ex post*) utility functions, *ex ante* utilities are employed and a welfarism theorem that is formulated in terms of *ex ante* utility functions is obtained. See Blackorby, Bossert, and Donaldson (2003) for details.

Variable population social choice is discussed, for example, in Blackorby and Donaldson (1984) and in Blackorby, Bossert, and Donaldson (2005*b*). As is the case for uncertainty, natural generalizations of welfarism can be characterized if the population is allowed to vary from one alternative to another. Moreover, the model can be extended to cover both uncertainty and variable population issues at the same time.

References

Arrow, K. 1951. *Social Choice and Individual Values*. New York: Wiley (2nd edn. 1963).
Blackorby, C., Bossert, W., and Donaldson, D. 2002. Utilitarianism and the theory of justice. Pp. 543–96 in *The Handbook of Social Choice and Welfare*, vol. i, ed. K. Arrow, A. Sen, and K. Suzumura. Amsterdam: Elsevier.
—— —— —— 2003. Harsanyi's theorem: a multi-profile approach and variable-population extensions. Discussion Paper 03–2003, Université de Montréal, CIREQ.

__ __ __ 2005a. Multi-profile welfarism: a generalization. *Social Choice and Welfare*, 24: 253–67.

__ __ __ 2005b. *Population Issues in Social-Choice Theory, Welfare Economics and Ethics.* Cambridge: Cambridge University Press.

__ and DONALDSON, D. 1982. Ratio-scale and translation-scale full interpersonal comparability without domain restrictions: admissible social evaluation functions. *International Economic Review*, 23: 249–68.

__ __ 1984. Social criteria for evaluating population change. *Journal of Public Economics*, 25: 13–33.

__ __ 1992. Pigs and guinea pigs: a note on the ethics of animal exploitation. *Economic Journal*, 102: 1345–69.

__ __ and WEYMARK, J. 1984. Social choice with interpersonal utility comparisons: a diagrammatic introduction. *International Economic Review*, 25: 327–56.

__ __ __ 1999. Harsanyi's social aggregation theorem for state-contingent alternatives. *Journal of Mathematical Economics*, 32: 365–87.

__ __ __ 2006. Social aggregation and the expected utility hypothesis. In *Justice, Political Liberalism, and Utilitarianism: Themes from Harsanyi and Rawls*, ed. M. Salles and J. Weymark. Cambridge: Cambridge University Press, forthcoming.

BLACKWELL, D., and GIRSHICK, M. 1954. *Theory of Games and Statistical Decisions.* New York: Wiley.

BLAU, J. 1957. The existence of social welfare functions. *Econometrica*, 25: 302–13.

BOSSERT, W., and WEYMARK, J. 2004. Utility in social choice. Pp. 1099–177 in *The Handbook of Utility Theory*, vol. ii: *Extensions*, ed. S. Barberà, P. Hammond, and C. Seidl. Dordrecht: Kluwer.

D'ASPREMONT, C. 1985. Axioms for social welfare orderings. Pp. 19–76 in *Social Goals and Social Organizations: Essays in Memory of Elisha Pazner*, ed. L. Hurwicz, D. Schmeidler, and H. Sonnenschein. Cambridge: Cambridge University Press.

__ and GEVERS, L. 1977. Equity and the informational basis of collective choice. *Review of Economic Studies*, 44: 199–209.

__ __ 2002. Social welfare functionals and interpersonal comparability. Pp. 459–541 in *The Handbook of Social Choice and Welfare*, vol. i, ed. K. Arrow, A. Sen, and K. Suzumura. Amsterdam: Elsevier.

DEMEYER, F., and PLOTT, C. 1971. A welfare function using "relative intensity" of preference. *Quarterly Journal of Economics*, 85: 179–86.

DESCHAMPS, R., and GEVERS, L. 1978. Leximin and utilitarian rules: a joint characterization. *Journal of Economic Theory*, 17: 143–63.

DIXIT, A. 1980. Interpersonal comparisons and social welfare functions. Unpublished manuscript, University of Warwick, Dept. of Economics.

GEVERS, L. 1979. On interpersonal comparability and social welfare orderings. *Econometrica*, 47: 75–89.

GOODIN, R. 1991. Utility and the good. Pp. 241–8 in *A Companion to Ethics*, ed. P. Singer. Oxford: Basil Blackwell.

GRIFFIN, J. 1986. *Well-Being: Its Meaning, Measurement, and Moral Importance.* Oxford: Clarendon Press.

HAMMOND, P. 1976. Equity, Arrow's conditions, and Rawls' difference principle. *Econometrica*, 44: 793–804.

__ 1979. Equity in two person situations: some consequences. *Econometrica*, 47: 1127–35.

HARSANYI, J. 1955. Cardinal welfare, individualistic ethics, and interpersonal comparisons of utility. *Journal of Political Economy*, 63: 309–21.

HARSANYI, J. 1977. *Rational Behavior and Bargaining Equilibrium in Games and Social Situations*. Cambridge: Cambridge University Press.

MASKIN, E. 1978. A theorem on utilitarianism. *Review of Economic Studies*, 45: 93–6.

MILNOR, J. 1954. Games against nature. Pp. 49–59 in *Decision Processes*, ed. R. Thrall, C. Coombs, and R. Davis. New York: Wiley.

MONGIN, P. 1994. Harsanyi's aggregation theorem: multi-profile version and unsettled questions. *Social Choice and Welfare*, 11: 331–54.

ROBERTS, K. 1980a. Possibility theorems with interpersonally comparable welfare levels. *Review of Economic Studies*, 47: 409–20.

—— 1980b. Interpersonal comparability and social choice theory. *Review of Economic Studies*, 47: 421–39.

SEN, A. 1970. *Collective Choice and Social Welfare*. San Francisco: Holden-Day.

—— 1974. Informational bases of alternative welfare approaches: aggregation and income distribution. *Journal of Public Economics*, 3: 387–403.

—— 1977. On weights and measures: informational constraints in social welfare analysis. *Econometrica*, 45: 1539–72.

—— 1979. Personal utilities and public judgements: or what's wrong with welfare economics?. *Economic Journal*, 89: 537–58.

—— 1986. Social choice theory. Pp. 1073–181 in *The Handbook of Mathematical Economics*, vol. iii, ed. K. Arrow and M. Intriligator. Amsterdam: North-Holland.

SUPPES, P. 1966. Some formal models of grading principles. *Synthese*, 6: 284–306.

WEYMARK, J. 1991. A reconsideration of the Harsanyi–Sen debate on utilitarianism. Pp. 255–320 in *Interpersonal Comparisons of Well-Being*, ed. J. Elster and J. Roemer. Cambridge: Cambridge University Press.

—— 1993. Harsanyi's social aggregation theorem and the weak Pareto principle. *Social Choice and Welfare*, 10: 209–22.

—— 1994. Harsanyi's social aggregation theorem with alternative Pareto principles. Pp. 869–87 in *Models and Measurement of Welfare and Inequality*, ed. W. Eichhorn. Berlin: Springer.

—— 1995. Further remarks on Harsanyi's social aggregation theorem and the weak Pareto principle. *Social Choice and Welfare*, 12: 87–92.

CHAPTER 24

FAIR DIVISION

STEVEN J. BRAMS

1 Introduction

The literature on fair division has burgeoned in recent years, with five academic books (Young 1994; Brams and Taylor 1996; Robertson and Webb 1998; Moulin 2003; Barbanel 2005) and one popular book (Brams and Taylor 1999b) providing overviews. In this review, I will give a brief survey of three different literatures: (i) division of a single heterogeneous good (e.g. a cake with different flavors or toppings); (ii) division, in whole or part, of several divisible goods; and (iii) allocation of several indivisible goods. In each case, I assume that different people, called *players*, may have different preferences for the items being divided.

For (i) and (ii), I will describe and illustrate procedures for dividing divisible goods fairly, based on different criteria of fairness. For (iii), I will discuss problems that arise in allocating indivisible goods, highlighting trade-offs that must be made when not all criteria of fairness can be satisfied simultaneously.

2 Single Heterogeneous Good

The metaphor I use for a single heterogeneous good is a cake, with different flavors or toppings, that cannot be cut into pieces that have exactly the same composition. Unlike a sponge or layer cake, different players may like different pieces—even if they are the same physical size—because they are not homogeneous.

* I am grateful to the editors for their valuable comments on an earlier draft.

Some of the cake-cutting procedures that have been proposed are discrete, whereby players make cuts with a knife—usually in a sequence of steps—but the knife is not allowed to move continuously over the cake. Moving-knife procedures, on the other hand, permit such continuous movement and allow players to call "stop" at any point at which they want to make a cut or mark.

There are now about a dozen procedures for dividing a cake among three players, and two procedures for dividing a cake among four players, such that each player is assured of getting a most valued or tied-for-most-valued piece (Brams, Taylor, and Zwicker 1995; Barbanel and Brams 2004). When a cake can be so divided, no player will envy another player, resulting in an *envy-free division*.

In the literature on cake-cutting, two assumptions are commonly made:

1. The goal of each player is to maximize the minimum-valued piece (*maximin piece*) he or she can guarantee for himself or herself, regardless of what the other players do. To be sure, a player might do better by not following such a *maximin strategy*; this will depend on the strategy choices of the other players. However, all players are assumed to be *risk averse*: They never choose strategies that might yield them larger pieces if they entail the possibility of giving them less than their maximin pieces.
2. The preferences of the players over the cake are continuous. Consider a procedure in which a knife moves across a cake from left to right and, at any moment, the piece of the cake to the left of the knife is A and the piece to the right is B. The continuity assumption enables one to use the intermediate value theorem to say the following: if, for some position of the knife, a player views piece A as being larger than piece B, and for some other position he or she views piece B as being larger than piece A, then there must be some intermediate position such that the player values the two pieces exactly the same.

Only two three-person procedures (Stromquist 1980; Barbanel and Brams 2004), and no four-person procedure, make an envy-free division with the minimal number of cuts ($n - 1$ cuts if there are n players). A cake so cut ensures that each player gets a single connected piece, which is especially desirable in certain applications (e.g. land division).

For two players, the well-known procedure of "I cut the cake, you choose a piece," or "cut-and-choose," leads to an envy-free division if the players choose maximin strategies. The cutter divides the cake 50–50 in terms of his or her preferences. (Physically, the two pieces may be of different size, but the cutter values them the same.) The chooser takes the piece he or she values more and leaves the other piece for the cutter (or chooses randomly if the two pieces are tied in his or her view). Clearly, these strategies ensure that each player gets at least half the cake, as he or she values it, proving that the division is envy free.

But this procedure does not satisfy other desirable properties. For example, if the cake is, say, half vanilla, which the cutter values at 75 per cent, and half chocolate, which the chooser values at 75 per cent, a "pure" vanilla–chocolate division would be better for both players than the divide-and-choose division, which gives each player

50 per cent vanilla and 50 per cent chocolate, or each exactly 50 per cent of the value of the cake.[1]

The moving-knife equivalent of "I cut, you choose" is for a knife to move continuously across the cake, say from left to right. Assume that the cake is cut when one player calls "stop." If each of the players calls "stop" when he or she perceives the knife to be at a 50–50 point, then the first player to call "stop" will produce an envy-free division if the cake is cut at this point and the first player gets the left piece, which as the cutter he or she values at 50 per cent, and the other player gets the right piece, which as the chooser he or she values more. (If both players call "stop" at the same time, the pieces can be randomly assigned to the two players.) To be sure, if the player who would truthfully call "stop" first knows the other player's preferences and delays calling "stop" until just before the knife would reach the other player's 50–50 point, the first player can obtain a greater-than-50 per cent share on the left. However, the possession of such information by the cutter is not generally assumed in justifying cut-and-choose, though it does not undermine an envy-free division.

Surprisingly, to go from two players making one cut to three players making two cuts cannot be done by a discrete procedure if the division is to be envy free.[2] The three-person discrete procedure that uses the fewest cuts is one discovered independently by John L. Selfridge and John H. Conway about 1960; it is described in, among other places, Brams and Taylor (1996) and Robertson and Webb (1998) and requires up to five cuts.

Although there is no discrete four-person envy-free procedure that uses a bounded number of cuts, Brams, Taylor, and Zwicker (1997) and Barbanel and Brams (2004) give moving-knife procedures that require up to eleven and five cuts, respectively. The Brams–Taylor–Zwicker (1997) procedure is arguably simpler because it requires fewer simultaneously moving knives. Peterson and Su (2002) give a four-person envy-free moving-knife procedure for chore division, whereby each player thinks he or she receives the least undesirable chores, that requires up to sixteen cuts.

To illustrate ideas, I will describe the Barbanel–Brams (2004) three-person, two-cut envy-free procedure, which is based on the idea of squeezing a piece by moving two knives simultaneously.[3] This procedure, however, is not as complex as Brams and Taylor's (1995) general n-person discrete procedure. Their procedure illustrates the price one must pay for an envy-free procedure that works for all n, because it places no upper bound on the number of cuts that are required to produce an envy-free division; this is also true of other n-person envy-free procedures (Robertson and Webb 1997; Pikhurko 2000). While the number of cuts needed depends on the players' preferences over the cake, it is worth noting that Su's (1999) approximate envy-free

---

[1] For different procedures to attenuate this and other problems, see Brams, Jones, and Klamler 2004.
[2] Robertson and Webb 1998, 28–9; additional information on the minimum numbers of cuts required to give envy-freeness is given in Even and Paz 1984, and Shishido and Zeng 1999.
[3] The Barbanel–Brams (2004) four-person, five-cut envy-free procedure also uses this idea, but it is considerably more complicated and will not be described here. For recent results on pie-cutting, in which radial cuts are made from the center of a pie to divide it into wedge-shaped pieces, see Barbanel and Brams 2006, and Brams, Jones, and Klamler 2006b.

procedure uses the minimal number of cuts at the cost of only small departures from envy-freeness.[4]

I next describe the Barbanel–Brams three-person, two-cut envy-free procedure, called the *squeezing procedure* (Barbanel and Brams 2004). I refer to players by number—player 1, player 2, and so on—calling even-numbered players "he" and odd-numbered players "she." Although cuts are made by two knives in the end, initially one player makes "marks," or virtual cuts, on the line segment defining the cake; these marks may subsequently be changed by another player before the real cuts are made.

Squeezing procedure. A referee moves a knife from left to right across a cake. The players are instructed to call "stop" when the knife reaches the 1/3 point for each. Let the first player to call "stop" be player 1. (If two or three players call "stop" at the same time, randomly choose one.) Have player 1 place a mark at the point where she calls "stop" (the right boundary of piece A in the diagram), and a second mark to the right that bisects the remainder of the cake (the right boundary of piece B). Thereby player 1 indicates the two points that, for her, trisect the cake into pieces A, B, and C, which will be assigned after possible modifications.

```
      A             B              C
/----------|-------------|-----------/
           1             1
```

Because neither player 2 nor player 3 called "stop" before player 1 did, each of players 2 and 3 thinks that piece A is at most 1/3. They are then asked whether they prefer piece B or piece C. There are three cases to consider:

1. If players 2 and 3 each prefer a different piece—one player prefers piece B and the other piece C—we are done: Players 1, 2, and 3 can each be assigned a piece that they consider to be at least tied for largest.
2. Assume players 2 and 3 both prefer piece B. A referee places a knife at the right boundary of B and moves it to the left. At the same time, player 1 places a knife at the left boundary of B and moves it to the right in such a way that the value of cake traversed on the left (by B's knife) and right (by the referee's knife) are equal for player 1. Thereby pieces A and C increase equally in player 1's eyes. At some point, piece B will be diminished sufficiently to a new piece, labeled B'—in either player 2's or player 3's eyes—to tie with either piece A' or C', the enlarged A and C pieces. Assume player 2 is the first, or tied for the first, to call "stop" when this happens; then give player 3 piece B', which she still thinks is the most valued or the tied-for-most-valued piece. Give player 2 the piece he thinks ties for most valued with piece B' (say, piece A'), and give player 1 the remaining piece (piece C'), which she thinks ties for most valued with the other enlarged piece (A'). Clearly, each player will think he or she received at least a tied-for-most-valued piece.

---

[4] See Brams and Kilgour 2001; Haake, Raith, and Su 2002; Potthoff 2002; and Abdul Kadiroglu, Sönmez, and Unver 2004 for other approaches, based on bidding, to the housemates problem discussed in Su 1999. On approximate solutions to envy-freeness, see Zeng 2000.

3. Assume players 2 and 3 both prefer piece C. A referee places a knife at the right boundary of B and moves it to the right. Meanwhile, player 1 places a knife at the left boundary of B and moves it to the right in such a way as to maintain the equality, in her view, of pieces A and B as they increase. At some point, piece C will be diminished sufficiently to C′—in either player 2's or player 3's eyes—to tie with either piece A′ or B′, the enlarged A and B pieces. Assume player 2 is the first, or the tied for first, to call "stop" when this happens; then give player 3 piece C′, which she still thinks is the most valued or the tied-for-most-valued piece. Give player 2 the piece he thinks ties for most valued with piece C′ (say, piece A′), and give player 1 the remaining piece (piece B′), which she thinks ties for most valued with the other enlarged piece (A′). Clearly, each player will think he or she received at least a tied-for-most-valued piece.

Note that who moves a knife or knives varies, depending on what stage is reached in the procedure. In the beginning, I assume a referee moves a single knife, and the first player to call "stop" (player 1) then trisects the cake. But, at the next stage of the procedure, in cases (2) and (3), it is a referee and player 1 that move two knives simultaneously, "squeezing" what players 2 and 3 consider to be the most valued piece until it eventually ties, for one of them, with one of the two other pieces.

3 SEVERAL DIVISIBLE GOODS

Most disputes—divorce, labor–management, merger–acquisition, and international—involve only two parties, but they frequently involve several homogeneous goods that must be divided, or several issues that must be resolved.[5] As an example of the latter, consider an executive negotiating an employment contract with a company. The issues before them are (1) bonus on signing, (2) salary, (3) stock options, (4) title and responsibilities, (5) performance incentives, and (6) severance pay (Brams and Taylor 1999a).

The procedure I describe next, called *adjusted winner* (AW), is a two-player procedure that has been applied to disputes ranging from interpersonal to international (Brams and Taylor 1996, 1999b).[6] It works as follows. Two parties in a dispute, after perhaps long and arduous bargaining, reach agreement on (i) what issues need to be settled and (ii) what winning and losing means for each side on each issue. For example, if the executive wins on the bonus, it will presumably be some amount that the company considers too high but, nonetheless, is willing to pay. On the other hand, if the executive loses on the bonus, the reverse will hold.

[5] Dividing several homogeneous goods is very different from cake-cutting. Cake-cutting is most applicable to a problem like land division, in which hills, dales, ponds, and trees form an incongruous mix, making it impossible to give all of one thing (e.g. trees) to one player. By contrast, in property division it is possible to give all of one good to one player. Under certain conditions, two-player cake division, and the procedure to be discussed next (adjusted winner), are equivalent (Jones 2002).

[6] Procedures applicable to more than two players are discussed in Young 1994; Brams and Taylor 1996, 1999b; Moulin 2003.

Thus, instead of trying to negotiate a specific compromise on the bonus, the company and the executive negotiate upper and lower bounds, the lower one favoring the company and the upper one favoring the executive. The same holds true on other issues being decided, including non-monetary ones like title and responsibilities.

Under AW, each side will always win on some issues. Moreover, the procedure guarantees that both the company and the executive will get at least 50 per cent of what they desire, and often considerably more.

To implement AW, each side secretly distributes 100 points across the issues in a dispute according to the importance it attaches to winning on each. For example, suppose the company and the executive distribute their points as follows, illustrating that the company cares more about the bonus than the executive (it would be a bad precedent for the company to go too high), whereas the reverse is true for severance pay (the executive wants to have a cushion in the event of being fired):

Issues	Company	Executive
1. Bonus	**10**	5
2. Salary	35	**40**
3. Stock Options	15	**20**
4. Title and Responsibilities	**15**	10
5. Performance Incentives	**15**	5
6. Severance Pay	10	**20**
Total	100	100

The boldface figures show the side that wins initially on each issue by placing more points on it. Notice that whereas the company wins a total of 10 + 15 + 15 = 40 of its points, the executive wins a whopping 40 + 20 + 20 = 80 of its points.

This outcome is obviously unfair to the company. Hence, a so-called *equitability adjustment* is necessary to equalize the points of the two sides. This adjustment transfers points from the initial winner (the executive) to the loser (the company).

The key to the success of AW—in terms of a mathematical guarantee that no win-win potential is lost—is to make the transfer in a certain order (for a proof, see Brams and Taylor 1996, 85–94). That is, of the issues initially won by the executive, look for the one on which the two sides are in closest agreement, as measured by the quotient of the winner's points to the loser's points. Because the winner-to-loser quotient on the issue of salary is 40/35 = 1.14, and this is smaller than on any other issue on which the executive wins (the next-smallest quotient is 20/15 = 1.33 on stock options), some of this issue must be transferred to the company.

But how much? The point totals of the company and the executive will be equal when the company's winning points on issues 1, 4, and 5, plus x per cent of its points on salary (left side of equation below), equal the executive's winning points on issues 2, 3, and 6, minus x per cent of its points on salary (right side of equation):

$$40 + 35x = 80 - 40x$$

$$75x = 40.$$

Solving for x gives $x = 8/15 = 0.533$. This means that the executive will win about 53 per cent on salary, and the company will lose about 53 per cent (i.e. win about 47 per cent), which is almost a 50–50 compromise between the low and high figures they negotiated earlier, only slightly favoring the executive.

This compromise ensures that both the company and the executive will end up with exactly the same total number of points after the equitability adjustment:

$$40 + 35(.533) = 80 - 40(.533) = 58.7.$$

On all other issues, either the company or the executive gets its way completely (and its winning points), as it should since it valued these issues more than the other side.

Thus, AW is essentially a winner-take-all procedure, except on the one issue on which the two sides are closest and which, therefore, is the one subject to the equitability adjustment. On this issue a split will be necessary, which will be easier if the issue is a quantitative one, like salary, than a more qualitative one like title and responsibilities.[7]

Still, it should be possible to reach a compromise on an issue like title and responsibilities that reflects the percentages the relative winner and relative loser receive (53 per cent and 47 per cent in the example). This is certainly easier than trying to reach a compromise on each and every issue, which is also less efficient than resolving them all at once according to AW.[8]

In the example, each side ends up with, *in toto*, almost 59 per cent of what it desires, which will surely foster greater satisfaction than would a 50–50 split down the middle on each issue. In fact, assuming the two sides are truthful, there is no better split for both, which makes the AW settlement *efficient*.

In addition, it is *equitable*, because each side gets exactly the same amount above 50 per cent, with this figure increasing the greater the differences in the two sides' valuations of the issues. In effect, AW makes optimal trade-offs by awarding issues to the side that most values them, except as modified by the equitability adjustment that ensures that both sides do equally well (in their own subjective terms, which may not be monetary). On the other hand, if the two sides have unequal claims or entitlements—as specified, for example, in a contract—AW can be modified to give each side shares of the total proportional to its specified claims.

Can AW be manipulated to benefit one side? It turns out that exploitation of the procedure by one side is practically impossible unless that side knows exactly how the other side will allocate its points. In the absence of such information, attempts at manipulation can backfire miserably, with the manipulator ending up with less than the minimum 50 points its honesty guarantees it (Brams and Taylor 1996, 1999*b*).

While AW offers a compelling resolution to a multi-issue dispute, it requires careful thought to delineate what the issues being divided are, and tough bargaining to

---

[7] AW may require the transfer of more than one issue, but at most one issue must be divided in the end.

[8] A procedure called *proportional allocation* (PA) awards issues to the players in proportion to the points they allocate to them. While inefficient, PA is less vulnerable to strategic manipulation than AW, with which it can be combined (Brams and Taylor 1996, 75–80).

determine what winning and losing means on each. More specifically, because the procedure uses an additive point scheme, the issues need to be made as independent as possible, so that winning or losing on one does not substantially affect how much one wins or loses on others. To the degree that this is not the case, it becomes less meaningful to use the point totals to indicate how well each side does.

The half-dozen issues identified in the executive-compensation example overlap to an extent and hence may not be viewed as independent (after all, might not the bonus be considered part of salary?). On the other hand, they might be reasonably thought of as different parts of a compensation *package*, over which the disputants have different preferences that they express with points. In such a situation, losing on the issues you care less about than the other side will be tolerable if it is balanced by winning on the issues you care more about.

4 INDIVISIBLE GOODS

The challenge of dividing up indivisible goods, such as a car, a boat, or a house in a divorce, is daunting, though sometimes such goods can be shared (usually at different times). The main criteria I invoke are *efficiency* (there is no other division better for everybody, or better for some players and not worse for the others) and *envy-freeness* (each player likes its allocation at least as much as those that the other players receive, so it does not envy anybody else).

But because efficiency, by itself, is not a criterion of fairness (an efficient allocation could be one in which one player gets everything and the others nothing), I also consider other criteria of fairness besides envy-freeness, including Rawlsian and utilitarian measures of welfare (to be defined).

I present two paradoxes, from a longer list of eight in Brams, Edelman, and Fishburn (2001),[9] that highlight difficulties in creating "fair shares" for everybody. But they by no means render the task impossible. Rather, they show how dependent fair division is on the fairness criteria one deems important and the trade-offs one considers acceptable. Put another way, achieving fairness requires some consensus on the ground rules (i.e. criteria), and some delicacy in applying them (to facilitate trade-offs when the criteria conflict).

I make five assumptions. First, players rank indivisible items but do not attach cardinal utilities to them. Second, players cannot compensate each other with side payments (e.g. money)—the division is only of the indivisible items. Third, players cannot randomize among different allocations, which is a way that has been proposed for "smoothing out" inequalities caused by the indivisibility of items. Fourth, all players have positive values for every item. Fifth, a player prefers one set S of items to

[9] For a more systematic treatment of conflicts in fairness criteria and trade-offs that are possible, see Brams and Fishburn 2000; Edelman and Fishburn 2001; Herreiner and Puppe 2002; Brams, Edelman, and Fishburn 2003; Brams and Kaplan 2004; Brams and King 2005.

a different set T if (i) S has as many items as T and (ii) for every item t in T and not in S, there is a distinct item s in S and not in T that the player prefers to t. For example, if a player ranks four items in order of decreasing preference, 1 2 3 4, I assume that it prefers

- the set {1, 2} to {2, 3}, because {1} is preferred to {3}; and
- the set {1, 3} to {2, 4}, because {1} is preferred to {2} and {3} is preferred to {4},

whereas the comparison between sets {1, 4} and {2, 3} could go either way.

Paradox 1: *A unique envy-free division may be inefficient.*

Suppose there is a set of three players, {A, B, C}, who must divide a set of six indivisible items, {1, 2, 3, 4, 5, 6}. Assume the players rank the items from best to worst as follows:

A: 1 2 3 4 5 6
B: 4 3 2 1 5 6
C: 5 1 2 6 3 4

The unique envy-free allocation to (A, B, C) is ({1, 3}, {2, 4}, {5, 6}), or for simplicity (13, 24, 56), whereby A and B get their best and third-best items, and C gets its best and fourth-best items. Clearly, A prefers its allocation to that of B (which are A's second-best and fourth-best items) and that of C (which are A's two worst items). Likewise, B and C prefer their allocations to those of the other two players. Consequently, the division (13, 24, 56) is envy free: all players prefer their allocations to those of the other two players, so no player is envious of any other.

Compare this division with (12, 34, 56), whereby A and B receive their two best items, and C receives, as before, its best and fourth-best items. This division *Pareto-dominates* (13, 24, 56), because two of the three players (A and B) prefer the former allocation, whereas both allocations give player C the same two items (56).

It is easy to see that (12, 34, 56) is Pareto optimal or efficient: no player can do better with some other division without some other player or players doing worse, or at least not better. This is apparent from the fact that the only way A or B, which get their two best items, can do better is to receive an additional item from one of the two other players, but this will necessarily hurt the player who then receives fewer than its present two items. Whereas C can do better without receiving a third item if it receives item 1 or item 2 in place of item 6, this substitution would necessarily hurt A, which will do worse if it receives item 6 for item 1 or 2.

The problem with efficient allocation (12, 34, 56) is that it is not *assuredly* envy-free. In particular, C will envy A's allocation of 12 (second-best and third-best items for C) if it prefers these two items to its present allocation of 56 (best and fourth-best items for C). In the absence of information about C's preferences for subsets of items, therefore, we cannot say that efficient allocation (12, 34, 56) is envy-free.[10]

---

[10] Recall that an *envy-free* division of indivisible items is one in which, no matter how the players value subsets of items consistent with their rankings, no player prefers any other player's allocation to its own. If a division is not envy free, it is *envy possible* if a player's allocation *may* make it envious of

But the real bite of this paradox stems from the fact that not only is inefficient division (13, 24, 56) envy free, but it is uniquely so—there is no other division, including an efficient one, that guarantees envy-freeness. To show this in the example, note first that an envy-free division must give each player its best item; if not, then a player might prefer a division, like envy-free division (13, 24, 56) or efficient division (12, 34, 56), that does give each player its best item, rendering the division that does not do so envy possible or envy ensuring. Second, even if each player receives its best item, this allocation cannot be the only item it receives, because then the player might envy any player that receives two or more items, *whatever* these items are.

By this reasoning, then, the only possible envy-free divisions in the example are those in which each player receives two items, including its top choice. It is easy to check that no efficient division is envy free. Similarly, one can check that no inefficient division, except (13, 24, 56), is envy free, making this division uniquely envy free.

Paradox 2: *Neither the Rawlsian maximin criterion nor the utilitarian Borda-score criterion may choose a unique efficient and envy-free division.*

Unlike the example illustrating paradox 1, efficiency and envy-freeness are compatible in the following example:

A: 1 2 3 4 5 6
B: 5 6 2 1 4 3
C: 3 6 5 4 1 2

There are three efficient divisions in which (A, B, C) each get two items: (i) (12, 56, 34); (ii) (12, 45, 36); (iii) (14, 25, 36). Only (iii) is envy free: Whereas C might prefer B's 56 allocation in (i), and B might prefer A's 12 allocation in (ii), no player prefers another player's allocation in (iii).

Now consider the following *Rawlsian maximin criterion* to distinguish among the efficient divisions: choose a division that maximizes the minimum rank of items that players receive, making a worst-off player as well off as possible.[11] Because (ii) gives a fifth-best item to B, whereas (i) and (iii) give players, at worst, a fourth-best item, the latter two divisions satisfy the Rawlsian maximin criterion.

Between these two, (i), which is envy possible, is arguably better than (iii), which is envy free: (i) gives the two players that do not get a fourth-best item their two best items, whereas (iii) does not give B its two best items.[12]

---

another player, depending on how it values subsets of items, as illustrated for player C by division (12, 34, 56). It is *envy ensuring* if it causes envy, independent of how the players value subsets of items. In effect, a division that is envy possible has the potential to cause envy. By comparison, an envy-ensuring division always causes envy, and an envy-free division never causes envy.

[11] This is somewhat different from Rawls's (1971) proposal to maximize the utility of the player with minimum utility, so it might be considered a modified Rawlsian criterion. We introduce a rough measure of utility next with a modified Borda Count.

[12] This might be considered a second-order application of the maximin criterion: If, for two divisions, players rank the worst item any player receives the same, consider the player that receives a next-worst item in each, and choose the division in which this item is ranked higher. This is an example of a *lexicographic decision rule*, whereby alternatives are ordered on the basis of a most important

Next consider a modified Borda Count, which also gives the nod to envy-possible division (i). Awarding 6 points for obtaining a best item, 5 points for obtaining a second-best item, ..., 1 point for obtaining a worst item in the example, (ii) and (iii) give the players a total of 30 points, whereas (i) gives the players a total of 31 points.[13] This criterion might be thought of as a measure of the overall utility or welfare of the players. Thus, neither the Rawlsian maximin criterion nor the *utilitarian Borda-score criterion* guarantees the selection of a unique efficient and envy-free division.

5 CONCLUSIONS

The squeezing procedure I illustrated for dividing up cake among three players ensures efficiency and envy-freeness, but it does not satisfy equitability. Whereas adjusted winner satisfies efficiency, envy-freeness, and equitability for two players dividing up several divisible goods, all these properties cannot be guaranteed if there are more than two players. Finally, the two paradoxes relating to the fair division of indivisible goods, which are independent of the procedure used, illustrate new difficulties—that no division may satisfy either maximin or utilitarian notions of welfare and, at the same time, be efficient and envy free.

Patently, fair division is a hard problem, whatever the things being divided are. While some conflicts are ineradicable, the trade-offs that best resolve these conflicts are by no means evident. Understanding these may help to ameliorate, if not solve, practical problems of fair division, ranging from the splitting of the marital property in a divorce to determining who gets what in an international dispute.

REFERENCES

ABDUL KADIROGLU, A., SÖNMEZ, T., and UNVER, U. 2004 Room assignment–rent division: a market approach. *Social Choice and Welfare*, 22: 515–38.
BARBANEL, J. B. 2005. *The Geometry of Efficient Fair Division*. Cambridge: Cambridge University Press.
—— and BRAMS, S. J. 2004. Cake division with minimal cuts: envy-free procedures for 3 persons, 4 persons, and beyond. *Mathematical Social Sciences*, 48: 251–69.
—— —— 2006. Cutting a pie is not a piece of cake. Preprint, Dept. of Politics, New York University.

criterion; if that is not determinative, a next-most important criterion is invoked, and so on, to narrow down the set of feasible alternatives.

[13] The standard scoring rules for the Borda Count in this six-item example would give 5 points to a best item, 4 points to a second-best item, ..., 0 points to a worst item. I depart slightly from this standard scoring rule to ensure that each player obtains some positive value for all items, including its worst choice, as assumed earlier.

BRAMS, S. J., EDELMAN, P. H., and FISHBURN, P. C. 2001. Paradoxes of fair division. *Journal of Philosophy*, 98: 300–14.

BRAMS, S. J., EDELMAN, P. H., and FISHBURN, P. C. 2003. Fair division of indivisible items. *Theory and Decision*, 55: 147–80.

—— and FISHBURN, P. C. 2000. Fair division of indivisible items between two people with identical preferences: envy-freeness, Pareto-optimality, and equity. *Social Choice and Welfare*, 17: 247–67.

—— JONES, M. A., and KLAMLER, C. 2006a. Better ways to cut a cake. Preprint, Dept. of Politics, New York University.

—— —— —— 2006b. Proportional pie-cutting. Preprint, Dept. of Politics, New York University.

—— and KAPLAN, T. R. 2004. Dividing the indivisible: procedures for allocating cabinet ministries in a parliamentary system. *Journal of Theoretical Politics*, 16: 143–73.

—— and KILGOUR, D. M. 2001. Competitive fair division. *Journal of Political Economy*, 109: 418–43.

—— and KING, D. R. 2005. Efficient fair division: help the worst off or avoid envy? *Rationality and Society*, 17: 387–421.

—— and TAYLOR, A. D. 1995. An envy-free cake division protocol. *American Mathematical Monthly*, 102: 9–18.

—— —— 1996. *Fair Division: From Cake-Cutting to Dispute Resolution*. Cambridge: Cambridge University Press.

—— —— 1999a. Calculating consensus. *Corporate Counsel*, 9: 47–50.

—— —— 1999b. *The Win-Win Solution: Guaranteeing Fair Shares to Everybody*. New York: W. W. Norton.

—— —— and ZWICKER, W. S. 1995. Old and new moving-knife schemes. *Mathematical Intelligencer*, 17: 30–5.

—— —— —— 1997. A moving-knife solution to the four-person envy-free cake division problem. *Proceedings of the American Mathematical Society*, 125: 547–54.

EDELMAN, P. H., and FISHBURN, P. C. 2001. Fair division of indivisible items among people with similar preferences. *Mathematical Social Sciences*, 41: 327–47.

EVEN, S., and PAZ, A. 1984. A note on cake cutting. *Discrete Applied Mathematics*, 7: 285–96.

HAAKE, C.-J., RAITH, M. G., and SU, F. E. 2002. Bidding for envy-freeness: a procedural approach to n-player fair-division problems. *Social Choice and Welfare*, 19: 723–49.

HERREINER, D., and PUPPE, C. 2002. A simple procedure for finding equitable allocations of indivisible goods. *Social Choice and Welfare*, 19: 415–30.

JONES, M. A. 2002. Equitable, envy-free, and efficient cake cutting for two people and its application to divisible goods. *Mathematics Magazine*, 75: 275–83.

MOULIN, H. J. 2003. *Fair Division and Collective Welfare*. Cambridge, Mass.: MIT Press.

PETERSON, E., and SU, F. E. 2002. Four-person envy-free chore division. *Mathematics Magazine*, 75: 117–22.

PIKHURKO, O. 2000 On envy-free cake division. *American Mathematical Monthly*, 107: 736–8.

POTTHOFF, R. F. 2002. Use of linear programming to find an envy-free solution closest to the Brams–Kilgour gap solution for the housemates problem. *Group Decision and Negotiation*, 11: 405–14.

RAWLS, J. 1971. *A Theory of Justice*. Cambridge, Mass.: Harvard University Press.

ROBERTSON, J. M., and WEBB, W. A. 1997. Near exact and envy-free cake division. *Ars Combinatoria*, 45: 97–108.

—— —— 1998. *Cake-Cutting Algorithms: Be Fair If You Can*. Natick, Mass.: A. K. Peters.

SHISHIDO, H., and ZENG, D.-Z. 1999. Mark-choose-cut algorithms for fair and strongly fair division. *Group Decision and Negotiation*, 8: 125–37.
STROMQUIST, W. 1980. How to cut a cake fairly. *American Mathematical Monthly*, 87: 640–4.
SU, F. E. 1999. Rental harmony: Sperner's lemma in fair division. *American Mathematical Monthly*, 106: 922–34.
YOUNG, H. P. 1994. *Equity in Theory and Practice*. Princeton, NJ: Princeton University Press.
ZENG, D.-Z. 2000. Approximate envy-free procedures. Pp. 259–71 in *Game Practice: Contributions from Applied Game Theory*. Dordrecht: Kluwer Academic.

PART VII

PUBLIC FINANCE AND PUBLIC ECONOMICS

CHAPTER 25

STRUCTURE AND COHERENCE IN THE POLITICAL ECONOMY OF PUBLIC FINANCE

STANLEY L. WINER

WALTER HETTICH

No one can quarrel with the requirement that the budget plan should be designed to maximize welfare...

(Musgrave and Peacock 1958, xi)

At first sight it might be argued that anyone who set himself up as a judge and wished to establish standards for the distribution of expenditure or amounts of revenue different from those approved by Parliament, must belong to one of three categories: either he must be mentally the equal of that average intelligence [in Parliament], in which case he could not

---

* For helpful comments we thank Timothy Besley, Tom Borcherding, Roger Congleton, Amihai Glazer, Randall Holcombe, Kai Konrad, Gary Miller, Paul Rothstein, Dan Usher, and editors Barry Weingast and Don Wittman, as well as participants in seminars at Carleton University, the Claremont Graduate School, and the University of Western Ontario. Winer's research was supported by a Canada-United States Fulbright Scholarship during the 2003–4 academic year and by the Canada Research Chair program. The hospitality extended to Winer by the Department of Economics and the Center for the Study of Democracy at UC Irvine is also gratefully acknowledged. Errors and omissions remain the responsibility of the authors.

arrive at a different judgment; or he must be inferior to it, in which case his opinion would be less reliable; or he must be superior to it, which could not be proved.

(Pantaleoni 1883, 17)

Economic journals continue to publish a steady stream of articles dealing with the public sector. Readers familiar with this literature will notice a crucial difference, however. The field is passing through a transitional phase. A central paradigm—the model of the social planner—is losing its long-held grip as an organizing principle. And although the search for a new coherence is apparent in much recent work, it has not yet resulted in a different analytical view that enjoys widespread acceptance.

The current tension is foreshadowed by the two quotations at the head of this chapter, although they belong to much earlier periods. Richard Musgrave and Alan Peacock wrote in mid-century. They expressed their belief in the importance of maximizing social welfare in the introduction to their famous collection of classic articles in public finance published in 1958, and there is little doubt that it was a view widely shared by economists of the day. In fact, it remained the dominant theoretical approach for another three decades or more in much of the literature dealing with public sector issues. The longevity of the social welfare approach occurred in large part because the early contributions to the theory of taxation, by Edgeworth (1897), Ramsey (1927), and Pigou (1951), and the work by Samuelson (1954) and others on public goods and the use of the social welfare function in public economics, were later reinforced and extended in important ways by the literature on optimal taxation.[1]

While Musgrave and Peacock provided a clear statement of the prevailing consensus, their collection of readings also had a second, quite different and somewhat subversive, effect.[2] The *Classics* introduced the English-speaking world to the writings of earlier European thinkers that had pursued a different approach, but who had little impact on the English and American economic literature. Two names—those of Knut Wicksell and Eric Lindahl—are now widely known, but other continental writers included in the collection, such as Maffeo Pantaleoni, have received less attention. Yet, like Wicksell and Lindahl, he recognized what would be revealed as the Achilles heel of social planning in a much later time. Because of the very nature of public sector activities, budgetary decisions have to be made by collective institutions, such as parliaments. A planner model, however elegant, cannot come to grips with this central fact.[3]

---

[1] The optimal tax approach is presented in Mirrlees 1971 and Atkinson and Stiglitz 1980. A more complete discussion of the relevant history of thought would of course have to mention many other significant contributions.

[2] The quote continues "but much needs to be added to give content to this formula," and the research published by the two writers covered a much wider range of topics than the above phrase would indicate. See especially Musgrave's *Theory of Public Finance* (1959) which heavily influenced the development of the field.

[3] In his discussion, Pantaleoni suggests that parliamentary decisions can be evaluated by comparing them to similar choices made by other legislatures, thus pointing toward the comparative study of institutions.

The work by the continental writers who had suffered neglect in the first half of the twentieth century became the source of a new and vigorous field of research in the second half dealing with collective choice and governing institutions. It developed largely alongside public finance and often had only limited influence on traditional writings, even though many of the questions raised by scholars using the new approach had direct relevance to matters of taxation and public expenditures. By the end of the century, work on collective choice provided a fully developed counterpoint to the social planning approach, and became one of the major reasons for the current unsettled state of public sector analysis.

The main criticisms of the social planning model may be summarized in three points. First, social planning does not provide any basis for empirical research designed to explain observed features of actual fiscal systems or policies. Second, there is a growing insistence among social scientists that behavioral assumptions in the public sector should be consistent with those stipulated for actions in the private economy. And third, there is a new challenge to social planning as the appropriate foundation for normative analysis.

The present chapter is written with this background in mind. We begin by outlining the structure of public sector economics when collective choice is regarded as an essential component of the framework of analysis, and point out the key issues that must be faced by economists and political scientists who insist that collective institutions cannot be ignored in research on public budgets and taxation. The analysis is comprehensive in the sense that both positive and normative aspects are considered in some detail. References to the vast literature on the political economy of public finance are necessarily selective; we attempt to provide a point of view on the field rather than a survey.

While the emphasis is on the role of collective choice in the analysis of the public sector, the discussion applies more broadly. The transitional phase mentioned earlier affects all analysis of public policy. The search for a new coherence is a wider effort that must of necessity extend beyond the limited scope of the present discussion.

1 THE STRUCTURE OF PUBLIC SECTOR ECONOMICS WHEN COLLECTIVE CHOICE MATTERS

The analysis of public finance in modern democratic societies usually begins with a discussion of what markets can and cannot do. This approach is a natural consequence of work based on the first theorem of welfare economics which links competitive private markets with efficiency in resource allocation. The public sector is treated as an adjunct to the private economy and as an aid to the efficient performance of competitive markets, which may fail when externalities or public goods are present.

Although it is acknowledged that there are prerequisites for the functioning of markets, their nature is analyzed only infrequently in the literature. Among the preconditions is the existence of secure property rights. They are needed both in the private economy and in the public sphere, where they include the rights to vote and to participate in other ways in public life. As in the case of all rights, those in the public sector must be well defined and be subject to conditions that circumscribe how and when they can be exercised.

Figure 25.1 gives a schematic presentation of the structure of public sector analysis. We begin with private and public property rights in the top box, which also lists behavioral assumptions concerning private agents, another necessary starting point for any empirical and theoretical examination. Given this basis, we can develop the analysis of markets and market equilibrium on the one hand, and of equilibrium outcomes in the public sector on the other. The diagram makes clear that consistency in approach is important for a successful understanding. Behavioral assumptions affect the analysis of both the private and the public economy, with scholars of collective choice arguing that human motivation must follow the same principles in both areas even though constraints facing individuals may systematically differ between private and public choice settings.

In accordance with our focus, the diagram gives more space to the public sector, while also pointing out the interdependence between public and private spheres. Since the public sector must deal with situations where markets fail partially or completely, other decision mechanisms are needed. This is indicated by the top box on the right side of the diagram, which lists collective choice together with the electoral institutions required for the functioning of democracy.[4] One should note that the enforcement of rights generally falls into the public sector, one of the crucial difficulties of democratic societies, since public as well as private property rights are usually enforced through public means.[5]

Market failure arises primarily because of non-excludability in the case of public goods and common-pool resources, and because of prices that do not reflect the welfare consequences of private decisions, in the case of externalities.[6] When of necessity markets are replaced with collective choice, other difficulties arise. Most prominent is the separation of spending and taxing, a term that refers to the severance of marginal benefits from marginal costs in consumption decisions for publicly provided goods. Because there is no complete revelation of preferences for public goods, and because of the corresponding difficulty of matching an individual's tax liabilities with his

---

[4] We refer here to "institutions *required* for the functioning of democracy" as our concern in this chapter is with collective choice in democratic societies. It should be noted that some of the important activities observed in democracies, such as the acquisition of information by the authorities about the preferences of citizens, will also occur in non-democratic regimes even though there are no elections and little civil liberty.

[5] Rights can also be privately enforced at higher cost. The study of such situations of "structured anarchy" is an area of public finance that has not been well explored. For further discussion and references, see Skaperdas 2003.

[6] Recent studies of market failure and the role for government include Salanié 2000 and Glazer and Rothenberg 2001.

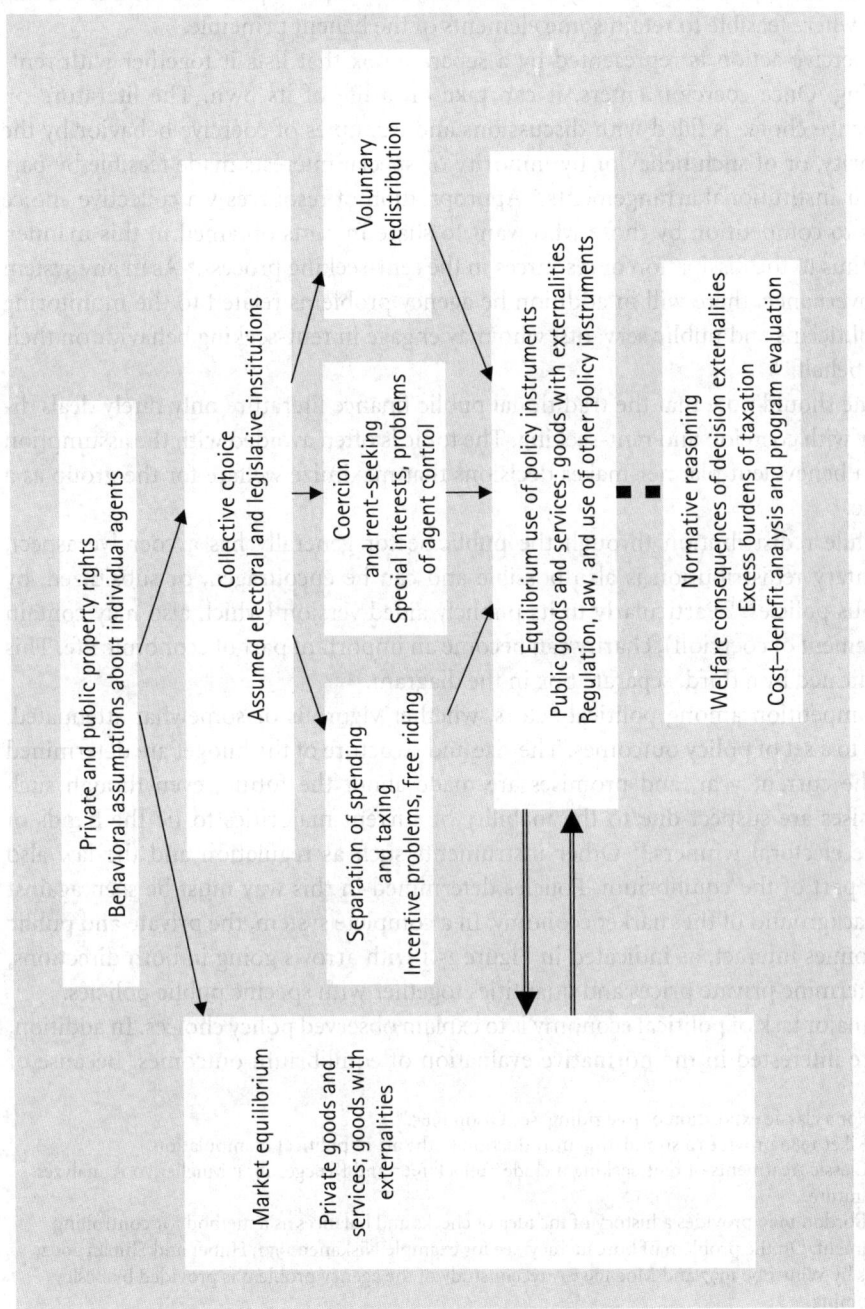

Fig. 25.1 The basic structure of public sector political economy

or her benefits, separation of spending and taxing and the attendant free riding become major problems.[7] The usual outcome is a system of compulsory taxes levied in accordance with ability to pay or other non-benefit principles, with user fees being used where feasible to retain some elements of the benefit principle.

Coercive action is represented by a separate box that lists it together with rent-seeking. Once coercion enters, it can take on a life of its own. The literature on collective choice is filled with discussions and examples of coercive behavior by the majority, or of such behavior by minority or special interests made feasible by particular institutional arrangements.[8] Appropriation of resources via collective choice leads to competition by those who want to share in rents obtained in this manner, and thus to the dissipation of resources in the rent-seeking process.[9] As in any system of governance, there will in addition be agency problems related to the monitoring of politicians and public servants, who may engage in rent-seeking behavior on their own behalf.[10]

One should note that the traditional public finance literature only rarely deals directly with coercion and rent-seeking. The topic is often avoided with the assumption that a benevolent planner makes decisions that maximize welfare for the group as a whole.

While redistribution through the public sector generally has a coercive aspect, voluntary redistribution is also possible and can be encouraged, or subsidized, by various policies.[11] Particularly in its publicly aided version (which also may contain an element of coercion), charity can become an important part of economic life. This is indicated by a third, separate box in the diagram.

Competition among political actors, whether vigorous or somewhat attenuated, leads to a set of policy outcomes. The size and structure of the budget are determined for the current year, and promises are made about the future, even though such promises are suspect due to the inability of current majorities to tie the hands of future electoral winners.[12] Other instruments such as regulation and the law also form part of the equilibrium. Policies determined in this way must be seen against the background of the market economy. In a complete system, the private and public economies interact, as indicated in Figure 25.1 with arrows going in both directions, to determine private prices and quantities together with specific public policies.

A major task of political economy is to explain observed policy choices. In addition, we are interested in the normative evaluation of equilibrium outcomes. Because of

---

[7] For a classic exposition of free riding, see Olson 1965.

[8] Riker 1986 provides a stimulating introduction to the art of political manipulation.

[9] Classic treatments of rent-seeking include Tullock 1967 and Krueger 1974. Mueller 2003 analyzes the literature.

[10] Gordon 1999 provides a history of the idea of checks and balances as a method for controlling government. On the problem of bureaucracy, see for example Niskanen 1971; Huber and Shipan 2002; surveys by Wintrobe 1997 and Moe 1997. A recent study of the agency problem is provided by Besley forthcoming.

[11] See, for example, Hochman and Rogers 1969; Andreoni 1990.

[12] The commitment problem is discussed at length by Drazen 2000. Marceau and Smart 2003 is a recent contribution, where vested interests attenuate the problem by engaging in political action to protect themselves from expropriation.

the absence of market prices for public goods, the measurement and evaluation of public sector outcomes raises difficult questions. The traditional literature on public finance has emphasized the excess burdens of taxation that are related directly to the separation of taxing and spending alluded to earlier. Benefit–cost analysis is a second tool that is often employed to evaluate policies, although observed prices must be complemented with a range of imputed ones in many cases.

As in other areas of economic life, inefficiencies in the public sector occur primarily when there is a divergence between private and social costs or benefits for particular decision-makers. The term "decision externalities," contained in the final box in Figure 25.1 referring to the public sector, thus summarizes a wide range of governing failures that arise in public life, much as market failures arise in the private economy. For example, because taxes paid and benefits received by each individual cannot be closely linked, there is a tendency for politicians in *all* electoral systems to view taxable activity as a common pool, and to overuse this pool in an attempt to deliver benefits to favored groups at the expense of the general taxpayer.[13]

Normative analysis of decision externalities generally relies on the planner model, in which ideal policies are those chosen to maximize social welfare. In this framework, all decision externalities can be internalized by the planner, subject to information and transactions costs that are part of the state of nature.

If we drop the planner and enter a world where collective institutions are needed because of the very nature of public goods, it becomes more difficult to define ideal conditions.[14] We are faced with hard choices between imperfect alternatives. This challenge is one of the reasons for the uncertain state of public finance, as discussed in greater detail in Section 3.

2 APPLIED GENERAL EQUILIBRIUM ANALYSIS AND THE FADING LUSTER OF THE MEDIAN VOTER

We begin our discussion of contemporary applications and issues by focusing on the equilibrium use of policy instruments. In the next section we consider normative issues that arise when we attempt to evaluate equilibrium policy outcomes.

Over four decades ago, Arnold Harberger (1954, 1962) enriched the field of public finance by showing how a practical equilibrium analysis of the incidence and excess

---

[13] This problem may be exacerbated by universalism—the tendency for legislators to agree to an excessive level of taxation in order to avoid the uncertainties of vote-cycling. See, for example, Shepsle and Weingast 1981. Ostrom 1990 considers how a variety of institutions may evolve so as to attenuate common-pool problems.

[14] In particular, it is no longer obvious what transactions costs are given by the state of nature, and what such costs are a result of social organization.

burden of taxation could be accomplished.[15] Harberger's framework could be used to uncover the long-run incidence of taxation, which differs from nominal incidence, and actually to value the excess burden associated with alternative tax blueprints. It filled a need for an analysis that incorporates general equilibrium theory yet is still simple enough to allow numerical calculations in policy-relevant situations.

Progress in political economy requires a similar advance.[16] Taxes, public services, regulations, and laws are jointly determined by political competition against the background of the market economy and political institutions. However, modeling this equilibrium structure in a realistic yet simple manner remains an outstanding challenge. Establishing a framework for applied analysis in the presence of collective choice is harder than the task faced by Harberger, since both political and economic margins are relevant to optimizing agents who operate in both sectors.

The situation in the 1960s and 1970s was less demanding. Following the seminal work of Bowen (1943) and Black (1958) on the median voter, it seemed that a marriage of the Harberger tradition and the median voter model could yield a manageable framework. If preferences are single peaked, the median voter is decisive, and we can solve for an economic and political equilibrium by maximizing the welfare of the median voter subject to the structure of the private economy. Notable examples of this approach include empirical models of the size of government by Borcherding and Deacon (1972), Bergstrom and Goodman (1973), and Winer (1983). It also forms the basis for analysis of coercive redistribution by Romer (1975) and Meltzer and Richard (1981, 1983) in which the response of labor supply to taxation limits the extent to which the median voter is successful in taking resources from the rich.

However, the luster of the median voter model is fading. Indeed, as Tullock (2004) notes, the single-peaked preference relation was a "broken reed" from its inception. Even when preferences are well behaved, the median voter model has no equilibrium under pure majority rule unless the issue space is unidimensional.[17] And most issues are more complex than can be represented by one dimension, at least in the minds of legislators and voters. Although a specific budget item may be debated, participants are aware of a multiplicity of links to other budgetary issues. No doubt the fading of the median voter was substantially hastened by the proofs by McKelvey (1976) and Schofield (1978) showing that vote-cycling is endemic when the issue space is multidimensional.

Work using a median voter model that we cited earlier is restricted to dealing with one issue, usually the size of government or an average tax rate that balances the budget. What should the analysis of the public finances include when policy issues are more complex? A reasonable answer is that a political economy of public

---

[15] The work of Harberger has been extended by Mieszkowski 1967 and Mieszkowski and Zodrow 1986 among many others. The Harberger-type model has also been implemented in a computable equilibrium context (e.g. Shoven and Whalley 1992).

[16] The paper by Besley and Coate (2003), accorded the Duncan Black prize for the year, represents an argument for the use of general equilibrium analysis in studying public policy in a collective choice setting.

[17] Attempts to extend the median voter to deal with complex policies using single-crossing restrictions on preferences have not been successful in going beyond two issues.

finance should concern itself with actual features of public activities and financing, and include analysis of at least some of the following issues:

  (i) the division between public and private activity;
 (ii) the size of government;
(iii) the structure of taxation, including the choice of bases, rate structures, and special provisions and the structure of public expenditure;
(iv) the incidence and full cost of fiscal systems, including excess burden and the cost of rent-seeking;
 (v) the nature and extent of redistribution, which necessarily raises multidimensional issues;
(vi) the relationship between fiscal and other policy instruments such as regulation and law;
(vii) interjurisdictional competition and the role of multilevel governance in federal systems;
(viii) international competition and the structure of national public sectors;
(ix) dynamic issues including the choice between current taxation and debt, intergenerational redistribution, and the consistency of public policy over time;
 (x) the relationship between electoral and legislative institutions and all of the issues listed above.

Although this list looks daunting, one should realize that successful research will focus on a few of these issues at any one time.

At present there are three promising approaches to replace the median voter model as a basis for analysis of these issues. We provide a brief introduction to these frameworks and to some of their applications below. Each of the models establishes an equilibrium where otherwise only a vote cycle would occur by introducing constraints on the ability of candidates to create winning platforms regardless of what the opposition has proposed. The models are distinguished by the nature of these constraints, by their treatment of party competition, and by the role that is formally assigned to interest groups.

2.1 Three Contemporary Approaches to Modeling Political Equilibrium

Probabilistic Spatial Voting

The most prominent of the recent frameworks builds on a long tradition in the study of spatial voting following the seminal work of Hotelling (1929) and Downs (1957). Probabilistic spatial voting models formalize the Downsian conception of party competition.[18] Two or more parties compete for votes by maximizing expected

---

[18] Contributions to spatial voting include, among others, Coughlin and Nitzan 1981; Hinich and Munger 1994; Merrill and Grofman 1999; McKelvey and Patty 2001.

electoral support. Individuals vote sincerely on the basis of how proposed policies will influence their welfare, and voting behavior is uncertain at least from the perspective of the parties. This uncertainty makes each party's objective continuous in its policies, and thus opens the door for a Nash equilibrium in pure strategies despite the complexity of the issue space.[19] If expected vote functions are also concave, so that parties can choose *optimal* strategies, an equilibrium will exist and may be unique.[20]

Since there is always a chance that a given voter may support any party, equilibrium policy choices reflect a balancing of the heterogeneous interests of the electorate. In some versions—e.g. Coughlin and Nitzan (1981) and Hettich and Winer (1999)—each person's welfare is weighted in equilibrium by the sensitivity of his or her vote to a change in welfare. (This result is important for the discussion of normative issues and we return to it below.) Party platforms converge in equilibrium, raising the question of how parties maintain their organizations.

An important variant of the spatial voting approach emphasizes the existence and role of interest groups and activists who offer political resources to particular parties in exchange for policy compromises.[21] Interest groups alter the weight placed on the welfare of various groups. Party platforms do not converge, as movement towards the center comes at the cost of contributions from activists who prefer less centrist policies. This opens the door for discrete changes in policy when the incumbent loses. Miller and Schofield (2003) suggest that party realignments and possibly large swings in policy may occur in response to the changing character of interest groups.

The models of Grossman and Helpman (1994, 2001) and of Dixit, Grossman, and Helpman (1997) are in essence similar to the spatial voting model with interest groups. This approach emphasizes the exchange of policies for resources between an incumbent and several interest groups using the menu-auction theory of Bernheim and Whinston (1986). The government plays off one group against the other in order to capture as much as possible of their surplus, which is then used to gain electoral advantage. The framework gives more limited attention to the modeling of the broader context in which electoral competition occurs.

The Citizen-Candidate

The citizen-candidate model of Osborne and Slivinsky (1996) and Besley and Coate (1997) deals with the instability of majority rule by modeling the number of competing citizen-candidates in an election.[22] The policy implemented is that most desired by the winning candidate; this feature ensures commitment to policies proposed by

---

[19] Lin, Enelow, and Dorussen 1999 show that a certain degree of uncertainty in voter preferences is required for equilibrium to exist. See also Lindbeck and Weibull 1987.

[20] Usher 1994 suggests that supremely contentious issues must be kept out of the political arena to preserve equilibrium: if policy platforms become highly polarized, the probability that some radical voters will support the more disliked party may fall to zero. In that case, expected vote functions may not be globally concave.

[21] See Aldrich 1983; Austen-Smith 1987; Schofield 2003, among others.

[22] Only the Besley–Coate version deals with issue spaces that are multidimensional, though the basic ideas in the two papers are similar.

candidates during the election. There are no political parties to deal with free rider problems in political organization or to establish consistency through reputation.

Every voter is considered a potential candidate. Equilibrium occurs when no voter wishes to change his or her vote, no citizen-candidate wishes to withdraw from the race, no one else wants to enter, and one of the candidates is destined to win by obtaining a plurality. It is not easy to become a winning candidate in this world, and most citizens will stay out of the race or face only the certain loss of fixed entry costs. For this reason, pure strategy Nash equilibria in this model often occur.[23]

The Party Coalition Model

A third type of model, due to Roemer (2001) and Levy (2004), emphasizes the formation and role of political parties. Parties are coalitions of individuals or interest groups having differing objectives. Levy's version emphasizes the role of parties in establishing a commitment to a range of policies that individual candidates cannot credibly propose on their own.

In Roemer's framework parties are coalitions of militants who want to announce a policy as close as possible to their ideal point, regardless of the probability of winning, and of opportunists who want to maximize the probability of election.[24] Party platforms represent a preference ordering on the issue space that is the intersection of the preference relations of each faction. Each party coalition by definition prefers its own policies to those of the opposition. An equilibrium in pure strategies may exist because it is hard for each party to alter its platform while still maintaining agreement among its own coalition members no matter what the opposition proposes.[25]

2.2 Applications to Public Finance

Analysis that is successful from both a theoretical and an empirical point of view has two components: First, it is based on an underlying model that confronts essential issues and stylized facts, especially the observed stability of multidimensional policy structures. Second, empirical work directly linked to this framework is carried out on one or more of the key topics in public finance.

Most applications when issues are multidimensional have used some type of probabilistic spatial voting model. Since it is reasonable to assume that expected support for a party will rise with the welfare it can deliver to voters and interest groups, every party has an incentive to make the excess burden that will result from its proposed platform as small as possible, subject to judgements about the distribution of political influence. Thus a spatial model in which parties maximize support from

---

[23] Usher 2003 argues that equilibria are so prevalent that the model is not sufficiently restrictive concerning possible policy choices. Roemer 2003 offers a similar criticism.

[24] There is a third group—the reformists—who maximize their expected utility. They do not alter the equilibrium since their preferences are a combination of those of militants and opportunists.

[25] Interestingly, an equilibrium exists only if there are at least two issues. Roemer does not consider this a limitation since most important issues are multidimensional.

a heterogeneous electorate is well suited to the study of how the full costs of taxation are reflected in the fiscal system. When there are information and administration costs attached to the use of policy instruments, tax and expenditure structures that economize on such costs emerge in the equilibrium (Hettich and Winer 1988, 1999).

This framework has been used successfully to study complete fiscal systems across space and time as well as more narrowly defined issues.[26] Applied work has also been carried out using the Grossman–Helpman model. This research is mainly directed at trade policy including the use of non-tariff barriers.[27]

As yet there is little empirical work that utilizes the citizen-candidate model or the party coalition framework. Although these models show promise for empirical research, the difficulties of applying them in practice have not yet been extensively explored. (But see Roemer 2001, and Lee and Roemer 2004.[28])

There are two challenging problems that are common to all of the models when they are applied to real data: (i) the difficulty of distinguishing between economic welfare and political influence; and (ii) the problem of identifying the role of electoral and legislative institutions. The distinction between economic welfare and political influence plays a central role in historical work on the evolution of tax systems, but it has proved difficult to separate the two empirically.[29] However, Rutherford and Winer (1990) and Hotte and Winer (2001) calibrate the political influence of several income classes in an applied probabilistic framework that incorporates the Gemtap tax model. Goldberg and Maggi (1999) and Gawande and Bandyopadhyay (2000) estimate the weights placed on contributions by special interests and by consumers in a Grossman–Helpman model of non-tariff barriers.[30]

The problem that arises concerning electoral systems is the implicit manner in which they usually enter the analysis. Modeling outcomes under proportional representation is especially difficult because of the need to deal with post-election coalition formation. Some progress has recently been made however. Persson, Roland, and Tabellini (2004) have constructed a spatial voting model in which the formation of coalitions under proportional representation and the emergence of single-party

---

[26] On fiscal systems see, for example, Kenny and Winer 2006; Hettich and Winer 1984, 1999, chs. 9 and 10; Ferris and Winer 2003. On more specific fiscal issues see, for example, Congleton and Shugart 1990 and Profeta 2002 on pensions, Chernick and Reschovsky 1996 on progressivity among US states, and Kenny and Toma 1997 on the choice between income taxation and the inflation tax.

[27] Applications of the Grossman–Helpman model to trade issues have recently been extensively reviewed by Feenstra (2004, ch. 9). The model has also been used to consider other types of polices, such as environmental taxation and regulation (e.g. Fredriksson 2001).

[28] Roemer (2001, ch. 10) applies his model of party unanimity Nash equilibrium to the long-standing question of why capitalists are not expropriated by the poor. The answer is that electorally successful coalitions usually require support from some people for whom income is not the only salient dimension and who do not, as a result, favor radical redistribution. Lee and Roemer apply a similar model empirically to consider the relationship of racism and redistribution in the United States—showing as a byproduct that two dimensions are required to understand the nature of redistribution.

[29] See for example Gillespie 1991 on Canadian tax history.

[30] Rutherford et al. find that the influence of lower-income voters in the USA increased over the decade of the 1970s, and the Goldberg–Maggi and Gawande–Bandyopadhyay papers show that consumers are more influential than special interests. Mueller and Stratmann 2003 also investigate the role of influence (with political participation as a proxy) using international panel data.

government in a majoritarian electoral system are explicitly represented.[31] Austen-Smith (2000) looks for conditions under which the fiscal system under PR may be more redistributive than in a majoritarian system. Baqir (2002) provides empirical evidence of the positive relationship between the number of legislators in a municipal system and the extent of the common-pool problem. Inman and Rubinfeld (1996) discuss the benefits of federalism as a means of attenuating the common-pool problem in national legislatures. And Hettich and Winer (1999, ch. 11) relate the size and frequency of tax changes to the greater transactions costs of legislative actions in the US system of checks and balances as compared to the Canadian parliamentary system.[32]

A balanced empirical view of the evolution of fiscal structure will include political influence, governance, and the more mundane factors that shape economic interests. It is not clear at this time what empirical importance should be attached to each of these elements, or even if such generalizations are possible. Further work on separating out the roles of political influence, electoral institutions, and narrowly defined economic interests is high on the research agenda.

3 NORMATIVE ANALYSIS, THE INVISIBLE HAND, AND THE PROBLEM OF CREEPING CONSTRAINTS

Normative analysis has a long tradition in public finance. In his massive and erudite *History of Economic Analysis* (1954), Joseph Schumpeter reviewed an extensive, and by now largely forgotten, literature created by those he called cameralists or consultant administrators. This diverse literature spanning more than 200 years had a central goal, namely to advise the sovereign on the management of the nation state.

Long-held attitudes die hard. When Knut Wicksell reviewed the literature on the public sector in 1896, a time when democratic governments had been in power for some time in the United States, England, and several European countries, he wrote, perhaps somewhat wistfully:

Even the most recent manuals on the science of public finance frequently leave the impression, at least upon me, of some sort of philosophy of enlightened and benevolent despotism, and they seem to represent a running commentary on the famous rule "Everything for the people, nothing by the people"—or, at most, with the faint-hearted addition "perhaps a little by the people" (p. 82).

---

[31] Their empirical results suggest that majoritarian systems have smaller public sectors, which they attribute to the ability of such systems to deal more easily with common-pool problems in public finance compared to coalition governments that often arise under PR.

[32] Kirchgässner 2002 more extensively reviews the evolving empirical literature on the effects of constitutional and legislative constraints on fiscal policy.

Many of those who created the modern literature on public finance never abandoned the goal of advising the sovereign on how to do the best *for the people*. It is true that questions were formulated more precisely and that the tools of analysis became more powerful. Yet, the enlightened sovereign somehow survived, having taken on the disguise of a benevolent social planner.[33]

Wicksell's challenge to the profession was profound; it was a call to create a positive and normative analysis of public policy *by the people*. Although the literature on collective choice has taken up the challenge, it has been more successful in dealing with the positive side. Normative analysis conducted from a collective choice perspective remains limited largely to the discussion of constitutional design and has failed so far to influence applied work dealing with taxation and public expenditure.[34] In most instances, quantitative analysis of a normative nature remains linked firmly to the social planner model.

In his own work, Wicksell focused on the optimality of decision procedures rather than of outcomes, an emphasis that later on led directly to the literature on constitutional choice. He was also concerned about coercion exercised through majority rule and proposed qualified unanimity as a solution.[35]

3.1 Efficiency and the Failure of Political Institutions

If we accept the existence of majority rule, the problem is different from the one formulated by Wicksell. A normative analysis of majority rule that parallels neoclassical welfare economics will include three elements: (i) an analog to the first theorem of welfare economics; (ii) a study of the failure of political or collective choice institutions (or "political market failure") that is derived from this theorem; and (iii) the measurement of departures from the first best. Only steps one and two have received much attention so far.

Probabilistic voting models have been used to develop analogs to the first theorem for political economies. Coughlin and Nitzan (1981), McKelvey and Patty (2001), and others show that political competition forces parties to adopt policy platforms that are consistent with Pareto efficiency. Chen (2000) extends this result to allow for bargaining among legislators. If people vote instrumentally and parties maximize expected support, competition forces parties to maximize a weighted sum of utilities, a result referred to as the *representation theorem*.[36] Otherwise, one of the parties could

---

[33] A balanced view of the ensuing literature will acknowledge Harsanyi's (1955, 1977) defense of utilitarianism as a basis for social action, a framework which relies in part on an organic view of the state (Mueller 1996, 64).

[34] On the constitutional approach, see Buchanan and Tullock 1962 and textbook treatments by Mueller 1996 and Cooter 2000.

[35] Lindahl 1919 went further and suggested a process that would result in an efficient allocation of public goods. Well aware of the assumptions necessary for the success of his model, he specified an equal distribution of power among participants. For a stimulating restatement of the Wicksellian approach, see Buchanan 1976.

[36] For further discussion see Hettich and Winer 1999, chs. 4 and 6.

increase some voters' welfare without reducing that of others, thereby improving its chance of electoral success. In a competitive equilibrium, no such Pareto improving policies will remain. The weighted sum of utilities that is maximized is *not* a social welfare function, since the weights are determined within the model by voting behavior.

In this world, the distribution of political influence matters. Parties are forced to a point on the Pareto frontier that will be more favorable to politically influential groups whose weights are relatively large. This fact is the source of some difficulty in assessing the normative properties of political equilibria: what may appear to be inefficiencies in taxation, such as inequalities in the marginal cost of funds across tax sources, may represent the minimum price of satisfying legitimately exercised political influence in a democratic society.[37]

The work shows that under certain conditions there *is* an invisible hand in democratic politics. Becker (1983) reaches a similar conclusion by arguing that those who lose from inefficient policy suffer losses that exceed the gains realized by the winners, and will spend more to push the equilibrium towards the Pareto frontier.[38] Based on empirical research, Lindert (2004) argues that the full cost of social welfare in advanced democracies has in fact been kept reasonably low. In a related way, Wittman (1995) argues that the public sector is as efficient as the market if one is careful to make a balanced assessment of private as well as of public failures.

The work by Becker and Wittman falls into the Chicago School, where emphasis is on the pervasive role of competition in pushing politicians to adopt welfare-improving policies.[39] In contrast, the Virginia School led by Buchanan sees political failure as endemic.[40] The latter group is largely concerned with the creation of constraints that limit coercion and rent-seeking and reduce the misuse of authority by elected officials and public servants.[41] A full argument will encompass both points of view. It would include a study of conditions under which equilibria are efficient, and a theory of political failure.

As an example of the analysis of political failure, consider the role of campaign advertising. If such advertising reduces private information costs about policy platforms or candidate quality without biasing the information received, it is welfare enhancing. According to the representation theorem mentioned, outcomes must then lie on the Pareto frontier (Hettich and Winer 1999, ch. 6). On the other hand, campaign advertising may affect voting behavior independently of the implications of platforms for welfare or of the quality of the candidates. In those cases, advertising may not be welfare enhancing, and restrictions on campaign finance may be warranted.

---

[37] A simple mathematical illustration of this point is found in Winer and Hettich 1998.

[38] Aidt 2003 provides further examination of Becker's approach by endogenizing political participation.

[39] See also Stigler 1972.

[40] For a recent debate between the two camps, see the exchange between Wittman and Niskanen in Winer and Shibata 2002, 101–22.

[41] Brennan and Buchanan 1980 and Buchanan and Congleton 1998 specify the nature of tax structures that will limit the extent of the damage.

The debate about the usefulness of advertising in private markets thus has its counterpart in the political context. The debate remains unsettled: Wittman (2004) argues that advertising on behalf of special interests helps uninformed voters to make better electoral choices; Coate (2004) studies situations in which the usefulness of advertising in allowing voters to better judge the quality of candidates is "too low" because voters think that excessive advertising reflects undesirable promises made to rich special interests. This debate has implications for the efficiency of equilibrium, the regulation of campaign finance, and the organization of political life in general. It shows that a type of welfare analysis is emerging in which the standard of reference is an equilibrium in a well-functioning democracy.

Besley and Coate (1997) also direct our attention to political failure using their citizen-candidate model. They explore a situation where there is one candidate who is more competent than the others (i.e. she can deliver more output per unit of revenue). But she loses to a less competent candidate because he can credibly promise a level of public services that is more in tune with a majority of voter preferences. No other candidates can enter the race and still expect to win.

Besley and Coate implicitly adopt a standard of reference where we always can find a competent candidate who shares the preferences of the majority. Questions that arise in this context relate to the supply of such candidates, and to the relative importance of competency in comparison with other factors. They call for specification of a first-best political equilibrium, thus taking us beyond the boundaries of the social planning model.

An important question in research of this type concerns measuring the "distance" from equilibrium. Rutherford and Winer (1990) suggest different metrics that could be used to evaluate the distance of a proposed policy from that in an existing equilibrium. Such metrics are required for a more formal statement about the democratic feasibility of alternative proposals.

3.2 Sustainability under Majority Rule

Another approach to normative work that takes account of collective choice focuses on the study of the compatibility of policies with democratic equilibria. An example is the work of Galasso and Profeta (2004), who consider the effect of aging on social security in selected OECD countries. Aging of the population leads to a rising dependency ratio making it more difficult to finance the system, and also has a political effect as older voters become more numerous and influential. The two effects are counterbalancing, and may or may not result in a pension system that is more generous. The authors look for policies that are likely to be able to cope with the tension between these two forces, and suggest that increasing the retirement age will be more acceptable to the electorate than a cut in benefits. Such an extension slows the growth in the dependency ratio and also reduces support for increasing the generosity of benefits.

Using a similar framework, Uebelmesser (2004) determines the latest point in time when a majority of voters would support pension reform, calculating that Italy has only a year or two, while Germany and France have until 2012 and 2014. Finally, in related work Buetler (2002) uses Swiss referenda data to test an empirical model that predicts support for and against extension of the retirement age.

3.3 Creeping Constraints

Proponents of social planning have responded to some of the criticism from work based on collective choice. An example is Boadway's (2002) scheme for politically constrained analysis that distinguishes among four stages: analysis at the constitutional, the legislative, the implementation, and the market response stage. At each level, participants take as given the outcomes of previous stages and anticipate the results of subsequent stages. Use of the planner model is advocated within this more restrictive framework *at each stage*.[42]

Boadway's framework gives formal recognition to the frequent use of ad hoc constraints in traditional analysis designed to relate outcomes more closely to the real world. Although the framework is a thoughtful response to the need for collective choice, it cannot avoid the underlying problem arising from specification of a standard of reference. A planner operating in a more limited context remains a planner. The question of whether advocated outcomes are efficient in comparison with an optimal political equilibrium remains unresolved. Boadway's observation that "it is not necessary for normative policy models to be realistic to be useful" does not deal with this point.

4 Concluding Remarks

The political economy of public finance stands at a crossroads. The planner model that has long dominated analysis is losing its hold on much of the literature, with the need for assuming consistent motivations of actors in both the public and private sectors being widely acknowledged.

Research on collective choice, by now a voluminous literature of its own, provides the means for including collective decision-making as an essential part in the examination of public sector issues. Until recently, it has appeared that the median voter model would readily serve this purpose, but the model has proven a fragile basis for theoretical and applied research because it cannot cope with the multidimensionality of budgetary choices.

After considering the nature of essential questions faced by researchers in the political economy of public finance, the chapter reviewed alternatives to the median voter model. These are frameworks that interpret public policies as equilibrium outcomes in a multidimensional setting. Most important among them are probabilistic spatial voting, the citizen-candidate model, and the party coalition model. All have

---

[42] Boadway also credits this scheme to Motohiro Sato.

the promise of leading to applied research, where observed data on taxation and expenditures are explained with formal statistical methods. However, only probabilistic spatial voting has been used so far to study actual public sector policies in considerable detail.

The challenge for empirical work is thus twofold: to choose a systematic approach from available models (or to develop a new model) and to adapt it to study specific questions concerning budgetary outcomes. The task is made more daunting by the complexity of general equilibrium analysis that incorporates an explicit political model, as well as a characterization of the private economy. The task is not impossible, however, as proven by a limited number of studies that achieve this aim.

A similar challenge applies to normative analysis. Once we abandon the construct of a central planner who maximizes a welfare function, we must develop an alternative that uses outcomes in an ideal collective choice framework as the basis against which to judge the efficiency of outcomes. While work on issues of this nature has started, it remains in its infancy and, at this time, serves mainly to critique the older planning approach. In particular, there is little work that connects particular political failures with *specific* observed features of existing fiscal systems.

The somewhat unsettled state of political economy of the public sector provides great opportunities for imaginative and innovative research. If we look at the history of economic thought, we discover that consensus in a field is often achieved after the most interesting possibilities have been exhausted and the path-breaking work has been done. Because of the complexity of issues, researchers in the field will be well advised to listen to Martin Shubik's dictum that "the suitability of a model depends as much on what is left out as on what is put in." With this in mind, the development and use of a unified framework to study the public sector in a multidimensional general equilibrium setting promises to be a rewarding task.

References

AIDT, T. 2003. Redistribution and deadweight cost: the role of political competition. *European Journal of Political Economy*, 19: 205–26.

ALDRICH, J. 1983. A Downsian spatial model with party activists. *American Political Science Review*, 77: 974–90.

ANDREONI, J. 1990. Impure altruism and donations to public goods: a theory of warm-glow giving. *Economic Journal*, 100: 464–77.

ATKINSON, A. B., and STIGLITZ, J. E. 1980. *Lectures on Public Economics*. New York: McGraw-Hill.

AUSTEN-SMITH, D. 1987. Interest groups, campaign contributions and probabilistic voting. *Public Choice*, 54: 123–39.

—— 2000. Redistributing income under proportional representation. *Journal of Political Economy*, 108: 1235–69.

BAQIR, R. 2002. Districting and government overspending. *Journal of Political Economy*, 110: 1318–54.

BECKER, G. S. 1983. A theory of competition among pressure groups for political influence. *Quarterly Journal of Economics*, 98: 371–400.

BERGSTROM, T. C., and GOODMAN, R. P. 1973. Private demands for public goods. *American Economic Review*, 63: 280–96.

BERNHEIM, B. D., and WHINSTON, M. D. 1986. Menu actions, resource allocation and economic influence. *Quarterly Journal of Economics*, 101: 1–31.

BESLEY, T. forthcoming. *Principled Agents? Motivation and Incentives in Politics*. Oxford: Oxford University Press.

—— and COATE, S. 1997. An economic model of representative democracy. *Quarterly Journal of Economics*, 112: 85–114.

—— —— 2003. On the public choice critique of welfare economics. *Public Choice*, 114: 253–73.

BLACK, D. 1958. *The Theory of Committees and Elections*. Cambridge: Cambridge University Press.

BOADWAY, R. 2002. The role of public choice considerations in normative public economics. Pp. 47–68 in *Political Economy and Public Finance: The Role of Political Economy in the Theory and Practice of Public Economics*, ed. S. Winer and H. Shitiata. Cheltenham: Edward Elgar.

BORCHERDING, T. F., and DEACON, R. T. 1972. The demand for the services of non-federal governments. *American Economic Review*, 62: 891–901.

BOWEN, H. R. 1943. The interpretation of voting in the allocation of economic resources. *Quarterly Journal of Economics*, 58: 27–48.

BRENNAN, G., and BUCHANAN, J. 1980. *The Power to Tax: Analytical Foundations of a Fiscal Constitution*. Cambridge: Cambridge University Press.

BRETON, A. 1996. *Competitive Governments: An Economic Theory of Politics and Public Finance*. Cambridge: Cambridge University Press.

BUCHANAN, J. M. 1976. Taxation in fiscal exchange. *Journal of Public Economics*, 6: 17–29.

—— and CONGLETON, R. D. 1998. *Politics by Principle, Not Interest: Towards a Nondiscriminatory Democracy*. New York: Cambridge University Press.

—— and TULLOCK, G. 1962. *The Calculus of Consent*. Ann Arbor: University of Michigan Press.

BUETLER, M. 2002. The political feasibility of increasing the retirement age: lessons from a ballot on the female retirement age. *International Tax and Public Finance*, 9: 331–48.

CHEN, Y. 2000. Electoral systems, legislative process and income taxation. *Journal of Public Economic Theory*, 2: 71–100.

CHERNICK, H., and RESCHOVSKY, A. 1996. The political economy of state and local tax structure. Pp. 253–72 in *Developments in Local Government Finance*, ed. G. Pola. G. France, and G. Levaggi. Cheltenham: Edward Elgar.

COATE, S. 2004. Pareto-improving campaign finance policy. *American Economic Review*, 94: 628–55.

CONGLETON, R., and SHUGART, W. 1990. The growth of social security expenditures: electoral push or political pull? *Economic Inquiry*, 28: 109–32.

COOTER, R. D. 2000. *The Strategic Constitution*. Princeton, NJ: Princeton University Press.

COUGHLIN, P. J., and NITZAN, S. 1981. Electoral outcomes with probabilistic voting and nash social welfare maxima. *Journal of Public Economics*, 15: 113–22.

DIXIT, A., GROSSMAN, G. M., and HELPMAN, E. 1997. Common agency and coordination: general theory and application to government policymaking. *Journal of Political Economy*, 105: 752–69.

DOWNS, A. 1957. *An Economic Theory of Democracy*. New York: Harper and Row.

DRAZEN, A. 2000. *Political Economy in Macroeconomics*. Princeton, NJ: Princeton University Press.

EDGEWORTH, F. Y. 1897. The pure theory of taxation. *Economic Journal*, 7. Repr. as pp. 119–36 in *Clasics in the Theory Poblic Finance*, ed. R. Musgrave and A. Peacock. New York: Macmillan, 1958.

FEENSTRA, R. C. 2004. *Advanced International Trade: Theory and Evidence*. Princeton, NJ: Princeton University Press.

FERRIS, S. J., and WINER, S. L. 2003. Searching for Keynes: with application to Canada, 1870–2000. Carleton University, Dept. of Economics working paper.

FREDRIKSSON, P. G. 2001. How pollution taxes may increase pollution and reduce net revenues. *Public Choice*, 103: 65–85.

GALASSO, V., and PROFETA, P. 2004. Lessons for an aging society: the political sustainability of social security reforms. *Economic Policy*, 63–115.

GAWANDE, K., and BANDYOPADHYAY, U. 2000. Is protection for sale? A test of the Grossman–Helpman theory of endogenous protection. *Review of Economics and Statistics*, 82: 139–52.

GILLESPIE, W. I. 1991. *Tax, Borrow and Spend: Financing Federal Spending in Canada, 1867–1990*. Ottawa: Carleton University Press.

GLAZER, A., and ROTHENBERG, L. 2001. *Why Government Succeeds and Why it Fails*. Cambridge, Mass.: Harvard University Press.

GOLDBERG, P. K., and MAGGI, G. 1999. Protection for sale: an empirical investigation. *American Economic Review*, 89: 1135–55.

GORDON, S. 1999. *Controlling the State: Constitutionalism from Ancient Athens to Today*. Cambridge, Mass.: Harvard University Press.

GROSSMAN, G. M., and HELPMAN, E. 1994. Protection for sale. *American Economic Review*, 89: 1135–55.

—— —— 2001. *Special Interest Politics*. Cambridge, Mass.: MIT Press.

HARBERGER, A. C. 1954. Monopoly and resource allocation. *American Economic Review: Papers and Proceedings*, 4: 77–87.

—— 1962. The incidence of the corporation income tax. *Journal of Political Economy*, 70: 215–40.

HARSANYI, J. C. 1955. Cardinal welfare, individualistic ethics and interpersonal comparison of utility. *Journal of Political Economy*, 63: 309–21.

—— 1977. *Rational Behavior and Bargaining Equilibrium in Games and Social Situations*. Cambridge: Cambridge University Press.

HETTICH, W., and WINER, S. L. 1988. Economic and political foundations of tax structure. *American Economic Review*, 78: 701–12.

—— —— 1999. *Democratic Choice and Taxation: A Theoretical and Empirical Analysis*. New York: Cambridge University Press.

HILLMAN, A. 2003. *Public Finance and Public Policy: Responsibilities and Limitations of Government*. Cambridge: Cambridge University Press.

HINICH, M., and MUNGER, M. 1994. *Ideology and the Theory of Political Choice*. Ann Arbor: University of Michigan Press.

HOCHMAN, H. M., and ROGERS, J. D. 1969. Pareto optimal redistribution. *American Economic Review*, 59: 542–57.

HOTELLING, H. 1929. Stability in competition. *Economic Journal*, 39: 41–57.

HOTTE, L., and WINER, S. L. 2001. Political influence, economic interests and endogenous tax structure in a computable equilibrium framework: with application to the United States, 1973 and 1983. *Public Choice*, 109: 66–99.

HUBER, J. D., and SHIPAN, C. R. 2002. *Deliberate Discretion: The Institutional Foundations of Bureaucratic Autonomy*. Cambridge: Cambridge University Press.

INMAN, R., and RUBINFELD, D. 1996. Designing tax policy in federalist economies: an overview. *Journal of Public Economics*, 60: 307–34.

KENNY, L. W., and TOMA, M. 1997. The role of tax bases and collection costs in the determination of income tax rates, seignorage and inflation. *Public Choice*, 92: 75–90.

―― and WINER, S. L. 2001. Tax systems in the world: an empirical investigation into the importance of tax bases, administration costs, scale and political regime. *International Tax and Public Finance*, 13: 181–215.

KIRCHGÄSSNER, G. 2002. The effects of fiscal institutions on public finance: a survey of the empirical evidence. Pp. 145–7 in *Political Economy and Public Finance: The Role of Political Economy in the Theory and Practice of Public Economics*, ed. S. Winer and H. Shibata. Cheltenham: Edward Elgar.

KRUEGER, A. O. 1974. The political economy of the rent-seeking society. *American Economic Review*, 64: 291–303.

LEE, W., and ROEMER, J. E. 2004. Racism and redistribution in the United States: a solution to the problem of American exceptionalism. Unpublished manuscript, Yale University.

LEVY, G. 2004. A model of political parties. *Journal of Economic Theory*, 115: 250–77.

LIN, T.-M., ENELOW, J. M., and DORUSSEN, H. 1999. Equilibrium in multicandidate probabilistic spatial voting. *Public Choice*, 98: 59–82.

LINDAHL, E. 1919. Just taxation: a positive solution. Pp. 168–76 in *Classics in the Theory of Public Finance*, ed. R. A. Musgrave and A. T. Peacock. London: Macmillan, 1958.

LINDBECK, A., and WEIBULL, J. W. 1987. Balanced-budget redistribution as the outcome of political competition. *Public Choice*, 52: 273–97.

LINDERT, P. 2004. *Growing Public: Social Spending and Economic Growth since the Eighteenth Century*. Cambridge: Cambridge University Press.

MCKELVEY, R. D. 1976. Intransitivities in multidimensional voting models and some implications for agenda control. *Journal of Economic Theory*, 12: 472–82.

―― and PATTY, J. W. 2001. A theory of voting in large elections. Unpublished manuscript, Dept. of Social Sciences, Carnegie Mellon University.

MARCEAU, N., and SMART, M. 2003. Corporate lobbying and commitment failure in capital taxation. *American Economic Review*, 93: 241–51.

MELTZER, A. H., and RICHARD, S. F. 1981. A rational theory of the size of government. *Journal of Political Economy*, 89: 914–27.

―― ―― 1983. Tests of a rational theory of the size of government. *Public Choice*, 41: 403–18.

MERRILL, S., III, and GROFMAN, B. 1999. *A Unified Theory of Voting: Directional and Proximity Models*. Cambridge: Cambridge University Press.

MIESZKOWSKI, P. M. 1967. On the theory of tax incidence. *Journal of Political Economy*, 75: 250–62.

―― and ZODROW, G. 1986. Pigou, Tiebout, property taxation and under-provision of local public goods. *Journal of Urban Economics*, 19: 356–70.

MILLER, G., and SCHOFIELD, N. 2003. Activists and party realignment in the United States. *American Political Science Review*, 97: 245–60.

MIRRLEES, J. A. 1971. An exploration in the theory of optimum income taxation. *Review of Economic Studies*, 38: 175–208.

MOE, T. M. 1997. The positive theory of public bureaucracy. Pp. 455–80 in *Perspectives on Public Choice: A Handbook*, ed. D. Mueller. Cambridge: Cambridge University Press.

MUELLER, D. C. 1996. *Constitutional Democracy*. Oxford: Oxford University Press.

―― 2003. *Public Choice III*. Cambridge: Cambridge University Press.

―― and STRATMANN, T. 2003. The economic effects of democratic participation. *Journal of Public Economics*, 87: 2129–55.

MUSGRAVE, R. 1959. *The Theory of Public Finance*. New York: McGraw-Hill.

―― and PEACOCK, A. (eds.). 1958. *Classics in the Theory of Public Finance*. New York: Macmillan.

NISKANEN, W. A., JR. 1971. *Bureaucracy and Representative Government*. Chicago: Aldine-Atherton.

OLSON, M., JR. 1965. *The Logic of Collective Action: Public Goods and the Theory of Groups*. Cambridge, Mass.: Harvard University Press.

OSBORNE, M. J., and SLIVINSKY, A. 1996. A model of political competition with citizen-candidates. *Quarterly Journal of Economics*, 111: 65–96.

OSTROM, E. 1990. *Governing the Commons: The Evolution of Institutions for Collective Action*. Cambridge: Cambridge University Press.

PANTALEONI, M. 1883. Contribution to the theory of the distribution of public expenditure. Repr. as pp. 16–27 in *Classics in the Theory of Public Finance*, ed. R. Musgrave and A. Peacock. New York: Macmillan, 1958.

PERSSON, T., ROLAND, G., and TABELLINI, G. 2004. How do electoral rules shape party structures, government coalitions, and economic policies? CESifo Working Paper No. 1115.

——and TABELLINI, G. 2000. *Political Economics: Explaining Economic Policy*. Cambridge, Mass.: MIT Press.

PIGOU, A. C. 1951. *A Study in Public Finance*, 3rd edn. London: Macmillan.

PROFETA, P. 2002. Retirement and social security in a probabilistic voting model. *International Tax and Public Finance*, 9: 331–48.

RAMSEY, F. P. 1927. A contribution to the theory of taxation. *Economic Journal*, 37: 47–61.

RIKER, W. H. 1986. *The Art of Political Manipulation*. New Haven, Conn.: Yale University Press.

ROEMER, J. E. 2001. *Political Competition: Theory and Application*. Cambridge, Mass.: Harvard University Press.

—— 2003. Indeterminacy of citizen candidate equilibrium. Cowles Foundation Discussion Paper No. 1410.

ROMER, T. 1975. Individual welfare, majority voting and the properties of a linear income tax. *Journal of Public Economics*, 4: 163–85.

RUTHERFORD, T., and WINER, S. L. 1990. Endogenous policy in a computational general equilibrium framework. Pp. 285–309 in S. Winer, *Political Economy in Federal States: Selected Essays of Stanley L. Winer*, Cheltenham: Edward Elgar, 2002.

SALANIÉ, B. 2000. *Microeconomics of Market Failure*. Cambridge, Mass.: MIT Press.

SAMUELSON, P. A. 1954. The pure theory of public expenditure. *Review of Economics and Statistics*, 36: 387–9.

SCHOFIELD, N. 1978. Instability of simple dynamic games. *Review of Economic Studies*, 45: 575–94.

—— 2003. Valence competition in the spatial stochastic model. *Journal of Theoretical Politics*, 15: 371–83.

SCHUMPETER, J. A. 1954. *History of Economic Analysis*. Oxford: Oxford University Press.

SHEPSLE, K. A., and WEINGAST, B. R. 1981. Structure-induced equilibrium and legislative choice. *Public Choice*, 37: 503–19.

SHOVEN, J. B., and WHALLEY, J. 1992. *General Equilibrium Modeling*. Cambridge: Cambridge University Press.

SKAPERDAS, S. 2003. Restraining the genuine homo economicus: why the economy cannot be divorced from its governance. *Economics and Politics*, 15: 135–62.

STIGLER, G. 1972. Economic competition and political competition. *Public Choice*, 13: 91–106.

TIEBOUT, C. M. 1956. A pure theory of local expenditures. *Journal of Political Economy*, 64: 416–24.

TULLOCK, G. 1967. The welfare costs of tariffs, monopolies and theft. *Western Economic Journal*, 5: 224–32.

_____ 2004. Problems of voting. Unpublished paper presented at the Public Choice Meetings, Baltimore.

UEBELMESSER, S. 2004. Political feasibility of pension reforms. *Topics in Economic Analysis and Policy*, 4: 1162.

USHER, D. 1994. The significance of the probabilistic voting theorem. *Canadian Journal of Economics*, 27: 433–45.

_____ 2003. Testing the citizen candidate model. Unpublished manuscript, Queen's University.

WICKSELL, K. 1896. A new principle of just taxation. Pp. 72–118 in *Classics in the Theory of Public Finance*, ed. R. Musgrave and A. Peacock. New York: Macmillan, 1958.

WINER, S. L. 1983. Some evidence on the separation of spending and taxing decisions. *Journal of Political Economy*, 91: 126–40.

_____ and HETTICH, W. 1998. What is missed if we leave out collective choice in the analysis of taxation. *National Tax Journal*, 51: 373–90.

_____ _____ 2004. The political economy of taxation: positive and normative analysis when collective choice matters. Pp. 173–91 in *Encyclopedia of Public Choice*, vol. i, ed. C. Rowley and F. Schneider. Dordrecht: Kluwer Academic.

_____ and SHIBATA, H. (eds.). 2002. *Political Economy and Public Finance: The Role of Political Economy in the Theory and Practice of Public Economics*. Cheltenham: Edward Elgar.

WINTROBE, R. 1997. Modern bureaucratic theory. Pp. 429–54 in *Perspectives on Public Choice: A Handbook*, ed. D. Mueller. Cambridge: Cambridge University Press.

WITTMAN, D. 1995. *The Myth of Democratic Failure: Why Political Institutions are Efficient*. Chicago: University of Chicago Press.

_____ 2004. Pressure groups and uninformed voters. Pp. 429–32 in *Encyclopedia of Public Choice*, vol. ii, ed. C. Rowley and F. Schneider. Dordrecht: Kluwer Academic.

CHAPTER 26

POLITICAL ECONOMY OF FISCAL INSTITUTIONS

JÜRGEN VON HAGEN

1 INTRODUCTION

THE core of public finances is that some people spend other people's money. In democracies, voters delegate the power over public spending and taxes to elected politicians. Two aspects of this are particularly important for the conduct of fiscal policy. The first is the principal–agent relationship between voters (the principals) and politicians (the agents). The second is the common-pool problem of public finances (von Hagen and Harden 1996).

The principal–agent relationship implies that politicians can extract rents from being in office. Voters might wish to limit these rents by subjecting politicians to strict rules. However, the uncertainty and complexity of economic and political developments prohibit the writing of complete contracts. Therefore, the principal–agent relation resembles an "incomplete contract" leaving politicians with considerable residual powers (Seabright 1996; Persson, Roland, and Tabellini 1997; Persson and Tabellini 1999a, 1999b, 2000; Tabellini 2000). The greater these residual powers

---

* I am grateful to Mark Hallerberg, Barry Weingast, and Donald Wittman for helpful comments and discussions.

are, the greater will be the divergence between voter preferences and actual policies. This basic claim has been tested and confirmed by comparing public finances under representative democracy and direct democracy, which gives voters more opportunities to express their preferences and more direct control over politicians, and hence fewer residual powers to politicians (Pommerehne 1978, 1990; Matsusaka 1995; Kirchgässner Feld, and Savioz 1999; Feld and Kirchgässner 1999; Feld and Matsusaka 2003).

The common-pool problem arises when politicians can spend money from a general tax fund on targeted public policies. The fact that the group of those who pay for specific targeted policies (the general taxpayer) is larger than the group of those who benefit from them implies a divergence between the net benefits accruing to the targeted groups and the net benefits for society as a whole. This divergence induces the targeted groups and the politicians representing them to demand more spending on such policies than what is optimal for society as a whole. Thus, the common-pool problem leads to excessive levels of public spending. Putting the argument into a dynamic context, one can show that it also leads to excessive deficits and government debts (Velasco 1999; von Hagen and Harden 1996). This tendency for excessive spending, deficits, and debt increases with the number of politicians drawing on the same general tax fund, a point empirically confirmed by Kontopoulos and Perotti (1999). Ideological and ethnic divisions or ethno-linguistic and religious fractionalization of societies increase the tendency of people on one side to neglect the tax burden falling on the other side, making the common-pool problem more severe. Thus, empirical studies showing that such schisms result in higher spending levels, deficits, and debt confirm the importance of the common-pool problem (Roubini and Sachs 1989; Alesina and Perotti 1995; Alesina, Baqir, and Easterly 1997; Annett 2000).

The common-pool problem also looms large behind vertical fiscal relations within countries. Transfers from the central to local governments imply that residents in one region benefit from taxes paid by residents in other regions. Bailouts of over-indebted local governments are a special form of such transfers. Careaga and Weingast (2000) show how vertical transfers distort local decisions towards excess spending and a bias in favor of public consumption. The studies collected in Rodden, Eskelund, and Litvack (2003) and Fernandez-Arias, Stein, and von Hagen (forthcoming) confirm the empirical relevance of bailouts in many countries.

The adverse consequences of the principal–agent problem and the common-pool problem can be mitigated by institutions governing the decisions over public finances. Three types of fiscal institutions are particularly relevant in this context: (1) *ex ante* rules such as constitutional limits on deficits, spending, or taxes, (2) electoral rules fostering political accountability and competition, and (3) procedural rules of the budget process. Studying the effects of these three types of fiscal institutions has been a very active field of research in the past fifteen years, stimulated by the need to rein in excessive spending and deficits in OECD and developing countries alike, and by the European Union's desire to find an adequate set of rules governing national fiscal policies in its monetary union.

This chapter reviews and discusses this research on fiscal institutions. Section 2 deals with *ex ante* rules. Section 3 discusses the roles of electoral institutions. Section 4 considers the budget process. Section 5 concludes.

2 *Ex Ante* Rules

We define *ex ante* fiscal rules as numerical constraints on certain budgetary aggregates. Prominent examples are the balanced budget constraints, numerical debt ceilings, and limits on (the growth of) taxes and spending that exist in almost all states of the USA and most provinces in Canada, and the numerical debt and deficit limits of the European Monetary Union. Historically, such rules were often imposed by taxpayers, who were angry about the spending profligacy of their elected representatives (Eichengreen and von Hagen 1996; Millar 1997) or rising taxes (Alm and Skidmore 1999). *Ex ante* rules are also frequently imposed on subnational governments to protect the central government against the risk of having to bail out highly indebted subnational governments with limited revenue sources of their own (von Hagen and Eichengreen 1996).

There is a fair amount of variation in the scope and strictness of *ex ante* rules (see ACIR 1987 and Strauch 1998 for the USA; Jones, Sanguinetti, and Tommasi 1999 for Argentine provinces; Hallerberg, Strauch, and von Hagen 2001 for European countries; and von Hagen and Eichengreen 1996, and Stein, Grisanti, and Talvi 1999 for other countries). At the national level, *ex ante* fiscal rules remain fairly rare (see Kennedy and Robbins 2001 and Kopits 2001). Germany, Italy, Japan, and the Netherlands introduced such rules after the Second World War to enhance the credibility of their macroeconomic stabilization programs. In the USA, the Gramm–Rudman–Hollings legislation of the 1980s is a prominent example of an unsuccessful *ex ante* rule. Canada and New Zealand introduced fiscal rules at the national level in the early 1990s, as did the member states of the European Monetary Union. In Switzerland, a constitutional-debt limit was voted into effect by public referendum in December 2001.

Ex ante rules seem straightforward to control politicians and attractive for simplicity and transparency. But how successful are they? Empirical evidence (Strauch 1998; Eichengreen 1990; von Hagen 1991) suggests that US state governments subject to stringent numerical deficit constraints tend to substitute debt instruments not covered by the legal rule for the debt instruments that are, leaving total debt unaffected. Kiewiet and Szakaly (1996) find that state governments subject to more restrictive borrowing constraints tend to substitute municipal debts for state debt. Fatas et al. (2003) find that the deficit limits of the European Monetary Union did not constrain deficits in the large member states effectively. Wolff and von Hagen (2004) show that member states of the European Monetary Union use creative accounting to circumvent the deficit limits. In US states, constitutional expenditure limits tend to induce a shift from the (constrained) current budget to the (unconstrained) investment budget (Strauch 1998). Rueben (1997) and Shadbegian (1996) find no significant effects of tax and expenditure limits on the level of spending in cross-section studies of US states. Controlling for the possible endogeneity of the rules, Rueben (1997) finds that the tax burden is slightly lower in the presence of tax limits. The key insight from this research is that the effectiveness of *ex ante* fiscal rules is limited at best, because the rules can be circumvented.

Furthermore, *ex ante* limits on subnational government deficits and debts can create a strategic dilemma for the central government, if the subnational governments do not own a sufficiently strong tax base. Bordignon (2000) shows that, in the 1970s and 1980s, Italian local governments frequently overran their budgets and turned to the national government for additional transfers, threatening to close down critical public services like hospitals and schools otherwise. Knowing that they could not borrow for legal reasons and had no tax-significant sources of their own, the national government had little choice but to give in to their demands. Several of the case studies of local government bailouts in Latin America collected in Fernandez-Arias, Stein, and von Hagen (forthcoming) describe similar strategic behavior by subnational governments. Von Hagen and Eichengreen (1996) find that central government debt ratios tend to be higher in countries where subnational governments are subject to *ex ante* borrowing constraints. This suggests that central governments accommodate demands from local governments to borrow on their behalf, exposing the central government to more financial fragility.

Several authors have suggested that *ex ante* limits on deficits and debts have beneficial effects on risk premia contained in government bond yields (Goldstein and Woglom 1992; Poterba and Rueben 1999). However, there may be harmful effects as well. Tight balanced budget constraints may prevent reforms because governments cannot smooth their fiscal costs over time. Razin and Sadka (2003) illustrate this point in the context of social security reform in an aging society, where the benefits and taxes of a pay-as-you-go system must be scaled back to keep the system viable. To be acceptable to both the current young and old generations, this reform must be financed in part by an increase in government debt. With a tight limit on government debt, the reform fails to win the required political support. In this case, the fiscal rules effectively undermine the financial stability of the government, because it focuses too narrowly on current and explicit debt and neglects future fiscal liabilities.

Poterba (1994) shows that states subject to more stringent numerical limits on deficits and debt tend have more pro-cyclical and, hence, less efficient fiscal policies and more macroeconomic volatility. In contrast, Fatas and Mihov (2003) find that *ex ante* rules prevent governments from engaging in discretionary policies creating unnecessary macroeconomic fluctuations. The result would be more efficient fiscal policies and less macroeconomic volatility. Fatas and Mihov (2004) provide econometric evidence suggesting that the second effect dominates. Thus, the implications of *ex ante* rules for macroeconomic stability remain an open question.

3 Political Competition and Accountability

According to the retrospective-voting paradigm, voters use elections to hold politicians accountable for past performance. They reappoint incumbents if they find their behavior satisfactory; otherwise, they vote for competing candidates. This suggests that rents can be limited by strict accountability and fierce competition. Political accountability and competition are determined by the rules governing political elections. Electoral rules are characterized by district magnitude, electoral formula, and ballot structure. District magnitude relates to the number of representatives elected from each electoral district. Electoral formula translates votes into seats. Ballot structure determines how citizens vote, e.g. they cast votes for individual candidates or they vote for entire party lists.

Different combinations of these three characteristics exist and they frequently do not conform neatly to stylized prototypes. A few tendencies can be identified, however. The combination of small district magnitude, plurality rule, and votes cast for individual candidates focuses the election on the personal performance of the candidates, maximizing personal accountability. In contrast, large district magnitude combined with proportional representation and votes cast for party lists focuses the election on the average performance of all candidates on the party list and weakens personal accountability. Thus, one should expect that the scope for extracting political rents from being in office is smaller with small district magnitude, plurality rule, and votes cast for individual candidates.

But electoral rules emphasizing personal accountability also give voters a greater opportunity to reward politicians for channeling general tax funds in their direction. If individual effort rather than average party effort is rewarded, each politician has a greater incentive to fight for policies benefiting his constituency. Furthermore, the winner-take-all structure of electoral outcomes under plurality rule implies that the minimum winning coalition of voters to gain a majority in parliament is smaller than under proportional representation. Plurality rule therefore induces politicians to target small but critical constituencies in individual electoral districts by providing the local public goods and services they demand. In contrast, proportional representation forces political parties to seek the support of broader shares of the electorate and, therefore, induces politicians to favor policies benefiting large groups of voters such as general public goods and welfare programs which benefit voters in many electoral districts (Persson and Tabellini 2004*a*; Milesi-Ferretti, Perotti, and Rostagno 2002; Lizzeri and Persico 2001).

The implications for public finance are threefold. First, by putting a check on rent extraction, electoral rules strengthening personal accountability should lead to lower levels of public spending. Second, proportional representation should lead to higher shares of broad-based welfare programs and general public goods in public spending than plurality rule. Third, both proportional representation and plurality rule contribute to the common-pool problem, although they promote different types of targeted policies. As discussed below, the extent to which the common-pool problem leads to excessive levels of spending, deficits, and debt depends on the design of the budget process. This implies that empirical tests of the first two implications should control for the prevailing budgetary institutions.

We now turn to the other aspect, competition. The need to gain a large share of votes in a district under plurality rule is an important barrier to entry for small parties. Political newcomers find it difficult to challenge incumbent politicians, because they need a majority to succeed from the start. In contrast, newcomers can win at least a small number of seats in parliament under proportional representation. Political competition is, therefore, more intense under the latter system, particularly when minimum vote thresholds are low. If contestants use the election campaign to identify waste and point to instances of rent extraction, one can expect more intense competition to lead to less waste and smaller rents. Thus, the consequences of weaker accountability under proportional representation may be compensated by more intense competition.

3.1 Empirical Evidence

The preceding discussion implies that detailed characterizations are necessary to capture the full details of electoral rules. As a result, one should not expect simple, clear-cut results. Some interesting evidence exists nevertheless. Persson and Tabellini (2004b) find that, in a panel of ninety democracies, countries with plurality rule have smaller governments than countries with proportional representation, and that the differences are economically significant. Persson and Tabellini (2003) find that, in a panel of sixty democracies, all countries expanded the size of government over the 1970s and 1980s, but countries with plurality rule experienced lower growth of government spending than countries with proportional representation.

Persson, Tabellini, and Trebbi (2003) find that proportional representation is associated with higher levels of corruption than plurality rule. If corruption is a proxy for rents, this is consistent with the theory. Persson and Tabellini (1999b, 2004b) and Milesi-Ferretti et al. (2002) also show that governments elected under plurality rule are characterized by lower shares of spending on general public goods and broad-based welfare programs than those elected under proportional representation.

Hallerberg (2000) argues that Italy's electoral reforms of 1994 were an important factor enabling the country to meet the fiscal requirements of European Monetary Union. Wibbels (2003) finds that, in the 1820s to 1840s, governments of US states where political competition was low had a greater tendency to accumulate large debt burdens than governments in more competitive states. Skilling (2001) reports a similar finding for a set of OECD countries after the Second World War. Hallerberg and Marier (2004) study a sample of Latin American states and find that the common-pool problem is more relevant in countries whose electoral rules focus on personal accountability. In sum, while the existing evidence is scant, it supports the view that electoral rules have important consequences for public spending.

4 LIMITING THE COMMON-POOL PROBLEM: THE BUDGET PROCESS

At the heart of the common-pool problem of public finances is an externality that results from using general tax funds to finance targeted public policies. Individual politicians perceive that an increase in spending on targeted policies will provide their constituencies with more public services at only a fraction of the total cost. The resulting spending and deficit biases can be reduced by inducing politicians to take a comprehensive view of the costs and benefits of their decisions. This is the main role of the budget process in our context. The budget process consists of the formal and informal rules governing budgetary decisions of the executive and legislative branches of government. A centralized budget process contains elements that induce decision-makers to internalize the common-pool externality by taking a comprehensive view of their decisions. A fragmented budget process fails to do that.

In this context, centralization refers to the internal organization rather than the geographical structure of budgetary decisions. Centralization of the budget process requires that all conflicts between competing claims on public finances are resolved within its scope. Four deviations from this principle result in fragmentation. The first is the use of off-budget funds allowing policy-makers to make financial decisions without being challenged by conflicting distributional interests. The second are non-decisions, which make budgetary expenditures dependent on developments exogenous to the budget process, such as the indexation of spending programs and open-ended welfare appropriations. Non-decisions degrade the budget process to a mere forecast of exogenous developments. The third deviation occurs when non-financial laws can make certain government expenditures compulsory, which implies that budgetary decisions are made outside the budget process. The fourth deviation results from unreported contingent liabilities such as guarantees for the liabilities of public or private enterprises or financial institutions. Contingent liabilities imply that the *ex post* distribution of public funds can differ significantly from the distribution negotiated in the budget process.

Transparency is another important prerequisite of centralization. It requires that the budget documents are comprehensive and that expenditures are clearly attributed to the relevant decision-making units within the government. Lack of transparency creates opportunities for collusion among self-interested policy-makers and prevents decision-makers from developing a comprehensive view of the consequences of their decisions.

Budget processes can be proximately divided into four stages, each involving different actors with different roles. The executive planning stage involves the drafting of the budget by the executive. The legislative approval stage includes the process of parliamentary amendments to the budget proposal, which may involve more than one house of parliament. The executive implementation stage covers the fiscal year to which the budget law applies. The *ex post* accountability stage involves a review of the final budget documents by a court of auditors or a similar institution checking their consistency with the legal authorization.

Reviewing budget processes in Europe, the USA, Latin America, and Asia reveals that centralization follows two basic approaches. The first is centralization based on delegation, the second is centralization based on contracts.

With delegation, the rules of the executive planning stage of the budget process lend special authority to a central agent who determines the broad parameters of the budget and enforces them using selective punishments for defecting spending ministers. Typically this agent is the finance minister, who can be expected to take the most comprehensive view of the budget among all members of the executive, and, therefore, to internalize the common-pool externality. At the legislative approval stage, the delegation approach lends large agenda-setting powers to the executive. At the implementation stage, centralization requires that the central agent be able to monitor and control the flow of expenditures during the year, to prevent spending departments from overspending their appropriations. Furthermore, centralization puts tight limits on any changes in the budget law during the fiscal year and limits the use of supplementary budgets.

In contrast, the contract approach emphasizes binding budgetary agreements on a set of fiscal targets negotiated among all members of the executive at the onset of the executive planning stage. Here, the bargaining process serves as a mechanism to internalize the common-pool externality. In practice, the targets are often derived from medium-term fiscal programs or coalition agreements among the ruling parties. The finance ministry's role under this approach is to evaluate the consistency of the individual departments' spending plans with these limits. Thus, the finance minister has information advantages but no extra strategic powers. At the legislative stage, the contract approach places more weight on the role of the legislature monitoring the faithful implementation of the fiscal targets and less on controlling parliamentary amendments. At the implementation stage, finally, the contract approach resembles the delegation approach in that it requires strong monitoring and control powers of the finance minister.

It is quite obvious that the delegation approach relies on hierarchical structures within the executive, and between the executive and the legislature, while the contract approach builds on a more even distribution of authorities in government. In democratic settings, hierarchical structures typically prevail within political parties, while relations between parties are more even. This suggests that the institutional choice between the two approaches depends on the number of parties in government. Delegation is appropriate for single-party governments, while the contracts approach is appropriate for multiparty coalition governments (Hallerberg and von Hagen 1999). There are two reasons behind this conjecture.

First, the delegation of strategic powers to the finance minister would create a new principal–agent problem for coalition governments. Cabinet members are likely to have very different views on spending priorities and the finance minister could abuse any special powers he has to promote the political interests of his own party at the cost of others. This problem does not arise in one-party governments, where spending ministers can be reasonably sure that the finance minister shares their basic spending preferences.

Second, delegation and contracts use different enforcement mechanisms. Under delegation, the ultimate punishment for a defecting spending minister is his dismissal from office. This punishment is heavy for the individual, but light for the government as a whole. It can be used, if the prime minister has the authority to select and replace cabinet members, which is typically not true in coalition governments. Breaking up the coalition is the ultimate punishment in coalition governments. This punishment is heavy for the entire coalition. Finally, commitment to fiscal targets is per se much less credible for one-party governments, who can always walk away from the targets with no further consequences.

These different enforcement mechanisms also explain the different relations between the executive and the legislature. When a single ruling party enjoys a majority in parliament, the main concern of the legislative stage is to limit the scope of defections from the budget proposals by individual members of parliament. This can be achieved by limiting the scope of parliamentary amendments to the budget proposal. With multiparty coalitions, in contrast, each party involved in the coalition will want to watch carefully that the executive sticks to the coalition agreement. Therefore, the contract approach typically vests the legislature with more information rights and stronger amendment power than the delegation approach (Hallerberg, Strauch, and von Hagen 2001).

Elections based on plurality rule promote the emergence of two-party systems and one-party majority governments (Duverger 1954; Taagepera and Shugart 1989, 1993). In contrast, proportional representation is consistently characterized by multiparty coalition governments (Lijphart 1984, 1994; Taagepera and Shugart 1989, 1993). This suggests that countries are more likely to opt for the contract approach if their elections are based on proportional representation (and low thresholds), while they are more likely to opt for delegation if their elections based on plurality rule. Hallerberg and von Hagen (1998) and Hallerberg, Strauch, and von Hagen (2001) test and confirm this hypothesis for the European Union states. Thus, different electoral rules demand different institutional solutions to the common-pool problem.

In presidential systems of government, the president does not rely directly on the legislature for his position as leader of the executive. Voters can, and often do, support a president from one party while denying his party a majority in the legislature. The role of the executive in the budget process is not much different in presidential systems. Since the president typically appoints the members of his administration—with confirmation by the legislature where applicable—the structure of the administration lends itself more to a delegation approach than to a contract approach to centralizing the budget process. The relationship between the president and the legislature, however, is often more difficult, since the two are conceived to be more equal political institutions than in parliamentary forms of governments.

As a result, centralization of the budget process in presidential systems emphasizes two institutional dimensions. One is the internal organization of the legislature. Here, centralization can be achieved by creating a strong leadership in parliament, through an elevated position of the speaker and through a hierarchical committee structure. The other dimension regards the relation between the executive and the legislature. The more the constitution puts the two institutions on an equal footing, the more budget agreements between the two must rely on the contract approach.

4.1 Empirical Evidence

The hypothesis that centralization of the budget process leads to lower government deficits and debts has been confirmed empirically in very different geographical and political settings. Von Hagen (1992) provides evidence from twelve European Union countries showing a significant negative association between the centralization of the budget process and general government deficits and debts relative to GDP. Von Hagen and Harden (1994b) extend and broaden the analysis and confirm the hypothesis that centralization of the budget process is associated with smaller deficits and debts. De Haan and Sturm (1994) work with EU data and show that the hypothesis holds up empirically even when a number of political factors such as the composition and stability of governments are controlled for. Hallerberg and von Hagen (1998, 1999) use panel data for fifteen EU countries and show that centralization of the budget process goes along with smaller annual budget deficits even when controlling for a number of economic determinants of the budget deficit and other political variables. Country studies for Belgium (Stienlet 2000), Sweden (Molander 2000), and Germany (Strauch and von Hagen 1999) point to the importance of centralization in achieving (or, in the case of Germany, losing) fiscal discipline.

Gleich (2002) studies the budget processes in ten central and east European countries, an interesting sample since a budget process in the proper sense did not exist under the socialist regime. All ten countries hold elections under various forms of proportional representation. Gleich shows that centralization conforms to the contract approach in these countries and that there is a strong negative association between the degree of centralization of the budget process and the public sector deficits and debts that emerged in the second half of the 1990s. His results are largely confirmed by Yläoutinen (2004a, 2004b).

Alesina et al (1999) and Stein, Grisanti, and Talvi (1999) use panel data from Latin America to show that centralization of the budget process goes along with lower government deficits. Jones, Sanguinetti, and Tommasi (1999) analyze Argentine provinces and confirm the same hypothesis. Lao-Araya (1997) provides similar results for eleven Asian countries. Strauch (1998) uses data from the fifty US state governments to show that centralization significantly reduces annual budget deficits. Finally, Strauch (1998) and Gleich (2002) show that centralization of the budget process is also associated with smaller levels of government spending, as the common-pool argument suggests. Other empirical studies, however, have failed to confirm this aspect of the theory. A suggestive explanation is that the common-pool problem implies that actual spending exceeds its efficient level, and that controlling for differences in the efficient level of spending is more difficult in cross-country studies than in the context of US state governments or the central and east European countries.

The possible endogeneity of institutions is an interesting and important issue in this context. Historical experience suggests that governments make efforts to centralize the budget process to overcome sharp fiscal crises. Relevant examples are France in the 1950s (Wildavsky 1986) and Sweden in the 1990s (Molander 2000). Studying the imposition of line-item vetoes in US state governments, de Figueiredo (2003) finds that fiscal conservatives strengthen the role of the executive in the budget process when they anticipate losing control over the legislature to fiscal liberals. Gleich and von Hagen (2002) find that states in central and east Europe characterized by greater social cleavages have adopted more centralized budget processes. This suggests that legislatures were willing to relinquish powers, anticipating that budgeting would be plagued by the consequences of severe common-pool problems otherwise. Hallerberg, Strauch, and von Hagen (2001) find that the choice between the delegation and the contracts approach to centralization among EU states confirms their prediction that the former is more adequate for single-party majority governments, while the latter is more adequate for coalition governments. Hallerberg (2004), in a study of EU countries since 1973, argues that countries with more intense political competition are more likely to adopt institutions that address the common-pool problem. All these studies indicate that institutional design responds to political factors and circumstances. More work is necessary to understand this interaction better.

5 Conclusions

The political economy of fiscal institutions has emerged as a fascinating and lively field of academic research in the last decade. Insights and implications of this research are of considerable practical relevance as they touch on important questions of the design and reform of constitutions, governments, and executive processes.

The research reviewed in this chapter takes the principal–agent relationship between the voter and the politicians and the common-pool property of public funds as the starting points. It strongly suggests that institutional design matters for fiscal performance. It also suggests that different political and constitutional environments demand different institutional solutions to these problems. More research is needed to explore this avenue. Furthermore, the research reviewed here has considered fiscal institutions of different kinds. Constitutional aspects such as electoral rules or the degree of political decentralization seem to be more fundamental than budgetary processes, but the latter should not be ignored. Future research into the fiscal effects of constitutions should pay more attention to controlling for the effects of these lower-level institutions. Furthermore, more research is needed on the endogeneity of constitutional aspects and how the factors that impinge on them affect the effectiveness of lower-level institutions.

References

ADVISORY COUNCIL FOR INTERSTATE RELATIONS (ACIR) 1987. The effect of constitutional restraints on government spending. In *Significant Features of Fiscal Federalism*. Washington, DC: ACIR.

ALESINA, A., BAQIR, R., and EASTERLY, W. 1997. Public goods and ethnic divisions. NBER Working Paper No. 6009.

—— and PEROTTI, R. 1995. Fiscal expansions and adjustments in OECD countries. *Economic Policy*, 207–48.

—— HAUSMAN, R., HOMMES, R., and STEIN, E. 1999. Budget institutions and fiscal performance in Latin America. *Journal of Development Economics*, 59: 253–73.

ALM, J., and SKIDMORE, M. 1999. Why do tax and expenditure limitations pass in state elections? *Public Finance Review*, 27: 481–510.

ANNETT, A. 2000. Social fractionalization, political instability, and the size of government. IMF Working Paper 00/82.

BORDIGNON, M. 2000. Problems of soft budget constraints in intergovernmental relationships: the case of Italy. Working paper, Catholic University of Milan.

CAREAGA, M., and WEINGAST, B. R. 2000. The fiscal pact with the devil: a positive approach to fiscal federalism, revenue sharing, and good governance. Working paper, Stanford University.

DE FIGUEIREDO, R. J. P. 2003, Endogenous budget institutions and political insulation: why states adopt the line item veto. *Journal of Public Economics*, 87: 2677–701.

DE HAAN, J., and STURM, J.-E. 1994. Political and institutional determinants of fiscal policy in the European Community. *Public Choice*, 80: 157–72.

DUVERGER, M. 1954. *Political Parties: Their Organization and Activity in the Modern State*. New York: Wiley.

EICHENGREEN, B. 1990. One money for Europe? Lessons from the US currency Union. *Economic Policy*, 10: 119–86.

—— and VON HAGEN, J. 1996. Fiscal policy and monetary union: federalism, fiscal restrictions, and the no-bailout rule. In *Monetary Policy in an Integrated World Economy*, ed. H. Siebert. Tübingen: JCB Mohr.

FATAS, A., and MIHOV, I. 2003. The case for restricting fiscal policy discretion. *Quarterly Journal of Economics*, 118: 1419–48.

—— —— 2004. The macroeconomic effects of fiscal rules in the U.S. states. Mimeo, INSEAD.

—— HALLETT, A. H., SIBERT, A., STRAUCH, R., and VON HAGEN, J. 2003. *Stability and Growth in Europe: Towards a Better Pact*. Monitoring European Integration 13. London: CEPR.

FELD, L. P., and KIRCHGÄSSNER, G. 1999. Public debt and budgetary procedures: top down or bottom up? In *Fiscal Institutions and Fiscal Performance*, ed. J. Poterba and J. von Hagen. Chicago: University of Chicago Press.

—— and MATSUSAKA, J. G. 2003. Budget referendums and government spending: evidence from Swiss cantons. *Journal of Public Economics*, 87: 2703–24.

FERNANDEZ-ARIAS, E., STEIN, E., and VON HAGEN, J. (eds.) forthcoming. *Subnational Government Bail-outs*.

GLEICH, H. 2002. The evolution of budget institutions in central and eastern European countries. Ph.D. dissertation, University of Bonn.

—— and VON HAGEN, J. 2002. The evolution of budget institutions: evidence from central and east European countries. Mimeo, ZEI, University of Bonn.

GOLDSTEIN, M., and WOGLOM, G. 1992. Market-based fiscal discipline in monetary unions: evidence from the U.S. municipal bond market. In *Establishing a Central Bank: Issues in Europe and Lessons from the US*, ed. M. Canzoneri, V. Grilli, and P. R. Masson. New York: Cambridge University Press.

HALLERBERG, M. 2000. The importance of domestic political institutions: why and how Belgium and Italy qualified for EMU. ZEI discussion paper, ZEI, University of Bonn.

—— 2004. *Domestic Budgets in a United Europe: Fiscal Governance from the End of Bretton Woods to EMU*. Ithaca, NY: Cornell University Press.

—— and MARIER, P. 2004. Executive authority, the personal vote, and budget discipline in Latin American and Caribbean countries. *American Journal of Political Science*, 48: 571–87.

—— and VON HAGEN, J. 1998. Electoral institutions and the budget process. In *Democracy, Decentralization, and Deficits in Latin America*, ed. K. Fukasaku and R. Hausmann. Paris: OECD Development Center.

—— —— 1999. Electoral institutions, cabinet negotiations, and budget deficits in the EU. In *Fiscal Institutions and Fiscal Performance*, ed. J. Poterba and J. von Hagen. Chicago: University of Chicago Press.

—— STRAUCH, R. R., and VON HAGEN, J. 2001. The use and effectiveness of fiscal norms and rules in the EU. Research Report to the Dutch Ministry of Finance, The Hague.

JONES, M. P., SANGUINETTI, P., and TOMMASI, M. 1999. Politics, institutions, and public sector spending in the Argentine provinces. In *Fiscal Institutions and Fiscal Performance*, ed. J. Poterba and J. von Hagen. Chicago: University of Chicago Press.

KENNEDY, S., and ROBBINS, J. 2001. The role of fiscal rules in determining fiscal performance. Dept. of Finance Working Paper 2001–16, Ottawa.

KIEWIET, D. R., and SZAKALY, K. 1996. Constitutional limits on borrowing: an analysis of state bonded indebtedness. *Journal of Law, Economics and Organization*, 12: 62–97.

KIRCHGÄSSNER, G., FELD, L. P., and SAVIOZ, M. R. 1999. *Die direkte Demokratie*. Basel: Helbing and Lichtenhahn.

KONTOPOULOS, Y., and PEROTTI, R. 1999. Government fragmentation and fiscal policy outcomes: evidence from OECD countries. In *Fiscal Institutions and Fiscal Performance*, ed. J. Poterba and J. von Hagen. Chicago: University of Chicago Press.

KOPITS, G. 2001. Useful policy framework or unnecessary ornament? IMF Working Paper 145.

LAO-ARAYA, K. 1997. The effect of budget structure on fiscal performance: a study of selected Asian countries. IMF working paper, Washington, DC.

LIJPHART, A. 1984. *Democracies: Patterns of Majoritarian and Consensus Government in Twenty-One Countries*. New Haven, Conn.: Yale University Press.

—— 1994. *Electoral Systems and Party Systems: A Study of Twenty-Seven Democracies 1945–1990*. Oxford: Oxford University Press.

LIZZERI, A., and PERSICO, N. 2001. The provision of public goods under alternative electoral incentives. *American Economic Review*, 91: 225–39.

MATSUSAKA, J. G. 1995. Fiscal effects of the voter initiative: evidence from the last 30 years. *Journal of Political Economy*, 103: 587–623.

MILESI-FERRETTI, G. M., PEROTTI, R., and ROSTAGNO, M. 2002. Electoral systems and public spending. *Quarterly Journal of Economics*, 117: 649–57.

MILLAR, J. 1997. The effect of budget rules on fiscal performance and macroeconomic stabilization. Bank of Canada Working Paper 97–115.

MOLANDER, P. 2000. Reforming budgetary institutions: Swedish experiences. In *Institutions, Politics, and Fiscal Policy*, ed. R. Strauch and J. von Hagen. Dordrecht: Kluwer Academic.

Persson, T., Roland, G., and Tabellini, G. 1997. Separation of powers and political accountability. *Quarterly Journal of Economics*, 112: 1163–202.

—— and Tabellini, G. 1999a. Political economics and public finance. Pp. 1549–659 in *The Handbook of Public Finance*, ed. A. Auerbach and M. Feldstein. Amsterdam: North-Holland.

—— —— 1999b. The size and scope of government: comparative politics with rational politicians. *European Economic Review*, 43: 699–735.

—— —— 2000. *Political Economics: Explaining Econimic Policy*. Cambridge, Mass.: MIT Press.

—— —— 2003. *The Economic Consequences of Constitutions*. Cambridge, Mass.: MIT Press.

—— —— 2004a. Constitutions and economic policy. *Journal of Economic Perspectives*, 18: 75–98.

—— —— 2004b. Constitutional rules and fiscal policy outcomes. *American Economic Review*, 94: 25–45.

—— —— and Trebbi, F. 2003. Electoral rules and corruption. *Journal of the European Economic Association*, 1: 958–89.

Pommerehne, W. 1978. Institutional approaches to public expenditure: empirical evidence from Swiss municipalities. *Journal of Public Economics*, 9: 255–80.

—— 1990. The empirical relevance of comparative institutional analysis. *European Economic Review*, 34: 458–69.

Poterba, J. 1994. State responses to fiscal crises: the effects of budgetary institutions and politics. *Journal of Political Economy*, 102: 799–821.

—— and Rueben, K. S. 1999. State institutions and the US municipal bond market. In *Fiscal Institutions and Fiscal Performance*, ed. J. Poterba and J. von Hagen. Chicago: University of Chicago Press.

—— and von Hagen J. (eds.) 1999. *Fiscal Institutions and Fiscal Performance*. Chicago: University of Chicago Press.

Razin, A., and Sadka, E. 2003. Privatizing social security under balanced budget constraints: a political economy approach. Mimeo, Tel Aviv University.

Rodden, J., Eskelund, G. S., and Litvack, J. 2003. *Fiscal decentralization and the challenge of the hard budget constraint*. Cambridge, Mass.: MIT Press.

Roubini, N., and Sachs, J. D. 1989. Political and economic determinants of budget deficits in the industrial democracies. *European Economic Review*, 33: 903–38.

Rueben, K. 1997. Tax limitations and government growth: the effect of state tax and expenditure limits on state and local government. Mimeo, California Institute of Public Policy.

Seabright, P. 1996. Accountability and decentralization in government: an incomplete contracts model. *European Economic Review*, 40: 61–89.

Shadbegian, R. J. 1996. Do tax and expenditure limits affect the size and growth of state government? *Contemporary Economic Policy*, 14: 22–35.

Skilling, D. 2001. Policy coordination, political structure, and public debt: the political economy of public debt accumulation in OECD countries since 1960. Ph.D. dissertation, Harvard University.

Stein, E., Grisanti, A., and Talvi, E. 1999. Institutional arrangements and fiscal performance: the Latin American experience. In *Fiscal Institutions and Fiscal Performance*, ed. J. Poterba and J. von Hagen. Chicago: University of Chicago Press.

Stienlet, G. 2000. Institutional reforms and Belgian fiscal policies in the 90s. In *Institutions, Politics, and Fiscal Policy*, ed. R. Strauch and J. von Hagen. Dordrecht: Kluwer Academic.

Strauch, R. R. 1998. Budget processes and fiscal discipline: evidence from the US states. Working paper, Zentrum für Europäische Integrationsforschung, Bonn.

____ and VON HAGEN, J. 1999. Tumbling giant: Germany's experience with the Maastricht criteria. In *From EMS to EMU*, ed. D. Cobham and G. Zis. London: Macmillan.

TAAGEPERA, R., and SHUGART, M. S. 1989. *Seats and Votes: The Effects and Determinants of Electoral Systems*. New Haven, Conn.: Yale University Press.

____ ____ 1993. Predicting the number of parties: a quantitative model of Duverger's mechanical effect. *American Political Science Review*, 87: 455–64.

TABELLINI, G. 2000. Constitutional determinants of government spending. Working paper, IGIER, Bocconi University.

VELASCO, A. 1999. Debts and deficits with fragmented fiscal policymaking. In *Fiscal Institutions and Fiscal Performance*, ed. J. Poterba and J. von Hagen. Chicago: University of Chicago Press.

VON HAGEN, J. 1991. A note on the empirical effectiveness of formal fiscal restraints. *Journal of Public Economics*, 44: 199–210.

____ 1992. Budgeting procedures and fiscal performance in the European Communities. *Economic Papers*, 96. Brussels: European Commission.

____ and EICHENGREEN, B. 1996. Federalism, fiscal restraints, and European Monetary Union. *American Economic Review*, 86: 134–8.

____ and HARDEN, I. 1994*a*. Budget processes and commitment to fiscal discipline. *European Economic Review*, 39: 771–9.

____ ____ 1994*b*. National budget processes and fiscal performance. *European Economy: Reports and Studies*, 3: 315–418.

____ ____ 1996. Budget processes and commitment to fiscal discipline. IMF working paper.

WIBBELS, E. 2003. Bailouts, budget constraints, and leviathans: comparative federalism and lessons from the early United States. *Comparative Political Studies*, 36: 475–508.

WILDASIN, D. 1997. Externalities and bail-outs: hard and soft budget constraints in intergovernmental fiscal relations. World Bank working paper, Washington, DC.

WILDAVSKY, A. 1986. *Budgeting*, 2nd edn. Oxford: Transaction.

WOLFF, G., and VON HAGEN, J. 2004. What do deficits tell us about debt? Empirical evidence on creative accounting with fiscal rules in the EU. CEPR discussion paper, London.

YLÄOUTINEN, S. 2004*a*. Fiscal frameworks in the central and eastern European countries. Finnish Ministry of Finance, Economics Department discussion paper 72.

____ 2004*b*. The role of electoral and party systems in the development of fiscal institutions in central and east European countries. Mimeo, University of Jyväskylä.

CHAPTER 27

VOTING AND EFFICIENT PUBLIC GOOD MECHANISMS

JOHN LEDYARD

Two neighbors are considering buying a street light. It costs $100 to install. Alice values the light at $70. Bart values it at $60. If they rely solely on the marketplace to make this decision and do not act together, neither will buy the lamp. However, it is clear that both would be better off if they acted together to make the purchase and split the cost. This street light is a public good—a good that cannot easily be denied to others once the allocation and payment for the good has been provided. Providing clear air and water or providing national security are examples of public goods. There are many others.

In this chapter, I am interested in processes for the allocation and financing of public goods. I begin by looking at markets. Market processes are widely used for the allocation of many types of goods. There are several theoretical rationales for this ubiquity. Stated concisely, they say "Markets Work." But, as the above example shows, markets won't necessarily "work" when asked to allocate public goods. Instead, voting processes are widely used for that task. There is little theoretical rationale for their ubiquity. In an effort to fill the gap, I am going to look for conditions under which we can say "Voting Works."

* In this chapter, I have relied heavily on past collaborations with Ted Groves, Tom Palfrey, and Marcus Berliant. I acknowledge each in the appropriate section below. They are responsible for aiding and abetting me in my research. They are not responsible for the flights of fantasy I have taken from our past work.

1 THE STORY BEHIND "MARKETS WORK"[1]

The rationale for the phrase "Markets Work" is contained in one of the most elegant results in economics, and one of the easiest to prove—the First Fundamental Theorem of Welfare Economics. It reads: if there are enough markets and if consumers and producers take prices as given when they optimize, then Walrasian allocations (where prices for all goods are announced simultaneously and supply equals demand in all markets) are Pareto optimal.[2] An important, but often unremarked, fact is that the Walrasian allocations are also individually rational.[3] Running counter to these results is the conventional wisdom that "in the presence of public goods, markets fail." Such wisdom is not a falsification of the First Welfare Theorem. As we were taught by Arrow (1969), even if there are public goods and other externalities, when enough markets are set up and when agents take prices as given, market allocations will be Pareto optimal and individually rational. Nevertheless there is a basis for the conventional wisdom. It lies in the understanding, described by Samuelson (1954), that once all of the markets needed to generate a First Welfare Theorem have been created, price-taking behavior is no longer compatible with the incentives of the agents—it is not *incentive compatible*. The assumption of price-taking behavior is just not believable in this context. Free riders will inevitably arise because each consumer is a monopsony buyer of their part of the public good. So, while the First Welfare Theorem remains true with public goods, it lacks interest because it is simply not applicable to the "real world."

In this chapter I take incentive compatible behavior seriously. In order to say that "a particular allocation mechanism works" I require the mechanism to be both efficient, in the sense that it select allocations that are Pareto optimal, and incentive compatible, in the sense that individuals will be willing to follow the prescribed behavior. Unfortunately finding mechanisms that are both efficient and incentive compatible is not an easy task. As Hurwicz (1972) taught us, even price-taking behavior is not incentive compatible in small private goods environments. He showed that any efficient, individually rational mechanism will not be incentive compatible. Myerson and Satterthwaite (1983) established a similar, but dual, result in a simple private good economy. They showed that any incentive compatible, individually rational mechanism will not be efficient. Hurwicz and Walker (1990) went further, dispensed with the requirement of individual rationality, and showed that there cannot be any mechanism which is simultaneously efficient and incentive compatible.

---

[1] In this section I use a number of terms from the economics and mechanism design literatures without definition. I apologize to those who are not familiar with the literature but I think the basic argument of this section is understandable even if certain words are not. All terms will eventually be defined later in the chapter and examples provided.

[2] Details, required assumptions, and proofs can be found in, e.g., Mas-Colell, Whinston, and Green 1995.

[3] Individual rationality requires that all participants be left at least as well off at the chosen allocation as they would have been able to accomplish on their own with just their initial endowments. Markets do this because property rights to the privately owned initial endowments are respected.

Does this mean one should conclude that markets don't work? Economists say no by taking refuge in numbers. They note that in large private goods economies, either price-taking is approximately incentive compatible and yields efficient allocations[4] or incentive compatible behavior is approximately price-taking and yields efficient allocations.[5] I will also take this approach and say that "a mechanism works" if it is approximately efficient and approximately incentive compatible in large economies. With this interpretation, "Markets do Work" in private goods economies.

But large numbers don't help us with public goods. "Markets don't Work" in public goods economies, even if they are large. For example, Roberts (1976) shows us that in large public goods economies any mechanism that is individually rational, as is certainly true of markets,[6] cannot be even approximately incentive compatible.[7] But if markets can't work, maybe something else will.

One is naturally led to ask: if we are prepared to dispense with a requirement of individual rationality, are there any mechanisms, other than markets, which "work" in public goods economies? In the following sections I provide some answers to this question. In Section 2, I look at two well-known processes for the allocation of public goods: majority rule and demand revealing processes. In Section 3, I ask whether there is anything significantly better and find that, in certain large environments, the answer is no. In Section 4, I look at voting in multidimensional issue spaces and explore whether there is anything better there. In Section 5, I provide some aggressive conclusions. In the process I establish several conditions under which one can say "Voting Works."

2 Imperfect Public Good Mechanisms

In this section I examine a number of processes that are either used or have been proposed for use in the allocation of public goods. Ultimately I end up focusing on two particularly interesting incentive compatible processes: majority rule and demand revelation. Neither of them produces efficient allocations. Neither of them guarantees individually rational allocations. They are imperfect but, as we will see later, they are about the best processes one can find.

But before I get to these processes I need to develop and illustrate a number of ideas and terms including the simple public good environment, mechanisms, consumer

---

[4] See, for example, Roberts and Postlewaite 1976. Various core-limit theorems also support this view. See, for example, Bewley 1973.

[5] McAfee 1992 provides an example of an incentive compatible mechanism for a simple private good economy which is approximately efficient in large economies.

[6] The canonical version of price-taking equilibrium in markets with public goods is Lindahl equilibrium. This equilibrium does satisfy individual rationality.

[7] There is another literature which also arrives at similar results when considering the core of a public goods economy. Muench 1972 provides a demonstration that the core with public goods need not shrink as numbers grow. See also Conley 1994. Here, also, a requirement of individual rationality plays a crucial role.

behavior, mechanism performance, allocative efficiency, and incentive compatibility. Readers familiar with these concepts can skip the next sub-section without missing anything necessary for the rest of the chapter.

2.1 Some Important Concepts

I start by introducing a simple *public good environment* we can use as a basis for most of this chapter. There is a public good of fixed size, it can either be produced or not, that costs K. There are n consumers, each with a utility function, $v^i y - t^i$. The parameter $v^i > 0$ is the voter's *type*. $y = 1$ if the public good is produced. $y = 0$ otherwise.[8] The amount t^i is the tax paid by the consumer. We call the vector $(y, t^1, \ldots, t^n)$ an *allocation*. An allocation is *feasible* if the sum of the taxes collected from all the consumers is at least equal to the cost of the public good. That is, $\sum_{i=1}^{n} t^i \geq Ky$.

> **Example 1:** *The opening example of the street lamp fits into this framework. The good costs 100. There are two consumers, A and B. A's utility function is $70y - t^A$ and B's is $60y - t^b$.*

> **Example 2:** *Here is an example we will return to later. $K = 10$. There are three consumers numbered 1, 2, and 3. 1's utility function is $u^1 = 2y - t^1$, 2's is $u^2 = 4y - t^2$, and 3's is $u^3 = 6y - t^3$. One possible feasible allocation is $y = 1$, $t^1 = 5$, $t^2 = 4$, $t^3 = 6$ since $(5 + 4 + 6) = 15 > 10$.*

In this world, a process or *mechanism* will take information from the consumers in the form of votes, demands, value statements, or other language and pick a level of public good and a vector of taxes, one for each consumer. Each voter i provides a *message* i denoted by m^i. The mechanism then translates the set of messages into a decision concerning how much is spent on the public good and how much each voter must pay in taxes $y(m^1, \ldots, m^n), t^1(m^1, \ldots, m^n), \ldots, t^n(m^1, \ldots, m^n)$.

> **Example 3:** *A very simple, well-studied mechanism is called the voluntary contribution mechanism (VCM for short). The consumer is asked to report how much she is willing to contribute towards the public good.[9] Let that amount be m^i. VCM then produces an allocation. The good is produced if and only if the contributions add up to at least the cost of the good. That is, $y = 1$ if and only if $m^1 + m^2 + \ldots + m^n \geq K$. Each consumer pays their contribution if the good is produced. That is, $t^i = m^i y$.*

> **Example 4:** *Another simple mechanism is the cost–benefit study with proportional taxation (CBS). Consumers are asked to report how much they value the public good (their true value is v^i). If the sum of the reported values, assumed to be a measure of the social benefits of the good, is bigger than the cost, K, then the public good is*

---

[8] In this section and much of the rest of the chapter I could deal with more general production and utility functions than these, but this environment is sufficient for illustrating the important concepts.
[9] They cannot request compensation. Contributions are not allowed to be negative. That is, $m^i \geq 0$.

produced. Taxes are then levied proportionately to the reported benefits. So $y = 1$ *if and only if* $\sum_{i=1}^{n} m^i \geq K$. *And,* $t^i = \left(\frac{m^i}{\sum_{i=1}^{n} m^i}\right) y$.

I am interested in mechanisms that "work." One standard definition of "work" requires a mechanism to select *Pareto optimal allocations* for all values of the parameters of the environment. The outcome from a mechanism is Pareto optimal in a particular environment if there is no way to increase the utility (welfare) of one participant without reducing the welfare of another participant. It is easy to see that, in the fixed size public good environment, an allocation $(y, t^1, \ldots, t^n)$ is Pareto optimal in the environment given by $(K, v^1, \ldots, v^n)$ if and only if *(a)* $y = 1$ if $\sum_{i=1}^{n} v^i \geq K$ and $y = 0$ otherwise, and *(b)* $\sum_{i=1}^{n} t^i = y$. We call *(a)* output efficiency and *(b)* resource efficiency.[10]

Example 5: *For the three-consumer Example 2, since* $(2 + 4 + 6) > 10$, *efficiency requires that* $y = 1$ *and* $\sum t^i = 10$.

The requirement that Pareto optimal allocations be selected is a minimal, but sensible, request. If there is a way to make everyone better off, it would seem natural to ask that the mechanism be modified to do so. But, to predict whether a mechanism will select Pareto optimal allocations, we need to factor in the *behavior* of the consumers—how they select the information they provide to the mechanism, m^i, as a function of what they know, v^i.[11] If consumers choose messages according to $m^i = b^i(v^i)$, then the outcome of a mechanism is $[y(b(v)), t^1(b(v)), \ldots, t^n(b(v))]$. Let us go back to our examples to see how this works.

Example 6: *Suppose, in the VCM, each consumer is asked to report their true value for the public good. If the consumers follow our request, then* $y = 1$ *if and only if* $\sum_{i=1}^{n} v^i = 1$. *Also,* $t^i = v^i$ *for each i. Notice that the VCM with this behavior is output efficient but not resource efficient in environments for which* $\sum_{i=1}^{n} v^i > K$.

Thus if we don't ask for and get the appropriate behavior, a mechanism may not select Pareto optimal allocations. But in many cases we can rescue the performance by asking for a different behavior.

Example 7: *Continuing with the VCM, suppose each consumer is asked to submit a message* m^i *so that* $v^i \geq m^i$ *and* $\sum_{i=1}^{n} m^i = K$ *if that is possible and to submit* $m^i = 0$ *otherwise.*[12] *Again* $y = 1$ *iff* $\sum_{i=1}^{n} v^i \geq K$ *but now* $\sum_{i=1}^{n} t^i = Ky$ *so that the VCM with this behavior does select Pareto optimal allocations.*

---

[10] *(a)* represents efficiency in the public good and *(b)* represents efficiency in the private good.

[11] For example, in the First Welfare Theorem, we not only need to know the market process (prices and allocations are set to equate supply and demand), we also need to know how consumers behave (they use demand functions derived from utility maximization taking prices as given).

[12] This is a version of VCM with rebate. Clearly this would require some iteration to accomplish. There is a way to do this in one iteration though. Modify the VCM mechanism so $y = 1$ iff $\sum_{i=1}^{n} m^i \geq K$ and $t^i = a^i$ where $m^i \geq a^i$ and $\sum_{i=1}^{n} a^i = Ky$. Then reporting $m^i = v^i$ will produce allocative efficient allocations.

There are many combinations of mechanisms and behavior that select Pareto optimal allocations. For example let's go back to the cost–benefit study.

Example 8: *In the CBS, each consumer is asked to report their true value. In this case, the outcome will be that $y = 1$ iff $\sum_{i=1}^{n} v^i \geq K$ and $t^i = \left(\frac{v^i}{\sum_{i=1}^{n} v^i}\right) y$. Thus the CBS under truthful reporting chooses Pareto optimal allocations.*

So far it seems as though finding mechanisms efficiently to allocate public goods and their costs is pretty easy. But all of this is not of much help unless the consumers actually follow the rules we suggest. So, I want to consider mechanisms in which self-interested individuals will want to follow the prescribed behavior no matter what the others are doing. That is, I want the prescribed behavior to be a dominant strategy for the consumers. If a mechanism and behavior have this property then I say that behavior and mechanism are *incentive compatible*. We illustrate this important concept by first considering some examples of mechanisms and behaviors which are not incentive compatible.

Example 9: *A simple example of a mechanism and behavior that are not incentive compatible is the CBS in Example 4 with truthful reporting. Suppose we are in the three-person Example 2. If all consumers report the truth, $m^i = v^i$, then consumer 2, say, gets $u^2 = v^2 - \left(\frac{v^2}{v^1+v^2+v^3}\right) 10 = 4 - \frac{40}{12} = \frac{2}{3}$, since $v^1 + v^2 + v^3 \geq 10$. But suppose 2 were to report $m^i = 2$ instead of 4. Since $m^1 + m^2 + m^3 = 2 + 2 + 6 \geq 10$, she would now get $u^2 = 4 - \frac{2}{10} 10 = 2 > \frac{2}{3}$. She is much better off than reporting truthfully. So following truthful reporting behavior is not incentive compatible for the CBS—there are times when a consumer is better off deviating from the requested behavior.*

Example 10: *The VCM mechanism is not incentive compatible for either of the reporting schemes introduced in Example 6 and in Example 7. Using Example 2, one can see why. For the behavior where consumers are asked to report truthfully, $m^i = v^i$. If consumer 2 reports the truth and the good is produced, she will end up with utility $u^2 = 4 - 4 = 0$. But if consumer 2 acts in a self-interested manner[13] then it is easy to see that she can improve her own utility by reporting a smaller number, no matter what the other consumers report. In fact, she is always best off reporting $m^i = 0$. If all three consumers do this, the combined effect of the VCM rules and the equilibrium of self-interested behavior is that $m^1 = m^2 = m^3 = 0$, and $y = t^1 = t^2 = t^3 = 0$ even if $v^1 + v^2 + v^3 > 10$. This is the classic example of free riding behavior and its corrosive effect on Pareto optimality.*

Example 11: *For a slightly more subtle example of mechanism and behavior that produce Pareto optimal allocations but are not incentive compatible, let us return to our very first story with Alice and Bart. Here we can see the difficulty that public goods create for the incentive compatibility of price-taking behavior. In order to have enough*

---

[13] Whether consumers will actually behave this way is an empirical question. Since this is simply an example I am not going to worry about this here. But the interested reader can see Ledyard 1995 for a survey of what was known at that time about actual behavior in the VCM.

markets to attain allocative efficiency, we need to charge Alice a different price from Bart and then pay the supplier of the lamp an amount equal to the sum of what they pay.[14] If Alice's price is $60 and Bart's is $40 and if each acts as if these prices are fixed, then each will demand the street lamp and, since the sum of the prices covers the cost, it will be supplied.[15] But there is a problem. Bart might guess that Alice has a value of around $70 and then act as if he only had a value of $30 for the street lamp when he submits his demand. Then the only equilibrium prices would be $70 for Alice and $30 for Bart. If Alice follows the same strategy as Bart and if she guesses that his value is $50 then she will act as if she only has a value of $50. But in doing so, the only equilibrium is a price of $50 for Alice, $30 for Bart, and no purchase of the lamp. Because price-taking was not compatible with their individual incentives, the market fails to produce Pareto optimal allocations.

At this point one might well ask whether there are any mechanisms and behavior that are incentive compatible. It turns out there are many.

Example 12: *A simple example of a mechanism that is incentive compatible under truthful reporting is the random dictator mechanism with constant per capita taxation (DPCTM). The mechanism asks everyone to report the level of public good they most want. It then randomly picks one consumer, say i, produces the requested amount m^i, and taxes everyone y/n. Given these messages, if i is chosen, the mechanism provides the amount of the item to person i that i says she wants. If i is not chosen, her message is ignored. Given this utility function and the rules of the mechanism, i will always want to tell the truth. So DPCTM is incentive compatible. In our fixed size public good environment, each i would like the public good to be produced, $y = 1$, if and only if $v^i \geq K/n$. They so report and they have no incentive to deviate from this.*

Example 13: *Another simple example of incentive compatible behavior in a mechanism can be crafted from the VCM mechanism. If we request all individuals to report $m^i = 0$ no matter what their value, then this is incentive compatible. It, of course, does not select Pareto optimal allocations.*

There are more interesting incentive compatible mechanisms. Two of these are voting under majority rule and the class of demand revealing mechanisms. I turn to those now.

2.2 Majority Rule

Consider a possibly complex political process in which it is agreed a priori that everyone will pay their per capita share of the cost of the public good. Suppose the equilibrium of this process is a public good level such that no other level is preferred

---

[14] I am describing the Lindahl equilibrium price system here. More information on this can be found in Mas-Colell, Whinston, and Green 1995.
[15] Of course, there are many possible prices, including $50 each, that would be Lindahl equilibrium prices.

by a majority. In the simple public goods environment such an equilibrium is the public good level desired by the median voter. I think of the reduced form of this voting process as majority rule with per capita taxes (MR).

We can think of the MR mechanism as follows. Each i is asked to report their ideal point. The mechanism then selects the median m^i and charges everyone $(\frac{1}{n})Ky$.

Example 14: *For the three-person environment, with per capita taxes, each consumer gets utility $u^i = v^i y - (\frac{1}{3})Ky = (v^i - \frac{1}{3}K)y$. It is easy to compute that $u^1 = \frac{-4}{3}y$, $u^2 = \frac{2}{3}y$, and $u^3 = \frac{8}{3}y$. So 1's preferred level of the public good, his ideal point, is 0, while 2 and 3 both prefer 1. Therefore, 1 is the outcome of the MR process.*

The performance of the MR mechanism is easy to determine and should be generally familiar to most readers of this chapter.

Proposition 1: *The MR mechanism is not individually rational.*

From the example we can see that, in equilibrium, $u^1 = -\frac{4}{3} < 0$. So 1 is clearly worse off under this mechanism than at his initial position. He will have to be "coerced" to pay his taxes.

Proposition 2: *The MR mechanism is incentive compatible.*

Under majority rule, if the utility functions satisfy single-peakedness, which they do for our fixed size public good environment, it is clear that no one will want to lie about their preferences. Suppose that i is the median voter. Since i is getting their most preferred allocation, i will not want to move from the median. At the same time, none of the others benefit by lying. If i's ideal point is to the right of the median voter, saying that she is further to the right than she actually is will not move the outcome. Saying she is further to the left than she actually is either does not change the outcome or changes it to a position that is worse for i. So there is no incentive to lie.

Proposition 3: *The MR mechanism does not produce Pareto optimal allocations.*

MR is resource efficient but not output efficient. The MR rule reacts to the median ideal point but output efficiency requires reaction to the mean ideal point. In our fixed size world the efficient output decision is $y = 1$ if and only if $\sum_{i=1}^{n} v^i \geq K$ or iff $(\sum_{i=1}^{n} v^i)/n \geq K/n$. But in MR, $y = 1$ if and only if the median value of v^i, call it v^m, is greater than or equal to K/n. There are only a few environments, vectors of (K, v), for which the median value, q^m, is equal to the mean. Only when the equality holds will the majority rule mechanism be efficient.[16]

One of the things that prevents voting from producing Pareto optimal allocations in this context is the restriction to per capita taxes. But, if we relax that constraint and let taxes also be part of the policy space over which votes are taken, there are in general no majority rule equilibria.

---

[16] To my knowledge this was first established in Bowen 1943. I thank Marcus Berliant for pointing this out to me.

Example 15: *Suppose the outcome of a majority rule process is that the public good be produced, $y = 1$, and taxes are assessed as follows. Consumer 1 pays $t^1 = 10$, consumer 2 pays $t^2 = 5$, and consumer 3 pays $t^3 = 15$. Assume the total collected just covers the cost of the public good, 30. Now consider a new proposal where $y = 1$, $t^1 = 5$, $t^2 = 0$, $t^3 = 25$. Both 1 and 2 are better off under the new proposal and will now vote for it over the previous outcome. It is easy to see that any vector of taxes can be beaten by a majority this way. So there will be new equilibria.*

Either with or without per capita taxes, voting appears to fail. However, before we give up on voting, we should at least find out whether we can do any better.

2.3 Demand-revealing Mechanisms

In a well-known collection of papers,[17] we were introduced to what are now called the Vickrey–Clarke–Groves (VCG) mechanisms. In these, each person is asked to report their demand function for (or utility function for) the public good. The good is then provided at the efficient output level for the reported functions. Each individual is assessed a tax equal to the per capita cost of the public good plus the impact they have on the rest of the group. It is this tax rule that makes the mechanism incentive compatible.

In the fixed-size public goods environment, the VCG mechanism reduces to the Pivot mechanism.[18] The rules of the Pivot mechanism are as follows. Everyone is asked to report their true value $m^i = v^i$. Then if $\sum_{i=1}^{n} m^i \geq K$

$$y = 1$$

$$t^i = \frac{K}{n} \text{ if } \sum_{j=1, j \neq i}^{n} \left(m^i - \frac{K}{n} \right) \geq 0$$

$$t^i = \frac{K}{n} - \sum_{j=1, j \neq i}^{n} \left(m^j - \frac{K}{n} \right) \text{ if } \sum_{j=1, j \neq i}^{n} \left(m^j - \frac{K}{n} \right) < 0$$

and if $\sum_{i=1}^{n} m^i < K$

$$y = 0$$

$$t^i = 0 \text{ if } \sum_{j=1, j \neq i}^{n} \left(m^i - \frac{K}{n} \right) < 0$$

$$t^i = \sum_{j=1, j \neq i}^{n} \left(m^j - \frac{K}{n} \right) \text{ if } \sum_{j=1, j \neq i}^{n} \left(m^j - \frac{K}{n} \right) \geq 0$$

---

[17] Vickrey 1961, Clarke 1971, and Groves 1973 are all credited with independently discovering a special class of dominant strategy mechanisms once called the demand-revealing mechanisms. They are now widely known as VCG mechanisms.

[18] See Green and Laffont 1979 for a full discussion of the Pivot mechanism in this very simple environment.

Basically this says that i pays (or receives) an extra tax (subsidy) only if they are pivotal; that is, only if their presence causes the public good decision to be changed from what the others would do. If they are pivotal they must compensate the others for that change. This has the effect of converting their utility function to $(v^i + \sum_{j=1, j\neq i}^{n} m^j - K)y$ which, if everyone tells the truth, is $(\sum_{i=1}^{n} v^i - K)y$. It is thus a dominant strategy to report the true v^i.

Example 16: *Consider a three-consumer example,[19] with $K = 18$, $v^1 = 2$, $v^2 = 8$, $v^3 = 10$. The VCG mechanism chooses $y = 1$ because $2 + 8 + 10 > 18$. Taxes are figured as follows. For person 1 for whom $v^1 = 2$, $\sum_{j=1, j\neq 1}^{n} \left(m^j - \frac{K}{n}\right) = v^2 + v^3 - 2(18/3) = 12 > 0$ so 1 is not pivotal and therefore $t^1 = 6 = (18/3)$. For person 2 for whom $v^2 = 4$, $\sum_{j=1, j\neq 2}^{n} \left(m^j - \frac{K}{n}\right) = (2 - 6) + (10 - 6) = 0$ so 2 is also, just, not pivotal. So $t^2 = 6$. For person 3 for whom $v^3 = 6$, $\sum_{j=1, j\neq 3}^{n} \left(m^j - \frac{K}{n}\right) = (2 - 6) + (4 - 6) = -4 < 0$ so 3 is pivotal. So $t^3 = 6 + 4$. One thing to note is that the total tax collected is $18 + 4 > K$.*

It is easy to prove that this mechanism is incentive compatible.

Lemma 1: *VCG is dominant strategy incentive compatible with truthful behavior, $m(v) = v$.*

For completeness, we add

Lemma 2: *The allocations of the VCG mechanism are generally not individually rational.*

Because it is incentive compatible, the output rule will generate allocations that are output efficient. It is sometimes erroneously claimed that "the VCG mechanism is efficient." That is certainly not true if by efficient we mean, as we should, that the outcomes are Pareto optimal. Because the VCG mechanism, as described above, collects more in taxes than necessary and must throw the surplus away so as to preserve incentive compatibility, the mechanism is not resource efficient and therefore is not Pareto optimal.

Lemma 3: *The allocations of the VCG mechanism are output efficient but are generally not resource efficient.*

Proof: The allocations are output efficient because $m(v) = v$ and, so, $y(m) = \arg\max_{y \geq 0} \sum_i [u^i(y, m^i) - ky]$. To see why they are generally not resource efficient, note that an individual's taxes are $t^i(v) = ky(v) + S^i(v_{-i})$. So $(\sum t^i) - C(y) = \sum S^i$ where

$$\sum S^i(v) = \sum \left\{ \left[\max_{y \geq 0} \sum_{j \neq i}(u(y, m^j) - ky\right] - \left[\sum_{j \neq i}(u(y(m), m^j) - ky(m)\right] \right\}$$

It is obvious that $S^i \geq 0$ for all v. It is easy to construct examples to confirm that, generically, $S^i(v) > 0$ for every i.

---

[19] I choose different values of K and v^i here because if the values are $K = 10$ and $v^i = 2, 4, 6$ then no one is pivotal and all pay only $10/3$. This is uncommon and so I change the example slightly.

So we have two interesting but imperfect processes: majority rule and VCG. Both are incentive compatible (under dominant strategies) and neither produce fully efficient (Pareto optimal) allocations.[20] This should not be a surprise. We know that there are no processes which are simultaneously dominant strategy incentive compatible and efficient over a reasonable range of possible environments even if we restrict those environments to ones with quasi-linear and quasi-concave utility functions.[21]

This leaves open at least two questions. Which of the two dominant strategy processes, VCG or MR, is the better? Is there a "best" dominant strategy mechanism? We turn to the first of these next.

2.4 Which is Better: MR or VCG?[22]

We already know that neither the VCG mechanism nor MR is efficient. Is it possible, however, that one of them is better than the other? One result that is easy to prove suggests that MR is better than VCG.

Lemma 4: *Majority rule majority dominates the VCG process.*[23]

Proof: I will only consider the case for which $\sum m^i > K$, the case in which VCG produces the public good. A symmetric argument works for the opposite situation. (Case 1) If the median value, v^m, is larger than k, then MR would also produce the public good and everyone would pay k. Since, in the Pivot mechanism, everyone pays k plus possibly a (positive) pivot tax, everyone will be at least as well off with majority rule. (Case 2) If $v^m < k$, then MR will not produce the good and no one pays any taxes. Those for whom $v^i > k$ are worse off under MR. Those for whom $v^i < k$ are better off under MR. Under the pivot rules they don't pay a pivot tax but they are forced to consume the public good. Since $v^m < k$, there are a majority of i such that $v^i < k$. QED

But if I look at large environments I can provide a result that suggests that VCG is better than MR.

---

[20] For symmetry, we should point out that there are processes which are efficient and not incentive compatible. In the simple environments, one such is the direct revelation mechanism which picks the output efficient allocation of the public good, y^*, and then charges per capita taxes, $t^i = ky^*$.

[21] This was established in a sequence of papers. Green and Laffont 1977 and Walker 1978 show that the only mechanisms for public goods which are simultaneously dominant strategy incentive compatible and output efficient are VCG mechanisms. Walker 1980 and Hurwicz and Walker 1990 show that, generically in environments, VCG mechanisms are not resource efficient. Hurwicz and Walker 1990 also show this impossibiltiy is true whether we are in a public goods economy or in a private goods economy.

[22] Much of this section is based on my joint work with Ted Groves. The paper that is most closely related is Groves and Ledyard 1977.

[23] In our 1977 paper raising questions about the viability of the VCG mechanism (then called the demand-revealing mechanism), Ted Groves and I showed this result for an environment with a variable size public good where $u^i = \theta^i \ln y$ for each consumer. I suspect it is true for any quasi-linear, quasi-concave utility functions for a single public good, but that remains to be proven. This result is of course not true (or, at the very least, is generically vacuous) for multidimensional public goods since MR equilibrium rarely exist. See for example McKelvey and Schofield 1987. We address this issue later in this chapter.

Lemma 5: *In large economies, without too many consumers at extreme values[24] of v^i, VCG is almost efficient. In large asymmetric economies[25] MR is generally not efficient.*

Proof: (for VCG) I will show that as $N \to \infty$, the total pivot taxes paid goes to zero. For an economy of size N let $a(N) = (1/N)(\sum v^i) - k$. For each i, let $c^i(N) = v^i - k$. Then, given a, there are two situations in which pivot taxes are paid by i. (1) $a > 0$, $c^i > Na$ where i pays $(c^i - Na)/(N-1)$ and (2) $a < 0$, $c^i < Na$ where i pays $(Na - c^i)/(N-1)$. Let's look at the case when $a > 0$. Then the total pivot taxes paid will be $\sum_{i \, \ni \, c^i > Na} (c^i - Na)/(N-1) = \frac{\#K(Na)}{N-1} \frac{\sum_{K(Na)} (c^i - Na)}{\#K(Na)}$ where $K(Na)$ is the number of i such that $c^i > Na$. Suppose that, as $N \to \infty$, the distribution of the c^i approaches $F(\cdot)$. So $\#K(Na)/(N-1) \to 1 - F(Na)$. Also $\frac{\sum_{K(Na)} (c^i - Na)}{\#K(Na)} \to$ expected value of $c^i - Na$ conditional on $c^i > Na$. that is it approaches $\frac{1}{1-F(Na)} \int_{Na} (c - Na) dF$. So the total pivot taxes approach $\int_{Na} (c - Na) dF$. If $\int_x cf(c)dc \to 0$ as $x \to \infty$, then $\int_{Na} (c - Na) dF \to 0$ as $N \to \infty$.

(For MR) If the median value of v^i, $v^m \neq \bar{v}$, the mean value of v^i, then MR is not efficient.

At this point the situation is a bit confusing. MR is majority preferred to VCG but, in large economies, VCG produces a higher level of aggregate welfare, $\sum v^i y(v) - t^i(v)$. So which is better?

2.5 Which Mechanisms are Best?

In order to answer this question, we need to decide what we mean when we say one mechanism is better than another. One might believe that mechanism A is better than mechanism B if and only if a majority would be willing to move [26] from B to A in all possible realizations of v. If so, then MR would be better than VCG. On the other hand, if one believes that mechanism A is better than mechanism B if and only if a unanimity would be willing to move from B to A in all possible realizations of v, then neither VCG nor MR is better than the other, since MR is never unanimously preferred to the VCG mechanism and there are always losers in a move from VCG to MR. Finally, if one believes that mechanism A is better than mechanism B if A always yields a higher aggregate payoff in all possible realizations of v, then VCG would be (approximately) better than MR in large economies, since it is almost efficient.

In this chapter, I accept the implication of Arrow's theorem that there is no universally acceptable way to completely rank all mechanisms. Instead, I will look

---

[24] By this I mean that $\lim_{x \to \infty} \int_x v^i f(v^i) dv^i = 0$ and $\lim_{x \to -\infty} \int^x v^i f(v^i) dv^i = 0$ where $f(\cdot)$ is the limiting density of types as $N \to \infty$.

[25] By this I mean that $F(\int v df(v) dv) \neq .5$: i.e. the median of the limiting distribution F is not equal to the mean.

[26] Those familiar with mechanism design will recognize that timing is important here. What the agents know when they make this decision is important. I am implicitly assuming here that they will know everything when they make their decision—all agents will have revealed their values. I am using an *ex post* analysis.

for mechanisms that are socially sensible. A minimal standard would be that it is common knowledge that there is no other mechanism such that everyone would be better off. To see how this works let us look at MR and VCG again. We do know, since neither chooses Pareto optimal allocations, that there are mechanisms that leave everyone better off. For example, let (y^{mr}, t^{mr}) be the MR process. Let (y^*, t^*) be any direct mechanism such that (a) $y^*(v) = 1$ iff $\sum(v^i - k) \geq 0$ (b) $\sum t^{*i}(v) = Ky^*(v)$, and (c) $v^i y^*(v) - t^{*i}(v) \geq v^i y^{mr}(v) - t^{mri}(v)$, with $>$ if possible. Since the allocations of MR are not efficient, we know such t^* exist. Therefore MR does not seem to survive our standard in very simple environments.[27] We can also do a similar thing for the VCG process so it also seems to fail our test.

So why don't we focus on efficient mechanisms like the (y^*, t^*) above instead of MR and VCG? Up to now we actually have been, by asking that our processes select Pareto optimal allocations in all environments. But, and this is a very important point, processes like (y^*, t^*) are not incentive compatible. Thus they are not implementable and so they really should not be considered to be viable challengers to either MR or VCG. We would be asking for too much.

I take a more forgiving approach and ask: what mechanisms are best among those that are incentive compatible? I will call a mechanism *incentive efficient* for a set of environments if it is incentive compatible and there is no other incentive compatible mechanism that is unanimously preferred to it over that set of environments.[28] Incentive efficient mechanisms are the best we can do within the reality of incentive constraints. If a mechanism is not incentive efficient, then one might expect it to be replaced by a more efficient, incentive compatible process. One would expect ubiquitous mechanisms, such as markets and voting, to have been able to survive such challenges. They would, therefore, be incentive efficient in exactly the sense I have chosen.

I can now rephrase my earlier question. Is either MR or VCG an incentive efficient mechanism over the simple public goods environments? Unfortunately I don't know the answer. In Roberts (1979), there is a characterization of the class of dominant strategy incentive compatible mechanisms for quasi-linear environments.[29] However, as far as I know, it remains an open problem to characterize the incentive efficient members of this class.

But it is too early to give up. It is time to try an indirect approach.

---

[27] To emphasize that the efficiency concept is not that weak I note that (y^*, t^*) is also "better" than MR under majority preference, unanimity preference, or aggregate value maximization.

[28] For those who are not familiar with mechanism design, Holmstrom and Myerson 1983 offer an excellent introduction to and discussion of efficient mechanisms in all their subtlety. They introduce the concept of incentive efficiency among many others also of importance.

Those familiar with mechanism design will recognize that in this section I am using the terms efficiency and incentive compatibility in the *ex post* sense, after everyone knows the entire vector v. I will take up the interim view in Section 3.

[29] If $u^i = u^i(y, v^i) - t^i$, then the class of dominant strategy direct revelation mechanisms is given by (a) $y(m) = \arg\max F(y) + \sum_i k_i u^i(y, m^i)$ and $t^i(m) = \frac{1}{k_i}[\sum_{j \neq i} k_j u^i(y, m^j) + F(y)] + h_i(v_{-i})$ where $k \geq 0$ and F are arbitrary. Note that VCG belongs to this class by letting $k_i = 1$ for all i and $F(y) = 0$ for all y. I do not know what values of k and F yield the MR mechanism.

3 CAN WE SAY "VOTING WORKS?"[30]

In this section, I raise the hurdle for a mechanism to be designated as incentive efficient by taking a Bayesian approach. I am going to broaden the class of mechanisms that will be considered to be incentive compatible and strengthen the criterion that must be satisfied for incentive efficiency. So it is now going to be harder for a mechanism to be incentive efficient. Such a mechanism will have to survive the challenge of more mechanisms and do it according to a stricter standard.

There is a price to pay for this strengthening. We will have to assume that there are prior beliefs, held by consumers, about the probability of any particular environment v. These beliefs will be common knowledge and, therefore, they can be used by the mechanism, creating even more challengers to potential incentive efficient mechanisms.

3.1 The Bayesian Approach

A very simple Bayes environment is described as follows. Begin with the very simple environment described in Section 2.1 where $u^i = v^i y - t^i$. The v^i are assumed to be drawn independently and identically from a distribution $F(v)$ on $[a, b]$ and this is common knowledge to the consumers and the mechanism. The density associated with F will be denoted by $f(v)$.

In this world, I will look for incentive efficient mechanisms among those that are Bayesian incentive compatible.

Definition 1: *A direct mechanism $[y(v), t(v)]$ is Bayesian incentive compatible (or interim incentive compatible) if and only if*

$$v^i \in \arg\max_{v'} \int \left[u^i(y(v/v'), v^i) - t^i(v/v') \right] dF(v|v^i)$$

where $(v/v') = (v^1, \ldots, v^{i-1}, v'^i, v^{i+1}, \ldots, v^N)$ and $dF = dF^1 \ldots dF^N$.

The use of the word "interim" denotes that the evaluation of possible misreporting and other issues is done at the time at which all agents know their own type but do not yet know the types of the others. This is to be contrasted with the previous section in which such evaluations were done after all agents knew everyone's type. For that reason the analysis of the previous section is often referred to as *ex post*. If a mechanism is dominant strategy (or *ex post*) incentive compatible then it will be Bayesian (or interim) incentive compatible. So, for instance, both MR and VCG are Bayesian incentive compatible mechanisms. This means I am enlarging the class of incentive compatible mechanisms relative to the set of dominant strategy incentive compatible mechanisms of the previous section. This will make it harder for any

---

[30] Much of this section is based on my joint work with Tom Palfrey. The paper that is most closely related is Ledyard and Palfrey 2002.

particular mechanism to emerge as incentive efficient since there are now more alternatives to compare it to.

I will look for mechanisms that are interim incentive efficient. These are mechanisms that are efficient when everyone knows their own type, v^i, but before anyone knows the other types.

Definition 2: *A mechanism $[y^*(v), t^*(v)]$ is interim incentive efficient iff there does not exist another mechanism $[y'(v), t'(v)]$ that is interim incentive compatible and for which*

$$\int u^i(y'(v), v^i) - t'^i(v) dF(v|v^i) \geq \int u^i(y^*(v), v^i) - t^{*i}(v) dF(v|v^i)$$

for all v^i, where the inequality is strict for a set of v^i of positive probability.[31]

There are at least three other equivalent definitions of interim incentive efficiency that can be helpful in understanding the concept. The first and most straightforward provides a simple reason why one should not expect interim incentive inefficient mechanisms to survive in practice.

Lemma 6: *A mechanism is interim incentive efficient iff it is common knowledge that there does not exist another interim incentive compatible mechanism that makes everybody better off.*

If a mechanism is not interim incentive efficient then it is common knowledge that everyone can be made better off with an alternative interim incentive compatible mechanism. So one should expect such an alternative to replace the current mechanism, even if all consumers know their own types.

The second definition is useful in searching for interim efficient mechanisms and can be derived from separating hyperplane theorems since the set of feasible and interim incentive compatible mechanisms is convex in the very simple Bayesian world.

Lemma 7: *A mechanism $[y^*(v), t^*(v)]$ is interim incentive efficient in the class of interim incentive compatible mechanisms iff there are $\lambda^i(v^i) > 0$ such that $[y^*(\cdot), t^*(\cdot)]$ solves*

$$\max \int \sum \lambda^i(v^i)[v^i y(v) - t^i(v)] dF(v)$$

subject to

$$\sum t^i(v) \geq K y(v)$$

and

$$v^i \in \arg\max \int v^i y(v/v'^i) - t^i(v/v'^i) dF(v|v^i).$$

---

[31] It is important to remember that I continue to forgo any individual rationality requirements. In Ledyard and Palfrey 2005 we considered interim efficient mechanisms that are individually rational.

The third alternative definition asserts that a mechanism is interim incentive efficient if and only if it is *ex ante* incentive efficient for all affine transformation of the utility functions.[32] It is this fact that convinces me, at least for a Bayesian analysis, that interim incentive efficiency is the right concept to use when trying to identify mechanisms that will survive and be used.

3.2 A Bayesian Characterization of Interim Incentive Efficient Mechanisms

In Ledyard and Palfrey (1999), we were able to characterize the class of interim incentive efficient mechanisms for the very simple Bayesian environment. In these, consumers announce their values, y is chosen according to a virtual cost–benefit rule, and taxes are computed using a rule discovered by d'Aspremont and Gerard-Varet (1979). We called these mechanisms virtual cost–benefit mechanisms.

Definition 3: *The VCB (virtual cost–benefit) mechanism, for given functions $\lambda^i(v^i)$, is given by $m^i \in M^i = V^i$, an output rule*

$$y^*(v) = 1 \text{ if } \sum_i w^i(v^i) \geq K$$

$$y^*(v) = 0 \text{ otherwise,}$$

where

$$w^i(v^i) = v^i + \{[F^i(v^i) - \Lambda^i(v^i)]/f^i(v^i)\},$$

$$\Lambda^i(v^i) = \int^{v^i} \lambda^i(s)ds$$

and a tax rule

$$t^{*i}(v) = ky^*(v) - [T^i(v^i) - Q^i(v^i)] + \left(\frac{1}{N-1}\right)\left\{\sum_{j \neq i}[T^j(v^j) - Q^j(v^j)]\right\}.$$

where

$$Q^i(v^i) = \int^{v^i} y^*(x)dF(x|v^i)$$

and

$$T^i(v^i) = \int^{v^i} s\, dQ^i(s).$$

---

[32] "*Ex ante*" refers to the analysis that is done prior to anyone knowing anything other than the common knowledge. A mechanism is *ex ante* efficient iff there are $\lambda^i > 0$ such that $[y^*(\cdot), t^*(\cdot)]$ solves $\max \int \sum \lambda^i[v^i y(v) - t^i(v)]dF(v)$ subject to feasibility and incentive compatibility. Compare this with the definition of interim efficiency to see that the difference is that the λ^i do not depend on the v^i. An affine transformation of utilities for each v^i yields $u^i = a^i(v^i)[v^i y(v) - t^i(v)] + b^i(v^i)$. This does not change either the feasibility or incentive constraints. But it does change the objective function to $\int \sum \lambda^i a^i(v^i)[v^i y(v) - t^i(v)]dF(v)$. So, letting $\lambda^i(v^i) = \lambda^i a^i(v^i)$, it is easy to see that a mechanism is *ex ante* efficient for all affine transformation of utilities iff it is interim efficient.

Myerson (1981) called the w^i virtual valuations which is why we refer to this as a virtual cost–benefit rule—the good is produced if and only if the virtual benefits outweigh the costs. The key result from Ledyard and Palfrey (1999) is

Lemma 8: *All interim incentive efficient mechanisms in the very simple Bayesian environment are VCB mechanisms for some λ.*

There are a couple of things to note. First, all interim incentive efficient mechanisms are resource efficient. That is, $\sum t^i(v) = Ky(v)$ for all v. One important implication of this is that VCG mechanisms will generally not be interim incentive efficient since they rarely satisfy resource efficiency. Second, output efficiency is neither necessary nor sufficient for interim incentive efficient mechanisms.[33] In fact, interim incentive efficiency implies output inefficiency for almost all weights λ. The only case in which output efficiency holds is for $\lambda^i(v^i) = 1$. In this singular case, the VCB mechanism selects Pareto optimal allocations. On the other hand, if λ is increasing in v, so that high-value types are weighted more heavily than low-value types, then the interim incentive efficient mechanisms for those λ will require the public good to be produced more often than is (*ex post*) efficient.[34] If λ is decreasing in v then interim-incentive-efficiency will require under-production of the public good.

At first glance the characterization does not bode well for the sought-after conclusion that "Voting Works." VCB mechanisms do not look very much like voting mechanisms. Further, since majority rule is interim incentive compatible and is not a VCB mechanism, it is not interim incentive efficient. I address this problem in two ways. I first broaden the class of voting mechanisms beyond simple MR, and then, as is done with markets for private goods, turn to large economies.

3.3 "Voting Works" in Large Bayesian Environments

In order more easily to explain why voting seems to work in large environments, we begin by looking at what the interim efficient VCB mechanisms look like in large economies. As $N \to \infty$, feasibility, quasi-linearity, and symmetry will imply that i's effect on i's conditional expected output, $dQ^i(v^i)/dv^i$, goes to zero. If that is true, then incentive compatibility requires that i's effect on i's conditional expected taxes, $dT^i(v^i)/dv^i$, should also go to zero.[35] This means that each individual's taxes must begin to look like per capita taxes.[36] It follows that, in large economies, all interim-incentive-compatible taxes are approximately per capita taxes.[37] This means that

---

[33] Over- and under-production are used, in VCB mechanisms, to relax the incentive compatibility constraints at a lower cost than using taxes as is done in VCG mechanisms.

[34] That means there will be times it is produced even if $\sum v^i - K < 0$.

[35] Incentive compatibility requires that $v^i dQ^i(v^i)/dv^i = dT^i(v^i)/dv^i$. So the right-hand side $\to 0$ as $N \to \infty$. Otherwise i will try to avoid taxes by misreporting her type.

[36] $T^i(v^i) \to kQ^i(v^i)$ and $t^i(v) \to ky(v)$ for all i as $N \to \infty$.

[37] This statement about the necessity of approximately constant per capita taxes for incentive compatibility in large environments holds considerably more broadly. It is true in public goods environments in which the public good is multidimensional and in which the types of the consumers are multidimensional.

voting procedures, if they can get the output decision right, have a chance to perform as well as the interim incentive efficient VCB mechanisms. There is a class that does.

Consider the class of voting processes, which I call q-referenda.[38] In these voting processes, each agent is asked to vote yes or no for the public good. The good is produced if and only if the proportion of yes votes is greater than or equal to q. Each agent pays the per capita cost of the public good.

Definition 4: [39] *A class of voting processes called q-referenda is given by:* $m^i \in M^i = \{0, 1\}$, *where 0 is a no vote and 1 is a yes vote, an outcome rule*

$$y(m) = 1 \text{ iff } \sum_i m^i \geq Nq,$$

and a taxation rule

$$t^i(m) = ky(m).$$

It is a dominant strategy to vote yes if and only if your value for the good is at least as much as the per capita cost of the good. So, all q-referenda are incentive compatible in both the dominant (*ex post*) and Bayesian (interim) senses. It is easy to show that q-referenda do not produce Pareto optimal allocations: they are resource efficient but not output efficient. But in large economies they begin to look very good. In particular, as $N \to \infty$, the set of q-referenda is virtually equivalent to the set of interim efficient mechanisms.

Using results from Ledyard and Palfrey (2002), one can show that for every λ, there is a q such that, as $N \to \infty$, the expected value of the q-referendum converges to the expected value of that λ-VCB mechanism.

Theorem 1: *Let* (y^λ, t^λ) *be the output and tax rules for the λ-VCB mechanism. Let* (y^q, t^q) *be the output and tax rules for the q-referendum. For every λ with* $\int \lambda^i dF^i(v^i) > 0$ *for all i, there is a $q \in [0, 1]$ such that as $N \to \infty$*

$$\int \sum \lambda^i(v^i)[v^i y^q(v) - t^{qi}(v)]dF \to \int \sum \lambda^i(v^i)[v^i y^\lambda(v) - t^{\lambda i}(v)]dF.$$

Proof: The q that works solves $qE\{\lambda v|v > k\} + (1-q)E\{\lambda v|v < k\} = k$.

A converse to this result also holds. For every q-referendum there is a λ-VCB mechanism that approximates it. This means that, in large economies, q mechanisms are approximately interim incentive efficient and any interim incentive efficient mechanism can be approximated with a q mechanism. In particular, in large economies, to an appropriate approximation, no mechanism—be it VCG or VCB—can replace a q-referendum and make everyone better off. On these grounds I would tentatively claim that "Voting Works" in an interim sense in a Bayesian context.[40]

[38] $q \in [0, 1]$ and represents the required plurality for acceptance of the referendum proposition that "the public good should be produced and financed with per capita taxes." If the required plurality is not achieved, "the public good is not produced and no one pays any taxes."
[39] A direct mechanism version of q-referenda is given by: $m^i \in V^i$, an outcome rule $y(v) = 1$ iff $\#\{v^i|v^i \geq k\} \geq Nq$, and a taxation rule $t^i(v) = ky(v)$.
[40] It is shown in Malath and Postlewaite 1990 that if we impose a requirement of interim individual rationality then as $n \to \infty$ the only feasible, incentive compatible, interim individually rational

3.4 "Voting Works" in Large Environments

But we can actually say more by recognizing two facts: (1) q-referenda are incentive compatible in dominant strategies and (2) any interim efficient mechanism is also an efficient mechanism. Using the first fact, if D is the set of all dominant strategy mechanisms and (y^q, t^q) is a q referendum, then

$$\int \sum \lambda^i(v^i)[v^i y^q(v) - t^{qi}(v)] dF \leq \max_D \int \sum \lambda^i(v^i)[v^i y(v) - t^i(v)] dF$$

and using the second fact, since $D \subset B$ where B is the set of all Bayesian incentive compatible mechanisms

$$\max_D \int \sum \lambda^i(v^i)[v^i y(v) - t^i(v)] dF \leq \max_B \int \sum \lambda^i(v^i)[v^i y(v) - t^i(v)] dF$$

where

$$\max_B \int \sum \lambda^i(v^i)[v^i y(v) - t^i(v)] dF = \int \sum \lambda^i(v^i)[v^i y^\lambda(v) - t^{\lambda i}(v)] dF$$

and y^λ, t^λ is the VCB mechanism for λ. Now stringing all of these together, it follows that, for the appropriate q, as $N \to \infty$ all of these expressions approach each other in value, because the largest and smallest do by Theorem 1. This means in particular that as $N \to \infty$

$$\int \sum \lambda^i(v^i)[v^i y^q(v) - t^{qi}(v)] dF \to \max_D \int \sum \lambda^i(v^i)[v^i y(v) - t^i(v)] dF$$

and so the q-referendum is approximately incentive efficient in large economies.[41]

I would claim that at this point we have ample grounds for saying that, if we forgo any requirement for individual rationality, "Voting Works" in large simple public goods environments.

3.5 Some Doubts

There are several reasons to pause here before declaring total victory.

In large economies, not only is reporting truth an incentive compatible behavior, so is almost anything else. If $dQ^i(v^i)/dv^i \approx 0$, and $dT^i(v^i) \approx 0$, then my report has virtually no effect on my utility. So almost any behavior, $m(v)$, will be incentive compatible in q-referenda. This means there are multiple equilibria in the mechanism which in turn means actual behavior is a bit unpredictable. This is a problem with many mechanisms. For example, the dynamic voluntary contributions game has

---

mechanisms do not produce the public good. We already know that the only feasible, incentive compatible mechanisms as $n \to \infty$ look like majority rule. And majority rule violates individual rationality unless unanimity is required, in which case nothing is ever produced.

[41] A warning is appropriate here. This does not mean that q-referenda are approximately equivalent to the set of incentive efficient mechanims. There may be incentive efficient mechanisms that cannot be approximated by a q-referendum.

equilibria that are Pareto optimal (see Marx and Matthews 2000), so it is an incentive compatible and efficient mechanism for public goods. But that mechanism also has multiple equilibria.[42]

Another reason to pause is that in large environments, as we have defined them, it is possible for command mechanisms to be interim incentive efficient. By a command mechanism, I mean a mechanism which does not ask for any information from consumers. Such mechanisms are really simple. Consider the following mechanism: $y = 1$ iff $\int \lambda(v) v \, dF(v) \geq k$ and $t^i = ky$. That is, if the prior beliefs are such that the expected weighted value of the public good is bigger than the per capita cost then produce the good. As $N \to \infty$, since the v^i are independently and identically distributed, the law of large numbers means that the probability that $\{y = 1 \text{ iff} \sum \lambda^i(v^i)[(v^i - k)] \geq 0\} \to 1$. It is trivially incentive compatible. That is, the command mechanism is almost interim incentive efficient. The force of this observation can be blunted by considering a more complex environment in which the types, v^i, are correlated. For example, let $v^i = r^i + c$ for all i where r^i is distributed independently and identically according to $F(r)$ and c is distributed according to $G(c)$. Then unilateral mechanisms will not be interim incentive efficient, even approximately, but Theorem 1 remains valid. So if values are correlated, q-referenda are almost interim incentive efficient but unilateral mechanisms are not.

Another reason to hesitate is that we do not know whether the results so far can be extended to simple environments with a variable quantity public good.[43] Ledyard and Palfrey (1999) provide the appropriate characterization of the VCB mechanisms for the case of a variable public good when the utility functions are linear in v^i. It is an open question whether any voting processes provide an approximation to these generalized VCBs.

3.6 Multidimensional Issues Spaces

Finally there is a question of what to do in multidimensional public goods problems. In the multidimensional policy spaces that arise when there is more than one public good or when the tax functions are up for grabs, there is rarely a median voter. This causes serious problems for many models of voting such as simple majority rule processes, as was illustrated earlier in Example 15. But one can still find voting processes that "work."[44]

Using techniques developed in Berliant and Ledyard (2004) and Ledyard (1984), one can find a mechanism which is interim incentive efficient in a world with multiple public goods, with non-linear tax schedules of income, and without quasi-linear utility functions. In this process, two candidates vie for election. Each wants to

---

[42] I thank Steve Matthews for reminding me about the issues surrounding multiple equilibria. I do not really confront this fully here.

[43] This is the case in which $u^i = g(y, v^i)$.

[44] My space is limited and so I have to forgo an extensive discussion at this point and just make the claim. The interested reader can pursue the details in Ledyard 2005.

maximize their probability of winning. It is costly to vote and that cost varies across consumers. A voter abstains if the expected benefits of voting do not outweigh the cost of voting. Voters take candidate positions as given and then turn out and vote given rational expectations about other voters. Candidates, knowing how voters behave, choose equilibrium platforms. Any equilibrium of the two-candidate election will be interim incentive efficient in the space of implementable platforms.[45]

4 AN AGGRESSIVE CONCLUSION

In this chapter, I have explored whether there were any conditions under which voting processes are good mechanisms for the allocation of and taxing for public goods. I was looking for something that compared to the central claim of welfare economics that "Markets Work" for the allocation of private goods. In that literature, it is demonstrated that, in large economies, there are market processes that are incentive compatible and almost efficient[46] and there are market processes that are efficient and almost incentive compatible.[47] Even though one cannot find mechanisms that are simultaneously incentive compatible and efficient in large economies (or small), these results are generally viewed as sufficient to provide a theoretical rationale for the ubiquitous nature of markets.

In this chapter I find similar results for voting and public goods. In large economies, voting is shown to be incentive compatible and almost incentive efficient, where the latter means that it is common knowledge that there is no other incentive compatible mechanism such that everyone is better off by more than a very small amount.

In large economies, if we dispense with the individual rationality constraint, "Voting Works."

REFERENCES

ARROW, K. J. 1969. The organization of economic activity: issues pertinent to the choice of market versus non-market allocation. Pp. 47–64 in *The Analysis and Evaluation of Public Expenditures: The PPB System*, ed. Joint Economic Committee. Washington, DC: Government Printing Office.
BERLIANT, M., AND LEDYARD, J. 2004. A direct approach to optimal income taxation. Manuscript.
BEWLEY, T. 1973. Edgeworth's conjecture. *Econometrica*, 41: 425–54.

---

[45] It would be nice also to have a result that characterized all interim efficient mechanisms in this world. I do not have such a theorem at this time.
[46] The examples can be found in McAfee 1992 and Gresik and Satterthwaite 1989.
[47] The canonical example is competitive equilibrium with price-taking behavior.

Bowen, H. 1943. The interpretation of voting in the allocation of economic resources. *Quarterly Journal of Economics*, 58: 27–48.

Clarke, E. 1971. Multi-part pricing of public goods. *Public Choice*, 11: 17–33.

Conley, J. 1994. Convergence theorems on the core of a public-goods economy: sufficient conditions. *Journal of Economic Theory*, 62: 161–85.

d'Aspremont, C., and Gerard-Varet, L. 1979. Incentives and incomplete information. *Journal of Public Economics*, 11: 25–45.

Green, J., and Laffont, J. J. 1977. Characterization of strongly individually incentive compatible mechanisms for the revelation of preferences for public goods. *Econometrica*, 45: 427–38.

——— ——— 1979. *Incentives in Public Decision Making*. Amsterdam: North-Holland.

Gresik, T., and Satterthwaite, M. A. 1989. The rate at which a simple market converges to efficiency as the number of traders increases: an asymptotic result for optimal trading mechanisms. *Journal of Economic Theory*, 48: 304–32.

Groves, T. 1973. Incentives in teams. *Econometrica*, 1: 617–31.

——— and Ledyard, J. 1977. Some limitations of demand revealing processes. *Public Choice*, 29: 107–24.

Holmstrom, B., and Myerson, R. 1983. Efficient and durable decision rules with incomplete information. *Econometrica*, 51: 1799–819.

Hurwicz, L. 1972. On informationally decentralized systems. Pp. 297–336 in *Decision and Organization*, ed. R. Radner and C. McGuire. Amsterdam: North-Holland.

——— and Walker, M. 1990. On the generic non-optimality of dominant-strategy allocation mechanisms: a general theorem that includes pure exchange economies. *Econometrica*, 58: 683–704.

Ledyard, J. 1984. The pure theory of large two candidate elections. *Public Choice*, 44: 7–41.

——— 1995. Public goods: a survey of experimental research. In *The Handbook of Experimental Economics*, ed. J. Kagel and A. E. Roth. Princeton, NJ: Princeton University Press.

——— 2005. Voting works. Manuscript.

——— and Palfrey, T. 1999. A characterization of interim efficiency with public goods. *Econometrica*, 67: 435–48.

——— ——— 2002. The approximation of efficient public good mechanisms by simple voting schemes. *Journal of Public Economics*, 83: 153–71.

——— ——— 2005. A General characterization of interim efficient mechanisms for independent linear environments. Manuscript.

McAfee, R. P. 1992. A dominant strategy double auction. *Journal of Economic Theory*, 56: 434–50.

McKelvey, R. D., and Schofield, N. 1987. Generalized symmetry conditions at a core point. *Econometrica*, 55: 923–33.

Malath, G., and Postlewaite, A. 1990. Asymmetric information bargaining problems with many agents. *Review of Economic Studies*, 57: 351–67.

Marx, L. M., and Matthews, S. A. 2000. Dynamic voluntary contribution to a public project. *Review of Economic Studies*, 67: 231, 327–58.

Mas-Colell, A., Whinston, M., and Green, J. 1995. *Microeconomic Theory*. Oxford: Oxford University Press.

Mirrlees, J. A. 1971. An exploration in the theory of optimal income taxation. *Review of Economic Studies*, 2: 175–208.

Muench, T. 1972. The core and the Lindahl equilibrium of an economy with a public good: an example. *Journal of Economic Theory*, 4: 241–55.

Myerson, R. 1981. Optimal auction design. *Mathematics of Operations Research*, 6: 58–73.

_____ and SATTERTHWAITE, M. A. 1983. Efficient mechanisms for bilateral trading. *Journal of Economic Theory*, 29: 265–81.

ROBERTS, J. 1976. The incentives for correct revelation of preferences and the number of consumers. *Journal of Public Economics*, 6: 359–74.

_____ and POSTLEWAITE, A. 1976. The incentives for price-taking behavior in large exchange economies. *Econometrica*, 44: 115–27.

ROBERTS, K. 1979. The characterization of implementable choice rules. Pp. 321–48 in *Aggregation and Revelation of Preferences*, ed. J.-J. Laffont. Amsterdam: North-Holland.

SAMUELSON, P. 1954. Pure theory of public expenditures. *Review of Economic Studies*, 36: 387–9.

VICKREY, W. 1961. Counterspeculation, auctions, and competitive sealed tenders. *Journal of Finance*, 16: 8–37.

WALKER, M. 1978. On the characterization of mechanisms for the revelation of preferences. *Econometrica*, 46: 147–52.

_____ 1980. On the nonexistence of a dominant-strategy mechanism for making optimal public decisions. *Econometrica*, 48: 1521–40.

CHAPTER 28

FISCAL COMPETITION

DAVID E. WILDASIN

1 INTRODUCTION

ANALYSES of fiscal competition seek to ascertain how fiscal policy-making is affected by competitive pressures faced by governments. Such analyses may be useful for normative evaluation, but, at base, the theory of fiscal competition requires a theory of policy choice. As such, it lies squarely in the realm of political economy. Does this theory have any operationally meaningful content? Does it offer useful guidance for empirical analysis? As will become clear, the answers to these questions are definitely "yes:" models of governments operating in a competitive environment typically predict policy outcomes different from those chosen by governments not facing competition. This is a far cry from saying that these implications are *readily* testable, however. At the most fundamental level, there is no settled operational basis on which to determine whether or to what degree any set of governments can be said to "compete," or whether the extent of competition has changed over time. The development of empirical tests for the effects of fiscal competition is an area of ongoing research, and will no doubt remain so for some time to come.

To help readers get their bearings in a rapidly developing branch of literature, this chapter presents a concise overview of some of the principal themes that have figured prominently in economic analyses of fiscal competition.[1] In addition to surveying some of the contours of existing research, I also try to identify significant gaps that

---

* I am grateful to the editors for helpful guidance in revising this chapter, but retain responsibility for errors and omissions.

[1] There are several literature surveys that interested readers may consult. These include Cremer et al. 1996; Wildasin 1998; Wilson 1999; Wilson and Wildasin 2004. Many key ideas can be found in Oates 1972.

warrant further attention and that may occupy the attention of investigators in the years to come.

1.1 What Is Fiscal Competition?

The term "fiscal competition" may evoke images of one state pitted in a contest with another for a high-stakes manufacturing project, with politicians serving up juicy packages of tax holidays, infrastructure projects, regulatory relief, and direct subsidies to entice a firm and advance the cause of "economic development," "jobs," or other supposedly desirable economic outcomes. However, events of this sort, sometimes rich in political drama, are not the only form of fiscal competition, just as the tales of buyouts, takeovers, and boardroom struggles that crowd the business pages are only one part of the process of commercial competition among business firms. The numerous producers in the wheat or corn industries, each reacting to market conditions that they cannot individually influence, are textbook examples of perfect competition in a market setting. Perfect competition, in a market context, limits the power of individual producers to affect market prices, creates powerful incentives to control costs and to respond to fluctuating market conditions, limits profits only to those pure rents that arise from the ownership of unique and non-replicable assets, and produces efficient allocations of resources in an otherwise undistorted economy. This type of market competition differs markedly from the rivalrous behavior that sometimes characterizes much more concentrated industries, in which a handful of captains of industry wheel and deal to snuff out, or perhaps to buy out, one or two other major competitors and thus secure market dominance. Textbook perfect competition deals with the rather more routine business of providing regular supplies of goods and services to numerous small customers who, though unable to dictate terms to any one supplier, can always turn to numerous competing suppliers.

Similarly, fiscal competition occurs, in its purest and probably most important form, in the routine daily decisions of numerous and usually small businesses, workers, consumers, and governments. To be sure, fiscal competition, like market competition, can certainly be investigated in cases of "imperfect competition," where governments, market agents (like firms), or both are small in number and large in size. The analysis of strategic interactions among small numbers of large agents— small numbers of governments, small numbers of firms, or small numbers of both— forms a rich and interesting branch of the literature on fiscal competition, but the case of perfect competition is always a useful and even essential benchmark. In order to limit its scope, most of the discussion in this chapter focuses on this benchmark "perfectly competitive" case in which many small governments compete for many small households and firms. In doing so, game-theoretic complexities arising from strategic interactions among governments are de-emphasized—undoubtedly a significant limitation in some contexts.[2]

---

[2] Brueckner 2000, 2003 surveys both the basic theory and the empirical testing of models of strategic fiscal competition in several different contexts.

Competition among governments can take many forms. The present chapter focuses just on those aspects of competition that arise from the (actual or potential) movement of productive resources—especially labor and capital, in their many forms—across jurisdictional boundaries. This type of fiscal competition is of great importance because the revenues of fiscal systems so often depend critically on the incomes accruing to capital and labor (or their correlates, including consumption) and their expenditures are so often linked to labor and capital (or their demographic and economic correlates, including populations and sub-populations of all ages). However, it should be kept in mind that competition may also result from trade in goods and services or simply from the flow of information among jurisdictions, as discussed in other branches of literature. In practice, these many types of competition should be expected to occur simultaneously. Analyses of these different types of competition are potentially complementary and are certainly not mutually exclusive.

1.2 Outline

This chapter is organized as follows. Section 2 discusses the basic economics of fiscal competition. Section 2.1 sketches a model that has been used frequently in theoretical and empirical analyses of fiscal competition, emphasizing how fiscal policies affect the welfare (real incomes) of various groups and how these impacts depend on the mobility of resources and thus providing the economic foundation for subsequent discussion. Section 2.2 shows how alternative versions of this model allow it to be exploited in diverse application contexts. The normative implications of fiscal competition are discussed briefly in Section 2.3.

Subsequent sections of the chapter address parts of the subject that are less well settled. Section 3 focuses on the political economy of fiscal competition, highlighting the fact that exit (or entry) options for mobile resources alter the payoffs from alternative fiscal policies among those who (rationally, under the circumstances) participate actively in the political process. Section 4 analyzes two intertemporal aspects of fiscal competition: the determination of the "degree" of factor mobility, especially for the purposes of empirical analysis, and the issue of time-varying policies, commitment, and dynamic consistency. Finally, Section 5 turns to the role of institutions, and particularly of higher- and lower-level governments (i.e. the vertical and horizontal structure of government), in fiscal competition. Section 6 concludes.

2 Models of Fiscal Competition: From Simple to Complex

Perhaps the most frequently utilized model of *tax* competition is one in which there is a *single* mobile factor of production, usually called "capital," that is the *single* source of revenue for a government that provides a *single* public good or service. Capital mobility implies that heavier taxation will drive capital to other jurisdictions, creating incentives for the government to limit the local tax burden. Since capital taxation is the sole source of local government revenue, capital mobility limits government expenditure.

In this model, competition for mobile capital may lead to under-provision of public services (sometimes described, with excessive rhetorical flourish, as a "race to the bottom") and can be harmful to economic welfare. At least, this can be true if public expenditures are used by *benevolent* local political decision-makers to provide public services valued by local residents—in the simplest case, by a *single* representative local resident. If, by contrast, self-interested politicians use government expenditure inefficiently—e.g. to overstaff the public sector, to overcompensate public sector workers, or to make sweetheart deals with the friends of corrupt officials—then capital mobility, by limiting public expenditures, also limits waste, e.g. by "Leviathans" (Brennan and Buchanan 1980; see also Keen and Kotsogiannis 2003). In this case, the welfare implications of capital mobility are ambiguous and it is possible that mobility of the tax base may be welfare improving.

As will be seen, it is easy to sketch a model in which these ideas can be developed more formally. However, it should already be apparent that simple "bottom-line" conclusions about the implications of "tax competition," such as the two opposing conclusions contained in the preceding paragraph (to state them as simply as possible, "tax competition puts downward pressure on public expenditures and is welfare harmful" and "tax competition puts downward pressure on public expenditures and is welfare improving"), rest on equally simple and highly debatable hypotheses. These hypotheses, when stated explicitly, are clearly anything but self-evident. In fact, it is possible to construct an entire series of models of fiscal competition that yield a wide range of positive and normative implications. As already suggested by the emphases in the preceding paragraphs, different assumptions may be made about the *types* of fiscal instruments utilized by governments, the *number* of fiscal instruments that they use, the underlying local economic structure (such as the *type* and *number* of mobile productive resources), and the *type* and *number* of agents in whose interest(s) policies are formulated. The present chapter cannot provide an exhaustive enumeration of all possible models of fiscal competition. However, equipped with a basic model, built on standard assumptions, it is relatively easy to see how the implications of fiscal competition can vary widely as critical assumptions are altered.

2.1 A Benchmark Model

The literature on fiscal competition owes much to the study of local government finance in the USA. It is worth recalling a few basic facts about these governments. First, they are numerous and, generally, small: there are about 90,000 local governments, including more than 3,000 counties, about 14,000 school districts, more than 20,000 municipalities, and tens of thousands of special districts and townships. Local education spending accounts for about 40 per cent of all local public expenditures (about half of all expenditures excluding public utility expenditures). Local property taxes account for about two-thirds of all local tax revenues. Historically, the local property tax has been, by far, the dominant element in local fiscal systems; even today, when many local governments have broadened their tax systems, it accounts for about 72 per cent of local government own-source tax revenue. Because property taxes have played such a dominant role as a source of local government revenues in the USA, and because education accounts for such a large part of local government spending, numerous early contributions to the literature on fiscal competition build upon the stylized assumption that governments use a *single* tax instrument to finance a *single* public service.

Modern studies of property tax incidence (that is, of the real economic burden of the property tax) provide much of the analytical foundation for the study of fiscal competition. The property tax is commonly viewed partly as a tax assessed on "raw" land and partly as a tax on the structures built on land. Land, per se, is perfectly inelastically supplied, but all of the other value of property—perhaps 90 per cent of the value of residential, commercial, and industrial property, in a modern urban setting—derives from investment in its improvement and development. These capital investments are durable resources that, while fixed in the short run (residential subdivisions, shopping malls, or industrial parks cannot be created instantaneously, and, once built, only depreciate gradually), are variable in the long run. A conventional view is that the burden of local property taxes falls on property owners in the short run because the supplies of both land and capital are inelastic. In the long run, however, the property tax discourages investment in the local economy, resulting in reduced local economic activity and lower returns to land or other fixed local resources, possibly including labor. Because of the quantitative importance of capital relative to land and because the variability of capital in the long run plays a critical role in the analysis of tax incidence, much of the literature on local property taxation simply ignores the land component of the property tax, treating it simply as a local tax on capital investment.

Figure 28.1 illustrates this model. Let k represent the amount of capital investment in the local economy. In the long run, this is determined by the profitability of local investment relative to investment opportunities elsewhere. The MP_K schedule shows the before-tax or gross rate of return on capital in the locality, based on its marginal productivity. Because capital combines with land, labor, or other immobile resources, this schedule is downward sloping, reflecting the idea that investments are very profitable when there is almost no capital in the local economy but that successive units of investment are decreasingly profitable as the local capital stock expands. If r^* is the *net* rate of return on investment elsewhere in the economy, and if there were no local property tax or other local policies that would influence investment, k^* would be the long-run equilibrium level of the local capital stock because the return on capital in the local economy would be just equal to the return earned elsewhere and there would therefore be no incentive for capital to flow into or out of the locality. The total value of local economic activity—all production of goods and services, including the rental value of residential property—is represented by the area $0ABk^*$, of which the amount $0r^*Bk^*$ is the return accruing to capital invested in the local economy and

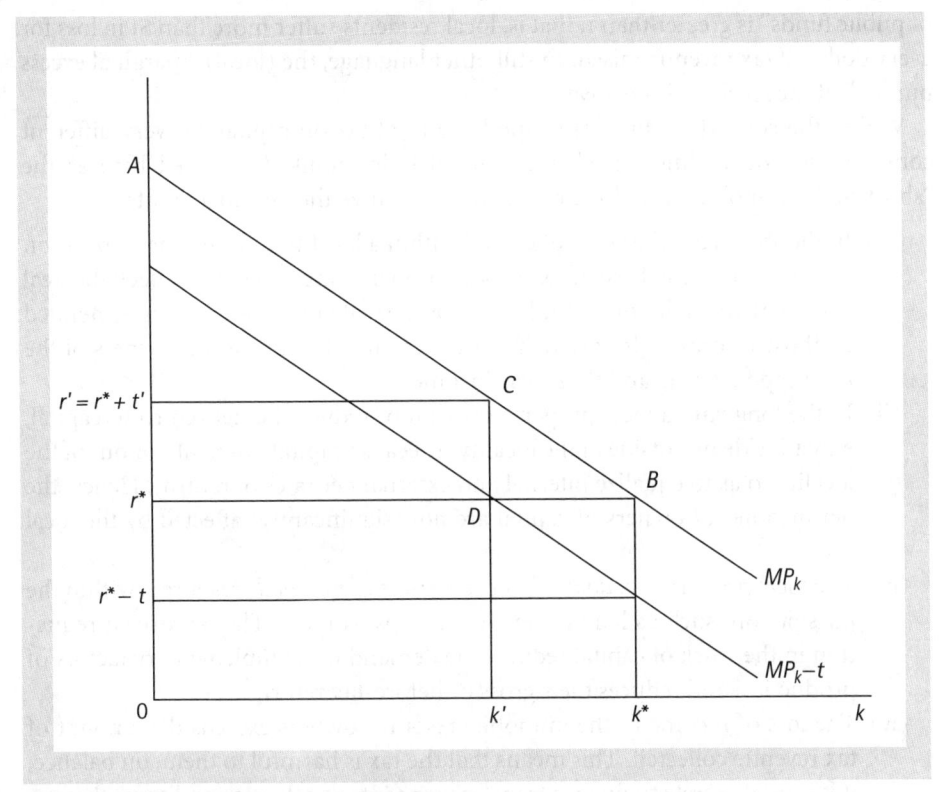

Fig. 28.1 Equilibrium allocation of a mobile factor of production in the presence of taxation

the remainder, r^*AB, is the income earned by local landowners, workers, or owners of other local resources.

If the capital stock is fixed at k^* in the short run and a local property tax is imposed, collecting t per unit of capital, the owners of local capital would suffer a loss in net income as the net rate of return falls to $r^* - t$. This is not a long-run equilibrium, however, since more profitable investments, earning r^*, are available outside the locality. Over time, the local capital stock would shrink to k', at which point the gross or before-tax rate of return in the local economy would have risen to r', that is, by the amount of the local tax t. With this higher local *before-tax* rate of return, the local *net* rate of return is equal to that available externally. In this post-tax situation, local production will have been reduced to $0ACk'$. The outflow of capital reduces the gross income of land, labor, or other local resources to $r'AC$ while the local government raises $r^*r'CB$ in tax revenues. If the entirety of this tax revenue is paid over to landowners or workers, either in cash or in the form of public services equal in value to the amount of tax revenue, their loss of income will be partly but not completely offset. On balance, they will lose the amount DCB in net income, that is, the collection of revenue through this tax is costly, on net, to local residents. To express this observation in a slightly different terminology, the (local) "marginal cost of public funds" is greater than 1, that is, local residents suffer more than $1 in loss for every dollar of tax revenue raised. In still other language, the (local) "marginal excess burden" of the local tax is positive.

Within the context of this simple model, a local tax on capital has very different consequences, depending on whether capital is immobile (identified here as the "short run") or mobile (the "long run"). To summarize the essential points:

(i) In the short run, the stock of capital within a locality is fixed. The imposition of a tax on capital, such as a local property tax, does not affect the real resources available within the locality or the real output and income generated by those resources. It does reduce the net rate of return to the owners of the local capital stock, and thus their incomes.

(ii) In the long run, a local property tax cannot reduce the net return to capital, either inside or outside of the locality[3] (because capital flows into or out of the locality so as to equalize internal and external net rates of return). Hence, the net incomes of owners of capital are not (significantly) affected by the local tax.

(iii) The local property tax *does* affect the owners of *immobile* resources within the jurisdiction, such as landowners or perhaps workers. The tax-driven reduction in the stock of capital reduces the demand for complementary factors of production and reduces their gross or before-tax returns.

(iv) The loss of income to the immobile resource owners exceeds the amount of tax revenue collected. This means that the tax is harmful to them, on balance, if it is used merely to finance transfer payments or other expenditures that are no more valuable than their cost. As a corollary, the only expenditures that will benefit local residents are those whose benefits exceed their direct cost.

So far, this analysis merely illustrates the effects of hypothetical policies without addressing the political economy of policy choice. But because it shows how different groups are affected by alternative policies, its potential lessons for politics are immediate. In particular, it shows how the mobility of a taxed resource changes the impact of fiscal policies on different groups, and thus on their incentives to influence the political process.

Assume for the moment that the local political process chooses policies that maximize the incomes of owners of resources other than capital—workers, say, or landowners. (Perhaps local residents elect politicians who pursue this goal on their behalf.) In the short run, a local tax on capital provides an opportunity for these agents to capture rents from the owners of capital—unless of course the capital is owned entirely by these agents themselves, in which case a tax on capital is just a tax on themselves. Provided, however, that there is some "foreign ownership" of capital, the local property tax is an attractive revenue instrument with which to finance local public services like schools. It can even provide a tool to transfer rents from capital owners to workers or landowners via direct cash transfers or

---

[3] More precisely, a local property tax does not *perceptibly* affect the net rate of return outside of the locality.

equivalent in-kind public expenditures. From a long-run perspective, however, the local economy has to compete for capital, and the incentive for local residents to use this tax to capture rents for themselves changes dramatically: in fact, it disappears altogether.

To forestall possible confusion, note that it is still *possible* to tax capital in the long run, even though it is freely mobile, and to use it to generate tax revenue. Mobility of the tax base does *not* mean that taxes cause the entire tax base to disappear; in Figure 28.1, the capital stock only shrinks to k', not 0, due to the tax, and the tax produces revenue equal to $r'C D r^*$. Mobility of capital does imply, however, that the *economic burden* of the tax on capital does not fall on the owners of capital, who must, in equilibrium, earn the same net rate of return r^* within the locality as without. Instead, the real burden of the tax now falls on the owners of land, labor, and other immobile resources, even though the tax is not imposed on these agents. The *economic incidence* of the tax is *shifted* from the owners of capital to the owners of resources that are "trapped" within the locality and cannot escape the burden of taxation. From a long-run perspective, the latter have no incentive to tax property in order to capture rents from the former. Indeed, a tax on capital that is used to finance transfers to the owners of locally fixed resources is not only not advantageous to them; on balance, it is harmful, because of the "deadweight loss" of the tax. This loss is absorbed by local residents—landowners or workers—in the form of reduced land rents or wages resulting from the flow of capital investment out of the local economy. If local residents *must* use the property tax to finance public service provision, they have an incentive to limit these services because raising local tax revenues is costly to them. They may end up providing lower levels of public services than would be true if they could, instead, use a tax on land rents or wages.

This discussion has relied on a series of highly stylized assumptions and a very simple model. In a stark form, it shows how the owners of immobile resources end up bearing the burden of local taxes imposed on mobile resources, including any (local) deadweight loss or excess burden associated with local taxes. This is true even if the owners of the immobile resources are not directly affected by the local tax. Likewise, capital mobility protects the owners of mobile capital from having to bear the burden of any local taxes imposed upon them. In this model, politicians acting on behalf of "immobile local residents"—landowners or workers—would not wish to impose taxes on mobile capital, even if the owners of this capital are outsiders with no voice whatsoever in local politics.

2.2 Further Interpretations and Applications of the Basic Model

These observations have important implications for the political economy of public policy. Before discussing these implications, however, let us pause to consider some variations on the very simple model developed above.

First, as we have seen, a tax on mobile capital that is used to finance transfer payments to local landowners or workers ends up harming the recipients of these payments, on net, by an amount equal to the excess burden from the tax on capital. They would therefore prefer a zero tax rate on capital to any positive tax. They would not, however, wish to *subsidize* capital investment, if they had to pay the taxes required to finance these subsidies. This policy, which is the reverse of a tax on capital used to finance transfer payments to the owners of immobile resources, is also harmful to the latter. It would attract capital and thus increase the level of before-tax income accruing to immobile resources (the size of the triangle in Figure 28.1) but this increased income would be more than offset by the taxes needed to finance the investment subsidy: in other words, this policy, too, creates an excess burden to be absorbed by local residents. If a tax or subsidy on capital investment merely involves offsetting transfers of cash (or its equivalent) to the owners of immobile resources, it imposes a net burden on them; from their viewpoint, such a policy should be eliminated. Competition for mobile capital does not imply that local governments will seek to *subsidize* capital investment.

Second, although the basic model can be applied to the analysis of property taxes levied by local school districts in the USA, nothing prevents its application to different types of tax or expenditure policies undertaken by higher-level governments. For instance, corporation income taxes are often viewed as source-based taxes on the income produced by business investment. These taxes are often imposed by state, provincial, and national governments. The benchmark model suggests that such taxes may impose net burdens on the incomes of corporations, and thus their owners, in the short run, but that their long-run burden falls on the owners of other, less mobile resources. Thus, the same model that has been used to analyze the taxation of property by local governments within a single country can also be used to analyze the taxation of business income by countries in an international context.

Third, although the mobile resource in the discussion so far has been called "capital," it should be clear that it is the mobility of the taxed or subsidized resource relative to other, immobile local resources that matters for the analysis. Depending on the context, the (potentially) mobile resource could also be people. In this case, the model shows that the real net income of mobile households is not affected by local fiscal policies, in the long run. A local tax on the incomes of the rich, for instance, would reduce their net incomes in the short run but, if they can move freely to other jurisdictions in the long run, the burden of such a tax would eventually fall on other, less mobile resources within the taxing jurisdiction.

Fourth, although the taxing powers of local school districts in the USA are often limited, both by law (for instance, a state constitution or statute may prohibit them from imposing any taxes other than a property tax) and by their limited capacity to administer income or other relatively complex taxes, higher-level governments, such as states, provinces, and nations, commonly have much more revenue autonomy and administrative capacity. On the expenditure side, higher-level governments can and do provide a wide array of public goods and services. Thus, although school districts in the USA may plausibly be described as jurisdictions that utilize a single tax (on property) to finance a single type of public good (primary and secondary education), most governments have many more fiscal policy instruments at their disposal. In such a context, the mobility of a single resource, such as capital, *may* result in a lower tax on that resource, but this need not imply a reduction in government spending; instead, it may mean that other sources of revenues are utilized more heavily. That is, fiscal competition may result not in less government spending but in a different *structure* of taxation, as governments substitute away from taxation of mobile resources and rely more heavily on taxation of less-mobile resources (Bucovetsky and Wilson 1991).[4]

Fifth, as a corollary of the preceding observation, note that fiscal competition may lead to *higher* public expenditures. In the simple model of Figure 28.1, there is only one fiscal instrument, a tax, that is applied to mobile capital. Often, however, government expenditures for public transportation, water, power, waste disposal, and other infrastructure may raise, rather than lower, the return to capital investment These expenditures may partially offset, or even more than offset, the negative impact of taxes on capital investment. It is the combined impact of *all* fiscal policies, positive and negative, that affects the location of capital or other mobile resources. The key message of the simple basic model is that fiscal competition provides incentives to reduce the *net* fiscal burden on a mobile resource; in practice, this may occur through tax reductions, subsidies that offset taxes, higher expenditures on selected public services that attract mobile resources, or possibly through even more complex policy bundles.

Finally, the simple model focuses on extreme polar cases in which one resource or another is either completely immobile or freely mobile, possibly depending on the time horizon under consideration (the "short run" or "long run"). Some resources, like mineral deposits, natural harbors, or rivers, may truly be immobile. Most other resources, like labor, capital, or cash in bank accounts, are at least potentially mobile but are seldom, if ever, truly costlessly mobile. Exactly how to determine the degree of resource mobility is not obvious, an issue that is discussed again in Section 4 below. In general terms, however, the fact that the extreme polar assumptions of the simple model are violated merely means that its predictions are expected only to be approximately rather than literally true.

In summary, the benchmark model of fiscal competition sketched in Section 2.1 lends itself to many variations and alternative interpretations, allowing it to be applied in a wide variety of contexts. Models of this type can thus be (and have been) used to study such diverse issues as welfare competition among US states, competition for the highly skilled or educated, competition for young workers, competition for old workers, or the effects of increased labor mobility in Europe resulting from successive expansions of EU membership or the prospective accession of still more countries—

---

[4] As one simple illustration of this possibility, note that few governments tax highly liquid financial assets such as bank account balances. When imposed, these taxes are usually levied at very low rates and they generate only modest revenues by comparison with taxes on household incomes, consumption, or fixed assets. This type of tax mix is readily understandable as a consequence of fiscal competition.

all in addition to the study of the competition among local governments in the USA, including school districts.

2.3 Normative Implications of Fiscal Competition

The normative implications of fiscal competition warrant at least brief mention. Early contributions to the literature on fiscal competition highlighted its potential benefits for economic efficiency as well as the constraints that it imposes on redistribution. Tiebout (1956) suggests that the sorting of people among localities (i.e. competition among localities for mobile households) could improve the efficiency of public expenditures. People with high demands for public services would be drawn to localities with high levels of public services and high levels of taxation, while low demanders would gravitate to localities with low taxes and low spending. Stigler (1957) argues that the mobility of resources limits the capacity of governments to redistribute income. A locality may tax the rich to subsidize the poor (in cash or in kind), but this policy will not effectively reduce the net incomes of the rich, nor raise the net income of the poor, if either or both groups are freely mobile.

These two ideas are related. Insofar as competition limits redistributive policies, it leads to public expenditures that are closely matched to taxes. Closer alignment between taxes and expenditures can result in greater efficiency of resource allocation. In the context of local public schooling in the USA, competition among jurisdictions for mobile households would be expected to lead to an equilibrium in which educational quality and expenditures vary among localities, with high demanders grouped in high-tax jurisdictions with good schools and low demanders grouped in low-tax jurisdictions with poor schools. This equilibrium, in which the benefits and costs of education are closely matched, may well be more efficient than one with no mobility of households. Given the abundant empirical evidence that education is a normal good (i.e. people demand more of it as their incomes rise), this equilibrium is also one in which children from rich families receive better educations than those from poor families. The same competitive forces that contribute to efficiency also preclude redistribution from rich to poor. Thus, the efficiency and equity effects of fiscal policy cannot, in general, be cleanly separated.

3 Fiscal Competition: Exit and Voice

Political decisions involve the resolution of conflicting interests. The mobility of labor, capital, or other resources is relevant for the analysis of political economy because it affects the payoffs to alternative fiscal policies, and thus the nature and extent of conflict. The Hirschman (1970) distinction between "voice" and "exit" provides a convenient lexicon with which to describe the key observations.

First, the payoffs to owners of resources that are truly freely mobile are unaffected by the policy choices of small jurisdictions. On the one hand, they are not adversely affected by local policies because they have an exit option: by relocating elsewhere, they can enjoy the same level of real income as is available externally. On the other hand, they cannot benefit from local policies, either, because others can enter from outside the jurisdiction to take advantage of the same benefits, and will have incentives to do so until those benefits are dissipated. The owners of freely mobile resources thus have no incentive to participate in or to influence the local political process, i.e. to exercise "voice." In one sense, they exert substantial power in the local political process: they do not need to defend their interests through voting, lobbying, or any other form of political action because market forces "do all the work" for them. In another sense, they are powerless: even full control over local policy-making does them no good. For the owners of truly immobile resources, the story is reversed. They have (by definition) no exit option: their resources are trapped in the local economy. For these agents, "voice" is essential. These agents do stand to gain or lose, depending on the outcome of the local political process.

To illustrate: consider the influences that may be brought to bear on policy-making in a town or city that is part of a major metropolitan area, and how this may depend on such factors as demographic structure and the form of housing tenure. One can imagine a city in which most residents are relatively young single people who rent their dwellings. Suppose that these dwellings, and the land on which they are situated, are owned by large real estate developers: individuals or businesses whose incomes depend on the profitability of local real estate investments. The people involved in these real estate activities may or may not reside in the city, but in any case have a powerful incentive to influence local policies in ways that improve the profitability of the real estate sector. One way to do this is to support taxes on real estate that are used to provide public services that are highly valued by renters, or to urge the restructuring of public expenditures toward services valued by renters, while limiting taxes and expenditures that are devoted to other uses. Landowners may influence local policy through lobbying, campaign contributions, or bribes, acting, in effect, as agents for the households from whom they collect rent. Renters may not vote or otherwise participate actively in the local political process and have little incentive to do so; nevertheless, their interests may be well represented in the local political process. Indeed, localities whose policies are, in effect, chosen by profit-maximizing landowners may produce fully efficient outcomes in which levels of public good provision satisfy the Samuelson condition.

As a variation on this model, residents could be homeowners rather than renters. Homeowners, too, might seek to maximize property values, if they are freely mobile. Home ownership may, however, raise the costs of moving, tying homeowners to the locality so that their personal preferences for local policy play a larger role and concern for property values diminishes. Of all the groups who exercise voice, however, none can impose burdens on the owners of freely mobile resources.

As a cautionary note, it should be remembered that resources that are relatively mobile in one context may be less so in a different context. Households newly arriving in a major metropolitan area can easily choose one locality over another in that area, almost at zero cost; the assumption that they can choose freely among them may be very plausible. The proportion of people who can easily relocate among much larger jurisdictions (like states, provinces, or countries) is normally much smaller, however. For such jurisdictions, it might be more appropriate (at least in the "short run") to assume that households are immobile rather than freely mobile. Even at the scale of larger jurisdictions, simple generalizations about the mobility of "labor" as a whole may be misleading, since mobility often differs by age, education, or other demographic types. In recent US experience, young and more highly educated people relocate relatively more frequently than those who are older and less educated, but this does not mean that such people are always intrinsically more mobile. For instance, black Americans exhibited a considerable degree of mobility during the period approximately 1915–50, which saw a substantial movement of low-skilled and poorly educated workers from the rural South into the industrial cities of the North, Midwest, and West. Observed flows of migration or capital are not necessarily good indicators of the degree of resource mobility.

4 Resource Mobility: The Importance of Dynamics

The theory of international trade conventionally draws a sharp distinction between "traded" and "non-traded" goods and services. Similarly, as noted earlier, much of the theoretical and empirical literature on fiscal competition sharply distinguished "mobile" and "immobile" resources. In neither case, however, can we be assured that reality falls neatly into line with these convenient distinctions. In particular, observed trade patterns do not necessarily determine whether or to what degree a commodity is tradeable, nor do flows of labor and capital among jurisdictions necessarily reveal the degree of factor mobility. In the simplest trade models, identical countries or regions will not trade simply because there is no incentive to do so, even if commodities can be transported across boundaries at zero cost. The same is true for factor mobility. Even if labor or capital is freely mobile among jurisdictions, there may be no differences in (net) rates of return and thus no incentive for resources to move. In Figure 28.1, the final equilibrium is indeed one in which net rates of return for capital or other mobile resources are equalized among jurisdictions; if and when such an equilibrium is reached, no further factor flows would be observed.

In general, then, how is one to determine which resources are mobile, and which are immobile? As the preceding discussion has made clear, this is a fundamental question for the analysis of fiscal competition. Building on the classical distinction between "short run" and "long run," it is reasonable to argue that the "degree" to which a resource is mobile depends critically on the time horizon over which mobility is to be assessed, and on the resource in question. For instance, modern technologies and the development of modern financial markets make it possible for financial capital to shift very rapidly within regions of a country as well as among countries. From the viewpoint of most aspects of fiscal policy-making, which occurs as a result of relatively slow-moving legislative or institutional change, a resource that can flow across jurisdictional boundaries within less than a year presumably qualifies as "mobile."

Far less mobile are the labor and capital, public and private, that constitute large urban agglomerations. These entities, though continuously evolving, grow or decline over decades or centuries. The slow pace of this process reflects the costs of adjustment both of stocks of real capital assets like factories, office buildings, apartment buildings, or houses, and of population and labor forces. For example, the growth of major modern cities—any of the largest 100 cities in the world, for example—can usually be traced to protracted periods of investment in real capital as well as inflows of population from other (often rural) areas. The size of a city's residential and non-residential capital stocks, population, and labor force certainly may and sometimes does decline over time, but sudden large-scale abandonment of existing stocks of real capital assets is rarely if ever observed. Annual growth or decline of populations and capital stock in the range of 2–10 per cent are not uncommon, however, and faster rates of change are certainly feasible.

Labor and capital are mobile on the largest geographic scales, as well, but, generally, over longer time horizons than is true for small geographical units. International migration and international flows of capital have played an important role in the economic and political development of the Western hemisphere, as is well illustrated by the work of Williamson (1998) and co-authors, who examine the simultaneous determination of capital and labor flows and wage and rate-of-return differentials between the Old and New Worlds during the nineteenth century. Of course, different *types* of labor and capital may be more or less mobile, to a degree that depends on information, transportation costs, the organization of markets, and other factors. For instance, world-class athletes, musicians, and other entertainers now commonly provide their services in more than one country, and perhaps in many different countries, in a single year. The same is true of world-class authors, scientists, entrepreneurs, and managers. These and other high-income people, or at least the taxable income streams that accrue to them, can probably relocate on a global basis with comparative ease.[5]

The above considerations suggest that the degree of factor mobility may be usefully characterized, operationally, by the speed with which factor movements occur. The geographic scope over which resources are mobile is likely to be rather small over very short time horizons, whereas mobility on a global scale is much less costly over long time horizons. In this perspective, polar extreme assumptions about "mobile" and "immobile" resources presumably bracket, but only imperfectly, most of the empirically relevant cases of resources that are "partially" mobile.

---

[5] The locational choices of such elite groups are of vital importance for public policy, far out of proportion to their numbers. In the USA, less than 0.2% of taxpayers receive about 10% of taxable income and pay about 20% of all personal income taxes.

In a dynamic setting, many of the basic implications of Section 2's benchmark model continue to hold, but in qualified form. Mindful of Keynes's observation that "in the long run we are all dead," we must note that participants in the political process care not only about the long-run effects of policies but also their short-run effects. In a world where economic agents discount the future, changes in incomes in the near term can be more important than long-run changes, even if the latter are larger in an undiscounted sense. A policy of taxation of capital investment or of high-income households may, in the long run, lead to outflows of capital or of high-income households. In the short run, however, it may be difficult for the owners of these taxed resources to escape the real burden of taxation. A policy that uses taxes on capital or high-income households to finance transfers to poor immobile or elderly households may thus be advantageous to the latter in present-value terms, even it is harmful "in the long run." Quasi-rents can be extracted from imperfectly mobile resources until the stock of these resources is gradually depleted sufficiently to raise their gross rate of return enough to equalize net rates of return with those available elsewhere. In a simple model of fiscal competition similar to that of Section 2, the optimal net fiscal burden on an imperfectly mobile resource is inversely proportional to the "half-life" of the dynamic adjustment process, i.e. very small, for a resource that adjusts very rapidly, but possibly very high for a resource that responds only sluggishly (Wildasin 2003).

Section 3's discussion of the political economy of fiscal competition can be reinterpreted in the context of dynamic factor mobility. Resources that are very mobile, such as highly liquid financial assets not subject to regulatory controls, earn very small quasi-rents. Those who can influence fiscal policy will not view these resources as very good fiscal policy "targets:" the modest gains from imposing significant fiscal burdens on them would be outweighed by the deadweight losses that ensue. Direct participation in the political process is unprofitable for the owners of such resources. Fixed capital investments or human resources, though perhaps highly mobile in the long term, adjust somewhat less rapidly to changes in policy. Favorable fiscal policies can produce positive changes in their incomes, in present-value terms, and adverse policies may harm them. Their owners have diminished "exit" or "entry" options and thus have a greater incentive to use "voice"—voting, lobbying, campaign financing—to affect fiscal policy.

These observations suggest that the time dimension of fiscal competition is of crucial importance, both because the speed with which resource stocks can adjust determines the degree of resource mobility and because policy-setting may involve trade-offs between short-run and long-run effects. This also implies that the problem of time consistency and credibility in policy-making is likely to play a critical role both in the economic analysis of fiscal competition and in the analysis of its implications for political economy.

Indeed, the problem of time consistency and commitment is already well recognized in the literature (Kydland and Prescott 1977). A now-classical problem in public finance concerns the means by which a government can commit itself not to expropriate capital investments either directly or, indirectly, through confiscatory taxation. A capital owner must incur the up-front costs of investment before a stream of returns can materialize, and these returns may be subject to taxation in future periods after the cost of investment is sunk. Today's incentive to invest depends on the expected tax treatment of the returns to capital investments in the future; the expectation of high tax burdens in the future would discourage investment in the present. To commit credibly not to tax capital heavily in the future is difficult because, when revenues are needed at future dates, the government will face the trade-off between taxing other revenue sources, such as earnings, or taxing the by-then historically determined stock of capital. A future tax on earnings or consumption would impose efficiency costs on the economy through distortions of behavior whereas a tax on the historically given stock of capital would not do so. Rational investors anticipate this problem and today's incentives to save and invest are harmed accordingly.

Kehoe (1989) explains how capital mobility can help to "solve" the problem of time-consistent taxation if capital is sufficiently mobile that it cannot be "trapped" in a high-tax jurisdiction. Specifically, Kehoe assumes that tax policies must be set prior to the decision about where to locate capital. In this case, fiscal competition prevents governments from capital expropriation. Other means by which governments can effectively "commit" to limited *ex post* taxation include up-front subsidies, investments in public infrastructure, or other special incentives that offset anticipated future increases in taxation (see, e.g., Keen and Marchand 1997), the development of reputation, and, of course, through constitutional constraints. These might include many forms of limits on governmental powers (e.g. enumeration of powers, due process, separation of powers) so as to constrain future demands for revenue or the capacity of government to collect it. It should be noted, however, that some commitment mechanisms might shift the balance of taxation *toward* rather than away from durable assets. For example, the establishment of an unfunded social security (public pension) system defers taxation to future periods and thus can undermine incentives for savings and investment.

5 COMPETITION AND INSTITUTIONAL CHANGE

Fiscal competition has significant implications for the organization of the public sector. In particular, jurisdictions with limited geographic scope (like the governments of small municipalities) are, in general, likely to face greater competitive pressures than larger ones (like large countries). While competition may limit the ability of small jurisdictions to redistribute income, it does not limit the underlying desire or demand for redistributive transfers. If interest groups or their representatives are unsuccessful at pursuing redistributive transfers at one level of government, they may move the locus of redistributive politics to a higher level of government at which such transfers may be more effective. Indeed, in his classic 1957 discussion, Stigler argued that the redistributive functions of government *should* be shifted to higher levels of government—in the US context, to the national government, away from local governments—precisely because of competitive pressures at the local level.

Normative arguments aside, it is empirically true that a great deal of the redistributive activities of the public sector do occur at the level of national governments rather than at the sub-national level. In the USA, welfare programs like Aid to Families with Dependent Children/Temporary Assistance to Needy Families and Medicaid, though implemented by state governments, have traditionally been generously supported by fiscal transfers (especially by open-ended matching grants) from the national government. Since the Second World War, state governments have taken a prominent role in local school finance, providing fiscal transfers to local governments in order to achieve greater uniformity of expenditures on elementary and secondary education—another instance in which higher-level governments pursue redistributive objectives that lower-level governments shun.

By providing insight into the comparative advantage of different levels of government in the redistributive activities of the public sector, the theory of fiscal competition can shed light on the organization of a federal system and thus on the institutions of the public sector. These evolve over time, and a topic worthy of further research concerns the relationship between institutional structures and changes in the degree of factor mobility over time. For example, the shifting balance of school financing away from local and toward state governments may be attributable, in part, to the increased stratification of metropolitan areas arising from increased mobility of households at the local level since the widespread introduction of automobiles and other forms of low-cost local transportation, and concomitant limits on the ability of local governments to finance relatively uniform levels of education to poor households by taxation of higher-income households. Over long historical periods, the mobility of labor and capital rises due to technological progress and it may also fall, sometimes rapidly, due to political change. These (possibly) exogenous changes provide a basis for an exploration of the effects of factor mobility on the institutions through which redistributive policies are implemented. As a broad working hypothesis, "upward reassignment" of redistributive functions over time would be anticipated. If no effective higher level of government is available to carry out redistributive functions, pressures may arise to bring new, higher-level governments into existence or to add new responsibilities to existing institutions. Recent debates and referenda concerning the EU constitution can be interpreted, at least partially, in this light.

6 CONCLUSION

The preceding discussion has shown how the economic impacts of fiscal policies depend on the mobility of the resources to which these policies are applied. Competition for resources changes the constraints under which governments operate, and the payoffs—to resident and non-resident households, the owners of firms, politicians, and political parties—from alternative fiscal policies. In this way, it affects the political economy of policy-making. Of course, it goes without saying that the political economy of policy-making is influenced by a host of other considerations, most notably the political institutions (dictatorships, parliamentary or "presidential" democracies, transparent or corrupt systems, etc.) through which policies are made.[6] In emphasizing the importance of resource mobility, I have focused on the *constraints under which* policies are made rather than on the *mechanisms through which* policies are made, but both are clearly important (and, as suggested in Section 5, interdependent).

Despite the considerable attention that it has recently received, there is much scope for fruitful additional analysis of fiscal competition. Clarifying the nature of "resource mobility" (perhaps through dynamic modeling, as suggested in Section 4) seems to be of fundamental importance. At present, conflicting and inconsistent assumptions about resource mobility are commonplace in both theoretical and empirical research. Perhaps the most challenging task on the research horizon is to investigate the nature of institutional change in a competitive environment. We live in a world in which the mobility of labor and capital appears to be increasing over time, in part due to secular trends (ever-falling transportation and communication costs, in particular), in part due to momentous political upheavals (especially the collapse of the Soviet Union and its satellite systems), and in part due to the liberalization of economic policies throughout the world (EU expansion, economic reforms in countries large and small). Students of institutional change are in the enviable position of being able to watch these events as they unfold. If successful in their efforts, they may achieve a better understanding of ongoing institutional evolution; they may even, in a modest way, help in the fashioning of new institutions and the policies that emerge from them.

REFERENCES

BRENNAN, G., and BUCHANAN, J. M. 1980. *The Power to Tax: Analytical Foundations of a Fiscal Constitution.* Cambridge: Cambridge University Press.

BRUECKNER, J. K. 2000. Welfare reform and the race to the bottom: theory and evidence. *Southern Economic Journal*, 66: 505–25.

──── 2003. Strategic interaction among governments: an overview of empirical studies. *International Regional Science Review*, 26: 175–88.

BUCOVETSKY, S., and WILSON, J. D. 1991. Tax competition with two instruments. *Regional Science and Urban Economics*, 21: 333–50.

CREMER, H., FOURGEAUD, V., LEITE-MONTEIRO, M., MARCHAND, M., and PESTIEAU, P. 1996. Mobility and redistribution: a survey. *Public Finance*, 51: 325–52.

HIRSCHMAN, A. O. 1970. *Exit, Voice, and Loyalty: Responses to Decline in Firms, Organizations, and States.* Cambridge, Mass.: Harvard University Press.

KEEN, M., and KOTSOGIANNIS, C. 2003. Leviathan and capital tax competition in federations. *Journal of Public Economic Theory*, 5: 177–200.

---

[6] See, e.g., Persson and Tabellini 2000 or Mueller 2003 for thorough treatments of this broad topic.

KEEN, M., and MARCHAND, M. 1997. Fiscal competition and the pattern of public spending. *Journal of Public Economics*, 66: 33–53.

KEHOE, P. J. 1989. Policy cooperation among benevolent governments may be undesirable. *Review of Economic Studies*, 56: 289–96.

KYDLAND, F., and PRESCOTT, E. 1977. Rules rather than discretion: the inconsistency of optimal plans. *Journal of Political Economy*, 85: 473–92.

MUELLER, D. C. 2003. *Public Choice III*. Cambridge: Cambridge University Press.

OATES, W. E. 1972. *Fiscal Federalism*. New York: Harcourt Brace Jovanovich.

PERSSON, T., and TABELLINI, G. 2000. *Political Economics: Explaining Economic Policy*. Cambridge, Mass.: MIT Press.

STIGLER, G. J. 1957. The tenable range of functions of local government. In Joint Economic Committee, *Federal Expenditure Policy for Economic Growth and Stability*. Repr. as pp. 167–76 in *Private Wants and Public Needs*, ed. E. S. Phelps, rev. edn. New York: Norton, 1965.

TIEBOUT, C. M. 1956. A pure theory of local expenditures. *Journal of Political Economy*, 64: 416–24.

WILDASIN, D. 1998. Factor mobility and redistributive policy: local and international perspectives. Pp. 151–92 in *Public Finance in a Changing World*, ed. P. B. Sorensen. London: Macmillan.

—— 2003. Fiscal competition in space and time. *Journal of Public Economics*, 87: 2571–88.

WILLIAMSON, J. G. 1998. Globalization, labor markets and policy backlash in the past. *Journal of Economic Perspectives*, 12: 51–7.

WILSON, J. D. 1999. Theories of tax competition. *National Tax Journal*, 52: 269–304.

—— and WILDASIN, D. E. 2004. Capital tax competition: bane or boon? *Journal of Public Economics*, 88: 1065–91.

PART VIII
POLITICS AND MACROECONOMICS

CHAPTER 29

THE NON-POLITICS OF MONETARY POLICY

SUSANNE LOHMANN

1 INTRODUCTION

Two puzzles drive political economy. First, economic policy deviates hugely and systematically from the normative prescriptions of economic theory. Second, economic performance changes over time and differs across countries to a degree that economic fundamentals cannot account for. The question is whether political factors—collective action and political institutions—can explain the discrepancy between policy and theory and the variations over time and across countries. Ultimately, the purpose is to devise political institutions that will shape economic policy and improve economic performance.

Macroeconomics and politics, or macro political economy, is the sub-field of political economy that is concerned specifically with monetary policy and monetary institutions. In recent decades, economists and political scientists have theoretically mapped out a range of issues such as the political vulnerability of monetary policy; proposed institutional solutions; and demonstrated empirically that monetary institutions make a difference over time and across countries for monetary policy and economic performance. In response to these findings, countries all over the world have adopted independent central banks, or granted their pre-existing central banks a higher degree of independence.

One indicator that the world has become a safer place, "monetarily speaking," is the fact that money and central banking have dropped off the domestic political agenda.

In the United States, Gallup regularly polls people on the question "What do you think is the most important problem facing this country today?" Inflation was at the top of the agenda in the two presidential campaigns that occurred in the immediate aftermath of the two oil price shocks, Ford v. Carter in 1976 and Carter v. Reagan in 1980 (and it is not a coincidence that in both cases the incumbent lost the election: inflation is *not* a vote-getter). Today, in 2005, inflation barely registers at all (only about 1 per cent of the respondents classify it as the most important problem). People do worry about some economic issues—unemployment and jobs (8 per cent), the state of the economy (10 per cent), and the federal budget deficit and federal debt (3 per cent)—but they do not generally hold monetary policy responsible; they blame globalization, or poor economic stewardship.

Meanwhile, people are preoccupied with non-economic issues such as war (25 per cent), social security (12 per cent), terrorism (9 per cent), health care (9 per cent), and education (6 per cent) (*USA Today* 2005).[1] Indeed, Thomas Frank's *What's the Matter with Kansas?* (2004) suggests that Bush vs. Kerry in 2004 was decided by people's moral values rather than their economic interests. Voters who are concerned about the morality of stem cell research, or the teaching of evolution in schools, will hardly obsess about money and central banking (though if they start obsessing, it looks like the gold standard could enjoy a comeback).

Americans have good reason not to be concerned about money and central banking—for now. (The future is another matter, as I shall argue.) Inflation is low, and has been for two decades; and output variability is down, arguably because the conduct of monetary policy has improved. Certainly, ill-conceived monetary theories and poorly devised monetary institutions no longer wreck the real economy the way they used to in the nineteenth century, when the value of the dollar was tied to a flaky bimetallic (gold and silver) standard, or in the Great Depression, when the real-bills doctrine required the central bank to slam on the brakes even as the economy was collapsing.

If the domestic arena is at peace, "money wise," the international arena is a different ball game altogether. After the two oil price shocks of the 1970s and the Mexican crisis of 1984–5, the 1990s brought a streak of international financial crises—the European Exchange Rate Mechanism crisis of 1992, the Mexican crisis of 1994–5, and the Southeast Asian crisis of 1997–8, which in turn triggered the Russian crisis of 1998 and the Brazilian crisis of 1999. Barry Eichengreen (2004) estimates that the typical international financial crisis claims 9 per cent of the gross domestic product (GDP) of the afflicted countries, and the worst crises wipe out as much as 20 per cent of GDP. With globalization it is becoming ever harder to contain financial turbulence neatly within a single country or continent.

It is all the more astonishing, then, that money and central banking have become non-issues in the international arena. The big themes are global climate change; global public health, including the AIDS/HIV crisis; and war, including

---

[1] The poll responses date 7–15 Mar. 2005.

ethnic conflicts that spill across national boundaries. When Björn Lomborg, author of *The Skeptical Environmentalist* (2001), convened a panel of leading economists to set priorities among a range of ideas for improving the lives of people in developing countries, the resulting Copenhagen Consensus, incredibly, was *not* to include international financial turbulence in the list of top priority concerns. Upon closer inspection, it turns out that the panel chose not to assign any priority to the idea of combating international financial turbulence not because they deemed international financial crises an unimportant problem, but because they felt that the research base was lacking for the panel to make an informed judgement (*Economist* 2000).

This pronouncement is as good an indicator as any that macro political economy is dead. It is dead in part because it was a success story; precisely because macro political economy made a difference in the world, political economists have moved on to the Next Big Thing, which is comparative political economy, or the political economy of development—its non-monetary aspects, that is. Macro political economy is dead in other part because it is intellectually stagnant; political economists should be developing the research base that would allow the world to combat international financial turbulence, and they aren't.

And so this chapter consists, first, of a eulogy for a dead sub-field. What was achieved, and what remains? I shall argue, second, that there is an urgent need for macro political economy to rise from the dead. Macro political economy, with its focus on game theory, is stuck with an impoverished understanding of political institutions. It must break out of its rut and develop a richer understanding that attends to history and culture. It must create a research base to support the development of monetary institutions that can address two looming challenges (there are surely more than two, but I have only so much space).

One challenge consists of the demographic time bomb in the developed countries. As the number of retirees balloons relative to the number of workers, monetary policy will get sucked into an intergenerational distributional conflict. In a given year, the working population produces a GDP pie, which gets split up between the working and retired populations. The share of older people depends on their entitlements (social security, state employee pensions, and the like). Monetary policy can, among other things, affect the real value of these entitlements, or the share of the GDP pie that goes to older people: to the extent that the entitlements are denominated in nominal currency and not indexed to inflation, they can be "inflated away."

Another challenge consists of the high likelihood that an extreme unforeseeable event will occur (the specific event is unforeseeble, but it is foreseeble that some such event will occur). For example, if a highly lethal disease spreads quickly and globally, much will depend on the intelligence of the monetary policy response—of an internationally coordinated response, that is—to avert global economic meltdown.

To deal with these challenges, domestic monetary institutions, which for the most part are in good working order, must be strengthened, and international monetary institutions, which are in terrible shape, must be reconceived from scratch.

2 The Life Cycle of Social Choice, Public Choice, and Political Economy

The twenty-year life cycle of macro political economy in the scientific literature, which describes the usual arc of vibrance and ossification, is embedded in the longer fifty-year life cycle of social choice, public choice, and political economy. Let us review the questions and answers that were bandied about in the longer life cycle, for these shed light on the questions and answers that emerged in the shorter life cycle.

Social choice was research-active from the 1950s through the 1970s; public choice, from the 1970s through the 1990s; political economy, from the 1980s through the 2000s. Macro political economy emerged in the late 1980s, peaked in the mid-1990s, and lost its mojo in the early 2000s. The definitive textbook for public choice, which also covers social choice, is Dennis Mueller's *Public Choice III* (2003).[2] The definitive textbooks for political economy and macro political economy are Torsten Persson and Guido Tabellini's *Political Economics* (2000) and Allen Drazen's *Political Economy in Macroeconomics* (2000). In comparison to these surveys, mine is not meant to be comprehensive, or balanced. My purpose is to illuminate the rise and fall of macro political economy and to lay out what remains to be done—in my judgement.

The overall research program is to merge economics and politics. The idea is, on the one hand, to apply the economics paradigm to the study of political phenomena. Why would rational self-interested individuals participate in costly collective action? The idea is, on the other hand, to account for political forces in models of economic phenomena. Might politics explain why real-world tax schedules deviate from the prescriptions of economic theory?

When social choice started out, the reigning practice in economics was to derive normative statements about economic policy by maximizing a social welfare function subject to a set of economic constraints. At the time, it was taken for granted that the people's preferences could be summarized by a social welfare function. Kenneth Arrow (1951) demonstrated, to the contrary, that if people's preferences are sufficiently diverse, it is impossible to summarize their preferences with a social welfare function that fulfills plausible criteria such as independence of irrelevant alternatives. (Independence of irrelevant alternatives means that the social preference over two alternatives should not "flip" if the individuals' preferences over the two alternatives stay the same even as a third—unrelated—alternative is added to, or dropped from, the set of alternatives under consideration.)

Social welfare functions subsequently went out of fashion among economists, or rather they snuck back in through the side door. In macroeconomics, the illegitimacy of assuming a social welfare function was elegantly circumvented by assuming that the economy could be summarized by a representative agent. Much of macro political economy would stick with the representative-agent assumption (Rogoff and Sibert

---

[2] *Public Choice III* is the third, and most comprehensive, edition of *Public Choice*, which was published in 1979.

1988). The occasional model will nod to diversity, for example, by assuming that two constituencies with different utility functions are represented by two parties that probabilistically succeed each other in power. Such minimal diversity can be neatly aggregated into a social welfare function by the simple means of weighting the two parties' utility functions with the two parties' election probabilities (Alesina 1987).

On a related note, social choice also demonstrated that voting rules affect voting outcomes. If people's preferences are sufficiently diverse, there exists no such thing as a neutral voting rule that will "simply" aggregate people's preferences. At first blush, this result seems rather worrisome because of its potential to undercut the legitimacy of outcomes arrived at by democratic means. But we shall see how this insight would get picked up productively—after all, if institutions can warp democratic decision-making, they can also serve a corrective function.

Social choice consisted largely of mathematical exercises with little economic content. Public choice, in comparison, employed microeconomic theory, and it was geared towards finding political explanations for the discrepancy between economic theory and practice. Before public choice entered the fray, economists were in the habit of spelling out what actions a benevolent dictator should take when he or she (or should we say, it?) encounters *market failure*. Public choice theorists, most prominently among them James Buchanan and Gordon Tullock, refused to see market failure behind every bush; in their minds, *government failure* loomed large (Tullock, Seldon, and Brady 2002).

These contrary approaches are nicely illustrated with reference to the income tax. Traditional public finance theory offered a model in which a benevolent dictator chooses a progressive income tax schedule that trades off the gains to social welfare that come with taxing the rich and distributing the proceeds to the poor against the deadweight losses that arise because taxes distort the economic choices of rich and poor (Atkinson and Stiglitz 1980). In contrast, public choice demonstrated that re-election-motivated policy-makers will devise an income tax schedule that is riddled with loopholes benefiting special interests, with the result that a nominally progressive income tax can end up being regressive in effect, and grossly inefficient to boot.[3]

Public choice also proposed institutional solutions to government failure. The typical proposal sought to tie the hands of elected policy-makers and to create transparency vis-à-vis voters or other audiences. The flat tax is a case in point (Hall and Rabushka 1995). It forgoes the benefits of progressivity and efficiency, but it also prevents policy-makers from piling on loopholes that benefit special interests precisely because voters, or other audiences, can easily monitor slippages and make a public fuss. The simplicity and transparency of the flat tax create a political cost of defecting from it.

Advanced democracies with complex economies have been reluctant to implement the institutional proposals coming out of public choice theory, perhaps because the proposals are seen as too crude; or might it be because they are inconveniently incorruptible? Interestingly, in the aftermath of the breakdown of Communism and

---

[3] See, for example, Hettich and Winer 1998.

the resulting democratic chaos, if you want to call it that, we find flat tax experiments going on in eastern European countries. When government failure is the dominant problem, rather than market failure, then simplicity and transparency are the way to go.

In the political spectrum of the United States, the flat tax proposal can be found on the right, as can other simple and transparent institutions, such as the gold standard. Public choice is occasionally written off as a right-wing enterprise (Lowi 1992). But it is worthwhile appreciating public choice for driving home this important point: when we compare flexible and complex institutions to simple and transparent institutions, we must take into account their relative political corruptibility.

What exactly does political corruptibility mean? Public choice spelled out how the policy process is warped by collective action and political institutions. For example, if small groups have an easier time solving the free-rider problem of collective action than do large groups, then policy will be biased in favor of special interests (Olson 1965). The power of special interests is also the result of congressional committees being captured by "high demanders," that is, members of Congress who represent constituencies (voters and campaign contributors) with a high demand for certain kinds of government handouts (Shepsle and Weingast 1987).

Where public choice applied microeconomic theory ("the supply and demand of collective action"), political economy made use of game theory ("greed, rationality, equilibrium"). The result was a higher standard of spelling out the rationality of political actors, including their informational states, and of making sure that all of their strategies and beliefs are consistent with each other so that the strategies and beliefs constitute an equilibrium.

For example, the story that policy-makers pander to special interests at the expense of voters does not necessarily make sense if voters follow a voting strategy by which they vote for the incumbent when they are well off and for the challenger when they are hurting. To make this story fly, one has to specify how a policy-maker can increase her re-election chances by taking something of value from the large mass of voters, losing a little of bit of it along the way (this is the deadweight loss created by redistribution, which generally distorts people's economic choices), and giving the remainder to special interests: why wouldn't the policy-maker lose more votes among the large mass of voters than she would gain among the special interests (Lohmann 1998a)? And if special interests are powerful because of campaign contributions, why wouldn't voters reject a policy-maker who is loaded with campaign contributions given that campaign contributions are a sign that the policy-maker is pandering to special interests at their expense? In the same vein, if special interest handouts are the result of high demanders hogging congressional committees, why would a majority in Congress go along with bills that benefit the constituents of the committee members at the expense of the majority's constituents? And why does a congressional majority allow high demanders to self-select on to congressional committees in the first place?

Political economy also differed from public choice by taking a balanced view of market and government failure, and it consequently was able to shake off the right-wing image of public choice. For example, when economic markets fail to aggregate distributed information about the mapping of economic policy into policy outcomes, then special interests or high demanders on congressional committees may well supply the requisite information, with the result that the quality of economic policy improves (because policy-makers are well informed) even though policy outcomes are biased (because policy-makers pander to special interests or high demanders) (Gilligan and Krehbiel 1987; Lohmann 1995). The implication is that we should not automatically assume that special interests and high demanders on congressional committees are a Bad Thing; we need to consider the workings of the economic and political system as a whole, in which case a Political Bad might cancel out an Economic Bad, and the net effect is a Good Thing. Because political economy traded off the gains and losses of imperfect markets *and* imperfect politics, it came up with more complex and more flexible institutions, compared to public choice.

To see how traditional economics, public choice, and political economy relate to each other, imagine a 2 × 2 matrix with two sides labeled "market failure YES/NO" and "government failure YES/NO," respectively. Traditional economics would inhabit the box "market failure YES, government failure NO," public choice, the box "market failure NO, government failure YES," and political economy, the box "market failure YES, government failure YES." There is one box left, "market failure NO, government failure NO," and inevitably it, too, came to be filled.

Donald Wittman, in "Why democracies produce efficient results" (1989), proposed that political markets, just like economic markets, tend to yield efficient outcomes.[4] If there is an externality, or some other source of potential market failure, the system of political and economic actors will endogenously adjust in the direction of solving the problem. Indeed, the Coase theorem implies that in the absence of transaction costs, the problem will be solved in full. For example, if the underlying problem in the political market consists of an information asymmetry, then information providers will have an incentive to enter the political market, and voters will have incentives to take information cues from them (Lupia 1994).

Buried here is an important point. Ever since the Coase theorem hit the books, we no longer assume automatically that economic actors are frozen in place in the face of externalities or other market failures, and in this regard we should treat political and economic actors symmetrically. That said, Wittman's argument ultimately did not prevail, perhaps because the persistence of both market failure and government failure is rather too obvious to be brushed off with reference to the Coase theorem. Wittman's argument was an intellectual exercise, and as such influential, for it forced political economists to refine their arguments as to *exactly why* failures, market or government, persist in the presence of rationality and equilibrium.

In the mid-1990s, behavioral and experimental economics relaxed the assumptions of greed and rationality (less so the assumption of equilibrium), thereby undercutting the political economy program of producing ever more refined rationality-and-equilibrium explanations of market-cum-government failure. Today, the extreme

---

[4] See also Wittman 1995.

application of the game theory paradigm to political phenomena is *passé*. The cutting edge lies in employing richer models of human behavior to understand the various forms of collective action we observe in reality, that is, in laboratory experiments and in the field.

Even as the one kind of political economy (the kind that applies game theory to political phenomena) is mired in a crisis, another kind of political economy (the kind that inserts politics into models of economic policy) has been busy expanding into comparative political economy, or the political economy of development. Whereas public choice was largely focused on the developed countries, or the rich capitalist democracies, political economy increasingly included the developing countries, many of which were governed (some still are) by tin-pot dictators, military cliques, and the like. Whereas public choice was concerned about the discrepancy between economic theory and practice in developed democracies, comparative political economy fretted over the disparities in economic performance across countries and sought to explain how some countries grew rich (why *these* countries, why *now*?) even as others remain poor (Landes 1998).

The differences are enormous—levels of per capita GDP in the richest and poorest countries differ by a factor of about fifty (Central Intelligence Agency 2004). The rich have become rich only in the last two centuries; for most of human history, they were about as poor as the poorest countries are today (DeLong 1998). What happened? One answer is collective action and political institutions.[5] The people of western Europe were lifted up by collective action (I have in mind the Glorious, Scientific, and French Revolutions) and political institutions (foremost among them limited and representative government), and they got rich. Countries that emulated the political and economic institutions of western Europe got rich, too.

Comparative political economists who pushed this story, or variants of it, naturally appreciated the fact that well-functioning market economies rely on well-functioning governments, just as they naturally appreciated that government in the developed countries is functioning extremely well, in both historical and cross-country comparison. Such appreciation is a 180-degree reversal of the anti-government bias that permeated the public choice program.

Thanks to the scholarship in public choice and political economy, our understanding of collective action and political institutions is light years ahead of where it was half a century ago. There is some question, however, whether internal scientific progress (improved understanding) has translated into external scientific progress (improved practice).

Take the developed countries. Germany, one of the richest countries in the world, suffers under a *Reformstau* (special interest gridlock), as does California, one of the richest states in the United States. In both cases, the underlying political logic is perfectly well understood, and yet nothing, apparently, can be done about it (Olson 1982; Lohmann 2003*a*).

---

[5] The question of what happened is a matter of great controversy among economists and historians. The contrary positions are represented by the *Economist* 1999 and Stokes 2001.

Government spending continues to be loaded with special interest pork. For example, in response to 11 September, Congress appropriated huge amounts of money to homeland security, and then promptly distributed the money according to the principles of pork-barrel politics. Thus, states get money not based on risk and vulnerability considerations, but based on population and state minimums. Wyoming, which is hardly in the sights of worldwide terrorist networks, gets seven times as many homeland security dollars, on a per capita basis, than does New York. Once again, the political logic is perfectly well understood, even the subject of a *New York Times* editorial, and yet nothing, apparently, can be done about it (*New York Times* 2005).

Let us continue with the 11 September theme and take a look at Joe Barton, who in 2005 chaired the House Energy and Commerce Committee. He used his clout to block chemical plant security legislation. Chemical plants are vulnerable to terrorist attacks. Two of the most dangerous facilities are located in Dallas, right next to Barton's district. They constitute a risk for more than one million people. A Texas Republican, Barton sides with the energy industry at the expense of his constituents— and forget about the constituents of his colleagues in Congress. Barton is the classical "high demander" on a congressional committee: before he was elected to Congress, he served as a consultant for an oil and gas company, and he has received more than $1.8 million in campaign contributions from the energy and chemical industries. Once again, the political logic is perfectly well understood, even the subject of a *New York Times* editorial, and yet nothing, apparently, can be done about it (Cohen 2005).

Looking back, one cannot help wondering whether public choice, with its insistence on simple and transparent institutions that might actually help slay the special interest dragon, had something important going on that got lost when political economy insisted on deriving ever more elaborate "optimal" institutions in a reductionist framework including hyper-rationality and equilibrium-*über-Alles*.

Next, take the developing countries. Today, in 2005, China stands out as the country with the largest population, ahead of India, and the second-largest economy, after the United States. In the last twenty-five years, after the Communist leadership embarked on a course of economic liberalization, China's real GDP increased close to eightfold, its real GDP per capita close to sixfold. This increase, with its speed and size, along with the huge number of people involved, has got to count as the single largest explosion in standards of living in human history. Several hundred million people were lifted out of the poverty of living on (the purchasing-power-parity equivalent of) one dollar a day, and some got very rich.

The nagging question is why China has outperformed India, which—in contrast to China—is a democracy. But if India is politically liberal, economically it is not; or rather, it was not until recently when it, too, caught the economic liberalization bug, no doubt in response to China's glowing success. After independence in 1947, India pursued policies that reflected a philosophy of government planning and economic self-sufficiency. Its economy was relatively stagnant until piecemeal economic reforms in the 1980s and some measure of economic liberalization in the 1990s improved economic growth rates. Today, in the 2000s, India appears poised for a take-off that might well end up outperforming China's.

What dragged India down, compared to China, were special interest politics of the kind that have been described by public choice theorists, including Mancur Olson in *Rise and Decline of Nations* (1982) (Diamond 2005). Large public works projects that were sold by politicians and run by bureaucrats were a magnet for bribes and special interest handouts. Then again, as Amartya Sen pointed out in *Poverty and Famines* (1981), democracies are less prone to man-made humanitarian disasters such as large-scale famines. The last Indian famine—the Bengal Famine—occurred in 1943, under British rule, and it killed three million people. China's Great Leap Forward Famine of 1958–61 cost 30 million lives. Let us not burn democracy just yet—the ideal, clearly, is economic *and* political liberalization.

The point I wish to make for now is that public choice dominates political economy when it comes to explaining the comparative performance of China and India. Economic liberalization combined with some degree of political stability (people need to know that they can keep the fruits of their entrepreneurial efforts) outperforms political liberalization combined with central planning. This is Hayekian thinking rather than Keynesian, and this is roughly the public choice credo: free the markets, limit the government, put in place a couple of simple and transparent rules, and let the people do their thing. In contrast, political economy comes across as fussing over market failures and deriving "optimal" institutions that will surgically correct the problem.

Interestingly, the developing countries that are in the firm grip of the economic experts at the IMF and the World Bank, especially the countries in Africa, have done spectacularly badly in comparison to China and India. This is not surprising. Even as the idea of top-down control has lost currency in the world, and ideas of decentralization and bottom-up governance have become popular, the IMF and the World Bank operate on the tried and untrue principle of "government by benevolent experts," or "father knows best"—and it shows.

3 Vibrance and Ossification in Macro Political Economy

Against this background, we can now assess the contribution of the sub-field of macro political economy. Before we examine the political vulnerability of monetary policy, we must cover an apolitical model that dominated the literature. Just as the larger political economy program addressed not just government failure but also market failure, macro political economy took as its starting point a model of market failure, in which a benevolent dictator produces a counter-productive inflation bias. The time-consistency problem in monetary policy was first described by Fynn Kydland and Edward Prescott in 1977, and it works as follows. Because nominal wage contracts do not get updated continuously, a monetary stimulus, by decreasing the real wage, increases employment and output. A benevolent dictator who would like to increase employment and output above the level that would obtain "naturally" in the labor market (that is, in the absence of government intervention) thus has an incentive to inflate. Unfortunately, wage-setters understand this incentive and write an inflation mark-up into their nominal wage contracts. The inflation mark-up is just high enough to give the benevolent dictator, who is also inflation averse, a disincentive to create surprise inflation. In equilibrium, inflation is equal to the inflation mark-up in the nominal wage contracts, which implies that the real wage, employment, and output are all realized at their natural levels. The benevolent dictator's attempt to stimulate employment and output is thus futile; all he achieves for his efforts is an inflation bias equal to the inflation mark-up.

One institutional solution would be for the benevolent dictator to tie his hands by committing to a monetary or inflation target. A fixed target, however, undercuts the stabilization role of monetary policy: sticky prices imply that monetary policy can offset the effects of real shocks to the economy.

Kenneth Rogoff in 1985 offered an institutional solution that traded off the goal of controlling inflation against the goal of stabilizing the real economy. The benevolent dictator could tie his hands by delegating monetary policy to an independent conservative central banker who places a higher weight on the inflation goal. The wage-setters, upon observing that an independent conservative central banker is in charge of monetary policy, would write a lower inflation mark-up into their wage contracts.

Delegation to a conservative central banker comes at a cost, however, namely that the conservative central banker, precisely because she places a lower weight on the output stabilization goal, under-responds to real shocks. The deadweight cost of delegation is low for small shocks and high for extreme shocks. A huge literature followed up on Rogoff to propose commitment devices that would improve the trade-off between the inflation and stabilization goals of monetary policy, that is, allow for some degree of commitment to low inflation (enough significantly to lower people's inflation expectations) along with some degree of flexibility especially when extreme output shocks are realized (to stabilize the economy when it most hurts). Thus, Susanne Lohmann in 1992 proposed that the optimal institution consists of a partially independent conservative central banker who will accommodate political pressures when extreme shocks hit the economy. Other solutions consist of an exchange rate target with an escape clause; multiperiod monetary targets with optimal targeting horizons; and optimal contracts for central bankers (Flood and Isard 1989; Garfinkel and Oh 1993; Walsh 1995).

Let me turn to models of the political vulnerability of monetary policy. Monetized economies are politically vulnerable for two reasons. The first consists of the incentive to fund government spending with increases in the money supply; the second, of the incentive to inflate to increase employment and output.

First, political pressures for government spending can translate into an excessive use of the money printing press. Government spending can be financed in three ways: taxing, borrowing, or printing money. If voter resistance places limits on tax increases, and financial markets or balanced budget rules place a limit on borrowing, then government spending will quickly translate into inflation, or even hyperinflation (Buchanan and Wagner 1977).

Political pressures to spend take on two forms, opportunistic and partisan. An opportunistic government might want to dole out special interest handouts just before the election to increase its chances of staying in power. Alternatively, the political party in power might be beholden to a partisan constituency that gains from certain kinds of government expenditures, such as farmers' associations or teachers' unions.

The second source of political vulnerability consists of sticky prices, or contracts denominated in nominal currency that are not inflation indexed and cannot be quickly adjusted. By inflating, the government can devalue such contracts.

Once again, the vulnerability can take opportunistic or partisan form. The government might have an incentive to stimulate employment and output before the election to improve its chances of re-election. Alternatively, one political party might be beholden to a group that benefits from easy money even as its opponent political party represents sound money interests. For example, in nineteenth century America, easy money benefited farmers because it reduced the real value of their debt, and so it will not surprise you to hear that banking and commercial interests stood for sound money; the Democratic Party represented the former interests, the Republican Party, the latter.

These two motives—opportunistic and partisan—were picked up by two models. The first one is due to William Nordhaus, who in 1975 coined the expression "political business cycle." He proposed that policy-makers increase the money supply before elections to stimulate employment and output and thereby improve their re-election prospects. The Nordhaus model was rationalized—that is, reformulated in a rational equilibrium model—by Kenneth Rogoff and Ann Sibert in 1988. Rogoff and Sibert triggered a huge follow-up literature that worked out their argument in further detail and spelled out institutional solutions.

The impetus for the rationalization originated in the internal dynamics of the scientific-literature life cycle, or the move from public choice to political economy. What does "rationalizing Nordhaus" entail? It requires, first of all, replacing adaptive inflation expectations with rational expectations. Adaptive expectations are mechanically updated: the wage-setters' period t expectation of period $t + 1$ inflation is a linear combination of the period $t - 1$ expectation for period t and the period t realization. Thus, if period $t + 1$ is a pre-election period, the wage-setters will be surprised by the pre-election monetary stimulus. Given their mechanical updating rule, they will then expect a higher inflation rate for the post-election period $t + 2$—only to be surprised again. This is a mess, obviously. Rational expectations are based on a correct understanding of the model: wage-setters expect inflation to be higher in period $t + 1$ if it is a pre-election period and lower if it is not.

Next, the assumption of sticky wages implies that the policy-maker can stimulate employment and output. Once again, rational expectations imply that wage-setters cannot be systematically fooled, and so wage-setters will write an inflation mark-up into their wage contracts. Meanwhile, the rationality assumption implies that voters cannot be fooled in equilibrium—why should they vote for a policy-maker whose futile and opportunistic attempt to stimulate employment and output yields an inflation bias? The (theoretical) answer is that unobservable policy-maker competence affects the real economy. Thus, the policy-maker has an incentive to stimulate the real economy to fool the voters into believing that she is more competent than she truly is. In equilibrium, the voters see through this incentive and anticipate the pre-election monetary stimulus and its effects on employment and output. Even though monetary stimulation is futile in equilibrium, the policy-maker is "forced" to go through with it because the voters expect it; a policymaker who fails to meet the voters' expectations will decrease employment and output relative to what the voters expect and thus come across as incompetent—and lose the election.

The opportunistic attempt to stimulate employment and output is necessarily futile in equilibrium, as a consequence of the rationality assumption, and it gives rise to a pre-election inflation bias over and above the standard inflation bias (the latter is due to the standard time-consistency problem in monetary policy).

Rational inflation expectations and voter rationality thus imply that pre-election monetary stimuli are futile and damaging, which in turn means that the policy-maker has an incentive to tie her hands. Not only does the policy-maker want to prevent herself from creating an opportunistic political business cycle; she needs the voters to know that her hands are tied. The policy-maker could, for example, delegate monetary policy to a central banker who shares her monetary policy goals but not her re-election goal. This can be achieved, for example, by granting the central banker a term in office that is longer than, or staggered relative to, the policy-maker's term in office (Lohmann 1998*b*).

The second political business cycle model is due to Douglas Hibbs who in 1977 offered a partisan variant whereby two political parties represent two constituencies, one of which prefers an easy monetary policy, or high inflation, the other a sound monetary policy, or low inflation. As the parties succeed each other in power, monetary policy will fluctuate over time for reasons unrelated to economic fundamentals, in tune with the partisan control of the government. Alberto Alesina in 1987 redid the Hibbs model by replacing adaptive inflation expectations with rational expectations. His contribution, too, triggered a huge follow-up literature.

In the partisan case, the willingness of the two parties to commit to a monetary institution that will implement an intermediate monetary policy in place of the partisan political business cycle depends on the time horizon of the two parties. If their time horizon is very short, say, if the party in office cares only about the current period, then the party in office would have no incentives to give up the power to set monetary policy. If both parties have long time horizons, then they can reach a consensus to lock in the intermediate policy. This can be achieved, for example, by setting up an independent central bank with a council that reflects the all-party consensus (Lohmann 1997; Waller 1989, 1992).

Once behavioral and experimental economics hit the system, the rationalization obsession of macro political economy seemed misplaced. Inflation expectations are surely less than fully rational, and the assumption of voter rationality is arguably flat-out wrong.

Even so, macro political economy was hugely influential, and its rationalization obsession played to its influence, but the exact way in which this happened is rather more convoluted than meets the eye. A useful precedent can be found with the monetarist revolution. In the 1960 and 1970s, monetarists proposed monetary targeting rules arguing that monetary policy matters rather than fiscal policy (their Keynesian opponents argued the opposite) and that stabilizing the money supply would serve to stabilize employment and output (ditto) (Mayer 1998). In other words, monetary targeting rules were celebrated for their economic properties and not their political properties. The reason why policy-makers adopted monetary targeting regimes in the 1970s, however, was because in the oil price shock era monetary targeting rules turned out to be a useful political device to fend off political pressures to inflate. In the political implementation of monetary targeting rules, their political properties prevailed.

And so it went with macro political economy. The message that filtered through to policy-makers and central bankers was that money cannot systematically raise employment and output. Moreover, political attempts to stimulate employment and output are futile and damaging—all they do is create inflation. For this reason, policy-makers themselves are better off delegating monetary policy to an independent central bank. Macro political economy thus made a successful case for the *depoliticization* of monetary policy.

The astonishing nature of this success becomes clear once you understand that essentially the same arguments apply to fiscal policy (the time-consistency problem and opportunistic and partisan political business cycles), and yet it is unthinkable for democratically elected policy-makers to give up the power to tax. In monetary policy, macro political economy made the unthinkable thinkable, and more: turned it into conventional wisdom.

But if macro political economy successfully depoliticized monetary policy, the question is how monetary institutions that emerged in an era of depoliticization will cope when distributional conflict returns to monetary policy. Let us take a closer look.

4 Total Special Interest Gridlock

One looming challenge consists of the rise of intergenerational distributional conflict in the developed countries and between the developed and developing countries.

In the developed countries, the proportion of older people, including the retired population, is ever increasing relative to the proportion of younger people, including the working population. Older people are formally entitled—"entitled on paper," that is—to an ever greater share of GDP.

The redistribution from the young working population, which produces the GDP pie, to the older retired population can be implemented through taxation. For example, the government might ask workers to pay social security contributions, which are then used to fund social security payments to retirees; or state governments might tax workers, and the tax revenue is then used to pay for state employee pensions. But if there are too few workers producing the GDP pie and too many retirees holding paper entitlements, the levels of taxation that are necessary to effect the redistribution will end up confiscatory and economically infeasible. (Workers will not simply continue working if, say, 95 per cent of their earnings are taxed away—they will work fewer hours, or participate in a worker riot, or emigrate to another country.)

Something will have to give, and the question is what role monetary policy will play in all of this. Monetary policy can, among other things, affect the real value of entitlements that are denominated in nominal currency and not indexed to inflation. The precise distributional effects of monetary policy depend in detail on which kinds of assets older people hold, which of those assets are indexed, and so on. Moreover, there may well be distributional effects within the group of older people, for example, because the rich and the poor among them hold different kinds of assets or are protected from inflation to different degrees. My purpose here is not to spell out the redistributional effects of monetary policy in detail. It is simply to say that because monetary policy is such a powerful tool of redistribution, monetary policy is likely to get dragged into the distributional conflict over the split of the GDP pie between the working population and the retired population.

If one part of the problem concerns the distribution of the GDP pie between the young and the old, the other part has to do with government spending on social security, health care for older people, and state employee pensions. If biotechnology increases lifespans to 120 years, then it will not help to increase the retirement age by a couple of years at the front end when at the other end people will be spending more time in retirement than they spent in the labor force. There will be pressures for government spending to benefit older people even as there are limits on the government's ability to tax and borrow, which translates into (you guessed it) pressures to print money. Once again, it appears inevitable that monetary policy will get dragged into this distributional conflict.

The deeper reason why an aging population is such a serious problem for advanced democracies is because of the disconnect between the economic and the political sides of the equation. On the economic side, there is no alternative to reneging on the promises made to older people, at least to some degree. Reneging can take various forms—increasing the retirement age, inflating away nominal entitlements, outright default, and so on. Different forms of reneging have different political and social costs, and the question is, what is the "least disastrous policy mix" taking into account the welfare of young and old alike? On the political side, however, older people will constitute a powerful voting bloc—there will be ever more of them; their participation rates in elections are way above average; they have relatively homogeneous interests compared to the young working population; they are relatively well informed, especially about the issues they care about (social security, health care); and in the United States they are exceedingly well represented by the American Association of Retired Persons (AARP), which is one of the most powerful lobbies in Washington, DC.

And make no mistake—older people are attached to their entitlements, and they will not let go of them without a (political) fight. It is no good to say that older people have no needs because their mortgages are paid off—as we speak, the needs are being created. People disproportionately make use of the health care system when they are old. Technological progress translates into expensive high-technology medicine—and once it is available, there will be a demand for it. Health care for older people also has a labor-intensive component, and labor-intensive services are subject to Baumol's disease. (The relative cost of delivering services in labor-intensive industries increases over time as other industries experience technological progress, employ labor-saving devices, and realize cost savings (Baumol and Bowen 1966)). And once older people live longer, they will want to get a life, which includes cosmetic surgery and second homes in warm places.

With such a powerfully united special interest group in place, it seems quite unlikely that the political system will be capable of reneging in the least disastrous way on promises made to older people. More likely, aging democracies will respond to the impossible tension between the economic and political sides of the equation by postponing hard decisions and remaining mired in total special interest gridlock.

What are the implications for money and central banking? On the one hand, monetary policy must help society avoid the non-solution of special interest gridlock, and it must contribute its share to the least disastrous policy mix; we can deplore inflation, but the question is: how destructive are alternatives such as outright default? On the other hand, monetary policy must remain aloof from counter-productive political pressures. How to square the circle? We do not know, and this is precisely why we need to develop a research base.

Intergenerational distributional conflict is first of all a domestic problem, but it does have international dimensions; first, because older people can disportionately be found in the developed countries, younger people, in the developing countries; second, because chronic American trade deficits imply that foreigners are accumulating formal entitlements to slices of future American GDP pies. Here, monetary policy can affect the real terms of trade and the real value of the entitlements held by foreigners by influencing real exchanges rates, capital movements, bond prices, and the like. There is an obvious political incentive to bring relief to the domestic redistribution problem by "taxing" foreigners. Here, too, monetary policy will inevitably get sucked into the distributional conflict.

Let me move on to another international threat that arguably requires cross-country collaboration and international institution-building. Many of the institutions in place today, such as the European Central Bank and the IMF, emerged in an era of (relative) peace and quiet. Are they equipped to deal with extreme unforeseen contingencies on the scale of, say, the Great Depression?

5 The Poverty of International Institutions

To fix ideas, imagine you could enter a time machine and return to the year 1900 to what was then the center of the world—western Europe. Looking back from the vantage point of 1900, you will encounter a couple of proud nations that have just experienced a century's worth of immense technological progress and an increase in material standards of living for which there exists no historical precedent. Now imagine you could tell the policy-makers of that era what to watch out for in monetary policy and central banking. What will you tell them?

Let us take a look what lies ahead. There is, first of all, the Great War (later renamed the First World War after it was followed by an even greater war). It was funded, in part, by war bonds whose value was subsequently eroded by inflation. In the aftermath of the First World War, the Weimar Republic responded to reparation demands by printing money, which led to a hyperinflation that impoverished and embittered the German middle class, which largely supported Hitler. The result was the Second World War and the Holocaust. Meanwhile, Britain returned to the gold standard at the pre-war parity—a stupid move that created economic hardship and for no obvious gain. Ill-conceived monetary theory and policy contributed to the Great Depression in the United States—which spread across the world and sank the system of international trade. The resulting worldwide depression contributed to the rise of Hitler.

Meanwhile, in eastern Europe, we find the Russian Revolution and the Gulag. Today, as we celebrate the supposed end of history, capitalism and liberal democracy having won out, it is easy to forget that the big ideological debate of the first half of the twentieth century was about capitalism versus socialism versus fascism (Fukuyama 1992; Caldwell 2003). People from all walks of life—not just the communists in the Soviet Union—believed that capitalism is inherently unstable and requires central planning to make it work; that the extreme inequities created by capitalism are immoral and require for their correction massive government intervention; and that capitalism contributed to the rise of fascism.

At the end of the Second World War, F. A. Hayek's ideas, as expressed in *The Road to Serfdom* (1994/1944), were seen as practically criminal, and they spelled professional death among economists. Hayek proposed that central planning was unworkable because central planners, as opposed to markets, cannot hope to pick up all of the distributed information they need to make good decisions; that government intervention, especially the surgical type, as opposed to the type that stands for the rule of the law, tends to make things worse; and that National Socialism is a form of socialism, and not a consequence of capitalism. It would take close to half a century before the Berlin Wall fell, and Hayek's ideas triumphed over John Maynard Keynes's.

In the second half of the twentieth century, western Europe was, blissfully, at peace. The process of European integration included repeated pushes for monetary integration: after the gold standard broke down, there emerged the European Snake, the European Monetary System, European Monetary Union, and the European Central Bank. Economists, by and large, opposed fixed exchange rate regimes and monetary union. Voters in many countries, especially Germany, were negatively disposed towards a common currency and central bank. But policy-makers like Helmut Kohl pushed ahead against both expert and voter opinion. By any reasonable measure, Kohl's actions were non-opportunistic and non-partisan. They were motivated by the idea that the peoples of Europe, who over the centuries have gone to war with each other to the tune of 100 million lost lives (give or take a couple of tens of millions), will find peace if they are tied together by a common set of institutions, including a common currency and central bank.

Kohl may well be right, and the issue here is not just war. The issue is that any extreme event that will require a coordinated response on the part of the European countries will now meet upon an elaborate set of institutions that can deliver such a response. This is not to say that the institutions of the European Community and European Monetary Union are a pretty sight—they are cumbersome and costly, and impossibly bureaucratic. It is simply to say that they will probably help avert large-scale disaster in Europe.

Today, the center of the world is the United States. We can look back at a century's worth of immense technological progress and an increase in material standards of living for which there is no precedent in history. But just as in 1900, if you look carefully, you can see portents of trouble. Religious conflict looms large within the United States and between the United States and Islam. Globalization is running strong—and so are extreme inequalities within and between countries, and not to forget identity politics and ethnic conflict. The Internet is creating unprecedented amounts of public information, but all of this public information is not exactly creating "one world," nor is it making people more tolerant. On the contrary, as people emigrate into chatrooms and virtual worlds, they self-select into like-minded groups that serve as echo chambers for their opinions. Religious and ideological conflict has not come to an end, and there is no guarantee that history is ever upward lifting.

We cannot tell for sure what the twenty-first century will bring us, obviously, but we can say with a high degree of certainty that something extreme will happen. The occurrence of further international financial crises is almost a given, but there is so much more that can happen, and much of it will require a coordinated monetary policy response. What if the global spread of a contagious disease triggers a global economic meltdown? What if global climate change leads to a sudden immersion under water of whole countries, or parts of countries, which in turn leads to large-scale population movements? What if a war breaks out driven by religious and ideological conflict over the distributional effects of globalization? And what will happen to people's *ideas* about capitalism and liberal democracy when the global economic and political system comes across as grossly dysfunctional—and what will happen when policy-makers *act* on the people's ideas? Are our international institutions equipped to respond adequately to extreme events, including ideological clashes over the way the world works?

In the early 1990s the International Monetary Fund (IMF) promoted reforms to liberalize capital and financial markets in east Asia that probably aggravated, and possibly caused, the 1997 crisis. Once the crisis was up and running, harsh policy measures prescribed by the IMF probably contributed to the spread and severity of the crisis. Ill-conceived macroeconomic theory met upon a poorly devised international institution, and the result is a repeat performance, now at the international level, of what we observed in the domestic sphere in the early nineteenth and twentieth centuries.

What kinds of institutions are needed? Three characteristics are essential. First, institutions must support an internal diversity of ideas and links to intellectual communities so they can pick up on competing theories about the way the world works. They must support elaborate internal collective decision-making processes that are capable of synthesizing conflicting ideas and moving the synthesis to the final decision-makers. (For example, lower-level staff might make a recommendation but attach to it minority opinions that serve as red flags.)

Second, institutions must have local listening posts allowing them to figure out what is happening "on the ground" and to pick up on failures of conventional wisdom. This information, too, must be synthesized and moved to decision-makers.

Third, institutions must develop external connections such that their decisions reflect the preferences of the peoples whose economic fortunes lie in their hands, and their decisions follow the people's preferences when those preferences change. In short, institutions must be politically responsive. And yet at the same time, the precise way in which they are politically responsive must allow them to resist counterproductive pressures (time-consistency problems, special interest gridlock, and the like).

If it sounds like an impossible task to design such institutions, the answer is that this is an impossible task for top-down institutional design. In well-functioning democracies, such institutions can evolve, and have evolved, in interplay with the pressures emanating from various political and economic actors and institutions. As a result, domestic monetary institutions have the characteristics listed above, at least in approximation.

The Federal Reserve System is a case in point. The geographically distributed district banks, which are somewhat beholden to local interests, represent some degree of intellectual and geographical diversity. The district bank presidents and their staff serve as local listening posts. There are elaborate internal processes in place by which diverse ideas about the way the economy works move to the decision-making center in Washington, DC, and by which distributed information is aggregated. Meanwhile, there are equally elaborate political processes in place—powers of appointment and budget approval, congressional hearings, and the like—by which the Federal Reserve is forced to attend to its political principals, who in turn are electorally connected to the people. Those political processes are sophisticated enough to include lags and buffers and political costs, as a result of which the president and Congress cannot simply reach into the Federal Reserve and order it to do their bidding, at least not instantaneously and in full (Lohmann 2003*b*).

International institutions look nothing like this. They lack intellectual diversity; they lack local listening posts; they lack bottom-up collective decision-making processes; they lack political accountability vis-à-vis the people whose economic fortunes they shape, and at the same time they are excessively beholden to the United States. The IMF in particular looks suspiciously like the monetary institutions of the nineteenth and early twentieth centuries, which regularly caused economic havoc (Adams 1991; Rich 1994; Lancaster 1999; Meltzer Commission 2000).

6 CONCLUSION

Two challenges loom before us: total special interest gridlock in the domestic sphere and extreme unforeseen events at the international level. To address them, we must strengthen domestic institutions and radically rethink our international institutions. Such institution-building requires a research base. Today, more than ever, there is an urgent need to combine public choice with macroeconomics to develop a deeper understanding of monetary institutions. How can we replicate at the international level what we have largely achieved in the domestic sphere? Institutions that, first of all, do no harm (that stabilize economies instead of wrecking them), and more: institutions that can negotiate model uncertainty, aggregate distributed information, and accommodate the preferences of the people but only up to a point.

REFERENCES

ADAMS, P. 1991. *Odious Debts: Loose Lending, Corruption and the Third World's Environmental Legacy*. London: Earthscan.
ALESINA, A. 1987. Macroeconomic policy in a two-party system as a repeated game. *Quarterly Journal of Economics*, 102: 651–78.
ARROW, K. J. 1951. *Social Choice and Individual Values*. New York: John Wiley.
ATKINSON, A. B., and STIGLITZ, J. 1980. *Lectures on Public Economics*. New York: McGraw-Hill.
BAUMOL, W. J., and BOWEN, W. G. 1966. On the performing arts: the anatomy of their economic problems. *American Economic Review*, 55: 495–502.
BUCHANAN, J. M., and WAGNER, R. E. 1977. *Democracy in Deficit: The Political Legacy of Lord Keynes*. New York: Academic Press.
CALDWELL, B. 2003. *Hayek's Challenge: An Intellectual Biography of F. A. Hayek*. Chicago: University of Chicago Press.
Central Intelligence Agency. 2004. Rank order—GDP—per capita. In *The World Factbook*, www.cia.gov/cia/publications/factbook/rankorder/2004rank.html; accessed 21 Mar. 2005.
COHEN, A. 2005. A lawmaker works, oddly enough, to keep his voters backyards dangerous: "Smokey Joe" and the politics of corporate profit. *New York Times*, 26 May: A28.
DELONG, J. B. 1998. *Estimating World GDP, One Million B.C.–Present*. Dept. of Economics, University of California, Berkeley, www.j-bradford-delong.net/TCEH/1998_Draft/World_GDP/Estimating_World_GDP.html; accessed 5 May 2005.

Diamond, L. 2005. *The Future of India: Politics, Economics and Governance.* New Delhi: Penguin India.
Drazen, A. 2000. *Political Economy in Macroeconomics.* Princeton, NJ: Princeton University Press.
Economist. 1999. The road to riches. 31 Dec.: 10–12.
—— 2004. Copenhagen Consensus: putting the world to right. 3 June.
Eichengreen, B. 2004. A remedy for financial turbulence? *Economist*, 15 Apr.
Flood, R., and Isard, P. 1989. Monetary policy strategies. *IMF Staff Papers*, 36: 612–32.
Frank, T. 2004. *What's the Matter with Kansas? How Conservatives Won the Heart of America.* New York: Metropolitan Books.
Fukuyama, F. 1992. *The End of History and the Last Man.* New York: Free Press.
Garfinkel, M. R., and Oh, S. 1993. Strategic discipline in monetary policy with private information: optimal targeting horizons. *American Economic Review*, 83: 99–117.
Gilligan, T., and Krehbiel, K. 1987. Collective decision-making and standing committees: an informational rationale for restrictive amendment procedures. *Journal of Law, Economics and Organization*, 3: 287–335.
Hall, R. E., and Rabushka, A. 1995. *The Flat Tax*, 2nd edn. Stanford, Calif.: Hoover Institution Press.
Hayek, F. A. 1994/1944. *The Road to Serfdom.* Chicago: University of Chicago Press.
Hettich, W., and Winer, S. L. 1998. *Democratic Choice and Taxation: A Theoretical and Empirical Analysis.* New York: Cambridge University Press.
Hibbs, D. 1977. Political parties and macroeconomic policy. *American Political Science Review*, 7: 1467–87.
Kydland, F. E., and Prescott, E. C. 1977. Rules rather than discretion: the inconsistency of optimal plans. *Journal of Political Economy*, 85: 473–91.
Lancaster, C. 1999. *Aid to Africa: So Much to Do, So Little Done.* Chicago: University of Chicago Press.
Landes, D. S. 1998. *The Wealth and Poverty of Nations: Why Some Are So Rich and Some So Poor.* New York: W. W. Norton.
Lohmann, S. 1992. Optimal commitment in monetary policy: credibility versus flexibility. *American Economic Review*, 82: 273–86.
—— 1995. Information, access and contributions: a signaling model of lobbying. *Public Choice*, 85: 267–84.
—— 1997. Partisan control of the money supply and decentralized appointment powers. *European Journal of Political Economy*, 13: 225–46.
—— 1998a. An information rationale for the power of special interests. *American Political Science Review*, 92: 809–27.
—— 1998b. Institutional checks and balances and the political control of the money supply. *Oxford Economic Papers*, 50: 360–77.
—— 2003a. Representative government and special interest politics (we have met the enemy and he is us). *Journal of Theoretical Politics*, 15: 299–320.
—— 2003b. Why do institutions matter? An audience-cost theory of institutional commitment. *Governance*, 16: 95–110.
Lomborg, B. 2001. *The Skeptical Environmentalist: Measuring the Real State of the World.* Cambridge, Mass.: Cambridge University Press.
Lowi, T. J. 1992. The state in political science: how we become what we study. *American Political Science Review*, 86: 1–7.
Lupia, A. 1994. Shortcuts versus encyclopedias: information and voting behavior in California insurance reform elections. *American Political Science Review*, 88: 63–76.

MAYER, T. 1998. The monetarist policy debate: an informal retrospective. In *Economics and Methodology: Crossing Boundaries*, ed. R. E. Backhouse, D. M. Hausman, U. Maki, and A. Salanti. New York: St Martin's Press.

MELTZER COMMISSION 2000. International financial institutions reform. Available at: www.house.gov/jec/imf/meltzer.htm; accessed 16 May 2005.

MUELLER, D. 2003. *Public Choice*, 3rd edn. Cambridge, Mass.: Cambridge University Press.

New York Times 2005. Editorial: an insecure nation. Real security, or politics as usual? 1 May.

OLSON, M. 1965. *The Logic of Collective Action*. Cambridge, Mass.: Harvard University Press.

—— 1982. *The Rise and Decline of Nations: Economic Growth, Stagflation, and Social Rigidities*. New Haven, Conn.: Yale University Press.

NORDHAUS, W. D. 1975. The political business cycle. *Review of Economic Studies*, 42: 169–90.

PERSSON, T., and TABELLINI, G. 2000. *Political Economics: Explaining Economic Policy*. Cambridge, Mass.: MIT Press.

RICH, B. 1994. *Mortgaging the Earth: The World Bank, Environmental Impoverishment, and the Crisis of Development*. Boston: Beacon Press.

ROGOFF, K. 1985. The optimal degree of commitment to an intermediate monetary target. *Quarterly Journal of Economics*, 100: 1169–89.

—— and SIBERT, S. 1988. Elections and macroeconomic policy cycles. *Review of Economic Studies*, 55: 1–16.

SEN, A. 1981. *Poverty and Famines*. New York: Clarendon Press.

SHEPSLE, K., and WEINGAST, B. 1987. The institutional foundations of committee power. *American Political Science Review*, 81: 86–108.

STOKES, G. 2001. Why the west? *Lingua Franca*, 11: 30–8.

TULLOCK, G., SELDON, A., and BRADY, G. L. 2002. *Government Failure: A Primer in Public Choice*. Washington, DC: Cato Institute.

USA Today. 2005. Gallup poll results. 15 Mar., www.usatoday.com/news/polls/tables/live/2005-03-15-poll.htm; accessed 26 Apr. 2005.

WALLER, C. J. 1989. Monetary policy games and central bank politics. *Journal of Money, Credit and Banking*, 21: 422–31.

—— 1992. A bargaining model of partisan appointments to the central bank. *Journal of Monetary Economics*, 29: 411–28.

WALSH, C. 1995. Optimal contracts for central bankers. *American Economic Review*, 85: 150–67.

WITTMAN, D. 1989. Why democracies produce efficient results. *Journal of Political Economy*, 97: 1395–424.

—— 1995. *The Myth of Democratic Failure: Why Political Institutions are Efficient*. Chicago: University of Chicago Press.

CHAPTER 30

POLITICAL-ECONOMIC CYCLES

ROBERT J. FRANZESE, JR.
KAREN LONG JUSKO

1 INTRODUCTION

WHEN economic policy-makers are directly elected (or appointed by directly elected officials), how do electoral and partisan incentives structure economic policy-making? Suppose, for example, that voters prefer candidates expected to deliver greater economic well-being. Voters may evaluate candidates on recent experience, perhaps on aggregate performance. As a result, incumbents seeking re-election have powerful incentives to improve voters' economic fortunes, or to signal or feign such ability. If voters weigh recent pasts more heavily than distant periods, the incentives to manipulate economic policy to improve the likelihood of re-election sharpen as elections approach. Such *electioneering* may result in cycles of economic expansion and contraction that follow electoral cycles.

Alternatively, voters may evaluate candidates primarily in partisan terms. Competing parties may, as a result, cultivate ties to different voter segments, and nurture reputations for policy-making that favors those segments. Under some conditions, partisan ties create incentives for incumbents of different parties to implement distinct economic policies. Patterns of *partisaneering*, i.e. the manipulation of economic policy to benefit a partisan constituency, are evident in cycles of emphasis on different macroeconomic policy tools that track shifts in the partisan composition of governments.

While political economists have long incorporated democratic policy-makers' strong electoral and partisan motivations into theoretical models of the strength, nature, and timing of economic policy-making (e.g. Nordhaus 1975; Hibbs 1977; Tufte 1978), supportive consensus generated through empirical research has been more limited. For example, evidence of partisan cycles in real economic performance is typically stronger than the evidence supporting similar electoral cycles, but Clark (2003) strongly dissents. More puzzling, perhaps, is that while there seems to be relatively strong and consistent evidence of electoral and partisan cycles in nominal outcomes (like inflation), the empirical evidence also seems to suggest that electoral and partisan cycles in fiscal policy are stronger than any in monetary policy (Drazen 2001). Although the more recent rational expectations (RE) models (Cukierman and Meltzer 1986; Rogoff and Sibert 1988; Rogoff 1990)—in which voters are rationally foresighted and therefore aware of incumbents' incentive to *electioneer* or *partisaneer*—may account for some of these empirical patterns, several questions remain. Most critically, how can one account for the great inconsistency in results across all these empirical explorations of such similar phenomena? Relatedly, (how) can one account for the apparent differences in relative strengths of electoral or partisan effects, and (how) can one explain incumbents' choices over different policy instruments?

At least in part, we argue, the neglect of variations in the *(a) international and domestic, (b) political and economic, (c) institutional, structural, and strategic contexts* in which elected, partisan incumbents make policy contributes to the limited empirical validation of both modern RE and classical political-economic cycle studies. (We use *context* or *contextual* to refer to this set of factors.) The magnitude, regularity, and content of political-economic cycles will vary with these *contexts*. Factors that vary across policies, countries, and times to yield such *contextual* effects include the nature and relative effective intensities of popular demands for economic policy and outcomes and of policy-makers' re-election and partisan incentives; the inter-, intra-, and extragovernmental allocation of policy-making control across multiple actors; and policy efficacy and maneuverability. For example, small, open economies, in which policy-makers retain less autonomy over some policies, or in which some policies may be less economically effective, likely lessen political-*macro*economic cycles. Where policy-making control is concentrated among a few highly disciplined partisan actors (e.g. Westminster), political-economic cycles may be sharp and clearly defined. Similarly, electoral rules may affect the relative political benefits of demographic v. geographic targeting of spending, and sharpen some political-economic cycles while blunting others. As these examples suggest, *contextual* variations structure policy-makers' incentives and abilities to manipulate policies and outcomes for electoral and partisan gain, and contextual variations modify the political-economic efficacy of such manipulations, again in many different ways across democracies, elections, and policies.

Political-economic cycles offer an ideal forum for exploring such *contextual* interactions: In all democracies, all policy-makers and policies ultimately must survive evaluation in partisan electoral contests. As a result, political-economic cycles should always emerge, but to degrees and in characters heavily *context conditioned*. Researchers, therefore, who wish to understand the implications of electoral and partisan incentives for economic policy-making should (Alt and Woolley 1982)—and increasingly have (as this review reveals)—incorporate the *context-conditionality* of electioneering and partisaneering in their analyses.

This entry surveys theoretical and empirical work on such *political-economic cycles*, i.e. cycles in economic outcomes induced by electoral and partisan competition.[1] In particular, we find the evidence to suggest that closer attention to the *context* in which economic policy decisions are made offers important and promising opportunities for future research. In the next section, we review, briefly, the literature on electoral cycles, building on Hibbs's discussion of electoral cycles (this volume), and emphasize how electoral context may heighten or inhibit incentives to electioneer. Then, turning to partisan cycles, we present a survey of the theoretical and empirical literature linking economic policy to partisan electoral motivations. Here too the opportunities for the incorporation of contextual factors, we suggest, seem very promising.

2 Electoral Cycles

Hibbs's discussion (this volume) presents details of important past and current developments in the theoretical and empirical study of electoral cycles. For our purposes—the review of political-economic cycles and evidence of their *context conditionality*—it will suffice to discuss this literature only briefly, emphasizing some features that Hibbs does not, and to refer our readers to Hibbs's chapter for a more thorough treatment.

2.1 Adaptive, Retrospective Citizens

Nordhaus (1975) showed how incumbents might use monetary policy to manipulate the well-known inverse relationship between inflation and unemployment (i.e. the Phillips curve) to win votes from myopic voters. Nordhaus's model of electoral cycles can be summarized in the following way: (1) Economic actors have adaptive expectations; that is, expected inflation rates are based (only) on past inflation. As a result, an expectations-augmented Phillips curve characterizes the economy. Simply put, Phillips curves give the relationship between inflation and unemployment; the expectations augmentation holds that only deviations of inflation from expectations, derived from past experience, will move unemployment rates. One implication of

---

[1] It borrows from and condenses Franzese 2002a. Some points made there are neglected here, and some points made here are elaborated and substantiated further there. Citations are also far more extensive there.

this set-up is that policy-makers can affect economic growth through the manipulation of inflation rates in the short run but not in the long run. (2) Voters are naive in the senses that they favor incumbents who preside over low inflation and high employment/growth without fully appreciating this economic relationship and that they weigh recent outcomes more heavily in their retrospective evaluations. (3) Incumbents (*a*) seek re-election and (*b*) control Phillips-curve stimulatory policies. Therefore, incumbents conduct stimulatory policy to improve real outcomes in pre-electoral periods, becoming contractionary post-election to combat the ensuing inflation and to prepare to stimulate again for the next election. Applying Tufte's (1978) murder-mystery analogy, 2 and 3*a* give *motive*; 1 gives *opportunity*; and 3*b* gives *weapons* for incumbents to *electioneer*. Drazen (2001) extends this logic formally to macroeconomic policies more generally, including fiscal policies.

As Hibbs (this volume) and others (e.g. Drazen 2001) make clear, that incumbents benefit from favorable economies has unequivocal empirical support (e.g. Kramer 1971; Tufte 1978; Fair 1978; and Hibbs 1987*a*, for presidential elections; Tufte 1975, 1978 for congressional elections; and Madsen 1980; Lewis-Beck 1988 for European democracies). In the United States, Alesina, Londregan, and Rosenthal (1993) find, notably, that voters reward/punish incumbents consistently with naive retrospective voting, rather than *rational* retrospective voting, in which voters may adjust their evaluations of incumbents' records in a way that acknowledges policy-maker incentives to electioneer (RE models are discussed below). Such *economic voting* being so well established, scholars moved to explore its *context conditionality* (e.g. *Electoral Studies* 2000). Hibbs (this volume) considers some of this research in his discussion of how "clarity of responsibility" may structure incentives to electioneer.

The strength of the evidence in support of economic voting stands in sharp contrast to evidence supporting electoral outcome cycles, especially evidence of cycles in real outcomes. Alt and Chrystal (1983), Alesina and colleagues,[2] and Hibbs (1987*a*), for instance, conclude that evidence from the USA or OECD democracies offers inconsistent support for electoral policy cycles and very little for outcome cycles, especially real-outcome cycles.[3] More widely viewed, the evidence for classic electoral outcome cycles is indeed mixed, but not uniformly unfavorable. For example, not counting Nordhaus and Tufte or these partisan-theory protagonists, Franzese (2002*a*) finds fourteen articles by ten authors reporting some cycles, and eight articles by six authors reporting weaker or no signs.

What is important for the purposes of our discussion, however, is a pattern that seems to pervade these seemingly inconsistent results. Nordhaus (1975), to take an example from the very start of this literature, found significant electoral unemployment cycles in just three of nine countries 1947–72, but the relative significance across countries suggests that closely contested elections, strong, unified executives, and

---

[2] Alesina and Sachs 1988; Alesina and Roubini 1992; Alesina, Cohen, and Roubini 1992, 1993; Alesina, Londregan, and Rosenthal 1993; Alesina, Roubini, and Cohen 1997; Alesina and Rosenthal 1995.

[3] Alesina and colleagues argue the post-election inflation they find may arise from RE pre-electoral policy cycles of the Rogoff 1990 sort. However, virtually any pre-electoral fiscal activism would spur post-electoral inflation (Drazen 2001).

domestic policy autonomy induce the strongest cycles. That is, empirical evidence hinted the importance of *context conditionality* for electoral cycles *ab initio*. Some of the inconsistencies in empirical evidence for electoral cycles likely emerged also from the implicit assumptions throughout these studies that all incumbents seek re-election equally in all elections and that all equally control policies equally effective toward that goal. Re-election incentives, control over policies, and political-economic policy efficacy are not constant, however; they vary considerably across *contexts*.

An even more serious limitation in these empirical searches for electoral cycles in macroeconomic outcomes derives from the following proposition: election-motivated incumbents will prefer policies that are more targetable and timeable (by incumbents, to voters), manipulable (by incumbents), palpable (to voters), and attributable (by voters, to incumbents) (Franzese 2002a). Following Tufte (1978), some policies that meet these criteria include direct benefits, such as transfers, tax cuts, or delayed hikes, spending increases or delayed cuts (especially public works), and public hiring/firing. In fact, only breadth of potential beneficiaries favors *macroeconomic* manipulation as an effective electioneering weapon, and, importantly, electioneering through policies that deliver direct benefits renders irrelevant the Phillips-curve exploitation on which the adaptive retrospective models rely and less relevant the distinction between adaptive and retrospective expectations entirely. And, indeed, evidence for electoral cycles in these sorts of policies is more consistently favorable.

Likewise, the timing of policy initiation or implementation and, in most parliamentary democracies, of elections themselves may be more easily manipulated by incumbents—and so more useful for electioneering—than either transfers or macroeconomic manipulation. Where incumbents can call early elections, policy-makers might more easily schedule elections to coincide with economic expansions than vice versa. Ito and Park (1988) and Ito (1990) find strong signs of strategic election timing in Japan (as do Alesina, Cohen, and Roubini 1993). Similarly, Chowdhury (1993) finds strategic timing in India, as do other more broadly comparative studies. Nevertheless, there remains little evidence of strategic election timing in other OECD democracies. As India and Japan are dominant-party systems, this pattern raises another possibility: early elections can occur for two reasons. On the one hand, as suggested above, incumbents may choose to call early elections to capitalize on favorable economic conditions. On the other hand, however, early elections may be forced upon incumbents because some of the coalition partners abandon the government, causing its collapse. If economic conditions are especially bad, coalition parties may try to avoid being punished at the polls by distancing themselves from the current government. Reasonably, therefore, we may expect economic conditions in endogenous election timing countries to exhibit greater variation across election years compared to non-election-year variance than that ratio in countries where elections are exogenously scheduled. Furthermore, opportunistic election timing to *strong* economies should be more prominent in single-party than in coalition government systems (Smith 1996, 2000). Finally, having endogenous election timing as an option should also (weakly) lessen the use of all other *electioneering weapons*; that is, given the additional weapon of moving the date of elections, other electioneering tools need be used less.

As that last consideration illustrates, all of this might imply a kind of *Ramsey Rule* for incumbents' electoral (and/or partisan) manipulation: assuming policies have decreasing marginal political-economic benefits, incumbents will manipulate all policies in direct proportion to their relative net-benefit elasticities (Franzese 2002a). Simply stated, incumbents will use all policy tools, in proportion to their effectiveness in satisfying their electoral goals. More specifically, an *electioneering Ramsey Rule* implies electoral cycles in policy composition as well as levels (Mani and Mukand 2000; Chang 2001), more prominent cycles in direct-delivery policies than less direct policies and outcomes, and that the degree and character of such policy composition *electioneering* are *context conditional*.

Returning to the example of coalition governments (or multiple sets of incumbents, more generally), incentives to *electioneer* may be modified by common-pool problems (in which total public revenue may be administered by several different and competing policy-makers; Goodhart 2000), agency problems (which arise when an actor, or set of actors, act on behalf of others, to further their goals and interests, e.g. Alt 1985), or veto-player problems (which arise when some actors can reject policy actions of others, e.g. Franzese 2002b). Similarly, coordination problems between central banks and governments (Cusack 2001) or other delegation and bargaining issues (Franzese 2003) may limit the *electioneering* effectiveness of different policy tools. Exchange rate regimes and international goods and financial market exposure (Franzese 2003; Clark 2003) and fiscal solvency also limit *electioneering* maneuverability (Blais, Blake, and Dion 1993; Franzese 2002b). Notably, Drazen's (2001) proposed active-fiscal/passive-monetary RE political cycles account is consistent with many of these expectations and empirical patterns.

Overall, this pattern—very strong support for direct transfers cycles, also strong in other policies and inflation around or after elections, and weakest in real outcomes—appears most clearly when specifications are conditioned by electoral competitiveness and other *contextual* variations, and it also receives more consistent support in developing than in developed democracies. The most promising approaches therefore, incorporate such *context conditionality* (Alt and Woolley 1982); conversely, factors like the presence of coalition partners, or autonomous central banks, when omitted, contribute to some of the apparent empirical weakness of electoral cycles. That is, when empirical specifications allow only unconditional electoral cycles, fail to control for competitiveness, and/or analyze less direct policies, support for policy cycles is weaker, although still stronger than for outcome cycles. Thus, electoral cycles do seem to be highly *context conditional*, rather than being of fixed magnitude and fixed content.

2.2 Rational, Prospective Citizens

Viewing this evidentiary pattern, economists naturally questioned the adaptive expectations and exploitable Phillips-curves assumptions. Voters and economic actors can easily foresee elections and policy-makers' incentives, so electoral cycles should not exist or should have no real effects under RE (although incentives for direct transfers may remain). If policy-makers do not possess any informational advantages over voters, then they cannot effectively signal their competence through pre-electoral stimulation, and, as a result, there are no incentives for Phillips-curve exploitations. However, if some actors apply adaptive expectations, then exploitable Phillips curves exist to that degree; likewise, if some voters evaluate naively retrospectively, their vote share gauges incumbents' broader *electioneering* incentives. Moreover, if some performance-affecting incumbent characteristics persist over time and if voters cannot fully observe these characteristics, rationally prospective actors would nonetheless evaluate retrospectively. Therefore, with incomplete citizen RE, classical electoral outcome cycle models should have some, albeit irregular or muted, validity.

As Hibbs (this volume) describes, RE competence signaling electoral cycle models are distinguished from complete information RE models in that elected policy-makers enjoy an information advantage—in particular, knowledge of their own competency—over voters. This informational advantage results in smaller, less regular cycles, especially in real outcomes. The empirical record may fit, but determining whether the correct degree of "smaller, less regular" cycles manifests, even if that degree were theoretically determinate, would be empirically difficult. Moreover, many *context-conditional* considerations would also imply smaller, less regular cycles, especially in an evidentiary record generated by studies that omitted such conditionality. Thus, empirical research does not contradict RE *competence*-signaling electoral cycles; cycles do seem less regular and smaller than models in which voters naively reward (or punish) policy-makers for good (or bad) economic performance suggest. However, the evidence is inconsistent with rational retrospective voting (Alesina, Londregan, and Rosenthal 1993); *context-conditional* cycles theories, whether RE or myopic, would also predict smaller, irregular cycles, especially as previously estimated; and smaller, irregular cycles would also obtain if political-economic actors in reality had *varying* information and rationality. The case for RE electoral cycles is more strongly theoretical than empirical: voters' prospective, RE evaluations probably do limit the degree to which incumbents manipulate economic policies and, a fortiori, outcomes for electoral advantage, but RE alone cannot (fully) explain the patterns in the accumulated empirical record. That is, observed cycles can be reconciled with RE, but RE may not (fully) explain observed cycles. *Context*, including the information environments in which political economic actors operate, remains a critical determinant of incentives to *electioneer*.

2.3 Further Discussion

One component of *context conditionality* that is especially neglected in electoral cycle studies is that of electoral challengers, who play little direct role in most models. Higher-quality challengers, for instance, may lead incumbents to expect closer elections, yielding greater *electioneering* in quality-challenger elections and in systems that usually produce such. Similarly, higher-quality challengers modify incumbent incentives to signal competence. More competent incumbents signal more because they can better distinguish themselves from expected average challengers, perhaps suggesting that quality challengers would incite *less* electioneering. This may offer some empirical leverage on (and bodes poorly for) *competence* signaling RE models.

Furthermore, *electioneering* seems to occur empirically both immediately before and after elections, and, indeed, is more pronounced and more certain just after (at least in transfers and deficits; Franzese 2002b). Challengers may explain this too. Incumbents can act on pre-electoral promises and therefore must do so to maintain credibility; winners can and almost always do fulfill their promises (Pomper 1971; Rose 1980; Alt 1985; Gallagher, Laver, and Mair 1995) for like reasons; and, *ceteris paribus*, candidates who promise more with greater credibility win. Therefore, given that electioneering may have some costs so that incumbents must estimate how much electioneering is optimal to undertake, the empirical pool of pre-electoral policy-makers will contain some incumbents who promised-cum-delivered too little/insufficiently credibly, and so lost; whereas post-electoral pools contain winners, returning incumbents and entering challengers, who (on average) will have promised, and so now must enact, greater largesse. Thus, the election essentially filters for credibility × promised largesse. Therefore, especially as newly seated governments are the most productive (*honeymoons*), post-electoral largesse is greater and more certain than pre-electoral. Note, finally, that this could also explain some weaknesses in early studies, which compared pre-electoral periods to all others, including immediate post-election periods.

In this section, we have considered empirical and theoretical research that evaluates the extent to which electoral cycles structure the incentives of economic policy-makers. While this has been a topic of extensive theoretical development, important inconsistencies in the support lent by empirical research remain. We have emphasized how the *context* in which policy-makers operate may structure their incentives to *electioneer*, and how failure to incorporate this context may generate misleading estimates of the effects of electoral incentives in economic policy-making. Although empirical evidence is more consistently supportive of partisan cycles, in which incumbent parties manipulate policy to benefit their constituencies (but see Clark 2003), the accounts provided there too are sensitive to these *contextual* considerations. In the next section, we review theoretical accounts of partisan incentives, as well as the related empirical research.

3 Partisan Cycles

3.1 Adaptive, Retrospective Citizens

In partisan models of political economics, candidates contest and voters adjudicate elections in partisan terms. Parties cultivate ties to different voter groups and nurture reputations for policy-making that favors those groups. Parties and voters value these ties and reputations, so incumbents conduct recognizably distinct partisan policies, yielding appreciably distinct economic outcomes. That parties do so distinguish themselves is somewhat unexpected theoretically: The Hotelling–Downs–Black (1929/1957/1958) model predicts that, in two-party competition at least, parties will converge, in policy terms, on the pivotal median voter. We might therefore expect the economic policies of all parties to reflect the interests of this voter.

Theoretically, however, partisan divergence can emerge as equilibria of several reasonable representations of electoral competition. Electoral uncertainty/incomplete information, especially regarding median voters' preferences, allows policy-interested parties to drift from *expected* medians at finite expected vote cost, yielding divergence, more as such uncertainty rises (Wittman 1977; Calvert 1985; Roemer 1992). Divergence can also arise if pre-electoral promises are not credible; candidates may find it optimal to renege on their promises post-election: with two parties, no entry, and one-stage games (e.g. no re-election), winners have no incentive to implement medians' preferences if theirs differ, so voters believe victors will enact victors' preferences whatever they might promise. Under these conditions, any degree of divergence is sustainable. In repeated games, however, parties can build reputations, which may foster some, but incomplete, convergence. With free entry, moreover, any number of candidates could enter anywhere, so low-cost-entry systems can sustain multiple parties of any divergence. More realistically, with some (non-preclusive) entry cost, multiple *citizen-candidate* equilibria (Besley and Coate 1997) arise. One, that only the median enters, returns the Hotelling–Downs–Black result, but the others, in which two candidates equidistant from the median enter, can sustain widening divergence as entry costs grow. Divergence, therefore, is an empirical matter.

Empirically, partisan economic policy/outcome differentiation is obvious. Tufte (1978), for example, finds US party platforms contrast *more* on economic and labor issues than on most others. Democrat and Republican voters divide similarly, though less sharply. Inflation and unemployment concerns, particularly, are highly cyclical and common to all, but persistent partisan differences manifest, mirroring the socio-economic characteristic of each party's constituency. Hibbs establishes left/right priorities most thoroughly, stressing relative unemployment/inflation aversion. Hibbs (1987a) shows, exhaustively and indisputably, that *lower* ends of occupational, income, and societal *hierarchies* face greater, more cyclical unemployment risk, and that tax-and-transfer systems only partly mitigate this risk. While unemployment's aggregate costs are large and obvious, Hibbs (and most others) find no evidence that inflation, *short of hyperinflation and distinct from relative prices and inflation variability*, harms almost any *real* outcome, including average income tax rates; aggregate real revenues, growth, investment, or savings; or the non-residential/housing investment mix. The only appreciably deleterious inflation effects appear in profitability, capital, and stock returns. Therefore, objectively, to the extent that these effects of inflation are felt more by upper classes, and to the extent that upper classes face less unemployment risk, they will have *relatively* more dislike of inflation than unemployment than do lower classes. Hibbs's partisan theory, in fact, requires only that this *ratio* of unemployment–inflation aversion among lower classes exceed that ratio among upper classes. Indeed only the ratio of perceived, and not necessarily objective, aversions matters, which Hibbs thoroughly demonstrates, estimating that Democratic voters penalize incumbents 1.1 times as much for 1 per cent unemployment as for 1 per cent inflation, substantively and statistically significantly greater than Republican voters' penalty ratio of .65.

Thus, different voter groups suffer disproportionately from unemployment or inflation; public perceptions reflect this objective difference; and incumbents' electoral approval follows suit, yielding differing partisan incentives to combat unemployment or inflation. More generally, party platforms differ on a range of economic issues; voters recognize and act on these differences; and parties enact policies accordingly. Therefore, left parties seek higher growth/employment and will accept higher inflation if need be to get them; right parties behave oppositely. (Left parties will also expend greater equalization efforts.) Hibbs assumes monetary, fiscal, and other policies have sizable short- to medium-term[4] impact, so these policy differences should manifest in outcomes also.

Supportive evidence is plentiful relative to that for electoral outcome cycles. Hibbs (1977, 1987a) estimates 1.5–2 per cent higher unemployment and 5.3–6.2 per cent lower real growth under US Republican administrations than under Democratic. Democrats also contributed 60± per cent of the 1948–78 reduction in 20/40-ratio income inequality. Beck (1982) finds these estimates inflated by about 1/3, but qualitatively concurs. Hibbs (1987b), Paldam (1989), and others find similarly in broader OECD samples. Alesina and his various colleagues (see n. 2 above) also find evidence of partisan cycles in the USA, as well as in the OECD countries. Several of these studies find *context-conditional* partisan cycles. Considerable consensus exists, therefore, about the role of partisanship in cycles of worsening nominal outcomes (like inflation) and improving real (unemployment, growth, etc.) and distributional outcomes under left governments, in US and comparative data. (Clark and colleagues[5] dissent, finding *context-conditional* cycles that favor electoral more than partisan models.)

An enormous literature analyzes empirical evidence of cycles in partisan policy. Imbeau, Petny, and Lamari (2001), for instance, meta-analyze 37 out of 600 partisan-policy studies that address economic policy, spanning welfare, education, health, social security, privatization, intervention, public employment, spending, revenue, debt/deficit, etc., yielding 545 coefficients of these, 72.5 per cent sign intuitively (e.g. left parties supporting policies favorable to their traditional constituencies), with 24.8 per cent significant at $p \leq .10$; 26.6 per cent have wrong sign, 8.3 per cent significantly; 0.9 per cent report no relation. This is a fair record, particularly when the varying and sometimes simplistic structure of the component studies is considered. The strongest partisan effects emerge from more sophisticated analyses, post-1973 samples, and regard government *size*: revenue, spending, employment (especially), or

---

[4] He explicitly denies any long-run inflation–unemployment trade-offs but stresses that stabilizing inflation and spurring growth/employment often conflict.

[5] Clark et al. 1998; Clark and Hallerberg 2000; Hallerberg, Vinhas de Souza, and Clark 2002; Clark 2003; Clark, Golder, and Golder 2002.

social welfare (less so). These results suggest that partisan cycles, like electoral cycles, follow a *Ramsey Rule:* all/most policy tools are used to meet partisan ends, although certain tools are preferred, and the extent and the mix of usage of policy tools exhibit strong *context* dependence.

Summarizing, empirical research demonstrates that nominal outcome effects exhibit partisan cycles most strongly, although partisan cycles in distributional outcomes are also evident and even real-outcome partisan cycles receive moderate support. Broad partisan policy cycles are also consistently and strongly evident, with strongest evidence for public employment but also some for spending and revenue. Finally, partisan cycles are found more consistently in social or welfare policies, tax structure, and monetary policy, than in fiscal policy. Naive left-deficit, right-surplus arguments,[6] for example, have least support.

In sum, empirical evidence of partisan policy and outcome divergence, in the expected directions, recurs frequently. Estimates vary and standard errors are sometimes large (statistical significance low), however, which could suggest that partisan divergence is small as Clark and colleagues (see n. 5 above) contend. To us, the more likely explanation for this variation in estimated coefficients and these sometimes large standard errors in the empirical record are the insufficient sample sizes/variations, the inappropriate/inadequate controls, and the mis-specification of *context-conditional* relations as unconditional characteristic of most empirical studies. We emphasize especially the last of these because, in all cases, and perhaps especially in monetary and fiscal policy, the overall pattern of empirical results suggests highly *context-conditional* partisan cycles.

3.2 Rational, Prospective Citizens

Unlike the electoral cycles case, empirical support for partisan cycles seemed strong, so no particular empirical puzzle motivated RE partisan theory. Rather, Alesina's (1987, 1988) *rational partisan theory (RPT)* filled theoretical needs, providing a framework logically consistent with modern RE economics, particularly with the latter's conclusion that fully expected macroeconomic policies (like those of the traditional political-macroeconomic policy cycles) are ineffective.

RPT's crucial insight is the *electoral surprise*. The minimal model can be summarized so: The economy is characterized by RE so that only unexpected policy affects outcomes; e.g. an RE-augmented Phillips curve, i.e. with forward-looking expectations that incorporate the full model rather than adaptive expectations. Two competing parties have or represent different preferences, and enact different policies if elected. Similarly, voters' preferences over inflation and unemployment vary, and they will vote for the party expected to deliver them highest utility. Under these conditions, economic actors' (voters') rational inflation expectations will average the two parties'

---

[6] Left-activist (counter-cyclical), right-passivist (less counter-, a-, or pro-cyclical) views find more support (Cusack 1999; Franzese 2005).

preferences (which are known), weighted by the rationally expected probability each wins. After the election, expectations adjust to the actual winning party but only as quickly as nominal contracting (e.g. wage-bargaining contracts) allows. Thus, unless winners were perfectly foreseen, actual election outcomes produce surprise policy, yielding short-term real-outcome shifts that fade as elections recede and contracts slowly adjust to the actual winner.[7]

Alesina and Rosenthal (1995) and Alesina, Roubni, and Cohen (1997) collect and advance Alesina and colleagues' (see n. 2 above) political-economic cycles work, contrasting evidence in support of electoral cycles and partisan cycles, in their RE and non-RE variants, from political-economic data across postwar US and OECD democracy samples. They find the data consistently favor RE models, indicate strong partisan, although few discernible electoral, cycles in macroeconomic outcomes, and suggest electoral and partisan macroeconomic-policy effects. The wider empirical literature, however, is more equivocal.

Recall that RE competence-signaling and non-RE electoral cycle theories have similar predictions, except that RE limit cycle size, regularity, or duration. The differences between RE and non-RE partisan theories of macroeconomic outcomes are also subtle: in non-RE partisan theory, policy-makers exploit stable Phillips curves to shift macroeconomic outcomes permanently. In *RPT*, only unexpected policy creates real effects, so when the left wins, inflation rises but real outcomes rise only insofar as the election winner and so the policy shift was unforeseen. Post-election, expectations adjust to incorporate the higher inflation, returning real outcomes to natural rates over time as new contracts come online, but inflation remains higher. The opposite pattern unfolds if the right wins. Thus, RE and non-RE partisan theories differ primarily in whether real partisan effects persist or fade. In US and/or OECD data, Alesina and colleagues (see n. 2 above) find indicators equal to $(1, -1)$ in the first $8\pm$ quarters ($2\pm$ years) of (left, right) governments empirically dominate traditional indicators equal to $(1, -1)$ over governments' whole terms. They interpret this as supporting the short-term real effects predicted by RE models. By contrast, inflation is permanently higher under left governments in both RE and non-RE models—a pattern which the data, explored in this manner, also support.

Empirical dominance of short-term indicators is indisputable; yet strongly concluding for *RPT* on this basis is premature (Franzese 2000). For one, the estimated cycles differ little substantively. More critically, much besides RE could explain shorter-term partisan effects. For example, Alesina, Roubini, and Cohen (1997) describe how left parties first apply expansionary policy, then, observing rising inflation, a potential electoral liability, switch to contractionary policies; rightist governments

---

[7] Two of the most interesting results from *RPT* logic lie beyond this article's scope. *Institutional balancing* (e.g. divided government) arises as moderate voters seek to produce moderate policies from polarized parties by giving control of different institutions (e.g. executive and legislature, central and local governments) to each. US *mid-term cycles* emerge because pre-electoral uncertainty about partisan control of the presidency leaves voters balancing against a weighted average in on-year congressional votes, but resolution of that uncertainty allows them to balance against a known president in off-year congressional elections, leading some moderate voters to switch their vote. Mid-term losses should therefore be larger after more unpredictable elections, which evidence supports (Scheve and Tomz 1999).

proceed oppositely. These paths, which the *mid-term balancing* of Alesina and Rosenthal (1995) would also produce, for instance, yield shorter-term cycles; *honeymoon* effects would also, as would any diminishing returns from stimulation. Finally, and most troubling for *RPT*, substantively and statistically stronger US real-growth partisan cycles emerge, before 1972, but significant right/left inflation differences, which produce *RPT*'s real cycles, emerged only after 1972.[8] Furthermore, Alesina, Roubini, and Cohen (1997) also explore US money growth, nominal interest rates, budget deficits, and transfers, finding some, but weak, partisan differences in monetary policy, though evidence is stronger in 1949–82 in nominal interest rates. (Evidence of pre-electoral monetary policy effects is also lacking, but possibly only because exchange rate regimes were ignored in that analysis.) Problematically, the partisan indicator in these policy studies lags two quarters, but the real-effects findings mentioned above assumed lags of just 1–2, implying that real effects emerge *before* monetary policy changes. This sequence directly suggests Drazen's (2001) active-fiscal/passive-monetary cycles in which fiscal policy drives partisan real-outcome cycles and nominal cycles arise from monetary accommodation of the fiscal manipulations. Also, the finding for monetary policy effects only in 1949–82 and the earlier finding of dampened inflation cycles through 1972 leave only a narrow 1973–82 window for partisan cycles to emerge from surprise inflation. Finally, the Phillips-curve slope required to produce the estimated real effects from the estimated monetary effects is implausibly steep.[9]

RPT also predicts more specifically that real-outcome effects should be proportional to electoral surprises. Alesina, Roubini, and Cohen (1997) very cleverly apply option-pricing theory to measure electoral surprises and find partisan unemployment effects in monthly US data proportional to these measures. However, they test for cycles proportional to surprise size (so measured) only against the absence of cycles; i.e. the alternative is no partisan effect rather than a simple partisan cycle. Moreover, *RPT* cycle amplitude actually depends on electoral surprises *times expected inflation differences between incumbents and challengers* rather than just the size of electoral surprises, as these models specified. The empirical models thus implicitly assume equal incumbent–challenger polarization across all elections. This would bias estimates if, e.g., victory probabilities relate to distances between candidates, which they would in *RPT* or most other reasonable models. Data from prior-office voting records of most presidential candidates, which could gauge the requisite distances, exist. Of course, the issues raised above—missing policy links behind the observed

---

[8] Under Bretton Woods (the pre-1972 system), the USA (as the Nth currency) retained autonomous and extremely effective monetary policy. Fiscal policy would have been less effective. So the real cycles should have come through strong partisan monetary cycles, which would have been clearly evident in inflation.

[9] In these policy cycle studies, Alesina and colleagues also find no pre-electoral deficit or transfers effects and few partisan transfers effects. However, they ignore post-electoral effects; samples here are small; and context conditionality is largely ignored. They do find statistically significantly higher deficits under the right, though, a result they attribute to the right strategically increasing debt to reduce any future left's fiscal maneuverability. Early empirical results directly addressing such strategic debt manipulation theories are not promising, though (Lambertini 2003; Franzese 2002a).

policy cycles, congressional influence, and varying exchange regime—apply to this analysis also.

Summarizing, Alesina and colleagues (see n. 2 above) clearly establish short-term real-outcome and long-term nominal-outcome partisan cycles, but the *RPT* model's explanation for these cycles is not well established empirically. In particular, monetary policy and nominal-outcome patterns cannot easily explain real-outcome patterns. Regarding policies, Alesina and colleagues find strongest partisan effects in two-party/bloc countries—which is intuitive since these systems produce greater right–left government alternations—and in redistributive policies like transfers—also completely intuitive. They find only weak signs of pre-electoral tax manipulation and, weaker still, of pre-electoral spending manipulation.

3.3 Further Discussion

Other empirical studies of *RPT* report more mixed results. Sheffrin (1989), for example, finds US monetary cycles, but not significantly consistent with *RPT* in the USA or elsewhere. Using over 100 years of American data, Klein (1996) finds political events associated with ends of slumps and booms, consistent with *RPT*, although Klein's study does not directly test *RPT*. Carlsen (1998, 1999) and Carlsen and Pedersen (1999) investigate nominal rigidities and electoral surprises, which *together* should produce *RPT* cycles, and compares measures reflecting their combination with those analogously derived from Hibbsian partisan theory. The results are weakly positive for US inflation cycles, supporting both versions of partisan theory, negative for US real outcomes, and mixed elsewhere; Carlsen and Pedersen (1999) find clear *RPT* support in the UK, some *RPT* support in Canada and Australia, classical partisan-theory support in the USA, and inconclusive findings in Sweden and Germany. Finally, Faust and Irons (1999) find evidence to support Alesina and colleagues' proposition that the first two years of new administrations exhibit the distinctive real outcomes *RPT* predicts (right-worse; left-better) but also that little of this distinctiveness can be attributed to partisan monetary policies, echoing some of the above discussion.

Others stress more theoretical limitations. Following Rogoff (1988), Garfinkel and Glazer (1994) ask whether US bargainers, in order to avoid election surprises that would alter the real terms of nominal contracts, would simply defer contracts to post-election, finding that some contracts do exhibit significant post-electoral kyphosis. This suggests that bargainers do perceive electoral-economic uncertainty sufficient to warrant altering their contracting behavior, supporting *RPT*'s theoretical basis, but that very alteration in behavior mutes any monetary-surprise-induced real cycles, weakening *RPT*'s explanation for partisan real-outcome cycles. Ellis and Thoma (1991) emphasize instead that, because election timing in most parliamentary systems is endogenous, partisan surprises there are more continuous and irregular, and likely somewhat smaller, than in exogenous election timing systems. Ellis and Thoma (1995) find evidence of current account, real exchange rate, and terms of trade cycles supporting hypotheses derived from their model reflecting this consideration.

Heckelman (2001), relatedly, models rational economic agents facing uncertainty regarding election timing and election winners. Real effects here depend on partisanship in current and previous periods, time since the last election, and incumbent popularity. In this RE model, unlike in Alesina's *RPT*, lefts/rights spur/dampen real output throughout their term, and these real effects rise rather than diminish over the term. Drazen (2001), finally, questions *RPT*'s emphasis on monetary policy, giving an active-fiscal/passive-monetary RE model that predicts political-economic cycles more consistent with the full policy and outcome evidentiary pattern described above.

4 Conclusion: *Context-conditional Political-Economic Cycles*

In all democracies, partisan electoral contests determine economic policy-makers. That partisan and electoral motivations influence economic policy-making, therefore, is not surprising. As discovered repeatedly above, however, cycles induced by electoral and partisan incentives receive strongest empirical support when researchers recognize their *context conditionality*. Franzese (2002a) summarizes this argument thusly: "Incentives and capacity for, and effects of, *electioneering* or *partisaneering* should vary predictably across policies and across domestic and international political-economic institutional, structural, and strategic *contexts*." Many specific hypotheses regarding *context-conditional* political-economic cycles are suggested there. To give a few examples here: given our *Ramsey Rule*, and subject to boundary conditions, policy-makers will use all instruments in proportion to their relative efficacy, producing cycles of varying amplitude in all policies and outcomes, and in policy composition (Chang 2001) and outcome mixes (Tufte 1978). Coalitions may have lesser *motive* given their collective-action/common-pool problems (Goodhart 2000) and lesser *opportunity* given their veto-actor problems (Franzese 2002b; Tsebelis 2002) to *electioneer*. Where political systems produce unified single-party governments, election timing may be an ideal *weapon*. Broad redistributive policies (e.g. transfers) may be good *weapons* given multimember districts, but distributive (pork-barrel) policies may be more effective given single-member districts, which make victory depend on winning narrower constituencies. *Motives* to *electioneer* per se, and relative to *motives* to *partisaneer* (Schneider and Frey 1988), vary with expected election competitiveness. Systems with less effective accountability mechanisms (see Powell 2000) may yield muted *electioneering/partisaneering motives* as well (Powell and Whitten 1993; Shi and Svensson 2001). *Motives* may also vary across elections with the share of power at stake (Tufte 1978), so systems that concentrate elections on key policy-makers (e.g. UK) would induce sharper cycles (Alt 1985; Goodhart 2000; Franzese 2002b). Incumbents' policies also depend on strategic *contexts* like opposition strength and partisanship or replacement risk (Hicks and Swank 1992; Franzese 2002b).

Opportunity to *electioneer/partisaneer* also varies, with multiple incumbents and internal and external constraints on policy maneuverability being central. Accumulated debt limits fiscal policy maneuverability (Blais, Blake, and Dion 1993; Franzese 2002b); government seat shares and party discipline augment it (Acosta and Coppedge 2001); private or public foreign-borrowing ability enhances it (Corsetti and Roubini 1997). Multiple policy-makers likely limit maneuverability in general (Tsebelis 2002; Alt 1985; Roubini and Sachs 1989; Perotti and Kontopoulos 1998; Franzese 2002b). Maneuverability also hinges on delegation, agency, and bargaining issues under shared policy control.[10] In monetary policy especially, many (Clark and colleagues (see n. 5 above) most thoroughly) have considered the implications of central bank independence, fixed exchange rates, and/or capital mobility in this regard. Fiscal policy contracts or delegation may have similar effects (Hallerberg and von Hagen 1998).

In sum, the empirical evidence surveyed here (see also Franzese 2002a) clearly supports models of political-economic cycles that are *context conditional*. Political economists should, therefore, recognize in the study of political-economic cycles generous opportunities to explore how international and domestic, political and economic institutions, structures, and strategic *contexts* shape the electoral and partisan incentives for public policy-making.

References

Acosta, A. M., and Coppedge, M. 2001. Political determinants of fiscal discipline in Latin America, 1979–1998. Paper presented at Latin American Studies Association, Annual Meetings.

Alesina, A. 1987. Macroeconomic policy in a two-party system as a repeated game. *Quarterly Journal of Economy*, 102: 651–78.

——1988. Macroeconomics and politics. *NBER Macroeconomics Annual*, 3: 13–61.

——Cohen, G., and Roubini, N. 1992. Macroeconomic policies and elections in OECD democracies. *Economics and Politics*, 4: 1–30.

——————1993. Electoral business cycles in industrial democracies. *European Journal of Political Economy*, 23: 1–25.

——Londregan, J., and Rosenthal, H. 1993. A model of the political economy of the US. *American Political Science Review*, 87: 12–33.

---

[10] Franzese 1999, 2002b, 2003 offers a useful empirical formulation for such scenarios, including probably all principal–agent relations. In abstract, specify the agent's policy-reaction function, $g(X)$, the principal's, $f(Z)$, and some function, $1 \geq h(I) \geq 0$, reflecting the theoretical arguments regarding *contexts* that determine the costs (monitoring, enforcement, opportunity, etc.) that the principal must pay to induce the agent to follow $f(Z)$ instead of $g(X)$. Then, in most strategic models, equilibrium policy will be $y = h(I) \cdot g(X) + \{1 - h(I)\} \cdot f(Z)$, which will be empirically estimable by non-linear least-squares or maximum likelihood for sufficiently distinct I, X, and Z and/or $f(\cdot), g(\cdot),$ and $h(\cdot)$.

―― and ROSENTHAL, H. 1995. *Partisan Politics, Divided Government, and the Economy*. Cambridge: Cambridge University Press.

―― and ROUBINI, N. 1992. Political cycles in OECD economies. *Review of Economy Studies*, 59: 663–88.

―― ―― and COHEN, G. 1997. *Political Cycles and the Macroeconomy*. Cambridge, Mass.: MIT Press.

―― and SACHS, J. 1988. Political parties and business cycle in the US. *Journal of Money, Credit, and Banking*, 20: 63–82.

ALT, J. E. 1985. Political parties, world demand, and unemployment: domestic and international sources of economic activity. *American Political Science Review*, 79: 1016–40.

―― and CHRYSTAL, K. A. 1983. *Political Economics*. Berkeley: University of California Press.

―― and WOOLLEY, J. 1982. Reaction functions, optimization and politics. *American Journal of Political Science*, 26: 709–40.

BECK, N. 1982. Parties, administrations, and American macroeconomic outcomes. *American Political Science Review*, 76: 83–93.

BESLEY, T., and COATE, S. 1997. An economic model of representative democracy. *Quarterly Journal of Economics*, 112: 85–114.

BLACK, D. 1958. *Theory of Committees and Elections*. Cambridge: Cambridge University Press.

BLAIS, A., BLAKE, D., and DION, S. 1993. Do parties make a difference? *American Journal of Political Science*, 37: 40–62.

CALVERT, R. 1985. Robustness of the multidimensional voting model: candidates' motivations, uncertainty, and convergence. *American Journal of Political Science*, 29: 69–95.

CARLSEN, F. 1998. Rational partisan theory: empirical evidence for the US. *Southern Economic Journal*, 65: 64–82.

―― 1999. Inflation and elections: theory and evidence for six OECD economies. *Economic Inquiry*, 37: 120–35.

―― and PEDERSEN, E. F. 1999. Rational partisan theory: evidence from seven OECD countries. *Economics and Politics*, 11: 12–32.

CHANG, E. C. C. 2001. Electoral budget cycles under alternative electoral systems. Unpublished manuscript, Michigan State University.

CHOWDHURY, A. R. 1993. Political surfing over economic waves. *American Journal of Political Science*, 37: 1100–18.

CLARK, W. R. 2003. *Capitalism Not Globalism*. Ann Arbor: University of Michigan Press.

―― GOLDER, M., and GOLDER, S. 2002. Fiscal policy and the democratic process in the European Union. Unpublished manuscript, New York University.

―― HALLERBERG, M. 2000. Mobile capital, domestic institutions, and electorally induced monetary and fiscal policy. *American Political Science Review*, 94: 323–46.

―― REICHERT, U. N., LOMAS, S. L., and PARKER, K. L. 1998. International and domestic constraints on political business cycles in OECD economies. *International Organization*, 52: 87–120.

CORSETTI, G., and ROUBINI, N. 1997. Politically motivated fiscal deficits. *Economics and Politics*, 9: 27–54.

CUKIERMAN, A., and MELTZER, A. 1986. A positive theory of discretionary policy, the cost of democratic government, and the benefits of a constitution. *Economic Inquiry*, 24: 367–88.

CUSACK, T. 1999. Partisan politics and fiscal policy. *Comparative Political Studies*, 32: 464–86.

―― 2001. Partisanship in the setting and coordination of fiscal and monetary policies. *European Journal of Political Research*, 40: 93–115.

Downs, A. 1957. *An Economic Theory of Democracy*. New York: Harper and Row.
Drazen, A. 2001. The political business cycle after 25 years. *NBER Macroeconomics Annual*, 15: 75–117.
Electoral Studies 2000. Vol. 19.
Ellis, C. J., and Thoma, M. A. 1991. Partisan effects in economies with variable electoral terms. *Journal of Money, Credit, and Banking*, 23: 728–41.
———— 1995. The implications for an open economy of partisan business cycles. *European Journal of Political Economy*, 11: 635–51.
Fair, R. 1978. The effect of economic events on votes for president. *Review of Economics and Statistics*, 60: 159–72.
Faust, J., and Irons, J. 1999. Money, politics, and the post-war business cycle. *Journal of Monetary Economics*, 43: 61–89.
Franzese, R. J. 1999. Partially independent central banks, politically responsive governments, and inflation. *American Journal of Political Science*, 43: 681–706.
———— 2000. Book review: *Political Cycles and the Macroeconomy*. *Journal of Policy Analysis Management*, 19: 501–9.
———— 2002a. Electoral and partisan cycles in economic policies and outcomes. *Annual Reviews of Political Science*, 5: 369–421.
———— 2002b. *Macroeconomic Policies of Developed Democracies*. Cambridge: Cambridge University Press.
———— 2003. Multiple hands on the wheel. *Political Analysis*, 11: 445–74.
———— 2005. Fiscal policy with multiple policymakers: veto actors and deadlock; collective action and common pools; bargaining and compromise. Forthcoming in *Veto Actor Analysis*, ed. H. Magara.
Gallagher, M., Laver, M., and Mair, P. 1995. *Representative Government in Modern Europe*, 2nd edn. New York: McGraw-Hill.
Garfinkel, M., and Glazer, A. 1994. Does electoral uncertainty cause economic fluctuations? *American Economic Review*, 84: 169–73.
Goodhart, L. M. 2000. Political institutions, elections, and policy choices. Thesis, Harvard University.
Hallerberg, M., Vinhas de Souza, L., and Clark, W. R. 2002. Political business cycles in EU accession countries. *European Union Politics*, 3: 231–50.
———— and von Hagen, J. 1998. Electoral institutions and the budget process. Pp. 65–94 in *Democracy, Decentralisation and Deficits in Latin America*, ed. K. Fukasaku and R. Hausmann. Paris: OECD.
Heckelman, J. C. 2001. Partisan business cycles under variable election dates. *Journal of Macroeconomics*, 23: 261–75.
Hibbs, D. 1977. Political parties and macroeconomic policy. *American Political Science Review*, 71: 1467–87.
———— 1987a. *The American Political Economy*. Cambridge, Mass.: Harvard University Press.
———— 1987b. *The Political Economy of Industrial Democracies*. Cambridge, Mass.: Harvard University Press.
Hicks, A. M., and Swank, D. H. 1992. Politics, institutions, and welfare spending in industrialized democracies, 1960–1992. *American Political Science Review*, 86: 658–74.
Hotelling, H. 1929. Stability in competition. *Economic Journal*, 39: 41–57.
Imbeau, L., Petry, F., and Lamari, M. 2001. Left–right party ideology and government policies. *European Journal of Political Research*, 40: 1–29.
Ito, T. 1990. The timing of elections and political business cycles in Japan. *Journal of Asian Economy*, 1: 135–56.

———— and PARK, J. H. 1988. Political business cycles in the parliamentary system. *Economic Letters*, 27: 233–8.
KLEIN, M. W. 1996. Elections and the duration of US business cycles. *Journal of Money, Credit, and Banking*, 28: 84–101.
KRAMER, G. 1971. Short-term fluctuations in US voting behavior. *American Political Science Review*, 65: 131–43.
LAMBERTINI, L. 2003. Are budget deficits used strategically? Boston College Dept. of Economics, Boston College Working Papers in Economics 578 (forthcoming in *Economics and Politics*).
LEWIS-BECK, M. 1988. *Economics and Elections*. Ann Arbor: University of Michigan Press.
MADSEN, H. 1980. Electoral outcomes and macroeconomic policies. Pp. 15–46 in *Models of Political Economy*, ed. P. Whitley. Beverly Hills, Calif.: Sage.
MANI, A., and MUKAND, S. 2000. Democracy and visibility. Unpublished manuscript, Vanderbilt University.
NORDHAUS, W. 1975. The political business cycle. *Review of Economic Studies*, 42: 169–90.
OATLEY, T. 1999. How constraining is capital mobility? *American Journal of Political Science*, 43: 1003–27.
PALDAM, M. 1989. Testing Hibbs' theory of partisan cycles. Aarhus University working paper.
PEROTTI, R., and KONTOPOULOUS, Y. 1998. Fragmented fiscal policy. NBER-ZEI Conference, Bonn.
PERSSON, T., and TABELLINI, G. 1990. *Macroeconomic Policy, Credibility and Politics*. London: Harwood Academic.
———— ———— 2000. *Political Economics*. Cambridge, Mass.: MIT Press.
POMPER, G. M. 1971. *Elections in America*. New York: Dodd, Mead.
POWELL, G. B. 2000. *Elections as Instruments of Democracy*. Cambridge, Mass.: Harvard University Press.
———— WHITTEN, G. D. 1993. A cross-national analysis of economic voting. *American Journal of Political Science*, 37: 391–414.
ROEMER, J. 1992. A theory of class differentatiated politics in an electoral democracy. Working Paper 384, Dept. of Economics, University of California, Davis.
ROGOFF, K. 1988. Comment. *NBER Macroeconomics Annual*, 3: 61–3.
———— 1990. Equilibrium political budget cycles. *American Economy Review*, 80: 21–36.
———— and SIBERT, A. 1988. Elections and macroeconomic policy cycles. *Review of Economic Studies*, 55: 1–16.
ROSE, R. 1980. *Do Parties Make a Difference?* Chatham, NJ: Chatham House.
ROUBINI, N., and SACHS, J. 1989. Government spending and budget deficits in the industrial countries. *Economic Policy*, 8: 99–132.
SCHEVE, T., and TOMZ, M. 1999. Electoral surprise and the midterm loss in US congressional elections. *British Journal of Political Science*, 29: 507–21.
SCHNEIDER, F., and FREY, B. S. 1988. Politico-economic models of macroeconomic policy. Pp. 239–75 in *Political Business Cycles*, ed. T. D. Willett. Durham, NC: Duke University Press.
SCHULTZ, K. A. 1995. The politics of the political business cycle. *British Journal of Political Science*, 25: 79–99.
SHEFFRIN, S. 1989. Evaluating rational partisan business cycle theory. *Economics and Politics*, 1: 239–59.
SHI, M., and SVENSSON, J. 2001. Conditional political budget cycles. Working paper, University of Wisconsin and IIES, Stockholm University.
SMITH, A. 1996. Endogenous election timing in majoritarian parliamentary systems. *Economics and Politics*, 8: 85–110.

_____ 2000. Election timing in majoritarian parliaments. Paper presented at APSA Annual Meetings.
TSEBELIS, G. 2002. *Veto Players*. Princeton, NJ: Princeton University Press.
TUFTE, E. 1975. Determinants of the outcomes of midterm congressional elections. *American Political Science Review*, 69: 812–26.
_____ 1978. *Political Control of the Economy*. Princeton, NJ: Princeton University Press.
WITTMAN, D. 1977. Candidates with policy preferences: a dynamic model. *Journal of Economic Theory*, 14: 180–9.
WRIGHT, G. 1974. The political economy of New-Deal spending. *Review of Economics and Statistics*, 56: 30–9.

CHAPTER 31

VOTING AND THE MACROECONOMY

DOUGLAS A. HIBBS, JR.

The people have been promised more than can be promised; they have been given hopes that it will be impossible to realize... The expenses of the new regime will actually be heavier than the old. And in the last analysis the people will judge the revolution by this fact alone—does it take more or less money? Are they better off? Do they have more work? And is that work better paid?

(Mirabeau [Honoré Gabriel Riquetti], 1791)

All Political history shows that the standing of the Government and its ability to hold the confidence of the electorate at a General Election depend on the success of its economic policy.

(Harold Wilson, 1968)

1 INTRODUCTION

THE proposition that support enjoyed by rulers among the ruled is decisively affected by economic conditions undoubtedly has been true since the formation of the first political communities. Empirical studies of systematic connections of voting and

---

* I am grateful to Nicola Acocella, Larry Bartels, John Ferejohn, Morris Fiorina, and Dennis Mueller for comments on drafts of this chapter.

the macroeconomy began to appear in the mid-1920s,[1] though by today's standards the early research applied quite casual statistical techniques, typically lacked well-articulated falsifiable hypotheses, and was not underpinned by any recognizable theoretical framework.

The landmark event in the modern history of research on macroeconomic conditions and election outcomes is Gerald Kramer's 1971 article on US voting behavior.[2] Kramer's work was inspired by the broader framework set out by Anthony Downs in *An Economic Theory of Democracy* (1957)—by a wide margin the most important work on the political economy of electoral democracies published in the twentieth century. Kramer proposed a clear model for macroeconomic voting, and its empirical predictions were subject to formal econometric tests. No one had done this before. Like Downs, Kramer viewed parties as alternative governing teams. Voters were presumed to be rational, self-interested, and future-oriented actors for whom acquiring and analyzing massive amounts of potentially relevant information was costly and impractical. Instead, he assumed that voters adopt a simple, efficient decision rule: if the incumbent's performance is "satisfactory," vote to retain the incumbent party; if not, vote for the opposition.[3]

Kramer calibrated "satisfactory" performance by favorable differences between realized and expected macroeconomic outcomes at the election year, on the assumption that the best readily available guide to future well-being was performance over the most recent year. Expected performance was in turn assumed to be given by outcomes realized the previous year. Accordingly, the macroeconomic arguments of Kramer's vote equations were election year growth rates of per capita real personal income and consumer prices, and the election year change in the unemployment rate. The dependent variable was the aggregate congressional vote share going to the president's party in non-presidential election years, and a weighted average of congressional and presidential vote shares in presidential election years, with the weights being a function of the estimated spillover from (especially strong or weak) presidential candidates to congressional candidates of the president's party.[4] Kramer's regression experiments showed that the growth of per capita real personal income exerted robust positive effects on aggregate voting outcomes from 1896 to 1964. In the presence of real income growth rates, inflation and changes in unemployment appeared to have little or no electoral

---

[1] See Monroe 1979 for a review of much of the early research. Reviews of research since 1970 include Nannestad and Paldam 1994 and Lewis-Beck and Stegmaier 2000. The most comprehensive recent guide to research on nearly all aspects of macro political economy and public choice is undoubtedly Mueller 2003. Another outstanding treatise, which covers a broad range of macro political economy and is lodged within a specific yet quite flexible analytical framework, is Drazen 2000. Gärtner 1994 masterfully reviews a narrower zone of the macro political economy field with exceptional pedagogical flair.

[2] In fact an efficient way to track the growth of the literature is to track citations to Kramer's 1971 paper.

[3] Years later, Ferejohn (1986, 1999) developed some micro-foundations for such simple voting rules in the context of pure retrospective voting theory. I discuss this work in Section 4.

[4] All by itself, the spillover mechanism was a significant contribution to voting theory, and it spawned a whole branch of research on presidential "coattails" which falls outside the scope of this chapter.

importance—a result that by and large has been sustained over a generation of subsequent empirical research.[5]

Key features of Kramer's model were part of the maintained hypothesis. He supplied no evidence that the stochastic properties of macroeconomic variables supported his assumption that the best forecast of future innovations to inflation and real income growth was current growth rates, or that the best forecast of innovations to unemployment was current changes in the rate. Nor did he undertake any tests supporting the assumption that economic voting was forward looking (prospective), as opposed to being purely retrospective, with past performance yielding electoral rewards and punishments regardless of the implications of past outcomes for the future. Furthermore, Kramer provided no mechanism mapping the behavior of individual, self-interested voters applying simple decision rules onto the aggregate vote shares populating his regression experiments. Treatment of those issues came during the decades afterward, on the back of Kramer's seminal contribution. Much of this chapter is a tour of the more important developments.

2 Aggregate Vote Shares and Individual Electoral Choices

The second major event in the emergence of sophisticated empirical analysis of voting and the macroeconomy is Ray Fair's famous 1978 article on economic voting for US presidents. Like Kramer, Fair adopted the Downsian environment of rational, self-interested voters whose electoral behavior is driven by maximization of expected future utility under the available political alternatives. Fair experimented with various combinations of within-term macroeconomic outcomes and outcomes observed during previous administrations of both the current incumbent and current opposition parties, and he concluded (as many others have since) that only within-term macroeconomic conditions affected voting. Fair revised his equations sequentially from one presidential election to the next in a quite openly ad hoc fashion, and from the start offered no explanation of how the various statistically significant, pre-election output growth and inflation variables in his regressions could rationally be informative about voters' "highest expected future utility." Perhaps Fair's most enduring contribution to applied macroeconomic voting theory was spelling out the strong assumptions necessary to get from individual, utility-maximizing voters to a linear aggregate voting equation.

---

[5] Kramer's estimates implied a 4 to 5 percentage point rise (decline) in the vote share for each 1 percentage point rise (decline) in the real income growth rate. Hibbs 2000 obtained nearly identical estimates of the effect of real income growth rates (sustained over the entire term, rather than just the election year) on aggregate postwar presidential voting outcomes—a consistency of results displaced by one branch of government, by twenty-nine years of research time, and by more than a half-century of electoral time from Kramer's ground-breaking paper.

Fair's derivation may be described as follows. Let U_{it}^I denote voter i's expected future utility under the incumbent party (political bloc) at election period t, and let U_{it}^O be the corresponding expected utility under the opposition party (political bloc). Let V_{it} equal 1.0 if voter i votes for the incumbent, and equal 0.0 otherwise. Utilities are determined by linear equations of the form

$$U_{it}^I = \mathbf{X}_t \mathbf{b} + v_{it}^I$$
$$U_{it}^O = \overline{\mathbf{X}} \mathbf{b} + v_{it}^O \quad (1)$$
$$Cov(\mathbf{X}, v^{I,O}) = 0$$

where $\mathbf{X}_t$ denotes a matrix of variables observed at periods during the incumbent's tenure, $\overline{\mathbf{X}}$ is a matrix of constants (the implicit standards against which the incumbent is evaluated), $\mathbf{b}$ is the associated vector of parameters, and $v_{it}^{I,O}$ are random events affecting utilities at each election that are unobserved by the investigator. $\mathbf{X}, \overline{\mathbf{X}}$, and $\mathbf{b}$ are common to voters.[6] Individual voting choices are determined by the party/candidate delivering the highest utility:

$$V_{it} = \begin{cases} 1 & \text{if } U_{it}^I \geq U_{it}^O \\ 0 & \text{if } U_{it}^I < U_{it}^O. \end{cases} \quad (2)$$

Letting $v_{it} = (v_{it}^O - v_{it}^I)$, the probability P of observing a vote for the incumbent is therefore

$$P(V_{it} = 1) = P\left[(\mathbf{X}_t - \overline{\mathbf{X}})\mathbf{b}\right] \geq v_{it}$$
$$= F_t\left[(\mathbf{X}_t - \overline{\mathbf{X}})\mathbf{b}\right] \quad (3)$$

where F_t is the cumulative distribution function of v_i at any election. Linearity of an aggregate voting equation is achieved by assuming the deviations $\tilde{v}_i = (v_i | t - \overline{v}_t)$ to be evenly distributed across voters at each election between some constants, say $\underline{d} < 0$ and $\overline{d} > 0$, with uniform probability density $f_t(\tilde{v}_i) = \frac{1}{\overline{d} - \underline{d}}$ and associated cumulative distribution function $F_t(\tilde{v}_i) = \frac{\tilde{v}_i - \underline{d}}{\overline{d} - \underline{d}}$.[7] The vote probabilities are then

$$P(V_{it} = 1) = \frac{-\underline{d} + (\mathbf{X}_t - \overline{\mathbf{X}})\mathbf{b} - \overline{v}_t}{(\overline{d} - \underline{d})}. \quad (4)$$

---

[6] For a K dimensional matrix of X's, $\mathbf{X}_t \mathbf{b}$ should then be understood to represent

$$\mathbf{X}_t \mathbf{b} = \sum_{k=1}^{K} \sum_j b_{kj} X_{kt-j}.$$

Fixing $\mathbf{b}$ over i (i.e. assuming that all voters react to macroeconomic outcomes and other variables in the same way) is of course an especially strong constraint. Alesina, Londregan, and Rosenthal 1993, however, show how imposing some regularity conditions on the distribution of individual sensitivities to $\mathbf{X}$ may give this assumption a degree of plausibility.

[7] The assumption of a uniform or even distribution is not all that restrictive in most settings. The distribution functions of more plausible bell-shaped alternatives, such as the normal and logistic, are quite flat over aggregate voting outcomes in the 35% to 65% range, which encompasses most election outcomes.

Taking averages over N voters (with N large enough to approximate an "infinity" of votes) to find $\frac{1}{N}\sum_{i=1}^{N} V_{it} \equiv V_t$, yields the aggregate, linear voting function most commonly used in empirical analysis

$$V_t = \alpha + \mathbf{X}_t \beta + u_t \qquad (5)$$

where $\alpha = \frac{-\underline{d}-\overline{\mathbf{X}}\mathbf{b}}{\overline{d}-\underline{d}}$, $\beta = \frac{\mathbf{b}}{\overline{d}-\underline{d}}$, $u_t = -\frac{\bar{v}_t}{\overline{d}-\underline{d}} \sim$ *white-noise*. Note that if the upper and lower bounds of the distribution of electoral shocks are equal in absolute value, i.e. $\overline{d} = -\underline{d}$, then the effects of $(\mathbf{X}_t - \overline{\mathbf{X}})$ would yield deviations of V_t from an expected vote share of $1/2$.

3 Two Views of Economic Voting: Prospective and Retrospective

Macroeconomic voting divides naturally into two main views defined by voters' time horizons: prospective and retrospective. In the prospective view, the expected future relative performance of contestants for office is all that matters. Prospective valuation is akin to the pricing of financial assets in efficient markets: The parties' stock of votes at elections (current asset values) is determined completely by rationally formed expectations of future benefits, calibrated in units of voter utility. Hence electoral choice is a political investment in the future to which a party's (candidate's, political bloc's) past performance per se has no relevance. As Downs put it: "Each citizen ... votes for the party he believes will provide him with higher utility than any other party during the coming electoral period" (1957, 38).

By contrast, under pure retrospective voting, elections are referenda on the governing party's performance in office. Voters reward "good" performance and punish "bad" performance. In the words of the original proponent of retrospective voting assessments, V. O. Key: "Voters may reject what they have known; or they may approve what they have known. They are not likely to be attracted in great numbers by promises of the novel or unknown" (1966, 61). For retrospective voters, bygones are never bygones (as they are under a purely forward-looking orientation), but rather comprise the driving force of political valuation and electoral choice.[8]

In the generation since the rational expectations revolution in economic theory, with its strong and often compelling emphasis on forward-looking behavior, pure retrospective voting frequently has been described as naive and irrational. Those characterizations have a certain normative, even messianic quality about them, but from a positive point of view are misguided. Building on a germinal paper of Barro (1973), Ferejohn (1986) constructed a well-known micro-founded model of Key's main arguments, with aggregate implications that have received much stronger support in

---

[8] See Fiorina 1981 for a comprehensive treatment of the history, mechanics, and survey-based evidence concerning retrospective voting in the United States.

data than prospective voting models. The central idea is that the electorate stands in a principal–agent relation to the incumbent party. Voters settle up with their agents by evaluating performance *ex post* for much the same reason—moral hazard—that insurance premiums are typically experience rated and that compensation of top corporate executives is generally heavily dependent upon past increases in share prices. Under pure retrospective valuation, promises to do better in the future are discounted completely, and exert no influence on voting choices. Instead, retrospective theory emphasizes the efficiency of inducing governing parties always to do their best in certain knowledge that voting settlements will be based on observed outcomes over the term, no matter how attractive are (inherently unenforceable) commitments to improve in the future. Opposition parties merely function as replacements on occasions when incumbents do not satisfy a fixed, attainable standard of performance.

In order for the underlying micro model to pass through, voters must react to macroeconomic performance, rather than to individual benefits ("sociotropic" voting), which in turn presumes implicit coordination among voters (and perhaps among party agents as well) in application of collectivist or utilitarian valuation standards.[9] If voting behavior were individualistic ("egotropic"), incumbents could pursue a divide and rule strategy by exploiting distributive conflicts in the electorate, and thereby mitigate, or perhaps avoid completely, the discipline of having to satisfy a minimal standard of macroeconomic performance augmenting aggregate welfare. A further implication of a principal–agent motivation of retrospective voting, though not a strict requirement, is that the electorate should evaluate performance over the incumbent's entire term of office, with little or no backward time discounting of performance outcomes.

4 Empirical Implementation

Consider a mandate period of duration T. A fairly general model encompassing both retrospective and prospective voting motivations would look like

$$V_t = a + \sum_{k=1}^{K} \sum_{j=0}^{T-1} \mu_{kj} X_{k,t-j} + E_t \left(\sum_{k=1}^{K} \sum_{j=1}^{T} \phi_{kj} X_{k,t+j} \right) + u_t \qquad u_t \sim white\text{-}noise$$

(6)

where E_t denotes expectations conditioned on voters' time t information set.[10] $\phi_k = 0$ yields pure retrospective voting; $\mu_k = 0$ implies that voting is purely prospective.[11] For

[9] Ferejohn 1999 elaborates upon his initial model and sketches a theory of how such coordination might arise among the constituent agents of parties, as well as among voters.
[10] The lag-lead sequences in (6) are based on the timing convention that elections yielding $V_t, V_{t+T}, \ldots$ occur after the realizations of outcomes $X_{k,t}, X_{k,t+T} \ldots$
[11] In systems with variable election dates, one cannot define the prospective time horizon in closed form. I arm-wave away the complication of endogenous election dates. Prospective voters could take

(6) to be operational we need to constrain the lag and lead parameters. The natural assumption for the prospective component is to impose a present discounted value with a constant rate of time preference. Stigler (1973) proposed the same approach to constraining retrospective evaluations. (See Section 4.3.) Simplified in those ways, the general model is:

$$V_t = a + \sum_{k=1}^{K} \sum_{j=0}^{T-1} \mu_k \lambda^j X_{k,\,t-j} + E_t \left(\sum_{k=1}^{K} \sum_{j=1}^{T} \phi_k \delta^j X_{k,\,t+j} \right) + u_t, \qquad (7)$$

where $\lambda, \delta \in [0, 1]$ are one-period discount factors.

4.1 Pure Prospective Voting

Consider first pure forward-looking, prospective voting ($\mu_k = 0$). Voting outcomes in this case are driven by:

$$V_t = a + E_t \left(\sum_{k=1}^{K} \sum_{j=1}^{T} \phi_k \delta^j X_{k,\,t+j} \right) + u_t. \qquad (8)$$

Empirical analysis of forward voting requires specification of how expectations are formed. The forecasting workhorses favored by time series specialists for most log real macroeconomic variables are random walks with drift and low-order autoregressions of first differences.[12] Alternatively, one could assume that expectations are based on forecasts from unconstrained multivariate autoregressions. Either way, using pre-election histories to forecast post-election realizations of relevant macroeconomic variables yields prospective voting equations that are observationally equivalent to retrospective equations.[13] Moreover, taking forecasts of future outcomes from past realizations of relevant variables implies that voters have no way of distinguishing, or make no attempt to distinguish, macroeconomic developments owing to competent, effective governance from what likely would occur in a neutral policy setting—a theoretical deficiency that was overcome by so-called "rational retrospective" models.

account of the consequences of performance during the post-election term for performance during periods afterward. (If macroeconomic variables have unit roots, then performance shocks persist indefinitely, and a rational voter's time horizon might accordingly span the indefinite future.) In analogous fashion, retrospective voters might look further back than the most recent term when forming electoral valuations, on the argument that current support can be viewed as a "political capital stock" of parties that accumulates over long periods of time. Fiorina 1977, 1981, and Hibbs 1982b advanced models with this feature.

As the discussion ahead should make clear, the first possibility is observationally equivalent to a one-term-ahead prospective time horizon. The retrospective possibility, however, is testable, and in the case of macroeconomic voting for US presidents it has been rejected in at least two studies: Hibbs 2000 and Peltzman 1990.

[12] See, for example, Mankiw and Shapiro 1985; Kormendi and Meguire 1990; Stock and Watson 2003.
[13] This point was developed by Blinder 1985 in his comments on Kirchgässner 1985.

4.2 Prospective Voting as "Rational" Retrospection

Rational retrospective voting set-ups originate with "signaling" models devised by Rogoff and Sibert (1988) and Rogoff (1990) to motivate fiscally driven political business cycles when incumbents face a forward-looking electorate endowed with rational expectations, as opposed to the backward-looking, "myopic" electorate relying upon adaptive expectations that was assumed in Nordhaus's (1975) path-breaking paper. The central idea is that economic voting is driven by the competence of the incumbent in producing favorable macroeconomic performance beyond what would be anticipated from the economy's development in a policy-neutral environment. The competence of elected authorities in managing the economy is persistent and, consequently, voters are able to infer useful information about unobserved post-election macroeconomic performance under the incumbent from observed pre-election performance. The mechanics of the rational decision-making process depend upon assumptions about the electorate's information set and the persistence of competence. Variations on what voters know and when they know it determine the specifics of closed-form solutions, but not the qualitative implications as long as voters are informed of within-term macroeconomic outcomes.[14]

Imagine that real output growth is the macroeconomic variable that voters are mainly concerned about, and that log output, q, evolves as a first-order moving average process with drift. For simplicity let period t denote half of the electoral term. The structure is:

$$q_t - q_{t-1} = \overline{q} + \varepsilon_t \tag{9}$$

$$\varepsilon_t = \eta_t + \psi_t, \quad \psi_t \sim white\text{-}noise, \ E\left(\eta_t, \psi_{t+j}\right)\}_{j=-\infty}^{+\infty} = 0 \tag{10}$$

$$\eta_t = \kappa_t + \theta \kappa_{t-1}, \quad \kappa_t \sim white\text{-}noise, \ \theta \in (0, 1]. \tag{11}$$

Output growth rates are determined by a constant drift of $\overline{q}$ per period, and by shocks ε_t that perturb the economy every period. ε_t is composed of a purely transitory component, ψ_t, which represents good or bad "luck" and, therefore, does not discriminate systematically between government and opposition, and a competency component, η_t, which does discriminate because it persists for the duration of a given incumbent team's term (here two periods). Luck and competence have zero covariance. The competency of parties currently in opposition is without loss of generality normalized to zero, and so η denotes the relative competence of the incumbent party during the present term. The *ex ante* expectation of $\eta(\kappa)$ is also normalized to zero without loss of generality. Further, competency is tied to parties in office, not individual office-holders. Consequently, if the incumbent party is re-elected, the effects of its competence spill over to growth rates realized during the following term (but no further), even if its dramatis personae are not seeking re-election (as, for example, when a sitting US president is not a candidate).

---

[14] If for some inexplicable reason voters had information only about election period performance then both traditional retrospective and rational retrospective models would be entirely notional, and voting necessarily could be affected only by election period outcomes.

If equation (8) is the operative vote function, rational retrospective voting implies that V_t is driven by the expected competence of the incumbent party in delivering favorable output growth rates over the next mandate period:

$$V_t = a + E_t(\phi \cdot (\delta \Delta q_{t+1}|\bar{q} + \delta^2 \Delta q_{t+2}|\bar{q})) + u_t$$
$$= a + E_t\left(\phi \cdot (\delta \eta_{t+1} + \delta^2 \eta_{t+2})\right) + u_t. \tag{12}$$

How are rational expectations of η_{t+1} and η_{t+2} formed at election period t? Voters understand the stochastic structure of the real macroeconomy generating output growth rates—equations (9)–(11) are common knowledge. However, voters observe only realizations of Δq and the composite shocks, ε, during the current term; i.e. at times t and $t-1$ in a two-period representation. Hence, although competence is not observed directly in the variant of the model laid out above, forward-looking voters gain some leverage on its future realizations under the incumbent from within-current-term performance.

Consider first expected competence during the latter half of the upcoming term, η_{t+2}. Voters know that:

$$\eta_{t+2} = \Delta q_{t+2} - \bar{q} - \psi_{t+2}$$
$$= \kappa_{t+2} + \theta \kappa_{t+1}. \tag{13}$$

Taking the time t conditional expectation yields:

$$E_t\left(\eta_{t+2}|\Delta q_t, \Delta q_{t-1}, \bar{q}\right) = E_t\left(\kappa_{t+2} + \theta \kappa_{t+1}\right)$$
$$= 0. \tag{14}$$

Although the incumbent's relative competence is persistent, in a two-period representation its effects on growth cannot carry over beyond the first period of the subsequent term, that is, to periods deeper into the post-election term than the duration of competence persistence.

Current-term performance is, however, informative about competence in the first part of the upcoming term, η_{t+1}. We have:[15]

$$\eta_{t+1} = \Delta q_{t+1} - \bar{q} - \psi_{t+1}$$
$$= \kappa_{t+1} + \theta \kappa_t. \tag{15}$$

$$E_t\left(\eta_{t+1}|\Delta q_t, \Delta q_{t-1}, \bar{q}\right) = \theta \cdot E_t\left(\kappa_t\right). \tag{16}$$

Equations (9)–(11) imply:

$$\kappa_t = \Delta q_t - \bar{q} - \theta \kappa_{t-1} - \psi_t. \tag{17}$$

---

[15] Note that at any election period t the conditional expectation of both η_{t+1} and η_{t+2} for a new government under the current opposition is zero, given that η norms the incumbent's competence relative to an opposition competence of nil. And should the opposition win the election at t, its ex post competence at the first period of the new term, η_{t+1}, would be just the first period realization κ_{t+1}, since at $t+1$ the lagged competency term $\kappa_t = 0$ when the governing party changes.

Substituting for $\kappa_{t-1} = \Delta q_{t-1} - \bar{q} - \theta \kappa_{t-2} - \psi_{t-1}$ gives:

$$\kappa_t = (\Delta q_t - \bar{q}) - \theta(\Delta q_{t-1} - \bar{q}) - (\psi_t - \theta \psi_{t-1} - \theta^2 \kappa_{t-2}) \qquad (18)$$

$$\Rightarrow (\kappa_t + \psi_t - \theta \psi_{t-1} - \theta^2 \kappa_{t-2}) = (\Delta q_t - \theta \Delta q_{t-1} - (1-\theta)\bar{q}). \qquad (19)$$

The linear projection of κ_t on $(\kappa_t + \psi_t - \theta \psi_{t-1} - \theta^2 \kappa_{t-2})$ yields:

$$\left(\frac{E\left(\kappa'_t \cdot (\kappa_t + \psi_t - \theta \psi_{t-1} - \theta^2 \kappa_{t-2})\right)}{E\left((\kappa_t + \psi_t - \theta \psi_{t-1} - \theta^2 \kappa_{t-2})' \cdot (\kappa_t + \psi_t - \theta \psi_{t-1} - \theta^2 \kappa_{t-2})\right)} \right) \qquad (20)$$

$$= \frac{\sigma_\kappa^2}{(1+\theta^4)\sigma_\kappa^2 + (1+\theta^2)\sigma_\psi^2}.$$

Hence the effect of the incumbent's competence on growth during the next mandate period implied by (16) is

$$E_t(\eta_{t+1}|\Delta q_t, \Delta q_{t-1}, \bar{q}) = \theta \cdot \frac{\sigma_\kappa^2}{(1+\theta^4)\sigma_\kappa^2 + (1+\theta^2)\sigma_\psi^2} \cdot \left[\begin{array}{c} \Delta q_t - \theta \Delta q_{t-1} \\ -(1-\theta)\bar{q} \end{array} \right], \qquad (21)$$

which in view of (12) implies the estimable regression relation

$$V_t = \tilde{\alpha} + \beta \cdot (\Delta q_t - \theta \Delta q_{t-1}) + u_t \qquad (22)$$

where $\tilde{\alpha} = [\alpha - \beta(1-\theta)\bar{q}]$, $\beta = \phi\delta\theta\left(\frac{\sigma_\kappa^2}{(1+\theta^4)\sigma_\kappa^2+(1+\theta^2)\sigma_\psi^2}\right)$. By contrast to conventional retrospective voting models, rational retrospective models therefore have the testable (and, at first blush, peculiar) requirement that the effects of pre-election growth rates on voting outcomes oscillate in sign.[16]

Rational retrospective, persistent competency models are quite ingenious but their influence has been confined wholly to the realm of detached theory. Such models have received no support in data. Alesina, Londregan, and Rosenthal (1993), and Alesina and Rosenthal (1995) appear to be the only serious empirical tests undertaken so far, and those studies found that US voting outcomes responded to observed output growth rates, rather than to growth rate innovations owing to persistent competence carrying over to the future.[17] As a result, the rational retrospective model was rejected empirically in favor of conventional retrospective voting. Yet competency models of

---

[16] In a model with more conventional periodicity (quarterly, yearly) and correspondingly higher-order moving average terms for the persistence of competence, the effects of lagged output growth rates on voting outcomes would exhibit the same damped magnitudes and oscillation of signs as one looks further back over the current term, that is, from election period t back to the beginning of the term at period $t - (T-1)$. See Hamilton (1994, ch. 4) for recursive computation algorithms for generating optimal forecasts from higher-order moving average models.

[17] The empirical analyses were based mainly on a variant of the rational retrospection model in which voters learn competency after a one-period delay. In a two-period set-up with first-order moving average persistence of competence, voters react to the weighted growth rate innovation:

$$E_t(\eta_{t+1}|\Delta q_t, \Delta q_{t-1}, \bar{q}) = \theta \cdot \frac{\sigma_\kappa^2}{\sigma_\kappa^2 + \sigma_\psi^2} \cdot [\Delta q_t - \bar{q} - \theta \kappa_{t-1}].$$

forward-looking electoral behavior have a theoretical coherence that is sorely lacking in much of the literature on macroeconomic voting, and the absence of more extensive empirical investigation is therefore rather surprising.[18] The econometric obstacles posed by theoretical constraints intrinsic to these models are probably part of the explanation.

4.3 Pure Retrospective Voting

Equation (7) evaluated at $\phi_k = 0$ gives a constrained model of pure retrospective voting suited to empirical testing:[19]

$$V_t = a + \sum_{k=1}^{K} \sum_{j=0}^{T-1} \mu_k \lambda^j X_{k,\,t-j} + u_t. \tag{23}$$

The basic functional form of this equation was to my knowledge first proposed by Stigler (1973) in his prescient critique of Kramer (1971). Stigler worked mainly with a single macroeconomic variable—changes in per capita real income—and he again was first to suggest that changes in "permanent" income,[20] calibrated over a substantial retrospective horizon, would logically be the place to look for macroeconomic effects on voting, although like so many ideas in macro political economy a rougher formulation of this hypothesis can be found in Downs (1957). Moreover, Stigler yet again was the first to connect instability of economic voting regression results to variation in the "powers or responsibilities" of the incumbent party[21]—an important research theme that did not receive systematic empirical attention until a generation

---

As I pointed out before, higher-order moving average processes also would generate damped magnitudes and oscillation of signs of coefficients for the lagged competence terms.

[18] Suzuki and Chappell 1996 investigated what they regarded as a rational prospective model of aggregate US voting outcomes. They applied various time series procedures to disentangle the permanent component of real GNP growth rates from the transitory component, and found some evidence that election year growth in the permanent component had more effect on aggregate voting outcomes than fluctuations in the transitory component. Unlike the Alesina et al. competency models, however, Suzuki and Chappell's regression set-ups are inherently unable to distinguish forward-looking voting from purely retrospective voting based on permanent innovations to output, as in the model of Hibbs 2000 discussed ahead.

[19] Many studies supplement the macroeconomic regressors of aggregate voting models with aggregated survey reports of presidential "job approval," policy "moods," economic "sentiments," party "attachments" ("party identification"), candidate "likes and dislikes," and related variables. (The most recent example I am aware of is Erikson, Mackuen, and Stimson 2002). Such perception-preference variables, however, are obviously endogenous to economic performance or voting choices or both, and consequently are logically unable to contribute any insight into the fundamental sources of voting behavior.

[20] "[T]he performance of a party is better judged against *average* [real per capita income] change"... "there is a close analogy between voting in response to income experience and the consumer theory of spending in response to durable ('permanent') income" (1973, 163, 165).

[21] "Per capita income falls over a year or two—should the voter abandon or punish the party in power? Such a reaction seems premature: the decline may be due to developments... beyond the powers or responsibilities of the party" (1973, 164).

later.²² Following Kramer, Stigler focused primarily on aggregate congressional vote shares going to the party holding the White House, and his results did not yield much evidence of stable macroeconomic voting from the turn of the twentieth century up to the mid-1960s.

However, about a decade afterward Hibbs (1982a) showed that the basic retrospective set-up of (23), specified with growth rates of per capita real disposable personal incomes over the fifteen post-inauguration quarters of a presidential term as the only regressors, explained postwar aggregate US presidential voting outcomes remarkably well. The biggest deviations from fitted vote shares were at the war elections of 1952 (Korea) and 1968 (Vietnam). A subsequent version of the basic set-up—Hibbs's (2000) "Bread and Peace Model"—took direct account of the electoral consequences of US involvement in undeclared wars by proposing the following simple retrospective equation, which was fit to data on aggregate presidential voting over 1952–96:

$$V_t = \alpha + \beta_1 \sum_{j=0}^{14} \lambda_1^j \, \Delta \ln R_{t-j} + \beta_2 \sum_{j=0}^{14} \lambda_2^j \, KIA_{t-j} \cdot NQ_t + u_t \qquad (24)$$

where V is the incumbent party's percentage share of the two-party presidential vote, R is quarterly per capita disposable personal income deflated by the Consumer Price Index, $\Delta \ln R_t$ denotes $\log(R_t/R_{t-1}) \cdot 400$ (the annualized quarter-on-quarter percentage rate of growth of R),²³ KIA denotes the number of Americans killed in action per quarter in the Korean and Vietnamese civil wars, and NQ is a binary nullification term equal to 0.0 for Q quarters following the election of a new president, and 1.0 otherwise. NQ defines the "grace period" for new presidents "inheriting" US interventions in Korea and Vietnam, that is, the number of quarters into each new president's administration over which KIA exerted no effect at the subsequent presidential election.²⁴

Hibbs (2000) found that real income growth rates accounted for around 90 per cent of the variance of presidential voting outcomes in the "non-war" elections, and were subject only to modest (if any) discounting over the term ($\hat{\lambda}_1 = 0.954$). The flow of American KIA was not discounted at all ($\hat{\lambda}_2 = 1.0$),²⁵ although the grace period for presidents inheriting the wars was estimated to be a full term ($\widehat{NQ} = 16$). Those estimates implied that that each sustained percentage point change in per capita real income yielded a 4 percentage-point deviation of the incumbent party's

---

²² I take up what has come to be known as the "clarity of responsibility" hypothesis in the next section.

²³ The growth rate of R is probably the broadest single aggregate measure of proportional changes in voters' personal economic well-being, in that it includes income from all market sources, is adjusted for inflation, taxes, government transfer payments, and population growth, and moves with changes in unemployment. R does not register, however, the benefits of government-supplied goods and services.

²⁴ As a practical matter, NQ determines the extent to which the 1956 vote for Dwight Eisenhower (who inherited American involvement in the Korean civil war from Harry Truman) was affected by US KIA in Korea after Eisenhower assumed office in 1953, and the extent to which the 1972 vote for Richard Nixon (who inherited US engagement in the Vietnamese civil war from Lyndon Johnson) was affected by US KIA in Vietnam after Nixon assumed office in 1969.

²⁵ The point estimate $\hat{\lambda}_1$ is also compatible with uniform weighting of income growth rates over the term, as the null hypothesis $\lambda_1 = 1$ could not be rejected at reasonable confidence levels.

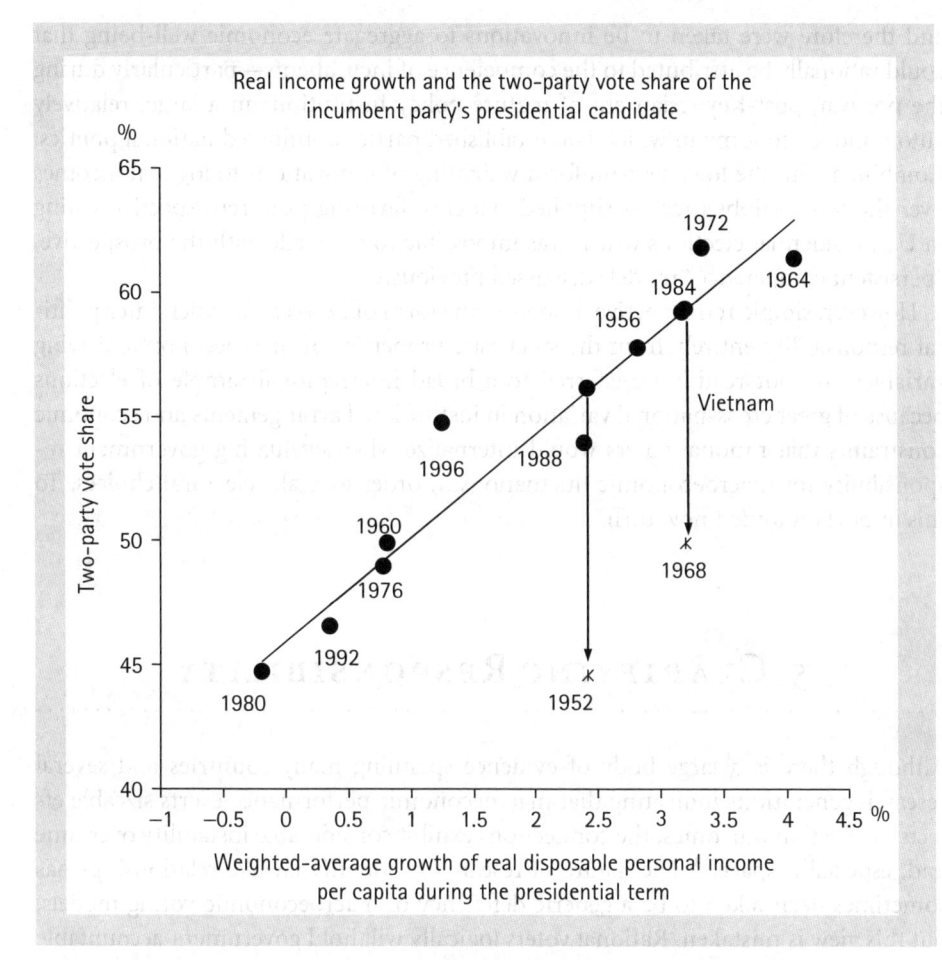

Real income growth and the two-party vote share of the incumbent party's presidential candidate

Fig. 31.1 US retrospective voting in the "Bread and Peace" model

vote share from a constant of 46 per cent ($\hat{\beta}_1 / \sum_{j=0}^{14} \hat{\lambda}_1^j = 4.1$, $\hat{a} = 46$), and that every 1,000 combat fatalities in Korea and Vietnam depressed the incumbent vote share by 0.37 percentage points ($1000 \cdot \hat{\beta}_2 = -0.37$). Cumulative KIA reduced the incumbent vote by around 11 percentage points in 1952 as well as in 1968, and almost certainly was the main reason the Democratic Party did not win those elections[26] (see Figure 31.1). No postwar event—economic or political—affected US presidential voting by anything close to this magnitude.

Hibbs (2000) took the political relevance of KIA to be self-evident. The statistical impact of real income growth rates was rationalized theoretically by establishing that log real per capita disposable personal income evolves as a random walk with fixed drift. Changes in ln R net of drift were shown to be unpredictable *ex ante*,

---

[26] The cumulative numbers of Americans killed in action at the time of the 1952 (Korea) and 1968 (Vietnam) elections were almost identical: 29,300 and 28,900, respectively, so re-estimation of the model with a binary war variable coded unity for 1952 and 1968 would yield results nearly identical to those discussed in the main text.

and therefore were taken to be innovations to aggregate economic well-being that could rationally be attributed to the competence of incumbents—particularly during the postwar, post-Keynesian era of mature policy institutions in a large, relatively autonomous economy in which two established parties dominated national politics. Combined with the low, near-uniform weighting of innovations to log real incomes over the term, Hibbs's results supplied evidence favoring pure retrospective voting in US presidential elections which was impossible to reconcile with the prospective, "persistent competence" models discussed previously.[27]

However, simple retrospective models in the form of (23)–(24), which infer political responsibility entirely from the stochastic properties of macroeconomic driving variables, are not readily transferred to a broad international sample of elections because of great cross-national variation in institutional arrangements and economic constraints that rational voters would internalize when evaluating government responsibility for macroeconomic fluctuations in order to make electoral choices. To this important topic I now turn.

5 Clarifying Responsibility

Although there is a large body of evidence spanning many countries and several research generations indicating that macroeconomic performance exerts sizeable effects on election outcomes, the connections exhibit considerable instability over time and, especially, space.[28] The failure of research to identify lawlike relationships has sometimes been taken to be a generic deficiency of macroeconomic voting models, but this view is mistaken. Rational voters logically will hold government accountable for macroeconomic outcomes that elected authorities have capacity to influence. Such capacity varies in time and space, depending, for example, upon national institutional arrangements, and the exposure of the national economies to external economic forces. This proposition forms the core of the "clarity of responsibility" hypothesis, which first was given sustained empirical attention in Powell and Whitten's (1993) comparative study of economic voting in nineteen industrial societies during the period 1969–88.

The empirical strategy pursued by Powell and Whitten and many who followed[29] amounts to allowing estimates of macroeconomic effects on voting to vary over

[27] Alesina and Rosenthal (1995, 202) claimed that their rational retrospective models have functional forms that "resemble the distributed lag empirical specifications of Hibbs (1987)." But this assertion is erroneous because, as shown earlier, their competence models always yield oscillation in the signs of the effects of lagged growth rates on current voting outcomes.

[28] The instability is documented by Paldam 1991. Mueller (2003, table 19.1) summarizes quantitative estimates of macroeconomic voting effects obtained in many studies.

[29] Examples include Anderson 2000; Hellwig 2001; Lewis-Beck and Nadeau 2000; Nadeau, Niemi, and Yoshinaka 2002; Pacek and Radcliff 1995; Taylor 2000; Whitten and Palmer 1999.

sub-groups of elections classified by institutional conditions believed to affect the "coherence and control the government can exert over [economic] policy" (Powell and Whitten 1993, 398).[30] This line of research has delivered persuasive evidence that macroeconomic effects on voting are indeed more pronounced under institutional arrangements clarifying incumbent responsibility—where clarity was taken to vary positively with the presence of single- as opposed to multiparty government, majority as opposed to minority government, high as opposed to low structural cohesion of parties, and the absence of strong bicameral opposition. The contribution to understanding instability of macroeconomic voting—particularly cross-national instability—has been substantial, yet mainly empirical, without reference to an explicit theoretical foundation.

The absence of a theoretical referent is odd because a compelling framework, which might have been used to practical advantage in empirical work on instability of economic voting, had emerged during the first part of the 1970s in the unobserved errors-in-variables and latent variables models of Goldberger (1972a, 1972b), Griliches (1974), Jöreskog (1973), Zellner (1970), and others, and those models had been applied to a wide variety of problems in economics, psychology, and sociology during the following twenty years.[31] Moreover, the errors-in-variables specification error model was applied directly to the problem of unstable economic voting a full decade before the appearance of Powell and Whitten (1993) in a brilliant paper by Gerald Kramer (1983), which was targeted mainly on the debate launched by Kinder and Kiewiet (1979) concerning the degree to which voting behavior is motivated by personal economic experiences ("egocentric" or "pocketbook" voting),[32] rather than by evaluations of government's management of the national economy ("sociotropic" or "macroeconomic" voting).[33]

Kramer's argument, which subsumed the responsibility hypothesis, was that voters rationally respond to the "politically relevant" component of macroeconomic performance, where, as in the subsequent empirical work of Powell and Whitten and others, political relevance was defined by the policy capacities of elected authorities. Suppose

---

[30] The responsibility thesis per se actually was proposed much earlier by researchers studying associations of voting behavior reported in opinion surveys to respondents' perceptions of personal and national economic developments; for example, Feldman 1982; Fiorina 1981; Hibbing and Alford 1981; Lewis-Beck 1988. The novel contribution of Powell and Whitten 1993 was to link "responsibility" to variation in domestic institutional arrangements in cross-national investigations of macroeconomic voting. Institutional determinants of economic voting motivated by the responsibility theme subsequently began to appear in a great many papers based on survey data, but this work falls outside the scope of this chapter.

[31] In fact, models with unobserved variables appeared as far back as the 1920s in the pioneering work of Sewell Wright. Goldberger 1972b gives a warm account of Wright's contributions, which were neglected outside his own domain of agricultural and population genetics until the late 1960s.

[32] This is the traditional *Homo economicus* assumption. In Downs's words, "each citizen casts his vote for the party he believes will provide him with more benefits than any other" (1957, 36).

[33] As Kinder and Kiewiet put it "The sociotropic voter asks political leaders not 'What have you done for me lately?' but rather 'What have you done for the country lately?' . . . sociotropic citizens vote according to the country's pocketbook, not their own" (1979, 156, 132).

voting is determined by

$$V = a + \sum_{k=1}^{K} \beta_k X_k^g + u \qquad u \sim white\text{-}noise \qquad (25)$$

where without loss of generality I drop time subscripts and abstract from dynamics. The variables determining voting outcomes, X_k^g, denote unobserved, politically relevant components of observed variables, X_k. The observables may be characterized by the errors in variables relations

$$X_k = X_k^g + e_k \qquad E\left(e_k, u\right) = E\left(e_k, X_k^g\right) = 0, k = 1, 2, \ldots K \qquad (26)$$

where e_k represent politically irrelevant components, beyond the reach of government policy.[34] Regression experiments based on observables take the form

$$V = \tilde{a} + \sum_{k=1}^{K} \tilde{\beta}_k X_k + \tilde{u} \qquad \tilde{u} = u - \sum_{k=1}^{K} \beta_k e_k, \qquad (27)$$

and they suffer from specification error because the true model (25) implies

$$V = a + \sum_{k=1}^{K} \beta_k X_k - \sum_{k=1}^{K} \beta_k e_k + u. \qquad (28)$$

It follows that least-squares estimation of the mis-specified equation (27) yields in the Yule notation

$$E\left(\tilde{\beta}_1\right) = \beta_1 - \beta_1 b_{e_1, x_1 | x_{k \neq 1}} - \beta_2 b_{e_2, x_1 | x_{k \neq 1}} - \ldots - \beta_K b_{e_K, x_1 | x_{k \neq 1}}$$
$$\vdots \qquad (29)$$
$$E\left(\tilde{\beta}_K\right) = \beta_K - \beta_1 b_{e_1, x_K | x_{k \neq K}} - \beta_2 b_{e_2, x_K | x_{k \neq K}} - \ldots - \beta_K b_{e_K, x_K | x_{k \neq K}}$$

where the b's denote partial regression coefficients obtained from (notional) auxiliary multiple regressions of each omitted e_k on $\sum_{k=1}^{K} X_k$.[35] The direction of the biases in principle can go in either direction. In general, however, in this errors-in-variables setting the partial coefficients will satisfy $b_{e_k, x_k | x_{j \neq k}} \simeq b_{e_k, x_k}$ and $b_{e_k, x_j | x_{k \neq j}} \simeq 0$. (Put to words, the partial association of each measurement error e_k, projected on the associated X_k and conditioned on the remaining $X_{j \neq k}$, will generally be nearly equal

---

[34] Kramer did not impose the restriction $E(e_k, X_k^g) = 0$ on the argument that government policies are sometimes designed to offset exogenous shocks to the macroeconomy. I believe a more appropriate view is that shocks to which government does or could respond are incorporated by voters to the politically relevant component X_k^g, leaving e_k as the politically irrelevant residual.

[35] Hence, in the partial b's the first subscript pertains to the omitted measurement error, the second subscript pertains to the included variable associated with the $\tilde{\beta}$ estimate, and the third subscript corresponds to all other included independent ("controlled") variables in the estimated voting equation. The number of terms contributing to the bias equals the number of omitted measurement errors.

to the corresponding bivariate projection.) It follows that asymptotically

$$\text{plim } \tilde{\beta}_k \simeq \beta_k - \beta_k \text{ plim} (b_{e_k, x_k}) \simeq \beta_k - \beta_k \cdot \frac{\sigma^2_{e_k}}{\left(\sigma^2_{e_k} + \sigma^2_{x^g_k}\right)} \qquad (30)$$

$$\simeq \beta_k \cdot \frac{\sigma^2_{x^g_k}}{\left(\sigma^2_{e_k} + \sigma^2_{x^g_k}\right)} \simeq \frac{\beta_k}{\left(1 + \frac{\sigma^2_{e_k}}{\sigma^2_{x^g_k}}\right)}, \quad k = 1, 2, \ldots, K$$

where σ^2 and σ denote population variances and standard deviations, respectively. Least-squares regressions therefore deliver estimates asymptotically biased downward in proportion to the reciprocal of the signal to noise ratio. Equations (25)–(30) supply a transparent specification error theoretical framework for interpretation of the instability of macroeconomic voting which has produced so much hand-wringing in the literature.

The implications of equation (30) for "clarity of responsibility" and political relevance are straightforward. One would expect, for example, that the politically relevant fraction of macroeconomic fluctuations would have lesser magnitude in small open economies with high exposure to international economic shocks than in large, structurally more insulated economies. The relevant fraction would logically also be comparatively low in countries in which prior political decisions divest government of important policy capacities; for instance, membership in the European Monetary Union, which deprives national authorities of monetary policy and unfettered deficit finance as instruments of macroeconomic stabilization.[36] The same reasoning implies that politically relevant variance would be low in systems with fractionalized parties and coalition governments, by comparison with two-party systems yielding one-party domination of policy during a typical government's tenure. Such considerations most likely explain why macroeconomic effects on voting outcomes generally are found to be more pronounced and more stable in two-party systems that are relatively insulated from international economic shocks (notably the United States[37]) than elsewhere.

---

[36] Rodrik 1998 showed that small open economies with high terms of trade risk tend to have comparatively large public sector shares of GDP, and comparatively large-scale public financing of social insurance against risk. Hibbs 1993 applied measurement specification error theory to evaluate research on Scandinavian and US economic voting, and conjectured that in big welfare states with weak aggregate demand policy capacities, macroeconomic fluctuations would logically have less impact on electoral outcomes than welfare state spending and policy postures. Pacek and Radcliff 1995 supplied aggregate evidence for seventeen developed countries observed over 1960–87, demonstrating that the effect of real income fluctuations on aggregate voting outcomes in fact declined with the size of the welfare state. Hellwig 2001 presented micro evidence covering nine developed democracies in the late 1990s indicating that economic voting declined with trade openness.

[37] I of course do not mean to suggest that the USA is immune to external economic shocks that logically are beyond the control of domestic political authorities. During the postwar period, the OPEC supply shocks of 1973–4 and 1979–81 are probably the most dramatic counter-examples. Hibbs (1987, ch. 5) devised a way to build those shocks into macroeconomic models of political support.

The domestic political-institutional variables featured in the research of Powell and Whitten (1993) and others, along with structural economic variables such as trade openness, domestic product concentration, and terms of trade risk featured in Rodrik's (1998) analysis of international variation in the size of government, appear to make excellent instruments for identifying the impact of politically relevant macroeconomic performance on voting outcomes when only gross performance is observed, which is of course always the case in national accounts data. It could be more illuminating, however, to entertain explicit latent structure models of the form

$$\mathbf{X} = \mathbf{X}^g + \mathbf{e} = \mathbf{Z}\boldsymbol{\gamma}_1 + (\mathbf{Z} \cdot \mathbf{X}_{-\tau})\boldsymbol{\gamma}_2 + \mathbf{e} \tag{31}$$

$$V = \alpha + \mathbf{X}^g \boldsymbol{\beta} + u \tag{32}$$

$$V = \alpha + \mathbf{X}^g \boldsymbol{\beta} + (\mathbf{X} - \mathbf{X}^g)\boldsymbol{\theta} + u \tag{33}$$

where $\mathbf{Z}$ represents a matrix of predetermined institutional and structural economic variables of the sort discussed above that are believed to affect political relevance. Equations (31) and (32) or (31) and (33) could be estimated either jointly by a full-information maximum-likelihood procedure, or in two-step fashion yielding reduced form voting equations such as[38]

$$V = \alpha + \hat{\mathbf{X}}^g \boldsymbol{\beta} + (\mathbf{X} - \hat{\mathbf{X}}^g)\boldsymbol{\theta} + \tilde{u} \tag{34}$$

where $\hat{\mathbf{X}}^g = \mathbf{Z}\hat{\boldsymbol{\gamma}}_1 + (\mathbf{Z} \cdot \mathbf{X}_{-\tau})\hat{\boldsymbol{\gamma}}_2$. Notice that models in the form of (33) and (34) permit direct tests of whether "politically relevant" variation in macroeconomic conditions dominate voting outcomes in the presence of "politically irrelevant" residuals. By comparison to current practice in the "clarity of responsibility" trade, empirical experiments based on test equations such as (31)–(34) hold excellent prospects of enhancing understanding of stability of macroeconomic voting over time and space.

6 Concluding Remarks

Research on voting and the macroeconomy emerged around three generations ago. However, all the way up until the end of the 1960s studies of macroeconomic voting were for the most part a-theoretical, and relied upon rudimentary graphical, tabular, and correlational analyses to investigate empirical regularities. The gradual integration of the General Linear Model—the statistical workhorse of social science—into graduate training programs beginning in the late 1950s, along with the appearance of Downs's monumental work in 1957, laid the foundations for econometrically sophisticated, theoretically grounded research. Yet for a decade or more following Kramer's

---

[38] It is not appropriate for me to get into identification and efficient estimation issues here. Pagan 1984 supplies an excellent analysis of various specific set-ups, including models like (31)–(34). The references cited earlier in this chapter to the econometric work in the 1970s on unobserved variables are also centrally relevant.

landmark 1971 paper, the lion's share of empirical studies were based mainly on free-form regressions only tenuously connected to a theory of electoral choice.

During the past dozen years theory, method, and knowledge have advanced significantly. The liveliest debates have centered on whether the electorate's valuation horizons are retrospective or prospective, and on the degree to which voters internalize domestic institutional arrangements and international economic forces that constrain the capacity of elected authorities to manage national economies. Research on institutional determinants of clarity of responsibility has exploded over the past decade, but testing formats are commonly ad hoc regressions populated by various interaction and conditioning variables that are not well motivated by either substantive or econometric theory. The potential leverage offered by unobserved, latent variable models, which were fully developed by the mid-1970s, remains unexploited. Some guidance, or at least commiseration, might be also be found in the analogous efforts to bring institutional factors to bear on measurement of "potential incomes" in neoclassical models of economic growth.[39] Nonetheless, the incorporation of institutional and international constraints to models of economic voting is an important development that is likely to progress steadily and productively.

Rational retrospective voting theory has appealing theoretical coherence, but it has not yet delivered any empirical value added. As matters stand, it gives every sign of going the way of the "surprise" macroeconomics paradigm generally—theoretical elegance devoid of empirical relevance, leading inevitably to abandonment. There is no reason in principle why voters might not apply mixed prospective and retrospective standards of political valuation and electoral choice, but no one has figured out how to implement the combination empirically, aside from studies based on perceptions about future outcomes obtained from opinion surveys.[40] But such survey data suffer

---

[39] I review a range of such efforts in Hibbs 2001.

[40] One can find regressions in the literature that allegedly test forward voting by using actual future outcomes as regressors. Such "perfect foresight" models have no logical foundation, because no one is endowed with perfect foresight; at best voters have rational expectations about the future. Considered at any election period t, rationality of expectations means that regressor(s) X satisfy

$$X_{t+T} = E_t(X_{t+T}) + e_{t+T}, \quad e_{t+T} \sim \text{white-noise}, \quad E[E_t(X_{t+T}), e_{t+T}] = 0 \qquad (35)$$

and that defensible voting models should be of the form:

$$V_t = \beta E_t(X_{t+T}) + u_t.$$

"Perfect foresight" models like

$$V_t = \beta(X_{t+T}) + u_t^*$$

are mis-specified because a logically admissible model, written in terms of actual future outcomes, implicitly would be

$$V_t = \beta[X_{t+T} - e_{t+T}] + u_t,$$

that is, $u_t^* = u_t - \beta e_{t+T}$. Clearly u_t^* is negatively correlated with regressors X_{t+T}. Consequently, perfect foresight models deliver estimates of β that are biased toward zero, and that could even have the wrong sign in more elaborate, mixed retrospective–prospective set-ups.

from severe problems of projection and rationalization, and for those reasons are viewed by many with profound skepticism. Devising models that bring forward-looking, competency models to macroeconomic data with statistical power poses one of the greatest challenges to future research.

REFERENCES

ALESINA, A., LONDREGAN, J., and ROSENTHAL, H. 1993. A model of the political economy of the United States. *American Political Science Review*, 87: 12–33.

―― and ROSENTHAL, H. 1995. *Partisan Politics, Divided Government and the Economy*. Cambridge: Cambridge University Press.

ANDERSON, C. 2000. Economic voting and political context: a comparative perspective. *Electoral Studies*, 19: 151–70.

BARRO, R. J. 1973. The control of politicians: an economic model. *Public Choice*, 14: 19–42.

BLINDER, A. 1985. Comments on "Rationality, causality, and the relation between economic conditions and the popularity of the parties" by Gebhard Kirchgässner. *European Economic Review*, 28: 269–72.

DOWNS, A. 1957. *An Economic Theory of Democracy*. New York: HarperCollins.

DRAZEN, A. 2000. *Political Economy in Macroeconomics*. Princeton, NJ: Princeton University Press.

ERIKSON, R., MACKUEN, M., and STIMSON, J. 2002. *The Macro Polity*. Cambridge: Cambridge University Press.

FAIR, R. 1978. The effect of economic events on votes for president. *Review of Economics and Statistics*, 60: 159–72.

FELDMAN, S. 1982. Economic self-interest and political behavior. *American Journal of Political Science*, 26: 446–66.

FEREJOHN, J. 1986. Incumbent performance and electoral control. *Public Choice*, 50: 5–25.

―― 1999. Accountability and authority: toward a theory of political accountability. In *Democracy, Accountability, and Representation*, ed. A. Przeworski, S. Stokes, and B. Manin. Cambridge: Cambridge University Press.

FIORINA, M. 1977. An outline for a model of party choice. *American Journal of Political Science*, 21: 601–28.

―― 1981. *Retrospective Voting in American National Elections*. New Haven, Conn.: Yale University Press.

GÄRTNER, M. 1994. Democracy, elections, and macroeconomic policy: two decades of progress. *European Journal of Political Economy*, 10: 85–109.

GOLDBERGER, A. 1972a. Maximum-likelihood estimation of regression models containing unobservable variables. *International Economic Review*, 13: 1–15.

―― 1972b. Structural equation models in the social sciences. *Econometrica*, 40: 979–1001.

GRILICHES, Z. 1974. Errors in variables and other unobservables. *Econometrica*, 42: 971–98.

HAMILTON, J. 1994. *Time Series Analysis*. Princeton, NJ: Princeton University Press.

HELLWIG, T. 2001. Interdependence, government constraints and economic voting. *Journal of Politics*, 63: 1141–62.

HIBBING, J., and ALFORD, J. 1981. The electoral impact of economic conditions: who is held responsible? *American Journal of Political Science*, 25: 423–39.

HIBBS, D. 1982a. President Reagan's mandate from the 1980 elections: a shift to the right? *American Politics Quarterly*, 10: 387–420.

———1982b. On the demand for economic outcomes: macroeconomic performance and mass political support in the United States, Great Britain and Germany. *Journal of Politics*, 44: 426–62.

———1987. *The American Political Economy: Macroeconomics and Electoral Politics in the United States*. Cambridge, Mass.: Harvard University Press.

———1993. *Solidarity or Egoism?* Aarhus: Aarhus University Press.

———2000. Bread and peace voting in U.S. presidential elections. *Public Choice*, 104: 149–80.

———2001. The politicization of growth theory. *Kyklos*, 54: 265–86.

JÖRESKOG, K. 1973. A general method for estimating a linear structural equation system. In *Structural Equation Models in the Social Sciences*, ed. A. Goldberger and O. D. Duncan. New York: Seminar Press.

KEY, V. O. 1966. *The Responsible Electorate: Rationality in Presidential Voting 1936–1960*. Cambridge, Mass.: Harvard University Press.

KINDER, D., and KIEWIET, D. 1979. Sociotropic politics: the American case. *British Journal of Political Science*, 11: 129–61.

KIRCHGÄSSNER, G. 1985. Rationality, causality, and the relation between economic conditions and the popularity of the parties. *European Economic Review*, 28: 243–68.

KORMENDI, R., and MEGUIRE, P. 1990. A multicountry characterization of the nonstationarity of aggregate output. *Journal of Money, Credit and Banking*, 22: 77–93.

KRAMER, G. 1971. Short-term fluctuations in U.S. voting behavior, 1896–1964. *American Political Science Review*, 65: 131–43.

———1983. The ecological fallacy revisited: aggregate- versus individual-level findings on economics and elections, and sociotropic voting. *American Political Science Review*, 77: 92–111.

LEWIS-BECK, M. 1988. *Economics and Elections: The Major Western Democracies*. Ann Arbor: University of Michigan Press.

——— and NADEAU, R. 2000. French electoral institutions and the economic vote. *Electoral Studies*, 19: 171–82.

——— and STEGMAIER, M. 2000. Economic determinants of electoral outcomes. *Annual Review of Political Science*, 3: 183–219.

MANKIW, N. G., and SHAPIRO, M. 1985. Trends, random walks and tests of the permanent income hypothesis. *Journal of Monetary Economics*, 16: 165–74.

MONROE, K. 1979. Econometric analyses of electoral behavior: a critical review. *Electoral Behavior*, 1: 37–73.

MUELLER, D. 2003. *Public Choice III*. Cambridge: Cambridge University Press.

NADEAU, R., NIEMI, R., and YOSHINAKA, A. 2002. A cross-national analysis of economic voting: taking account of political context across time and nations. *Electoral Studies*, 21: 403–23.

NANNESTAD, P., and PALDAM, M. 1994. The VP function: a survey of the literature on vote and popularity functions after twenty-five years. *Public Choice*, 79: 213–45.

NORDHAUS, W. 1975. The political business cycle. *Review of Economic Studies*, 42: 169–90.

PACEK, A., and RADCLIFF, B. 1995. Economic voting and the welfare state: a cross-national analysis. *Journal of Politics*, 57: 44–61.

PAGAN, A. 1984. Econometric issues in the analysis of regressions with generated regressors. *International Economic Review*, 25: 221–47.

PALDAM, M. 1991. How robust is the vote function? A study of seventeen nations over four decades. In *Economics and Politics: The Calculus of Support*, ed. H. Norpoth, M. Lewis-Beck, and J. D. Lafay. Ann Arbor: University of Michigan Press.

PELTZMAN, S. 1990. How efficient is the voting market? *Journal of Law and Economics*, 33: 27–63.

POWELL, G. B., and WHITTEN, G. 1993. A cross-national analysis of economic voting: taking account of political context. *American Journal of Political Science*, 37: 391–414.

Rodrik, D. 1998. Why do more open economies have bigger governments? *Journal of Political Economy*, 106: 997–1032.

Rogoff, K. 1990. Equilibrium political budget cycles. *American Economic Review*, 80: 21–36.

—— and Sibert, A. 1988. Elections and macroeconomic policy cycles. *Review of Economic Studies*, 55: 1–16.

Stigler, G. 1973. General economic conditions and national elections. *American Economic Review: Papers and Proceedings*, 63: 160–7.

Stock, J., and Watson, M. 2003. Forecasting output and inflation: the role of asset prices. *Journal of Economic Literature*, 41: 788–829.

Suzuki, M., and Chappell, H. 1996. The rationality of economic voting revisited. *Journal of Politics*, 58: 224–36.

Taylor, M. 2000. Channeling frustrations: institutions, economic fluctuations, and political behavior. *European Journal of Political Research*, 38: 95–134.

Whitten, G., and Palmer, H. 1999. Cross-national analyses of economic voting. *Electoral Studies*, 18: 49–67.

Zellner, A. 1970. Estimation of regression relationships containing unobservable independent variables. *International Economic Review*, 11: 441–54.

CHAPTER 32

THE POLITICAL ECONOMY OF EXCHANGE RATES

J. LAWRENCE BROZ

JEFFRY A. FRIEDEN

THE exchange rate is the most important price in any economy, for it affects all other prices. In most countries, policy toward the national currency is prominent and controversial. Economic epochs are often characterized by the prevailing exchange rate system—the Gold Standard Era, the Bretton Woods Era. Contemporary developments, from the creation of an Economic and Monetary Union in Europe to successive waves of currency crises, reinforce the centrality of exchange rates to economic trends.

The analysis of the *political economy* of currency policy has focused on two sets of questions. The first is global, and has to do with the character of the international monetary system. The second is national, and has to do with the policy of particular governments towards their exchange rates. These two interact. National policies, especially of large countries, have an impact on the international monetary system. By the same token, the global monetary regime influences national policy choice.

At the frontiers of research, political economists are grappling with the complexities of this interaction, analyzing the linkages between the international and domestic aspects of exchange rate policy-making. In this chapter, we start by separating the analysis of the international monetary system from the analysis of the policy choices of national governments. This allows us to simplify the issues in each area and present them in generic political economy terms. We then discuss how the issues might be analyzed jointly, across the domains, in the next phase of research.

1 THE INTERNATIONAL POLITICAL ECONOMY OF EXCHANGE RATE POLICY

International monetary regimes tend toward one of two ideal types. The first is a fixed rate system, in which currencies are tied to each other at publicly announced rates. Some fixed rate systems involve a common link to a commodity such as gold or silver; others peg to a national currency such as the US dollar. The second ideal-typical monetary regime is free floating, in which national currency values vary with market conditions and national macroeconomic policies. There are many potential gradations between these extremes.

In the past 150 years, the world has experienced three broad international monetary orders. For about fifty years before the First World War, and again in modified form in the 1920s, most of the world was on the classical gold standard, a quintessential fixed rate system. Under the gold standard, governments committed to exchange gold for currency at an announced rate. From the late 1940s until the early 1970s, the capitalist world was organized into the Bretton Woods monetary order, a modified fixed rate system. Under Bretton Woods, currencies were fixed or "pegged" to the US dollar and the US dollar was fixed to gold. However, national governments could change their exchange rates when they deemed it necessary. Under this "adjustable peg" system, currencies were not as firmly fixed as under the classical gold standard. Since 1973 the reigning order has been one in which the largest countries have had floating national currencies, while smaller countries have tended either to fix their currencies against one of the major currencies or to allow their currencies to float with varying degrees of government management.

Monetary regimes can be regional as well as global. Within the international monetary free-for-all that has prevailed since 1973, a number of regional fixed rate systems have emerged. Some countries have fixed their currency to that of a larger nation: the franc zone of the African Financial Community, or "CFA franc zone," ties the currencies of fourteen African countries to each other and to the French franc (now to the euro). Several countries in Latin America and the Caribbean have pegged their exchange rates to the US dollar. European monetary integration began with a limited regional agreement, evolved into a Deutschmark link, and eventually became a monetary union with a single currency and a common central bank. Countries in the eastern Caribbean and southern Africa have also developed monetary unions.

Analyses of international monetary regimes treat nation states as decision-making units (like "firms" in microeconomics) and consider how these units deal with standard *coordination* and *cooperation* problems. Coordination entails interaction among governments to converge on a focal point—for example, linking national currencies to gold or to the dollar. This implies the existence of a Pareto improving equilibrium (often more than one), such as is the case in an assurance game, in which each actor wants to choose the same strategy as other actors. In this case, each country wants to choose the same currency regime as other countries—nobody wants to be the only country on gold, or the only country to float—but may disagree over which one to choose. Cooperation among nation states involves the adjustment of national policies to support the regime—such as joint intervention in currency markets. This implies the existence of a Pareto inferior Nash equilibrium, which can be improved upon (i.e. to a Nash bargaining solution), such as is the case in a prisoner's dilemma game: countries can work together to improve their collective and individual welfare. The two problems are not mutually exclusive; indeed, the resolution of one usually presupposes the resolution of the other. But for purposes of analysis it is helpful to separate the idea of a fixed rate system as a focal point, for example, from the idea that its sustainability requires deliberately cooperative policies.

Coordination in international monetary relations. An international or regional fixed rate regime, such as the gold standard or the European Monetary System, has important characteristics of a focal point around which national choices can be coordinated (Meissner 2005; Frieden 1993). Such a fixed rate system can be self-reinforcing: the more countries that were on gold, or pegged to the Deutschmark, the greater the benefits to other countries of also choosing to go along. This can be true even if the motivations of countries differ: one might particularly appreciate the monetary stability of a fixed rate, the other the reduction in currency volatility. It does not matter, so long as the attractions of the regime increase with its membership (Broz 1997).

Most fixed rate regimes appear to grow in this way, as additional membership attracts ever more members. This was the case of the pre-1914 gold standard, which owed its start to gold-standard Britain's centrality to the nineteenth-century international economy, and its eventual global reach to the accession of other nations to the British-led system. European monetary integration also progressed in this manner, as the Deutschmark zone of Germany, Benelux, and Austria gradually attracted more European members. The focal nature of a fixed rate system can lead to a "virtuous circle" as more and more countries sign on, but the unraveling of the regime can lead to a "vicious circle." The departure of important countries from the system can reduce its centripetal pull, as with the collapse of the gold standard in the 1930s: British exit began a stampede which led virtually the rest of the world off gold within a couple of years.

We have illustrated coordination problems by reference to fixed rate regimes, but similar problems arise in floating rate regimes. Members of a floating regime can benefit—individually and jointly—by committing to a common standard on payments and exchange restrictions (Simmons 2000). A focal point in this respect is the voluntary standard on payments restrictions embodied in the International Monetary Fund's Articles of Agreement. The IMF standard proscribes governments from rationing or limiting access to foreign exchange when citizens request it to pay for imports or service a foreign debt. This promotes international trade, which benefits all members. Simmons (2000) finds strong evidence of regional diffusion effects, suggesting that the gains of adopting the standard increase with the number of nations in a region that do so.

Cooperation in international monetary relations. International monetary relations may require the resolution of problems of cooperation. A fixed rate system may give governments incentives to "cheat," such as to devalue for competitive purposes while taking advantage of other countries' commitment to currency stability. Even a system as simple as the gold standard sometimes relied on agreements among countries to support each others' monetary authorities in times of difficulty. An enduring monetary system, in this view, requires explicit cooperation among its principal members.

The welfare gains associated with interstate collaboration in the international monetary realm are several. First, reduced currency volatility almost certainly increases international trade and investment. Second, fixed rates tend to stabilize *domestic* monetary conditions, so that international monetary stability reinforces domestic monetary stability. Third, predictable currency values can reduce trade conflicts: a rapid change in currency values often leads to an import surge, protectionist pressures, and commercial antagonism.

These joint gains may be difficult to realize because they can require national sacrifices. Supporting the fixed rate system may require painful adjustment policies to sustain a country's commitment to its exchange rate. Governments may be forced to raise interest rates to high levels in order to defend an overvalued currency, and the domestic economic and political consequences can lead to conflict over the international distribution of adjustment costs. For example, under Bretton Woods and the European Monetary System, one country's currency served as the system's anchor. This forced other countries to adapt their monetary policies to the anchor country, and led to pressures on the key-currency government to bring its policy more in line with conditions elsewhere. Under Bretton Woods, from the late 1960s until the system collapsed, European governments wanted the United States to implement more restrictive policies to bring down American inflation, while the US government refused. In the EMS in the early 1990s, governments in the rest of the European Union wanted Germany to implement less restrictive policies to combat the European recession, while the German central bank refused. Generally speaking, the better able countries are to agree about the distribution of the costs of adjustment, the more likely they are to be able to create and sustain a common fixed rate regime.

Historically, intergovernmental cooperation has been crucial to the durability of fixed rate monetary systems. Barry Eichengreen (1992) argues that credible cooperation among the major powers before 1914 was the cornerstone of the classical gold standard, while its absence explains the interwar failure to revive the regime. Many regional monetary unions, too, seem to obey this logic: where political and other factors have encouraged cooperative behavior to safeguard the common commitment to fixed exchange rates, the systems have endured, but in the absence of these cooperative motives, they have decayed (Cohen 2001).

Two recent regional ventures, Economic and Monetary Union in Europe (EMU) and dollarization in Latin America, illustrate these international factors. Dollarization appears largely to raise coordination issues, as national governments consider independent choices to adopt the US dollar. The principal attraction for dollarizers is association with dollar-based capital and goods markets; the more countries dollarize, the greater this attraction will be. The course of EMU from 1973 to completion did have features of a focal point, especially in the operation of the European Monetary System as a Deutschmark bloc, but the transition to EMU went far beyond this. Participants bargained over the structure of the new European Central Bank, the national macroeconomic policies necessary for membership in the monetary union, and a host of other issues. These difficult bargains were unquestionably made much easier by the small number of central players, the institutionalized EU environment, and the network of policy linkages between EMU and other European initiatives.

Despite the importance of international factors, international monetary cooperation and coordination rest on the foundation of national currency policies, which are subject to an array of political economy pressures.

2 THE DOMESTIC POLITICAL ECONOMY OF EXCHANGE RATE POLICY

Political factors *within* nations give rise to two basic types of pressures for—or against—coordination and cooperation in the international arena. On the one hand, exchange rate policies involve trade-offs with domestic *distributional* implications. International coordination or cooperation may not find sufficient support within a nation, if the losers are sufficiently powerful. On the other hand, exchange rate policies have *electoral* implications. The exchange rate is such an important price that politicians may wish to manipulate it for the purpose of winning elections, rather than stabilizing an international regime. We suggest ways in which distributional politics and electoral politics might interact with external monetary conditions to shape exchange rate outcomes.

Two fundamental currency decisions confront policy-makers, and each has distributional consequences. First, policy-makers must decide whether to heed external signals and join the dominant international or regional regime. This *regime decision* involves choosing whether to allow the currency to float freely, to be fixed against some other currency, or to adopt a system in between a hard fix and a pure float. Second, for all but irrevocably fixed rate regimes, policy-makers also confront choices involving the level of the exchange rate, the price at which the national currency trades in foreign exchange markets. *Level decisions* fall along a second continuum that runs from a more depreciated to a more appreciated currency. Although regime and level decisions are interconnected, we treat them separately to illustrate their distinct political economy implications.

Choice of exchange rate regime. Regime decisions involve trade-offs among desired national goals, whose benefits and costs fall unevenly on actors within countries. Fixed rate regimes have two main national benefits. First, they promote trade and investment by reducing exchange rate risk. Countries that share a common currency or have a long-term peg appear to trade much more than comparable countries with separate currencies (Rose 2000). Second, fixed rates promote domestic monetary stability. By anchoring the value of the domestic currency to a low-inflation currency (or gold), monetary officials are constrained to follow a time-consistent path of low inflation (Giavazzi and Pagano 1988; Canavan and Tommasi 1997). The cost of fixing is the flip side of this benefit: forfeiture of domestic monetary policy independence. When local monetary conditions cannot differ from conditions in the anchor country, monetary policy cannot be used for domestic macroeconomic stabilization.

The distributional effects of regime choice follow from these aggregate costs and benefits: groups involved in foreign trade and investment (international banks and investors, exporters) should favor fixed rate systems because exchange rate stability promotes trade and investment (Frieden 1991). By contrast, groups whose economic activity is limited to the domestic economy (non-tradeables producers, import-competing sectors) should prefer a floating regime that allows the government to stabilize domestic economic conditions.

Scholars have examined the role of interest groups in exchange rate regime determination in a variety of contexts, from the historical gold standard to contemporary currency politics in Europe and Latin America. Many have found that interest groups line up as anticipated, and that they seem to have an impact on policy outcomes (Hefeker 1995; Eichengreen 1995; Frieden 1997; Frieden, Ghezzi, and Stein 2001; Frieden 2002). However, research on the role of distributionally motivated interest groups in currency relations is not well developed. The determinants of interest group preferences require more detailed analysis, to specify more precisely how economic characteristics of firms and industries relate to their exchange rate preferences. More attention also needs to be paid to organizational characteristics of such interest groups, to show how their features relate to their ability to engage in collective political action.

In many instances, interest group preferences are relevant inasmuch as they are mediated through political parties (Bearce 2003). Some have argued that centrist and rightist parties are likely to support fixed regimes as their business constituencies benefit from the credible commitment to low inflation, and from the expansion of trade and investment made possible by fixing (Simmons 1994). Left-wing parties, by contrast, favor flexible regimes since labor bears the brunt of adjusting the domestic economy to external conditions. However, the character of partisan influences on exchange rate policy is not straightforward and further analysis will need to clarify their operation, and how they, in turn, relate to differences in electoral and legislative institutions.

Another suggestion for future work is to give more attention to how international regime conditions affect domestic lobbying. For example, an implication of the focal point interpretation of international regimes is that interest group pressures might be the mechanism by which nations coordinate on a certain international regime, as suggested by Frieden (1993) and Broz (1997). In this account, the reason why the attraction of joining an international regime increases with the number of members is that interest group lobbying intensifies with the growth of a regime. Researchers have also recognized that regime choice has electoral implications, which vary with the structure of political institutions (Bernhard and Leblang 1999). It is easy to envision scenarios in which an office-seeking politician would be loath to join a fixed-rate international regime, as it would mean depriving himself of a tool to influence the economy for electoral purposes. In countries where the stakes in elections are high (e.g. single-member plurality systems), politicians may prefer a floating regime as a means to preserve the use of monetary policy to engineer greater support before elections. Where elections are not as decisive (e.g. proportional representation systems), fixing has smaller electoral costs, implying that fixed regimes are more likely to be chosen. When the timing of elections is predetermined, governing parties are less likely to surrender monetary policy by pegging, since it can be a useful tool for winning elections. When election timing is endogenous, there is less need for monetary flexibility, so pegging is more likely.

In the developing world, it may be the absence of democracy, rather than its form, that matters. One regularity is that non-democracies are more likely to adopt a fixed regime for low inflation purposes than democracies (Broz 2002; Leblang 1999). Non-democracies may peg because they are more insulated from domestic audiences, and bear lower political costs of adjusting the economy to the peg. Or they may peg because other alternatives, like central bank independence (CBI), are less viable in a closed political system. More generally, if fixed exchange rates and CBI are alternative forms of monetary commitment, then it is necessary to analyze the decision as a joint policy choice in which governments weight the costs and benefits of *all* alternatives (Bernhard, Broz, and Clark 2003). Analysts might pursue the idea that currency regimes and domestic monetary institutions are policy substitutes, and try to explain why some nations prefer exchange rate-based sources of low inflation credibility while others adopt domestic rules and institutions. Part of the explanation may reside outside the scope of domestic institutions and politics, in the character of the international monetary regime. At the margins, the existence of a large global or regional fixed rate regime may tip the decision toward an exchange rate-based stabilization, by adding the political economy benefits of greater trade to the extant credibility gains.

To appreciate or depreciate? As with the regime decision, the choice of the level of the exchange rate has distributional and electoral implications. Of course, governments cannot directly set the real exchange rate, but they can affect trends in the real exchange rate over a period long enough to be of political and economic significance—typically estimated at three to five years. Thus a government must decide whether it prefers a relatively appreciated or a relatively depreciated currency. This choice involves a basic political-economy trade-off between *competitiveness* and *purchasing power*.

The real exchange rate affects the relative price of domestically produced goods in local and foreign markets, and it also affects the purchasing power of those who earn the currency. A real appreciation increases the purchasing power of local residents, by lowering the relative price of foreign (more generally, tradeable) goods. However, by making domestic goods more expensive relative to foreign goods, it reduces the "competitiveness" of local tradeables producers. A real depreciation has the opposite effects, reducing purchasing power but improving competitiveness by lowering the price of domestically produced goods.

There is no clear economic guideline as to the appropriate level of the exchange rate. A relatively depreciated currency encourages exports and expenditure switching from imports to domestic goods, thereby boosting aggregate output. However, depreciation can have contractionary effects that follow from higher prices. While the net effect on overall national welfare is very hard to calculate, the level of the exchange rate has clear distributive consequences domestically. Export and import competing industries lose and domestically oriented (non-tradeables) industries gain from currency appreciation (Frieden 1991). Domestic consumers/voters also gain as the domestic currency price of imported (and tradeable) goods falls, lowering the cost of living. Currency depreciations have the opposite effects, helping exporting and import competing industries at the expense of domestic consumers and non-traded industries.

Group currency preferences are affected by economic factors, and their ability to turn these preferences into policy is affected by political institutions. Economically, the distributional impact of exchange rate changes is contingent on economic characteristics of industries and firms, for example the sensitivity of product prices to currency movements. Many goods prices do not respond rapidly to changes in currency values, a phenomenon associated with the fact that foreign producers are reluctant to "pass through" the exchange rate change to local consumers for fear of losing market share. Producers of goods with low pass-through—specialized, highly differentiated products, such as automobiles—will be less concerned with the exchange rate than producers of goods with high pass-through, typically more standardized products. By the same token, the extent to which an industry relies on imported intermediate inputs will also determine whether it is harmed or helped by appreciation (Campa and Goldberg 1997).

A number of regularities about preferences over the currency level can be identified. These are related to points made above about regime preferences. For example, the argument that producers of simple tradeables are relatively insensitive to currency volatility complements the argument that they are very sensitive to the level of the exchange rate: producers of commodities and simple manufactures will prefer a flexible regime and a tendency for a depreciated currency. On the other hand, the argument that producers of complex and specialized tradeables are very sensitive to currency volatility complements the argument that they are relatively insensitive to the level of the exchange rate: these producers will prefer a fixed regime. Capturing an industry's (or an entire nation's) sensitivity to exchange rate changes involves measuring the extent to which it sells products to foreign markets, uses foreign-made inputs, and, more indirectly, competes with foreign manufacturers on the basis of price (Frieden, Ghezzi, and Stein 2001).

The panoply of interests in the exchange rate makes the political institutions within which they are expressed particularly important to explaining policy outcomes.

Political institutions affect the impact of special interests on economic policy, including on exchange rate policy. By the same token, exchange rate policies are likely to be affected by varieties of electoral institutions, and by election timing. This is because the real exchange rate affects broad aggregates like purchasing power, growth rates, and the price level, and these broad aggregates are almost certainly relevant to elections. Indeed, governments tend to maintain appreciated currencies before elections, delaying a depreciation/devaluation until after the election (Klein and Marion 1997; Frieden, Ghezzi, and Stein 2001; Leblang 2002). Electoral cycles in exchange rate policy help explain some characteristics of the currency crises that have been common over the past twenty years. Although the causes of currency crises are controversial (Corsetti, Pesenti, and Roubini 1999), delaying devaluation certainly makes the problem worse. Given the political unpopularity of a devaluation-induced reduction in national purchasing power, governments may face strong incentives to avoid devaluing even when the result is a more severe crisis than would otherwise be expected. In Mexico in 1993–4 and Argentina in 1999–2001, for example, electorally motivated delays almost certainly led to far more drastic currency collapses than would have otherwise been the case. The electoral cycle is likely to be muted in countries where the central bank has sufficient insulation from political pressures, or the government has a time horizon long enough to endogenize the higher costs of delayed action on the exchange rate. Political institutions condition the extent to which politicians are willing or able to respond to short-run electoral incentives.

Interest group activity on the level of the exchange rate varies greatly over time and across country, and its impact on policy is a function of national political institutions. Analyses of the politics of exchange rate policy evaluate both special and mass-political interests, and the institutions within which they are expressed, and have found strong evidence of interest group and election cycle effects on policy.

One research frontier is the role of exchange rate policy as a substitute for other policies (and vice versa). For example, currency policy and trade policy are close substitutes: a 10 per cent real depreciation is equivalent to a 10 per cent import tax plus a 10 per cent export subsidy. Hence, the tradeables sector can organize on an industry-by-industry basis to seek trade barriers or export subsidies, or as a whole to attempt to obtain a depreciation. This requires careful consideration of the organizational, political institutional, and other factors that might lead private actors to pursue one policy or the other, and public policy-makers to use one policy or the other. Exchange rate policies are similarly closely related to policies toward capital flows, financial regulation, and many other arenas. A full analysis of the political economy of exchange rate policy requires consideration of its alternatives.

Another research challenge is to integrate the external regime environment into analyses of the domestic politics of exchange rate levels. The character of the extant regional or international exchange rate regime may condition national policy decisions on whether to appreciate or depreciate the currency. On the one hand, an external regime with explicit rules and sanctions regarding members' exchange rate policies can make it difficult for a nation pressured by weak-currency interests to depreciate for competitive purposes. On the other, regime rules and monitoring mechanisms may limit the ability of national politicians to manipulate exchange rates for electoral purposes, especially if such manipulations impose costs on other governments.

3 CONCLUSIONS

Exchange rates are prominent features of economic life, and the study of their political economy is important. Scholars have made substantial progress in understanding how regional and international currency regimes emerge and evolve, and why governments pursue the exchange rate policies they do.

At the international level, the study of global and regional monetary regimes has incorporated developments in the analysis of international coordination and cooperation to explain the origin and operation of such systems over the past two centuries. At the domestic level, there is a reasonably well-developed set of arguments about the economic interests at stake, and about how political institutions affect currency policy choices.

Future research confronts several challenges. First, it needs to continue to integrate international and domestic sources of exchange rate policy. Just as national policymakers take the international regime into account when deciding how to manage their currencies, so too should our models. Second, it needs to clarify and refine the theoretical and empirical uncertainties that remain in existing scholarship. Third, in concert with scholars in other areas of political economy, it needs to incorporate the impact of such closely related issue areas as trade and financial policy on international monetary affairs. These are substantial challenges, but the past ten years have seen impressive progress in the study of exchange rate politics, and there is no reason to doubt that the coming decades will be just as fruitful.

REFERENCES

BEARCE, D. 2003. Societal preferences, partisan agents, and monetary policy outcomes. *International Organization*, 57: 373–410.

BERNHARD, W., BROZ, J. L., and CLARK, W. R. 2003. *The Political Economy of Monetary Institutions*. Cambridge, Mass.: MIT Press.

—— and LEBLANG, D. 1999. Democratic institutions and exchange-rate commitments. *International Organization*, 53: 71–97.

BROZ, J. L. 1997. The domestic politics of international monetary order: the gold standard. Pp. 53–91 in *Contested Social Orders and International Politics*, ed. D. Skidmore. Nashville: Vanderbilt University Press.

—— 2002. Political system transparency and monetary commitment regimes. *International Organization*, 56: 861–87.

CAMPA, J., and GOLDBERG, L. S. 1997. The evolving external orientation of manufacturing: a profile of four countries. *Federal Reserve Bank of New York Economic Policy Review*, 3: 53–70.

CANAVAN, C., and TOMMASI, M. 1997. On the credibility of alternative exchange rate regimes. *Journal of Development Economics*, 54: 101–22.

COHEN, B. J. 2001. Beyond EMU: the problem of sustainability. Pp. 179–204 in *The Political Economy of European Monetary Unification*, 2nd edn., ed. B. Eichengreen and J. Frieden. Boulder, Colo.: Westview Press.

CORSETTI, G., PESENTI, P., and ROUBINI, N. 1999. What caused the Asian currency and financial crisis? *Japan and the World Economy*, 11: 305–73.

EICHENGREEN, B. 1992. *Golden Fetters*. Oxford: Oxford University Press.

—— 1995. The endogeneity of exchange rate regimes. Pp. 3–33 in *Understanding Interdependence*, ed. P. Kenen. Princeton, NJ: Princeton University Press.

FRIEDEN, J. A. 1991. Invested interests: the politics of national economic policy in a world of global finance. *International Organization*, 45: 425–51.

—— 1993. The dynamics of international monetary systems: international and domestic factors in the rise, reign, and demise of the classical gold standard. Pp. 137–62 in *Coping with Complexity in the International System*, ed. R. Jervis and J. Snyder. Boulder, Colo.: Westview Press.

—— 1997. Monetary populism in nineteenth-century America: an open economy interpretation. *Journal of Economic History*, 57: 367–95.

—— 2002. Real sources of European currency policy: sectoral interests and European monetary integration. *International Organization*, 56: 831–60.

—— GHEZZI, P., and STEIN, E. 2001. Politics and exchange rates: a cross-country approach to Latin America. Pp. 21–63 in *The Currency Game: Exchange Rate Politics in Latin America*, ed. J. A. Frieden and E. Stein. Baltimore: Johns Hopkins University Press.

GIAVAZZI, F., and PAGANO, M. 1988. The advantage of tying one's hands: EMS discipline and central bank credibility. *European Economic Review*, 32: 1055–75.

GOWA, J. 1988. Public goods and political institutions: trade and monetary policy processes in the United States. *International Organization*, 42: 15–32.

HEFEKER, C. 1995. Interest groups, coalitions and monetary integration in the nineteenth century. *Journal of European Economic History*, 24: 489–536.

KLEIN, M. W., and MARION, N. P. 1997. Explaining the duration of exchange-rate pegs. *Journal of Development Economics*, 54: 387–404.

LEBLANG, D. 1999. Democratic political institutions and exchange rate commitments in the developing world. *International Studies Quarterly*, 43: 599–620.

—— 2002. The political economy of speculative attacks in the developing world. *International Studies Quarterly*, 46: 69–91.

MEISSNER, C. M. 2005. A new world order: explaining the international diffusion of the gold standard, 1870–1913. *Journal of International Economics*, 66: 385–406.

ROSE, A. 2000. One money, one market: estimating the effect of common currencies on trade. *Economic Policy*, 30: 7–46.

SIMMONS, B. 1994. *Who Adjusts?* Princeton, NJ: Princeton University Press.

—— 2000. International law and state behavior: commitment and compliance in international monetary affairs. *American Political Science Review*, 94: 819–35.

PART IX

DEMOCRACY AND CAPITALISM

CHAPTER 33

CAPITALISM AND DEMOCRACY

TORBEN IVERSEN

1 INTRODUCTION

A QUESTION permeates much comparative political economy from the classics to contemporary scholarship: how it is possible to combine capitalism with democracy? The former produces stark inequalities in the distribution of property and income, while the latter divides power in a manner that is in principle egalitarian (one person, one vote). So why don't the poor soak the rich? And if they do, how can capitalism be viable as an economic system?

The answer to the first question depends a great deal on how economic interests are aggregated into public policies. We know from Arrow's impossibility theorem that getting a well-behaved "social welfare function" when there are multiple dimensions and no dictator is, well, impossible (Arrow 1951). In the case of distributive politics the policy space is inherently multidimensional since there are as many dimensions as there are agents fighting for a piece of the pie. Distributive politics under democratic rules—who gets how much, including whether the poor soak the rich—is therefore anything but straightforward. Like the proverbial elephant in the corner of the room that everyone ignores, most of the existing political economy literature on democracy has skirted the issue. But it cannot be ignored. It is fundamental to how we understand distributive politics under democracy.

Answering the second question requires an understanding of how economic agents respond to the democratic pressures for redistribution. If the state undermines the market, as commonly assumed, how can we explain the economic success of countries that spend well over half their gross domestic products on social protection and redistribution? If the welfare state is built on the shoulders of an unwilling capitalist class, should we not expect capitalists to shun productive investment, stage coups, or move their money abroad? Yet the welfare state has not collapsed, democracy is spreading, and globalization has not resulted in convergence around laissez-faire capitalism. If we want to understand how democracy and capitalism coexist, therefore, we need a model of capitalism that goes beyond a simple dichotomy between state and market.

This chapter discusses three different approaches to the study of democratic redistribution, and then considers the recent literature on capitalism as an economic system and how economic and democratic institutions may relate to each other. The first approach assumes that democratic politics is structured around a single left–right redistributive dimension. The central issue in this literature is how democratic politics affects who sets public policies, and much of the debate centers on the question of partisanship: Does "Who Governs" matter, and if so, in what ways? This is a key question for political economy because it goes to the heart of whether democratic politics makes a difference: Do the poor ever get a chance to try to soak the rich, and how successful are they when they do? In Section 3 I discuss some plausible answers.

The main weakness of this approach is that it largely ignores the question of what happens when several political agents compete in a multidimensional distributive space (the elephant in the corner). It is hard to understand why politicians should limit themselves to pursuing redistribution in a single predetermined policy dimension, and when they do not, opportunities to form distributive coalitions abound. The work that puts coalitional politics at the center of the analysis, which I discuss in Section 4, paints a richer and more realistic picture of the politics of redistribution. But the cost may be theoretical intractability, and much of the coalitional literature falls into the trap of *post hoc* description. Description, no matter how accurate, will not produce explanation. At the end of the section I discuss two recent attempts to move beyond such description.

The third approach explains distributive politics as a function of the specific design of democratic institutions—including electoral rules and federalism. The strategy here is to replace ad hoc model assumptions, such as unidimensionality, with ones that are rooted in careful observation of actual institutional designs. This approach moves beyond the partisan literature by explicitly considering how economic preferences are aggregated into policies, at the same time as it avoids the chaotic world of unconstrained coalitional politics. As I argue in Section 5, this combination has produced a vibrant research program that helps answer key questions such as the conditions under which the poor are more likely to soak the rich.

The modern study of capitalism as an economic system has also taken an institutionalist turn, building on transaction costs economics rather than neoclassical models. The "varieties of capitalism" approach, in particular, illuminates the relationship between redistributive politics and economic performance and helps explain why there is no necessary contradiction between state and market. The work also helps make sense of the observed institutional diversity of modern capitalism, and why such diversity persists in the face of global market integration. But the tradition has thus far produced few insights into the relationship between economic and political institutions, and it has little to say about the political origins of economic institutions—focusing instead on economic-organizational efficiency as a cause.

The lack of a theory of institutional origins also haunts the literature on political institutions. As Riker (1980) argued many years ago, institutions are "congealed tastes" which themselves have to be explained. Some of the latest literature on democracy and capitalism seeks to endogenize institutions, including the institution of democracy itself, by modeling these as a function of class interests. This brings us right back to the elephant in the corner because without institutional constraints, the issues of multidimensionality and preference aggregation re-emerge. In the concluding section I suggest that there is a new structuralist turn in political economy, where the parameters for our models of institutional design are derived from the specific historical conditions that shaped capitalism in different parts of the world. But I start with a brief discussion of some of the most important precursors for the contemporary literature.

2 Precursors for the Contemporary Literature

In a seminal article, Przeworski and Wallerstein (1982) give a simple answer to the question of why the poor don't soak the rich. Any attempt at radical redistribution, or socialism, they argue, would be met by massive disinvestment and possibly violence by the upper classes. So even if the poor would ultimately be better off in a system where private property rights were suspended (itself a big if, of course), the "valley of transition" would dissuade any rational government with a limited time horizon from attempting it. Conversely, the rich might consent to democracy and redistribution because the costs of repression or the threat of revolution would otherwise be too high. "Class compromise," in other words, could be an equilibrium. This model wiped out the notion in the Marxist literature that capitalism could only survive if the lower classes were repressed or misinformed.

Class compromise has survived as a central concept (e.g. Swenson 1991; Garrett 1998; Acemoglu and Robinson 2005), but conceptualizing capitalist democracy as a class compromise does not itself take us very far in explaining the variance in policies and outcomes across countries. Although it is easy to think that democracy—as a particular form of government—and capitalism—as a particular type of economic system—would produce similar policies and outcomes, one of the most striking facts about capitalist democracies is the enormous cross-national variance in inequality, social spending, redistribution, and the structure of social protection. A full-time Norwegian worker in the top decile of the income distribution, for example, earns about twice as much as someone in the bottom decile, whereas in the United States this ratio is well over four (based on 2000 data from the OECD). The extent to which democratic governments redistribute also varies to a surprising degree. According to data from the Luxembourg Income Study the reduction in the poverty rate in the United States as a result of taxation and transfers was 13 per cent in 1994 whereas the comparable figure for Sweden was 82 per cent.

There are two standard approaches to explaining this variance, which frame much of the current debate (even as the literature has moved beyond the original formulations). One is Meltzer and Richard's (1981) model of redistribution, which has been the workhorse in the political economy for two decades (see also Romer 1975). The model is built on the intuitively simple idea that since the median voter tends to have below-average income (assuming a typical right-skewed distribution of income) he or she has an interest in redistribution. With a proportional tax and flat rate benefit, and assuming that there are efficiency costs of taxation, Downs's median voter theorem can be applied to predict the extent of redistribution. The equilibrium is reached when the benefit to the median voter of additional spending is exactly outweighed by the efficiency costs of such spending. This implies two key comparative statics: spending is higher (*a*) the greater the skew in the distribution of income, and (*b*) the greater the number of poor people who vote.

The latter suggests that an expansion of the franchise to the poor, or higher voter turnout among the poor, will shift the decisive voter to the left and therefore raise support for redistribution. Assuming that the median voter's policy preference is implemented, democratization will therefore lead to redistribution. There is some support for this proposition (see Rodrik 1999 on democracy and Franzese 2002, ch. 2 on turnout), although the evidence is contested (see Ross 2005).

The first implication—that inegalitarian societies redistribute more than egalitarian ones—has been soundly rejected by the data (see Bénabou 1996; Perotti 1996; Lindert 1996; Alesina and Glaeser 2004; Moene and Wallerstein 2001). Indeed, the pattern among democracies appears to be precisely the opposite. As noted in the example above, a country with a flat income structure such as Sweden redistributes much more than a country like the USA with a very inegalitarian distribution of income. Sometimes referred to as the "Robin Hood paradox," this is a puzzle that informs much contemporary scholarship.

The other main approach to the study of capitalism and democracy focuses on the role of political power, especially the organizational and political strength of labor. If capitalism is about class conflict, then the organization and relative political strength of classes should affect policies and economic outcomes. There are two variants of the approach. *Power resources theory* focuses on the size and structure of the welfare state, explaining it as a function of the historical strength of the political left, mediated by alliances with the middle classes (Korpi 1983, 1989; Esping-Andersen 1990; Huber and Stephens 2001). *Neo-corporatist theory* focuses on the organization of labor and its relationship to the state—especially the degree of centralization of unions and their incorporation into public decision-making processes (Schmitter 1979; Goldthorpe 1984; Cameron 1984; Katzenstein 1985).

Both variants have come under attack for not paying sufficient attention to the role of employers. Research by Martin (1995), Swenson (2002), and Mares (2003), for example, suggests that employers did not simply oppose social policies, but in fact played a proactive role in the early formation of such policies. Also, if the welfare state is built on the shoulders of employers, we should expect investment and economic performance to suffer. But the remarkable fact is that there is no observed relationship between government spending, investment, and national income across advanced democracies (Lindert 1996). Or if there is one, it is so weak that it does not appear to have imposed much of a constraint on governments' ability to spend and regulate labor markets. The neo-corporatist variant is more satisfactory in this respect because it suggests how encompassing unions may choose wage restraint, which leads to higher profits and investment. But this cannot be the whole story since corporatist arrangements were dismantled in the 1980s, often led by export-oriented employers who presumably care deeply about wage restraint (Pontusson and Swenson 1996; Iversen 1996).

A more fundamental question is why conflict should be organized around class and not, say, around sector or occupational group. When people make investments in specific assets, which may be physical or human capital, their interests will be tied up with those investments rather than the collective interest broader class to which they belong (Frieden 1991; Iversen 2005). There is also no systematic account of how distributive conflict between different groups of wage earners gets worked out politically. Dividing a pie invites the formation of redistributive coalitions, and such coalitions cannot be modeled as simply a function of interests. This is clearly also a problem for the Meltzer–Richard model where the median voter is assumed to be king.

3 DEMOCRACY AND PARTISANSHIP

Median voter models are very simple to use, but as the Robin Hood paradox suggests, they do not provide much leverage on explaining the observed variance in redistributive politics. Power resources theory points to one potential source of such variation that has been subject to much research: government partisanship. If center-left governments *simultaneously* promote pre-fisc income equality and redistribution, partisanship may not only explain distributive outcomes but solve the Robin Hood paradox.[1] If partisanship is important in explaining distributive outcomes, we would expect equality and redistribution to go hand in hand.

Partisanship may also explain why corporatist institutions are not always conducive to good economic performance. In Lange and Garrett's (1985) well-known model of economic growth, "encompassing" unions that organize all or most workers are not likely to restrain wages if right partisan governments are in power that are not

---

[1] Governments may affect the primary distribution of income through public education (Boix 1998), through the facilitation corporatist bargains that promote wage equality (Cameron 1984; Katzenstein 1985; Garrett 1998), or through minimum wage legislation.

attentive to the long-term interests of labor. As I discuss in Section 5, this idea of "congruence" between policies and institutions is an important topic for contemporary models of capitalist institutions.

For partisanship to matter, the median voter theorem must be systematically violated, so there must be some explanation for why this should be the case. It is by no means obvious. Although Downs only applied his argument to majoritarian two-party systems, the median voter theorem also applies to multiparty systems where the median legislator can make take-it-or-leave-it proposals. Since no majority can be formed without the support of the median legislator, those proposals will become government policy. In simple unidimensional models of government formation the government always includes the party with the median legislator and does not even need a majority to govern since no viable alternatives can be formed (Laver and Schofield 1990). Yet, the comparative evidence seems to imply that partisanship matters (see, for example, Hicks and Swank 1992; Iversen 1998; Huber and Stephens 2001; Cusack 1997; Allan and Scruggs 2004; Kelly 2005; Kwon and Pontusson 2005).

One explanation is suggested by Wittman's (1973) model of probabilistic voting.[2] If two parties represent constituencies with distinct interests on any set of issues, and if they face uncertainty about the election outcome, the platforms that maximize the implementation of the parties' preferred policies will be away from the median. Since their expected utility is the product of the probability of winning times the proximity of policies to parties' ideal point, parties trade off a lower probability of winning for a policy that is closer to their preference. The Wittman model has found wide application in the study of two-party systems, where one of its attractive features is that it can handle multidimensional spaces (more on this below).

Another explanation for partisanship is that political parties, to be electorally successful, have to appeal to core constituents who provide the money and activists required to run effective electoral campaigns (Hibbs 1977; Schlesinger 1984; Kitschelt 1994; Aldrich 1993, 1995). Aldrich (1983) has formalized this idea in a Downsian model with party activists in which party leaders exchange policy influence to relatively extreme core constituents for unpaid work during campaigns.[3] The logic is illustrated by the American primary system where successful presidential candidates first have to win the support of the parties' core constituents before they can contest the general election. In the general election they have an incentive to moderate their image to appeal to the median voter, but since they were chosen as candidates on different platforms, the perception among voters of real policy differences is accurate.

Aldrich's amended Downsian model raises a critical issue of commitment in politics—an issue that is also important for understanding partisanship. If the winning electoral platform in an election is the median voter preference, but candidates

---

[2] For a more exhaustive discussion of the different possibilities in two-party systems, see Grofman 2004.

[3] An interesting model along these lines has been developed by McGann 2002. In the McGann model voters sort themselves into parties based on their platforms, and the platforms of parties are determined by their members (the median members to be precise). Needless to say, this set-up produces policy divergence.

represent partisan constituencies, how can their commitment to the median voter be credible? Downs largely skirted this issue by assuming that party platforms had to be consistent over time, but it is now standard to assume that such commitments cannot be credible (Persson and Tabellini 1999, 2000). In modern political macroeconomics, for example, governments have a short-term incentive before elections to make the economy look better by using inflationary policies, even as such policies are unsustainable and have deleterious long-run effects (Alesina, Cohen, and Roubini 1992; Franzese 2002; Adolph 2005; Clark 2003).[4] This creates room for partisan politics.[5]

"Citizen-candidates" models takes this idea to its logical conclusion by assuming that candidates cannot commit to anything other than their own preferred policies (Osborne and Slivinski 1996; Besley and Coate 1997). With two candidates and costs of running, the equilibrium is away from the median voter because otherwise one citizen would not find it worthwhile to enter the race (why run if someone is already representing you?). With strategic voting this divergence can be quite large because voters may not want to switch from an existing candidate to a more moderate entrant in the fear that this may cause the least preferred candidate to win.

Turning from party competition to government formation, new bargaining models also do not bear out the idea that the median legislator can dictate policy. If there is real bargaining taking place, Rubinstein bargaining theory essentially implies that parties will split their policy differences. The threat to break off negotiations and initiate bargaining with another party cannot easily be used by the median party to get its way. The reason is that if there are *any* costs of switching (which may simply be the cost of a delay), the new bargaining partner has no incentive to offer a bargain that is better than the original *minus* the cost of switching.[6] As long as parties have different policy preferences, as in the citizen-candidate model, governments will therefore be away from the median.

But while there are compelling reasons why partisanship matters, a critical issue that has largely been skirted is why some countries are dominated by center-left governments and others by center-right governments. In the absence of such dominance we may get partisan political business cycles, as argued by Alesina and others (Alesina, Cohen, and Roubini 1992), but partisanship could no longer explain persistent cross-national differences in policies and outcomes. Nor could partisanship serve as a credible commitment mechanism as it does in the Lange–Garrett model (since partisanship would change in the future). In fact, government partisanship *does* vary significantly across democracies (see Powell 2002; Iversen and Soskice 2002), and much of the evidence for the importance of partisanship is cross-national.[7]

---

[4] Stokes 1999 offers an interesting alternative in which parties appeal to the short-term interests of voters in the election only to pursue longer-term group interests after the election.

[5] There is a very large literature on the political economy of macroeconomics that is not discussed here. Much of this literature originates with Hibbs's seminal 1977 article and is discussed by Hibbs in his contribution to this volume.

[6] This can be inferred from the "outside option principle" in bargaining theory (Osborne and Rubinstein 1994, 128), although the only proof I am aware of is in Soskice and Iversen 2005.

[7] Power resource theory implies that this is due to differences in the strength of the labor movement. But unionization, or the size of the industrial working class, are in fact poor predictors of partisanship.

Rather surprisingly, most of the literature also fails to distinguish between the preferences of parties and the preferences of voters. Observed policy differences between left and right governments could be due to either. There are methodological fixes to this problem—such as comparing the ideological composition of the government to that of the legislature, or focusing on "natural experiments" where the outcome approximates a random assignment of the partisan "treatment" (say, in very close elections)—but we also need a theory of voter preferences. Since voters have an incentive to be "rationally ignorant," as argued by Downs many years ago, it is not really satisfactory to assume that parties simply reflect the interests of citizens. Partisan models must also explain how interests are defined and become common knowledge—a major agenda for future research.

4 Multiple Dimensions and Coalitional Politics

As noted in the introduction, distributive politics is inherently multidimensional because a pie can be divided along as many dimensions as there are political agents vying for a piece. It is therefore hard to understand why politicians should constrain themselves to contest a single policy instrument such as the proportional tax/flat rate benefit in the Meltzer–Richard model. And when alternative tax-benefit schedules are considered the results change. In Snyder and Kramer (1988), for example, the choice is over different—linear and non-linear—tax schedules, and the majority choice is no longer redistribution that benefits the poor. The Snyder–Kramer model is itself restricted to one dimension (because it limits the choice to single-parameter schedules subject to an exogenously given revenue target), but it demonstrates the sensitivity of model predictions to the tax-benefit assumptions they make.[8]

One of the first to recognize the importance of multidimensional distributive politics was Esping-Andersen (1990). He distinguishes three different "worlds" of welfare capitalism—each associated with a distinct tax-benefit structure. In the most redistributive (social democratic) type, progressive taxation is coupled with flat rate benefits; in the "liberal" type means-tested benefits are targeted to the poor; while in the "conservative" type benefits are tied to income and occupation. Esping-Andersen makes a plausible (and interesting) argument that the structure of benefits is associated with, and perhaps causes, different social divisions and political patterns: the poor against the middle class in the means tested, insiders versus outsiders in the conservative, and public against private sector in the social democratic. To explain redistributive politics, political economy therefore has to endogenize the structure of benefits.

[8] The winner in the Snyder–Kramer model is the middle class—a result that is echoed in some multidimensional models discussed below.

Clearly this task can be accomplished neither with a median voter model, nor with a simple left–right partisan model. Building on the majestic work of Moore (1971), Esping-Andersen instead suggests that the answer lies in historically unique class coalitions. Red-green coalitions in Scandinavia forced socialist parties (which lacked stable majorities) to accept universalism. State-corporatist coalitions in continental Europe were forged by autocrats like Bismarck to stem the rise of the labor movement. In countries such as Britain and the USA, where the state and the left were both relatively weak, social issues were essentially dealt with through an extension of the old poor laws, allying the middle class with higher income groups.

Echoing the recent literature on path dependence (Pierson 2000), Esping-Andersen then suggests that the structure of the benefit system re-produces the political support for each type. But neither the origins of the three worlds, nor their stability, can be said to be *explained* since there is no argument to preclude alternative outcomes. For example, why would it not be possible for liberal welfare states to expand redistribution towards the middle class? Or why does the middle class not try to exclude the poor from sharing in the generous benefits of the social democratic model? Or why can outsiders not offer a deal to a subset of insiders in the conservative model that would cause the coalition to break up? Without any explicit theory, much of Esping-Andersen's analysis comes across as *post hoc* description.

One could make a similar charge against Lowi's (1964) account of public policy-making. Like Esping-Andersen's work, however, it provides a convincing account of the numerous forms that distributive politics can take. Specifically, Lowi distinguishes between distributive, regulatory, and redistributive politics. Distributive politics refers to a situation where narrowly defined groups or constituencies, such as congressional districts, seek to maximize their share of appropriations. Since most of the cost can be externalized, everyone pushes for more spending and no one has a sufficiently strong incentive to prevent others from doing the same: "I agree to spend on your project if you agree to spend on mine." The result is what Olson terms "distributive coalitions," characterized by excessive and wasteful spending.

Unlike the quiet, behind-the-scenes logrolling of distributive politics, regulatory politics pits losers against winners as some are advantaged and others disadvantaged by public policies (public procurement decisions, licensing, and other regulatory decisions). Redistributive politics of the Meltzer–Richard variety is also contentious, but the divisions are now across class instead of sector. In a sense, therefore, the nature of public policy (distributive, regulatory, or redistributive) can be predicted by the policy area. Yet, it is hard to see how "policy area" can be treated as a truly exogenous variable any more than the benefit structure in Esping-Andersen's story can. Sure, we know that the New Deal involved class politics and major redistribution, and it clearly contrasts to Lowi's other types, but to move beyond *post hoc* description needs a theory of why distributive politics takes on particular forms at particular times.

Dixit and Londregan's (1996, 1998) model of transfer spending takes us one step in this direction. Assuming probabilistic voting, if two parties do not know individual voter preferences but do know the distribution of such preferences by groups, and if loyalty to different parties varies across groups, vote-maximizing parties will concentrate transfers on the groups with the most "swing" voters. The principle is to distribute transfers so that the marginal vote gain for each dollar spent is exactly the same across all groups. Not surprisingly, groups that have a lot of swing votes will be advantaged because the returns (in terms of votes) of investing in these groups are higher than in other groups. With the additional assumption that loyalists are concentrated among the rich and the poor (those with "extreme" preferences), the implication is that middle class will receive most of the transfers [9]—a result that is known as "Director's Law".

An assumption that is not explained is why parties cannot compete for the loyalty of ideologically committed voters. For example, if African-Americans are loyal to the Democrats because of the party's position on affirmative action (or for any other reason for that matter), then there is no reason Republicans cannot appeal to these voters by adopting a more pro-affirmative action platform. Yet, if loyalty is endogenous to party strategies we are right back into strange world of multidimensional politics without a core. The same is true if we drop the two-party assumption since the "divide the pie" game then does not predict any stable coalition. What is lost by adopting restrictive model assumptions is therefore the ability to consider more complex patterns of coalition formation, and that limits the usefulness of the model for comparative purposes.

Modeling multidimensional coalitional politics is at the center of several new attempts to understand distribution in democracies. In Roemer's (1997, 2001) model, people have intrinsic preferences on some ascriptive dimension such as race or religion, in addition to preferences over redistribution. If the redistributive dimension was the only one that mattered, the analysis would essentially collapse to a Meltzer–Richard model. When a second dimension is introduced, however, the right party can appeal to poor religious or racist voters, and the left party is forced to respond by attracting more wealthy anticlerical or anti-racist voters. As this "exchange" of voters takes place, the two constituencies will tend to become more similar in terms of income. The original pro-welfare coalition is thus broken apart by appeals to commonalities on another, non-economic, dimension. As Riker (1986) recognized informally many years ago, the (re-)bundling of issues is a critical component of coalitional politics, and it helps explain why the poor often don't soak the rich.[10]

Alesina and Glaeser (2004) make a related argument for why racial politics may undermine redistribution. If people feel altruistic only towards people of their own race, they will not redistribute to a minority that constitutes a disproportionate share of the poor. Of course, if solidarity with the poor is a "taste" then we need a theory of why people acquire this taste, and Alesina and Glaeser go on to argue that

---

[9] Not *necessarily* all because if utility is declining in income, and hence transfers, marginal vote gain of giving to groups with many swing voters will also be declining.

[10] The model is in fact more complicated because, once again, there is no equilibrium with majority voting in a multidimensional space. Roemer solves this problem in two alternative ways. In the first formulation one party gets to select its platform before the other party, producing a Stackelberg equilibrium. In another, different factions of both parties must all agree to the policy platform, and this reduces the feasible policy space to a single point.

elites that oppose redistribution can use the "race card" to undermine support for redistribution. This is similar to the logic in Roemer's model.

Austen-Smith and Wallerstein (2003) provide a quite different story about the importance of race. In their model people have "race-blind" preferences and are simply trying to maximize their net income. Yet the mere existence of a second dimension (here affirmative action) can cause a legislative coalition in favor of redistribution to break up. The reason (loosely speaking) is that the rich in the majority can offer a bargain to the minority that strengthens affirmative action but reduces redistribution to the poor. Of course, other coalitions are also feasible, but none that generate as much redistribution as bargaining over a single redistributive policy would.

The Roemer and Austen-Smith models are both very complex, but they suggest that countries with a higher dimensionality of the policy space also tend to have less redistribution. Przeworski and Sprague (1986) proposed a similar idea when they argued that left policies would become less prominent as party competition became more influenced by non-economic issues. Yet, to my knowledge no systematic comparative test of the effect of multidimensionality on redistribution has been carried out. Alesina and Glaeser present cross-national correlations between spending and racial, ethnic, and religious heterogeneity, but this is an area ripe for empirical research.

5 DEMOCRATIC INSTITUTIONS

As we have seen, some of the literature has dealt with the complexity of democratic politics by using highly simplifying model assumptions. The Meltzer–Richard model is a prominent example. Such simplifications lead to clear and deductively valid inferences, but they often come at a considerable cost in terms of realism. Those who believe that this cost is too great have turned to history and "thick description." Much of this work, such as Esping-Andersen's influential book on welfare capitalism, underscores the importance of coalitional politics and leads to compelling accounts of cross-national differences in policy regimes. Yet, *post hoc* description is not explanation and the few attempts to model the complexity of coalitional politics, while promising, are themselves complex and have so far produced little comparative research.

In the view of many scholars, focusing on the role of institutions strikes an attractive middle ground. Instead of ad hoc model assumptions, the constraints on political behavior are derived from observed characteristics of political and economic institutions, and instead of *post hoc* descriptions of behavior, outcomes are predicted from the interaction of purposeful behavior and institutional constraints.[11] The approach has been highly successful in explaining cross-national differences in economic policies and outcomes.

---

[11] "Institutions" defined broadly as the "rules of the game" (North 1990).

Other contributions to this volume go into considerable detail on the role of particular institutions. Here I pick some prominent examples that focus on either democratic institutions (this section) or economic institutions (the next section).[12] These examples are meant to be illustrative of the institutionalist approach, not an exhaustive discussion of the literature. I begin with a discussion of the role of the electoral system because it is a feature of democracies that varies a great deal *and* covaries with government spending, redistribution, and income equality (Persson and Tabellini 2005). This covariation has become the focus of intense scrutiny in recent work in comparative political economy.

In a path-breaking article, Carey and Shugart (1995) propose one way to understand the effects of electoral rules. They argue that the electoral system shapes the incentives of politicians either to toe the party line or to use their influence over public policies to cultivate a personal following. Confirming a long-standing intuition among students of political parties, the incentives for politicians to campaign on a broad party platform depends on the ability of parties to control politicians' re-election chances. The best-known means to accomplish such control is a closed party list system where a candidate's rank on the list determines that candidate's likelihood of re-election. By contrast, in systems where candidates are chosen through primaries, such as elections to the US Congress, political parties cannot directly control who gets on the ballot and politicians have a stronger incentive to pursue their own agendas and appeal to location-specific interests.

Carey and Shugart do not fully spell out the implications of their argument for economic policy, but an obvious hypothesis is that systems that encourage politicians to cultivate a personal following will lead to a targeting of public money to local projects and narrowly defined groups. An example is the pre-1994 Japanese system where candidates from the same party competed against each other for a single non-transferable vote, and therefore produced strong incentives for politicians to spend on their districts while ignoring the public interest. The consequence was a highly fragmented fiscal policy (Cox and Thies 1998; Rosenbluth and Thies 2001). This resonates with Lowi's notion of distributive politics, but in the Carey–Shugart framework the nature of the policy-making process is a function of the political system, which varies across time and space. Put another way, Carey and Shugart help explain differences in countries with respect to their use of policies across Lowi's categories.

In Persson and Tabellini's (1999, 2000) account, the critical institutional feature is the electoral formula. In majoritarian systems, they argue, if middle-class swing voters are concentrated in particular districts, parties have an incentive to ignore completely other districts that are leaning one way or the other ideologically. These districts are "safe" and therefore not worth fighting over. Similarly to Dixit and Londregan's model, money therefore flows to swing votes in middle-class districts. In single-district PR systems, by contrast, there are no safe districts so politicians cannot ignore the loss of support among other groups by concentrating transfers on

---

[12] For a comprehensive review of the "new" institutionalist literature see Hall and Taylor 1996.

the middle class. The result is greater dispersion of spending across classes (or more spending on broad public goods).

PR systems, however, tend to spend more on *both* transfers and public goods. To explain this Persson and Tabellini point to a "second-order effect" of PR, namely that PR systems tend to have more parties and be ruled by multiparty governments (see Ordeshook and Shvetsova 1994; Neto and Cox 1997 for the evidence). If each party wants to spend on its own group (so that the space is multidimensional), this can lead to a common-pool problem with excessive spending as a result (see also Bawn and Rosenbluth 2002; Crepaz 1998). Again, Lowi's distributive politics is here linked to an institutional feature that varies across countries.

Electoral systems also appear to be systematically related to class politics. Iversen and Soskice (2006) argue that when parties representing different classes have to form coalitions to govern, as is typically the case under PR, the center and left have an incentive to get together to soak the rich. This is not true in two-party majoritarian systems where parties are coalitions of classes. In this situation, middle-class voters can be soaked by the poor if the center-left party deviates from a median voter platform. Assuming that the right cannot engage in regressive redistribution, incomplete platform commitment therefore puts the median voter at risk and the center-left at an electoral disadvantage. The implication is that partisanship and redistribution, class politics in Lowi's scheme, systematically covary with electoral system.

Another democratic institution that has generated intense scholarly scrutiny is federalism. Much of the research in this area originates with Brennan and Buchanan's (1980) argument that competition between local governments for mobile sources of revenue undermines the ability of predatory governments to impose excessive taxation. Coupled with the potential ability of states to secede, which restricts the ability of central governments to exploit member states, federalism may also constitute a credible commitment to property rights—what Weingast (1995) calls "market-preserving federalism." Viewed from the left, this logic suggests that federalism may undermine the welfare state and lead to under-provision of social welfare or a "race to the bottom" (Pierson 1995).

A related argument is that federalism makes it harder to pass new legislation because it has to be ratified in two legislative assemblies. The implication is a status quo bias, which is sometimes argued to have slowed the expansion of the welfare state (Huber, Ragin, and Stephens 1993). But while federalism does appear to be associated with smaller governments, there is in fact a striking amount of variance across federalist states (Obinger, Leibfried, and Castles 2005). Swiss and US federalism seems to be linked to low spending, but this is not true of German or Austrian federalism.

To account for this variation, Rodden (2003, 2005) has proposed to distinguish between federalist systems with different fiscal institutions. If local spending is locally financed, tax competition puts a damper on spending, but if local spending is financed through central or intergovernmental grants, local politicians have little incentive to contain spending. This argument applies more generally to political systems where there is a division of labor between local governments and the center (a unitary system like Sweden, for example, exhibits a lot of local policy autonomy).

Revenue-sharing may be seen as a source of common-pool problems (or Lowi's distributive politics), or it may be seen as a method to reduce the power of those with mobile assets and empowering governments to pursue redistribution. Whatever the normative perspective, if there are two different types of federalism, one with a "soft" and one with a "hard" budget constraint, then a key issue is why some governments have adopted hard budget constraints while others have not (Wibbels 2003; Wildasin, this volume). Alternatively, there is a wealth of interesting variation in revenue-sharing between local governments and states that seems critical to fiscal policy, yet is not treated as an object of explanation. There *is* a literature on fiscal discipline and its consequences (see von Hagen and Harden 1995 and the von Hagen chapter in this volume), but budgetary rules are for the most part treated as exogenous.

By anchoring model assumptions in the rich details of actual political institutions, the new institutionalist literature enables the coupling of formal reasoning with the realism of inductive research. It reduces the indeterminism of democratic policy-making and suggests promising ways to endogenize partisanship, coalition formation, and styles of policy-making. Our understanding of fiscal policies and distributive outcomes has been greatly advanced in the process. But by highlighting the critical importance of institutional detail, one cannot help but wonder if the real task is not the explanation of the institutions themselves. I return to this question below. But first I turn to another successful branch of institutionalism that focuses on modern capitalism as an economic system.

6 Varieties of Capitalism

It is common to portray democratic capitalism as a system where markets allocate income according to efficiency while governments redistribute income according to political demand. This suggests a convenient intellectual division of labor between economists and political scientists, but it is based on a neoclassical view of the economy that few today believe. Instead, the dominant approach to the study of capitalism as an economic system builds on new institutional economics and is known as the "varieties of capitalism" (or VoC) approach (Hall and Soskice 2001). Just as democracy has been shown to divide into institutional subspecies, so has capitalism. As I discuss at the end of this section, there is in fact a close empirical association between political and economic institutions, although the reasons for this association are not well understood.

The VoC approach assumes that economic institutions are designed to help firms and other economic agents make the best use of their productive assets (Hall and Soskice 2001). As argued by Williamson (1985), North (1990), and others, when an economy is characterized by heavy investment in co-specific assets, economic agents are exposed to risks that make market exchange problematic.[13] A precondition for such an economy to work efficiently is therefore a dense network of institutions that provide information, offer insurance against risk, and permit continuous and impartial enforcement of complex contracts. In the complete absence of such institutions, exchange is possible only at a small scale in local trading communities where repeated face-to-face interactions enable reputational enforcement of contracts. At a larger scale, or with a greater division of labor, markets that are left to their own devices will either be accompanied by costly and continuous haggling, or be restricted to exchanges of very homogeneous goods.

Another central feature of the VoC approach is the idea that an institution has to be understood in relation to other institutions. Institutional complementarity means that the effectiveness of one institution depends on the design of another. Precursors for this idea are Lange and Garrett's (1985) congruence model (that I discussed above), as well as Streeck's (1991) account of the German model and Aoki's (1994) account of the Japanese. The VoC approach generalizes the idea and argues that *all* major institutions of capitalism are complementary to each other: the industrial relations system, the financial and corporate governance system, the training system, and the innovation system. For example, if firms make investments in their workers' skills, unions gain hold-up power that can be levied against the firms. This necessitates an industrial relations system where such hold-up power can be managed. Conversely, workers will be reluctant to acquire firm-specific skills unless firms can make credible long-term commitments, which require a financial system that provide access to "patient" capital, and a corporate governance system where workers are given influence, and so on.

Because of these institutional complementarities, one is not likely to find every logically conceivable combination of institutions in the real world. In fact, Soskice (1999) makes the claim that there are only two dominant types: one called liberal market economies (LMEs) and another called coordinated market economies (CMEs). Each is characterized by the extent to which institutions protect and encourage investment in assets that assist firms in pursuing particular product market strategies. In CMEs where firms and workers have invested heavily in assets that are specific to particular companies, industries, or jobs, institutions are designed to protect those investments.[14] In LMEs where such institutional protection is missing or weak, market competition encourages economic agents to make investments in general assets since, in the absence of protection, mobility is the best insurance against risks. This does not eliminate specific assets, but it will reduce their relative importance.

The VoC argument suggests a very different explanation for the welfare state than power resources theory. Mares (2003), for example, argues that companies and industries that are highly exposed to risk will favor a social insurance system where cost and

---

[13] Polanyi 1944 is an important precursor for many of these arguments.
[14] For example, unionized workers with specific skills possess very considerable potential hold-up power over firms, and firms will be unlikely to rely on workers with specific skills unless individual unions are constrained through an interfirm collective bargaining system. In turn there is strong evidence that such collective bargaining systems lead to a compression of wages (Rueda and Pontusson 2000; Wallerstein 1999).

risk are shared, leading employers to push universalistic unemployment and accident insurance. Although low-risk firms will oppose such spending, it is remarkable that universalism has been promoted by groups of employers since the literature associates it so closely with policies imposed on employers by unions and left governments. Manow (forthcoming) argues that social insurance systems shape the structure of production systems, and Estevez-Abe, Iversen, and Soskice (2001) and Iversen (2005) suggest that social protection (including job protection, unemployment benefits, income protection, and a host of related policies such as public retraining programs and industry subsidies) encourages workers to acquire specific skills, which in turn enhances the ability of firms to compete in certain international market segments.[15] The welfare state is thus linked to the economy in a manner that creates beneficial complementaries. This may help explain the lack of evidence for the deleterious effects of social spending on growth, and why globalization has not spelled the end to the welfare state.

A mostly unexplored topic in the VoC literature is the relationship between economic and political institutions. It is striking, for example, that the distinction between LMEs and CMEs is almost perfectly collinear with the distinction between PR and majoritarian electoral systems. One possible explanation, which goes back to Katzenstein's (1985) work on corporatism, is that PR promotes the representation of specialized interests in the legislature and its committees. At least this would be true if parties have incentives to accommodate each other's specific interests.[16] Majoritarian systems, by contrast, encourage parties to elect strong leaders in order to convince the median voter that they are not beholden to special interests. Such "leadership parties" are consequently not conducive to the protection of specialized interests and therefore encourage economic agents to make investments in more portable assets (say, college degrees as opposed to extensive vocational training).

Another reason for the coupling of electoral and economic systems may be that PR serves as a credible commitment to social protection because of its effect on class coalitions and redistribution. A high level of insurance will encourage investment in risky assets and hence support a particular type of firm.[17] This is a conjecture that still awaits careful empirical corroboration. In particular, it will need to be shown that the correlation between electoral systems and production regimes is not

[15] The skill argument may also account for some of the variation in labor market segregation between the sexes. Women appear to find it much harder than men to enter into specific skills jobs, and this may have to do with the differential ability of men and women to commit to uninterrupted careers (Estevez-Abe 1999; Iversen and Rosenbluth 2006).

[16] This logic may build on Laver and Shesple's (1996) model of government formation, since policies of multiparty governments in their theory reflect the distinct interests of the participating parties. Parties representing agriculture dominate the agricultural ministry, parties representing industry the industrial ministry, etc. It does require, however, that parties representing significant specific interests are not permanently excluded from policy influence.

[17] Although redistribution and insurance are analytically distinct, in practice they are closely related. The unemployed, the sick, the old, and those with low pre-fisc income more generally, will support redistribution and benefit from it. But for those who are currently employed, healthy, young, and enjoying a high income such redistribution is insurance against many of the vagaries of the capitalist economy.

a historical accident, but the result of a deliberate design of political institutions by representatives of particular economic interests.

The question of institutional origins, of course, is a matter that concerns the entire institutionalist approach to political economy. The more successful political economy is in explaining economic policies and outcomes with reference to the institutional design, the more pressing it is to explain why one design was chosen rather than another (Thelen 1999; Pierson 2000). But the question then is how we can approach this task without being overwhelmed by the complexity of institution-free politics. In the concluding section I ask whether the answer may lie in a structuralist approach.

7 Conclusion: Towards a New Structuralism?

A decade ago nearly all comparative political economists would have called themselves institutionalists. Today an increasing number of scholars are convinced that only way forward is by going back—back to the origins of institutions and the conditions that gave rise to them. The questions that are being asked by these scholars are fundamental: under which structural-economic conditions do autocracies move to democracy (Acemoglu and Robinson 2005; Boix 2003)? How do institutions emerge that will protect property rights and produce prosperity (North and Weingast 1989)? What are the origins of modern skill systems (Thelen 2004)? What accounts for differences in the structure of social programs (Mares 2003; Swenson 2002)? What are the origins of federalism (Wibbels 2003) and of electoral institutions (Boix 1999; Cusack, Iversen, and Soskice 2004)?

In a recent paper, Rogowski and MacRay (2003) conjecture that many of the institutional effects that have been documented in painstaking detail by decades of institutional research are in fact epiphenomenal to the structural conditions and interests that gave rise to them. If this is true, it puts a premium on understanding the "pre-strategic" policy preferences of agents and the circumstances that determine them. But if we make this move we need to understand that this could bring us head to head with that elephant in the corner: the chaos of institution-free politics. If we take this path, is there a way to avoid *post hoc* description or ad hoc modeling?

Take the example of Acemoglu and Robinson's (2005) theory of democratic transitions. This is one of the most sophisticated attempts to model democracy, yet it relies heavily on the simplifying assumptions of the Meltzer–Richard model. Understandably, Acemoglu and Robinson replace the lack of well-defined institutional constraints with the safe familiarity of a model that is easy to understand, but may omit important aspects of the coalitional dynamics.

There is however the outline of an alternative in Acemoglu and Robinson's book that I will loosely refer to as "new structuralism" (to distinguish it from Marxist structuralism, structural functionalism, and other previous uses of the term). In their model, inequality and the size of the middle class powerfully shape the incentives that political agents have to compromise. A sizeable middle class essentially serves as a buffer against radical demands for redistribution under democracy. Or to put the matter in more general terms: the structure of the pre-democratic economy places constraints on political agents that may help to explain their behavior.

This idea of rooting actors in the structure of the capitalist economy can clearly be taken further. Rogowski (1989), who has made one of the most influential structural arguments to date, focuses on variation in trade exposure and relative factor endowments. Others imply that political interests are defined not only by factor endowments, but by the specificity of these factors (e.g. Frieden 1991; Alt et al. 1996; Iversen and Soskice 2001). In a different context, Mares (2003) emphasizes the size of firms and their exposure to risk when explaining preferences over social policy. Swenson (2002) similarly traces employer-driven social policy initiatives to product market conditions. In explaining modern skill and production systems, Thelen (2004) argues that the strength of the guild system at the dawn of the industrial revolution powerfully shaped subsequent developments. Thelen also makes a convincing case that institutions are rarely created *de novo* but grow out of existing institutions, which shape the direction of change even as they are transformed. In other words, institutions often belong on both sides of the causal equation.

These examples do not add up to a single coherent approach to the study of institutional design. The point is simply that as we move "behind" the institutions to explain their genesis, an important task will be to identify the key structural attributes of capitalist economies (including old "obsolete" institutions), and the agents that populate them, so that they can serve as parameters in our models of institutional design and change. Similarly to the institutionalist project, the success of the new structuralism will depend on combining carefully identified historical constraints with rigorous theorizing. If this can be done, we may be able to leave the elephant in peace for a while longer.

References

ACEMOGLU, D., and ROBINSON, J. 2005. *Political Origins of Dictatorship and Democracy*. Cambridge: Cambridge University Press.
ADOLPH, C. 2005. The dilemma of discretion: career ambitions and the politics of central banking. Ph.D. dissertation, Department of Government, Harvard University.
ALDRICH, J. H. 1983. A Downsian spatial model with party activism. *American Political Science Review*, 77: 974–90.
―― 1993. Rational choice and turnout. *American Journal of Political Science*, 37: 246–78.
―― 1995. *Why Parties? The Origins and Transformation of Party Politics in America*. Chicago: University of Chicago Press.
ALESINA, A., COHEN, G., and ROUBINI, N. 1992. Macroeconomic policy and elections in OECD democracies. *Economics and Politics*, 4: 1–30.

_____ _____ 2004. *Fighting Poverty in the US and Europe: A World of Difference.* Oxford: Oxford University Press.

_____ ROSENTHAL, H. 2000. Polarized platforms and moderate policies with checks and balances. *Journal of Public Economics*, 75: 1–20.

ALLAN, J., and SCRUGGS, L. 2004. Political partisanship and welfare state reform in advanced industrial societies. *American Journal of Political Science*, 48: 493–512.

ALT, J., FRIEDEN, J., GILLIGAN, M. J., RODRIK, D., and ROGOWSKI, R. 1996. The political economy of international trade: enduring puzzles and an agenda for inquiry. *Comparative Political Studies*, 29: 689–717.

AOKI, M. 1994. The Japanese firm as a system of attributes: a survey and research agenda. Pp. 11–40 in *The Japanese Firm: Sources of Competitive Strength*, ed. M. Aoki. Oxford: Clarendon Press.

ARROW, K. 1951. *Social Choice and Individual Values.* New York: John Wiley (2nd edn. 1963).

AUSTEN-SMITH, D., and WALLERSTEIN, M. 2003. Redistribution in a divided society. Unpublished paper.

BAWN, K., and ROSENBLUTH, F. 2002. Coalition parties versus coalitions of parties: how electoral agency shapes the political logic of costs and benefits. PIEP Working Paper Series, WCFIA, Harvard University.

BÉNABOU, R. 1996. Inequality and growth. Pp. 11–74 in *National Bureau of Economic Research Macro Annual*, 11, ed. B. S. Bernanke and J. J. Rotemberg. Cambridge, Mass.: MIT Press.

BESLEY, T., and COATE, S. 1997. An economic model of representative democracy. *Quarterly Journal of Economics*, 112: 85–114.

BOIX, C. 1998. *Political Parties, Growth and Equality.* New York: Cambridge University Press.

_____ 1999. Setting the rules of the game: the choice of electoral systems in advanced democracies. *American Political Science Review*, 93: 609–24.

_____ 2003. *Democracy and Redistribtuion.* Cambridge: Cambridge University Press.

BRENNAN, G., and BUCHANAN, J. 1980. *The Power to Tax: Analytical Foundations of a Fiscal Constitution.* New York: Cambridge University Press.

CAMERON, D. 1984. Social democracy, corporatism, labor quiescence, and the representation of economic interest in advanced capitalist society. Pp. 143–78 in *Order and Conflict in Contemporary Capitalism*, ed. J. Goldthorpe. Oxford: Clarendon Press.

CAREY, J. M., and SHUGART, M. S. 1995. Incentives to cultivate a personal vote: a rank ordering of electoral formulas. *Electoral Studies*, 14: 417–39.

CLARK, W. R. 2003. *Capitalism, Not Globalism: Capital Mobility, Central Bank Independence, and the Political Control of the Economy.* Ann Arbor: University of Michigan Press.

Cox, G. 1990. Centripetal and centrifugal incentives in electoral systems. *American Journal of Political Science*, 34: 903–35.

_____ and THIES, M. F. 1998. The cost of intraparty competition: the single, non-transferable vote and money politics in Japan. *Comparative Political Studies*, 31: 267–91.

CREPAZ, M. M. L. 1998. Inclusion versus exclusion: political institutions and welfare expenditures. *Comparative Politics*, 31: 61–80.

CUSACK, T. 1997. Partisan politics and public finance: changes in public spending in the industrialized democracies, 1955–1989. *Public Choice*, 91: 375–95.

_____ IVERSEN, T., and SOSKICE, D. 2004. Specific interests and the origins of electoral systems. Paper prepared for presentation at the American Political Science Associations Meetings, Chicago, Aug.

DIXIT, A., and LONDREGAN, J. 1996. The determinants of success of special interests in redistributive politics. *Journal of Politics*, 58: 1132–55.

_____ _____ 1998. Ideology, tactics, and efficiency in redistributive politics. *Quarterly Journal of Economics*, 113: 497–529.

Esping-Andersen, G. 1990. *The Three Worlds of Welfare Capitalism*. Princeton, NJ: Princeton University Press.

Estevez-Abe, M. 1999. Comparative political economy of female labor participation. Paper prepared for presentation at the Annual Meetings of the American Political Science Association, Atlanta, 2–5 Sept.

—— Iversen, T., and Soskice, D. 2001. Social protection and the formation of skills: a reinterpretation of the welfare state. Pp. 145–83 in *Varieties of Capitalism: The Institutional Foundations of Comparative Advantage*, ed. P. A. Hall and D. Soskice. Oxford: Oxford University Press.

Franzese, R. 2002. *Macroeconomics of Developed Democracies*. Cambridge: Cambridge University Press.

Frieden, J. 1991. Invested intersts: the politics of national economc policies in a world of global finance. *International Organization*, 45: 425–51.

Garrett, G. 1998. *Partisan Politics in the Global Economy*. Cambridge: Cambridge University Press.

Goldthorpe, J. (ed.). 1984. *Order and Conflict in Contemporary Capitalism*. Oxford: Clarendon Press.

Grofman, B. 2004. Downs and two-party convergence. *Annual Review of Political Science*, 7: 25–46.

Hall, P. A., and Soskice, D. 2001. An introduction to varieties of capitalism. Pp. 1–68 in *Varieties of Capitalism: The Institutional Foundations of Comparative Advantage*, ed. P. A. Hall and D. Soskice. Oxford: Oxford University Press.

—— and Taylor, R. 1996. Political science and the three new institutionalisms. *Political Studies*, 44: 936–57.

Hibbs, D. 1977. Political parties and macroeconomic policy. *American Political Science Review*, 71: 1467–87.

Hicks, A., and Swank, D. 1992. Politics, institutions, and welfare spending in industrialized democracies, 1960–82. *American Political Science Review*, 86: 649–74.

Huber, E., Ragin, C., and Stephens, J. 1993. Social democracy, Christian democracy, constitutional structure and the welfare state. *American Journal of Sociology*, 99: 711–49.

—— and Stephens, J. D. 2001. *Development and Crisis of the Welfare State: Parties and Policies in Global Markets*. Chicago: University of Chicago Press.

Iversen, T. 1996. Power, flexibility and the breakdown of centralized wage bargaining: the cases of Denmark and Sweden in comparative perspective. *Comparative Politics*, 28: 399–436.

—— 1998. Equality, employment, and budgetary restraint: the trilemma of the service economy. *World Politics*, 50: 507–46.

—— 2005. *Capitalism, Democracy and Welfare*. Cambridge: Cambridge University Press.

—— and Rosenbluth, F. 2006. The political economy of gender: explaining cross-national variation in the gender division of labor and the gender voting gap. *American Journal of Political Science*, 50: 1–19.

—— and Soskice, D. 2001. An asset theory of social policy preferences. *American Political Science Review*, 95: 875–93.

—— —— 2002. Electoral institutions, parties, and the politics of class: why some democracies redistribute more than others. Paper presented at the Annual Meetings of the American Political Science Association.

—— —— 2005. Why governments diverge from the preferences of the median legislator. Manuscript, Dept. of Government, Harvard University.

Katzenstein, P. 1985. *Small States in World Markets*. Ithaca, NY: Cornell University Press.

KELLY, N. J. 2005. Political choice, public policy, and distributional outcomes. *American Journal of Political Science*, 49: 865–80.

KITSCHELT, H. 1994. *The Transformation of European Social Democracy*. Cambridge: Cambridge University Press.

KORPI, W. 1983. *The Democratic Class Struggle*. London: Routledge and Kegan Paul.

―― 1989. Power, politics, and state autonomy in the development of social citizenship: social rights during sickness in 18 OECD countries since 1930. *American Sociological Review*, 54: 309–28.

KWON, H. Y., and PONTUSSON, J. 2005. The zone of partisanship: parties, unions and welfare spending in OECD countries, 1962–99. Unpublished manuscript, Dept. of Political Science, Cornell University.

LANGE, P., and GARRETT, G. 1985. The politics of growth: strategic interaction and economic performance, 1974–1980. *Journal of Politics*, 47: 792–827.

LAVER, M., and SCHOFIELD, N. 1990. *Multiparty Government: The Politics of Coalition in Western Europe*. Oxford: Oxford University Press.

―― and SHEPSLE, K. 1996. *Making and Breaking Governments: Cabinets and Legislatures in Parliamentary Democracies*. Cambridge: Cambridge University Press.

LINDERT, P. H. 1996. What limits social spending? *Explorations in Economic History*, 33: 1–34.

LOWI, T. 1964. American business, public policy, case studies, and political theory. *World Politics*, 16: 677–715.

McGANN, A. J. 2002. The advantages of ideological cohesion: a model of constituency representation and electoral competition in multiparty democracies. *Journal of Theoretical Politics*, 14: 37–70.

MANOW, P. Forthcoming. *Social Protection and Capitalist Production: The Bismarckian Welfare State and the German Political Economy, 1880–1990*. Amsterdam: Amesterdam University Press.

MARES, I. 2003. *The Politics of Social Risk: Business and Welfare State Development*. Cambridge: Cambridge University Press.

MARTIN, C. J. 1995. Nature of Nuture? Source of firm preferences for national health reform. *American Political Science Review*, 89: 898–913.

MELTZER, A. H., and RICHARD, S. F. 1981. A rational theory of the size of government. *Journal of Political Economy*, 89: 914–27.

MOENE, K. O., and WALLERSTEIN, M. 2001. Inequality, social insurance and redistribution. *American Political Science Review*, 95: 859–74.

MOORE, B. 1971. *Social Origins of Democracy and Dictatorship: Lord and Peasant in the Making of the Modern World*. Boston: Beacon Press.

NETO, O. A., and COX, G. W. 1997. Electoral institutions, cleavage structures, and the number of parties. *American Journal of Political Science*, 41: 149–74.

NORTH, D. 1990. *Institutions, Institutional Change and Economic Performance*. Cambridge: Cambridge University Press.

―― and WEINGAST, B. R. 1989. Constitutions and commitment: the evolution of institutions governing public choice in the 17th-century England. *Journal of Economic History*, 49: 803–32.

OBINGER, H., LEIBFRIED, S., and CASTLES, F. G. (eds.). 2005. *Federalism and the Welfare State: New World and European Experiences*. Cambridge: Cambridge University Press.

ORDESHOOK, P., and SHVETSOVA, O. 1994. Ethnic heterogeneity, district magnitude, and the number of parties. *American Journal of Political Science*, 38: 100–23.

OSBORNE, M. J., and RUBINSTEN, A. 1994. *A Course in Game Theory*. Cambridge, Mass.: MIT Press.

OSBORNE, M. J. and SLIVINSKI, A. 1996. A model of political competition with citizen-candidates. *Quarterly Journal of Economics*, 111: 65–96.
PEROTTI, R. 1996. Growth, income distribution and democracy: what the data say. *Journal of Economic Growth*, 1: 149–87.
PERSSON, T., and TABELLINI, G. 1999. The size and scope of government: comparative politics with rational politicians. *European Economic Review*, 43: 699–735.
_____ 2000. *Political Economics: Explaining Economic Policy*. Cambridge, Mass.: MIT Press.
_____ 2005. *The Economic Effects of Constitutions*. Cambridge, Mass.: MIT Press.
PIERSON, P. 1995. Fragmented welfare states: federal institutions and the development of social policy. *Governance*, 8: 449–78.
_____ 2000. Path dependence, increasing returns, and the study of politics. *American Political Science Review*, 94: 251–67.
POLANYI, K. 1944. *The Great Transformation*. New York: Rinehart.
PONTUSSON, J., and SWENSON, P. 1996. Labor markets, production strategies, and wage bargaining institutions: the Swedish employer offensive in comparative perspective. *Comparative Political Studies*, 29: 223–50.
POWELL, B. 2002. PR, the median voter, and economic policy: an exploration. Paper presented at the Annual Meetings of the American Political Science Association, Boston.
PRZEWORSKI, A., and SPRAGUE, J. 1986. *Paper Stones: A History of Electoral Socialism*. Chicago: University of Chicago Press.
_____ and WALLERSTEIN, M. 1982. Structural dependence of the state on capital. *American Political Science Review*, 82: 11–29.
RIKER, W. H. 1980. Implications for the disequilibrium of majority rule for the study of institutions. *American Political Science Review*, 74: 432–46.
_____ 1986. *The Art of Political Manipulation*. New Haven, Conn.: Yale University Press.
RODDEN, J. 2003. Reviving Leviathan: fiscal federalism and the growth of government. *International Organization*, 57: 695–729.
_____ 2005. *Hamilton's Paradox: The Promise and Peril of Fiscal Federalism*. Cambridge: Cambridge University Press.
RODRIK, D. 1999. Democracies pay higher wages. *Quarterly Journal of Economics*, 114: 707–38.
ROEMER, J. E. 1997. The democratic political economy of progressive taxation. *Econometrica*, 67: 1–19.
_____ 2001. *Political Competition: Theory and Applications*. Cambridge, Mass.: Harvard University Press.
ROGOWSKI, R. 1989. *Commerce and Coalitions: How Trade Affects Domestic Political Alignments*. Princeton, NJ: Princeton University Press.
_____ and MACRAY, D. 2003. Does inequality determine institutions? What history and (some) data tell us. Paper presented in the Political Institutions and Inequality Study Group, Center for European Studies, Harvard University, Oct.
ROMER, T. 1975. Individual welfare, majority voting, and the properties of a linear income tax. *Journal of Public Economics*, 14: 163–85.
ROSENBLUTH, F. M., and THIES, M. F. 2001. The electoral foundations of Japan's financial politics: the case of Jusen. *Policy Studies Journal*, 29: 23–37.
ROSS, M. 2005. Is democracy good for the poor? Unpublished manuscript, UCLA Dept. of Political Science.
RUEDA, D., and PONTUSSON, J. 2000. Wage inequality and varieties of capitalism. *World Politics*, 52: 350–83.
SCHLESINGER, J. 1984. On the theory of party organization. *Journal of Politics*, 46: 369–400.

SCHMITTER, P. 1979. Modes of interest intermediation and models of societal change. Pp. 43–94 in *Trends toward Corporatist Intermediation*, ed. P. Schmitter and G. Lehmbruch. Beverly Hills, Calif.: Sage.

SNYDER, J. M., and KRAMER, G. H. 1988. Fairness, self-interest, and the politics of the progressive income tax. *Journal of Public Economics*, 36: 197–230.

SOSKICE, D. 1999. Divergent production regimes: coordinated and uncoordinated market economies in the 1980s and 1990s. Pp. 101–34 in *Continuity and Change in Contemporary Capitalism*, ed. H. Kitschelt, P. Lange, G. Marks, and J. D. Stephens. Cambridge: Cambridge University Press.

—— and IVERSON, T. 2005. *Why Governments Diverge from the Prefrences of the Median Voter*. Manuscript. Harvard University.

STOKES, S. 1999. Political parties and democracy. *Annual Review of Political Science*, 2: 243–67.

STREECK, W. 1991. On the institutional conditions of diversified quality production. Pp. 21–61 in *Beyond Keynesianism*, ed. E. Matzner and W. Streeck. Aldershot: Elagar.

SWENSON, P. 1991. Bringing capital back in, or social democracy reconsidered: employer power, cross-class alliances, and centralization of industrial relations in Denmark and Sweden. *World Politics*, 43: 513–44.

—— 2002. *Employers against Markets* Cambridge: Cambridge University Press.

THELEN, K. 1999. Historical institutionalism in comparative politics. *Annual Review of Political Science*, 2: 369–404.

—— 2004. *How Institutions Evolve: The Political Economy of Skills in Germany, Britain, the United States and Japan*. Cambridge: Cambridge University Press.

VON HAGEN, J., and HARDEN, I. 1995. National budget processes and commitment to fiscal discipline. *European Economic Review*, 39: 771–9.

WALLERSTEIN, M. 1999. Wage-setting institutions and pay inequality in advanced industrial societies. *American Journal of Political Science*, 43: 649–80.

WEINGAST, B. R. 1995. The economic role of political institutions: market-preserving federalism and economic development. *Journal of Law, Economics, and Organization*, 1: 1–31.

—— and MARSHALL, W. J. 1988. The industrial organization of Congress: or, why legislatures, like firms, are not organized as markets. *Journal of Political Economy*, 96: 132–63.

WIBBELS, E. 2003. Bailouts, budget constraints, and Leviathans: comparative federalism and lessons from the early United States. *Comparative Political Studies*, 36: 475–508.

WILLIAMSON, O. E. 1985. *The Economic Institutions of Capitalism: Firms, Markets, Relational Contracting*. New York: Free Press.

WITTMAN, D. 1973. Parties as utility maximizers. *American Political Science Review*, 67: 490–8.

CHAPTER 34

INEQUALITY

EDWARD L. GLAESER

1 INTRODUCTION

THE insight that economics impacts politics as much as politics impacts economics lies at the heart of political economy. This circle of causation is at the center of research on the political economy of inequality. Democracy, political stability, and executive constraints all appear to be more feasible in more equal societies. Public policies towards redistribution and human capital can make societies more equal.

In Section 2 of this chapter, I review the causes of inequality. Recent increases in inequality in the developed world are in part the result of skill-biased technological change (Katz and Murphy 1992), but government policies influence how these technological changes impact different developed countries (Hanratty and Blank 1992). Long-standing differences in inequality across countries may reflect colonialism and patterns of agriculture, but initial differences in inequality also influenced political institutions, policies, and structures, which may have exacerbated economic inequality (as in Moore 1996; Engerman and Sokoloff 2002).

In Section 3 I review the second half of the causal chain between inequality and politics—the impact of inequality on government. In median voter models, inequality predicts more redistribution. However, greater inequality also means that the wealthy have more resources to influence the political outcome. Great gaps between rich and poor may also hurt democracy and rule of law if elites prefer dictators who will protect their interests or if the disadvantaged turn to a dictator who promises to ignore property rights.

In the last section of this review, I turn to the special question of "American exceptionalism," which in this context refers to the question of why there is so much

---

* I am grateful to the editors, Barry Weingast and Donald Wittman, for extensive comments and editing.

less redistribution and more inequality in the USA than in Europe. The differences between the USA and Europe in inequality and redistribution have troubled authors like Friedrich Engels, Werner Sombart, and Martin Lipset for more than a century. American exceptionalism appears to be the result of ethnic heterogeneity and a stable constitutional history, in contrast to European political institutions, which have been influenced by numerous revolutions and two world wars. A large body of evidence supports the hypothesis that ethnic heterogeneity reduces support for welfare, and the USA is far more ethnically heterogeneous than Europe. The USA also has political institutions, including a majoritarian government, federalism, and checks and balances, which have limited the expansion of the American welfare state, while European countries lack comparable institutions. These institutional differences are not exogenous, but rather reflect the fact that many European constitutions were rewritten in the twentieth century by left-wing politicians when earlier monarchies were defeated militarily.

2 THE POLITICAL AND ECONOMIC CAUSES OF INEQUALITY

Most studies of inequality focus on income, but inequality can also be calculated based on wealth, consumption, or any other reasonable proxy for well-being. Wealth or consumption have the advantage that they are less subject to short-term income shocks, and the inequality of lifetime earnings is probably more important than the inequality of transitory earnings. However, because wealth and consumption data are not available in enough circumstances, most of the empirical work focuses on inequality of annual income. Consequently, I focus my empirical discussion on that variable. Nevertheless, improving inequality measures by improving the measurement of permanent well-being is certainly one research frontier.

Measuring income inequality also requires transforming the distribution of income or wealth or consumption into a single measure that can be used in standard empirical work. The literature on this issue parallels the industrial organization literature on market concentration. The most popular measure of income inequality is the Gini coefficient, which is the difference between the 45-degree line and the Lorenz curve that shows the cumulative distribution of income. A second measure is the share of total national income possessed by various sub-groups of the population, e.g. the share of total wealth owned by the richest 5 per cent of the population. In some cases, these variables will actually reveal much more than a Gini coefficient, especially if we are interested in knowing whether inequality matters because the rich are particularly rich or because the poor are particularly poor. As different measures are usually highly correlated, different empirical studies that use these different measures

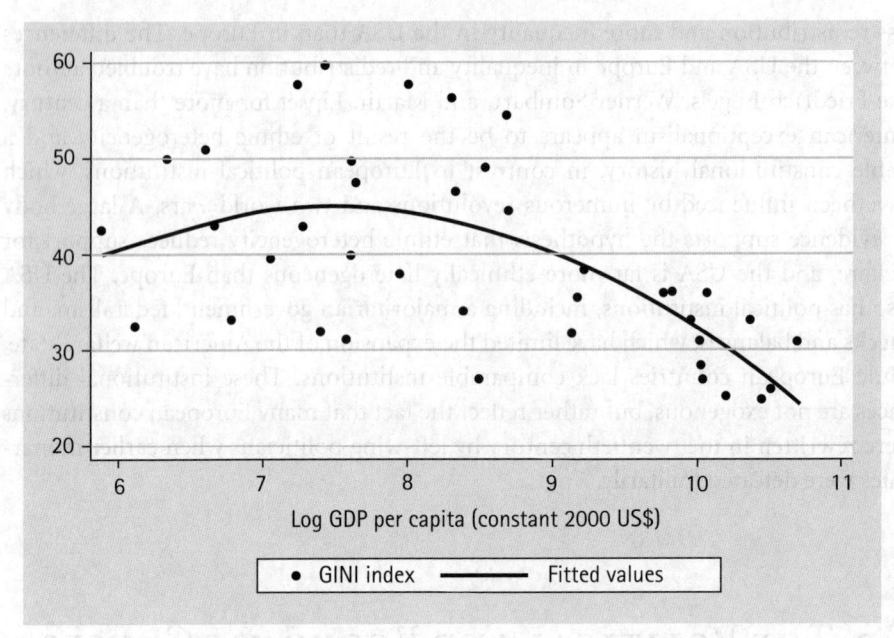

Fig. 34.1 Inequality and income

often produce quite similar results (e.g. compare Persson and Tabellini 1994 with Alesina and Rodrik 1994).

2.1 Inequality over Time

These empirical measures are then used by empirical researchers, who have provided a series of facts about the correlates of inequality. Perhaps the most famous relationship is the Kuznets (1955) curve shown in Figure 34.1. Income inequality first rises and then falls as countries get richer. This curve points to the initial period of industrialization as the point of development where inequality is maximized. Indeed, US history shows a "great compression" during the middle decades of the twentieth century (Goldin and Margo 1992) as the relatively equal period between 1950 and 1975 followed the far greater inequality of the Gilded age and pre-depression America. Figure 34.1 also illustrates American exceptionalism as the USA is much more unequal than other countries of comparable income.

The Kuznets curve is not just an economic phenomenon; it also reflects political factors. The general pattern in industrializing nations is that there are few public efforts to redistribute during early industrialization. During this period, traditional private providers of charity (churches, charities, families) are expected to look after the bottom end of the income distribution. As industrialization proceeds, governments almost universally started taking a more active role in redistribution, which is one reason why inequality declines with development. Development increases redistribution for at least three reasons: development is generally associated with greater government size, probably due to increasing governmental competence; development is associated with greater education and political skill on the part of poorer citizens; and development transforms a dispersed agrarian workforce into clustered industrial workers who can readily be organized.

Somewhat surprisingly, given the Kuznets curve, the great compression was followed within the United States, and elsewhere, by a significant increase in inequality since 1975. Katz and Murphy (1992) conclude that the period of rising inequality in the USA appears to have been driven by rising demand for more skilled workers. The rise in demand for the skilled might be the result of a number of different changes including skill-biased technological change, increasing trade and globalization, the decline of manufacturing, and unions. Pride of place appears now to be given to changing technology (Autor, Katz, and Krueger 1998) as the cause of greater inequality, but other factors also matter.

While most authors seem to believe that rising inequality within the USA is the result of economic as opposed to political changes, the impact of these economic changes is determined in part by a political filter. Technological changes and increases in world trade should impact most developed countries in similar ways. Yet the USA has experienced a much more striking increase in inequality than most other comparable countries (Picketty and Saez 2003; Blau and Kahn 1996; Hanratty and Blank 1992), and economic forces alone do not appear to explain why inequality rose so much more within the USA.

Political factors surely played some role in the greater increase in inequality within the USA. At the top of the income distribution, less progressive taxation in the USA made it easier for Americans to become rich and increased the incentives for Americans to acquire large fortunes (Picketty and Saez 2003). Stronger unions in Europe increased equality there among the many European workers whose salaries are determined by collective bargaining (Blau and Kahn 1996). Unions have generally fought inequality among their members, perhaps because heterogeneity breaks down union cohesion or because of the quasi-democratic nature of most unions. At the bottom of the income distribution, general unemployment benefits and restrictive labor market regulations ensure that more of the less productive European workers leave the workforce and are therefore excluded from measures of wage inequality.

2.2 Inequality across Countries

If changes in inequality within the USA and other countries are primarily the result of changing returns to skills and government responses to those changing returns to skill, then differences in inequality across countries reflect differences in the distribution of skills. In particularly egalitarian countries, like those of Scandinavia, the population is generally well educated and the distribution of skills is quite compact. Conversely, particularly unequal developing countries like Brazil have enormously heterogeneous skill levels between educated urban elites and less-educated agricultural workers.

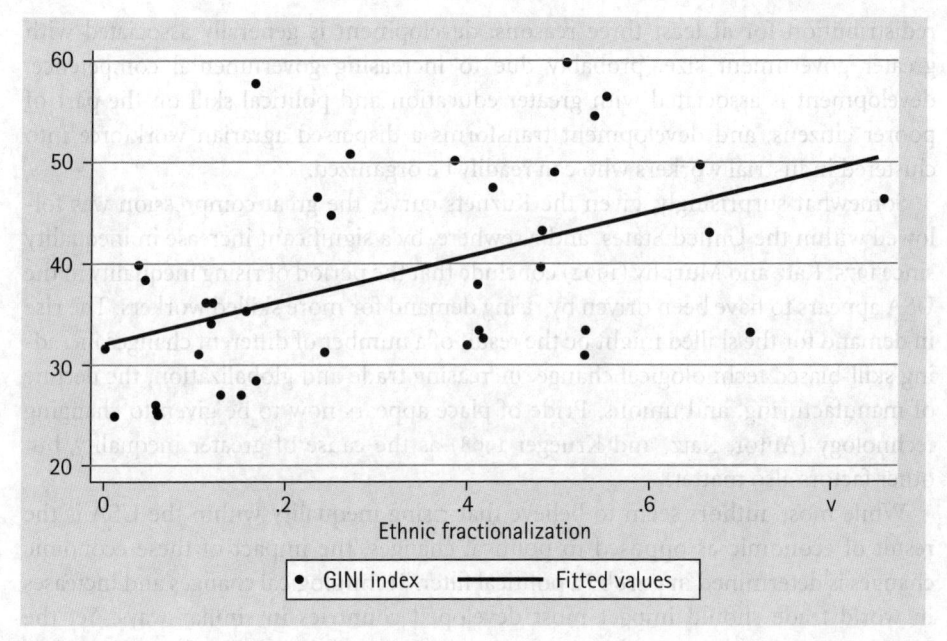

Fig. 34.2 Fractionalization and inequality

But if the inequality of skills underlies the inequality of income, then the primary puzzle becomes understanding why skill inequalities are so different across countries. Skill levels today are themselves the result of both government policies and long-standing cultural forces, like religion or ethnicity, but patterns of national inequality appear to pre-date the era of large-scale government schooling (the nineteenth century). As high levels of inequality often pre-date significant government redistribution or schooling, cultural and religious causes are probably the first causes of inequality across countries.

Protestant churches sought legitimacy in the Bible (as opposed to the traditions of the Catholic Church), and these churches encouraged literacy to increase familiarity with the Bible (Weber 2001). Protestant communities worked to create widespread education that would ensure that everyone could read, which both increased the level of education and decreased its variance by raising the lower tail of the distribution.

More importantly, skill inequality seems to come mostly from the juxtaposition of ethnicities with different educational traditions, and in particular the extent to which New World countries are made up primarily of Europeans or of mixtures of Europeans and non-Europeans. As Figure 34.2 shows, the correlation between ethnic fractionalization and income inequality is quite strong. Europeans who came to the New World had a significant educational advantage over the natives they conquered, at least in terms of skills that became valuable in developed economies. Even the great empires of the pre-Columbian Americas lacked basic modern skills; the Incas had no alphabet.

Inequality then depends significantly on the extent to which nations are populated by Europeans or mixtures of Europeans and natives. Engerman and Sokoloff (2002) argue that countries with a comparative advantage in cash crops, such as sugar or tobacco, attracted small numbers of Europeans who then relied on local and slave labor to farm these crops. Those countries are less equal to this day. Acemoglu, Johnson, and Robinson (2001) argue that settler mortality determined whether countries attracted large European migrations (which then largely eradicated the existing native populations) or smaller-scale migrations that then interacted with native and slave labor. Galor, Moav, and Vollrath (2004) present a more general theory of land distribution and long-run inequality.

If populations with heterogenous educational backgrounds are the initial condition determining modern inequality, the actual distribution of income today also depends on a large number of government policies towards schooling and redistribution since that point. Many Asian countries, which once had small European elites and large masses of uneducated natives, are now both well-educated and egalitarian. These transformations reflect the results of government policies towards education in countries like Singapore, Taiwan, and South Korea. By contrast, initial skill differences in countries in ethnically heterogeneous countries were often widened, not eliminated, by subsequent educational policies, which favored the European elites.

Figure 34.3 shows the strong negative correlation between inequality and social welfare spending across countries. This correlation reflects both that social welfare reduces inequality and that more initial inequality leads to less redistribution. While some of this relationship reflects reverse causality, and omitted variables (like income

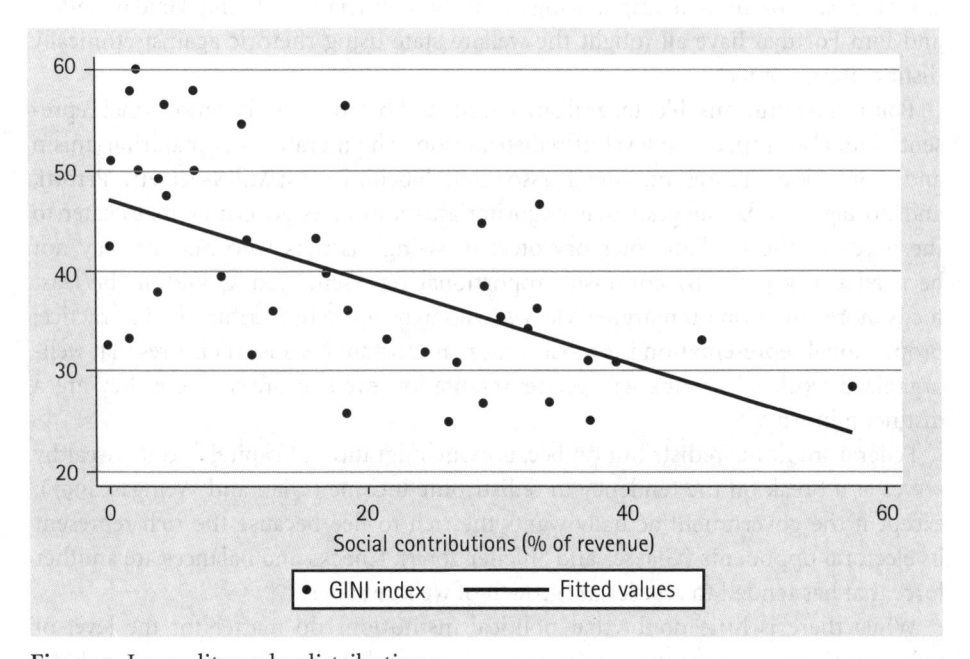

Fig. 34.3 Inequality and redistribution

and fractionalization) that drive both variables, there is little doubt that governments have the power through tax policy and through spending to alter the income distribution of their country.

Understanding income inequality across countries also requires understanding the reasons that a government decides to invest in its children, or to invest in redistribution more generally. Two factors, apart from inequality itself, appear to be important: ethnic heterogeneity and political institutions. Ethnic and racial fractionalization limits the tendency to redistribute income either because people are less willing to support transfers to those who are ethnically different, or because ethnic differences provide a means of demonizing policies that help the poor (Alesina and Glaeser 2004). Individual data on opinion polls and voting behavior, cross-state outcomes within the USA, cross-national data, and history all support the view that ethnic heterogeneity reduces redistribution. Luttmer (2001) shows that people are more likely to support redistribution when they live around poor people of the same race and less likely to support redistribution when they live around poor people of a different race. Holding income constant, there is also a huge impact of race on the willingness to support redistribution and vote Democratic, suggesting the significance of race in politics.

Across states within the USA, the percentage of the population that is black strongly predicts less-generous welfare systems; and across countries, ethnic heterogeneity strongly predicts less redistribution; across countries, redistribution also declines with ethnic heterogeneity (Alesina and Glaeser 2004). The history of redistribution within the USA points to the important role that race has played at several critical junctures, such as the fight against the Populists in the 1890s (see Woodward 1955). Over the past twenty years, right-wing European politicians including Haidar, LePen, and Pim Fortuyn have all fought the welfare state using rhetoric against ethnically distinct immigrants.

Political institutions, like federalism, checks and balances, and proportional representation, also impact the level of redistribution. The literature on majoritarianism and proportional representation (Persson and Tabellini 2003; Miles-Ferretti, Perotti, and Rostagno 2002) suggests that majoritarianism induces governments to cater to the needs of the median voter or voters in swing districts who may or may not be particularly poor. By contrast, proportional representation should at the least focus more attention on marginal classes, who may desire redistribution. In practice, proportional representation is probably more important because it ensures that well-organized workers' groups will get representation even in areas where they are a distinct minority.

Federalism limits redistribution because out-migration of capital and the wealthy serves as a break on the tendency to redistribute income (Qian and Weingast 1997), except if the government actually wants the rich to flee because the rich represent its electoral opponents (Glaeser and Shleifer 2004). Checks and balances are another force that has tended to restrict the growth of welfare states.

While there is little doubt that political institutions do matter for the level of redistribution in society, the greater question is whether these institutions should be taken as first causes or as endogenous factors that reflect deeper social forces (Glaeser et al. 2004). Political institutions are hardly all that permanent. France acquired proportional representation in 1946, with the Fourth Republic, lost it after the failed right-wing coup that ended that government and put DeGaulle in power, reacquired it under Mitterrand, and then lost it when the socialists realized that proportional representation was helping right-wing extremists. The relative stability of Anglo-American traditions has often led scholars to overstate vastly the degree to which political institutions are durable. I will turn to the causes of institutional change in Section 4 when I compare the USA and Europe.

3 THE IMPACT OF INEQUALITY ON POLITICS

Inequality might impact political outcomes in three different ways. First, rising economic inequality should impact the level of post-tax inequality because of an increased preference for redistribution by the median voter. Second, higher inequality might reduce redistribution and public good provision because economic resources determine not only preferences, but the ability to influence political outcomes as well. Third, economic inequality might influence the whole structure of political institutions (like democracy) themselves.

The most straightforward prediction of the median-voter literature (summarized by Londregan in this volume) is that redistribution will be popular when the mean income is higher than the median income (Meltzer and Richard 1981). If income follows a Pareto distribution, then an increase in variance will be associated with an increase in the gap between mean and median income. Two of the more influential papers that examine inequality within a median voter context are Persson and Tabellini (1994) and Alesina and Rodrik (1994), which both argue that greater inequality will lead to greater preferences for redistribution, and show a negative empirical connection between inequality and growth.

The open question with these papers is whether inequality actually increases redistribution. As shown in Figure 34.3, empirically there is a strong negative relationship between inequality and social welfare spending, which seems to contradict this claim. While this negative correlation might reflect that more redistribution reduces inequality, it is also possible that more inequality leads to less redistribution rather than more because in unequal societies the poor lack the resources to push their political agenda.

The median voter model can also explain a connection between inequality and public good provision. Greater inequality should work like any form of heterogeneity and decrease the demand for common public goods (Alesina, Baqir, and Easterly 1999). For example, the rich might want a legal system focused on protecting property while the poor might be more concerned with preventing interpersonal violence in disadvantaged areas. Because these groups disagree, there is less willingness to invest in a common legal system than there would be if the population shared a common set of legal needs.

This is certainly one interpretation of the finding that crime is higher in more unequal societies (Fajnzylber, Lederman, and Loayza 2002). One natural interpretation of this connection might be that as inequality rises, the returns to crime increase for the poor (because rich victims are richer) and the opportunity costs of crime are lower (because the poor are poorer), but many researchers doubt this hypothesis because most crime is poor-on-poor not poor-on-rich, and because the cross-national evidence suggests that the aspect of inequality that matters most for crime is the amount of inequality among the upper income quintiles. Another interpretation that squares with those facts is that more unequal societies have less public policing because rich private individuals invest in private policing and choose not to support public safety. In this view, because in highly unequal societies the very rich are so different from everyone else, they have no interest in supporting public goods (like public safety) but rather invest in private alternatives. This view explains why, for example, there are only 12,000 police officers in Bogotá, Colombia, and 28,000 police officers in New York City. These two cities have similar populations, but Colombia is a particularly unequal nation (of course Colombia is also poorer).

While the most cited papers on inequality and policy outcomes have focused on results within a median-voter context, inequality of resources will also change the political clout of different groups. Indeed, the most important impact of inequality may be changing the power with which the rich and poor can impact outcomes. For example, if the rich can influence political outcomes through lobbying activities or membership in special interest groups (Prat in this volume discusses the influence of pressure groups), then more inequality could lead to less redistribution rather than more. This negative correlation can be seen in Figure 34.3. According to this view, as the rich become richer, they acquire a greater ability to influence policy and achieve the policy goals that they want.

Glaeser, Scheinkman, and Shleifer (2003) provide one connecting inequality of resources with the ability to manipulate political institutions. This model focuses on bribing judges. It suggests that when the judicial system is sufficiently weak, so that the expected penalty facing a judge who accepts a bribe is small, then the ability to bribe will determine the outcome in court. This work emphasizes the subversion of legal and political processes and argues that this subversion will be more likely in societies where different actors have unequal access to the resources needed for subversion. Inequality may lead courts to break down or, as in the Engerman and Sokoloff examples, rich magnates may use their economic power to make a mockery of popular democracy.

These arguments are related to a third literature on the connection between inequality and political outcomes which emphasizes that inequality will lead to different political institutions, and in some cases less democracy (the Przeworski chapter in this volume discusses the determinants of democracy). Indeed, stable democracy is much more common in highly equal societies (and in richer societies, as Przeworski illustrates in his chapter). Dividing the world into more and less equal countries based on World Bank Gini coefficients shows that 95 per cent of the more equal countries are classified as democracies by Jaggers and Marshall (2000) and only 75 per cent of the less equal societies are classified as democracies.

The correlation between inequality and democracy might be the result of reverse causality where democracy reduces inequality, but Engerman and Sokoloff (2002) provide some historical evidence showing that in the Americas initial inequality seems to deter the development of democracy. Inequality, which was itself the result of long-run economic factors, led many seemingly progressive groups to oppose extending the franchise. Educated urban workers feared extending the franchise in many cases because this would empower rural magnates who would totally control the votes of their poor employees. On the other hand, the historical patterns in Asia and Africa appear much less consistent with the view that initial differences in inequality drive the development of democracy.

Many models predict a causal link between equality and democracy. It may be that in less equal countries, elites are less willing to share power with the poor because of fear of expropriation. Alternatively, potential enemies of democracy may find it easy to build support among the poor. While there is a great deal of history providing support for both phenomena (Finer 1962), little empirical work exists to assess the relative importance of the different stories.

Inequality is not only correlated with dictatorship, but also with other measures of political problems. For example, Figure 34.4 shows that inequality is positively correlated with subjective assessments of the risk of governments expropriating private

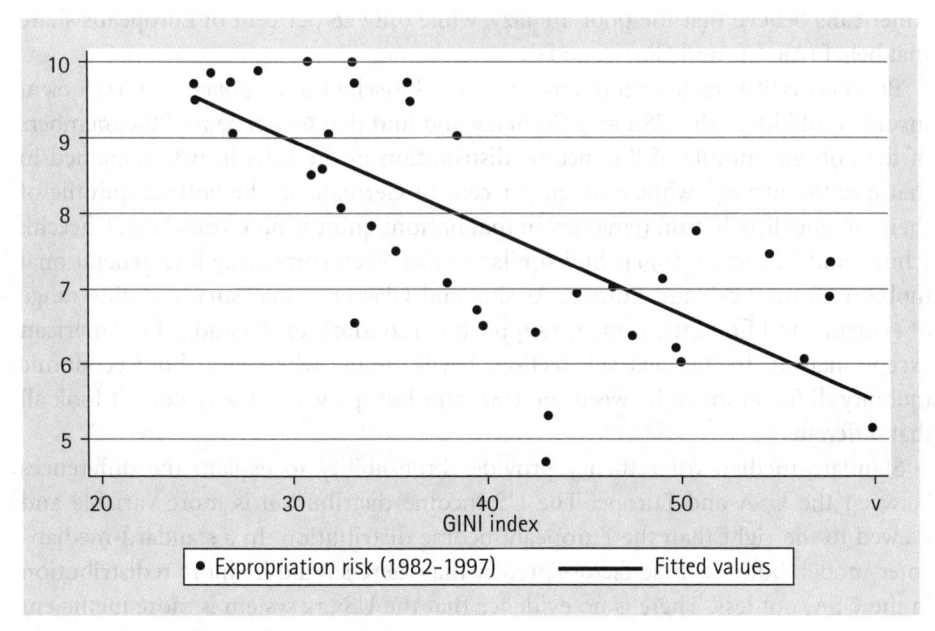

Fig. 34.4 Inequality and expropriation

wealth. Most similar measures of property rights protection show a negative correlation with inequality. You and Khagram (2004) indeed find a connection between inequality and corruption. Again, causal inference is impossible, but these correlations are strong and suggestive, and they at least raise the possibility that inequality may be causing bad government.

4 AMERICAN EXCEPTIONALISM

Few topics in the political economy of inequality have as rich a heritage as the study of American exceptionalism, which in the context of inequality means why the USA is less equal than Europe and why the USA never developed a full-fledged European welfare state. Although de Tocqueville (1835) is rightly seen as the first scholar of American exceptionalism, the modern literature really begins with Friedrich Engels (1959) and Werner Sombart (1976), who asked "Why is there no socialism in the United States?" Seymour Martin Lipset (1966) continued this tradition and became the expert in understanding why socialism never flourished within the USA.

Economic, political, and sociological factors could all potentially explain American exceptionalism. The economic explanations focus on the allegedly higher levels of economic opportunity within the USA. Americans do believe that they live in an open society, and Europeans believe that they live in a rigid class-bound society. After all, only 29 per cent of Americans surveyed believe that the poor are trapped in poverty while 60 per cent of Europeans believe that the poor are trapped. Sixty per cent of Americans believe that the poor are lazy, while only 26 per cent of Europeans share that belief (Alesina and Glaeser 2004).

But there is little reality behind those views. Gottschalk and Spolaore (2002) look at income mobility in the USA and Germany and find that 60 per cent of the members of the bottom quintile of the income distribution in the USA in 1984 remained in that quintile in 1993, while only 46 per cent of Germans in the bottom quintile of their income distribution remained in that bottom quintile nine years later. Checchi, Ichino, and Rustichini (1999) find similar results when comparing intergenerational mobility in the USA and Europe. Alesina and Glaeser (2004) survey a wide range of evidence and find little evidence supporting economic explanations for American exceptionalism. In the next sub-section, I will discuss why views about economic mobility differ so much between the USA and Europe when reality doesn't look all that different.

Standard-median-voter theory provides little ability to explain the differences between the USA and Europe. The US income distribution is more variable and skewed to the right than the European income distribution. In a standard-median-voter model, both of these factors predict that there should be more redistribution in the USA, not less. There is no evidence that the US tax system is more inefficient than European tax systems. Privately, Americans are much more generous than their European counterparts, so it is hard to believe that the lack of an American welfare system just reflects some lack of American generosity.

Two factors appear to explain America's low level of redistribution and greater level of inequality: ethnic heterogeneity and political institutions. As I discussed above, ethnic fractionalization appears to be strongly correlated with low levels of redistribution across countries, and America is far more ethnically heterogeneous than Europe. European countries are remarkably homogeneous, either because nations engaged in strong homogenizing policies or because current nations reflect ethnically homogeneous areas that broke away from former empires. America is a nation of immigrants and kidnapped slaves, and there has never been a policy of homogenization comparable to that followed in France, for example, in the late nineteenth century.

The importance of ethnic fractionalization is not only seen in cross-national regressions. As mentioned above, there is a significant correlation between the percentage of the population that is black in a state and less-generous welfare payments. Opinion polls within the USA also confirm the role of race in attitudes towards redistribution. Perhaps most convincingly, there are many examples where left-wing movements were stemmed because of racial divisions. For example, the New York City Draft riot, which was both America's bloodiest riot and in a sense its biggest labor uprising, petered out in part because the German rioters turned on the Irish. Between 1870 and 1920, conflicts between natives, immigrants, and African-Americans bedeviled the labor movement. During this period, Friedrich Engels himself emphasized the divisions between natives, immigrants, and blacks as a reason why America didn't have a socialist party.

In the 1890s, Southern conservatives used racism to discredit their populist opponents whose policies would have enriched poor blacks in addition to poor whites. In 1928, anti-Catholicism was used against Democrat Al Smith in the election. In the 1960s, the powerful Democratic political coalition fell apart over issues of race and civil rights in the South. Racial divisions do not automatically breed dislike, but they do make it possible for political entrepreneurs to build distrust and even hatred. Using the coefficient from an international regression where redistribution is regressed on ethnic heterogeneity and other controls, the differences in ethnic heterogeneity between the USA and Europe can explain one-half of the difference in redistribution between these two regions.

But racial heterogeneity is not the only reason for American exceptionalism. A number of differences in political institutions between the USA and Europe also help explain the smaller US welfare state. As discussed earlier, there is a strong link across developed countries between proportional representation and the level of redistribution. This link shouldn't surprise any student of European history—in the early twentieth century, workers' parties regularly lobbied for the introduction of proportional representation because they thought that this would strengthen their electoral chances. Using the coefficient on proportional representation from cross-country regressions, the difference in this one institution between the USA and

Europe can explain the smaller US social welfare state (holding majoritarianism constant; Alesina, Glaeser, and Sacerdote 2001).

The strong relationship between proportional representation and redistribution across countries reflects more than just a causal effect of this one institution. Proportional representation tends to accompany a wide range of institutions, which together supported the rise of the welfare state in Europe, while American majoritarianism is accompanied by many other political institutions which have helped stem the growth of American redistribution. For example, the US tradition of federalism, which gave power of welfare to the states, seems to have checked the rise of welfare spending as states limit redistribution to keep rich people in and poor people out. Checks and balances within the USA, which are often weaker in many European countries, also appear to check the growth of redistribution. In the 1930s, the conservative bloc in the Senate (combining southern Democrats and northern Republicans) blocked the continuing expansion of the New Deal. Alston and Ferrie (1993) show that southern Democrats only allowed the New Deal policies to impact the South in the 1950s, when technological change made these policies less problematic for their core elite supporters. In the 1990s, the interactions between Gingrich's House of Representatives and Clinton's presidency ended "welfare as we know it."

America also has institutions that are not particularly majoritarian and that represent past political views more than current popular enthusiasms. Both the Senate and the Supreme Court have at various times presented serious roadblocks to the growth of the American welfare state, particularly in the 1930s, but also in the nineteenth century when the Supreme Court repeatedly declared that the income tax was unconstitutional. In the late twentieth century, conservatives railed against a liberal activist court, but prior to 1950, the Supreme Court was a steady brake on the growth of government regulation, taxation, and redistribution.

While there seems little doubt that American political institutions help us to understand why the USA has much less redistribution and more inequality, these institutions are themselves hardly the root causes of the differences across the Atlantic. Institutions are rarely the first causes of anything, but rather just reflect more exogenous differences between countries. A comparison of European and American political institutions in 1870 would surely tell us that the USA had the most liberal, not the most conservative, institutions among wealthier countries. The United States had widespread suffrage and gave more power to democratically elected representatives than most European nations. France had an emperor, Prussia its king, and even England had a powerful, entrenched House of Lords. In the nineteenth century, the USA had institutions that were particularly progressive, not particularly conservative.

The big difference in political institutions between the USA and Europe is the result of radical change of political institutions in nineteenth-century Europe and the relative stability of the USA. Almost every major country in continental Europe had either a full-fledged revolution (as in Germany, Austria, Portugal, Russia), a general strike whose impact was quasi-revolutionary (as in Belgium, Sweden, Finland, Switzerland), a civil war (Spain), or a postwar constitutional revision that completely revamped pre-existing institutions (France, Italy). Some European countries had more than one of these events.

In small, dense countries, these violent uprisings succeeded in forcing institutional change even without externally produced chaos. Belgium, Finland and Portugal all revamped their institutions (and established proportional representation) before the First World War. In larger countries, big armies made up of soldiers who were socially isolated from strikers or revolutionaries served to repress domestic uprisings before 1914. The real watershed was the First World War, when ancient dynasties were first defeated in battle and then upended by domestic uprisings. Demoralized armies that were made up of civilian draftees rather than professional soldiers were unwilling or unable to suppress revolution or strikers in Russia, Germany, Austria-Hungary, Turkey, and Italy. As left-wing groups gained control at the expense of defeated dynasties, they crafted political institutions that would entrench left-wing power for decades to come. The European welfare state is, in many cases, built on political institutions which are the legacy of the chaos and defeats of 1918.

The USA then is exceptional, not because it lacked violent strikers or because it lacked a labor movement, but rather because these groups were unable to force change in the American Constitution through strikes or revolutions. In the late nineteenth century, in the New York City Draft riots, in the Homestead strike, and in the Haymarket riots, police and Pinkerton agents successfully stopped uprisings. Moreover, because of America's vast size, these uprisings happened far from the corridors of power, so they did not really threaten America's political leadership. In the twentieth century, when the Bonus marchers moved on Washington, the undefeated, professional America easily dispersed these straggling veterans with force. America kept its eighteenth-century Constitution, with its strong respect for property rights, because the country did not lose a war on its home soil and the forces of the government were always easily up to the task of repressing left-wing uprisings. In Europe, political institutions reflect the chaos of twentieth-century Europe and the power of socialist forces during that chaos.

4.1 Beliefs about Inequality

This discussion still leaves one final puzzle: why do Americans and European have such different beliefs about the nature of inequality in their countries? One thing is clear. Differences across countries in beliefs about the nature of inequality don't reflect reality. As mentioned above, the available evidence suggests that the American poor work harder than their European equivalents and have a lower probability of exiting from poverty. Yet 60 per cent of Americans believe that their poor are lazy and have tremendous opportunities, while 60 per cent of Europeans believe that the poor are trapped.

A far better explanation is that beliefs about inequality reflect political power of the left and right working through indoctrination and the formation of beliefs. Left-wing leaders find it in their interest to convince people that the poorer beneficiaries from left-wing policies are good people sadly beset by forces outside of their control. Right-wing leaders find it equally in their interest to convince people that the poor are cheats and wastrels and that money spent on welfare is useless spending on morally deficient individuals.

While there is little direct evidence on the impact of indoctrination, two sets of facts are clear. First, a vast abundance of evidence from psychology (starting with Asch 1955) has shown that beliefs are extraordinarily malleable, at least in contexts where error isn't privately costly. Second, across countries Alesina and Glaeser (2004) show that political variables, like proportional representation, that seem to increase the power of the left (as discussed above) also predict beliefs about inequality. Somewhat remarkably, geographic variables that seem to increase the political power of the left (like little land area) also predict beliefs about income inequality, even though they have no correlation with the relevant economic reality.

Indoctrination works through both political speeches and education. Right-wing American inaugural speeches are filled with comments like "no one can deny the equality of opportunity that made us what we are" (Harding 1921) and "there are no limits to growth and human progress when men and women are free" (Reagan 1985). By contrast, left-wing European leaders say things like "the society in which we live is founded on privilege" (Blum 1946), and "In countries where the capital system of production prevails the masses of people are forced down to the condition of proletarians" (Kautsky 1910).

Almost surely, teaching in schoolrooms shapes economic views more strongly than political speeches, and again here, there is a clear difference between the USA and Europe. In the nineteenth-century USA, schoolbooks like McVickar (1846) taught that "even the poorest boy in our country ... has as good a chance of becoming independent and respectable, and perhaps rich, as any man in the country." Still today, high school textbooks emphasize that the USA remains the land of opportunity. Significantly, when Europe was actually more aristocratic and less open, its textbooks were more likely to teach that children were growing up in a land of opportunity. For example, the textbooks of the French Third Republic taught that "hard work and rectitude were bound to bring improvement, internal and external," and featured a shoemaker named Grégoire whose hard work was leading towards success. The Kaiser was just as adamant that his schools taught people that working hard will lead to success.

The difference between American and European indoctrination appeared with the triumph of the European left. Already in the 1890s, German teachers' unions fought with the Kaiser to teach a different ideological message. In the aftermath of the First World War, schools in Europe came steadily to spread Marxist messages of class immobility and consciousness (details in Alesina and Glaeser 2004). The steady use of education to build "class consciousness" appears to have formed economic beliefs in Europe and can provide at least one explanation of why beliefs in the USA and Europe are so different. As such, beliefs about income mobility and inequality reflect indoctrination and the political success of the right in the USA and the left in Europe, more than they do anything about reality.

5 CONCLUSION

Inequality remains a fascinating topic of research. Across countries, inequality levels differ wildly and inequality is correlated with a number of important variables. Inequality appears to be determined by the level of development in a non-monotonic manner. Inequality also seems to be the result of ethnic heterogeneity, which impacts inequality both directly, since different ethnicities have different skill levels, and indirectly through political channels, as people seem less eager to transfer money to people from a different ethnic group. Inequality is correlated with dictatorship and with governments that fail to respect property rights. These correlations at least raise the possibility that inequality is actually a causal variable that leads to worse political outcomes, but we are far from confident that causality runs from inequality to politics.

The implications of inequality research for public policy are far from clear. Alesina and Rodrik (1994) suggest that inequality deters growth because inequality leads to costly redistributionary policies. Even if this were the right interpretation of the small inequality–growth correlation, then it would hardly make sense to try to fight inequality with redistribution since, according to this model, redistribution is the problem that inequality creates. The literature on the political economy of inequality does not give clear answers on policies, but it does suggest that shifts in inequality may influence polities in far-ranging, substantial, and often unpredictable ways.

REFERENCES

ACEMOGLU, D., JOHNSON, S., and ROBINSON, J. 2001. The colonial origins of economic development: an empirical investigation. *American Economic Review*, 91: 1369–401.

ALESINA, A., BAQIR, R., and EASTERLY, W. 1999. Public goods and ethnic divisions. *Quarterly Journal of Economics*, 114: 1243–84.

―― and GLAESER, E. 2004. *Fighting Poverty in the U.S. and Europe: A World of Difference.* Oxford: Oxford University Press.

―― ―― and SACERDOTE, B. 2001. Why doesn't the U.S. have a European-style welfare state? *Brookings Papers on Economic Activity*, 2: 187–278.

―― and RODRIK, D. 1994. Distributive politics and economic growth. *Quarterly Journal of Economics*, 109: 465–90.

ALSTON, L., and FERRIE, J. 1993. Paternalism in agricultural labor contracts in the U.S. South: implications for the growth of the welfare state. *American Economic Review*, 83: 852–76.

ASCH, S. 1955. Opinions and social influence. *Scientific American*, 193: 31–55.

AUTOR, D., KATZ, L., and KRUEGER, A. 1998. Computing inequality: have computers changed the labor market? *Quarterly Journal of Economics*, 113: 1169–213.

BLAU, F., and KAHN, L. 1996. International differences in male wage inequality: institutions versus market forces. *Journal of Political Economy*, 104: 791–837.

BLUM, L. 1946. *For All Mankind*. New York: Viking Press.

CHECCHI, D., ICHINO, A., and RUSTICHINI, A. 1999. More equal and less mobile? Education financing and intergeneration mobility in Italy and in the U.S. *Journal of Public Economics*, 74: 351–93.

DE TOCQUEVILLE, A. 1835. *Democracy in America*. London: Saunders and Otley.

ENGELS, F. 1959. Why there is no large socialist party in America. In *Marx and Engels: Basic Writings on Politics and Philosophy*, ed. L. S. Feuer. Garden City, NY: Anchor.

ENGERMAN, S. L., and SOKOLOFF, K. L. 2002. Factor endowments, inequality, and paths of development among New World economies. *Economia*, 3: 41–102.

FAJNZYLBER, P., LEDERMAN, D., and LOAYZA, N. 2002. Inequality and crime. *Journal of Law and Economics*, 45: 1–40.

FINER, S. 1962. *The Man on Horseback: The Role of the Military in Politics*. London: Pall Mall.

GALOR, O., MOAV, O., and VOLLRATH, D. 2004. Land inequality and the origin of divergence and overtaking in the growth process: theory and evidence. Brown Economics Working Paper 2003–04.

GLAESER, E., SCHEINKMAN J., and SHLEIFER, A. 2003. The injustice of inequality. *Journal of Monetary Economics*, 50: 199–222.

—— and SHLEIFER, A. 2004. The Curley effect: the economics of shaping the electorate. *Journal of Law, Economics and Organization*, 21: 1–19.

GOLDIN, C., and MARGO, R. A. 1992. The great compression: the U.S. wage structure at mid-century. *Quarterly Journal of Economics*, 108: 1–34.

GOTTSCHALK, P., and SPOLAORE, E. 2002. On the evaluation of income mobility. *Review of Economic Studies*, 69: 191–208.

HANRATTY, M., and BLANK, R. 1992. Down and out in North America: recent trends in poverty rates in the United States and Canada. *Quarterly Journal of Economics*, 108: 233–54.

HARDING, W. 1921. Inaugural address. 4 March. Available at: www.yale.edu/lawweb/avalon/presiden/inaug/harding.htm.

JAGGERS, K., and MARSHALL, M. 2000. Polity IV Project, Center for International Development and Conflict Management, University of Maryland.

KAUTSKY, K. 1910. *The Class Struggle*. Chicago: Charles H. Kerr.

KATZ, L., and MURPHY, K. 1992. Changes in relative wages, 1963-1987: supply and demand factors. *Quarterly Journal of Economics*, 107: 35–78.

KUZNETS, S. 1955. Economic growth and income inequality. *American Economic Review*, 65: 1–28.

LIPSET, S. M. 1966. *American Exceptionalism*. New York: W. W. Norton.

LUTTMER, E. 2001. Group loyalty and the taste for redistribution. *Journal of Political Economy*, 109: 500–28.

MCVICKAR, REV. J. 1846. *First Lessons in Political Economy for the Use of Schools and Families*. Boston: Hillard, Gray & Co.

MELTZER, A., and RICHARD, S. 1981. A rational theory of the size of government. *Journal of Political Economy*, 89: 914–27.

MILES-FERRETTI, G. M., PEROTTI, R., and ROSTAGNO, M. 2002. Electoral rules and public spending. *Quarterly Journal of Economics*, 117: 609–58.

MOORE, B. 1996. *Social Origins of Dictatorship and Democracy: Lord and Peasant in the Making of the Modern World*. Boston: Beacon Press.

PERSSON, T., and TABELLINI, G. 1994. Is inequality harmful for growth? *American Economic Review*, 84: 600–21.

—— 2003. *The Economic Effects of Constitutions*. Cambridge, Mass.: MIT Press.

PICKETTY, T., and SAEZ, E. 2003. Income inequality in the United States: 1913–1998. *Quarterly Journal of Economics*, 118: 1–39.

REAGAN, R. 1985. Second inaugural address. 21 January. Available at: www.yale.edu/lawweb/avalon/presiden/inaug/reagan2.htm.
QIAN, Y., and WEINGAST, B. R. 1997. Federalism as a commitment to preserving market incentives. *Journal of Economic Perspectives*, 11: 83–92.
SOMBART, W. 1976. *Why is there no Socialism in the United States?* London: Macmillan.
TASK FORCE ON INEQUALITY AND AMERICAN DEMOCRACY 2004. American democracy in an age of rising inequality. Washington, DC: American Political Science Association.
WEBER, M. 2001. *The Protestant Ethic and the Spirit of Capitalism*. London: Routledge.
WOODWARD, C. V. 1955. *The Strange Career of Jim Crow*. New York: Oxford University Press.
YOU, J., and KHAGRAM, S. 2004. Inequality and corruption. Hauser Center for Nonprofit Organizations Working Paper 22, KSG Working Paper Series RWP04–001.

CHAPTER 35

COMPARATIVE PERSPECTIVES ON THE ROLE OF THE STATE IN THE ECONOMY

ANNE WREN

In his influential work on "Political Control of the Economy," Tufte (1978, 104) concludes that:

> The single most important determinant of variations in macroeconomic performance from one industrialized democracy to another is the location on the left-right spectrum of the governing party...the governing political party is very much responsible for major macroeconomic outcomes—unemployment rates, inflation rates, income equalization, and the size and rate of expansion of the government budget.

This statement is significant in two respects. First, in its assignment of a high level of control over important economic outcomes to the state. Second, in its identification of governing parties as the most powerful political actors in the economic policy-making process. Reviewed nearly three decades later, the strength of these conclusions appears surprising. In the period since Tufte wrote, both the instrumental capacity of the state to shape economic activity and outcomes, and the extent of the influence of elected governments in the policy-making process, have been the subject of debate in the comparative political economy literature. In this chapter we will review these debates, outline how they have influenced current thinking about the role of the state in the economy, and suggest several important avenues for future research.

We will begin by describing the challenges posed to the thesis that state actors possess the *instrumental capacity* to engage in *macroeconomic demand management* by the rational expectations revolution in economics; by arguments about the contingency of the effectiveness of government interventions in this area on the structure of socioeconomic institutions; and, more recently, by considerations of the limits placed on state capacities by the international integration of trade and capital markets. We will then discuss the increasingly important literature analyzing the capacity of state actors to intervene effectively on the *supply side* of the economy to create the conditions for growth, expansion, and stability. We will consider the extent to which interventions in these areas also may be constrained by the structure of existing socioeconomic institutions, and by processes of international economic integration.

Finally we will outline how these debates lead to important questions about the relative explanatory power of arguments, emphasizing the long-term economic impact of states' socioeconomic institutional structures, and those focusing on the more immediate influence of governing political parties. We will suggest that the assessment of the relative economic importance of state structures and government policy has important implications for the future direction of the field and, in particular, for the choices which we make in modeling the impact of politics on the economy.[1]

1 STATES' INSTRUMENTAL CAPACITIES

1.1 The State's Role in Macroeconomic Demand Management

The first critique of governments' abilities to engage in successful demand management emerged from the rational expectations revolution in economics. Building on the work of Friedman (1968) it was argued that, in a monetary policy game between governments and rational economic agents, governments could no longer be assumed to control more than the nominal value of monetary instruments. Any anticipated change in nominal values would be compensated for by instantaneously adjusting wages and prices, so that real economic outcomes could not be diverted from their long-run equilibrium values. This argument challenged claims of the existence of a

---

[1] Obvious reasons of space have compelled us to limit the number of research questions which we consider. Among the literatures which we have been forced to exclude, but which clearly also bear relevance to the issue of the state's economic role, we would include the new and exciting literature relating economic policy and performance directly to the structure of the state's political institutions (e.g. the electoral system) rather than the socioeconomic institutions considered here (some of this material is covered in Iversen, this volume, and Persson and Tabellini, this volume); as well as the literature on the constraints placed on politicians' policy choices by the actions of autonomous, or semi-autonomous, bureaucratic agents (some of this material is covered in Huber and Shipan, this volume).

stable negative relationship between unemployment and inflation rates—the Phillips curve (Phillips 1958)—and as a result undermined the influential contributions of Hibbs (1977) and Tufte (1978) to the literature on the economic significance of government partisanship. For an exploitable Phillips curve to exist, governments would have to be capable of systematically "fooling" economic agents—a violation of the rationality assumption (Lucas 1972; Sargent and Wallace 1975; and Franzese, this volume, for a further discussion). Thus it was impossible for left- and right-wing governments to simply "select" different Phillips-curve locations in response to the distributional preferences of their electoral constituencies, as postulated by Tufte and Hibbs.

Later Alesina's "rational partisan" model reintroduced the possibility of observing real effects of partisanship, as a result of institutional rigidities in wage and price-setting, and of uncertainty regarding electoral outcomes (see Alesina, Roubini, and Cohen 1997). Still, Alesina's model predicted that the real economic effects (in terms of output and employment) of partisanship would be temporary (disappearing once wages and prices adapt to the post-electoral environment). Only their effects on inflation were expected to persist.

A different line of argument, meanwhile, considered how the process of macroeconomic demand management is influenced by the broader institutional environment in which it takes place. Alvarez, Garrett, and Lange (1991), for example, identify a non-neutral role for government in influencing the wage-setting behavior of politically powerful union movements. Centralized union movements are more likely to internalize the effects of their wage demands on the economy as a whole (Calmfors and Driffill 1988). They also have considerable institutional capacity to deliver economy-wide wage restraint. However, the real benefits to labor of delivering this restraint are uncertain, unless credible assurances can be obtained that public policy will encourage the productive reinvestment of profits in the domestic economy, and will safeguard the welfare of workers (Przeworski and Wallerstein 1982; Lange 1984).

This uncertainty implies that governments can potentially play an important role in influencing wage behavior. Common knowledge about parties' ideological and electoral commitments, renders left governments more credible as guarantors of the protection of labor interests. Thus, the argument goes, in a centralized environment, left governments are more capable than governments of the right of encouraging wage restraint and achieving superior growth and inflation performance. Under a right-wing government, uncertainty about the distribution of the economic benefits of wage restraint will reduce the incentive for powerful centralized unions to act cooperatively. In contrast, in a more decentralized environment, common knowledge about the ideological and electoral commitments of left governments renders them more likely to be taken advantage of by opportunistic fragmented unions, so that their economic performance will tend to be worse than that of governments of the right. Thus the appropriate role for the government, and the economic effectiveness of governments of different partisan hues, is expected to vary depending on the institutional context.

Lange and Garrett's "institutional partisan" model is quite successful in explaining variations in cross-national growth performance in response to the oil shocks of the 1970s. In recent years, however, in response to the increased trend towards the delegation of monetary policy to independent central banks, a new set of arguments has been developed which model inflation and unemployment rates as emerging from the interaction between independent monetary authorities and the parties to the wage negotiation process (unions and employers' organizations) (Hall and Franzese 1998; Iversen 1999).

Again these models are designed to show how the impact of policy intervention can vary depending on the institutional context, but in this instance the government's role is more restricted. While it bears responsibility for the selection of the monetary regime, it may have limited powers to alter it once it is in place. If its selection involves the delegation of monetary authority to an independent central bank, for example, this implies that in future iterations of the game, the principal political actors engaged in the macroeconomic management of the business cycle will be central bankers, and the representatives of unions and employers' organizations. Their behavior, in turn, is dictated by the system of incentives emerging from the institutional environments in which they operate. In these arguments, macroeconomic outcomes are principally determined by the interaction between the socioeconomic institutions of the state, and the impact of their structures on the behavior of economic actors, rather than by the direct actions of democratic governments.

Additional constraints on the ability of governments effectively to pursue macroeconomic demand management policies are identified in the growing literature on the domestic economic impact of trade and capital market liberalization. On the monetary policy side, for example, it is argued that the ability of large financial institutions to transfer funds rapidly across borders creates a strong impetus for cross-national convergence in policy outcomes (see, for example, Kurzer 1993; Moses 1994; Keohane and Milner 1996; Simmons 1998). Where exchange rates are fixed, cross-national convergence in interest rates will be induced by the free movement of capital in search of the highest returns (Mundell 1961). Where exchange rates are allowed to float, states retain some capacity to engineer monetary expansions via currency depreciations, but such expansions are rendered less effective by associated increases in the cost of imports, and increase the prospect of economically damaging speculative currency attacks (McKinnon 1988). Similarly, on the fiscal side, increased trade and capital market openness creates a number of problems with the pursuit of counter-cyclical deficit-financed expansions. First, trade openness reduces the effectiveness of such policies, since the multiplier effect associated with domestic expansions is diminished where large components of domestic demand are international. Second, capital market openness increases their cost, since higher levels of debt lead to higher expected rates of inflation and are thus likely to be associated with capital flight unless nominal interest rates are allowed to rise.

These arguments have given rise to an extensive empirical literature which attempts to estimate the extent of these constraints in practice, and in particular, their impact on patterns of monetary and fiscal policy-making across parties. The findings of this literature, while mixed, tend to support the hypothesis that the capacities of governments in this area have been reduced by economic openness. While the evidence does not indicate that the constraints on the ability of governments to pursue independent monetary and fiscal policies are overwhelming, it does appear as though the size of partisan effects in these areas has declined in recent decades, and is associated in particular with the increased liberalization of capital markets and the introduction of fixed exchange rate regimes (Oatley 1999; Boix 2000). These findings provide some support for the hypothesis that the feasibility of Keynesian demand management policies favored traditionally by left-wing governments has been compromised by the globalization process.

1.2 The State's Role in Managing the Supply Side of the Economy

In light of critiques of their capacity to engage in macroeconomic demand management, students of the politics of state intervention have turned their attention to the range of supply-side strategies available to governments with which they can influence economic outcomes. Boix (1998), for example, focuses on policies aimed at providing the investment in physical and human capital needed for growth. He points out that in this area social democratic governments have traditionally favored interventionist strategies based on public sector-led investment in both physical and human capital, placing particular emphasis on strategies aimed at upgrading the skills of previously low-skilled workers in order to reduce market-based inequities. Conservative governments, on the other hand, have tended to rely on market-based strategies to maximize the incentives for private investment in both physical and human capital, with less regard for their impact in terms of equality.

Iversen and Wren (1998), meanwhile, investigate the effects of labor market policies on the development of services sectors. They point out that processes of market saturation and technical change, combined with increased exposure to trade with the developing world, have significantly reduced the relative size and economic significance of industrial sectors in the advanced economies.[2] Since this process of deindustrialization tends to be associated with significant job losses in traditional industrial sectors, they argue, a primary goal of governments in all advanced industrial democracies has now become the expansion of service sector employment. Low capacities for productivity growth in many areas of service production, however, imply that employment expansion in these sectors is hard to achieve when these countries tie the wages of sevice sector workers to those in more productive sectors. A trade-off exists, therefore, between the potential policy goals of equality and private service sector employment creation. The alternative, public sector, route to service employment expansion comes at its own cost in terms of government spending, which must be financed by taxes or debt. This results in a "trilemma," or three-way choice, between

---

[2] See Rowthorn and Rawaswamy 1997, 1998, for useful analyses of this process.

the policy goals of service employment creation, equality, and fiscal restraint (low levels of spending), whose structure implies that at most two of these goals can be pursued successfully at the one time.

Iversen and Wren argue that social democratic, neoliberal, and Christian democratic parties have tended to select divergent responses to the distributional trade-offs contained in the trilemma. Social democratic governments, for example, tend to prioritize the goals of employment creation and equality, at a cost of relatively high levels of state spending (generally financed by taxation). Neoliberal governments have tended to embrace a more market-driven approach, prioritizing the goals of private sector employment creation and fiscal restraint, at a cost of higher levels of inequality. Finally, European Christian democratic governments have typically combined the pursuit of the goal of equality with an emphasis on fiscal restraint, leading to poor performance in the area of service employment creation.

Finally, an extensive literature exists on the role of governments in the development of welfare states. Through the creation of regulatory welfare systems aimed at insuring citizens against social risk, and, in particular, at guaranteeing their compensation for the dislocations associated with economic change, governments (in conjunction with employers and union organizations) have sought to engineer the economic and social stability required for investment in physical and human capital, and for growth (Sinn 1995; Iversen and Soskice 2001; Moene and Wallerstein 2001; Mares 2003). In doing so, however, governments have also pursued their own redistributive goals, and this has led to the observation of significant variations in the types of welfare state policies pursued by governing parties of diverging ideological backgrounds. In this regard, the path-breaking work of Esping-Andersen (1990) identified three distinct "worlds" of welfare capitalism emerging in the process of welfare state development: a social democratic one emphasizing equality and market-replacing public service provision, a Christian democratic one emphasizing occupational and income-graduated public transfer payments, and a liberal one emphasizing market-based self-reliance supplemented by a limited needs-based transfer system.

State actors also face constraints in the pursuit of supply-side economic strategies, however. Here again, the structure of socioeconomic institutions impacts the range of effective strategies from which they may choose. Consider, for example, government policies aimed at reducing wage inequality. Recent research indicates that the ability of governments to influence levels of equality is constrained by the structure of wage-bargaining institutions. In particular, negotiated outcomes emerging from centralized wage negotiations, as opposed to decentralized or sector-by-sector negotiations, tend to result in more compressed wage structures (Iversen 1999; Wallerstein 1999).

Of course, governments also possess a considerable range of policy instruments with which they can influence wage structures directly—for example, by setting minimum wage and benefit levels, or by imposing legal extensions on collectively bargained agreements. However, the effect of these policies will always be constrained by the existing institutional environment. For example, in highly centralized environments, even neoliberal governments can be expected to preside over relatively high levels of wage equality, unless they engage in a full frontal assault on the institutional structure of wage bargaining (a challenging political task).

In addition to these institutional constraints, governments also face new challenges in designing supply side strategies for an increasingly open economic environment. The mechanisms through which the constraints of openness are felt on the supply side are slightly different from those affecting governments' capacities to engage in demand management. Consider, for example, the supply-side strategies pursued by social democratic governments in the areas of capital investment, service sector development, and welfare state protection described earlier (see Boix 1998; Iversen and Wren 1998; Esping-Andersen 1990). All of these strategies involve the pursuit of public sector expansions, and the maintenance of relatively egalitarian incomes structures. Critically, however, they have traditionally been financed largely through taxation rather than deficits and, as such, have been less directly impacted by the constraints on deficit spending associated with the liberalization of capital markets. This does not mean that the constraints of economic openness are removed in this case; rather it means that they center around the effects of taxation and labor market regulation on economic competitiveness, and on the threat of investment capital to "exit" the domestic economy in the face of policies which reduce the efficiency of their investments (Kurzer 1993; Rodrik 1997; Alesina and Perotti 1997).

Several scholars have pointed out that the grounds for arguing (as conventional wisdom sometimes assumes) that these effects will lead to a cross-national convergence in favor of neoliberal outcomes are not particularly strong. First, as pointed out by Garrett (1998), it cannot be assumed that the cost–benefit analyses of capital investors will lead them to reject all forms of public investment and social policy. The observation by endogenous growth theorists that the market is likely to under-provide some of the public goods required for growth—such as investment in infrastructure, and in the skills and health of the workforce—suggests positive benefits to capital of their public provision (Romer 1994; Barro 1997). Given the right institutional environment, therefore, social policy can generate positive externalities—such as higher rates of productivity growth, and political, economic, and social stability—which the owners of capital find it cost effective to fund.[3] Second, several scholars have argued that the economic dislocation which openness creates simultaneously increases citizen demand for welfare state protection from economic uncertainty and risk. The development and expansion of welfare states in advanced industrial economies in the 1960s and 1970s can be interpreted at least partly as a result of the responsiveness of state actors to these demands (Cameron 1978) and there is ample evidence of the generation of similar political pressures in the current era of globalization (Rodrik 1997).

The globalization process, therefore, does not rob state actors of the policy instruments necessary for the provision of public investment or welfare. Rather it alters the calculus of political decision-making over economic policy. State actors must

---

[3] Indeed, new research has explicated the positive role played by employers in the development of the welfare state (Swenson 2002; Mares 2003).

now weigh demands for redistribution and public spending against potential new economic costs associated with the pursuit of interventionary policies—namely the risks of reduced competitiveness and an increased risk of capital flight associated with high levels of taxation and regulation. The outcome of this process clearly depends critically on the structure of *political* incentives facing state actors.

Empirical examinations of the extent of the constraints under which governments operate in the pursuit of supply-side strategies have produced mixed results. The most consistent empirical result in this area is the observation of a large degree of structural continuity over time. In the areas of welfare and labor market policy, for example, several authors provide convincing evidence of the long-term persistence of social democratic, Christian democratic, and neoliberal "regime types" and their continued influence on economic outcomes, in the face of increased economic openness (Esping-Andersen 1990; Pierson 1994, 2001; Iversen and Wren 1998; Huber and Stephens 2001).

The task of establishing the independent economic effects of *current* government partisanship and inherited institutional structures has proved more difficult for methodological reasons. High levels of correlation between many key variables— such as, for example, the degree of centralization of wage-bargaining institutions, the strength of social democratic welfare state regime "characteristics," and the current and historical electoral strength of social democratic parties—enhanced by the small size of the sample on which most empirical investigations have focused (eighteen or fewer OECD nations over a period of thirty or forty years), create problems of multicollinearity in the conduct of cross-national regression analyses.[4] As a result, measures of the independent effects of theoretically relevant institutional variables are omitted from many analyses. Unfortunately these problems have tended to restrict our ability to separate the influence of democratically elected governments on economic activity from that of the socioeconomic institutional environment in which they operate.

2 STATE STRUCTURES AND STATE ACTORS: THE ROLE OF GOVERNMENTS

In spite of challenges to Tufte's original characterization of the nature of political control of the economy, therefore, developments in the comparative political economy literature over the last three decades have served to reaffirm the instrumental capacity of the state to influence economic outcomes. At the same time, as described in the last section, analyses of *government intervention* on both the demand and the supply sides of the economy have increasingly emphasized the contingency of their effectiveness on the structure of the socioeconomic institutions of the state. These

---

[4] See Huber and Stephens 2001 for a careful discussion of these issues.

arguments follow a common logic which identifies the influence of the structure of socioeconomic institutions on the behavior of important economic actors (such as employers and labor unions), and its resulting impact on their behavioral responses to different kinds of policies. Reflecting this emphasis on the significance of socioeconomic institutional configurations, several authors have identified powerful long-run effects of institutional structures on patterns of economic activity, which persist even in an increasingly economically integrated international environment.

This emphasis on the persistence of socioeconomic "regime" types, and their importance in accounting for variations in patterns of economic development and performance, reaffirms the significance of the state's economic role. At the same time, it calls into question the extent of the capacity of *governing political parties* to influence economic outcomes independently. Perhaps the most comprehensive set of arguments emphasizing the long-term significance of states' socioeconomic institutional structures is contained in the new, and influential, "varieties of capitalism" approach developed by Hall and Soskice (2001).[5] Scholars adopting this approach have identified the existence of *complementarities* between a broad range of socioeconomic institutions concerned *with both supply- and demand-side economic strategies*— including, for example, the institutions of union and employer representation; of education and training; of the financial system; and of the welfare state. The existence of these complementarities implies that some institutional configurations are likely to be more economically successful than others.

Hall and Soskice identify two specific "varieties of capitalism," both of which have the capacity for strong economic growth, but which rely on very different models of socioeconomic organization. The liberal market economy (LME) relies on arm's-length exchange and formal contracting—in short, on the institutions of competitive markets—to coordinate the activities of firms, and other socioeconomic actors. In the coordinated market economy (CME), in contrast, economic actors rely more heavily on non-market relationships to coordinate their activities. Cooperative equilibrium outcomes are reached through repetitive interactions between economic actors involved in long-term relationships with each other in a context of closely monitored networks. An important difference between the CME model and the more traditional competitive market model embodied in LME, is the CME's reliance on a set of appropriately designed and stable intermediate institutions—such as employers' organizations, strong unions, and cross-shareholding networks—which allow both the exchange of information, and the monitoring, and if necessary sanctioning, of behavior, which are necessary to enable actors to make credible commitments to cooperative outcomes.

The authors argue that comparative institutional advantages in different types of production flow from these differences in organization, rendering LMEs more competitive in the production of goods requiring flexibility and radical innovation (for example, in high-tech sectors such as biotechnology or semiconductors), while CMEs compete more effectively in the production of goods requiring incremental

[5] Iversen (this volume) covers some related issues.

innovation and the maintenance of high levels of quality in production over long periods of time (for example, in many areas of consumer durables). They argue that, given the apparently successful integration of both of these models into the international economy, there are no grounds to expect cross-national institutional convergence as a result of increasing international economic integration.

Within the "varieties of capitalism" approach the capacity of government actors independently to influence economic outcomes, or the direction of economic development, seems particularly tightly constrained. The argument suggests that the economic effectiveness of a given policy or institution is heavily contingent on the structure of the broader institutional configuration in which it is embedded. This implies that government actors face a restricted menu of potential policy choices. Attempts to engage in reform in one area of policy, without simultaneously reforming the many other socioeconomic institutions with which it interacts, are likely to lead to disimproved economic outcomes. Within this framework, there appears to be little scope for governments to exert a significant independent influence on economic outcomes. Rather, states are expected to continue to diverge along their existing equilibrium paths unless they experience a significant external economic shock.

Attempts by governments to engage in more wide-ranging reforms in the institutional environment aimed at shifting a political economy entirely from one institutional equilibrium to another, meanwhile, are likely to be politically infeasible given the vested interests of citizens and socioeconomic actors in the existing system. Firms and workers base a range of investment decisions (for example, in the development of their production profiles, or in education and training) on the institutional environments in which they are operating. As a result, they develop policy preferences which favor the support and improvement of existing institutions (a strategy which promises to protect the value of the returns to existing assets) over radical institutional change (a strategy which increases the uncertainty associated with these returns).[6]

For example, Estevez-Abe, Iversen, and Soskice (2001) argue that workers who have invested in firm- and sector-specific skills through participation in the highly developed systems of on-the-job and vocational training present in CMEs are more likely to support high levels of employment and unemployment protection. This is because they require insurance against the relatively high levels of risk associated with specific asset investments of this type. (Workers with specific skills face greater threats to their income from, for example, a sectoral shock, than those who have invested in more general skills which can be easily transported across firms and sectors). Meanwhile firms operating in CMEs, whose production profiles rely on workers

---

[6] Note that, within this framework, it is possible for an economy to be moved away from its existing equilibrium path by a significant external shock. Under these circumstances the returns to existing investments (or at least the uncertainty associated with them) may be sufficiently altered as to allow the implementation of more radical reforms. It is important to note, however, that the authors of the varieties of capitalism volume do not consider that the increased economic openness of the current period has created a shock of this type for either CMEs or LMEs. This is because, according to their argument, both models have shown themselves equally capable of adapting to the new international economic environment.

with specific skills, are also likely to support both the vocational training and social protection systems which facilitate their acquisition (Hall and Soskice 2001). Firms' and workers' decisions to invest in a particular set of production profiles and skills, therefore, create vested interests in the set of interacting institutions which maximize the expected returns to these investments.

These theoretical arguments have two implications of relevance to this chapter which are of particular importance to the future of the field of comparative political economy. First, they imply that governing political parties are in fact tightly constrained in their selection of socioeconomic policies by the structure of the inherited socioeconomic institutional environment in which they are operating. Second, they imply that socioeconomic actors' policy preferences should be considered endogenous in our models of institutional evolution—defined by the structure of the institutions themselves.

If these arguments are true they indicate that in attempting to identify the impact of politics on economic outcomes, there may be more explanatory power to be gained by investigating the political factors contributing to institutional choice at certain key moments of historical discontinuity, and by understanding processes of political path dependence in institutional evolution (as exemplified, for example, in the work of North 1990), than by the development of increasingly sophisticated models of the structure of electoral opportunities and constraints faced by governing political parties (as exemplified in the research agenda initiated by Tufte).

Before any conclusions on this issue can be drawn, however, it is critical that the open *empirical* question of the relative importance of government partisanship and the state's socioeconomic institutional structure be resolved. Unfortunately, as outlined above, this task has proved somewhat problematic methodologically, given the high levels of correlation between many key variables, and the small size of the sample on which most empirical investigations have focused. These problems can only be expected to worsen in the face of the expanded network of socioeconomic institutions theorized to impact interactively on economic outcomes in the "varieties of capitalism" approach. Effective resolution of these methodological issues will require a broadening of the sample on which such analyses are conducted, or the pursuit of more detailed case study analysis. This research is essential to the goal of separating the effects of state structure and political agency on economic outcomes.

3 Conclusion

In conclusion, let us consider what new light has been shed on Tufte's original characterization of the nature of political control of the economy by subsequent developments in the comparative political economy literature. On the one hand, new arguments in this literature (as well as in economics) suggest increasing constraints on the capacities of governments to engage in effective macroeconomic demand management. On the other hand we still see significant evidence of state influence in the development of supply-side strategies. On both the supply and the demand side, however, we find a range of new arguments which emphasize how governments are constrained in their selection of policies by the existing socioeconomic institutional configuration of the state. These arguments are coupled with empirical evidence identifying significant long-term effects of states' socioeconomic institutional structures on patterns of economic development and performance. By emphasizing the impact of *state structures* on patterns of economic activity, these arguments tend to downplay the significance of the economic role played by elected *governments*.

Ultimately the question of the significance of government influence on economic policy-making in the face of inherited institutional constraints is an empirical one, which can only be resolved through methodological innovation. However, as we have described, it has important normative and positive implications. Stated in the most general terms, the important question which we need to address is whether we should see "states" as sets of equilibrium socioeconomic institutions, relatively immune to the actions of governments (aside from their historical role in the selection of institutions at the point of creation), or whether governing political parties should also be considered important state actors—retaining the capacity significantly to influence economic outcomes, and the welfare of citizens.

REFERENCES

ALESINA, A., and PEROTTI, R. 1997. The welfare state and competitiveness. *American Economic Review*, 87: 921–39.
—— and ROUBINI, N., with COHEN, G. 1997. *Political Cycles and the Macroeconomy*. Cambridge, Mass.: MIT Press.
ALVAREZ, R. M., GARRETT, G., and LANGE, P. 1991. Government partisanship, labor organization, and macroeconomic performance. *American Political Science Review*, 85: 539–56.
BARRO, R. 1997. *Determinants of Economic Growth*. Cambridge, Mass.: MIT Press.
BOIX, C. 1998. *Political Parties, Growth and Equality*. Cambridge: Cambridge University Press.
—— 2000. Partisan governments, the international economy, and macroeconomic policies in OECD countries, 1964–93. *World Politics*, 53: 38–73.
CALMFORS, L., and DRIFFILL, J. 1988. Centralization of wage bargaining. *Economic Policy*, 6: 14–61.
CAMERON, D. 1978. The expansion of the public economy: a comparative analysis. *American Political Science Review*, 72: 1243–61.
ESPING-ANDERSEN, G. 1990. *The Three Worlds of Welfare Capitalism*. Princeton, NJ: Princeton University Press.
ESTEVEZ-ABE, M., IVERSEN, T., and SOSKICE, D. 2001. Social protection and the formation of skills: a re-interpretation of the welfare state. In *Varieties of Capitalism: The Institutional Foundations of Comparative Advantage*, ed. P. A. Hall and D. Soskice. Oxford: Oxford University Press.
FRIEDMAN, M. 1968. The role of monetary policy. *American Economic Review*, 58: 1–17.
GARRETT, G. 1998. *Partisan Politics in the Global Economy*. Cambridge: Cambridge University Press.

HALL, P. A., and FRANZESE, R., JR. 1998. Mixed signals: central bank independence, coordinated wage bargaining and European Monetary Union. *International Organization*, 52: 505–35.

——and SOSKICE, D. (eds.). 2001. *Varieties of Capitalism: The Institutional Foundations of Comparative Advantage*. Oxford: Oxford University Press.

HIBBS, D. 1977. Political parties and macroeconomic policy. *American Political Science Review*, 71: 1467–87.

HUBER, E., and STEPHENS, J. D. 2001. *Development and Crisis of the Welfare State*. Chicago: University of Chicago Press.

IVERSEN, T. 1999. *Contested Economic Institutions*. Cambridge: Cambridge University Press.

——and SOSKICE, D. 2001. An asset theory of social policy performances. *American Political Science Review*, 95: 875–93.

——and WREN, A. 1998. Equality, employment and budgetary restraint: the trilemma of the service economy. *World Politics*, 50: 507–74.

KEOHANE, R., and MILNER, H. 1996. *Internationalization and Domestic Politics*. Cambridge: Cambridge University Press.

KURZER, P. 1993. *Business and Banking*. Ithaca, NY: Cornell University Press.

LANGE, P. 1984. Unions, workers and wage regulation: the rational bases of consent. In *Order and Conflict in Contemporary Capitalism*, ed. J. H. Goldthorpe. New York: Oxford University Press.

LUCAS, R. E. 1972. Expectations and the neutrality of money. *Journal of Economic Theory*, 4: 103–24.

MCKINNON, R. I. 1988. Monetary and exchange rate policies for financial stability. *Journal of Economic Perspectives*, 2: 83–103.

MARES, I. 2003. *The Politics of Social Risk*. Cambridge: Cambridge University Press.

MOENE, K. O., and WALLERSTEIN, M. 2001. Inequality, social insurance and redistribution. *American Political Science Review*, 95: 859–74.

MOSES, J. 1994. The abdication of national policy autonomy: what's left to leave? *Politics and Society*, 22: 125–48.

MUNDELL, R. A. 1961. A theory of optimal currency areas. *American Economic Review*, 51: 657–65.

NORTH, D. 1990. *Institutions, Institutional Change, and Economic Performance*. Cambridge: Cambridge University Press.

OATLEY, T. 1999. How constraining is capital mobility? The partisan hypothesis in an open economy. *American Journal of Political Science*, 43: 1003–27.

PHILLIPS, A. W. 1958. The relation between unemployment and the rate of change of the money wage rates in the United Kingdom. *Economica*, 25: 283–99.

PIERSON, P. 1994. *Dismantling the Welfare State? Reagan, Thatcher and the Politics of Retrenchment*. Cambridge: Cambridge University Press.

——(ed.). 2001. *The New Politics of the Welfare State*. Oxford: Oxford University Press.

PRZEWORSKI, A., and WALLERSTEIN, M. 1982. The structure of class conflict in democratic capitalist societies. *American Political Science Review*, 76: 215–38.

RODRIK, D. 1997. *Has Globalization Gone Too Far?* Washington, DC: Institute for International Economics.

ROMER, P. 1994. The origins of endogenous growth. *Journal of Economic Perspectives*, 8: 3–22.

ROWTHORN, R., and RAMASWAMY, R. 1997. Deindustrialization: causes and implications. IMF Working Paper 97:42. Washington, DC.

————1998. Growth, trade and deindustrialization. IMF Working Paper 98: 60. Washington, DC.

SARGENT, T., and WALLACE, N. 1975. Rational expectations, the optimal monetary instrument, and the optimal money supply rule. *Journal of Political Economy*, 83: 241–54.
SIMMONS, B. 1998. The internationalization of capital. In *Continuity and Change in Contemporary Capitalism*, ed. H. Kitschelt, P. Lange, G. Marks, and J. Stephens. Cambridge: Cambridge University Press.
SINN, H. W. 1995. A theory of the welfare state. *Scandinavian Journal of Economics*, 97: 495–526.
SWENSON, P. 2002. *Capitalists against Markets*. Oxford: Oxford University Press.
TUFTE, E. R. 1978. *Political Control of the Economy*. Princeton, NJ: Princeton University Press.
WALLERSTEIN, M. 1999. Wage-setting institutions and pay inequality in advanced industrial societies. *American Journal of Political Science*, 43: 649–80.

CHAPTER 36

DEMOCRATIZATION

POST-COMMUNIST IMPLICATIONS

ANNA GRZYMALA-BUSSE
PAULINE JONES LUONG

Why do some countries successfully democratize, while others fail to establish firmly the rules and practices of democracy? Scholars have approached this question from two distinct perspectives. The first one focuses on the role of structural preconditions for democracy: a given society's levels of economic development, urbanization, or literacy. These are not easily influenced by any one individual, develop over decades if not centuries, and act as a fundamental constraint on elite behavior. The second concentrates instead on political agency, and argues that elite actors can "craft democracies:" when authoritarian governments and their opponents confront each other, they bargain over the distribution of power and authority. As a result, these actors can write new democratic rules and create the legislative and judicial structures to support and enforce these rules.

We argue here that the artificial divisions and unrecognized overlaps between the two perspectives have hampered our understanding of democratization. Drawing upon the experience of post-Communist countries, we show how structural preconditions enable elite action as much as they constrain it. Elites deliberately use existing structural legacies to construct new regimes. The rules and practices critical to democracy are both formal and informal, and they are as much a product of pre-existing state structures as of societal preconditions.

The chapter proceeds as follows. We first review and contrast the two approaches. We then focus on the post-Communist experience to synthesize the two perspectives.

We conclude by evaluating the success of these approaches in explaining the variation in democratization outcomes.

1 Approaches To Democratization

Most of the scholarship views either structural preconditions or elite agency as the critical factor behind the success of democratization. This dichotomy is often portrayed as mutually exclusive, if not jointly exhaustive. Below, we examine each approach in turn.

1.1 Structure

Structural accounts have emphasized broad societal preconditions for democracy, such as economic development and subsequent urbanization, or the development of a middle class and greater literacy. Scholars have highlighted these particular preconditions because they increase the demands for participation and for accountability that lead authoritarian regimes to democratize (e.g. Lipset 1960; Lerner 1958; Kilson 1987). They arise slowly, over decades and generations, and cannot be easily influenced by any one individual's beliefs or actions.

Such approaches portray these structures as formidable constraints on human behavior, which range from broad socioeconomic conditions, such as the level of economic development and class interests (e.g. Luebbert 1991; Moore 1966), to more immediate factors such as the path of extrication from the previous regime or economic conditions (e.g. Karl and Schmitter 1991; Haggard and Kaufman 1995). They also include specific institutions that shape governance and the relationship between state and society, such as legislatures or judiciaries (e.g. Bratton and van de Walle 1992; Widener 1994). The international political context can also greatly influence democratization, as democratic norms are exported abroad, and one country's citizens learn that it is possible to democratize similarly repressive regimes (e.g. O'Loughlin et al. 1998; Starr 1991).[1]

Others argue that economic performance can determine democratization outcomes. Sustained economic growth has long been viewed as a democratic stimulus, while low levels of economic development and the absence of a middle class, for example, have long been viewed as impediments to democratization (e.g. Moore 1966; Huntington 1991).[2] More recent scholarship has confirmed that economic wealth helps to maintain both authoritarian and democratic regimes; in other words,

---

[1] Not all subscribe to this notion, of course. On the other extreme, for example, Przeworski and Limongi 1997 argue that democratic transitions occur randomly.

[2] Larry Diamond argues that although the correlation has weakened, it remains robust. See Diamond 1992.

all regimes acquire a renewed stability beyond a certain GDP-per-capita threshold (Przeworski et al. 2000). Yet these findings are cold comfort for countries undergoing simultaneous democratization and market reforms: newly empowered electorates can lash out against governments that implement economic reforms that are painful in the short term (e.g. Callaghy 1994). Short-term losers of the transition can thus subvert the long-term processes of continued economic reform and its benefits (Przeworski 1991). The pessimistic conclusion is that political and economic transformation, if undertaken simultaneously, are likely to undermine one another.

Such broad phenomena, which occur at the level of entire societies and economies, are said to form powerful constraints on elite action and institutional innovation. Historical legacies of authoritarian regimes are especially likely to undermine the chances for successful and stable democratization.[3] For example, where the authoritarian regime has violently oppressed society, even the most democratic of successor regimes have to contend with the "torturer problem:" punishing the powerful perpetrators of past evil without letting them undermine the fragile new democracies (Huntington 1991; Fatton 1999). As a result, the survival of actors and institutions from the previous regime makes the transition to democracy more difficult. This pessimism has been echoed by some studies of the former Soviet Union and eastern Europe, who argued that the "Leninist legacy" of empire, one-party rule, and forced participation could doom both political and economic reform to failure for lack of widespread popular experience with and support for pluralism (e.g. Jowitt 1992; Motyl 1997).

1.2 Agency

If structural accounts view democratization as influenced primarily by the preconditions inherited from the *ancien régime*, agency-based accounts view it as a sharp and deliberate break with the authoritarian past. Where structuralist accounts talk of thresholds beyond which democratization is likely, agency-based accounts see unpredictable and contingent events that cascade into regime collapses. And, where structure-based models rely on societies and economies as the levels of analysis, agency-based accounts focus on individuals and their ability to enact their preferences for regime change or the status quo. As a result, democratization in this perspective can be both radical and rapid.

For agency-based accounts, therefore, the catalyst for democratization is often a regime crisis. Such crises can be external in origin (e.g. wars and occupations, or radical changes in trade patterns) or arise from domestic sources (e.g. the inability of

---

[3] The exceptions include those who argue that the particular configuration of political and economic institutions inherited from colonial rule has a direct impact on both the rate and the degree of liberalization. Thus, for example, francophone Africa experienced an earlier transition to democracy than the former British colonies in Africa due to the legacy of corporatism, which not only fostered interest group formation but also lowered the transaction costs of various interest groups to mobilize in support of political reform (Widener 1994).

governments to deliver goods and services to the populace, the death of an authoritarian ruler, the rise of local opposition to the government.)

In responding to these crises, elites and the societal groups they mobilize determine the outcomes of democratization. In one schematic, radicals and moderates (often identified as "softliners" and "hardliners") arise within both the government and the opposition (O'Donnell and Schmitter 1986; Huntington 1991). Under certain circumstances, these groups begin to bargain over the rules by which politics will be played. If centrists from both groups emerge as the most powerful actors, then such bargains can conclude in pacts that establish new democratic rules that allow for free competition, the expression of popular interests, and the protection of both *ancien régime* actors and new democratic rights. If, on the other hand, hardliners from either group emerge triumphant, a stable democratic pact is unlikely. The formal political institutions that follow thus reflect both the preferences and the power bases of these bargaining elites (e.g. Di Palma 1990; Linz and Stepan 1996).

Partly owing to its focus on elite bargaining and the ability of the bargainers to enact their preferences, this literature also emphasizes the construction of formal democratic institutions such as legislatures, electoral systems, or judiciaries. Since they were set up to favor the more powerful of the negotiating sides, moreover, the composition of these institutions reflects the distribution of power during the transition. Such explanations have been especially popular among scholars analyzing institutional change in post-Communist states (e.g. Colomer 1994; Geddes 1996). For example, they can account for the initial power of the Polish presidency (set up to favor Lech Wałęsa, the wildly popular anti-Communist leader) or the complex Hungarian electoral system (which reflected the calculations of the weak but radical opposition during the democratic transition) (Bernhard 2000).

As a result, the rise of these formal institutions, the backbone of functioning democracies, has also become one of the chief indicators of both transition to democracy and its consolidation. Especially salient debates were waged over the impact of formal electoral institutions on representation and government stability, and the specificities of electoral systems, political party regulations, and the choice of parliamentary versus presidential systems (e.g. Lardeyret 1991; Quade 1991). For example, an overwhelming consensus developed that parliamentary systems are more likely to promote democratic consolidation than presidential systems (e.g. Linz 1990; Stepan and Skach 1993). Numerous studies have also evaluated post-Communist transitions to democracy by solely examining the configurations of formal democratic institutions (e.g. Elster, Offe, and Preuss 1998; Frye 1997).

2 THE POST-COMMUNIST EXPERIENCE

Structural explanations highlight the broader context in which regime transition takes place, specifically the institutional constraints on the process of democratization. They are ill equipped, however, to explain the strategic behavior that often drives this process. Conversely, agency-based explanations go a long way in analyzing the thrust and parry of the transition period, as multiple actors struggle for survival and dominance. Yet they have been aptly criticized for suffering "from a myopia of the moment" (Bratton and van de Walle 1997, 27) and lack of attention to the limitations and opportunities inherited from the past. One resolution has been a division of labor: "structuralist approaches are good at accounting for the general causes of regime breakdown and the consolidation of new democracies. Process approaches may explain the timing of breakdown and transition as well as the specific trial-and-error process of searching for a new viable regime" (Kitschelt 1992, 1029).

Yet the most recent wave of democratization, which followed the collapse of Communism in 1989–91 in the Soviet Union and its east European satellites, shows that these two perspectives have much to contribute to each other. First, several structural preconditions inherited from the authoritarian regimes act to foster democratization, rather than constrain it. Moreover, elite agency matters long after the initial bargaining and well into the subsequent "consolidation" period. Second, elites can deliberately use these legacies to construct democratic regimes—subject to constraints from both elite competition and informal institutions. Third, the formal institutions of the *state* are as important as those of participation and electoral competition. Indeed, if there is a dominant lesson to be learned from the experience of post-Communism, it is that weak states threaten both democratic freedoms and the rule of law (e.g. Holmes 1997).

2.1 Structures Enabling Elites

First, both structure- and agency-based accounts tend to assume that structure constrains elites. It is only in moments of crisis that elites can act more freely. Yet if elite actors are the central agents of democratization, then where do their relative power, preferences, and strategies come from? Classifying elites "hardliners," "softliners," or "liberalizers" often leads to tautologies: the actors concluding the bargains are centrists, and we know they are centrists because they concluded the bargain. Just as importantly, why are some elites so much more successful than others in implementing their strategies?

Post-Communist cases demonstrate that the key to elite action is their cognitive, organizational, and social endowments: skills and experiences, reputations, informal alliances and networks. Ironically, for the elites involved in democratization, these resources have their origin in the authoritarian *anciens régimes* and they can be used to facilitate or obstruct democratization. In central Asia, for example, regional leaders empowered by their control over scarce resources and, hence, ability to distribute patronage under Soviet rule dominated the negotiations for institutional change following the regimes' collapse. Not surprisingly, facing almost no popular opposition, they opted to change little of the system with which they continued strongly to identify and from which they continued to benefit disproportionately (Jones Luong 2002). But such elite endowments can also have more subtle effects: for example, the post-1956 Hungarian consensus on the need for stability, and the Communist regime's subsequent cooptation of many of its intellectual opponents, weakened the anti-Communist opposition and left it without a broad support base—which then paradoxically emboldened the opposition (Bruszt and Stark 1991).

As a result, it is not only democrats who can establish democracy. The actors most likely to support the transition to democracy, no matter what their political pedigree, are those with portable resources: skills, reputations, and networks that allow these elites to function easily in both authoritarian and democratic regimes. Such elites can be found both among the functionaries of the old regime, and among the opposition firebrands. For example, those Communist elites in east–central Europe who were recruited into the party on the basis of their managerial skills and put in charge of implementing liberalizing reforms have proven to be the most successful democratic competitors of post-Communist political contests (Grzymala-Busse 2002).

Similarly, committed democrats may not be the best ones to establish and consolidate democracy. There are several cases of opposition elites who have been unable to manage successfully the transition to liberal democratic politicians as a result of their patchy skill set: Lech Wałęsa in Poland is perhaps the most illustrative example. A popular leader of the opposition to Communist rule and Nobel Peace Prize winner, he was unable to adapt to his new role as Poland's democratically elected president, fomenting a destructive "war at the top," fragmenting elites, negating foreign policy commitments, and questioning the legitimacy of other elected officials.

Critically, then, structural preconditions are not simply a constraint on elites— nor are they simply found at the level of societies or economies. The practices and structures of the authoritarian past can enable democratization by providing elites with the skills, reputations, and networks necessary to create and then credibly commit to the new rules and practices of democracy. The rise of legacies that enable democratization calls into question the widespread assumptions that the legacies of the authoritarian past undermine democratization, and that the survival of actors from the previous regime makes the transition to democracy more difficult.

2.2 The Deliberate Use of Structure

If structural preconditions do not necessarily constrain elites, they are also subject to deliberate use and exploitation by political elites. The opportunities to gain political and economic advantage in the new democratic regimes from the inherited structural legacies are manifold. Subsequently, political elites continue to exploit and transform the new democratic institutions they have created, as their constituencies, identities, and interests change over time.

First, as noted earlier, some of the elites were endowed with skills and resources that were highly portable to the new regime. In one example, former Communist party elites endowed with these resources radically transformed the Communist parties after the collapse of their rule into successful democratic competitors. In Hungary, Poland, Slovenia, and Lithuania, highly experienced and worldly technocrats took over the party leaderships, centralized power within the parties, streamlined extensive memberships and organizations, and committed themselves to democracy. The result was that these parties re-entered power within a few years of the Communist collapse, this time by winning democratic elections with appeals to secularism, moderation, and technocratic competence.

In a second example, both the former authoritarian elites and their opponents can build in informal economic and political advantages for themselves that last long beyond the transition. In the post-Communist setting, control over the enormous assets of the state (which comprised almost the entire industrial and service sectors of the economy) began to slip as the Communist regime began to collapse. As a result, there were numerous instances of "spontaneous privatization," as managers and party hacks took advantage of murky property rights to claim entire state enterprises at fire prices. The most notorious examples of such practices have occurred in the former Soviet Union, where entire sectors of the economy were bought at below-market prices by individuals (known widely as "the oligarchs") who gained enormous economic power and political influence under President Boris Yeltsin (e.g. Hoffman 2002).

Nor is the deliberate use of such structures confined to the years surrounding the regime collapse. Once new democratic institutions are in place, elites can continue deliberately to exploit any loopholes to their advantage, leading the way back to authoritarian practice in some cases. The letter, if not the spirit, of the democratic law is followed. For example, in Russia, President Vladimir Putin's steady move to gain greater control and authority over the media, and to discredit potential competitors, did not actually violate the country's formal legal institutions and in some cases has actually strengthened them (Smyth 2002). Similarly, Slobodan Milošević in Serbia and Vladimir Meciar in Slovakia proceeded largely by exploiting legal loopholes and interpreting them in distinctly favorable ways, and rarely proceeded by obviously or directly violating formal institutions.

This is not to say that all structural legacies will either have the same impact on elite action, or be as available for exploitation. These structural legacies are not uniform. First, no transition is a tabula rasa, but neither is it ineffably determined by the overwhelming weight of the past. The legacies of authoritarian regimes vary in their half-lives, with some disappearing virtually overnight (for example, consumer behavior and self-censorship), and others persisting well into the new regime (Grzymala-Busse 2002). Second, these legacies differ by regime: even within the supposedly homogeneous Communist empire, distinct economic, political, military, cultural, and geographic legacies continued to make their mark and launch these countries on divergent trajectories (e.g. Kopstein and Reilly 2002; Ekiert and Hanson 2003).

Moreover, elites are constrained in their use and exploitation of the institutions they have created—not necessarily by other institutions or structures, but by elite competition itself. Where *ancien régime* elites never had to exit power, or even to expand their existing constituency and basis for legitimacy, both economic and democratic reforms are stifled, as entrenched political actors continue to seek private rents and to extract resources from the state and its assets (e.g. Ganev 2001; Motyl

1997). Where elites never faced a threat of replacement from a credible and well-organized set of opposition forces, this despoilation could go on unchecked, as in central Asia (Jones Luong 2002). Indeed, the post-Communist context demonstrates that democratic contestation, rather than undermining economic reform, enables it (e.g. Hellman 1998; Fish 1998).

Representative elite competition, then, is one key to the successful introduction of both market reform and democracy (Grzymala-Busse and Jones Luong 2002). This is not simply a question of elite turnover, but of a mutual holding in check, and the generation of incentives to appeal to broader constituencies. This effect is predicated on the representativeness of elites, and on their contestation, not simply on fragmentation or divisions among elites. As both Latin American and African cases show, political fragmentation per se can pose major obstacles to economic reform.[4] In contrast, an active and well-organized opposition limits the excesses of the governing elites, by creating a credible threat of replacement to the government.

2.3 The Roles of the State and Informal Institutions

Both structure- and agency-based accounts of democratization have tended to focus on the formal institutions of representation and accountability. Given that without elections and contestation, we cannot speak of democratization, this is not an unreasonable emphasis. However, it overlooks the other institutional aspects of successful democratization: specifically, the role of the state and informal institutions.

First, with few exceptions, the state has long been ignored in the study of democratization and of market reforms.[5] The emphasis has been on the pluralization of politics, economics, and civil society (e.g. Dahrendorf 1990; Fatton 1999), rather than on the institutions of the state, such as centralized bureaucracies and the networks of security, redistribution, and market regulation, that they administer.

Yet, the post-Communist experience demonstrates that the type and extent of state structures found in the countries undergoing transition profoundly influence democratization (e.g. Carothers 2002; Grzymala-Busse and Jones Luong 2002; O'Donnell 1996). For example, a clear division between state and society generates powerful incentives both for elites to appeal to outside constituencies, and for these constituencies to hold elite despoilation in check. Moreover, the more the state had grown independent of the party during Communist rule, and the more it developed the capacity to administer (through implementing economic reforms, co-opting potential opposition, etc), the more successfully it could navigate the simultaneous transition to market and democracy. And a more apolitical state whose representatives have experience in administering liberalization has been a key contributor to the success of democratization.

---

[4] Similar arguments have been raised about the lack of reform progress in Ukraine (Motyl 1997). Haggard and Kaufman 1995 and van de Walle 1999 go as far as to argue that in these contexts, dominant party systems are more likely to initiate and sustain reform.

[5] These exceptions include Linz and Stepan 1996 and O'Donnell 1993.

A focus on the state can also resolve a key puzzle for scholars of democratization: why has rapid and simultaneous economic and political liberalization been a recipe for success in the post-Communist world, in contrast to other regions including Africa (e.g. Bienen and Herbst 1996) and Latin America? All the leaders of post-Communist reforms, Hungary, Slovenia, Estonia, Poland, and the Czech Republic, underwent simultaneous and radical reforms of both the planned economy and the authoritarian polity. In contrast, the notorious laggards on economic reform in the former Soviet Union (e.g. Belarus, Uzbekistan, and Turkmenistan) opted for gradual political liberalization, if any. The answer lies in the strong correlation with state organizational capacity and impartiality. The relatively strong and impartial states in east–central Europe made rapid and simultaneous transitions a far more manageable challenge than in the former Soviet Union where the state is subservient to entrenched interests and unable to administer public goods. In Africa, where the state is further weakened by low population density and competing sources of authority, the challenge of simultaneous market and democratic reforms becomes next to impossible to meet.

A second and related omission is that of informal institutions. In the context of rapid regime change, informal institutions—unwritten and unenforced by the state—are often the ones that exert greater influence on elite behavior and popular expectations.[6] For example, where they did not inherit the central state institutions that previously governed their respective states, post-Communist elites have relied primarily on informal structures (such as patronage networks and unofficial policy-making channels) to establish their authority. As a result, there is little of the procedural predictability necessary for initiating, let alone establishing, a democratic system. Similarly, the real purpose of formal institutions may be to serve informal ends: in nearly all of the post-Communist states, for example, electoral systems have been designed with precision and multiple elections have been held since 1989. Yet in several cases, such rules only stabilized the existing distribution of power and secured the privileged political and economic status of the participating elites (Jones Luong 2002).[7] Thus, the termination of scheduled elections and the increasing use of referenda to extend presidential rule throughout central Asia is not evidence of a failure to consolidate democracy. Rather, it reflects the lack of any intention to build democracy in the first place. More broadly, the focus on formal democratic institutions tends to conflate formal institutions, in particular elections and electoral institutions, with a transition to democracy (Carothers 2002). Elections are viewed as both the initiation of the democratization process and the hallmark of successful democratization.[8] However, elections and electoral rules themselves tell us far less than we would like about the level of elite commitment to democratization.

[6] Note that this is not only true of "new democracies," as others have argued (see e.g. Bunce 2000; O'Donnell 1998) but also of many with long histories, for example, Argentina (Levitsky and Murillo 2004).

[7] In other cases (e.g. Moldova), democratization was the unintended consequence of a polity in which elections could produce no clear winners (Way 2003).

[8] Variants of the notions of "founding elections" and the need for a peaceful transfer of power, which were introduced by O'Donnell and Schmitter 1986, have continued to be used (see, e.g., Huntington 1991; Przeworski 1991).

3 CONCLUSION

In the end, then, which approach better explains the variation in democratization? Both structural preconditions and elite agency have been found to play critical roles in democratization. Yet, if elite action and mass mobilization catalyze democratization, structural preconditions profoundly influence its eventual success. They do so in two ways: first, structural legacies *enable* elite action by determining individual elite capacities to forge a successful democratic transition. Second, they provide elite agency with organizational resources and strategic templates, such as state administrations and informal institutions, respectively, which implement, enforce, and legitimize elite democratization projects.

REFERENCES

BERNHARD, M. 2000. Institutional choice after communism: a critique of theory-building in an empirical wasteland, *East European Politics and Societies*, 14: 316–47.
BIENEN, H., and HERBST, J. 1996. The relationship between political and economic reform in Africa. *Comparative Politics*, 29: 23–42.
BRATTON, M., and VAN DE WALLE, N. 1992. Popular protest and political reform in Africa. *Comparative Politics*, 24: 419–42.
—— 1997. *Democratic Experiments in Africa: Regime Transition in Comparative Perspective*. Cambridge: Cambridge University Press.
BRUSZT, L., and STARK, D. 1991. Remaking the political field in Hungary: from the politics of confrontation to the politics of competition. *Journal of International Affairs*, 45: 201–45.
BUNCE, V. 1994. Should transitologists be grounded? *Slavic Review*, 54: 111–27.
—— 1998. Regional differences in democratization: the east versus the south. *Post-Soviet Affairs*, 14: 187–211.
—— 2000. Comparative democratization: big and bounded generalizations. *Comparative Political Studies*, 33: 703–34.
CALLAGHY, T. 1994. Africa: back to the future? *Journal of Democracy*, 5: 133–45.
CAROTHERS, T. 2002. The end of the transition paradigm. *Journal of Democracy*, 13: 5–21.
COLLIER, D., and LEVITSKY, S. 1997. Democracy with adjectives: conceptual innovation in comparative research. *World Politics*, 49: 430–51.
COLOMER, J. M. 1994. The Polish games of transition. *Communist and Post-Communist Studies*, 27: 275–94.
COLTON, T. J., and HOUGH, J. F. (eds.) 1998. *Russia's Protodemocracy in Action: Perspectives on the Election of 1993*. Washington, DC: Brookings Institution Press.
—— and MCFAUL, M. 2003. Russian democracy under Putin. *Problems of Post-Communism*, 50: 12–21.
DAHL, R. 1971. *Polyarchy: Participation and Opposition*. New Haven, Conn.: Yale University Press.
DAHRENDORF, R. 1990. *Reflections on the Revolution in Europe*. London: Chatto and Windus.
DIAMOND, L. 1992. Economic development and democracy reconsidered. *American Behavioral Scientist*, 35: 450–99.

―― 1996. Illusions about consolidation. *Journal of Democracy*, 7: 34–51.
―― 2002. Thinking about hybrid regimes. *Journal of Democracy*, 13: 21–35.
Di Palma, G. 1990. *To Craft Democracies: An Essay on Democratic Transitions*. Los Angeles: University of California Press.
Easter, G. M. 1997. Preference for presidentialism: postcommunist regime change in Russia and the NIS. *World Politics*, 49: 184–211.
Ekiert, G. 1991. Democratization processes in east central europe: a theoretical reconsideration. *British Journal of Political Science*, 21: 285–313.
―― and Hanson, S. 2003. *Capitalism and Democracy in Central and Eastern Europe*. New York: Cambridge University Press.
Elster, J., Offe, C., and Preuss, U. K. 1998. *Institutional Design in Post-communist States: Rebuilding the Ship at Sea*. New York: Cambridge University Press.
Fatton, R. 1999. The impairment of democratization: Haiti in comparative perspective. *Comparative Politics*, 31: 209–30.
Fish, M. S. 1994*a*. *Democracy from Scratch: Opposition and Regime in the New Russian Revolution*. Princeton, NJ: Princeton University Press.
―― 1994*b*. Russia's fourth transition. *Journal of Democracy*, 5: 31–42.
―― 1998. The determinants of economic reform in the postcommunist world. *East European Politics and Societies*, 12: 31–78.
―― 2001. Putin's path. *Journal of Democracy*, 12: 71–8.
Freedom House 2003. *Nations in Transit 2003: Democratization in East Central Europe and Eurasia*. Savage, Md.: Rowman and Littlefield.
Frye, T. 1997. A politics of institutional choice: post-communist presidencies. *Comparative Political Studies*, 30: 523–52.
Ganev, V. I. 2001. The Dorian Gray effect: winners as state breakers in postcommunism. *Communist and Post-Communist Studies*, 34: 1–25.
Geddes, B. 1996. Initiation of new democratic institutions in Eastern Europe and Latin America. In *Institutional Design in New Democracies: Eastern Europe and Latin America*, ed. A. Lijphart and C. H. Waisman. Boulder, Colo.: Westview Press.
Gel'man, V. 1999. Second Europe-Asia lecture. Regime transition, uncertainty and prospects for democratization: the politics of Russia's regions in comparative perspective. *Europe–Asia Studies*, 51: 939–56.
Gill, G. J., and Markwick, R. D. 2000. *Russia's Stillborn Democracy? From Gorbachev to Yeltsin*. Oxford: Oxford University Press.
Grzymala-Busse, A. 2002. *The Regeneration of Communist Successor Parties in East Central Europe: Redeeming the Past*. Cambridge: Cambridge University Press.
―― 2003. Political competition and the politicization of the state in east central Europe. *Comparative Political Studies*, 36: 1123–47.
―― 2004. Transforming the party-state: formal reform and informal practices. Unpublished manuscript.
―― and Jones Luong, P. 2002. Reconceptualizing the state: lessons from post-communism. *Politics and Society*, 30: 529–54.
―― and Innes, A. 2003. Great expectations: the EU and domestic political competition in east central Europe. *East European Politics and Societies*, 17: 64–73.
Haggard, S., and Kaufman, R. R. 1995. *The Political Economy of Democratic Transitions*. Princeton, NJ: Princeton University Press.
Hahn, J. W. 1997. Democratization and political participation in Russia's regions. In *Democratic Changes and Authoritarian Reactions in Russia, Ukraine, Belarus, and Moldova*, ed. K. Dawisha and B. Parrott. Cambridge: Cambridge University Press.

HELLMAN, J. 1998. Winners take all: the politics of partial reform in postcommunist transitions. *World Politics*, 50: 203–34.

HOFFMAN, D. 2002. *The Oligarchs: Wealth & Power in the New Russia*. New York: Public Affairs.

HOLMES, S. 1997. What Russia teaches us now: how weak states threaten freedom. *American Prospect*, 33: 30–9.

HUNTINGTON, S. P. 1991. *The Third Wave: Democratization in the Late Twentieth Century*. Norman: University of Oklahoma Press.

ISHIYAMA, J. T. 1997. Transitional electoral systems in post-communist eastern Europe. *Political Science Quarterly*, 112: 95–115.

JONES LUONG, P. 2002. *Institutional Change and Political Continuity in Post-Soviet Central Asia: Power, Perceptions, and Pacts*. Cambridge: Cambridge University Press.

—— 2003a. Economic decentralization in Kazakhstan: causes and consequences. In *The Transformation of Central Asia: States and Societies from Soviet Rule to Independence*, ed. P. Jones Luong. Ithaca, NY: Cornell University Press.

—— 2003b. The Middle Easternization of Central Asia. *Current History*, Oct.: 333–40.

—— 2003c. Political obstacles to economic reform in Uzbekistan, Kyrgyzstan, and Tajikistan: strategies to move ahead. Paper prepared for the Lucerne Conference of the World Bank CIS-7 Initiative.

JOWITT, K. 1992. *New World Disorder: The Leninist Legacy*. Los Angeles: University of California Press.

—— 1996. Dizzy with democracy. *Problems of Post-Communism*, 43: 3–8.

KARL, T. L., and SCHMITTER, P. 1991. Modes of transition in Latin America, southern, and eastern Europe. *International Social Science Journal*, 128: 269–84.

KILSON, M. 1987. The anatomy of African class consciousness. In *Studies in Power and Class in Africa*, ed. I. L. Markovitz. New York: Oxford University Press.

KIRKOW, P. 1995. Regional warlordism in Russia: the case of Primorskii Krai. *Europe–Asia Studies*, 47: 923–47.

KITSCHELT, H. 1992. Structure and process-driven explanations of political regime change. *American Political Science Review*, 86: 1028–34.

KOPSTEIN, J., and REILLY, D. 2000. Geographic diffusion and the transformation of the post-communist world. *World Politics*, 53: 1–37.

LARDEYRET, G. 1991. The problem with proportional representation. *Journal of Democracy*, 2: 30–5.

LERNER, D. 1958. *The Passing of Traditional Society*. Glencoe, Ill.: Free Press.

LEVITSKY, S., and MURILLO, M. V. 2004. Theory building in a context of institutional instability. In *The Politics of Institutional Weakness: Argentine Democracy in Comparative Perspective*, ed. S. Levitsky and M. V. Murillo. Unpublished manuscript.

LIJPHART, A. 1991. Constitutional choices for new democracies. *Journal of Democracy*, 2: 72–84.

—— 1992. Democratization and constitutional choices in Czecho-Slovakia, Hungary and Poland, 1989-91. *Journal of Theoretical Politics*, 4: 207–23.

LINZ, J. 1990. The perils of presidentialism. *Journal of Democracy*, 1: 51–69.

—— and STEPAN, A. 1996. *Problems in Democratic Transition and Consolidation: Southern Europe, South America, and Post-Communist Europe*. Baltimore: Johns Hopkins University Press.

LIPSET, S. M. 1960. *Political Man: The Social Bases of Politics*. Garden City, NY: Doubleday.

LUEBBERT, G. M. 1991. *Liberalism, Fascism, or Social Democracy: Social Classes and the Political Origins of Regimes in Interwar Europe*. New York: Oxford University Press.

McFAUL, M. 1999. The perils of a protracted transition. *Journal of Democracy*, 10: 4–18.

McFaul, M., Petrov, N., and Ryabov, A. 2004. *Between Dictatorship and Democracy: Russian Post-Communist Political Reform.* Washington, DC: Carnegie Endowment for International Peace.

McMann, K. 2000. Symbiotic transitions: democratic development and economic independence in post-Soviet provinces. Ph.D. dissertation, University of Michigan.

Mainwaring, S. 1993. Presidentialism, multipartism, and democracy: the difficult combination. *Comparative Political Studies*, 26: 198–228.

Moore, B. 1966. *Social Origins of Dictatorship and Democracy: Lord and Peasant in the Making of the Modern World.* Boston: Beacon Press.

Motyl, A. 1997. Structural constraints and starting points: the logic of systemic change in Ukraine and Russia. *Comparative Politics*, 29: 433–47.

Munck, G., and Leff, C. S. 1997. Modes of transition and democratization: South America and eastern Europe in comparative perspective. *Comparative Politics*, 29: 343–62.

O'Donnell, G. 1993. On the state, democratization, and some conceptual problems: a Latin American view with glances at some postcommunist countries. *World Development*, 21: 1355–69.

——— 1994. Delegative democracy. *Journal of Democracy*, 5: 55–69.

——— 1996. Illusions about consolidation. *Journal of Democracy*, 7: 34–51.

——— 1998. Horizontal accountability in new democracies. *Journal of Democracy*, 9: 112–26.

——— and Schmitter, P. 1986. *Transitions from Authoritarian Rule: Tentative Conclusions about Uncertain Democracies.* Baltimore: Johns Hopkins University Press.

O'Loughlin, J., Ward, M. D., Lofdahl, C. L., Cohen, J. S., Brown, D. S., Reilly, D., Gleditsch, K. S., and Shin, M. 1998. The diffusion of democracy, 1946-1994. *Annals of the Association of American Geographers*, 88: 545–74.

Orttung, R. 1995. *From Leningrad to Saint Petersburg: Democratization in a Russian City.* New York: St Martin's Press.

Przeworski, A. 1991. *Democracy and the Market.* Cambridge: Cambridge University Press.

——— and Limongi, F. 1997. Modernization: theories and facts. *World Politics*, 49: 155–83.

——— Alvarez, M. E., Cheibub, J., and Limongi, F. 2000. *Democracy and Development: Political Institutions and Well-Being in the World 1950-1990.* Cambridge: Cambridge University Press.

Quade, Q. L. 1991. Proportional representation and democratic statecraft. *Journal of Democracy*, 2: 36–41.

Reddaway, P. 2001. Will Putin be able to consolidate power? *Post-Soviet Affairs*, 17: 23–44.

Schmitter, P., with Karl, T. L. 1994. The conceptual travels of transitologists and consolidationologists: how far should they attempt to go? *Slavic Review*, 53: 173–85.

Schumpeter, J. 1950. *Capitalism, Socialism and Democracy.* New York: Harper and Row.

Shevtsova, L. 2001. Russia's hybrid regime. *Journal of Democracy*, 12: 65–70.

Smyth, R. 2002. Building state capacity from the inside out: parties of power and the success of the president's reform agenda in Russia. *Politics and Society*, 30: 555–78.

Starr, H. 1991. Democratic dominoes: diffusion approaches to the spread of democracy in the international system. *Journal of Conflict Resolution*, 35: 356–81.

Stepan, A., and Skach, C. 1993. Constitutional frameworks and democratic consolidation: parliamentarism versus presidentialism. *World Politics*, 46: 1–22.

Vachudova, M. 2001. The leverage of international institutions on democratizing states: the European Union and eastern Europe. RSCAS Working Paper No. 2001/33.

van de Walle, N. 1999. Economic reform in democratizing Africa. *Comparative Politics*, Oct.: 21–41.

——— 2002. Africa's range of regimes. *Journal of Democracy*, 13: 66–80.

WAY, L. 2003. Weak states and pluralism: the case of Moldova. *East European Politics and Societies*, 17: 454–82.

WIDENER, J. 1994. Political reform in anglophone and francophone African countries. In *Economic Reform and Political Liberalization in Sub-Saharan Africa*, ed. J. Widener. Baltimore: Johns Hopkins University Press.

ZAKARIA, F. 1997. The rise of illiberal democracy. *Foreign Affairs*, 76: 22–43.

PART X

HISTORICAL AND COMPARATIVE DEVELOPMENT AND NON-DEMOCRATIC REGIMES

CHAPTER 37

PATHS OF ECONOMIC AND POLITICAL DEVELOPMENT

DARON ACEMOGLU
JAMES A. ROBINSON

1 INTRODUCTION

OVER the last half millennium different societies have moved onto distinct paths of political and economic development. For example, beginning in the seventeeth century, Britain experienced a series of changes in political institutions which led to the emergence of a constitutional monarchy and a much greater stability of property rights. In consequence, the British economy began to develop rapidly and was at the forefront of the industrial revolution in the nineteenth century. As Britain grew rich it also became more democratic. Starting with the First Reform Law in 1832 and culminating with the Representation of the People Act in 1919, British political elites gradually created a fully democratic polity. In 2006 Britain was a rich democracy.

Other societies experienced dramatically different development paths over this period. In the late eighteenth century Haiti, then called Saint-Domingue, was a colony of France known as the "pearl of the Caribbean" which produced sugar cane with the help of an army of African slaves. At the time of the slave uprising in 1794 it was

* We are grateful to the editors for their detailed comments on a first draft.

possibly the richest country in the world. However, during the following 200 years per capita income declined and the country experienced extensive political instability, social chaos, and civil wars interrupted only by the reign of unenlightened despots like the Duvaliers. In 2006 Haiti was a desperately poor non-democracy.

The huge variation we see in the world today in both economic and political outcomes is the result of long-run historical processes. To understand why Haiti is how it is today we need to understand how its history placed it on the particular development path that it did. Similarly with Britain. Though some countries do change their development path, for example Japan after the Meiji Restoration in 1868, Turkey after the First World War, Russia after the 1917 Revolution and again after 1989, the preponderance of evidence suggests that once a society gets onto a particular path it stays on it.

Within these different paths lie some of the most important questions in political science and economics. Why are some countries prosperous and others not? Why are some countries democratic and others not? In this chapter we first develop a simple theoretical framework for integrating the study of political and economic development. In Section 3 we apply this framework to develop a theory of the creation and consolidation of democracy. In Section 4 we discuss comparative statics, emphasizing how this framework implies that prosperity and democracy may covary in a rather specific way. Section 5 provides an in-depth case study to show our theory in action—the rise of prosperity and democracy in Britain. Section 6 concludes.

2 A Theoretical Framework

The basic argument of this chapter can be summarized as follows:

1. Economic institutions matter for economic growth because they shape the incentives of key actors in society. In particular, they influence investments in physical and human capital and technology, and the organization of production. Although cultural and geographical factors may also matter for economic performance, differences in economic institutions are the major source of cross-country differences in economic growth and prosperity.[1] Economic institutions not only determine the aggregate economic growth potential of the economy, but also how this pie is divided among different groups and individuals now and in the future. We summarize these ideas schematically as (where the subscript t refers to current period and $t + 1$ to the future):

$$\text{economic institutions}_t \Rightarrow \begin{cases} \text{economic performance}_t \\ \text{distribution of resources}_{t+1} \end{cases}$$

[1] See Acemoglu, Johnson, and Robinson 2001, 2002.

2. Economic institutions are endogenous. They are determined as collective choices of the society, in large part for their economic consequences. However, there is no guarantee that all individuals and groups will prefer the same set of economic institutions because, as noted above, different economic institutions lead to different distributions of resources. Consequently, there will typically be a *conflict of interest* among various groups and individuals over the choice of economic institutions.

   So how are equilibrium economic institutions determined? If there are, for example, two groups with opposing preferences over the set of economic institutions, which group's preferences will prevail? The answer depends in part on the *political power* of the two groups. Although the efficiency of one set of economic institutions compared with another may play a role in this choice, political power will be the ultimate arbiter. Whichever group has more political power is likely to secure the set of economic institutions that it prefers. This leads to the second building block of our framework:

   $$\text{political power}_t \Rightarrow \text{economic institutions}_t$$

3. Implicit in the notion that political power determines economic institutions is the idea that there are conflicting interests over the distribution of resources and therefore indirectly over the set of economic institutions. But why do the groups with conflicting interests not agree on the set of economic institutions that maximize aggregate growth (the size of the aggregate pie) and then use their political power simply to determine the distribution of the gains? Why does the exercise of political power lead to economic inefficiencies and even poverty? We argue that this is because there are commitment problems inherent in the use of political power. Individuals who have political power cannot commit not to use it in their best interests, and this commitment problem creates an inseparability between efficiency and distribution because credible compensating transfers and side payments cannot be made to offset the distributional consequences of any particular set of economic institutions (Weingast 1997; Acemoglu 2003a).

4. The distribution of political power in society is also endogenous, however. In our framework, it is useful to distinguish between two components of political power, which we refer to as *de jure (institutional)* and *de facto political power*. Here *de jure* political power refers to power that originates from the *political institutions* in society. Political institutions, similarly to economic institutions, determine the constraints on and the incentives of the key actors, but this time in the political sphere. Examples of political institutions include the form of government, for example, democracy vs. dictatorship or autocracy, and the extent of constraints on politicians and political elites. For example, in a monarchy, political institutions allocate all *de jure* political power to the monarch, and place few constraints on its exercise. A constitutional monarchy, in contrast, corresponds to a set of political institutions that reallocates some of the political power of the monarch to a parliament, thus effectively constraining the political

power of the monarch. This discussion therefore implies that:

$$\text{political institutions}_t \Rightarrow \textit{de jure} \text{ political power}_t$$

5. There is more to political power than political institutions, however. A group of individuals, even if they are not allocated power by political institutions, for example as specified in the constitution, may nonetheless possess political power. Namely, they can revolt, use arms, hire mercenaries, co-opt the military, or use economically costly but largely peaceful protests in order to impose their wishes on society. We refer to this type of political power as de facto political power, which itself has two sources. First, it depends on the ability of the group in question to solve its collective action problem, i.e. to ensure that people act together, even when any individual may have an incentive to free ride. For example, peasants in the Middle Ages, who were given no political power by the constitution, could sometimes solve the collective action problem and undertake a revolt against the authorities. Second, the de facto power of a group depends on its economic resources, which determine both their ability to use (or misuse) existing political institutions and also their option to use force against different groups. Since we do not yet have a satisfactory theory of when groups are able to solve their collective action problems, our focus will be on the second source of de facto political power, hence:

$$\text{distribution of resources}_t \Rightarrow \text{de facto political power}_t$$

6. This brings us to the evolution of one of the two main *state variables* in our framework, political institutions (the other state variable is the distribution of resources, including distribution of physical and human capital stocks, etc.). Political institutions and the distribution of resources are the state variables in this dynamic system because they typically change relatively slowly, and more importantly, they determine economic institutions and economic performance both directly and indirectly. Their direct effect is straightforward to understand. If political institutions place all political power in the hands of a single individual or a small group, economic institutions that provide protection of property rights and equal opportunity for the rest of the population are difficult to sustain. The indirect effect works through the channels discussed above: political institutions determine the distribution of *de jure* political power, which in turn affects the choice of economic institutions.

Political institutions, though slow changing, are also endogenous. Societies transition from dictatorship to democracy, and change their constitutions to modify the constraints on power-holders. Since, like economic institutions, political institutions are collective choices, the distribution of political power in society is the key determinant of their evolution. This creates a tendency for persistence: political institutions allocate *de jure* political power, and those who hold political power influence the evolution of political institutions, and they will generally opt to maintain the political institutions that give them political power. However, de facto political power occasionally creates changes in political institutions. While these changes are sometimes discontinuous, for example when an imbalance of power leads to a revolution or the threat of revolution leads to major reforms in political institutions, often they simply influence the way existing political institutions function, for example whether the rules laid down in a particular constitution are respected as in most functioning democracies, or ignored as in current-day Zimbabwe. Summarizing this discussion, we have:

$$\text{political power}_t \Longrightarrow \text{political institutions}_{t+1}$$

Putting all these pieces together, a schematic (and simplistic) representation of our framework is as follows:

$$\left.\begin{array}{c}\text{political}\\\text{institutions}_t\\\\\text{distribution}\\\text{of resources}_t\end{array}\right\}\Longrightarrow\left.\begin{array}{c}\text{de jure}\\\text{political}\\\text{power}_t\\\&\\\text{de facto}\\\text{political}\\\text{power}_t\end{array}\right\}\begin{array}{c}\Longrightarrow\text{economic institutions}_t\Longrightarrow\\\\\\\Longrightarrow\text{political institutions}_{t+1}\end{array}\left\{\begin{array}{c}\text{economic}\\\text{performance}_t\\\&\\\text{distribution}\\\text{of resources}_{t+1}\end{array}\right.$$

The two state variables are political institutions and the distribution of resources, and the knowledge of these two variables at time t is sufficient to determine all the other variables in the system. While political institutions determine the distribution of *de jure* political power in society, the distribution of resources influences the distribution of de facto political power at time t. These two sources of political power, in turn, affect the choice of economic institutions and influence the future evolution of political institutions. Economic institutions determine economic outcomes, including the aggregate growth rate of the economy and the distribution of resources at time $t + 1$. Although economic institutions are the essential factor shaping economic outcomes, they are themselves endogenous and determined by political institutions and the distribution of resources in society.

There are two sources of persistence in the behavior of the system: first, political institutions are durable, and typically, a large change in the distribution of political power is necessary to cause a change in political institutions, such as a transition from dictatorship to democracy. Second, when a particular group is rich relative to others, this will increase its de facto political power and enable it to push for economic and political institutions favorable to its interests. This will tend to reproduce the initial relative wealth disparity in the future. Despite these tendencies for persistence, the framework also emphasizes the potential for change. In particular, "shocks," including changes in technologies and the international environment, that modify the balance of (de facto) political power in society can lead to major changes in political institutions and therefore in economic institutions and economic growth.

It is worth returning at this point to two critical assumptions in our framework. First, why do the groups with conflicting interests not agree on the set of economic institutions that maximize aggregate growth? So, for example, in the case of the conflict between President Robert Mugabe and the white farmers in Zimbabawe, why does Mugabe not set up secure property rights to encourage economic growth and tax some of the benefits? Second, why do groups with political power want to change political institutions in their favor? The answers to both questions revolve around issues of *commitment* and go to the heart of our framework.

The distribution of resources in society is an inherently conflictual, and therefore political, decision. As mentioned above, this leads to major commitment problems, since groups with political power cannot commit to not use their power to change the distribution of resources in their favor. For example, economic institutions that increased the security of property rights for land and capital owners during the Middle Ages would not have been credible as long as the monarch monopolized political power. He could promise to respect property rights, but then at some point renege on his promise, as exemplified by the numerous financial defaults by medieval kings (e.g. Veitch 1986). Credible secure property rights necessitated a reduction in the political power of the monarch. Although these more secure property rights would foster economic growth, they were not appealing to the monarchs who would lose their rents from predation and expropriation as well as various other privileges associated with their monopoly of political power. This is why the institutional changes in England as a result of the Glorious Revolution of 1688 were not simply conceded by the Stuart kings. James II had to be deposed for the changes to take place (North and Weingast 1989; Acemoglu, Johnson, and Robinson 2005).

The reason why political power is often used to change political institutions is related. In a dynamic world, individuals care not only about economic outcomes today but also in the future. In the example above, private citizens such as merchants who were threatened by the predation of the king were interested in their profits and therefore in the security of their property rights, not only in the present but also in the future. During the late sixteenth and early seventeenth centuries, various factors changed the balance of de facto power in Britain (see Section 4), strengthening the hand of those opposed to the king and in favor of different economic institutions. These groups, primarily merchants and capitalist farmers, would have liked to use their (de facto) political power to secure benefits in the future as well as the present. However, commitment to future allocations (or economic institutions) was not possible because decisions in the future would be decided by those who had political power in the future with little reference to past promises. If the merchants had been sure of maintaining their de facto political power, this would not have been a problem. However, de facto political power is often transient, for example because the collective action problems that are solved to amass this power are likely to resurface in the future, or other groups, especially those controlling *de jure* power, can become stronger in the future. Therefore, any change in policies and economic institutions that relies purely on de facto political power is likely to be reversed in the future. Using political power to change political institutions then emerges as a useful strategy to make gains more durable. The framework that we propose, therefore, emphasizes the importance of political institutions, and changes in political institutions, as a way of manipulating future political power, and thus indirectly shaping future, as well as present, economic institutions and outcomes.

We now show how, following Acemoglu and Robinson (2000, 2001, 2005), this general framework can provide a theory of the origins of democracy.

3 A Theory of Democracy

Democracy is a particular set of political institutions. Relative to some type of non-democratic regime the key aspect of democracy is that it is a situation of *relative political equality*.[2] In a non-democracy some non-representative elite dominates the political institutions and this elite will use their power to make collective choices and economic institutions that benefit them. This elite is different in different countries. For example, in present-day China it is the Chinese Communist Party. In Burundi it is the Tutsi-dominated military. In nineteenth-century Britain it was the rich and landed aristocracy. In a non-democracy the preferences of most people are not taken into account in collective decision-making except to the extent that the disenfranchised can exercise de facto power.

We can now consider how the framework we developed in the last section can be applied more specifically to think about the origins of democracy. Consider the simplest dynamic world we can imagine: there is a "today" and a "tomorrow," and the elite, who control non-democracy, and the citizens care about both policies and economic institutions today and tomorrow. Suppose we are in a non-democratic society, which generally looks after the interests of the elite, and the citizens have de facto political power today. By this we mean that the disenfranchised have solved the collective action problem and can threaten to impose costs on the elite and in the limit depose it in a revolution. However, though the disenfranchised have de facto power today they are unsure whether they will have the same political power tomorrow. Given that we are in a non-democratic society, tomorrow the citizens may no longer have the same political power. Can they ensure the implementation of the policies and economic institutions they like both today and tomorrow?

Imagine now that the citizens do not simply use their de facto political power today to obtain what they like now, but they also use it to change the political system from non-democracy to democracy. If they do so, they will have effectively increased their *de jure* political power in the future. Instead of non-democracy, we are now in a democratic regime where there will be voting by all. With their increased *de jure* political power, the citizens are therefore more likely to secure the economic institutions and policies they like tomorrow as well.

---

[2] We do not distinguish between different non-democratic regimes (see Linz and Stepan 1996 for a typology). The nature of a non-democratic regime may be important for specific comparative static results but it does not alter the basic mechanisms that lead to the creation or consolidation of democracy (see Acemoglu and Robinson 2005, ch. 4).

In this account transitions to democracy, or more generally a change in political institutions, emerges as a way of regulating the future allocation of political power. The citizens demand democracy so that they can have more political say and political power tomorrow. Note here the importance of *the transitory nature of de facto political power*. The citizens are presumed to have political power today, but are uncertain about whether they will have similar power tomorrow. The balance between the elite and the citizens fluctuates. This is reasonable in the dynamic and uncertain world we live in. A real threat from the citizens requires the juxtaposition of many unlikely factors: the masses need to solve the collective action problem necessary to organize themselves, they need to find the momentum to turn their organization into an effective force against the regime, and the elite, who are controlling the state apparatus, should be unable to use the military to suppress the uprising effectively. It is therefore very reasonable that such a challenge against the system would be only transitory: in non-democracy, if the citizens have political power today, they most likely will not have it tomorrow.

It is precisely the transitory nature of political power, that citizens have it today and may not have it tomorrow, that creates a demand for a change in political institutions. The citizens would like to lock in the political power they have today by changing political institutions, specifically by introducing democracy and greater representation for themselves, because without the institutional changes their power today is unlikely to persist.

Transitions to democracy take place when the elite controlling the existing regime change political institutions and extend voting rights. Why would they do so? After all, the transfer of political power to the majority may lead to social choices that the elite don't like. Faced with the exercise of de facto power and perhaps the threat of disorder and even a revolution, wouldn't the elite like to try other types of concessions, even giving the citizens the policies they want, rather than give away their power? Alternatively, why doesn't the elite simply use the military to repress the citizens?

The first option for the elite is to give them what they want today: adopt economic institutions or policies favorable to the majority. But suppose that concessions today are not sufficient to dissuade the citizens from revolution. What can the elite do to prevent an imminent and, for themselves, extremely costly revolution? They can of course promise the same thing tomorrow. And yet these promises may not be *credible*. Changing economic institutions or altering policies in the direction preferred by the citizens is not in the immediate interest of the elite. Today they are doing so to prevent a revolution. Tomorrow, the threat of revolution may be gone, so why should they keep their promises? If such promises are non-credible, then they are worth little. To prevent a revolution the elite have to make a credible commitment to future pro-majority policies and economic institutions. A credible promise means that the decision should not be theirs, but placed in the hands of groups that actually prefer such institutions. Or in other words, they have to transfer political power to the citizens. That is precisely what a transition to democracy does: it shifts future political power away from the elite to the citizens, thereby creating *a credible commitment to future pro-majority policies and institutions*.

The second option for the elite is to use force and repression. For example, the white South African regime rejected calls for democracy and kept itself in power for decades by using the military to repress demonstrations and opposition. Similarly Argentine military regimes of the 1960s and 1970s killed thousands of people to avoid reintroducing democracy and this has been a pattern in many other Latin American countries, for example Guatemala and El Salvador. In Asia, non-democratic regimes in China and Burma have used force to block demands for democracy, and this was also true in eastern European countries during the dominance of the Soviet Union, for example in Hungary in 1956 and Czechoslovakia in 1968. Repression is attractive for elites since it allows them to maintain power without having to make any type of concessions to the disenfranchised. Nevertheless, repression is both costly and risky for elites. It leads to the loss of life and the destruction of assets and wealth and, depending on the international climate of opinion, it may lead to sanctions and international isolation, as happened in South Africa during the 1980s. In a related discussion Dahl (1971, 79) notes the "enormous limitations, costs and inefficiencies of violence, coercion and compulsion in managing an advanced society where incentives and complex behavior are needed that cannot be manipulated by threats of violence." Moreover, repression may fail which could cause a revolution, the worst possible outcome for the elite. Finally, to use repression the elite has to have a strong military, but such a military is itself a threat to elites (Finer 1976).

These considerations imply that only in certain circumstances will repression be attractive. When we incorporate this into the analysis we shall see that democracy arises when concessions are not credible and repression is not attractive because it is too costly.

A theory of democratization is of course not sufficient to understand why some countries are democratic while some others are ruled by dictatorships. Many countries become democratic, but eventually revert back to a non-democratic regime as a result of a military coup. This has been an especially common pattern in Latin America. Why has democracy been so hard to consolidate in much of Latin America? To answer this question, we need to develop a theory of coups, or alternatively a theory of democratic consolidation.

A democracy is consolidated if the set of institutions which characterize it endure through time. Our theory of democratic consolidation and coups builds on the different attitudes of the elite and the citizens towards democracy. Once again, the citizens are more pro-democratic than the elite (because democracy is more pro-citizen than non-democracy). Consequently, when there is a situation with the military on the side of the elite and sufficient turbulence to allow a military takeover, the elite might support or sponsor a coup to change the balance of power in society.

The reason that the elite might want to change political institutions, from democracy to non-democracy, is similar to why the citizens want democratization. What the elite care about is to change institutions in their favor. Political turbulence and the alignment between their interests and those of the military might give them a window of opportunity for doing so. But there is again the issue of the transitory nature of de facto political power. They may have this opportunity today, but not necessarily tomorrow. Any promise by the citizens to make policies less anti-elite in the future is not necessarily credible within the context of democratic politics. Tomorrow, the threat of a coup may be gone, and democratic politics may again cater to the needs of the majority, who will choose the policies they prefer without worrying about the elite undermining their power via a coup. But this is precisely what made democracy so costly for the elite in the first place. To change economic institutions and policies in a credible way the elite need political power. A coup is their way of increasing their *de jure* political power so that they can pursue the policies they like. In other words, a coup enables the elite to turn their transitory de facto political power into more enduring *de jure* political power by changing political institutions.

4 COMPARATIVE STATICS

The framework of Section 2, though abstract and highly simplified, enables us to provide some preliminary answers to two central questions: why do some societies choose "good economic institutions" and become prosperous; and why do some societies become democracies? We think of good economic institutions as those that provide security of property rights and relatively equal access to economic resources to a broad cross-section of society. Although this definition is far from requiring equality of opportunity, it implies that societies where only a very small fraction of the population have well-enforced property rights do not have good economic institutions.

Given this definition of good economic institutions our framework leads to a number of important comparative statics which predict when they might arise. First, political institutions that place checks on those who hold political power, for example, by creating a balance of power in society, are useful for the emergence of good economic institutions. This result is intuitive; without checks on political power, power-holders are more likely to opt for a set of economic institutions that are beneficial for themselves and detrimental for the rest of society, which will typically fail to protect the property rights of a broad cross-section of people.

Second, good economic institutions are more likely to arise when political power is in the hands of a relatively broad group with significant investment opportunities. The reason for this result is that, everything else equal, in this case power-holders will themselves benefit from secure property rights.[3]

Third, good economic institutions are more likely to arise and persist when there are only limited rents that power-holders can extract from the rest of society, since such rents would encourage them to opt for a set of economic institutions that make the expropriation of others possible. This comparative static suggests that the

---

[3] The reason why we inserted the caveat of "a relatively broad group" is that when a small group with significant investment opportunities holds power, they may sometimes opt for an oligarchic system where their own property rights are protected, but those of others are not (see Acemoglu 2003*b*)

structure of the economy may be important for good economic institutions. For instance, if coercive labor market institutions, such as slavery, are more feasible in agriculture than industry (see Fogel 1989; Eltis 2000) then an agrarian economy may have worse economic institutions. This may happen because human capital is less valuable in agriculture, or because unobservable effort is much more important in industry. Factor endowments such as the presence of oil and other natural resources may also be important in promoting bad economic institutions since they generate large rents without necessitating the development of good economic institutions (an argument frequently made in the context of Africa, e.g. Leonard and Strauss 2003). They therefore reduce the opportunity cost of extractive institutions.

These comparative statics emphasize political institutions. Political institutions are essential both because they determine the constraints on the use of (de facto and *de jure*) political power, and also because they determine which groups hold *de jure* political power in society. These factors may all influence the costs and benefits of good economic institutions. We emphasize however that, since institutions tend to persist over time, large changes in institutions are rather rare events and only happen at important "critical junctures." Nevertheless, all of the above factors may be important in maintaining and even occasionally, in the right circumstances, creating good or bad economic institutions.

What can these comparative statics tell us about whether or not a society is likely to be democratic? The most fundamental link stems from the fact that in moving from a non-democracy to a democracy one moves towards greater political equality. Bad economic institutions typically arise because they happen to concentrate resources in the hands of some politically powerful group. For instance, equality before the law may be critical for guaranteeing the property rights of all agents in society and thus allowing people with good ideas or opportunities to invest. Nevertheless, general equality before the law also makes it more difficult for groups in control of society to get what they want. A movement from non-democracy to democracy changes the balance of political power away from narrow elites and in the direction of the majority of the population. Such a change in the balance of power will tend to undermine the economic institutions favored by non-democratic elites. There is thus a complementarity between good economic institutions and democracy. Our framework therefore implies that the circumstances that give rise to good economic institutions will also tend to give rise to democracy. Democracy is therefore likely to emerge in the same circumstances as good economic institutions arise so that the comparative statics derived above with respect to good economic institutions ought to tell us something about when democracy is created and consolidated.

First, we would expect a society to be democratic when there are checks on the use of political power or a balance of political power in society. Democracy is itself a political institution which produces a balance of political power relative to non-democracy, but in the absence of democracy power can nevertheless be relatively balanced. The United States was not a democracy when it adopted its constitution in the late eighteenth century, but the checks and balances built into this document helped to facilitate subsequent democratization by guaranteeing that political elites were relatively unthreatened by democracy.

Many factors can also lead to a balance of de facto power. For instance, a high degree of equality in the distribution of economic resources may lead de facto power to be balanced. Equally all groups may be well organized and able to solve the collective action problem. Alternatively, the relevant political institutions may not just be formal institutions such as the nature of the constitution or who has voting rights. There may also be important "informal" political institutions which help to regulate the allocation of power (which is one interpretation of the work of Putnam 1993). Checks on the use of power make it likely that elites benefit less from non-democracy while at the same time, by reducing what the majority can do, they make democracy less threatening to non-democratic elites. Both factors promote democracy. A balance in the distribution of de facto power also makes it more costly or difficult for elites to avoid democratizing by using repression or overthrowing democracy subsequently by mounting coups.

Second, democracy will be facilitated when a broad group in society has good investment opportunities. In this case, democracy, since it gives political power to relatively numerous groups, will be complementary to good economic performance since it will enfranchise exactly those people with a vested interest in good economic institutions.

Third, democracy will tend to arise when factor endowments and the structure of the economy are such that there are only limited rents to be extracted with bad economic institutions. For example, an elite which dominates an agrarian society will be in a very different position from one which holds physical capital and where the disenfranchised have human capital which is complementary to the capital of the elites (a connection clearly seen by Moore 1966). This is for several reasons. First, as we discussed before, bad economic institutions such as slavery may be much more attractive in an agrarian society. Second, repression and coups are likely to be much more costly in a society dominated by physical and human capital and this tilts the balance of de facto power towards the disenfranchised, thus promoting democracy. Third, land is much easier to tax or redistribute than capital and thus in a society dominated by land, the preferences of the elite and the disenfranchised over economic institutions may be very different. This makes democracy potentially very bad for landowning elites and thus leads them to oppose it strenuously. Finally, economies dominated by natural resources, such as oil, create large rents from monopolizing political power which make elites reluctant to surrender it to democrats. The presence of such rents may therefore make repression and coups more attractive (Ross 2001).

Our framework suggests that the level of per capita income, its rate of growth, and the extent of democracy are jointly determined as part of a political economic equilibrium. Existing empirical studies have not attempted to take into account this joint endogeneity and thus can say little about whether democracy causes prosperity or vice versa, though they do of course establish some important partial correlations and robust facts to be explained. Our framework does suggest that because democracy, other things equal, redistributes political power to the mass of people with an interest in broad-based property rights, it ought to be good for prosperity. However, there are no unambiguous implications for the impact of income per capita or economic growth on democracy. Indeed, Acemoglu et al. (2005) show that once the historical determinants of the development path are properly controlled for, income per capita has no causal effect on democracy, a finding which suggests that while there is a correlation between income and democracy, as noted by Lipset (1959), there is no causal relationship running from income to democracy.

5 THE THEORY IN ACTION: HOW BRITAIN BECAME RICH AND DEMOCRATIC

5.1 Narrative

We now illustrate our framework in action with an example, based on Acemoglu and Robinson (2000, 2001, 2005): the economic growth and the rise of mass democracy in Britain. In 1500 Britain (or the countries which subsequently came to constitute Britain) was a relatively backward society. In terms of per capita income northern Italy and the Low Countries were significantly more prosperous (Maddison 2001, table B-21) and Britain, which had only recently emerged from a devastating civil war (the "War of the Roses"), was ruled by an absolutist monarchy. Yet by the early nineteenth century Britain had become the richest nation in the world and remained so for most of the century. At the same time, after 1832 a series of Reform Acts were passed which eventually culminated in democracy. What drove these processes and how were they interrelated?

The origins of British economic supremacy stem from a series of institutional changes which took place from the middle of the seventeenth century onwards (see North and Thomas 1973; North and Weingast 1989; O'Brien 1993; Acemoglu, Johnson, and Robinson 2005). These changes emerged out of the Civil War of 1642–51 and Glorious Revolution of 1688 and led to a dramatic change in the political institutions. Conflict between the Stuart monarchs intent on maintaining and expanding their absolutist powers, and a Parliament intent on reigning them in, ended with parliamentary victories. The outcome was a restructuring of political institutions that severely limited the monarchy's power and correspondingly increased that of Parliament. The change in political institutions led to much greater security of property rights, since people no longer feared predation by the state. In particular it placed power into the hands of a Parliament in which were represented merchants and landowners oriented towards sale for the market. This basic change also had many spin-offs which were crucial for economic expansion, particularly the expansion of financial markets (North and Weingast 1989).

By the late eighteenth century sustained economic growth had begun in Britain. Yet the political system which emerged from the Glorious Revolution was not a democracy. While there were regular parliaments, the franchise was severely restricted, both by feudal notions of status, and also by property requirements (O'Gorman 1997). There was also widespread electoral corruption in the absence of a secret ballot and many elections were unopposed.

The first important move towards democracy in Britain came with the First Reform Act of 1832. This Act removed many of the worst inequities under the old electoral system, in particular the "rotten boroughs" where several Members of Parliament were elected by very few voters. The 1832 reform also established the right to vote based uniformly on the basis of property and income and was passed in the context of rising popular discontent at the existing political status quo in Britain.

By the 1820s the industrial revolution was well under way and the decade prior to 1832 saw continual rioting and popular unrest. Notable were the Luddite Riots of 1811–16, the Spa Fields Riots of 1816, the Peterloo Massacre in 1819, and the Swing Riots of 1830 (see Stevenson 1979). Another catalyst for the reforms was the July Revolution of 1830 in Paris. Much of this was led and orchestrated by the new middle-class groups who were being created by the spread of industry and the rapid expansion of the British economy. For example, under the pre-1832 system neither Manchester nor Sheffield had any members in the House of Commons.

There is little dissent amongst historians that the motive for the 1832 Reform was to avoid social disturbances (e.g. Lang 1999, 36). In presenting his electoral reform to the British Parliament in 1831, Prime Minister Earl Grey was well aware that this was a measure necessary to prevent a likely revolution. He argued: "The Principal of my reform is to prevent the necessity for revolution . . . reforming to preserve and not to overthrow" (quoted in Evans 1983, 212).

The 1832 Reform Act increased the total electorate from 492,700 to 806,000, which represented about 14.5 per cent of the adult male population. Yet, the majority of British people still could not vote. There is also evidence of continued corruption and intimidation of voters until the Ballot Act of 1872 and the Corrupt and Illegal Practices Act of 1883. The Reform Act therefore did not create mass democracy, but rather was designed as a strategic concession.

Unsurprisingly therefore, the issue of parliamentary reform was still very much alive after 1832. But as Lee (1994, 137) notes, "The House of Commons was largely hostile to reform because, at this stage, it saw no need for it." This had changed by 1867, largely due to a juxtaposition of factors, including the sharp business cycle downturn that caused significant economic hardship and the increased threat of violence. Also significant was the founding of the National Reform Union in 1864 and the Reform League in 1865, and the Hyde Park riots of July 1866 provided the most immediate catalyst.

Lang (1999, 75) sums up his discussion by saying, "The Hyde Park affair, coupled with other violent outbursts, helped to underscore the idea that it would be better to keep the goodwill of the respectable workers than to alienate them." Reform was initially proposed by the Liberal Prime Minister Russell in 1866 but was defeated by the Conservatives and dissident MPs. As a result Russell's government fell, and the Conservatives formed a minority administration with Lord Derby as their leader in the House of Lords, and Disraeli in charge of the House of Commons. It was Disraeli who then constructed a coalition to pass the Second Reform Act in 1867.

As a result of these reforms, the total electorate was expanded from 1.36 million to 2.48 million, and working-class voters became the majority in all urban constituencies. The electorate was doubled again by the Third Reform Act of 1884, which extended the same voting regulations that already existed in the boroughs (urban constituencies) to the counties (electoral constituencies in the rural areas). The Redistribution Act of 1885 removed many remaining inequalities in the distribution of seats and after 1884 about 60 per cent of adult males were enfranchised. Once again social disorder appears to have been an important factor behind the 1884 act.

In Britain, the Reform Acts of 1867–84 were a turning point in the history of the British state. Economic institutions also began to change. In 1871 Gladstone reformed the civil service, opening it to public examination, making it meritocratic. Liberal and Conservative governments introduced a considerable amount of labor market legislation, fundamentally changing the nature of industrial relations in favor of workers. During 1906–14, the Liberal Party, under the leadership of Asquith and Lloyd George, introduced the modern redistributive state into Britain, including health and unemployment insurance, government-financed pensions, minimum wages, and a commitment to redistributive taxation. As a result of the fiscal changes, taxes as a proportion of national product more than doubled in the thirty years following 1870, and then doubled again. In the mean time, the progressivity of the tax system also increased (Lindert 2004). Finally, there is also a consensus amongst economic historians that inequality in Britain fell after the 1870s (see Lindert 2000, 2004).

Meanwhile, the education system, which was either primarily for the elite or run by religious denominations during most of the nineteenth century, was opened up to the masses; the Education Act of 1870 committed the government to the systematic provision of universal education for the first time, and this was made free in 1891. The school leaving age was set at eleven in 1893, then in 1899 it increased to twelve and special provisions for the children of needy families were introduced (Mitch 1993). As a result of these changes, the proportion of ten-year-olds enrolled in school that stood at 40 per cent in 1870 increased to 100 per cent in 1900 (Ringer 1979, 207). Finally, a further Act in 1902 led to a large expansion in the resources for schools and introduced the grammar schools which subsequently became the foundation of secondary education in Britain.

Following the Great War, the Representation of the People Act of 1918 gave the vote to all adult males over the age of twenty-one, and women received the vote on the same terms as men in 1928. The measures of 1918 were negotiated during the war and may reflect to some extent a quid pro quo between the government and the working classes who were needed to fight and produce munitions. Nevertheless, Garrard (2002, 69) notes, "most assumed that, if the system was to survive and 'contentment and stability prevail', universal citizenship could not be denied men, perceived to have suffered so much and to have noticed Russia's Revolution."

5.2 Interpretation

Overall, the picture which emerges from British economic and political history is clear. In the seventeenth century a series of political conflicts were won by those interested in introducing political institutions which limited the *de jure* power of the monarchy. This change in political institutions greatly improved economic institutions. By reducing the risk of state predation, property rights became more stable which encouraged investment. Also *de jure* political power in the new system was in the hands of men with commercial and capitalistic interests and this led to large induced changes in economic institutions, for instance in capital and financial markets, that were important for further economic expansion.

The reason that these institutional changes arose in Britain (and not, say, in France or Spain) appears to be twofold. First, at the start of the early modern period Britain had political institutions which limited the powers of the monarchs more than in other places (Ertman 1997). Why this was so seems to be the outcome of a complex historical process of the building of dynasties and invasions. Second, various significant changes took place in the structure of the economy which greatly strengthened the interest of various groups, particularly capitalistic farmers (the so-called "gentry") and merchants, in different economic institutions. Also significant was the early collapse of feudal institutions in Britain (Brenner 1976). These same changes also increased the de facto power of these same interests which critically influenced the outcome of the Civil War and Glorious Revolution (Tawney 1941; Brenner 1993; Acemoglu, Johnson, and Robinson 2005).

The outcome of the seventeenth-century conflicts in Britain was a set of economic institutions which gave property rights to a broad set of people (see Thompson 1975). The result was the ending of the Malthusian cycle and the beginning of modern economic growth. Yet the structural changes that in consequence began, for instance urbanization and the rise of the factory system, had further implications for the distribution of de facto political power. In particular they began to make the exercise of de facto power by the poor and politically disenfranchised much easier (Tilly 1995 and Tarrow 1998 document the changing qualitative nature of collective action over this period). The rise in the de facto political power of the poor necessitated a change in political institutions in their favor to defuse the threat of revolution. In consequence, the future allocation of *de jure* political power was tilted in favor of the citizens making more likely economic institutions and policies consistent with their interests. This is exactly what the process of democratization did.

Beginning in 1832, the British political elite made a series of strategic concessions aimed at incorporating the previously disenfranchised into politics since the alternative was seen to be social unrest, chaos, and possibly revolution. The concessions were gradual because in 1832, social peace could be purchased by buying off the middle classes, and even in 1867 the government could get away with making fewer concessions than those demanded by organizations such as the Reform League. Moreover, although challenged during the 1832 reforms, the House of Lords provided an important bulwark for the wealthy against the potential of radical reforms emanating from a democratized House of Commons. Later, as the working classes reorganized, further concessions had to be made. The Great War and the fallout from it sealed the final offer of full democracy. Though the pressure of the disenfranchised played less of a role in some reforms than others, and other factors, such as strategic calculations about electoral advantage, were possibly important, the threat of social disorder was the main driving force behind the creation of democracy in Britain.

Why did elites in Britain create a democracy? Our discussion makes it clear that democracy did not emerge from the voluntary acts of an enlightened elite. Democracy was, in many ways, forced on the elite, because of the threat of social disorder and revolution. Nevertheless, democratization was not the only potential outcome in the face of pressure from the disenfranchised, or even in the face of the threat of revolution. Many other countries faced the same pressures and political elites decided to repress the disenfranchised rather than make concessions to them. This happened with regularity in Europe in the nineteenth century, though by the turn of the twentieth century most had accepted that democracy was inevitable. Repression lasted much longer as the favorite response of elites in Latin America, and it is still the preferred option for current political elites in China and Burma.

The problem with repression is that it is costly. Confronted with demands for democracy political elites face a trade-off. If they grant democracy, then they lose power over policy and face the prospect of, possibly radical, redistribution. On the other hand, repression risks destroying assets and wealth. In the urbanized environment of nineteenth-century Europe (Britain was 70 per cent urbanized at the time of the Second Reform Act), the disenfranchised masses were relatively well organized and therefore difficult to repress. Moreover, industrialization had led to an economy based on physical, and increasing human, capital. Such assets are easily destroyed by repression and conflict, making repression an increasingly costly option for elites. In contrast, in predominantly agrarian societies like many parts of Latin America earlier in the century or current-day Burma, physical and human capital are relatively unimportant and repression is easier and cheaper. Moreover, not only is repression cheaper in such environments, democracy is potentially much worse for the elites because of the prospect of radical land reform. Since physical capital is much more costly to redistribute, elites in Britain found the prospect of democracy much less threatening.

Repression is attractive not just when it is relatively cheap, but also when there is a lot at stake. Our discussion suggests that the very changes in economic and political institutions that allowed sustained economic growth to emerge also ameliorated the threat of democracy to British elites. Democracy did bring changes in economic institutions away from those preferred by the elite. In the nineteenth century, economic institutions, particularly in the labor market, disadvantaged the poor. For example, trade unions were illegal and as late as 1850 in Britain workers trying to organize a trade union could be shipped to the penal colony in Tasmania, Australia. As we noted above, this and many other things changed, particularly after 1867 when economic institutions were altered to cater to the demands of the newly enfranchised. Though these changes were significant, they represent much smaller changes in economic institutions than those faced by Russia or Austria-Hungary in the nineteenth century, or Guatemala and El Salvador in the twentieth.

Faced with the threat of revolt and social chaos, political elites may also attempt to avoid giving away their political power by making concessions, such as income redistribution or introducing other pro-poor policies or institutions. The problem with concessions however is their credibility. We argued that the extent of credibility is intimately linked to the persistence of collective action and de facto power. The promise of concessions which people know to be non-credible is unlikely to defuse collective action. Hence, Acemoglu and Robinson (2000, 2001, 2005) argue that democratization occurs as a way of making credible commitments to the disenfranchised. Democratization is a relatively credible commitment to future pro-majoritarian institutions and policies because it reallocates *de jure* political power away from the elites to the mass of citizens. In a democracy, the poorer segments of society are relatively more powerful and can use their *de jure* political power to implement economic institutions and policies consistent with their interests. Therefore, democratization is a way of transforming the transitory de facto power of the disenfranchised poor into more durable *de jure* political power.

Our rendering of British political and economic history illustrates the dynamic framework of Section 2. We see the interplay of *de jure* and de facto political power. We see how economic and social changes alter the underlying balance of de facto power leading to changes in *de jure* power and economic institutions and how the processes set in motion in the early modern period moved Britain onto a virtuous circle of prosperity and democracy. Obviously other paths are possible, including those where an elite persists, where it sets economic institutions and policies to enrich itself at the expense of society, and where poverty and dictatorship persist. Such has been the lot of Haiti since independence.

6 Conclusion

In this chapter we have developed a framework for thinking about the determinants of prosperity and democracy. Our approach emphasizes that economic institutions are the primary determinant of prosperity, but that what economic institutions arise in equilibrium depends on the distribution of political power. A key determinant of political power is the political institutions, with democracy being one important subset of such institutions. Economic institutions which promote prosperity are those that provide incentives for the broad mass of society, and such institutions may be associated with democratic political institutions since democracy, relative to various types of non-democracy, tends to give political power to the broad mass of people. This framework then suggests that prosperity and democracy may indeed be related, as Lipset (1959) first systematically documented. Nevertheless, this does not mean that income causes democracy, nor that democracy causes a society to be prosperous.

Though democracy does play a role in allocating political power and thus sustaining certain sets of economic institutions, we stressed that of more importance is the historically determined underlying structure of political and economic institutions.

In essence, the extent of prosperity and democracy in a society is determined by its institutional organization, and different societies get on different paths of economic and political development as a consequence of historical shocks or critical junctures. Acemoglu, Johnson, and Robinson (2001, 2002) emphasize that European colonialism was one such juncture with particularly large and persistent effects on economic and political institutions. Nevertheless, there are many other such junctures in history.

References

ACEMOGLU, D. 2003a. Why not a political Coase theorem? *Journal of Comparative Economics*, 31: 620–52.

——2003b. The form of property rights: oligarchic versus democratic societies. NBER Working Paper #10037.

——JOHNSON, S., and ROBINSON, J. A. 2001. The colonial origins of comparative development: an empirical investigation. *American Economic Review*, 91: 1369–401.

—— —— ——2002. Reversal of fortune: geography and institutions in the making of the modern world income distribution. *Quarterly Journal of Economics*, 118: 1231–94.

—— —— ——2005. The rise of Europe: Atlantic trade, institutional change and economic growth. *American Economic Review*, 95: 546–79.

——and ROBINSON, J. A. 2000. Why did the west extend the franchise? Growth, inequality and democracy in historical perspective. *Quarterly Journal of Economics*, 115: 1167–99.

—— ——2001. A theory of political transitions. *American Economic Review*, 91: 938–63.

—— ——2005. *Economic Origins of Dictatorship and Democracy*. Cambridge: Cambridge University Press.

——JOHNSON, S., ROBINSON, J. A., and YARED, P. 2005. Income and democracy. NBER Working Paper #11205.

BRENNER, R. 1976. Agrarian class structure and economic development in preindustrial Europe. *Past and Present*, 70: 30–75.

——1993. *Merchants and Revolution: Commercial Change, Political Conflict, and London's Overseas Traders, 1550–1653*. Princeton, NJ: Princeton University Press.

DAHL, R. A. 1971. *Polyarchy: Participation and Opposition*. New Haven, Conn.: Yale University Press.

ELTIS, D. 2000. *The Rise of African Slavery in the Americas*. New York: Cambridge University Press.

ERTMAN, T. 1997. *Birth of the Leviathan: Building States and Regimes in Medieval and Early Modern Europe*. New York: Cambridge University Press.

EVANS, E. J. 1983. *The Forging of the Modern State: Early Industrial Britain, 1783–1870*. New York: Longman.

FINER, S. E. 1976. *The Man on Horseback: The Role of the Military in Politics*, 2nd edn. Baltimore: Penguin.

FOGEL, R. W. 1989. *Without Consent or Contract: The Rise and Fall of American Slavery*. New York: Norton.

GARRARD, J. 2002. *Democratization in Britain: Elites, Civil Society and Reform since 1800*. Basingstoke: Palgrave.

Lang, S. 1999. *Parliamentary Reform, 1785–1928*. New York: Routledge.
Lee, S. J. 1994. *Aspects of British Political History, 1815–1914*. New York: Routledge.
Leonard, D. K., and Strauss, S. 2003. *Africa's Stalled Development: International Causes and Cures*. Boulder, Colo.: Lynne Rienner.
Lindert, P. H. 2000. Three centuries of inequality in Britain and America. In *The Handbook of Income Distribution*, ed. A. B. Atkinson and F. Bourguignon. Amsterdam: North-Holland.
—— 2004. *Growing Public: Social Spending and Economic Growth since the Eighteenth Century*, 2 vols. Cambridge: Cambridge University Press.
Linz, J. J., and Stepan, A. 1996. *Problems of Democratic Transition and Consolidation: Southern Europe, South America, and Post-communist Europe*. Baltimore: Johns Hopkins University Press.
Lipset, S. M. 1959. Some social prerequisites for democracy: economic development and political legitimacy. *American Political Science Review*, 53: 69–105.
Maddison, A. 2001. *The World Economy: A Millenial Perspective*. Paris: Development Centre of the OECD.
Mitch, D. 1993. The role of human capital in the first industrial revolution. In *The British Industrial Revolution: An Economic Perspective*, ed. J. Mokyr. San Francisco: Westview Press.
Moore, B. 1966. *The Social Origins of Dictatorship and Democracy: Lord and Peasant in the Making of the Modern World*. Boston: Beacon Press.
North, D. C., and Thomas, R. P. 1973. *The Rise of the Western World: A New Economic History*. Cambridge: Cambridge University Press.
—— and Weingast, B. R. 1989. Constitutions and commitment: the evolution of institutions governing public choice in seventeenth-century England. *Journal of Economic History*, 49: 803–32.
O'Brien, P. K. 1993. Political preconditions for the industrial revolution. In *The Industrial Revolution and British Society*, ed. P. K. O'Brien and R. Quinault. New York: Cambridge University Press.
O'Gorman, F. 1997. *The Long Eighteenth Century: British Political and Social History 1688–1832*. New York: Oxford University Press.
Putnam, R. H., with Leonardi, R., and Nanetti, R. 1993. *Making Democracy Work: Civic Traditions in Modern Italy*. Princeton, NJ: Princeton University Press.
Ringer, F. 1979. *Education and Society in Modern Europe*. Bloomington: University of Indiana Press.
Ross, M. L. 2001. Does oil hinder democracy? *World Politics*, 53: 325–61.
Stevenson, J. 1979. *Popular Disturbances in England, 1700–1870*. New York: Longman.
Tarrow, S. 1998. *Power in Movement: Social Movements and Contentious Politics*, 2nd edn. New York: Cambridge University Press.
Tawney, R. H. 1941. The rise of the gentry, 1558–1640. *Economic History Review*, 11: 1–38.
Thompson, E. P. 1975. *Whigs and Hunters: The Origin of the Black Act*. New York: Pantheon.
Tilly, C. 1995. *Popular Contention in Britain, 1758–1834*. Cambridge, Mass.: Harvard University Press.
Veitch, J. M. 1986. Repudiations and confiscations by the medieval state. *Journal of Economic History*, 46: 31–6.
Weingast, B. R. 1997. The political foundations of democracy and the rule of law. *American Political Science Review*, 91: 245–63.

CHAPTER 38

AUTHORITARIAN GOVERNMENT

STEPHEN HABER

From the time of the first recorded states in the third millennium BCE, the vast majority of the world's governments have been authoritarian. Nevertheless, we understand far less about the political economy of authoritarian governments than we do about democracies.

This is not to say that there are not sets of agreed-upon facts. But it is to say that those facts do not easily square with one another. For example, there is a broad consensus that authoritarian governments enforce property rights more weakly (Keefer and Knack 1997) and provide fewer public goods than democracies (Lake and Baum 2001). One would therefore expect countries ruled by authoritarians to grow more slowly than democracies. Nevertheless, since 1970, authoritarian countries have experienced average rates of economic growth the same as democracies, even controlling for the fact that they started with lower absolute levels of economic development (Barro 1997). One explanation for this surprising outcome is that there is much higher variance in the rate of economic growth under authoritarianism than under democracy: a subset of authoritarian countries performs extraordinarily well, pushing up an otherwise low average. This fact, however, replaces one puzzle with another: why are some authoritarian countries able to grow at breakneck paces, while others languish?

Our lack of understanding of authoritarian governments extends beyond their economic performance. Indeed, there are a number of empirical puzzles central to the

---

* This article benefited from discussions with Noel Maurer. Latika Chaudhary, Victor Menaldo, Terry Moe, Robert Packenham, Armando Razo, James Robinson, Paul Sniderman, and Barry Weingast made helpful comments on earlier drafts. Latika Chaudhary, Victor Menaldo, Diane Raub, and Scott Wilson provided invaluable research assistance. The usual caveats apply.

study of comparative political economy that are unresolved: why are some authoritarian governments motivated to provide social welfare programs, while others provide little in the way of public goods; why do some authoritarian governments practice widespread repression, while others permit a surprisingly broad range of civil rights; why are some authoritarian governments marked by corruption and nepotism, while others have efficient bureaucracies; why are some authoritarian governments able to transition to democracy, while others simply replace one dictator with another?

Resolving these empirical puzzles requires a theoretical framework that can organize what we already know and that can serve as a guide to future research. The purpose of this chapter is therefore to advance such a theory—to construct a logic of authoritarianism. In order to demonstrate the advantages of this theory concretely, I focus on its implications for property rights and economic growth. Nevertheless, the framework I advance has implications for a number of issues beyond economic performance, some of which I will address briefly in the conclusion.

In building this framework I draw on two, seemingly disparate, literatures—one influenced by political sociology, the other by economics.

The political sociology literature focuses on patterns of behavior in authoritarian governments, and generates typologies based on those patterns. This literature includes many of the classic works in comparative political development such as Huntington (1968) and Linz (2000). It also includes virtually all of the case studies of dictatorships written by political scientists, was well as the comparative studies of regime types, such as Huntington and Moore (1970), O'Donnell (1979, 1988), Remmer (1989), Chehabi and Linz (1998), Ottaway (2003), Geddes (2004), Magaloni (2004), and Simpser (2005).

Owing to its origins in sociology, this literature organizes dictatorships into categorical types based on their ascriptive characteristics. Because it is not rooted in a consensus theory, however, the literature has generated a jumble of regime "types," such as neo-sultanistic, neo-patrimonial, personal, bureaucratic authoritarian, military, inclusive military, exclusive military, single party, dominant (or hegemonic) party, semi-authoritarian, autocratic, and totalitarian—to name some of the most commonly used. These typologies are subject to easy criticism: many of them are neither exclusive nor exhaustive, some are based on ad hoc criteria; and at least one of them (bureaucratic authoritarianism) contains a regime "type" that appears to include only one case. Nevertheless, this literature does contain an important insight: there is a high degree of variance in the behavior of authoritarian regimes.

The economics literature rejects the notion that there are categorical "types" of dictators, and instead builds generalizable theories based on the common goals and incentives that face all dictators. The origins of this literature go back to Tullock (1987), who argued that all dictators share the same primary goal: hold on to office for dear life because failing to do so will result in jail, exile, or a bullet in the back of the head. Holding on to office is, however, extremely difficult because dictators cannot know who supports them and who does not: virtually all constituents and colleagues in dictatorships—at least those who value their necks—profess loyalty to the dictator, even as they conspire to depose him. The net effect is a paradox: dictators are inherently insecure.

A number of scholars have built upon Tullock's basic insight about the insecurity of dictators. Wintrobe (2000), for example, explores how dictators deploy either of two instruments, repression or economic redistribution, to resolve the problem of their insecurity. Bueno de Mesquita et al. (2003) depart from Wintrobe by assuming that dictators do not face a general threat from the rest of society, but instead face a threat from a subset of society (which they term the selectorate). This selectorate can therefore veto policies proposed by the dictator, and thus shape a wide variety of economic and political outcomes.[1]

Both Wintrobe and Bueno de Mesquita et al. are vague about who, exactly, can threaten to remove a dictator from power. Wintrobe assumes that anyone in society may do so. Bueno de Mesquita et al. argue that the group that can lodge a credible threat is a subset of society (the selectorate), that the size of the selectorate (and the size of the minimum winning coalition within it) varies across countries, and that differences in the size of the selectorate and minimum winning coalitions determine a broad range of outcomes. They do not specify, however, how the selectorate comes into existence, how it solves collective action problems, and why its size varies across polities.

Haber, Razo, and Maurer (2003) explore the question of who can threaten a dictator with removal from power, and the mechanism that they use to do so. They argue that in order to lodge a credible sanction against a dictator, a political entrepreneur must have a leadership role in an organized group that can accomplish two things: serve as a forum to coordinate with other political entrepreneurs; and mobilize a rank and file against the dictatorship. They also explore how the dictator and the political entrepreneurs that can sanction him can create a stable regime by creating a property rights system that is based on the generation and distribution of economic rents, and they demonstrate that such systems can generate impressive rates of economic growth—at least in the short run.

The framework that I advance is very much in the economics tradition in that it seeks to derive a theory from first principles. Nevertheless, it demonstrates that rational choice reasoning can be used to derive a logic of authoritarianism that generates a typology of sorts—three very different institutional arrangements, each with its own implications for political repression, property rights, economic growth, and democratic transitions.

1 An Organizational Theory of Dictatorship

One of the insights of Haber, Razo, and Maurer (2003) is that dictators are insecure because they face political entrepreneurs who lead organized groups. This presents

[1] Bueno de Mesquita (this volume) summarizes this approach.

us, however, with a paradox: if dictators fear political entrepreneurs and the groups they lead, why don't they simply stamp them out?

The answer is twofold. First, dictators need an organized group in order to take power. Some of these groups, such as the military, a political party, or a royal family, are formally constituted, have rules governing their internal workings, and may already be part of a pre-existing government. Others, such as a revolutionary movement, a military splinter group, or a federation of warlords, are less institutionalized.

Second, the dictator needs this launching organization, as well as the other organizations within the state that the launching group permeates, because without them he cannot run the country. This organization is made up of self-interested individuals. Its members therefore quickly populate the formal organizations of the government—the courts, police, bureaucracy, and legislature (if there is one). Thus, the dictator cannot simply declare the dissolution of the launching group: it is integrated into the state.

Precisely because the launching organization was able to solve the collective action problems inherent in putting the dictator into office, it can solve the collective action problem of removing him from office. Indeed, its control of the apparatus of government facilitates its ability to remove him. As a consequence, the dictator lives in fear that the organization's self-interested leaders will use it to launch their own bids for power. The dictator's fears are not without foundation: military coups are attempted against dictatorships twice as frequently as they are attempted against democracies (Brooker 2000) and succeed so frequently that the vast majority of dictators are removed not by popular uprisings but by internal coups (Tullock 1987).

The implication is clear: the dictator's political survival requires that he either find a way to commit credibly to do the bidding of the launching organization's leadership—to accept the fact that they can sanction him with removal from office if he pursues policies that they dislike—or he find a way to curb their power. If he follows the first strategy, he knows that he will always be insecure—and may end up a puppet. If he follows the second strategy, however, the leaders of the launching organization will resist him, because they know that their political futures (and perhaps their lives) are over if he succeeds. The early years of dictatorships therefore tend to be characterized by a power struggle—a game as it were, with the stakes being tenure in office—between the dictator and the leadership of the organized group that launched him.

Neither side in this game plays from a state of nature. They inherit an economy, a system of property rights, a class of wealth-holders, and a range of pre-existing organizations and institutions—not the least of which are constitutions, legislatures, political parties, opposition political movements, trade unions, police forces, and militaries. Thus, when the dictator and the leadership of the organization that launched him sit down to play they find that some of the pieces have already been moved—they cannot play any strategy that they like. Because the set-up of the board varies from one dictatorship to the next, the games played by dictators and the organized groups that launch them have multiple solutions.

This is not to say, however, that there are not commonalities in the winning strategies played by dictators. As an empirical matter, there appear to be three broad classes of outcomes: the dictator terrorizes the leadership of the launching organization; the dictator co-opts the leadership of the launching organization; or the dictator creates a set of rival or complementary organizations, the purpose of which is to raise the cost of collective action for the leadership of the launching organization.

There is no guarantee that a dictator will necessarily hit upon one of these solutions. He may fail to do so—and be overthrown. Indeed, the comparative case study and cross-country regression literatures indicate that there is a class of countries—those with very low levels of GDP whose political organizations and institutions have only recently taken shape, such as Spanish America in the nineteenth century or sub-Saharan Africa since the 1960s—in which the process of sorting through dictators may take quite some time (Londregan and Poole 1990; Campos and Nugent 2002, 2003; North, Summerhill, and Weingast 2000; Bates 2004). Nevertheless, even in these countries, at some point a dictator emerges who figures out an appropriate strategy and consolidates his rule.

Each one of these solutions generates a property rights system. Some of the resulting property rights systems severely limit the number of people that can enforce their property and contract rights. Others confer economic rights on a very large percentage of the population. Given the central role played by contract and property rights in the process of economic growth (Keefer and Knack 1997), the result is a high degree of variance in economic performance across dictatorships.

2 WHY ARE THERE SO FEW STATIONARY BANDITS?

A skeptical reader might scratch his head and ask why dictators and the organizations that launch them have to engage in a power struggle. Why can't the dictator offer to be a benign despot, and the leadership of the launching organization accept his offer?

This benign despot outcome is at the heart of Olson's (2000) widely cited stationary bandit model of dictatorships, and is the underlying mechanism that explains economic growth under authoritarianism in Przeworski et al. (2000). In Olson's framework, dictators are assumed to face no threat to their survival, and thus operate as "stationary bandits." They therefore have long time horizons, giving them fiscal incentives to enforce property rights universally, invest in public goods, and tax at the long-run revenue-maximizing rate. They then spend all tax revenues in excess of that necessary to enforce property rights and create public goods on conspicuous consumption. Przeworski et al. (2000) advance a similar argument, but make even stronger claims. They agree with Olson's view that a long-lived dictator will have an incentive to defend property rights, but then go on to argue that the real threat to property rights comes from democracies, because organized social groups can vote in favor of income redistribution. They assert, in fact, that most non-communist dictatorships are committed to defending private property, and further claim that the probability that a democracy will fail actually increases investment (pp. 209–11).

As Acemoglu et al. (2004) have shown, the strong claims made by Przeworski et al. are a product of mis-specified regressions: their econometric results fall apart as soon as researchers control for omitted variables in simple ways, such as adding country fixed effects.

Moreover, as a matter of history, the kind of benign despots/stationary bandits that figure in Olson's and Przeworski's theories are quite rare. The case study literature about long-lived dictatorships indicates, in fact, that they are highly predatory (Lewis 1980; Miranda 1990; Hutchcroft 1991; Thompson 1995; Chehabi and Linz 1998; Vatikiotis 1999; Turtis 2002; Razo 2003; Haber, Razo, and Maurer 2003; Mackey 2003). For every benign despot like Lee Kuan Yew (Singapore), there are a dozen predators like Juan Vicente Gómez (Venezuela), Fulgencio Batista (Cuba), Ferdinand Marcos (Philippines), Rafael Trujillo (Dominican Republic), Anastasio Somoza (Nicaragua), François and Jean Claude Duvalier (Haiti), Idi Amin (Uganda), Mobutu Sese Seko (Zaire), Suharto (Indonesia), Robert Mugabe (Zimbabwe), and Blaise Campaore (Burkina Faso), whose modus operandi is to appropriate everything they can.

There are theoretical reasons why the benign despot/stationary bandit solution occurs so rarely. First, the stationary bandit model assumes that the dictator can see how the exercise of his power in the short run diminishes his long-run accumulation of wealth. Second, it assumes that dictators have infinite time horizons. The problem is, of course, that no one lives forever. The older the dictator grows, the more he will discount the future, and as his discount factor increases the more likely he will be to increase taxes and seize property. Finally, it assumes that the dictator's allies—the leadership of the group that helped bring him to power—are lacking in self-interest: the dictator may extract social surplus by keeping for himself the difference between what he obtains from taxes and spends on public goods; but his allies seek nothing more than the opportunity to compete on a level playing field against everyone else in the economy. In short, the stationary bandit solution is rare because it has an underlying model of politics in which, as Razo (2003) points out, there are no politics.

3 THE LOGIC OF TERROR

The most direct strategy to curb the launching organization is to terrorize its leadership through murder, show trials, torture, and purges. One key element of the terror strategy is that it foments distrust: organization members have incentives to denounce one another in order to save their own skins, making it exceedingly difficult for them to coordinate their actions against the dictator. It also means, however, that the dictator cannot know whether the denunciations of organization members reflect accurate information, or are strategically motivated. Hence he purges indiscriminately, which only heightens everyone's sense of uncertainty (Tullock 1987).

Perhaps the most intensively studied case of a terror strategy was Stalin's purges of the Soviet Communist Party and the Red Army in the 1930s, which murdered 1.5 to 2.5 million party members and senior military officers (Conquest 1991; Azrael 1970). Other examples of this strategy include the purges of the Korean Communist Party carried out by Kim Il Sung and Kim Jong Il, Mao Tse-tung's Cultural Revolution, the killing fields of Cambodia's Pol Pot, and the bloody purge of Iraq's Baath Party by Saddam Hussein.

The terror strategy is not, however, frequently used, and there are three good reasons why. First, it is a very high-stakes game that leaves little room for error and experimentation: the dictator needs to be absolutely certain that he will quickly get the upper hand; if he fails to do so, the leaders of the organization that he is terrorizing have every incentive to put aside their differences and depose him.

Second, a campaign of terror requires the creation of a specialized terror organization, a secret police. This organization itself, however, looms as a threat to the dictator—and thus its own leadership must be terrorized. Stalin, for example, moved successively against the two heads of the NKVD who carried out the 1930s purges, both of whom he executed (Linz 2000).

Third, torture, terror, and political murder not only undermine the organization that launched the dictator; they undermine the ability of the government, which is populated by the organization's terrorized members, to function. Not surprisingly, the efficiency of government in countries characterized by political terror tends to be notoriously low. If the purge has been directed against the armed forces, the government's ability to defend itself from foreign invasion or internal rebellion is particularly damaged. Stalin, for example, murdered so many of his own generals and colonels that when Germany invaded in 1941 there was scarcely anyone to lead the Red Army (Azrael 1970).

What implications does a successful terror strategy have for property rights? If the dictator succeeds in terrorizing the organization that launched him, he has unconstrained authority and discretion. To put it in the vocabulary of Bueno de Mesquita et al., the selectorate has one person in it, the dictator. There is nothing to keep him from taking virtually everything that is worth taking in pursuit of his personal or ideological goals. Paradoxically, this generates a problem for the dictator: the lack of secure property rights dampens investment, thereby denying him the tax base he needs to run the country. The dictator cannot resolve this problem by promising to respect property and contract rights: because there is no sanction for breaking his promises, no promise he makes is credible. Thus, the logic of the situation pushes the dictator to expropriate private assets: he needs resources to run the government and the only ready source of funds is the stock of assets of the country's private wealth-holders.

Are there any areas of the economy that are safe from expropriation? There will still be private investment so long as investors believe that the rate of return in a particular enterprise exceeds the probability of expropriation (Maurer and

Gomberg forthcoming). The problem is, however, that high rates of return increase the dictator's motivation to expropriate the enterprise. Thus, private investment will only occur if the probability of expropriation is low because of some asset-specific factor.

One class of investment where asset-specific factors provide protection for property rights is enterprises that can escape detection by the government, because they do not require the judicial system to enforce contracts, can hide income from taxation, and are able to evade the registration of property sales. These factors mean, however, that these enterprises are likely to be of very modest scale: small farms, artisan workshops, and petty traders.

A second class of enterprises that have a low probability of expropriation are those in which virtually all of the assets are in the form of human capital. They include firms that provide medical, legal, and accounting services, as well as manufacturing firms that use non-mechanized technologies operated by highly skilled craftsmen (diamond-cutting is a classic example). These enterprises, however, are also likely to be of modest scale. Indeed, their lack of physical and financial capital is why we tend to think of them not so much as business enterprises, but as professions.

A third class of enterprises that have a low probability of expropriation are those that have large amounts of physical capital, but the efficient operation of that capital requires proprietary knowledge of markets or technologies. Investors in these enterprises know that the government can neither credibly threaten to expropriate them nor allocate their property rights to another firm—because neither the government nor that firm can operate the enterprise efficiently enough to yield tax income higher than that provided by the incumbent investors. One type of firm characterized by high levels of proprietary knowledge is those engaged in natural resource extraction. Successfully finding, extracting, refining, and distributing petroleum and minerals requires skilled personnel with knowledge of geology, hydrology, chemistry, metallurgy, and engineering. It also requires access to, and knowledge of, foreign markets, because the vast majority of the output of these industries is consumed in a small number of industrialized countries (Haber, Maurer, and Razo 2003). Not surprisingly, foreign companies that specialize in resource extraction often invest in even the most brutal of dictatorships, while their counterparts in banking and manufacturing stay away.

With private investment relegated to these three areas of the economy—a low-productivity "informal sector," a specialized set of service and manufacturing firms that use extremely low levels of physical or financial capital, and an enclave economy dedicated to the extraction of natural resources—it is unlikely that the country will experience rapid rates of economic growth. Indeed, such an economy is likely to be missing one economic sector that is crucial for growth—a banking system (King and Levine 1993), because the liquid nature of its assets makes it an attractive target for expropriation. As an empirical matter, the countries where dictators have ruled through terror, the Soviet Union under Stalin, Iraq under Saddam Hussein, China under Mao, and Korea under Kim Il Sung and Kim Jong Il, have performed very weakly.

4 THE LOGIC OF CO-OPTATION

Far more common than the strategy of terrorizing the leadership of a launching organization is the strategy of co-opting it by buying its loyalty. The stream of rents paid to the leadership of the organization convinces them that they are better off cooperating with the regime than overthrowing it. They will only join a coup attempt if they believe that the stream of rents they will earn post-coup, multiplied by the probability of the coup's success, minus the cost of losing their heads if the coup fails, exceeds the stream of rents they earn already.

The key to a co-optation strategy is a source of rents. These rents can conceivably come from state-owned firms. This strategy was played, for example, by Argentina's military dictators in the 1970s and 1980s, who bought the loyalty of senior officers by allowing them to run state-owned enterprises (Rock 1987, 371). The problem with this strategy, however, is that the source of rents and the government are one and the same. This means that coup leaders can credibly promise to maintain the pre-coup rent-sharing arrangements, which puts the dictator at risk.

A rent-sharing arrangement with more than two parties creates greater uncertainty about the post-coup generation and division of rents. As a practical matter, most rent-sharing arrangements under stable authoritarian governments tend to have three parties: the dictator, the leadership of the organized group that can sanction him, and a group of investors who generate a stream of rents in privately owned enterprises.

As Haber, Razo, and Maurer (2003) demonstrate, the heart of this system is the creation of economic rents by reducing competition through regulatory barriers to entry, such as selectively allocated import permits, preferential tax treatment, or the requirement of licenses or concessions to enter particular lines of economic activity. The dictator has an incentive to create these regulatory barriers, because it coaxes capital into production, thereby creating a tax base for him. Investors in these favored firms know, however, that the dictator has no real commitment to them. In fact, the monopoly rents they earn give him an incentive to expropriate their firms. They therefore share some of the rents with the dictator, as well as with his government in the form of tax revenues, in order to reduce his incentives to expropriate them. In addition, they also seek out individuals and groups that can provide them with protection from the dictator, and they have something that they can offer those individuals or groups by way of compensation: a share of the rents generated by regulated entry. The mechanisms that investors employ to transfer these rents are not complicated: they appoint the very same political entrepreneurs who can sanction the dictator to the boards of directors of the favored firms; employ them as consultants; make them loans with no expectation of repayment; or hire their family members. In short, this property rights system not only permits rent-seeking, it requires it.

Rent-sharing arrangements of this variety are extremely common in dictatorships. Examples include Taiwan under Chiang Kai-shek, the Dominican Republic under Trujillo, Venezuela under Gómez, the Philippines under Marcos, Nicaragua under the

Somoza dynasty, Indonesia under Suharto, Cuba under Batista, Brazil under Vargas, and Mexico under Porfirio Díaz.

Over the short run, the allocation of property rights to a small group of people can create impressive rates of economic growth. The Porfirio Díaz regime in Mexico (1876–1911) is a classic, and intensively studied, case in point. During his thirty-five-year dictatorship, Díaz built a rent-sharing system that co-opted the political entrepreneurs who opposed him. It also provided investors with incentives to build a railroad network, banking system, manufacturing industries, and vibrant mining, petroleum, and export agriculture sectors. Indeed, under Díaz, Mexico actually grew at a faster rate than the United States. (Haber, Razo, and Maurer 2003; Razo 2003).

Over the long term, however, rent-sharing systems weigh on economic growth. First, the requirement that rents be generated and distributed through the political system means that resources are misallocated: industries exist in which the country has no comparative advantage; monopolies and oligopolies exist in industries that should be characterized by near-perfect competition; and opportunities are denied to entrepreneurs with the required skills and assets, but without political access or protection (Fisman 2001; Haber, Razo, and Maurer 2003). Second, the rents necessary to sustain this system must come from somewhere: usually everyone and anyone outside the coalition that effectively governs the country—the dictator, investors in favored enterprises, and the leadership of the organization that can sanction the dictator. This has negative distributional consequences, which limit the size and depth of the domestic market.

5 THE LOGIC OF ORGANIZATIONAL PROLIFERATION

The organized group that can sanction the dictator may also be undermined, paradoxically, by creating yet more organizations. The goal of this strategy is to raise the cost of collective action within the launching organization through either of two mechanisms: it forces its leadership to coordinate with the leadership of the other, newly created, organizations (which might otherwise come to the rescue of the dictator during a coup); and/or it raises the cost of coordination within the launching organization by aligning the incentives of its membership with the leadership of another organization. An example of the first mechanism is the creation of multiple branches of the military. Adolf Hitler, for example, created three different armies: the regular army; a militarized branch of the secret police, the Waffen SS; and a ground force of 300,000 soldiers that was under the command of the air force. An example of the second mechanism is the creation of an official party by a military government. The party is then used to reward military officers who are loyal party members, thereby aligning their incentives with the dictator, instead of with the military chain of command. Alfredo Stroessner, the military strongman who ruled Paraguay from 1954 to 1989, for example, took over a debilitated political party, the Colorados, and turned it into an immense patronage machine designed to align the incentives of the officer corps with his regime (Lewis 1980; Miranda 1990).

Neither the membership of the dictatorship's organizations, nor their leadership, work for free. Property rights to secure jobs, loans from government-run banks, and the opportunity to receive bribes and kickbacks must be provided to rank and file members, while the selective allocation of trade protection, tax preferences, or contract enforcement must be provided to the organizations' leaders.

Dictatorships that are characterized by organizational proliferation therefore confer economic rights and opportunities on a very broad percentage of the population, as compared to dictatorships that employ strategies of terror or cronyism. This creates incentives for the members of those organizations to invest in productive enterprises, and the result is impressive rates of economic growth. This growth is hampered, of course, by the fact that those individuals who are not protected by organization membership are fair game for organization members: their property rights can be preyed upon, and contracts with them may be abrogated with impunity. Nevertheless, the resulting property rights system more closely approximates that found in democracies (where property rights and public goods are allocated and enforced universally) than it does those of authoritarian regimes characterized by co-optation (where property rights are allocated narrowly) or by terror (where property rights are vested in the dictator).

Perhaps the most fully developed economic system based on a strategy of organizational proliferation was Mexico between 1929 and 2000. In the aftermath of the Mexican Revolution of 1910, numerous warlords-turned-politicians jockeyed for power, producing coups, rebellions, and civil wars that stretched through the 1920s. In 1929, one of these warlords, General Plutarco Elias Calles, hit upon the idea of creating a political party, the Partido Nacional Revolucionario (PNR), whose initial purpose was to arbitrate disputes among the warlords, thereby allowing Calles to maintain de facto political control of the country. Later Mexican presidents transformed the PNR, however, into a mass party organized on corporatist lines (the Partido Revolucionario Institucional, known by its Spanish acronym, PRI), which was not only successful in checking Calles's ambitions but also managed to create a regularized, non-violent process by which party elites would rotate the presidency and other "elected offices" among themselves. The key to the PRI's success was that it sat at the center of a network of organizations, which were designed to align the incentives of a wide variety of organized corporate groups, making it extremely difficult for any one of them to mount a credible challenge to the party's monopoly on power (Simpser 2005; Magaloni forthcoming). They also managed to create an economic system that produced real per capita rates of economic growth roughly double that of the United States for a period of nearly five decades.

The result of organizational proliferation in Mexico was that a sizable percentage of the population had enforceable economic rights. Manufacturers, for example, obtained rights to trade protection that protected them from foreign competition.

The lack of competition, in turn, allowed industrial workers in PRI-affiliated labor unions to have a property right to lifetime job security, as well as rights to a range of social welfare benefits that were not available to the general population, such as health care, subsidized housing, and retirement pensions. Even groups as disparate as Mexico City's collective taxi drivers, who were members of the PRI's National Confederation of Popular Organizations, obtained a special property right: they were given exclusive routes that prevented the development of a competitive fringe of collective taxis (Haber et al. 2005).

6 Conclusions and Implications

The literature on authoritarianism has tended to fall into either of two broad camps, one written by scholars influenced by sociology, the other written by scholars influenced by economics. This chapter has argued that these literatures can be integrated into a unified framework that explains variance in economic performance across dictatorships.

The heart of this framework is the notion that there is an inevitable set of strategic interactions—a game—among dictators and the organized groups that launch them to power. Neither side in this game plays from a state of nature: they inherit a pre-existing set of political institutions and organizations, along with an economy and society. This means that the game has multiple outcomes. A close reading of the case study literature indicates, however, that the set of the dictator's winning strategies is small. He may terrorize the launching organization's leadership, co-opt them by providing them with private goods, or raise their costs of collective action by proliferating yet more organizations. Each of these strategies generates quite different property rights systems, and each of those property rights systems has consequences for economic growth and distribution.

One implication of this framework is that the vast literature on the "resource curse" has perhaps mis-specified the causal connection between high levels of natural resource exports and authoritarian government. Researchers such as Ross (2001) have identified an important empirical pattern: there is a strong correlation between having an authoritarian government and having an economy that is heavily weighted toward the export of natural resources. Researchers usually interpret this correlation as an indication that causality runs from having a large stock of natural resources to authoritarianism (Karl 1997; Wantchekon 1999). The framework I advance suggests, however, that causality runs the other way: when dictators have unconstrained authority and discretion, investment tends to cluster in enterprises that are difficult to expropriate because running them requires proprietary knowledge of markets and technologies—such as petroleum and mineral extraction. The result is that a large proportion of the economy's GDP is composed of oil and mineral exports—independent of the extent of the country's natural resource endowment.

Recent research by Haber, Maurer, and Razo (2003), Wright and Czelusta (2004), and Robinson, Torvik, and Verdier (forthcoming) supports this view. Nevertheless, the study of which way causality runs is still not a settled matter, and warrants additional investigation.

The implications of this framework extend beyond issues related to economic growth. One central question of the field of comparative politics is why some dictatorships are able to transition to democracy, while others replace one dictator with another. There is as yet no consensus answer to that question, although it has been argued by Przeworski et al. (2000) that the success of a democratic transition is a function of per capita income: all authoritarian countries periodically experiment with democracy, but democracy only endures once a country has reached a minimum standard of living.

The framework advanced here suggests that the relationship between successful democratic transitions and per capita income is endogenous to the outcome of the power struggle between dictators and the organizations that launch them. Dictatorships in which the power of the launching organization was curbed by terrorizing or co-opting its leadership tend to allocate property rights to a restricted set of individuals. As a result, the economies of these countries tend to grow very slowly, and their levels of per capita income remain low. Dictatorships in which the power of the launching organization was curbed by proliferating yet more organizations, however, tend to allocate property rights to a much larger set of individuals. As a result, the economies of these countries tend to grow more rapidly. Democratic transitions are more likely, therefore, to be successful in those countries in which the dictatorship was characterized by organizational proliferation, rather than terror or co-optation.

Countries that are characterized by organizational proliferation have an additional advantage, beyond that conferred by higher per capita incomes, in the process of democratic transition. The steps necessary to create democratic institutions in these polities are incremental: the dictatorship itself has created a party (or parties), the military cannot easily overthrow the government, and a large number of citizens have already been vested with political and economic rights. But, when the strategic interaction of dictators and the organized groups that launch them produces dictatorial strategies of terror or co-optation, the additional steps necessary to create democratic institutions are gargantuan. Given the importance attached by both political scientists and policy-makers to the spread of democracy, testing this hypothesis is of obvious importance.

References

Acemoglu, D., Johnson, S., Robinson, J., and Yared, P. 2004. Income and democracy. Mimeo.

Azrael, J. R. 1970. The internal dynamics of the CPSU, 1917–1967. Pp. 261–83 in *Authoritarian Politics in Modern Society: The Dynamics of Established One-Party Systems*, ed. S. P. Huntington and C. Moore. New York: Basic Books.

Barro, R. J. 1997. *Determinants of Economic Growth: A Cross-Country Empirical Study.* Cambridge, Mass.: MIT Press.

Bates, R. 2004. On "The politics of property rights" by Haber, Razo, and Maurer. *Journal of Economic Literature,* 42: 494–500.

Brooker, P. 2000. *Non-democratic Regimes: Theory, Government, and Politics.* New York: St Martin's Press.

Brownlee, J. 2004. Ruling parties and durable authoritarianism. Center for Democracy, Development, and the Rule of Law working paper.

Bueno de Mesquita, B., Smith, A., Silverson, R. M., and Morrow, J. D. 2003. *The Logic of Political Survival.* Cambridge, Mass.: MIT Press.

Campos, N. F., and Nugent, J. B. 2002. Who is afraid of political instability? *Journal of Development Economics,* 67: 157–72.

——— ——— 2003. Investment and instability: an econometric investigation. *Economica,* 70: 533–49.

Chehabi, H. E., and Linz, J. J. (eds.). 1998. *Sultanistic Regimes.* Baltimore: Johns Hopkins University Press.

Conquest, R. 1991. *The Great Terror: A Reassessment.* Oxford: Oxford University Press.

Fisman, R. 2001. Estimating the value of political connections. *American Economic Review,* 91: 1095–102.

Friedrich, C. J. 1970. The failure of a one-party system: Hitler Germany. Pp. 239–60 in *Authoritarian Politics in Modern Society: The Dynamics of Established One-Party Systems,* ed. S. P. Huntington and C. Moore. New York: Basic Books.

Geddes, B. 2004. Authoritarian breakdown. Mimeo, University of California, Los Angeles.

Haber, S., Maurer, N., and Razo, A. 2003. When the law does not matter: the rise and decline of the Mexican oil industry. *Journal of Economic History,* 63: 1–31.

——— Razo, A., and Maurer, N. 2003. *The Politics of Property Rights: Political Instability, Credible Commitments, and Economic Growth in Mexico, 1876–1929.* Cambridge: Cambridge University Press.

——— Klein, H. S., Maurer, N., and Middlebrook, K. J. 2005. *The Second Mexican Revolution.* Unpublished book manuscript.

Huntington, S. P. 1968. *Political Order in Changing Societies.* New Haven, Conn.: Yale University Press.

——— and Moore, C. 1970. *Authoritarian Politics in Modern Society: The Dynamics of Established One-Party Systems.* New York: Basic Books.

Hutchcroft, P. D. 1991. Oligarchs and cronies in the Philippine state: the politics of patrimonial plunder. *World Politics,* 43: 414–50.

Karl, T. L. 1997. *The Paradox of Plenty: Oil Booms and Petro-States.* Berkeley: University of California Press.

Keefer, P., and Knack, S. 1997. Why don't poor countries catch up? A cross-national test of an institutional explanation. *Economic Inquiry,* 35: 590–602.

King, R. G., and Levine, R. 1993. Finance and growth: Schumpeter might be right. *Quarterly Journal of Economics,* 108: 717–38.

Lake, D. A., and Baum, M. A. 2001. The invisible hand of democracy: political control and the provision of public services. *Comparative Political Studies,* 34: 587–621.

Lewis, P. H. 1980. *Paraguay under Stroessner.* Chapel Hill: University of North Carolina Press.

Linz, J. J. 2000. *Authoritarian and Totalitarian Regimes.* Boulder, Colo.: Lynne Rienner.

Londregan, J. B., and Poole, K. T. 1990. Poverty, the coup trap, and the seizure of executive power. *World Politics,* 42: 151–83.

MACKEY, S. 2003. *The Reckoning: Iraq and the Legacy of Saddam Hussein*. New York: W. W. Norton.

MAGALONI, B. 2004. Hegemonic party autocracies in the world. Mimeo, Stanford University.

—— forthcoming. *Voting for Autocracy: The Politics of Party Hegemony and its Demise*. New York: Cambridge University Press.

MAURER, N., and GOMBERG, A. forthcoming. When the state is untrustworthy: public finance and private banking in Porfirian Mexico. *Journal of Economic History*.

MIRANDA, C. 1990. *The Stroessner Era: Authoritarian Rule in Paraguay*. Boulder, Colo.: Westview Press.

NORTH, D. C., SUMMERHILL, W. R., and WEINGAST, B. R. 2000. Order, disorder, and economic change: Latin America versus North America. Pp. 17–58 in *Governing for Prosperity*, ed. B. Bueno de Mesquita and H. L. Root. New Haven, Conn: Yale University Press.

O'DONNELL, G. 1979. *Modernization and Bureaucratic-Authoritarianism: Studies in South American Politics*. Berkeley: Institute for International Studies, University of California.

—— 1988. *Bureaucratic Authoritarianism: Argentina, 1966–73, in Comparative Perspective*. Berkeley: University of California Press.

OLSON, M. 2000. *Power and Prosperity: Outgrowing Communist and Capitalist Dictatorships*. New York: Basic Books.

OTTAWAY, M. 2003. *Democracy Challenged: The Rise of Semi-Authoritarianism*. Washington, DC: Carnegie Endowment for International Peace.

PRZEWORSKI, A., ALVAREZ, M., CHEIBUB, J. A., and LIMONGI, F. 2000. *Democracy and Development: Political Institutions and Material Well-Being in the World, 1950–1990*. New York: Cambridge University Press.

RAZO, A. 2003. Social networks and credible commitments in dictatorships: political organization and economic growth in Porfirian Mexico, 1876–1991. Ph.D. dissertation, Stanford University.

REMMER, K. L. 1989. *Military Rule in Latin America*. London: Routledge.

ROBINSON, J., TORVIK, R., and VERDIER, T. forthcoming. Political foundations of the resource curse. *Journal of Development Economics*.

ROCK, D. 1987. *Argentina, 1516–1987: From Spanish Colonization to Alfonsin*. Los Angeles: University of California Press.

ROSS, M. 2001. Does oil hinder democracy? *World Politics*, 53: 235–61.

SIMPSER, A. 2005. Making votes not count: strategic incentives for electoral corruption. Ph.D. dissertation, Stanford University.

THOMPSON, M. R. 1995. *The Anti-Marcos Struggle: Personalistic Rule and Democratic Transition in the Philippines*. New Haven, Conn: Yale University Press.

TULLOCK, G. 1987. *Autocracy*. Boston: Kluwer Academic.

TURTIS, R. L. 2002. *Foundations of Despotism: Peasants, the Trujillo Regime, and Modernity in Dominican History*. Stanford, Calif.: Stanford University Press.

VATIKIOTIS, M. 1999. *Indonesian Politics under Suharto: The Rise and Fall of the New Order*. London: Routledge.

WANTCHEKON, L. 1999. Why do resource dependent countries have authoritarian governments? Mimeo, Yale University.

WINTROBE, R. 2000. *The Political Economy of Dictatorship*. Cambridge: Cambridge University Press.

WRIGHT, G., and CZELUSTA, J. 2004. The myth of the resource curse. *Challenge*, 47: 6–38.

CHAPTER 39

THE ROLE OF THE STATE IN DEVELOPMENT

ROBERT H. BATES

ADDRESSING the role of the state in development, this chapter seeks both to synthesize and to innovate. So vast is the literature—it runs from anthropology (e.g. Colson 1974) through international relations (e.g. Keohane 1984) and comparative politics (e.g. Kang 2002) and on to political economy (e.g. Evans 1995)—that any synthesis must of necessity be selective. To structure to my treatment of this literature, I therefore advance a blunt thesis—"no state, no development." Before elaborating my argument, I first clarify my terms and intentions and defend against criticisms implicit in the literature. After fully developing my argument, I conclude by noting its implications for future research.

1 BACKGROUND

So bald a thesis demands clarification. I ground my conception of development in political economy and regard it as the achievement of political security and economic prosperity. My goal is purposefully minimalist: I focus on the transformation of the

* The research reviewed in this chapter was supported by the National Science Foundation (Grant SES 9905568), the Carnegie Corporation, and the Center for International Development and Weatherhead Center for International Affairs at Harvard University. I wish to thank Barry Weingast for the tough and supportive comments made on earlier versions of this chapter. The deficiencies that remain are my responsibility alone.

use of power from a means of appropriating wealth into an instrument of its creation and demur from addressing such topics as the politics of industrial policies (Fishlow et al. 1994; Amsden 1989) or of the welfare state (Hall and Soskice 2001).

This chapter can therefore be viewed as a contribution to the program pioneered by Douglass North (e.g. North and Thomas 1973). For North, the key to development was the creation of institutions. While political rather than economic in nature, institutions, he argued, were sources of value. Institutions that equated the private with the social rate of return set in place incentives that would deter rational individuals from taking actions that were privately profitable but socially harmful and encourage them to undertake activities that while privately costly would be socially beneficial. By noting that any agency powerful enough to create such institutions would also be powerful enough to dismantle them, Weingast (1995) pointed to a major lacuna in North's argument: the absence of a theory of politics or, more precisely, a theory as to why political agents would use power to elicit the creation of wealth rather than to engage in predation.[1]

In arguing "no state, no development," I will seek the conditions under which the provision of security and the creation of wealth become rational political acts. Under these conditions, those who control the means of violence will (if a citizen) put it aside or (if a ruler) employ it to defend the property of others. When these choices form an equilibrium, then, I will argue, there is a state. And when there is a state, I further argue, the equilibrium can support the attainment of both security and prosperity. Indeed, it can support a (Pareto) welfare maximum. When organized as a state, coercion underpins development.

1.1 Defending on One Front: The Writings of Anthropologists

One possible challenge to such an argument originates from the ranks of anthropologists, who, as noted by Almond and Coleman (1960), demonstrate that societies can generate security even though they lack states. To view the state as necessary for the provision of security is thus to confound form with function, they would argue, treating the state as necessary when its function can in fact be performed by other social structures. It is Gluckman (1955) who provides the best gloss: In societies without states, he contends, peace is achieved in the shadow of the feud. Families provide protection for their kin and it is fear of retaliation by one's kin that safeguards a person's security.

While documenting that people who dwell in societies without states can in fact be secure, anthropologists fail to stress a second key feature of these societies: their poverty. More precisely, they fail to recognize that poverty may result from statelessness. I argue that the state provides a means of securing peace *with* prosperity, whereas in polities based on kinship, people must trade the one value off against the other.

---

[1] It was Margaret Levi 1981, 1988, who provided the most coherent neoclassical theory of governance.

1.2 Defending One Another: The Literature on International Relations

A second challenge emanates from students of international relations. At the global level, there is no state; but as emphasized by Keohane and Nye (1989) there can nonetheless be order. A host of scholars (consult, for example, Martin and Simmons 2001) have demonstrated that even in the absence of an international government there can still be peace and, indeed, high levels of cooperation.

The substantive findings in this field thus pose a second challenge to my argument. So too do the analytics that generate them: the logic of non-cooperative, repeated games. Appealing to the so-called folk theorem of repeated games (Fudenberg and Maskin 1986), students of international relations argue that socially productive behavior can be elicited and socially destructive behavior discouraged even in stateless (i.e. non-cooperative) environments. In repeated games, people can play trigger strategies. That is, they can condition the actions they take on previous actions by others. The degree to which retaliation will deter is a function of its relative severity, its duration, and the degree to which the potential defector discounts the future. According to the folk theorem, even in prisoner's dilemma games, for a given set of payoffs, the benefits from cooperation can be secured as an equilibrium if the rate of discount renders future losses from the punishments inflicted by trigger strategies greater than the one-period gains from an opportunistic defection.

I too acknowledge the power of the folk theorem. But I demur from endorsing the optimistic implications drawn by students of international relations. At the core of development lie dynamics; the very term "development" implies change over time. Either because of increases in capital (in the relatively short run) or of changes in technology (in the relatively longer run), the payoffs for a given set of strategies can change. A rate of discount may render cooperation an equilibrium choice of strategy, given the initial payoffs; but it will later fail to do so, should payoffs alter and, in particular, should the rewards for defection increase in value. The folk theorem thus does not offer the assurance of cooperation to students of development that it offers to students of international relations. Even while appropriating the analytics employed in that field, I shall therefore continue to argue: no state, no development.

To lay the foundations for my claim, I return to the terrain of the anthropologists and to behavior in stateless societies.

2 STATELESS SOCIETIES

The hallmark of a stateless society is the decentralized control of the means of coercion. In the absence of an agency that possesses a monopoly over the use of force, each person—each family—retains control over the instruments of violence and provides its own security. The decentralized provision of violence characterizes village and kinship societies (Sahlins 1968; Wolff 1966); medieval cities (Greif 1998); and feudal societies (Bloch 1970). In such societies, the roots of political order lie in the capacity to deter. The system is based on the certainty of retaliation: it is "fear of the feud" (Gluckman 1955) that dissuades people from behaving opportunistically.

The literature on stateless societies thus yields a counterintuitive result: that people who do not possess states can nonetheless be orderly. The finding has informed the work of anarchists (e.g. Taylor 1987) and libertarians (e.g. Buchanan and Tullock 1962), who for contrasting reasons seek to limit the reach of public power.

A closer analysis suggests that while there may be order in these societies, it comes at a high cost.[2] People value both income and leisure; but when stateless, people have to provide their own protection and they therefore must divert resources to military preparation. The sacrifice of income and leisure implies a decline in welfare. In addition, while the threat of retaliation may be designed to deter, once triggered, retaliation provokes disorder; the initial costs are therefore compounded. That the subsequent losses may exceed in value those resulting from the initial harm points to a third deficiency: fearing to trigger a costly feud, people may have to tolerate "minor" infractions. They may have to live at a level of security lower than that which they would prefer.

While highlighting the imperfections of a system in which security is privately provided, these observations fall short of demonstrating the inability of stateless societies to secure development. As shown by the folk theorem, given a sufficiently low rate of discount, cooperation can be achieved as an equilibrium choice of strategies and even first-best level of welfare secured in equilibrium. Retaining the logic that underlies this claim, hold constant the discount rate and let the payoffs from defection increase; that is, let there be growth. Without an offsetting increase in the severity of the punishments, the actors will then find that the joys of immediate gratification outweigh future losses from retaliation. For social order to be stable, the growth in prosperity will therefore require a modification of political arrangements. Failing that, the likelihood of opportunistic defection will rise.

To cut deeper, focus on the conditions under which people in stateless societies might nonetheless be willing to disarm. To be willing to disarm, a family must have no reason to fear its neighbor; the neighbor must therefore have no reason to wish to steal the family's property. The conclusion therefore appears inescapable: the price of disarmament is having nothing worth stealing. There may be peace; there also may be leisure; but there is also poverty in stateless societies.

We can look as well for conditions under which prosperity *can* be achieved in stateless societies. As Bates, Greif, and Singh (2002) demonstrate, the condition is that people be prepared to fight. The price of prosperity is that people be willing to sacrifice leisure. They must amass military resources sufficient to deter others from appropriating the fruits of their labor.

---

[2] See Axelrod 1984 for further insights into the costs of this system.

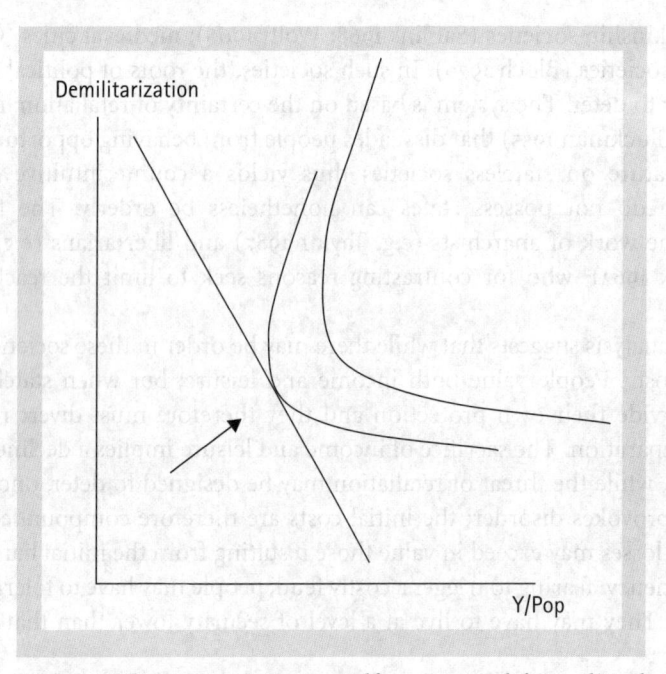

Fig. 39.1 The constraints on welfare imposed by political institutions

Figure 39.1 provides a visual portrayal of the implications of this argument. The vertical axis designates the level of demilitarization; the x-axis marks the level of prosperity. People want higher levels of both: utility therefore increases as one moves northeast in the plane framed by the two axes. The first-best outcome would locate in the upper right-hand corner, representing the achievement of both high income and demilitarization. As suggested by the downward-sloping line, the cost of prosperity is greater levels of military preparation; by the same token, the cost of demilitarization is poverty. The political institutions of stateless societies, the figure suggests, thus impose a trade-off between prosperity and security. Because development implies higher levels of both, the downward-sloping line can also be viewed as a constraint on the level of development that such societies can attain. The origin of this constraint is the society's political institutions. In their search for higher levels of welfare, people in stateless societies are limited by the nature of their institutions.

3 Societies With States

Thus far I have defended the thesis: "No state, no development." By demonstrating how power can be organized in a way that engenders both security and prosperity, I now turn to the positive case for the role of the state in development.

To launch the argument, I introduce a figure, G (think "government"), who is a specialist in the use of violence. In contrast to the private citizens, G does not secure his income from productive labor: rather, he secures it by using force. In seeking the "primitive" conditions for the state, I seek the conditions under which G would find it preferable to earn an income by employing his command over the military arts to safeguard rather than to seize the wealth of others.

Now there are three actors: G and the two private agents. Each values both leisure and income. G can gain an income from predation or from payments made by citizens in exchange for protection; the private agents, by working or raiding. To draw closer to the conditions that define the properties of the state, I ask three questions:

1. Under what conditions would G choose to employ force to defend the citizens rather than to prey upon them?
2. Under which conditions will citizens choose to disarm, leaving the government to protect their life and property?
3. And when will these choices prevail as an equilibrium?

By equilibrium, is meant:

I. No private agent should be able to gain by raiding or refusing to pay taxes.
II. Nor should an agent be able to gain by altering the allocation of her resources between work, leisure, and military preparation.
III. G's threat to predate must be credible.
IV. And G must find it optimal *not* to predate if the economic agents adhere to their strategies.

The structure of repeated play helps to define this equilibrium for it opens up the possibility of punishment should any player deviate. In the punishment phase, G would earn his income from predation rather than protection; the citizens would reallocate resources from production to defense and to leisure, the former so as to deter those who might raid and the latter so as to render raiding unattractive. Society would therefore be poor and its members insecure. As stated by Hobbes, the life of man would be "poor, nasty, brutish, and short."

To illustrate the conditions that support adherence to the equilibrium path of play, I first focus on the incentives that shape the choices of G, the specialist in violence. I stress the incentives that prevail in equilibrium and those that arise should a deviation occur (Figure 39.2). I then turn to the behavior of the citizens.

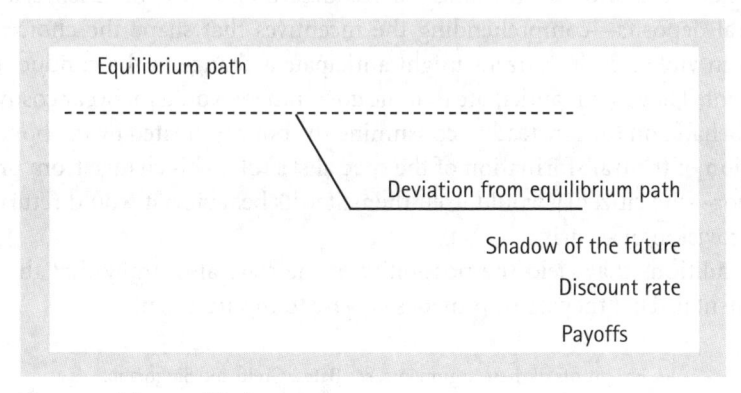

Fig. 39.2 The equilibrium path

G's incentives to adhere to the equilibrium choice of strategies derive from the revenues he can secure from taxation. To induce G to refrain from predation, the level of revenues he earns from the provision of protection needs to be high enough that G finds it optimal, given the private agents' choice of strategies, to refrain from confiscating the agents' wealth if they pay taxes. But the revenues must also be sufficiently low that private agents prefer to purchase the services of G rather than to incur the costs of providing their own security. The level of revenues must satisfy both G's and the citizens' participation constraints, where the latter is defined by a capacity to revert to the private provision of security and to the taking up of arms.

G's willingness to adhere to the equilibrium path also depends upon his payoffs in the punishment phase. The magnitude of these payoffs constitute the shadow of the future, to use Axelrod's phrasing (Axelrod 1984). This shadow will be the dimmer and the punishment phase therefore less of a deterrent to predation should G be assured of a prosperous future even should the state break down. Should, for example, G be able to retain control over oil fields, gold mines, or other assets, then he need not fear the loss of taxes, should he abandon his role as a guardian. The shadow will dim as well should G more heavily discount the future and thus the losses during the punishment phase. Should his future become less certain or his level of impatience rise, then G will come to weigh the prospects of immediate gain more highly than future pain. He will find the immediate rewards (even given the attendant punishment) from predation more attractive than the steady but moderate future flow of earnings from the provision of protective services. Both the magnitude of these rewards in the punishment phase and the degree to which the payoffs are discounted thus determine the strength of G's incentives to behave like the government of a state rather than like a warlord.[3]

I have focused on the incentives facing G. But note too the behavior of the private citizens. If public revenues decline, then, understanding G's incentives, the citizens might fear their government's behavior. They might expect the specialist in violence to begin to behave as a predator, using his power to extract resources from the private economy. So too if G's hold on power becomes less secure: the citizens might then fear that their government—now facing greater prospects of the loss of power—would now begin to despoil rather than to protect the private economy. And should a major new source of wealth arise—a resource boom, say; or discoveries of oil or mineral deposits—comprehending the incentives that shape the choices of the specialist in violence, the citizens might anticipate a change in the conduct of their government. They might anticipate that the government would forswear costly efforts on their behalf and turn instead to consuming the bounty created by the bonanza. In anticipation of the transformation of the specialist's role—his change from protector to predator—the citizenry would itself then alter its behavior: it would return to the private provision of security.

The conditions that yield the possibility of the state also imply that the state is developmental. That they do so provides closure to my argument.

---

[3] For proofs of these arguments, see Bates, Greif, and Singh 2002.

When G is willing and able to punish those who engage in raiding, then private citizens need no longer divert resources from productive effort. And when G can gain a higher income by protecting the creation of wealth than by engaging in predation, citizens need not fear that increases in prosperity will trigger political expropriation. Given the security of their property and the fruits of their labors, citizens will therefore be willing to shift resources into productive endeavors. The citizens will enjoy security and their incomes will grow.

If G is little tempted to deviate from its role as guardian, then it can be shown that as the rate at which he discounts the future declines, the level of taxes necessary to secure his services approaches "0" (Bates, Greif, and Singh 2002). Put another way, as the rate at which G discounts the future declines, fewer resources need be diverted from the private to the public economy to keep the society on the equilibrium path, and the magnitude of the distortions created by the need to pay for the services of G therefore declines. The fewer the distortions, the greater the total product.

The properties of these political arrangements thus contrast with those that characterize stateless societies. People in the society can enjoy both security *and* prosperity. Society can reach regions in the space described in Figure 39.1 which previously were unattainable. The conditions that lead to the possibility of the state lead as well to the possibility of development.

4 STATE FAILURE

The conditions that support adherence to the equilibrium path and the possibility of the state also define the circumstances under which states will fail. When these conditions fail to hold, specialists in violence become warlords and civilians take up arms. For evidence of the plausibility of my argument, I turn to the literatures on state failure.

One branch of this literature addresses the political costs of democratization. As noted by Snyder (2000), when authoritarian regimes face the prospect of being overthrown, they then turn predatory; in response, political challengers then seek to mobilize the citizenry. Because the Third Wave rendered authoritarian regimes insecure, Snyder (2000) argues, it therefore produced not only democracy but also nationalism, ethnic conflict, and state failure. Snyder's argument is echoed by Chua (2003), Zakaria (1997), and defended more rigorously by Hegre et al. (2001) and others (e.g. Goldstone et al. 2003). It suggests that, in keeping with my argument, as the future becomes uncertain, the possibility of the state declines.

A second relevant literature addresses the so-called "resource curse." Originally coined to highlight a surprising lack of connect between natural endowments and economic growth, the phrase has acquired political as well as economic meaning. Through the work of Karl (1997), Ross (1999), and others, it has come to refer to transformation of political incentives brought on by natural resource booms. Given access to extraordinary opportunities for wealth, public servants turn from providers of services to consumers of public revenues, these scholars contend; they use their access to power to privatize the public domain. The state becomes a rentier state (Mahdavy 1970; Beblawi and Giacomi 1987; Chaudry 1994; Shambayati 1994), organizing the consumption rather than the creation of wealth. And the non-resource economy withers, not only as a result of macroeconomic distortions resulting from an ill-managed boom but also from the inefficiency and corruption of the public services, including those whose job is to secure rights in property. In its most pernicious form, the resource curse takes the form of violence—a possibility investigated in the extensive literature on "greed and grievance" (Reno 1995; Klare 2002; Collier et al. 2003).

A last relevant portion of the literature on state failure focuses on the political impact of economic decay. It focuses in particular on the impact of the late century recession triggered by the oil price shocks of the 1970s, the Mexican default of 1982, and the subsequent debt crisis (see, for example, Sachs 1989; Haggard et al. 1993). One result was a sharp drop in the incomes of developing countries. A second was a decline in public revenues. In the developing areas, economic activity moved from the formal to the informal economy, where entrepreneurs could shed high fixed costs, employ flexible modes of production, and avoid paying taxes (see MacGaffey 1991; Soto 1990). While the private economy thus adjusted to the recession, it did so at the expense of the public economy.

When starved of funds as a result of the recession, this literature shows, some governments turned predatory. When civil servants were poorly paid, many turned to corruption. If unpaid, soldiers mutinied or staged coups in protest against the erosion of the salaries and conditions of service (Dianga 2002). When governments could no longer afford the transfers that bind powerful groups to the center, then those groups rebelled. Thus Acemoglu and Robinson's (2001) theory of revolution and Azam and Mesnard's theory (2003) of regional succession (see also Centeno 2002). The result of the crisis of public revenues was state failure.

These literatures—on the impact of resource booms, democratization, and global economic shocks—thus address the changes in the very variables that circumscribe the possibility for the state. That these literatures link changes in the values of these variables to the failure of states provides support for my argument.

5 THE DEVELOPMENT OF THE STATE

On the one hand, then, stand stateless societies, wherein security is traded off against prosperity. On the other stand societies with states, wherein—under a specific set of conditions—people can enjoy both. An additional question therefore arises: how do societies move from the one set of institutions to the other and so enhance their prospects for development? The literature offers three different approaches to this question.

5.1 Demand-driven Explanation

The first answer stresses the importance of the welfare losses associated with the lack of political order. These are depicted in Figure 39.1 by the region of desirable outcomes that remain unattainable, given the constraint imposed by decentralized political institutions. Historical accounts of state formation in medieval and early modern Europe document the calls for order that underpinned the popularity of the Angevin dynasty after the collapse of Norman rule in England (Bartlett 2002; Hyams 2003); the cries for the king's justice that led to the propagation of instruments of centralized rule—the courts, the bailiffs, and the rule of law—in medieval England (Hyams 2003); and the demands for the extension of the king's peace in the provinces of France, wherein order had been disrupted by feuds between branches of the aristocratic families (Duby 1987).

To marshal an additional example: in medieval England, back-country magnates recruited muscular youths to their households, thereby providing protection for their domains. These retainers formed liveried companies: bands of warriors bearing the colors of their lords. But when attending parliament, the very magnates who had formed these companies called for their disbanding (Hicks 1995). Aware of the violence and disorder they spread throughout the countryside, the magnates pleaded for the king to suppress the liveried companies. Their behavior, I would argue, reflects the nature of the payoffs that confront private citizens in stateless societies. Each magnate, acting alone, had incentives to create a military band; but because all had the same incentives, each devoted too many resources to protection and too few to production. The role of the king was to coordinate the movement toward demilitarization—a movement that was collectively desirable but privately perilous.

6 THE STANDARD ACCOUNT

More common than accounts based on contract are those based on conquest. In anthropology, the so-called "standard account" of state formation begins with families clustering in locations that have been richly endowed by nature: in the alluvial soils near rivers, for example, or in rich volcanic highlands. When the productivity of the region significantly exceeds that in neighboring regions, then families will be loath to exit the favored locale. And when those who possess political power seek to increase their incomes, they therefore can extract tribute and services in exchange for property rights and, in particular, rights in land. Stratification based on differences in wealth and power then replaces the rough democracy of kinship (e.g. Feinman and Marcus 1998). In this way politics is transformed from one of decentralized, egalitarian interaction to centralized and forceful redistribution.[4]

---

[4] See Carneiro 1970 and Feinman and Marcus 1998. For a powerful illustration of the use of this reasoning, see Vansina 2004.

6.1 Competition, Security and Fitness

A third literature suggests an evolutionary account. The selection mechanism is military competition and the level of fitness is determined by the capacity to pay the costs of warfare.

The followers of Hintze (Gilbert 1975) propose such an account. Military competition, as McNeil (1982) and others stress, inspires a search for new technologies, such as the refinement and casting of metals, the development of ships, and the creation of instruments for navigation. As argued by van Creveld (1977), military competition spurs economic change. Behind the "head" of every army trails a logistical "tail" that provides clothing, shelter, food, and munitions. Without logistical support, soldiers remained a part of the productive economy; i.e. they fed themselves. Armies therefore disbanded at the time of planting and harvesting. A competitive advantage therefore accrued to commanders who could feed their armies and so keep them in the field while their opponents disbanded. An advantage therefore accrued to those with a strong economic base. Not only could they acquire better weapons but they could also support a large body of unproductive labor: men who trained to fight.

Warfare demands finance. Revenues have to be levied from the private economy, thus requiring taxation. The tax base itself thus has to be nurtured, requiring the selection of proper policies. By this account, the origins of the state lie in military competition. And those that survive are those that are most fit, i.e. those that are developmental (see Levi 1988; Skocpol 1979; Rosenthal 1998).

7 Conclusion

Arguing "no state, no development," this chapter has sought both to cut deep and to range widely. While seeking to provide a review of the relevant literature, it has also sought to mount a distinctive argument. Just as economic historians have sought the act of "primitive accumulation"[5] that fueled the growth of the industrial economy, so too have I sought the "primitive conditions" that lead to the transformation of power from a means of predation into a force for development.

The argument of this chapter highlights areas ripe for empirical investigation. One is the politics that takes place on a knife edge from which some polities descend into predation while others turn developmental. On the one side, the winning political strategy is to extract wealth; on the other, it is to promote its creation. As in North's early work (North and Thomas 1973), much could be learned from historical research, but in this instance focusing on states poised on the cusp. How did England draw back from the chaos of Stephen and Matilda and transit to the relative order of the Angevins—a lineage as much inclined to despoil as any other but who instead

---

[5] The phrase of course comes from Marx 1906. See also Crouzet 1972.

promoted order and prosperity? Much could be learned as well by investigating the transformation of the Kuomintang, whose leaders behaved as warlords on the mainland but who turned developmental in Taiwan.

I sketched out three paths that descend from the knife edge. Research into each would yield bountiful rewards. To focus on but one, consider the evolutionary account. Much could be learned by comparing two regions, one with high levels of military competition and another in which warfare has been suppressed. A comparison between Europe and China would be apt.[6] So too would a study of economic development in Africa, especially in the traditional states, before and after the imposition of colonial "order."

Such suggestions take as their premiss the argument of this chapter and respond to the priorities that it implies. More valuable in the longer run, however, would be a reformulation of that argument. I have in mind a program of research into what could be termed "the industrial organization" of violence.

The production of coercion requires the inputs of labor and capital. By harnessing a technology of violence (in the words of the old theory of the firm) or by forging a "nexus of contracts" (in the words of contemporary theories), managers transform these inputs into physical force. In doing so, they are subject to constraints (e.g. mountainous terrain: Fearon and Laitin 2003); and they have to act in anticipation of the best response of their opponent. The research program I endorse would view conflict in this manner.

Adopting this perspective, consider the difference between decentralized and centralized societies. In the competition for scarce resources, one strategy might be to disperse and to infiltrate (as in Sahlins 1961) while another might be to bunch up and to invade. The first response would lead to societies that appear stateless; the second, to those in apparent possession of a state. To understand the manner in which such choices are made, scholars might well turn to literature on industrial organization, with its analyses of the strategic choice of competitive behavior, or to biology, with its models of the conditions under which populations disperse or swarm.

Or, to return once again to history, consider the Thirty Years War.[7] On the one hand stood (Albrecht Wenzel Eusebius von) Wallenstein. Recruiting, supplying, and moving large forces, he became one of the most formidable commanders in the conflict. While successful economically and militarily, Count Wallenstein did not create a state. He favored "spot contracts" for soldiers and supplies, abjured incomplete contracts, and failed to build organizations that were longer lived than those that staffed them. On the other stood Gustavus Adolphus, an equally formidable commander. While receiving aid from France, Sweden was poor and the resources at his command paled by comparison with those available to Wallenstein. But although facing the same hostile terrain as Wallenstein, Gustavus Adolphus forged relationships that endured. The political order he helped to forge outlived him and those he commanded. By viewing the "contract" offered by Gustavus Adolphus to his followers through the

---

[6] Philip Hoffman and Jean-Laurant Rosenthal are undertaking such a comparison.
[7] A more fruitful subject for this enquiry than others, such as the First World War, which political scientists more frequently ponder.

lens of the modern theory of organizations, and by comparing its properties with those offered by Wallenstein, we could deepen our understanding of how coercion can be organized—and thus of the properties of the state.[8]

REFERENCES

ACEMOGLU, D., and ROBINSON, J. A. 2001. A theory of political transitions. *American Economic Review*, 91: 938–63.
ALMOND, G. A., and COLEMAN, J. S. (eds.). 1960. *The Politics of the Developing Areas*. Princeton, NJ: Princeton University Press.
AMSDEN, A. H. 1989. *Asia's Next Giant: South Korea and Late Industrialization*. New York: Oxford University Press.
AXELROD, R. 1984. *The Evolution of Cooperation*. New York: Basic Books.
AZAM, J.-P., and MESNARD, A. 2003. Civil war and the social contract. *Public Choice*, 115: 455–75.
BARTLETT, R. 2002. *England under the Norman and Angevin Kings, 1075–1225*. New York: Oxford University Press.
BATES, R. 2004. *State Failure in Africa*. Cambridge, Mass.: Center for International Development, Harvard University.
BATES, R. H., GREIF, A., and SINGH, S. 2002. Organizing violence. *Journal of Conflict Resolution*, 46: 599–628.
BEBLAWI, H., and GIACOMI, L. (eds.). 1987. *The Rentier State*. London: Croom Helm.
BLOCH, M. 1970. *Feudal Society*. Chicago: University of Chicago Press.
BUCHANAN, J., and TULLOCK, G. 1962. *The Calculus of Consent*. Ann Arbor: University of Michigan Press.
CARNEIRO, R. L. 1970. A theory of the origin of the state. *Science*, 169: 733–8.
CENTENO, M. A. 2002. *Blood and Debt: War and the Nation-State in Latin America*. University Park: Pennsylvania State University Press.
CHAUDRY, K. A. 1994. Economic liberalization and the lineages of the rentier state. *Comparative Politics*, 27: 1–24.
CHUA, A. 2003. *World on Fire*. New York: Doubleday.
COLLIER, P., ELLIOTT, V. L., et al. 2003. *Breaking the Conflict Trap*. Washington, DC: World Bank and Oxford University Press.
COLSON, E. 1974. *Tradition and Contract: The Problem of Order*. Chicago: Aldine.
CROUZET, F. 1972. *Capital Formation and the Industrial Revolution*. London: Methuen.
DIANGA, J. W. 2002. *Kenya, 1982: The Atttempted Coup*. London: Penn Press.
DUBY, G. 1987. *France in the Middle Ages, 987–1460*. Oxford: Blackwell.
EVANS, P. 1995. *Embedded Autonomy: States and Industrial Transformation*. Princeton, NJ: Princeton University Press.
FEARON, J., and LAITIN, D. 2003. Ethnicity, insurgency and civil war. *American Political Science Review*, 97: 75–90.
FEINMAN, G. M., and MARCUS, J. 1998. *Archaic States*. Santa Fe, N. Mex.: School of American Research Press.
FISHLOW, A., GWIN, C., et al. 1994. *Miracle or Design? Lessons from the East Asian Experience*. Washington, DC: Overseas Development Council.

---

[8] For an intriguing probe at the issues raised herein, see Singer 2003.

FUDENBERG, D., and MASKIN, E. 1986. The folk theorem in repeated games with discounting or with incomplete information. *Econometrica*, 54: 533–54.
GILBERT, F. (ed.). 1975. *The Historical Essays of Otto Hintze*. New York: Oxford University Press.
GLUCKMAN, M. 1955. *Custom and Conflict in Africa*. Oxford: Blackwell.
GOLDSTONE, J., MARSHALL, M., et al. 2003. State failure task force project, phase III report. McLean, Va., SAIC.
GREIF, A. 1998. Self-enforcing political systems and economic growth: late medieval Genoa. Pp. 23–63 in *Analytic Narratives*, ed. R. H. Bates, A. Greif, J.-L. Rosenthal, M. Levi, and B. Weingast. Princeton, NJ: Princeton University Press.
HAGGARD, S., LEE, C. H., et al. (eds.). 1993. *The Politics of Finance in Developing Countries*. Ithaca, NY: Cornell University Press.
HALL, P. A., and SOSKICE, D. W. 2001. *Varieties of Capitalism: The Institutional Foundations of Comparative Advantage*. Oxford: Oxford University Press.
HEGRE, H., GATES, S., et al. 2001. Toward a democratic civil peace? Democracy, political change and civil war, 1816–1992. *American Political Science Review*, 95: 33–48.
HICKS, M. 1995. *Bastard Feudalism*. London: Longman.
HYAMS, P. 2003. *Rancour and Reconciliation in Medieval England*. Ithaca, NY: Cornell University Press.
KANG, D. 2002. *Crony Capitalism*. Cambridge: Cambridge University Press.
KARL, T. L. 1997. *The Paradox of Plenty*. Berkeley: University of California Press.
KEOHANE, R. 1984. *After Hegemony*. Princeton, NJ: Princeton University Press.
—— and NYE, J. S. 1989. *Power and Interdependence*. New York: HarperCollins.
KLARE, M. T. 2002. *Resource Wars*. New York: Henry Holt.
LEVI, M. 1981. The predatory theory of rule. *Politics and Society*, 10: 431–66.
—— 1988. *Of Rule and Revenue*. Berkeley: University of California Press.
MACGAFFEY, J. 1991. *The Real Economy of Zaire*. Philadelphia: University of Pennsylvania Press.
MCNEIL, W. 1982. *The Pursuit of Power*. Chicago: University of Chicago Press.
MAHDAVY, H. 1970. The patterns and problems of economic development in rentier states: the case of Iran. Pp. 428–67 in *Studies in Economic Histroy of the Middle East*, ed. M. A. Cook. New York: Oxford University Press.
MARTIN, L. L., and SIMMONS, B. A. (eds.). 2001. *International Institutions*. Special Issue, International Organization. Cambridge, Mass.: MIT Press.
MARX, K. 1906. Part VIII: the so-called primitive accumulation. Pp. 784–855 in *Capital*. New York: Modern Library.
NORTH, D. C., and THOMAS, R. P. 1973. *The Rise of the Western World*. Cambridge: Cambridge University Press.
RENO, W. 1995. *Corruption and State Politics in Sierra Leone*. Cambridge: Cambridge University Press.
ROSENTHAL, J.-L. 1998. The political economy of absolutism reconsidered. Pp. 64–108 in *Analytic Narratives*, ed. R. H. Bates, A. Greif, M. Levi, J.-L. Rosenthal, and B. R. Weingast. Princeton, NJ: Princeton University Press.
ROSS, M. L. 1999. The political economy of the resource curse. *World Politics*, 51: 325–61.
SACHS, J. D. (ed.). 1989. *Developing Country Debt and the World Economy*. Chicago: University of Chicago Press for the National Bureau of Economic Research.
SAHLINS, M. D. 1961. The segmentary lineage: an organization of predatory expansion. *American Anthropologist*, 63: 322–45.
—— 1968. *Tribesmen*. Englewood Cliffs, NJ: Prentice Hall.
SHAMBAYATI, H. 1994. The rentier state, interest groups, and the paradox of autonomy. *Comparative Politics*, 26: 307–31.

SINGER, P. 2003. The ultimate military entrepreneur. *Military History Quarterly*, 15: 6–15.
SKOCPOL, T. 1979. *States and Social Revolutions*. Cambridge: Cambridge University Press.
SNYDER, J. 2000. *From Voting to Violence*. New York: W. W. Norton.
SOTO, H. DE 1990. *The Other Path*. New York: Perennial Library.
TAYLOR, M. 1987. *The Possibility of Cooperation*. New York: Cambridge University Press.
VAN CREVELD, M. L. 1977. *Supplying War: Logistics from Wallenstein to Patton*. Cambridge: Cambridge University Press.
VANSINA, J. 2004. *Antecedents to Modern Rwanda: The Nyiginya Kingdom*. Madison: University of Wisconsin Press.
WEINGAST, B. 1995. The economic role of political institutions. *Journal of Law, Economics, and Organization*, 7: 1–31.
WOLFF, E. R. 1966. *Peasants*. Englewood Cliffs, NJ: Prentice Hall.
ZAKARIA, F. 1997. The rise of illiberal democracy. *Foreign Affairs*, 76: 22–43.

CHAPTER 40

ELECTORAL SYSTEMS AND ECONOMIC POLICY

TORSTEN PERSSON

GUIDO TABELLINI

WHAT is the effect of the constitution on economic policy choices? This issue is often at the heart of debates on constitutional reform. Recently, Italy replaced its system of proportional representation, where legislators were elected according to the proportions of the popular national vote received by their parties, with one that includes ingredients of plurality rule, where legislators are elected in each district according to who receives the highest number of votes. Italian political leaders are now considering proposals to replace the current parliamentary regime with elements of presidentialism, where the head of government is elected by direct popular vote. An important motivation for these reforms was the idea that they would reduce political corruption and the propensity of Italian governments to run budget deficits.

In recent years, a number of other countries have implemented related reforms. For instance, New Zealand altered its system of plurality rule in single-member districts to a system mixing elements of proportional representation. Japan moved to a system that mixes elements of proportional and plurality representation from its special form of plurality rule (the so-called single non-transferable vote). The UK has debated similar proposals. What are the effects of these reforms on economic policy outcomes and economic performance?

* We are grateful to the editors of this *Handbook*, Barry Weingast and Don Wittman, for helpful comments and to the Canadian Institute of Advanced Research for financial support.

It is only recently that this question has been addressed by social scientists. Political scientists specializing in comparative politics have described the fundamental features of constitutions and their political effects. Yet they have mainly focused on political phenomena, failing to study how constitutional rules shape economic policies. Although economists in the field of political economics have studied the determinants of policy choices, they rarely study constitutional details and their implications for policy choice and economic performance.

This chapter discusses recent theoretical and empirical research on one feature of modern democracies: the electoral rule. Our central conclusion is that the electoral rule systematically shapes economic policy. We show that to understand the extent of political corruption, the devil is in the details of electoral systems, such as the ballot structure or district magnitude. In the case of the size of government and fiscal policy outcomes, the effects are associated with the broad distinction between proportional and majoritarian systems. The effects are often large enough to be of genuine economic interest.

A closely related question concerns the effects on economic policy of the constitutional rules that define the form of government, especially the crucial distinction between parliamentary and presidential systems. We do not address this topic here and refer the interested reader to Persson and Tabellini (2003, 2004a).

We develop our arguments as follows. Section 1 outlines some key objectives of electoral rules and notes the stability and systematic selection that characterize real-world constitutions. Section 2 introduces the main concepts that categorize different electoral rules. Section 3 explains how these elements shape the accountability of government and the size of political rents and corruption. Section 4 deals with representation in government and a variety of fiscal policy choices. Section 5 offers our conclusions and brief comments on emerging research.

1 Electoral Systems: Motives, Stability, and Selection

In a representative democracy, elected officials determine policy. Electoral systems decide how well voters can hold politicians accountable and which groups in society are more likely to see their interests represented.

Economists in the field of corporate finance show that alternative rules of corporate governance entail a trade-off between agency problems and representation of minority interests. Rules that concentrate powers in the hands of a dominant shareholder reduce managerial discretion and limit the scope of the agency problem, but this control is likely to come at the expense of minority shareholders (cf. for instance Becht, Bolton, and Röell 2003).

A similar trade-off between accountability and representation arises in the design of electoral rules. Indeed, this idea is familiar to political scientists in the field of comparative politics (see e.g. Bingham Powell 2000; Prezworski, Stokes, and Manin 1999). Compared to proportional representation, plurality rule in single-member districts translates swings in voter sentiment into larger changes in legislative majorities. This leverage effect of plurality rule strengthens the incentives of politicians to please the voters, leading to smaller political rents and less corruption. But since it makes political candidates more responsive to the wishes of pivotal groups of voters, stronger accountability also raises the propensity to target benefits to narrow constituencies. This targeting comes at the expense of broad spending programs that benefit many citizens. Hence the design of electoral rules entails a trade-off between accountability and representation.

Overall features of electoral systems change very seldom. In the sample of sixty democracies studied by Persson and Tabellini (2003), only two enacted important reforms of the electoral system between 1960 and 1990 (Cyprus and France)—though more reforms are observed if one considers marginal changes and transitions from autocracy to democracy. At the same time, the electoral system is strongly correlated with stable country characteristics: former British colonies tend to have UK-style plurality rule in single-member districts, while continental Europe predominantly has proportional representation.

These patterns make it difficult to draw causal inferences from the data. Electoral stability means that reforms are very seldom observed; but cross-country comparisons risk confounding the effects of the constitution with other country characteristics, since the electoral rule itself could be selected on the basis of unobserved variables that also influence policy outcomes.

In our own work, we have exploited econometric techniques developed by labor economists to estimate the causal effects of non-random treatments from cross-sectional comparisons. For us, treatment is the electoral reform. We have relied on three estimation methods. First, we isolate exogenous variation in electoral rules through instrumental variables. If change is very rare, it may be largely determined by historical circumstances (whatever was "fashionable" at the time). The broad period in which the current constitution was adopted can thus be used as an instrument for the electoral system. The identifying assumption is that, controlling for other determinants of policy (including the age of democracy), the birth period of the constitution is not directly related to current policy outcomes. Second, we adjust the estimates for possible correlation between the random components of policy outcomes and the selection of electoral systems, as suggested by Heckman and others. Third, we exploit so-called "matching methods" where countries are ranked by the probability of adopting a specific electoral system, called a propensity score. Comparisons of countries with similar propensity scores, but with different actual systems, receive more weight. This third method avoids biased estimates due to heterogeneous treatment effects. Persson and Tabellini (2003) discuss these three estimation methods in context, while Acemoglu (2005) provides a critical review.

2 Categorizing Electoral Systems

Political scientists commonly emphasize three aspects of electoral rules for legislatures.

Electoral formulas translate votes into seats. Under plurality rule, only the winner(s) of the highest vote share(s) are elected in a given district. In contrast, proportional representation awards legislative seats in proportion to votes in each district. To ensure closeness between overall vote shares and seat shares, a district system of plurality rule is often amended by a system of "adjustment seats" at the national level.

District magnitudes reflect the number of legislators (given the size of the legislature) acquiring a seat in a typical voting district. One polar case is where all districts have a single seat, as in the US House of Representatives; the other polar case is where legislators are all elected in a single, all-encompassing district, such as the Israeli Knesset. See Grofman (this volume) for a more extended discussion.

Ballot structures determine how citizens cast their ballot. One possibility is that they choose among individual candidates. Another common possibility is that each voter chooses from a set of closed lists of candidates drawn up by the parties participating in the election. In the latter, if an electoral district has ten seats and party A wins, say, four of these seats, the first four candidates on the list of party A get elected.[1]

Although these three aspects are theoretically distinct, their use is correlated across countries. Anglo-Saxon countries often implement plurality rule with voting for individual candidates in single-member districts. Others implement proportional representation though a system of closed party lists in large districts, sometimes a single national district. In the wake of this pattern, many observers have classified countries into two archetypical electoral systems, labeled "majoritarian" and "proportional" (or "consensual"). These correlations are nonetheless not perfect, and several countries employ "mixed" electoral systems. German voters, for instance, cast two ballots, electing half the Bundestag by plurality in single-member districts, and the other half by proportional representation at a national level, to achieve proportionality between national vote and seat shares. Furthermore, some proportional representation systems, such as the Irish, do not rely on party lists.[2] Blais and Massicotte (1996) and Cox (1997) present overviews of world electoral systems.

3 Accountability

How do electoral rules affect accountability? In this section, we consider only policies evaluated in roughly the same way by all voters (so-called valence issues), leaving

---

[1] The distinction between open and closed party lists is discussed further below.
[2] To achieve proportionality, the Irish "single transferable vote" system (also used in Malta) relies on votes over individuals in multimember districts where each voter can only vote for a single candidate, and a complicated procedure where seats are awarded sequentially and votes for losing candidates are transferred from one seat to the next.

the problem of how elected officials react to disagreement among voters for the next section that focuses on representation. Accountability in this context refers to two things. It gives voters some control over politicians who abuse their power: voters can punish or reward politicians through re-election or other career concerns, and this creates incentives for good behavior. Accountability also refers to the ability of voters to select the most "able" candidate, where ability can be interpreted as integrity, technical expertise, or other intrinsic features valued by voters at large. As the emphasis of this chapter is on economic policy-making, we focus on how the electoral rule affects corruption, rent-seeking, and electoral budget cycles.

The details of electoral rules have *direct* effects on the incentives of politicians. They also have *indirect* effects through party structure and, more generally, who holds office. We consider the direct and indirect effects of the three aspects of electoral rules mentioned above: ballot structure, district magnitude, and the electoral formula.

3.1 Direct Effects

Politicians have stronger direct incentives to please the voters if they are held accountable individually, rather than collectively. Because they disconnect individual efforts and re-election prospects, party lists discourage effort by office-holders. Persson and Tabellini (2000) formalize this idea and predict that political rents will be higher under electoral systems that rely on list voting than in systems where voters directly select individual candidates. The same argument also implies that *open* lists (voters can modify the order of candidates) should be more conducive to good behavior than *closed* lists (non-amendable by voters), as should preferential voting (voters are asked to rank candidates of the same party).

What does the evidence say? If higher political rents are associated with illegal benefits, then we can study whether corruption by public officials in different countries is systematically correlated with the electoral rule. Of course, corruption is only an imperfect proxy for political rents. Furthermore, corruption is measured with error and is determined by many other country features.

Cross-sectional and panel data suggest some connections. Persson and Tabellini (2003) and Persson, Tabellini, and Trebbi (2003) study about eighty democracies in the 1990s. They measure corruption as perceived through surveys assembled by the World Bank, Transparency International, and private risk services. They also control for country characteristics that earlier studies have found to correlate with corruption, notably per capita income, openness to international trade, the citizens' education and religious beliefs, a country's history as captured by colonial heritage, and geographic location as measured by a set of dummy variables. The ballot structure is indeed strongly correlated with corruption: a switch from a system with all legislators elected on party lists, to plurality rule with all legislators individually elected, would reduce perceptions of corruption by as much as 20 per cent. This is about twice the estimated effect of being in Latin America. The decline in corruption is stronger when individual voting is implemented by plurality rule, rather than by using preferential voting or open lists in proportional electoral systems. Of course, the result could also reflect effects of the electoral formula (as discussed below), rather than just the ballot structure. Kunicova and Rose Ackerman (2001) obtain similar empirical results, although they single out closed-list, proportional representation systems as the most conducive to corruption.

Some of these conclusions run counter to those in Carey and Shugart (1995) and Golden and Chang (2001), who instead emphasize the distinction between inter-party and intra-party competition. These scholars argue that competition between parties is desirable, as it leads to legislation that pleases voters at large. In contrast, competition within parties is not desirable, as it leads candidates to provide favors to their constituencies, through patronage and other illegal activities. The Italian and Japanese electoral systems before the 1990s reforms are deemed to exemplify this problem. Measuring corruption by judicial inquiries against Italian members of parliament, Golden and Chang (2001) show that corruption is more frequent in districts with more intense intra-party competition. They conclude that open-list systems are worse than closed-list systems, and claim that the empirical results by Kunicova and Rose Ackerman (2001) reflect a mis-specified model (see also Golden and Chang 2003).

Summarizing the argument so far, both theory and evidence suggest that individual accountability under plurality rule strengthens the incentives of politicians to please the voters and is conducive to good behavior. But the effects of individual accountability under proportional representation, implemented with open rather than closed lists, are more controversial.

The electoral formula, including district magnitude, seems to affect the incentives for politicians also in other ways. Under plurality rule, the mapping from votes to seats becomes steep when electoral races are close. This connection ought to create strong incentives for good behavior: a small improvement in the chance of victory would create a large return in terms of seats. The incentives under proportional representation are weaker, as additional effort has a lower expected return on seats (or on the probability of winning). If electoral races have likely winners, however, incentives may instead be weaker under plurality than proportional representation: if seats are next to certain, little effort goes into pleasing the voters of those districts.[3] Aggregating over all districts (and thus over races of different closeness), the relative incentives to extract rents under different electoral formulas become an empirical question. Strömberg's (2003) results bear on these arguments. Employing a theoretical and structurally estimated model of the US Electoral College, he studies the effects of a (hypothetical) reform to a national vote for president. Given the empirical distribution of voter preferences, he finds that the incentives for rent extraction are basically unaffected by such a reform.

---

[3] Of course, districts can be redesigned at will at some intervals, which makes the closeness of elections an endogenous choice. This possibility opens up the door for strategic manipulation (gerrymandering) where protection of incumbents is one of several possible objectives.

3.2 Indirect Effects

Electoral rules (and in particular district magnitude) also have indirect effects on accountability, by altering the set of candidates that have a chance to be elected, or more generally by changing the party system.

Myerson (1993) presents a model in which barriers to entry allow dishonest candidates to survive. He assumes that parties (or equivalently, candidates) differ in two dimensions: honesty and ideology. Voters always prefer honest candidates, but disagree on ideology. With proportional representation and multimember districts, honest candidates are always available for all ideological positions, so dishonest candidates have no chance of being elected. But in single-member districts, only one candidate can win the election. Voters may then cast their ballot, strategically, for dishonest but ideologically preferred candidates, if they expect all other voters with the same ideology to do the same: switching to an honest candidate risks giving the victory to a candidate of the opposite ideology. Thus, plurality rule in single-member districts can be associated with dishonest incumbents, whom it is difficult to oust from office.

But electoral systems that make it easy for political parties to be represented in parliament (for example, multimember districts and proportional representation) may actually encourage rent-seeking, through another channel. If many factions are represented in parliament, the government is more likely to be supported by a coalition of parties, rather than by a single party. Under single-party government, voters know precisely whom to blame or reward for observed performance. Under coalition government, voters may not know whom to blame, and the votes lost for bad performance are shared amongst all coalition partners; this dilutes the incentives of individual parties to please the voters. These ideas are discussed by Persson, Roland, and Tabellini (2003) and Bingham Powell (2000).

Do the data shed light on these alternative predictions? The hypothesis that coalition governments are associated with more corruption remains untested, as far as we know, though some of the blatant corruption scandals in Europe—Belgium and Italy—have been intimately associated with such governments. Other evidence supports the idea that barriers to entry raise corruption, however. Persson and Tabellini (2003) and Persson, Tabellini, and Trebbi (2003) find corruption to be higher in countries and years with small district magnitude (that is, few legislators elected in each district), again with large quantitative effects. Alt and Lassen (2002) show that restrictions on primaries in gubernatorial elections, which raise barriers to entry for new candidates, are positively associated with perceptions of corruption in US states.

We have thus far emphasized the implications of the electoral rule for political rents and corruption. A strong incentive of political representatives to please the voters can also show up in electoral policy cycles, however. Persson and Tabellini (2003) consider panel data from 1960 covering about 500 elections in over fifty democracies. They classify countries in two groups according to the electoral formula and estimate the extent of electoral cycles in different specifications, including fixed country and time effects and other regressors. Governments elected under plurality rule tend to cut taxes and government spending during election years, by about 0.5 per cent of GDP.

In proportional representation democracies, tax cuts are less pronounced, and no spending cuts are observed. This finding is consistent with better accountability under plurality rule, allowing voters to punish governments for high taxes and spending either because they are fiscal conservatives (as in Peltzman 1992) or because they are subject to a political agency problem (as in Persson and Tabellini 2000 or Besley and Case 1995).

3.3 Summing up

What does all of this imply about the consequences of electoral reforms for corruption? Because it would entail changing several features of the electoral rule, a large-scale reform from "proportional" to "majoritarian" elections would have ambiguous effects. A switch from proportional representation to plurality rule, accompanied by a change in the ballot structure from party lists to voting over individuals, would strengthen political incentives for good behavior, both directly and indirectly through the type of government. But these welfare-improving effects might be offset if the reform diminishes district magnitude, thus erecting barriers to entry to the detriment of honest or talented incumbents. The net effects of electoral reform thus depend on which channel is stronger, and on the precise architecture of reform. The empirical evidence in Persson and Tabellini (2003) and Persson, Tabellini, and Trebbi (2003) supports this nuanced conclusion. After controlling for other variables and taking into account the self-selection of countries into constitutions, they find no robust difference in corruption across a broad classification of majoritarian vs. proportional electoral systems.

4 REPRESENTATION

Economic policy generates conflicts of interest. Individuals and groups in society differ in many dimensions: they have different levels and sources of income, work in different sectors and occupations, live in different geographic areas, and possess different ideologies. As a result, people differ in their views about public policies: the appropriate level and structure of taxation, the preferred structure of tariffs, subsidies, and regulations, the support for programs aimed at different regions, and so on. Electoral rules help aggregate such conflicting interests into public policy decisions, but the weight given to specific groups varies with the system. In this section, we discuss how this influences fiscal policy choices.

4.1 Direct Effects on the Composition of Government Spending

Single-member districts and plurality vote both tend to pull in the direction of narrowly targeted programs benefiting small geographic constituencies. Conversely, multimember districts and proportional representation induce politicians to provide benefits for broad groups of voters. Building on this insight, some recent papers have studied the influence of district magnitude and the electoral formula on the composition of government spending.

Persson and Tabellini (1999; 2000, ch. 8) study electoral competition between two opportunistic and office-seeking parties. Multimember districts and proportional representation diffuse electoral competition, giving the parties strong incentives to seek electoral support from broad coalitions in the population through general public goods or universalistic redistributive programs (e.g. public pensions or other welfare programs). In contrast, single-member districts and plurality rule typically make each party a sure winner in some of the districts, concentrating electoral competition in the other pivotal districts. Both parties thus have a strong incentive to target voters in these swing districts. Strömberg (2003) considers the effect of the Electoral College on the allocation of campaign resources or policy benefits in his aforementioned structural model of the election for US president. He shows empirically that this election method implies a much more lopsided distribution across states, where spending is focused on states where a relatively small number of votes might tip the entire state, compared to a (counterfactual) system of a national vote.

Moreover, the winner-takes-all property of plurality rule reduces the minimal coalition of voters needed to win the election. Under plurality rule, a party can control the legislature with only 25 per cent of the national vote: half the vote in half the districts. Under full proportional representation, 50 per cent of the national vote is needed, which gives politicians a stronger incentive to provide benefits for many voters. This point has been made in different frameworks. Lizzeri and Persico (2001) study a model with binding electoral promises, where candidates can use tax revenue to provide either (general) public goods or targeted redistribution. Persson and Tabellini (2000, ch. 9) consider a broad or narrow policy choice by an incumbent policy-maker trying to win re-election. Milesi-Ferretti, Perotti, and Rostagno (2002) obtain similar results in a model where policy is set in post-election bargaining among the elected politicians. They also predict that proportional elections lead to a larger overall size of spending.

Is the evidence consistent with the prediction that proportional electoral systems lead to more spending in broad redistributive programs, such as public pensions and welfare spending? Without controlling for other determinants of welfare spending, legislatures elected under proportional electoral systems spend much more on social security and welfare compared to majoritarian elections: on average, the difference is about 8 per cent of GDP. Controlling for other determinants of social security and welfare spending, such as demographics, per capita income, the age and quality of democracy, this magnitude shrinks to 2–3 per cent of GDP and remains statistically significant. This estimate is robust to the sample of countries and to taking into account the non-random nature of electoral systems (cf. Milesi-Ferretti, Perotti, and Rostagno 2002; Persson and Tabellini 2003, 2004*b*).

If politicians have stronger incentives to vie for electoral support through broad spending programs under proportional representation than under plurality rule, we might expect to observe systematic differences around election time in the two systems. Persson and Tabellini (2003) indeed find a significant electoral cycle in welfare state spending—expansions of such budget items in election and post-election years—in proportional representation systems, but not in plurality systems.

4.2 Indirect Effects on the Overall Size of Government Spending

The papers discussed so far in this section focus on the incentives of individual candidates, in a two-party system. Many studies of comparative politics, however, observe that electoral rules also shape party structure and types of government. Plurality rule and small district magnitude produce fewer parties and a more skewed distribution of seats than proportional representation and large district magnitude (for example, Duverger 1954; Lijphart 1990). Moreover, in parliamentary democracies few parties means more frequent single-party majority governments, and less frequent coalition governments (Taagepera and Shugart 1989; Strom 1990). Evidence presented in Persson, Roland, and Tabellini (2003) suggests that these political effects of the electoral rule may be large. In about fifty parliamentary democracies, proportional electoral rule is associated with a more fragmented party system, more frequent coalition governments, and less frequent governments ruled by a single-party majority.

It would be surprising if such large political effects did not also show up in the economic policies implemented by these different party systems and types of government. Indeed, a few recent papers have argued that the more fractionalized party systems induced by proportional elections lead to a greater overall size of government spending. For example, Austen-Smith (2000) studies a model where redistributive tax policy is set in post-election bargaining. He assumes that there are fewer parties under plurality rule (two parties) than under proportional representation (three parties). The coalition of two parties spends and taxes more compared to the single party. But here the number and size of parties is not allowed to depend on policy choices, imposing an artificial constraint on political competition.

Persson, Roland, and Tabellini (2003) and Bawn and Rosenbluth (2003) also predict that proportional representation leads to more government spending than plurality rule; but they treat the number of parties as endogenous and stress how the type of government determines the nature of electoral competition. When the government relies on a single-party majority, the main competition for votes is between the incumbent and the opposition; this pushes the incumbent towards efficient policies, or at least towards policies that benefit the voters represented in office. If instead the government is supported by a coalition of parties, voters can discriminate between the parties in government and this creates electoral conflict inside the coalition. Under plausible assumptions, inefficiencies in bargaining induce excessive government spending.

These theoretical predictions are supported by the data: without conditioning on other determinants of fiscal policy, legislatures elected under proportional representation spend about 10 per cent of GDP more than legislatures elected under plurality rule. Careful estimates obtained from cross-country data confirm this result. Persson and Tabellini (2003, 2004*b*) consider a sample of eighty democracies in the 1990s, controlling for a variety of other policy determinants (including the distinction between presidential and parliamentary democracy), and allow for self-selection of countries into electoral systems. Their estimates are very robust, and imply that proportional representation rather than plurality rule raises total expenditures by central government by a whopping 5 per cent of GDP.[4]

Persson, Roland, and Tabellini (2003) focus on fifty parliamentary democracies, identifying the effect of electoral rules on spending either from the cross-sectional variation, or from the time series variation around electoral reforms. They find spending to be higher under proportional elections by an amount similar to that found by Persson and Tabellini (2003, 2004*b*). But here the effect seems to be entirely due to a higher incidence of coalition governments in proportional electoral systems. This conclusion is reached by testing an over-identifying restriction that follows from the underlying theoretical model. Several features of the electoral rule—such as the electoral formula, district magnitude, and minimum thresholds for being represented in parliament—are jointly used as instruments for the type of government. The data cannot reject the restriction that all these measures of electoral systems are valid instruments for the type of government; that is, the electoral rule only influences government spending through the type of government, with no direct effects of the electoral rule on spending. Earlier empirical papers that treated the type of government as exogenous also find evidence that larger parliamentary coalitions spend more (e.g. Kontopoulos and Perotti 1999; Baqir 2002).

As noted above, the selection of countries into electoral systems is certainly not random, and some of the empirical research takes account of this (in particular, Persson and Tabellini 2003, 2004*b*). But Ticchi and Vindigni (2003) and Iversen and Soskice (2003) note a particularly subtle problem: at least in the OECD countries, proportional electoral rule is frequently associated with center-left governments, while right-wing governments are more frequent under majoritarian elections. This correlation, rather than the prevalence of coalition governments, could explain why proportional representation systems spend more.

But why should the electoral rule be correlated with government ideology? These papers argue that majoritarian elections concentrate power, which tends to favor the wealthy. In such systems, the argument goes, minorities (groups unlikely to benefit from spending, irrespective of who holds office) would rather see fiscal conservatives than fiscal liberals in office, since this reduces their tax burden. Hence, in winner-takes-all systems, conservative parties have an electoral advantage. If electoral rules are chosen on the basis of the policies they will deliver, this might explain the observed correlation: where the center-left voters dominate, proportional systems have

---

[4] Variables held constant in the underlying regressions include per capita income, the quality and age of democracy, openness of the economy, the size and age composition of the population, plus indicators for federalism, OECD membership, colonial history, and continental location. Various estimation techniques produced similar results.

been selected, whereas majoritarian systems have been selected where conservatives dominate. The empirical results by Persson, Roland, and Tabellini (2003) cast some doubt on this line of thought, however. If indeed the electoral rule influences policy through the ideology of governments, rather than through the number of parties in government, the electoral rule cannot be a valid instrument for the incidence of coalition governments in a regression on government spending—contrary to the findings discussed above.

4.3 Indirect Effects on Budget Deficits

Finally, if bargaining inefficiencies inside coalition governments lead to high spending, they may also produce other distortions. Several papers have studied intertemporal fiscal policy, treating the type of government as exogenous, but arguing that coalition governments face more severe "common-pool problems." The latter concept refers to the tendency for over-exploitation when multiple users make independent decisions on how much to exploit a common resource such as fish; the analogy to this common resource is current and future tax revenue. In reviewing the extensive work on government budget deficits, Alesina and Perotti (1995) draw on the work by Velasco (1999) to argue that coalition governments are more prone to run deficits. Hallerberg and von Hagen (1998, 1999) and von Hagen (this volume) explicitly link the severity of the common-pool problem to electoral systems and argue that this has implications for the appropriate form of budgetary process.

The experiences of European and Latin American countries suggest a second reason why coalition governments might be prone to run budget deficits. As coalition governments have more players who could potentially veto a change, they may be less able to alter policy in the wake of adverse shocks (Roubini and Sachs 1989; Alesina and Drazen 1991). These ideas are related to those in Tsebelis (1995, 1999, 2002), where a large number of veto players tends to "lock in" economic policy and reduce its ability to respond to shocks. In Tsebelis's conception, proportional elections often lead to multiple partisan veto players in government and thus to more policy myopia, even though the electoral rule is not the primitive in his analysis.

Finally, changes of government or the threat of government crisis are more frequent under proportional elections (due to the greater incidence of minority and coalition governments). And governments facing a vote on their own survival are more likely to behave myopically and run large budget deficits (Grilli, Masciandaro, and Tabellini 1991). A priori, this argument could also go the other way, however. In a coalition government, some parties will remain in government for a long time, despite changes in the coalition. With plurality rule, the party in power this time may be completely out of power next time. So the party in power today will take the money and run. In other words, political instability (i.e. large swings in political majorities), rather than government instability, undermines fiscal prudence (Alesina and Tabellini 1990).

The empirical evidence confirms that proportional electoral systems behave more myopically. In the raw data, budget deficits are larger by about 1 per cent of GDP in legislatures elected under proportional representation, compared to those elected under plurality rule. Persson and Tabellini (2003) show that, when controlling for other determinants of policy, this difference grows to about 2 per cent of GDP and is statistically significant in a large sample of democracies. There is also evidence that the electoral rule is correlated with government reaction to economic shocks: in proportional democracies, spending as a share of GDP rises in recessions but does not decline in booms, while cyclical fluctuations tend to have symmetric impacts on fiscal policy under other electoral systems.

5 Discussion

One of the principal conclusions of this chapter is that electoral reforms entail a trade-off between accountability and representation, as political scientists have suggested, and this has sharp implications for economic policy outcomes. This trade-off shows up in the direct effects of the electoral rule on the incentives of political candidates, as well as the indirect effects on party structure and type of government.

Plurality rule strengthens accountability. It does so directly, by reinforcing the incentives of politicians to please the voters, which results in smaller political rents and less corruption. But plurality rule also makes political candidates more responsive to the wishes of pivotal groups of voters, which increases the propensity to target benefits to narrow constituencies, at the expense of broad and universalistic programs such as welfare state spending and general public goods. We surveyed a range of evidence suggesting that both effects are quantitatively important.

Electoral rules also have indirect effects on policy outcomes, through the party structure. Small district magnitude combined with plurality rule results in fewer political parties. This makes it more difficult to oust dishonest or incompetent incumbents, because voters often support such incumbents over honest but ideologically opposed challengers. Fewer parties also reduce the incidence of coalition governments (in parliamentary democracies), and this is likely to lead to more efficient policies. As these indirect effects work in opposite directions, the overall impact on accountability is ambiguous. The approach also reveals that the overall size of government and budget deficits is much larger under coalition governments, and the latter are promoted by proportional representation and large district magnitude.

Whether economists or political scientists, at the end of the day we are interested not only in economic policies, but also in their overall effects on economic performance. The interaction between electoral systems, other political institutions, and economic development is one of the most exciting new areas of research at the boundary between economics and political science. As discussed by Helpman (2004), progress in this area will have to combine insights not only from these two disciplines, but also from sociology, and from many branches of economics, such as macroeconomics, economic development, political economics, and economic history. This line of research will also have to focus on the distinction between democratic and autocratic forms of government, trying to understand which features of democratic institutions make democracy more stable, and how the quality of democracy interacts with specific institutional features. Although it is still premature to review this rapidly evolving line of research, one thing is sure. When such a review is written a few years down the line, the state of our knowledge in economics and political science will be very different from what it is today.

References

Acemoglu, D. 2005. Constitutions, politics and economics: a review essay on Persson and Tabellini's "The economic effects of constitutions." *Journal of Economic Literature*, 43: 1025–48.

Alesina, A., and Drazen, A. 1991. Why are stabilizations delayed? *American Economic Review*, 81: 1170–88.

——— and Perotti, R. 1995. The political economy of budget deficits. *IMF Staff Papers*, 42: 1–31.

——— and Tabellini, G. 1990. A positive theory of fiscal deficits and government debt. *Review of Economic Studies*, 57: 403–14.

Alt, J., and Lassen, D. 2002. The political economy of institutions and corruption in American states. EPRU Working Paper Series 02–16, University of Copenhagen.

Austen-Smith, D. 2000. Redistributing income under proportional representation. *Journal of Political Economy*, 108: 1235–69.

Baqir, R. 2002. Districting and government overspending. *Journal of Political Economy*, 110: 1318–54.

Bawn, K., and Rosenbluth, N. 2003. Coalition parties vs. coalition of parties: how electoral agency shapes the political logic of costs and benefits. Mimeo, Yale University.

Becht, M., Bolton, P., and Röell, A. 2003. Corporate governance and control. European Corporate Governance Institute, Working Paper No. 02/2002.

Besley, T., and Case, A. 1995. Does political accountability affect economic policy choices? Evidence from gubernatorial term limits. *Quarterly Journal of Economics*, 110: 769–98.

——— ——— 2003. Political institutions and policy choices: evidence from the United States. *Journal of Economic Literature*, 41: 7–73.

Bingham Powell, G. 2000. *Elections as Instruments of Democracy: Majoritarian and Proportional Visions*. New Haven, Conn.: Yale University Press.

Blais, A., and Massicotte, L. 1996. Electoral systems. Pp. 49–82 in *Comparing Democracies: Elections and Voting in Global Perspective*, ed. L. LeDuc, R. Niemei, and P. Norris. Beverly Hills, Calif.: Sage.

Carey, J., and Shugart, M. 1995. Incentives to cultivate a personal vote: a rank ordering of electoral formulas. *Electoral Studies*, 14: 417–39.

Cox, G. 1997. *Making Votes Count*. Cambridge: Cambridge University Press.

Duverger, M. 1954. *Political Parties: Their Organization and Activity in the Modern State*, trans. B. North and R. North. New York: John Wiley.

Golden, M., and Chang, E. 2001. Competitive corruption: factional conflict and political malfeasance in postwar Italian Christian democracy. *World Politics*, 53: 558–622.

——— ——— 2003. Electoral systems, district magnitude and corruption. Mimeo, UCLA.

GRILLI, V., MASCIANDARO, D., and TABELLINI, G. 1991. Political and monetary institutions and public financial policies in the industrialized countries. *Economic Policy*, 13: 342–92.

HALLERBERG, M., and VON HAGEN, J. 1998. Electoral institutions and the budget process. Pp. 65–94 in *Democracy, Decentralization and Deficits in Latin America*, ed. K. Fukasaka and R. Hausmann. Paris: OECD Development Center.

―― ―― 1999. Electoral institutions, cabinet negotiations, and budget deficits in the European Union. Pp. 209–32 in *Fiscal Institutions and Fiscal Performance*, ed. J. Poterba and J. von Hagen. Chicago: University of Chicago Press.

HELPMAN, E. 2004. *The Mystery of Economic Growth*. Cambridge, Mass.: Harvard University Press.

IVERSEN, T., and SOSKICE, D. 2003. Electoral systems and the politics of coalitions: why some democracies redistribute more than others. Mimeo, Harvard University.

KONTOPOULOS, Y., and PEROTTI, R. 1999. Government fragmentation and fiscal policy outcomes: evidence from the OECD countries. Pp. 81–102 in *Fiscal Institutions and Fiscal Preference*, ed. J. Poterba and J. von Hagen. Chicago: University of Chicago Press.

KUNICOVA, J., and ROSE ACKERMAN, S. 2001. Electoral rules as constraints on corruption: the risks of closed-list proportional representation. Mimeo, Yale University.

LIJPHART, A. 1990. The political consequences of electoral laws 1945–85. *American Political Science Review*, 84: 481–96.

LIZZERI, A., and PERSICO, N. 2001. The provision of public goods under alternative electoral incentives. *American Economic Review*, 91: 225–45.

MILESI-FERRETTI, G.-M., PEROTTI, R., and ROSTAGNO, M. 2002. Electoral systems and the composition of public spending. *Quarterly Journal of Economics*, 117: 609–57.

MYERSON, R. 1993. Effectiveness of electoral systems for reducing government corruption: a game theoretic analysis. *Games and Economic Behavior*, 5: 118–32.

PELTZMAN, S. 1992. Voters as fiscal conservatives. *Quarterly Journal of Economics*, 107: 329–61.

PERSSON, T., ROLAND, G., and TABELLINI, G. 2003. How do electoral rules shape party structures, government coalitions and economic policies? Mimeo, Bocconi University.

―― and TABELLINI, G. 1999. The size and scope of government: comparative politics with rational politicians, 1998 Alfred Marshall Lecture. *European Economic Review*, 43: 699–735.

―― ―― 2000. *Political Economics: Explaining Economic Policy*. Cambridge, Mass.: MIT Press.

―― ―― 2003. *Economic Effects of Constitutions*. Cambridge, Mass.: MIT Press.

―― ―― 2004a. Constitutions and economic policy. *Journal of Economic Perspectives*, 18: 75–98.

―― ―― 2004b. Constitutional rules and economic policy outcomes. *American Economic Review*, 94: 25–46.

―― ―― and TREBBI, F. 2003. Electoral rules and corruption. *Journal of the European Economic Association*, 1: 958–89.

POTERBA, J., and VON HAGEN, J. (eds.) 1999. *Fiscal Rules and Fiscal Performance*. Chicago: University of Chicago Press.

PRZEWORSKI, A., STOKES, S., and MANIN, B. 1999. *Democracy, Accountability and Representation*. Cambridge: Cambridge University Press.

ROUBINI, N., and SACHS, J. 1989. Political and economic determinants of budget deficits in the industrial democracies. *European Economic Review*, 33: 903–33.

STROM, K. 1990. *Minority Government and Majority Rule*. Cambridge: Cambridge University Press.

STRÖMBERG, D. 2003. Optimal campaigning in presidential elections: the probability of being Florida. Mimeo, IIES.

TAAGEPERA, R., and SHUGART, M. 1989. *Seats and Votes: The Effects and Determinants of Electoral Systems.* New Haven, Conn.: Yale University Press.

TICCHI, D., and VINDIGNI, A. 2003. Endogenous constitutions. Mimeo, IIES, University of Stockholm.

TSEBELIS, G. 1995. Decision-making in political systems: veto players in presidentialism, parliamentarism, multicameralism and multipartyism. *British Journal of Political Science,* 25: 289–326.

—— 1999. Veto players and law production in parliamentary democracies. *American Political Science Review,* 93: 591–608.

—— 2002. *Veto Players: How Political Institutions Work.* Princeton, NJ: Princeton University Press.

VELASCO, A. 1999. A model of endogenous fiscal deficit and delayed fiscal reforms. Pp. 37–58 in *Fiscal Rules and Fiscal Performance,* ed. J. Poterba and J. von Hagen. Chicago: University of Chicago Press for the NBER.

CHAPTER 41

ECONOMIC GEOGRAPHY

ANTHONY J. VENABLES

1 Introduction

THE study of spatial relationships has, until recently, been conspicuously absent from mainstream economics. International economics characterized countries as points in space, defined by their endowments of immobile factors or political jurisdictions, but not by their spatial relationships with other countries. Regional economics followed a path largely outside modern economics, eschewing the tools of rigorous economic analysis. Urban economics modeled the internal structure of cities, but not the relationship between them. Yet just as some popular writers have started to write about globalization as the "death of distance" (Cairncross 2001) so distance has now re-entered mainstream economics in the form of "new economic geography." The purpose of this chapter is to outline some of the main issues and ideas in this emergent field.[1] Understanding spatial relationships is, we shall argue, a key part of understanding relationships in the world economy. It offers new insights into the "great divergence" of the nineteenth and early twentieth centuries and into the current process of globalization. It is also central to understanding one of the pre-eminent institutions of the modern economy—the city.

Our focus of attention—indeed our definition of "geographical economics"—is the study of spatial relationships between economic actors. Defining the field in this way immediately rules out much that falls under a wide definition of geography.

---

* Thanks to the editors for valuable comments.
[1] See Krugman 1991b; Fujita, Krugman, and Venables 1999; and Fujita and Thisse 2002 for detailed and more technical coverage of this material.

Physical geography has been crucial in shaping human history; modern man crossed out of Africa when a cold climatic episode 85,000 years ago lowered water levels in the southern Red Sea, and made it to Europe when a south–north fertile corridor opened during a warm episode some 50,000 years ago (Oppenheimer 2003). The spread of domesticated crops and animals depended on geography (Diamond 1998) and propensity to disease is a function of climate (Sachs 2001). Patterns of settlement by European emigrants, and the institutions that went with them, were determined largely by the geographical characteristics of the host regions (Acemoglu, Johnson, and Robinson 2001).

While these episodes illustrate the fundamental importance of geography, our narrower definition leads us to focus on two sorts of questions. The first is: given the location of the main centers of economic activity, how do economic activity and levels of income depend on proximity—in an appropriate economic sense—to these centers? The second is: what drives the existence and determines the location of centers of activity? Standard economic reasoning, with diminishing returns to activities, suggests that economic activity will tend to spread out uniformly across space. This is patently not so: the world is characterized by spatial clustering of population, of prosperity, and of poverty.

Both these types of question can be addressed at very different spatial scales. The first one can be directed at the determinants of land rents in cities—why do they fall from the center to the edge? It can also be directed at the world economy; how great is the cost penalty suffered by a land-locked African economy relative to an economy in central Europe? So too the second question. The spatial interaction between economic actors can be used to explain residential ghettos or industrial districts within cities; to explain the development of systems of cities within countries; or to explain the emergence and persistence of international income inequalities in the world economy. Clearly, modeling approaches need to be tailored to each of these specific contexts, but they all require two building blocks. One is an understanding of the costs of distance, and the other is a description of the mechanisms that cause activity to cluster.

The next two sections of the chapter lay out these building blocks. The remainder of the chapter then draws out their implications; Section 4 looks at patterns of development in the world economy, and Section 5 turns to urban systems. Section 6 concludes—and endeavours to answer the question: why is all this important for students of political economy?

2 Costs of Distance

The fundamental premiss is that geographical distance is a barrier to economic interaction. Most of our interactions are local, this applying to our workplace, our consumption of goods and services, and our sources of information and ideas. Costs

Table 41.1 Economic interactions and distance (flows relative to their magnitude at 1,000 km)

	Trade	Equity flows	FDI	Technology
1,000 km	1	1	1	1
2,000 km	0.42	0.55	0.75	0.65
4,000 km	0.18	0.31	0.56	0.28
8,000 km	0.07	0.17	0.42	0.05

Sources: See text.

of distance are made up partly of direct travel or freight costs, and also time and information costs. Time in transit is expensive, because of the direct time costs and also because of associated inflexibility; production decisions have to be made early if it takes time to ship the goods to market (Harrigan and Venables 2003). Information exchange and learning often requires repeated close interaction and face-to-face contact.

It is worth reporting some facts that illustrate the importance of distance. Table 41.1 shows the rate at which a number of forms of economic interaction decline with distance, relative to their intensity between two points 1,000 km apart. The trade column is based on estimates of the gravity model on international trade data. The numbers indicate that doubling distance from 1,000 km to 2,000 km reduces trade flows by more than half; at 4,000 km trade volumes are down by 82 per cent and by 8,000 km down by 93 per cent.[2] Other columns of the table report effects for other forms of economic interaction. Portes and Rey (1999) study cross-border equity, finding that flows at 8,000 km are less than one-fifth those at 1,000 km. Foreign direct investment (FDI) flows are studied by Di Mauro (2000) who finds a less steep decline, although international flows more than halve as distance goes from 1,000 km to 8,000 km. Keller (2002) looks at the dependence of total factor productivity on R&D stocks for twelve industries in the G-7 countries. Productivity depends on both own and foreign stocks of R&D, with stocks in distant countries having much weaker effects on productivity than do those in closer countries, so that the effect at 8,000 km is only 5 per cent of that at 1,000 km.

Several further comments are in order. One is that raw distance, as used in these estimates, is only a part of the barrier to interactions. Infrastructure matters, as do international borders. Trade costs within countries—even large ones—reduce interactions much less than do international borders with their associated differences in fiscal, legal, linguistic, and cultural standards. Even the most benign border, that between the USA and Canada, has the effect of choking off trade ten to twenty times more than do provincial borders within Canada (Helliwell 1998; Anderson and van Wincoop 2004). The cost of economic interactions has obviously changed

---

[2] Using a representative gravity estimate of the elasticity of trade with respect to distance of −1.25. Similar results apply at a finer spatial scale, e.g. doubling from 250 km to 500 km. See Anderson and van Wincoop 2004 for a comprehensive survey.

dramatically through time, and part of the economic geography story is that these changes have been important in shaping the world economy. How are they changing now? Some modes of interaction have become very much cheaper; falling air-freight rates mean that around 30 per cent of US imports now go by air. However, studies based on these data indicate an implicit willingness to pay for time saved at the rate of around 0.5 per cent of the value of goods shipped for each day saved, indicating the massive premium on proximity (Hummels 2001). Information and communication technology means that some activities—those that can be digitized—can now be shipped at essentially zero cost. However, the share of expenditure going on digitally supplied services is extremely small, partly because once an activity is digitized it also becomes cheap. Indeed the argument can be made that the economic importance of distance has increased. This is because expenditure has shifted to sectors where trade across wide distances is difficult, such as personal services, creative industries, design, and media, all activities in which proximity and face-to-face contact are important.

What are the implications of these costs of spatial interaction for the economic structure and income levels of remote economies? They have direct effects of increasing import prices and depressing export earnings in remote economies. Impacts on income and on the structure of activity can be derived by identifying the "market access" of locations (Harris 1954). Recent studies take into account the fact that it is not only market access, but also the costs of imported goods and equipment that are important for income.[3] They find that distance-based measures of access to markets and to suppliers are a statistically robust and quantitatively important determinant of a country or region's per capita income, even when other factors (such as institutions and education) are controlled for. For example, Redding and Venables (2003) find that halving the market access of a country—loosely interpreted as doubling the distance between a country and its main markets—reduces per capita income by around 25 per cent.

3 AGGLOMERATION MECHANISMS

Given the cost of spatial interactions, what pattern of economic activity do we expect to see in the world economy? The assumptions of neoclassical economics imply that activities will be dispersed, and spread quite evenly across locations. This is because production that is not subject to increasing returns to scale will be broken up to supply local demands. In the limit, this is "backyard capitalism"—a little bit of everything is produced in everyone's backyard. Clearly, this is not a good description of the world, and the key problem lies in the treatment of returns to scale. Only in the presence of increasing returns is there a trade-off between producing everywhere (low trade costs but small scale) and producing in few locations (high trade costs

[3] See for example Leamer 1997; Hanson 1998; Redding and Venables 2004.

and low production costs). Essentially, efficiency (from the division of labor, *inter alia*) is limited by the extent of the market, and the extent of the market is shaped by geography. Once this is recognized it is possible—although not automatic—that spatial clustering and agglomeration will occur.

3.1 Market Size and Labor Mobility

A satisfactory and tractable model of increasing returns to scale—and the concomitant imperfectly competitive market structures—entered common use in economics in the 1970s and 1980s, and was taken up rapidly in industrial, international, and spatial economics. As noted above, increasing returns to scale force firms to choose where to locate production (as opposed to putting some production everywhere). Rather unsurprisingly it turns out that, other things being equal, it is more profitable to produce in a place with good market access than one with bad market access. For example, suppose that there are two locations (countries or cities), one with a larger population than the other, and that trade between them is possible, although costly. The larger location then has better market access (more consumers can be accessed at low cost) and will be the more attractive location for production. Firms are attracted to the location, bidding up wages (and the prices of other inputs such as land) until, in equilibrium, both locations are equally profitable but the larger one pays higher wages. The advantages of good market access have been shifted to workers and other factors of production.

The next stage in the argument is clear. Locations with large populations have good market access so offer high wages; if labor is mobile, then high wages will attract inward migration, in turn giving them large population and good market access. As Krugman's (1991a) "core–periphery" model showed, it is possible that two locations are *ex ante* identical, but in equilibrium all activity will agglomerate in just one of them. Positive feedback (from population to market size to firms' location to wages to population) creates this agglomeration force. Pulling in the opposite direction are forces for dispersion, such as variation in the prices of immobile factors of production (e.g. land) and the need to supply any consumers who remain dispersed. The resultant economic geography is determined by the balance between these forces.

The story outlined above is simple, but provides an economical way of explaining the uneven dispersion of economic activity across space. There are two key messages that come from this and more sophisticated economic geography models. One is that even if locations are *ex ante* identical, *ex post* they can be very different. "Cumulative causation" forces operate so that very small differences in initial conditions can translate into large differences in outcomes, as initial advantage is reinforced by the actions of economic agents. The other message is that there is path dependence and "lock-in." Once established, an agglomeration will be robust to changes in the environment. For example, a change in circumstances may mean that a city is in the "wrong place." However, it is not rational for any individual to move, given that others remain in the established agglomeration.

3.2 Linkages and Externalities

While the preceding sub-section outlined agglomeration mechanisms based on population movement, most other mechanisms are based on efficiency gains in production. This literature dates from Marshall (1890), who described three types of mechanism, each of which has now been developed in the modern literature.

The first is based on linkages between firms. Firms that supply intermediate goods want to locate close to downstream customer firms (the same market size effect as we saw in the previous sub-section) and the downstream firms want to locate close to their suppliers. In Marshall's words:

> Subsidiary trades grow up in the neighbourhood, supplying it with implements and materials, organising its traffic, and in many ways conducing to the economy of its material ... the economic use of expensive machinery can sometimes be attained in a very high degree in a district in which there is large aggregate production of the same kind ... subsidiary industries devoting themselves each to one small branch of the process of production, and working it for a great many of their neighbours, are able to keep in constant use machinery of the most highly specialised character, and to make it pay its expenses.

These ideas were the subject of a good deal of attention in the development economics literature of the 1950s and 1960s, as writers such as Myrdal (1957) and Hirschman (1958) focused on the role of backward linkages (demands from downstream firms to their suppliers) and forward linkages (supply from intermediate producers to downstream activities) in developing industrial activity. But as we saw above, rigorous treatment requires that the concepts are placed in an environment with increasing returns to scale. This was done by Venables (1996), who showed how the interaction of these linkages does indeed create a positive feedback, so tending to cause clustering of activity. If linkages are primarily intrasectoral then there will be clustering of firms in related activities, as described in much of the work of Porter (1990). Alternatively, if the linkages are intersectoral then the forces may lead to clustering of manufacturing as a whole. We return to this case in Section 4 below.

The second of Marshall's mechanisms is based on a thick labour market:

> A localized industry gains a great advantage from the fact that it offers a constant market for skill. Employers are apt to resort to any place where they are likely to find a good choice of workers with the special skill which they require; while men seeking employment naturally go to places where there are many employers who need such skill as theirs and where therefore it is likely to find a good market. The owner of an isolated factory, even if he has good access to a plentiful supply of general labour, is often put to great shifts for want of some special skilled labour; and a skilled workman, when thrown out of employment in it, has no easy refuge.

In the modern literature this idea has surfaced in a number of forms. One is risk-pooling (Krugman 1991b), as risks associated with firm-specific shocks are pooled by a cluster of firms and workers with the same specialist skills. Another is that incentives to acquire skills are enhanced if there are many potential purchasers of such skills, avoiding the "hold-up" problem that may arise if workers find themselves faced with a monopsony purchaser of their skills.[4]

The third mechanism is geographically concentrated technological externalities:

> The mysteries of the trade become no mystery; but are as it were in the air ... Good work is rightly appreciated, inventions and improvements in machinery, in processes and the general organisation of the business have their merits promptly discussed; if one man starts a new idea, it is taken up by others and combined with suggestions of their own; and thus it becomes the source of further new ideas.

This idea is applied in much of the regional and urban literature (see for example Henderson 1974), as well as in some older trade literature (Ethier 1979), and there is debate as to the extent to which these effects operate within or between sectors (as argued by Jacobs 1969). It is perhaps best viewed as a black box for a variety of important yet difficult-to-model proximity benefits.

4 PATTERNS OF DEVELOPMENT

With these building blocks in place, we now turn to their implications for the location of activity and for spatial disparities in economic performance.

4.1 The Great Divergence

Once these clustering forces are put in a full general equilibrium model of trade and location, what happens, and what predictions are derived for spatial disparities? A sweeping view of world history is provided by the model of Krugman and Venables (1995) which studies the effects of falling trade costs on industrial location and income levels. Their model has just two countries (North and South), endowed with equal quantities of internationally immobile labor. There are two production sectors, perfectly competitive agriculture and manufacturing. Manufacturing is monopolistically competitive, with firms operating under increasing returns to scale, and also contains forward and backward linkages arising as firms produce and use intermediate goods as well as producing final output.

The Krugman and Venables story is summarized in Figure 41.1, which has trade costs on the horizontal axis and real wages in North and South on the vertical axis. At very high trade costs the two economies have the same wage rates ($w_N = w_S$), reflecting the fact that they are identical in all respects. The linkages between manufacturing firms create a force for agglomeration but when trade costs are high these are dominated by the need for firms to operate in each country to supply local consumers. As trade costs fall (moving left on the figure) so the possibility of supplying consumption

---
[4] For a recent survey see Duranton and Puga 2004.

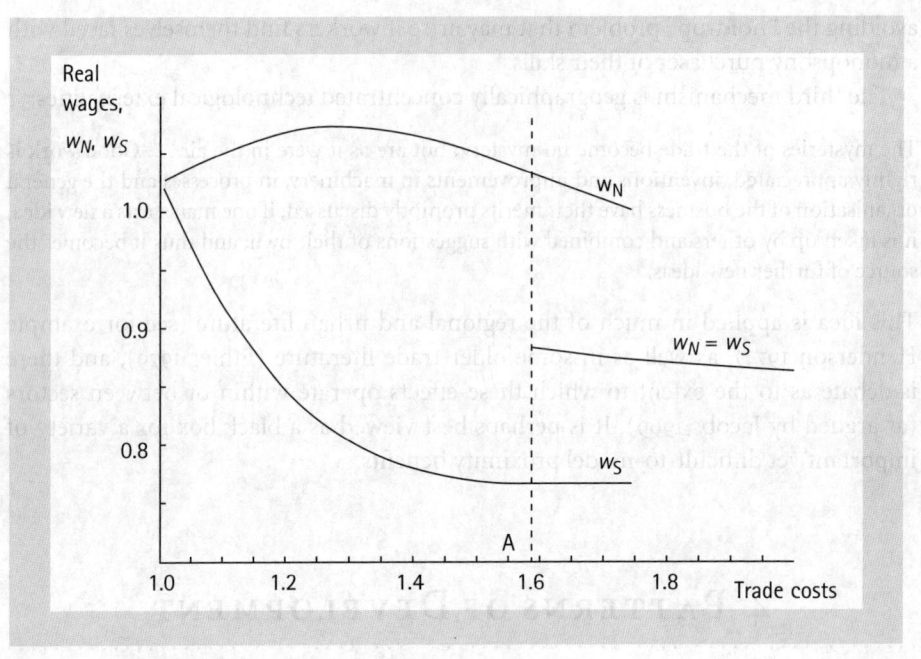

Fig. 41.1 History of the world

through trade rather than local production develops, and clustering forces become relatively more important. At point A clustering forces come to dominate, and the equilibrium with equal amounts of manufacturing in each country becomes unstable; if one firm relocates from S to N then it *raises* the profitability of firms in N and *reduces* the profitability of remaining firms in S, causing further firms to follow. Four forces are at work. Two are dispersion forces: by moving to N the firm raises wages in N and increases supply to N consumers, these forces tending to reduce profitability of firms in N. But against this there are two agglomeration forces. A firm that moves increases the size of the N market (the backward linkage, creating a demand for intermediate goods). It also reduces the costs of intermediates in N (the forward linkage, since it offers a supply of intermediates). The last two effects come to dominate and we see agglomeration of industry in one country, raising wages as illustrated.[5]

For a range of trade costs below A, the world necessarily has a dichotomous structure. Wages are lower in S, but it does not pay any firm to move to S as to do so would be to forgo the clustering benefits of large markets and proximity to suppliers that are found in N. However, as trade costs fall it becomes cheaper to ship intermediate goods; linkages matter less so the location of manufacturing becomes more sensitive to factor price differences. Manufacturing therefore starts to move to S and the equilibrium wage gap narrows. In this model wage gap goes all the way to factor price equalization when trade is perfectly free—the "death of distance."

---

[5] There is a range in which agglomeration (with $w_N > w_S$) and dispersion (with $w_N = w_S$) are both stable equilibria. See Fujita, Krugman, and Venables 1999 for details.

The model is intended to be suggestive of some of the forces driving the "great divergence" of the nineteenth and twentieth centuries. Between 1750 and 1880 western Europe's share of world manufacturing production went from less than 20 per cent to more than 65 per cent; together with North America, their share approached 75 per cent in the interwar period, before falling back to around 50 per cent by the beginning of the twenty-first century. Per capita incomes diverged, and are only now showing—for some regions—convergence. The model provides a single mechanism that can capture both these phases. Falling transport costs in a setting in which there are agglomeration forces in industry means that one region—the North—comes to deindustrialize the South and create inequality in the world economy. Only once transport costs become low enough—the globalization phase—does industry flow back and income convergence take place.

Of course, other mechanisms are also important, and there is probably a complementarity between mechanisms. Levels of education and institutional quality are determinants of income, but are in turn determined by income. The incentives to invest in education or develop institutions that support modern economic activity are low in an economy that is unable to compete with imports from the Northern manufacturing cluster.

4.2 Migration and the New World

The nineteenth century saw mass emigration from Europe to the new worlds of the Americas and Australasia. Just one of these booming regions—the northeast of the USA—made a successful transition from agriculture to manufacturing. Why was this so? The historical literature gives a number of explanations, largely based around institutional quality. Differing colonial legacies are important (North, Summerhill, and Weingast 2000), as are the different patterns of land tenure supported by climatic as well as colonial factors (Engerman and Sokoloff 1997). What additional and complementary mechanisms are provided by new economic geography?

Once again, it is helpful to think in a very stylized way in order to draw out some possibilities.[6] Suppose that there is an established economic center with manufacturing activity (Europe) and some number of other locations (in the New World) that can trade with the center. The new locations have high land–labor ratios, so export primary products and import manufactures. This endowment ratio also means that they offer high wages, attracting an inflow of migrants. The question is, at what stage—if at all—do these new economies attract manufacturing activity? The answer depends on trade costs (including tariff policies), market size, and competition from other sources of supply. Suppose that all New World economies are identical to each other, and all attracting immigrants at the same rate. Then there comes a point at which the local market is large enough to support manufacturing. However, simultaneous growth of manufacturing in all of these regions is not a possible

---

[6] This draws on Crafts and Venables 2003.

outcome—there would be oversupply of manufactures. Given the presence of agglomeration forces, what happens is that if one region gets just slightly ahead (perhaps by random chance) then cumulative causation forces take over. This region attracts manufacturing at the expense of the others, and is the only one of the New World regions to industrialize. The region also becomes more attractive for migrants, so attains larger population and economic size. The world supply of manufactures is then met by two clusters (Europe and northeast America) with the rest of the world specialized in agriculture, as in the example of the preceding sub-section. Comparing Argentina and the USA, North, Summerhill, and Weingast (2000) comment that "no deus ex machina translates endowments into ... outcomes;" in this simple story one does, and it plays dice.

Of course, this picture is oversimplified. Competing regions are not identical *ex ante*; market size, location, endowments, and institutions are all important in determining the success of the modern sector. However, the insight from the theory is that even if differences in initial conditions are small, they may translate into large differences in outcomes. A small advantage can give a location the advantage of being the next to start industrializing. The industrialization process is then rapid—a "take-off" as increasing returns and cumulative causation cut in. Furthermore, the industrialization of one New World region depresses the prospects for others, due simply to the overall supply of manufactures in the world economy. These other regions may experience failed industrialization, or industrialization that serves only the domestic market and remains internationally uncompetitive.

4.3 The Spread of Industry: Globalization and Integration

We outline one further application of this line of reasoning, extending the arguments developed above. As globalization reduces trade costs it breaks down some (although not all) of the clustering mechanisms outlined in Section 3, thereby facilitating movement of industry to low wage regions. What form does this "spread of industry" take? More or less steady convergence, with most countries catching up at a steady rate, or alternatively rapid growth of some countries, while others stagnate? Comparison of east Asian performance with much of the rest of the developing world seems to support the former view, as does the empirical work of Quah (1997) pointing to the development of "twinpeaks" in the world income distribution—an emptying of the low–middle range of the income distribution, as some countries grow fast and others are left in a low-income group.

The economic geography approach to this should now be apparent, and was formalized by Puga and Venables (1999). Let the world be divided between countries that have manufacturing activity and those that do not. Some growth process is going on in the world economy—e.g. technical progress—which is raising demand for manufactures. This demand growth raises wages in the economies with manufacturing until at some point it is profitable for a firm to relocate; the cost advantages of being in an existing cluster are outweighed by the higher wages this entails. Where do firms go? If there are linkages between relocating firms then they will cluster in a single newly emergent manufacturing country. A situation in which all countries gain a little manufacturing is unstable; the country that gets even slightly ahead will have the advantage, attracting further firms. Running this process through time a sequence of countries join the group of high-income nations. Each country grows fast as it joins the club, and is then followed by another country, and so on. As before, the order in which countries join is determined by a range of factors to do with endowments, institutions, and geography. Proximity to existing centers may be an important positive factor, as with development in eastern Europe and with regions of Mexico, east Asia, and China.[7] Of course, the strict sequence of countries should not be taken literally. The key insight is that the growth mechanism does not imply more or less uniform convergence of countries, as has been argued by some economic growth theorists (e.g. Lucas 2000). Instead, growth is sequential, not parallel, as manufacturing spreads across countries and regions.

5 Urban Structures

We commented earlier that economic geography insights apply at different sectoral and spatial levels. Sectorally, it offers approaches to thinking about the location of modern activity as a whole, and also about sectoral clusters of financial, R&D, or industrial activities. Spatially, it provides insights for international economics, and also for regional and urban studies. In this section we make a few remarks on the last of these topics.

Cities can derive their existence from a spatially concentrated endowment (a port or mineral deposit) or a spatially concentrated source of employment (a seat of government). But for most modern cities increasing returns to scale—driven by the agglomeration mechanisms outlined in Section 3—are a key reason for their existence and for their success. There is considerable evidence that productivity increases with city size, a doubling of size typically raising productivity by between 3 and 8 per cent, although the exact mechanism through which this operates remains contentious.[8] Historically, the role of agglomeration was central to Marshall's account of the success of some UK cities, and David's (1989) study of Chicago confirmed that its phenomenal growth was founded on agglomeration effects.

Pulling in the opposite direction have been transport costs. Transport costs between cities and rural areas reduced the market access of cities and made food supply to large cities costly. And within cities, commuting costs take a large part of

---

[7] The implications of market size and trade barriers are investigated by Puga and Venables 1999 who assess the alternatives of export-oriented versus import-substituting manufacturing development.

[8] See the survey by Rosenthal and Strange 2004.

people's time and expenditure and account for substantial center–edge rent gradients. Furthermore, city transport systems are frequently congested, so that further city growth creates negative congestion externalities for residents.

Equilibrium city size is given by the balance of these forces, when individuals are indifferent between living in alternative locations. However, this private trade-off between agglomeration economies and diseconomies does not, in general, create an outcome that is socially efficient. The decision of a migrant to live and work in a city, or of a firm making its location choice, is based on private returns and fails to take into account external effects. New entrants to the city do not internalize either the productivity externalities associated with city growth, or the negative externalities due to congestion. In a city of a given size congestion externalities raise policy questions for organization of transport and land use. In addition, the fact that these are reciprocal externalities—each resident exerting effects on all others—may create coordination failures. It is then difficult to establish new cities or to regenerate city districts, since there is no incentive for a single small economic agent to move into a low-rent area.

The presence of these market failures raises important questions about city governance. One important strand of literature argues that the externalities can all be internalized by "private government." This government is provided by large developers who develop land, receiving the payoff from city development in the form of land rent. It turns out that if there is a competitive supply of such developers then the equilibrium that they support is socially efficient. Rents just cover the subsidies that are required to align private incentives with public ones—the "Henry George" theorem (Stiglitz 1977). However, it seems unlikely that there are many situations in which large developers play this role. Even in countries where such developers have a significant presence they are typically tightly circumscribed. An efficient outcome can also be achieved by city governments that are able to tax 100 per cent of land rents, and in which incumbent city residents vote on subsidy and tax payments in a way that internalizes externalities. However, these results are typically dependent on the tax instruments available and on cities' ability to borrow in perfect capital markets (Henderson and Venables 2004).

These issues are of importance in countries with established urban structures, where they are typically manifest in the contexts of urban regeneration, suburban sprawl, and the development of transport systems. They are vastly more important in developing countries, where urban population is projected to increase by some 2 billion in the next thirty years. Will this population all go into existing mega-cities or can new cities be developed? Reciprocal externalities mean that a new city may be difficult to establish; initial residents do not reap benefits of scale in the short run and may also be uncertain about the long-run prospects of a new town. In this case mega-cities may expand vastly beyond the size that is socially efficient.

Much work remains to be done on the design of economic policy in these situations. The political economy of implementing it, and in particular the extent to which fiscal responsibility and decision-taking should be centralized or devolved, then becomes crucial.[9]

6 CONCLUSIONS

Ideas from new economic geography provide a different lens through which to view many aspects of the world economy. We suggest that there are several main messages for students of political economy.

First, the literature suggests that spatial disparities are a normal economic outcome. These disparities show up in different ways. If labor is fully mobile then income differences will be eliminated but activity will have a spatially lumpy distribution as population becomes concentrated in cities. If labor is immobile the disparities may be manifested through spatial income inequalities. Thus, the approach provides a rigorous analytical foundation for notions of "core" and "periphery" in the world economy, as put forward by other writers (e.g. Wallerstein 1974). Of course, the approach does not claim to be the only mechanism supporting such inequalities. Endowments of human and physical capital and of natural environment matter, as does the quality of institutions, emphasized in the work of North (1990), Acemoglu, Johnson, and Robinson (2001, 2002), and others.

The second message is cumulative causation. If increasing returns to scale are spatially concentrated then we expect to see regions with small initial advantages performing substantially better than other regions. There is path dependence so that, once established, the advantages of these cities, regions, or countries are relatively difficult to overtake. New economic geography offers an economic basis for cumulative causation and, once again, this mechanism is complementary to others based on political economy and institutional inertia. The incentives to develop education and business-friendly institutions are greater in regions where economic opportunities are larger, while the development of education and institutions are themselves self-reinforcing processes. Conversely, bad institutions may restrict interaction with the world economy, increasing a country's economic remoteness. Interactions between these mechanisms, all of them operating in a cumulative rather than a linear manner, means that it is difficult—and possibly futile—to seek to quantify the relative importance of each.

Third, this view of the world suggests that externalities, arising from the agglomeration mechanisms outlined in Section 3, are all pervasive. Individually they are small—no one individual has a great effect on the productivity of his urban

---

[9] See Helsley 2004 for a survey of urban political economy. There is a substantial literature on fiscal federalism (see the survey by Rubinfeld 1988) although this is typically based in simple environments without the returns to scale and externalities that are crucial to understanding cities and regional disparities.

neighbours—but collectively they add up to substantial productivity effects. Given these externalities market outcomes are generally inefficient. Institutions are required not just to secure basic rights, but also to provide governance in this complex situation. A major challenge for urban and regional analysis is to combine economics and political economy to create a better understanding of policy design and implementation in this environment.

REFERENCES

ACEMOGLU, D., JOHNSON, S., and ROBINSON, J. 2001. Colonial origins of comparative development: an empirical investigation. *American Economic Review*, 91: 1369–401.
—— —— —— 2002. Reversal of fortune: geography and modern institutions in the making of the modern world income distribution. *Quarterly Journal of Economics Review*, 117: 1231–94.
ANDERSON, J., and VAN WINCOOP, E. 2004. Trade costs. *Journal of Economic Literature*, 42: 691–751.
CAIRNCROSS, F. 2001. *The Death of Distance*. Boston: Harvard Business School Press.
CRAFTS, N. F. R., and VENABLES, A. J. 2003. Globalization and geography in historical perspective. In *Globalization in Historical Perspective*, ed. M. D. Bordo, A. M. Taylor, and J. G. Williamson. Chicago: NBER–University of Chicago Press.
DAVID, P. A. 1989. The Marshallian dynamics of industrial localization: Chicago, 1850–1890. Mimeo, Stanford University.
DIAMOND, J. 1998. *Guns, Germs and Steel*. London: Jonathan Cape.
DI MAURO, F. 2000. The impact of economic integration on FDI and exports: a gravity approach. CEPS Working Document No. 156.
DURANTON, G., and PUGA, D. 2004. Micro-foundations of urban agglomeration economies. In *The Handbook of Urban and Regional Economics*, vol. iv, ed. V. Henderson and J. Thisse. Amsterdam: North-Holland.
ENGERMAN, S. L., and SOKOLOFF, K. L. 1997. Factor endowments, institutions, and differential paths of growth among New World economies. In *How Latin America Fell Behind*, ed. S. Haber. Stanford, Calif.: Stanford University Press.
ETHIER, W. J. 1979. Internationally decreasing costs and world trade. *Journal of International Economics*, 9: 1–24.
FUJITA, M., KRUGMAN, P. R., and VENABLES, A. J. 1999. *The Spatial Economy: Cities, Regions and International Trade*. Cambridge, Mass.: MIT Press.
—— and THISSE, J. 2002. *The Economics of Agglomeration*. Cambridge: Cambridge University Press.
HANSON, G. 1998. Market potential, increasing returns and geographic Concentration. NBER Working paper No. 6249.
HARRIGAN, J., and VENABLES, A. J. 2003. Timeliness, trade and agglomeration. CEPR Discussion Paper No. 4294.
HARRIS, C. 1954. The market as a factor in the localisation of industry in the US. *Annals of the Association of American Geographers*, 44: 315–48.
HELLIWELL, J. 1998. *How Much do National Borders Matter?* Washington, DC: Brookings Institute.
HELSLEY, R. W. 2004. Urban political economics. In *The Handbook of Urban and Regional Economics*, vol. iv, ed. V. Henderson and J. Thisse. Amsterdam: North-Holland.

HENDERSON, J. V. 1974. The sizes and types of cities. *American Economic Review*, 64: 640–56.
────1988. *Urban Development: Theory, Fact and Illusion*. Oxford: Oxford University Press.
──── and VENABLES, A. J. 2004. The dynamics of city formation: finance and governance. CEPR Discussion Papers 4638, Centre for Economic Policy Research, London.
HIRSCHMAN, A. 1958. *The Strategy of Economic Development*. New Haven, Conn.: Yale University Press.
HOHENBERG, P. M., and LEES, L. H. 1985. *The Making of Urban Europe*. Cambridge, Mass.: Harvard University Press.
HUMMELS, D. J. 2001. Time as a trade barrier. Mimeo, Purdue University.
JACOBS, J. 1969. *The Economy of Cities*. New York: Vintage.
KELLER, W. 2002. Geographic location of international technology diffusion. *American Economic Review*, 92: 120–42.
KRUGMAN, P. R. 1991a. Increasing returns and economic geography. *Journal of Political Economy*, 49: 137–50.
────1991b. *Geography and Trade*. Cambridge, Mass.: MIT Press.
──── and VENABLES, A. J. 1995. Globalization and the inequality of nations. *Quarterly Journal of Economics*, 110: 857–80.
LEAMER, E. 1997. Access to western markets and eastern effort. In *Lessons from the Economic Transition: Central and Eastern Europe in the 1990s*, ed. S. Zechini. Dordrecht: Kluwer Academic.
LUCAS, R. E. 2000. Some macro-economics for the twenty-first century. *Journal of Economic Perspectives*, 14: 159–68.
MARSHALL, A. 1890. *Principles of Economics*. London: Macmillan (8th edn. 1920).
MYRDAL, G. 1957. *Economic Theory and Under-developed Regions*. London: Duckworth.
NORTH, D. C. 1990. *Institutions, Institutional Change and Economic Performance*. Cambridge: Cambridge University Press.
──── SUMMERHILL, W. R., and WEINGAST, B. R. 2000. Order, disorder, and economic change: Latin America vs North America. In *Governing for Prosperity*, ed. B. Bueno de Mesquita and H. L. Root. New Haven, Conn: Yale University Press.
OPPENHEIMER, S. 2003. *Out of Eden: The Peopling of the World*. London: Constable and Robinson.
OVERMAN, H. G., REDDING, S. J., and VENABLES, A. J. 2003. The economic geography of trade, production and income: a survey of empirics. In *The Handbook of International Trade*, ed. K. Choi and J. Harrigan. Oxford: Blackwell.
PORTER, M. E., 1990. *The Competitive Advantage of Nations*. New York: Macmillan.
PORTES, R., and REY, H. 1999. The determinants of cross-border equity flows. NBER Working Paper No. 7336.
PRED, A. C. 1977. *City-Systems in Advanced Economies*. New York: John Wiley.
PUGA, D., and VENABLES, A. J. 1999. Agglomeration and economic development: import substitution versus trade liberalisation. *Economic Journal*, 109: 292–311.
QUAH, D. T. 1997. Empirics for growth and distribution: stratification, polarization, and convergence clubs. *Journal of Economic Growth*, 2: 27–60.
REDDING, S., and VENABLES, A. J. 2004. Economic geography and international inequality. *Journal of International Economics*, 62: 53–82.
ROSENTHAL, S. S., and STRANGE, W. C. 2004. Evidence on the nature and sources of agglomeration economies. In *The Handbook of Urban and Regional Economics*, vol. iv, ed. V. Henderson and J. Thisse. Amsterdam: North-Holland.
RUBINFELD, D. 1988. Economics of the local public sector. In *The Handbook of Public Economics*, vol. ii, ed. A. Auerbach and M. Feldstein. Amsterdam: North-Holland.

SACHS, J. D. 2001. Tropical underdevelopment. NBER Working Paper No. 8119.
STIGLITZ, J. E. 1977. The theory of local public goods. In *The Economics of the Public Services*, ed. M. S. Feldstein and R. P. Inman. London: Macmillan.
VENABLES, A. J. 1996. Equilibrium locations of vertically linked industries. *International Economic Review*, 37: 341–59.
WALLERSTEIN, I. 1974. *The Modern World System: Capitalist Agriculture and the Origins of the European World Economy in the Sixteenth Century*. New York: Academic Press.

PART XI

INTERNATIONAL POLITICAL ECONOMY

CHAPTER 42

INTERNATIONAL POLITICAL ECONOMY

A MATURING INTERDISCIPLINE

DAVID A. LAKE

THE world is "globalized." Among developed countries, international trade now accounts for nearly 38 per cent of gross domestic product (GDP). For developing economies, imports plus exports comprise nearly 49 per cent of all national output. Over the last two decades, global flows of foreign direct investment have more than doubled relative to GDP. As journalist Thomas Friedman (2000, 9) has famously described it, globalization now allows "individuals, corporations, and nation-states to reach around the world farther, faster, deeper and cheaper than ever before."

The field of international political economy (IPE) pre-dates the current era of globalization, but not by much; perhaps more accurately, it was created by scholars trying to grasp the fundamentals of this nascent age. Nonetheless, this young field is rapidly maturing. From a range of early perspectives, a dominant approach, referred to as Open Economy Politics (OEP), now structures and guides research.[1] Although political scientists are more apt to identify themselves as "international political economists," OEP bridges the disciplines of political science and economics

---

* I am grateful for comments on an earlier draft of this chapter from J. Lawrence Broz, Jeffry Frieden, Gordon Hanson, and Marc Muendler.

[1] The term comes from Bates 1997.

and provides a vehicle for synthesizing the interesting work being done in both areas. Although there remain some significant differences between disciplines, and scholars are too often unaware of parallel developments in the other field, IPE is emerging as a true interdiscipline.

This chapter provides an overview of IPE. It begins with an outline of the early origins of the field, and then provides one of the first comprehensive statements of the OEP approach. It concludes by identifying areas for future research.

1 ORIGINS

As a distinct field, IPE focuses on the politics of international economic exchange. Unlike some of the other areas surveyed in this *Handbook*, IPE is a substantive topic of enquiry, rather than a methodology in which economic models are applied to political phenomena—although scholars are, in fact, increasingly drawn to such methods. The field is primarily informed by two sets of key questions. First, how, when, and why do states choose to open themselves to transborder flows of goods and services, capital, and people? In other words, what are the political determinants of what we now call globalization? In this first set of questions, openness is the dependent variable, or outcome to be explained, and politics (defined broadly) is the independent or causal variable. Economic theory posits that free and unrestricted international commerce is, with limited exceptions, welfare improving; many politically naive analysts, in turn, expect countries to evolve toward free trade. By contrast, IPE begins with the reality that openness is historically rare, politically problematic, and a phenomenon that needs to be explained.

Second, how does integration (or not) into the international economy affect the interests of individuals, sectors, factors of production, or countries and, in turn, national policies? Here, government policy is the dependent variable and how the actor is situated in the international economy is the independent variable. In reality, of course, these two sets of questions are themselves integrated. For pragmatic purposes, however, nearly all analysts study just one half of the causal circle.

Although these questions were central to political economists of the late eighteenth and early nineteenth centuries, they fell into an intellectual limbo with the split between economics and political science into two separate disciplines in the late nineteenth century. As economics underwent the "marginalist" revolution and slowly transformed itself into an axiomatic science and political science turned to the study of formal-legal constitutions and institutions, both disciplines grew increasingly introspective. Questions concerning the political foundations of markets and the economics of politics were left to languish—or were happily consigned to ostracized Marxists.[2] Some scholars addressed questions relevant to IPE—witness

---

[2] For an analysis of the early years of political economy and its trajectory, see Caporaso and Levine 1992.

E. E. Schattschneider's (1935) famous study of the political logrolling that produced the Smoot–Hawley Tariff or Wolfgang Stolper and Paul Samuelson's (1941) definitive proof of the distributional implications of liberalizing trade—but their studies were primarily oriented toward their respective disciplines and failed, at the time, to generate much interdisciplinary interest. What little cross-disciplinary research emerged remained highly descriptive (Bauer, Pool, and Dexter 1972; Preeg 1970).

IPE emerged as a new and distinct interdisciplinary field beginning in the late 1960s and early 1970s as a result of two contradictory, real-world developments. Together, these trends forced scholars to grapple anew with the same questions that had occupied earlier political economists. First, the success of the postwar international economic regime constructed at Bretton Woods, and embodied in the postwar institutions of the International Monetary Fund, World Bank, and General Agreements on Tariffs and Trade (GATT), ushered in an era of increasing economic interdependence. By the end of the 1960s, as the tariff cuts negotiated at the Kennedy Round of the GATT took full effect, trade as a percentage of all economic activity began to rise rapidly in all advanced countries, leading to a new focus on the political impact of deepening economic ties (Cooper 1968; Keohane and Nye 1972). This new era was expected by some to transform the nature of international politics, with economic historian Charles Kindleberger (1969, 207) famously proclaiming that "the nation-state is just about through as an economic unit" and political scientists Robert Keohane and Joseph Nye (1977) unveiling a new model of international politics characterized by "complex interdependence." We now recognize this surge of interdependence as the nascent phase of the present era of globalization, more frequently dated from the removal of capital controls in many developed economies in the early 1980s. Many today still believe that globalization carries the same transformative potential (see below).

Second, at nearly the same time that interdependence was "taking off," the political foundations of this open international economy began to crack, revealing for all that economic exchange rested on unstable political ground.[3] In August 1971, facing the huge dollar "overhang" first theorized by economist Robert Triffin (1960) and the consequences of a decade of fiscal and monetary mismanagement, President Richard Nixon formally ended the convertibility of the dollar into gold, closing the door on the Bretton Woods regime (Gowa 1983). Two years later, the postwar exchange rate regime collapsed when the major currencies began to float against one another. Contributing to this monetary instability, the Arab boycott begun during the 1973 Middle East war transformed oil into a coercive weapon. Breathing life into the Organization of Petroleum Exporting Countries (OPEC), first formed in 1960, the factious states began to operate effectively as a cartel, raising oil prices fifteenfold between 1973 and 1980. Envying OPEC's success, even while suffering under higher oil prices, the developing world called for a New International Economic Order through which other commodity producers hoped to exercise similar market power with the acquiescence or hopefully support of northern consumers. Finally, in response to the growth of imports unleashed by liberalization and rising interdependence, American

---

[3] An early and forceful statement of this insight was Gilpin 1972.

industry began clamoring for increased or renewed trade protection. Trying to satisfy industry without undermining its commitment to free trade, the United States adopted a series of innovative non-tariff barriers to trade including "voluntary export restraints," directed primarily at Japan (Goldstein 1988).

As international economic relations were politicized, it became apparent that international exchange was not an autonomous sphere—a natural phenomenon beyond political machinations—but was itself a product of the pulling and hauling of politics within and between countries. Just as property rights later came to be understood as both central to economic growth and a product of redistributive politics within countries, early international political economists realized that an open international economy rested on highly contested national policy decisions. As analysts struggled to understand the simultaneous growth and conflict in international markets, the field of IPE was born.

2 EARLY CURRENTS[4]

Perhaps the earliest approach to IPE was *dependency theory*, developed largely by Latin American scholars writing in the 1960s and popular in North America and Europe in the 1970s.[5] Described even by its adherents as a school rather than a single theory (Palma 1978), the many variants of dependency theory are unified by the idea that the economy and prospects for development in poor countries (the periphery) are conditioned by a global economy dominated by already developed states (the core). In the view of Andre Gunder Frank (1966), one of the more strident advocates of the approach, today's poor countries are not just undeveloped, as had been the case for the core centuries earlier, but are underdeveloped by an international economy that is forever biased against them. It follows that underdeveloped countries cannot follow the same path as the already industrialized states, as posited by modernization theory, but that they must pursue new and more autonomous strategies of development.

Despite its early prominence, dependency theory waned by the 1980s for two reasons. First, its proponents failed to develop a unified, logically consistent, and empirically robust theory of underdevelopment, or at least one that could compete in rigor and explanatory power with neoclassical economic theories of growth and development. Second, the theory was essentially falsified by the rise of the so-called newly industrializing economies, who despite all expectations of dependency theory "took off" in the 1970s using an export-led growth strategy (see Haggard 1990). Nonetheless, dependency theory taps into issues of international inequality, uneven growth, and national control over international economic forces that remain central

---

[4] An alternative typology divides theories into Marxist, Liberal, and Realist approaches. See Gilpin 1975.

[5] The cornerstone of dependency theory is Cardoso and Faletto 1979, first published in Spanish in 1967. An early approach was Prebisch 1964. See also Marini 1972; Furtado 1973; Sunkel 1969.

to contemporary debates about globalization. Even if the theory is broadly rejected, the real-world concerns that lent it credence endure.

A second early approach to IPE is hegemonic stability theory (HST), again more a school than a unified theory.[6] Based largely on the experiences of Great Britain in the mid-nineteenth and the United States in the mid-twentieth centuries, the key intuition behind this approach is that a single hegemonic state is necessary and sufficient for international economic openness to arise.

One variant of HST, which I have elsewhere called leadership theory, derives largely from the economic literature on collective action (see Pahre 1999). Kindleberger (1973, 305) first identified a series of what we would now call international market failures that caused the Great Depression of the 1930s, and concluded "that for the world economy to be stabilized, there has to be a stabilizer, one stabilizer." Economists Beth Yarbrough and Robert Yarbrough (1992) extend this basic insight to argue that an international division of labor necessarily produces greater relationship-specific assets and the risk of costly opportunism. Building on Oliver Williamson's (1985) work on markets and hierarchies, they treat hegemony as a form of hierarchy necessary to enforce contracts and maintain international order so that international exchange and investment can occur. Leadership theory nonetheless fails to demonstrate that privileged groups able and willing to provide international public goods necessarily have to consist of one and only one state (see Lake 1988; Snidal 1985). In principle, at least, small groups of countries are equally capable, undermining the theoretical case for the observed correlation between hegemony and stability.

A second variant, which I call hegemony theory, posits that large dominant states possess strong preferences for free and open international exchange and, in turn, coerce, induce, or persuade other states into opening their markets to foreign trade and investment (Gilpin 1975, 1977). Rather than focusing on collective action problems, hegemony theory posits that states have different preferences over international economic policy and outcomes are a result of strategic bargaining. Hegemony theorists argue that either states have more complex utility functions, including not just national wealth but power and stability (Gowa 1994; Krasner 1976), or their large internal markets and increasing returns to scale industries give hegemons strategic trade advantages that they attempt to lock in by encouraging others to adopt free trade (Lake 1988). Although plausible, these alternative intuitions have yet to produce a body of well-specified theory. Nor has hegemony theory successfully challenged orthodox international trade theory, especially the axioms that in a world of constant returns free trade remains the optimal policy for nearly all countries nearly all the time and that small countries benefit disproportionately from free trade.

As America's hegemony declined in the 1970s and 1980s, both variants of HST expected the international economy to become more fragile and, ultimately, to collapse into renewed protectionism and exclusive economic blocks (Gilpin 1987). The rising problems and tensions in the international economy, and America's own slide into new forms of protectionism, gave backing to this view. Yet, the open international economy did not fall apart—and, indeed, new and unprecedented forms of

---

[6] HST is reviewed in greater detail in Lake 1993.

macroeconomic policy cooperation emerged in the late 1970s. In the early 1980s, scholars turned to regimes and institutions to explain the unexpectedly robust international economy (Keohane 1984; Krasner 1983). By the early 1990s, the Soviet Union had collapsed, the European and Japanese economies had slipped into a decade of stagnation, and the United States was once again hegemonic—but HST was nearly forgotten. Central to this approach, however, was the recognition that not all countries are "created equal," that some are more important to the openness of the world economy than others, and that large countries have particularly large effects on others. Although seldom appreciated by theorists building new models of interstate economic cooperation, the intuitions and set of ideas that motivated HST are now reprised in OEP's focus on terms of trade effects within the international economy (see below).

A final early approach to IPE focuses on domestic interests largely in the advanced industrialized economies and, especially, in the United States.[7] Practical observers of politics and, of course, scholars as early as Schattschneider (1935) had emphasized the importance of interest groups in trade policy. Yet, domestic theories of international political economy emerged only recently. An early foundation was Kindleberger's (1951) essay on "Group behavior and international trade," followed by, in political science, Peter Gourevitch's (1977) study of the first great depression and, in economics, Richard Caves's (1976) evocative rendering of different models of trade policy-making. In the ferment of the early years of IPE, political scientists built on these works to construct a demand-side or societal-based theory of trade policy (see Cassing, McKeown, and Ochs 1986; Frieden 1988b; McKeown 1984; Milner 1988). At about this same time, economists developed a parallel "endogenous tariff theory," which also emphasizes the importance of domestic interests and lobbying (Baldwin 1985; Grossman and Helpman 1994; Lavergne 1983; Magee, Brock, and Young 1989; Pincus 1975). Key to much of this work was the differential ability of actors to solve their collective action problems and then build majority coalitions with, ultimately, importers triumphing politically over exporters, producers over consumers, and concentrated over diffuse interests. Less important than how groups define their interests (see below) is how they are structured and organized for political action. This early work on domestic interests nonetheless created the foundation for our contemporary approach to IPE.

3 THE STATE OF THE ART

Out of these early currents, and as a direct descendant of the domestic interest approach, OEP emerged and came to dominate the study of IPE in the 1990s. OEP adopts the assumptions of neoclassical economics and international trade theory. But

---

[7] Complementing this domestic interest group approach, at least in political science, is a domestic structures model that seeks to characterize and capture institutional variations across developed countries (Ikenberry, Lake, and Mastanduno 1988; Katzenstein 1978).

by incorporating political variables more explicitly into its analysis, OEP provides a bridge between modern economics and political science—although the span is not yet fully closed.

OEP begins with firms, sectors, or factors of production as the units of analysis, derives their interests over economic policy from each unit's position within the international economy, conceives of institutions as mechanisms that aggregate interests (with more or less bias) and condition the bargaining of competing societal interests, and, finally, introduces when necessary bargaining at the international level between states with different societally produced interests. Few theories give equal weight to all steps in this analysis. Most focus on one step—for instance, how institutions aggregate societal interests—and treat others in "reduced form," or as analytic simplifications that are unmodeled in the theory at hand.[8] In principle, the broadly shared assumptions allow the components to be connected together into a more complete whole, although in practice synthesis remains imperfect for reasons I will explain below.

3.1 Interests

The fundamental building block of OEP is interest, or how an individual or group is affected by a particular policy. In what may now be regarded as the canonical model (Grossman and Helpman 1994, 2002), actors that benefit from a policy are expected to expend resources in the political arena to obtain that policy (as a shorthand, to lobby) up to the point where the marginal cost of that effort equals the marginal benefit (defined either as "more" of the policy or an increased probability of obtaining a fixed policy). Conversely, actors that lose from a policy are expected to lobby against it. In short, politics is fundamentally about winners and losers from alternative policies.

Theories differ in what they assume to be the relevant unit of analysis. Although nearly all theories are fundamentally individualist, for pragmatic purposes theorists bundle individuals into groups that can be reasonably assumed to share (nearly) identical interests. In other words, when a policy affects a set of individuals in the same way, they are typically treated as if they constitute a homogeneous group or, for purposes of analysis, a single actor. In some OEP theories, individuals are primary but in most, firms, sectors, or factors of production are taken to be the relevant units.

OEP uses economic theory to deduce what types of individuals can be reasonably assumed to share identical interests.[9] A key divide within the approach is between the Ricardo–Viner or specific factors theory of international trade, which assumes that, typically, capital and labor are fixed in particular occupations and, thus, will tend to have similar interests over trade policy, and the Heckscher–Ohlin theory of international trade, which assumes that all factors are mobile across occupations and, therefore, capital, land, and labor will possess opposing interests. Stephen Magee (1980) attempted to discern which assumption was more appropriate by studying the lobbying behavior of capital and labor in the trade bill of 1973, and found support

---

[8] OEP is a subset of strategic choice theory, discussed in Lake and Powell 1999.
[9] Alternatives attempt to derive groups and interests from institutional structure (Verdier 1994) or see interests as socially constructed (Abdelal 2001; Simmons and Elkins 2003).

for the specific factors approach in his observation that capital and labor almost always testified on the same side of the proposed legislation. This implied that sectors were the appropriate unit of analysis for theories of trade policy.[10] More recently, Michael Hiscox (2002) has used cross-industry variations in rates of return as a proxy for factor mobility. In his small sample of industrialized countries, he finds that for the late nineteenth to the mid-twentieth centuries, as mass production was introduced, factor mobility for capital and labor generally increased, and from the mid-twentieth century until today factor mobility has generally decreased, which in turn is broadly confirmed by the changing structure of political interests on trade over the last century. This implies that the relevant units evolved from sectors, to factors, and back to sectors over the course of the last century or more.

Having defined the relevant unit of analysis, OEP goes further to derive interests—preferences over alternative policies—from the distributional implications of different economic policies and, in turn, how a group is located relative to others in the international economy.[11] Firms vary by whether they are in the tradeable or nontradeable sectors, produce import-competing or export-competing goods, use imported components, and so on. By knowing a firm's production profile (Gourevitch 1986), OEP predicts how it will be affected, for instance, by policies to increase international openness. Sectors vary by similar characteristics. Factors of production, in turn, vary by their scarcity relative to the world economy (Rogowski 1989; Stolper and Samuelson 1941). Using Mundell's (1957) equivalence condition—that flows of goods and factors across international borders are equivalent in their effects on relative rates of return—we can derive expectations about how factors will be affected by a large range of economic policies and, thus, identify their interests over those same policies. Although OEP first derived these distributional implications for trade policy, and the deductions remain clearest for this issue, the same method has now been used to identify the distributional effects of international finance and exchange rate policies (Frieden 1988a, 1991, 1997; O'Mahony 2003). The distributional implications of foreign direct investment, and especially the ownership of assets and production that such investment implies, remain the research frontier (Pinto 2004).

Deducing interests from economic theory was a fundamental innovation for OEP, one that makes the approach unique in political economy. Rather than treating them simply by assumption or inferring them from the political actions we often want to explain, interests are derived from a prior, falsifiable, and empirically robust theory—putting the whole approach on a sound deductive footing. It is on this innovation that the distinctive nature and, indeed, explanatory power of OEP rests.

3.2 Institutions

Institutions aggregate conflicting societal interests, with varying degrees of bias, and condition the bargaining between opposing groups. In weakly institutionalized

---

[10] Baldwin and Magee 2000 find more support for the Heckscher–Ohlin model.
[11] On studying preferences more generally, see Frieden 1999.

political systems, like the international system or "failed states," coercive strength is expected to determine political outcomes; on average, and simplifying somewhat, we expect the side with the most guns to win. In highly institutionalized settings, like most domestic political systems, established rules and procedures generally reflect group strength over the long term. But because they often do other valuable things for society, like enhance the credibility of commitments, institutions can develop an independent standing and structure, channel, and sometimes offset brute force in the short term. At any moment, institutions serve to define what political power means in a particular society, whether the competition over policy will be conducted via votes, normally expected to favor labor, via contributions and bribes, often in capital's comparative advantage, or via ideas and argument. In short, institutions determine the rules of the political game.

Political scientists and, increasingly, economists are studying in detail how institutions aggregate interests. The findings are surveyed elsewhere in this volume (Parts II–V), and will not be reviewed extensively here. But among the more relevant findings for IPE are:

- Large constituencies—at the extreme, a single electoral district for the entire country—incline policy towards the general welfare, assumed to be the free flow of goods, services, and factors of production, while small constituencies bias policy toward more protectionist groups (Rogowski 1987).
- The more veto points within a political system (actors with the authority to block the enactment of policy), the more likely the status quo is to prevail, reducing the credibility of any promise to adopt political or economic reforms (Cowhey 1993) and, at the same time, reducing the ability of a government to respond effectively to external shocks (MacIntyre 2001).
- Proportional representation systems produce policy stability and inflexibility, implying less credible commitments to reform and less ability to respond effectively to external shocks, whereas majoritarian electoral systems tend toward policy flexibility and instability, with the opposite effects on credibility and effective response (Rogowski 1999).

Our understanding of how institutions aggregate interests is far more advanced for democracies than for democratizing or autocratic states. Interest aggregation in nondemocratic or newly democratic states remains an important area for future research.

Institutions also condition the bargaining between groups, largely by setting the reversion point for policy in the absence of some compromise and defining possible side payments, cross-issue deals, and logrolls. For instance, Peter Katzenstein (1985) argues that the small open economies of Europe developed corporatist institutions to facilitate economic adjustment, capital–labor cooperation to moderate wage demands, and compensatory social welfare systems to ease the costs to individuals of economic adversity. Dani Rodrik (1997), Geoffrey Garrett (1998), and others have generalized this argument to all states, finding substantial evidence of an "embedded liberal" compromise (Ruggie 1983) in which social welfare policies are the "price" capital pays for economic openness. Similarly, multimember electoral districts, as in

Japan, promote particularistic interests and policies, creating socially inefficient rent-seeking and economic inflexibility (Ramseyer and Rosenbluth 1993).

OEP recognizes, in a way that the earlier domestic interests approach did not, that interests are not enough. However well specified, interests are refracted through political institutions that often have an independent effect on policy choices. The focus on institutions is not, of course, unique to OEP, and in fact it is this emphasis that ties OEP into the larger literature on political economy reviewed elsewhere in this volume. What remains distinctive about OEP, however, is its insistence on explicit theorizing of both interests and institutions.

3.3 International Bargaining

With domestic interests aggregated through institutions into a national "policy"—or, more accurately, a national interest or ideal point—states then bargain when necessary to influence one another's behavior and to determine the joint outcome of their actions.[12] This is the third and final step in the OEP approach.

International bargaining commonly arises when the policies of one state create externalities for others. In many situations, externalities arise from the collective choices of many small economic actors. In these so-called market failures, individually optimal choices lead to collectively suboptimal results. These are well-studied dilemmas, even if they remain difficult to resolve.[13] In other situations, however, understanding the externality requires relaxing the "small country" assumption of traditional international trade theory, which holds that any individual state's production or consumption is sufficiently small relative to world supply and demand that its actions cannot affect world prices. Under this assumption, the unilateral actions of states do not affect the welfare of others and, it follows, unilateral free trade is the first-best policy. In a world of "large" countries, on the other hand, unilateral actions can affect world prices (for at least some commodities) and, as Kyle Bagwell and Robert Staiger (2002) demonstrate, negotiated movements toward freer trade can be superior.[14] Although important, externalities are not a necessary condition for international bargaining to arise. Even when they are not directly affected by the actions of others, states may promote international norms and may be willing to pay some price to gain adherents or alter the behavior of possible violators. The effort to promote the "Washington Consensus" on development may be one example of norm-driven behavior in the IPE (Stiglitz 2002), and attempts to regulate child sex tourism

---

[12] This includes unilateral actions that impose costs or benefits on others. In this case, the absence of overt negotiations can still be understood as bargaining.

[13] Among others, see Frey 1984, ch. 7; Sandler 1997.

[14] Empirical work on the magnitude of these terms of trade effects is rare and controversial. Whalley (1985, 246) notes that tariff levels reached during the Great Depression might well have been "optimal." Given the costs of retaliatory policies adopted by many states following the Smoot–Hawley Tariff of 1930, this is implausible.

a possible second (Martin 2003).[15] Nonetheless, most theories of IPE continue to assume that bargaining occurs mostly as a result of some material externality.

Much research in OEP focuses on how international institutions, like their domestic counterparts, structure bargaining and affect outcomes. There are essentially two approaches that, as Stephen D. Krasner (1991) reminds us, capture different but complementary dimensions of the bargaining game. The first, often referred to as neoliberal institutionalism, sees institutions as sets of rules that facilitate cooperation. By providing information, creating issue linkages, and reducing transactions costs, institutions help states reach Pareto improving bargains (Bagwell and Staiger 2002; Keohane 1984). Current research has moved well beyond the sterile debates that dominated political science in the 1990s over whether international institutions "matter," and now focuses on how institutions are designed to achieve the aims of member states.[16]

A second approach focuses on bargaining over the gains from cooperation. If the first approach sees institutions as moving states closer to the Pareto frontier, this school emphasizes (the zero sum) movement along the frontier. As in most bargaining models, the key variables in this redistributive game are the relative cost of the reservation point to the parties, their time horizons (discount rates), and their ability to make credible threats and promises. James Fearon (1998) demonstrates that a long "shadow of the future," which in the first approach promotes cooperation via the folk theorem, can also inhibit cooperation by raising the stakes over which the parties are bargaining.

In focusing on distributional conflict, this second line of enquiry implies that cooperation may not necessarily improve social welfare. The logic parallels ideas first developed in the "Chicago School" of economic regulation (Peltzman 1976; Stigler 1971). Groups may use their national governments to create international institutions that limit competition and produce rents they can appropriate. Robert Bates (1997) describes the International Coffee Organization as a cartel of large coffee producers allied with the large coffee roasters in developed countries that limited supply and raised prices at the expense of coffee consumers. John Richards (1999) finds similar cartel-like behavior in the international aviation regime.

This third level of OEP, however, remains less than fully integrated into the other levels. Clearly, as Robert Putnam (1988) and Helen Milner (1997) have shown, domestic interests and institutions can affect international bargaining and cooperation. The "Schelling conjecture" that domestic constraints improve a leader's bargaining strength abroad generally appears to hold (Milner 1997; Tarar 2001). But as these examples suggest, the levels of OEP are typically assumed to cumulate in one

---

[15] We can convert normative principles into externalities simply by adding into an individual's utility function a desire, say, not to see children exploited. Yet when there is no direct or indirect impact on a person's welfare other than through the unobservable normative principle, the concept of externality is stretched almost to breaking point. Nearly any observed behavior can then be "explained" by appeal to externalities.

[16] See the special issues of *International Organization* on *Legalization and World Politics*, ed. J. Goldstein, M. Kahler, R. O. Keohane, and A.-M. Slaughter (Vol. 54, Summer 2000), and *The Rational Design of International Institutions*, ed. B. Koremenos, C. Lipson, and D. Snidal (Vol. 55, Autumn 2001).

direction—from interests to institutions to international bargaining. Less attention has been paid to how international institutions affect the constellation of domestic interests or institutions.

Perhaps most important, domestic interest models, the bedrock of the OEP approach, continue to rest exclusively on the small country assumption. To the extent that terms of trade effects are present—by no means a constant—and actions and agreements at the international level do affect relative prices, the strategic horizons of groups within countries are lengthened. No longer are groups merely struggling against domestic policy rivals, and taking the rest of the world as fixed, but they are pursuing their aims in combination with other similarly strategic actors at home and abroad. As Scott James and David Lake (1989) have shown in the case of Britain's repeal of the Corn Laws in 1846, these strategic linkages existed even in the most important unilateral trade liberalization in history.[17] The terms of trade effects on others were not the primary reason behind repeal. But British free traders nonetheless understood that eliminating tariffs on grain would benefit farmers in the American Midwest and, hopefully, lead them to defect from their protectionist coalition with the northeastern industrialists for a free trade coalition with the cotton-exporting South. With repeal, this realignment did, in fact, occur and led to the passage of the dramatically freer trade Walker Tariff by Congress later that same year.

Integrating terms of trade effects into models of domestic interest formulation is, in my view, the most important research frontier in OEP. As noted above, HST and the concerns that gave rise to that theory resonate with contemporary attempts to theorize more rigorously about how national actions affect relative international prices and how these prices, in turn, alter domestic interests and policy. Although the prior focus on hegemony failed to mature into sound theory, this earlier work may yet prove to be fertile soil for new models of international bargaining in IPE.

4 Beyond the State (of the Art)

There are many research frontiers in IPE, including those already noted above. In this closing section, I highlight three topics that are emerging as important areas of research that will, I expect, attract considerable attention in the years ahead. The issue areas, moreover, are not now linked to OEP, but are compatible with that approach and would benefit from a self-conscious application of its insights.

4.1 Endogenous State Formation

International trade theory assumes that state size is fixed and exogenous, even though the size of a country's internal market is a primary determinant of the relative gains

---

[17] The definitive study of the repeal of the Corn Laws from an OEP approach is Schonhardt-Bailey 2006. Nye 1991 argues that repeal was not a dramatic policy reversal and that, in fact, French tariffs were lower than Britain's throughout this period.

from international exchange. We also know that state size is highly variable across countries and over time. Indeed, the average size of states more than doubled over the nineteenth century, paralleling the rise in overseas empires, and then shrank back to previous levels (Lake and O'Mahony 2004), all the while approximating a log-normal distribution (Cederman 2003). Relaxing the assumption of static borders, allowing states to vary in size, and explaining the observed variations is a critically important question not only for policy-makers who are concerned with the future of states, but also for analysts attempting to understand better political and economic outcomes.

In recent years, several models have been introduced to explain the size of states. This literature is reviewed more extensively in the chapter by Enrico Spolaore in this volume. The best known of these models, developed by Alberto Alesina and Spolaore (2003), rests on the intuition that the per capita costs of government fall with state size, while preference heterogeneity and, thus, dissatisfaction with the uniform policies of the central government increases with size. Larger states distribute the costs of public goods over more taxpayers, create greater military power to fight or deter others, prosper from larger internal markets, and insure against regional economic fluctuations, but are limited by more citizens who desire different baskets of these goods. Alesina and Spolaore predict that democratization, trade liberalization, and the reduction of warfare will lead to a world of smaller states, whereas protectionism, autocracy, and wars will produce larger states.

The models developed thus far are, for the most part, functionalist and expect only that states will evolve toward their most efficient size. At most, political institutions vary, in a gross way, from democratic to autocratic ideal types. Richer and, hopefully, more empirically robust models can be built on the insights of OEP. Rather than relying on highly abstract assumptions that restrict preferences to vary in an orderly way over an even plane, OEP suggests which groups in which countries ought to be most supportive of, say, broader confederations or, conversely, of secession and smaller states. Extending Mundell's (1957) equivalence theorem further, the central tenets of OEP appear to imply that scarce factors of production should prefer smaller, and more abundant factors should favor larger states, contingent on the level of international openness. Similarly, institutions that privilege one group or another should also influence state size in systematic ways. Analyzing the distributional implications of state size may well propel this nascent literature in important new directions.

4.2 Global Governance

Many analysts expect globalization to transform the structure of global governance. Continuing a theme first raised by interdependence theorists in the early 1970s on the imminent demise of the nation state, globalization today is seen as forcing a convergence of state institutions and practices, often in a lowest common denominator "race-to-the-bottom," and prompting significant shifts in sites of political authority upwards to newly empowered supranational institutions, downwards to revitalized regions, provinces, and municipalities, and laterally to private corporations and non-governmental organizations that acquire previously "public" responsibilities.

These trends are poorly documented—often resting on just a couple of vivid anecdotes—and controversial. Explanations tend toward the journalistic, of which Friedman's (2000) description of globalization as a "golden straitjacket" is perhaps the best known. Like models of endogenous state formation, the evolving structure of global governance is typically explained in functional or efficiency terms.

Once again, however, OEP provides a more political way of understanding and, hopefully, explaining trends in governance. As Miles Kahler and David Lake (2003) suggest, OEP provides a useful foundation for theory-building. Paraphrasing the Prussian military strategist Carl von Clausewitz, they begin from the premiss that governance is politics by other means. If economic integration produces distributive outcomes that favor some groups and disadvantage others, political actors will possess distinct preferences over policies toward globalization itself (more or less economic openness) and policies to redistribute the benefits of globalization. Since institutions shape the politics of choice and the outcomes observed, concerned parties will attempt to align governance structures with their interests. That is, the politics of designing, building, and overturning institutions of governance at all levels is really about policy choices. Thus, debates about convergence, or its absence, and alternative sites of political authority are typically struggles over institutions that will produce results favoring some groups or interests at the expense of others. In this way, issues of global governance can be brought into the purview of OEP, with the nature and effects of institutions themselves being the object of struggle rather than policy per se.

Kahler and Lake (2003) outline how OEP can be applied to questions of global governance, but there are many fruitful areas for continuing research. Critical questions focus on the coalitional and institutional characteristics that allow the losers from policy at the national level to succeed in shifting policy to another arena. When is a political minority at one level likely to be a majority at another? Do institutions like "supremacy" and "direct effect," which have been so important in allowing disaffected groups to sidestep their national legislatures and affect policy through the European Court of Justice, generalize outside the European Union (Alter 1998)? Overall, it is obvious why the losers would want to shift the site of governance, but why would the national-level winners allow this to occur? Specifying when and how such shifts in the sites of governance occur remains a serious task.

4.3 Political Economy of Conflict

In recent years, political scientists have drawn upon similar work in economics (Hirshleifer 1987, ch. 10) to construct what is widely known as the rationalist approach to war (RAW). This emergent literature is reviewed in Part XII of this volume. Briefly, RAW describes war and civil war as "bargaining failures." Like strikes (Ashenfelter and Johnson 1969) or court battles (Schweizer 1989), wars are costly to all participants and, therefore, Pareto improving bargains that the parties would prefer to actually fighting must always exist. Violence arises when (1) at least one party possesses private information with incentives to misrepresent its knowledge, (2) at least one party cannot make a credible commitment to the possible bargain, or (3) the issue under dispute is indivisible, sufficiently lumpy to preclude satisfactory division, or not amenable to side payments (Fearon 1995). RAW has revolutionized the study of war and civil war and stimulated important new research agendas.[18]

This approach, however, typically treats states—or, in the case of civil wars, the "sides"—as unitary actors. For many disputes, this may be a reasonable assumption. As above, the test of this analytic simplification is whether it is plausible to assume that all individuals who comprise the relevant unit share relatively similar preferences. OEP suggests several ways, however, in which the core logic of RAW can be usefully applied at a more disaggregated group level. First, the issues under dispute may have distributional implications for groups within states (sides). Depending on the relative scarcity of land, for instance, traditional aristocracies may have more or less intense preferences for territorial expansion—providing a firmer footing for Schumpeter's (1951) famous explanation of imperialism as the product of "atavistic elites." In addition, although the state (side) as a whole might lose from fighting, particular groups may benefit, especially if they succeed in redistributing the costs of war onto others. Even groups that themselves receive no direct benefit from the forcible resolution of a dispute may still gain from forming a redistributive majority coalition (Snyder 1991; Solingen 1998).

Second, war may impose differential costs on groups within a state (side). As Rogowski (1989) notes, war typically represses international trade, lowering returns to the abundant factor of production and, over time, decreasing its political power (Lobell 2003). Similarly, if there is a single "best practice" in warfare, not only will states (sides) whose factor endowments are favored by the technology have a lower relative cost for war but mobilization will penalize some groups and benefit others disproportionately (Rowe 1999). The current revolution in military affairs, for example, promotes a capital-intensive form of warfare that benefits rich, developed countries overall and disproportionately rewards owners of capital within those states.

The basic notion that issues in dispute and war itself have differential effects on groups has long been prominent in the literature on conflict. But until now, analysts have identified groups inductively and have lacked any theoretical means for identifying appropriate groups and their interests. OEP provides a solid foundation on which to rebuild this old insight in new and, hopefully, more productive directions. RAW, in turn, has not yet begun to incorporate group differences into its theoretical core. Marrying OEP to RAW promises to open new and important research avenues.

5 CONCLUSION

In three short decades, but a moment in academic time, IPE has grown into a true interdiscipline, combining some of the best of political science and economics.

---

[18] Reviewed in Reiter 2003.

From a welter of competing approaches, IPE has now centered on, if you will, a hegemonic approach that structures knowledge, generates puzzles, and identifies areas likely to yield profitable future research. Despite its successes, OEP is not perfect. Many refinements and extensions are possible and, indeed, can be expected in the years ahead. Nonetheless, OEP is a powerful approach that promises future rewards.

The sources of this success are threefold, and may be usefully emulated by other sub-fields and approaches. First, OEP is disciplined by a strong empirical foundation. From its inception, IPE has focused on historical trends in the international economy, both political and economic. Analysts have generally been careful not to mistake a single cross-section for all possible states of the world, but have mined the rich history available to them to test their theories. In turn, considerable attention has been devoted to developing appropriate indicators of trade protection, non-tariff barriers to trade, exchange rate regimes, and so on. Where IPE was originally constrained to case studies or, at best, statistical tests based on very limited data, some of the best new research employs very large time series data-sets and powerful econometric tools. Whatever the method, however, IPE remains a strongly empirical science.

Second, OEP emphasizes deductive rigor. Political scientists, especially, have benefited from powerful theories developed in economics. Economists, in turn, have been prompted to take politics and political institutions seriously, and to integrate realistic understandings of political processes into their models. Scholarly debate has forced all to clarify the assumptions they make, revealing strengths and limitations, and to state propositions in clear and falsifiable ways, thereby opening arguments to empirical test. By working within agreed standards of scientific enquiry, scholarly interactions and cumulative knowledge are facilitated.

Finally, OEP draws upon and is integrated into broader bodies of theory. Theorists have grounded their analyses in the pure theory of international trade, theories of collective action, and theories of political institutions—all developed in larger disciplines and for other purposes. This not only links OEP to broader research programs and facilitates cross-fertilization, but prevents analysts from reinventing the wheel each time they sit down at their computers.

Norms of theoretical rigor disciplined by empirical facts are now deeply inculcated in scholars of IPE. For the same reasons that substantial intellectual progress has occurred in the past, I remain optimistic about the future of this emerging inter-discipline.

References

ABDELAL, R. 2001. *National Purpose in the World Economy*. Ithaca, NY: Cornell University Press.
ALESINA, A., and SPOLAORE, E. 2003. *The Size of Nations*. Cambridge, Mass.: MIT Press.
ALTER, K. J. 1998. Who are the "masters of the treaty?" European governments and the European Court of Justice. *International Organization*, 52: 121–47.

ASHENFELTER, O. A., and JOHNSON, G. E. 1969. Bargaining theory, trade unions, and industrial strike activity. *American Economic Review*, 59: 35–49.

BAGWELL, K., and STAIGER, R. W. 2002. *The Economics of the World Trading System*. Cambridge, Mass.: MIT Press.

BALDWIN, R. E. 1985. *The Political Economy of U.S. Import Policy*. Cambridge, Mass.: MIT Press.

——and MAGEE, S. P. 2000. Is trade policy for sale? Congressional voting on recent trade bills. *Public Choice*, 105: 79–101.

BATES, R. H. 1997. *Open-Economy Politics: The Political Economy of the World Coffee Trade*. Princeton, NJ: Princeton University Press.

BAUER, R. A., POOL, I DE S., and DEXTER, A. 1972. *American Business and Public Policy*, 2nd edn. Chicago: Aldine-Atherton.

CAPORASO, J. A., and LEVINE, D. P. 1992. *Theories of Political Economy*. New York: Cambridge University Press.

CARDOSO, F. H., and FALETTO, E. 1979. *Dependency and Development in Latin America*. Berkeley: University of California Press.

CASSING, J. H., McKEOWN, T. J., and OCHS, J. 1986. The political economy of the tariff cycle. *American Political Science Review*, 80: 843–62.

CAVES, R. E. 1976. Economic models of political choice: Canada's tariff structure. *Canadian Journal of Economics*, 9: 278–300.

CEDERMAN, L.-E. 2003. Generating state-size distributions: a geopolitical model. Unpublished manuscript, Zurich.

COOPER, R. N. 1968. *The Economics of Interdependence: Economic Policy in the Atlantic Community*. New York: McGraw-Hill.

COWHEY, P. F. 1993. Domestic institutions and the credibility of international commitments: Japan and the United States. *International Organization*, 47: 299–326.

FEARON, J. D. 1995. Rationalist explanations for war. *International Organization*, 49: 379–414.

——1998. Bargaining, enforcement, and international cooperation. *International Organization*, 52: 269–305.

FRANK, A. G. 1966. The development of underdevelopment. *Monthly Review*, 28: 17–31.

FREY, B. S. 1984. *International Political Economics*. New York: Basil Blackwell.

FRIEDEN, J. A. 1988a. Capital politics: creditors and the international political economy. *Journal of Public Policy*, 8: 265–86.

——1988b. Sectoral conflict and U.S. foreign economic policy, 1914–1940. *International Organization*, 42: 59–90.

——1991. Invested interests: the politics of national economic policies in a world of global finance. *International Organization*, 45: 425–51.

——1997. Monetary populism in nineteenth-century America: an open economy interpretation. *Journal of Economic History*, 57: 367–95.

——1999. Actors and preferences in international relations. Pp. 39–76 in *Strategic Choice and International Relations*, ed. D. A. Lake and R. Powell. Princeton, NJ: Princeton University Press.

FRIEDMAN, T. L. 2000. *The Lexus and the Olive Tree: Understanding Globalization*, updated and expanded edn. New York: Anchor.

FURTADO, C. 1973. The concept of external dependence in the study of underdevelopment. Pp. 118–23 in *The Political Economy of Development and Underdevelopment*, ed. C. K. Wilber. New York: Random House.

GARRETT, G. 1998. *Partisan Politics in the Global Economy*. New York: Cambridge University Press.

GILPIN, R. 1972. The politics of transnational economic relations. Pp. 48–69 in *Transnational Relations and World Politics*, ed. R. O. Keohane and J. S. Nye. Cambridge, Mass.: Harvard University Press.

—— 1975. *U.S. Power and the Multinational Corporation: The Political Economy of Foreign Direct Investment*. New York: Basic Books.

—— 1977. Economic interdependence and national security in historical perspective. Pp. 19–66 in *Economic Issues and National Security*, ed. K. Knorr and F. N. Trager. Lawrence: Regents Press of Kansas.

—— 1987. *The Political Economy of International Relations*. Princeton, NJ: Princeton University Press.

GOLDSTEIN, J. 1988. Ideas, institutions, and American trade policy. *International Organization*, 42: 179–217.

GOUREVITCH, P. A. 1977. International trade, domestic coalitions, and liberty: comparative responses to the crisis of 1873–1896. *Journal of Interdisciplinary History*, 8: 281–300.

—— 1986. *Politics in Hard Times: Comparative Responses to International Economic Crises*. Ithaca, NY: Cornell University Press.

GOWA, J. 1983. *Closing the Gold Window: Domestic Politics and the End of Bretton Woods*. Ithaca, NY: Cornell University Press.

—— 1994. *Allies, Adversaries, and International Trade*. Princeton, NJ: Princeton University Press.

GROSSMAN, G. M., and HELPMAN, E. 1994. Protection for sale. *American Economic Review*, 84: 833–50.

—— —— 2002. *Interest Groups and Trade Policy*. Princeton, NJ: Princeton University Press.

HAGGARD, S. 1990. *Pathways from the Periphery: The Newly Industrializing Countries in the International System*. Ithaca, NY: Cornell University Press.

HIRSHLEIFER, J. 1987. *Economic Behavior in Adversity*. Chicago: University of Chicago Press.

HISCOX, M. J. 2002. *International Trade and Political Conflict: Commerce, Coalitions, and Mobility*. Princeton, NJ: Princeton University Press.

IKENBERRY, G. J., LAKE, D. A., and MASTANDUNO, M. (eds.). 1988. *The State and American Foreign Economic Policy*. Ithaca, NY: Cornell University Press.

JAMES, S., and LAKE, D. A. 1989. The second face of hegemony: Britain's repeal of the Corn Laws and the American Walker Tariff of 1846. *International Organization*, 43: 1–29.

KAHLER, M., and LAKE, D. A. (eds.). 2003. *Governance in a Global Economy: Political Authority in Transition*. Princeton, NJ: Princeton University Press.

KATZENSTEIN, P. J. (ed.). 1978. *Between Power and Plenty: Foreign Economic Policies of Advanced Industrial States*. Madison: University of Wisconsin Press.

—— 1985. *Small States in World Markets: Industrial Policy in Europe*. Ithaca, NY: Cornell University Press.

KEOHANE, R. O. 1984. *After Hegemony: Cooperation and Discord in the World Political Economy*. Princeton, NJ: Princeton University Press.

—— and NYE, J. S., JR. (eds.). 1972. *Transnational Relations and World Politics*. Cambridge, Mass: Harvard University Press.

—— —— 1977. *Power and Interdependence: World Politics in Transition*. Boston: Little, Brown.

KINDLEBERGER, C. P. 1951. Group behavior and international trade. *Journal of Political Economy*, 59: 30–46.

—— 1969. *American Business Abroad*. New Haven, Conn.: Yale University Press.

—— 1973. *The World in Depression, 1929–1939*. Berkeley: University of California Press.

Krasner, S. D. 1976. State power and the structure of international trade. *World Politics*, 28: 317–47.
—— (ed.) 1983. *International Regimes*. Ithaca, NY: Cornell University Press.
—— 1991. Global communications and national power: life on the Pareto frontier. *World Politics*, 43: 336–66.
Lake, D. A. 1988. *Power, Protection, and Free Trade: The International Sources of American Commercial Strategy, 1887–1939*. Ithaca, NY: Cornell University Press.
—— 1993. Leadership, hegemony, and the international economy: naked emperor or tattered monarch with potential? *International Studies Quarterly*, 37: 459–89.
—— and O'Mahony, A. 2004. The incredible shrinking state: explaining change in the territorial size of countries. *Journal of Conflict Resolution*, 48: 699–722.
—— and Powell, R. 1999. *Strategic Choice and International Relations*. Princeton, NJ: Princeton University Press.
Lavergne, R. P. 1983. *The Political Economy of U.S. Tariffs: An Empirical Analysis*. Toronto: Academic Press.
Lobell, S. E. 2003. *The Challenge of Hegemony: Grand Strategy, Trade, and Domestic Politics*. Ann Arbor: University of Michigan Press.
MacIntyre, A. 2001. Institutions and investors: the politics of economic crisis in Southeast Asia. *International Organization*, 55: 81–122.
McKeown, T. J. 1984. Firms and tariff regime change: explaining the demand for protection. *World Politics*, 36: 215–33.
Magee, S. P. 1980. Three simple tests of the Stolper–Samuelson theorem. Pp. 138–53 in *Issues in International Economics*, ed. P. Oppenheimer. London: Oriel Press.
Magee, S. P., Brock, W. A., and Young, L. 1989. *Black Hole Tariffs and Endogenous Policy Theory: Political Economy in General Equilibrium*. New York: Cambridge University Press.
Marini, R. M. 1972. Brazilian subimperialism. *Monthly Review*, 23: 14–24.
Martin, L. L. 2003. The leverage of economic theories: explaining governance in an internationalized industry. Pp. 33–59 in *Governance in a Global Economy: Political Authority in Transition*, ed. M. Kahler and D. A. Lake. Princeton, NJ: Princeton University Press.
Milner, H. V. 1988. *Resisting Protectionism: Global Industries and the Politics of International Trade*. Princeton, NJ: Princeton University Press.
—— 1997. *Interests, Institutions, and Information: Domestic Politics and International Relations*. Princeton, NJ: Princeton University Press.
Mundell, R. A. 1957. International trade and factor mobility. *American Economic Review*, 47: 321–35.
Nye, J. V. 1991. The myth of free-trade Britain and Fortress France: tariffs and trade in the nineteenth century. *Journal of Economic History*, 51: 23–46.
O'Mahony, A. 2003. Monetary regimes: the interrelated choice of monetary policy and the exchange rate. Ph.D. dissertation, University of California, San Diego.
Pahre, R. 1999. *Leading Questions: How Hegemony Affects the International Political Economy*. Ann Arbor: University of Michigan Press.
Palma, G. 1978. Dependency: a formal theory of underdevelopment or a methodology for the analysis of concrete situations of dependency. *World Development*, 6: 881–924.
Peltzman, S. 1976. Towards a more general theory of regulation. *Journal of Law and Economics*, 19: 211–40.
Pincus, J. J. 1975. Pressure groups and the pattern of tariffs. *Journal of Political Economy*, 83: 757–78.

PINTO, P. M. 2004. Domestic coalitions and the political economy of foreign direct investment. Ph.D. dissertation, University of California, San Diego.

PREBISCH, R. 1964. *Towards a New Trade Policy for Development*. New York: United Nations.

PREEG, E. H. 1970. *Traders and Diplomats: An Analysis of the Kennedy Round of Negotiations under the General Agreement on Tariffs and Trade*. Washington, DC: Brookings Institution.

PUTNAM, R. D. 1988. Diplomacy and domestic politics: the logic of two-level games. *International Organization*, 42: 427–60.

RAMSEYER, J. M., and ROSENBLUTH, F. M. 1993. *Japan's Political Marketplace*. Cambridge, Mass.: Harvard University Press.

REITER, D. 2003. Exploring the bargaining model of war. *Perspectives on Politics*, 1: 27–43.

RICHARDS, J. 1999. Toward a positive theory of international institutions: regulating international aviation markets. *International Organization*, 53: 1–37.

RODRIK, D. 1997. *Has Globalization Gone Too Far?* Washington, DC: Institute for International Economics.

ROGOWSKI, R. 1987. Trade and the variety of democratic institutions. *International Organization*, 41: 203–23.

——1989. *Commerce and Coalitions: How Trade Affects Domestic Political Alignments*. Princeton, NJ: Princeton University Press.

——1999. Institutions as constraints on strategic choice. Pp. 115–36 in *Strategic Choice and International Relations*, ed. D. A. Lake and R. Powell. Princeton, NJ: Princeton University Press.

ROWE, D. M. 1999. World economic expansion and national security in pre-World War I Europe. *International Organization*, 53: 195–231.

RUGGIE, J. G. 1983. International regimes, transactions, and change: embedded liberalism in the postwar economic order. Pp. 195–231 in *International Regimes*, ed. by S. D. Krasner. Ithaca, NY: Cornell University Press.

SANDLER, T. 1997. *Global Challenges: An Approach to Environmental, Political, and Economic Problems*. New York: Cambridge University Press.

SCHATTSCHNEIDER, E. E. 1935. *Politics, Pressures, and the Tariff*. New York: Prentice Hall.

SCHONHARDT-BAILEY, C. 2006. *From the Corn Laws to Free Trade: Interests, Ideas, and Institutions in Historical Perspective*. Cambridge, Mass.: MIT Press.

SCHUMPETER, J. A. 1951. *Imperialism and Social Classes*, trans. H. Norden. New York: A. M. Kelley.

SCHWEIZER, U. 1989. Litigation and settlement under two-sided incomplete information. *Review of Economic Studies*, 56: 163–77.

SIMMONS, B. A., and ELKINS, Z. 2003. Globalization and policy diffusion: explaining three decades of liberalization. Pp. 275–304 in *Governance in a Global Economy: Political Authority in Transition*, ed. M. Kahler and D. A. Lake. Princeton, NJ: Princeton University Press.

SNIDAL, D. 1985. The limits of hegemonic stability theory. *International Organization*, 39: 579–614.

SNYDER, J. 1991. *Myths of Empire: Domestic Politics and International Ambition*. Ithaca, NY: Cornell University Press.

SOLINGEN, E. 1998. *Regional Orders at Century's Dawn: Global and Domestic Influences on Grand Strategy*. Princeton, NJ: Princeton University Press.

STIGLER, G. J. 1971. The theory of economic regulation. *Bell Journal of Economic and Management Science*, 2: 3–21.

STIGLITZ, J. E. 2002. *Globalization and its Discontents*. New York: W. W. Norton.

STOLPER, W., and SAMUELSON, P. A. 1941. Protection and real wages. *Review of Economic Studies*, 9: 58–73.

SUNKEL, O. 1969. National development policy and external dependence in Latin America. *Journal of Development Studies*, 6: 23–48.
TARAR, A. 2001. International bargaining with two-sided domestic constraints. *Journal of Conflict Resolution*, 45: 320–40.
TRIFFIN, R. 1960. *Gold and the Dollar Crisis*. New Haven, Conn.: Yale University Press.
VERDIER, D. 1994. *Democracy and International Trade: Britain, France, and the United States, 1860-1990*. Princeton, NJ: Princeton University Press.
WHALLEY, J. 1985. *Trade Liberalization among Major World Trading Areas*. Cambridge, Mass.: MIT Press.
WILLIAMSON, O. E. 1985. *The Economic Institutions of Capitalism: Firms, Markets, and Relational Contracting*. New York: Free Press.
YARBROUGH, B. V., and YARBROUGH, R. M. 1992. *Cooperation and Governance in International Trade: The Strategic Organizational Approach*. Princeton, NJ: Princeton University Press.

CHAPTER 43

NATIONAL BORDERS AND THE SIZE OF NATIONS

ENRICO SPOLAORE

1 INTRODUCTION

THE formation, consolidation, and break-up of states has been at the center of human history for thousands of years, from Hammurabi's unification of Mesopotamia to the recent collapse of the Soviet Union and Yugoslavia. Currently in the world there are almost 200 nations, some as large as China or India, others as small as San Marino or Tuvalu.[1]

Questions on the number and size of states have been debated for almost as long as states themselves exist.[2] Plato in *The Laws* even calculated the "optimal size" of a polity (5,040 heads of family), although he also pointed out that "the number of citizens should be sufficient to defend themselves against the injustice of their neighbors." Aristotle in *The Politics* argued that a state should be no larger than a size in which everybody knows each other, and claimed that "experience has shown that it is difficult, if not impossible, for a populous state to be run by good laws." Montesquieu in *The Spirit of the Laws* wrote that "in a small republic, the public good

---

* I am grateful to the University of Munich's Center for Economic Studies (CES) for its hospitality while I completed the first draft of this chapter. I thank the editors, and seminar participants at George Mason University, for useful comments. The usual disclaimer applies.

[1] By "nation" in this chapter we mean internationally recognized "sovereign state," as commonly understood in English when one speaks of inter*national* trade or United *Nations*.

[2] For a discussion of the older political literature on the size of states see Dahl and Tufte 1973. Historical studies of nationalism include Hobsbawn 1990 and Anderson 1991.

is more strongly felt, better known, and closer to each citizen." Issues of "optimal" size and centralization were at the core of the debate during the American Constitutional Convention in 1787, when Madison and the other Federalists provided celebrated arguments in defense of a large federal polity against the objections of the Anti-Federalists.

Sovereignty, independence, and border redrawing have been paramount issues throughout the nineteenth and twentieth centuries, and remain very prominent today, from Quebec to the Basque countries and Catalonia, from Ireland to Belgium and Corsica, from the Middle East to Kashmir and Indonesia.

While these issues have traditionally been the preserve of political philosophers and historians, in recent years they have also been addressed by a growing analytical literature within political economy. Understanding the formation and break-up of nations is a natural development of political economy's research program. A central goal of contemporary political economy is the endogenization of political institutions, and sovereign states are perhaps the most important political institutions in the world.

2 Literature on Size of Nations and Related Areas of Research

In this chapter I will briefly review some ideas and results from the political economy literature on the size of nations. Earlier contributions are Friedman (1977) and Wittman (1991). More recent analytical work includes Alesina and Spolaore (1997, 2003, 2005, 2006), Alesina, Spolaore, and Wacziarg (2000, 2005), Bolton and Roland (1997), Bordignon and Brusco (2001), Casella (2001), Casella and Feinstein (2003), Dagan and Volij (2000), Ellingsen (1998), Findlay (1996), Goyal and Staal (2004), LeBreton and Weber (2001, 2003), Haimanko, LeBreton, and Weber (2005), Spolaore (1995, 2004), and Wittman (2000), among others. An earlier discussion of the literature is provided by Bolton, Roland and Spolaore (1996). Alesina and Spolaore (2003) cover most of the materials discussed in this chapter and also provide discussions of the empirical and historical evidence, which must be omitted here because of space limitations.

Recent contributions have studied the determination and change of political borders in different political and economic environments, and using various concepts of solutions and equilibria. For example, in his pioneering paper Friedman (1977) studied the formation of borders as set by rent-maximizing Leviathans. Bolton and Roland (1997) studied the break-up of nations by direct majority vote, when income distributions differ across regions, and median voters in different regions have different preferences over redistribution policies. LeBreton and Weber (2003) among others have analyzed equilibria when groups of individuals can secede unilaterally and form their own country. Wittman (2000) has focused on efficient (i.e. welfare-maximizing) solutions. In Alesina and Spolaore (1997, 2003) the number and size of countries have been derived and compared under different solution concepts: efficient borders, voting equilibria, equilibria under unilateral secessions, and equilibria in a world of rent-maximizing Leviathans.

The recent political economy literature on national borders is connected to other related bodies of research. An important link is to the literature on local public goods and clubs, pioneered by Tiebout (1956) and Buchanan (1965).[3] In Buchanan's analysis, clubs are modeled as voluntary associations in which individuals have identical tastes for both public and private goods. The optimal club size is determined where the marginal cost of an additional member from crowding equals the reduction in the other members' dues from spreading the fixed costs of the public goods over the extra club member.[4] In Tiebout's analysis, different bundles of public goods are offered at different locations, and people sort themselves in homogeneous local "clubs" by voting with their feet. A necessary condition to ensure global optimality in a Tiebout world is the absence of economies of scale in producing the public good.

There are many points of contact between the literature on clubs and local public goods and the literature on nations: in a way nations, from a global perspective, do provide "local" public goods. However, national public goods—unlike local public goods—have high economies of scale from sharing the costs with a large population. Moreover, in the traditional theory of local public goods local jurisdictions are not completely autonomous, while the analysis of nations explicitly focuses on *sovereign* states that can impose direct barriers to economic exchange and/or use force in settling disputes with their neighbors.[5]

The literature on the formation of nations is also linked to the large literature on customs unions, trade blocs, and preferential trade agreements.[6] Modern national states tend to promote free trade within their own borders, while all their regions tend to face the same barriers to trade with other countries. In that respect, countries can be seen as "trade blocs" of regions. On the other hand, countries are much more than trade blocs: they are not only economically integrated, but also politically integrated. In fact, one could think of free trade areas, customs unions, supranational associations, and sovereign states as points on a continuum of increasing coordination and integration of political functions. Hence, while the study of nation formation and break-up benefits from a close connection to the analysis of trade blocs, the study of trade blocs could also benefit from using some of the tools, concepts, and results

---

[3] This literature studies public goods that are jointly supplied but excludable either through some technological device or because of spatial distance. For a survey see Inman and Rubinfeld 1997 and Scotchmer 2002. Schmidtchen 1994 explicitly studies national borders in the context of Buchanan's theory of clubs and constitutional rules.

[4] The stable distribution of club sizes and benefits was studied in classic contributions by Pauly 1967, 1970. Formally, this approach to voluntary clubs is analogous to the study of the core with externalities.

[5] An interesting approach to jurisdictions based on voluntary association has been proposed by Frey and Eichenberger 1999, who have stressed voluntary mechanisms for the creation of clubs of public goods (their "functional, overlapping,and competing jurisdictions," or FOJC). Issues of legal monopoly of coercion and free riding are usually not addressed in this context.

[6] The classical reference is Viner 1950. For a survey of the literature see, for instance, Baldwin and Venables 1995.

developed in the study of nations. The European Union, with its intermediate nature between a free-trade area and a fully-fledged political union, represents a promising case study.[7]

A third body of research that is highly relevant for the study of nations is the economic analysis of conflict and appropriation, developed by Boulding (1962), Tullock (1974), Hirshleifer (1989, 1991, 1995a, 1995b), Grossman (1991), Skaperdas (1992), and others. This work is also related to the formal study of conflict by international relations scholars (see Powell 1999). Links between this formal literature on conflict and the study of the size of nations have been developed by Wittman (2000) and Alesina and Spolaore (2005, 2006). While in most formal work on conflict and wars the identity and number of agents and groups engaging in conflict have to be taken as given, the fundamental objective of the literature on nations is to endogenize those collective organizations. In this respect, the literature on nations is related to the literature on the formation of military alliances, from which it differs for its focus on centralization of defense in sovereign institutions (nations).[8] The mechanisms through which governments manage (or fail) to establish an effective monopoly on the means of coercion within their borders is an important area of enquiry that is likely to receive increasing attention in the future.

3 BENEFITS AND COSTS OF NATIONAL SIZE

When considering the equilibrium size of nations, a natural starting point is the trade-off between benefits and costs from a larger size. There are several benefits from a larger national size. A key role for nations is the provision of a set of public goods to their citizens. The per capita cost of many public goods is lower in larger countries, where more taxpayers pay for them. Economies of scale can be expected in the provision of general-policy coordination and administration, defense and foreign policy, a legal and judicial system, police and crime prevention, a monetary and financial system, infrastructure for communications, public health, and so on. Empirically, the share of government spending over GDP is decreasing in population (smaller countries have larger governments).[9] Larger countries can also better internalize cross-regional externalities, a point extensively studied in the literature on decentralization and fiscal federalism.[10] An additional benefit from size comes from insurance via interregional transfers. When international capital markets are imperfect, larger countries can better provide insurance to regions affected by imperfectly

---

[7] On European integration see, for example, Alesina and Wacziarg 1999; Alesina and Spolaore 2003, ch 12. See also the chapter on the political economy of European integration by Eichengreen in this volume. For a discussion of the effects of European integration on European nation states and regions, see Drèze 1993.

[8] A classic reference is Olson and Zeckhauser 1966. A survey is provided by Murdoch 1995.

[9] See Alesina and Wacziarg 1998; Alesina and Spolaore 2003, ch 10.

[10] For a survey see Oates 1999.

correlated shocks. Larger countries can also build redistributive schemes from richer to poorer regions, therefore achieving distributions of after-tax income which would not be available to individual regions acting independently.[11] Finally, larger nations mean larger domestic markets when political borders are associated with barriers to international exchange. In principle, the size of the market may or may not coincide with the political size of a country as defined by its borders. It does coincide with it if a country is completely autarkic; that is, if it does not engage in exchanges of goods or factors of production with the rest of the world. By contrast, market size and political size would be uncorrelated in a world of perfect free trade in which political borders imposed no costs on international transactions. So, in models in which the scale of markets matters, market size depends both on country size and on the trade regime. In a regime of free trade, small countries can prosper, while in a world of trade barriers, being large is much more important for economic success.[12]

Size also comes with costs. As countries become larger, administrative and congestion costs may overcome the benefits of size mentioned above. More importantly, larger populations are associated with higher heterogeneity of preferences of different individuals. Being part of the same country implies sharing jointly supplied public goods and policies in ways that cannot satisfy everybody's preferences. Decentralization of some public goods and policies can offer a partial response to such heterogeneity. The current move towards decentralization in many parts of the world has been partly explained as a response to increasing secessionist pressures.[13] Nonetheless, some essential national policies that characterize a sovereign state (defense, foreign policy, basic characteristics of the legal system) are indivisible and must be shared among the whole population. The costs of heterogeneity in the population have been documented empirically in a recent literature on the political and economic effects of ethnolinguistic fractionalization, which is shown to be inversely related to measures of economic performance, economic freedom, and quality of government.[14] As noted by Wittman (2000), such political costs are likely to depend not only on the degree of heterogeneity of preferences, but also on the quality of institutions through which preferences are mediated and turned into policy. While in some societies and political systems there exist effective mechanisms to integrate populations with diverse preferences, in other societies heterogeneity brings about high political and economic costs. On the other hand, the quality of institutions itself is likely to depend on heterogeneity of preferences.[15] Further research is needed to provide insights and evidence on the complex relationships and causal links among heterogeneity of preferences, formation of jurisdictions, and the nature and quality of political institutions.

[11] However, as we will see below, these redistribution schemes may also induce political fragmentation when there is political disagreement between voters in different regions. Redistribution also increases the possibility of wasteful rent-seeking.
[12] This point will be further discussed in Section 8
[13] See Bardhan 2002; de Figueiredo and Weingast 2002.
[14] See Easterly and Levine 1997; La Porta et al. 1999; Alesina et al. 2003.
[15] Moreover, heterogeneity of preferences in the long run may be an endogenous function of variables under the direct or indirect control of the government (see Alesina and Spolaore 2003, 76–8).

4 Borders, Voting, and Efficiency in a Simple Framework

In this section we will present a simple analytical framework for understanding some basic issues about the formation and break-up of nations.[16]

We assume that governments come in different "types," with different legal structures, different policies, different official languages, etc. To keep things simple, we collapse all these characterictics into one dimension, and denote a "type" of government as a point on the interval $[0, 1]$. For instance, we can say that a country has a government of "type 1/4" while another country has a government of "type 3/4." We assume that physical space is also unidimensional, and all individuals are distributed over a unidimensional interval, also denoted by $[0, 1]$. So, we can say that Mr X is "located" at 1/4 while Ms Y is "located" at 3/4. Finally, we assume that there exists a *perfect correlation* between an individual's location and his or her most preferred type of government. This means that Mr X, who is located at 1/4, prefers a government of type 1/4, while Ms Y, who is located at 3/4, prefers a government of type 3/4. To fix ideas, picture the interval as the East Coast of the United States between Boston and Savannah, and assume that all the American population is located along that coast (not a bad approximation for the USA right after independence in 1776). Interpret the "type" of government as the location of the country's "capital city." A perfect correlation between an individual's location and his or her preference for the "type of government" means that people in Boston would like a "Bostonian" type of government, with "Bostonian" policies, laws, rules, and rights. An independent country with the "capital city" in Boston would be a country with the type of government most preferred by the inhabitants of Massachusetts. Bostonians would be less happy with a "New-York-City" type of government, but may still prefer that to a government "located" in South Carolina or in Georgia, which would be a "Southern" type of government. As we will see, when people with different "preferred types" form a country, their "capital city" will reflect the median preferences of the relevant population. For instance, the location of Washington, DC, and, more importantly, the "type of government" of the newly formed United States, would reflect "median" preferences for location and type of government in the original thirteen colonies.[17] Of course, we all know that the real world is not unidimensional, and geographical locations are not always perfectly correlated with ideological preferences.[18] But, as it is often the case,

---

[16] Because of space limitation, formal proofs are omitted.

[17] More precisely, the original "type of government" in the USA did not reflect the preferences of the whole population (including slaves), but of that subset of the American population with political rights and power at the time.

[18] For instance, some individuals in San Francisco may have preferences for the type of government which are "far" from those of some of their neighbors while closer to the preferences of some other individuals who live further away—say, in New York. However, political maps of the USA (and elsewhere) show a strong correlation between political preferences and geographical location. Especially strong correlations tend to hold when preferences for types of government are affected by ethnolinguistic differences across populations.

drastic analytical simplifications provide useful insights on the trade-offs involved in border formation that can generalize to more complex settings.[19] Therefore, we will assume that the whole population, of mass equal to P, is distributed over a geographical *and* ideological interval $[0, 1]$. Nations are geographically connected (no "holes"), and of size $P_1, P_2, \ldots P_j \ldots P_N$.[20]

Each individual i has income y_i and pays taxes equal to t_i. In this section we will assume that everybody has the same exogenous income y.[21] Private consumption is $c_i = y - t_i$. Public goods provide individual i with services denoted by g_i. Individual i's utility is increasing both in c_i and in g_i:

$$U_i = u(c_i) + g_i \qquad (1)$$

where $u'(c_i) > 0$ and $u''(c_i) \leq 0$. Government services have different utilities for different individuals depending on the type of public policy selected by the government. As mentioned above, each individual i's location x_i also denotes his or her preferred public policy. $\theta_{j(i)}$ is the type of public policy chosen in the country j in which individual i lives. We assume

$$g_i = g - h|x_i - \theta_{j(i)}| \qquad (2)$$

The parameter h plays a key role in the analysis of national size.[22] It captures the costs associated with policies far from one's preferred policy—e.g. the political costs from heterogeneous preferences over types of governments and public policies. The parameter h may also reflect institutional quality: a lower h can be associated with institutions that are better at reducing the political costs of heterogeneity within the population.[23]

In order to provide government services, the government of the nation j in which individual i lives must pay a cost $k_{j(i)}$, which includes a fixed part $f > 0$ and a variable part, proportional to the size of the nation $P_{j(i)}$ (the mass of nation j's population):

$$k_{j(i)} = f + v P_{j(i)} \qquad (3)$$

where v is a non-negative parameter. If the costs of government are equally shared by all citizens in the nation of size $P_{j(i)}$, we can calculate individual i's taxes by dividing

---

[19] For a broader discussion of the meaning and limits of these assumptions, see Alesina and Spolaore 2003.

[20] For example, if population P is uniformly distributed on the interval $[0, 1]$ and is divided in two countries of equal size, all people in the first country, of size $P_1 = P/2$, will be located between 0 and 1/2, and all people in the second country, also of size $P_2 = P/2$, will be located between 1/2 and 1.

[21] We will consider the case of income inequality in Section 6

[22] In the rest of the analysis we will normalize $g = 0$.

[23] As mentioned above, the model can be given a simple geographical interpretation by defining the type of a government as the "location" of the country's "capital." Then the heterogeneity costs can be reinterpreted as a political analogue of "transportation costs." See Fujita and Thisse 2002 for a useful survey of spatial models, including models of "capital cities."

the total costs $k_{j(i)}$ in equation (3) by the size of the country's population $P_{j(i)}$:

$$t_i = \frac{f}{P_{j(i)}} + v \qquad (4)$$

The parameter f captures the benefits from belonging to a larger country where the costs of government can be spread over a larger population, therefore reducing taxes per capita. For example, an individual who lives in a country that has size $P_{j(i)} = 1{,}000{,}000$ pays taxes equal to $\frac{f}{1{,}000{,}000} + v$, but an individual who lives is a *larger* country—say, twice that size, with $P_{j(i)} = 2{,}000{,}000$—pays lower taxes equal to $\frac{f}{2{,}000{,}000} + v$, because the fixed cost f is shared among twice as many people.

But a larger country also means, on average, a larger distance from a citizen's preferred policy. Suppose that the whole population P is uniformly distributed on the interval $[0, 1]$ and belongs to a unified country with one government and one public policy. A government that aims at maximizing average utility would choose the type of government preferred by the median individual, i.e. by the individual located at $1/2$. The same outcome is obtained if the type of government is chosen directly by majority vote (median voter's theorem). With a uniform distribution the government is located at $1/2$, average distance from the government is $1/4$, and average utility is:

$$U_a = u\left(y - v - \frac{f}{P}\right) - \frac{h}{4} \qquad (5)$$

Now, consider the case in which population P is divided into two countries of equal size $P/2$. Then the cost of government will increase: everybody will pay higher taxes ($\frac{2f}{P} + v$). But average distance will go down to $1/8$, because the two governments will be located at $1/4$ and $3/4$, respectively, and more people will be "closer" to each government. Average utility when the population is divided into two separate countries is given by:

$$U_b = u\left(y - v - \frac{2f}{P}\right) - \frac{h}{8} \qquad (6)$$

Let $\Delta(f, v, y)$ denote the change in utility from private consumption that each person experiences when we compare a two-country outcome and a one-country outcome:

$$\Delta\left(y, v, \frac{f}{P}\right) \equiv u\left(y - v - \frac{f}{P}\right) - u\left(y - v - \frac{2f}{P}\right) \qquad (7)$$

$\Delta(f, v, y)$ measures the net benefits (per person) from economies of scale in public-good provision: it is always non-negative, and strictly positive if and only if $f > 0$. The benefits from scale are increasing in the fixed cost of the public good f. For a positive f and a strictly concave utility function, they are also increasing in the variable cost v, because a higher v increases taxes and reduces disposable income, therefore raising the marginal utility of tax savings from unification.[24]

---

[24] For the same reason, the economies of scale in the provision of the public good have a bigger impact on utility at lower levels of income.

Average utility is higher in the unified country than in two separate countries (i.e. $U_a > U_b$) if and only if

$$\Delta\left(y, v, \frac{f}{P}\right) > \frac{h}{8} \tag{8}$$

which means that the benefits from scale $\Delta(y, v, \frac{f}{P})$ must exceed the costs associated with a higher distance from the government, measured by $h/8$. That is, the left-hand side shows the benefits from scale, and the right-hand side shows the average "heterogeneity costs." When the economies of scale are higher than the heterogeneity costs, average utility is higher in a unified country than in two separate countries. Therefore, when inequality (8) holds, it is "efficient" (i.e. average utility maximizing) to keep the country together. However, if citizens can choose whether to form one or two countries by majority vote, inefficient break-ups may occur. One can show that a majority of voters will strictly prefer a unified country to a break-up if and only if the individual at location 1/4 prefers unification; that is, if and only if:

$$\Delta\left(y, v, \frac{f}{P}\right) > \frac{h}{4} \tag{9}$$

The above equation (9) has a similar structure to equation (8), but the heterogeneity costs on the right-hand side are *higher*. That means that the median voter will accept a break-up even when economies of scale are high enough to make unification efficient. Specifically, for all values of the parameters such that

$$\frac{h}{8} < \Delta\left(y, v, \frac{f}{P}\right) < \frac{h}{4} \tag{10}$$

we have majorities in favor of an inefficient break-up. This result is due to the unequal distribution of the benefits from having a larger country: the individuals at the margins do not fully internalize those benefits, since they pay a disproportionate share of heterogeneity costs, and are therefore willing to break up the country, even if that means higher taxes per capita for everybody and a reduction of average utility overall.

The result that majority voting might lead to inefficient break-up of countries extends to the more general case in which individuals can vote on any number and size of countries Alesina and Spolaore (1997, 2003) consider the case in which utility from private consumption is linear ($u(c_i) = c_i$), the mass of population is normalized to one ($P = 1$—an assumption we will maintain in the rest of this chapter), and majority voting takes place on configurations of countries of equal size in order to satisfy a stability condition. Under those assumptions, they find that the unique number of countries in their majority voting equilibrium is given by the integer that is closest to the following number:

$$N^v = \sqrt{\frac{h}{2f}} \tag{11}$$

By contrast, the efficient number of countries is the integer closest to:

$$N^e = \sqrt{\frac{h}{4f}} < N^v \qquad (12)$$

Both numbers capture the trade-off between heterogeneity of preferences (higher h—more nations of smaller size) and economies of scale in public-good provision (higher f—fewer, bigger nations), but the voting equilibrium presents an inefficiently large number of nations. N^v does not maximize average welfare, but the utility of the individual at the border (the individual with the lowest utility). In fact, the majority vote equilibrium N^v would be chosen as the "optimal" solution by a Rawlsian social planner with the goal of maximizing minimum utility, assuming that taxes are identical across individuals with different preferences.

In specific cases it might be possible to obtain efficient borders by direct majority rule. Consider a modification of the above framework in which political costs are modeled as a *quadratic* function of an individual's distance from the government, a specification used by Wittman (2000) in his analysis of efficient national borders. Now:

$$U_i = u(c_i) - h(x_i - \theta_{j(i)})^2 \qquad (13)$$

Individuals are still uniformly distributed over [0, 1], and world population size P is normalized to one. Because of the symmetric distribution, for all configurations of borders mean and median locations coincide, and the median voter's favored location of government is identical to the mean location, which now maximizes average utility.[25] In a unified country, the sum of everybody's utility can be calculated by adding up the utility from consumption, which is identical for all individuals and equal to $u(y - v - f)$ (i.e. utility of income y minus taxes $v + fi$), and all the "heterogeneity costs" associated with individuals being far from the government (which is located at $1/2$). These costs vary across individuals, and can be calculated by integrating (that is, summing up) all individual costs. With a uniform distribution and a population size $P = 1$, we have that the density $f(x) = 1$, and we can write the sum of all squared distances from 0 to 1 as $\int_0^1 (x_i - \frac{1}{2})^2 dx_i$. Hence, the sum of everybody's utilities in a unified country is given by:

$$\overline{U}_1 = u(y - v - f) - h \int_0^1 \left(x_i - \frac{1}{2}\right)^2 dx_i \qquad (14)$$

---

[25] An interesting issue is what happens when mean and median do not coincide. Wittman 2000 argues in favor of the mean rather then the median as the appropriate solution concept in this case, using two arguments: (*a*) average welfare is maximized by the mean, and with appropriate transfers across voters, everybody would prefer that solution; (*b*) in a symmetric probabilistic-voting framework an opportunist policy-maker in competition for a representative office would maximize his votes by targeting mean preferences. As briefly discussed below, analogous issues are important when one considers not just the efficiency of policy choice (type of government) for given borders, but also the efficient determination of the borders themselves.

When people are split into two separate countries, their utility from consumption is lower because of higher taxes: taxes are now $v + 2f$ and utility is $u(y - v - 2f)$. On the other hand, total heterogeneity costs are lower, because now we have to sum up the costs associated with the distance from 1/4 (the "capital city" of the first country) of all individuals who are located between 0 and 1/2, and the distance from 3/4 (the "capital city" of the second country) of all individuals located between 1/2 and 1. Therefore, the sum of everybody's utilities when people are divided in two separate countries is:

$$\overline{U}_2 = u(y - v - 2f) - h \int_0^{1/2} \left(x_i - \frac{1}{4}\right)^2 dx_i - h \int_{1/2}^1 \left(x_i - \frac{3}{4}\right)^2 dx_i \quad (15)$$

A unified country provides higher average utility than two separate countries if an only if: $\overline{U}_1 > \overline{U}_2$. By solving the integrals in equations (13) and (14), and using equation (7) for $P = 1$, we have that $\overline{U}_1 > \overline{U}_2$ holds if an only if:

$$\Delta(y, v, f) > \frac{h}{16} \quad (16)$$

The above inequality shows, as usual, the benefits of scale on the left-hand side and the heterogeneity costs on the right-hand side. As before, average utility is higher in a unified country than in two separate countries when the benefits of scale are high enough to offset the heterogeneity costs. A majority of citizens will be in favor of maintaining a unified country if and only if the individual at location 1/4 prefers a unified country,[26] which happens to imply the same condition $\Delta(y, v, f) > \frac{h}{16}$. Therefore in this example a democratic vote over border replicates the efficient outcome. The result depends on the quadratic specification of the political costs. In general, direct voting over borders brings about inefficient outcomes, unless appropriate tax-and-transfer schemes are in place.

5 COMPENSATIONS

Can individuals with preferences "far from the government" receive compensations, and can such compensations sustain efficient borders? Sometimes we can observe "border regions" with different preferences and characteristics from the "center" that have received a relatively favorable fiscal treatment—for instance, special-status regions in Italy, northern regions in Sweden, some provinces of Canada and Argentina, etc. However, in general the implementation of these transfer schemes may be economically costly, distortive, or, as briefly discussed below, non-credible.[27] The feasibility of transfer schemes as means to prevent secessions and implement efficient border configurations has been studied by LeBreton and Weber (2001, 2003), who

---

[26] As in the case of linear costs, it is easy to check that if the individual at location 1/4 prefers a unified country, so do all individuals between 0 and 1/4 and all individuals between 3/4 and 1.

[27] These issues are discussed in Alesina and Spolaore 2003, ch. 4.

explore the case in which a non-linear transfer scheme can prevent unilateral secessions in a country of optimal size, and generalize the analysis to populations distributed over bounded and unbounded intervals.[28]

In the case of linear utility from consumption ($u(c_i) = c_i$), an efficient solution would be achieved via majority voting if taxes could be set according to a "full-compensation" formula, in which individuals who are "far" from the government pay lower taxes as compensation for the "political costs" they suffer. In principle, by appropriately lowering the taxes of individuals in proportion to the "political harm" they receive because of their location, it is possible to ensure that all voters have equal utility. Specifically, individual i's taxes in a "full-compensation" formula are given by:

$$t_i = Q_{j(i)} - h|x_i - \theta_{j(i)}| \tag{17}$$

For each country of size P_j (with $j = 1, 2, \ldots, N$) with borders between $\underline{b}_j$ and $\overline{b}_j$, Q_j is set in order to satisfy the budget constraint (that is, total taxes equal to total costs):

$$\int_{\underline{b}_j}^{\overline{b}_j} t_i \, di = f + v P_j \tag{18}$$

When the world is divided into N countries all of equal size $\overline{P} = 1/N$, all individuals in the world will receive the same utility, which can be calculated as follows:[29]

$$U(\overline{P}) = y - \frac{f}{\overline{P}} - v + g - \frac{h\overline{P}}{4} \tag{19}$$

The above equation shows that, *for all individuals*, utility is given by consumption (income minus the costs per capita of the government $\frac{f}{\overline{P}} + v$) plus the average benefits of government services, which take into account the *average* "political costs" $\frac{h\overline{P}}{4}$. The above utility is maximized for $\overline{P} = 1/N^e$ Hence all individuals will unanimously choose the configuration of borders for which $\overline{P} = 1/N^e$, i.e. the efficient configuration of borders. In this version of the model, linear full compensation would work perfectly, in principle, to ensure efficient and equitable borders.

Practical problems with this scheme include costs, feasibility in the presence of imperfect information about individual preferences (an issue from which we have abstracted in the model), and credibility. In our example if there are any costs, even very small, associated with this scheme, voters would reject the scheme *after* borders are set, unless there exists a persistent and credible threat of secession. Haimanko, LeBreton, and Weber (2005) show that even in the absence of an appropriate commitment technology, linear transfer schemes may be supported by a majority of the

---

[28] In this chapter we have mainly focused on break-up via majority voting. However, equal or even greater attention in the literature has been given to the concept of unilateral secessions by groups of individuals—a concept related to the study of the core. For an earlier contribution on secession threats and taxation in a different context, see Buchanan and Faith 1987. Characterizations of secession-proof configurations of countries for the linear version of our basic framework are provided in Alesina and Spolaore 1997; 2003, ch. 3. See also Bordignon and Brusco 2001.

[29] It is also easy to verify that all parameters Q_j will be identical and equal to $\frac{f}{\overline{P}} + v + \frac{h\overline{P}}{4}$.

population in *polarized* societies in which the median distance from the government is higher than the average distance. However, even in this case, there is no assurance that the feasible redistributive scheme enforces the optimal size of countries. In fact, in a political economy equilibrium in which compensation schemes are decided via majority voting, "excessive" compensation may induce a "secession of the center."[30]

6 INCOME INEQUALITY, REDISTRIBUTION, AND BREAK-UP OF NATIONS

Bolton and Roland (1997) study a model of country break-up by majority vote when individuals differ in productivity and income. Then differences in income across region are at the roots of different preferences over public policies (redistribution), and may generate incentives to break up, even in the absence of other forms of heterogeneity. Bolton and Roland's model can be illustrated with a simple modification of our basic framework. Again, we focus on the potential break-up of a unified country into two countries of size 1/2 each. The distribution of income in the first half of the unified country (region 1) is represented by a probability density function $\phi_1(y_i)$, while the distribution of income in the second half of the unified country (region 2) is denoted by a probability density function $\phi_2(y_i)$. Income distribution in the unified country formed by region 1 plus region 2 is defined by $\phi_u(y_i)$. y_1, y_2, and y_u denote average income levels in region 1, region 2, and the unified country. As before, governments provide public goods with fixed cost equal to f.[31] Government's functions also include redistribution of income across individuals. Each individual i receives lump-sum transfers R. Public goods and transfers are financed by a proportional income tax at rate τ. Taxation is costly: a dollar of tax revenues provides only $(1 - \frac{\tau}{2})$ dollars for transfers and public goods. Individual i's utility is:[32]

$$U_i = c_i = (1 - \tau)y_i + R \qquad (20)$$

If a region $j = 1, 2$ is independent, each individual in the region receives

$$R_j = \left(\tau - \frac{\tau^2}{2}\right) y_j - 2f - v \qquad (21)$$

while if everybody is part of a unified country transfers per capita are:

$$R_u = \left(\tau - \frac{\tau^2}{2}\right) y_u - f - v \qquad (22)$$

Let y_1^m, y_2^m, and y_u^m denote median incomes in region 1, region 2, and the unified country. Let the tax rate preferred by the median voters (i.e. the voters with median

---
[30] A numerical example is discussed in Alesina and Spolaore 2003, 60–3.
[31] To simplify notation and without loss of generality, we will assume $v = 0$ and $u(c_i) = c_i$.
[32] Here we abstract from heterogeneity of preferences over types of public goods, and focus on heterogeneity of income.

income) in region 1, region 2, and the unified country be, respectively, τ_1, τ_2, and τ_u. If the median income is lower than average income (as usually the case empirically) we can calculate the preferred tax rate by the median voter as:

$$\tau_j = 1 - \frac{y_j^m}{y_j} \tag{23}$$

The above equation shows that the median voter's preferred tax rate is higher the larger the gap between median income and average income, since a poorer median voter has more to gain from higher taxes. Will voters prefer unification or separation? The median voter's theorem applies: a majority of individuals in region j will strictly prefer unification if and only if unification is preferred by the individual with median income in the region, that is, if and only if

$$U_u(y_j^m) > U_j(y_j^m) \tag{24}$$

which can be written as:[33]

$$f > \frac{(y_u^m - y_j^m)^2}{2y_u} + \left[\frac{y_j - y_u}{2} + \frac{(y_j^m)^2}{2y_j} - \frac{(y_j^m)^2}{2y_u}\right] \tag{25}$$

Three effects can be identified. The first effect is captured by the the term f: it comes from the *economies of scale* from forming a union. The larger is f, the more likely it is that unification will be preferred to separation. The second effect (*political effect* in Bolton and Roland's terminology) is captured by $\frac{(y_u^m - y_j^m)^2}{2y_u}$, which is the difference in desired fiscal policy between the median voter in region j and the median voter in the unified country. From the perspective of the median voter in region j, this effect is always positive (that is, it raises the appeal of a separation), as long as $y_j^m \neq y_u^m$. The third term ($\frac{y_j - y_u}{2} + \frac{(y_j^m)^2}{2y_j} - \frac{(y_j^m)^2}{2y_u}$) captures the "tax base effect." This effect increases the likelihood of secession if region j is richer than the unified country ($y_j > y_u$), while it subtracts from the political effect (i.e. it makes unification more appealing) if region j is poorer than the unified country. However, if the political effect is large enough, the regional median voter may prefer secession even if his or her region is *poorer* than the unified country. In other words, while a richer region is more likely to secede than a poorer region, sufficiently large differences in preferences over redistribution may also induce secessions by poorer regions. Bolton and Roland (1997) show that even when using a compensatory fiscal policy, the national median voter cannot always prevent a break-up when faced with large differences in desired redistribution policies. The study of the relationships among redistribution policies, income inequality, and secessions is a promising area of theoretical and empirical research within the literature on political borders.

---

[33] This equation is analogous to a similar equation (12) in Bolton and Roland 1997, 1064. However, this equation differs from the Bolton–Roland equation because we assume economies of scale in public good provision, while Bolton and Roland assume that separation reduces everybody's income proportionally.

7 Nations in a World of Rent-seeking Governments

Borders set efficiently or by direct majority rule are useful benchmarks that help identify important trade-offs between benefits and costs of size. However, it is unlikely that actual borders have ever been determined through those mechanisms. More often, border changes have been the outcomes of actions by rulers—kings, emperors, dictators—entering into peaceful negotiations and/or violent wars over territories and populations.[34] Even when governments are elected democratically, they rarely allow their citizens to make direct decisions over borders by referendum. In the literature on nations, the drawing of borders by rent-seeking Leviathans has been analyzed by Friedman (1977), who first proposed that in a world of rent-seeking governments, actual borders in the long run will maximize the net rents of Leviathans.

The concept of a "Leviathan solution" has been formalized by Alesina and Spolaore (1997). In particular, they have assumed that Leviathans are constrained by the need to provide utility above a given threshold to a fraction of their population (δ) in order to stay in power. Under this constraint, the equilibrium number of nations that maximizes Leviathans' net rents is given by:

$$N^\delta = \sqrt{\frac{h\delta}{2f}} \tag{26}$$

The result implies that countries are too few and too large when Leviathans are "real dictators" who only need the support of a minority of the population ($\delta < 1/2$). Efficiency is achieved with Leviathans who need to keep into account the preferences of exactly half of the population, while for $\delta = 1$ a world of Leviathans has the same (inefficient) borders that would have been chosen by voters in direct referenda.

In summary, non-democratic governments are associated with excessive size and centralization, while democratization should go hand in hand with break-up of countries and secessions—unless efficient compensation schemes and/or mechanisms that reduce political costs are introduced along with the democratization process.

The historical record on the break-up of empires—including the former Soviet Union—the empirical evidence on the size of capital cities in dictatorships (Ades and Glaeser 1995), and cross-country evidence on democracy and decentralization (Panizza 1999), are consistent with this view of "centralizing Leviathans."

---

[34] An interesting analysis of the expansion of empires has been provided by Findlay 1996. A more recent study is Grossman and Mendoza 2004.

8 BORDERS AND BARRIERS: INTERNATIONAL OPENNESS AND THE SIZE OF NATIONS

The relationship between international economic integration and the size of nations has been at the forefront of the recent literature on endogenous national borders. A survey of these topics, which also focuses on the implications for growth and development, is provided by Alesina, Spolaore, and Wacziarg (2005), who build on previous work by Alesina and Spolaore (1997), Alesina, Spolaore, and Wacziarg (2000), Spolaore (1995), and Spolaore and Wacziarg (2005). The topic is also covered in detail by Alesina and Spolaore (2003, esp. chs. 6, 10). Therefore in this section I will very briefly review some general points, while referring the reader to the survey and book chapters for analytical details and for discussions of the empirical and historical evidence.

This work suggests that economic integration and political disintegration tend to go hand in hand. The reason is that, as already mentioned, the benefits of a large domestic market go down as international economic integration increases. Conversely, the benefits of trade openness and economic integration are larger, the smaller the size of a country. This is confirmed by empirical evidence from cross-country regressions (Alesina, Spolaore, and Wacziarg 2001; Alcalá and Ciccone 2003; Spolaore and Wacziarg 2005), where measures of economic performance (income per capita, growth, productivity) depend positively on a country's size, positively on a country's openness (appropriately instrumented), but negatively on the interaction between size and openness, showing that the benefits from size are larger for less open countries, and the benefits from openness are bigger for smaller countries. As the world economy becomes more integrated, one of the benefits of large countries (the size of domestic markets) tends to vanish. Hence the trade-off between size and heterogeneity shifts in favor of smaller and more homogeneous countries. In the model presented by Alesina, Spolaore, and Wacziarg (2005), this effect tends to be larger in more developed economies. By contrast, technological progress in a world of *high* barriers to trade should be associated with the formation of *larger* countries.

We can also think of the reverse source of causality. Small countries have a particularly strong interest in maintaining free trade, since so much of their economy depends upon international markets. When openness is endogenized, the analysis can be extended to capture two possible worlds: a world of large and relatively closed economies, and one of more numerous, smaller, more open economies. Spolaore (1995, 2004) provides models with endogenous openness and multiple equilibria in the number of countries. Spolaore and Wacziarg (2005) also treat openness as an explicitly endogenous variable, and show empirically that larger countries tend to be more closed to trade. In the real world both directions of causality between size of nations and international openness are likely to coexist. *Ceteris paribus*, smaller countries tend to adopt more open trade policies, so that a world of small countries will be more open to trade.[35] Conversely, changes in the average degree of openness in the world should be expected to lead to more secessions and smaller countries.

These effects abstract from the role of factor mobility (labor and capital). Capital and labor mobility introduce potential competition among governments and may affect the size of nations through several channels. For example, in Friedman's (1977) analysis national borders are set by rent-maximizing Leviathans who want to prevent migration, and Friedman argues that trade, by increasing labor productivity, leads to larger countries so that the rulers can capture higher monopoly rents. By contrast, Wittman (2000) develops a model of efficient size of nations in which individuals can migrate across countries. Wittman does not model international trade explicitly, but allows for economies of scale in production, and argues that such economies would be zero under perfect free trade and perfect cross-country enforcement of property rights, but are positive when intracountry transaction costs are higher than intercountry transaction costs. Hence in Wittman's framework a reduction in the economies of scale in production–due, for example, to increasing economic integration—would lead to smaller, more numerous countries, consistently with the above-mentioned results in Alesina and Spolaore (1997, 2003), Spolaore (1995), and Alesina, Spolaore, and Wacziarg (2000, 2005). Analyzing trade and factor mobility in microfounded models with international trade, endogenous international barriers, and endogenous borders represents an interesting and promising area for future research.

9 Conflict, Defense, and the Size of Nations

Conflict, defense and security have historically been paramount in the determination and redrawing of national borders. Contributions to the formal literature of endogenous borders have explicitly modeled provision of defense by governments, international conflicts, and wars, building on the formal literature on conflict and appropriation that we mentioned in Section 2. In particular, conflict and defense are at the center of the analysis in Alesina and Spolaore (2005, 2006) and Spolaore (2004), and are also modeled by Wittman (2000).

In these papers the size of nations is affected by the fact that a country's military power matters in the settlement of international disputes. Defense and national power are public goods, and, at least in principle, larger countries can provide better and cheaper security for their citizens.[36] In a more bellicose world, larger, more centralized

---

[35] The effect might be partially or totally offset if a regime of international free trade also requires investments in some "international public good." Then smaller countries might have stronger incentives to free ride.
[36] For a contrary view see Thomson 1974.

countries may be at an advantage, while a reduction in international conflict reduces the incentives to form larger political unions, and may lead to break-ups and secessions.[37] For example, in Alesina and Spolaore (2006), defense spending per capita in equilibrium is an inverse function of country size, and the number of nations in a world of Leviathans is given by

$$N^\delta = \sqrt{\frac{h\delta - pe}{2f}} \tag{27}$$

where p is the probability that force will be used in an international dispute, and e measures the stakes of the dispute.[38] In a world where conflict is more likely and/or matters more (higher p and/or e), there are fewer, larger countries. The larger is our measure of "democratic constraint" δ (i.e. the fraction of the population whose preferences must be taken into account by the Leviathan), the smaller is the impact of p on the size of nations. Vice versa, the less conflictual the world is (smaller p), the larger is the impact of democratization on the size of countries.[39] In other words, democratization and *reduction* in conflict both lead to a break-up of countries, and also mutually reinforce their respective effects.

However, a decrease in p, while reducing the incentives for citizens and rulers to form larger political units, might not reduce the total "mass" of conflict in the world. When borders are endogenous, a lower p, by leading to more political fragmentation, may indeed increase the number of observed conflicts in the world, because, even if the use of force is less likely in each specific international dispute, the formation of more numerous, smaller countries may increase the probability that some countries will enter into a confrontation. In other words, since a lower probability of having to use force in international relations increases the number of nations in equilibrium, it can be associated with an overall increase in the number of international interactions that are resolved through conflict and the use of national power. In particular, a reduction in global conflict between larger political units may lead to an increase in more localized conflict between smaller political units (Alesina and Spolaore 2006). By the same token, improvements in the enforcement of control rights by countries through a more effective rule of international law reduce the need for defense and force, and therefore may cause a break-up of nations, and lead to more rather than less conflict in equilibrium (Alesina and Spolaore 2005).

In general, economies of scale in defense and military exploitation, and other aspects of military technology, have played a key role in the dynamics of national borders, in interaction with the other important variables identified in the literature, that is: heterogeneity and political costs, economies of scale in the provision of other public goods, democratization and internal organization of governments,

[37] For example, the expansion in the scale and costs of international wars has been emphasized by Tilly 1990 as the key force behind the consolidation of modern European national states and the decline of alternative political organizations (city-states, federations).

[38] The parameter e in this model is related to Wittman's (2000) parameter g (general military effectiveness), a variable that depends on both military technology and the spoils of war.

[39] Formally, $\frac{\partial^2 \overline{P}^\delta}{\partial p \partial \delta} < 0$ where $\overline{P}^\delta = \frac{1}{N^\delta}$.

tax-and-transfers schemes and ability to provide side payments and compensations across regions, income inequality and redistribution policies, benefits from the extent of the market, and effects of increasing economic integration in goods and factors of production.[40] The study of the complex interrelations among all these variables and mechanisms, and the assessment of their relative weights in actual episodes of border redrawing, represent challenging and stimulating tasks for political economists who want to gain insights into the endogenous formation and break-up of nations.

References

ADES, A., and GLAESER, E. 1999. Evidence on growth, increasing returns and the extent of the market. *Quarterly Journal of Economics*, 114: 1025–45.

ALCALÁ, F., and CICCONE, A. 2003. Trade, the extent of the market and economic growth 1960-1996. Unpublished manuscript, Universitat Pompeu Fabra.

ALESINA, A., and SPOLAORE, E. 1997. On the number and size of nations. *Quarterly Journal of Economics*, 112: 1027–56.

—— —— 2003. *The Size of Nations*. cambridge, Mass.: MIT Press.

—— —— 2005. War, peace and the size of countries. *Journal of Public Economics*, 89: 1333–54.

—— —— 2006. Conflict, defense spending, and the number of nations. *European Economic Review*, 50: 91–120.

—— —— and WACZIARG, R. 2000. Economic integration and political disintegration. *American Economic Review*, 90: 1276–96.

—— —— —— 2005. Trade, growth, and the size of countries. In *The Handbook of Economic Growth*, ed. P. Aghion and S. Durlauf. Amsterdam: North-Holland.

—— and WACZIARG, R. 1998. Openness, country size and the government. *Journal of Public Economics*, 69: 305–21.

—— —— 1999. Is Europe going too far? *Carnegie-Rochester Conference Series on Public Policy*, 51: 1–42.

—— DERLEESCHAUWEN, A., EASTERLY, W., KURLAT, S., and WACZIARG, R. 2003. Fractionalization. *Journal of Economic Growth*, 8: 155–94.

ANDERSON, B. 1991. *Imagined Communities: Reflections on the Origin and Spread of Nationalism*. London: Verso.

BALDWIN, R. E., and VENABLES, A. 1995. Regional economic integration. In *The Handbook of International Economics*, vol. iii, ed. G. Grossman and K. Rogoff. Amsterdam: North-Holland.

BARDHAN, P. 2002. Decentralization of governance and development. *Journal of Economic Perspectives*, 16: 185–205.

BOLTON, P., and ROLAND, G. 1997. The breakups of nations: a political economy analysis. *Quarterly Journal of Economics*, 112: 1057–89.

—— —— and SPOLAORE, E. 1996. Economic theories of the break-up and integration of nations. *European Economic Review*, 40: 697–705.

---

[40] For example, as analyzed in a vast economic and political literature, trade may affect conflict, and conflict may affect trade, and both interact with border redrawing. For a formal analysis of these issues, see Spolaore 2004.

BORDIGNON, M., and BRUSCO, S. 2001. Optimal secession rules. *European Economic Review*, 45: 1811–34.

BOULDING, K. E. 1962. *Conflict and Defense: A General Theory*. New York: Harper.

BUCHANAN, J. M. 1965. An economic theory of clubs. *Economica*, 32: 1–14.

—— and FAITH, R. L. 1987. Secessions and the limits of taxation: towards a theory of internal exit. *American Economic Review*, 77: 1023–31.

CASELLA, A. 2001. The role of market size in the formation of jurisdictions. *Review of Economic Studies*, 68: 83–108.

—— and FEINSTEIN, J. S. 2002. Public goods in trade: on the formation of markets and political jurisdictions. *International Economic Review*, 43: 437–62.

DAGAN, N., and VOLIJ, O. 2000. Formation of nations in a welfare-state minded world. *Journal of Public Economic Theory*, 2: 157–81.

DAHL, R. A., and TUFTE, E. R. 1973. *Size and Democracy*. Stanford Calif.: Stanford University Press.

DE FIGUEIREDO, R., and WEINGAST, B. 2002. Self-enforcing federalism. Mimeo, Stanford University.

DRÈZE, J. H. 1993. Regions of Europe: a feasible status, to be discussed. *Economic Policy*, 8: 206–307.

EASTERLY, W., and LEVINE, R. 1997. Africa's growth tragedy: policies and ethnic divisions. *Quarterly Journal of Economics*, 111: 1203–50.

ELLINGSEN, T. 1998. Externalities and internalities: a model of political integration. *Journal of Public Economics*, 68: 251–68.

FINDLAY, R. 1996. Towards a model of territorial expansion and the limits of empires. In *The Political Economy of Conflict and Appropriation*, ed. M. Garfinkel and S. Skaperdas. Cambridge: Cambridge University Press.

FREY, B., and EICHENBERGER, R. 1999. *The New Democratic Federalism for Europe: Functional, Overlapping, and Competing Jurisdictions*. London: Edward Elgar.

FRIEDMAN, D. 1977. A theory of the size and shape of nations. *Journal of Political Economy*, 85: 59–77.

FUJITA, M., and THISSE, J. F. 2002. *Economics of Agglomeration: Cities, Industrial Location, and Regional Growth*. Cambridge: Cambridge University Press.

GOYAL, S., and STAAL, K. 2004. The political economy of regionalism. *European Economic Review*, 48: 563–93.

GROSSMAN, H. I. 1991. A general equilibrium model of insurrections. *American Economic Review*, 81: 912–21.

—— and MENDOZA, J. 2004. Annexation or conquest? The building of the Roman Empire. Mimeo, Brown University.

HAIMANKO, O., LE BRETON, M., and WEBER, S. 2005. Transfers in a polarized country: bridging the gap between efficiency and stability. *Journal of Public Economics*, 89: 1277–303.

HIRSHLEIFER, J. 1989. Conflict and rent-seeking success functions: ratio versus difference models of relative success. *Public Choice*, 63: 101–12.

—— 1991. The technology of conflict as an economic activity. *American Economic Review: Papers and Proceedings*, 81: 130–4.

—— 1995a. Theorizing about conflict. In *The Handbook of Defense Economics*, ed. K. Hartley and T. Sandler. Amsterdam: North-Holland.

—— 1995b. Anarchy and its breakdown. *Journal of Political Economy*, 103: 26–52.

HOBSBAWN, E. 1990. *Nations and Nationalism since 1870*. Cambridge: Cambridge University Press.

INMAN, R. P., and RUBINFELD, D. L. 1997. The political economy of federalism. In *Perspecitves on Public Choice*, ed. D. C. Mueller. Cambridge: Cambridge University Press.

LA PORTA, R., LOPEZ DE SILANES, F., SHLEIFER, A., and VISHNY, R. 1999. The quality of government. *Journal of Law, Economics and Organization*, 15: 222–79.

LE BRETON, M., and WEBER, S. 2003. The art of making everybody happy: how to prevent a secession? *IMF Staff Papers*, 50: 403–35.

MURDOCH, J. C. 1995. Military alliances: theory and empirics. In *The Handbook of Defense Economics*, ed. K. Hartley and T. Sandler. Amsterdam: North-Holland.

OATES, W. E. 1999. An essay on fiscal federalism. *Journal of Economic Literature*, 37: 1120–49.

OLSON, M., and ZECKHAUSER, R. 1966. An economic theory of alliances. *Review of Economics and Statistics*, 48: 266–79.

PANIZZA, U. 1999. On the determinants of fiscal centralization: theory and evidence. *Journal of Public Economics*, 74: 97–139.

PAULY, M. 1967. Clubs, commonality and the core: an integration of game theory and the theory of public goods. *Economica*, 34: 314–24.

—— 1970. Cores and clubs. *Public Choice*, 9: 53–65.

POWELL, R. 1999. *In the Shadow of Power: States and Strategies in International Politics*. Princeton, NJ: Princeton University Press.

SCHMIDTCHEN, D. 1994. International contracting and territorial control: the boundary question. *Journal of Institutional Economics*, 150: 272–8.

SCOTCHMER, S. 2002. Local public goods and clubs. In *The Handbook of Public Economics*, vol. iv, ed. A. Auerbach and M. Feldstein. Amsterdam: North-Holland.

SKAPERDAS, S. 1992. Cooperation, conflict and power in the absence of property rights. *American Economic Review*, 82: 720–39.

SPOLAORE, E. 1995. Economic integration, political borders and productivity. Prepared for the CEPR-Sapir conference on "Regional integration and economic growth," Tel Aviv University, Dec.

—— 2004. Economic integration, international conflict and political unions. *Rivista di politica economica*, Sept.–Oct.: 3–41.

—— and WACZIARG, R. 2005. Borders and growth. *Journal of Economic Growth*, 10: 331–8.

TIEBOUT, C. 1956. A pure theory of local expenditures. *Journal of Political Economy*, 64: 416–24.

TILLY, C. 1990. *Coercion, Capital, and European States, AD 990-1992*. Cambridge, Mass.: Blackwell.

THOMSON, E. A. 1974. Taxation and national defense. *Journal of Political Economy*, 82: 755–82.

TULLOCK, G. 1974. *The Social Dilemma: The Economics of War and Revolution*. Blacksburg, Va.: University Publications.

VINER, J. 1950. *The Customs Union Issue*. New York: Carnegie Endowment for International Peace.

WITTMAN, D. 1991. Nations and states: mergers and acquisitions; dissolutions and divorce. *American Economic Review: Papers and Proceedings*, 81: 126–9.

—— 2000. The wealth and size of nations. *Journal of Conflict Resolution*, 6: 885–95.

CHAPTER 44

EUROPEAN INTEGRATION

BARRY EICHENGREEN

EUROPEAN integration has long fascinated scholars of political economy. Understanding the economic initiatives at the heart of this process—the European Payments Union, the European Coal and Steel Community, the European Economic Community, the Single Market, and now the euro—and their institutional counterparts—the European Parliament, the Court of Justice, the Commission, the Council of Ministers, and the European Central Bank—has been a challenge for both economists and political scientists, neither of which have been reluctant to take up the gauntlet.

The development of scholarship in this area, not surprisingly, mirrors developments in the wider world. In the early years following the Second World War, the process of European integration seemed unique. The pace of integration and the development of supranational institutions were unprecedented; they were unrivaled in other parts of the world. The member states of today's European Union showed an unparalleled willingness to pool authority and create collective institutions. This encouraged theories and interpretations of European integration that treated the case as *sui generis* (see Section 1 below). Impetus derived, it was said, from Europe's history of hostilities, or its geography of economic interdependence, or its inheritance of social democracy, preconditions that did not exist in other parts of the world. Once the process of integration started, it was driven forward by the founding generation of intellectual and political leaders, dynamized by the operation of positive feedbacks, and locked in by institutionalization. Because the preconditions were distinctive and the process took on a life of its own, European integration was one of a kind.

But as one decade gave way to the next, initiatives to promote freer trade and closer relations appeared in North America, South America, Asia, and elsewhere, and it became evident that the regional impulse was by no means exclusively European. To be sure, these regional arrangements differed from Europe's in their particulars. Still, the growth of regionalism in other parts of the world reopened the question of whether the political economy of European integration was unique or whether Europe's experience was in fact just one more manifestation of a more general phenomenon.

This encouraged what might be called the normalization of European integration studies (see Section 2 below). Instead of searching for respects in which Europe was unique, researchers sought to identify a common set of factors—the expansion of trade, the rise of capital mobility, the difficulty of liberalization negotiations at the global level—encouraging regional integration throughout the world. They sought to identify subtle variations that might explain why Europe embarked on this process earlier than other regions, which in this new view was all that really needed to be explained.

But, all the while, there remained a vague and inchoate sense that the European case was unique. Integration in Europe proceeded faster and further than integration in other regions. European integration had a more prominent institutional aspect. And there was more talk of a political dimension. These observations encouraged efforts to rehabilitate early views of the political economy of European integration by recasting them in the language of modern economic theory, and specifically in terms of models of non-ergodic processes (see Section 3 below). By invoking concepts from economics like network externalities, lock-in, and path dependence, this new work sought to formalize and update notions that had been at the heart of early studies of the political economy of European integration.

This, then, was an effort to explain how regionalism in Europe could differ from regionalism elsewhere even if these processes all responded broadly to the same preferences, endowments, and constraints. It was an attempt to reintroduce a role for history into the study of European integration.

In this chapter, I discuss conceptions of the political economy of European integration in terms of these three generations of academic work. In the conclusion I ask where the subject should go from here.

1 The Uniqueness of European Integration

Early studies of European integration focused on national governments and leaders engaged in negotiations with their foreign counterparts, logically enough insofar as the most visible early manifestations of the European Community were agreements between governments. Quickly, however, there developed an alternative approach focusing on the institutions of European integration themselves. These two approaches acquired the sobriquets "intergovernmentalism" and "institutionalism" as a way of distinguishing them from one another (Keohane and Hoffmann 1991).

Already in discussions of the first integrationist initiative of the 1950s, the European Payments Union (EPU), there had been hints of the tension between these competing views. The EPU was negotiated to address the payments problems associated with the restoration of current account convertibility following the Second World War. While the arrangement was intergovernmental, it also had a prominent institutional component, notably a managing board comprised of financial experts reporting to the Council of the Organization of European Economic Cooperation, which oversaw the policies of member states and made recommendations regarding the provision of temporary financial assistance.

The question, then, was how to understand this institutional dimension. One answer was framed in purely instrumental terms. The EPU addressed the coordination problem facing countries seeking to liberalize—the fact that it paid to relax restrictions on imports only if other countries did likewise so that the newly liberalizing country had markets to which to export. In more theoretically oriented terms, it was a mechanism to facilitate the coordination of liberalization initiatives across countries and to lock in the commitment to avoid backsliding by monitoring the compliance of governments with the terms of their agreement, by sharing information on such compliance, and by providing adjustment assistance. Already, then, analysis of the EPU sounded several themes that would resonate through studies of European integration for the next fifty years, such as the use of regional arrangements to solve coordination problems and the role of institutions in forming credible commitments (see e.g. Keohane 1984).

Yet, there was also a sense that the institutions associated with this initiative had a deeper and wider impact than suggested by this instrumentalist perspective. For one thing, while the EPU was first and foremost an economic initiative directed at problems of trade and payments, it also involved cold war politics, since seed money was provided by the United States through the Marshall Plan. This observation suggested that neither textbook economic models, which explain policy decisions on the basis of distributional interests, nor political analyses framed exclusively in terms of security concerns, sufficed to account for the initiative. Instead, some new, more distinctive analysis blending politics and economics might be required.

The continent's next regional initiative was the European Coal and Steel Community (ECSC). Coal and steel remained consequential industries in the 1950s, but that the creation a European free trade area started with these sectors reflected not so much their economic significance per se as their importance for collective security. Coal and steel had been the backbone of the German army in the Second World War, leading France to insist on restrictions on the production of these commodities following the conclusion of hostilities. But coal and steel were important as well for the fabrication of capital goods, the traditional comparative advantage of German industry. The ECSC can thus be thought of as a deal in which Germany sacrificed autonomy over its coal and steel industries in return for freedom from restrictions on industrial production (Berger and Ritschl 1995). Germany received economic concessions (the removal of ceilings on permissible levels of industrial production, which was essential for the postwar recovery of its economy) in return for security guarantees (in the form of an agreement to share management of its coal and steel industries with other countries).

Thus, early analyses of the ECSC, like those of the EPU, pointed up issues that came to dominate European integration studies for several decades. Diplomatic historians and European foreign policy specialists developed the argument that security concerns were the ulterior motive for economic integration, applying it subsequently to everything from the Single Market to the single currency. International relations specialists noted the synergy of economic and security concerns and generalized those connections into a theory of "issue linkage" in which European integration became a mechanism for facilitating Pareto improving policy trades across issue areas. In the 1990s, for example, they explained Germany's agreement to the creation of a monetary union (and, specifically, the country's willingness to sacrifice the Bundesbank's disproportionate influence over monetary conditions in Europe) as a quid pro quo for acquiescence on the part of its European neighbors to German reunification (Garrett 2001). At an analytical level they explored the conditions under which such mutually advantageous cross-issue policies trades are possible, such as divergences in the value that different countries place on different issues.

In addition, observers of European integration again noted the institutionalized nature of the ECSC, which entailed a joint High Authority to monitor compliance with the terms of the agreement, a Common Assembly of parliamentarians to hold the High Authority accountable, and a Community Court to adjudicate disputes between the High Authority and member states. They were struck by the fact that from these modest beginnings evolved the European Commission, the European Parliament, and the European Court of Justice, institutions that came to play an increasingly prominent role in the continent's integration. These scholars thus sought to develop further their explanation for the institutional dimension of the process.

One rationale for the highly institutionalized nature of European integration was the fact that not all linked policies could be undertaken simultaneously. This made a key challenge for linkage arguments the identification of mechanisms preventing governments from reneging on deferred components of their bargain. While Germany could promise demilitarization as a quid pro quo for reindustrialization at the beginning of the 1950s, for example, what was to prevent the German government from remilitarizing later, once reindustrialization was an accomplished fact? Or, to draw an example from the 1990s, what ensured that Germany would not renege on its commitment to support monetary unification once German reunification was a fait accompli? And, if such guarantees did not exist, what made the bargain viable in the first place? Institutions as mechanisms for making credible commitments came to be seen as a response to this problem (see e.g. Moravcsik 1998).

This early experience encouraged two further themes in the literature on the political economy of European integration. One was the notion of neofunctionalist spillovers associated with Haas (1958). This was the thesis that integration in one functional sphere increased the likelihood of integration in others. An example was how the EPU, by encouraging the reconstruction of intra-European trade, expanded the economic constituency for a common market in goods and services. A subsequent example was the Common Agricultural Policy (CAP), not the proudest but arguably the most consequential achievement of the European Community in the 1960s other than the Common Market itself. The CAP created pressure for monetary coordination, since the exchange rate fluctuations that might otherwise arise threatened to wreak havoc with the compatibility of domestic-currency-denominated support prices in different member countries. Similarly, the Single Market Program of the 1980s, by prompting the removal of capital controls, undermined the viability of pegged but adjustable exchange rates and can be seen as encouraging EU member states to push ahead to monetary union in the 1990s. Because of the interdependence of issues, this logic ran, initiatives in one area encouraged initiatives in others. Consequently, European integration (in the neofunctionalist view) acquired a momentum of its own.

The other theme was the role of elites in pushing forward the integration process. Observing the influence of prominent individuals like the French technocrat Jean Monnet in the 1950s and the French politician Jacques Delors in the 1990s, analysts highlighted the existence of an epistemic community of European policy entrepreneurs who advanced the integrationist process faster than it would have proceeded otherwise. These individuals, according to an influential strand of writing on the European Community, were able to use an increasingly powerful transnational bureaucracy headquartered in Brussels to set the policy agenda and limit the options available to national governments. (See for example Ross 1994.) They were able to compel national leaders and their constituents to engage in a forced march to deeper integration.

This formulation was appealing because it preserved a role for human agency while at the same time pointing to the institutions of the European Community in answer to the question of why a few obscure technocrats might have such disproportionate sway. Together with theories of neofunctionalist spillover, it seemed to explain how decisions by a few could influence outcomes for the many, and why small, calculated actions could have large, unanticipated consequences. But the more scholars reflected on these analyses, the less satisfied they became. If the logic of neofunctionalist spillovers was so compelling, then surely elected officials and their constituents understood their operation. If neofunctionalist spillovers were so prevalent, why then didn't governments realize that integration in one area might lead irresistibly to integration in others? And if officials like Monnet and Delors could wield such influence, then why didn't national governments rein them in?

Consider for example a popular argument concerning the political economy of monetary unification in the 1990s, to the effect that Delors and his colleagues pushed monetary integration because they saw it as the camel's nose under the tent. Monetary unification might or might not be desirable in itself. The theory of optimal currency areas as applied to Europe was ambiguous; Delors himself apparently was ambivalent on the question. But Delors and his colleagues understood that the creation of the euro and the European Central Bank (ECB) would ratchet up the pressure to develop political mechanisms capable of holding Europe's monetary policy-makers accountable. It would create pressure to expand the prerogatives of the European Parliament as a way of applying political checks and balances to the independent European Central Bank. In the extreme version of the argument, monetary integration would lead ineluctably to political union, which was the federalists' ultimate goal. That the creation of the ECB was followed rather quickly by a constitutional convention designed to strengthen the accountability of EU institutions is at least superficially consistent with this interpretation of events.

But, in agreeing to monetary unification, did the national leaders and citizens of EU member states really permit themselves to be painted into a federalist corner that they would have preferred to avoid? Chiefs of government and even the man in the street could see the logic running from monetary integration to political integration. After all, reservations about the implications for political integration were part of what informed popular resistance to the single currency in Britain and certain other European countries. But if national leaders and voters understood this logic and anticipated these repercussions, how then was it possible, asked authors like Martin (1993), to sustain the argument that Delors and his colleagues, operating through institutions like the European Commission, were able to produce unintended results?

One can imagine some elements of an answer. It is most difficult for constituents to control the actions of politicians and officials (that is, what theorists refer to as "principal–agent slack" is greatest) when those constituents find it difficult to monitor the actions of their agent and anticipate their consequences (in other words, when information is "asymmetric"). It is plausible that principal–agent slack was considerable in the case of policy entrepreneurs like Monnet and Delors and the national governments in whose service they worked. Technical matters like the rationalization of the coal and steel industries, the regulation of intra-European exchange rates, and the design of European-wide policy toward mergers and acquisitions are complex and obscure. National governments lack the resources necessary painstakingly to monitor EU-level initiatives in such areas (Pierson and Leibfried 1995). Voters have difficulty monitoring and understanding the actions taken by their governments to monitor and understand the actions taken by their delegates in Brussels, creating multiple layers of principal–agent slack. In addition, there was the problem of the "democratic deficit," the underdevelopment of mechanisms for holding the EU's technocracy accountable for its actions. The European Parliament could tender a vote of no confidence in the European Commission only on grounds of incompetence and dereliction of duty, not over policy disagreements, giving the latter additional room to act autonomously. Conceivably, this constellation of circumstances allowed technocrats in Brussels to take actions with not widely understood consequences that pushed forward the process of European integration faster than it would have proceeded otherwise.

In early studies of the political economy of European integration, these ideas, while implicit in the analysis, were never fully spelled out. The plausibility of their underlying assumptions about, *inter alia*, the imperfect nature of the information environment were not systematically addressed. Moreover, with the creation of the Council of

Ministers, an intergovernmental grouping of heads of state and ministers, as a competing power center to the European Commission, questions arose about whether a model of principal–agent slack between Brussels and national capitals was the right framework for analyzing these developments. For all these reasons, the literature on the political economy of European integration seemed ready for a new direction.

2 THE NORMALIZATION OF EUROPEAN INTEGRATION STUDIES

Meanwhile, regional integration of a sort not entirely unlike Europe's began developing in other parts of the world, raising questions about the validity of these one-of-a-kind arguments. Memories of the Second World War and the special circumstances that had invigorated the early stages of European integration grew less vivid, weakening the presumption that European circumstances were, in some fundamental sense, unique. On the principle that sometimes a cigar is only a cigar, analysts began taking at face value the economic initiatives on which the process focused. The major European states agreed to create a free trade area, or an exchange rate mechanism, or a single market, or a monetary union, this new generation of observers posited, because they saw doing so as in their economic self-interest, pure and simple. The specific terms of their bargain depended on the leverage that governments exercised over negotiations, together with their fallback options or "threat points" (the credibility of their threat to withdraw from negotiations if certain terms were not met)—that is, on the standard determinants of equilibrium solutions to game-theoretic models.

This new work (see e.g. Garrett 1992; Lange 1993; Moravcsik 1993) thus focused on the structural characteristics of economies—their dependence on trade, their sensitivity to exchange rate fluctuations, the share of employment in agricultural production—as determinants of their bargaining positions. To explain why European integration unfolded as it did, it thus sought to explain changes over time in these economic conditions, pointing for example to the rise in capital mobility in the 1980s and 1990s as an explanation for the growing urgency of discussions of monetary cooperation. And in a throwback to the intergovernmental approach, it encouraged analysts to treat member states, which were the parties engaged in these negotiations, as unitary entities.

This did not rule out a role for EU institutions in shaping outcomes, especially as decision-making became increasingly structured and routinized. Authors like Martin (2001) suggested that the design of decision-making processes could independently influence the outcome of negotiations. For example, EU voting rules requiring unanimous consent might increase the leverage of small countries whose size allows them to make only relatively minor contributions to the union's common endeavors but which can still veto collective efforts, allowing them to extract favorable terms. Of course, this just pushed the question back another step, to why the large countries agreed to such voting rules in the first place. One answer is that large countries like Germany and France valued European integration more than some of their smaller counterparts; they were therefore willing to give their smaller neighbors disproportionate leverage in order to get them on board. But if this is the explanation, then the underlying preferences of these countries and the intensity with which those preferences are felt, and not voting rules, ultimately shape the outcome of negotiations. The implication of this view is that institutional arrangements play no independent role.

At the same time, national referenda on the Maastricht Treaty, not all of which went smoothly, and persistent complaints about the democratic deficit seemed to suggest that interest groups and individual voters cared deeply about European integration and sought to influence it through conventional political channels. These observations were consistent with the presumption that countries and constituencies, by making their preferences felt, were ultimately driving the integration process. They encouraged attempts to understand European integration not in terms of negotiations between unitary states but as a reflection of interest group politics at the national and international levels.

In a study representative of these efforts, Frieden (2002) sought to analyze national attitudes toward monetary integration in terms of variables suggested by economic models of how different sectors and factors of production are affected. He argued that export-oriented producers perceive themselves as among the principal beneficiaries of measures promising to limit exchange rate volatility; he therefore took exports to Germany, Belgium, Luxembourg, and the Netherlands, the countries comprising the so-called "DM bloc" at the core of the European Monetary System, as his principal explanatory variable. In addition he argued that producers experiencing an intensification of import competition (a surge in imports) will be reluctant to forgo the option of depreciating the currency and took the change in the trade balance (as a percentage of GDP) as a proxy for this effect. In an econometric analysis covering the early 1970s through the mid-1990s, both variables had their predicted effect on the variability and rate of depreciation of European currencies vis-à-vis the German Deutschmark. This was true even after controlling for the standard arguments of the theory of optimum currency areas, the political orientation of the government in power, and the demand for credibility as captured by a country's inflationary history. Frieden took these results as an indication of the influence of sectoral interests over the process of European integration.

To be sure, these are simple tests of complex hypotheses. The association between exports and exchange rate stability is open to alternative interpretations. Both variables could reflect the influence of a common omitted factor, say, the depth of financial ties between countries. Or greater exchange rate stability could encourage exports rather than the other way around. In any case, an exchange rate stabilization arrangement like the Snake of the 1970s or the European Monetary System of the 1980s and 1990s is very different from the creation of a common currency, the momentous policy decision to which these results are implicitly applied. They have different institutional corollaries and political consequences, as we have seen. Authors like Rose (2000) suggest that they have different economic effects as well.

One response to these objections was to consider survey data on attitudes toward European integration. Eurobarometer surveys have been used to study attitudes toward everything from the single market to the euro and a common foreign policy. To stick with the preceding example, Gabel (2001) analyzed survey data on attitudes toward monetary union (specifically, answers to a question posed in 1993–4 of whether the currencies of all EU member states should be replaced by a single European currency). To test the sectoral interests hypothesis, he related individual answers to each person's sector of employment (industry, services, government, nationalized industry). To test class- or factor-content-based explanations, he related answers to measures of the skilled–unskilled nature of employment and to whether individuals had high or low incomes (the assumption being that high-income individuals tend to own capital that benefits disproportionately from both capital-account liberalization and monetary integration—two phenomena that presumably go together). His findings are broadly consistent with the hypothesis of self-interested attitude formation, suggesting in the main that domestic political agents form opinions and exhibit behaviors consistent with a desire to further their economic goals.

To the extent that the opinions and behaviors of individuals manifest themselves in voting on EU referenda and national elections, this work is a challenge to scholarship emphasizing European elites and institutions. Its limitations include the fact that sharp shifts in economic characteristics like the sectoral distribution of employment or the functional distribution of income are rarely observed over short periods. This makes it hard to understand the repeated sharp bursts of integrationist activity, separated by interludes of stasis, that are seemingly characteristic of the European process. It also makes it hard to understand how Europe could have pushed ahead with initiatives like the single currency when opinion polls consistently show that the majority of European voters are opposed.

Such observations led some scholars to attempt to synthesize these different views. Moravcsik (1998) is representative of this effort. He first explains the preferences of governments in terms of special interest politics (as the outcome of how different interest groups at the national level are affected by policy options). He next analyzes the ability of national governments to translate those preferences into EU policy by treating states as unitary and analyzing their negotiating leverage in terms of threat points and fallback options. Finally he explains the heavily institutionalized aspect of European integration in terms of the need of the negotiators to make credible commitments to the policies on which they agree. On this basis he explains the important landmarks in the process of European integration: the Common Market, the Common Agricultural Policy, the European Monetary System, etc. The institutions of the European Union are thus seen in largely instrumental terms—as a way of allowing governments to strengthen their own bargaining power by enabling them to make credible commitments; other than this, EU institutions play no role. The preferences of governments, in turn, are grounded in the preferences of their constituents. The governments of member states similarly play no autonomous role. In the language of neoclassical economics, there is little principal–agent slack at either level.

3 THE REVENGE OF NEOFUNCTIONALISM

This synthetic view was not universally accepted. European scholars (see e.g. Majone 1992; Dehousse 1994) continued to insist that focusing on interest group politics at the national level and on the leverage of chiefs of government over interstate negotiations missed what is distinctive about European integration. EU institutions were seen as having a capacity to impinge on national politics in ways that could not be understood simply in terms of self-interested negotiations among autonomous member states. This reflected more than just the rise of transnational coalitions of like-minded interest groups across EU member states. These European scholars detected something resembling the development of a multilevel, quasi-federalist European state in which decisions taken by EU bureaucracies and leaders had a disproportionate impact on policy outcomes.

Studies responding to these observations (e.g. Krasner 1989; Pierson 1996) can be seen as attempting to rehabilitate older neofunctionalist arguments. The neofunctionalists had emphasized cross-issue spillovers and the influence of semi-autonomous EU institutions in shaping European integration. Many of the examples they invoked seemed to display the positive feedback loops and cumulative dynamics characteristic of the path-dependent processes popularized by economic theorists like Brian Arthur (see Arthur 1988, 1989). More generally, the concept of path dependence appeared to capture the prevalence of unintended consequences and the exceptional influence ascribed to individuals in the process of European integration. It provided a rationale for how transitory events, often resulting from human agency, could have long-lived, even permanent effects.

Path dependence is an elastic concept. There is sometimes a tendency to invoke it as the explanation for everything that is not readily explained by standard models. It is hard to exonerate the defendant by discrediting the witness—by showing that models of interest group politics and intergovernmental negotiations are not up to the task—since it is always possible to redefine the preferences of interest groups in ways that are consistent with observed outcomes *ex post*. Thus, to establish the path-dependent character of European integration, one must demonstrate that the phenomenon satisfies the necessary and sufficient conditions for such a process. These are lock-in (that once the process starts off on a particular trajectory there is no turning back) and positive feedback (that once a branch in the road is taken there is a tendency to proceed ever further along it). Unfortunately, whether a specific process exhibits path-dependent characteristics tends to be difficult to verify empirically (as evidenced by the controversy over the classic instance of a supposedly path-dependent process in economics, namely, the development of technology and the now-standard example of the Qwerty typewriter keyboard—see David 1985; Leibowitz and Margolis 1990).

Not all studies of European integration invoking the concept of path dependence have convincingly established the existence of lock-in and positive feedback. This criticism can be levied at even the best of these studies, e.g. Pierson (1996). Pierson focuses on the role of institutions like the European Commission and the Court of Justice in determining the direction of integrationist initiatives and sustaining their momentum. He analyzes why gaps emerge in member-state control of these institutions, how those gaps allow institutions to shape events in ways that were not anticipated by their founders, and what prevents those gaps from being closed. Pierson attributes growing gaps in member-state control of these institutions to the efficiency advantages of delegating decision-relevant powers as the EU has grown from its founding six members. He points to additional pressure to delegate as the range of competencies assumed by the EU has expanded from economics to social policy, internal security, foreign policy, and other issues, rendering infeasible direct management by the national governments of member states. The result has been to endow EU institutions with growing agenda-setting and process-managing power. Given the ability of the agenda-setter and process-manager to influence outcomes, a growing gap has opened up between EU institutions and the governments of the member states.

At its root, this perspective is very similar to that informing early neofunctionalist models emphasizing the roles of elites and institutions in the process of European integration. The difference is that underlying assumptions are now made explicit and discussed systematically. Whether they constitute an adequate rationale for the importance assigned to EU institutions in the process of integration can still be questioned. Their adequacy hinges on the existence of a convincing explanation for what prevents gaps in member-state control of EU institutions from being closed. In other words, while the explanation for the development of such gaps may be convincing enough, why don't the governments of member states force those gaps to be closed and their unintended consequences to be reversed when they diverge significantly from national preferences?

Consider the case of EU foreign policy. The development of a common EU foreign policy entails many complex issues. Steps to preserve European security might have to be taken more quickly than can be agreed in meetings of twenty-five ministers or heads of state in the Council. These are arguments for delegating some responsibility for these matters to the Commission, which can cut through complexity and react quickly. They can help to explain why gaps open up between the decisions of the Commission and the control of the member states. But imagine that the Commission takes decisions that conflict with the preferences of a majority of governments and attempts to extend its authority over foreign policy still further. What then prevents the Council from taking back control of foreign policy and assigning it to its own delegate? This case is not simply hypothetical: the division of responsibility for foreign policy between the High Representative for Common Foreign and Security Policy, appointed and directly accountable to the Council (constituted and directed controlled by the member states), and the Commissioner for External Relations was a key issue in the constitutional convention of 2002–3. That there already existed a Commissioner for External Relations did not prevent member states from reassigning a significant share of such powers to the President of the Council and therefore, ultimately, to themselves.

The question, then, is what prevents the member states from taking back such powers even when they have been delegated to an EU institution previously? And what allows EU institutions to sustain actions that run counter to the preferences of national governments and to expand their powers still further? In answer to these questions, Pierson cites the short time horizon of national politicians, the high density of the issues that arise in European Union politics, and the sunk costs of participating in the European Union. The short time horizons of national politicians, who rarely look beyond the next election, are invoked to explain why governments do not make expensive investments in institutional reform now in order to prevent EU bureaucrats from running away with the policy agenda later. Closing the gap between principal and agent would presumably yield a stream of benefits over time but require a costly up-front investment, which politicians with high discount rates are reluctant to make. But it is not clear that this argument is sufficient to explain path dependence. If their constituents look far into the future, even politicians with high discount rates will be forced to do the same to avoid being thrown out of office immediately. And, in practice, the members of the Commission and other EU institutions serve limited terms that are not always significantly longer than those of national chiefs of government. It may be that the long time horizon of EU institutions somehow derives from the rules and procedures of those institutions, not from the individuals involved. But this argument remains to be developed and defended.

Similarly, the density, number, and complexity of issues provides an efficiency argument for delegation—for why a gap between principal and agent may open up— but not for why the decision to delegate is not reversed if the agent pursues policies that are at variance with the preferences of the principals. The sunk costs of EU membership can explain why the threat of exit is not effective for reining in renegade institutions, but exit is not the only mechanism for addressing such problems. Indeed, when an EU institution takes actions that are inconsistent with the preferences of the majority of member states, exit is not the most obvious or relevant mechanism.

Consider the case of the European Central Bank. The ECB is a relatively autonomous EU institution; among other things, it has an independent source of income, and its statute prohibits the board from taking instructions from national governments. The ECB has very significant influence over economic conditions in the member states. Imagine now that it takes monetary policy decisions that strongly and persistently conflict with the preferences of national governments and that it attempts to expand its competencies still further by acquiring additional influence over, say, the supervision and regulation of financial markets and the formulation of European fiscal policies. What would prevent the member states from overriding and reversing its decisions?

To be sure, amendments to the central bank's state and mandate, which are incorporated into the Treaty of European Union, would have to surmount the high hurdle of unanimous consent (plus, conceivably, ratification at the national level), which is cited by authors like Pollack (1997) as a reason why institutional arrangements may be "sticky." But it is not clear that their high discount rates would prevent politicians from calling the ECB to task in the press, something that has effectively "disciplined" other central banks, or even seeking to modify its statute and procedures to, say, give governments a mandate to set the general orientations of monetary policy (something that has been actively proposed in the literature on inflation targeting). To the contrary, their concern with the present and immediate future might incline political leaders to press for such changes more urgently. To be sure, exiting the monetary union over dissatisfaction with ECB policy, while not inconceivable, would be difficult given the high density of issues in the EU (that exiting the monetary union might cast into doubt a country's other treaty obligations to its partners and even jeopardize its participation in the union itself). In addition, the economy will presumably have adapted to life with the single currency (business cycles will have grown more symmetric with those of the rest of the euro area, trade with other euro area countries will have expanded, etc.), diminishing the benefits of monetary autonomy relative to those of monetary union—even when the common monetary policy is not to a particular country's liking. But if ECB policy consistently conflicted with the preferences of a large majority of member states (the case at hand), governments would have other means short of exit of disciplining the bank, such as public statements that make life difficult for its president and other board members.

Thus, while models of path dependence suggest an appealing way of formalizing long-standing arguments for the autonomous influence of EU institutions, the case for path dependence remains to be convincingly made.

4 Where We Go From Here

Given the rich and varied nature of this literature, it is tempting to say that we now have the pieces in place for a coherent interpretation. Because the European Union remains a union of sovereign nation states, its progress continues to reflect the interplay of its principals (the citizens of these states) and their agents (national officials and Eurocrats). In an obvious sense, citizens and governments support further integration when they see the benefits as dominating the costs. The pace of integration thus accelerates and slows with changes in the external environment and in the structure of the European economy and polity itself, changes that make themselves felt through self-interested voting and intergovernmental negotiation.

But in a world where information is costly and politicians are not easily monitored, there is scope for principal–agent slack and for individuals to shape outcomes by setting and pursuing personal agendas. This is an avenue through which the values of the elite, which seem to have played an important role in the history of European integration, can enter the process. Similarly, the increasingly prominent institutional dimension of the integration process works to condition the effects of these interest group politics and intergovernmental negotiations. These observations help to explain why the progress of European integration has taken its particular form, one which has not always been fully anticipated by the member states.

In recent historical-institutionalist accounts, the point has been put more strongly: institutions "as the carriers of history" (in the words of David 1994) are said to be responsible for the path-dependent character of European integration. But, as evaluated in this chapter, this effort to rehabilitate early interpretations of the dynamics of European integration as a process characterized by path dependence, spillovers, and positive feedbacks has not been entirely successful. The preconditions for the existence of a non-ergodic process have not been identified satisfactorily. Testable implications of this view, which can be used to distinguish it from the alternatives, have not been adequately specified.

Much of the literature on the political economy of European integration seeks to establish the incompatibility of these views instead of exploring how they fit together. Methodologically, these different strands of work approach the problem in very different ways—some rely on narrative, others on econometrics—which may help to explain the inability of their advocates to appreciate one another's contributions. More effectively bringing together these different strands of work, analytically and empirically, will help to push this research agenda forward.

References

Arthur, B. 1988. Self-reinforcing mechanisms in economics. Pp. 9–32 in *The Economy as an Evolving Complex System*, ed. P. W. Anderson, K. J. Arrow, and D. Pines. Reading, Mass.: Addison Wesley.

—— 1989. Competing technologies, increasing returns and lock-in by historical events. *Economic Journal*, 99: 116–32.

Berger, H., and Ritschl, A. 1995. Germany and the political economy of the Marshall Plan, 1947–52: a re-revisionist view. Pp. 199–245 in *Europe's Postwar Recovery*, ed. B. Eichengreen. Cambridge: Cambridge University Press.

David, P. A. 1985. Clio and the economics of qwerty. *American Economic Review: Papers and Proceedings*, 75: 332–7.

—— 1994. Why are institutions the "carriers of history?" Path-dependence and the evolution of conventions, organizations and institutions. *Structural Change and Economic Dynamics*, 5: 205–20.

Dehousse, R. 1994. Community competences: are there limits to growth? Pp. 103–25 in *Europe after Maastricht: An Ever Closer Union*, ed. R. Dehousse. Munich: Beck.

Frieden, J. A. 2002. Real sources of european currency policy: sectoral interests and European monetary integration. *International Organization*, 56: 831–60.

GABEL, M. 2001. Divided opinion, common currency: the political economy of public support for EMU. Pp. 49–76 in *The Political Economy of European Monetary Unification*, ed. B. Eichengreen and J. Frieden. Boulder, Colo.: Westview Press.

GARRETT, G. 1992. International cooperation and institutional choice: the European Community's internal market. *International Organization*, 46: 533–58.

—— 2001. The politics of Maastricht. Pp. 111–30 in *The Political Economy of European Monetary Unification*, ed. B. Eichengreen and J. Frieden. Boulder, Colo.: Westview Press.

HAAS, E. 1958. *The Uniting of Europe*. Stanford, Calif.: Stanford University Press.

KEOHANE, R. 1984. *After Hegemony*. Princeton, NJ: Princeton University Press.

—— and HOFFMANN, S. 1991. Institutional change in Europe in the 1980s. Pp. 1–39 in *The New European Community: Decisionmaking and Institutional Change*, ed. R. Keohane and S. Hoffmann. Boulder, Colo.: Westview Press.

KRASNER, S. D. 1989. Sovereignty: an institutional perspective. Pp. 69–96 in *The Elusive State: International and Comparative Perspectives*, ed. J. A. Caporaso. Newbury Park, Calif.: Sage.

LANGE, P. 1993. The Maastricht social protocol: why did they do it? *Politics and Society*, 21: 5–36.

LEIBOWITZ, S., and MARGOLIS, S. 1990. The fable of the keys. *Journal of Law and Economics*, 33: 1–26.

MAJONE, G. 1992. Regulatory federalism in the European Community. *Environment and Planning C: Government and Policy*, 10: 299–316.

MARTIN, L. 1993. International and domestic institutions in the EMU process. *Economics and Politics*, 5: 125–44.

—— 2001. International and domestic institutions in the EMU process and beyond. Pp. 131–55 in *The Political Economy of European Monetary Unification*, ed. B. Eichengreen and J. Frieden. Boulder, Colo.: Westview Press.

MORAVCSIK, A. 1993. Preferences and power in the European Community: a liberal intergovernmentalist approach. *Journal of Common Market Studies*, 31: 473–524.

—— 1998. *The Choice for Europe: Social Purpose and State Power from Messina to Maastricht*. Ithaca, NY: Cornell University Press.

PIERSON, P. 1996. The path to European integration: a historical institutionalist analysis. *Comparative Political Studies*, 29: 123–63.

—— and LEIBFRIED, S. 1995. Multi-tiered institutions and the making of social policy. Pp. 1–40 in *European Social Policy*, ed. S. Leibfried and P. Pierson. Washington, DC: Brookings Institution.

POLLACK, M. A. 1997. Obedient servant or runaway Eurocracy? Delegation, agency and agenda setting in the European Community. *International Organization*, 51: 99–134.

ROSE, A. 2000. One money, one market: estimating the effect of common currencies on trade. *Economic Policy*, 15: 8–45.

ROSS, G. 1994. *Jacques Delors and European Integration*. Oxford: Polity Press.

SANDHOLTZ, W. 1993. Choosing union: monetary politics and Maastricht. *International Organization*, 47: 1–39.

CHAPTER 45

TRADE, IMMIGRATION, AND CROSS-BORDER INVESTMENT

RONALD ROGOWSKI

POLITICAL economists have understood since the famous Stolper–Samuelson essay of 1941 that increasing international trade—whether in products (e.g. grain, steel) or in factors of production (labor, capital)—can have strong distributional consequences, benefiting some groups domestically and internationally but harming others. By now four distinct models in international political economy offer specific predictions about the distributional consequences, between and among nations, of cross-border exchange.[1] While virtually all models conclude that trade improves *world* welfare,[2] some allow that trade can diminish welfare in particular *countries*, chiefly the advanced industrial ones. One of the models predicts *factoral* within-country effects

---

[1] The between-nation impact is usually called a *welfare effect*, and trade in factors of production is commonly labeled *migration* or *foreign investment*. I argue below that the full social and political impact of lowered barriers to trade—what is commonly called "globalization"—can be understood only if we look at these effects as a whole, and if we consider trade both in products and in factors.

I omit any discussion of the familiar Ricardo (or, as some would have it, Ricardo–Pangloss) single-factor, single-good model, since it predicts no distributional consequences: every group in every country gains from trade.

[2] I note one small, but potentially important, exception below.

(e.g. workers win, capital loses), the other three mainly *sectoral* effects (computers win, textiles lose).

By now most political scientists, but not all, will be familiar with (if not totally sympathetic to) the approach that this chapter embodies, namely deriving explicit *political* implications from what were originally devised as *economic* models. In this case, economic models yield definite predictions about who will win and who will lose from increasing trade in goods or factors; the political side of the task is to figure out, at a minimum, (*a*) the political pressures that are likely to arise from these distributional consequences, and (*b*) the kinds of coalitions that form, or that can be formed by smart political entrepreneurs, on behalf of particular trade-related policies.

In what follows, I will discuss the implications of the four models, the empirical evidence for and against them, and what all this suggests for future research. I will focus particularly on the *anomalies*—i.e. the seeming violations of theoretical prediction—that have arisen in recent work, and on the efforts to modify theory in response to those anomalies.

I shall label the four main models (1) *Heckscher–Ohlin (HO)*, (2) *specific factors, including Samuelson–Jones (SJ) and Ricardo–Viner (RV)*, (3) *neo-Ricardian*, and (4) *Economies of Scale (EOS)*. As the name given to the last model implies, the first three all assume constant returns to scale (doubling all inputs exactly doubles output). All but the neo-Ricardian model normally assume, in addition, that the same production technology is available in all countries, i.e. all countries have identical production functions; but the models differ (obviously) in their assumption about whether factors are mobile among sectors, an issue that also becomes important within the neo-Ricardian model. All models make the conventional assumption of diminishing marginal returns to any individual factor.

We consider these models in turn, focusing in each case first on trade in products and then on cross-border migration and investment.

1 HECKSCHER–OHLIN

(*a*) *Trade in products*. In the simplest two-factor, two-good variant of this workhorse model, trade in goods and services benefits every country as a whole—to put it concretely, trade raises GDP per capita. Hence, obviously, trade also improves world welfare; but it harms, in every country, owners of locally scarce resources.[3] The well-known Mayda–Rodrik paper (1999) accurately applies this model to a world

---

[3] The classic example asks us to imagine Japan (densely populated) and Australia (thinly populated) in autarky: in Japan, both land and grain (a land-intensive product) will be expensive, i.e. will trade for many hours of labor, or of labor-intensive products (e.g. cloth). In Australia, land and grain will be cheaper in isolation, i.e. will require fewer hours of labor, or of labor-intensive products, to buy. If trade now opens between Japan and Australia, Japan will export steel and import grain; Australia will export grain and import steel. Trade will harm Japanese landowners and benefit Japanese workers; but it will benefit Australian landowners and harm Australian workers.

in which the only factors are human capital and labor: in the developed countries, abundant in human capital, trade would harm (and be opposed by) the unskilled; in developing countries, abundant in unskilled labor, opposition to trade would come from the owners of (scarce) human capital. Since the model assumes costless mobility of factors among sectors (e.g. workers displaced in apparel or automobiles can with no difficulty go into computers or financial services) sectoral employment does not matter: in developed countries *all* unskilled, in developing ones *all* skilled, workers are harmed. Again following the basic model, in developed economies globalization would increase the returns to human capital, the incentives to acquire it, and the extent of economic inequality; while in developing economies all of these would diminish. Since in each country the gains to the abundant factor outweigh the losses to the scarce one (otherwise trade could not be welfare improving for the country as a whole), smart politicians and credible institutions can shape compensation schemes that sustain free trade.

(*b*) *Migration and investment.* Imagine, however, a Heckscher–Ohlin world in which no products, but only factors of production, can move. Locally abundant factors will seek the higher returns of areas in which they are scarce; and migration and investment, just like trade in products, will benefit locally abundant factors, harm locally scarce ones, and improve world welfare. The classical illustration of these points is the simple two-country, two-factor model presented in Figure 45.1. We imagine that the "world" population is divided between countries A and B, with everybody to the left of the vertical line residing in A, everybody to the right in B. Pre-migration, the wage (equivalent, in any competitive market, to the marginal productivity of labor, or MPL) in country A, w_A, is higher than in country B, w_B.

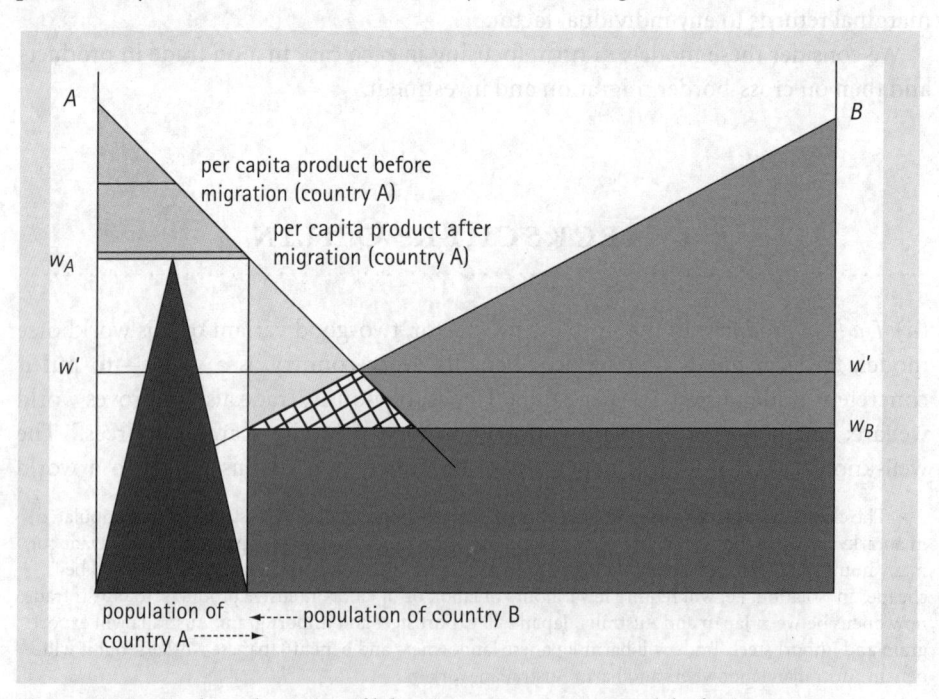

Fig. 45.1 Marginal productivity of labor in a two-country model of migration

Under the general principle of declining marginal productivity of each factor, MPL in each country decreases as the country's population increases. Again before migration, the total product in country A is just the sum of all the marginal products, or the total area under the MPL curve; labor in country A receives its wage times its total labor, or the area of the darkly shaded left-side rectangle; owners of capital receive the remainder, or the area of the lightly shaded left-side triangle. Similarly labor in country B receives the area of the darkly shaded right-side rectangle, capital the area of the medium-shaded right-hand triangle.

If labor can migrate freely between the two countries (and assuming that no capital moves with it), labor will flow from B to A (shifting the vertical line of division between the two countries to the right) until the wage is equalized in the two countries at w'. The wage in country A will fall, that in country B will rise; country A capitalists will benefit, country B capitalists will be harmed. But *world* production will increase, since after migration world product will include the diagonally striped center triangle that, before migration, was forgone. Hence migration, for the world as a whole, is unambiguously welfare improving. Exactly the same analysis would hold for movements of capital, save that *ex ante* capital would have the higher return in the less capital-abundant (i.e. poorer) country and would migrate from rich countries to poor ones.

Less often noted, however, is that in advanced economies not just the wages of the unskilled, but *per capita income*, can fall as a result of migration and foreign investment; that is, the losses to the scarce factor can actually outweigh the gains to the abundant one(s). Again, this can readily be seen in the simple terms of Figure 45.1. Recall that total product in each country is the area under the MPL (marginal product of labor) line: the MPL tells us how much *additional* product we get from each new unit of labor, and the sum of all those marginal products is the total product.[4] Then per capita total product in each country is just that area under the MPL curve divided by the population segment (represented, remember, by the x-axis). This is the same thing as the average height of the trapezoid composed of (for our high-wage country in Figure 45.1) the medium-shaded triangle and the dark-shaded rectangle on the left-hand side. As population moves from country B to country A, per capita product— the average height of this trapezoid—must fall in A and rise in B. The point can be generalized: in the simplest Cobb–Douglas production function, with only capital and labor as inputs, per capita output $y(=Y/L)$ is always increasing in the capital–labor ratio $k(=K/L)$.[5] As trade in factors opens, capital-abundant countries export capital and import labor, decreasing k. Since, in the model, the marginal gain in productivity in the capital-scarce countries outweighs the marginal loss in the capital-abundant ones, world welfare improves;[6] but, in theory, developed-country welfare can easily decline.

---

[4] Similarly, if we graphed each student's weight against her or his height, we would have a "marginal" curve; if we take the sum of all those weights—i.e. the area under the weight–height curve, or the cumulative distribution—we will know the total poundage of all students below a specific height.

[5] In the standard Cobb–Douglas notation, $Y = AK^{\alpha}L^{1-\alpha}$; $\alpha \in (0,1)$; hence, where $y = Y/L$ and $k = K/L$, $y = Ak^{\alpha}$. Whatever decreases the capital–labor ratio must decrease per capita output.

[6] In the notation used immediately above, $dy/dk = \frac{A\alpha}{k^{1-\alpha}}$; i.e. the marginal per capita gain in output from any given increase in the capital–labor ratio will be higher, the *lower* is the initial capital–labor ratio.

Add to this what is suggested by the impressive historical work of O'Rourke and Williamson (2001), namely that migration has equalized factor prices more quickly and thoroughly than either investment or trade, and we perhaps begin to see why: (*a*) developed-country politicians have found it far harder to construct pro-immigration than pro-free trade coalitions; and (*b*) only highly undemocratic regimes (think the Berlin Wall) have been able to restrict *emigration*.

But the *pattern* of trade, whether in products or factors, predicted by the HO theory has increasingly seemed at odds with reality. This is the first major anomaly we must face. Even in the 1980s, HO would have predicted capital to have earned about 60 times as much in India as in the USA, making it something of a marvel that, even allowing for a lot of political risk, capital did not flood from the rich countries to the poor ones (Lucas 1990). Today, HO predicts with equal clarity that skilled labor should be migrating in droves from the rich countries (where skilled workers are abundant) to the poor ones (where they are scarce: cf. Davis and Weinstein 2005, discussed at greater length below).

That important issue to one side, the HO model predicts the same *factoral* coalitions on migration and investment as it does on trade: in developed countries, all unskilled workers should oppose immigration and outward foreign investment; in poor countries, all skilled workers and capitalists should oppose emigration and inward foreign investment. As a first approximation of the alignments that have emerged on the issue of the new, and now seemingly stillborn, European Constitution, this does not do badly.[7]

2 Specific Factors

As was emphasized above, the Heckscher–Ohlin model, like Ricardo's classical picture, assumes that factors of production (labor, capital, land) can redeploy costlessly between sectors. Workers, or machinery or land, that are displaced by import competition move frictionlessly into exporting sectors. What happens if, somewhat more realistically, we replace this assumption of "mobile factors" with one in which at least some factors are "specific," i.e. can be used *only* in a particular sector, or can be adapted to others only at considerable cost?

(*a*) *Trade in products*. The *Ricardo–Viner* (RV) specific-factors model is straightforward, indeed obvious: factors specific to import-competing sectors will embrace protection, those specific to exporting sectors will favor free trade. Thus, while American capitalists generally should favor free trade (because capital is abundant in the USA), owners of textile factories, swamped by Third-World imports and unable to convert their factories to other uses, will (and do) advocate protection. A more interesting

---

[7] In Paris, wealthy districts voted overwhelmingly yes, poor ones no. In France as a whole, farmers, blue-collar workers, public sector employees, and the unemployed all voted no by more than 60%. A major issue was the likelihood of increasing immigration from the new member countries. See the *New York Times*, 30 May 2005.

prediction of this model, emphasized for example in Hiscox (2002), is that, as factors become more specific—i.e. less able to move between sectors—politics will divide less along factoral lines (workers vs. capitalists) and more along sectoral ones (textiles vs. computers).

In sharp contrast, however, the *Samuelson–Jones* (SJ) specific-factors model, which is the more widely accepted modern treatment,[8] emphasizes the ambiguous distributional consequences for the *mobile* factor (depending, in essence, on its owners' consumption preferences). In the SJ model, effects on *specific* factors, but not necessarily *mobile* ones, continue to be governed by conventional factor-abundance considerations.

Imagine for example an advanced economy with abundant physical capital, above-average human capital, but scarce unskilled labor, producing two kinds of goods: high tech and low tech. The physical capital can be used only in the high-tech sector, the unskilled labor only in low-tech production; skilled labor is used in both sectors and is fully mobile between them. Then freeing up trade will benefit owners of physical capital and harm unskilled workers; but it will have ambiguous effects on skilled workers (i.e. owners of human capital), depending chiefly on their relative propensity to consume high-tech products (which will rise in price as trade increases) vs. low-tech ones (which will become cheaper). Certainly one possible political scenario, in such an SJ world, is a protectionist coalition of unskilled and (at least some) skilled workers; and the current outsourcing anxieties of developed-country skilled workers, seemingly one of the advanced economies' most mobile groups, make this version of the specific-factors model seem quite relevant.

More generally, where the RV model predicts that increasing specificity of factors will lead to *sectoral* coalitions, the SJ one predicts increasingly anomalous *factoral* coalitions, e.g. the possibility that skilled labor in a developed economy, despite being abundant, may wind up advocating protection—or, equally, that scarce skilled labor in a developing economy could favor free trade. Exactly as in the HO model, however, trade improves all countries' (and hence world) welfare.

As an aside, it seems that human capital is inherently more specific than physical capital. Smart owners of physical capital can nowadays diversify their portfolios with a few mouse-clicks, but investment in human capital is arduous, focused, and long term, be it the learning of a specific skill or the attainment of a university degree. Moreover, Estevez-Abe, Iversen, and Soskice (2001) have emphasized that decisions about specificity of human capital are to a large extent *endogenous*, conditioned on subsidies to training and social insurance mechanisms: an eighteen-year-old, forced to choose between a general and easily redeployable form of human capital (e.g. a university education) and a much more specific one (e.g. mastering the production processes of a particular firm), is likelier to choose the latter if she knows that generous unemployment and retraining benefits will kick in if the firm or sector subsequently fails.

---

[8] See Samuelson 1971; Jones 1971; or any conventional textbook treatment, e.g. Krugman and Obstfeld 1994, ch. 3.

(*b*) *Migration and investment*. Here, too, the SJ and the RV variants of specific factors come to interestingly opposed conclusions. In SJ, group preferences regarding immigration and foreign investment will remain exactly as in HO: scarce factors opposed, abundant ones in favor, whether they are mobile or specific. Coalitions on this issue will remain wholly *factoral* and wholly predicted by relative factor abundance. Under the RV model, however, preferences on immigration will be uniform (and pro-immigration) in exporting sectors, but divided along *factoral* lines in import-competing sectors; or, to put it another way, all owners of abundant factors will favor immigration, while *some* owners of scarce (but export-specific) factors will also be pro-immigrant.

For simplicity, suppose that a developed-country economy consists of only two sectors: textiles, heavily pressured by import competition, and software, characterized by booming exports. Each is produced by only two factors, each specific to its sector: textile-specific capital and labor; software-specific capital and labor. Assuming that immigrants can no more easily master the skills of the software sector than can domestic labor, software workers, despite the relative scarcity of labor in their economy overall, will favor immigration as much as they do free trade: if anything immigration will drive down the costs of their textiles.[9] By the same token, textile workers will hate immigration even more than they do free trade. But textile *owners*, pressured already by low-wage competition from abroad, will favor immigration as a way of lowering their costs. Hence in the RV picture of the world, we should expect to see: (*a*) some groups where preferences over trade and immigration diverge (e.g. favoring both protection and immigration, or free trade and restricted immigration); and (*b*) uniformly sectoral coalitions on trade, but some factoral ones on migration.

In the specific-factors model, as in the HO one, trade in factors improves world and poor-country welfare; it may, however, not raise per capita real income in developed countries.

3 THE NEO-RICARDIAN MODEL

In an important recent paper, Davis and Weinstein (2005) stress the peculiar implications of the HO model noted earlier in this chapter. Since the return to each factor must equal its marginal product (e.g. the wage is just the marginal product of labor), and since the marginal product should always diminish with relative abundance of that factor, returns to factors should always be lower where the factor is most abundant.[10] Thus skilled labor, clearly abundant in the USA, should earn a *higher*

---

[9] If, that is, we consider only the factor-returns story. In a recent paper, Hanson, Scheve, and Slaughter (2005) emphasize that, at least in tolerably generous welfare states, the post-redistribution implications of migration may depart considerably from those of free trade.

[10] In the simple two-factor Cobb–Douglas production function discussed earlier (n. 5), $Y = AK^{\alpha}L^{1-\alpha}$ implies that the wage will equal the marginal productivity of labor, i.e. $w = \partial Y/\partial L = A(1-\alpha)k^{\alpha}$, where (as before) $k = K/L$. Hence, assuming identical production

real wage where skills are scarce (e.g. India); and American skilled workers should be *emigrating* to India. And the fact of skilled migration into the USA and other advanced economies is a second major anomaly that we must address.

In fact, Davis and Weinstein (DW) argue persuasively, the USA may well offer higher returns than the rest of the world to virtually *all* factors, including many that it holds abundantly; and they suggest that the only explanation must lie in US *technological and legal-system superiority*. In short, they advocate (as, to be sure, have many students before them) abandonment of the traditional HO assumption of identical production functions in all countries and an admission that total factor productivity, the *A* term in most production functions (e.g. Cobb–Douglas: above, n. 5), is simply higher in advanced economies.

As Davis and Weinstein note, however, the distributional, welfare, and pattern of trade implications of assuming between-nation differences in technology are often at least as strange as those of the HO model, and sometimes are downright alarming. Trade in products continues to be welfare improving for all countries, just as in the original Ricardo model (although of course, exactly as in that model, factor prices no longer equalize between countries); but *migration*, while it improves world and sending-country welfare, may (and, in their empirical estimation, does) harm *all* sectors in the receiving country, chiefly by eroding the more productive country's terms of trade advantage.

(*a*) *Trade in products*. Since in the DW model there is only one factor, labor, which can move costlessly among sectors, distributional effects within countries disappear: everybody will favor free trade. If (as DW do not do), one assumed instead that labor was differentiated and specific to sectors, the neo-Ricardian model predicts an ordinal relationship: the more productive the given sector, the likelier it would be to benefit from, and to favor, free trade. This is not an altogether empty prediction, but it is less informative than we might wish, both because the source of the productivity advantage remains a black box, and because productivity must to some extent be endogenous.

(*b*) *Migration and investment*. [11] Here the DW model has its real bite. Because trade can no longer equalize wages between countries, migration will continue (if allowed) even under costless trade in products, until wages equalize; and production will then locate according to absolute, not comparative, advantage. Migration is unambiguously welfare lowering for the more productive country, but welfare improving for the less productive one and for the world as a whole. If labor is freely mobile between sectors, everybody in the advanced country will oppose immigration (even as all favored free trade); to the extent that labor is immobile among sectors, presumably immigration will be most opposed by those sectors in which the country's

---

functions across countries, the wage will (in isolation) be higher where labor is scarcer. The same will hold true for any factor: the relatively scarcer (more abundant) it is, the higher (lower) will be its return in the given economy.

[11] In the strict DW model, there is no capital, hence no cross-border investment; but obviously if *K* were the only factor instead of *L*, the same logic would apply: all owners of capital (which is to say, everybody) within the advanced economy would oppose cross-border investment.

absolute advantage is *greatest* (since precisely those sectors have wages most above world levels and hence will attract the most immigrants and see their terms-of-trade advantage erode most quickly).[12] Conversely, in LDCs: (*a*) if labor is mobile, all should *favor* migration; and (*b*) if labor is immobile among sectors, emigration should be favored most by those whose comparative *dis*advantage is greatest.

The testable implication of note is that, quite in contrast to the HO, SJ, or even RV models, attitudes toward free trade and free migration in advanced economies will in general be *negatively* correlated. More precisely, the specific-factor version of the DW model suggests for such economies that, the more productive any given sector, the more it should (*a*) favor free trade, but (*b*) oppose immigration.

4 Economies of Scale Trade

While these models[13] have somewhat lost favor in recent years, and while the Krugman monopolistic competition variant predicts unambiguous welfare gains from broader trade via greater variety,[14] two other classes of such models may still be relevant and do predict unambiguous distributional effects. First, one cannot understand something like the USA–EU conflict over Boeing and Airbus without a picture of economies of scale internal to the firm. In essence, it appears, world demand for big civilian aircraft intersects the firm average-cost curve well before it minimizes, so that in the end only one firm will survive. As in the older Brander–Spencer picture, sizable monopoly rents will accrue to the firm (and the country) that wins the competition, motivating both firms and governments, not to protect against imports, but to subsidize exports. Most scholars no longer see this model as having very general applicability, but we cannot leave it altogether out of consideration.

More important are probably models of *locational* or *network* economies of scale: for the former, think Hollywood; for the latter, the Qwerty keyboard or the Windows operating system. In these cases, there can be a lot of competition among firms—Hollywood has many studios and even more producers of such intermediate services as casting, editing, lighting; and lots of vendors offer Windows-based software—but it's just too daunting, at least for a long time, for anybody to set up a rival Hollywood (Bollywood? China?) or a rival operating system (*pace* Linux). Welfare losses can easily ensue, as the dominant locale or network extracts monopoly rents (Hollywood wages, Microsoft prices), and these losses can actually grow as barriers to trade erode. In the Qwerty version of this story, an inferior and/or higher-cost product or locale

---

[12] A particularly counterintuitive implication is that brain drain—migration of highly skilled labor from less to more productive societies—should be *opposed* by high-skill workers in the developed countries but *favored* by high-skill ones in LDCs.

[13] Common to all of them is the assumption that, whether at the level of the firm, the locale, or the country, there are increasing returns to scale, i.e. doubling all inputs more than doubles output. Hence, taking factor prices as fixed, the biggest producer can always produce most cheaply.

[14] For the standard textbook treatment, see Krugman and Obstfeld 1994, ch. 6.

repeatedly crushes superior and cheaper rivals. There is probably no easy answer to this story, as the EU's antitrust efforts against Microsoft suggest; but it seems clear that the countries, locales, and even firms that wind up losing such a struggle are *harmed* and, in the strongest variant of the story, world welfare is suboptimal also: we'd all be more productive (allegedly) with Linux, or would get cheaper watches from Thailand than from Switzerland, if we could just make the switch.

In the locational variants of this model, incentives to immigration persist even (or especially) under free trade: migration and trade are complements, not substitutes, and a NAFTA or an expanded EU can actually *increase* migration into, and investment in, existing centers of production (cf. Krugman 1991). Such migration improves world, national, and likely even sectoral welfare.

5 SUMMARY

Looking at all of this another, and perhaps more helpful, way, we can see effects at the level of the world, the country, the factor, and the sector; and we can think of the coalitional and redistributional mechanisms that might ameliorate distributional conflicts.

(*a*) The *world* is better off from trade and migration except in some locational and network economies-of-scale cases. This means that, in theory, *global* redistribution, were it possible, could nearly always handle the distributional issues surrounding globalization—although, in something like the Davis–Weinstein picture, the redistribution would have to be from poor to rich countries!

(*b*) In the great majority of models, each *country* is also made better off by migration and trade, i.e. per capita income rises. Only in the economies of scale models does trade sometimes make a nation worse off; but *migration* can reduce the welfare of receiving countries even in the classical HO model, and definitely does so in the neo-Ricardian cases. Concretely, this means that coalitions in favor of free migration will be harder to build than ones in favor of free trade in products, and will be virtually impossible where trade is based on technological superiority rather than differences in factor endowments.

(*c*) Gains and losses from trade, and hence preferences over trade, will divide along *factoral* lines in the HO and in the SJ specific-factors models, abundant factors normally favoring, and scarce factors normally opposing, free movement of products and factors. (In the SJ case, the position of the mobile factor cannot be predicted *ex ante* by its relative abundance: skilled workers in the USA, precisely because of their mobility in an otherwise specific-factors economy, can conceivably lose from trade.) Perhaps more importantly, however, factor owners' preferences on trade will correlate almost perfectly with their preferences on migration and foreign investment: free traders will favor free migration (again, abstracting away from any fiscal or cultural impact) and free movement of capital, and protectionists will also oppose migration and foreign investment. The difference, as indicated earlier, is that under free trade the winners' gains will outweigh the losers' losses; under migration this need not be the case.

(*d*) In the RV, the neo-Ricardian specific factors, and the firm-specific EOS models, gains and losses from trade will divide very much along *sectoral* lines, but with very different specific implications. In both the RV and the neo-Ricardian pictures of the world, the most productive, export-successful sectors should most favor free trade; the least productive, most import-threatened ones should be protectionist. Under RV, however, workers should most oppose immigration (and owners should most favor it) in the least productive, most import-pressured sectors; while workers in a neo-Ricardian specific-factors world will most oppose immigration in precisely the economy's most productive sectors.

Where economies of scale are internal to the firm (again, think Boeing or Airbus) workers and owners should again unite, not on behalf of protection but in favor of the subsidies and opening of foreign markets that will permit them to achieve an eventual world monopoly. Where EOS are external to the firm, workers and owners will favor free trade and, in most cases, free immigration.

6 Important Research Questions

Given this theoretical background, we can isolate several topics as important for current and future research.

(*a*) *What kind of trade?* Some trade in factors and products is driven by differences in factor endowments, some by differences in technology, some by economies of scale. Surely China's exports of labor-intensive toys and Mexico's of low-skill labor are driven by factor endowments; but America's or Sweden's imports of high-skill labor, with which they are already abundantly endowed, must be a result of technological superiority or of locational economies of scale. The theories imply unambiguously that these different kinds of trade will have different distributional effects, and hence quite different political consequences: factor-endowments trade (e.g. with China) is likely to alienate low-skill workers in advanced economies, but it should prove possible (see below) to blunt their resistance through compensation; immigration, particularly where it is based on technological superiority, may not be politically resolvable; while trade based on economies of scale will ignite few domestic conflicts but major ones between nations.

(*b*) *How specific are the factors?* This has been a major line of enquiry, implicated for example in the work of Scheve and Slaughter, Mayda and Rodrik, and most prominently Michael Hiscox. Fortunately both direct and indirect measures (cross-sectoral differences in wage and profit rates; observed patterns of sectoral vs. factoral opinion and lobbying) can be deployed to good effect. But recent work reminds us also that the extent of factor specificity is in large part endogenous (conditioned by welfare and labor-market mechanisms, educational systems, capital markets, social insurance, union contracts, etc.); and these may themselves be affected by the pressures of global competition.

Generous welfare states and retraining subsidies, for example, or powerful unions, make it less risky for young workers to invest in sector-specific skills, even where the odds are high that these will soon be obsolete. American printing trade apprentices, for example, rushed out of linotype training as soon as computers began to show their word-processing skills; but German apprentices, confident that printers' unions could hold back the new technology, or if that failed that the state would provide generous unemployment insurance and retraining support, continued to master what would soon be the equivalent of the horse and buggy. On the other hand private companies, aware of the moral hazards, will not insure against technological skill obsolescence (how do I *prove* that technology, and not merely my own laziness, has made me unemployable?); so it is likely that, in terms of social welfare, a stingy welfare state like that of the USA encourages too little investment in specific skills.

At the same time, increasing global competition arguably makes it harder for countries to maintain generous social insurance schemes—implying, if this perspective is correct, that many countries where workers once invested extensively in specific skills will now switch to a more general skill portfolio, at least among younger workers or those still in the educational system.

The interesting research question is the degree of endogeneity, i.e. how rapidly do people readjust their investment patterns (particularly in human capital) when incentives change. The most traction on this question may be gained by looking particularly at cases where the degree of specificity has recently changed or is changing (Denmark, Germany, France, China, Japan).

(c) *Do gender and age matter, and if so how?* A fascinating recent finding, due to Burgoon and Hiscox (2004), is that women, controlling for virtually all other factors, including particularly education, tend to be more protectionist than men. The most plausible explanation, though one that is hard to pin down empirically, is simply women's greater vulnerability to rapid economic change: for family or personal reasons, most are still less likely to move to a job in a new region, have fewer private savings to fall back on when a job is lost, and worry more about the effects of economic dislocation on present or future children. One test of this hypothesis, which so far as I know has not yet been done, is to compare attitudes of women in stingy welfare states (e.g. the USA) with those of women in generous, and particularly in family-friendly welfare states (e.g. Christian democratic Europe), where women are more cushioned against economic disruption.

According to most factor-endowments models, *age* should also matter: pensioners, or even those approaching retirement age, should be concerned mostly about the economy's productivity, hence should favor free trade—*except* where important retirement benefits (e.g. pensions, health care) are linked to the fate of a particular firm or sector. Hence in countries with generous state pension schemes, financed by taxes on the whole economy (e.g. a VAT), the older the worker, the more she or he should support free trade; while in less generous countries, and particularly among workers with defined-benefit pensions funded by individual firms (e.g. General Motors or United Airlines), we might expect rising age to correlate weakly or even negatively with support for free trade.

(*d*) *What are existing compensation mechanisms, and how efficient and reliable are they?* Losers from globalization may accept it if they will be compensated from the social gains (assuming those exist, as in most theories they do). On the other hand generous mechanisms may make factors more specific or impede adjustment. It's important to gauge (*a*) how generous the mechanisms are, (*b*) what incentives they create, and (*c*) how effective and reliable people judge them to be (i.e. are they confident that they will be compensated for any losses from trade or migration?).

Regimes clearly differ in the credibility and reliability of their promises of compensation. Iversen and Soskice (2002, 2004) argue that disciplined parties and proportional representation (PR) combine to make long-term promises credible. Persson and Tabellini (2003) show that PR regimes offer more general compensation, while majoritarian electoral systems focus on geographically separable "pork-barrel" spending; and Fiona McGillivray (2004) suggests why such spending will flow, in majoritarian systems, predominantly to marginal districts. A logical implication of both strands of work is that, when the marginality of a district changes, whether from a shift in preferences or via gerrymandering, previous assurances may be abandoned. Most recently, and in a similar vein, Grossman and Helpman (2004) find, in an elegant and convincing modeling exercise, that protection increases under majoritarian electoral institutions as party discipline weakens. To the extent that this line of research is correct, and that certain regime types impede or favor welfare-improving bargains in trade policy—e.g. by making promises of compensation more reliable—a question of "feedback" obviously arises: as globalization increases countries' exposure to world markets, and thus raises the welfare losses from protection, do political entrepreneurs find incentives to change political institutions (cf. Hiwatari 2001)? Or does increasing inequality, very likely a consequence of globalization in the advanced economies, lead more indirectly to change in political institutions (cf. Ticchi and Vindigni 2003)?

Again, empirical research can focus most usefully on recent changes, whether in institutions (the shift from PR to largely majoritarian electoral systems in Italy and Japan, the reverse shift in New Zealand, the expansion of the European Union) or in policies (tightening of the welfare state in the Netherlands and, more controversially, in Germany; the whole issue of "structural reform" throughout the European economies). Have the policy shifts been driven by trade-related issues, by global competition, or more indirectly by growing inequality? Have they resulted from, or been connected with, changes in (or proposals to change) institutions?

(*e*) *Support for/opposition to free trade, migration, investment.* Obviously this is the meat of the matter. Popular attitudes have usually not been well tapped by survey instruments (or, to put it another way, framing effects are enormous) but have nonetheless given some extremely useful insights. Voting behavior, elite opinion, lobbying, and politicians' positions and maneuvering have been even less reliably ascertained. Fortunately a major effort is under way, led by Michael Hiscox and Helen

Milner, to undertake more reliable cross-national research on all of these aspects. The basic question is clear: are the observed patterns well predicted by the theories, and does the accuracy depend, in the way argued, on country, factor, and industry characteristics? Do positions (e.g. on trade and migration) correlate with one another as predicted?

7 CONCLUSION

I take for granted that the backdrop to all of this is growing global economic integration. But it may also be worth noting that the *pace* of that integration has varied greatly, even in recent years, and that the pace of integration has varied significantly across countries. The great majority of the developed economies have been open for decades, but a few have opened more recently and with astonishing rapidity: Canada, New Zealand. In the developing world, even more countries have opened, recently and more rapidly: China and the former Soviet-bloc countries of course, but even more recently Mexico and India. Have the distributional conflicts and the political alignments, coalitions, and compensation schemes in such cases accorded with theoretical predictions, or do they call them into question? (One issue that has attracted most attention is the seeming failure of rapid opening to diminish inequality in developing countries—for the HO model, as already noted, certainly predicts exactly such a diminution in inequality.)

Empirical research will succeed in this area to the extent that it is informed by, and sheds light on, the well-developed theories of IPE. Precisely because our theories of the distributional consequences are so good, and so linked to specific assumptions about things like technology, economies of scale, and factor specificity, well-designed enquiries can rapidly advance (and in many cases have rapidly advanced) our overall understanding of trade's political effects.

REFERENCES

BURGOON, B., and HISCOX, M. J. 2004. The mysterious case of female protectionism: gender bias in attitudes toward international trade. Available at: www.people.fas.harvard.edu/~hiscox/BurgoonHiscoxFemaleProtectionism.pdf.

DAVIS, D. R., and WEINSTEIN, D. E. 2005. Technological superiority and the losses from migration. Available at: www.international.ucla.edu/cms/files/DavisMigrationDraft.pdf.

ESTEVEZ-ABE, M., IVERSEN, T., and SOSKICE, D. 2001. Social protection and the formation of skills: a reinterpretation of the welfare state. Ch. 4 in *Varieties of Capitalism: The Institutional Foundations of Comparative Advantage*, ed. P. A. Hall and D. Soskice. Oxford: Oxford University Press.

GROSSMAN, G. M., and HELPMAN, E. 2004. A protectionist bias in majoritarian politics. Available at: www.princeton.edu/~grossman/protectionistbias120804gg.pdf.

Hanson, G. H., Scheve, K. F., and Slaughter, M. J. 2005. Public finance and individual preferences over globalization strategies. NBER Working Paper 11028. Available at: www.nber.org/papers/w11028.

Hiscox, M. J. 2002. *International Trade and Political Conflict: Commerce, Coalitions, and Mobility*. Princeton, NJ: Princeton University Press.

Hiwatari, N. 2001. Why electoral reform and party system reorganization? The impact of global capital mobility on the consensus democratic institutions of Italy and Japan. Tokyo: Institute of Social Sciences, University of Tokyo. Available at: http://web.iss.u-tokyo.ac.jp/~hiwatari/papers/010802.pdf.

Iversen, T., and Soskice, D. 2002. Political parties and the time-inconsistency problem in social welfare provision. Paper presented at the Annual Meeting of the Public Choice Society.

—— —— 2004. Electoral institutions, parties, and the politics of class: why some democracies redistribute more than others. Paper presented at the Annual Meeting of American Political Science Association. Available at: www.people.fas.harvard.edu/~iversen/Iversen-Soskice2004d.pdf.

Jones, R. W. 1971. A three-factor model in theory, trade and history. Pp. 3–21 in *Trade, Balance of Payments, and Growth*, ed. J. Bhagwati et al. Amsterdam: North-Holland.

Krugman, P. 1991. *Geography and Trade*. Leuven: Leuven University Press.

—— and Obstfeld, M. 1994. *International Economics: Theory and Policy*, 3rd edn. New York: HarperCollins.

Lucas, R. 1990. Why doesn't capital flow from rich to poor countries? *American Economic Review*, 80: 92–9.

McGillivray, F. 2004. *Privileging Industry: The Comparative Politics of Trade and Industrial Policy*. Princeton, NJ: Princeton University Press.

Mayda, A. M., and Rodrik, D. 1999. Why are some people (and countries) more protectionist than others? NBER Working Paper 8461. Available at: http://ideas.repec.org/p/nbr/nberwo/8461.html.

O'Rourke, K., and Williamson, J. 2001. *Globalization and History*. Cambridge, Mass.: MIT Press.

Pagano, M., and Volpin, P. 2004. The political economy of corporate governance. CSEF Working Paper 29. Available at: www.dise.unisa.it/WP/wp29.pdf.

Persson, T., and Tabellini, G. 2003. *The Economic Effects of Constitutions*. Cambridge, Mass.: MIT Press.

Redding, S., and Schott, P. K. 2003. Distance, skill deepening and development: will peripheral countries ever get rich? *Journal of Development Economics*, 72: 515–41.

Samuelson, P. 1971. Ohlin was right. *Swedish Journal of Economics*, 73: 365–84.

Ticchi, D., and Vindigni, A. 2003. Endogenous constitutions. Available at: www.iies.su.se/publications seminarpapers/726.pdf.

PART XII

INTERNATIONAL RELATIONS AND CONFLICT

CHAPTER 46

CENTRAL ISSUES IN THE STUDY OF INTERNATIONAL CONFLICT

BRUCE BUENO DE MESQUITA

1 INTRODUCTION

THE study of international conflict is undergoing a rapid and dramatic transformation. Some of the field's most venerable beliefs now confront fundamental challenges to their logic and their empirical reliability. For example, the idea that a balance of power promotes peace and an imbalance war traces back more than two millennia to Thucydides' *History of the Peloponnesian War*. It is a belief that continues to permeate the thinking of secretaries of state or defense in the United States and of foreign ministers and defense ministers throughout the world. Yet careful research makes it clear that the distribution of power, whether balanced or not, by itself bears neither a logically nor an empirically compelling relationship to the likelihood of international instability or conflict (Niou, Ordeshook, and Rose 1989; Bueno de Mesquita and Lalman 1992; Kim and Morrow 1992; Powell 1996).

The study of conflict was long thought of as high politics, with states as the central actors pursuing grand strategies designed to maximize national security. In fact, the view of the state as the key player in the international arena is so strong that the English language does not provide a common word or phrase to describe inter*national* relations without invoking the *nation* as the object of study. Now the subject is being recast as part of the everyday pulls and tugs of domestic affairs, integrating the study of conflict into investigations of all other aspects of politics. Where once national interest was at the forefront of research on international affairs, increasingly the study of the political ambitions of and institutional constraints faced by leaders is supplanting concern about the national interest. Indeed, insights from spatial models and other approaches to domestic politics challenge the fundamental meaning of "the national interest." When it is possible to assemble many majority coalitions around competing interests within the same population of national decision-makers it is difficult to say that the interests backed by one coalition are closer to the national interest than the policies backed by another coalition (McKelvey 1976, 1979; Schofield 1978).

In this chapter I touch upon some debates regarding international affairs and the ways we go about studying conflict and peace. International relations scholarship can loosely be divided into those who focus on such structural aspects of the international system as the global distribution of power, or the alignment of nations into two blocs—the bipolar world of the cold war—or many blocs and those who attend to the ways in which domestic political dynamics shape international relations. For much of the post–Second World War years, structural perspectives including neo-realism (Waltz 1979; Glaser 1992; Schweller 1994, 1997), liberalism (Keohane and Nye 1977; Keohane 1984), and power transition theory (Organski 1958; Organski and Kugler 1980; Tammen et al. 2000; Lemke 2002) have contended for domination as explanations of variance in cooperative and conflict-prone behavior. By structural perspectives I mean theories, such as those just listed, for which the central concern is how aggregate characteristics of the international system such as the distribution of power or distribution of wealth among states (as rational unitary actors) determines interactions leading to international conflict or cooperation.

Neorealism treats international affairs as anarchic; that is, a self-help system lacking a dominant power that can enforce agreements. It hypothesizes that political stability in the form of the survival of states is ensured by national efforts to maximize security through alignments. Its focus is on explaining conflict and constancy in relations among states under the supposition that war is the natural state of affairs. Liberalism countered by assuming that international relations are hierarchic rather than anarchic and that a hegemonic power, such as the United States, stands atop the international system. Its focus is on the prevalence of cooperation rather than conflict and so naturally draws researchers into investigations of such international political economy arenas as trade policy, the use of economic sanctions, and international banking policy. The power transition shares with liberalism a focus on hierarchical power relations but centers its attention on how domestic economic growth might influence the risk of system-transforming wars; that is, wars that fundamentally alter who is on top and, therefore, what policies or norms of action are imposed on the community of nations.

During the past decade there has been a shift away from structural perspectives toward ones that look at how domestic political institutions constrain and create incentives that shape cooperation and conflict (Putnam 1988; Bueno de Mesquita and Lalman 1992; Fearon 1994; Downs and Rocke 1995; Schultz 1998, 2001a; Bueno de Mesquita et al. 1999; Werner 1996; Goemans 2000; Bueno de Mesquita et al. 2003; Gartzke and Gleditsch 2004).

The purpose of this chapter is to survey both categories of perspectives and to highlight how different the view of international politics is when focused on political leaders responding to domestic political incentives rather than unitary states responding to aggregate characteristics of the collectivity of states. To this end, this chapter proceeds as follows. Section 2 examines structural perspectives. Section 3 discusses the evolving research programs that look inside the state to grasp how conflict or cooperation relates to ordinary politics. Section 4 illustrates the differences across approaches by selecting two empirical issues, briefly evaluating how different approaches address these issues. The two empirical puzzles are (1) the difference between the record of nation-building following military intervention and the claimed intentions of interveners, and (2) reconciliation of the existence and use of foreign aid as a policy instrument and the record of its ineffectiveness in alleviating poverty.

2 Structural Theories

In this section I summarize key claims and evidence from the two most prominent structural theories: neorealism and the power transition. Although liberalism is an equally important strand of theorizing, its focus on cooperation places it somewhat outside my purview. Therefore, other than in passing commentary, I overlook the strengths and weakness of this approach. Those interested in this aspect of international relations research might see Morrow (1994), Levy (1998), and Simmons (1998) for insights into alternative ways to think about problems of coordination and cooperation. Space constraints preclude discussing other structural perspectives.

2.1 Neorealism

The structural point of view is most prominently represented in Kenneth Waltz's (1979) neorealist theory. Neorealism begins with a handful of seemingly straightforward, innocuous, and parsimonious assumptions. These include the view that international politics is anarchic, states seek to maximize their security against threats to sovereignty; bipolar environments produce substantially less uncertainty about the responses of other states to crises than do multipolar environments; and states seek to increase their power unless doing so is expected to put their security at risk later on.

By definition, an anarchic international system, as intimated earlier, is one in which states cannot make binding commitments enforced by some supernational authority or hegemonic state. Therefore, international politics is best characterized as a non-cooperative game. It is a game in which all states are assumed to share common goals: to make themselves secure and, subject to achieving security, to make themselves more powerful. Neorealists also assume that international interactions arise in a prisoner's dilemma setting (Waltz 1979, 109; Gowa and Mansfield 1993), but, incongruously, also argue that because power is relative, gains for one state must mean losses for others (Waltz 1979, 170–1; Grieco 1988), suggesting a zero sum game. Of course, one cannot logically hold simultaneously that international affairs are characterized as a prisoner's dilemma and as a zero sum game. Some have tried to repair this contradiction by introducing additional parameters into a simple game form that allows the game, under different parameter values, to morph into either the prisoner's dilemma or a zero sum game (Snidal 1991; Powell 1991). In the end there is not much evidence to support the belief that much insight into international affairs is acquired by focusing on the extent to which decision-maker utility functions revolve around relative gains or absolute gains.

Neorealists go on to argue that to improve security or to gain power, states cluster together in blocs that serve as self-help mechanisms. When all states are aligned into only two blocs with each bloc dominated by one especially powerful state, everyone can be certain about how everyone else will react to a crisis. With more than two blocs and more than two large powers, crises engender more uncertainty because a pair of states in a dispute involving two blocs cannot be certain about how those in other blocs will respond. Here, the literature conflates the idea of bipolarity or multipolarity with complete and perfect information or uncertainty.

The core hypotheses of neorealism are generally thought to be that:

1. Bipolar systems, because they involve little or no uncertainty, are more stable than multipolar systems (Waltz 1979);
2. Power tends to become balanced because imbalances place some states' survival at greater risk (Niou, Ordeshook, and Rose 1989); and
3. Alliance partners' responses to threats in a multipolar environment depend on perceived dependence on one's allies or complacency toward the alliance structure (Christensen and Snyder 1990).

Several formal models attempt to capture essential elements of neorealism. One reason why there is more than one such model is that neorealists tend to disagree about the exact meaning of some fundamental concepts, such as security or stability (Elman and Vasquez 2003; Volgy and Bailin 2003). Different formalizations emphasize different meanings attributed to core concepts while placing the informal arguments of neorealists in a political economy framework that helps uncover precise implications and potential sources of inconsistency.

Niou, Ordeshook, and Rose (1989), for instance, present a model of an anarchic, self-help system in which states seek survival above all else. Their model demonstrates that stability has two distinct characteristics that are conflated in informal examinations of neorealism and the balance of power. One, which they call system stability, refers to environments in which no states—that is, no members of the international system—cease to exist so that the composition of the system remains fixed. The other, which they call resource stability, is achieved when the distribution of power does not change among the states in the international system.

They note that the international system can experience system stability without resource stability.

Niou et al. deduce four theorems that seem consistent with neorealist expectations about the stability of the international system. These theorems, stated informally here, indicate that essential states—states whose resources are necessary to avoid such an imbalance of power that there is system instability—are never eliminated from the international system; essential states never become inessential; inessential states never become essential; and inessential states are always eliminated from the international system. They also show that an infinite variety of distributions of power are consistent with system stability though not necessarily resource stability in a multipolar setting. These distributions of power all meet the criteria for being balances of power in the logical, if not the intuitive, sense of that term. Thus, the phrase "balance of power" appears to have little discriminatory power in their formal representation of neorealism. What is more, all four of the theorems that follow from their formalization are empirically false.

By way of illustration, we can surely agree that the Soviet Union and Austria-Hungary were essential states that no longer exist. The United States, inessential in the late 1700s or early 1800s, is obviously essential today. Contrary to the theorems, states rise and decline in their essentialness and states come and go in terms of existence. Indeed, so prevalent is state failure that it is a topic of current research (Beck, King, and Zeng 2000).

Robert Powell's (1993) formalization of neorealism shows that under conditions of anarchy, pursuit of national security is unlikely to dominate state resource allocations. Contrary to views expressed by Waltz (1979) and earlier realists, peace and stability can be achieved while spending relatively little on defense. Contrary to a basic tenet of realist thought, neither war nor its imminent threat is the normal state of affairs in anarchy. Powell examines the trade-off between consumption spending and defense spending and demonstrates that equilibrium defense spending in a bipolar system is rather modest if the environment is anarchic. He shows that a small amount of military spending is sufficient to deter the threat of an attack by a would-be attacker who is interested in improving her people's future consumption and that, since this holds for both parties to a potential arms race, neither has an incentive to spend above the minimal amount needed to achieve successful deterrence.

Additionally, Powell demonstrates that a long shadow of the future (i.e. patience) can decrease cooperation and increase the risk of conflict. His result depends on the timing of costs and benefits. By giving up some consumption now to spend more on arms—that is, adopting a strategy of defection—a state can create a first-strike advantage that improves its chances of gaining a future stream of consumption benefits if the adversary does not sacrifice current consumption for arms. Thus, unlike the well-known folk theorem applied to repeated prisoner's dilemmas, Powell presents a game in which defection—arms rather than consumption—today yields greater benefits tomorrow because of a current military advantage instead of yielding a larger benefit today (the PD temptation payoff P) resulting in long-term punishment and, therefore, loss of expected benefits over time. This latter result contradicts a central claim in the research agenda put forward by neoliberals (Axelrod 1984; Axelrod and Keohane 1986).

Bueno de Mesquita and Lalman (1992) construct a realist and a domestic variant of their international interaction game from which they deduce several propositions. In keeping with neorealist expectations, they show that an imbalance of power is a logically necessary, but not sufficient, condition for war in the realist variant. Additionally, they show that regardless of information conditions, it is impossible in the realist variant for one state ever to choose to acquiesce to the demands of another state. Finally, they demonstrate that war in the realist variant can only arise as a consequence of uncertainty in keeping with Waltz's hypothesis about the different risks of instability under bipolarity and multipolarity. This is in contrast to their demonstration that commitment problems can lead to war even with complete and perfect information. Fearon (1995), in fact, identifies three rationalist explanations for war: asymmetric information, commitment problems, and a dispute over indivisible goods. Chiozza and Goemans (2004) suggest that when we focus on individual decision-makers rather than states the number of rationalist explanations for war proliferates still further.

The empirical record contradicts the three neorealist hypotheses Bueno de Mesquita and Lalman (1992) deduce from their realist variant of the international interaction game and supports at least partially the propositions that follow from their domestic variant (Bueno de Mesquita and Lalman 1992; Signorino 1999; Smith 1999; Bennett and Stam 2000), thereby reinforcing the evidence associated with Niou et al.'s formalization, suggesting that the realist account is poorly supported by evidence.

2.2 Power Transition

Power transition theory was first developed by A. F. K. Organski (1958) and then refined by Organski and Kugler (1980), Tammen et al. (2000), Lemke (2002), and others. It views international politics as hierarchic rather than anarchic. It assumes that all states are interested in imposing international organizations, institutions, rules, and regulations that govern international intercourse on the international system. States are assumed to maximize their control over "the rules of the game" or the status quo norms and policies in the international system, ideas also echoed by Gilpin (1981) and by Krasner (1983) in developing the literature on international regimes.

Power—or relative material resources—is taken as exogenously given and is assumed to be the determinant of who controls international affairs. The most powerful state sits at the apex of a power pyramid in which those below the apex aspire to rise to challenge the dominant state for control of the "rules of the game." States are assumed to be divided into two broad coalitions. Those in the satisfied coalition find the dominant state's rules and norms acceptable while those in the dissatisfied coalition do not. The opportunity to challenge for control arises when a dissatisfied state's internal growth rate is fast enough relative to the dominant state's that the "challenger" can be expected to pull equal in power to and then overtake the dominant state. In the temporal window during which this power transition occurs, war is predicted to be likely if the challenger is dissatisfied (as in the Franco-Prussian War of 1870–1). A peaceful transition is anticipated if the challenger is part of the satisfied coalition (as between the UK and the USA in the twentieth century).

Two formalizations of power transition suggest important modifications to this theory. Kim and Morrow (1992) show that the likelihood of war is not materially influenced by differences in the growth rates between challengers and the dominant state. This is so because a more rapid growth rate for the so-called challenger makes waiting to attack more attractive. The longer the challenger waits, the better its chances of prevailing. At the same time, rapid growth by the challenger makes delay risky for the declining dominant state because that state's odds of victory are decreasing with time. Who will move first and whether the contenders will fight or resolve their transition peacefully depends on their respective willingness to take risks as it is the degree of asymmetry in the shape of their utility functions, and not growth rates per se, that determines the trade-off between fighting now, fighting later, or never fighting. Kim and Morrow's formalization also shows that equality of power is not an inherently critical factor determining the risk of war. Their theoretical claims are buttressed by substantial empirical tests that are consistent with their formalization and that depart significantly from claims made in informal statements of the power transition theory.

Powell (1996) replicates the theoretical structure of the power transition in his investigation of the consequences of appeasement and the risks of what he calls salami tactics by which the dominant state slowly gives very small bits of value away until eventually nothing is left. Except under special conditions that include the anticipation of a reversal in the declining fortunes of the dominant state, Powell demonstrates that with incomplete information about the demanding state's satiation point for extracting resources from the rival, there are numerous conditions that lead to or away from war and that with complete information war never arises as an equilibrium outcome in his power transition/appeasement game. Like Kim and Morrow, Powell fails to find support for the central tenets of the power transition theory or for balance of power theory.

2.3 Summary

Neorealism and power transition focus on states as the central actors in international politics. For neorealists, what happens within states is largely irrelevant for understanding the stability of the international system or the security of states. Each state is assumed to have an abiding interest that any leader follows. For power transition theorists, conditions within states matter to the extent that they influence growth rates, but those conditions are assumed to be exogenously fixed and immutable. The two theories differ in their view of international politics, with neorealists assuming that international politics is anarchic and power transition theorists assuming it is hierarchic. They also disagree about what the goals are that are pursued by states: security or control over the "rules of the game." Although the power transition assumes that different states have different policy goals in mind (i.e. different rules), its predictions are not driven by the substantive differences in goals. Thus, domestic political competition over national policy plays no part in either power transition theory or neorealism.

The empirical record does not support the main claims of neorealism and only partially supports the core claims of power transition theory. One apparently well-established empirical regularity in particular—the democratic peace—has raised serious doubts about the centrality of these and other theories concerned with system structure or with theories that treat the state as a unitary actor. Several empirical regularities are associated with what has come to be called the democratic peace. Foremost among these is the observation that democracies rarely, if ever, fight wars with each other while democracies and autocracies fight with one another (and autocracies with other autocracies) with regularity. The evidence for these and other democratic peace regularities highlights the realization that domestic characteristics of regimes lead to sharply different patterns of foreign policy behavior, a fact that cannot be true if states are rational unitary actors whose patterns of behavior are determined by factors outside the domestic politics of the state as argued by structuralists.

3 Domestic Politics and International Relations

The state-centric view has been challenged by those who contend that international politics is a product of the normal pulls and tugs of domestic affairs; that leaders—not nations—make policy decisions and do so to maximize their prospects of staying in office. Leaders' decisions are therefore strategic and, taking into account expected responses by adversaries and supporters, designed to maximize the leader's (not the state's) welfare. In this perspective, the motivations, interests, and constraints imposed on individual decision-makers are what shape how political leaders, acting in the name of their states, interact with one another.

This research ties together international politics, foreign policy, and domestic politics; as such, it leads to implications incompatible with the received wisdom of realism or the power transition. The various models that tie domestic politics directly to international relations, for instance, provide little basis for believing that the distribution of power is crucial for understanding the likelihood, severity, or resolution of disputes. Domestic approaches give scant attention to whether alliances are organized to create a bipolar or multipolar international environment. And such an approach dismisses the tenet that states seek to maximize power, security, control over the rules governing international interactions, or the national interest.

In place of a focus on states as decision-makers, the domestic perspective, as I will call it here, draws attention to the taxing and spending incentives and constraints created by different domestic governing institutions and to how those institutions help shape variations in international and domestic policy choices. I briefly summarize the key ideas, and then offer some examples of how these ideas work in elucidating international politics and the study of conflict in particular.

Let us suppose that political leaders want to maximize their prospects of gaining and staying in power (Downs 1957; Riker 1962; Downs and Rocke 1995; Bueno de Mesquita and Siverson 1995; Bueno de Mesquita et al. 1999, 2003; Goemans 2000). They choose actions, therefore, that help advance that objective. If those actions happen also to be beneficial for the rest of the people in the society they lead, so much the better, but that which makes leaders better off need not also make their subjects better off (Robinson 1998; Bueno de Mesquita and Root 2000). Indeed, it is difficult to see how we can explain the actions of totalitarians and even petty dictators if their interests and the state's interests—that is, the welfare of the citizenry—are taken as being the same. Even when the state faces war, the interests of leaders and citizens can diverge markedly depending on how governing institutions influence the tie between victory or defeat in war and political survival for the incumbent leadership (Bueno de Mesquita et al. 2004; Chiozza and Goemans 2003, 2004). Of course, these disparate interests are taken as the same in theories that treat the state as a unitary actor.

Different theories—some complementary and some in competition with one another—suggest explanations of international conflict from the perspective of domestic politics, a topic also closely examined by Stam and Reiter in this volume. Maoz and Russett (1993), Russett (1993), and others suggest a norms-based theory of international conflict. Bueno de Mesquita et al. (1999, 2003) suggest what they call the selectorate theory of politics to explain how political institutions shape leaders' policy decisions. Fearon (1994) offers a perspective on crisis escalation grounded in what he calls audience costs, with those costs varying as a function of key features of a state's institutional set-up. Smith (1996) points to selection effects overlooked in Fearon's treatment and that help refine predictions about the impact of audience costs on conflict. Schultz (1998, 2001a) reflects on the role of opposition parties in democracies in disciplining foreign policy choices in a way fundamentally different from what one expects in autocracies, or other institutional arrangements that make political opposition especially costly. These approaches lead to propositions—many of which are testable and have been tested—that suggest empirical patterns that ought not to be observed if neorealist or other structural perspectives are correct.

3.1 Normative Explanation of Conflict and Regime Differences

The literature on the democratic peace creates a critical challenge to the core ideas behind theories that treat the state as a unitary actor. In the latter theories, the internal workings of states are thought to be irrelevant to decisions related to challenges to national survival. Yet the empirical record indicates that war involvement and war fighting differ markedly depending on whether a state is organized as a democracy or an autocracy. These observations have given rise to numerous domestic political explanations of empirical regularities regarding war.

The normative explanation of the democratic peace argues that people in democracies are experienced with compromise and negotiation and so use these modes of conflict resolution rather than war when confronting one another (Maoz and Abdolali 1989; Maoz and Russett 1993; Russett 1993). The normative account goes on to argue, in a quasi-realist fashion, that when democrats confront autocrats, democrats adopt the norms of aggression and bullying used by autocrats lest they put their own national survival at risk by seeking compromise with adversaries who prefer force over concessions.

The normative account is consistent with the observation that democratic dyads rarely, if ever, fight wars; that autocratic dyads fight; and autocrats and democrats fight each other. But, putting aside the danger that the normative account appears to assume the answer to these puzzles, it suffers from important empirical problems. For instance, the normative domestic account fails to explain why democrats use force against much weaker societies as in many wars of imperial and colonial expansion. Since the targets in those wars did not represent a threat to the survival of the democrats who initiated conflict, the normative account does not explain the choice by democrats to adopt non-democratic norms of behavior. Because of these weaknesses, the normative account has been challenged by more formalized models of domestic politics that rely on structure-induced equilibria.

3.2 Institutional Constraints

Portions of the democratic peace have also been studied from the perspective that institutional arrangements constrain the range of available responses to conflict. Morgan and Campbell (1991), for instance, argue that democracies have a harder time choosing actions because of their procedures for making policy decisions. Maoz and Russett (1993, 626; emphasis added) elaborate on this point, maintaining that:

> due to the complexity of the democratic process and the requirement for securing a broad base of support for risky policies, democratic leaders are reluctant to wage wars, except in cases wherein war seems a necessity or when the war aims are seen as justifying the mobilization costs. *The time required for a democratic state to prepare for war is far longer than for nondemocracies.* Thus, in a conflict between democracies, by the time the two states are militarily ready for war, diplomats have the opportunity to find a nonmilitary solution to the conflict.

Evidence regarding the time it takes democrats to prepare for war compared to non-democrats is just beginning to appear in the literature so that this hypothesis about institutional constraints remains an open question. It is a proposition challenged by at least one domestic theory that examines institutionally induced incentives as distinct from constraints.

An alternative, more fully formalized theory of institutional constraints examines what Fearon (1994) calls audience costs. The contention here is that when democratic leaders threaten military action they pay a heavy domestic political cost if they subsequently back down. Because autocrats do not depend on re-election they are less vulnerable to these domestic audience costs. Fearon demonstrates theoretically that audience costs create important selection effects in disputes involving a democracy. Democratic leaders must be careful about the disputes in which they become involved and, if the dispute is not resolved peacefully to their satisfaction, they are more likely than autocrats to escalate in pursuit of a successful outcome.

Although there have been empirical efforts to test the audience costs argument (e.g. Partell and Palmer 1999), Schultz (2001b) cautions that empirical tests are likely to be misleading. He notes that selection effects operate so that the observed cases of audience costs are drawn from a distribution with a smaller expected mean than one would expect in the full population of conflict opportunities for democracies. Therefore, it is difficult to draw inferences about audience costs from the inherently biased sample of observed cases.

Schultz (1998, 2001a) offers an alternative argument to explain differences in the willingness of democrats and autocrats to take foreign policy risks. He notes that democracies make political opposition in pursuit of political power relatively cheap compared to opposition in autocracies. That is, autocrats are prone to oppress and even kill opponents (Poe and Tate 1994; Poe, Tate, and Keith 1999; Bueno de Mesquita et al. 2003), while political opposition is a normal, routine aspect of democratic politics. Because would-be domestic opponents are more effectively deterred in non-democratic regimes, leaders under such institutions are deprived of the informational benefits of opposition if they choose foreign policies that others anticipate will lead to bad outcomes.

Schultz maintains that opposition parties in democracies are unlikely to oppose a foreign policy pursued by the incumbent leader if that policy is expected to succeed. After all, opposition to a successful policy is unlikely to attract support to the rival party and so does not improve the prospects of election. But if the foreign policy is expected to fail, then the political opposition is likely to speak out against it in order to gain political support. Seeing such opposition, the incumbent can infer that the policy is believed to be unlikely to succeed and so is compelled by personal political ambition to review it closely. Sometimes, of course, the review will not produce a change in policy, but sometimes it will. Thus, the presence of opposition acts as a signal that can discipline the incumbent not to be overly venturesome in foreign policy (or stimulate foreign rivals to take advantage of caution on the part of democratic incumbents). The absence of such a legitimate opposition mechanism in autocracies means that autocrats are likely to choose foreign actions with higher variance in the *ex post* outcome and with limited consequences for their domestic political survival. Schultz's argument, then, offers a domestic perspective from which leadership survival considerations under different institutional arrangements influence the direction of international politics while also implying that a norm of nonpartisan foreign policy can increase the risks of conflict involvement.

3.3 Institutional Incentives

Bueno de Mesquita et al. (1999, 2003) suggest an institutional theory in which all states can be seen as governed by a tenure-maximizing leader who relies on a coalition of core supporters to remain in power. The core supporters—the winning coalition—are drawn from a larger pool that they call the selectorate. They examine how institutions alter the incentives of leaders in domestic affairs and international politics. Their so-called selectorate theory posits that leaders want to maximize their survival time in office (and secondarily their income from office). Leaders are responsible for raising revenues and spending those revenues in the name of the state, with their taxing and spending decisions driven by their interest in staying in power. This theory focuses on how different political arrangements—like democracy (i.e. a system in which leaders depend on a large winning coalition) or autocracy (in which leaders depend on a small coalition, possibly drawn from a large or a small selectorate)—shape how incumbents tax, allocate revenues, and choose courses of foreign policy action.

All leaders raise and allocate revenues to three basic spending categories according to the selectorate theory:

1. Public goods that benefit all members of society (e.g. national defense, rule of law, protection of civil liberties);
2. Private goods that benefit those whose support is essential to keep the leader in office (e.g. the use of nepotism, privileged access to contracts, rent-seeking opportunities, discriminatory tax policies to benefit the so-called winning coalition); and
3. Discretionary funds that are at the disposal of the incumbent leader (e.g. secret bank accounts, lavish lifestyles, political rainy-day funds).

When leaders rely on only a few people to keep them in office then it proves most efficient for the incumbent to buy their support by providing the coalition's members with lots of private benefits in exchange for loyalty. When domestic political institutions compel a leader to have a broad base of support—as is true in democracies—then purchasing loyalty through private rewards is an inefficient way to stay in power (Lake 1992; Robinson 1998; Robinson and Verdier 2002; Bueno de Mesquita et al. 2003). Democratic leaders would have to spread the private rewards across so many people that each would receive too little to be influenced to remain loyal to the incumbent. In such a situation, it is more efficient for leaders to rely on public goods as their best means to retain office. But when a leader needs many supporters, each supporter knows that he or she also has excellent prospects of being essential to the political success of a politician who challenges the incumbent for office. Conversely, when a leader only needs backing from a few people to stay in power, those few people are loyal both because they are getting well rewarded for their support and because they face a high risk of losing their privileges if another politician succeeds in toppling the incumbent regime. Thus, autocrats spend more resources on private goods than on public goods as compared to democrats; they enjoy strong loyalty from their coalition; and this loyalty allows them to spend less than the total pool of revenue on their backers even when facing a credible political rival. What small coalition leaders do not spend to maintain the loyalty of their supporters remains as discretionary funds for their own use, in essence, a rainy-day fund to get out of political trouble if it arises.

Democratic leaders, in contrast, emphasize public goods over private goods. Consequently, membership in a democratic winning coalition confers only a small private goods edge over the public goods rewards that go to everyone. Furthermore, because the winning coalition is a large portion of the selectorate, the risk of exclusion following political defection is small. Thus, in democracies, leaders must spend more to maintain coalition loyalty than in autocracies; they can reserve less to compensate for an exogenous shock; and so they are more susceptible to be turned out of office than are their small coalition counterparts. Autocrats, then, can rule by theft and yet stay in office for a long time while democrats rule based on good public policy and are easily defeated by political rivals.

Consider now what the selectorate argument implies about the inclination to fight wars. State-centric theories, like realism or liberalism, lack a clear way to explain the generally accepted observation that democracies tend not to fight wars with one another even though they are not especially reluctant to fight with autocratic regimes. According to the selectorate logic, democratic leaders cannot afford to pursue overly risky foreign policies because democratic leaders are judged primarily in terms of how good a job they do in providing public benefits. Democrats, therefore, become involved in wars only when they believe at the outset that their chances of victory are very high or when all efforts at negotiation fail.

Autocrats, in contrast, are not retained or deposed by their domestic supporters primarily because of the job they do in providing successful public policies. They are judged by their ability to deliver private benefits to their cronies. As a result, autocrats are not as selective as democrats about the disputes they participate in or the wars they fight and they do not make as great a marginal effort as democrats do to win wars that prove to be tougher than initially expected or to find negotiated settlements to their disputes.

Except for two special circumstances, to survive in office, autocrats need to be sure that they can pay their essential supporters enough that they do not defect while democrats, if faced with war, need victory or a negotiated settlement before fighting breaks out. For autocrats, extra money that goes into trying to win a war is money that could have been better spent by using it to buy the loyalty of cronies. For democrats, saving money to bribe backers is not nearly as politically beneficial as is spending money to assure policy success, including victory in war.

This idea is readily shown with a simple, stylized example based on the limiting case in which all available resources are devoted either to the war effort or to private goods for members of the winning coalition. Suppose a leader must choose between putting all the available revenue (R) into fighting a war or retaining all of the revenue to distribute as private rewards to W members of his or her winning coalition. Further, assume that victory (V) is assured if all revenue is put into the war effort and defeat in the war is assured if all revenue is retained for use as private rewards to coalition members. Suppose $V = v + r$ where v is the public goods component of victory enjoyed by everyone in the society and r represents the additional resources (i.e. the spoils of war) that can be extracted from the vanquished state and allocated to the leader's coalition members following victory. Defeat has a value of 0. Let the per capita cost of waging war be k whether the war is won or lost. If a leader makes an all-out effort to ensure victory, then the public and private benefits of winning are worth $v + r/W - k$ for each member of her coalition. Alternatively, if the leader chooses to retain resources for use as private benefits to her coalition at the expense of losing the war for sure, then the payoff to her coalition is $R/W - k$. The leader prefers additional effort when $v > (R - r)/W$, the latter term of which is decreasing in W provided that $R > r$; that is, national resources (R) exceed the value of postwar spoils (r). We see, then, that small W systems—like autocracies and juntas—are more likely to induce leaders to choose to make relatively little extra effort to win a war, and large coalition systems, like democracies, are relatively more likely to induce leaders to give up paying their coalition private rewards in exchange for relatively more extra, marginal effort put into achieving victory in war (Bueno de Mesquita et al. 1999, 2004).

Empirical evidence reveals that democrats need victory relatively more than autocrats to survive in office and so make the extra effort described above (Bueno de Mesquita and Siverson 1995; Bueno de Mesquita et al. 2004). This implies that leaders of large coalition systems are more selective than autocrats about the circumstances under which they are prepared to fight, and, further, helps explain why they almost always win the wars they initiate. In fact, democracies win 93 per cent of the wars they initiate while autocrats win only about 60 per cent of the time (Reiter and Stam 2002). The cases of observed war outcomes, of course, represent a biased sample as many disputes are resolved through negotiation. The above summary statistics presumably reflect the situations in which autocrats thought (*a*) they had an acceptable chance of victory; the dispute was over (*b*) a policy concession, such as deposition of the rival, that the autocrat could not agree to; or over (*c*) a proposed concession—like the autocrat going into exile—that the democrat could not credibly commit to honor *ex post*. This commitment problem, of course, is the issue faced by Chile's deposed dictator Augusto Pinochet; and it may have been an issue in Saddam Hussein's decision to fight rather that negotiate a deal with the United States in 2003.

Allowing for the small advantage gained by striking first, autocrats basically have even odds of winning when they start a war while for democrats victory is practically certain. But if two democrats are at loggerheads, then war is unlikely. The reason is that each democratic leader has similar incentives, including an incentive to try hard if war ensues. Each must provide policy success in order to be retained by his or her constituents. The likelihood is practically naught that leaders of two rival democracies each believes at the same time about the same dispute that their prospects of victory are nearly certain. When democrats do not think they are nearly certain of victory they opt for negotiations over fighting. Thus leaders of two democracies are unlikely to find that the circumstances are right for them to gamble on war over negotiations.

Autocrats do not face the same circumstances. Autocrats generally do not need to try especially hard to win most of their wars; they are prepared to fight even when the chances of victory are not exceptionally good; and they are more likely to be overthrown if they do not retain adequate resources for their cronies than if they lose the war, unless the defeat is horrendous (Goemans 2000). Thus it is that we observe democracies fighting with autocracies; autocracies fighting with one another; democracies not fighting with each other; democracies winning most of the wars in which they get involved; and democracies showing greater eagerness than autocracies to resolve disputes through negotiations (Bueno de Mesquita et al. 2003).

There are two exceptional circumstances when domestic institutionally induced incentives do not make democrats try harder than autocrats. One arises when the opponent is so weak that victory is assured without extra effort. The other occurs when the conflict is about the deposition of the defeated foreign rival. In that case, all leaders try hard. The first exception characterizes wars of imperial or colonial expansion. The latter characterizes the effort in the last stages of the Second World War, when it was evident that an allied victory meant the removal of the axis's leaders.

In the selectorate theory's account of the so-called "democratic peace," democratic leaders are not more civic minded, nor are they inherently better at fighting wars than other types of political leaders. Instead, their desire to stay in office shapes their choices and makes them highly selective about escalating disputes to violence. Likewise, autocrats were not assumed to have different motivations from democrats; just different institutionally induced incentives. State-centric approaches to international relations simply have no basis for explaining the pattern of behavior just described and yet historical, case study, and statistical analyses support the implications of the coalition-selectorate explanation or some of the other domestic accounts.

4 Nation-building, Foreign Aid, and Domestic Politics

Models of domestic politics provide a way to explain broad patterns and detailed nuances of foreign policy and international politics. What is more, they offer a microfoundation for arguments about what happens at the system or structural level (Kadera, Crescenzi, and Shannon 2003). In this section I consider insights into nation-building and foreign aid policy provided by domestic models. It will be evident that even when theoretical conclusions are reached that seem consistent with a realist viewpoint, the microfoundations and logic of action are completely different.

When it comes to nation-building following military intervention or to foreign aid as a policy instrument, domestic perspectives offer accounts that do not at first appear very different from the view of realists. In each case, there is little reason to be sanguine about nation-building or foreign aid as exercises oriented toward developing new democracies or improving individual welfare except under special circumstances. The logic leading to policy implications, however, is radically different. To illustrate how the logic of the domestic perspective works when it comes to nation-building, consider the incentives American political leaders have to shape governments in other countries following a military intervention such as occurred in Iraq in the spring of 2003.

A president of the United States acts as a self-interested (or political party interested) leader. As such, the president always has a strong policy motive driven by re-election incentives. This colors not only his decision of where and when to intervene but also of how to intervene. From the domestic perspective, a factor determining whether to intervene is whether the president believes that the policies pursued by the other state's government are good or bad from the perspective of the president's core constituents; that is, the American voter or at least those who might be persuaded to support (or oppose) the president's (or his party's) re-election. In cases where the policies are viewed as poor from the point of view of his supporters, the president is pulled by his need to produce effective public policy toward changing the other state's leadership and possibly its governing institutions so as to improve his own re-election prospects. When American voters view the policies in the target state favorably, US intervention is generally motivated by a desire to prop up the target government and ward off domestic forces opposing it. The domestic perspective helps us recognize that democracies, including the United States, even when partially motivated to spread democracy, are also motivated by other goals in the world. Sometimes furthering those other goals through intervention or other foreign policy choices necessarily implies working against democracy in some states (Bueno de Mesquita and Downs 2006).

The problem with erecting a true democracy following military intervention arises when the policies desired by the citizens of the defeated state are incommensurate with the policies desired by the core constituents of the democratic intervener, whether it is the United States or some other democracy. The key is that a quasi-autocratic puppet government can credibly commit to deliver the policies desired by the intervener in exchange for sufficient funds to remain in power (e.g. by providing adequate financial returns to their small group of coalition members). Thus there is a critical trade-off decision to be made by the democratic victor: obtain a preferable policy outcome by maintaining or imposing a friendly autocrat in power or risk a future stream of hostile policies by promoting democracy in the defeated state, leaving policy choices to its citizens rather than imposing the policies desired by the victor's constituents. Since autocratic leaders need not satisfy the policy ambitions of a broad constituency, the policy interests of the general populus becomes a commodity autocrats can sell in exchange for the resources they need to satisfy the private goods demands of their small coalition. If a democratic government were installed, its leaders could not make such a commitment because those leaders would need to satisfy the policy wishes of their own constituents to stay in office. As an empirical matter, most countries that have experienced military intervention are no more—and often less—democratic ten to twenty years after the intervention than they were before. This is true whether the intervener is a democracy, an autocracy, a multilateral effort, or the United Nations.

Foreign aid follows a similar pattern. Aid-giving, like military intervention, can be a useful approach to achieving policy gains for domestic constituents. Democracies are more likely to give aid than are autocracies. Aid is more likely to be received by autocrats than by needy democrats according to the domestic perspective because democratic donors and autocratic recipients have something to trade; namely, policy concessions from the recipient in exchange for money from the donor.

An autocratic prospective aid recipient can more readily afford to make policy concessions to the democratic donor than can democratic prospective recipients of aid. Autocrats are maintained in power based on their distribution of private goods to their small group of supporters rather than on their emphasis on providing public goods in the forms of generally desired policies. Autocrats can get money needed to maintain their coalition of backers by entering into an aid for policy deal.

Democratic leaders seeking aid bear a higher political cost for making policy concessions in exchange for money than do autocratic recipients. The core backers of a democrat depend on public policy benefits more than private benefits in choosing whether to continue to support the democratic incumbent or switch to another candidate. Consequently, a democrat seeking aid in exchange for policy concessions must receive more aid than an autocrat because the political costs associated with making a policy concession are greater in democracies than in autocracies.

Democratic donors survive in office by satisfying their constituents through policy choices. At the margin, gaining policy concessions on salient issues (e.g. help with the war on terrorism) from other states can improve a democrat's political survival prospects. If it happens that the people in a democracy particularly desire a policy that alleviates poverty in recipient countries, then there is not much constraint on granting aid to a democracy, but if the donor's domestic constituents seek policy concessions, as often seems to be the case, then they face a trade-off between promoting economic well-being and policy gains through aid.

Substantial evidence supports the dismal conclusion that aid has had only a small impact on improving economic growth, health care, education, social welfare, freedom, or governmental accountability (Easterly 2001). Perhaps this is because aid agencies like USAID, the World Bank, or the IMF do not understand how to promote economic growth. That interpretation, however, is inconsistent with another body of evidence that shows that aid is most likely to go to small coalition, poor autocratic regimes but that the largest amount of per capita aid goes to the larger/coalition and/or to relatively well-off countries (e.g. Egypt, Israel, Marshall Plan) rather than to the poorest countries. As Bueno de Mesquita and Smith (2004) show theoretically and empirically, foreign aid is most likely to be given by wealthy polities whose government depends on the support of a large coalition. Aid is most likely to be given to poor governments dependent on a small coalition so that the leaders can commit to follow policies the donor (democratic or otherwise) wants even if the recipient's citizens do not like the policy. From this domestic perspective, foreign aid is a deal between those who value a policy concession on the one hand—public goods-oriented regimes—and those who value money for use as rewards for cronies—the private goods-oriented regimes. A consequence of such aid for policy deals is that citizens in recipient countries often have their own welfare diminished as a result of aid even as their failed leaders are helped by democratic donors to sustain themselves in office. No wonder such aid for policy arrangements are popular with recipient leaders but unpopular with the exploited citizenry in recipient countries.

5 CONCLUSIONS

Structural theories cannot predict how regime type influences the following: either who gets or who gives aid; how nation-building unfolds; differences in war fighting or war outcomes; or a host of other empirically observed regularities in the domain of international relations. Domestic politics-oriented theories provide clear formal deductions about such questions. The evidence seems more consistent with deductions from domestic models than from implications drawn from structural theoretical approaches. Indeed, the domestic perspective and its attendant theories and models contradict the idea that there is a sharp distinction to be drawn between foreign policy and international politics, yet this is one of the core ideas behind neorealist theorizing.

With the advent of political economy models of the domestic perspective the study of international conflict is now firmly embedded in the broader context of political theory, with the microfoundations of action being laid out and the ties between individual choices and aggregate consequences becoming clearer. Increasingly, international politics and conflict research fall within the domain of comparative political economy rather than being seen as outside the mainstream of political theorizing. As one recent title suggests, we have entered the period of *Dissolving Boundaries* (Werner, Davis, and Bueno de Mesquita 2005) when all aspects of international politics can be studied as problems in comparative politics.

REFERENCES

AXELROD, R. 1984. *The Evolution of Cooperation*. New York: Basic Books.
──── and KEOHANE, R. 1986. Achieving cooperation under anarchy. In *Cooperation under Anarchy*, ed. K. Oye. Princeton, NJ: Princeton University Press.
BECK, N., KING, G., and ZENG, L. 2000. Improving quantitative studies of conflict: a conjecture. *American Political Science Review*, 94: 21–36.
BENNETT, D. S., and STAM, A., III. 2000. A cross-validation of Bueno de Mesquita and Lalman's international interaction game. *British Journal of Political Science*, 30: 541–61.
BUENO DE MESQUITA, B., and DOWNS, G. W. 2006. Intervention and democracy. *International Organization*, 60.

—— and LALMAN, D. 1992. *War and Reason*. New Haven, Conn.: Yale University Press.

—— and ROOT, H. (eds). 2000. *Governing for Prosperity*. New Haven, Conn.: Yale University Press.

—— and SIVERSON, R. M. 1995. War and the survival of political leaders. *American Political Science Review*, 89: 841–55.

—— and SMITH, A. 2004. Foreign aid: a theory and tests. Working Paper, New York University Dept. of Politics.

—— MORROW, J. D., SIVERSON, R. M., and SMITH, A. 1999. An institutional explanation of the democratic peace. *American Political Science Review*, 93: 781–807.

—— —— SIVERSON, R. M., and MORROW, J. D. 2003. *The Logic of Political Survival*. Cambridge, Mass.: MIT Press.

—— —— —— —— 2004. Testing novel implications from the selectorate theory of war. *World Politics*, 56: 363–88.

CHIOZZA, G., and GOEMANS, H. E. 2003. Peace through insecurity: tenure and international conflict. *Journal of Conflict Resolution*, 47: 443–67.

—— —— 2004. International conflict and the tenure of leaders: is war still *ex post* inefficient? *American Journal of Political Science*, 48: 604–19.

CHRISTENSEN, T., and SNYDER, J. 1990. Chain gangs and passed bucks: predicting alliance patterns in multipolarity. *International Organization*, 44: 137–68.

DOWNS, A. 1957. *An Economic Theory of Democracy*. New York: Harper.

DOWNS, G., and ROCKE, D. 1995. *Optimal Imperfection? Uncertainty and Institutions in International Relations*. Princeton, NJ: Princeton University Press.

EASTERLY, W. 2001. *The Elusive Quest for Growth*. Cambridge, Mass.: MIT Press.

ELMAN, C., and VASQUEZ, J. (eds). 2003. *Realism and the Balancing of Power: A New Debate*. Englewood Cliffs, NJ: Prentice Hall.

FEARON, J. D. 1994. Domestic political audiences and the escalation of international disputes. *American Political Science Review*, 88: 577–92.

—— 1995. Rationalist explanations for war. *International Organization*, 49: 379–414.

GARTZKE, E., and GLEDITSCH, K. S. 2004. Regime type and commitment: why democracies are actually less reliable allies. *American Journal of Political Science*, 48: 775–95.

GILPIN, R. 1981. *War and Change in World Politics*. Cambridge: Cambridge University Press.

GLASER, C. 1992. Political consequences of military strategy. *World Politics*, 44: 497–538.

GOEMANS, H. 2000. *War and Punishment*. Princeton, NJ: Princeton University Press.

GOWA, J., and MANSFIELD, E. 1993. Power politics and international trade. *American Political Science Review*, 87: 408–20.

GRIECO, J. M. 1988. Realist theory and the problems of international cooperation: analysis with an amended prisoner's dilemma model. *Journal of Politics*, 50: 600–24.

KADERA, K. M., CRESCENZI, M. J. C., and SHANNON, M. L. 2003. Democratic survival, peace, and war in the international system. *American Journal of Political Science*, 47: 234–47.

KEOHANE, R. O. 1984. *After Hegemony*. Princeton, NJ: Princeton University Press.

—— and NYE, J. S. 1977. *Power and Interdependence*. Boston: Little, Brown.

KIM, W., and MORROW, J. D. 1992. When do power shifts lead to war? *American Journal of Political Science*, 36: 896–922.

KRASNER, S. D. 1983. *International Regimes*. Ithaca, NY: Cornell University Press.

LAKE, D. 1992. Powerful pacifists: democratic states and war. *American Political Science Review*, 86: 24–37.

LEMKE, D. 2002. *Regions of War and Peace*. Cambridge: Cambridge University Press.

LEVY, J. 1998. The causes and the conditions of peace. *Annual Review of Political Science*, 1: 139–66.

McKelvey, R. 1976. Intransitivities in multidimensional voting models and some implications for agenda control. *Journal of Economic Theory*, 12: 472–82.
—— 1979. General conditions for global intransitivities in formal voting models. *Econometrica*, 47: 1085–112.
Maoz, Z., and Abdolali, N. 1989. Regime type and international conflict, 1816–1976. *Journal of Conflict Resolution*, 33: 3–36.
—— and Russett, B. M. 1993. Normative and structural causes of the democratic peace. *American Political Science Review*, 87: 624–38.
Morgan, T. C., and Campbell, S. H. 1991. Domestic structure, decisional constraints, and war. *Journal of Conflict Resolution*, 35: 187–211.
Morrow, J. D. 1994. Modeling the forms of cooperation. *International Organization*, 48: 387–423.
Niou, E., Ordeshook, P., and Rose, G. 1989. *The Balance of Power*. New York: Cambridge University Press.
Organski, A. F. K. 1958. *World Politics*. New York: Alfred Knopf.
—— and Kugler, J. 1980. *The War Ledger*. Chicago: University of Chicago Press.
Partell, P. J., and Palmer, G. 1999. Audience costs and interstate crises. *International Studies Quarterly*, 43: 389–405.
Poe, S. C., and Tate, N. 1994. Repression of rights to personal integrity in the 1980s. *American Political Science Review*, 88: 853–72.
—— —— and Keith, L. C. 1999. Repression of the human right to personal integrity revisited. *International Studies Quarterly*, 43: 291–313.
Powell, R. 1991. Absolute and relative gains in international relations theory. *American Political Science Review*, 85: 1303–20.
—— 1993. Guns, butter, and anarchy. *American Political Science Review*, 87: 115–32.
—— 1996. Uncertainty, shifting power, and appeasement. *American Political Science Review*, 90: 749–64.
Putnam, R. 1988. Diplomacy and domestic politics: the logic of two-level games. *International Organization*, 42: 427–60.
Reiter, D., and Stam, A., III. 2002. *Democracies at War*. Princeton, NJ: Princeton University Press.
Riker, W. H. 1962. *The Theory of Political Coalitions*. New Haven, Conn: Yale University Press.
Robinson, J. A. 1998. Theories of bad policy. *Policy Reform*, 1: 1–46.
—— and Verdier, T. 2002. The political economy of clientelism. DELTA mimeo.
Russett, B. M. 1993. *Grasping the Democratic Peace*. Princeton, NJ: Princeton University Press.
Schofield, N. 1978. Instability of simple dynamic games. *Review of Economic Studies*, 45: 575–94.
Schultz, K. A. 1998. Domestic opposition and signaling in international crises. *American Political Science Review*, 92: 829–44.
—— 2001*a*. *Democracy and Coercive Diplomacy*. Cambridge: Cambridge University Press.
—— 2001*b*. Looking for audience costs. *Journal of Conflict Resolution*, 45: 32–60.
Schweller, R. L. 1994. Bandwagoning for profit: bringing the revisionist state back in. *International Security*, 19: 72–107.
—— 1997. New realist research on alliances: refining, not refuting Waltz's balancing proposition. *American Political Science Review*, 91: 927–30.
Signorino, C. 1999. Strategic interaction and the statistical analysis of international conflict. *American Political Science Review*, 93: 279–98.
Simmons, B. A. 1998. Compliance with international agreements. *Annual Review of Political Science*, 1: 75–94.

SMITH, A. 1996. To intervene or not to intervene: a biased decision. *Journal of Conflict Resolution*, 40: 16–40.
—— 1999. Testing theories of strategic choice. *American Journal of Political Science*, 43: 1254–83.
SNIDAL, D. 1991. Relative gains and the pattern of international cooperation. *American Political Science Review*, 85: 701–26.
TAMMEN, R., KUGLER, J., LEMKE, D., STAM, A., III, ALSHARABATI, C., ABDOLLAHIAN, M. A., EFIRD, B., and ORGANSKI, A. F. K. (eds.) 2000. *Power Transitions*. Chatham, NJ: Seven Bridges Press.
VOLGY, T., and BAILIN, A. 2003. *International Politics and the Strength of States*. Boulder, Colo.: Lynne Rienner.
WALTZ, K. 1979. *Theory of International Politics*. Reading, Mass.: Addison Wesley.
WERNER, S. 1996. Absolute and limited war. *International Interactions*, 22: 67–88.
—— DAVIS, D., and BUENO DE MESQUITA, B. 2005. *Dissolving Boundaries*. London: Blackwell.

CHAPTER 47

ETHNIC MOBILIZATION AND ETHNIC VIOLENCE

JAMES D. FEARON

1 INTRODUCTION

WHY are political coalitions, movements, and structures of patron–client relations so often organized along ethnic lines? Why is ethnicity politicized in these ways in some countries more than others, and what accounts for variation over time within particular countries? Under what conditions is the politicization of ethnicity accompanied by significant ethnic violence?

The sizable body of work on these questions contains few analyses that use tools or ideas from microeconomic theory, the hallmarks of "political economy" as conceived in this volume. In what follows I briefly review the main answers advanced in the broader literature, and situate and discuss the contributions of several political economy analyses.

The chapter has four main sections. In the first two I review some of the salient empirical patterns concerning cross-national and temporal variation in the politicization of ethnicity and ethnic violence. In the third and fourth I discuss attempts to explain the prevalence and variation of politicized ethnicity, and then arguments proposing to explain the occurrence of ethnic violence.

Some definitional matters must be addressed before starting. In ordinary English usage, the term "ethnic group" is typically used to refer to groups larger than a family in which membership is reckoned primarily by a descent rule (Fearon and Laitin 2000a; Fearon 2003). That is, one is or can be a member of an ethnic group if one's parents were also judged members (conventions and circumstance decide cases of mixed parentage). There are some groups that meet this criterion but that intuition may reject as "ethnic," such as clans, classical Indian castes, or European nobility. But even in these cases analysts often recognize a "family resemblance" to ethnic groups based on the use of descent as the basis for membership.[1]

Members of the *prototypical* ethnic group share a common language, religion, customs, sense of a homeland, and relatively dense social networks. However, any or all of these may be missing and a group might still be described as "ethnic" if the descent rule for membership is satisfied.[2] In other words, while shared cultural features often distinguish ethnic groups, these are contingent rather than constitutive aspects of the idea of an "ethnic group." Becoming fluent in the language, manners, and customs of Armenia will not make me "ethnically Armenian." The key constitutive feature is membership reckoned primarily by descent.

This observation helps explain why groups considered "religious" in one context may be reasonably considered "ethnic" in another. In the United States, Protestants and Catholics are religious rather than ethnic groups because membership is reckoned by profession of faith rather than descent; one can become a member of either group by conversion. In Northern Ireland, descent rather than profession of faith is the relevant criterion for deciding membership, even though religion is the main cultural feature distinguishing the two main social groups. Protestants and Catholics in Northern Ireland can thus reasonably be described as ethnic groups despite common language, appearance, many customs, and genetic ancestry (in some sense). This contrast also makes clear that ethnic distinctions are not a matter of biology but rather are conventions determined by politics and history.

2 Some Stylized Facts About the Politicization of Ethnicity

Ethnicity is *socially relevant* when people notice and condition their actions on ethnic distinctions in everyday life. Ethnicity is *politicized* when political coalitions are organized along ethnic lines, or when access to political or economic benefits depends on ethnicity. Ethnicity can be socially relevant in a country without it being much politicized, and the degree to which ethnicity is politicized can vary across countries and over time.

---

[1] Horowitz 1985 and Chandra 2004, for example, argue for coding Indian castes as ethnic groups.

[2] For instance, Roma and other nomadic groups have no real sense of homeland; Germans profess multiple religions; Jews speak multiple first languages; and Somali clans are not distinguished from each other by any notable cultural features. Each of these groups might or might not be considered an "ethnic group" by some, but they are all at least candidates so considered by others.

Ethnicity is socially relevant in all but a few countries whose citizens have come to believe that they are highly ethnically homogeneous (such as Ireland, Iceland, and North or South Korea). In most countries, citizens consider that there are multiple ethnic groups, and in some they largely agree on what the main ethnic groups are. For example, in eastern Europe and the former Soviet republics ethnicity was officially classified and enumerated by the state, which seems to have yielded a high degree of consensus on the category systems. By contrast, in many countries, such as the United States and India, there is less agreement on how to think about what the "ethnic groups" are, although everyone agrees that they exist. In the USA, for example, the current census categories include White, African-American, Asian, Hispanic, Native American, and Pacific Islanders.[3] But why not separate out Arab-Americans, Mexican Americans, Cuban Americans, Peruvian Americans, German Americans, Scottish Americans, and so on? This sort of problem is almost infinitely worse for India and very bad for many countries, rendering it difficult to make more than quite subjective estimates of the number of ethnic groups in many countries.

One could argue for attempting to base estimates on the way that most people in the country think about what the main ethnic groups are. Using secondary sources rather than survey data (which are not available), Fearon (2003) attempts this for about 160 countries, considering only groups with greater than 1 per cent of country population. Table 47.1 provides some basic descriptive statistics by region.[4] By these estimates the average country has about five ethnic groups greater than 1 per cent of population, with a range from 3.2 per country in the West to 8.2 per country in sub-Saharan Africa. Sub-Saharan Africa stands out as the only region in which fewer than half of the countries have an ethnic majority group, and it has only one country with a group comprising at least 90 per cent of the population (Rwanda).[5] The West stands out for having an ethnic majority in every single country, and three out of five with a "dominant" ethnic group (90 per cent or more). Interestingly, countries with a "dominant" group in this sense are rare in the rest of the world. Socially relevant ethnic distinctions are thus extremely common.

The politicization of ethnicity varies markedly, in a pattern that to some extent reflects variation in the prevalence of socially relevant ethnic distinctions. Ethnically based parties are common in sub-Saharan Africa, and access to political and economic benefits is frequently structured along ethnic lines. This is also the case for most of the more ethnically diverse countries of South and Southeast Asia. Ethnic parties are less common in eastern Europe, the former Soviet Union, and north Asia. However, at least during the Communist era the allocation of political and economic benefits was often formally structured along ethnic lines in eastern Europe and the former Soviet Union (Slezkine 1994; Suny 1993); the same seems true, more informally, of China, Korea, and Japan. Ethnic parties are rare in the more homogeneous Western countries, excepting Belgium and to a lesser extent Spain, Britain,

---

[3] The US government insists on a distinction between "race" and "ethnicity," though without really explaining why or on what basis.
[4] The figures in the table are based on a slightly updated version of the data used in Fearon 2003.
[5] I coded the major Somali clans as ethnic groups, though some might not see them as such.

Table 47.1 Descriptive statistics on ethnic groups larger than 1% of country population, by region

	World	West[a]	NA/ME	LA/Ca	Asia	EE/FSU	SSA[b]
# countries	160	21	19	23	23	31	43
% total		.13	.12	.14	.14	.19	.27
# groups	824	68	70	84	108	141	353
% total		.08	.08	.10	.13	.17	.43
Groups/country	5.15	3.24	3.68	3.65	4.7	4.55	8.21
Avg. pop. share of largest group	.65	.85	.68	.69	.72	.73	.41
% countries with a group ≥ 50%	.71	1	.84	.78	.78	.90	.28
% countries with a group ≥ 90%	.21	.62	.21	.17	.22	.19	.02

[a] Includes Australia, New Zealand, and Japan.
[b] Includes Sudan.

and Canada. Access to political and economic benefits can certainly be influenced by ethnicity in the Western countries (for example, in labor markets and often in urban politics), though to an extent that generally seems small when compared to most countries in other regions.

Traditionally, political cleavages in Latin America were understood in terms of class rather than ethnicity, despite ample raw material for ethnic politics in the form of socially relevant ethnic distinctions in most countries (indigenous versus mestizo versus whites, and in some cases intra-indigenous ethnic distinctions). It is an interesting question why Latin American countries have seen so little politicization of ethnicity in the form of political parties and movements, especially when political and economic benefits have long been allocated along ethnic lines in many countries of the region.[6] Middle Eastern and North African countries with marked linguistic or religious heterogeneity such as Cyprus, Lebanon, Turkey, Iraq, and Iran have experienced political mobilization along ethnic lines, while in many countries in this region politics among Arabs is structured by clan and tribal distinctions.

[6] Since the end of the cold war, there has been a notable increase in political mobilization on the basis of ethnicity in some Latin American countries (Yashar 2005). The resolution of the puzzle may have something to do with the fact that, even today, in many Latin American countries an "indigenous" person can choose to become "mestizo" simply by language and lifestyle choices. That is, the categories are not understood as unambiguously descent based.

The politicization of ethnicity also varies a great deal over time. In the broadest terms, a large literature on the origins of nationalism observes that until the last 100 to 200 years (depending on where you look), ethnic groups were not seen as natural bases for political mobilization or political authority. As Breuilly (1993, 3) notes, in the fourteenth century Dante could write an essay identifying and extolling an Italian language and nation without ever imagining that this group should have anything to do with politics. Indeed, he also wrote an essay arguing for a universal monarchy in which it never occurs to him that the monarchy should have any national basis or tasks. In early modern Europe, religion and class were the most politicized (and violent) social cleavages, and except in a few places religion was not simply a marker for ethnicity. (For example, religious conversion was possible, common, and often put family members on different sides of a divide.) Moreover, ethnic distinctions were not politicized in pre- and early modern Europe despite the fact that European countries were far more ethnically fractionalized in that period, at least if measured by linguistic diversity (see Weber 1976 on France, for example). During the nineteenth century, national homogenization projects pursued by European states via school systems and militaries paralleled a secular increase in the politicization of nationality understood in ethnic terms. The success of nationalist doctrine is now so complete that almost no one questions whether cultural groups (and in particular "nations" understood as ethnic groups) form the proper basis for political community (Gellner 1983).

The politicization of ethnicity can also vary on shorter timescales. A striking stylized fact, noted by Horowitz (1985) and Bates (1983) among others, concerns the production or reformulation of ethnic groups in response to changed political boundaries. For instance, a great many ethnic groups in Africa did not exist as such prior to the colonial period. The groups now called the Yoruba or the Kikuyu (to give just two examples) are amalgams of smaller groups that spoke related dialects but had no common social or political identity (on the Yoruba, see Laitin 1986; and more generally Vail 1991). The sense of Yoruba and Kikuyu ethnicity, identity, and political interest developed in the context of the new colonial states, which enlarged the field of political and economic competition and oriented it towards colonial capitals.

Shrinking political boundaries can have the opposite effect. Horowitz (1985, 66) mentions the 1953 reorganization of Madras state in India which led to the separation of Tamil Nadu from Andra Pradesh. In Madras state, "with large Tamil and Telugu populations, cleavages within the Telugu group were not very important. As soon as a separate Telugu-speaking state was carved out of Madras, however, Telugu subgroups—caste, regional, and religious—quickly formed the bases of political action." Posner (2005) shows how in Zambia ethnic coalitions have formed along lines of either language or tribe, depending on whether the elections were national or local. Young (1976) famously observed that individuals" perceptions of ethnic group memberships were "situational" in the sense that they might identify with and mobilize according to multiple different ethnic categorizations, shifting identifications depending on the political context (e.g. one might identify as a Yoruba in the north of Nigeria but as an Oyo, a sub-group of the Yoruba, in the south).

Finally, a number of authors have noted that violence can have powerful effects on the politicization of ethnicity. Violent attacks made along ethnic lines have often caused rapid and extreme ethnic polarization in societies in which ethnicity had not been much politicized (Laitin 1995; Kaufmann 1996; Mueller 2000; Fearon and Laitin 2000*b*).

3 SOME STYLIZED FACTS ABOUT ETHNIC VIOLENCE

Many different sorts of violent events may be referred to as "ethnic," from bar fights to hate crimes to riots to civil wars. Generally speaking, a violent attack might be described as "ethnic" if either (*a*) it is motivated by animosity towards ethnic others; (*b*) the victims are chosen by ethnic criteria; or (*c*) the attack is made in the name of an ethnic group.[7]

Compared to the myriad opportunities for conflict between contiguous ethnic dyads in the world's numerous multi-ethnic states, low-level societal ethnic violence is extremely rare (Fearon and Laitin 1996). At least since the Second World War, the vast majority of ethnic killing has come from either state oppression or fighting between a state and an armed group intending to represent an ethnic group (typically a minority). Of the 709 minority ethnic groups in Fearon's (2003) list, at least 100 (14.1 per cent) had members engaged in significant rebellion against the state on behalf of the group at some time between 1945 and 1998.[8] In the 1990s alone, almost one-in-ten of the 709 minorities engaged in significant violent conflict with the state. Table 47.2 shows great variation across regions. More than one-quarter of the relatively few ethnic minorities (greater than 1 per cent of country population) in Asia and North Africa/Middle East were involved in significant violence, whereas only one in ten of the many minorities in sub-Saharan Africa were. Across countries, there is no correlation between percentage of ethnic groups experiencing violence with the state and the number or fractionalization of ethnic groups in the country.

Cross-national statistical studies find surprisingly few differences between the determinants of civil war onset in general, versus "ethnic" civil wars in particular. Once one controls for per capita income, neither civil wars nor ethnic civil wars are significantly more frequent in more ethnically diverse countries; nor are they more likely when there is an ethnic majority and a large ethnic minority (Collier

---

[7] See Fearon and Laitin 2000*a* for a fuller discussion.
[8] I matched the groups in Fearon 2003 with the Minorities at Risk (MAR) groups (Gurr 1996), and then counted the number of matched groups that scored 4 or higher on the MAR rebellion scale (i.e. "small," "intermediate," or "large-scale" guerrilla activity, or "protracted civil war" for at least one five-year period since 1945). This underestimates the number of ethnic groups in violent conflict, since the non-MAR groups are not considered. But because MAR tends to select on violence, the underestimate is probably not very far off.

Table 47.2 Ethnic minorities involved in significant violence with the state since 1945 and 1990

Region	# minorities	% with signif. violence in 1945–98	% with signif. violence in 1990–98
West	47	0.0	0.0
LAm/Carib.	66	6.1	4.6
SSA	339	11.8	8.4
EEur/FSU	113	12.4	11.8
N.Afr/M.E.	54	27.8	13.0
Asia	90	30.0	20.0
World	709	14.1	9.8

Note: "Significant violence" means that Gurr (1996) codes the group as having been involved in a small-scale guerrilla war or greater with the state at some point in the relevant period.

and Hoeffler 2004; Fearon and Laitin 2003).[9] Both ethnic and non-ethnic civil wars have occurred more often in countries that are large, poor, recently independent, or oil rich (Fearon and Laitin 2003). Ethnic wars may tend to last longer than others on average, though this is probably due to the fact that they are more often fought as guerrilla wars (Fearon 2004). Greater ethnic diversity does not appear to be associated with higher casualties in civil conflict (Lacina 2004).

4 Explanations for the Politicization of Ethnicity

On one view, described as "primordialist," no explanation is needed for why ethnicity often forms the basis for political mobilization or discrimination. Ethnic groups are naturally political, either because they have biological roots or because they are so deeply set in history and culture as to be unchangeable "givens" of social and political life. In other words, primordialists assume that certain ethnic categories are always socially relevant, and that political relevance follows automatically from social relevance. The main objection to primordialist arguments is that they can't make sense of variation in the politicization of ethnicity over time and space.

In political economy work, ethnic groups are sometimes treated as an extreme form of interest group whose members share enduring common preferences over all public policies. Rabushka and Shepsle (1972) pioneered this approach, arguing that democracy is infeasible in an ethnically divided society because polarized ethnic

[9] But see Sambanis 2001 for an analysis that finds some differences.

preferences will lead to "ethnic outbidding" and polarized policies, which in turn makes ethnic groups unwilling to share power through elections (see also Horowitz 1985, ch. 8). Alesina, Baqir, and Easterly (1999) argue that ethnic groups have different preferences over types of public goods, and that such diversity leads to lower aggregate provision. Fearon (1998) shows that if minority and majority ethnic groups in a new state anticipate having conflicting preferences over some public policies, then the majority may have trouble credibly committing to a compromise policy that both sides would prefer to a violent conflict.

In such models, ethnic politicization follows in part from an assumption about the polarization and stability of ethnic preferences. This may be reasonable in the short run for particular cases, but it is dubious as a general proposition. It is also questionable whether, in many cases, ethnic groups disagree that much about the *types* of public goods that should be provided. In multi-ethnic Africa, for instance, schools, roads, health care, and access to government jobs are universally desired. Ethnic conflict arises when ethnic coalitions form to gain a greater share of commonly desired goods, which is hard to explain in models where "the action" comes from assumptions about conflicting preferences over types of goods.[10]

In contrast to primordialist arguments, "modernists" see ethnic groups as political coalitions formed to advance the economic interests of members (or leaders). Variation in the politicization of ethnicity is then explained by an argument about when it makes economic sense to organize a coalition along ethnic lines.

The most influential of these arguments propose to explain why ethnicity and nationality were apolitical in the premodern world, but became the foundation for international organization and much domestic political contention by the late nineteenth century. Deutsch (1953), Gellner (1983), and Anderson (1983) all find the root cause in economic modernization. Economic modernization increased social mobility and created political economies in which advancement depended increasingly on one's cultural capital. When Magyar- or Czech-speaking young men from the countryside found themselves disadvantaged in the German-using Habsburg bureaucracy or in the new industrial labor markets of Bohemia on account of their first language, they became receptive to political mobilization along ethnic ("national") lines (Deutsch 1953; Gellner 1983). The central idea is that ascriptive barriers to upward mobility—that is, discrimination according to a criterion that an individual acquires more or less at birth, such as ethnicity—gives political entrepreneurs an eager constituency.[11]

Why did states and societies increasingly discriminate along cultural lines in polity and economy, especially if this would provoke separatist nationalisms? Gellner sees cultural discrimination arising from the nature of modern economies. Because these require literate workers able to interpret and manipulate culturally specific symbols,

---

[10] Ethnic groups often have sharply conflicting preferences over national language policies, although Laitin 2001 argues that these have been highly amenable to peaceful, bargained solutions.

[11] Anderson 1983 observes that the relevant ascriptive barrier for the New World nationalisms of South America was not cultural difference but the Spanish empire's refusal to let creoles (those born in the New World) progress beyond a certain point in the imperial bureaucracy.

culture matters in the modern world in a way it never did in the premodern, agrarian age. So why not just learn the language and culture of those who control the state or the factories? Gellner, Deutsch, and Anderson all suggest that such assimilation may be possible, but only when preexisting cultural differences are not too great. France, where various regional dialects were mutually unintelligible into the nineteenth century (Weber 1976), is the leading example. Where the differences were greater, as in Austria-Hungary, the pace of assimilation may be too slow relative to economic modernization (Deutsch 1953), or psychological biases may lead advanced groups to attribute backwardness to the ethnic differences of less modernized groups (Gellner 1983). Anderson (1983) also suggests that the development of biological theories of race contributed to acceptance of ethnicity as a natural criterion for political and economic discrimination.[12]

Because they focus on the slow-moving variable of economic modernization, modernist theories of the rise of nationalism have trouble explaining the rapid politicization of ethnicity after independence in most former British and French colonies. Political coalitions shifted quickly from, for example, Kenyans versus British to Kikuyu versus Luo. Certainly the colonizers often prepared the ground for ethnic politics (Laitin 1986). British colonial rule displayed a remarkable zeal for "racial" classification, enumeration, and discrimination (see Fox 1985, or Prunier 1995 on the Belgians in Rwanda). But why do we sometimes observe *rapid* shifts in politically relevant ethnic groups when political boundaries or institutions (such as the level of elections) change?

Initiated by Bates (1983), another line of research argues that ethnicity can provide an attractive basis for coalition formation in purely distributional conflicts over political goods. Bates argued that African ethnic groups—as opposed to the much more local, precolonial formation of "tribes"—developed as political coalitions for gaining access to the "goods of modernity" dispensed by the colonial and postcolonial states. Drawing on Riker (1962), Bates proposes that "Ethnic groups are, in short, a form of minimum winning coalition, large enough to secure benefits in the competition for spoils but also small enough to maximize the per capita value of these benefits."[13] Bates's and related arguments might be termed "distributive politics" theories of ethnification.

Because changes in political boundaries or the level of elections can change the size of a minimum winning coalition, this approach can help to explain both situational and temporal shifts in ethnic politicization.[14] Posner (2004b) shows that the distinction between Chewas and Tumbukas is sharply politicized in Malawi but not

[12] Anderson seems to join Deutsch and Gellner in relying on the extent of preexisting cultural differences to explain the upward barriers to mobility in the Old World (see, for example, his explanation for the weakness of Scottish nationalism: 1983, 90). It is not entirely clear what he thinks is behind the refusal of the *peninsulares* in Spain to allow the upward progress of the New World creoles.

[13] "Minimum winning coalition" should be interpreted somewhat metaphorically here, since a minority group might be pivotal and thus influential depending on the nature of coalition politics in a country.

[14] Horowitz 1985 had explained the phenomenon as a result of a perceptual bias—that the perceived extent of cultural difference between two groups decreases with the range of available contrasts. Thus an

next door in Zambia because these groups are large enough to be political contenders in small Malawi but are too small to form winning coalitions in much larger Zambia. Similarly, Zambians have mobilized in ethnic groups defined in terms of broad language commonalities for multiparty elections where control of the presidency was at issue, while in single-party elections they have identified along tribal lines (Posner 2005). Chandra (2004) shows that similar dynamics occur in elections and in the formulation and reformulation of caste categories in India.

To work, such arguments need to explain when and why political coalitions form along ethnic rather than some other lines, such as class, religion, region, district, or political ideology. Bates (1983) made two suggestions. First, shared language and culture make it easier for political entrepreneurs to mobilize "intragroup" rather than across ethnic groups. Second, ethnic and colonial administrative boundaries tended to coincide, and modern goods like schools, electricity, and water projects tend to benefit people in a particular location. Lobbying for these goods along ethnic lines was thus natural.

Surely both arguments are often a part of the story, but neither ties the constitutive feature of ethnic groups—membership by a descent rule—to the reason for ethnic coalition formation. There are many cases of ethnic politicization between groups with a common language and much common culture (for instance, Serbs and Croats, Somali clans, Hutus and Tutsis), and of ethnic politicization behind leaders who could barely speak the ethnic group's language (for instance, Jinnah, founder of the Muslim League and Pakistan). And if coalition formation is simply a means to obtain spatially distributed goods, then why should ethnic as opposed to other, possibly arbitrary criteria define the optimal geographic coalition? In fact, we often observe ethnic politicization within administrative districts with highly mixed ethnic populations. Bates (1983) himself gives a number of examples of politicization in ethnically mixed African urban areas.

Fearon (1999) argues that distributive politics on a mass scale favors coalitions based on individual characteristics that are difficult to change, because changeable characteristics would allow the expansion of the winning coalition so that it becomes less close to "minimum winning." For example, if "pork" in an American city is dispensed solely to precincts that voted Democrat in the last mayoral election, then there are strong incentives for all precincts to vote Democrat, and thus less pork per winner. Ethnicity is almost by definition unchangeable for an individual (since it is defined by a descent rule), and "passing" can be very difficult. Thus ethnicity may be favored as a basis for coalitions in distributive politics because it makes excluding losers from the winning coalition relatively easy.[15] It follows that in countries or jurisdictions where politics is mainly about the distribution of "pork"

Ibo and Yoruba might come to see each other as having a shared Nigerian ethnicity/nationality if they live in New York.

[15] In most societies the sex ratio among adults is slightly skewed in favor of males, which implies that a coalition of males against females would be almost perfectly minimum winning under pure majority rule. This has the downside of dividing families. Various other characteristics acquired at birth, like hair and eye color, suffer from the same problem.

rather than choosing the type of public policy from a continuum (like a tax rate or policy on abortion), we might expect to see more ethnic and less ideological politics.

Caselli and Coleman (2002) formally investigate how the ability to "pass" affects incentives for coalition formation in a distributive politics problem. They consider a model in which individuals choose whether to mobilize for conflict along a particular cleavage, anticipating that in the second stage they will have the opportunity to switch identities at a utility cost of $c \geq 0$. Zero cost might be a case like party identification. A large (or infinite) cost might represent an ethnic cleavage across which there is no possibility of passing. They show that mobilization and conflict does not occur when switching identities is easy since it is anticipated that the winning coalition would expand. Caselli and Coleman suggest that higher switching costs obtain for members of groups that are distinguished by skin color or other somatic features. There are a great many counterexamples, cases of intense ethnic conflict between groups whose members can't be reliably distinguished by physical features or even language alone. But it is unclear what a systematic empirical investigation would reveal on this point.

Chandra (2004) argues that ethnic coalitions are favored in the electoral politics of "patronage democracies" (that is, democracies with large, pork-ridden state sectors) because voters find it easier to code the beneficiaries of patronage by ethnicity than by other social categories, as the information is more readily available. She suggests that as a result politicians can most easily develop a reputation as a provider by distributing patronage goods along ethnic lines.

5 EXPLANATIONS FOR ETHNIC VIOLENCE

Horowitz (1985) maintains that conflicts along ethnic lines are more likely to turn violent than are conflicts along ideological and other political cleavages. He suggests that because ethnic brethren are understood as metaphorical family members, ethnic conflicts engage intense emotions and a sense of existential threat. Killing may then appear a more reasonable and justified reaction.

While many authors have proposed explanations for ethnic violence, Horowitz's argument is one of relatively few in which ethnicity per se does explanatory work. For example, consider a country in which two or more ethnic groups are already mobilized and can be treated as "unitary actors" because they have leaderships acting for them. Then the usual rationalist explanations for violent conflict are potentially available—bargaining failure due to private information, and problems of credible commitment (Fearon 1995). In these cases the only thing "ethnic" about the explanation is the type of actors and possibly what they are bargaining over. The distinguishing features of ethnic groups (and in particular descent rules of membership) play no role in explaining violence.

Thus, Cetinyan (2001, 2002) models ethnic groups as represented by unitary actors who bargain over the terms of the minority's treatment in the state. If the minority group has private information about its willingness to fight, the majority group may demand too much, leading to a violent fight. Cetinyan stresses that this implies that while observable measures of the balance of power between two ethnic groups should predict the *terms* of a bargain they reach, they should not predict the probability of violence (since a weaker minority will simply face tougher demands).[16]

Fearon (1994, 1998, 2004) considers models in which a majority ethnic group may not be able to commit credibly to a regional autonomy deal or constitution that would protect minority rights in the future. Ethnic war may occur when the minority anticipates that its ability to fight for a better deal will decline in the future. One could argue that ethnicity per se appears here in the implicit assumption that political coalitions and preferences over public policies will, in the future, continue to divide along ethnic lines. If there were salient cross-cutting cleavages, then being in the minority today would not imply being in the minority next year.

Another set of rationalist explanations for ethnic violence drops the unitary actor assumption, focusing instead on how interethnic violence may emerge as a consequence of *intra*ethnic politics (see Fearon and Laitin 2000b for a general discussion). These develop the common claim that ethnic violence is a tool by which political elites maintain or increase their public support (e.g. Gagnon 1994–5). The central theoretical puzzle for such "diversionary" arguments is why publics would increase their support for a leader who takes actions, such as provoking ethnic violence, that by hypothesis make them worse off.[17]

Sociological and social psychological arguments invoke biases or non-rational human tendencies, such as a tendency for external threat to increase in-group cohesion (Coser 1956) or a tendency to discount negative news about those in one's in-group (Tajfel 1982). De Figueiredo and Weingast (1999) show that if members of an ethnic group are unsure about which side is to blame for an escalation of ethnic conflict, then they may rationally increase their support for the leadership out of increased fear of the other group. Thus the leadership may find it rational to provoke ethnic violence if it can do so without clear attribution.[18] Somewhat similarly, Kydd and Walter (2002) analyze the conditions in which extremists in group B can use ethnic violence so that group A will come to doubt the commitment of moderates in group B to a peace process. In their model, group A cannot observe whether extremist violence occurred because moderates in group B lacked the capability or the will to prevent it. One implication is that terrorist attacks undermine trust to a greater extent when

---

[16] As Cetinyan notes, this argument also appears in the game-theoretic literature on interstate conflict (Wittman 1979; Wagner 1994; Powell 1996).

[17] If the public is made better off by the ethnic violence, then it makes no sense to blame the "manipulative" elites for doing what publics would want.

[18] An observable implication of their argument that differs from those of the psychological tradition is that on seeing an escalation of violence or failure of negotiations, the public should increase their belief that their *own* leadership is aggressive and the cause of the trouble as well.

the moderates of group B are seen as strong relative to extremists. Kydd and Walter show evidence that Palestinian terrorist attacks in the 1990s were timed in a manner consistent with the implications of their model.

Laitin (1995) and Fearon and Laitin (2000b, 2003) observe that would-be insurgent groups often hope that their attacks on the state will provoke harsh, indiscriminate retaliation that will increase anger against the state and thus support for their cause. Moreover, this expectation often appears justified. While various arguments can be made (including those just sketched), it remains a puzzle why people do not more consistently blame the insurgents for bringing the government down on their heads. Kalyvas (1999a, 1999b) suggests that rebel and government attacks politicize highly local, often personal grievances and feuds that are unconnected to the larger ethnic or ideological struggle. In his analysis, what may appear as "ethnic" or "ideological" violence mislabels what is better understood as the arming and escalation of village-level feuds and grudges (see also Brass 1997).

As noted above, apart from Horowitz's psychological conjecture none of these arguments use ethnicity per se to explain ethnic violence. Instead, they adapt more general explanations for violent conflict for cases where combatants are organized (or would like to promote organization) along ethnic lines. This is not necessarily a problem. It may be that as an empirical matter such theories can do a good job of revealing the conditions under which ethnic violence is likely. Still, many have the intuition that there is something different about ethnic violence—that its unspeakable cruelties mean that it springs from distinct roots. Horowitz (1985, 140) famously wrote that "A bloody phenomenon cannot be explained by a bloodless theory" (referring to rationalist and economic theories of ethnic conflict).

Kalyvas's research raises some questions about this supposition as well. The patterns of extreme violence and cruelty found in ethnic conflict are characteristic of guerrilla warfare in general, whether or not a society is ethnically divided (Kalyvas 1999a).

6 Conclusion

The politicization of ethnicity attracts our attention in the first instance because it violates the classical liberal norm that political distinctions should not depend on inherited designations or attributes per se. Liberals view harmful discrimination along ethnic lines as morally wrong. This is enough to justify the study of politicized ethnicity, which is extremely common in an age that, paradoxically, views ethnic groups as natural bearers of sovereignty. In addition, many view politicized ethnicity or simply ethnic differences as causing other bad outcomes, such as poor economic performance, dictatorship rather than democracy, or violence.

The body of empirical work documenting these associations, and of theoretical work explaining them, is small but growing. We have several papers examining the relationship between ethnic diversity and economic growth or public goods provision. The results are mixed but generally find a negative relationship (Easterly and Levine 1997; Alesina, Baqir, and Easterly 1999; Miguel 2004; Miguel and Gugerty 2005; Posner 2004a). Rabushka and Shepsle (1972) and Horowitz (1985) discussed cases that they argued showed a tendency for ethnic polarization to undermine democracy, but the recent wave of cross-national statistical work on determinants of democracy has not closely examined the effect of ethnic variables.[19] As noted, there does not appear to be a strong cross-national association between various measures of ethnic diversity or demography and the onset of civil war (Fearon and Laitin 2003; Collier and Hoeffler 2004).

For all three dependent variables—economic performance, violence, and especially democracy—basic empirical work remains to be done. Regarding the first, we know little about the mechanisms linking ethnic demographies to economic outcomes, and we do not know whether ethnic demographies can reasonably be taken as exogenous in studies of economic performance or economic policy. If, as suggested by the European experience, strong states make ethnic homogeneity as much as the reverse, then the negative relationships found in the small empirical literature may not be fully causal. Regarding violence, we need systematic work on whether and when state policies that discriminate against particular groups are associated with violent conflict.[20] Also, there is no work to date systematically comparing the propensity of ethnic as opposed to other political cleavages to cause violence. Regarding democracy, even fairly basic cross-national analyses remain to be undertaken. Work on all three dependent variables might be helped if we had cross-national survey data on how people think about their ethnicity and what role it plays in their thinking about politics.[21]

As discussed above, theoretical work on the politicization of ethnicity and onset of ethnic violence has proposed a number of logics for why and when these may occur. Missing, with a few exceptions, are developed formalizations of these arguments that would allow a deeper understanding of how the logics work and relate to one another. Models examining how ethnic divisions affect democratic stability and performance are almost completely absent, and as noted most models examining ethnicity and violence could just as well be models of, say, class and violence. Finally, we lack a good baseline model that would formalize the intuition that particular ethnic distinctions are matters of social coordination and convention rather than simply given by history and culture for all time.[22] Much remains to be done.

---

[19] Przeworski et al. 2001 find little evidence for a direct impact of ethnic fractionalization on either democratic onset or persistence, whereas Boix 2003 finds that democracy is less stable in ethnically diverse middle-income countries. Fish and Brooks 2004 find no cross-national relationship. Generalizing from her analysis of India, Chandra 2005 argues that under the right institutional conditions ethnic diversity might actually support democracy and democratic stability.

[20] Cederman and Girardin 2005 find some evidence that countries in which ethnic minorities control the state apparatus are more civil war prone.

[21] See Bannon, Miguel, and Posner 2004 for an interesting analysis of this sort.

[22] Fearon 1999 and Posner 2005 propose simple models of this sort, but neither is fully developed and analyzed.

References

Alesina, A., Baqir, R., and Easterly, W. 1999. Public goods and ethnic divisions. *Quarterly Journal of Economics*, 114: 1243–84.

Anderson, B. 1983. *Imagined Communities*. London: Verso.

Bannon, A., Miguel, E., and Posner, D. N. 2004. Sources of ethnic identification in Africa. Afrobarometer Working Paper No. 44.

Bates, R. H. 1983. Modernization, ethnic competition, and the rationality of politics in contemporary Africa. Pp. 152–71 in *State versus Ethnic Claims: African Policy Dilemmas*, ed. D. Rothchild and V. A. Olunsorola. Boulder, Colo.: Westview Press.

Boix, C. 2003. *Democracy and Redistribution*. Cambridge: Cambridge University Press.

Brass, P. R. 1997. *Theft of an Idol*. Princeton, NJ: Princeton University Press.

Breuilly, J. 1993. *Nationalism and the State*. Chicago: University of Chicago Press.

Caselli, F., and Coleman, W. J. 2002. On the theory of ethnic conflict. Manuscript, Harvard University.

Cederman, L.-E., and Girardin, L. 2005. Beyond fractionalization: mapping ethnicity onto nationalist insurgencies. Manuscript, Swiss Federal Institute of Technology.

Cetinyan, R. 2001. Intrastate ethnic relations: the role of private information and uncertainty. Mimeo, University of Pittsburgh.

—— 2002. Ethnic bargaining in the shadow of third-party intervention. *International Organization*, 56: 645–77.

Chandra, K. 2004. *Why Ethnic Parties Succeed: Patronage and Head Counts in India*. Cambridge: Cambridge University Press.

—— 2005. Ethnic parties and democratic stability. *Perspectives on Politics*, 3: 235–52.

Collier, P., and Hoeffler, A. 2004. Greed and grievance in civil war. *Oxford Economic Papers*, 56: 563–95.

Coser, L. 1956. *The Functions of Social Conflict*. Glencoe, Ill.: Free Press.

de Figueiredo, R., and Weingast, B. R. 1999. The rationality of fear: political opportunism and ethnic conflict. Pp. 216–302 in *Civil War, Insecurity, and Intervention*, ed. J. L. Snyder and B. F. Walter. New York: Columbia University Press.

Deutsch, K. W. 1953. *Nationalism and Social Communication*. Cambridge, Mass.: MIT Press.

Easterly, W., and Levine, R. 1997. Africa's growth tragedy: policies and ethnic divisions. *Quarterly Journal of Economics*, 112: 1203–50.

Fearon, J. D. 1994. Ethnic war as a commitment problem. Paper presented at the Annual meetings of the American Political Science Association, New York, 30 Aug.–2 Sept.; available at: www.stanford.edu/~jfearon/.

—— 1995. Rationalist explanations for war. *International Organization*, 49: 379–414.

—— 1998. Commitment problems and the spread of ethnic conflict. Pp. 107–26 in *The International Spread of Ethnic Conflict*, ed. D. A. Lake and D. Rothchild. Princeton, NJ: Princeton University Press.

—— 1999. Why ethnic politics and "pork" tend to go together. Mimeo, Stanford University.

—— 2003. Ethnic and cultural diversity by country. *Journal of Economic Growth*, 8: 195–222.

—— 2004. Why do some civil wars last so much longer than others? *Journal of Peace Research*, 41: 275–301.

—— and Laitin, D. D. 1996. Explaining interethnic cooperation. *American Political Science Review*, 4: 715–35.

—— —— 2000a. Ordinary language and external validity. Paper presented at the Annual Meetings of the American Political Science Association, Washington, DC, Sept.

—— —— 2000b. Violence and the social construction of ethnic identity. *International Organization*, 54: 845–77.

—— —— 2003. Ethnicity, insurgency, and civil war. *American Political Science Review*, 97: 75–90.

Fish, M. S., and Brooks, R. S. 2004. Does diversity hurt democracy? *Journal of Democracy*, 15: 154–66.

Fox, R. G. 1985. *Lions of the Punjab: Culture in the Making*. Berkeley: University of California Press.

Gagnon, V. P. 1994–5. Ethnic nationalism and international conflict: the case of Serbia. *International Security*, 19: 130–66.

Gellner, E. 1983. *Nations and Nationalism*. Ithaca, NY: Cornell University Press.

Gurr, T. R. 1996. Minorities at Risk III dataset: user's manual. CIDCM, University of Maryland; available at: www.cidcm.umd.edu/inscr/mar/home.htm.

Horowitz, D. L. 1985. *Ethnic Groups in Conflict*. Berkeley: University of California Press.

Kalyvas, S. 1999a. Wanton and senseless? The logic of massacres in Algeria. *Rationality and Society*, 11: 243–85.

—— 1999b. Violence in civil war: is discrimination between ethnic and non-ethnic cleavages useful? Manuscript, University of Chicago.

Kaufmann, C. 1996. Possible and impossible solutions to ethnic civil wars. *International Security*, 20: 136–75.

Kydd, A., and Walter, B. F. 2002. Sabotaging the peace: the politics of religious violence. *International Organization*, 56: 263–96.

Lacina, B. 2004. Why civil wars come in different sizes. Mimeo, PRIO, Oslo.

Laitin, D. D. 1986. *Hegemony and Culture: Politics and Religious Change among the Yoruba*. Chicago: University of Chicago Press.

—— 1995. National revivals and violence. *Archives européennes de sociologie*, 36: 3–43.

—— 2001. Language conflict and violence. *Archives européennes de sociologie*, 41: 97–137.

Miguel, E. 2004. Tribe or nation? Nation building and public goods in Kenya versus Tanzania. *World Politics*, 56: 327–62.

—— and Gugerty, M. K. 2005. Ethnic diversity, social sanctions, and public goods in Kenya. *Journal of Public Economics*, 89: 2325–68.

Mueller, J. 2000. The banality of "ethnic war." *International Security*, 25: 42–70.

Posner, D. N. 2004a. Measuring ethnic fractionalization in Africa. *American Journal of Political Science*, 48: 849–63.

—— 2004b. The political salience of cultural difference: why Chewas and Tumbukas are allies in Zambia and adversaries in Malawi. *American Political Science Review*, 98: 529–45.

—— 2005. *Institutions and Ethnic Conflict in Africa*. New York: Cambridge University Press.

Powell, R. 1996. Stability and the distribution of power. *World Politics*, 48: 239–67.

Prunier, G. 1995. *The Rwanda Crisis: History of a Genocide*. New York: Columbia University Press.

Przeworski, A., Alvarez, M. E., Cheibub, J. A., and Limongi, F. 2001. *Democracy and Development: Political Institutions and Well-Being in the World, 1950–1990*. Cambridge: Cambridge University Press.

Rabushka, A., and Shepsle, K. A. 1972. *Politics in Plural Societies: A Theory of Democratic Instability*. Columbus, Ohio: Merrill.

Riker, W. H. 1962. *The Theory of Political Coalitions*. New Haven, Conn.: Yale University Press.

Sambanis, N. 2001. Do ethnic and non-ethnic civil wars have the same causes? A theoretical and empirical inquiry (part 1). *Journal of Conflict Resolution*, 45: 259–82.

SLEZKINE, Y. 1994. The USSR as a communal apartment, or how a socialist state promoted ethnic particularism. *Slavic Review*, 53: 414–52.
SUNY, R. G. 1993. *The Revenge of the Past*. Stanford, Calif.: Stanford University Press.
TAJFEL, H. (ed.). 1982. *Social Identity and Intergroup Relations*. Cambridge: Cambridge University Press.
VAIL, L. (ed.). 1991. *The Creation of Tribalism in Southern Africa*. Berkeley: University of California Press.
WAGNER, R. H. 1994. Peace, war, and the balance of power. *American Political Science Review*, 88: 593–607.
WEBER, E. J. 1976. *Peasants into Frenchmen*. Stanford, Calif.: Stanford University Press.
WITTMAN, D. 1979. How a war ends: a rational model approach. *Journal of Conflict Resolution*, 23: 743–63.
YASHAR, D. 2005. *Contesting Citizenship in Latin America: The Rise of Indigenous Movements and the Postliberal Challenge*. Princeton, NJ: Princeton University Press.
YOUNG, C. 1976. *The Politics of Cultural Pluralism*. Madison: University of Wisconsin Press.

CHAPTER 48

DEMOCRACY, PEACE, AND WAR

DAN REITER
ALLAN C. STAM

Why do wars start, and what accounts for their nature? The traditional realpolitik answer to this question focuses on the distribution of power among nations. However, much of the recent scholarship on interstate conflict has moved beyond the realist's myopic focus on power and begun to explore the role of domestic politics in shaping the nature of war. The result has been the generation of wide-ranging ideas and findings about this vital connection. The group of those still doubtful that domestic institutions systematically affect states' foreign policies is small and dwindling (see Gowa 1999; Mearsheimer 2001; Desch 2002).

This chapter focuses on how variations in domestic political institutions affect states' foreign policy behavior. While scholars have not agreed on a single theory of how institutions affect foreign policy, they agree on the general framework. In this chapter, we lay out that general framework, and then some specific theories within the framework which express different visions of how exactly domestic politics affect matters of war and peace.

1 A General Framework for Domestic Politics and War

Why do wars occur? A commonly held view in the international relations literature is that when states disagree about the nature of a potential war, they will be unable to reach a mutually agreeable bargain when presenting competing claims on the distribution of international goods, such as the placement of an international border or the distribution of military power between them (Fearon 1995; Smith and Stam 2004). A state dissatisfied with the territorial status quo or the local balance of military capabilities may demand that another state make concessions or face war. The target of the demand may accede or refuse, and from refusal, war may follow. Critically, state leaders take the steps to war mindful of the costs and benefits of each individual step: doing nothing, posing a demand, accepting or refusing the demand, and choosing war or backing down.

Within this conventional approach to war, the traditional realist perspective assumes that calculations of costs and benefits take into account only the state's national interest. The domestic politics approach poses a fundamental challenge to this assumption, arguing that when national leaders make foreign policy decisions that may lead to war they will consider domestic politics as well as the national interest. The general proposition of the domestic politics approach is that variations in domestic political conditions, especially variation in domestic political institutions, can affect decisions for war or peace.

To understand how domestic politics affect foreign policy decisions, the domestic politics framework begins with three assumptions. The first is that all leaders seek to maintain their hold on office, and will make foreign policy choices to improve and defend their domestic political fortunes as well as advance the national interest (Bueno de Mesquita et al. 2003).

The second assumption of the domestic politics framework is that political institutions matter because they determine how leaders gain and retain office. In democracies, for example, regular, competitive, and free elections provide the means by which publics can hold political leaders accountable for their foreign policy decisions. In dictatorships, the absence of electoral institutions means that leaders face fewer constraints on their choices, but may also face different domestic costs for perceived policy failures. If domestic political institutions (such as elections) allow publics to change their leaders frequently and with relatively low cost, then leaders will be more likely to adopt foreign policies that are popular with voters. Conversely, in states where it is difficult and/or costly for the public to reselect a leader, then the leader will feel freer to adopt unpopular policies, knowing that public anger will be less likely to cause him or her to lose office.

The third assumption is that political leaders and voters may often have quite different preferences for various foreign policies (see Russett and Oneal 2000). Democratic institutions provide a means for voters to force leaders to act on the public's rather than on the leader's preferences.

Thus far, the discussion of institutions and selection has focused on the probability of losing office. Institutions can also matter by determining the consequences of losing office. Elected leaders may face relatively benign personal consequences from losing office, as they can look forward to a comfortable retirement writing memoirs and giving public lectures. Leaders of other states such as dictatorships may face more dire consequences, such as exile, prison, or even execution (Goemans 2000).

As we noted at the outset there is no unanimous consensus over any single domestic politics model of war. Scholars focus on different components of the war process and employ different assumptions to construct models that in some cases make different predictions. We next describe two major variants within this general framework: public opinion constraints and audience costs. Our goals are to lay out the basic principles of these models, describe their predictions, and review how well the empirical record supports them. We should emphasize that these two variants share important similarities, but we hope that by distinguishing them and avoiding the temptation to combine them into a single model, the reader will get a sense of the intellectual depth and ferment within this area of scholarship.

1.1 Public Opinion Constraints

The first variant focuses on how institutions can affect the relationship between public opinion and foreign policy. The essence of this perspective is that of representative democracy, that political leaders try to maintain their position by serving the public's interests which the leaders gauge by measuring public opinion. Many, but not all of these arguments are decision theoretic in nature, assuming, for example, that states targeted for war will necessarily fight back (Reiter and Stam 2002). A critical question for this variant is: what foreign policies do people prefer? There are three general answers to this question. First, cheaper policies are commonly more popular. The principal costs of wars are casualties and the diversion of resources from other priorities. Because society bears these costs more directly than its leaders, when the people have more influence, a state's foreign policy will reflect greater cost sensitivity. Democracies should therefore be less likely to initiate wars or disputes, and when democracies do fight, they should try to do so quickly and cheaply (Bennett and Stam 1996; Slantchev 2004).

Second, people want success, and elected leaders fear failure. In democracies, voters often react to past or anticipated policy failure by voting leaders out of office. This means that democratic leaders are more fearful than autocrats of policy failure such as defeat in war, as for the former it means the costs of bad policy outcomes and a greater risk of losing political power, whereas for the latter it means only the cost of bad policy outcomes. The principal predictions of this argument are that democracies are more conservative in launching military ventures, doing so only when they are confident of cheap victory, whereas authoritarian leaders are more inclined to engage in risky wars, knowing that even in defeat they are likely to remain in power. Some, such as Bueno de Mesquita et al. (2003), focus on the constraints imposed by leaders anticipating the costs of voters acting prospectively at elections to select leaders out of office. Reiter and Stam (2002) focus on the constraint imposed by a need to generate contemporaneous consent among likely voters for policies leaders would prefer to choose. By generating consent in advance, leaders can inoculate themselves against the possible costs of policy failures. In the prospective voting set-up, voters use information drawn from past events to make judgements about the likely competence of leaders in the future.

The need for policy success may introduce perverse incentives. Leaders facing dwindling political fortunes due to failing policies may feel impelled to resort to war or adopt suboptimal military strategies, "gambling for resurrection," since winning might increase their chances of retaining power, while a loss would not matter for domestic political fortunes because the leader would lose power or face even greater sanction anyway (Smith 1996; Goemans 2000). Others argue that leaders of newly formed democracies may initiate conflicts with their neighbors to consolidate their domestic political support (Mansfield and Snyder 2002).

A third line of research concerns the stakes of war. Most public constraint theories do *not* propose that democracies are more or less likely to fight wars of empire or genocide. Sometimes those wars are profitable and popular (Bueno de Mesquita et al. 2003; Reiter and Stam 2002; Henderson 2002). One model predicts that democracies are more likely to pursue war aims best characterized as public goods, while autocracies are more likely to pursue aims more easily translated into private goods (Bueno de Mesquita et al. 2003).

Public constraints arguments have attracted substantial empirical support. The popularity of elected leaders declines as casualties mount (Gartner and Segura 1998), though publics are willing to accept casualties for important stakes and when victory seems likely (Feaver and Gelpi 2004). Anticipation of the electoral consequences of declining support for war in the face of mounting casualties also affects the nature of war. Democracies fight shorter wars (Bennett and Stam 1996) in part because of the strategies they fight with (Reiter and Meek 1999) and in part because of the type of wars they choose to fight in the first place (Slantchev 2004). In these wars, democracies suffer fewer casualties (Siverson 1995; Goemans 2000, 65) and more readily compromise in longer wars (Bennett and Stam 1998).

Studies show that leaders understand how political institutions shape the domestic political consequences of military defeat. This leads elected leaders to be much more likely to win the international crises (Rioux 1998; Gelpi and Griesdorf 2001) and wars (Reiter and Stam 2002) they start. Dictators are less likely to win the crises and wars they start because they are more likely to launch risky ventures with *ex ante* lower probabilities of victory. These findings are quite robust (Reed and Clark 2000; Clark and Reed 2003; Reiter and Stam 2003a). Consistent with the rational expectations view, because democracies anticipate the electoral consequences of war, they avoid disastrous wars and, as a result, we do not observe that elected leaders lose power faster than non-elected leaders after wars (Chiozza and Goemans 2004). Some theoretical models that extend the public opinion logic in a strategic setting predict that authoritarian states may seek to exploit this democratic cost sensitivity, and may be especially likely to initiate international disputes against democracies, hoping the democracy will back down rather than risk war (Filson and Werner 2004).

Though democracies are less likely to fight each other, the evidence on whether democracies are generally more peaceful is mixed. Recognizing that publics may be motivated to fight for nationalistic reasons, Braumoeller (1997) argues that liberalism may provide fewer protections against war than many surmise. Some have found that democracies are more conflictual in their relations with non-democratic states than non-democratic states are with each other (Werner 2000; Reiter and Stam 2003*a*; Bennett and Stam 2004). Some found that democracies are more likely to be targeted by other states (Rousseau et al. 1996; Schultz 2001, 135), though others report different results (Pickering 2002; Huth and Allee 2002, 153; Bennett and Stam 2004, 128–31). Gelpi and Grieco (2001) found that after controlling for leaders' tenure, democracies are no more likely to be the target of other states' aggression. Some claim that democracies are less likely to initiate crises or the use of force (Schultz 2001, 135; Huth and Allee 2002, 152).

The evidence on other implications derived from the public opinion constraints approach is also mixed. Regarding whether democracies extract more during wartime, Bueno de Mesquita et al. (2003, 2004) found that in certain cases democracies do extract more during wartime, though other tests report the opposite (Reiter and Stam 2002). Some have speculated that representative political institutions may make citizens more willing to consent to conscription (Levi 1997). Others have argued that the soldiers of democracies are no more or less willing to sacrifice themselves, though they may fight with better initiative and leadership (Reiter and Stam 2002, ch. 3). An intriguing twist on this line of reasoning is that representative institutions may push democracies to invest more and more broadly in education (Lake and Baum 2001) and better-educated soldiers and officers appear to fight better (Biddle and Long 2004).

The evidence on exactly how institutional variations affect conflict behavior is also mixed. Some have proposed that elected leaders with broader legislative support might be less vulnerable to domestic political challenges, and hence might be more willing to take risks and initiate force. Though there is some supportive evidence for this claim (Howell and Pevehouse 2005; Clark 2000; Ireland and Gartner 2001), other studies found no relationship between legislative support and proclivity to use force (Reiter and Tillman 2002; Leblang and Chan 2003; Palmer, London, and Regan 2004). Others have proposed that the key institutional check lies in the state's need to serve the preferences of the fraction of society whose support the leader needs to stay in power (Bueno de Mesquita et al. 2003; Reiter and Tillman 2002).

The evidence that declining political fortunes cause leaders to initiate conflict is also weak and inconsistent (Fordham 2002; Meernik 2001; Miller 1995; Gelpi 1997). Others find evidence that potential attackers are less likely to initiate conflict against democracies facing internal strife, suggesting that these potential attackers anticipate that troubled leaders are more inclined to escalate conflict, and hence avoid giving such roiled states an excuse for war (Leeds and Davis 1997; Miller 1999; Clark and Reed 2003). Many authors are skeptical of the claim that states with newly minted democratic institutions are more conflict prone (Russett and Oneal 2000), though there is empirical support for the narrower claim that states with new partly democratic institutions are more conflict prone (Mansfield and Snyder 2002).

1.2 Audience Costs

Fearon's (1994) "audience costs" model is closely related to but theoretically distinct from the public constraints argument. Starting from a somewhat different premiss from the public opinion literature, the "audience costs" literature begins with the assumption that war is an inefficient solution to a bargaining problem (Fearon 1995). One reason states might adopt an inefficient policy is because state A cannot credibly signal to state B what A's true resolve or cost tolerance is. This line of reasoning is explicitly strategic, in that the problem or cause of war or peace lies in one side's strategic incentives to misrepresent its own capabilities. The theoretical focus is on leaders' ability or lack thereof to decipher their opponent's resolve.

The audience costs permutation of the signaling model of war is based on the indirect effects of anticipated electoral punishments, and assumes that during international crises states are uncertain about each other's resolve for war (resolve here refers to how willing the opposing sides are to fight and therefore bear the high costs of war to defend their interests). Because a state's costs of fighting are related to both its own resolve as well as its opponent's, states have incentives to adopt policies short of war to try to force their opponents to reveal credible information about their levels of resolve. Escalating a diplomatic crisis by mobilizing one's military forces is one way in which a state can attempt to communicate its resolve to the other side, that it will fight to defend its interests, and in doing so, hopefully get the other side to back down.

In the audience costs approach, domestic politics enters the picture when leaders consider what might happen if they back down after precipitating or escalating a crisis. The audience costs model proposes that potential voters will view backing down in a crisis as a policy failure, and when able, will therefore punish at the polls leaders that back down in a crisis. Institutions matter in that citizens of authoritarian states are less able to inflict political costs on their leaders than voters are in states with elected leaders. Notably, some audience costs models have focused on the political opposition rather than on the public (Schultz 2001).

From the audience costs perspective, all leaders know that dictators are freer to back down, and hence more likely to bluff, than are elected leaders. In turn, according to this logic, because a democratic leader will suffer greater punishment from backing down than an authoritarian counterpart will, the democrat will be likely to step up the escalatory ladder only when he or she is unlikely to back down; that is, when he or she has a high resolve for war. Ironically, this becomes an advantage for democracies, as a democracy's decision to escalate a crisis is a stronger signal of its resolve for war than is an autocrat's decision to escalate. When democracies escalate they really "mean it," but when autocrats escalate, they are more likely than democracies to be bluffing. Relatedly, some have proposed that democratic domestic audiences are more likely to punish political leaders for reneging on international agreements like alliances, which in turn makes cooperation between democracies more likely (Leeds 1999).

Empirical testing of audience costs models is at this stage preliminary. However, one central audience costs hypothesis is that when a democracy escalates a crisis, the other side should be significantly more likely to back down, as the prospective audience costs to a democracy of escalating and then backing down are high enough that a democracy would only escalate if it had a high resolve for war The empirical evidence in support of this prediction, however, is mixed. Schultz (2001) finds that escalatory moves made by democratic states, such as increasing the level of military mobilization in a crisis, are less likely to meet resistance by non-democratic opponents than is the case in pairs of non-democracies in similar settings. There are, however, limits to the empirical reach of this result. Eyerman and Hart (1996) found that crises involving two democracies involve fewer steps, offering indirect support for the audience costs proposition that democracies communicate during crises more effectively. Partell and Palmer (1999) also found that democracies are less likely to back down in crises, and that democracies are less likely to launch so-called "limited probes" of opponents' resolve. However, using an improved research design, Lai (2004) found that democrats' opponents are more likely to back down in the face of a democratic crisis initiation but *not* escalation. Further, democracies are significantly less likely to become involved in non-violent international disputes, meaning that democracies are not using such disputes to signal resolve to each other (Kinsella and Russett 2002). The evidence on democratic alliance behavior is also mixed, as some have found that democracies are more likely to ally with each other and honor alliance agreements (Leeds et al. 2002; Leeds 2003), while others have found a weak or negative relationship (Lai and Reiter 2000; Gibler and Sarkees 2004; Gartzke and Gleditsch 2004; Reiter and Stam 2002).

Some of the work grounded in the public opinion constraint model offers direct theoretical challenges to the audience costs perspective. In an intriguing paper linking bargaining and war, Filson and Werner (2004) challenge the audience costs view that targets of democratic challenge and escalation are more likely to back down because they are convinced that the democracies are resolved for war. Filson and Werner propose that such episodes of democratic challenges are more likely to end peacefully because democracies make lower demands, which their opponents are more likely to accept, not because the democracies are more capable or resolved.

2 NEW DIRECTIONS

Many theoretical and empirical gaps remain in the study of domestic politics and war. One major undeveloped area concerns how political institutions may affect the quality of information provided to leaders. When leaders have higher-quality information, they may be able to assess more accurately international conditions, including the resolve of the opponent, the likely costs of a prospective war, and the chances of victory if war does come. Some have proposed that because democracies protect freedoms of speech and press, they enjoy a more vibrant marketplace of ideas. These in turn provide liberal leaders with more robust policy debates and analyses, enabling elected leaders to be more likely to avoid military disasters. Authoritarian leaders do not enjoy these benefits. Further, tyrants may suffer greater intelligence shortcomings because their fears of domestic political threats may cause them to purge their militaries, and surround themselves with yes-men and toadies rather than apolitical professionals (Reiter and Stam 2002; Snyder 1991; Quinlivan 1999). The role of the marketplace of ideas informing foreign policy has received only the barest empirical attention, though one study argued that the marketplace in the USA failed in the months before the 2003 Iraq War (Kaufmann 2004).

Other important areas of enquiry remain. Scholars are just beginning to understand the causal arrow reversed: how international factors affect democracy (Gleditsch 2002; Russett and Oneal 2000; Reiter 2001; Pevehouse 2002). Oddly, authoritarianism itself besides being portrayed as the opposite of democracy is only just beginning to receive study, and one useful path is the exploration of how different kinds of authoritarianism lead to different foreign policy behaviors (Lai and Slater 2006; Peceny and Beer 2003). In the public opinion and signaling debates, there is no consensus about the timing of the constraint, whether voters evaluate policy prospectively, retrospectively, or contemporaneously. Smith and Stam (2004) develop a model of war built on disagreement with non-common priors that calls into question the logic of the signaling games from which the audience cost literature evolved.

One last puzzle is the odd tendency of democracies to perform quite well in crises and wars, but also to attract attackers. If democracies are quite powerful, and this is well known, this fact should deter potential predators. Instead, they seem to be more likely to strike. If the audience costs perspective is correct, then democracies ought to do quite well at fending off attackers by demonstrating their resolve effectively and efficiently. As noted, Filson and Werner (2004) speculate that the presumed higher casualty sensitivity of democracies trumps increased audience costs credibility. This effect works counter to the audience effect and suggests that autocratic leaders may believe that democrats will back down quickly rather than fight or settle for lesser gains in wars under way (Bennett and Stam 1998). However, the repeated willingness of democracies to stand, fight, and win seems to be a lesson ignored by autocrats, as potential attackers look to the occasional instance of apparent democratic faintheartedness for encouragement. This puzzle deserves closer examination. In a related vein, the rational expectations approach implies that we should see little advantage accrue to states that initiate wars, as being willing to initiate should signal to potential targets that the target is likely to lose, and so should sweeten its offer in order to prevent the costs associated with fighting a losing war. Empirically, however, war initiators in general, and democratic ones in particular, enjoy a significant edge in the disproportionate number of wars they go on to win (Reiter and Stam 1998, 2002).

Scholarly consideration of the connection between domestic politics and war is far from complete. Several different theoretical perspectives compete with each other, and the substantial body of empirical results resembles a tangled ball of yarn rather than a completed sweater. Students and scholars of international relations should not see this as a sign of a dying argument, but rather as an open invitation to participate in the debate and help advance our understanding in this crucial area.

References

Bennett, D. S., and Stam, A. C., III. 1996. The duration of interstate wars, 1816–1985. *American Political Science Review*, 90: 239–57.

——— 1998. The declining advantages of democracy: a combined model of war outcomes and duration. *Journal of Conflict Resolution*, 42: 344–66.

——— 2004. *The Behavioral Origins of War*. Ann Arbor: University of Michigan Press.

Biddle, S., and Long, S. B. 2004. Democracy and military effectiveness: a deeper look. *Journal of Conflict Resolution*, 48: 525–46.

Bueno de Mesquita, B., Smith, A., Siverson R. M., and Morrow, J. D., 2003. *The Logic of Political Survival*. Cambridge Mass.: MIT Press.

——— 2004. Testing novel implications from the selectorate theory of war. *World Politics*, 56: 363–88.

Braumoeller, B. F. 1997. Deadly doves: liberal nationalism and the democratic peace in the Soviet successor states. *International Studies Quarterly*, 41: 375–402.

Cederman, L.-E. 2001. Back to Kant: reinterpreting the democratic peace as a macro historical learning process. *American Political Science Review*, 95: 15–31.

Chiozzi, G., and Goemans, H. E. 2003. Peace through insecurity: tenure and international conflict. *Journal of Conflict Resolution*, 47: 443–67.

——— 2004. International conflict and the tenure of leaders: is war still ex post inefficient? *American Journal of Political Science*, 48: 604–19.

Clark, D. H. 2000. Agreeing to disagree: domestic institutional congruence and U.S. dispute behavior. *Political Research Quarterly*, 53: 375–400.

——— 2003. Can strategic interaction divert diversionary behavior? A model of U.S. conflict propensity. *Journal of Politics*, 65: 1013–39.

——— and Reed, W. 2003. A unified model of war onset and outcome. *Journal of Politics*, 65: 69–91.

Desch, M. C. 2002. Democracy and victory: why regime type hardly matters. *International Security*, 27: 5–47.

Dixon, W. J. 1994. Democracy and the peaceful settlement of international conflict. *American Political Science Review*, 88: 14–32.

——— and Senese, P. 2002. Democracy, disputes, and negotiated settlements. *Journal of Conflict Resolution*, 46: 547–57.

Eyerman, J., and Hart, R. A., Jr. 1996. An empirical test of the audience cost proposition. *Journal of Conflict Resolution*, 40: 597–616.

Fearon, J. D. 1994. Domestic political audiences and the escalation of international disputes. *American Political Science Review*, 88: 577–92.

——— 1995. Rationalist explanations for war. *International Organization*, 49: 379–414.

Feaver, P. D., and Gelpi, C. 2004. *Choosing your Battles: American Civil–Military Relations and the Use of Force*. Princeton, NJ: Princeton University Press.

Filson, D., and Werner, S. 2004. Bargaining and fighting: the impact of regime type on war onset, duration, and outcomes. *American Journal of Political Science*, 48: 296–313.

Fordham, B. O. 2002. Another look at "Parties, voters, and the use of force abroad." *Journal of Conflict Resolution*, 46: 572–96.

Gartner, S. S. 1997. *Strategic Assessment in War*. New Haven, Conn.: Yale University Press.

——— and Segura, G. 1998. War, casualties, and public opinion. *Journal of Conflict Resolution*, 42: 278–300.

Gartzke, E., and Gleditsch, K. 2004. Why democracies may actually be less reliable allies. *American Journal of Political Science*, 48: 775–95.

GELPI, C. 1997. Democratic diversions: governmental structure and the externalization of domestic conflict. *Journal of Conflict Resolution*, 41: 255–82.
———— and GRIECO, J. M. 2001. Attracting trouble: democracy, leadership tenure, and the targeting of militarized challenges, 1918–1992. *Journal of Conflict Resolution*, 45: 794–817.
———— and GRIESDORF, M. 2001. Winners or losers? Democracies in international crisis, 1918–94. *American Political Science Review*, 95: 633–47.
GIBLER, D., and SARKEES, M. 2004. Measuring alliances: the correlates of war formal interstate alliance dataset, 1816–2000. *Journal of Peace Research*, 41: 211–22.
GLEDITSCH, K. S. 2002. *All International Politics is Local: The Diffusion of Conflict, Integration, and Democratization*. Ann Arbor: University of Michigan Press.
GOEMANS, H. E. 2000. *War and Punishment: The Causes of War Termination and the First World War*. Princeton, NJ: Princeton University Press.
GOWA, J. 1999. *Ballots and Bullets: The Elusive Democratic Peace*. Princeton, NJ: Princeton University Press.
HENDERSON, E. A. 2002. *Democracy and Peace: The End of an Illusion?* Boulder, Colo.: Lynne Rienner.
HOWELL, W., and PEVEHOUSE, J. 2005. Presidents, Congress, and the use of force. *International Organization*, 59: 209–32.
HUTH, P. K., and ALLEE, T. L. 2002. *The Democratic Peace and Territorial Conflict in the Twentieth Century*. Cambridge: Cambridge University Press.
IRELAND, M. J., and GARTNER, S. S. 2001. Time to fight: government type and conflict initiation in parliamentary systems. *Journal of Conflict Resolution*, 45: 547–68.
KAUFMANN, C. 2004. Threat inflation and the failure of the marketplace of ideas: the selling of the Iraq War. *International Security*, 29: 5–48.
KINSELLA, D., and RUSSETT, B. 2002. Conflict emergence and escalation in interactive international dyads. *Journal of Politics*, 64: 1045–68.
LAI, B. 2004. Resolve, bargaining costs, and international crisis: the effects of military mobilization and democracy. Unpublished manuscript.
———— and REITER, D. 2000. Democracy, political similarity, and international alliances, 1816–1992. *Journal of Conflict Resolution*, 44: 203–27.
———— and SLATER, D. 2006. Institutions of the offensive: domestic sources of dispute initiation in authoritarian regimes, 1950–1992. *American Journal of Political Science*, 50: 113–26.
LAKE, D. A., and BAUM, M. A. 2001. The invisible hand of democracy: political control and the provision of public services. *Comparative Political Studies*, 34: 587–621.
LEBLANG, D., and CHAN, S. 2003. Explaining wars fought by established democracies: do institutional constraints matter? *Political Research Quarterly*, 56: 385–400.
LEEDS, B. A. 1999. Domestic political institutions, credible commitments, and international cooperation. *American Journal of Political Science*, 43: 979–1002.
———— 2003. Alliance reliability in times of war: explaining state decisions to violate treaties. *International Organization*, 57: 801–27.
———— and DAVIS, D. R. 1997. Domestic political vulnerability and international disputes. *Journal of Conflict Resolution*, 41: 814–34.
———— RITTER, J. M., MITCHELL, S. M., and LONG, A. G. 2002. Alliance treaty obligations and provisions, 1815–1944. *International Interactions*, 28: 237–60.
LEVI, M. 1997. *Consent, Dissent, and Patriotism*. Cambridge: Cambridge University Press.
MANSFIELD, E. D., and SNYDER, J. 2002. Democratic transitions, institutional strength, and war. *International Organization*, 56: 297–337.
MEARSHEIMER, J. J. 2001. *The Tragedy of Great Power Politics*. New York: Norton.
MEERNIK, J. 2001. Domestic politics and the political use of military force by the United States. *Political Research Quarterly*, 54: 889–904.

MILLER, R. A. 1995. Domestic structures and the diversionary use of force. *American Journal of Political Science*, 39: 760–85.

―― 1999. Regime type, strategic interaction, and the diversionary use of force. *Journal of Conflict Resolution*, 43: 388–402.

PALMER, G. H., LONDON, T. R., and REGAN, P. M. 2004. What's stopping you? The source of political constraints on international conflict behavior in parliamentary democracies. *International Interactions*, 30: 1–24.

PARTELL, P. J., and PALMER, G. 1999. Audience costs and interstate crises: an empirical assessment of Fearon's model of dispute outcomes. *International Studies Quarterly*, 43: 389–405.

PECENY, M., and BEER, C. 2003. Peaceful parties and puzzling personalists. *American Political Science Review*, 97: 339–42.

PEVEHOUSE, J. C. 2002. Democracy from the outside-in? International organizations and democratization. *International Organization*, 56: 515–49.

PICKERING, J. 2002. Give me shelter: reexamining military intervention and the monadic democratic peace. *International Interactions*, 28: 293–324.

QUINLIVAN, J. T. 1999. Coup-proofing: its practice and consequences in the Middle East. *International Security*, 24: 131–65.

REED, W., and CLARK, D. H. 2000. War initiators and war winners: the consequences of linking theories of democratic war success. *Journal of Conflict Resolution*, 44: 378–95.

REITER, D. 2001. Does peace nurture democracy? *Journal of Politics*, 63: 935–48.

―― 2003. Exploring the bargaining model of war. *Perspectives on Politics*, 1: 27–43.

―― and MEEK, C. 1999. Determinants of military strategy, 1903–1994: a quantitative empirical test. *International Studies Quarterly*, 43: 363–87.

―― and STAM, A. C. 2002. *Democracies at War*. Princeton, NJ: Princeton University Press.

―― ―― 2003a. Identifying the culprit: democracy, dictatorship, and dispute initiation. *American Political Science Review*, 97: 333–7.

―― ―― 2003b. Understanding victory: why political institutions matter. *International Security*, 28: 168–79.

―― and TILLMAN, E. 2002. Public, legislative, and executive constraints on the democratic initiation of conflict. *Journal of Politics*, 64: 810–26.

RIOUX, J.-S. 1998. A crisis-based evaluation of the democratic peace proposition. *Canadian Journal of Political Science*, 31: 263–83.

ROUSSEAU, D. L., GELPI, C., REITER, D., and HUTH, P. K. 1996. Assessing the dyadic nature of the democratic peace, 1918–1988. *American Political Science Review*, 90: 512–33.

RUSSETT, B., and ONEAL, J. 2000. *Triangulating Peace: Democracy, Interdependence, and International Organizations*. New York: Norton.

SCHULTZ, K. A. 2001. *Democracy and Coercive Diplomacy*. Cambridge: Cambridge University Press.

SIMMONS, B. 2002. Capacity, commitment, and compliance: international institutions and territorial disputes. *Journal of Conflict Resolution*, 46: 829–47.

SIVERSON, R. M. 1995. Democratic and war participation: in defense of the institutional constraints argument. *European Journal of International Relations*, 1: 481–9.

SLANTCHEV, B. 2004. How initiators end their wars: the duration of warfare and the terms of peace. *American Journal of Political Science*, 48: 813–29.

SMITH, A. 1996. Diversionary foreign policy in democratic systems. *International Studies Quarterly*, 40: 133–53.

―― and STAM, A. C. 2004. Bargaining and the nature of war. *Journal of Conflict Resolution*, 48: 783–813.

SNYDER, J. 1991. *Myths of Empire: Domestic Politics and International Ambition*. Ithaca, NY: Cornell University Press.

STAM, A. C. 1996. *Win, Lose, or Draw*. Ann Arbor: University of Michigan Press.

WENDT, A. 1999. *A Social Theory of International Politics*. Cambridge: Cambridge University Press.

WERNER, S. 2000. The effects of political similarity on the onset of militarized disputes, 1816–1985. *Political Research Quarterly*, 53: 343–74.

CHAPTER 49

ANARCHY

STERGIOS SKAPERDAS

RELATIONS between states are often characterized as anarchic, in the sense that there is no ultimate authority regulating these relations. Especially in the realist and neo-realist traditions of international relations thought, states are viewed as purposive actors with material interests and objectives; their interactions under anarchy would thus appear amenable to the formal modeling typically pursued by economists and other social scientists who follow a rational choice approach. Up until relatively recently, though, there had been surprisingly little such work on formally modeling anarchy in general, and there is still even less work on modeling anarchy in international relations specifically. This could be partly explained by the rooting of neoclassical economics in the liberal tradition of thought that assumes away anarchy, any imperfections in contracting, or the costly enforcement of property rights. For example, all received models of international trade abstract away from security considerations and thus the possible connections between trade and security policies cannot even be considered within such models.

In this chapter I will introduce recent research from economics that models anarchy. Although relations between states are not its main concern, this research clearly has implications for thinking about interstate relations and there are indications that such relations are becoming a greater as well as a fruitful concern. The starting point of the approach is that under anarchy parties cannot write enforceable contracts that would eliminate arming and the possibility of using violence. That starting point goes against a long tradition of neoclassical economics that assumes property rights are perfectly and costlessly enforced but it is consistent with the more basic assumption

---

* I am thankful to the editors for their helpful comments and to Michelle Garfinkel for her very careful reading that prevented a number of errors appearing in the final version of this chapter. My research was partly supported by a research and writing grant from the John D. and Catherine T. MacArthur Foundation.

of self-interest, for a genuine *Homo economicus* would not be restrained from using force if using force were to enhance his material interests.

To enhance accessibility, I will present only simplified versions of models and only discuss the intuition of many results. The reader who is interested in more detail is referred to the particular items in the references. Questions that will be discussed include: how is power under anarchy determined and distributed? What are some of the determinants of open conflict versus settlement under the threat of conflict? How can trade and security policies be related? How do norms and institutions of governance affect the outcome under anarchy? What kind of governance can be expected to emerge out of anarchy? Obviously, some of these are fundamental questions of social science—not just of political science or economics—and it would be presumptuous to assume the literature reviewed here provides new answers. Nevertheless, the hope is that this formal modeling approach reframes such old questions in ways that can help clarify the nature of the different possible answers that have been offered in the past.

1 THE BASICS: GUNS V. BUTTER

Under anarchy there is no higher authority—laws, courts, police—to enforce contracts externally. Any contracts made by individual parties have to be enforced by the parties themselves. As with contracts enforced by the state, the ultimate power to do so comes out of the threat of using force. Norms, informal and formal agreements, whatever international laws and institutions might exist could well restrain and shape the use of force, but the extent of a party's capability with guns can be reasonably considered the most important determinant in the party getting better terms under anarchy. While guns can enhance one party's position relative to others, they are expensive to produce and reduce material welfare in other ways. Thus, in examining interaction under anarchy, the basic trade-off between guns and butter is central.

Over the past few decades, Jack Hirshleifer was the first economist to argue that, in making a living, there is a basic trade-off between production and appropriation— between producing and taking away the production of others, or between guns and butter. The basic approach presented here follows Hirshleifer and related contributions.[1] To organize my discussion, I will present a basic model of anarchy. For now, suppose there are just two countries, labeled 1 and 2. Each country $i = 1, 2$ has a total amount of resources R_i that can be considered a composite of its labor, capital, land, and other inputs that can be used in producing guns and butter. In particular, the basic trade-off between the production of guns (G_i) and butter (B_i) is given by the

---

[1] Hirsheifer 1988 was the first paper to allow for that trade-off. Hirshleifer's other work in the area includes Hirshleifer 1989, 1991, 1995 and the collection of his articles in Hirshleifer 2001. Haavelmo 1954 has the first model in which production and appropriation are allowed. Other contributors to the more recent literature include Garfinkel 1990; Grossman 1991; Skaperdas 1992; Grossman and Kim 1996; Esteban and Ray 1999; Wittman 2000; Mehlum, Moene, and Torvik 2000. Hirshleifer 1994 provides an argument for importance of the approach in general, whereas Skaperdas 2003 has a critical review of the literature. A special issue of the *Journal of Conflict Resolution* included some relevant papers (Sandler 2000 has the overview).

following constraint:

$$R_i = G_i + \frac{1}{\beta_i} B_i \qquad (1)$$

where $\beta_i > 0$ is a productivity parameter for country i. Given this constraint, for any given choice of guns, country i's production of butter would equal:

$$B_i = \beta_i(R_i - G_i) \qquad (2)$$

From this equality it is clear that a country's production of butter would be higher, (i) the lower is its production of guns, G_i; (ii) the higher is the country's resource, R_i; and (iii) the higher is its productivity, β_i.

We suppose that each country and its population materially value what they can directly consume, which in this benchmark model is butter and not guns. In a world with perfectly secure property rights—the opposite extreme to anarchy—each country would therefore have no need for guns and could devote all of its resources to the production of butter and consume all of that production. Under anarchy, though, the butter a country were to produce would not be secure and some or all of it could be subject to capture by the other country in the event of conflict or be extorted away under the threat of it. Likewise, the country could decide that it is more profitable to go after the other country's butter rather than produce much butter. Guns, not butter, are the currency that ultimately counts under this ideal type of anarchy. Then, before considering how the countries would allocate their resources between guns and butter, we need to establish how exactly the currency of guns is cashed in.

1.1 Technologies of Conflict

Guns affect the chances that each country has in prevailing if conflict were to occur. Then, given a choice of guns by the two countries, G_1 and G_2, we can denote the probability of country 1 winning as $p_1(G_1, G_2)$ and the probability of country 2 winning as $p_2(G_1, G_2)$. Clearly, the probability of each country winning can be expected to be higher, the higher is its own quantity of guns and the lower is the quantity of guns of its opponent. How these expenditures on guns affect the winning probabilities of each party depend on the state of the military technology. With both countries having access to the same military technology, a reasonable property for the winning probabilities is to have $p_1(G_1, G_2) = p_2(G_2, G_1)$. A wide class of functional forms that has been examined is the following:

$$p_1(G_1, G_2) = \frac{f(G_1)}{f(G_1) + f(G_2)} \qquad (3)$$

provided G_1 or G_2 is positive (otherwise, $p_1(G_1, G_2) = 1/2$) and where $f(.)$ is a non-negative, increasing function.[2] The most commonly used functional form is the

---

[2] A major property of this class of functional forms is the "independence from irrelevant alternatives" property, whereby the probability of winning of either side does not depend on the guns possessed by third parties to the conflict. Hirshleifer 1989 has examined two important functional forms and Skaperdas 1996 has axiomatized the class.

one in which $f(G_i) = G_i^m$, where $m > 0$ (and often, for technical reasons, $1 \geq m$), so that:

$$p_1(G_1, G_2) = \frac{G_1^m}{G_1^m + G_2^m} \quad (4)$$

For this form the probability of winning depends on the ratio of guns expenditures by the two parties. Some effects of different military technologies can be captured by the parameter m; for example, the technology of seventeenth-century warfare during the Thirty Years War, with its large armies and artillery units, can be thought of as having a higher value for this parameter than the feudal levies of medieval Europe. Such factors have consequences for the size of political units.

1.2 How Power is Determined

We can now examine how the two countries can be expected to distribute their resources between guns and butter in this simple setting. We abstract away from all the collective action problems as well as those of strategic interaction between domestic political groups, and suppose that each country behaves as a unitary actor. With both countries caring about how much butter they will consume and supposing that they are risk neutral,[3] the expected payoffs in the event of war, in which the winner receives all the butter and the loser receives nothing, would be the following:

$$W_1(G_1, G_2) = p_1(G_1, G_2)(B_1 + B_2) = p_1(G_1, G_2)[\beta_1(R_1 - G_1) + \beta_2(R_2 - G_2)]$$

$$W_2(G_1, G_2) = p_2(G_1, G_2)(B_1 + B_2) = p_2(G_1, G_2)[\beta_1(R_1 - G_1) + \beta_2(R_2 - G_2)] \quad (5)$$

Note that these two payoffs are thought of as depending on the expenditures on guns by the two parties, since given (2) the choice of guns by each party determines the quantity of butter as well. Furthermore, because these payoffs are derived on the condition that the two countries are risk neutral, the probability of winning for each country, $p_1(G_1, G_2)$ and $p_2(G_1, G_2)$, can also be interpreted as the share of total butter each country receives in the shadow of war.

We are interested in deriving Nash equilibrium strategies for guns—that is, a combination (G_1^*, G_2^*) such that $W_1(G_1^*, G_2^*) \geq W_1(G_1, G_2^*)$ for all G_1 and $W_2(G_1^*, G_2^*) \geq W_2(G_1^*, G_2)$ for all G_2. At a Nash equilibrium there is no incentive for any party to deviate in their strategies. At that equilibrium the marginal benefit of each country's choice of guns equals its marginal cost so that:

$$\frac{\partial p_1(G_1^*, G_2^*)}{\partial G_1}(B_1^* + B_2^*) = p_1(G_1^*, G_2^*)\beta_1$$

$$\frac{\partial p_2(G_1^*, G_2^*)}{\partial G_2}(B_1^* + B_2^*) = p_2(G_1^*, G_2^*)\beta_2 \quad (6)$$

---

[3] Under risk neutrality there is neither aversion towards risk nor love of risk. Clearly, this is a strong assumption that is nevertheless analytically very convenient that is almost always adopted when a certain problem is first modeled. We discuss the effects of risk aversion in Section 2.

The marginal benefits in the right-hand side include the total butter that is contested multiplied by the marginal increase in the probability of winning. The marginal cost includes the probability of winning times the productivity parameter of each country. That is, the higher is the productivity of a country (in the production of butter), the higher is its marginal cost of producing guns. Therefore, the more usefully productive country has an incentive to produce fewer guns whereas the less usefully productive country has an incentive to produce more guns. That is, the less usefully productive party has a comparative advantage in gun production.

In fact, in this specific model it can be shown that, as long as both countries produce some butter, the country with lower productivity will produce more guns (i.e. $G_1^* < G_2^*$ if and only if $\beta_1 > \beta_2$). The less productive country would then have a higher probability of winning or, if the countries were to settle in the shadow of conflict, a bigger share of the total amount of butter. In the latter case, typically the more productive country would provide tribute in butter to the less productive and more powerful one.[4] There are numerous historical examples in which marcher states or tribal federations, characterized by low productivity, have subjugated more productive and established states. Central Asia, for instance, has been the breeding ground for successive invasions and conquests, all the way from the western and eastern Roman empires, to states in the Middle East, to India, China, and even Japan. The Arab twelfth-century philosopher-historian Ibn Khaldun (1967) even built a theory of the cycles of history based on successive waves of barbarians, with little useful productivity other than being good at warfare, conquering settled, productive areas and then, after they themselves become civilized and soft, being conquered by a fresh wave of uncouth warriors from the steppes.

We should not, however, take this result that productivity and power are always inversely related literally both because it does not always hold formally and because empirically there are cases in which those who are more usefully productive can also be more powerful. Formally, if we were to allow a more general production function for butter than we have done in (2), the less productive country would not be necessarily more powerful. Nevertheless, there would be a strong tendency for improvements in productivity leading to less power, in the sense that a higher β_i would lead to a lower probability of winning or share for country $i(p_i(G_1^*, G_2^*)^i)$.[5]

In related work that examines the dynamic incentives for innovation, Gonzalez (2003) has found a range of conditions under which butter consumption would be reduced if a country were to adopt a superior technology (i.e. one with a higher β_i). Under such conditions, superior technologies available at zero cost would not be adopted because they would confer a disadvantage on those who adopt them, an outcome that Gonzalez argues is relevant to many instances of slow adoption or the outright rejection of superior technologies in history.

One curious result of the interaction described by (3) is that the initial resources can be shown to have minimal effect on power. For example, under the conflict

---

[4] The only exception to this outcome is when the resource of the more productive country is not too much smaller than the resource of the less productive country.

[5] Skaperdas and Syropoulos 1997 describe general conditions under which this outcome occurs.

technology in (4) the ratio of guns of the two countries depends only on the ratio of productivities and on the parameter m (in particular, we have $G_1^* = (\beta_2/\beta_1)^{\frac{m}{m+1}} G_2^*$), as long as these expenditures on guns are lower than the resources of each country. Nevertheless, this result does not generalize when there is risk aversion or when there is complementarity in consumption or production so that, for instance, the two countries produce different types of outputs. In any of those more general settings and under a wide set of conditions, a higher level of resource R_i would lead to more power for country i (Skaperdas and Syropoulos 1997 derive such results).

Finally, in discussing this simple benchmark model of anarchy, higher levels of the "effectiveness" parameter m in the conflict technology (4) always lead to higher levels of guns and thus lower production of butter and material welfare. In the remainder of this chapter we will discuss additional questions that can explored using the approach just introduced.

2 Settlement in the Shadow of Conflict

The "power" of each country i, $p_i(G_1^*, G_2^*)$, has been interpreted either as a probability of winning in the event of conflict or as a share of total output in the shadow of conflict. That equivalence has been derived under the assumption of risk neutrality as well as other conditions that we will shortly mention. In practice, interactions under anarchy typically involve a great degree of accommodation by the interacting parties with warfare being only a last resort, and the outcomes under conflict and under settlement are rather different. When, then, will there be a negotiated settlement (a "cold" war) and when conflict (a "hot" war)? First, in order to be clear, we will consider the following protocol of moves:

1. The two countries choose their respective levels of guns and butter.
2. The two countries negotiate in the shadow of conflict about how to divide the total butter available for division. If they agree on a division, the division takes place and each country consumes its share.
3. In the event of no peaceful division, conflict takes place with one side winning the whole available quantity of butter.

The decision whether to go to war is taken at stage 2. Obviously, both sides would have to agree on a negotiated settlement but just one side can make the decision to have war. There are a number of compelling reasons that both sides would prefer a settlement at stage 2 and we list some major ones below:

1. War is destructive. Contrary to our implicit assumption in the previous section, in which we assumed that war does not destroy any of the butter produced by the two countries, war is typically destructive in output, resources, and the use of arms beyond those that would be necessary for a negotiated settlement. In the absence of other benefits to war then, it appears that a negotiated settlement would be feasible, provided of course that the two sides have open channels of communication.

To illustrate the possibilities for a negotiated settlement, consider any particular choice of guns that might have been made in stage 1, say (G'_1, G'_2) with associated choices of butters (B'_1, B'_2). Furthermore, suppose that if war were to occur, only a fraction $\phi(< 1)$ of total butter would be left for the winner with the remainder fraction, $1 - \phi$, destroyed during war. Then, the expected payoff in the event of war for country i would be $p_i(G'_1, G'_2)\phi(B'_1 + B'_2)$. Then, consider the possibility of peacefully dividing the total quantity of butter according to the winning probabilities. Then, under risk neutrality the (deterministic) payoff for country i would be $p_i(G'_1, G'_2)(B'_1 + B'_2)$ which, given that $\phi < 1$, is strictly higher than the expected payoff under war. Thus, both sides would have an incentive to agree on the division of the total pie in accordance with the winning probabilities. There are also other possible ways of dividing the pie—an issue that can lead to other problems associated with the bargaining problem. However, the threat of war limits the number of possible settlements acceptable to both parties and the threat of war provides an enforcement device for whatever settlement that the parties may arrive at.

2. *Risk aversion and the uncertainty of war's outcome.* As we have modeled it and as it is in practice, the outcome of war is typically uncertain. Thus far, we have maintained that the two sides are risk neutral—that they do not care about the risk entailed in the outcome of war. However, when it comes to big uncertain outcomes that affect people's jobs, careers, health, and lives, most people are risk averse—they do not like taking big risks and, if they face them and insurance is available, they will insure against them. That risk aversion can be expected to transfer to political and military leaders and to the risk preferences expressed at the country level. Because war is uncertain but a particular settlement is not, a range of negotiated settlements can be expected to be preferable to both parties.

Again, to illustrate the basic point, suppose particular choices have been made for guns (G'_1, G'_2) and butter (B'_1, B'_2) at stage 1. Under risk aversion, suppose both countries have strictly concave von Neumann–Morgenstern utility functions $U(.)$. Then, the expected payoff in the event of war for country i is $p_i(G'_1, G'_2)U(B'_1 + B'_2) + (1 - p_i)(G'_1, G'_2)U(0)$. (The second term reflects the expected payoff in the event of losing the war.) On the other hand, the payoff under a negotiated settlement in which each party receives a share of butter that equals its winning probability would be $U[p_i(G'_1, G'_2)(B'_1 + B'_2)] = U[p_i(G'_1, G'_2)(B'_1 + B'_2) + (1 - p_i)(G'_1, G'_2)0]$, which by the strict concavity of $U(.)$ is strictly greater than the expected payoff under war. Thus, both sides would strictly prefer to divide the pie according to their winning probabilities than go to war. Again, a range of other divisions of the pie would be preferable to the two sides over going to war.

The modeling approach we have followed has one source of uncertainty—who will win and who will lose—that, moreover, is expressed by probabilities that are common knowledge to both sides. That is a lot of knowledge to possess and in its absence there would be additional sources of uncertainty: different expectations, unforeseen contingencies, and so on. The presence of such additional sources of uncertainty in the presence of risk aversion would normally make the two sides more conservative and more willing to negotiate. However, this does not always need to be the case for two reasons: First, we simply have not examined the effect of risk aversion in such more complicated environments formally in order to confirm the conjecture. And, second, in the presence of incomplete information whereby each side has different beliefs about the nature of their interaction, the choice of war can actually be an equilibrium as is well known from an extensive literature (see e.g. Brito and Intriligator 1985; Bester and Warneryd 2000).

3. *Complementarities in production or consumption.* Another consequence of wars having winners and losers is that the goods with which each side ends up could easily be far from what would be optimal for production or consumption. In the case of war over territory, the winner could get all the contested land minus its people who might become refugees on the loser's remaining territory. Then, it is highly likely that the winner would have too much land relative to the labor that it has available whereas the loser would have too little land relative to its available labor. A negotiated settlement could avoid this imbalance and make both sides better off than they would be in expected terms under war. As there is complementarity between factors of production, so there is between final consumption goods, and a similar argument can be made in favor of negotiated settlements when there are such complementarities in consumption.

In order to take account of complementarities formally, the benchmark model would have to be enriched. One possibility is to have final production or consumption being a function $F(B, L)$ where B is butter and L is another good that is non-appropriable, and the function is increasing and has diminishing returns in both of its arguments. Suppose each side has an endowment of L_i and, again, consider that in stage 1 they have chosen a certain quantity of guns (G'_1, G'_2) and butter (B'_1, B'_2). Then, the expected payoff of country i under war would be $p_i(G'_1, G'_2)F(B'_1 + B'_2, L_i) + (1 - p_i)(G'_1, G'_2)F(0, L_i)$. Under a negotiated settlement with each country receiving a share of butter equal to its winning probability, the payoff would be $F[p_i(G'_1, G'_2)(B'_1 + B'_2), L_i]$, which by the property of diminishing returns in butter can be shown to be strictly higher than the war payoff. Thus, a negotiated settlement is again superior to war for any given choice of guns and butter.

2.1 How Much Arming? Settlement under Different Rules of Division

We have shown a wide range of variations in the benchmark model that make a negotiated settlement in stage 2 always better for both sides. That is, settlement is part of any perfect equilibrium of games with the protocol of moves that we specified above. We have not touched upon, though, the issue of arming under settlement.

Since the two countries cannot make firm commitments on arming, any settlement they arrive at depends on the relative amount of guns the two sides possess. Does the fact that the countries can be expected to reach a negotiated settlement reduce their arming compared to the case of war? Given that there are many possible negotiated settlements and rules of division, which ones would the two sides be expected to use? Are there any rules of division that are better than others and in what sense?

The answer to the first question is "not in general," and answering it is related to the other two questions just posed. For how many guns (and how much butter) the two sides decide to produce in stage 1 critically depends on the rule of division they expect to follow in stage 2, the stage of negotiations.

To illustrate some possibilities consider a model that allows for destructive war. In particular, suppose that a resource of total T is contested by the two sides and side i pays a cost of guns of G_i regardless of whether they win, lose, or settle. In the case of war a fraction $1 - \phi$ of T is lost. In addition, suppose that in stage 2 the contested resource is divided in accordance with the winning probabilities; that is, country i receives the share $p_i(G_1, G_2)$.

Then, the payoff function under war would be: $p_i(G_1, G_2)\phi T - G_i$. The payoff function under settlement would be $p_i(G_1, G_2)T - G_i$. For simplicity, let $m = 1$. Then, the equilibrium guns under war would be the same for both sides and equal to $G^w = \frac{\phi}{4}T$ which, given that $\phi < 1$, is less than $\frac{1}{4}T$. Guns under settlement would also be the same for both sides and equal to $G^s = \frac{1}{4}T > \frac{\phi}{4}T = G^w$. That is, in this case *arming under settlement is higher than arming under war*. The total "pie" under settlement is higher than that under war because of the destruction brought about by war, whereas the way the two pies are divided are the same. The two sides just jockey for a better bargaining position under settlement by allocating more resources in guns than under war. It should be noted however that, even though more guns are produced under settlement, both sides receive higher payoffs under settlement than they have expected payoff under war, as the higher costs of arming under settlement are lower than the lost part of the contested resource in the case of war.

The division of the pie according to the winning probabilities is only one possible rule of division. In fact, this rule is not consistent with any of the bargaining solutions and non-cooperative bargaining games that have been extensively analyzed in the economic theory literature (see Muthoo 1999). And, for the benchmark model with destruction, all symmetric bargaining solutions would lead to the following share for country i: $\phi p_i(G_1, G_2) + (1 - \phi)\frac{1}{2}$. Note that according to this rule the more destructive is conflict (i.e. the higher is ϕ), the less guns matter in negotiated settlement. Actually, the equilibrium guns under this rule of division is the same as those under war noted in the previous paragraph ($G^w = \frac{\phi}{4}T$). With this rule, then, guns under settlement and under war are the same.

This example illustrates that *different rules of division lead to different levels of arming*. And the differences across different rules can be rather dramatic. For more general classes of problems, different bargaining solutions do not coincide as they do in the benchmark model. As Anbarci, Skaperdas, and Syropoulos (2002) have shown, a number of bargaining solutions themselves can be ranked in terms of the amount of arming they induce and in terms of material efficiency, with those that put less weight to the threat utilities (which are the payoffs of going to war) inducing in less arming. Thus, *norms against threats* that are enshrined in international law, in international institutions, or simply in the culture of interactions among states *can have real effects on arming and material welfare* without fundamentally changing the relative positions of states. That is, anarchy, far from necessarily leading to just one outcome, can lead to widely differing sets of outcomes, depending on the underlying norms of conduct by the states. Despite the absence of ultimate authority and enforcement, anarchy can be governed with norms and institutions that can provide different measures of commitment towards arming. While arming cannot be expected to disappear, it can be largely supplanted by diplomacy and politics. Even if ultimately arming might have the final say in the event everything else were to fail, to sustain such a shift to politics requires wide recognition of the norms, institutions, and organizations relevant to settling disputes.

The analysis we have followed thus far has been static or, equivalently, a steady state of a long-run process without any feedback through time. Over the past few decades the evolution of norms, institutions, and organizations has been modeled in much of rational choice social science as implementing cooperative equilibria of indefinitely repeated supergames, with the "shadow of the future" (Axelrod 1984) being of prime importance. That is, the more different participants value the future, the greater are the sets of superior alternatives to war that could be self-enforcing. Such an approach could provide a rationale for the adoption of different norms that bring about fewer guns and more butter under anarchy. A longer shadow of the future, however, can well make the more conflictual equilibria even worse, as Powell (1993) and Skaperdas and Syropoulos (1996) have demonstrated in different settings. In fact, a longer shadow of the future may well have the opposite effect in encouraging not just costlier negotiated settlements but also outright warfare, a topic to which we now turn.

3 CONFLICT AND THE ROLE OF THE FUTURE

Given all the reasons in favor of negotiated settlement and coexistence of rival states, why are there wars at all? Incomplete and asymmetric information, as we have already mentioned, as well as simple misperceptions and the difficulties in attaining common knowledge of the relevant game that is being played (see Chwe 2000), have been extensively analyzed over the past two decades as major sources of war. Typically these are the main reasons given for the occurrence of wars. In addition to those, however, Fearon (1995) has discussed an additional class of reasons that he identifies as the inability of different sides to make credible commitments.

In particular, within the models we have examined, each state is unable to commit to a certain level of arming. Negotiated settlements take place only with the backing up of each party's guns. But because the settings that we have examined are static, we have not allowed for the possibility of war altering the conditions for future interactions, of altering the balance of power between adversaries well into the future. Then, by pursuing war now, one party could weaken its adversaries permanently or even possibly eliminate them and take control well into the future. Therefore, a party that values the future highly could indeed take the chance of war instead of pursuing negotiation and compromise, despite the short-term benefits of compromise, because the expected long-run profits could be higher in case the opponents become permanently weakened or eliminated. In environments in which those who win gain an advantage in the future, both the intensity of conflict and the choice of overt conflict over negotiation become more common (Garfinkel and Skaperdas 2000) as the future becomes more important.

To illustrate how this argument goes through consider the following simple example. Suppose there are two states and they care about what happens *today* and about what happens in the *future*; that is, for simplicity, we can think of the game as having two periods. In each period there is total butter of 100 units. Because of incomplete contracting on arming, each side has to devote 20 units of resources to guns in each period. Given the guns they have there are two options, war and settlement. If they were to settle, each side would receive half of the butter for a net payoff of 30 units ($\frac{1}{2}100 - 20$). If they were to engage in war, each adversary would have half a chance of winning and half a chance of losing all the butter, which would however be reduced by 20 units as a result of the destruction that war would bring. The expected payoff of each side under war in a particular period would then be $\frac{1}{2}(100 - 20 - 20) + \frac{1}{2}(0 - 20) = 20$. Therefore, because war is destructive both sides would have a short-term incentive to settle. War, however, has long-term effects on the relative power of the adversaries. For simplicity and starkness suppose that if there were war *today*, the loser would be eliminated and the winner could enjoy all the surplus by itself in the *future* and do that without having to incur the cost of arming. Letting $\delta \in (0, 1)$ denote the discount factor for the *future*, the expected payoff from compromise as of *today*—which would also imply settlement in the *future*—would be $30 + \delta 30$. The expected payoff from war, again as of *today*, would be $20 + \delta(\frac{1}{2}100 + \frac{1}{2}0) = 20 + \delta 50$. Thus, war would be preferable to settlement by both adversaries if $20 + \delta 50 > 30 + \delta 30$ or if (and only if) $\delta > \frac{1}{2}$. That is, war would be induced if the "shadow of the future" were long enough, whereas settlement and peace would ensue only if the future were not valued highly.

Wars of conquest, including those of Xerxes, of Alexander the Great, of Roman senators and emperors, of the various central Asian federations, of medieval lords and potentates, of absolutist European monarchs, of the Habsburgs, Napoleon, Hitler, and many others, could well be accounted for by the combination of the inability to make long-term treaties that reduce arming and a long shadow of the future on the part of these rulers. They were calculated gambles that, if they turned out well initially, could lead to a bandwagon effect of greater power. Although we tend to know more about the winners of such gambles, because they are the ones who are more prominent in the historical record, that record is also strewn with a lot more less successful individuals as well as states who have been on the losing side of these gambles. Asymmetry of information, of course, is present in one form or another and could account for cases in which a tribute was not agreed and instead a battle had to take place, but overall the inability to commit along with a long shadow of the future is, I think, a very underrated source of conflict and its persistence.

4 Other Topics in Brief and Future Prospects

Because of space limitations we will now briefly refer to some important topics that have been examined thus far, as well as discuss possible fruitful directions that such research could take.

4.1 Alliance Formation

States have rarely viewed all other states the same way. They are usually allied with some and not with others. What are the determinants of alliance formation? Is there a tendency for bipolarity (i.e. have two grand alliances) or not? The approach reviewed in this chapter could be promising in trying to answer such questions, and there have been some initial attempts in such a direction.

In studying the problem, there are two critical modeling issues that need to be confronted. First, once an alliance has formed, how do members of the alliance divide the total pie? In particular, does relative arming determine at all members' shares and how are these shares determined otherwise? Thus, Bloch, Sanchez-Pages, and Sonbeyran (2002) suppose members of the alliance do not use arms at all in determining shares whereas Skaperdas (1996) analyzes the case in which shares are determined through arming. Second, there is no unique concept of equilibrium of different alliance structures (comparable, say, to Nash equilibrium) and, when there is, there can be more than one alliance structure that would be predicted (Ray and Vohra 1999). Perhaps, as can be expected given these issues, there are no universal predictions about how alliances form or about bipolarity. Bloch, Sanchez-Pages, and Sonbeyran (2002), with restrictions on the possible stability of alliances that favor the formation of large coalitions, predict the grand alliance; Skaperdas (1996) who analyzes the case of three countries finds a critical role for the technology of conflict in determining whether any alliances form; and Garfinkel (2004), who employees a solution concept that is not as advantageous to large coalitions, finds a number of different plausible outcomes other than the grand alliance.[6]

---

[6] Sandler and Hartley 2001 survey the literature on burden-sharing in already established alliances.

The multiplicity of possible outcomes suggests a critical role for history and path dependence, something that has not been incorporated into current models, primarily because the problem of alliance formation is computationally rather complex already in static settings. Clever ways of introducing dynamics could thus yield new insights into this important problem.

4.2 Trade Openness and Insecurity

From a classical liberal perspective—which by default is the perspective of neoclassical economics as well—international trade alleviates the problems with anarchy and is enough of a carrot to bring together potential adversaries. From a realist perspective, though, trade openness with adversaries can be anathema, especially when the "relative" gains from trade go to the adversary. Conventional models of international trade assume all resources and trade itself are perfectly enforceable without leaving any room for arming and conflict, whereas our benchmark model allows for arming and conflict but not for trade. In order to examine the validity of the claims made by classical liberals and realists, however, we need to allow for both trade and conflict. One possibility is to analyze a model with complementarities in production or consumption like the one that was briefly specified in Section 2. Findlay and Amin (2000) and Skaperdas and Syropoulos (2001) have analyzed such models. They find conditions under which free trade can be better than autarky as well as the other way around.

The key in making such comparisons is whether security costs (defense expenditures and other costs of conflict) under autarky can be lower than the same costs under trade. If they are and they are greater than the gains from the trade, then autarky can be better than trade. Security costs could be higher under trade if a disputed territory or resource (like oil or diamonds) has much higher value internationally than it would have domestically and thus induces higher security costs on the part of the adversaries. When, however, the disputed resource has less value internationally that it would have under autarky, security costs are lower under trade and free trade is unambiguously superior to autarky.

4.3 Restraints and Governance

As we have discussed extensively in Section 2, anarchy does not imply warfare or economically crippling cold wars and high levels of arming. Norms, international law, institutions, and organizations can limit the resources that are devoted to arming. An alternative to the anarchy of the international system is a more hierarchical, even imperial, form of governance. Without being able to get into any detail here, certainly that has been one major way that lower-levels of anarchy have evolved into states. In this context there has been a debate about the effects of hierarchical governance. Findlay (1990) and Grossman and Noh (1994) first examined settings in which the state is "proprietary;" that is, it is owned by someone who taxes and provides services so as to maximize profits. McGuire and Olson (1996) argued that such an arrangement can be nearly efficient but Moselle and Polak (2001) have found several problems with that argument. Furthermore, Konrad and Skaperdas (1999) have argued that monopolistic governance invites competition, and competition between different proprietors would eliminate all efficiencies and lead to a higher level of organized anarchy (see also Greif, Bates, and Singh 2000, for another comparative treatment of the emergence of governance through violence). That is, breaking down anarchy by creating a hierarchical order does not look theoretically promising in addition to the objections one might have on empirical grounds.

4.4 Future Prospects

One main weakness of the approach reviewed in this chapter is the conception of states not only as unitary actors but also as not responding to concerns that are not material in nature. That might have been true up to about two centuries ago, when the state was indeed largely owned by king or emperor and fighting to defend it was his private affair. Beginning with Napoleon, who managed to motivate Frenchmen to fight for their own country, and the emergence of nationalism which is an integral element of the modern state, the world appears to have become more complex. Notions like "ideology," "legitimacy," or "sovereignty" do not have a place in the approach reviewed in this chapter, or at least they do not have one yet beyond those of norms for rules of division, but they do appear important in practice. As far as I can tell, and as an outsider to the relevant debates I cannot be completely sure, these are also concerns directed against the realist school. It would be advisable at least to attempt thinking about how such notions could modify any insights that might come out of the approach reviewed here.

References

ANBARCI, N., SKAPERDAS, S., and SYROPOULOS, C. 2002. Comparing bargaining solutions in the shadow of conflict: how norms against threats can have real effects. *Journal of Economic Theory*, 106: 1–16.

AXELROD, R. 1984. *The Evolution of Cooperation*. New York: Basic Books.

BESTER, H., and WARNERYD, K. 2000. Conflict resolution. Working paper, Stockholm School of Economics.

BLOCH, F., SANCHEZ-PAGES, S., and SOUBEYRAN, R. 2002. When does universal peace prevail? Secession and group formation in conflict. Universitat Autonoma de Barcelona.

BRITO, D., and INTRILIGATOR, M. 1985. Conflict, war and redistribution. *American Political Science Review*, 79: 943–57.

CHWE, M. 2000. Communication and coordination in social networks. *Review of Economic Studies*, 67: 1–16.

ESTEBAN, J. M., and RAY, D. 1999. Conflict and distribution. *Journal of Economic Theory*, 87: 379–415.

FEARON, J. D. 1995. Rationalist explanations for war. *International Organization*, 49: 379–414.

FINDLAY, R. 1990. The new political economy: its explanatory power for the LDCs. *Economics and Politics*, 2: 193–221.

——and AMIN, M. 2000. National security and international trade: a simple general equilibrium model. Columbia University, Dept. of Economics, Nov.

GARFINKEL, M. R. 1990. Arming as a strategic investment in a cooperative equilibrium. *American Economic Review*, 80: 50–68.

——2004. Stable alliance formation in distributional conflict. *European Journal of Political Economy*, 20: 829–52.

——and SKAPERDAS, S. 2000. Conflict without misperception or incomplete information: how the future matters. *Journal of Conflict Resolution*, 44: 793–807.

GONZALEZ, F. M. 2003. Poor protection of property rights and the choice of technological backwardness. Dept. of Economics, University of British Columbia.

GREIF, A., BATES, R., and SINGH, S. 2000. Organizing violence: wealth, power, and limited government. Paper presented at the World Bank–Princeton Workshop on the Economics of Political Violence, Mar.

GROSSMAN, H. I. 1991. A general equilibrium model of insurrections. *American Economic Review*, 81: 912–21.

——and KIM, M. 1996. Predation and accumulation. *Journal of Economic Growth*, 1: 333–51.

——and NOH, S. J. 1994. Proprietary public finance and economic welfare. *Journal of Public Economics*, 53: 187–204.

HAAVELMO, T. 1954. *A Theory of Economic Evolution*. Amsterdam: North-Holland.

HIRSHLEIFER, J. 1988. The analytics of continuing conflict. *Synthese*, 76: 201–33.

——1989. Conflict and rent-seeking success functions. *Public Choice*, 63: 101–12.

——1991. The paradox of power. *Economics and Politics*, 3: 177–200.

——1994. The dark side of the force. *Economic Inquiry*, 32: 1–10.

——1995. Anarchy and its breakdown. *Journal of Political Economy*, 103: 26–52.

——2001. *The Dark Side of the Force*. New York: Cambridge University Press.

KHALDUN, I. 1967. *The Muqaddimah: An Introduction to History*, trans. F. Rosenthal, ed. and abr. N. J. Dawood. Princeton, NJ: Princeton University Press.

KONRAD, K. A., and SKAPERDAS, S. 1999. The market for protection and the origin of the state. CEPR working paper.

MCGUIRE, M., and OLSON, M. 1996. The economics of autocracy and majority rule: the invisible hand and the use of force. *Journal of Economic Literature*, 34: 72–96.

MEHLUM, H., MOENE, K., and TORVIK, R. 2000. Predator or prey? Parasitic enterprises in economic development. Dept. of Economics, University of Oslo.

MOSELLE, B., and POLAK, B. 2001. A model of a predatory state. *Journal of Law, Economics, and Organization*, 17: 1–33.

MUTHOO, A. 1999. *Bargaining Theory with Applications*. New York: Cambridge University Press.

POWELL, R. 1993. Guns, butter, and anarchy. *American Political Science Review*, 87: 115–32.

RAY, D., and VOHRA, R. 1999. A theory of endogenous coalition structures. *Games and Economic Behavior*, 26: 286–336.

SANDLER, T. 2000. Economic analysis of conflict. *Journal of Conflict Resolution*, 44: 723–9.

——and HARTLEY, K. 2001. Economics of alliances: the lessons for collective action. *Journal of Economic Literature*, 39: 869–96.

SKAPERDAS, S. 1992. Cooperation, conflict, and power in the absence of property rights. *American Economic Review*, 82: 720–39.
―――― 1996. Contest success functions. *Economic Theory*, 7: 283–90.
―――― 1998. On the formation of alliances in conflict and contests. *Public Choice*, 96: 25–42.
―――― 2003. Restraining the genuine *homo economicus*: why the economy cannot be divorced from its governance. *Economics and Politics*, 15: 135–62.
―――― 1996. Can the shadow of the future harm cooperation? *Journal of Economic Behavior and Organization*, 29: 355–72.
―――― 1997. The distribution of income in the presence of appropriative activities. *Economica*, 64: 101–17.
―――― 2001. Guns, butter, and openness: on the relationship between security and trade. *American Economic Review: Papers and Proceedings*, 91: 353–7.
WITTMAN, D. 2000. The wealth and size of nations. *Journal of Conflict Resolution*, 44: 868–84.

PART XIII

METHODOLOGICAL ISSUES

CHAPTER 50

ECONOMIC METHODS IN POSITIVE POLITICAL THEORY

DAVID AUSTEN-SMITH

1 INTRODUCTION

ECONOMICS and political science share a common ancestry in "political economy" and both are concerned with the decisions of people facing constraints, at the individual level and in the aggregate. But while rational choice theory in some form or other has been a cornerstone of economic reasoning for over a century, with the mathematical development of this theory beginning in the middle of the nineteenth century, its introduction to political science is relatively recent and far from generally accepted within the discipline.[1] Three books proved seminal with respect to the application

---

[1] A suggestion (first made to me in conversation many years ago by Barry Weingast) as to why the two disciplines differ so markedly with respect to the use of mathematical modeling is that political science has no analogous concept to that of the *margin* in economics. And the importance of the margin in this respect lies less with its substantive content than with the amenability of its logic to elementary diagrammatic representation. Economic theorizing evolved into its contemporary mathematical form through a diagrammatic development of the logic of the margin, whereas positive political theory, almost of necessity, bypassed any such graphical development and jumped directly to applied game theory.

of economic methods in political science, the first of which is Kenneth Arrow's *Social Choice and Individual Values* (1951, 1963).[2]

Although mathematical models of voting can be found at least as far back as the thirteenth century (McLean 1990) and despite Paul Samuelson's claim, in the foreword to the second edition of the book, that the subject of Arrow's contribution was "mathematical politics," an appreciation within political science (as opposed to economics) of the significance of both Arrow's possibility theorem itself or, more importantly for this chapter, the axiomatic method with which it is established was slow in coming. An exception was William Riker, who quickly understood the depth of Arrow's insight and the significance of an axiomatic theory of preference aggregation, both for normative democratic theory and for the positive analysis of agenda-setting and voting.

The remaining two of the three seminal books are Anthony Downs's *An Economic Theory of Democracy* (1957) and William Riker's *The Theory of Political Coalitions* (1962). These books were distinguished for political science by their use of rational choice theory and distinguished for rational choice theory by their explicit concern with politics.

Downs's 1957 volume covers a wide set of issues but is perhaps most noted for his development of the spatial model of electoral competition and for the decision-theoretic argument suggesting rational individuals are unlikely to vote. The spatial model builds on an economic model of retail location due to Hotelling (1929) and Smithies (1941). Approximately a decade after the publication of Downs's book, Davis and Hinich (1966, 1967) and Davis, Hinich, and Ordeshook (1970) described the multidimensional version of the (political) spatial model, the mathematics of which has given rise to a remarkable series of results, exposing the deep structure of a variety of preference aggregation rules, most notably, simple plurality rule (e.g. Plott 1967; McKelvey 1979; Schofield 1983; McKelvey and Schofield 1987; Saari 1997). Similarly, Downs's decision-theoretic approach to turnout elicited a variety of innovations as authors sought variations on the theme to provide a better account of participation in large elections (e.g. Riker and Ordeshook 1968; Ferejohn and Fiorina 1975). But although treating voters as taking decisions independent of any consideration of others' behaviour (as the Downsian decision-theoretic approach surely does) yields some insight, the character of most if not all political behavior is intrinsically strategic, for which the appropriate model is game theoretic.[3]

Riker understood the importance not only of Arrow's theorem and a mathematical theory of preference aggregation, he also recognized that game theory, the quintessential theory of strategic interaction between rational agents, was the natural tool with which to analyze political behaviour. In his 1962 book, Riker exploited a cooperative game-theoretic model, due to von Neumann and Morgenstern (1944), to develop an

---

[2] Duncan Black's *The Theory of Committees and Elections* (1958) has some claim to be included as a fourth such book. However, although Black considers similar issues to those taxing Arrow, his concern was more limited than that of Arrow and his particular contribution to political science was generally recognized only after the importance of Arrow's work had begun to be appreciated.

[3] Palfrey and Rosenthal 1983 and Ledyard 1984 provide the earliest fully strategic models of turnout.

understanding of coalition structure and provide the first thoroughgoing effort to apply game theory to understand politics. Cooperative game theory is distinguished essentially by the presumption that if gains from cooperation or collusion were available to a group of agents, then those gains would surely be realized. As such, it is closely tied to the Arrovian approach to preference aggregation and much of the early work stimulated by Riker's contribution reflected concerns similar to those addressed in the possibility theorem. An important concept here is that of the *core* of a cooperative game.

Loosely speaking, if an alternative x is in the core, then any coalition of individuals who agree on a distinct alternative y that they all strictly prefer, cannot be in a position to replace x with y. For example, the majority rule core contains only alternatives that cannot be defeated under majority voting. Similarly, if we imagine that a group uses a supramajority rule requiring at least 2/3 of the group to approve any change, then x is in the core if there is no alternative y such that at least 2/3 of the group strictly prefer y to x. So if a group involves nine individuals, five of whom strictly prefer x to y and the remaining four strictly prefer y to x, then the majority rule core (when the choice is between x and y) is x alone whereas both x and y are in the 2/3 rule core.

The concept of the core is intuitively appealing as a predictor of what might happen. Given the actions available to individuals under the rules governing any social interaction, and assuming that coalitions can freely form and coordinate on mutually advantageous courses of action, the core describes those outcomes that cannot be overturned: even if a coalition does not like a particular core outcome, the very fact that the outcome is in the core means that the coalition is powerless to overturn it. On the other hand, when the core is empty (that is, fails to contain any alternatives) then its use as a solution concept for a cooperative game-theoretic model is suspect. For example, suppose a group of three persons has to use majority rule to decide how to share a dollar and suppose every individual cares exclusively about their own share. Then every possible outcome (that is, division of the dollar) can be upset by a majority coalition. To see this, suppose a fair division of $(1/3)$ to each individual is proposed; then individuals (say, A and B) can propose and vote to share the dollar evenly between themselves and give nothing to individual C; but then A and C can propose and vote to give $(2/3)$ to A and $(1/3)$ to C. Because A and C care only about their own shares, this proposal upsets the proposal favoring A and B. But by the same token, a division that shares the dollar equally between C and B, giving nothing to A, upsets the outcome that gives B nothing; and so on. In this example, the core offers no guidance about what to expect as a final outcome. Furthermore, it does not follow that the core being empty implies instability or continued change. Rather, core emptiness means only that every possible outcome can in principle be overturned; as such, the model offers *no* prediction at all. It is an unfortunate fact, therefore, that, save in constrained environments, the core of any cooperative game-theoretic model of political behavior is typically empty, attenuating the predictive or explanatory content of the model.

Discovering the extent to which the core failed to exist was disappointing and induced at least some pessimism about the general value of formal economic reasoning as a tool for political science. Things changed with the development of techniques within economics and game theory that greatly extended the scope and power of *non-cooperative* game theory, in which there is no presumption that the existence of gains from cooperation are realized. And at least at the time of writing this chapter, it is non-cooperative game theory that dominates contemporary positive political theory.

This chapter concerns economic methods in political science. It is confined exclusively to positive (formal) political theory, paying no attention to econometric methods for empirical political science. Furthermore, I adopt the perspective that a central task for positive political theory is to understand the relationship between the preferences of individuals comprising a polity and the collective choices from a set of possible alternatives over which the individuals' preferences are defined.[4] The next section sketches the two canonical approaches to developing a positive political theory, collective preference theory and game theory. I briefly argue that despite some clear formal differences, these two techniques are essentially distinguished by the trade-off each makes with respect to a minimal democracy constraint and a demand that well-defined predictions are generally guaranteed. Moreover, the attempt to develop collective preference theory as an explanatory framework for political science reveals two important analytical characteristics, distinctive to political science rather than economics. The subsequent section, therefore, considers some more specific techniques within the game-theoretic approach designed to accommodate these characteristics. A third section concludes.

2 Two Approaches From Economics

Economics is rooted in the choices of individuals, albeit with a broad notion of what counts as an "individual" when useful, as in the theory of markets where firms are often treated as individuals. And the basic economic model of individual choice is decision theoretic: in its simplest variant, individuals are assumed to have preferences over a set of feasible alternatives that are complete (every pair of alternatives can be ranked) and transitive (for any three alternatives, say x, y, z, if x is preferred to y and y is preferred to z, then x must be preferred to z) and to choose an alternative (e.g. purchasing bundles of groceries, cars, education, ...) that maximizes their preferences, or payoffs, over this set. The predictions of the model, therefore, are given

---

[4] Of course, this understanding itself reflects a largely consequentialist perspective intrinsic to economics. Insofar as there is consideration with any economic process, it is rarely with the process per se but with respect to the outcomes supported or induced by that process. This remains true for normative analysis. For example, axiomatic characterizations of procedures for dispute resolution (such as bargaining or bankruptcy) rarely exclude all references to the consequences of using such procedures: Pareto efficiency and individual rationality are common instances of such consequentialist properties. In contrast, a consequentialist perspective is less well accepted within political science at large, where (*inter alia*) there is widespread concern with, say, the legitimacy of procedures independent of the outcomes they might induce.

by studying how the set of maximal elements varies with changes in the feasible set. Now it is certainly true that individuals make political decisions but those decisions of interest to political science are not primarily individual consumption or investment decisions; rather, they are decisions to vote, to participate in collective action, to adopt a platform on which to run for elected office, and so forth. In contrast to canonical decision-making in economics, therefore, what an individual chooses in politics is not always what an individual obtains (e.g. voting for some electoral candidate does not ensure that the candidate is elected). Thus, the link between an individual's decisions in politics and the consequent payoffs to the individual is attenuated relative to that for economic decisions: the basic political model of individual choice is game theoretic.

The preceding observations suggest two approaches to understanding how individual preferences connect to political, or collective, choices and both are pursued: a *direct* approach through extending the individual decision-theoretic model to the collectivity as a whole, an approach essentially begun with Arrow (1951, 1963) and Black (1958); and an *indirect* approach through exploring the consequences of mutually consistent sets of strategic decisions by instrumentally rational agents, an approach with roots in von Neumann and Morgenstern (1944) and Nash (1951).

Under the direct (*collective preference*) approach to social choice, individuals' *preferences* are directly aggregated into a "social preference" which, as in individual decision theory, is then maximized to yield a set of best (relative to the maximand) alternatives, the collective choices. But although individual preferences surely influence individual decisions such as voting, there is no guarantee that individuals' preferences are revealed by their decisions (for example, an individual may have strict preferences over candidates for electoral office, yet choose to vote strategically or to abstain). Under the indirect (*game-theoretic*) approach to social choice, therefore, it is individuals' *actions* that are aggregated to arrive at collective choices. Faced with a particular decision problem, individuals rarely have to declare their preferences directly but instead have to take some action. For example, in a multicandidate election under plurality rule, individuals must choose the candidate for whom to vote and may abstain; the collective choice from the election is then decided by counting the recorded votes and not by direct observation of all individuals' preferences over the entire list of candidates. It is useful to be a little more precise.

A preference profile is a list of preferences, one for each individual in the society, over a set of alternatives for that society. An abstract collective choice rule is a rule that assigns collective choices to each and every profile; that is, for any list of preferences, a collective choice rule identifies the set of outcomes chosen by society. Similarly, a preference aggregation rule is a rule that aggregates individuals' preferences into a single, complete, "social preference" relation over the set of alternatives; that is, for any profile, the preference aggregation rule collects individual preferences into a social preference relation over alternatives. It is important to note that while the theory (following economics) presumes individual preferences are complete and transitive, the only requirement at this point of a social preference relation is that it is complete. For any profile and preference aggregation rule, we can identify those alternatives (if any) that are ranked best by the social preference relation derived from the profile by the rule. With a slight abuse of the language, this set is known as the *core* of the preference aggregation rule at the particular profile of concern.[5] Taken together, therefore, a preference aggregation rule and its associated core for all possible preference profiles is an instance of an abstract collective choice rule. Thus, the extension of the classical economic decision-theoretic model of individual choice to the problem of collective decision-making, the direct approach mentioned above, can be described as the analysis of the abstract collective choice rules defined by the core of various preference aggregation rules.

The analytical challenge confronted by the direct approach is to find conditions under which preference aggregation relations exist and yield well-defined, that is, nonempty, cores. This approach has focused on two complementary issues: delineating classes of preference aggregation rule that are consistent with various sets of *desiderata* (for instance, Arrow's possibility theorem (1951, 1963) and May's theorem (May 1952) characterizing majority rule) and describing the properties of particular preference aggregation rules in various environments[6] (for instance, Plott's characterization of majority cores (Plott 1967) in the spatial model and the chaos theorems of McKelvey 1976 1979, and Schofield 1978, 1983). Contributions to the first issue rely heavily on axiomatic methods whereas contributions to the second have, for the most part, exploited the spatial voting model in which the feasible set of alternatives is some subset of (typically) k-dimensional Euclidean space and individuals' preferences can be described by continuous quasi-concave (loosely, single peaked in every direction) utility functions.

From the perspective of developing a decision-theoretic approach to prediction and explanation at the collective level, the results from collective preference theory are a little disappointing. There exist aggregation rules that justify treating collective choice in a straightforward decision-theoretic way only if the environment is very simple, having a minimal number of alternatives from which to choose or satisfying severe restrictions on the sorts of preference profiles that can exist (for instance, profiles of single-peaked preferences over a fixed ordering of the alternatives), or if the preferences of all but a very few are ignored in the aggregation (as in dictatorships). Moreover, in the context of the spatial model, most of the aggregation procedures observed in the world are, at least in principle, subject to chronic instability unless politics concerns only a single issue.[7] Nevertheless, a great deal has been learned from the collective preference approach to political decision-making about the properties and implications of preference aggregation and voting rules,

---

[5] The abuse arises since, strictly speaking, the core is defined with respect to a given family of coalitions. To the extent that a preference aggregation rule can be defined in terms of so-called decisive, or winning coalitions, the use of the term is standard. But not all rules can be so defined in which case the set of best elements induced by such a rule is not a core in the strict sense (see, for example, Austen-Smith and Banks 1999, ch. 3). The terminology in these instances is therefore an abuse but a useful and harmless one nevertheless.

[6] That is, various admissible classes of preference profiles and sorts of feasible sets of alternatives.

[7] See Austen-Smith and Banks 1999 for an elaboration of these claims.

and about the normative and descriptive trade-offs inherent in choosing one rule over another.[8]

Unlike the direct collective preference approach, the indirect approach to collective choice through the aggregation of the strategic decisions of instrumentally rational individuals begins by specifying the collection of possible decision, or strategy, profiles that could arise. A strategy for an individual specifies what the individual would do in every possible contingency that could arise in the given setting. A strategy profile is then a list of individual strategies, one for each member of the polity. An outcome function is a rule that identifies a unique alternative in the set of possible social alternatives with every feasible strategy profile. A specification of all possible strategy profiles along with an outcome function is called a *mechanism*. An abstract theory of how individuals make their respective decisions under any mechanism is a rule that associates a strategy profile with every preference profile; that is, for any given preference profile, an abstract decision theory assigns a set of possible strategy profiles consistent with the theory when individuals' preferences are described by the given list of preferences.[9] For any preference profile, mechanism, and decision theory, we can identify those alternatives that could arise as outcomes from strategy profiles consistent with the decision theory at that preference profile. This is the set of *equilibrium outcomes* under the mechanism at the preference profile. Then the indirect approach to preference aggregation can be described as the analysis of the collective choice rules defined by the sets of equilibrium outcomes of various mechanisms and theories of individual decision-making.

There is no effort under the indirect approach to treat collective decision-making as in any way analogous to individual decision-making. Instead, individuals make choices (vote, contribute to collective action, and so forth) taking account of the choices of others and the likely consequences of various combinations of the individuals' decisions. Although such choices are expected to reflect individual preferences, there is no presumption that they do so in any immediately transparent or literal fashion. The approach therefore requires both a theory of how individuals make their decisions (the abstract theory of decision-making considered above) and a description of how the resulting decisions are mapped into collective choices (a specification of the outcome function). Putting these two components together with preferences then yields a model of collective choice through the aggregation of individual decisions.

Unlike the collective preference approach, there is little difficulty with developing coherent predictive models of collective choice within the game-theoretic framework. That is, while the social choice mapping derived from a preference aggregation rule rarely yields maximal elements, the mapping derived from a mechanism and theory of individual behavior is typically well defined. This fact, coupled with the flexibility

---

[8] It is worth pointing out here, too, that the typical emptiness of the core has stimulated work on solutions concepts other than the core for collective preference theory (e.g. Schwarz 1972; Miller 1980; McKelvey 1986).

[9] Examples of such decision theories include Nash equilibrium and its refinements. See Fudenberg and Tirole 1991 or Myerson 1991.

of the approach with respect to modeling institutional details, uncertainty, and incomplete information, has led to game theory dominating contemporary formal theory. Indeed, it has been argued that the adoption of (in particular) non-cooperative game-theoretic techniques represents a fundamental shift in methodology from those of collective preference theory (e.g. Baron 1994; Diermeier 1997). Yet, at least from a formal perspective, the difference between the collective preference and the game-theoretic approaches is not so stark.

Both approaches to collective choice, the direct and the indirect, yield social choice rules, taking preference profiles into collective choices. Thus any result concerning such rules must apply equally to both. In particular, it is true that a social choice rule is generally guaranteed to yield a non-empty core only if it violates a "minimal democracy" property, where "minimal democracy" means that if all but at most one individuals strictly prefer some alternative x to another y, then y should not be ranked strictly better than x under the choice rule (Austen-Smith and Banks 1998). Whence it follows that the indirect approach ensures existence of well-defined solutions by violating minimal democracy, whereas the direct approach insists on minimal democracy at the expense of ensuring non-empty cores in any but the simplest settings. On this account, the direct and the indirect approaches to understanding collective decision-making are complementary rather than competitive. Which sort of model is most appropriate depends on the problem at hand and, in some important cases, their respective predictions are intimately related (Austen-Smith and Banks 1998, 2004). Moreover, the collective preference approach has revealed two general analytical characteristics of collective decision-making peculiar to political science relative to economics, characteristics that have stimulated important methodological and substantive innovations in the game-theoretic approach. It is to these characteristics and the innovations they have induced that I now turn.

3 Two Analytical Characteristics

The first characteristic exposed by collective preference theory involves the role of opportunities for trade. In economics, it is typically the case that, for any given society, the greater are the opportunities for trade the more likely it is that welfare-improving trade takes place. The analogue to increasing opportunities for trade in politics is increasing the dimensionality of the policy space in the spatial model or the number of alternatives in the finite-alternative model. As the number of alternatives or issue dimensions on which the preferences of a given population can differ grows, so too does the number of opportunities for winning coalitions to agree on a change from any policy; with one dimension, for example, coalitions must agree either to "move policy to the left" or to "move policy to the right" but, with two dimensions, there are uncountable directions in which to change policy, and preferences can be distributed over the plane, permitting more coalitions to form against any given policy. But it is precisely in such complex settings that preference aggregation rules are most poorly behaved: with one dimension the median voter theorem ensures a well-defined collective choice under majority rule (Black 1958) but, with two dimensions, the existence of such a choice is an extremely rare event and virtually any pair of alternatives can be connected by a finite sequence of majority-preferred steps (McKelvey 1979). Thus increasing "opportunities for trade" in the political setting exacerbate the problems of reaching a collective choice rather than ameliorate them.

The second characteristic concerns large populations. In economics it is the market that aggregates individual decisions into a collective outcome. As the number of individuals grows, the influence of any single agent becomes negligible and, in the limit, instrumentally rational individuals act as price-takers; moreover, large populations tend to smooth over non-convexities and irregularities at the individual level, justifying an approximation that all members of the population act as canonic economic theory presumes. These nice properties do not hold in political settings. Individual decisions are aggregated through voting and although the likelihood that any individual is pivotal vanishes as the electorate grows, for any finite society that likelihood is not zero: under majority rule in the classical Downsian spatial model, the median voter is pivotal whether there are three voters or three billion and three. So not only can the collective choice depend critically on a single person's decision, it is unjustified to treat each agent analogously to a "price-taker" and non-convexities and irregularities can matter a great deal depending on precisely where they are located in the population. The "correct" model of decision-making here is therefore to presume individuals condition their choices on being pivotal and act as if their vote or contribution or whatever tips the balance in favour of one or other collective choice: either they are not in fact pivotal in which case their decision is irrelevant, or they are pivotal in which case their decision determines the collective choice.[10]

The conclusion that rational individuals condition their vote decisions on the event that they are pivotal is a strategic, game-theoretic, perspective and it is within this framework that efforts to tackle the problems raised by each characteristic have been undertaken.

3.1 Institutions and Explanation

A virtue of the collective preference methodology (and, to a large extent, the cooperative game-theoretic methodology exploited by Riker 1962 and others) is that it is essentially "institution free," focusing exclusively on how domains of preference profiles are mapped into collective choices without attention to how the profiles might be recorded, from where the alternatives might arise, and so on. The idea underlying the axiomatic method of collective preference theory is to abstract from empirical and

---

[10] While this applies to any large finite electorate, proceeding to the limit in which each voter is infinitesimally small removes even this prescription regarding how strategically rational agents may behave, on which more below.

detailed institutional complications and study whole classes of possible institution-satisfying particular properties. A limitation of this method for an explanatory theory, however, is the typical emptiness of the core in complex settings, that is, those with many issues or alternatives over which to choose. And although non-cooperative game theory typically requires an exhaustive description of the relevant institutional details in any application, it is rarely hampered by questions of the existence of solutions. This observation prompted a shift in emphasis away from a collective preference methodology tailored to avoid concerns with the details of any application, to a non-cooperative game-theoretic approach that embraces such details as intrinsic to the analysis.

Two illustrations of the role of institutional detail in finessing problems of existence in complex political environments are provided by the use of particular sorts of agenda in committee decision-making from finite sets of alternatives (see Miller 1995 for an overview) and the citizen-candidate approach to electoral competition in the spatial model, whereby the candidates contesting an election are themselves voters who strategically choose whether or not to run for office at some cost (Osborne and Slivinsky 1996; Besley and Coate 1997).

In the classical preference profile to illustrate the instability of majority rule (the Condorcet paradox), three committee members have strict preferences over three alternatives such that each alternative is best in one person's ordering, middle ranked in a second person's ordering, and worst in a third person's ordering. There is no majority core in this example, with every alternative being beaten by one of the others under majority *preference*. However, committee decisions are often governed by rules, such as the amendment agenda. Under the amendment agenda, one alternative is first voted against another and the majority winner of the *vote* (not preference) is then put against the residual alternative in a final majority vote to determine the outcome. It is well known that the unique subgame perfect Nash equilibrium (an instance of a theory of individual decision-making in the earlier language) prescribes that individuals vote with their immediate (sincere) preferences at the final division to yield two conditional outcomes, one for each possible winner at the first division, and then vote sincerely at the first division with respect to these two conditional outcomes. Assuming majority preference is always strict, this backwards induction procedure invariably produces a unique prediction which in general depends on the ordering of the alternatives as well as the distribution of individual preferences per se.[11] Moreover, the set of possible outcomes from amendment agendas (on any given finite set of alternatives and any finite committee) as a function of the preference profiles inducing a strict majority preference relation is now completely characterized (Banks 1985).

Similar to the difficulty with many alternatives illustrated by the Condorcet paradox, the majority rule core in the multidimensional spatial model is typically empty, and core emptiness means the model offers *no* positive predictions beyond the claim

---

[11] It is worth noting in this example that the equilibrium outcome surely violates minimal democracy because, for every possible decision, there is an alternative that is strictly preferred by two of the three individuals.

that for every policy, there exists an alternative policy and a majority that strictly prefers that alternative. But policies are offered by candidates and candidates are themselves members of the electorate. It is natural, therefore, to treat the set of potential candidates as being exactly the set of citizens. Furthermore, since citizens are endowed with policy preferences, other things equal and conditional on being elected, a successful candidate has no incentive to implement any platform other than his or her most preferred policy. In turn, rational voters recognize that whatever a candidate drawn from the electorate might promise in the campaign, should the candidate be elected then that person's ideal policy is the final outcome. When the set of potential candidates coincides with the set of voters, therefore, there is no essential difference between the problem of electoral platform selection and the problem of candidate entry: explaining the distribution of electoral policy platforms in the citizen-candidate model is equivalent to explaining the distribution of citizens who choose to run for electoral office. And assuming that it is costly to run for office, individuals weigh the expected gains (which depend, *inter alia*, on who else is running) from entering an election against this cost when deciding whether to run for office. It follows that alternatives are costly to place on the agenda in the citizen-candidate model and it is not hard to see, then, that these institutional details introduce sufficient stickiness to ensure the existence of equilibria. Moreover, by varying parameters such as the cost of entry, the electoral rule of concern, and so forth, various comparative predictions concerning policy outcomes and electoral system are available.[12]

3.2 Information and Large Populations

Beyond questions of core existence, the application of the collective preference model to environments in which individuals face considerable uncertainty, either about the implications of any collective decision (imperfect information) or about the preferences of others (incomplete information), is awkward. Non-cooperative game theory, however, can readily accommodate uncertainty and informational variations.[13] And whereas uncertainty is unnecessary for developing a coherent theory of economic behavior among large populations (in particular, the theory of perfect competition), it is uncertainty that provides a hook on which to develop a coherent theory of political behavior among large populations.

As remarked above, a peculiarity of political decision-making relative to economic decision-making is that consideration of large populations greatly complicates rather than simplifies the analysis of individual decisions. In markets, each consumer becomes negligible with respect to influencing price as the number of consumers grows

[12] The contemporary literature on game-theoretic models of comparative institutions is large and growing. Examples include Austen-Smith and Banks 1988; Cox 1990; Persson, Roland, and Tabellini 1997; Myerson 1999; and Diermeier, Eraslan, and Merlo 2003.

[13] The theoretical foundations were laid by Harsanyi 1967–8. Two particularly important papers since then for political science are Spence 1973, who introduced the class of signaling games, and Crawford and Sobel 1982, who extended this class to include cheap-talk (costless) signaling.

and, therefore, is properly conceived as taking prices as given; in electorates, however, while it remains true that the likelihood that any single vote tips the outcome becomes vanishingly small as the number of voters grows, it is not true (at least for finite electorates) that the behavior of any given voter should be conditioned on the almost sure event that the voter's decision is consequentially irrelevant. This is not usually a problem for classical collective preference theory which, as the name suggests, focuses on aggregating given preference profiles, not vote profiles. Nor is it any problem for Nash equilibrium theory insofar as there are a huge number of equilibrium patterns of voting in any large election (other than with unanimity rule), most of which look empirically silly. But empirical voting patterns are not arbitrary. And once account is taken of the fact that preferring one candidate to another in an election does not imply voting for that candidate (individuals can abstain or vote strategically), there is clearly a severe methodological problem with respect to analysing equilibrium behavior in large electorates.

One line of attack has been by brute force, using combinatorial techniques to compute the probability that a particular vote is pivotal, conditional on the specified (undominated) votes of others (Ledyard 1984; Cox 1994; Palfrey 1989). But this is cumbersome and places considerable demands on exactly what it is that individuals know about the behavior of others. In particular, individuals are assumed to know the exact size of the population. Myerson (1998, 2000, 2002) relaxes this assumption and develops a novel theory of Poisson games to analyse strategic behavior in large populations.

Rather than assume the size of the electorate is known, suppose that the actual number of potential voters is a random variable distributed according to a Poisson distribution with mean n, where n is large. Then the probability that there is any particular number of voters in the society is easily calculated. As a statistical model underlying the true size of any electorate, the Poisson distribution uniquely exhibits a very useful technical property, *environmental equivalence*: under the Poisson distribution, any individual in the realized electorate believes that the number of other individuals in the electorate is also a random variable distributed according to a Poisson distribution with the same mean. And because the number and identity of realized individuals in the electorate is a random variable, it is enough to identify voters by *type* rather than their names, where an individual's type describes all of the strategically relevant characteristics of the individual (for example the individual's preferences over the candidates seeking office in any election). If the list of possible individual types is fixed and known, then the distribution of each type in a realized population of any size is itself given by a Poisson distribution.

The preceding implications of modeling population size as an unobserved draw from a Poisson distribution allow a relatively tractable and appealing strategic theory of elections. Because only types are relevant, individual strategies are appropriately defined as depending only on voter type rather than on voter identity. Thus individuals know only their own types, the distribution of possible types in the population, that the population size is a random draw from a Poisson distribution, and that all individuals of the same type behave in the same way. Call such a strategic model a

Poisson game. An equilibrium to a Poisson game is then a specification of strategies, one for each type, such that, for any individual of any type, the individual is taking a best decision taking as given the strategies of all other types, conditional on his or her beliefs regarding the numbers of individuals of each type in the electorate. Such equilibria exist and have well-defined limits with strictly positive turnout as the mean population size increases. Myerson proposes using these limiting equilibria as the basis of predictions about political behavior in large populations. And to illustrate the relative elegance of the method over the usual combinatoric approach, in Myerson (2000) he provides a version of a theorem on turnout and candidate platform convergence due to Ledyard (1984) and, in Myerson (1998), he establishes a Condorcet jury theorem (see also Myerson 2002 for a comparative analysis of three-candidate elections under scoring rules using a Poisson game framework).[14]

In economics, markets also serve to aggregate information through relative prices. There are no relative prices explicit in elections, yet it is not only implausible to presume voters know the true size of the electorate, it is also implausible that they know the full implications of electing one candidate rather than another. Because the likelihood that any single vote is pivotal in a large election is negligible, the incentives for any one voter in a large electorate to invest in becoming better informed regarding the candidates for election are likewise negligible. Thus Downs (1957) argued that voters in large populations would be "rationally ignorant." But just as is the case with his theory of participation, Downs's argument is decision-theoretic and does not necessarily apply once the strategic character of political behavior is made explicit. In particular, an instrumentally rational voter conditions her vote on the event that she is pivotal; and in the presence of asymmetric information throughout the electorate, conditioning on the event of being pivotal can yield a great deal of information about what others know. To see this, consider an example in which two candidates are competing for a majority of votes in a three-person electorate. Suppose each voter receives a noisy private signal correlated with which of the two candidates would be best and (for simplicity) suppose further that all voters share identical full-information preferences. Now if the first two voters are voting sincerely relative to their signals and the third voter is pivotal, it must be the case that the first two voters have received conflicting information about the candidates, in which case the third voter can base her vote on all of the available information distributed through the electorate, even though that distribution was not publicly known.

Exactly what are the information aggregation properties of various electoral schemes is currently subject to much research. In some settings, the logic sketched above can yield quite perverse results; for example, Ordeshook and Palfrey (1988) provide an example in which an almost sure Condorcet winner (that is, an alternative against which no alternative is preferred by a strict majority) is surely defeated in an amendment agenda with incomplete information. And in other settings, it turns

---

[14] Condorcet jury theorems address the problem of choosing one of two alternatives when voters are uncertain about which is most in their interests. Typically, the theorems connect the size of the electorate (jury) to the probability that majority voting outcomes coincide with the majority choice that would be made under no uncertainty.

out that elections are remarkably efficient at aggregating information; Feddersen and Pesendorfer (1996) prove a striking full-information equivalence theorem for two-candidate elections with costly voting under any majority or super-majority rule shy of unanimity, namely despite the fact that a significant proportion of the electorate might abstain, the limiting outcome as the population grows is almost surely the outcome that would arise if all individuals voted under complete information.[15]

4 Conclusion

To all intents and purposes, the methods of contemporary positive political theory coincide with the methods of contemporary economic theory. The most widespread framework for models of campaign contributions at present derives from the common agency problem introduced by Bernheim and Whinston (1986); Rubinstein's model of alternating offer bargaining (Rubinstein 1982) has been developed and extended to ground a general theory of legislative decision-making and coalition formation; Spence's theory of costly signaling games (Spence 1974) and Crawford and Sobel's (1982) extension of this theory to costless (cheap-talk) signaling provide the tools for a theory of legislative committees, delegation, informational lobbying, debate, and so on. More recently, the growth of interest in behavioral economics, experimental research, and so forth is beginning to appear in the political science literature. Rather than sketch these and other applications of economic methods to political science, this chapter attempts to articulate a broader (likely idiosyncratic) view of positive political theory since the importation of formal rational choice theory to politics. After all, political decision-making has at least as much of a claim to being subject to rational choice as economic decision-making; political agents make purposive decisions to promote their interests subject to constraints. It would be odd, then, to discover that the methods of economics are of no value to the study of politics.

References

Arrow, K. J. 1951. *Social Choice and Individual Values*. New Haven, Conn.: Yale University Press.
—— 1963. *Social Choice and Individual Values*, 2nd edn. New Haven, Conn.: Yale University Press.

---

[15] The logic of this result is that the while, as Downs suggested, the *relative* number of voters voting informatively declines as the electorate grows due to the diminishing likelihood of being pivotal, the *absolute* number of voters voting informatively increases as the electorate grows at a faster rate, and it is the latter that dominates the information aggregation.

Austen-Smith, D., and Banks, J. S. 1988. Elections, coalitions and legislative outcomes. *American Political Science Review*, 82: 405–22.

—— —— 1998. Social choice theory, game theory and positive political theory. In *Annual Review of Political Science*, vol. i, ed. N. Polsby. Palo Alto, Calif: Annual Reviews.

—— —— 1999. *Positive Political Theory*, i: Collective Preference. Ann Arbor: University of Michigan Press.

—— —— 2004. *Positive Political Theory*, ii: Strategy and Structure. Ann Arbor: University of Michigan Press.

Banks, J. S. 1985. Sophisticated voting outcomes and agenda control. *Social Choice and Welfare*, 1: 295–306.

Baron, D. 1994. A sequential choice perspective on legislative organization. *Legislative Studies Quarterly*, 19: 267–96.

Bernheim, D., and Whinston, M. 1986. Common agency. *Econometrica*, 54: 923–42.

Besley, T., and Coate, S. 1997. An economic model of representative democracy. *Quarterly Journal of Economics*, 112: 85–114.

Black, D. 1958. *The Theory of Committees and Elections*. Cambridge: Cambridge University Press.

Cox, G. W. 1990. Centripetal and centrifugal incentives in electoral systems. *American Journal of Political Science*, 34: 903–935.

—— 1994. Strategic voting equilibria under the single nontransferable vote. *American Political Science Review*, 88: 608–21.

Crawford, V., and Sobel, J. 1982. Strategic information transmission. *Econometrica*, 50: 1431–51.

Davis, O. A., and Hinich, M. J. 1966. A mathematical model of policy formation in a democratic society. In *Mathematical Applications in Political Science*, ii, ed. J. Bernd. Dallas, Tex. Southern Methodist University Press.

—— —— 1967. Some results related to a mathematical model of policy formation in a democratic society. In *Mathematical Applications in Political Science*, iii, ed. J. Bernd. Dallas, Tex. Southern Methodist University Press.

—— —— and Ordeshook, P. C. 1970. An expository development of a mathematical model of the electoral process. *American Political Science Review*, 64: 426–48.

Diermeier, D. 1997. Explanatory concepts in formal political theory. Mimeo, Stanford University.

—— Eraslan, H., and Merlo, A. 2003. A structural model of government formation. *Econometrica*, 71: 27–70.

Downs, A. 1957. *An Economic Theory of Democracy*. New York: Harper.

Feddersen, T. J., and Pesendorfer, W. 1996. The swing voter's curse. *American Economic Review*, 86: 408–424.

Ferejohn, J. A., and Fiorina, M. P. 1975. Closeness counts only in horseshoes and dancing. *American Political Science Review*, 69: 920–5.

Fudenberg, D., and Tirole, J. 1991. *Game Theory*. Cambridge, Mass.: MIT Press.

Harsanyi, J. 1967–8. Games with incomplete information played by "Bayesian" players, parts I, II and III. *Management Science*, 14: 159–82, 320–34, 486–502.

Hotelling, H. 1929. Stability in competition. *Economic Journal*, 39: 41–57.

Ledyard, J. 1984. The pure theory of large two-candidate elections. *Public Choice*, 44: 7–43.

McLean, I. 1990. The Borda and Condorcet principles: three medieval applications. *Social Choice and Welfare*, 7: 99–108.

McKelvey, R. D. 1976. Intransitivities in multidimensional voting models and some implications for agenda control. *Journal of Economic Theory*, 12: 472–82.

McKelvey, R. D. 1979. General conditions for global intransitivities in formal voting models. *Econometrica*, 47: 1086–112.

——1986. Covering, dominance and institution-free properties of social choice. *American Journal of Political Science*, 30: 283–314.

—— and Schofield, N. J. 1987. Generalized symmetry conditions at a core point. *Econometrica*, 55: 923–34.

May, K. O. 1952. A set of independent necessary and sufficient conditions for simple majority decision. *Econometrica*, 20: 680–4.

Miller, N. R. 1980. A new solution set for tournaments and majority voting. *American Journal of Political Science*, 24: 68–96.

——1995. *Committees, Agendas and Voting*. Chur: Harwood Academic.

Myerson, R. B. 1991. *Game Theory: Analysis of Conflict*. Cambridge, Mass.: Harvard University Press.

——1998. Population uncertainty and Poisson games. *International Journal of Game Theory*, 27: 375–92.

——1999. Theoretical comparisons of electoral systems. *European Economic Review*, 43: 671–97.

——2000. Large Poisson games. *Journal of Economic Theory*, 94: 7–45.

——2002. Comparison of scoring rules in Poisson voting games. *Journal of Economic Theory*, 103: 217–51.

Nash, J. F. 1951. Noncooperative games. *Annals of Mathematics*, 54: 289–95.

Ordeshook, P., and Palfrey, T., 1988. Agendas, strategic voting and signaling with incomplete information. *American Journal of Political Science*, 32: 441–66.

Osborne, M. J., and Slivinski, A. 1996. A model of political competition with citizen-candidates. *Quarterly Journal of Economics*, 111: 65–96.

Palfrey, T. R. 1989. A mathematical proof of Duverger's Law. In *Models of Strategic Choice in Politics*, ed. P. C. Ordeshook. Ann Arbor: University of Michigan Press.

—— and Rosenthal, H. 1983. A strategic calculus of voting. *Public Choice*, 41: 7–53.

Persson, T., Roland, G. and Tabellini, G. 1997. Separation of powers and political accountability. *Quarterly Journal of Economics*, 112: 310–27.

Plott, C. R. 1967. A notion of equilibrium and its possibility under majority rule. *American Economic Review*, 57: 787–806.

Riker, W. H. 1962. *The Theory of Political Coalitions*. New Haven, Conn: Yale University Press.

—— and Ordeshook, P. C. 1968. A theory of the calculus of voting. *American Political Science Review*, 62: 25–43.

Rubinstein, A. 1982. Perfect equilibrium in a bargaining model. *Econometrica*, 50: 97–109.

Saari, D. G. 1997. The generic existence of a core for q-rules. *Economic Theory*, 9: 219–60.

Schofield, N. J. 1978. Instability of simple dynamic games. *Review of Economic Studies*, 45: 575–94.

——1983. Generic instability of majority rule. *Review of Economic Studies*, 50: 695–705.

Schwartz, T. 1972. Rationality and the myth of the maximum. *Nous*, 7: 97–117.

Smithies, A. 1941. Optimum location in spatial competition. *Journal of Political Economy*, 49: 423–39.

Spence, A. M. 1974. *Market Signaling: Informational Transfer in Hiring and Related Screening Processes*. Cambridge, Mass.: Harvard University Press.

Spence, M. 1973. Job market signaling. *Quarterly Journal of Economics*, 87: 355–79.

Von Neumann, J., and Morgenstern, O. 1944. *Theory of Games and Economic Behaviour*. Princeton, NJ: Princeton University Press.

CHAPTER 51

LABORATORY EXPERIMENTS

THOMAS R. PALFREY

1 INTRODUCTION AND OVERVIEW

MUCH of the laboratory research in political science follows the style that was pioneered in experimental economics a half-century ago by Vernon Smith. The connection between this style of political science experimentation and economics experimentation parallels the connection between economic theory and formal political theory.

This is no accident. In both cases, researchers who were trained primarily as theorists—but interested in learning whether the theories were reliable—turned to laboratory experiments to test their theories, because they felt adequate field data were unavailable. These experiments had three key features. First, they required the construction of isolated (laboratory) environments that operated under specific, tightly controlled, well-defined institutional rules. Second, incentives were created for the participants in these environments in a way that matched incentives that existed for the imaginary agents in theoretical models. Third, the theoretical models to be studied had precise *context-free* implications about behavior in any such environment so defined, and these predictions were quantifiable and therefore directly testable in the laboratory.

One of the key innovators of political science experimentation is Charles Plott, who conducted early economics experiments as well, to test the effect of

---

* The financial support of the National Science Foundation and the Center for Economic Policy Studies at Princeton University is gratefully acknowledged. I wish to thank many co-authors for sharing their insights about political economy experiments. I am especially indebted to Richard McKelvey. The editors provided helpful comments on an earlier draft.

economic institutions and rules on trade and exchange. It was a short but important step to use the same methods to compare different political institutions and rules vis-à-vis policy outcomes. Just as economic theory used models that made *quantitative* predictions about behavior in markets, formal political theories had begun to make precise quantitative predictions about behavior in non-market settings, such as elections, committees, and juries.

It is also no accident that this brand of experimentation followed rather than preceded similar research in economics. The lag in political science experimentation relative to economics reflects a similar lag in developing rigorous theory.

This chapter will be organized around a rough classification of four kinds of political science experiments that use the political economy/formal theory approach. This is obviously not an exhaustive list, and the discussion is intended to draw out the main insights from these experiments rather than being comprehensive (this would require a book-length chapter). They are: (1) *committee decision-making*; (2) *elections and candidate competition*; (3) *information aggregation*; and (4) *voter turnout and participation games*.

The initial political economy experiments investigated the most fundamental principle of the theory of committees: *committees operating under majority rule will choose Condorcet winners when they exist*. At first glance, this seems an obvious point, but it turns out to depend in very subtle ways on what is meant by "operating under majority rule." Testing this basic hypothesis is as fundamental to political science as the discoveries by Vernon Smith that markets organized as double auctions result in competitive equilibrium prices and quantities—and that markets organized in other ways may not converge to competitive equilibrium. The bottom line for both kinds of experiments—the first political science experiments and the first economics experiments—was that quantitative equilibrium theories work pretty well in some settings, but institutions matter. While there existed lots of casual evidence and qualitative historical analysis, laboratory experiments provided the first non-circumstantial evidence that institutions matter—and identified exactly how. Besides being non-circumstantial evidence, it also provided *replicable* evidence, and *precise comparative static tests* about how changing preferences and institutions lead to changes in committee outcomes. And these effects could be clearly identified as causal, in the sense that preferences and institutions created in the laboratory are, by design, *exogenously specified and controlled*, while with the inherent limitations of historical data, one can only make weaker claims about correlations between preferences, institutions, and outcomes. Controlled laboratory experimentation circumvents problems of spurious correlation and endogeneity.

The next section of this chapter will examine two quite different approaches to the study of committee decision-making. First it will explore and discuss in more detail the findings from this first line of political science experiments, which, in addition to studying institutions, also focus on questions of testing or improving *cooperative* game-theoretic solution concepts. Second, we will discuss more recent experiments on committee bargaining designed to test theories from *non-cooperative* game theory, focusing mainly on questions of distributive politics where Condorcet winners do not exist, in contrast to the earlier focus on the Downs–Hotelling spatial model.

The second wave of political science experiments, which followed quickly after the experiments on the majority rule core, investigated the question of Condorcet winners in the context of competitive elections rather than small committees. These studies address a wide range of questions, all of which have received the attention of empirical political scientists for decades. The key questions we will focus on here are: retrospective voting; the Downsian model of spatial convergence of candidate platforms in competitive elections; the importance of polls in transmitting information to voters and coordinating voting behavior in multicandidate elections; and asymmetric competition that leads to candidate divergence.

More recently, both formal theorists and experimentalists have become interested in the problem of information aggregation. The problem was posed originally by Condorcet and has become known as the Condorcet jury problem. Each member holds a piece of information about the true state of the world. The committee is charged with making a decision, and the correct decision depends on the state of the world. We will discuss briefly the experimental findings for Condorcet juries, and related issues of information aggregation through social learning.

An independent line of research, but one which has significant implications for mass elections, investigates factors affecting voter turnout. More generally, this includes participation games, and a wide range of related phenomena involving coordination problems such as the volunteer's dilemma. Experimental studies of abstract games, in particular the game of chicken and the battle of the sexes, are also closely related. The third section of this chapter will try to highlight some of the insights and regularities across this wide range of experimental research.

2 Experiments in Committee Decision-making

This section discusses: (i) the earliest experiments that study the majority rule core and other concepts central to cooperative game theory; and (ii) more recent experiments that study committee bargaining under majority rule. Both of these kinds of experiments study allocation problems where the members have conflicting preferences over the possible outcomes.

2.1 Committee Bargaining in Multidimensional Policy Spaces

This line of research, beginning with the landmark article by Fiorina and Plott (1978), explores two distinctly different kinds of questions. First, it tests the basic theory of the core in small committees, and examines its robustness with respect to the fine details of committee procedure.[1] This can be thought of as a "comparative statics" question. The theory says that as preferences and/or procedures change in certain ways, outcomes from committee deliberation should change in corresponding ways. Second, it explores what happens in case the core fails to exist. We know from Plott (1967), McKelvey (1976, 1979), and Schofield (1983) that non-existence problems are rampant in these environments.

The basic theoretical structure in most of these experiments is the following. The set of feasible alternatives, A, is a convex concave subset of $\Re^2$, usually a square or rectangle.[2] There is a finite set of members of the committee, $I = \{1, \ldots, i, \ldots, n\}$ with Euclidean preferences, where n is an odd number for most experiments. Therefore, the environment is fully specified by $[A, I, x]$, where $x = (x^1, \ldots, x^i, \ldots, x^n) \subseteq A^n$ is the profile of members' ideal points. For any such environment, we can define the simple majority rule binary relation. For any pair of alternatives, $a, b \in A$, we write $a \succ b$ if a majority of the members of I strictly prefer a to b. In this case, we say a defeats b under majority rule. If a does not defeat b, we write $b \succeq a$. The majority rule *core*, or the set of *Condorcet winners*, $C \subseteq A$, includes precisely those alternatives that are undefeated under majority rule. That is $C = \{c \in A | c \succeq a \forall a \in A\}$. An implication of the results in Plott (1967) is that in these environments, if n is odd and the x^i are all distinct, then (i) the core coincides with one of the member's ideal points, call it x^{i^*}, and (ii) the other members can be paired up in such a way that for each pair, the line connecting the ideal points of the pair pass through x^{i^*}. The condition is sometimes referred to as *pairwise symmetry*, and has a natural generalization to environments with arbitrary quasi-concave and continuous preferences with ideal points, in terms of pairs of utility gradients at the core point.[3]

2.2 Fiorina and Plott (1978)

Fiorina and Plott (1978) created sixty-five five-member laboratory committees, each of which deliberated under a simplified version of Roberts' Rules. The policy space included a fine grid of points in a two-dimensional policy space. The two dimensions in the model correspond to policy choices, such as spending on defense and tax rates, but no labels as such were used in the experiments in order to maintain a neutral context. The policy space was, literally, the blackboard. Preferences were induced using monetary payments that depended on the outcome and differed across subjects. Iso-payment contours (indifference curves) were either concentric circles or ellipses,

---

[1] The core is a concept developed in cooperative game theory as the set of outcomes that are stable with respect to coalitional deviation under some well-defined institution. This is often modeled as a game in characteristic function form. An outcome is in the core if there doesn't exist some alternative feasible outcome that makes some subset (coalition) of individuals better off and that cannot be blocked by the other members.

[2] In the actual experiments, the outcome space is given by a finite grid of points on the plane.

[3] Some experiments have been conducted using elliptical indifference curves, rather than circular (Euclidean). In this case the gradient version of pairwise symmetry applies.

so this method extended to committee environments the *induced value* approach pioneered by Smith (1976) in market settings. Deliberation by each committee started at a status quo point that generated low payoffs for all members. Members could raise their hands and propose alternative points; a vote between the status quo and the alternative ensued, with the alternative replacing the new status quo point if it passed by receiving a majority of votes. This process could continue indefinitely, as long as members made new proposals. At any point, a member could make a motion to adjourn. If the motion to adjourn passed, the session ended and subjects were paid based on the last alternative that had passed (or the original status quo, if no alternative ever passed). The main treatment variable in the initial experiment was the preference profile, using two preference profiles for which a core existed and one where a core did not exist.[4] In the treatment where a core point did not exist, the ideal point of one voter was shifted a small distance, breaking pairwise symmetry. Thus, this treatment was designed to test whether the discontinuous nature of core existence would lead to a discontinuous change in committee outcomes. It was an important variation to investigate, since results by McKelvey on global cycling (or "chaos") were widely interpreted at the time as implying anything can happen in the absence of a core point.

The principal findings were:

1. *Core clustering.* When it exists, the core is the best predictor among sixteen competing hypotheses to explain committee outcomes. While few outcomes are *exactly* at the core point, the outcomes tend to cluster nearby the core point, when it exists.
2. *Robustness.* The secondary treatments had little effect, although there was greater variance of outcomes when payoff magnitudes were low (low incentives).
3. *Continuity.* When the core point did not exist, but the preference profile was close to admitting a core point, the outcomes still clustered around a region in the policy space in much the same way as was observed when a core point existed! Thus, it appears that the distribution of committee outcomes varies continuously with the preference profile of the members.

The third of these observations is perhaps the most important. Why? The theory of the core is not a behavioral theory, but simply a property of the majority rule binary relation. The deliberation procedure, while simple to describe, is virtually impossible to model as an extensive form game. There is no theory of who makes proposals, no theory of how people vote on proposals, no theory of adjournment, and so forth. That is, Fiorina and Plott (1978) *and subsequent studies along the same line* investigate environments and procedures for which there is no accepted *behavioral* model to describe or predict individual actions. These are experiments that test axiomatic theories of social choice, not behavioral theories.[5]

---

[4] There are also some some minor treatment variations regarding payoff magnitudes and communication limitations.
[5] Fiorina and Plott and later studies suggest alternative hypotheses that are suggestive of a behavioral model (such as fairness), but do not construct or test such models.

2.3 The Robustness of Core Clustering

With few exceptions, subsequent research has reinforced most of the conclusions above. Berl et al. (1976) investigate some variations on the original Fiorina and Plott (1978) study, showing robustness to a number of factors including additional variations in preferences (using city block metric preferences).[6] In a later study, McKelvey and Ordeshook (1984) restrict agendas to issue-by-issue voting; they find that outcomes still cluster around the core. This, together with the findings about limitations on debate/communication, illustrates how robust core clustering is with respect to significant procedural variation.[7]

Rick Wilson and his co-authors have conducted a range of different variations on Fiorina and Plott. One of the most interesting assessed everyone on the committee a fixed cost (called an "agenda access cost") whenever a proposal is successful (Herzberg and Wilson 1991). This has two interesting and countervailing effects. First, it expands the set of core outcomes. For example in the Fiorina and Plott environment without a core, a core point exists even with small access costs. The second effect is more subtle. Because changes are more costly, members are more reluctant to vote for *any* change, and this creates a drag on the process. Voters might vote against a change that makes them better off in the short run, because they fear the change will lead to further changes incurring additional costs. The findings therefore are mixed. For example, if a core already exists in the absence of access costs, then imposing access costs leads to more dispersion in the final outcomes, a negative effect. Outcomes still cluster near the core, but with more scatter, and occasionally the process fails entirely, without ever moving away from the initial (bad) status quo. These experiments are instructive because they suggest behavioral models of individual behavior, such as risk aversion. They also suggest that individuals are not myopic in their voting decisions, but anticipate the future consequences of current votes.

Plott conducted additional experiments showing that the results replicate to larger committees[8] and also for committees where there was agenda control by one or more of its members. In Kormendi and Plott (1982), one member of a five-member committee served as a gatekeeper (called a "convener" in the paper) who was allowed to offer or unilaterally block proposals, in an environment with the same preferences as one of the Fiorina and Plott core treatments. This agenda power restriction changes the core, since blocking coalitions must include the agenda-setter. The core expands and becomes the line segment between the original core point and the agenda-setter's ideal point. The outcomes line up closely with the core predictions. Hence these experiments show that the majority rule core, modified to account for changes in proposal procedures, continues to predict committee outcomes. An important corollary

---

[6] In spite of the earlier publication date, the experiments reported in Berl et al. 1976 were motivated by an early version of Fiorina and Plott 1978.
[7] With issue-by-issue voting, a new alternative can amend the status quo on only one dimension.
[8] Plott 1991 replicates the FP results for committees with between twenty-three and forty-five members.

is that subtle changes in procedures can cause dramatic changes in outcomes, as predicted by game theory.

There are some exceptions to the robustness of core clustering. One striking result is described in Eavey and Miller (1984a), which follows up on an earlier experiment by Isaac and Plott (1978).[9] Isaac and Plott studied three-person committees with a convener, but with only a small finite set of possible outcomes, so the environment was not framed to the subjects as a two-dimensional policy space. There is a unique core, which predicts outcomes very well. Eavey and Miller point out that the core in that experiment was also a *fair* outcome that gives something to everyone. They designed a "critical" experiment in which the fair outcome is different from the core, and both are unique. They find that fair outcome was selected eight out of ten times, and the core was only selected twice. Eavey and Miller conclude that interpersonal comparisons (fairness, altruism, universalism) can affect outcomes in committees. Their result presaged the recent wave of social preference models in behavioral economics.

2.4 Committee Bargaining with Fixed Extensive Forms

Eavey and Miller (1984b) modified the convener design by allowing the convener to make exactly one proposal, and then the committee adjourns. That is, an agenda-setter makes a take-it-or-leave-it offer to the committee, which then decides between the offer and the status quo, according to majority rule. This is precisely the game form studied in Romer and Rosenthal (1978), called *the setter model*. It is modeled as an extensive form game in two stages. In the first stage, the setter makes a proposal. In the second stage, there is a vote by the committee to accept or reject the setter's proposal. Then the game ends. The perfect equilibrium of the game is for the setter to propose the alternative he prefers most, among those proposals that at least a majority (weakly) prefers to the status quo. This proposal passes in equilibrium.

Eavey and Miller used both a discrete setting and a one-dimensional policy space and found little support for the setter model. Rather than extracting all the rents, the monopolistic setter offers proposals that leave something on the table for other committee members; another indication of fairness, and possibly social preferences.

This mirrors similar findings for two-person committees with strict majority rule, otherwise known as the *ultimatum bargaining game*. In that game, one player proposes a split of a fixed amount of money. The second person either accepts the split or rejects it. If he rejects, both players receive 0. The subgame perfect equilibrium is for the proposer to offer either zero or the smallest positive amount, and for the responder to accept the offer. That rarely happens. The modal offer is an equal split and the mean offer is about 60–40. Many explanations have been offered for this clear violation of subgame perfect equilibrium.

The Rubinstein (1982) and Baron–Ferejohn (1989) bargaining models are comparable to the ultimatum game and the setter model, respectively, but in a divide-the-pie,

---

[9] McKelvey and Ordeshook 1981 also find evidence that core selection depends on fine details of the preference profile.

or distributive politics, environment. The only difference is that the game does not end after the proposer makes a proposal, but continues in some fashion (usually with the proposer changing over time) in the event the proposal is rejected. In versions of these games that have been conducted in the laboratory, the theoretical equilibrium has three essential properties:

1. *Proposer advantage.* A committee member is better off if they are the proposer than if they are not the proposer.
2. *No delay.* The first proposal is always accepted in equilibrium.
3. *Full rent extraction.* The offer to the other members of the committee (or the other bargainer in the two-person case) is such that those voting for the proposal are exactly indifferent between voting for and against. Coalitions should be minimal winning.

There have been several laboratory studies of the Baron–Ferejohn bargaining model, and all have reached qualitatively similar conclusions that were foreshadowed by the Eavey–Miller experiment with the setter model. *Models that predict full rent extraction predict poorly if responders are allowed to veto the outcome, either individually, or as part of a blocking coalition.* This means the proposer in all of these settings must trade off the value of better proposal against the risk of having it voted down. But this risk implies that there must be delay, due to the unpredictability of the responder's behavior, and because different proposers will tolerate risk differently and have different beliefs. But there should still be a proposer advantage; and there is, although diminished somewhat because of the blocking threat.

There is insufficient space to cover the vast number of experimental studies of bargaining, both bilateral and multilateral. For bilateral bargaining, recommended reading is Roth (1995) and Camerer (2004, ch. 4). For committee bargaining à la Baron–Ferejohn, see McKelvey (1991), Diermeier and Morton (2005), and Fréchette, Kagel, and Morelli (2005). In all these experiments, where members often have different voting weights, one observes the same three qualitative findings: proposer advantage, delay, and only partial rent extraction.

3 Elections and Candidate Competition

The second wave of political science experiments, which followed quickly on the heels of committee experiments on the majority rule core, investigated the question of Condorcet winners in the context of competitive elections rather than small committees. These studies address many of the same questions that have received the attention of empirical political scientists. The key questions we will focus on here are: spatial convergence of candidate platforms in competitive elections; retrospective voting; and the importance of polls in transmitting information to voters and coordinating voting behavior in multicandidate elections.

3.1 Competitive Elections and the Median Voter Theorem

The median voter theorem says that under certain conditions, in two-candidate winner-take-all elections, candidate platforms will converge to the ideal point of the median voter. The theorem applies under fairly general conditions in one-dimensional policy spaces with single-peaked preferences, and under more stringent conditions in multidimensional policy spaces. Basically, if Condorcet winners exist, they are elected. Does this happen? Casual evidence indicates significant divergence of candidate and party platforms, even in winner-take-all elections. Laboratory experiments can help us understand why this may happen by informing us about what conditions are essential for convergences and which are inessential.

There has been extensive work on candidate competition in the one-dimensional world with single-peaked preferences and various conditions of information. The main contributors to this effort are McKelvey and Ordeshook, and much of this is detailed in their 1990 survey. I will cover only the basics here. First, in two-dimensional policy spaces when a Condorcet winner exists, the candidates converge to that point. There is a process of learning and adjustment over time, but, just as competitive markets eventually converge to the competitive price, platforms in competitive elections converge to the Condorcet winner. Their original experiments showing this (McKelvey and Ordeshook 1982) were conducted with full information. Candidates knew the preferences of all voters and voters knew the platforms of the candidates. Candidates did not have policy preferences.

Through an ingenious series of subsequent experiments on spatial competition, McKelvey and Ordeshook (1985a, 1985b) pursued a variety of issues, mostly related to the question of how much information was required of voters and candidates in order for competitive elections to converge to the Condorcet winner. Perhaps the most striking experiment was reported in McKelvey and Ordeshook (1985b). That experiment used a single policy dimension, but candidates had no information about voters, and only a few of the voters in the experiment knew where the candidates located. The key information transmission devices explored were polls and interest group endorsements. In a theoretical model of information aggregation adapted from the rational expectations theory of markets, they proved that this information alone is sufficient to reveal enough to voters that even uninformed voters behave optimally—i.e. as if they were fully informed.[10] A corollary of this is that the candidates will converge over time to the location of the median voter. They find strong support for the hypothesis of full revelation to voters, and also find support for candidate convergence. However, in an extension of this experiment to two dimensions, candidate convergence is slower; only half the candidates converge to the Condorcet winner with replication.

A second set of experiments explores whether median outcomes can arise purely from retrospective voting. The earlier set of experiments with rational expectations and polls was forward looking and evaluation of candidates was prospective. In

---

[10] Voters also are assumed to know approximately where they stand relative to rest of the electorate on a left–right scale. But they don't need any information about the candidates per se.

Collier et al. (1987), voters observe only the payoff they receive from the winning candidate after the fact—not even the platform adopted by the winning candidate, nor the platform of the losing candidate! There are no campaigns or polls. Voters either re-elect the incumbent or elect an unknown challenger. Candidates are better informed: they observe all the platforms that their opponent has adopted in the past, as well as the past election results. But candidates are given no information about the distribution of voter ideal points. They find that on average candidates converge to the median, even without much information.

One of the implications of these results is that it is irrational for voters to gather costly information, if other sources of information such as polls, endorsements, and word of mouth are virtually free. This point is made in Collier, Ordeshook, and Williams (1989). That paper and Williams (1991) explore voter behavior and candidate convergence through extending these experimental environments by giving voters the option to gather costly information about candidates.

These experiments establish two important facts. First, even in laboratory elections where the stakes are low, election outcomes are well approximated by median voter theory. The Condorcet winner (core) is an excellent predictor of competitive election outcomes. Second, this result is robust with respect to the information voters have about candidates and the information candidates have about voters. Precious little information is needed—a result that mirrors laboratory demonstrations that markets converge quickly to competitive equilibrium prices and quantities, even with poor information and few traders.

There has been great concern voiced by political scientists and pundits about low levels of information in the electorate. One reason for this concern is a widely shared belief that these information failures can doom competitive democratic processes. The McKelvey and Ordeshook series of experiments dispels this doomsday view. Just as financial markets can operate efficiently with relatively few informed traders, or with many slightly informed traders, the forces of political competition can lead to election outcomes that reflect public opinion, even in information-poor environments.

3.2 Multicandidate Elections

In many elections, more than two candidates are competing for a single position using plurality rule. In these *multicandidate* elections, there is a natural ambiguity facing voters and in fact, almost anything can happen in equilibrium. The reason is that there are many Nash equilibrium voting strategies. To see this, just consider a three-candidate election, with the candidates A, B, and C having three distinct positions on a one-dimensional issue scale, say the interval $[-1, 1]$. Suppose there is a very large number of voters with ideal points scattered along the interval. Voters know their own ideal point, but have only probabilistic information about the other voters. Then, for any pair of candidates $\{i, j\}$ there is a Bayesian equilibrium in which only these two candidates receive any votes, with each voter voting for whichever of the two is closer to their ideal point. This is an equilibrium because it never (instrumentally) pays to vote for a candidate whom nobody else is voting for. Indeed there can be some other equilibria, too (Palfrey 1989; Myerson and Weber 1993), but two-candidate equilibria are the only ones that are stable (Fey 1997). Voters face a coordination problem. Which two candidates are going to be receiving votes? Will a Condorcet winner be chosen if it exists?

Forsythe et al. (1993, 1996) explore these and other questions in a series of experiments. Their laboratory elections had three categories of voters defined by different preference orders over the three candidates. One group preferred A to B to C. The second group preferred B to A to C, and the third group ranked C first and was indifferent between A and B. The third group was the largest, but was less than half the population. Groups 1 and 2 were the same size. Hence, if voters voted for their first choice, C will win, but C is a *Condorcet loser*,[11] since it is defeated by both A and B in pairwise votes. There are many equilibria, including the three two-candidate equilibria noted above, but because of a special configuration of preferences and because there is complete information, sincere voting is also an equilibrium.

First, they note that without any coordinating device, there is coordination failure. Some voters in groups 1 and 2 vote strategically (i.e. for their second choice, trying to avoid C) but many don't, and the strategic behavior is poorly coordinated, so as a result the Condorcet loser wins 90 per cent of the elections!

Second, they look at three kinds of coordinating devices: polls, past elections, and ballot position. Polls allow the voters in groups 1 and 2 to coordinate their votes behind either candidate A or candidate B. This is indeed what happens. The Condorcet loser wins only 33 per cent of the elections. Moreover, when either A or B is first ranked in the poll, the Condorcet loser wins only 16 per cent of the time. Election history also helped with coordination. There was a small bandwagon effect between A and B. Whichever was winning in past elections tended to win in future polls. Ballot position had an effect on voting strategies, but the effect was too small to affect election outcomes.

Their second paper looks at alternative voting procedures, comparing plurality rule to the Borda Count and Approval Voting. Both procedures worked better than plurality rule, in the sense that the Condorcet loser was more easily defeated. Both procedures tended to result in relatively close three-way races with A or B usually winning. Plurality, in contrast, produced close three-way races, but with C usually winning.

This line of work has been extended in a number of directions. For example, Gerber, Morton, and Rietz (1998) look at cumulative voting in multimember districts to see if it can ameliorate problems of minority under-representation. Theoretically, it should, due to the similar problems of strategic voting and coordination. They run an experiment and find it makes a difference, and the data support the main theoretical results.

In these studies, only voter behavior is examined, since there are no candidates in the experiment. Plott (1991) reports experiments with three-way plurality races where candidates choose positions in a policy space, and voter ideal points are located so an equilibrium exists. He finds that candidates tend to cluster near the equilibrium point.

[11] A Condorecet losing candidate is one who is defeated in a pairwise vote with any of the other candidates.

3.3 Asymmetric Contests

In many elections, candidates are asymmetric. A widely cited source of asymmetry is incumbency. It is generally thought that incumbents have a significant advantage over challengers, above and beyond any advantage (or disadvantage) they may have due to spatial location. Other sources of asymmetries include valence characteristics of candidates, such as a familiar name, movie or athletic star status, height, articulateness, and personality traits. The two key aspects of these valence characteristics are: (1) most voters value them, independent of the candidate platforms; and (2) they are fixed, rather than being chosen by the candidates. With strategic competition, candidate asymmetries have interesting and systematic implications for equilibrium platforms. These asymmetric contests have been studied recently both theoretically and empirically in game-theoretic models by Erikson and Palfrey (2000), Ansolabehere and Snyder (1999), Groseclose (2001), Aragones and Palfrey (2002, 2005), and others.

Groseclose (2001) and Aragones and Palfrey (2002, 2005) show that valence asymmetries lead to candidate *divergence*, even in one-dimensional spatial models. The equilibria, which can be either mixed strategy equilibria or pure strategy equilibria (if candidates have policy preferences and there is enough exogenous uncertainty), have two interesting features. First, a disadvantaged candidate will tend to locate at more extreme locations in the policy space than the advantaged candidate. Second, the extent to which this happens depends on the distribution of voters, in a systematic way. As the distribution of voter ideal points becomes more polarized (e.g. a bimodal distribution), the disadvantaged candidate moves toward the center, while the advantaged candidate moves in the opposite direction, and adopts more extreme positions.

Aragones and Palfrey (2004) report the results of an experiment designed to test whether these systematic effects can be measured in a simplified spatial competition environment. Candidates simultaneously choose one of three locations {L, C, R}. The location of the median voter is unknown, but they both know the distribution of voters. The median is located at C with probability a, and located at either L or R with probability $(1-a)/2$. Candidate 1 is the advantaged candidate; he wins if the median voter is indifferent (in policy space) between the two candidates, which happens if the candidates locate in the same position, or if one chooses L and the other R. Their main treatment variable is a, the probability the median is located at C, which in different sessions takes on values of either 1/5, 1/3, or 3/5. The equilibrium is characterized by a pair of probabilities of locating at the central location, one for the advantaged candidate (p) and one for the disadvantaged candidate (q). These equilibrium probabilities are ordered as follows:

$$0 < q_{3/5} < q_{1/3} < q_{1/5} < \frac{1}{3} < p_{3/5} < p_{1/3} < p_{1/5} < 1$$

The data perfectly reproduce this ordering of candidate locations, for all treatments. The result appears to be robust, and has been replicated successfully with different subject pools and instruction protocols.

4 Information Aggregation

The standard model for information aggregation in committees is one in which a likeminded group of individuals must choose a policy whose (common) payoff depends on an unknown state of the world. But the committee has limited information about the state of the world. To compound matters, this information is decentralized, with each member having some piece of information. The task of the committee is to try to boil down this information into a decision that would be as efficient as the decision of a rational Bayesian who had access to all the scattered pieces of information. Using a model with two states of the world and two alternatives, Condorcet argued that majority rule would be the most efficient voting method to solve this problem. While his 2×2 model has become standard, his approach and conclusions about the superiority of majority rule has met with criticism because he assumed voters would vote sincerely. That is, if a voter's private information indicates policy A is probably better than B, they will vote for A regardless of the voting rule. However, since the work of Austen-Smith and Banks (1996), this assumption is now known to be flawed, in the sense that rational players would not necessarily vote that way. Nash equilibria of the voting game can involve complicated strategies, and can lead to perverse outcomes. Moreover, the equilibrium strategies are highly sensitive to the voting rule itself.

The key experimental paper in this line of research is Guarnaschelli, McKelvey, and Palfrey (2000). That paper was inspired by the Feddersen and Pesendorfer (1998) result that the rule of unanimity in juries is flawed, since the Nash equilibrium may lead to a higher probability of convicting the innocent than sub-unanimity rules, including majority rule. Furthermore, the problem can be worse in larger juries than smaller juries. This directly contradicts the standard jurisprudential argument for unanimity rules and large (twelve-member) juries. Naive intuition suggests that raising the hurdle for conviction will reduce the chances of a false conviction. But that intuition relies on an assumption that voting behavior is unaffected by the voting rule, in particular, voters are non-strategic. Game-theoretic reasoning says the opposite: when the hurdle for conviction is raised, voters are less willing to vote to acquit.

There are at least three reasons to be skeptical of the behavioral predictions of Nash equilibrium in this setting. First, if the pure intuition of legal scholars and great thinkers like Condorcet is that voters will be sincere, then why wouldn't voters also follow the same intuitive reasoning? Second, the strategic reasoning underlying the Nash equilibrium is quite complicated, and its computation requires, among other things, repeated application of Bayes's rule and conditioning on low probability events (pivot probabilities). There is ample evidence from experimental psychology that judgements of low probability events are flawed, and that individuals often fail to apply Bayes's rule correctly. Third, the equilibrium is in mixed strategies, and there are laboratory data in other contexts indicating that Nash equilibrium does not predict that well in games with mixed strategy equilibria.

In fact, it was a fourth reason that motivated the experiment: *quantal response equilibrium* (or QRE; McKelvey and Palfrey 1995, 1998) makes much different predictions about the effects of size and the voting rule compared to Nash equilibrium. The QRE model assumes the players are strategic, and are aware other players are also strategic, but players are not perfect maximizers.[12] Rather than always choosing optimally, players choose better strategies more often than worse strategies, but there is a stochastic component to their choices, so inferior strategies are sometimes selected. With the additional stochastic term in the picture, standard jurisprudential arguments emerge as properties of the equilibrium: majority rule should lead to more false convictions than unanimity, and larger unanimous juries produce fewer false convictions than smaller unanimous juries.

A central finding in Guarnaschelli, McKelvey, and Palfrey (2000) is that the predictions of QRE capture the main features of the data quite well, both with respect to comparative statics and quantitatively, and most of the Nash equilibrium comparative static predictions fail. But perhaps more interesting is what the data say about the three "obvious" reasons to be suspicious of the Nash equilibrium behavior. (1) Do voters follow the same naive intuition as legal scholars and great thinkers? No. They behave strategically.[13] (2) Is the strategic reasoning too complicated for voters in the laboratory to behave according to theory? No. Their strategic behavior is consistent with the Logit version of QRE, which requires even more complicated computation than the Nash equilibrium. (3) Does the fact that the equilibrium is in mixed strategies lead to problems? No. In fact, QRE assumes that behavior is inherently stochastic and accurately predicts the probability distribution of aggregate behavior. Analysis of individual behavior in these experiments uncovers a wide diversity of patterns of individual choice behavior. Aggregate behavior is consistent with the interpretation of mixed strategy equilibria (or QRE) as an "equilibrium in beliefs."

Others have investigated variations on this basic jury model. Hung and Plott (2001) look at majority rule juries that vote sequentially rather than simultaneously and obtain results similar to earlier experiments with simultaneous voting.[14] This provides some support for the theoretical result of Dekel and Piccione (2000) that the order of voting does not matter in this game.

Morton and Williams (1999, 2001) run experiments that are a hybrid of the Hung–Plott sequential elections and earlier experiments described above on multicandidate elections. Just as polls coordinate information for voters, so can sequential elections. Indeed this is exactly the idea behind bandwagons in primary campaigns. Voters of the same party converge on the candidate who seems most likely to win in the general election (*ceteris paribus*). Different voters have different hunches about the electability of the candidates and so the question is whether this information is

---

[12] The model reduces to Nash equilibrium if players are perfect maximizers.
[13] Ladha, Miller, and Oppenheimer 1995 also find evidence of strategic voting in information aggregation experiments.
[14] In these experiments the majority rule Nash equilibrium is sincere voting.

gradually aggregated over sequential elections. Their experiments show that voters do indeed learn from earlier results.[15]

A related set of questions falls under the heading of social learning and information cascades. These information aggregation problems are relevant to political science, economics, sociology, and finance. Using the same information structure as Condorcet juries, a sequence of decision-makers chooses a private action, whose payoff depends on the state of the world. They have a piece of information, and are able to observe the choices of some subset of the other decision-makers. In the canonical version (Bikhchandani, Hirshleifer, and Welch 1992), the decision-makers move in sequence and can observe all the previous choices. In these models, it is easy to have information traps, where after a few moves all decision-makers choose the same action, regardless of their private signal. This happens because the information contained in the actions by a few early movers quickly swamps the information content of the small piece of private information. These are called *herds*, or *information cascades*. Several experiments have been conducted to test whether these information cascades can be observed in the laboratory. Anderson and Holt (1997) do observe such phenomena, even though they only consider sequences of six decision-makers.

However, these herds turn out to be quite fragile. A subsequent experiment by Goeree, Palfrey, and Rogers (2004) looks at longer sequences of twenty and forty decision-makers. They find that while herds do form, they usually collapse very quickly, leading to a cycle of herd formation and collapse. Beliefs apparently do not become stuck, so the information trap seems to be avoided. For example, they find that herds on the "correct" action are more durable than herds on the incorrect action, and as a result there is a tendency for information cascades to "self-correct." Furthermore, they find a decreasing hazard rate: the probability a cascade collapses is a decreasing function of how long it has already lasted. In a companion paper Goeree, Palfrey, and Rogers (2006) prove that these features of the cascade cycles are consistent with the same QRE model that was applied earlier to the jury experiments. In a QRE, there is full information revelation in the limit, as the number of decision-makers becomes large.

5 VOTER TURNOUT AND PARTICIPATION

Fiorina (1990) dubbed it "The paradox that ate rational choice theory." A typical statement of the paradox is the following. In mass elections, if a significant fraction of voters were to turn out to vote, the probability any voter is pivotal is approximately equal to zero. But if the probability of being pivotal is zero, it is irrational to vote because the expected benefits will be outweighed by any tiny cost associated with voting.

---

[15] A somewhat different bandwagon model (more closely aligned with the standard jury set-up) has been studied theoretically by Fey 1997 and Callander 2003.

Hence the fact that we see significant turnout in large elections is inconsistent with rational choice theory. A common (but misguided) inference from this is that rational choice theory is not a useful approach to understanding political participation.

Palfrey and Rosenthal (1983) take issue with the logic of the paradox. They point out that turnout should be modeled as a "participation game," and that zero turnout is *not* an equilibrium of the game, even with rather high voting costs. In fact, as the number of eligible voters becomes large (even in the millions or hundreds of millions), they prove the existence of Nash equilibria where two-party elections are expected to be quite close and in some cases equilibrium turnout can be nearly 100 per cent. Those high turnout equilibria also have some other intuitive properties; for example, the minority party turns out at a higher rate than the majority party.

Schram and Sonnemans (1996) present results from an experiment designed not only to test the Palfrey–Rosenthal theory of turnout, but also to compare turnout in winner-take-all (W) elections to turnout in proportional representation (PR). They studied two-party elections with twelve, fourteen, or twenty-eight voters in each election. The main findings were:

1. Turnout in the early W elections started around 50 per cent, and declined to around 20 per cent by the last election. The decline was steady, and it's not clear whether it would have declined even further with more experience.
2. Turnout in the early PR elections started around 30 per cent, and declined to around 20 per cent in the last two elections. The decline was very gradual in these elections, and it's not clear whether it would have declined even further with more experience.
3. The effects of electorate size and party size are negligible.

One puzzling feature of their data is that initial turnout rates in the PR elections were so much lower than initial turnout rates in the W elections. A possible explanation is coordination failure and multiple equilibria. While both voting rules have multiple equilibria, it is only the W elections for which equilibria exist with *high* turnout rates (above 50 per cent). My interpretation of these experiments is that the severe multiple equilibrium problems identified by the theory present tremendous strategic ambiguity to the subjects and render the data almost useless for evaluating the effect of voting rules and electorate size on turnout. Despite this shortcoming, the experiments provide an interesting source of data for understanding coordination failure and the dynamics of behavior in coordination games.

Levine and Palfrey (2005) take a different approach to addressing comparative statics questions about the effect of electorate size, relative party size, and voting cost on turnout in W elections. Their design follows Palfrey and Rosenthal (1985), where all voters in a party have the same benefit of winning, but each voter has a privately known voting cost that is an independent draw from a commonly known distribution of costs. The equilibria of these games involve cut-point strategies, whereby voters in party j with costs less than a critical cost c_j^* vote and voters with costs greater than c_j^* abstain.

Table 51.1 Comparison of Nash equilibrium turnout rates and data (p = turnout)

N	N_A	N_B	p_A^{Data}	p_A^{Nash}	p_B^{Data}	p_B^{Nash}
3	1	2	.530 (.017)	.537	.593 (.012)	.640
9L	3	6	.436 (.013)	.413	.398 (.009)	.374
9T	4	5	.479 (.012)	.460	.451 (.010)	.452
27L	9	18	.377 (.011)	.270	.282 (.007)	.228
27T	13	14	.385 (.009)	.302	.356 (.009)	.297
51L	17	34	.333 (.011)	.206	.266 (.008)	.171
51T	25	26	.390 (.010)	.238	.362 (.009)	.235

Source: Levine and Palfrey 2005.

They conduct an experiment where electorate size can take on values of 3, 9, 27, and 51 and the cost distribution is chosen so as to avoid multiple equilibria. For each electorate size, N, there are two party size treatments, called *toss-up* (T) and *landslide* (L). In the T treatment, the larger party has $\frac{N+1}{2}$ members and the smaller party has $\frac{N-1}{2}$ members. In the L treatment, the larger party has $\frac{2N}{3}$ members and the smaller party has $\frac{N}{3}$ members. This produces a 4 × 2 design.[16] In all elections, there is a unique Bayesian Nash equilibrium. The comparative statics of the equilibrium are simple and intuitive. There are three main effects.

1. *The size effect.* Turnout should be decreasing in N for both parties.
2. *The competition effect.* Turnout should be higher for both parties in the T treatment than in the L treatment.
3. *The underdog effect.* Turnout should be higher for the smaller party than the larger party, with the exception of $N = 3$, an unusual case where the larger party has higher equilibrium turnout.

The aggregate results are conclusively supportive of the Bayesian Nash equilibrium comparative statics. All differences in turnout rates have the theoretically predicted sign, except for $27T - 51T$, where the differences for both parties are negligible (less than 0.01). Table 51.1 compares the observed turnout rates to the Bayesian Nash equilibrium predictions.

All of the predicted qualitative comparative statics results are observed. The results are also very close quantitatively to the equilibrium predictions, with one caveat. The turnout probabilities are slightly less responsive to the treatment parameters than equilibrium theory predicts. This is particularly noticeable for the largest electorate, where the turnout probabilities are significantly greater than the predicted ones. These attenuated treatment effects are consistent with QRE, which, in particular, predicts *higher* turnout than the Nash predictions for large electorates, and *lower* turnout in the $N = 3$ treatment.

[16] When $N = 3$, the toss-up and landslide treatments are the same.

There are two other kinds of laboratory experiments that are related to the voter turnout question. The first of these is voluntary contribution public good games, where individuals can sacrifice some personal earnings for the benefit of other group members. The most striking results are seen in experiments where it is a dominant strategy to contribute nothing, as in the prisoner's dilemma. This has a long tradition, and the interested reader is referred to the excellent (but now somewhat dated) survey by John Ledyard (1995). This research has identified an array of environmental, institutional, psychological, and sociological factors that influence the degree of cooperation in these games. This variety reflects the many disciplines that have contributed (and continue to contribute) to experimental research in this area.

The second group of related experiments examine threshold public goods games. In these games, there is a single group and each member faces a participation cost. If the total number of participants exceeds a known fixed threshold, then everyone in the group receives a prize, and the value of the prize exceeds the participation cost. These are generalizations of the game of chicken and the stag hunt games, rather than the prisoner's dilemma game. The voter turnout game is only slightly more complicated, with the threshold of each party being endogenously determined by the turnout choices of the other party. Thus it is as if there were a random threshold.[17] A series of experiments by Palfrey and Rosenthal (1991a, 1991b, 1994) study incomplete information versions of these games (analogous to the Levine–Palfrey incomplete information versions of the turnout game) and explore the effects of communication and repeated play. They find that the Nash predictions are fairly accurate, but there is strong evidence that the players have biased beliefs about the contribution behavior of their opponents: they behave as if they think the other members of the group are more generous than is actually the case. Goeree and Holt (2005) investigate a more general class of games that include these threshold games.

6 Concluding Thoughts

The short length of this chapter required leaving some gaping holes in the political economy laboratory experimental literature. To complete the picture of political science experimentation (or at least the "economic" brand of such) would require a much deeper discussion of all the above topics, especially the early experiments on committee bargaining in a spatial setting.

What is on the horizon in the coming decade of laboratory research in political economy? Using history as a guide, laboratory experiments in political economy will follow the current trends in theory. Thus, for example, new experiments relating to *the design of optimal voting procedures in committees* are a good bet, since there has been a flurry of theoretical research on this recently. In fact, we are beginning to see

---

[17] See Suleiman et al. 2001.

some experiments along this line, such as Hortala-Vallve (2004), Casella, Gellman, and Palfrey (2006), and Casella, Palfrey, and Riezman (2005), which explore the behavior of laboratory committees using novel voting methods that allow members to express strength of preference. The research on *deliberation and information transmission in committees with conflicting preferences* (e.g. Austen-Smith and Feddersen 2005; Meirowitz 2004) suggests a wave of experiments that would be a hybrid of the early committee experiments and the more recent experiments on information aggregation in juries. A third set of experiments is suggested by theoretical models of *endogenous candidate entry*. These could blend insights from the earlier experiments on candidate spatial competition and more recent experiments on entry and coordination in abstract games. Fourth, in the study of both politics and economics, there is a new behavioral revolution in theory that relaxes the model of perfect rationality, borrowing liberally from results in experimental psychology. This theoretical approach will surely be complemented and enriched even more by laboratory experiments in the coming years.

References

ANDERSON, L., and HOLT, C. 1997. Information cascades in the laboratory. *American Economic Review*, 87: 797–817.

ANSOLABEHERE, S., and SNYDER, J. M., JR. 2000. Valence politics and equilibrium in spatial election models. *Public Choice*, 103: 327–36.

ARAGONES, E., and PALFREY, T. R. 2002. Mixed equilibrium in a Downsian model with a favored candidate. *Journal of Economic Theory*, 103: 131–61.

———— 2004. The effect of candidate quality on electoral equilibrium: an experimental study. *American Political Science Review*, 98: 77–90.

———— 2005. Spatial competition between two candidates of different quality: the effects of candidate ideology and private information. In *Social Choice and Strategic Decisions*, ed. D. Austen-Smith and J. Duggan. Berlin: Springer.

AUSTEN-SMITH, D., and BANKS, J. 1996. Information aggregation, rationality, and the Condorcet jury theorem. *American Political Science Review*, 90: 34–45.

———— and FEDDERSEN, T. 2005. Deliberation and voting rules. In *Social Choice and Strategic Decisions*, ed. D. Austen-Smith and J. Duggan. Berlin: Springer.

BARON, D. P., and FEREJOHN, J. A. 1989. Bargaining in legislatures. *American Political Science Review*, 83: 1181–206.

BERL, J., McKELVEY, R. D., ORDESHOOK, P. C., and WINER, M. 1976. An experimental test of the core in a simple N-person cooperative nonsidepayment game. *Journal of Conflict Resolution*, 20: 453–79.

BIKHCHANDANI, S., HIRSHLEIFER, D., and WELCH, I. 1992. A theory of fads, fashion, custom, and cultural change as information cascades. *Journal of Political Economy*, 100: 992–1026.

CALLANDER, S. 2003. Bandwagons and momentum in sequential voting. Working paper, Northwestern University.

CAMERER, C. 2004. *Behavioral Game Theory*. Princeton, NJ: Princeton University Press.

CASELLA, A., GELMAN, A., and PALFREY, T. R. 2006. An experimental study of storable votes. *Games and Economic Behavior*.

———— PALFREY, T. R., and RIEZMAN, R. 2005. Minorities and storable votes. Working paper, Princeton University.

COLLIER, K. E., ORDESHOOK, P. C., and WILLIAMS, K. C. 1989. The rationally uninformed electorate: some experimental evidence. *Public Choice*, 60: 3–29.

———— McKELVEY, R. D., ORDESHOOK, P. C., and WILLIAMS, K. C. 1987. Retrospective voting: an experimental study. *Public Choice*, 53: 101–30.

DEKEL, E., and PICCIONE, M. 2000. Sequential voting procedures in symmetric binary agendas. *Journal of Political Economy*, 108: 34–55.

DIERMEIER, D., and MORTON, R. 2005. Experiments in majoritarian bargaining. In *Social Choice and Strategic Decisions*, ed. D. Austen-Smith and J. Duggan. Berlin: Springer.

EAVEY, C., and MILLER, G. 1984a. Bureaucratic agenda control: imposition or bargaining? *American Political Science Review*, 78: 719–33.

———— ———— 1984b. Fairness in majority rule games with a core. *American Journal of Political Science*, 28: 570–86.

ERIKSON, R., and PALFREY, T. R. 2000. Equilibrium effects in campaign spending games: theory and data. *American Political Science Review*, 94: 595–609.

FEDDERSEN, T., and PESENDORFER, W. 1998. Convicting the innocent: the inferiority of unanimous jury verdicts. *American Political Science Review*, 92: 23–36.

FEY, M. 1997. Stability and coordination in Duverger's Law: a formal model of preelection polls and strategic voting. *American Political Science Review*, 91: 135–47.

———— 1998. Information cascades and sequential voting. Working paper, University of Rochester.

FIORINA, M. 1990. Information and rationality in elections. In *Information and Democratic Processes*, ed. J. Ferejohn and J. Kuklinski. Champaign: University of Illinois Press.

———— and PLOTT, C. R. 1978. Committee decisions under majority rule: an experimental study. *American Political Science Review*, 72: 575–98.

FORSYTHE, R., MYERSON, R., RIETZ, T., and WEBER, R. 1993. An experiment on coordination in multi-candidate elections: the importance of polls and election histories. *Social Choice and Welfare*, 10: 223–47.

———— ———— ———— ———— 1996. An experimental study of voting rules and polls in three-way elections. *International Journal of Game Theory*, 25: 355–83.

FRÉCHETTE, G., KAGEL, J., and MORELLI, M. 2005. Gamson's Law versus noncooperative bargaining theory. *Games and Economic Behavior*, 51: 365–90.

GERBER, E., MORTON, R., and RIETZ, T. 1998. Minority representation in multimember districts. *American Political Science Review*, 92: 127–44.

GOEREE, J., and HOLT, C. 2005. An explanation of anomalous behavior in models of political participation. *American Political Science Review*, 99: 201–13.

———— ———— and PALFREY, T. R., 2004. Self-correcting information cascades. Social Science Working Paper 1197, California Institute of Technology, Pasadena.

———— ———— ———— and ROGERS, B. 2006. Social learning with private and common values. *Economic Theory*, 28: 245–64.

GROSECLOSE, T. 2001. A model of candidate location when one candidate has a valence advantage. *American Journal of Political Science*, 45: 862–86.

GUARNASCHELLI, S., McKELVEY, R. D., and PALFREY, T. R. 2000. An experimental study of jury decision rules. *American Political Science Review*, 94: 407–23.

HERZBERG, R., and WILSON, R. 1991. Costly agendas and spatial voting games: theory and experiments on agenda access costs. In *Contemporary Laboratory Research in Political Economy*, ed. T. Palfrey. Ann Arbor: University of Michigan Press.

HORTALA-VALLVE, R. 2004. A first experiment on qualitative voting. Working paper, London School of Economics.

HUNG, A., and PLOTT, C. R. 2001. Information cascades: replication and an extension to majority rule and conformity-rewarding institutions. *American Economic Review*, 91: 1508–20.

ISAAC, R. M., and PLOTT, C. R. 1978. Cooperative game models of the influence of the closed rule in three person, majority rule committees: theory and experiment. In *Game Theory and Political Science*, ed. P. Ordeshook. New York: New York University Press.

KORMENDI, R., and PLOTT, C. R. 1982. Committee decisions under alternative procedural rules. *Journal of Economic Behavior and Organization*, 3: 175–95.

LADHA, K., MILLER, G., and OPPENHEIMER, J. 1995. Information aggregation by majority rule: theory and experiments. Working paper, Washington University, St Louis.

LEDYARD, J. O. 1995. Public goods experiments. In *Handbook of Experimental Economics*, ed. J. Kagel and A. Roth. Princeton, NJ: Princeton University Press.

LEVINE, D., and PALFREY, T. R. 2005. The paradox of voter participation? A laboratory study. Working paper, Princeton University.

MCKELVEY, R. D. 1976. Intransitivities in multidimensional voting models and some implications for agenda control. *Journal of Economic Theory*, 12: 472–82.

——1979. General conditions for global intransitivities in formal voting models. *Econometrica*, 47: 1085–112.

——1991. An experiment test of a stochastic game model of committee bargaining. In *Contemporary Laboratory Research in Political Economy*, ed. T. Palfrey. Ann Arbor: University of Michigan Press.

——and ORDESHOOK, P. C. 1981. Experiments on the core: some disconcerting results for majority rule voting games. *Journal of Conflict Resolution*, 25: 472–82.

——1982. Two-candidate elections without majority rule equilibria: an experimental study. *Simulation and Games*, 13: 311–35.

——1984. Rational expectations in elections: some experimental results based on a multidimensional model. *Public Choice*, 44: 61–102.

——1985a. Elections with limited information: a fulfilled expectations model using contemporaneous poll and endorsement data as information sources. *Journal of Economic Theory*, 36: 55–85.

——1985b. Elections with limited information: a fulfilled expectations model using conemporaneous poll and endorsement data as information sources. *Journal of Economic Theory*, 36: 55–85.

——1990. A decade of experimental research on spatial models of elections and committees. In *Government, Democracy, and Social Choice*, ed. M. J. Hinich and J. Enelow. Cambridge: Cambridge University Press.

——and PAGE, R. T. 2000. An experimental study of the effects of private information in the Coase Theorem. *Experimental Economics*, 3: 187–213.

——and PALFREY, T. R. 1992. An experimental study of the centipede game. *Econometrica*, 60: 803–36.

——1995. Quantal response equilibria for normal form games. *Games and Economic Behavior*, 10: 6–38.

——1998. Quantal response equilibria for extensive form games. *Experimental Economics*, 1: 9–41.

MEIROWITZ, A. 2004. In defense of exclusionary deliberation. Working Paper, Princeton University.

MORTON, R., and WILLIAMS, K. 1999. Information asymmetries and simultaneous versus sequential voting. *American Political Science Review*, 93: 51–67.

—— —— 2001. *Learning by Voting*. Ann Arbor: University of Michigan Press.

MYERSON, R., and WEBER, R. 1993. A theory of voting equilibria. *American Political Science Review*, 87: 102–14.

PALFREY, T. R. 1989. A mathematical proof of Duverger's Law. In *Models of Strategic Choice in Politics*, ed. P. C. Ordeshook. Ann Arbor: University of Michigan Press.

—— and ROSENTHAL, H. 1983. A strategic calculus of voting. *Public Choice*, 41: 7–53.

—— —— 1985. Voter participation and strategic uncertainty. *American Political Science Review*, 79: 62–78.

—— —— 1991a. Testing game-theoretic models of free riding: new evidence on probability bias and learning. In *Contemporary Laboratory Research in Political Economy*, ed. T. Palfrey. Ann Arbor: University of Michigan Press.

—— —— 1991b. Testing for effects of cheap talk in a public goods game with private information. *Games and Economic Behavior*, 3: 183–220.

—— —— 1994. Repeated play, cooperation, and coordination: an experimental study. *Review of Economic Studies*, 61: 545–65.

PLOTT, C. R. 1967. A notion of equilibrium under majority rule. *American Economic Review*, 57: 787–806.

—— 1991. A comparative analysis of direct democracy, two-candidate elections and three-candidate elections in an experimental environment. In *Contemporary Laboratory Research in Political Economy*, ed. T. Palfrey. Ann Arbor: University of Michigan Press.

ROMER, T., and ROSENTHAL, H. 1978. Political resource allocation, controlled agendas, and the status quo. *Public Choice*, 33: 27–45.

ROTH, A. 1995. Bargaining experiments. In *Handbook of Experimental Economics*, ed. J. Kagel and A. Roth. Princeton, NJ: Princeton University Press.

RUBINSTEIN, A. 1982. Perfect equilibrium in a bargaining model. *Econometrica*, 50: 97–109.

SCHOFIELD, N. 1983. Generic instability of majority rule. *Review of Economic Studies*, 50: 695–705.

SCHRAM, A., and SONNEMANS, J. 1996. Voter turnout as a participation game: an experimental investigation. *International Journal of Game Theory*, 25: 385–406.

SMITH, V. L. 1976. Experimental economics: induced value theory. *American Economic Review*, 66: 274–9.

SULEIMAN, R., BUDESCU, D., and RAPOPORT, A. 2001. Provision of step level public goods with uncertain threshold and continuous contribution. *Journal of Group Decision and Negotiation*, 10: 253–74.

WILLIAMS, K. C. 1991. Candidate convergence and information costs in spatial elections: an experiment analysis. In *Contemporary Laboratory Research in Political Economy*, ed. T. Palfrey. Ann Arbor: University of Michigan Press.

CHAPTER 52

THE TOOL KIT OF ECONOMIC SOCIOLOGY

RICHARD SWEDBERG

WHILE the standard definition of economic sociology—*the application of the sociological perspective to economic phenomena*—shows that economic sociologists are primarily interested in analyzing the economy and its main institutions, here I will argue that the field also brings important insights into politics and the interrelationship between the political and economic spheres. This goes for the classics—Marx, Weber, Schumpeter—as well as for recent studies in economic sociology (e.g. Fligstein 1990; Evans 1995; Beckert 2004).

To analyze what happens at the interface between politics and economics is clearly not the exclusive task of economic sociology; it also is something that e.g. political economy does. An important difference, however, is that political economy draws on a type of analysis that is deeply influenced by analytical economics. Political economy, in contrast to contemporary economic sociology, makes use of a variety of economic ideas, such as constitutional economics, game theory, and so on. One may even define the field of political economy as the logic of economics applied to political phenomena.

In this chapter I will argue that economic sociology would do well in some respects to follow the example of political economy and pay more attention to analytical economics and its general approach to what is central to economic behavior. Contemporary economic sociology, I argue, focuses far too much on social relations. What is wrong with this approach is that it disregards the importance of *interests* or

---

* For helpful comments I thank the editors of *The Oxford Handbook of Political Economy*.

the forces that drive human behavior, not least in the economy, but also in the political sphere. What needs to be done—and this will be the red thread throughout this chapter—is to *combine* social relations and interests in one and the same analysis. If we do this, I argue, we may be able to unite some of the basic insights from economics, with some of the basic insights from sociology (e.g. Swedberg 2003).

As opposed to modern economics, economic sociology does not have a core of basic concepts and ideas, welded together over a long period of time. Instead economic sociology, mirroring sociology itself, consists of a number of competing perspectives, some more coherent than others. Many economic sociologists, for example, draw on a social constructivist perspective, others draw on a Weberian perspective; some follow Mark Granovetter in emphasizing embeddedness, while still others follow Pierre Bourdieu in approaching the analysis of the economy with the concepts of field, habitus, and different types of capital. The reader who is interested in an introduction to these different perspectives is referred to *The Handbook of Economic Sociology* (Smelser and Swedberg 1994; 2nd edition 2005). In what follows I shall first discuss two of the most important concepts in modern economic sociology—*embeddedness* (including networks) and *field*. I will then proceed to a discussion of two concepts that I argue should be at the center of contemporary economic sociology: *a sociological concept of interest* and *an interest-based concept of institutions*.

1 Embeddedness (Including Networks)

The most famous concept in today's economic sociology is by far that of *embeddedness*. While the term itself can be found in the work of Karl Polanyi, it was rarely used by him and had to wait till the 1980s and Mark Granovetter to be thrust to prominence. While the centrality of embeddedness to what has become known as the "new economic sociology" (mid-1980s–) is beyond doubt, its analytical status is, on the other hand, contested. While some see it as a useful tool with which to show what is distinctive about the sociological approach, a number of economic sociologists also question its usefulness.

One reason why the concept of embeddedness is so controversial may well be its many meanings, which range all the way from simply being a slogan that proclaims the superiority of the sociological approach over the economic approach, to a more analytical vision, as in Granovetter's work (Granovetter 1985; cf. Granovetter 1992). Polanyi used embeddedness as part of his attack on liberalism and market-oriented approaches more generally. The first half of his argument is well known: in pre-capitalist society the economy is integrated into (or embedded in) the rest of society, especially in its political and religious institutions; but with the advent of capitalism the economy was separated out and has come to dominate the rest of society. The second half of Polanyi's argument is less known, but follows logically from its first half: for society to become healthy again, the economy has to be re-embedded or integrated into society. Political and other collective institutions have to acquire precedence over the market.

Through a much cited article in the mid-1980s Granovetter introduced a different and analytically more useful concept of embeddedness (Granovetter 1985). He first of all challenged the political dimension of Polanyi's ideas by arguing that a pre-capitalist economy was just as embedded as a capitalist economy is, in the sense that both are *social* or embedded in the social structure. Secondly, he brought analytical sharpness to the concept of embeddedness by insisting that all economic actions are embedded in *networks of social relations*. There is no embeddedness of the economy in general; all economic actions take an interpersonal expression; and thanks to network theory, this expression can be traced with precision.

One may finally also speak of a third way in which the term embeddedness is used. This may well be the most popular (and least interesting) meaning, since embeddedness here is simply synonymous with "social." The general hostility that sociologists feel towards economic analysis may well be at the root of this usage. Whatever the reason, the analytical content of this meaning is close to zero.

Critics of the embeddedness approach in its strongest version (that is, in the version that Granovetter represents) have pointed out that it ignores the political and cultural dimensions of society; that it is unable to handle economic phenomena at the macro level; and that the term "embeddedness" is inadequate and confusing as a metaphor (e.g. Zukin and DiMaggio 1990; Nee and Ingram 1998; Krippner 2001). To this should be added that the embeddedness perspective does not single out and theorize the role of interest, and thereby runs the risk of attaching too much importance to the role of social relations in economic and political life.

What nonetheless makes the concept of embeddedness quite useful is its close links to network theory. This type of method, which has become popular in current economic sociology, provides the analyst with a metric to analyze social interactions, including economic ones (for a technical introduction, see e.g. Wasserman and Faust 1994). Through its reliance on a method with a strikingly visual dimension, network theory also provides the researcher with a tool that can quickly communicate complex social relations.

It is, for example, quite easy to communicate the gist of Granovetter's famous thesis of weak ties with the help of a graph: an actor who is connected through a casual link to one member in many different groups (weak ties) is in a much better position to acquire information than an actor who has long-standing links to each of the members in a single group (strong ties; Granovetter 1973).

A special mention should also be made of a European version of networks theory, so-called actor-network-theory (ANT), which is considerably less technical than conventional networks theory of the type that is popular in the United States (e.g. Callon 1989; Law and Hassard 1999). The basic idea here is that not only individuals and firms can be actors but also objects. What is meant with this paradoxical statement is that the analysis must not exclusively focus on social relations but also include objects; and the rationale for this is that objects can be part of social interactions or steer social interaction in some special direction. As examples one can mention the way that, say, surveillance technology enables supervisors to track employees or how an assembly line presupposes that the workers coordinate their actions in a certain way.

Conventional networks theory covers a host of different topics. One of these has to do with interlocks or the links between corporations that are created when directors are members of more than one board. While big hopes were initially attached to this type of study, it has by now been realized that interlocks do not automatically translate into control or co-optation, but rather constitute potentially important conduits of communication between corporations—which in some cases may mean control or co-optation (Mizruchi 1996, 2004).

Firms can also be connected in the form of business groups—a topic that has been pioneered by economic sociologists and by Granovetter in particular (1994, 2005). Business groups can be defined as "sets of legally separate firms bound together in persistent formal and/or informal ways" (Granovetter 2005, 1). They are located somewhere on a spectrum between firms that are bound together by short-term strategic alliances and firms that are legally to be considered a single entity. Business groups play a major role in many economies around the world, such as India, Japan, China, and Taiwan. Their absence in the United States Granovetter ascribes to antitrust legislation.

Networks theory is a handy tool for analyzing not only corporate actors and their interactions but also individuals. Ronald Burt, for example, has suggested that the entrepreneur can be conceptualized as a person who connects two groups of people (say, sellers and buyers) who otherwise would be disconnected (Burt 1993). In his capacity as a middleman, the entrepreneur straddles a so-called "structural hole," in Burt's terminology. Economic sociologists have also shown that consumers not only use their personal networks to gather information about buyers and sellers, but also select buyers and sellers from their personal networks in certain situations (DiMaggio and Louch 1998). Consumers use their friends and acquaintances in particular when it comes to acquiring second-hand cars and real estates where no realtor is involved.

The concept of embeddedness can be used to analyze what happens at the interface of the economy and politics. Polanyi, for example, developed the concept of embeddedness precisely to give voice to his discontent with the way that the economic sphere and the political sphere are separated from each other in capitalist society. Granovetter's concept of embeddedness is, however, considerably more useful than Polanyi's ideas on this score and also less normative. The reason for their usefulness has much to do with the close link between embedddedness and networks analysis in Granovetter's work.

As an example of how a networks approach to embeddedness can be of help in analyzing the interaction of economics and politics, one can mention *The Structure of Corporate Political Action* by Mark Mizruchi (1992). Rejecting the assumption that the business community is either united (elite theory) or that it contains many divergent interests (pluralist theory), Mizruchi argues that one should instead treat business unity as a dependent variable. Drawing on a sample of contributions by large manufacturing corporations to PACs in 1980, he shows that firms that are connected to one another via financial intermediaries, as well as firms that are economically interdependent, are more likely to be in agreement with one another on political questions.

2 THE FIELD

After embeddedness, the concept of *field* may well be the most important concept in contemporary economic sociology. This term denotes a distinct area of social space, in which all the relevant actors are influenced by the overall structure. This definition is admittedly somewhat vague, and just like embeddedness, the concept of field has its critics.

There currently exist two versions of the concept of the field: one that has emerged in the sociology of organizations in the United States, and another that has Pierre Bourdieu as its author. While they overlap to some extent, these two versions also differ on important points. Sociologists of organization basically use the concept of field in the sense of an *organizational field*—that is, to analyze phenomena in social life that can be conceptualized as a number of similar and related organizations. A field, from this perspective, typically denotes a number of organizations that belong together, either by virtue of directly interacting with one another or because they take each other into account in some other way. To cite a standard text in organizational sociology: "by *organizational field* we mean those organizations that, in the aggregate, constitute a recognized area of institutional life: key suppliers, resource and product consumers, regulatory agencies, and other organizations that produce similar services or products" (Powell and DiMaggio 1991, 64–5). Examples of fields include industries, professions, and nations.

For Bourdieu, in contrast, a field is not so much a middle-range concept as an integral part of his general theory of society. The field, in all brevity, constitutes together with the concepts of *habitus* and different types of capital (social capital, symbolic capital, and so on) the basic building stones of Bourdieu's theory of society. There exist a huge variety of fields in society, according to Bourdieu, such as the fields of art, photography, literature, the economy, an industry, a firm, and so on (e.g. Bourdieu and Wacquant 1992, 94–115).

The main function of the concept of field, Bourdieu argues, is to represent *the structure* of some part of society. This structure is primarily important in that it assigns a specific place to each actor; it also exerts pressure on the actor to remain in his or her position. Each field is centered around a specific interest; and the actors in a field all basically pursue the same interest—be it prestige in the field of art, market share in an industry, or political power in a democracy.

One advantage with the concept of field, according to its advocates, is that it is not restricted to what happens in direct interactions. If you rely primarily on networks and the concept of embeddedness, you are restricted to actual interactions, and thereby miss the impact of the structure of the field (e.g. Bourdieu 2000, 242). But it is also well understood in sociology that it is hard to trace the exact impact of a field, and that the social mechanisms that translate the power of the overall structure into pressure on the actor are often unknown. Even the advocates of "field theory" agree that this is the case, though they emphasize that the positive outweighs the negative (e.g. Martin 2003).

Can the concept of the field be of help in addressing issues at the interface of the economy and politics? Its advocates in economic sociology say "yes." While they acknowledge that politics constitutes its own distinct field in modern society, just as the economy does, they also note that the political field impinges on the economic field in important ways. As an example of this, one may mention Bourdieu's argument that the French state has deeply influenced the country's construction industry by introducing various loans for private home ownership (Bourdieu 2005).

While Bourdieu may be correct that the concept of field is of help in establishing the important influence that the French state has had on the private building sector, it is not difficult to think of other theoretical approaches that can accomplish the same. It is, on the other hand, considerably more difficult to duplicate the results that Neil Fligstein gets when he uses the concept of field in *The Transformation of Corporate Control* (1990). Fligstein's study is centered around an analysis of the thousand largest corporations in the United States from 1880 to the 1980s; and he basically attempts to show how their strategies for making a profit have shifted over the years in response to changing political and legal circumstances.

To some extent Fligstein uses the concept of field in a way that is reminiscent of Bourdieu. He similarly argues, for example, that most of the firms in a field look to the most powerful firms as their reference group. But Fligstein also adds a dimension of his own to the concept of field, namely that each field is structured in accordance with the world-view of the leading firms—what Fligstein terms their "conception of control." This world-view lays out what a successful strategy for making a profit should look like and also how competition can be controlled.

According to Fligstein, there have been four periods with different conceptions of control during the last century in the United States; and these are: "direct control of competition" (1880–1900), "manufacturing control" (1900–25), "sales and marketing control" (1925–55), and "finance control" (1955–80s). During the first period, profit was made and markets were held stable through direct control of one's competitors, e.g. with the help of trusts. During the second period, the emphasis was instead on controlling the price through power over the whole production process. During the third period, the way to exert control shifted to market share; and from the mid-1950s and onwards, the firm has increasingly been seen as a money-making machine. Today "the shareholder value conception of control" is dominant (e.g. Fligstein and Shin 2004). According to this conception of control, the firm is primarily seen as a way of making profit for the shareholder.

What is interesting about Fligstein's type of analysis for a discussion of the interface of the polity and the economy is that the US state, including the legal system, has often played a key role in changing the conception of control. Direct control of competition, for example, was stopped by the Sherman Antitrust Act (1890) and the Clayton Act (1914); while it was the Depression that put an end to the attempt to control competition and profits via the price. Sales and marketing control was ended by the Celler–Kefauver Act (1950), in combination with some other factors; and the finance conception of control has laid the foundation for the current shareholder value conception of control through the termination of the Glass–Seagall Act (1933) and more generally through the deregulation efforts by the Reagan administration and onwards.

3 A Sociological Concept of Interest

While the concepts of embeddedness and field are central to contemporary economic sociology, this is not the case with the concept of interest. Sociologists typically ignore this concept and happily leave it to the economists. I take a different stand on this issue: in order to advance economic sociology as well as set it on a sound foundation, the concept of interests must be explicitly introduced into the sociological analysis.

The first task in an economic-sociological analysis should be to figure out which interests are involved and how the actors attempt to realize their interests, typically with the help of social relations. To do this, I argue, you need *a sociological concept of interest*, and such a concept is somewhat different from the concept of interest that is used in mainstream economics. The motivation for starting out with interests is nevertheless the same: you first of all need to establish the basic motives of the actor or the basic forces that drive the actor.

The emphasis in the type of economic sociology that I advocate should not be on rational choice as *consistency* (to speak with Amartya Sen), but on rational choice as *interest realization* (Sen 1986). What is of primary importance is the existence of an interest and that the actor attempts to realize this interest—not that the actor knows how to realize his or her interest or that the actor does so in a rational way. Sen's formal terms for the former type of analysis is "the interest *consistency approach*," and for the latter "the *interest correspondence approach*." Another reason why the interest consistency approach may be less suitable for economic sociology is that the actor's perception of his or her interest is in principle an empirical question. While an actor can be in a position to order his or her preferences in a consistent order in certain situations, this may not be the case in others.

While economics and sociology share the insight that interests are essential to the analysis of society, they nonetheless differ on a few points. For one thing, economics tends to take only one type of interests into account, and that is economic interests (or, alternatively, cast non-economic interests directly in the mold of how they treat economic interests). Economics also has a tradition of operating with a non-sociological concept of interest (which it is currently trying to overcome). Both points need some explication.

Economists tend to cast all interests in the same mold—namely, that of economic interest—and to follow the interest consistency approach, while economic sociologists who favor an interest-based type of analysis proceed in another way. Different types of interests, they argue, cannot be analyzed using the same metric. The sociologist has to proceed empirically and in particular investigate how the actors perceive their different interests. A religious interest, for example, can be considerably stronger than an economic interest in certain situations and so can a political or an erotic interest. The nature of the interest must not be assumed before the analysis, but should be determined through research. While interests are sometimes based in human nature, they are only acknowledged and negotiated in society—in their social form—and it is this social form that must be established empirically.

Interests can only be realized through social relations. While the role of social relations in explaining economic phenomena is explicitly denied in early neoclassical economics, and while it is increasingly acknowledged in today's mainstream economics, it has been at the core of economic sociology from the very beginning. Many difficult problems no doubt arise for sociologists by taking this position, and one way to approach these would be to make the assumption that interests drive actions, while social relations give them their direction. Or to paraphrase Weber's well-known formulation:

Not social relations, but material and ideal interests, directly govern men's conduct. Yet very frequently the social structures that have been created by social relations have, like switchmen, determined the tracks along which action has been pushed by the dynamic of interest. (cf. Weber 1946, 280)

One example that can illustrate how the perspective of a sociological concept of interest may be of help in analyzing problems at the intersection of politics and the economy can be found in Weber's theory of *political capitalism* (see in particular Weber's studies of antiquity in e.g. Weber 1976; cf. Love 1991). In various writings Weber contrasts what he terms rational capitalism to other forms of capitalism, especially traditional capitalism and political capitalism. In traditional capitalism, economic interests can only be realized through accepted and long-standing forms of interaction (such as traditional work forms, non-dynamic competition, slow-moving markets, and so on). In rational capitalism, economic interests are primarily realized through impersonal markets, with the state in the background, guaranteeing the rules of the market. Finally, in political capitalism profit is made through contacts in the state or under the direct umbrella of the state's intervention in another country, as in classical imperialism. The result is a form of capitalism that is prone to corruption and closely bound to the fortunes of the political power.

Another example of how actors typically need to take social relations into account in order to realize their interests can be found in a classic in economic sociology, Stewart Macaulay's "Non-contractual relations in business" (1963). In a preliminary study based on interviews with representatives for manufacturing firms in Wisconsin, Macaulay found that businessmen often prefer *not* to go to court when a contract has been broken. The reason for this is that going to court would once and for all destroy the relationship between the two parties. Subsequent studies have confirmed Macaulay's findings, even if the decision not to go to court may not be as common as Macaulay had found in 1963.

4 AN INTEREST-BASED CONCEPT OF INSTITUTIONS

The concept of institution is absolutely indispensable to economic sociology. Even though this concept is obviously not unique to economic sociology, it is well worth discussing in this chapter since it is increasingly being realized in the different social sciences that institutions play a key role in society. Moreover, a new approach to the concept of institutions is currently being developed in economic sociology—what may be termed *an interest-based concept of institutions*.

Sociologists have emphasized the role of institutions ever since the birth of sociology; and the relevant sociological literature on this concept is consequently enormous. Instead of providing an overview (see e.g. Powell and DiMaggio 1991; Stinchcombe 1997), I shall only make the following summary observation. While early sociologists tended to restrict the concept of institution to central aspects of society (such as politics, the economy, and the family), recent sociology tends to use it in a much broader sense. According to the view of so-called new institutionalism in sociology, pretty much anything constitutes an institution, including a dance and a handshake (see e.g. Jepperson 1991). Another key feature in this approach is the emphasis on the role of culture, sense-making, and the diffusion of distinct models of behavior. New institutionalism downplays the concept of interest and instead focuses on those aspects of institutions that are not related to interests (e.g. DiMaggio 1988). It is argued, for example, that firms are not run in a rational manner; firms just want to appear rational since rationality is an important value in contemporary Western culture (e.g. Meyer and Rowan 1977; cf. Powell and DiMaggio 1991).

The new institutionalist view, as I see it, takes the analytical edge out of the concept of institution, and is therefore of limited use. For the concept of institutions to be useful, I argue, it should be restricted to areas of society where interests come into play in an important and direct manner—such as politics, the economy, and the family. The strength of institutions comes precisely from the fact that they channel interests or, to put it differently, that they present dominant models for how interests can be realized. These models are also typically seen as legitimate or they would not be stable.

From this perspective, institutions are typically enforced by law because of their centrality to society. They may be consciously designed—say, through a constitution—but usually develop in a gradual and largely unintended manner, along the lines first suggested by Menger and Hayek (e.g. Menger 1892; Hayek 1982). Since institutions regulate areas of society that are of great importance to the individuals, they are often contested. Rather than directly reflect interests, they may reflect the outcome of struggles over interests.

Together with my colleague Victor Nee, I suggest the following definition of an institution:

An institution may be conceptualized as a dominant system of interrelated informal and formal elements—customs, shared beliefs, norms, and rules—which actors orient their actions to, when they pursue their interests.[1]

In this view, institutions are dominant social structures that provide a conduit for social and collective action by facilitating and structuring the interests of actors. It follows from this interest-related definition of institutions that institutional change involves not simply remaking the formal rules in the various centers of society, but the realignment of interests, norms, and power. Institutions that are seen as legitimate are, to repeat, stronger than institutions that are directly based on, say, force or interest.

The concept of institutions that is advocated here is especially close to that of Douglass North, and Victor Nee and I advocate that economic sociology adopt what we term an institutionalist perspective in its analysis (e.g. North 1990). North's distinction between institutions as rules, on the one hand, and organizations as players, on the other, is especially useful to our mind; we also agree with North that institutions are related to incentive structures.

But we are also of the opinion that one may proceed further than North on a few crucial points. One of these is, to repeat, that the concept of interest should be at the very center of what we mean by institution; another is that the current literature on institutions makes a much too sharp distinction between actor and structure—to the detriment of the understanding of institutions. I shall briefly elaborate on both of these points.

Interests represent the basic forces that drive the individual, and must for this reason also be at the very center of the concept of institution. One way of prioritizing interests in this context is to conceptualize institutions as dominant models for how interests should be realized. The individual who wants to realize her interests will, following this approach, typically orient her actions to the relevant institution; meaning by this that if she wants to realize her interests she will have to follow the general rules or prescriptions for how to behave. The individual may also choose *not* to follow the institutional model, in which case sanctions will typically occur. By emphasizing the independence of the actor (through the notion of "orienting oneself to rules," rather than simply "following rules"), we proceed in the spirit of methodological individualism.

When one presents the concept of institution as a dominant model for how to realize interests, it is important not to emphasize the element of model to the point that the individual disappears. The reason for this is that society does not consist of models or rules but of ongoing activities, and similarly there are no institutions per se but only *institutions in action*. This means that ongoing institutions are invested with the power that comes from a number of individuals acting out their patterns of behavior in an effort to realize certain interests, and it is precisely *this* that gives

---

[1] Victor Nee and I are currently developing an interest-related approach to comparative institutional analysis at the Center for the Study of Economy and Society at Cornell University (see www.economyandsociety.org).

institutions their enormous force and importance in society. If institutions are resistant to change, it is not only because models of behavior are hard to change because of inertia (an important topic in its own right), but because they are invested with the force that comes from interests in action.

Can this interest-based concept of institution add to the understanding of what goes on at the intersection of politics and economics? The answer is in principle "yes," even though it should be emphasized that this concept is currently under construction and has not yet been applied to concrete cases in a stringent manner. Nonetheless, it would seem clear that introducing interests into the sociological analysis of the interaction between politics and economics will first of all augment its realism, primarily by emphasizing the strength of the interests involved and the related difficulty in changing ongoing institutions.

By way of an illustration of why it is important to have an interest-centered concept of institutions, as opposed to one that is exclusively centered around rules, one can take the current discussion in the United States about the structure of boards of public corporations. What is at issue is what the new rules or models for behavior should look like. Who should be allowed to nominate new board members—the CEO, existing board members, and/or shareholders? Who should be allowed to be a member of the compensation committee and the audit committee, and what should the relationship of this member be to the CEO and the board? In order to understand how these questions will be answered, however, it is not enough to focus exclusively on the rules, as many theories of institutions suggest that we do; the interests of the various actors must also be taken into account. We would, for example, expect that the CEO, who today is typically the head of the board and controls its members, will clash with shareholders and actors like the SEC, New York Stock Exchange, and Nasdaq, who are all currently arguing for having a majority of independent board members.

5 Concluding Remarks: Continuing Role of the Classics in Economic Sociology

In the main text of this chapter I have focused on what I consider to be the two most important concepts in contemporary economic sociology (embeddedness, field). I have also discussed two new concepts in economic sociology that I consider crucial for this field to move ahead (the sociological concept of interest, the interest-based concept of institutions). As emphasized in the introduction, there also exist several other important concepts that are part of economic sociology, and something needs to be said about these. This is particularly the case with some of the concepts that are associated with the early figures in this field. The main reason for drawing the reader's attention to these is that they have proven their usefulness.

One of these classical concepts is Max Weber's concept of economic-social action, which is introduced and discussed in Weber's main theoretical text on economic sociology, to be found in *Economy and Society*. This text is a book-length chapter entitled "Sociological categories of economic action," which is still unsurpassed in the literature on economic sociology for its theoretical sophistication as well as comprehensiveness (Weber 1978, 63–211; cf. Swedberg 1998 for an introduction to these ideas). What Weber wanted to accomplish with the concept of economic-social action was to construct a sociological equivalent to the concept of economic action in standard economic analysis. In Weber's days, it should be noted, mainstream economics of the analytical type did not theorize the social dimension of economic action, and Weber's concept of economic-social action should be judged from this perspective.

In constructing the social dimension of economic action, Weber drew to some extent on the insights of the institutionalists, but he was also careful to take the analytical economics into account. He essentially defined economic-social action as a type of action which (1) has utility as its goal and (2) is also oriented to other actors (Weber 1978, 4, 63). What makes this type of economic action "social," Weber explicates, is the fact that economic action is *oriented to other actors*. Similar to what game theory several decades later would suggest, an economic relationship can be conceptualized, according to Weber, as a situation in which two economic actors orient their actions to one another.

That Weber's concept of economic-social action can be applied to the intersection of economics and politics is clear from the fact that a social action can be oriented to several different actors simultaneously. In a complex market deal, for example, the two parties may not only orient their behavior to one another but also to the legal order, as represented by their lawyers. Weber was also the first to insist that what rational capitalism first and foremost needs from the legal system is predictable action; arbitrary action by a ruler is incompatible with large and long-term investments.

A second set of classical concepts that are frequently used in today's economic sociology are *reciprocity–redistribution–exchange*, as introduced by Polanyi (Polanyi et al. 1971). These three ways of organizing the economy, it has increasingly been realized, are especially handy in analyzing different economic systems. There is also the fact that each concrete economy is typically a mixture of these three types. The modern capitalist economy, for example, is centered around the corporate sector, but also has a state-dominated sector and a household economy. Of Polanyi's three categories, redistribution is clearly the one that is the most useful when it comes to analyzing the role of the state in the economy.

All in all, economic sociology, while lacking a cohesive theoretical core of the type that mainstream economics has, nonetheless has at its disposal a number of concepts that help untangle the impact of social relations and social structures. In particular, as argued here, these concepts can be used to approach the interactions between the political and the economic spheres in modern society. What is primarily needed to advance economic sociology beyond its current state is to make room for the concept of interest, to make it easier to get at the forces that drive the economic actions of individual actors.

REFERENCES

BECKERT, J. 2004. *Unverdientes Vermögen: Soziologie des Erbrechts*. Berlin: Campus Verlag.
BOURDIEU, P. 2005. *Social Structures of the Economy*. Cambridge: Polity Press.
—— and WACQUANT, L. 1992. *An Invitation to Reflexive Sociology*. Chicago: University of Chicago Press.
BURT, R. 1993. The social structure of competition. Pp. 65–103 in *Explorations in Economic Sociology*, ed. R. Swedberg. New York: Russell Sage Foundation.
CALLON, M. 1989. Society in the making: the study of technology as a tool for sociological analysis. Pp. 83–103 in *The Social Construction of Technological Systems*, ed. W. Bijker et al. Cambridge, Mass.: MIT Press.
DIMAGGIO, P. 1988. Interest and agency in institutional theory. Pp. 3–21 in *Institutional Patterns and Organizations*, ed. L. Zucker. Cambridge: Ballinger.
—— and LOUCH, H. 1998. Socially embedded consumer transactions: for what kind of purchases do people most often use networks? *American Sociological Review*, 63: 619–37.
EVANS, P. 1995. *Embedded Autonomy: States and Industrial Transformation*. Princeton, NJ: Princeton University Press.
FLIGSTEIN, N. 1990. *The Transformation of Corporate Control*. Cambridge, Mass.: Harvard University Press.
—— and SHIN, T. 2004. Shareholder value and the transformation of the American economy: 1984–2001. Working Paper Series 19, Center for the Study of Economy and Society, Cornell University.
GRANOVETTER, M. 1973. The strength of weak ties. *American Journal of Sociology*, 78: 1360–80.
—— 1985. Economic action and social structure: the problem of embeddedness. *American Journal of Sociology*, 91: 481–510.
—— 1992. Economic institutions as social constructions: a framework for analysis. *Acta Sociologi*, 35: 3–11.
—— 1994. Business groups. Pp. 453–75 in *The Handbook of Economic Sociology*, ed. N. Smelser and R. Swedberg. New York: Russell Sage Foundation and Princeton University Press.
—— 2005. Business groups. Pp. 429–50 in *The Handbook of Economic Sociology*, 2nd expanded edn., ed. N. Smelser and R. Swedberg. New York: Russell Sage Foundation and Princeton University Press.
HAYEK, F. 1982. *Law, Legislation and Liberty*. London: Routledge.
JEPPERSON, R. 1991. Institutions, institutional effects, and institutionalism. Pp. 143–63 in *The New Institutionalism in Organizational Analysis*, ed. W. Powell and P. DiMaggio. Chicago: University of Chicago Press.
KRIPPNER, G. 2001. The elusive market: embeddedness and the paradigm of economic sociology. *Theory and Society*, 30: 775–810.
LAW, J., and HASSARD, J. (eds.). 1999. *Actor Network Theory and After*. Oxford: Blackwell.
LOVE, J. 1991. *Antiquity and Capitalism: Max Weber and the Sociological Foundations of Roman Civilization*. London: Routledge.
MACAULAY, S. 1963. Non-contractual relations in business: a preliminary study. *American Sociological Review*, 28: 55–67.
MARTIN, J. L. 2003. What is field theory? *American Journal of Sociology*, 109: 1–49.
MENGER, C. 1892. On the origin of money. *Economic Journal*, 2: 39–55.
MEYER, J., and ROWAN, B. 1977. Institutionalized organizations: formal structure as myth and ceremony. *American Journal of Sociology*, 83: 340–63.

Mizruchi, M. 1992. *The Structure of Corporate Political Action: Interfirm Relations and their Consequences*. Cambridge, Mass.: Harvard University Press.

——1996. What do interlocks do? An analysis, critique, and assessment of research on interlocking directorates. *Annual Review of Sociology*, 22: 271–98.

——2004. Berle and Means revisited: the governance and power of large U.S. corporations. *Theory and Society*, 33: 579–617.

Nee, V., and Ingram, P. 1998. Embeddedness and beyond: institutions, exchange, and social structure. Pp. 19–45 in *The New Institutionalism in Sociology*, ed. M. Brinton and V. Nee. New York: Russell Sage Foundation.

North, D. 1990. *Institutions, Institutional Change and Economic Performance*. Cambridge: Cambridge University Press.

Polanyi, K., et al. (eds.) 1971. *Trade and Markets in Early Empires*. Chicago: Henry Regnery.

Powell, W., and DiMaggio, P. (eds.) 1991. *The New Institutionalism in Organizational Analysis*. Chicago: University of Chicago Press.

Sen, A. 1986. Rationality, interest, and identity. Pp. 343–53 in *Development, Democracy, and the Art of Trespassing*, ed. A. Foxley et al. Notre Dame, Ind.: University of Notre Dame Press.

Smelser, N., and Swedberg, R. (eds.) 1994. *The Handbook of Economic Sociology*. New York: Russell Sage Foundation and Princeton University Press.

—— —— (eds.) 2005. *The Handbook of Economic Sociology*, 2nd expanded edn. New York: Russell Sage Foundation and Princeton University Press.

Stinchcombe, A. 1997. On the virtues of the old institutionalism. *Annual Review of Sociology*, 23: 1–18.

Swedberg, R. 1998. *Max Weber and the Idea of Economic Sociology*. Princeton, NJ: Princeton University Press.

——2003. *Principles of Economic Sociology*. Princeton, NJ: Princeton University Press.

Wasserman, S., and Faust, K. 1994. *Social Network Analysis: Methods and Applications*. Cambridge, Mass.: Cambridge University Press.

Weber, M. 1946. *From Max Weber*, ed. H. Gerth and C. Wright Mills. New York: Oxford University Press.

——1976. *The Agrarian Sociology of Ancient Civilizations*. London: New Left Books.

——1978. *Economy and Society: An Outline of Interpretive Sociology*. Berkeley: University of California Press.

Zukin, S., and DiMaggio, P. 1990. Introduction. Pp. 1–36 in *Structures of Capital*, ed. S. Zukin and P. DiMaggio. Cambridge, Mass.: Cambridge University Press.

CHAPTER 53

THE EVOLUTIONARY BASIS OF COLLECTIVE ACTION

SAMUEL BOWLES
HERBERT GINTIS

1 INTRODUCTION

MANY aspects of political behavior have been illuminated by standard models in which political actors maximize self-interested preferences. The works of Downs (1957), Buchanan and Tullock (1962), Buchanan, Tollison, and Tullock (1980), and Becker (1983), as well as those inspired by these seminal contributions, have contributed to our understanding of voter, party, and policy preferences, interest group politics, rent-seeking, coalition formation, bargaining, and other aspects of political behavior. Using this framework, works on electoral support for the welfare state (Bénabou and Ok 2001; Moene and Wallerstein 2002), informal enforcement of contracts (Greif 1994; Greif, Milgrom, and Weingast 1994), the efficiency of democratic governance (Wittman 1989), nationalism (Breton et al. 1995), and ethnic conflict (Varshney 2003) have produced important and sometimes surprising insights.

* We would like to thank the John D. and Catherine T. MacArthur Foundation and the Behavioral Sciences Program of the Santa Fe Institute for financial support.

Yet as Ostrom (1998) and others have pointed out, a number of critical aspects of political behavior remain difficult to explain within this framework. These include the fact that people bother to vote at all, and electoral support for costly redistributive programs from which the voter concerned is unlikely to benefit and for which he will certainly pay additional taxes (Luttmer 2001; Fong 2001; Fong, Bowles, and Gintis 2004), and many forms of political violence (Stern 2003). Among the more striking examples of the shortcomings of the standard model is the large class of political behavior that takes the form of voluntary contribution to public goods. Included is participation in joint political activities and other forms of collective action (Moore 1978; Wood 2003; Scott 1976), the adherence to social norms (Young and Burke 2001; Andreoni, Erard, and Feinstein 1998), and the punishment of those violating social norms (Mahdi 1986; Harding 1978; Boehm 1993; Wiessner 2003).

When one is motivated to bear personal costs to help or to hurt others we say that one has *other-regarding* preferences, meaning that affecting the states experienced by someone other than oneself is part of one's motivations. Unlike the conventional self-regarding preferences of *Homo economicus*, social preferences are other regarding. Generosity towards others and punishing those who violate norms are commonly motivated by other-regarding preferences.

We use the term self-regarding rather than "selfish" to describe the standard assumptions about preferences to avoid the circularity arising from the fact that all uncoerced actions are motivated by preferences and hence might confusingly be termed selfish, leaving only those actions that violate one's preference ordering to be called unselfish (but which would better be called non-rational). To explain behavior, both other-regarding and self-regarding preferences must be transitive, and when they are (as we assume) the actions they motivate are rational in the strict sense typically adopted in economics and decision theory. The common designation of generous behavior as "irrational" is based on a gratuitous conflation of rationality and self-regarding preferences.

We explore two problems in the study of the political behaviors supporting collective action. The first concerns the view frequently advanced by economists and biologists that cooperative behaviors can be fully explained on the basis of self-interested motivations, once one takes account of the repeated nature of interactions and the degree of genetic relatedness among members of a cooperating group. We show that repeated interactions and kin-based altruism, while strong influences on behavior in many settings, do not provide an adequate account of the forms of cooperation observed in natural and experimental settings.

These and other types of political behavior are based on preferences that include a concern for the well-being of others and a taste not only for fairness but also for retribution. We review recent behavioral experiments documenting the variety and extent of these so called social preferences and the manner in which the existence of even a minority of individuals with social preferences can dramatically affect group behavior (see Bowles and Gintis 2005*b*; Gintis et al. 2005; and Henrich et al. 2004 for a more extensive review of this evidence).

The second is the puzzle of how these social preferences could have evolved by means of genetic transmission and natural selection, or cultural learning and socialization, or both. The puzzle arises because the political behaviors motivated by social preferences are often altruistic in the biological sense—of conferring gains on others in one's group while entailing costs—and altruistic behaviors will be disadvantaged in most evolutionary processes that favor higher payoff types. Our treatment of these topics is necessarily cursory, drawing extensively on work presented more fully in Bowles and Gintis (2007), Gintis et al. (2005), and Henrich et al. (2004).

2 The Cooperative Species

Cooperation among humans is unique in nature, extending to a large number of unrelated individuals and taking a vast array of forms. By cooperation we mean engaging with others in a mutually beneficial activity. Cooperative behavior may confer benefits net of costs on the individual cooperator, and thus may be motivated by entirely self-regarding preferences. In this case, cooperation is a form of what biologists call *mutualism*, namely an activity that confers net benefits both on the actor and on others.

But, cooperation may also incur net costs to the individual. In this case cooperative behavior constitutes a form of *altruism*. In contrast to mutualistic cooperation, altruistic cooperation would not be undertaken by an individual whose motives were entirely self-regarding and thus did not take account of the effects of one's actions on others.

While the high frequency of altruistic cooperation in humans relative to other species could be an evolutionary accident, a more plausible explanation is that altruistic cooperation among humans is the result of capacities that are unique to our species and that strongly promote our relative reproductive fitness. Thus we seek an explanation of cooperation that works for humans, but which, because it involves capacities that are unique to humans, does not work for other species, or works substantially less well.

Central to our explanation will be human cognitive, linguistic, and physical capacities that allow the formulation of general norms of social conduct, the emergence of social institutions regulating this conduct, the psychological capacity to internalize norms, and the capacity to base group membership on such non-kin characteristics as ethnicity and linguistic differences, which in turn facilitates costly conflicts among groups. Also important is the unique human capacity to use projectile weapons, a consequence of which is to lower the cost of punishing norm violators within a group, and to render intergroup conflicts more lethal.

Thus, our account of human sociality and its evolution hinges critically on a reconsideration of the canonical economic model of self-interested behavior. But more than individual motivation is involved. The extraordinary levels of cooperation observed in human society cannot be attributed simply to our generosity towards those with whom we interact or our capacity to favor the advancement of our nation or ethnic group over our individual well-being. The regulation of social interactions by group-level norms and institutions plays no less a role than altruistic individual motives in understanding how the cooperative species came to be. The institutions that regulate behaviors among non-kin affect the rewards and penalties associated with particular behaviors, often favoring the adoption of cooperative actions over others. In the social environments common to human interactions, the self-regarding are often induced to act in the interest of the group. Of course it will not do to posit these rules and institutions a priori. Rather, we show that these could have co-evolved with other human traits in a plausible representation of the relevant ecologies and social environments.

Cooperation is not an end to be valued in its own right, but rather is a means that under some conditions may contribute to human well-being. In other settings, competition plays no less essential a role. Similarly, the individual motives and group-level institutions that account for cooperation among humans include not only the most elevated—a concern for others, fair-mindedness, and democratic accountability of leaders, for example—but also the most venal: vengeance, exclusion of "outsiders," and frequent warfare among groups, for example.

Our reasoning is disciplined in three ways. First, the forms of cooperation we seek to explain are confirmed by natural observation, historical accounts, and behavioral experiments. Second, our account is based on a plausible evolutionary dynamic involving some combination of genetic and cultural transmission, the consistency of which can be demonstrated through formal modeling. Third, agent-based simulations show that our models can account for human cooperation under parameter values consistent with what can be reasonably inferred about the environments in which humans evolved.

3 MUTUALISTIC COOPERATION

Because mutualistic cooperation will be sustained by individuals with entirely self-regarding preferences, it is treated in standard biological and economic models as an expression of self-interest. "Natural selection favors these ... behaviors," wrote Robert Trivers in his "The evolution of reciprocal altruism" (1971), "because in the long run they benefit the organism performing them. ... two individuals who risk their lives to save each other will be selected over those who face drowning on their own" (pp. 34–5). Cooperation, in Trivers's interpretation, is simply symbiosis with a time lag. Trivers's explanation initially found favor among biologists and economists because it is consistent with both the common biological reasoning that natural selection will not favor altruistic behaviors and with the canonical economic assumption of self-interest.

Trivers identified the conditions under which assisting another would be reciprocated in the future with a likelihood sufficient to make mutual assistance a form of mutualism. These conditions favoring reciprocal altruism included an extended lifetime, mutual dependence, and other reasons for limited dispersal so that groups remain together, extended periods of parental care, attenuated dominance hierarchies, and frequent combat with conspecifics and predators. Foraging bands of humans, he pointed out, exhibit all of these conditions. Michael Taylor (1976) and Robert Axelrod and William Hamilton (1981) subsequently formalized Trivers's argument using the theory of repeated games. In economics, analogous reasoning is summarized in the folk theorem, which shows that cooperation among self-regarding individuals can be sustained as long as interactions are expected to be repeated with sufficient frequency and individuals are not too impatient (Fudenberg and Maskin 1986; Fudenberg, Levine, and Maskin 1994).

But, in many important human social environments, Trivers's conditions favoring reciprocal altruism do not hold, yet cooperation among non-kin is commonly observed. These include contributing to common projects when community survival is threatened, and cooperation among very large numbers of people who do not share common knowledge of one another's actions. In fact, the scope of application of the folk theorem is quite restricted, especially in groups of any significant size, once the problem of cooperation is posed in an evolutionary setting and account is taken of "noise" arising from mistaken behaviors and misinformation about the behaviors of others.

A plausible model of cooperation must satisfy the following five conditions. First, it must be *incentive compatible*. In particular, those who provide the rewards and inflict punishments dictated by the rules for cooperation must have the motivation to do so. Second, a model must be *dynamically stable*, in the sense that random fluctuations, errors, and mutations (the emergence of novel strategies) do not disrupt cooperation or entail excessive efficiency losses. Third, the organizational forms and incentive mechanisms deployed in the model must reflect the types of strategic interaction and incentives widely observed in human groups. In particular, the model should work well with group sizes on the order of ten to twenty, and the incentive to punish defectors should reflect those deployed in real-world public goods game settings. Fourth, the model should not require extraordinary *informational requirements*. Finally the model should work with *plausible discount factors*. It is reasonable to suppose that within a group faced by a public goods game, there will be a distribution of discount factors among members, and average discount factors can be high in some periods and low in others, as the probability of group dissolution rises an falls.

A careful analysis shows that all models of cooperation based on tit-for-tat and related repeated game strategies, when played among self-interested individuals violate at least one of these conditions, and hence fail to solve the problem of cooperation among unrelated agents.[1] First, reciprocal altruism fails when a social group is threatened with dissolution, since members who sacrifice now on behalf of group members do not have a high probability of being repaid in the (highly uncertain) future.

Second, many human interactions in the relevant evolutionary context took the form of n-person public goods games—food sharing and other co-insurance, upholding social norms among group members, information sharing, and common defense—rather than dyadic interactions. The difficulty in sustaining cooperation in public goods games by means of the standard tit-for-tat and related repeated game strategies increases exponentially with group size (Boyd and Richerson 1988; Bowles and Gintis 2007), even if interactions are repeated with high probability. The reason is that in groups larger than two, withdrawing cooperation in response to a single defection imposes a blanket punishment on all, defectors and cooperators alike. But, targeting punishment on defectors alone does not work in large groups unless members have unrealistically accurate information about the actions taken by others.

Third, the contemporary study of human behavior has documented a large class of social behaviors inexplicable in terms of reciprocal altruism. For instance, there is extensive support for income redistribution in advanced industrial economies, even among those who cannot expect to be net beneficiaries (Fong, Bowles, and Gintis, 2005). Under some circumstances group incentives for large work teams are effective motivators even when the opportunity for reciprocation is absent and the benefits of cooperation are so widely shared that a self-interested group member would gain from free riding on the effort of others (Ghemawat 1995; Hansen 1997; Knez and Simester 2001). Finally, laboratory and field experiments show that other-regarding motives are frequently robust causes of cooperative behavior, even in one-shot, anonymous settings.

4 Strong Reciprocity: Evidence from Behavioral Experiments

A more direct reason for doubting the interpretation that most cooperation is mutualistic is given by the compelling evidence that many (perhaps most) people behave in ways inconsistent with the assumption that they are motivated by self-regarding preferences. A suggestive body of evidence points to the importance of a suite of behaviors that we call *strong reciprocity*. A strong reciprocator comes to a new social situation with a predisposition to cooperate, is predisposed to respond to cooperative behavior on the part of others by maintaining or increasing his level of cooperation,

---

[1] This analysis is presented in full in Gintis (2004) and Bowles and Gintis (2007), which also shows that recent game-theoretic extensions of these models using repeated game theory (Fudenberg and Maskin 1986; Fudenberg et al. 1994; Sekiguchi 1997; Piccione 2002; Ely and Välimäki 2002; Bhaskar and Obara 2002; Matsushima 2000; Kandori 2002) do not alter this conclusion. These contributions, while important in their own right, either suffer the same problems discussed in the text, or are not stable in a dynamic setting.

and responds to antisocial behavior on the part of others by retaliating against the offenders, even at a cost to himself, and even when he cannot not reasonably expect future personal gains from such retaliation. The strong reciprocator is thus both a *conditionally altruistic cooperator* and a *conditionally altruistic punisher* whose actions benefit other group members at a personal cost. We call this "strong reciprocity" to distinguish it from "weak" (i.e. self-regarding) forms of reciprocity, such as Trivers's reciprocal altruism.

Strong reciprocity is an example of a larger class of so-called *social preferences* which describe the motivations of people who care (one way or the other) about the well-being of others, and not only have preferences over the states they and others experience but also care about how the states came about.

In the ultimatum game, under conditions of anonymity, two players are shown a sum of money, say $10. One of the players, called the "proposer," is instructed to offer any number of dollars, from $1 to $10, to the second player, who is called the "responder." The proposer can make only one offer. The responder, again under conditions of anonymity, can either accept or reject this offer. If the responder accepts the offer, the money is shared accordingly. If the responder rejects the offer, both players receive nothing.

Since the game is played only once and the players do not know each other's identity, a self-interested responder will accept any positive amount of money. Knowing this, a self-interested proposer will offer the minimum possible amount, $1, and this will be accepted. However, when actually played, *the self-interested outcome is never attained and never even approximated*. In fact, as many replications of this experiment have documented, under varying conditions and with varying amounts of money, proposers routinely offer respondents very substantial amounts (50 per cent of the total generally being the modal offer), and respondents frequently reject offers below 30 per cent (Camerer and Thaler 1995; Güth and Tietz 1990; Roth et al. 1991).

Strong reciprocity emerges in many other experimental games, some of which are described in Table 53.1 (from Camerer and Fehr 2004). In all cases, given the one-shot, anonymous nature of the game, self-regarding agents would neither contribute to the common good, nor reward others for so contributing. Nor would they punish others for failing to contribute. Yet, in each game, under many different conditions and in different cultures, a considerable fraction of agents contributes, and enough agents punish free riding that even the self-regarding agent often contributes simply to avoid punishment.

5 THE EVOLUTION OF STRONG RECIPROCITY

If preferences were entirely self-regarding, the extent of human cooperation would indeed be puzzling. But if social preferences are common, the puzzle takes a somewhat different form: how might strong reciprocity and other altruistic preferences

Table 53.1 Seven experimental games useful for measuring social preferences

Game	Definition of the game	Real-life example	Predictions with selfish players	Experimental regularities, references	Interpretation
Prisoner's Dilemma Game	Two players, each of whom can either cooperate or defect. Payoffs are as follows: 		Cooperate	Defect
---	---	---
Cooperate	H,H	S,T
Defect	T,S	L,L | $H > L, T > H, L > S$	Production of negative externalities (pollution, loud noise), exchange without binding contracts, status competition.	Defect.	50% choose to cooperate. Communication increases frequency of cooperation. Dawes (1980).[a]	Reciprocate expected cooperation.
Public Goods Game	n players simultaneously decide about their contribution g_i. $(0 \leq g_i \leq y)$ where y is players' endowment; each player i earns $\pi_i = y - g_i + mG$ where G is the sum of all contributions and $m < 1 < mn$.	Team compensation, cooperative production in simple societies, over-use of common resources (e.g. water, fishing grounds).	Each player contributes nothing; that is, $g_i = 0$.	Players contribute 50 % of y in the one-short game. Contributions unravel over time. Majority chooses $g_i = 0$ in final period. Communication strongly increases cooperation. Individual punishment opportunities greatly increase contributions. Ledyard (1995).[a]	Reciprocate expected cooperation.
Ultimatum Game	Division of a fixed sum of money S between a proposer and a responder. Proposer offers x. If responder rejects x both earn zero; if x is accepted the proposer earns $S - x$ and the responder earns x.	Monopoly pricing of a perishable good; '11th hour' settlement offers before a time deadline.	Offer $x = \varepsilon$ where ε is the smallest money unit. Any $x > 0$ is accepted.	Most offers are between 0.3 and 0.5S. $x < 0.2S$ rejected half of the time. Competition among proposers has a strong x-increasing effect; competition among responders strongly decreases x. Güth, Schmittberger, and Schwartze (1982);[b] Camerer (2003).[a]	Responders punish unfair offers; negative reciprocity.

Dictator Game	Like the UG but the responder cannot reject; that is, the "proposer" dictates $(S - x, x)$.	Charitable sharing of a windfall gain (lottery winners giving anonymously to strangers).	No sharing; that is, $x = 0$.	On average "proposers" allocate $x = 0.2S$. Strong variations across experiments and across individuals. Kahneman, Knetsch, and Thaler (1986);[b] Camerer (2003).[a]	Pure altruism.
Trust Game	Investor has endowment S and make a transfer y between 0 and S to the trustee. Trustee receives $3y$ and can send back any x between 0 and $3y$. Investor earns $S - y + x$. Trustee earns $3y - x$.	Sequential exchange without binding contracts (buying from sellers on eBay).	Trustee repays nothing: $x = 0$. Investor invests nothing: $y = 0$.	On average $y = 0.5S$ and trustees repay slightly less than $0.5S$. x is increasing in y. Berg, Dickhaut, and McCabe (1995);[b] Camerer (2003).[a]	Trustees show positive reciprocity.
Gift Exchange Game	"Employer" offers a wage w to the "Worker" and announces a desired effort level $\hat{e}$. If Worker rejects $(w, \hat{e})$ both earn nothing. If worker accepts, he can choose any e between 1 and 10. Then Employer earns $10e - w$ and Worker earns $w - c(e)$. $c(e)$ is the effort cost which is strictly increasing in e.	Non-contractibility or non-enforceability of the performance (effort, quality of goods) of workers or sellers.	Worker chooses $e = 1$. Employer pays the minimum wage.	Effort increases with the wage w. Employers pay wages that are far above the minimum. Workers accept offers with low wages but respond with $e = 1$. In contrast to the UG, competition among workers (i.e. responders) has no impact on wage offers. Fehr, Kirchsteiger, and Reidl (1993).[b]	Workers reciprocate generous wage offers. Employers appeal to workers' reciprocity by offering generous wages.
Third-party Punishment Game	A and B play a DG. C observes how much of amount S is allocated to B. C can punish A but the punishment is also costly for C.	Social disapproval of unacceptable treatment of others (scolding neighbors).	A allocates nothing to B. C never punishes A.	Punishment of A is higher, the less A allocates to B. Fehr and Fischbacher (2004).[b]	C sanctions violation of a sharing norm.

[a] Denotes survey papers.
[b] Denotes papers that introduced the respective games.

Source: Camerer and Fair 2004.

that support cooperation have evolved over the course of human history? The puzzle is posed especially clearly if the processes of cultural and genetic evolution favor behavioral traits that on average are associated with higher levels of material success. We think that this assumption of what is called a *payoff monotonic dynamic* is not entirely adequate. But Gintis (2000) and Bowles and Gintis (2004) adopt just such an evolutionary model to show that individuals behaving as strong reciprocators can proliferate in a population in which they were initially rare, and that their presence in a population could sustain high levels of cooperation among group members.

One intuition behind these models is that in groups with strong reciprocators present, group members whose self-regarding preferences lead them to shirk on contributing to common projects will be punished by being ostracized from the group. Strong reciprocators bear the cost not only of contributing to common projects, but also of punishing the shirking of the self-interested members. If reciprocators are common enough, however, the self-interested members will conform to cooperative norms in order to escape punishment, thereby reducing or eliminating the fitness differences between the reciprocators and the self-interested members. A second argument supporting strong reciprocity is that groups with a sufficient proportion of strong reciprocators will be better able to survive such group crises as war, pestilence, and adverse climatic conditions. In such situations, a group of self-regarding agents would simply disband, since each member will do better to bear the personal costs of abandoning the group rather than bearing the even heavier costs of attempting to preserve the group, most of the gains of which would accrue to other group members. Since strong reciprocators enforce cooperation without regard for the possibility of extinction, a sufficient proportion of strong reciprocators can enhance the possibility of group survival.

Group-level characteristics—such as relatively small group size, limited migration, or frequent intergroup conflicts—have co-evolved with cooperative behaviors. Cooperation is thus based in part on the distinctive capacities of humans to construct institutional environments that limit within-group competition and reduce phenotypic variation within groups, thus heightening the relative importance of between-group competition, and hence allowing individually costly but in-group-beneficial behaviors to coevolve with these supporting environments through a process of interdemic selection.

The idea that the suppression of within-group competition may be a strong influence on evolutionary dynamics has been widely recognized in eusocial insects and other species. Alexander (1979), Boehm (1982), and Eibl-Eibesfeldt (1982) first applied this reasoning to human evolution, exploring the role of culturally transmitted practices that reduce phenotypic variation within groups. Group-level institutions thus are constructed environments capable of imparting distinctive direction and pace to the process of biological evolution and cultural change (Friedman and Singh 2001).

Bowles, Choi, and Hopfensitz (2003) models an evolutionary dynamic along these lines. They show that intergroup conflicts may explain the evolutionary success of both altruistic forms of human sociality towards non-kin, and group-level institutional structures such as resource-sharing that have emerged and diffused repeatedly in a wide variety of ecologies during the course of human history.

6 PROXIMATE MOTIVES: INTERNALIZED NORMS AND SOCIAL EMOTIONS

An *internal norm* is a pattern of behavior enforced in part by internal sanctions, including shame and guilt. Individuals follow internal norms when they value certain behaviors for their own sake, in addition to, or despite, the effects these behaviors have on personal fitness and/or perceived well-being. The ability to internalize norms is nearly universal among humans. All successful cultures foster internal norms that enhance personal fitness, such as future orientation, good personal hygiene, positive work habits, and control of emotions. Cultures also widely promote altruistic norms that subordinate the individual to group welfare, fostering such behaviors as bravery, honesty, fairness, willingness to cooperate, and empathy with the distress of others (Brown 1991).

If even a fraction of society internalizes the norms of cooperation and punish free riders and other norm violators, a high degree of cooperation can be maintained in the long run. The puzzles are two: why do we internalize norms, and why do cultures promote cooperative behaviors? Gintis (2003) provides an evolutionary model in which the capacity to internalize norms develops because this capacity enhances individual fitness in a world in which social behavior has become too complex to be learned through personal experience alone. It is not difficult to show that if an internal norm is fitness enhancing, then for plausible patterns of socialization, the allele for internalization of norms is evolutionarily stable. This framework implements the suggestion in Simon (1990) that altruistic norms can "hitchhike" on the general tendency of internal norms to be fitness enhancing.

Pro-social emotions are physiological and psychological reactions that induce agents to engage in cooperative behaviors as we have defined them above. The pro-social emotions include some, such as shame, guilt, empathy, and sensitivity to social sanction, that induce agents to undertake constructive social interactions, and others, such as the desire to punish norm violators, that reduce free riding when the pro-social emotions fail to induce sufficiently cooperative behavior in some fraction of members of the social group (Frank 1987; Hirshleifer 1987). Without the pro-social emotions we would all be sociopaths, and human society would not exist, however strong the institutions of contract, governmental law enforcement, and reputation. Sociopaths have no mental deficit except that their capacity to experience shame, guilt, empathy, and remorse is severely attenuated or absent.

Pro-social emotions function like the basic emotion, "pain," in providing guides for action that bypass the explicit cognitive optimizing process that lies at the core of the standard behavioral model in economics. Antonio Damasio (1994, 173) calls these "somatic markers," that is, a bodily response that "forces attention on the negative outcome to which a given action may lead and functions as an automated alarm signal which says: beware of danger ahead if you choose the option that leads to this outcome.... the automated signal protects you against future losses." Emotions thus contribute to the decision-making process, not simply by clouding reason, but in beneficial ways as well. Damasio continues: "suffering puts us on notice. ... it increases the probability that individuals will heed pain signals and act to avert their source or correct their consequences" (p. 264).

Does shame serve a purpose similar to that of pain? If being socially devalued has fitness costs, and if the amount of shame is closely correlated with the level of these fitness costs, then the answer is affirmative. Shame, like pain, is an aversive stimulus that leads the agent experiencing it to repair the situation that led to the stimulus, and to avoid such situations in the future. Shame, like pain, replaces an involved optimization process with a simple message: whatever you did, undo it if possible, and do not do it again.

Since shame is evolutionarily selected and is costly to use, it very likely confers a selective advantage on those who experience it. Two types of selective advantage are at work here. First, shame may raise the fitness of an agent who has incomplete information (e.g. as to how fitness reducing a particular antisocial action is), limited or imperfect information-processing capacity, and/or a tendency to undervalue costs and benefits that accrue in the future. Probably all three conditions conspire to react suboptimally to social disapprobation in the absence of shame, and shame brings us closer to the optimum. Of course the role of shame in alerting us to negative consequences in the future presupposes that society is organized to impose those costs on rule violators. The emotion of shame may have co-evolved with the emotions motivating punishment of antisocial actions (the reciprocity motive in our model).

The second selective advantage to those experiencing shame arises through the effects of group competition. Where the emotion of shame is common, punishment of antisocial actions will be particularly effective and as a result seldom used. Thus groups in which shame is common can sustain high levels of group cooperation at limited cost and will be more likely to spread through interdemic group selection (Bowles and Gintis 2004; Boyd et al. 2003). Shame thus serves as a means of economizing on costly within-group punishment.

While we think the evidence is strong that pro-social emotions account for important forms of human cooperation, there is no universally accepted model of how emotions combine with more cognitive processes to affect behaviors. Nor is there much agreement on how best to represent the pro-social emotions that support cooperative behaviors.

Bowles and Gintis (2005b) considers a public goods game where subjects maximize a utility function that captures five distinct motives: personal material payoffs, one's valuation of the payoffs to others, which depend both on ones' altruism and one's degree of reciprocity, and one's sense of guilt or shame when failing to contribute one's fair share to the collective effort of the group. We have evidence of shame if players who are punished by others respond by behaving more cooperatively than is optimal for a material payoff-maximizing agent. We present indirect empirical evidence suggesting that such emotions play a role in the public goods game.

Direct evidence on the role of emotions in experimental games remains scanty. The forms of arousal associated with emotions are readily measured, but they do not readily allow us to distinguish between, say, fear and anger. Self-reports of emotional states are informative but noisy. Recent advances in brain imaging, however, can identify the areas of the brain that are activated when an experimental subject is confronted with a moral dilemma or unfair treatment by another experimental subject. This use of fMRI and related technology may eventually allow us to distinguish among the emotional responses of subjects in experimental situations.

7 Conclusion

The study of collective action and other forms of cooperative behaviors exhibits a curious disparity among social scientists. In the Marxian tradition, and among many historians, sociologists, anthropologists, and political scientists, the fact that people often behave pro-socially in the pursuit of common objectives, even when this involves cooperating in an n-person prisoner's dilemma game, is frequently invoked to explain social structures and their dynamics. Among economists, biologists, and others influenced by their models, by contrast, self-regarding actors will rarely, if ever, cooperate in such a setting.

It may be thought that the key difference accounting for this divergence is the methodological individualism adopted by economists and biologists, in contrast to the more holist or structural approaches adopted by historians and many social scientists outside of economics. According to this view, if anthropologists, sociologists, Marxists, and others were only to ask the obvious question—why would an individual engage in a costly activity to benefit others?—they would agree with the economists. But this is not the case.

The question needs an answer, but in light of what we now know about the nature of social preferences, it is not that altruistic forms of collective ction are likely to be an ephemeral and unimportant aspect of political life and that most forms of seemingly altruistic cooperation are just self-interest in disguise. Like adherence to social norms and punishment of those who violate them, collective action is an essential aspect of political behavior and one which is readily explained by the fact that strong reciprocity and other social preferences are sufficiently common in most human populations to support high levels of cooperation in many social settings.

References

ABREU, D., PEARCE, D., and STACCHETTI, E. 1990. Toward a theory of discounted repeated games with imperfect monitoring. *Econometrica*, 58: 1041–63.

ALEXANDER, R. D. 1979. *Biology and Human Affairs*. Seattle: University of Washington Press.

ANDREONI, J., ERARD, B., and FEINSTEIN, J. 1998. Tax compliance. *Journal of Economic Literature*, 36: 818–60.

AUMANN, R. J. 1987. Correlated equilibrium and an expression of Bayesian rationality. *Econometrica*, 55: 1–18.

AXELROD, R., and HAMILTON, W. D. 1981. The evolution of cooperation. *Science*, 211: 1390–6.

BECKER, G. 1983. A theory of competition among pressure groups for political influence. *Quarterly Journal of Economics*, 98: 71–400.

BÉNABOU, R., and OK, E. A. 2001. Social mobility and the demand for redistribution: the Poum hypothesis. *Quarterly Journal of Economics*, 116: 47–87.

BERG, J., DICKHAUT, J., and MCCABE, K. 1995. Trust, reciprocity, and social history. *Games and Economic Behavior*, 10: 122–42.

BHASKAR, V., and OBARA, I. 2002. Belief-based equilibria: the repeated prisoner's dilemma with private monitoring. *Journal of Economic Theory*, 102: 40–69.

BOEHM, C. 1982. The evolutionary development of morality as an effect of dominance behavior and conflict interference. *Journal of Social and Biological Structures*, 5: 413–21.

—— 1993. Egalitarian behavior and reverse dominance hierarchy. *Current Anthropology*, 34: 227–54.

BOWLES, S., CHOI, J. K., and HOPFENSITZ, A. 2003. The co-evolution of individual behaviors and social institutions. *Journal of Theoretical Biology*, 223: 135–47.

—— —— 2004. The evolution of strong reciprocity: cooperation in heterogeneous populations. *Theoretical Population Biology*, 65: 17–28.

—— —— 2007. *A Cooperative Species: Human Reciprocity and its Evolution*. Manuscript in preparation.

—— —— 2005a. Social preferences, *Homo economicus*, and *zoon politikon*. In *The Oxford Handbook of Contextual Political Analysis*, ed. R. E. Goodin and C. Tilly. Oxford: Oxford University Press.

—— and GINTIS, H. 2005b. Prosocial emotions. In *The Economy as an Evolving Complex System III*, ed. L. E. Blume and S. N. Durlauf. Santa Fe, N. Mex.: Santa Fe Institute.

BOYD, R., GINTIS, H., BOWLES, S., and RICHERSON, P. J. 2003. Evolution of altruistic punishment. *Proceedings of the National Academy of Sciences*, 100: 3531–5.

BRETON, A., GALEOTTI, G., SALMON, P., and WINTROBE, R. 1995. *Nationalism and Rationality*. Cambridge: Cambridge University Press.

BROWN, D. E. 1991. *Human Universal*. New York: McGraw-Hill.

—— and TULLOCK, G. 1962. *The Calculus of Consent: Logical Foundations of Constitutional Democracy*. Ann Arbor: University of Michigan Press.

BUCHANAN, J., TOLLISON, R., and TULLOCK, G. 1980. *Toward a Theory of the Rent-Seeking Society*. College Station: Texas A&M University Press.

CAMERER, C. 2003. *Behavioral Game Theory: Experiments in Strategic Interaction*. Princeton, NJ: Princeton University Press.

—— and FEHR, E. 2004. Measuring social norms and preferences using experimental games: a guide for social scientists. Pp. 55–95 in *Foundations of Human Sociality: Economic Experiments and Ethnographic Evidence from Fifteen Small-Scale Societies*, ed. J. Henrich, R. Boyd, S. Bowles, C. F. Camerer, E. Fehr, and H. Gintis. Oxford: Oxford University Press.

—— and THALER, R. 1995. Ultimatums, dictators, and manners. *Journal of Economic Perspectives*, 9: 209–19.

DAMASIO, A. R. 1994. *Descartes' Error: Emotion, Reason, and the Human Brain*. New York: Avon.

DAWES, R. M. 1980. Social dilemmas. *Annual Review of Psychology*, 31: 169–93.

DOWNS, A. 1957. *An Economic Theory of Democracy*. Boston: Harper and Row.

EIBL-EIBESFELDT, I. 1982. Warfare, man's indoctrinability and group selection. *Journal of Comparative Ethnology*, 60: 177–98.

ELY, J. C., and VÄLIMÄKI, J. 2002. A robust folk theorem for the prisoner's dilemma. *Journal of Economic Theory*, 102: 84–105.

FEHR, E., and FISCHBACHER, U. 2004. Third party punishment and social norms. *Evolution and Human Behavior*, 25: 63–87.

—— KIRCHSTEIGER, G., and RIEDL, A. 1993. Does fairness prevent market clearing? *Quarterly Journal of Economics*, 108: 437–59.

FONG, C. M. 2001. Social preferences, self-interest, and the demand for redistribution. *Journal of Public Economics*, 82: 225–46.

—— BOWLES, S., and GINTIS, H. 2004. Reciprocity and the welfare state. In *Moral Sentiments and Material Interests: On the Foundations of Cooperation in Economic Life*, ed. H. Gintis et al. Cambridge, Mass.: MIT Press.

FRANK, R. H. 1987. If *Homo economicus* could choose his own utility function, would he want one with a conscience? *American Economic Review*, 77: 593–604.

FRIEDMAN, D., and SINGH, N. 2001. Negative reciprocity: the coevolution of memes and genes. *Evolution and Human Behavior*, 25: 155–73.

FUDENBERG, D., LEVINE, D. K., and MASKIN, E. 1994. The Folk Theorem with imperfect public information. *Econometrica*, 62: 997–1039.

—— and MASKIN, E. 1986. The folk theorem in repeated games with discounting or with incomplete information. *Econometrica*, 54: 533–54.

GINTIS, H. 2000. Strong reciprocity and human sociality. *Journal of Theoretical Biology*, 206: 169–79.

—— 2003. The Hitchhiker's Guide to altruism: genes, culture, and the internalization of norms. *Journal of Theoretical Biology*, 220: 407–18.

—— 2004. Modeling cooperation among self-interested agents: a critique. Manuscript, Santa Fe Institute.

—— BOWLES, S., BOYD, R., and FEHR, E. 2005. *Moral Sentiments and Material Interests: On the Foundations of Cooperation in Economic Life*. Cambridge, Mass.: MIT Press.

GREIF, A. 1994. Cultural beliefs and the organization of society: an historical and theoretical reflection on collectivist and individualist societies. *Journal of Political Economy*, 102: 912–50.

—— MILGROM, P., and WEINGAST, B. R. 1994. Coordination, commitment, and enforcement: the case of the merchant guild. *Journal of Political Economy*, 104: 745–76.

GÜTH, W., SCHMITTBERGER, R., and SCHWAT, B. 1982. An experimental analysis of ultimatum bargaining. *Journal of Economic Behavior and Organization*, 3: 367–88.

_____ and TIETZ, R. 1990. Ultimatum bargaining behavior: a survey and comparison of experimental results. *Journal of Economic Psychology*, 11: 417–49.

HARDING, S. 1978. Street shouting and shunning: conflict between women in a Spanish village. *Frontiers*, 3: 14–18.

HARSANYI, J. C. 1973. Games with randomly distributed payoffs: a new rationale for mixed-strategy equilibrium points. *International Journal of Game Theory*, 2: 1–23.

HENRICH, J., BOYD, R., BOWLES, S., CAMERER, C., FEHR, E., and GINTIS, H. 2004. *Foundations of Human Sociality: Economic Experiments and Ethnographic Evidence from Fifteen Small-Scale Societies*. Oxford: Oxford University Press.

HIRSHLEIFER, J. 1987. Economics from a biological viewpoint. Pp. 319–71 in *Organizational Economics*, ed. J. B. Barney and W. G. Ouchi. San Francisco: Jossey-Bass.

KAHNEMAN, D., KNETSCH, J. L., and THALER, R. H. 1986. Fairness as a constraint on profit seeking: entitlements in the market. *American Economic Review*, 76: 728–41.

KANDORI, M. 2002. Introduction to repeated games with private monitoring. *Journal of Economic Theory*, 102: 1–15.

LEDYARD, J. O. 1995. Public goods: a survey of experimental research. Pp. 111–94 in *The Handbook of Experimental Economics*, ed. J. H. Kagel and A. E. Roth. Princeton, NJ: Princeton University Press.

LUTTMER, E. F. P. 2001. Group loyalty and the taste for redistribution. *Journal of Political Economy*, 109: 500–28.

MAHDI, N. Q. 1986. Pukhtunwali: ostracism and honor among the Pathan hill tribes. *Ethology and Sociobiology*, 7: 295–304.

MATSUSHIMA, H. 2000. The folk theorem with private monitoring and uniform sustainability. CIRJE Discussion Paper F-84, University of Tokyo.

MILGROM, P. R., NORTH, D. C., and WEINGAST, B. R. 1990. The role of institutions in the revival of trade: the law merchant, private judges, and the champagne fairs. *Economics and Politics*, 2: 1–23.

MOENE, K. O., and WALLERSTEIN, M. 2002. Inequality, social insurance and redistribution. *American Political Science Review*, 95: 859–74.

MOORE, B., JR. 1978. *Injustice: The Social Bases of Obedience and Revolt*. White Plains, NY: M. E. Sharpe.

OSTROM, E. 1998. A behavioral approach to the rational choice theory of collective action. *American Political Science Review*, 92: 1–21.

PICCIONE, M. 2002. The repeated prisoner's dilemma with imperfect private monitoring. *Journal of Economic Theory*, 102: 70–83.

ROTH, A. E., PRASNIKAR, V., OKUNO-FUJIWARA, M., and ZAMIR, S. 1991. Bargaining and market behavior in Jerusalem, Ljubljana, Pittsburgh, and Tokyo: an experimental study. *American Economic Review*, 81: 1068–95.

SCOTT, J. C. 1976. *The Moral Economy of the Peasant: Rebellion and Subsistence in Southeast Asia*. New Haven, Conn.: Yale University Press.

SEKIGUCHI, T. 1997. Efficiency in repeated prisoner's dilemma with private monitoring. *Journal of Economic Theory*, 76: 345–61.

SIMON, H. 1990. A mechanism for social selection and successful altruism. *Science*, 250: 1665–8.

STERN, J. 2003. *Terror in the Name of God*. New York: HarperCollins.

TAYLOR, M. 1976. *Anarchy and Cooperation*. London: John Wiley and Sons.

TRIVERS, R. L. 1971. The evolution of reciprocal altruism. *Quarterly Review of Biology*, 46: 35–57.

VARSHNEY, A. 2003. Nationality, ethnic conflict, and rationality. *Political Science and Politics*, www.apsanet.org, 1: 85–99.

WIESSNER, P. 2005. Norm enforcement among the Ju/'hoansi bushmen: a case of strong reciprocity? *Human Nature*, 16: 115–45.

WITTMAN, D. 1989. Why democracies produce efficient results. *Journal of Political Economy*, 97: 1395–424.

WOOD, E. J. 2003. *Insurgent Collective Action and Civil War in El Salvador*. Cambridge: Cambridge University Press.

YOUNG, P., and BURKE, M. 2001. Competition and custom in economic contracts: a case study of Illinois agriculture. *American Economic Review*, 91: 559–73.

PART XIV

OLD AND NEW

CHAPTER 54

QUESTIONS ABOUT A PARADOX

KENNETH J. ARROW

1 Editors' Introduction

We approached Kenneth Arrow with the possibility of writing some reflections on his contributions to social choice theory and related themes. Unfortunately, we were not the first to make this request. Arrow demurred, saying he had already written such pieces (see, e.g., Arrow forthcoming). We suggested instead that we might engage him in a dialogue, to which he agreed.

We asked a number of political economy scholars, "If you had one question you could ask of Ken Arrow, what would it be?"

What follows are the questions and Arrow's thoughts and responses.

2 Arrow's Introduction

I wish to begin with a general remark concerning the issues of the impossibility theorem and voting paradoxes that come up frequently in the questions below. My attitude toward paradoxes has shifted over the years, especially under the stress by Herbert Simon and others on the boundedness of rationality.

Consider someone who holds two contradictory beliefs. How can that be? The answer is in part the limits on cognition—it takes time to work out the internal differences. Therefore an individual can go along with two contradictory beliefs because the situation in which they would collide doesn't arise. If it did arise, the different implications would become apparent.

A related implication of cognitive limits is that computation takes time and effort. This implies that we don't really make complete plans or sets of decisions for the future. Indeed, it is not cognitively possible. Once you grant that, each individual knows that she will make decisions in the future. All decisions today are partial plans.

These remarks have an implication for the paradox of voting. Even if cycles exist, they may not manifest themselves. Either they do not exist (or at least are not at the top) for the given preference profile or an agenda-setting or electoral mechanism yields an outcome without revealing the cycle.

This idea will bear on several of the points below.

3 Questions and Answers: Impossibility Theorems and Social Choice Theory

[1] If non-dictatorial social choice mechanisms are more prone to indecision (cycling) and poor decision-making (chaos) than dictatorial systems, why are democracies so commonplace these days?

One aspect of political decision-making that I didn't consider in my approach to social choice theory is that the political process includes communication, not just decision-making. Information is critical. Hence the recent emphasis on deliberative democracy is important. Yet, it seems clear that even after an intense deliberative phase, irreconcilable differences will remain. Indeed, deliberation may make differences of opinion clearer.

Consider dictatorships. My work implies that dictators should be efficient at running the social choice mechanism, if largely for themselves. What this misses is that dictatorships also tend to be poorer on communication.

Further, a real-life dictator has to involve others and take their interests into account, so that social choice theory is not irrelevant even in so-called dictatorships.

Finally, I would not want to assume that the current prevalence of democracy is permanent. Many democracies have ceased to be. Indeed, several, such as Germany in 1933, have made a conscious choice to set aside democracy. Venezuela has made a somewhat similar move, and other Latin American democracies are very shaky. Even in the stablest democracies, the United States and several countries of Europe, there is a mismatch between the issues in the political arena and the actual concerns of the voters. The rejection of the European Union constitution in France and the Netherlands, against the unanimous views of the political elites, is one example. In the United States, observers have noted that the partisan divisions in elections and in the legislatures are more extreme than the actual views of the electorates. One symptom of the disconnect is low participation in voting.

[2] In light of the findings of social choice, a field launched by your work, what care must we exercise in speaking about collectivities? What constraints must we observe in our discourse about collective preferences, such as the "public interest?"

We must take care when considering collectivities, but I believe they can be meaningful under certain circumstances. Take the notion that "something is in the United States' interest." For example, it's in the country's interest to lower tariff barriers even though some are worse off. Efficiency is a good place to start, but alone is not adequate because of distributional arguments. For any policy, we should also ask something like what happens for the seventy-fifth percentile worker. Hence I would like to see more attention to the losers when we evaluate policy.

[3] When did the analogy between collective choice processes and individual multi-criterion choice processes occur to you and how do you view that analogy today?

The analogy occurred to me right away. I saw that choice under uncertainty, with comparisons of different states, was very much like social choice theory, though with some differences. The analogy was even clearer before L. J. Savage made Bayesianism respectable. In the Neyman–Pearson and Wald minimax approaches, the different states were not really comparable. In the Savage reduction of statistical inference to decision theory, there is interstate comparability of utility. The analogy was the inspiration behind my work with Hervé Reyaud, *Social Choice and Multicriteria Decisionmaking* (1986).

[4] What lessons should constitution-writers seek in the theory of social choice and mechanism design?

I believe that constitutions should provide some way of ensuring decisiveness, even at the expense of transitivity. From time to time society faces a compelling problem that must be addressed. Sometimes, benign neglect is fine, but at other times it is not. At these times, it is important to have a clear, impartial, and acceptable view of both the status quo (what policies are currently in place, so that you know when you're changing things) and the range of possible alternative policies. The uncertainty over the results of the 2000 election provides an example of when the United States needed a decisive answer.

[5] Your general possibility theorem is, indeed, general (not in the sense of the use in the title of the theorem, but in the sense of broadly applicable). Its application, however, has tended to focus on democratic institutions in particular. One might infer that the theorem is of central concern for democratic institutions while its application to economic or social institutions has more of an "interesting intellectual curiosity" flavor. Is this how you see the importance of the general possibility theorem, of demonstrating a deep series of concerns about political institutions but of logical relevance though lesser importance for other institutional settings? Or do

you see it as revealing something profound across a larger array of institutional settings?

Let me concentrate on the question of whether the impossibility theorem is as significant in interpreting economic outcomes as it is with politics. In the usual formulations, economies tend toward an equilibrium among a variety of preferences and technologies. Markets do not compel people toward uniformity of behavior. Indeed, economics helps us understand how differences among people persist and are compatible. Politics is different because of power, especially the coercion implied in having one law for everyone.

The more specific question is, does the impossibility theorem apply to markets, the general equilibrium model in particular? I think this is something of an open problem. General equilibrium defines one way of choosing among social states. As already suggested, there are differences in the set-up between economic and political models. Nonetheless, I believe an aspect of general equilibrium has the same impossibility problem. Consider the question, is it better to adopt a new technology, specifically, a technology that involves trade-offs, so that something gained, but something else is lost? If we set up the problem right, then the impossibility theorem applies. But this set-up is somewhat artificial, i.e. the context may not be so natural as it seems in politics. In contrast to the above assumption about technology, some new technologies instead push out the frontier without involving a trade-off. In this circumstance, the choice is between a set and a bigger set, so no paradox arises.

[6] Was social choice theory, as you originally conceived of it, intended to be positive (i.e. predictive)?

Originally, I saw it as a normative program. Yet as I've lived with it, more and more I think of it as descriptive. In *Social Choice and Individual Values* (1951), I cited proposals for federal support of education, which had clear support of majorities. Yet the issue of desegregation was used to defeat this.

Similarly, Frank Easterbrook (1982) and Maxwell Stearns (2000) have applied this analysis to the Supreme Court. When you look at the reasons behind the decisions, different majorities rely on different and contradictory logic, even when individual justices are consistent.

4 Questions and Answers: Economics and Political Economy

[1] Do you believe economic efficiency can be a meaningful and useful concept (and why do you believe what you do)?

Like pornography, I know it when I see it. Measures of economic efficiency suffer from the social choice problem. Nevertheless, it is better to consider efficiency than not. Take benefit–cost analysis as an example of applying the efficiency criterion. It may not be utterly conclusive, but it provides an important piece of information for public decision-making. For example, going back to the 1950s, benefit–cost analysis has been used in water resource decisions. Its use has not prevented projects with benefit–cost ratios of less than one. But those with ratios of .3 are much harder to do even with political pressures.

> [2] *In your 1963* American Economic Review *article on moral hazard in health care provision (Arrow 1963), you stressed the importance of trust—i.e. ongoing relationships—as a means around our inability to contract fully for all possible outcomes. Might trust play a similar role in a group's allocative choices, such as those we find in committees and legislatures? Might trust work in small groups but not in large groups (à la Olson 1965)?*

In group choice, trust relates to the deliberative phase, not the choice phase. For example, one member of the group tells the others something, and they believe him even though they have different interests. Trust implies that members count on the others not to mislead them. This parallels the question of cooperation.

In my paper on the medical profession, I argued that the professions were designed to signal trust. An interesting empirical question is whether this form of trust has broken down—many of the factors I listed in that paper as engendering trust may no longer hold. (1) The proportion of for-profit hospitals among all hospitals has risen sharply. (2) Advertising of drugs and even of medical services has become prominent, where it was previously virtually non-existent. (3) The rise of managed care means that the institutions that deliver medical treatment no longer give primacy to the individual physician.

> [3] *What does economics have to say about intrapersonal and interpersonal mechanisms of preference formation?*

The short answer is nothing, though we should say something. There has been some formalization. Economics can learn.

A considerable literature exists on interpersonal effects, such as peer effects. For example, Glaeser, Sacerdote, and Scheinkman (1996) have written about peer effects in criminality. Our usual explanatory variables, such as poverty or education, explain very little of the variability in crime across metropolitan areas and even less of that across nations. Glaeser et al. argue that crime is a game with multiple equilibria, a form of coordination on preferences, not behavior. People have a desire to conform. There are two equilibria: one in which everyone is a criminal, the other in which no one is. This model appears to explain a lot of variance. Yet these and related models are very simple; the cost of departing from the local norm is a concave quadratic function. Yet they have considerable statistical explanatory power.

I'm persuaded that there's something important about peer effects, yet important difficulties remain. The simplest version of the peer effect hypothesis—"I want to be like others"—is too naive. A useful formulation has yet to be found. Moreover, how important is context? Clearly peer effects are not universal. A parallel set of models have been studied to deal with the diffusion of innovations: the models frequently cause an innovation to be adopted if it is being adopted by others without regard to whether the innovation is good or bad. In a similar fashion, the adoption of a locally current norm may depend on its interaction with other elements of the individual's preferences and opportunities.

> *[4] Does economics inevitably require a political foundation? Specifically, the economy depends on property rights system, legal regimes, protection against expropriation, a stable macroeconomy, and a host of other regulatory policies. All these decisions have a direct effect on the economy and economic development; and all are endogenous to the political system. Does this imply that a mature theory of economics and economic performance requires that economics gain a political foundation?*

The premise in this question is obviously correct. But we should also mention the legal and social foundations of economics along with the political ones. Each of these four realms—economic, political, legal, and social—has a different set of institutions that interact, but they are not the same. Just as economic problems can affect the political agenda, so too can social problems affect economics and politics. Under social foundations, I include groups and their effects, including social norms; and generally, how people behave when they interact.

This issue arises in the study of economic development, where a major question is, do institutions matter? And, in a collateral version of the question, maybe institutions matter, but they are endogenous. Describing institutions is not very easy. Commodities are easier to describe, but are still hard. Institutions are more like services, where so many difficult questions arise. For example, is a physician-hour the same now as fifty years ago?

Moreover, the study of institutions faces significant problems of measurement and empirical testing. For example, we expect the effects of many institutions to have very long lags. This implies that it is hard to use cross-country data to study institutions. The latter have yielded a very intensive study of the last thirty years of economic experience, but data limitations mean we cannot study longer periods in the same way.

The effect of the economy on the political system is equally worth talking about. For example, I went to the former Soviet Union in 1991. One of the questions we faced was, should we recommend that they adopt contract law and accounting systems? I wondered, do we have to recommend that? It seems so straightforward. And yet, the Soviets did not have either of these things. On the empirical side, the Russians subsequently did begin to provide these while the Chinese have not. Yet which is doing better—and why?

Returning to the question: the trouble is, we have a relatively strong theory of economics, but our theories of politics are weaker, and so adding a theory of politics to economics under the current circumstances only weakens it. Similarly, in principle we should also add to economics very important social components. But theory in that area is even worse than in politics.

Next let me raise a point about the influence of psychology on economics, which has been quite substantial in recent years. In many ways, research in psychology is more rigorous than in politics and sociology. So, even though psychology is not as important for economics as politics and social interaction, economists have found the theory and methodology much more useful.

[5] Do you have any thoughts on the striking parallels and contrasts between the 1950–1970s economics and social choice/theoretical political economy? In general equilibrium theory you and others showed that, under general conditions without any reference to characteristics of specific markets, a general equilibrium exists. The two fundamental theorems of welfare economics also contributed to the view that economic systems have nice properties.

Things worked out differently in theoretical political economy. First, your impossibility theorem suggested that at a general level systems with rational individuals were not likely to exhibit social rationality. Second, in parallel with general equilibrium, students of majority rule sought in the 1960s and 1970s to study the equilibrium properties of majority rule and ended up proving the opposite of general equilibrium in markets—that in general majority rule lacks any equilibrium.

Theory demonstrates real differences between politics and economics. The theory of economics has nice theorems with good properties. The competitive context, for example, produces automatic pressures for efficiency. But as soon as you have large aggregations of power—whether in economics or politics—analysis becomes difficult. Moreover, assumptions such as self-interest play a bigger role; and departures from self-interest become more important.

In politics, the absence of the existence of a political equilibrium makes theorizing very inconvenient. The use of single-dimensional models to study politics is useful, but problematic.

5 Questions and Answers: Methodological and Miscellaneous

[1] What is the big question in political economy that you would advise young researchers to pursue?

There are lots of questions to which we need answers. How do individuals in the political system coalesce to form groups, such as pressure groups? How do these groups form? Second, once formed, how do they work within the system to have influence? A specific instance of this has always concerned me: why is the political influence of farmers inversely proportion to their numbers?

[2] What are the prospects and limitations for a more behavioral (or boundedly rational) approach to the study of political economy?

We now have real concrete work on bounded rationality. But there is a trouble with theories of bounded rationality: they are very difficult to use. Moreover, some of the behavioral anomalies arise in experiments, but the situations in which they arise don't occur in real life. Consider, for example, anchoring. An individual is asked to estimate a magnitude after being given a clearly irrelevant observation; the observation has a distinct effect. But this is an experimental paradigm, not one likely to occur naturally. This means that some of the problems emphasized in the literature are not surprising.

But other behavioral problems and anomalies are obviously important. Consider the issue of framing, especially important in politics. But how does it work? We have no theory. An obvious place to start: does the frame that is ultimately chosen reflect mere chance? Are some people much better at creating frames? Might an evolutionary theory of survival of frames be appropriate?

[3] With the publication and wide dissemination of results, such as your general possibility theorem, many scholars in economics and political science opine that cooperative game theory, and particularly social choice theory, is now a "dead field." The implication is that we will learn more by focusing our theoretical energies on non-cooperative game theory, particularly in its newer behavioral and computational guises. Do you agree with this characterization of cooperative game theory and, in particular, of social choice theory?

Non-cooperative game theory is individually based and elegant. Nevertheless, it does not provide an adequate or full theory. Consider, for example, the experimental evidence that people cooperate far more than predicted by prisoner's dilemma models. As soon as the prisoner's dilemma is repeated in an experimental setting, even a little, people tend to cooperate. People can see collective rationality even though the only non-cooperative equilibrium in a finitely repeated prisoner's dilemma game is the one-shot defect-defect equilibrium. We also see this type of cooperation in real life.

We don't yet have a good theory of this type of cooperation.

Take the Hobbes/Coasian view: people will bargain to a more efficient agreement. Many theoretical impediments arise to efficient bargaining: holdouts and an empty core. I find all sorts of reasons that collective rationality is not compelling. Yet people do seem to cooperate. For example, competitors in an industry form research alliances even when they compete intensely. As Brandenburger and Nalebuff (1998) emphasize, you get competition and cooperation at the same time. We have no good formalization of this process. Yet it is clearly important. Cooperation and conflict in the political world should be the same.

To summarize, it's clear that the cooperative phenomenon is there. We can't abandon the problem of cooperative theory even though we have no good theory.

[4] Do you see any significant costs in the mathematization of political economy that occurred over the course of your career?

Resources are scarce, so devoting attention to mathematization means less time devoted to something else, like data collection. We can never really know what these costs are. Hence I feel we should let people make their own decisions in a decentralized way. Everything has costs, but we have no way of making an *ex ante* prescription.

[5] How can we be more effective in bringing the implications of our research to the attention of policy-makers to help them make better-informed policy choices?

I'm the last one to answer that question! I just finished making a policy recommendation about the financing of new malaria-reducing drugs. So far, it's been ineffective. The report took two years of hard work, and it's not obvious that anything will happen.

6 CONCLUDING REMARK

I may spend the rest of my life working on these problems.

REFERENCES

ARROW, K. J. 1951. *Social Choice and Individual Values.* New Haven, Conn.: Yale University Press (2nd edn. 1963).
—— 1963. Uncertainty and the welfare economics of medical care. *American Economic Review*, 53: 941–73.
—— forthcoming. The subject-matter of social choice theory. In *The Handbook of Social Choice and Welfare*, vol. ii, ed. K. J. Arrow, A. K. Sen, and K. Suzumura. Amsterdam: Elsevier.
—— and REYNAUD, H. 1986. *Social Choice and Multicriteria Decisionmaking.* Cambridge, Mass.: MIT Press.
BRANDENBURGER, A. M., and NALEBUFF, B. J. 1998. *Co-opetition.* New York: Doubleday.
EASTERBROOK, F. 1982. Ways of criticizing the court. *Harvard Law Review*, 95: 802–32.
GLAESER, E. L., SACERDOTE, B., and SCHEINKMAN, J. 1996. Crime and social interactions. *Quarterly Journal of Economics*, 111: 507–48.
OLSON, M. 1965. *Logic of Collective Action.* Cambridge, Mass.: Harvard University Press.
STEARNS, M. 2000. *Constitutional Process: A Social Choice Analysis of Supreme Court Decisionmaking.* Ann Arbor: University of Michigan Press.

CHAPTER 55

POLITICS AND SCIENTIFIC ENQUIRY

RETROSPECTIVE ON A HALF-CENTURY

JAMES M. BUCHANAN

1 INTRODUCTION

As the new century moves forward, the ranks of those who can personally recall the state of play in political analysis at the middle of the last century are rapidly thinning. And without personal recollection, which must itself sometimes be forcefully imposed on what seems best forgotten, it remains impossible to appreciate the depth of confusion that described the then-prevailing "science" of politics. To modern scholars who must work within the constraints of published works, the glaring failure of social scientists to dispel the fog, or even to recognize that the fog exists, seems both inexplicable and inexcusable. They should recognize, however, that while with modern tools of analysis the fog may seem to lift, thereby offering more satisfying explanatory results, many of the sources of the basic confusion have not been fully displaced. Potential value has been extracted from the "science of politics" as it has developed over a half-century, but this "science" itself has generated its own critics, perhaps an indirect measure of some success.

I entitled an early paper "An economist's approach to 'scientific politics'" (Buchanan 1968). The two parts of this title, properly understood, can be used to describe, in summary, what has happened to scholarly discourse on politics over the last half of the twentieth century. The study of politics became "scientific" in the authentic meaning of this term. At the same time, the economists' approach—incorporating methodological individualism and rational choice—came to dominate explanatory enquiry.

Science is systematic enquiry into that which is. Two thresholds must be crossed before any such enquiry can make progress: first, agreement must emerge on the object of enquiry, on the categorical definition of "that which is;" second, "that which is" must be separated from "that which ought to be." Interrelated failures along both these dimensions of enquiry have continued to be major barriers to understanding.

2 What Is the State?

In the paper referenced above, I recounted the parable of the blind men and the elephant. If they agree that their task is to come to a composite understanding of an elephant, these blind persons (men and women) can, by using their active senses of touch, smell, and hearing and by comparing notes, reach an adequate and comprehensive result. Suppose, however, that some members of the group think that they are aiming at understanding the structure of an ostrich. In this case, the result will be incoherent.

Continuing confusion as to what politics is, as a potential subject for systematic enquiry, has plagued discussion through the ages, and, by the nature of the case, must continue to make analysis difficult. To the economist, and perhaps to most modern social scientists, the initial concentration of attention must be placed on the behavior of the persons who make political-collective choices for the organized polity. Even such an innocuous starting point bypasses, however, the whole tradition of enquiry that commences with the state, or collectivity, as such, treated as an organic and monolithic unity independent of those persons who occupy agency or subject roles.

This organic model, or rather conceptualization, cannot be so readily dismissed as economists might be wont to do. "The state," as an acting unit, does exist, if for no other reason than that it is treated as such in common parlance. And, by necessity, the isolated individual, as subject, confronts this entity in its various manifestations. Regardless of how its internal decision processes are organized and the results are generated, the collectivity, as such, becomes a reality beyond the behavioral control of the individual, who is reduced to parametric reaction only.

It is plausible, therefore, for the putative scientist to commence enquiry with the collective unit, as such, and to examine how states have acted throughout history;

how they may be predicted to act under differing circumstances; and how analytical models of state action might generate scientifically falsifiable hypotheses to be tested. An empirically based macropolitics might be constructed in some such fashion and with some claim to genuinely scientific standing.[1]

A science limited to the exposing of regularities in patterns of state action, without some grounding of these regularities in the behavior of those persons who act as agents of and for the collective unit, however, would be too truncated for the modern investigative mindset. The organic state, as a metaphysical unit, is simply not philosophically meaningful, and not only to the would-be scientist. To be sure, elements of the "state as God" mentality may have been force fed during the socialist epoch, and residues of such mentality may remain descriptive over some spectra of public attitudes, but a science of "politics without politicians" will be almost universally rejected. Any political science must be constructed on microfoundations.

History is not helpful here. With some notable exceptions, political units have evolved from origins that locate authority in identifiable autocratic leaders, whose choices are made without necessary or formal inputs from those who are externally affected by such choices. In this setting, the monolithic political agent, the embodiment of the state, is, quite simply, acting as an isolated individual who might be modeled as maximizing an objective function subject to whatever constraints are faced. Micro- and macropolitics merge into one. "The prince" becomes the ideal type for any analysis, and Machiavelli becomes the direct precursor of any scientific enquiry.

It is perhaps not surprising that those who ventured into enquiries about politics shied away from the approach taken by Machiavelli and his Italian peers. The ultimate normative purpose or motivation for science is control aimed at reform or improvement, and Machiavelli's advice to the prince did not sit well with those whose interests were not coincident with those of the prince. One avenue of escape involved the rejection of the scientific approach itself, a withdrawal of efforts aimed at explaining how princes do, in fact, behave, and intensification of discourse about how princes "should" behave.

3 THE "OUGHT" REPLACES THE "IS"

Ethical norms for the guidance of the behavior of those who make decisions for the collectivity became center stage in discourse on politics, and Plato was recognized as the fountainhead of ideas in the political theory that was to dominate enquiry until the middle of the last century. Such elevation of normative discussion, to the comparative neglect of positive analysis, might possibly have been justified so long as political units were best described as principalities, under the authority of single

---

[1] For two efforts that could be classified in this category, see de Jasay 1985, and van Creveld 1999.

rulers. Surprisingly, however, the mindset that conceives the whole exercise as that of proffering advice to a benevolent despot was retained as autocratic regimes were being replaced by democratic structures of governance. Those persons elected in democratic processes were implicitly modeled as "temporary princes" immunized from constituency pressure. There seems to have been a generalized failure, on the part of those who concentrated scholarly attention on politics, to recognize that decisions emergent from the processes involving multiple participants are simply not amenable, even on some "as if" basis, to unitary models of choice behavior. This unwillingness to factor down the observed outcomes of complex political processes in which many persons make "public choices," and in varying agency roles, was strengthened, and especially in English-language scholarship, by the dominance of utilitarianism, throughout political economy. This normative structure appeared to provide a common measuring standard which, if adhered to by agents in differing roles, would allow even the most complex institutions to generate outcomes that would be equivalent to those emergent from some "behind the curtain" force that aimed to maximize "social welfare" or "the public interest." It continues to be amazing that, even into this new century, welfare economists have never ceased their search for "social welfare functions."

Note that in the several settings mentioned here, whether that of the organic state, the single ruler, or the existence of a common standard for all political agents, discussion and analysis could proceed, either positively or normatively, based on a model of a single or unitary mind. A methodological individualism, of sorts, could provide the psychological framing for efforts aimed at understanding political actions. And, within this structure, precepts of rationality may or may not be considered applicable to the choices that are analyzed.

4 Unitary and Multiple Sovereigns

A categorical distinction must be made between all such models that, either directly or indirectly, analyze political choices as if they emerge from a monolithic unitary mind and those models that involve multiple participants in the generation of any result. A major element in the continuing confusion in political analysis has been the failure to recognize even the existence of this distinction.

In any unitary-mind model, the alternative outcomes are within the choice set of the entity that makes the choice. There is a one-to-one relationship between "that which is chosen" and "that which emerges from choice." The chooser is uniquely responsible for the result or outcome of the choice that is made. This relationship cannot exist in any model that involves more than one participant in the selection process.

Consider the simple case with only two persons, A and B, locked in a collective unit, who are confronted with alternatives that must be jointly available (say, dormitory roommates who must live with a single thermostat setting). In any unitary model, either A or B must be the ruler or dictator. If, however, both are participants in the decision process, neither A nor B can uniquely determine which alternative is to be chosen. The alternatives, as such, are not within the choice set of either participant. The participants can, of course, order the alternatives and agreement may be reached on some process or rule for making a selection.

It seems evident that the disjuncture between a person's ordering of the alternatives and that same person's expressed "choices" (votes) in processes in which other persons are known to participate becomes a possible source for differences in behavior. Further, it seems clear that characteristics or attributes of a person's ordering of alternatives need not necessarily correspond to the characteristics or attributes of that same person's "choice" behavior in the process of selection. In different words, there is no necessary mapping between the individual's evaluative orderings of the collective alternatives and the ranking of the choices that would be made as participation in the institutions of collective selection, including voting, takes place. There is a logically derived attenuation between these two orderings that stems from the absence of full responsibility for choice.[2]

Methodological clarity, if nothing else, would seem to dictate that these categorically differing models of state or collective action be separately analyzed in parallel tracks, rather than incoherently intermingled. In this respect, only the Italian fiscal theorists who developed their primary contributions over the course of a century, roughly, 1850–1950, are deserving of special commendation. These scholars, among whose names would be placed Ferrara, Pantaleoni, Mazzola, de Viti de Marco, Einaudi, Puviani, Fasiani, Cosciani, Barone, along with others, did not neglect attention to the model of the collective unit subject to analysis. De Viti de Marco and Fasiani, in particular, wrote treatises in which the two models, that of the unitary or monopoly state and that of the cooperative or democratic state, were presented side by side.[3] Interestingly enough, Duncan Black and I, who were early contributors to the "new" approach to the analysis of politics in mid-century and later, were both exposed, early in our own research programs, to this Italian tradition in fiscal theory.

5 Theory of "Democratic" Politics

As noted, residues of the organic state model of collective action remain in modern analyses, and especially in the sense that much enquiry seems to be informed by a longing for patterns of collective action that would, in fact, be comparable to those

---

[2] For early discussion, see Buchanan 1954. Note that the disjuncture here does not depend, in any way, on the logical grounds for expressive voting that emerge only in large-number electoral settings. For discussion of expressive voting, see Brennan and Buchanan 1984 and Brennan and Lomasky 1993.

[3] For a general summary overview of the whole Italian tradition in public finance, see Buchanan 1960. The only major work in English translation is de Viti de Marco 1936. In Italian, see Fasiani 1951.

that would emerge from a unitary decision-maker. For the most part, however, modern analyses commence from the presumption that politics is a process, or processes, that involve multiple participants, who may influence, variously, the collective outcomes that are observed. To this extent, the models introduced are almost exclusively "democratic." Attention is focused on the behavior of the individual, as a participant in the process of collective decision-making and on the ways through which the separate individual behaviors are combined or aggregated so as to generate definitive collective outcomes.

What is "an individual" for purposes of providing the starting point for analysis of collective action? For comparison, think of the comparable question as put to the economist who aims to analyze private behavior in the idealized marketplace. The individual is readily defined as a two-set combination of preferences and endowments (capacities). In stylized collective action settings that are "democratic," individuals are equally endowed with the authority over final outcomes. The definition of the individual reduces, therefore, to the set of preferences possessed. Hence, the abstracted person that becomes the basis for analysis of collective action is a set of preferences, nothing more. It is perhaps worth noting that, for the pure theory of politics at this level of enquiry, a presumption that persons have equal preferences eliminates totally any problems of aggregation.[4]

The individual, defined as an abstract set of preferences, became the explicitly recognized starting point for the pioneering work of Duncan Black (1948, 1958), for the somewhat earlier and much neglected work of Howard Bowen (1943), and for the more general analysis of Kenneth Arrow (1951). It is noteworthy that all of these early contributors were economists by training, and the concentration of attention on the behavior of the individual, as a participant in collective action, presumably stemmed from the methodological individualism that was, and remains, characteristic of economic analysis.

The second step in any construction of an abstract theory of politics requires the specification of the structure within which individuals, as participants in the process through which collective outcomes are generated, are presumed to act. Here it was perhaps understandable that majority voting was placed at center stage, despite the institutional complexities that seem to remove observed politics far from any simple majoritarian models. Duncan Black commenced his research program in an effort to analyze majority voting in small committee settings, and Howard Bowen seemed to incorporate majority rule as a natural element in any collective decision process. Kenneth Arrow's approach was much more general, and majority voting was only one among the many processes that failed to pass the test imposed in the general impossibility theorem. As Arrow's analysis was interpreted in the scientific community, however, concentration was centered on the failure of majoritarian processes, on the possible instability of democracy itself, translated as the institutionalization of majority rule.

---

[4] The Stigler–Becker 1977 setting in which persons have equal preferences as one basis for analyzing behavior in markets could not be carried over into politics.

6 The Objects of Collective Action

What are the alternatives among which collective "choices" are made? This area of enquiry has been surprisingly neglected.[5] Analysis has proceeded "as if" the alternatives for collective action are exogenously determined outside the processes which generate the results.[6]

Duncan Black was interested in explaining how persons, primarily in small committees, make collective selections among alternative motions, candidates, or party platforms. His attention did not extend to the larger questions as to the domain of collective options. Kenneth Arrow's seminal analysis offered mathematical tractability but at the expense of specificity. The domain for collective choice includes the whole set of alternative "social states," each member of which embodies a complete description of the allocation and distribution of value among all members of the polity. By inference, Arrow's domain for collective or political action becomes all inclusive.

Politics, as observed, is not, however, the inclusive domain for social interaction. At some base level of choice, persons enter into collective action when they consider that in such action they can secure more of that which they value (utility) than they can secure in non-collective interactions. The ultimate logic of collective action finds its *raison d'être* in the potentiality for shared gains. These strictures apply, of course, only to consensual politics, at least at the level of constitutional structure. They do not apply to regimes of governance that are non-democratic in the sense that, for some sub-sectors of the membership, the "game" is negative sum over the whole anticipated sequence of play. The scientific developments in our understanding are almost totally concentrated on the presumption that political regimes are broadly "democratic," at least in this limited sense.

Analysis was greatly clarified by Samuelson's articulation of the concept of pure "public goods" at mid-century (Samuelson 1954). In the stylized limiting case, a pure public or collective-consumption good or service is non-rivalrous in usage or consumption over large numbers of potential users. The costs of provision to any user-consumer remain unchanged as others are added to the using-consuming group. In any such setting, the value-enhancing potential for collective, as opposed to non-collective, action in providing such a good is evident, made especially so if the exclusion of users-consumers is itself costly. In the early analyses derivative from Samuelson's contribution, emphasis was placed primarily on why markets tend to fail in producing efficient quantities of goods that embody publicness characteristics. Relatively little attention was focused on the implications of the analysis for the domain for political action, as such.

Critics suggested, correctly, that goods exhibiting the pure publicness characteristics are rare indeed, and that the dividing line between the market and collective choice domains was likely to be determined by other considerations. In particular,

---

[5] For an effort to remedy the neglect, see Buchanan 1995.

[6] Economists may be charged with a comparable neglect in analyses of market choices. "Goods" are more or less presumed to be defined exogenously to the processes of market interaction.

distributional attributes alongside shared value potential are omnipresent in those goods and services actually supplied and financed through collective auspices. Collectively supplied goods, like all others, cost something, and when the taxing side of the public account is reckoned with, distributional conflict may swamp any underlying collective action logic.

Further, public and social choice analysts were slow to recognize that the alternatives for collective "choice" are themselves critically dependent on the processes and rules through which such "choices" are made. Two elementary examples: (1) the institutions of majority rule introduce a necessary discriminatory bias toward alternatives that benefit members of majority coalitions at the expense of those persons in the minority; (2) the absence of party supremacy and discipline, contrasted with the presence in parliamentary systems, tends to generate logrolling among special constituency coalitions, exemplified by the "pork-barrel" politics of the United States.

7 Toward an Operational Science of Politics

By concentrating attention on individual behavior in stylized majoritarian voting processes, with some understanding of both the institutional complexity of structures and the origins of collective action alternatives, analysts have developed an operational science of politics or collective action. We do, indeed, understand more about how politics works than we did at the half-century. Problems arise and criticisms emerge when analysis is extended to efforts to develop a *predictive* science, which must impute specific objectives to participants. What do persons seek to achieve through political action?

Direct transposition of the motivations imputed to persons in their private market behavior to behavior in politics allows for the generation of readily falsifiable hypotheses. But is net wealth, in some objectively measurable sense, comparably plausible as a motive for behavior when participants recognize both that the alternative finally selected is "public," and hence applicable to all members of the polity, and, further, that the individual who votes in the processes of selection is one among many whose action determines the final outcome? Overly zealous extension of the economic models of behavior to political settings has provided soft targets for critics of the whole modern enterprise, often described under the "rational choice" rubric.

These critics do not advance effective explanatory alternatives, and they fail to understand that their arguments apply only to the predictive elements in the positive science. The arguments do not undermine the basic rational choice postulates, which do not require the elevation of net wealth to a position of dominance among the motives for political actors. Practitioners in public choice–social choice should, however, acknowledge the limits of their explanatory models. The rational choice perspective, whether or not net wealth is included as an important motivating force, is one among several perspectives, each of which may yield some understanding of the very complex reality that is "politics."

8 Toward Normative Relevance

As noted, science is aimed at understanding what is. But one ultimate purpose of any such understanding is improvement; and, primarily, we seek to understand in order to "make things better." For the linkage here to function, however, we require a scalar that will tell us what "betterness" is. We have little or no difficulty with many ordinary scientific endeavors. Medical science has as its ultimate purpose the improvement of the health of women and men. Physical science (with some exceptions) aims at improvements in our ability to utilize natural sources of energy more fully. Information science and technology allow us to transmit information more quickly.

There is no comparable criterion for improvement in the social sciences. What, then, is the ultimate normative purpose of achieving scientific understanding in economics or political science, or, inclusively, in political economy? By understanding more about how social interaction processes work, we can say that improvements or reforms in these processes can allow participants in the polity to secure more value. But there is no independent criterion for what value is. We are reduced to saying that reform involves change that will allow persons to generate more of whatever it is that they value.

Classical utilitarianism circumvented this problem by elevating utility to the position of *the* criterion for improvement. The social sciences found their ultimate purpose in discovering institutional changes to be made that would increase utility, which was both objectively measurable and interpersonally comparable. Utilitarianism remained the dominating normative foundation for neoclassical economics in particular and residues remain in modern analysis. By the 1930s, however, and specifically with the powerful arguments from Robbins (1932), the emptiness of utilitarianism was laid bare. There was no ultimate criterion against which reforms might be evaluated.

Economists seemed to be placed in the position where their science had no normative implications. Fortunately, however, Pareto was discovered, who had recognized the problem early in the century and who had provided a basis from which a "new" welfare economics could be constructed. This branch of enquiry, sometimes called "theoretical welfare economics," offered the normative base for the economics of the middle-century decades.

The Pareto criterion was profoundly individualistic in a basic philosophical sense, making it categorically different from utilitarianism. Since aggregation over separate individuals was not possible, the criterion for improvement became the enhancement of value for each and every person, considered separately, and value as determined within the psyche of the person alone. Somewhat interestingly, however, this highly restrictive condition did not totally eliminate normative implications from economic science. Economists could infer that value enhancement for all parties becomes possible when exchanges are voluntary and when entry and exit into exchanges are free. Economic policy aimed at the opening up of exchange or market opportunities was normatively justified as value enhancing, even when values are only those expressly shown by voluntary actions of separate persons. The science of economics, which produced a better and better potential understanding of this relationship, was put on all fours with the other sciences.

As noted earlier in connection with the mid-century development of public goods theory, the welfare economists of those decades were primarily concerned with demonstrating when and under what conditions voluntary exchange relationships, or markets, fail to ensure increases in value, as assessed against the Pareto criterion. To the extent that elements of "publicness" are technologically embedded in the qualities of goods, or, to put the same thing differently, that extra-exchange externalities are present, voluntary exchanges, as normally interpreted, will increase the values for some individuals, but, at the same time, may reduce or increase values for others outside the exchanges. Potential values may remain unexploited.

Modern public choice theory made it clear that the welfare theorists of mid-century moved too quickly from their diagnoses of market failure to the challenges involved in politicized or collectivized corrections for such failures, and without explicit effort to analyze the working of politics. There are two separate but related avenues of enquiry to be followed up for those settings where voluntary exchanges, as normally interpreted, are acknowledged to be incomplete in the exhaustion of potential values. The first, which we may associate with the work of R. H. Coase (1960), involves an extension of the notion of voluntary exchanges to encompass more than the simple two-party traders in goods and services conventionally considered. The second, which we may associate with Knut Wicksell (1896), involves a transposition of the logic of exchange to politics itself, precursory to the late-century development of constitutional political economy or, possibly, labeled as welfare politics. These two research programs may be discussed in turn.

9 EXTENDING THE EXCHANGE NEXUS

If persons are free to enter into exchanges, one with another, and if exchanges offer prospects for mutual gains, such exchanges will occur. This elementary insight is the starting point for Coase's critique of neoclassical welfare economics, with its emphasis on market failures. From the Coasian perspective, the existence of an externality is a signal that unexploited gains from further possible exchange remain, and, if persons are at liberty to enter such exchanges, externalities will be internalized. Markets will not fail to exhaust potential values. If apparent externalities seem to be observed, failure to exploit these opportunities may be traced to the presence of prohibitive transactions costs barriers.

The normative implications are clear; participants in the economy will be able to secure more of that which they separately value if barriers to possible exchanges are removed or reduced. Particular focus is to be placed on the facilitation of exchanges in legal rights to undertake or to prevent activities, often treated as beyond the conventional nexus of exchange in goods and services. The implications of the Coasian analytical thrust for the development of a science of politics are largely indirect. To the extent that the exchange or market nexus can be extended by the clarification of rights and improved enforcement of contracts, any value-based argument for politicization or collectivization becomes less convincing. On the other hand, the argument for collective or political provision of protective state services, those that involve guarantees of freedom to enter and exit exchanges, along with protection of person and property and enforcement of voluntary contracts, is strengthened. In the idealized setting that may be inferred from the Coasian analytical structure, the protective state would be strong, and the productive state would be quite limited in scope.[7]

10 Wicksell and the Unanimity Benchmark

Knut Wicksell's seminal contribution was written well before the twentieth-century developments in welfare economics and in public choice (Wicksell 1896). His interest was in extending the analytical framework of neoclassical economic theory, which he had been instrumental in constructing, to the public or collective sector of economic interaction. Wicksell started from the presumption that members of an organized polity, through their representative agents, will seek to secure values potentially promised by shared goods and services. But how will the collective action be organized when the costs of providing such goods and services necessarily involve distributional considerations? Wicksell was under no delusion to the effect that representative agents seek out some general or public interest rather than that of their own constituents. And he stressed that majority voting in legislative assemblies contained no protection against exploitation of minorities and no guarantee that the aggregate benefits of collective action exceed the costs.

How could the decision structure be constructed so as to ensure that the values promised by shared goods and services could be secured in such fashion to ensure that all members of the sharing group receive net gains? How could both economic efficiency and justice be guaranteed? These questions made it necessary for Wicksell

---

[7] For an explicit discussion of the distinction between the protective and productive state, see Buchanan 1975.

to challenge the normative legitimacy of majority voting, as the dominating instrument of "democracy." And, although he did not himself appreciate the implications, Wicksell's contribution becomes precursory to later developments in constitutional enquiry.

If all members of a sharing group are to be ensured net gains, how must the costs be distributed? Clearly costs must be distributed in some relation to the distribution of gains. The ultimate test can be found only in agreement among all members of the group. If all persons in the sharing group agree to a distribution of the costs, this agreement in itself becomes the criterion for efficiency. The voting rule must be that of unanimity, which becomes the benchmark institution.

Wicksell recognized that, even in a stylized limiting case, strict implementation of the unanimity rule would be difficult, since each member of the decision-making group would be placed in a position of potential veto power. In practice, some fallback rule, between simple majority on the one hand and unanimity on the other, would be the best that could be expected to work. Wicksell's analysis establishes the legitimacy of qualified majority rules. Majority rule is effectively dethroned as the be-all and end-all of democratic politics.

It is worth noting that Wicksell's unanimity criterion for collective action is identical to the Pareto criterion for assessing the efficacy of any change in the constraints within which persons engage in exchanges. All members of the relevant political group must be brought into agreement, or at the least acquiescence, on a proposed change in order to ensure against discriminatory exploitation. Both efficiency and justice dictate that consensus be attained before collective action, with its necessarily attendant coercion, be taken.

11 THE CALCULUS OF CONSENT

The Wicksellian analysis suggests that, absent agreement, there is no basic normative legitimacy for collective action. Developments in scientific understanding of how politics work offer little justification for the whole enterprise. Clearly, general agreement is rarely observed to be present in any collective action; almost always there are net losers as well as net gainers.

Viewed in retrospect, the primary contribution of Buchanan and Tullock, in their 1962 book *The Calculus of Consent*, was to offer at least a partial resolution of the Wicksellian dilemma. If politics is conceptualized as a two-stage or two-level process (the constitutional and post-constitutional), with a separation between the politics of selecting the basic rules and the ordinary action taken within these rules, the agreement criterion may be applied differently, with more acceptable implications. The Wicksellian criterion may be shifted from the level of ordinary politics to that of the rules that constrain such politics—to the constitution, inclusively defined. And while there may be net losers in almost any collective action taken at the second stage, and especially if majority voting is operative, there may exist generalized consensus at the constitutional level. The rules in prospect or in being may secure widespread adherence and acceptance if, over an anticipated whole sequence of particular actions, all members of the polity expect to secure positive benefits.

For scientific analysis, the focus shifts from questions concerning the desirability of this or that particular policy proposal, as it moves through the complex institutional structure through which political outcomes finally emerge, to questions concerning the efficacy of the structure, as described by the rules of the political game, by the constitution. *Constitutional political economy* emerges as a research program on its own.

This program involves analyses of processes through which constraints are selected, as opposed to analyses of processes through which choices are made among exogenously determined and imposed constraints. Such research becomes relatively unfamiliar territory, especially to economists. The enterprise does require acceptance of the presumption that the basic structures of rules, the inclusive constitution of a society, are subject to deliberatively designed and implemented change. These structures become variables, and the working properties of alternative sets of rules become direct objects of enquiry. Also, as a normatively meaningful program, constitutional political economy does rest on the proposition that constitutions, as such, can constrain the excesses of politics.

Practical examples of the relevance of this research program emerged in the discussions concerning the prospects for selecting a constitution for the European Union in the early years of the new century, and in the efforts to design constitutions for the republics that were components of the Soviet Union. Questions as to the relative efficacy of parliamentary and republican systems of governance, of unicameral and bicameral legislatures, of plurality and proportional representation, of federal and unified structures, remain active objects of enquiry, along with many other less inclusive ones.

12 POLITICS AS EXCHANGE

In Section 1, I stated that enquiry into politics over the half-century incorporates the economists' approach to social interaction, and specifically in the concentration on the behavior of individual actors in political processes—actors who are modeled as furthering identifiable interests in accordance with precepts of rationality. Almost exclusive emphasis has been on the development of a micro- rather than on a macro-politics. A "positive" science of politics need go no further; the objective may be limited to the politics that is observed, whether this be described by the behavior of the autocratic ruler, the participant in large-number electoral settings, the bureaucratic rent-seeker, the party chairman, the representative agent in any of several roles, or any other of the many public choice situations that require individual action.

As also noted, however, for most practitioners, science has as its ultimate normative purpose some improvement or betterment in the human condition. In this sense, a pure science of politics limited to an understanding of that which is observed would be of limited value. Normative relevance emerges only as the purpose of politics is specified, thereby allowing assessment of the observed against some scalar. At this level, there is still another element that links development in political enquiry with the economists' approach. In some meaningful sense, the whole enterprise of politics must be interpreted as a complex process of *exchange*, in which participants agree to give up liberties of independent action and secure, in return, the benefits of shared goods and services, including, importantly, the protective shield for person, property, and contract.

The political nexus and the economic nexus are necessarily coincident, and the central subject matter for enquiry becomes the institutional structure within which persons seek to secure mutual gains. This basic element in modern political economy implies, of course, that the philosophical foundations are in the theories of social contract. In game-theoretic formulations, and relating to the Paretian–Wicksellian criteria discussed above, the great game of politics must be modeled not only as positive rather than zero or negative sum in some aggregative sense, but as positive sum as evaluated by every participant.

The distributional conflict that seems to describe so much of the politics observed must not be elevated to a position as the exclusive explanatory element. Distributional conflict will, of course, be omnipresent in the operation of post-constitutional or ordinary politics. But politics must be modeled as being more than a simple struggle among interests. (Politics is not, and cannot be, conceived of as war by other means.) There is conflict among interests, yes, but always within a consensual structure that ensures against permanent or locked-in discrimination against any set of interests as evaluated over a sequence of electoral periods, and that guarantees open entry into political competition, and that imposes no prohibition on exit.

13 THE SCIENCE AS SUCH

In the introduction, I also stated that enquiry into politics had become more "scientific" over the course of the half-century, with the word enclosed in quotation marks. And, in Section 7, I suggested that an operational science, of sorts, has emerged, a science that meets the conventional criteria. We do know more about how the political economy works, and we can advance falsifiable predictions as to the effects of this or that change in the institutional structure. The important development was, however, the break-out from the dominant mindset that modeled politics as the search for the *summum bonum*, whether carried out by a benevolent despot, by agents motivated by utilitarian norms, or by citizens who generally subsume their separate interests within some generalized public interest. This mindset was unable to respond to the important Marxian challenge that viewed politics "before the revolution" as aimed at advancing the interests of the ruling class. In a very real sense, the half-century generated escapes from these countervailing visions and produced in scholarly and public attitudes both an ability and a willingness to look at politics "without romance," or politics, "warts and all."

As noted, an ultimate test of science is whether or not the human condition is bettered by some applications of its findings. A few decades are perhaps too short for the full impact of the new political economy, the modern science of politics, on the organization of social interaction to be felt. On the other hand, having cleared up the intellectual-scientific brush, so to speak, the way should be clear to examine constructively the complex web of political processes, with a view toward identifying perverse incentive arrangements, the removal of which would allow participants to secure more of whatever it is that they value. Agreement should converge, among both scientists and citizens, on the dissipation of value potential observed in rent-seeking efforts to garner differential gains for specialized interests. The incorporation of some equivalent of the generality principle into practical politics might indeed work wonders.[8]

Residues of both the romantic and Marxian visions of politics remain, and critics will continue to express yearnings for a politics that can only be imagined rather than realized. But genuine scientific progress has been made; definitive research programs have emerged that share a common hard core that seems unlikely to be successfully challenged.

References

ARROW, K. 1951. *Social Choice and Individual Values*. New York: Wiley.
BLACK, D. 1948. On the rationale of group decision making. *Journal of Political Economy*, 56: 23–34.
—— 1958. *The Theory of Committees and Elections*. Cambridge: Cambridge University Press.
BOWEN, H. 1943. The interpretation of voting in the allocation of economic resources. *Quarterly Journal of Economics*, 58: 27–49.
BRENNAN, G., and BUCHANAN, J. M. 1984. Voter choice: evaluating political alternatives. *American Behavioral Scientist*, 28: 185–201.
—— and LOMASKY, L. E. 1993. *Democracy and Decision: The Pure Theory of Electoral Preference*. Cambridge: Cambridge University Press.
BUCHANAN, J. M. 1954. Individual choice in voting and the market. *Journal of Political Economy*, 62: 334–43.
—— 1960. "La scienza delle finanze:" the Italian tradition in fiscal theory. Pp. 24–74 in *Fiscal Theory and Political Economy: Selected Essays*. Chapel Hill: University of North Carolina Press.
—— 1968. An economist's approach to "scientific politics." Pp. 77–88 in *Perspectives in the Study of Politics*, ed. M. Parsons. Chicago: Rand-McNally.

[8] See Buchanan and Congleton 1998 for extensive discussion.

―― 1975. *The Limits of Liberty: Between Anarchy and Leviathan*. Chicago: University of Chicago Press.
―― 1995. Foundational concerns: a criticism of public choice theory. Pp. 3–20 in *Current Issues in Public Choice*, ed. J. Casas Pardo and F. Schneider. Cheltenham: Edward Elgar.
―― and CONGLETON, R. D. 1998. *Politics by Principle, Not Interest: Toward Nondiscriminatory Democracy*. New York: Cambridge University Press.
―― and TULLOCK, G. 1962. *The Calculus of Consent: Logical Foundations of Constitutional Democracy*. Ann Arbor: University of Michigan Press.
COASE, R. 1960. The problem of social cost. *Journal of Law and Economics*, 3: 1–44.
DE JASAY, A. 1985. *The State*. Oxford: Basil Blackwell.
DE VITI DE MARCO, A. 1936. *First Principles of Public Finance*, trans. E. P. Marget. London: Harcourt Brace.
FASIANI, M. 1951. *Principii di scienza delle finanze*. Turin: G. Giappichelli.
ROBBINS, L. 1932. *The Nature and the Significance of Economic Science*. London: Macmillan.
SAMUELSON, P. A. 1954. The pure theory of public expenditures. *Review of Economics and Statistics*, 36: 387–9.
STIGLER, G. J., and BECKER, G. S. 1977. De gustibus non est disputandum. *American Economic Review*, 67: 76–90.
VAN CREVELD, M. L. 1999. *The Rise and Decline of the State*. Cambridge: Cambridge University Press.
WICKSELL, K. 1896. *Finanztheoretische Untersuchungen*. Jena: Gustav Fisher (repr. as pp. 72–118 in *Classics in the Theory of Public Finance*, ed. R. A. Musgrave and A. T. Peacock. New York: St Martin's Press, 1958).

CHAPTER 56

THE FUTURE OF ANALYTICAL POLITICS

MELVIN J. HINICH

1 Introduction

THE development of a science of political economy has a bright future in the long run. But the short run will most likely be similar to what has transpired these last thirty years in academia—a stumbling in the dark. I will address in this chapter some serious problems with the recent research agenda in political economy that are likely to continue on in the near future. The problem with present research is that it too often ignores the following interrelated issues: (1) multidimensional political choices, (2) the lack of equilibrium in political games, (3) the lack of common knowledge, and (4) the complex non-linear dynamics of the political/economical system. Making significant progress requires addressing these problems. Moreover, the solution to these problems will be found in integrating various strands of social science research into a new formulation that deals with these issues. My discussion will be within the context of electoral politics.

2 The Past

The influence of analytical political economy[1] has greatly increased since *An Economic Theory of Democracy* by Anthony Downs, *The Theory of Committees and Elections*

[1] I use the terms "analytic politics" and "analytical political economy" rather than "political economy" by itself because there are two conflicting meanings of the term. To some the field of political

by Duncan Black, and *The Calculus of Consent* by James Buchanan and Gordon Tullock were first published. A Google search on the words "political economy" yields 36,900,000 links, and similar searches on "formal theory in political science" and "analytical politics" yield 12,300,000 and 2,630,000 links respectively. In contrast the well-established field of comparative politics in academic political science yields 8,700,000 links for a Google search of "comparative politics."

When I first started working in analytical politics with Otto Davis, the median voter result in one of the chapters of Downs's thesis was hardly known. The dominant paradigm amongst political scientists interesting in voting behavior in those days was "party identification," abbreviated as PI. Voters vote for a party because they identify with that party based on sociological reasons. PI is similar to what is called "brand loyalty" in marketing. A consumer buys a product with a brand that the consumer trusts. The idea of having choices based on utility functions was almost strictly confined to microeconomic theory and statistical decision theory until so-called "formal theorists" successfully made inroads in the contentious field of political science. In the face of this success, many political scientists outside of formal theory argue that the major journals of the field such as the *American Political Science Review* and the *American Journal of Political Science* publish too many papers using mathematics and statistics that they cannot understand.[2]

The problem is that, after this fine start, much of the research did not progress in a meaningful way. For example, too many papers continue to assume a single dimension when this assumption clearly does not hold. Furthermore the assumption of common knowledge borrowed from modern game theory is much too strong and the game models ignore the non-linear dynamics of the system.

3 Problems for Future Academic Research

The interdisciplinary nature of research on social choice problems that was standard among the top scholars in economics, psychology, and sociology in the 1950s and early 1960s has been replaced by the frantic effort to publish in top journals. If we

---

economy is the development of theory of the interrelationship between politics and economics using the model of rational individual choice based on utility theory. To others "political economy" is a Marxist-based theory. Another possible alternative term is "public choice." This term is perceived by many scholars to be the type of public finance economics developed by James Buchanan, Gordon Tullock, and their students and colleagues. I believe that the field of public choice is a subset of analytical politics.

[2] Some but not all important past contributions to analytical politics besides Arrow, Black, Buchanan and Tullock, and Downs are in the following papers and books: Aldrich 1994; Coughlin 1992; Cox 1987; Cox and McCubbins 1993, 1994; Denzau and Mackay 1981; Denzau and Parks 1977, 1979; Feld and Grofman 1987; Kadane 1972; Kramer 1972, 1973; McKelvey 1976, 1986; McKelvey and Ordeshook 1990; Miller 1980; Ordeshook 1986, 1997; Poole and Rosenthal 1996; Shepsle 1979; Slutsky 1977; and Riker and Ordeshook 1968.

are to make significant advances in political economics that will allow policy-makers to follow and predict shifts in the political structure of democracies, we will have to build interdisciplinary research teams. The models we have now have to be expanded and extended and their implications have to be tested with solid empirical analysis involving data.

The typical paper today uses a spatial model that is still based on a single dimension whose interpretation alternates between a single political issue and a latent ideological dimension, usually called a Downsian dimension. Even though multidimensional utility-based choice models have been an integral part of economic theory for a long time, papers on analytical politics in economics usually employ game theory based on the median voter model where the political choices are confined to the unit interval. This problem should be overcome by a generalization of the theory.

An especially creative application of single-dimensional theory in a multidimensional setting is the structurally induced model of legislatures developed by Kenneth Shepsle and Barry Weingast (1981, 1987). Each committee or subcommittee is restricted to a single issue and the median voter model is applied to the committee voting decisions. One problem with the original theory is that it requires that the legislators have separable preferences for the issues that are dealt with by other committees. The structurally induced equilibrium theory should be generalized to allow for the politicians to have non-separable preferences for the issues dealt with during a legislative session.

The extensive use of single-dimensional models is surprising, as a number of multidimensional models have been developed in the past. The work (cited in the references) that I have done with Otto Davis, Peter Ordeshook, James Enelow, and Michael Munger is based on a theory where issues spaces are linked to a low-dimensional latent ideological space. This work is confined to explaining plurality rule systems. Laver and Schofield have developed a theory of multiparty politics with multiple dimensional spaces in the context of proportional representation systems. Because this approach relies on multiple rather than single-dimensional models, their work may serve as a basis for future research.

Most models of political games assume that the politicians are solely driven by their desire to get elected and re-elected. One major exception to this crucial assumption was the work of Donald Wittman (1973, 1977, 1983). Wittman argues that candidate and party preferences are part of the larger political game. This approach should be incorporated in a general theory of political competition.

Another problem that must be addressed is the oversimplification of political game theory. Political economic models are mainly developed by game theorists who apply the same assumption of common knowledge to political games as they do to economic games. Economists who model politics rarely cite relevant papers in the political science journals that do not conform to the styles that are demanded by economic theorists. The fashion these days is to develop a model that is so highly simplified that the model has little or no relationship with the complex reality of politics, nor does it have a relationship with analytical work published in political science journals.

The future for the development of analytical politics in academic economics is also limited by the rigid adherence in the profession to strict rationality. I expect that the developments in the new field of evolutionary economics will be incorporated in analytical politics. An important contribution in this field is a recent working paper by Andrew Lo. Lo argues that "much of what behavioralists cite as counterexamples to economic rationality—loss aversion, overconfidence, overreaction, mental accounting, and other behavioral biases—are, in fact, consistent with an evolutionary model of individuals adapting to a changing environment via simple heuristics." Modeling decision heuristics in the chaotic world of political games is an especially important challenge for the advancement of analytical politics. His paper is directed to a revision of the theory of market efficiency but his discussion applies to any decision process.

We also have to admit that economic science can only make very limited forecasts about economic systems especially in light of the fact that economics systems are non-linear, a fact supported by empirical evidence (see Brooks, Hinich and Molyneux 2000; and Brooks and Hinich 2001). A non-linear process is path dependent and non-scalable. This means that the reaction to a shock at time t_1 can be radically different from the reaction of the same process to the same level of a shock at time $t_2 > t_1$ even though the parameters of the system remain constant. This property of non-linear systems makes it very difficult to develop good predictions even in the short run. The simplified game-theoretic models in economics fail to capture this aspect of the economy. Likewise, simplified game-theoretic models of political systems cannot capture their non-linear dynamics.

The linear modeling and fitting approach may yield useful forecasts of a non-linear process but there is no way to know when the linear forecasts are very wrong. The usefulness of a linear approach to forecasting an episodic non-linear process is even more questionable than the use of a linear approach to forecasting a stationary non-linear process.

Political systems are not only highly non-linear, they have a fundamental uncertainty due to the lack of a majority rule core that has been studied for a variety of voting mechanisms by numerous scholars over the last forty years. It is time that we faced up to the theoretical results about the lack of equilibrium in political systems. Let us leave equilibrium analysis behind us and start on the quest to develop dynamic models of political systems that have the power to make non-trivial short-run forecasts beyond "tomorrow will be like today unless there is a surprise."

The study of politics is the hardest task in the social sciences. The political system defines the scope of the economics system while taking resources from the economy in order to run campaigns and produce the types of compromises that are required of a stable economic and political system. Politics involves group choices as well as individual choices. Emotions are as important in politics as self-interest.

Political and social games are so complex that the assumption of common knowledge that all actors know all the states of nature in the games and the conditional joint density of the states is grossly false. The future is unknowable and the fundamental uncertainties in politics are as much a part of political life as in economics, sociology, and war.

Life is complex and so we must simplify our analysis to obtain useful insights. The art of research involves creation of simplifications that provide insights based on evidence and observations. Advances in analytic political economy will have to deal with the issues that I have raised in this chapter, but at the same time the models will have to make the appropriate simplifications.

4 Speculation about the Future of Analytical Political Theory for National Policy

An organized program to develop a scientific approach to analyzing political systems would play an important role in support of a nation's defense and foreign policies. A political leadership in some nation will eventually decide to set up and fund a research institute to manage a continuing research program on these topics from an analytical perspective.

A research institute designed to make significant progress in our understanding of politics must have the following characteristics. Such an institute has to be independent of the day-to-day policy struggles that are a fact of life in any nation's government. The director of this institute should have a classical liberal arts education with a strong background in the natural sciences and a deep interest in the social sciences literature. The director should of course have experience in managing scientists and engineers working on projects that have well-defined goals, such as putting men on the moon and getting them back alive. I do not imply that the moon project goal is a model for the development of an analytical political system program, but practical and achievable goals must be set in order to avoid turning the institute into a report-generating machine.

I have no idea which country and what type of funding agency will carry out such a task nor when it will happen. I believe that it will happen, and that if one country does, then others will follow.

References

Aldrich, J. 1994. A model of a legislature with two parties and a committee system. *Legislative Studies Quarterly*, 19: 313–40.
Arrow, K. 1951. *Social Choice and Individual Values*. New Haven, Conn.: Yale University Press.
Black, D. 1958. *The Theory of Committees and Elections*. Dordrecht: Kluwer Academic.
—— and Newing, R. A. 1951. *Committee Decisions with Complementary Valuation*. London: Lowe and Brydon.

BROOKS, C., and HINICH, M. 2001. Bicorrelations and cross-bicorrelations as tests for nonlinearity and as forecating tools. *Journal of Forecasting*, 20: 181–96.

—— —— and MOLYNEUX, R. 2000. Episodic nonlinear event detection: political epochs in exchange rates. Pp. 83–98 in *Political Complexity*, ed. D. Richards. Ann Arbor: University of Michigan Press.

BUCHANAN, J., and TULLOCK, G. 1962. *The Calculus of Consent: Logical Foundations of Constitutional Democracy*. Ann Arbor: University of Michigan Press.

COUGHLIN, P. 1992. *Probabilistic Voting Theory*. New York: Cambridge University Press.

COX, G. 1987. The core and the uncovered set. *American Journal of Political Science*, 31: 408–22.

—— and MCCUBBINS, M. 1993. *Legislative Leviathan: Party Government in the House*. Berkeley: University of California Press.

—— —— 1994. Bonding, structure, and the stability of political parties: party government in the house. *Legislative Studies Quarterly*, 19: 215–32.

DAVIS, O., DEGROOT, M., and HINICH, M. 1972. Social preference orderings and majority rule. *Econometrica*, 40: 147–57.

—— and HINICH, M. 1966. A mathematical model of policy formation in a democratic society. Pp. 175–208 in *Mathematical Applications in Political Science*, ii, ed. J. Bernd. Dallas, Tex.: Southern Methodist University Press.

—— —— 1967. Some results related to a mathematical model of policy formation in a democratic society. Pp. 14–38 in *Mathematical Applications in Political Science*, iii, ed. J. Bernd. Charlottesville: University of Virginia Press.

—— —— 1968. On the power and importance of the mean preference in a mathematical model of democratic choice. *Public Choice*, 5: 59–72.

—— —— and ORDESHOOK, P. C. 1970. An expository development of a mathematical model of the electoral process. *American Political Science Review*, 64: 426–48.

DENZAU, A., and MACKAY, R. 1981. Structure induced equilibrium and perfect foresight expectations. *American Journal of Political Science*, 25: 762–79.

—— and PARKS, R. 1977. A problem with public sector preferences. *Journal of Economic Theory*, 14: 454–7.

—— —— 1979. Deriving public sector preferences. *Journal of Public Economics*, 11: 335–52.

DOWNS, A. 1957. *An Economic Theory of Democracy*. New York: Harper and Row.

ENELOW, J., and HINICH, M. 1983*a*. Voting one issue at a time: the question of voter forecasts. *American Political Science Review*, 77: 435–45.

—— —— 1983*b*. On Plott's pairwise symmetry condition for majority rule equilibrium. *Public Choice*, 40: 317–21.

—— —— 1984. *The Spatial Theory of Voting: An Introduction*. New York: Cambridge University Press.

—— —— 1989. A general probabilistic spatial theory of elections. *Public Choice*, 61: 101–13.

—— —— (eds.) 1990. *Advances in the Spatial Theory of Voting*. New York: Cambridge University Press.

FELD, S., and GROFMAN, B. 1987. Necessary and sufficient conditions for a majority winner in n-dimensional spatial voting games: an intuitive geometric approach. *American Journal of Political Science*, 31: 709–28.

HINICH, M. J. 1977. Equilibrium in spatial voting: the median voting result is an artifact. *Journal of Economic Theory*, 16: 208–19.

—— LEDYARD, J., and ORDESHOOK, P. A. 1973. Theory of electoral equilibrium: a spatial analysis based on the theory of games. *Journal of Politics*, 35: 154–93.

—— and MUNGER, M. 1994. *Ideology and the Theory of Political Choice*. Ann Arbor: University of Michigan Press.

—— —— 1997. *Analytical Politics*. New York: Cambridge University Press.

KADANE, J. 1972. On division of the question. *Public Choice*, 13: 47–54.
KRAMER, G. 1972. Sophisticated voting over multidimensional choice spaces. *Journal of Mathematical Sociology*, 2: 165–80.
——1973. On a class of equilibrium conditions for majority rule. *Econometrica*, 41: 285–97.
LAVER, M., and SCHOFIELD, N. 1998. *Multiparty Government: The Politics of Coalition in Europe*. Ann Arbor: University of Michigan Press.
LO, A. 2004. The adaptive markets hypothesis: market efficienty from an evolutionary perspective. Working paper, MIT Sloan School of Management, 15 Aug.
MCKELVEY, R. 1976. General conditions for global intransitivities in formal voting models. *Econometrica*, 47: 1085–111.
——1986. Covering, dominance, and institution-free properties of social choice. *American Journal of Political Science*, 30: 283–314.
——and ORDESHOOK, P. 1990. A decade of experimental results on spatial models of elections and committees. Pp 99–144 in *Advances in the Spatial Theory of Voting*, ed. J. Enelow and M. Hinich. New York: Cambridge University Press.
MILLER, N. 1980. A new solution set for tournament and majority voting. *American Journal of Political Science*, 24: 68–96.
ORDESHOOK, P. C. 1986. *Game Theory and Political Theory*. New York: Cambridge University Press.
——1997. The spatial analysis of elections and committees: four decades of research. Pp. 247–70 in *Perspectives on Public Choice: A Handbook*, ed. D. Mueller. Cambridge: Cambridge University Press.
POOLE, K., and ROSENTHAL, H. 1996. *Congress: A Political-Economic History of Roll-Call Voting*. New York: Oxford University Press.
SCHOFIELD, N. 1978. Instability of simple dynamic games. *Review of Economic Studies*, 65: 575–94.
——1983. Generic instability of majority rule. *Review of Economic Studies*, 50: 696–705.
SHEPSLE, K. 1979. Institutional arrangements and equilibrium in multidimensional voting models. *American Journal of Political Science*, 23: 27–59.
——and WEINGAST, B. 1981. Structure induced equilibrium and legislative choice. *Public Choice*, 37: 503–19.
—— ——1987. The institutional foundations of committee power. *American Political Science Review*, 81: 85–104.
SLUTSKY, S. 1977. A voting model for the allocation of public goods: existence of an equilibrium. *Journal of Economic Theory*, 14: 299–325.
RIKER, W., and ORDESHOOK, P. C. 1968. A theory of the calculus of voting. *American Political Science Review*, 62: 25–42.
WITTMAN, D. 1973. Parties as utility maximizers. *American Political Science Review*, 67: 490–8.
——1977. Candidates with policy preferences: a dynamic model. *Journal of Economic Theory*, 14: 180–9.
——1983. Candidate motivation: a synthesis. *American Political Science Review*, 77: 142–57.

CHAPTER 57

WHAT IS MISSING FROM POLITICAL ECONOMY

DOUGLASS C. NORTH

As the title suggests, this chapter is about what is missing from the literature on political economy.[1] The lion's share of political economy models in both political science and economics focus on formal institutions in the high-income countries of the developed West. As many of the surveys in this *Handbook* attest, this work has produced elegant models of how legislatures work, how and why bureaucratic delegation takes place, and why developed countries sometimes choose poor economic policies. These scholars have also modeled the role of interest groups and, more generally, the degree to which developed countries redistribute income.

Yet this approach misses a series of bigger questions, the most important of which is, why aren't all countries in the world advanced industrialized nations? Why do legislatures produce relatively secure property rights and the rule of law in the developed world, but not in the developing world? The answer reflects the failure of both modern economics and political science.

Both economic and political science approaches are built on models with a powerful embedded assumption. This assumption is that developing countries developed through series of gradual, incremental changes. For example, by adding this (e.g. democracy) or adding that (e.g. financial markets).

History, however, does not seem to present us with a wide spectrum of societies gradually making a transition from old to new political and economic institutions.

---

[1] This chapter draws on my recent work with John Wallis and Barry Weingast. See North, Wallis, and Weingast 2006.

Historically, social systems have persistently limited entry into political and economic activities. The economic and political rents created by limited entry have been the glue holding social systems together. Providing for social order by limiting entry, however, has come at an increasingly high cost.

Over the last three centuries, a handful of societies have made a transition to open access political and economic systems. In reality, these systems enjoy a greater degree of internal competition. This competition corresponds to the theoretical constructs of democracy and civil society created by political scientists, and theoretical models of competitive markets created by economists. These societies are called open access orders because they allow open access in both politics and economics: in politics, there is open entry into politics, competition for political power, and all citizens have rights by virtue of being citizens; in economics, there is open entry into markets, and markets are competitive rather than systematically restricted by the state.

We have begun to understand how open access societies work to produce better defined and enforced political rights and more productive economic systems. But we are far from understanding how a social order makes the transition from limited to open access.

In short, we have yet to figure out what makes the non-developing countries so stable that, even with a generation's worth of the best advice and substantial aid, few developing countries are significantly further down the road of political and economic development than they were in 1980. Moreover, those states that have made significant progress—such as Korea, Taiwan, and Singapore—have not done so by taking the advice of development specialists.

The current state of political economy theories and applications is lacking in two areas. First, they do not adequately address the problem of non-incremental change. Second, they do not take into consideration the nature of human cognition. Each of these omissions is addressed in turn.

1 THE NEED FOR A DYNAMIC THEORY

A natural starting point for social science theories is to assume that today's world looks pretty much the same as yesterday's world. We implicitly assume that we live in an ergodic world, that there is a fundamental underlying structure to the world that is stable and that we can figure out. This assumption implies that changes in the world around us occur incrementally, at the margin.

The incremental approach to economic reform is wrong. Instead, development requires that a country change its entire structure. Theoretical political economy needs to address this question: what is the structure of developing countries that makes them so stable? Only then can you begin to understand how you might change it.

Incrementalism also fails to explain history. History doesn't repeat itself. Instead, polities and economies are continually evolving. This point doesn't imply that political and economic theories are wrong, but that they cover a subset of the problem of the evolution of societies over time. We must recognize that the non-ergodic nature of the world implies that it cannot be modeled completely in the standard way.

The non-ergodic nature of the world causes problems for humans. The brain consolidates information from the past based on pattern-based reasoning.[2] In novel situations, individuals look for patterns from their experience to apply to the new situations. In truly novel situations, individuals are likely to misunderstand what they are seeing—e.g. apply a pattern from the past that turns out, *ex post*, to be inappropriate to the new situation.

The emergence of open access orders in a few countries over the last few centuries is a prime example of the non-ergodic nature of social change. Individuals in open access societies assume that competitive forces will produce market prices that can be relied on and governments that they can trust (at least in relative terms). One of the main results of the growing cross-country growth literature in both economics and political science is that citizens "trust" their governments and social institutions much more in the developed world (e.g. Knack and Keefer 1995).

How are we to account for the change from a social equilibrium in which individuals rationally trust neither the economic nor the political institutions they live under to one where open access institutions enable individuals to trust in viable and fair social outcomes?

The main implication is that solving novel problems requires that economic and political actors must be self-aware of what is happening to them. In truly novel situations, where past patterns and solutions cannot work, the only path to a solution is a dynamic one involving trial and error and feedback in an attempt to find something that works; in a word, fumbling. There is no alternative. This is why Hayek's adaptive efficiency is so important.

2 THE CENTRALITY OF BELIEFS AND LEARNING

The dynamic nature of history implies that the centrality of beliefs—how humans form their beliefs and how they learn (North 2005)—is fundamental to a new social science. This in turn leads us to two enquiries: first, how the mind and brain work to understand the environment; second, how humans learn from one another, for example though culture.

We also need to understand that studying the mind is not like studying the physical sciences—"it's all in your head" as they say. This makes all knowledge, at least at the first step, subjective. But lest you think we're going in the direction of postmodernism, we're not. Social scientists try to test their theories. But even the tests have subjective

---

[2] North 2005 elaborates on this theme.

elements, because they are in your heads. This doesn't make it postmodern, but that the social sciences are more imprecise than the sciences. Understanding these limits is a necessary first step toward understanding what social sciences can do.

So a beginning requirement is understanding how the mind and brain work. How we translate evidence from the exterior world through the senses and combine it with beliefs and previous knowledge to create explanations for the social science world.

Social science has an advantage: we have explicit tests of logic and evidence. This implies we should do a better job, but not always.

Beliefs also require that we consider learning: We learn both from the environment and from each other. The latter includes culture, the accumulated beliefs and inherited institutions from the past that provide the framework within which we begin thinking about problems.

In some situations, we are exposed to new ideas and experiences, and some of the latter force us to think differently. We have no good theories about how humans form beliefs, how we evolve existing patterns of understanding into new ones. Hence we have only the rudiments of the tools needed to study the problem of behavior in the face of novel problems.

This process is never automatic, and many societies fail to resolve the new challenges they face.

3 THREE APPLICATIONS

Consider three examples. In the early 1760s, American colonists had lived within the British Empire for over a century and considered themselves British.[3] To the extent that Americans thought about the metropole, it was that Britain was a benign, if remote, presence. Although Britain controlled the system-wide policies of the empire—trade and security—Americans exercised self-government for nearly all domestic affairs, including property rights, social policy, religion, economic regulation, and the enforcement of contracts. Nothing in the American experience suggested otherwise.

And yet events over the dozen years after the end of the Seven Years War in 1763 shocked Americans because they were inconsistent with these long-held beliefs. For the first time, Britain sought to make domestic colonial policy. Many of the initial policies, such as the stamp tax, were relatively trivial in magnitude. But some colonists—those who later became radicals—declared that these policy changes represented a fundamental sea change in British attitudes and intentions.

Drawing on the Whig tradition in seventeenth-century England, the theory of the British constitution that dominated among the colonists held that practice enshrined over the generations attained constitutional status (Greene 1986; Reid 1995). This view

---

[3] This example draws on Rakove, Rutten, and Weingast 2005.

implied that acquiescing in the British attempt to impose the stamp tax—no matter how trivial in itself—gave them the right to impose any policy. To many radicals, this implied that Britain sought to undo the credible commitment to honoring American property rights: In short, the British had become a great threat. The radicals read malevolence into British behavior—Great Britain was out to subjugate the American colonies.

In the mid-1760s, most Americans did not agree. Although they did not approve of the British behavior, they did not see it as the beginnings of malevolence and subjugation. Nothing in their previous experience suggested anything like what the radicals were suggesting. And yet, nothing in their experience allowed them to understand what the British were doing and why they were doing it.

In the face of their failure to convince most Americans, the radicals made a prediction: the British would attack the source of American liberty, the colonial assemblies that had protected their rights. Indeed, the British did just that. In the face of New York's refusal to quarter British troops, Britain suspended the New York Colonial Assembly. A few years later, when Americans in Boston dumped tea in the harbor to protest the British, reaction was far more forceful, passing what became known in the colonies as the Intolerable Acts. These closed the port of Boston, imposed martial law, and annulled the Massachusetts Colonial Charter. In short order, the British had acted exactly as the radicals had predicted: they had disbanded the Colonial Assembly and with it Massachusetts law protecting colonial property rights. Pivotal moderates became sufficiently convinced of British malevolence that they supported a revolution.

The point of this example is that Americans faced a problem that was unique given their experience. Nothing from the past allowed them easily to interpret this challenge. Initially, most people thought the problem relatively small while a smaller group argued that it represented the end of the world as they had known it. As the colonists and the British interacted, more evidence was produced, eventually leading a sufficient coalition to support a revolution. Even so, most Americans could not be sure a war was necessary.

Second, consider Timur Kuran's (1992) brilliant point in his essay "Why revolutions are better understood than predicted." The idea is that in authoritarian regimes (think of Poland in the 1970s), most citizens hate the regime and, moreover, this is common knowledge. And yet each citizen knows that if she acts alone against the regime, she risks severe punishment. Only if a great many citizens act in concert do they have a hope of overthrowing the regime. This is a coordination game; specifically, a tipping game.

Authoritarian regimes understand this strategic environment, so they spend a large portion of their resources suppressing the ability of citizens to coordinate. These regimes typically drastically curtail the freedom to speak, to assemble, and to form organizations. As Kuran observes, the regime acts to defend against all actions that it can reliably predict will foster citizen coordination.

This point implies that the only events that can spark citizen coordination are those that the regime fails to recognize for what they are. In other words, revolutions cannot be repeated: smart authoritarians will defend against means for coordination used in previous revolutions.

Third, 9/11 dramatically transformed the United States' view about its security and vulnerability. The solution to this new form of terrorism is not obvious at this point. Although not likely, it is possible that the rise of terrorism over the coming decades will dramatically transform the developed world, shrinking economies. At the current moment, policy-makers have no real idea how to solve this problem, indeed, whether or not there is a solution to this problem.

These examples illustrate several points. First, they demonstrate the need for a dynamic theory of the world. Major events in history—perhaps all major turning points in history—occur when a novel issue arises where existing patterns of knowledge are inadequate to understand the world. In each of these examples, a society faced a novel problem where the solution was not obvious, and, in the case of Kuran's revolutions, not even recognized as a problem.

Second, existing theories are useful because they help us learn about human nature (for example, that politics typically involves a mix of self-interest and the importance of beliefs) and about basic principles that hold under all circumstances (such as the principles of economics). But these lessons are about a subset of all problems. The non-ergodicity implies novel problems are always emerging, necessarily that existing "lessons" are inadequate guides. This forces us to ask a much tougher question: how are we evolving and can we understand novel change in the world? This requires that we have a theory about the dynamics of the process of change, which we do not have.

4 Conclusions

We have an inadequate understanding of why the developed world is developed; how it made the transition from non-developed countries to developed ones; why it can sustain democratic constitutions; and why both economic development and democracy typically fail in the so-called developing world. This chapter argues that the failure to understand these fundamental questions reflects that social science fails to have a truly dynamic theory that takes into account the non-ergodic nature of the world.

References

Greene, J. P. 1986. *Peripheries and Center: Constitutional Development in the Extended Polities of the British Empire and the United States, 1607–1788*. New York: Norton.

Knack, S., and Keefer, P. 1995. Institutions and economic performance: cross-country tests using alternative institutional measures. *Economics and Politics*, 7: 207–27.

Kuran, T. 1992. Why revolutions are better understood than predicted. *Contention*, 1: 199–207.

North, D. C. 2005. *Understanding the Process of Economic Change*. Princeton, NJ: Princeton University Press.
—— Wallis, J. J., and Weingast, B. R. 2006. A framework for understanding recorded human history. Unpublished working paper, Hoover Institution, Stanford University.
Rakove, J., Rutten, A., and Weingast, B. R. 2005. Ideas, interests, and credible commitments in the American Revolution. Working paper, Hoover Institution, Stanford University.
Reid, J. P. 1995. *Constitutional History of the American Revolution*, abridged edn. Madison: University of Wisconsin Press.

CHAPTER 58

MODELING PARTY COMPETITION IN GENERAL ELECTIONS

JOHN E. ROEMER

1 Introduction

POPULAR elections are the central political act of democracies,[1] and citizens in all advanced democracies organize their political competition through parties that compete in general elections. While political historians have studied parties for many years, it is remarkable that only in the last decade or so have there been serious attempts at abstract conceptualizations—that is, formal models—of inter- and intraparty competition in a democracy. In this chapter, I will report on the attempts to model political equilibrium among parties and its applications. Indeed, it appears that a satisfactory model of interparty competition can only be constructed by paying careful attention to *intra*party competition between conflicting interests or factions.

In the advanced democracies, between 27 and 50 per cent of the gross national product is collected through taxation and disbursed by the state, and state policies are decided, ultimately, by popular elections. We no longer view the state as a benevolent social planner, which maximizes some social welfare function whose arguments are the utilities of its citizens; rather, in the new political economy, the state is pictured as

[1] After William Riker 1982.

implementing the favored policies of whichever coalition of citizens manages to win control of it. (In one extreme view, that coalition could be the bureaucrats who run the state.) Thus, the theory of political competition should be, and is becoming in fact, a sub-field of public economics.

Furthermore, the issues with which the state deals are myriad, involving law, religion, language, and ethnic and racial conflict, as well as traditional economic issues of taxation and the provision of public goods. This means that any realistic theory of political competition must represent parties as taking positions in a *multidimensional policy space*.

Yet the most commonly used theory of political competition, of Harold Hotelling (1929), later elaborated by Anthony Downs (1957), with its principal result, the so-called median voter theorem, posits unidimensional political competition. Moreover, many believe that the Arrow impossibility theorem tells us that there can be no theory of multidimensional political competition—that there is no satisfactory procedure whereby citizens can aggregate their preferences to decide upon which multidimensional policy will be implemented. Our aim in this chapter is to rectify these Downsian and Arrovian pessimisms.

We will begin by introducing some notation, and then proceed to a review of the two main theories of political competition when it is assumed that the policy space is unidimensional. We will then note the problems involved in generalizing these theories to the multidimensional context, and propose a resolution to these problems, a theory of multidimensional political competition. Finally we will discuss some applications of this theory, and pose some open questions.

2 THE POLITICAL ENVIRONMENT

We model a polity as follows. There is a *policy space T*, a subset of some n-dimensional real space. There is a set of *voter types*, denoted H, which is a sample space endowed with a probability measure F. A voter of type h has preferences over the policy space represented by a utility function $v(\cdot\,;h)$, on T.

In the simplest economic application, we might think of h as describing a citizen's income or wealth and her preference for public goods, and T as a set of vectors each of which specifies some tax policy and supply of public goods. Given any tax policy t, the voter's after-tax income will be determined, as will be the supply of public goods, engendering a utility level for this citizen. $v(t;h)$ is the utility citizen h enjoys at policy t; the function v is thus an indirect utility function, derived from the citizen's direct utility function over consumption of private and public goods.

Suppose the voters face two policies, t^1 and t^2. The set of voter types who prefer the first policy to the second is denoted:

$$W(t^1, t^2) = \{h | v(t^1, h) > v(t^2, h)\}.$$

If everyone votes, then the fraction voting for t^1 should be $F(W(t^1, t^2))$, and if these are the only two policies in the election, then t^1 wins exactly when $F(W(t^1, t^2)) > 0.5$.[2] In reality, however, the outcomes of elections are uncertain, because not everyone votes, not everyone is rational, random shocks may occur, and so on. We wish to capture this uncertainty in a simple way. We suppose that the fraction who will, in the event, vote for policy t^1 is $F(W(t^1, t^2)) + X$, where X is a random variable that is uniformly distributed on some interval $[-\delta, \delta]$, where δ is a (fairly small) positive number. Think of δ as the error term that newspapers report, when they say "We estimate that 53% will vote Democratic, but our forecast is subject to a 4% margin of error." Translation: $F(W(t^1, t^2)) = 0.53$ and $\delta = .04$. We can now compute the probability that t^1 will win the election; it is:

$$prob\left[F(W(t^1, t^2)) + X > \tfrac{1}{2}\right] =$$
$$prob\left[X > \tfrac{1}{2} - F(W(t^1, t^2))\right]$$

$$= \begin{cases} 0 \text{ if } F(W(t^1, t^2)) \leq \tfrac{1}{2} - \delta \\ \dfrac{\delta + F(W(t^1, t^2)) - \tfrac{1}{2}}{2\delta}, \text{ if } \tfrac{1}{2} - \delta \leq F(W(t^1, t^2)) \leq \tfrac{1}{2} + \delta \\ 1 \text{ if } F(W(t^1, t^2)) \geq \tfrac{1}{2} + \delta \end{cases} \quad (1)$$

This formula is derived as follows. The fraction of the vote for policy t^1 can fall anywhere between $F(W(t^1, t^2)) - \delta$ and $F(W(t^1, t^2)) + \delta$, and it is uniformly distributed on this interval, by hypothesis. We simply compute the fraction of this interval that lies above 0.5; this produces formula (1). We denote the above probability by $\pi(t^1, t^2)$.

If we apply formula (1) to the newspaper report quoted above, then we see that the probability of Democratic victory is 0.875. When the fraction of voters voting for t^1 ranges from 49 to 57 per cent, 7/8 or 87.5 per cent of the time the fraction will be larger than 50 per cent.

Although I suggested that δ is a small number, note that it is really appropriate to measure uncertainty, from the parties' viewpoints, at the time that they announce their policies. The party manifestos, or the party conventions, typically take place months before the elections, when uncertainty may be substantial. Consequently, the appropriate δ could be fairly large; there could be at that time substantial uncertainty concerning the election outcome.

Because we wish to model large polities, where no type is of noticeable size in the entire population, the default assumption is that H is a continuum of types, and F is a continuous probability measure. Note that, even with a continuum of types, uncertainty in the outcome of voting does not disappear in our model. We assume that the random variable X applies, as defined above. The interpretation must be that the "misbehavior" of voters is correlated; it is not i.i.d. across voters. This may be because a scandal occurs in a campaign, which will cause some unpredictable fraction of voters to vote "against" their supposed preferences, or because one candidate is

---

[2] F is a probability measure, not a distribution function. Thus $F(A)$ is the fraction of the polity whose type is in the set A.

more telegenic than another. In sum, it is reasonable that uncertainty concerning the outcome of the elections is produced by shocks that correlate deviations by voters from "rational" behavior in the same direction. So even when there is a very large number of voter types, and large numbers of voters in each type, uncertainty does not disappear. Because of uncertainty, it will sometimes be appropriate to assume that $v(\cdot\,;h)$ is a von Neumann–Morgenstern (vNM) utility function on the policy space.

3 Unidimensional Political Competition

We now specialize to the case that T is an interval of real numbers: a unidimensional policy space. For example, T might be the interval $[0, 1]$, and $t \in [0, 1]$ could be proportional income tax rate.

Suppose that the functions $\{v(\cdot\,;h)|h \in H\}$ are all *single peaked* on T: that is, each function has a unique local maximum on T, which is also its global maximum. Suppose there are two political candidates: each wishes to propose the policy that will maximize his probability of victory, given what the other candidate is proposing. In other words, if Candidate 2 proposes t^2, then Candidate 1 will choose

$$t \text{ to maximize } \pi(t, t^2)$$

and if Candidate 1 chooses t^1 then Candidate 2 will choose

$$t \text{ to maximize } 1 - \pi(t^1, t).$$

A Nash equilibrium in this game is a pair of policies (t^1, t^2) such that:

$$t^1 \text{ solves } \max_t \pi(t, t^2)$$
$$t^2 \text{ solves } \max_t (1 - \pi(t^1, t))$$

If the functions $\{v(\cdot\,;h)|h \in H\}$ are single peaked, then Hotelling (1929) showed there is a unique such equilibrium: both candidates must play the policy that is the median in the set of ideal policies of all voters: that is, $t^1 = t^2 = t^*$, where t^* has the property that exactly one-half of the set of types has an ideal policy at least large as t^* and exactly one-half of the set of types has an ideal policy no larger than t^*.

Neither Hotelling nor Downs had uncertainty in the model, as we do, but the extension of the "median voter theorem" to our environment, with uncertainty, is immediate. Writing before Nash, Hotelling of course did not speak of Nash equilibrium. In fact, the Hotelling equilibrium is a dominant strategy equilibrium, a simpler concept than Nash equilibrium. However, when we introduce uncertainty, we must resort to the full power of Nash equilibrium to deduce the "median voter theorem."

There are two central problems with Hotelling–Downs equilibrium as a conceptualization of political competition: the first is its realism, the second is mathematical. The reality problem is that political parties, the soul of democracy, have not been modeled. In fact, as Downs tells the story, the two candidates are completely opportunist: they have no interest in policies per se, and use them only as vehicles for winning the election. To be precise, Downs *does* speak of parties, but his parties are evidently controlled completely by venal opportunistic politicians who have no accountability to constituents. He writes:

[Party members] act solely in order to obtain the income, prestige, and power which comes from being in office. Thus politicians in our model never seek office as a means of carrying out particular policies; their only goal is to reap the rewards of holding office per se.... Upon this reasoning rests the fundamental hypothesis of our model: parties formulate policies in order to win elections, rather than win elections to formulate policies. (Downs 1957, 28)

Historically, however, parties are associated with particular ideologies—presumably the views, or preferences, of the coalition of citizens whom they, in some way, represent. So the Downsian model is missing something important—perhaps the essence—of democratic competition.

Indeed, it is interesting—and puzzling—to compare the development of general equilibrium theory and formal political equilibrium theory, with respect to the issue of agency. In the Arrow–Debreu model, no agency problem is mentioned: it is assumed that firms maximize profits, without any friction between owners/shareholders and managers. Not until the early 1970s did the principal–agent problem enter into *formal* economic theory—although, of course, Berle and Means (1932) had discussed the problem of ownership vs. control much earlier. In contrast, the first formal model of political competition, the Downs model, assumes that political parties are completely in control of the *agents*, the political entrepreneurs, who, somehow, completely escape supervision by their collective principal, the parties' constituents.

In Downsian equilibrium, both candidates play a *Condorcet winner* in the policy space, a policy that defeats or ties all other policies. Each candidate wins with probability one-half, if we assume that every voter casts her vote randomly, and the policies of both candidates are identical.

The mathematical problem I alluded to above is that Downsian equilibrium does not generalize to the case of a multidimensional policy space. If T is a subset of $\mathbf{R}^2$ or some higher-dimensional space, there is in general no Nash equilibrium (in pure strategies) of the game in which each politician has, as her payoff function, her probability-of-victory function. Only in a singular case, first observed by Plott (1967), will an interior Nash equilibrium in this game exist. (There may be a Nash equilibrium on the boundary of the policy space, if it is compact. See Roemer 2001, ch. 6 for details.)

Although historians and political scientists had (informally) studied parties with ideological commitments for many years, it appears that the first formal model of ideological parties was proposed by Donald Wittman (1973). In that model, each party has a (von Neumann–Morgenstern) utility function on policies, and seeks to maximize its expected utility, given the policy played by the opposition party. Given parties called A and B, with utility functions $v^A : T \to \mathbf{R}$, $v^B : T \to \mathbf{R}$, a *Wittman equilibrium* is a pair of policies (t^A, t^B) such that

$$t^A \text{ solves } \max_t \pi(t, t^B)v^A(t) + (1 - \pi(t, t^B))v^A(t^B), \text{ and}$$

$$t^B \text{ solves } \max_t \pi(t^A, t)v^B(t^A) + (1 - \pi(t^A, t))v^B(t).$$

In other words, it is a Nash equilibrium of the game played by expected-utility-maximizing parties, where utility depends on policy outcomes.

Perhaps the central weakness in Wittman's concept is that the parties' utility functions are exogenous, so the model is incomplete. To put it politically, parties do not *represent* citizens in the Wittman model. Ortuño-Ortin and Roemer (1998) remedied this as follows. For any partition of the set of types, $A \cup B = H$, $A \cap B = \emptyset$, define the utility functions

$$V^A(t) = \int_{h \in A} v^h(t)dF(h), \quad V^B(t) = \int_{h \in B} v^h(t)dF(h);$$

these are utility functions of two parties, should coalitions A and B form parties. We say that a partition (A, B) and a pair of policies (t^A, t^B) comprise an *endogenous-party Wittman equilibrium* (EPW) if

1. (t^A, t^B) is a Wittman equilibrium for the utility functions (V^A, V^B), and
2. $h \in A \Rightarrow v^h(t^A) \geq v^h(t^B)$,
   $h \in B \Rightarrow v^h(t^B) \geq v^h(t^A)$.

Condition (1) says that each party maximizes the expected utility of an "average constituent" of the party, facing the policy of the other party. Condition (2) states that each citizen (weakly) prefers the policy of her own party to the policy of the other party. This condition means that each citizen will vote (modulo the uncertainty element) for the party that, by hypothesis, accepts him as a constituent.[3] In other words, at an EPW equilibrium, the set of *voters* for a party comprise exactly its *constituency*, and the party represents its constituency in the sense of maximizing their average expected utility.

There is (to date) no simple proof of equilibrium existence for EPW equilibrium, as there is for Downs equilibrium. (There are some difficult proofs that are not completely general: e.g. see Roemer 2001, ch. 3.) The difficulty comes from the fact that even with the kind of simple specification of the probability function that we have given, the conditional payoff functions of the parties are not quasi-concave, and so the premises of the usual fixed-point theorems do not hold. Still, in practice, it seems that EPW equilibria exist whenever one has a specific environment to work with.

The EPW equilibrium is a self-contained concept: given only the political environment defined in Section 2, equilibrium can be calculated. In this sense, the concept has the same informational standing as Downs equilibrium. Unlike Downs equilibrium,

---

[3] Readers will note that for the integration of member utility functions, in constructing the party utility function, to be meaningful, member utility functions should be cardinally unit comparable. There are other ways of aggregating member preferences into party preferences which avoid this, but I will not discuss them here (see Roemer 2001, sec. 5.3).

parties play different policies (generically) in EPW equilibrium, and so the concept provides an escape from the tyranny of the median voter. It is also the case that, generically, parties do not win with probability one-half in EPW equilibrium: this, too, provides a realistic contrast to the Downsian prediction.[4]

Naturally, the EPW equilibrium concept is harder to work with than Downsian equilibrium: for applications that arise from particular economic environments, such as the determination of tax rates to finance public goods, it is usually easy to compute the EPW equilibrium (on a computer), but the comparative statics are often difficult to deduce analytically: one must resort to simulation. Political economists are in the habit of constructing politico-economic models that are quite complex on the economic side, and simplistic (that is, Downsian) on the political side. To replace the political module of these models with EPW equilibrium will often complicate the analysis substantially. I believe, however, that the extra effort is worth taking, because the EPW concept is the simplest model of *party competition* that we have. Of course, it formulates an ideal view of representation—every citizen "belongs" to, or is represented by, a party, and each citizen's influence on his party's utility function is equal. It is, however, a far better approximation to democratic reality than the Downs model.

I summarize one application, taken from Lee and Roemer (2005), to show the payoff of using EPW equilibrium in political economy. The polity consists of workers and capital owners. A worker's type is her real wage or skill level; the distribution of real wages is given. There is a trade union that represents all workers. Two political parties form endogenously, which jointly represent all citizens. In the equilibrium to be described, one party (the "left") represents all workers whose real wage is less than some endogenously determined value, and the other party ("right") represents all more skilled workers and all capital owners. A game will be played between the two parties and the union. The union's strategy is a mark-up on the Walrasian equilibrium wage, w, of the worker whose skill is unity. (Thus, if a worker's skill is s, her Walrasian real wage will be sw.) The mark-up determines the degree of unemployment, since firms choose their labor demand to maximize profits. The income tax rate, set by political competition, determines the size of government revenues, which are used to finance an unemployment benefit for those who cannot find work at the non-Walrasian wages.

An *endogenous party Wittman equilibrium* is, in this case:

(a) a skill level s^*, defining two parties, L, consisting of all workers whose skill level is $s \leq s^*$, and R, consisting of all other workers and all capital owners;
(b) payoff functions for the two parties and the union, defined on vectors (t^L, t^R, λ), where t^J is the tax rate proposed by party $J = L, R$, and λ is the rate of unemployment, which can be viewed as the union's strategy choice. A party's payoff function is the average expected utility of its members, and the union's payoff function is the average expected utility of its members.

---

[4] One reason that I have introduced uncertainty is that, under certainty, EPW equilibrium also consists in both parties proposing the same policy. So to escape the unrealistic prediction of the Downsian model, one must introduce *both* parties that care about policies, *and* uncertainty.

(c) a Nash equilibrium $(t^{L*}, t^{R*}, \lambda^*)$ in the game played among the two parties and the union;[5]

(d) each party member (weakly) prefers her party's policy to the opposition's, given the equilibrium unemployment rate and mark-up.

We compare the welfare of citizens, in this equilibrium, to their welfare in a full-employment Walrasian equilibrium. This allows us to say something about why some societies have a highly unionized labor market, and some (such as the USA) one with much less union strength. We view the choice of "labor market regime" as made by citizens. If the majority of citizens fare better in the Walrasian equilibrium, we expect to have a quite unregulated labor market, whereas if the majority fare better in the union equilibrium described above, we expect to have highly regulated labor markets. The main result is with regard to a comparative static that alters the *degree of skill inequality* among workers: when that inequality coefficient is low or high, the majority of citizens prefer the unionized regime; when it has an intermediate value, the majority prefer the Walrasian equilibrium. Thus, the mapping from degree of skill inequality to choice of labor market regime is U shaped. We test for this result econometrically, and find support for it.

We also study the relationship between inequality and tax rates. A number of authors have studied this question, using the Downsian model (Alesina and Rodrik 1994; Persson and Tabellini 1994). In those models, increasing inequality of skill engenders increasing tax rates. There is, however, an extensive empirical literature arguing that this does not hold in reality (for example, Alvarez, Garrett, and Lange 1991). In our model, the result is more nuanced: we find that as inequality of skill increases among workers, the left party proposes higher tax rates, while the right party proposes *lower* tax rates. Not only do the two parties propose different tax rates (unlike the Downsian model), but their proposals move in different directions as inequality changes. We test this result econometrically, and find support for it.

Thus the feature of Wittman equilibrium, that parties generically propose different policies as long as there is some uncertainty, becomes important in explaining a "puzzle" in the empirical literature.

The Downsian model, in other words, mis-specifies the problem. We claim that an understanding of the relationship between taxation and inequality requires specifying, as well, whether the left or the right party holds power.

4 Multidimensional Generalizations

As I said earlier, multidimensional political competition is ubiquitous. And even if one is interested only in, say, tax policy, it would mis-specify the model to work with a

---

[5] There are two forms of uncertainty represented in the payoff function: first, the uncertainty associated with a citizen's being unemployed or not, and second the uncertainty concerning the size of the tax rate and the unemployment benefit, deriving from electoral uncertainty.

unidimensional policy space, because the positions of voters on *other* issues will affect the equilibrium in tax policy. As we will see, the preferences of voters on the religious issue or the race issue will significantly affect the equilibrium policies that emerge on economic issues. So a proper specification of political competition requires a theory where parties compete on multidimensional policy spaces.

Unfortunately, neither the Downs nor the Wittman model generalizes in what I think is a satisfactory way to multidimensional policy spaces.[6] Wittman equilibrium, or EPW equilibrium, sometimes exists on multidimensional policy spaces but existence is undependable. Interested readers are referred to Roemer (2001, sec. 8.5) for the details. Besides crafting the "probabilistic voting" models referred to in the previous footnote, political scientists responded to the non-existence of Downsian equilibrium in the multidimensional environment in the following ways:

- mixed strategy equilibrium;
- sequential games;
- institutions;
- the uncovered set;
- cycling.

A quick summary: often a game without pure strategy equilibria possesses mixed strategy equilibria. But mixed strategy equilibrium is best justified by assuming that players do not know the types of other players. In our case, the players are political parties, which are public institutions. It is, I submit, not reasonable to say that parties do not know each other's preferences. In the sequential game approach, one party moves first, and the other second, giving a Stackelberg equilibrium. These often exist in multidimensional policy spaces. But I submit that it is more appropriate to model the game as one of simultaneous moves, and so I have not found the sequential-game approach to public elections convincing. Shepsle (1979) is associated with the view that political equilibrium exists, in multidimensional contexts, because institutions restrict the moves that players can make. Actually, Shepsle's model is one of legislative equilibrium, not general elections. In the legislative context, his approach is credible. But concerning general elections, one still faces the fact that parties seem to be playing a fairly straightforward game with two players and simultaneous moves. The uncovered set is a "cooperative" kind of solution concept; its logical foundations are suspect, and it is not strategic. The uncovered set always contains the Condorcet winner if one exists, so it is, mathematically, a generalization of Downsian equilibrium. (For critique, see Roemer 2001, sec. 8.1.) Finally, many political scientists took the non-existence of multidimensional equilibrium in the known models to mean that *in reality* there was no equilibrium in the party competition game, and hence one should

---

[6] Two very similar models of multidimensional Downs equilibrium were indeed proposed by Lindbeck and Weibull 1987 and Enelow and Hinich 1989. Coughlin 1992 also proposed a model of this type. Existence is secured by having voters behave probabilistically, in a way which "convexifies" the conditional payoff functions of the Downsian parties. Uncertainty exists about electoral outcomes, but only when the set of voters is finite. Moreover, the equilibria have both parties playing the same policy, an unrealistic prediction that we wish to avoid.

observe *cycling*: each party plays its best response to the previous move of the other party, and this generates a sequence of moves which end only with the election.

An equilibrium theorist, however, does not conclude that if her model fails to produce equilibrium, there *is* no equilibrium in the real world; this would be a last resort. Instead, she looks for another model. The failure of the Downs and Wittman models does not necessarily tell us something about the world, but rather, something about the models. For we *do* seem to observe equilibrium in real-world party competition.

In the last decade, two models have been offered that do produce political equilibrium with multidimensional policy spaces, in which parties propose different policies: the party-faction model of Roemer (1998, 1999, 2001), and the citizen-candidate model of Osborne and Slivinski (1996) and Besley and Coate (1997). I will spend most of the remaining space discussing the party-faction model, because it appears to be more realistic, easier to work with, and has more applications at present than the citizen-candidate model. I will discuss the citizen-candidate model only briefly.

The party-faction model is a generalization of both the Downsian model and the EPW model: it contains both of them as special cases. We assume, now, that the decision-makers in parties form factions. Each faction possesses its own payoff function in the game of party competition. Thus, as in the EPW model, let (A, B) be a partition of the space of types: $A \cup B = H$, $A \cap B = \emptyset$. As before, we define the average utility functions of these two coalitions:

$$V^A(t) = \int_{h \in A} v(t; h) dF(h), \quad V^B(t) = \int_{h \in B} v(t; h) dF(h).$$

The first faction in party A are the Opportunists; as in the Downsian model, they wish only to maximize the probability of their party's victory against party B. Thus, the payoff function of the Opportunists in A is:

$$^{Opp}\Pi^A(t^A, t^B) = \pi(t^A, t^B). \tag{2}$$

The second faction in A are the Reformists: they are the characters of the Wittman model, who wish to maximize the expected utility of the average party member. Thus, their payoff function is:

$$^{Ref}\Pi^A(t^A, t^B) = \pi(t^A, t^B)V^A(t^A) + (1 - \pi(t^A, t^B))V^A(t^B). \tag{3}$$

The third faction in A are the Militants (or the Guardians): they are concerned with ideology only, and want to play a policy as close as possible to the ideal policy of the "average" party member. Their payoff function is:

$$^{Mil}\Pi^A(t^A, t^B) = V^A(t^A). \tag{4}$$

In like manner, party B has the analogous three factions.

Party factions are not to be associated with particular voter types. The factions are formed by professional party activists, and are small relative to the size of the population.

The idea is that, while parties *compete* with each other strategically, factions within parties *bargain* with each other over policy. I state the equilibrium concept and then explain it:

A partition of types (A, B) and a pair of policies (t^A, t^B) comprise a *party-unanimity Nash equilibrium* (PUNE) if:

1. Given the policy t^B, there is no policy t that all three factions of party A would prefer to play, instead of t^A;
2. Given the policy t^A there is no policy t that all three factions of party B would prefer to play, instead of t^B;
3. Every member of each party (weakly) prefers the policy of his party to the policy of the other party.

The phrase "that all three factions would prefer to play" is shorthand for: "that all three factions would weakly prefer to play and at least one would prefer to play."

Requirement (1) means that, given policy t^B, policy t^A is Pareto optimal for the three factions in A: there is no policy choice that would increase all their payoffs. We can thus think of t^A as the outcome of *efficient bargaining* among the factions of A, when facing t^B. In like manner, (2) means that policy t^B is the outcome of efficient bargaining among the factions of B, when facing t^A.

There is much historical evidence to justify the choice of these factions. One could quibble, and define other factions. These three, however, seem fairly canonical. It is the Militants who seem the most surprising. Yet there are many examples of Militants in history. The Militants' strategy seems to be to use the elections as a platform for advertising the party's preferences—perhaps with an eye to changing the preferences of voters for future elections.

The interesting fact is that the Reformists are expendable (or gratuitous) in this equilibrium concept: that is to say, *we get exactly the same set of equilibria* if only the Opportunist and Militant factions are active in the parties. The Reformists are, in an appropriate mathematical sense, just a convex combination of the Opportunists and the Militants.

Although there is no satisfactory *general* existence theorem (as in the case with endogenous-party Wittman equilibrium), in all applications that I have studied on multidimensional policy spaces, PUNEs exist. Moreover, there is a two-dimensional manifold (set) of equilibria. We can understand this as follows.

It turns out (see Roemer 2001, sec. 8.3) that the bargaining that takes place in the intraparty faction struggle can be represented as generalized Nash bargaining, when appropriate convexity properties hold. Take the threat point of the intraparty bargaining game in our party to be the bad situation that the opposition party wins for sure, because our party does not succeed in solving its bargaining problem and defaults. In generalized Nash bargaining, the bargainers maximize the product, raised to some power, of their utility gains from the threat point. Thus, for the Militants and Opportunists in A, this means:

$$\max_{t \in T}[\pi(t, t^B) - 0]^a [V^A(t) - V^A(t^B)]^{1-a}. \tag{5}$$

Party B's factions do the same thing. So I am claiming that a PUNE can be expressed as a pair of policies (t^A, t^B) such that

$$t^A = \arg\max_{t \in T} [\pi(t, t^B)]^\alpha [V^A(t) - V^A(t^B)]^{1-\alpha},$$
$$t^B = \arg\max_{t \in T} [1 - \pi(t^A, t)]^\beta [V^B(t) - V^B(t^A)]^{1-\beta},$$

for *some* numbers α, β in $[0,1]$.

In words, recall that, if party A fails to propose a policy, then its probability of victory is zero, and the utility of its average constituent will be $V^A(t^B)$ since party B will win for sure. Thus expression (5) states that bargaining maximizes the weighted product of the "utility" gains from the threat point of the Opportunist and Militant factions. This, as I said earlier, is the upshot of the Nash bargaining game.

We call $\alpha(\beta)$ the *relative strength* of the Opportunists in party A (resp., B). Now if such a pair of policies exists for a particular pair of numbers (α, β) then the implicit function theorem tells us (generically) that there will exist solutions for all values of the relative strengths in a small neighborhood of (α, β). This describes the two-dimensional manifold of PUNEs: each equilibrium is indexed by a pair of relative strengths of the factions in the intraparty bargaining game.

In other words, if we wanted to specify a particular pair of relative strengths of the factions in the two parties as a datum of the problem, we would have a unique equilibrium. The problem is that, *we cannot be guaranteed* that an equilibrium will exist with any *pre-specified* pair of bargaining strengths.

In fact, it is easy to deduce that an endogenous party Wittman equilibrium is a PUNE where $\alpha = \beta = \frac{1}{2}$, in other words, a PUNE where the Opportunists and Militants *have equal strengths*. This is a nice characterization of Wittman equilibrium—indeed, one that applies as well in the unidimensional model. Unfortunately, there is no guarantee that a PUNE with *this* pair of relative strengths exists when the policy space is multidimensional. For some environments it does, and for others it does not.

Hence, PUNE is a generalization of Wittman equilibrium. It is also a generalization of a Downs equilibrium: set $\alpha = \beta = 1$ for Downs equilibrium. We know, however, that this equilibrium rarely exists.

Here is a second story that gives rise to exactly the same equilibrium concept.[7] Each party has two factions, the Opportunists and the Guardians. The Opportunists are as above; the Guardians insist that, whatever the Opportunists do, they (Guardians) will not accept a policy that would give their party's constituents, on average, too low a utility. Thus, we can express the bargaining problem in party A as follows:

$$\max_{t \in T} \pi(t, t^B) \tag{6}$$
$$s.t. \quad V^A(t) \geq k^A.$$

The bigger the number k^A, the tougher are the Guardians. In like manner, party B's bargaining problem is characterized by a number k^B. It is easy to see that there is a

---

[7] It was remarked by Gérard Debreu that formal models often, virtuously, support several interpretations of reality. Here is a case in point.

2-manifold of equilibria of this game, indexed by pairs of numbers (k^A, k^B), and that this manifold is identical to the PUNE manifold.[8]

Therefore we have the freedom to conceptualize the "tough" guys in party bargaining as either Militants (who use the party as a platform to advertise) or Guardians (who hold the fort in the interest of constituents). Perhaps the Guardian story is more appealing.

As I said, I have no suitably general existence theorem for PUNE: all I can say is that in many applications that I have studied, PUNEs exist. The intuition for existence is that it is much harder to find a successful deviation to a proposal in the PUNE game than in the Wittman or Downs game. To deviate, two payoff functions must be satisfied—and the Militants and Opportunists have sufficiently "orthogonal" preferences that that is often hard to do. So many pairs of policies survive the deviation test necessary to qualify as a Nash equilibrium.

I now briefly describe citizen-candidate equilibrium, which is the second equilibrium concept that survives the generalization to multidimensional policy spaces and produces differentiated policies at equilibrium. We begin with the same data ($H, \mathbf{F}, v, T$), which define the environment. Each citizen now considers whether or not to stand for election. If a citizen enters the contest, she pays a cost, and if she wins, she enjoys a benefit from holding office, as well as deriving utility from implementing the policy upon which she ran. It is assumed that, if a candidate stands for election, she must announce her ideal policy; to do otherwise would not be credible in this one-shot game. An equilibrium consists of a set of citizens each of whom enters the race, and each announces her ideal policy. Once the policies have been announced, we can compute the coalitions of citizens that will vote for each candidate, absent uncertainty. We can then append an element of uncertainty as we have above. The equilibrium is a Nash equilibrium; to be so, it must satisfy two tests. First, each candidate must not have higher expected utility, should he decide not to run. (Under that deviation, he does not have to pay the cost of running, but forfeits the expected gain from winning.) Secondly, each non-candidate must not have higher utility should she throw her hat into the ring. The model generally possesses pure-strategy equilibria with a small set of candidates, even when the policy space is multidimensional. Thus, both limitations of the Downs model are overcome, because candidates are explicitly "ideological," as well as caring about the spoils of office, and equilibria exist.

I see two problems with the model. First, it is not a model of party competition, and so ignores the central institutions of democratic political competition. Second, the element of compromise in political competition is ignored, in the sense that each candidate proposes her ideal policy. The justification of this move is that the game is one-shot, and candidates cannot commit themselves to do otherwise. This strikes me as unrealistic, even if it is logically consistent within the framework of a one-shot game. In the PUNE model, parties do compromise, although we ignore the credibility of their proposing non-ideal policies in a one-shot game. (There is, indeed, a (locally)

---

[8] One can check the claim that the two stories engender the same equilibria by noting that the first-order conditions for the solution of (5) and (6) are equivalent. Of course, the same holds for the corresponding FOCs for the B party.

unique equilibrium in the PUNE model where both parties play the ideal point of their average member, but I consider this to be an uninteresting equilibrium.)

5 APPLICATIONS

Two of the virtues of the PUNE model are that it is often possible to derive interesting analytical results in specific applications, and it is possible to estimate the model econometrically, which enables one to conduct policy experiments for specific polities. In this section I present four applications of PUNE.

5.1 Progressive Taxation

We observe that, in all advanced democracies, income taxation is progressive, in the sense that marginal tax rates rise with income. Why is this so? A standard answer has been that progressive taxation seems fair. Many, however, would consider this explanation not to be parsimonious: it would be better to have a completely "political" explanation, one that did not presuppose any assumption that citizens are motivated by a sense of justice or fairness. Thus, one can ask, will the income tax proposals that survive in cut-throat democratic competition be progressive ones? An early discussion of this problem is due to Kramer and Snyder (1988), which takes a Downsian approach, and places an ad hoc assumption on the nature of the policy space in order to produce equilibria. The unidimensional Downsian and Wittman models are ill equipped to answer this question. The standard unidimensional policy space of tax regimes consists of the set of affine income tax functions, characterized by a constant marginal tax rate (in the interval $[0, 1]$) and a lump-sum transfer to all, financed by that tax rate. None of these tax regimes have increasing marginal tax rates. Now one could work with a unidimensional policy space constructed to possess both convex and concave tax functions, but the unidimensional restriction is really too constraining. The ideal model is one that poses a space of tax policies that is genuinely multidimensional, and contains both progressive and regressive tax functions.

In Roemer (1999), the tax-function space contains all quadratic income tax functions, constrained to require that no citizen pay a tax greater than her income, and that after-tax income be non-decreasing in pre-tax income (an incentive compatibility constraint). This is a two-dimensional policy space. We posit a distribution of income-earning capacities (wages). Citizens desire only to maximize their after-tax income—they have no desire for leisure—and so everyone works at his full capacity. The income tax is purely redistributive (no public goods). We study the two-party PUNEs of this model. It is shown that, if the median income is less than mean income, then in *every* PUNE,[9] the probability that a progressive tax scheme wins the election is unity. (In other words, either both parties propose progressive schemes, or if not, the one proposing a regressive scheme wins with probability zero.) Here, then, is a completely "positive" explanation of the ubiquity of progressive taxation.[10]

5.2 The Effect of Non-economic Issues on Taxation

In the introduction, I wrote that a central reason to model political competition as multidimensional is that apparently non-economic issues can affect political outcomes on economic issues. Suppose that the electorate is concerned with two issues, taxation and religion. (Religion is a place-holder for many other issues, of course.) Thus, voters have preferences over the tax policy and the religious policy of the state, and parties compete on this policy space. To be specific, let us suppose that a voter's type is a pair (w, ρ), a policy is a pair (t, r), mean income is μ, and the voter's utility function is:

$$v(t, r; w, \rho) = (1 - t)w + t\mu - a(r - \rho)^2. \tag{7}$$

Thus, w is this voter's income, ρ is the voter's religious position, t is an affine income tax which distributes the lump-sum $t\mu$ to all citizens, and the voter's preferences over the religious issue are Euclidean (she suffers a quadratic loss as the state's policy becomes further away from her religious view). We call a the *salience* of the religious issue, which is here assumed to be the same for all citizens.

Here the space of types is two dimensional, as is the policy space. Given a distribution of types F, the environment is complete, and we can study the two-party PUNEs. The question is: when do citizens' views on the religious issue affect the equilibrium tax rates proposed by the parties in PUNEs?

If $a = 0$, this model reduces to a unidimensional model on tax policies, and it is not hard to show that in the endogenous-party Wittman equilibrium, the two parties consist of the "poor" and the "rich," and they propose tax rates of one and zero, respectively. This is the benchmark. We can ask: is it ever the case that, when a is positive, *both* parties propose a tax rate of zero (or a tax rate of one)? That would show that religious views can have an extreme effect on economic policy.

The answer is there is such a case. Suppose the following condition on the distribution F holds:

Condition A. The mean income of the cohort of voters who hold the median religious view is greater than mean income in the population as a whole.

Then it can be shown (see Roemer 1998, 2001) that if a is sufficiently large, and if uncertainty is sufficiently small, then in *all* PUNEs, both parties propose a tax rate of

---

[9] There is, as usual, a 2-manifold of PUNEs.
[10] An extension for future research would be to study this problem on a small-dimensional space of piecewise linear tax functions, which are prevalent in reality. The problem of characterizing PUNEs on such a space is much harder than on the space of quadratic functions.

zero! Correspondingly, if we change "greater" to "less" in the statement of Condition A, then the conclusion is that, in all PUNEs, both parties propose a tax rate of one.

An intuition behind this result is as follows. As a gets large, the model approaches one where political competition is unidimensional, and the only policy is the religious issue. If uncertainty is small, then in such competition, both parties will propose policies close to the ideal policy of the voter(s) with the median religious view. But if this cohort of voters has income greater than the mean, on average, then they want zero taxation. Conversely, if this cohort has mean income less than the mean, they want a tax rate of one.

The substantial result is that convergence of both parties to proposing a tax rate of zero, if Condition A holds, happens at finite a and with a positive degree of uncertainty.

More generally, the comparative static is that as a increases, the tax rates proposed in PUNEs fall. In other words, we should see economic policy moving to the right (left), as the salience of the religious increases, if Condition A (resp., its negation) holds.

The applications of this result seem myriad. The religious issue could be nationalism, racism, language policy, civil rights, etc. In Section 5.4 below, I discuss an application where the second issue is "racial policy" in the USA.

5.3 The Flypaper Effect

It has been noted by many authors that an increase in the wealth of a community by one unit engenders a smaller increase in the level of locally financed public goods than an increase by one unit of a federal grant to the community engenders: Hines and Thaler (1995) find that a federal grant increases the financing of public goods by about $637 per thousand dollars of the grant, a substantially greater increment than occurs with an increase in the community's average wealth by an equivalent amount. This has been dubbed the flypaper effect. Many authors have viewed it as an anomaly, because if the community is assumed to be composed of homogeneous citizens, the increase in the supply of the public good should be identical in the two cases.

However, if the community is heterogeneous in income, but homogeneous in preferences over income and the public good, the flypaper effect is predicted theoretically.

How should one model the political problem here? There are two things to be decided: the tax policy and the value of the public good. This can be done on a unidimensional policy space, if one restricts taxation to be proportional to income, and finances the public good from the tax revenues. So a Downsian formulation is possible. Indeed, with a Downsian formulation, we do predict the flypaper effect, with heterogeneous incomes.

But proportional taxation is unusual. More realistically, tax policy is affine—a constant marginal tax rate and a transfer payment to all citizens. Thus, here we have, naturally, a two-dimensional policy space: three variables must be chosen—the income tax rate, the lump sum transfer payment to all citizens, and the value of the public good. The budget constraint states that tax revenues must equal the sum of transfers and the public good, so the policy space is two dimensional.

Roemer and Silvestre (2002) model the problem using PUNE. We parameterize the model to the US income distribution, and choose some reasonable values for the parameters of the utility function, which determine the relative preference of citizens for private income and the public good. We compute PUNEs for three economies:

E1. An economy at date zero, with a given distribution of income;
E2. An economy at date one, with the same distribution of income and a external subsidy of $1,000 per capita;
E3. An economy at date one, with the distribution of income whose mean is $1,000 more than in E1, and no external subsidy.

Each PUNE consists of two policy proposals (by the two parties) and the probability of left victory. We take the expected expenditure on public goods as the value to examine. There is a 2-manifold of PUNEs: we take the average of the expected expenditures on public goods over this manifold. We find that the political equilibria in E2 have expected expenditures on public goods that are $635 higher than the political equilibria in E1: this is almost exactly the average found in the Hines and Thaler (1995) studies. It is substantially more than the increase in expected expenditures in the move from E1 to E3, which is $157.

5.4 The Effect of Racism on Redistribution in the USA

In Lee and Roemer (2006), we take the "religious" issue of Section 5.2 above to be the race issue in the United States. We fit a model of citizen preferences to the US polity, and attempt to compute the effect of racism in the electorate on the degree of redistribution that takes place through income tax policy, where the policy space is two dimensional, representing income taxation and the position of the party on the race question. We fit the model to the data for every presidential election in the period 1976–92, achieving an excellent fit. We then conduct counterfactual experiments, asking what the equilibrium would be on the tax rate dimension, if the degree of voter racism should decline. (The distribution of voter racism is estimated from the American National Election Studies.) The punchline is that (we predict) the marginal tax rate would increase by at least ten points, were American voters not racist, making the US fiscal system much closer in size to that of the northern European democracies.

6 Conclusion

We have argued that in modern democracies, an understanding of the apparatus of political competition, whereby citizens with divergent interests organize to battle for control of state policy, is of the highest importance. In this chapter, we have discussed only one of the several arenas of political competition: general popular elections. Indeed, contemporary practice lags reality: the vast majority of scholarly papers in political economy model political competition using the Hotelling–Downs apparatus, one which predicts that, in two-party competition, both parties propose the same policy. Were this indeed the case, it is hard to understand how parties would finance themselves: what motivation would the rational citizen have to contribute to one party over another in such a situation? Moreover, the Hotelling–Downs model is incapable of describing political competition which is complex, in the sense of taking place over several issues. All general elections are concerned with a multitude of issues.

We argued that a variation on Wittman's model provides a superior description of reality to Hotelling–Downs in the unidimensional context. The basic data of a political environment—preferences of citizens and the policy space—determine a partition of citizens into two parties, an equilibrium pair of policy proposals, and a probability that each party wins the election. The model can be estimated and its predictions tested.

Neither the Hotelling–Downs model nor the endogenous-party Wittman model generally possess equilibria, however, when the policy space is multidimensional. We proposed that the way to solve this problem is not to complexify the concept of Nash equilibrium (to a stage game, for instance) but rather to articulate further the conception of what a party is. Parties are, in reality, complex institutions, and they are the soul of modern democracy: hence, good modeling impels us to think carefully about what parties are. We proposed to think of the decision-makers in parties as forming factions, with different concerns: Opportunists, Reformists, and Militants or Guardians. *Inter*party competition is strategic, in the sense of Nash equilibrium; *intra*party competition is "cooperative" in the sense of Nash bargaining among factions. (Thus our PUNE can be thought of as a "Nash–Nash" equilibrium.) Formally, the PUNE is a generalization of both Hotelling–Downs and endogenous-party Wittman equilibrium, but unlike those two special cases, PUNEs exist with multidimensional policy spaces. We argued that interesting analytical results can be derived about PUNE in specific applications, and moreover, the model can be fit to data, in order to study policy and comparative statics for actual political economies.

The models described here have all been ones of *perfectly representative democracy*. In the PUNE, every citizen is a member (constituent) of one party, and each party aggregates the preferences of its constituent types according to their population sizes. This is an ideal type of party behavior. In the USA, where private financing of parties is the norm, one might expect that parties would represent their *contributors* according to their *contributions*, rather than their constituents according to their numbers. The models of this chapter can be generalized to study that kind of imperfectly representative democracy (see Roemer 2006).

Moreover, we have stayed with the assumption of two parties. The citizen-candidate model allows the number of candidates to be endogenous: however, there are many equilibria so that it can hardly be said to have *determined* the number of candidates. PUNE can be generalized to deal with more than two parties. But it must be said that models with more than two parties are inherently more complex, because the natural political game then has two stages: first, an election, and second, the formation of a government among a set of parties that comprise a majority coalition.[11] That coalition-formation process must be modeled, and then the citizen-voter must take into account the nature of that process when she votes. There is no conceptual problem in using the PUNE concept to study multidimensional political competition with several parties: the main conceptual issue, about which disagreement among political scientists persists, is the nature of the coalition formation process in the second stage.

Many open questions are posed by the factional approach to party competition. What are the microfoundations of the formation of the particular factions I have presumed to exist? Do voters form factions? How do candidates emerge from factional bargaining? Can we formulate a theory of how the results of primary elections influence the bargaining powers of factions? More generally, how can one endogenize the relative bargaining powers of the factions? In a federal system, one might conceive of factions in national parties as representing different regional interests. This, too, would suffice to provide existence of equilibria in multidimensional competition, as long as the regional interests were suitably different.

Finally, to return to a point alluded to much earlier, how does the Arrow impossibility theorem fit into all this? To see, we must first formulate the political environments described here as Arrovian environments. Thus, let the set of *social alternatives* be lotteries whose elements are policy pairs taken from the given policy space. A *profile* is a function $\{v(\cdot\,;h)|h \in H\}$ where h is distributed according to F. A *social choice function* maps a profile into orderings of social alternatives. We could take the ordering of lotteries associated with a given profile to be as follows: all lotteries that are engendered by PUNEs are socially indifferent, and all other lotteries are socially indifferent, and inferior to the ones generated by PUNEs. This social choice function violates the Arrow postulates as follows:

- it is not defined on *preferences* but on *utility functions*, which must be cardinally unit comparable (or else adding up [integrating] members' utilities to form the party's utility function makes no sense);
- it is not Pareto efficient (in fact, each party proposes, in a PUNE, a policy that *is* a Pareto efficient social alternative, but the *lottery* between these policies, engendered because of uncertainty, might not be Pareto efficient, because of risk aversion);
- the axiom of binary independence of alternatives fails.

In the *modified* Arrovian framework, where utility functions are cardinally unit comparable, the unique social choice function to satisfy the Arrovian axioms is utilitarianism:[12] but certainly the PUNE is not the utilitarian rule.

---

[11] Reality is still more complex. There are times when governments are formed by coalitions that together won less than one-half of the votes.
[12] See d'Aspremont and Gevers 1977, theorem 3; also Roemer 1996, theorem 1.4.

Does this mean that political equilibrium, as we have described it in this chapter, is not a legitimate way for a society to aggregate its members' preferences? Hardly; it means the Arrovian framework is not the right abstraction to capture the nature of political competition. (Let me simply note that if Nash equilibrium is involved in political competition, we cannot expect outcomes to be Pareto efficient, immediately violating an Arrovian axiom.) Although it is *desirable* to have Pareto efficient outcomes, that might not be compatible with democratic competition.

To put the same point somewhat differently, defining the set of feasible allocations for a society in the classical way is an apolitical approach. Why should some allocations be "feasible" if there are no political institutions that could bring them about? The same point has been made with regard to asymmetric information: Why should an allocation be regarded as "feasible"[13] if asymmetric information makes it impossible for it ever to be brought about? The constraint of asymmetric information is just as real as a technological constraint; similarly, a complex society must have politics, and it is therefore myopic to conceive of feasibility apolitically.

References

ALESINA, A., and RODRIK, D. 1994. Distributive politics and economic growth. *Quarterly Journal of Economics*, 109: 465–90.
ALVAREZ, R., GARRETT G., and LANGE, P. 1991. Government partisanship, labor organization and economic performance. *American Political Science Review*, 85: 539–56.
BERLE, A., and MEANS, G. 1932. *The Modern Corporation and Private Property*. New York: Harcourt, Brace and World (repr. 1968).
BESLEY, T., and COATE, S. 1997. An economic model of representative democracy. *Quarterly Journal of Economics*, 112: 85–114.
COUGHLIN, P. 1992. *Probabilistic Voting Theory*. New York: Cambridge University Press.
D'ASPREMONT, C., and GEVERS, L. 1977. Equity and the informational basis of collective choice. *Review of Economic Studies*, 44: 199–209.
DOWNS, A. 1957. *An Economic Theory of Democracy*. New York: HarperCollins.
ENELOW, J., and HINICH, M. 1989. A general probabilistic spatial theory of elections. *Public Choice*, 61: 101–13.
HINES, J. R., JR., and THALER, R. H. 1995. The flypaper effect. *Journal of Economic Perspectives*, 9: 217–26.
HOTELLING, H. 1929. Stability in competition. *Economic Journal*, 39: 41–57.
KRAMER, G., and SNYDER, J. 1988. Fairness, self-interest, and the politics of the progressive income tax. *Journal of Public Economics*, 36: 197–230.
LEE, W., and ROEMER, J. E. 2005. The rise and fall of unionised labour markets: a political economy approach. *Economic Journal*, 115: 28–67.
—— —— 2006. Racism and redistribution in the United States: a solution to the problem of American exceptionalism. *Journal of Public Economics*.
LINDBECK, A., and WEIBULL, J. 1987. Balance budget redistribution as the outcome of political competition. *Public Choice*, 52: 273–97.

---

[13] For instance, one achieved through certain kinds of lump-sum taxation.

ORTUÑO-ORTIN, I., and ROEMER, J. E. 1998. Endogenous party formation and the effect of income distribution on policy. Section 5.2 in J. Roemer, *Political Competition*. Cambridge. Mass.: Harvard University Press.

OSBORNE, M., and SLIVINSKI, A. 1996. A model of political competition with citizen-candidates. *Quarterly Journal of Economics*, 111: 65–96.

PERSSON, T., and TABELLINI, G. 1994. Is inequality harmful for growth? *American Economic Review*, 84: 600–21.

PLOTT, C. 1967. A notion of equilibrium and its possibility under majority rule. *American Economic Review*, 57: 787–806.

RIKER, W. 1982. *Liberalism against Populism: A Confrontation between the Theory of Democracy and the Theory of Social Choice*. San Francisco: W. H. Freeman.

ROEMER, J. E. 1996. *Theories of Distributive Justice*. Cambridge, Mass.: Harvard University Press.

——1998. Why the poor do not expropriate the rich in democracies: an old argument in new garb. *Journal of Public Economics*, 70: 399–442.

——1999. The democratic political economy of progressive income taxation. *Econometrica*, 67: 1–19.

——2001. *Political Competition*. Cambridge, Mass.: Harvard University Press.

——2006. Political equilibrium under private and public campaign financing: a comparison of institutions. *Advances in Theoretical Economics*.

——and SILVESTRE, J. 2002. The "flypaper effect" is not an anomaly. *Journal of Public Economic Theory*, 4: 1–17.

SHEPSLE, K. 1979. Institutional arrangements and equilibrium in multidimensional voting models. *American Journal of Political Science*, 23: 27–59.

WITTMAN, D. 1973. Parties as utility maximizers. *American Political Science Review*, 67: 490–8.

CHAPTER 59

OLD QUESTIONS AND NEW ANSWERS ABOUT INSTITUTIONS

THE RIKER OBJECTION REVISITED

KENNETH A. SHEPSLE

THE last quarter-century has witnessed an intense scrutiny of constitutions and institutions—as abstract principles of governance and as real ways of doing things collectively. The veritable explosion of democratization during this period has provided both theoretical rationales and empirical laboratories for this scrutiny. In this chapter I want to revisit some old issues to suggest some new considerations, and to resurrect some old answers as possible solutions to new problems.

I motivate the discussion with three questions:

- What are institutions?
- How are institutions chosen?
- Once chosen, how are institutions maintained or changed?

With these as motivation, I take up what has come to be known in the political science literature as the *Riker Objection*. By far the lion's share of analyses in the institutional revolution takes political institutions as given and studies their effects.

* The author is grateful to the two editors for their incisive comments through several revisions of this chapter. He also appreciates the research support of the National Institute of Aging (RO1-AG021181-02).

Riker's objection is essentially that institutions, like the policies subsequently chosen under them, are endogenous. Riker (1980) praised early post-behavioral explorations (e.g. Shepsle 1979) for reintroducing institutions into formal analysis, but reprimanded them for treating decision-making arrangements as fixed exogenous constraints rather than as changeable features of the political landscape.

The last few decades have witnessed some progress on the endogenous treatment of institutions, but standard comparative statics analysis has proven to be insufficient because institutional changes are dynamic rather than one-time changes. Constitutions, after all, are said to be "living." Old regimes segue into new ones which, in turn, may segue into still newer ones. Rules are changed, constitutions amended, procedures suspended, institutions reformed, emergency powers invoked. Institutional arrangements at any particular point in time, in short, are possibly no more than way-stations in an evolving sequence. As a consequence, the treatment of institutions as exogenous and stable is riddled with perplexing issues, and the Riker Objection reminds us that this approach is at best a first step in a longer analytical project. The remainder of the chapter focuses on some of these dynamic considerations.

1 WHAT ARE INSTITUTIONS?

The focus in this chapter is on micro-analytical aspects of institutions, so I intend to put to one side macrohistorical conceptions that treat broad phenomena like culture, law, and slavery as institutions (in one version likening them to coral reefs that form and re-form without apparent human agency—see Sait 1938).[1] Rather I want to focus on interpretations of institutions that are micro-analytical, game theoretic, and explicitly involve human agency. I discuss two interpretations in particular—institutions as game forms and as equilibria of more fundamental strategic interaction.

Institutions as game forms. "Institutions are the rules of the game in a society or, more formally, are the humanly devised constraints that shape human interaction" (North 1990, 3; also see Mantzavinos, North, and Shariq 2004). This definition takes an institution as a *game form*, and North (1990, 46) urges us to think flexibly of this as ranging from informal constraints like those found in taboos, customs, conventions, codes of behavior, and traditions, to formal rights, responsibilities, and constraints as are contained in modern contracts, official procedures, and written constitutions. The institution qua game form specifies the set of players, what actions players may take (must take, may not take, etc.), informational conditions under which they make their choices, the timing of moves, the role and timing of exogenous events, and the

---

[1] A fine modern treatment of historical institutionalism may be found in Hall and Taylor 1996. For a more elaborate conceptual discussion of institutions generally, see Crawford and Ostrom 1995, and Ostrom 2005.

outcome that results from a distribution of choices and the realization of all random factors. Once player preferences are added to the mix, the game form becomes a *game*. For North, the players are often organizations and the entrepreneurs that create and maintain them. Organizations—firms or political parties or legislative committees or interest groups or public bureaux or military units—exploit their institutional environment in order to pursue entrepreneurial objectives. An institution, then, is a venue for strategic social interaction and choice.

Where do these venues for strategic interaction come from? No single answer will do, since institutions may be the explicit product of choice and design (like the US Constitution of 1787, or the 1975 revision of Rule 22 of the US Senate modifying the vote requirement to shut down filibusters and close debate), or may have evolved in complex and possibly inexplicable ways shrouded in the mists of time (for example, "Who is the architect of Roman Law?" asks Sait 1938). I think it is fair to say, however, that most uses of the game-form conception of institution are focused mainly on the *consequences* of institutional arrangements, not their origins. Attention is riveted on the play of the game and its outcome—what I elsewhere called a *structure-induced equilibrium* (Shepsle 1979), or simply an *institutional equilibrium* (Shepsle 1986). It is a description of the set of strategies in (subgame perfect Nash) equilibrium, given player tastes and rules of engagement.

Institutions as equilibria. Rather than take an institution as an exogenously provided game form that induces equilibrium outcomes—the classic Downsian model of two-party electoral competition under plurality rule is an exemplar—one might instead think of the game form itself as an equilibrium—as an endogenous product of a more primal setting, or what may be called an *equilibrium institution* (Shepsle 1986). It is a relationship of a set of arrangements to the elemental features of its environment, or an adaptation of these arrangements to them. For example, one would ask in which political circumstances a plurality electoral system will emerge. The electoral rules, treated as fixed and exogenous parameters in Downs, now become variables that are the product of a more encompassing game. In effect, the primal strategic setting is characterized parametrically, but these parameters may change in response to shocks or perturbations.

Typically shocks to the primal parameters are taken to be exogenous. For example, the accidental discovery of mineral deposits may boost the private demand for military assets (protection of oil fields or diamond mines), and thus increase the potential political influence of military groups on a regime. However, there are times when the institution itself may affect the distribution of shocks to primal parameters. A regime of well-defined property rights and well-worked-out mineral law, for example, will encourage exploration and thus affect the likelihood of "accidental" discovery. In either case, these changes in the primal strategic environment will influence the viability of existing institutional arrangements.

The institution-as-equilibrium perspective takes the behavioral equilibrium induced by the primal environmental circumstances as the institution. It was articulated early on by Schotter (1981), and then elegantly elaborated by Calvert (1995). This approach regards "an institution as an equilibrium of behavior in an underlying game... It must be rational for nearly every individual to almost always adhere to the behavioral prescriptions of the institution, given that nearly all other individuals are doing so" (Calvert 1995, 58, 60).

This contrasts with the institutions-as-constraint approach which *takes for granted the rationality of conforming to institutional practices*. That is, the institutions-as-constraint approach assumes away the prospect of defection and the necessity of enforcement; the institutions-as-equilibrium approach always allows the prospect of defection and requires as part of the equilibrium the possibility of adverse off-the-equilibrium-path consequences as a credible deterrent against defection. Calvert (1995, 73–4) describes this as follows:

[T]here is, strictly speaking, no separate animal that we can identify as an institution. There is only rational behavior, conditioned on expectations about the behavior and reactions of others. When these expectations about others' behavior take on a particularly clear and concrete form across individuals, when they apply to situations that recur over a long period of time, and especially when they involve highly variegated and specific expectations about the different roles of different actors in determining what actions others should take, we often collect these expectations and strategies under the heading of *institution* . . . *Institution* is just a name we give to certain parts of certain kinds of equilibria. (emphasis in original)

The real advantage of this approach is that the basis for understanding an institution is the same as that for understanding behavior within it. Optimal behavior within the rules, and obeying the rules in the first place rather than defecting from them, are accounted for by the very same appeal to rationality.

Even if we grant the institution-as-equilibrium approach intellectual priority over the institution-as-constraint approach—I am a recent convert to this point of view—it is nevertheless possible to see how the two approaches fit together. When a set of arrangements is in equilibrium with its environment—either in the sense that it has adapted to a relatively calm and unchanging environment or is robust to perturbations experienced by that environment—then the behaviors it fosters appear to be equilibrium responses to the opportunities provided by this (equilibrium) arrangement. The "institution" looks like a game form, and behavior looks like an optimizing response to this stable strategic environment. The institution-as-constraint approach would capture things quite satisfactorily. If, on the other hand, the institution were not robust—small perturbations in the environment unraveled it—then it makes far less sense to refer to the institution as constraining. The very next shock to the environment contains seeds for the institution's destruction, i.e. incentives for players to deviate from institutional prescriptions. A historic legislative chamber like the US Senate or the British House of Commons appears to consist of players optimizing in a well-defined game because the institution is well adapted to its environment. Its players are understood as optimizing according to *given* rules rather than contemplating moving outside the rules altogether. The opportunity to depart from the nominal "rules of the game"—to make things up as they go along—seems so much more attractive, on the other hand, to the legislators in the modern Russian

Duma (see Andrews 2002). Its members constantly test how much they can get away with. Indeed, it may constitute an abuse of terminology in the institutions-as-equilibria approach to call the Duma an institution—it hardly seems "institutionalized" at all (Polsby 1968).[2]

2 HOW ARE INSTITUTIONS CHOSEN?

In the literature there are both historical and analytical approaches to the "choice" of institutions. Choice is put in quotation marks because some institutional arrangements cannot literally be said to have been chosen, but instead to have evolved and taken hold. Having said that, however, I still insist that even these are the product of choices—that "taking hold" reflects choices by individuals to abide by, not defect from, behavioral conventions.

Uncertainty in various guises is an important feature in most depictions of institutional origins. Perhaps the most famous of these is the Rawlsian *veil of ignorance* (Rawls 1972). In a (fictitious) constitutional moment, Rawlsian deliberators deliberate about prospective institutional arrangements in ignorance of their own physical, material, and intellectual endowments. Deliberators are therefore also ignorant of who stands as the decisive decision-maker in any institutional arrangement they might craft. So, according to Rawls, deliberators are unable to pursue institutions that maximize a private utility function, and thus are free to act on behalf of alternative objectives—maximizing the welfare of the "average," the most advantaged, or the least advantaged, for instance, even if they don't know that person's identity. Rawls offers a normative brief for "maximin justice" under these circumstances, structuring institutions so as to maximize the welfare of the least well off.

As a normative treatise, *A Theory of Justice* is a milestone of twentieth-century thinking about constitutional moments. As a basis for a historical or positive analytical treatment of actual constitution writing, it possesses problems. Once deliberation is completed, the Rawlsian veil lifts and the distribution of endowments becomes common knowledge. Then the tests for the new order are implementation and enforcement, and possibly the delicate matters of defection, punishment, and renegotiation. Why don't the biggest, the richest, or the smartest, who now know

[2] What Calvert 1995 points out is that the institutions-as-constraints approach never entertains the possibility of a change in the game. In most circumstances where this approach is appropriate, this failure is not fatal. The reality, however, is that strategic players may wake up each morning and indeed ask themselves whether today is the day to make an unexpected move. The Speaker of the US House, for example, may decide one day *not* to draw most members of a conference committee from the standing committee of original jurisdiction—a move that would come as a bolt from the blue but one surely within the strategic reach of the Speaker in the "primal" majoritarian game (in which all his behavior requires in order to stick is support of a chamber majority). Indeed, in mid-2005 the Republican leadership in the US Senate considered just such a move, dubbed the "nuclear option," in which the rules governing debate would be radically reinterpreted.

who they are, threaten to defect or insist on renegotiation? A Rawlsian deliberation, in short, is not strategically compelling; it is a normative approach that is not predicated on equilibrium behavior and so fails either the institutions-as-constraints or institutions-as-equilibrium test. Rawls responds that his is an arrangement requiring integrity—if it is normatively satisfactory before the veil is lifted, then honorable people should behave honorably after the veil is lifted. This may be satisfactory in a normative exercise, but it is not helpful if one is trying to come to grips with actual constitutions and institutional arrangements.

The empirical problem with the Rawlsian veil is its lack of descriptive authenticity. In constitutional moments, deliberators are not often plagued by the sort of uncertainty supposed by Rawls. They often *do* know their own endowments. Thus, to a first-order approximation at least, winning coalitions (Riker 1962), veto players (Tsebelis 2002), and decisive political agents in any institutional arrangement will also be widely recognized. As Aghion, Alesina, and Trebbi (2004, 17) observe, "Veils of ignorance have large holes in them."

To deny the Rawlsian veil, however, is not to deny the significance of uncertainty in choosing institutions. Downs and Rocke (1995) make a basic point. Even if uncertainty about individual endowments is not problematical, the realization of random shocks may still affect the distribution of attractive opportunities. The real source of ignorance concerns opportunities, not endowments; institutions will often appear endogenously in response to this kind of uncertainty. A society of healthy people, for example, is still subject to unexpected afflictions and infirmities. These, in turn, will affect their productive opportunities in the future. They all know their present health, but a particularly unlucky person faces a grim future. Medical insurance institutions may arise if people are sufficiently risk averse about these unexpected possibilities and occurrences are sufficiently random so that insuring people is a profitable undertaking.

This is clearly not uncertainty of the Rawlsian kind—which consists of incomplete information about current endowments (Tirole 1999; Battigalli and Maggi 2002)—but rather uncertainty about the future. Deliberators *are* aware of the present distribution of physical and material endowments. Moreover, from any institutional arrangements they design at time *t* they are able to map their own "place" in the society at that time. The politicians of the founding era in the USA, for instance—Federalists and Anti-Federalists alike—had well-formed beliefs about what their places in the society and economy of 1787 would be as a result either of implementing the newly drafted Constitution or leaving the existing Articles of Confederation in place. But what about 1797? 1807? The veil of ignorance is not about current endowments but rather about future developments.

It is from this non-Rawlsian veil that Fernandez and Rodrik (1991) deduce a *status quo bias*. Changing an institutional arrangement may, in principle, produce a sum of gains that exceeds all losses, and maybe even more gainers than losers. But *ex ante* it is not always possible to identify who is which. This ignorance about who will gain from reform is sufficient in some circumstances to defeat reform. (This was the bias that had to be overcome by the Federalists in convincing enough state conventions to ratify the newly created Constitution in late eighteenth-century America. For an excellent analysis of the ratification campaign, see Riker 1996.[3])

Another source of uncertainty is *preference drift*. Today's "decisive deliberator" might well be able to select the institutional design that befits her preferences now. But her preferences will "drift" in uncertain ways over future periods. Indeed, whether her assets and tastes change or not, those of others may so that she need no longer remain decisive. It is this uncertainty about tomorrow that she will want to take on board as she plays the role of decisive deliberator today. In effect, her contemporaneous assessment of any institutional arrangement will be informed not only by today's payoff, but also by its present value over a relevant time horizon discounted for both risk and time. This theme is developed by Messner and Polborn (2004).[4]

In sum, a constitutional moment is one in which uncertainty figures prominently in the minds of deliberators, but it is not the Rawlsian kind. Deliberators often know their own endowments, and thus their own interests, and sometimes even those of relevant others. But they may be less confident in their interests over a more extended time horizon owing to preference drift, unforeseen contingencies, and even foreseen contingencies that arise stochastically but have not yet been realized.

3 How are Institutions Maintained (or Not)?

This last point provides a transition to the next question on our agenda. Institutions arise under conditions of uncertainty in the primal strategic environment. Over time the environment generates events, some anticipated and others unforeseen. It also generates changes in preferences. Institutions are robust if they still support the same equilibrium behavior despite the changed circumstances.[5] Alternatively,

[3] The Fernandez–Rodrik argument reminds us that institutions, whether explicitly chosen or not, must survive the test of time against proposals for "reform." Their message is that uncertainty may sustain an institution, a point also developed in Shepsle 1986.

[4] They begin with the puzzle of why, at a constitutional moment, a simple majority would agree to a supermajority decision rule, as is often the case on bond referenda in local school districts. Why, that is, would the median voter (who is decisive in the *simple* majority-rule model they explore) agree to a non-simple majority decision rule that did not make her decisive? They offer an interesting dynamic argument in which the median voter today is allowed to imagine how her preferences will change over time so that she may not be the decisive voter tomorrow. They formulate the optimization problem implied by this kind of preference drift as one in which the decisive voter chooses a decision rule that maximizes the utility of her *average future self*. They deduce that she will opt for a supermajority decision rule.

[5] That is, an institution may prove workable not only in the circumstances (the primal context) in which it was originally crafted, but also for changes in these circumstances. The larger the range of changes in context for which the institution continues to induce more or less the same equilibrium behavior, the more robust it is. It may exhibit this robustness because the outcomes it produces prove acceptable in a wide range of circumstances. Then again, it may be robust because the institution is very hard to alter, with the transaction costs of change exceeding the benefits of change.

changes in the strategic environment may invite deviation to a new equilibrium. This new equilibrium, given the changed environment, may prove satisfactory to those involved in the sense that no individuals or groups with the power to change the institution have an incentive to do so. Less satisfactory outcomes following departures from the initial conventional behavior, however, may provoke some to seek change in the institution itself. Institutional agents, that is, may not only change their own responses in light of the changed circumstances, but change the "rules of the game" as well. Indeed, some institutions possess self-referential mechanisms of adaptation and reformation—internal thermostats, so to speak—enabling them to adjust either to the "discovery of gaps" in their own make-up (Hayek 1979, 125), or to poor adaptation, by providing a course of correction and a way forward. For example, constitutional courts often reinterpret constitutional language to accommodate novel circumstances that had not been anticipated by the drafters of the document.

Before considering these internal mechanisms of change, let us first examine a case illustrating just how an unexpected or unforeseen circumstance can shake up an institutional relationship. De Figueiredo, Rakove, and Weingast (2000) contemplate this possibility in their discussion of events leading up to the American Revolution. The interesting feature of this historical episode is a mutually inconsistent appreciation of the colonial relationship of which neither colonialists nor the imperial center was aware—a difference in understanding that exogenous events made necessary to reconcile. A long-standing interaction had been founded on a misunderstanding that had not become apparent to the parties until the status of colonists became a paramount issue. The latter was a bolt out of the blue.

According to de Figueiredo et al. some forms of interaction are in equilibrium *because* of incomplete information. I may do x and you do y and each is seen to be a best response to the other by both parties. That is, my understanding of our strategic interaction allows me to appreciate that my choice of x is best against your choice of y, and that your choice of y is your best response against my choice of x. Likewise, your understanding of the situation allows you to appreciate precisely the same things about these choices. Best responses, however, are in equilibrium even if our modes of understanding are not the same. All that matters is that our possibly different understandings about the world nevertheless lead both of us to believe that x and y are best responses to one another. So long as this equilibrium is undisturbed, then it simply does not matter that we may have different underlying models of the world. Off the equilibrium path (involving choices not taken and situations not encountered) our differing understandings of how the world works may have significant consequences; so long as we "don't go there," it doesn't affect our best-response behavior and beliefs. Nothing that occurs disconfirms either of our views about our own strategies or those played by others. Our respective choices constitute a *self-confirming equilibrium*. Our strategic interaction leads each of us to have our respective underlying models of the world confirmed.

This, de Figueiredo et al. claim, constituted (roughly speaking) the equilibrium between colony and imperial power for more than 100 years in seventeenth- and eighteenth-century America. The English colonists enjoyed the protection of the empire, and the relative freedom of distant colonies, while the imperial center, distracted by war and intrigue on the European continent, tolerated elements of self-government as long as the colonies did not drain the Treasury. Continental wars of the Old World, however, spread to the New World. It grew expensive to protect the English colonists from the predations of the French and their native allies. To raise revenues to cover some of these rising costs following the Seven Years War (1756–63), parliament imposed new taxes on the colonies. The imposition of these taxes was unexpected by the colonists, and distasteful. They objected, standing on their "rights as Englishmen," claiming that this constituted a departure from the previous rules of self-government, and insisting on a role in decisions affecting their well-being. "Of what relevance are 'rights of Englishmen'?" queried confused politicians in London attempting to cope with fiscal stresses. The Americans are not Englishmen, they are colonists. Here were two different understandings of exactly what the strategic interaction comprised. The colonists thought of themselves as Englishmen with rights of representation and self-government. To the imperial center, the colonists were *colonists* with no rights except what the center permitted and tolerated. So long as behaviors preferred by the colonists were within the realm of imperial toleration, as they more or less had been for more than a century before 1763, the differing understandings did not matter. Once events redefined what could be tolerated, the center felt unconstrained in responding to this redefinition (the supremacy of parliament). These differences became all consuming. The institutions comprising the colonial relationship were damaged—that is, no longer in equilibrium. Deviation from conventional behavior on each side of the previous relationship now looked attractive—revolt and repression. It is in this sense that a previous equilibrium, founded on incomplete awareness about inconsistent beliefs by the parties concerned but made transparent by unfolding events, fell apart.

In many institutional settings, however, various kinds of incompleteness are acknowledged and appreciated *ex ante* (Tirole 1999): it is known that contingencies will arise that were not anticipated, and it is also recognized that it is often too costly to specify appropriate behavior even in some contingencies that can be anticipated, at least probabilistically. In such circumstances there is often a reversion strategy: "If one of these unplanned for or unexpected circumstances arises, then here's what we do." I take this issue up more fully in Section 5. For now, though, let me make some brief remarks about maintaining institutions in the presence of "surprises."

In the absence of shocks or unplanned-for occurrences, an institution consists of well-defined behavior arising out of strategies in equilibrium. It is self-maintaining, as it were. Taking it one step further, if there are shocks to the environment but they do not disrupt the equilibrium, then it is a robust institution. Taking it one step further still, there may be occasions in which shocks do disrupt the equilibrium, but reversion features of the institution allow it to transform itself, bringing it back into equilibrium so to speak. There are many such features on which I provide details shortly. These features may be thought of not so much as the means by which to maintain an institution no longer "appropriate" to its environment, but rather as the means to transform the institution. It is "merely" definitional as to whether we consider this transformed institution a *different* institution or not. What is clear is that the *equilibrium* is different. This prospect of self-generating institutional revision is the basis now for taking up the Riker Objection.

4 THE RIKER OBJECTION AND SOME RESPONSES

> [T]he distinction between constitutional questions and policy questions is at most one of degree of longevity.
>
> (Riker 1980, 445)

> Should the choice of a choice rule be treated as a special type of decision, or is it just one more instance of many issues that a society has to face?
>
> (Barbera and Jackson 2004, 2)

During the debates at the Constitutional Convention of 1787, in various exchanges traded during the subsequent ratification campaigns, and in retrospective assessments, numerous activists and scholars defended the procedure for amending the Constitution as outlined in Article V. In Philadelphia, Madison's *Notes* records Charles Pinckney as stating the positive case for this Article: "It is difficult to form a Government so perfect as to render alterations unnecessary; we must expect and provide for them." Madison asserted in *Federalist 43*, "That useful alterations will be suggested by experience, could not but be foreseen. It was requisite therefore that a mode for introducing them should be provided." Writing a half-century later about the Founding Fathers, Joseph Story observed in his *Commentaries on the Constitution*, "They believed, that the power of amendment was ... the real effective instrument to control and adjust the movements of the machinery, when out of order, or in danger of self-destruction."[6] These observers acknowledged that constitution-writers are incompletely informed about the world around them, can only anticipate and make provision for some of what is likely to transpire—either because it is impossible to anticipate or simply is too costly to accommodate in advance—and thus are wise to supply ways to revise and otherwise "adjust the movements of the machinery" in light of events and experiences.

Riker (1980, 445) offers a less benign, less mechanical view of amendments: "One can expect that losers on a series of decisions under a particular set of rules will attempt ... to change institutions and hence the kind of decisions produced under them." Making provision for an amendment procedure is not merely the prudent

---

[6] The quotations in this paragraph come from Kurland and Lerner 1987, iv, 578, 579, and 584, respectively.

ex ante recognition by constitution-writers of the probable *ex post* necessity for future adjustments. Constitution-writers surely recognize that unforeseen contingencies will be experienced, and revision procedures surely provide the means for addressing these. But a process for amending a body of rules is also a strategic weapon that potentially allows "losers" the means to become "winners" (Shepsle 2003).

This is an instance of the *Riker Objection* to the institutions-as-constraints, institutions-as-game-form perspective. The rules of the game are not fixed and inflexible. The constraints are not etched in stone. Even if no unforeseen contingencies are experienced, even if there are no *ex ante* uncertainties that come to be realized *ex post* in unexpected ways, there still is a role for amendment procedures to play. The *positivist* fact of the matter is that they provide strategic opportunities, quite apart from any welfare-enhancing justification for their utility in a constitution. The Riker Objection is both a recognition of the endogeneity of rules and procedures—they cannot be taken as preset and unvarying—and an acknowledgement of their strategic potential.

If an institutional arrangement is altered, then this reflects that while it may originally have been in equilibrium, it had been disequilibrated by some change in the underlying strategic context. When, then, is an institutional arrangement in equilibrium? Barbera and Jackson (2004) provide two ideas about *self-stability* that depend upon whether policy decisions and procedural decisions differ "only in degree," as Riker would have it, or are distinctly different kinds of decisions.

Riker (1980, 445) assumes policy and procedural decisions are essentially of the same type: "[R]ules or institutions are just more alternatives in the policy space and the status quo of one set of rules can be supplanted with another set of rules." For this circumstance Barbera and Jackson (2004, 4) describe an institution entirely in terms of a *decision rule, s*. For an institution consisting of n decision-makers, a decision rule $s(1/2 < s \leq 1)$ requires that the proportion of decision-makers necessary to approve a measure be at least s. Suppose a group operates according to s-majority rule. Then, "Given a majority size s, will it be the case that no alternative majority size s' is preferred over s by s or more votes? If s is not so defeated by any other rule, we say that the rule s is *self-stable*."[7]

As just defined, Barbera–Jackson *self-stability* takes decisions on procedures and decisions on policies under those procedures as governed by the same body of rules; this captures Riker's idea that procedures and policies are essentially the same—they are just things about which the decision-making body decides.

Suppose, on the other hand, rules are *not* merely "more alternatives in the policy space" but rather that the method of making a decision on rules differs from making a decision on policy. Specifically, suppose we describe a body of rules in terms of two voting rules, s and S. As before, s is the voting rule for ordinary policy decisions of the group or society. A "special majority," S, however, is required to change the rules. Then the rules are self-stable if no majority of size S or larger prefers some alternative set of rules to them.

---

[7] Without abusing the concept too much, we could say that the rule is an *s-Condorcet winner*.

Suppose, as is empirically the case most of the time, that $s < S$. A *simple* majority is often all that is required for normal business, but an *extraordinary* majority is necessary for procedural changes and other constitutional matters. It is quite possible for a simple majority to wish to conduct business differently, but they fall short of the special majority required to revise the rules.

In a setting in which policy and procedure were subject to the same decision rule, Riker felt that dissatisfied decisive coalitions on policy would not long sustain the prevailing consensus on procedure. Since a winning policy coalition is also a winning procedural coalition, the denial of their policy preferences on procedural grounds would not persist. After experiencing defeats for a time perhaps, they will learn what procedures require change and implement them; they have both the means and the motivation. Preferences over institutions/procedures are *inherited* from preferences over policies (Shepsle 1986, 57). The decisive policy coalition can re-form itself as a procedural coalition, make the institutional changes, and thus obtain their policy preference.

The tension is acute, however, and potentially persistent, when winning policy coalitions fail to be winning procedural coalitions. If an s-majority suffices to prevail on a substantive vote, but an extraordinary S-majority is required to "shut off debate," as in the US Senate under Rule 22 for example, then s-majorities are limited by the tolerance of every coalition of size greater than $1 - S$ that prevents an S-coalition from supporting the closure of debate and thus permitting a substantive vote to take place. Riker is on much weaker grounds in this second context. This means that it will pay dividends to examine the various ways in which procedures may be altered.

5 MODES OF PROCEDURAL CHANGE

Suppose there were no way to alter a procedural agreement. Once in place it remains in place. This is problematical in two respects. First, there are prospective gaps in the agreement too costly to fill in advance as well as contingencies unforeseen altogether. If either of these arises, then the contracting parties may be worse off living under the agreement than abandoning it altogether.[8] Defection from the agreement becomes a real possibility. Second, as Rosendorff and Milner (2001) describe in the context of international trade agreements, an *ex post* inability to "escape" unexpectedly onerous burdens imposed by an agreement produces *ex ante* obstacles to reaching agreement in the first instance.

But there is a trade-off. An agreement with loopholes and escape clauses and easy routes to obviating its terms is hardly an agreement at all. The slightest inconvenience

[8] Mr Iredell, in the North Carolina ratifying convention of the US Constitution as reported in Kurland and Lerner 1987, 582, spoke to this point: "The Constitution of any government which cannot be regularly amended when its defects are experienced, reduces the people to this dilemma—they must either submit to its oppressions or bring about amendments, more or less, by a civil war."

becomes a pretext for non-compliance. Unlimited discretion is a condition making it hardly worthwhile to enter into such agreements. Rosendorff and Milner (2001, 834) argue for *costly* escape clauses—"rules with costly discretion" rather than "no discretion at all." [9] Including costly escape clauses in agreements makes them easier to reach on the one hand, and restricts the circumstances in which their terms will not be honored on the other.[10]

In the remainder of this section alternative forms of costly flexibility and revision are examined. I provide this brief catalogue to display how institutions in the real world actually build in a capacity to reform themselves. This underscores Riker's objection to taking institutions as fixed and unchangeable. They may not be like ordinary policies, subject to ordinary change. But this does not mean they cannot be changed at all.

Amendment procedures. In the debates on the US Constitution in the Virginia ratifying convention, Madison addressed the amendment mechanism contained in Article V by asking, "Does not the thirteenth article of the [Articles of] Confederation expressly require that no alteration should be made without the unanimous consent of all the states? Could anything in theory be more perniciously improvident and injudicious than this submission of the will of the majority to the most trifling minority?" (Kurland and Lerner 1987, 582). In the Constitutional Convention itself, Charles Pinckney had bemoaned the high cost of flexibility in the Articles of Confederation: "[D]ifficult as the forming a perfect Government would be, it is scarcely more so, than to induce Thirteen separate legislatures, to think and act alike upon one subject" (Kurland and Lerner 1987, 578). And Blackstone, in his *Commentaries*, notes: "Nor can we too much applaud a constitution, which thus provides a safe, and peaceable remedy for its own defects" (Kurland and Lerner 1987, 583). Most bodies of rules provide for endogenous revision, typically requiring a greater consensus than on ordinary decisions—$s < S$ in Barbera and Jackson's formulation. The institution thus contains the very seeds of its own reform.

Interpretative courts. Explicit amendment procedures are not the only way to change a body of rules. Justice Oliver Wendell Holmes once said of the US Supreme Court that "the job of this Court is to say what the law means." The interpretation of law, both statutory and constitutional, is an alternative road to reform; it is a complement to official amendment processes. And the activist role for the court in judicial review first charted by Chief Justice John Marshall is undoubtedly responsible in part for the

---

[9] Downs and Rocke 1995, 77, complement this reasoning by suggesting that, instead of formal "exceptions" or "escapes" in a constitution, it is sometimes more effective simply to permit non-compliance, punish it, but to make these costs low enough that violations may occur from time to time in equilibrium. This may be simpler than struggling to craft exceptions in a more complete agreement.

[10] Joseph Story, in his *Commentaries on the Constitution* (1833), suggests: "The great principle to be sought is to make change practicable, but not too easy." Battigalli and Maggi 2002 show that for various cost conditions an optimal agreement will possess different degrees of flexibility—that is, different mixes of discretionary and rigid delegations to agents. There are large literatures on *renegotiation* in game theory and *optimal breach* in contract theory that bear a close resemblance to these issues.

fact that the US Constitution has, since the Bill of Rights, been amended fewer than twenty times in 200 years.

Judicial review, either by extending the jurisdiction of a meaning or altering the meaning altogether, provides a less costly means of altering constitutional practice than amendment. In doing so, however, it must be noted that this arrangement empowers judges and, as Riker would surely remind us, this is not necessarily a benign development. Constitutional courts, in other words, are not merely procedural devices for "fixing" institutions whose equilibria have been perturbed by a change in the underlying strategic setting. While admitting that judges may be something more than mere politicians—"legislators in robes" (Shepsle and Bonchek 1997) so to speak—they surely *are* politicians with agendas of their own.

Suspension of the rules. In the US House of Representatives there is a body of standing rules, adopted by a new Congress as one of its first orders of business but then rarely followed! Legislation almost always passes in two ways that deviate from "normal procedure." First and most typical, the Committee on Rules proposes a "special rule," crafted especially for the legislation at hand. This rule, if adopted by a simple majority, specifies the special circumstances that are to prevail in the consideration of the bill—limiting legislative debate, naming amendments that are in order, and making points of order against the bill out of order. A second device to expedite proceedings literally suspends the rules. In considering a bill, it is in order to move to "suspend the rules and pass" the bill in question. Debate is compressed, the ordinary rules are suspended, no amendments are in order, and the legislation is approved if the motion is supported by two-thirds of those present and voting. The standing rules, in other words, constitute reversion procedures that obtain only if special circumstances like suspension and special rules haven't been arranged for.

The US Senate also has a body of standing rules. Like the House, its "normal" procedures are so convoluted and burdensome to follow as effectively to prevent action in many instances. To escape this perplexing problem without having to craft an entire new body of rules with their own flaws, the Senate typically observes *unanimous consent* on matters of procedure. Unanimous consent agreements, like suspension and special-rule procedures in the House, are mechanisms for cutting the Gordian knot and getting on with business in a manner short of formal amendment of the rules. Such agreements, in both chambers, empower veto players and position them to extract concessions in exchange for lifting their veto.

Escape clauses and nullification. The Articles of Confederation required a form of unanimity for many formal actions by the Articles Congress. (A modern example is the Council of Ministers of the European Union.) This arrangement provided each state delegation with veto power, and proved to be a disaster in the face of growing threats. (Shays's Rebellion and the inability of the Confederation to respond militarily to it was the straw that broke the camel's back for many who assembled in Philadelphia in July 1787 to explore alternatives.)

Nullification limits the scope of an action (whereas veto power prevents action altogether). It is an *ex post* restriction on the reach of a policy and in effect locates ultimate sovereignty in the constituent units empowered to nullify rather than in the collectivity. It allows a constituent unit to escape the consequences of policies adversely affecting it. For example, it would have permitted nineteenth-century South Carolina to nullify a high tariff on manufactured goods by permitting it to import those goods through the port of Charleston at lower rates.

Via backward induction, a nullification power would induce policy-makers to take into account prospective *ex post* actions by constituent units. The prospective nullification of a tariff by a constituent unit, for example, to the extent that it would have national repercussions in effectively undercutting the rate structure on imports, might induce legislators to lower the offending rates. That is, nullification power enhances the *ex ante* bargaining leverage of constituent units.

Nullification, as Chen and Ordeshook (1994) remind us, is an alternative to secession (see below), and looks very much like escape clauses in international trade agreements (Rosendorff and Milner 2001). At the point of negotiating an agreement, the opportunity to escape its strictures may enhance its prospects of being entered into in the first place, especially in high-variance environments where uncertainties loom large and some of their realizations have the potential to wreak havoc. Having witnessed the Tariff of Abominations, for example, South Carolina's John Calhoun promoted nullification as a protection for the South against the possibility of an out-of-control national legislature—one dominated by Northern economic and anti-slavery interests (Herzberg 1992). Rosendorff and Milner (2001, 831) claim that these constitute efficient responses in international trade negotiations to conditions of domestic uncertainty, reducing domestic pressure on governments to withdraw altogether from agreements during periods of protectionist sentiment.

Nullification and escape, especially if they are exercised at a cost to their initiator, may be superior to the failure to reach any agreement at all. Moreover, in multilateral settings an agreement that prompts a "local" evasion may nevertheless generate benefits to those remaining in the fold. So, the presence of an escape clause, or the opportunity to nullify, may have three distinct effects. They may reassure *ex ante*, thereby improving the prospects for an agreement. In order to discourage nullification or escape, they may dissuade a temporarily decisive coalition from extracting maximal advantage. And third, they may provide for agreement even if *ex post* uses of escape and nullification can be expected from time to time in equilibrium (Downs and Rocke 1995). Nullification opportunities, of course, may entirely unravel an agreement; but then an agreement without the nullification option may not have been on the cards in the first place. To avoid the use of nullification in every circumstance that makes a constituent unit worse off, it cannot be cost or risk free.

Secession. Secession by a constituent unit is a mode of institutional change *in extremis*. It alters the nature of strategic interaction. In transforming the original game, the remaining players find themselves in an altogether different strategic setting. Their domestic affairs now have a different profile of interests and a revised set of decisive coalitions. The secessionist now has a domestic politics wholly different from what it had been originally. And now there are strategic relations between sovereigns that hadn't previously existed. Chen and Ordeshook (1994) show that secession may be "constitutionally permitted," i.e. others will not seek to prevent it, or "constitutionally prohibited," yet attempted. Both of these are equilibria of the Secession Game they analyze.

Admission of new members. The addition of players, like the subtraction, alters the strategic complexion of a game. The nominal practice in the United States was to have a geographic region first apply for territorial status, then write a territorial constitution that met with congressional approval, and finally apply for statehood when its population reached that of the average congressional district. Yet, as Stewart and Weingast (1992) show, the timing and sequencing of admission decisions by Congress were fraught with strategic calculation. As North and South moved in different directions on slavery and other economic issues in antebellum America, the admission of new states produced some of the most spectacular congressional roll calls in the history of that institution. The admission of Maine and Missouri as part of the Compromise of 1820 began a pattern of "balance" in admissions between slave and free territories. The acquisition of new territory (e.g. the Mexican War) posed further strategic issues. Each new player in national politics meant a potential redefinition of winning coalitions and possibly dramatic swings in policy. Even after the Civil War, the late nineteenth-century admission of western states had implications for national politics and presidential elections, depending on their partisan coloration. This did not go unnoticed by Congress.[11] In short, as a game form an institution is sensitive to the number of players and their strategic opportunities. Changes, whether by addition or subtraction, change institutions.

Emergency powers. "Regimes of exception," as Loveman (1993) calls them, are constitutional orders with processes for partial self-suspension. The Romans, for example, conferred emergency powers upon dictators for limited periods. "The dictator could not initiate the state of emergency but rather was charged by the legitimate government with emergency powers and could not legally alter the existing constitutional order—only defend it" (Loveman 1993, 19). Loveman suggests the "historical landmark" of modern emergency powers is the British Riot Act of 1714, empowering the forces of order to disperse a riotous crowd first by "reading them the Riot Act" and then resorting to force if necessary, their actions fully indemnified against civil prosecution for any harm done. His book is a broad survey of emergency powers in Latin American constitutions. Hayek (1979, 124–6) warns against conflating the declaration of a state of emergency with the actual exercise of emergency powers, arguing that the two should be held separate to minimize their use for self-serving purposes. (This was true of the Roman practice, but the separation did not hold over time and emergency powers lapsed into dictatorship—see Loveman 1993, 19.)

Emergency powers exercised during states of emergency, siege, public disorder, public disturbance, or internal commotion are normally interpreted as instances of

---

[11] A contemporary illustration of these same observations is the ongoing expansion of the European Union.

a constitutional equilibrium upset by events. The powers are, in principle, defensive of the constitutional order and are deployed in order to remove the disruptive conditions that took affairs off the equilibrium path. However, the causality may be reversed—it is an out-of-equilibrium constitution that triggers public disorder which, in turn, precipitates the exercise of emergency powers. This latter interpretation brings emergency powers closer to endogenous amendment procedures in that both seek to restore equilibrium by adapting the constitution to the new circumstances.[12]

6 Conclusion

The endogenous forms of institutional change reviewed in the previous section highlight the importance of the Riker Objection in contexts even richer than he considered. There are a variety of ways for a decisive procedural coalition to adjust the institutional machinery. The decisive procedural coalition, however, need not be the same as one of the decisive policy coalitions that ultimately makes policy choices. The tools of institutional engineering are not always available to a "mere" policy coalition. So institutions may still structure equilibrium (Shepsle 1979), because the means for a policy coalition to alter the machinery to secure their preferred results either are not at hand or are too costly to employ (Calvert 1995). In effect, institutions have a life of their own and are decisive as long as they stay within the transaction-cost boundary that changing to a new institution would require.

Making this claim limits the impact of Riker's objection; however, it does not undermine the *political* thrust of Riker's line of reasoning. Endogenous sources of institutional revision are more than *ex ante* provisions to cope with a changing environment or to accommodate the "discovery of gaps." They provide alternative routes by which groups try to get what they want; they privilege particular coalitions of agents with procedural advantages; they may be deployed for reasons limited only by political imagination.

The Riker Objection was first formulated twenty-five years ago. In retrospect it may be seen as a static and narrow statement. It did not differentiate policy coalitions (*s*) from procedural coalitions (*S*). It did not give credit to institution designers for anticipating dynamic developments or for inserting self-revising features. The last decade or so has produced research that brings a great number of these elements into play. There is, however, a second facet of the Riker Objection—one focusing less on "failure correction" and other shortcomings of incomplete contracts in uncertain environments. Institutional revision is not merely an adjustment to imperfect design and unreliable settings. It is, as I have noted several times, a way forward for whatever

[12] The modes of procedural adjustment described here may be extended. Additional modes include redistricting, expansion of the (s)electorate, and devolution.

purposes a decisive coalition sets for itself. Much less progress has been made on this political dimension.

References

AGHION, P., ALESINA, A., and TREBBI, F. 2004. Endogenous political institutions. *Quarterly Journal of Economics*, 119: 565–612.
ANDREWS, J. 2002. *When Majorities Fail: The Russian Parliament, 1990–1993*. New York: Cambridge University Press.
BARBERA, S., and JACKSON, M. O. 2004. Choosing how to choose: self-stable majority rules. *Quarterly Journal of Economics*, 119: 1011–48.
BATTIGALLI, P., and MAGGI, G. 2002. Rigidity, discretion, and the costs of writing contracts. *American Economic Review*, 92: 798–818.
CALVERT, R. 1995. Rational actors, equilibrium, and social institutions. Pp. 57–95 in *Explaining Social Institutions*, ed. J. Knight and I. Sened. Ann Arbor: University of Michigan Press.
CHEN, Y., and ORDESHOOK, P. C. 1994. Constitutional secession clauses. *Constitutional Political Economy*, 5: 45–60.
CRAWFORD, S. E. S., and OSTROM, E. 1995. A grammar of institutions. *American Political Science Review*, 89: 582–600.
DE FIGUEIREDO, R., RAKOVE, J., and WEINGAST, B. R. 2000. Rationality, inaccurate mental models, and self-confirming equilibrium: a new understanding of the American Revolution. Unpublished manuscript.
DOWNS, G. W., and ROCKE, D. M. 1995. *Optimal Imperfection? Domestic Uncertainty and Institutions in International Relations*. Princeton, NJ: Princeton University Press.
FERNANDEZ, R., and RODRIK, D. 1991. Resistance to reform: status quo bias in the presence of individual-specific uncertainty. *American Economic Review*, 81: 1146–55.
GREIF, A., and LAITIN, D. D. 2004. A theory of endogenous institutional change. *American Political Science Review*, 98: 633–53.
HALL, P. A., and TAYLOR, R. C. R. 1996. Political science and the three new institutionalisms. *Political Studies*, 44: 936–57.
HAYEK, F. 1979. *Law, Legislation, and Liberty*, vol. iii. Chicago: University of Chicago Press.
HERZBERG, R. 1992. An analytic choice approach to concurrent majorities: the relevance of John C. Calhoun's theory of institutional design. *Journal of Politics*, 54: 54–81.
KURLAND, P. H., and LERNER, R. 1987. *The Founders Constitution*. Indianapolis: Liberty Fund Press.
LOVEMAN, B. 1993. *The Constitution of Tyranny: Regimes of Exception in Spanish America*. Pittsburgh, Pa.: University of Pittsburgh Press.
MANTZAVINOS, C., NORTH, D. C., and SHARIQ, S. 2004. Learning, institutions, and economic performance. *Perspectives on Politics*, 2: 75–84.
MESSNER, M., and POLBORN, M. K. 2004. Voting on majority rules. *Review of Economic Studies*, 71: 115–32.
NORTH, D. C. 1990. *Institutions, Institutional Change and Economic Performance*. New York: Cambridge University Press.
OSTROM, E. 2005. *Understanding Institutional Diversity*. Princeton, NJ: Princeton University Press.
PERSSON, T., and TABELLINI, G. 2000. *Political Economics*. Cambridge, Mass.: MIT Press.
POLSBY, N. W. 1968. The institutionalization of the U.S. House of Representatives. *American Political Science Review*, 62: 148–68.

Rawls, J. 1972. *A Theory of Justice*. Cambridge, Mass.: Harvard University Press.
Riker, W. H. 1962. *The Theory of Political Coalitions*. New Haven, Conn.: Yale University Press.
―― 1980. Implications from the disequilibrium of majority rule for the study of institutions. *American Political Science Review*, 74: 432–46.
―― 1996. *The Strategy of Rhetoric: Campaigning for the American Constitution*, ed. R. L. Calvert, J. Mueller, and R. K. Wilson. New Haven, Conn.: Yale University Press.
Rosendorff, B. P., and Milner, H. V. 2001. The optimal design of international trade institutions: uncertainty and escape. *International Organization*, 55: 829–57.
Sait, E. M. 1938. *Political Institutions: A Preface*. New York: Appleton-Century-Crofts.
Schotter, A. 1981. *The Economic Theory of Social Institutions*. New York: Cambridge University Press.
Shepsle, K. A. 1979. Institutional arrangements and equilibrium in multidimensional voting models. *American Journal of Political Science*, 23: 23–57.
―― 1986. Institutional equilibrium and equilibrium institutions. Pp. 51–82 in *Political Science: The Science of Politics*, ed. H. F. Weisberg. New York: Agathon.
―― 2003. Losers in politics (and how they sometimes become winners): William Riker's heresthetic. *Perspectives on Politics*, 1: 307–15.
―― and Bonchek, M. 1997. *Analyzing Politics*. New York: W.W. Norton.
Stewart, C., and Weingast, B. R. 1992. Stacking the Senate, changing the nation: Republican rotten boroughs and American political development in the late 19th century. *Studies in American Political Development*, 6: 223–371.
Story, J. 1833. *Commentanies on the Constitution of the: United States*. Boston: Hilliard, Gray.
Ticchi, D., and Vindigni, A. 2003. Endogenous constitutions. Unpublished manuscript.
Tirole, J. 1999. Incomplete contracts: where do we stand? *Econometrica*, 67: 741–81.
Tsebelis, G. 2002. *Veto Players: How Political Institutions Work*. Princeton, NJ: Princeton University Press.

NAME INDEX

Note: Includes all referenced authors.

Abdelal, R 763 n9
Abdolali, N 840
Aberbach, J D 263
Abraham, H 282
Abrams, S 251
Abreu, D 956
Acemoglu, D 603, 617, 629, 674 n1, 675, 678, 679, 682 n3, 685, 688, 690, 691, 716, 725, 740, 751
Acosta, A M 560
Adams, J 111
Adams, P 542
Ades, A 792
Adolph, C 607
Advisory Council for Interstate Relations (ACIR) 466
Aghion, P 99 n24, 1036
Aidt, T 455 n38
Alaminos, A 314
Alcalá, F 793
Alchian, A 17
Aldrich, J 37, 146 n7, 157, 209 n4, 450 n21, 606, 997 n2
Alesina, A 21, 124 n4, 322, 324 n18, 465, 473, 527, 535, 548, 549, 551, 555, 556, 557, 568 n6, 574, 578 n27, 604, 607, 610–11, 630, 631, 634, 636, 638, 639, 644, 648, 734, 769, 779, 780, 781, 782 n14, 782 n15, 784 n19, 786, 788 n27, 789 n28, 790 n30, 792, 793, 794, 795, 859, 865, 1017, 1036
Alexander, R D 961
Alexander the Great 20
Alford, J 579 n30
Allan, J 606
Allee, T L 873
Alm, J 466
Almond, G A 325, 709
Alston, L 636
Alt, J 152, 548, 550, 552, 559, 560, 729
Alter, K J 770
Alvarez, R M 644, 1017
Amin, Idi 698
Amin, M 893
Amorim Neto, O 145, 153
Amsden, A H 709
Anbarci, N 890
Anderson, B 778 n2, 859, 860
Anderson, C 578 n29
Anderson, J 741
Anderson, L 929
Andreoni, J 446 n11, 952
Andrews, J 146 n7, 1035

Annett, A 465
Ansolabehere, S 32 n5, 35 n7, 36, 45 n11, 46, 50, 95, 172 n24, 190, 191, 926
Aragones, E 926
Aranson, P 77 n10
Aristotle 778
Arrow, K J 103, 373, 405, 409, 413, 417, 419, 480, 526, 601, 900, 903, 904, 974, 975, 985, 986
Arthur, B 808
Asch, S 638
Ashenfelter, O A 770
Ashworth, S 52, 57 n11, 59
Asquith, H 687
Atkinson, A B 314 n4, 442 n1, 527
Aumann, R J 88, 89–90, 956
Austen-Smith, D 52 n5, 66, 87–8, 165 n8, 167, 170 n17, 172 n27, 193 n20, 450 n21, 453, 611, 732, 904 n5, 904 n7, 906, 909 n12, 927, 933
Ausubel, L M 385
Autor, D 627
Axelrod, R 163–4, 711 n2, 714, 836, 890, 955
Azam, J-P 716
Azrael, J R 699

Bagwell, Kyle 766, 767
Bailey, M 52, 248
Bailin, A 834
Baldwin, R E 762, 764 n10, 780 n6
Balla, S J 261, 263 n3
Bandyopadhyay, U 452
Banerjee, A 314 n4
Banks, J 66, 74, 75, 81–2, 165 n8, 167, 170 n17, 172 n27, 193 n20, 215 n8, 904 n5, 904 n7, 906, 908, 909 n12, 927
Bannon, A 865 n21
Baqir, R 453, 465, 631, 733, 859, 865
Barbanel, J B 425, 426, 427, 428
Barberà, S 383, 384, 1040, 1041
Bardhan, P 782 n13
Baron, D P 12, 32 n6, 85, 150, 157, 162, 164, 168–70, 172, 173, 187–8, 190, 362, 906, 921, 922
Barro, R J 569, 648, 693
Barry, Brian 290, 293, 296, 297, 306
Bartlett, R 717
Barton, Joe 531
Bates, R 697, 711, 714 n3, 715, 757 n1, 767, 856, 860, 861, 894
Batista, Fulgencio 698, 702
Battigalli, P 1036, 1043 n10

NAME INDEX

Bauer, R A 759
Baum, M A 693, 873
Baumol, W J 538
Bawn, K 154, 215 n8, 260, 261, 263, 613, 732
Bearce, D 592
Beblawi, H 716
Becht, M 724
Beck, N 554, 835
Becker, G S 455, 951, 985 n4
Beckert, J 937
Bednar, J 359
Beer, C 876
Beer, S H 304
Ben Zion, U 12
Bénabou, R 314 n3, 604, 951
Bendor, J 260, 266, 268
Benhabib, J 314–16, 325
Bennett, D S 836, 871, 872, 873, 876
Benoit, K 138
Beramendi, P 366
Berg, J 959
Berger, H 801
Bergstrom, T C 448
Berl, J 920
Berle, Adolph 304, 305, 1014
Berleson, Bernard 40
Berliant, M 486 n16, 498
Berlin, I 374, 379
Bernhard, M 659
Bernhard, W 264 n5, 593
Bernheim, B D 450, 912
Bernstein, M H 212
Bertrand, J 88
Besley, T 37, 81, 132, 323, 362, 446 n10, 448 n16, 450, 456, 553, 607, 730, 908, 1019
Bester, H 888
Bewley, T 481 n4
Bhaskar, V 956
Bickel, A M 208
Biddle, S 873
Bienen, H 664
Bikhchandani, S 385, 929
Binder, S 134, 146, 157, 184, 204
Bingham Powell, G 725, 729
Binmore, K 171 n20
Bismarck, Otto von 609
Black, D 103, 182, 224, 448, 553, 900 n2, 903, 907, 984, 985, 986, 996–7
Blackorby, C 408, 413, 417, 418, 420, 422
Blackstone, W 342 n1, 1043
Blackwell, D 421
Blair, Tony 129
Blais, A 550, 560, 726
Blake, D 550, 560
Blank, R 624, 627
Blau, F 627
Blau, J 419
Blinder, A 571 n13
Bloch, F 892
Bloch, M 711
Blondel, J 126
Blum, L 638
Boadway, R 457

Boehm, C 952, 961
Bohte, J 262, 263
Boix, C 103, 315 n5, 365, 605 n1, 617, 646, 648, 865 n19
Bolton, P 22, 365, 724, 779, 790, 791
Bonchek, M 1044
Bonfield, A E 214
Borcherding, T F 448
Bordignon, M 467, 779, 789 n28
Bossert, W 376, 413, 420, 422
Boucher, R L 211
Boudreau, C 277
Boulding, K E 781
Bourdieu, Pierre 938, 941, 942
Bowen, H R 448, 486 n16, 985
Bowen, W G 538
Bowler, S 115, 126 n5
Bowles, S 952, 953, 956 n1, 960, 961, 963
Boyd, R 19 n22, 963
Brady, D W 182, 224, 228, 247, 252 n15
Brady, G L 527
Brady, H 33, 35, 44
Brams, S 107 n8, 396, 397, 404, 425, 426, 427, 428, 429, 431, 432
Brandenburger, A M 978
Brass, P R 864
Bratton, M 657, 660
Braumoeller, B F 872
Brennan, G 290, 330 n1, 331 n2, 332 n4, 336, 340 n6, 360, 363, 455 n41, 505, 613, 984 n2
Brenner, R 688
Breton, A 951
Breuilly, J 856
Brito, D 888
Brock, W A 762
Brooker, P 696
Brooks, C 999
Brooks, R S 865 n19
Brown, D E 961
Browne, E C 165, 172 n22, 173
Broz, J L 589, 593
Brueckner, J 360, 503 n2
Brusco, S 779, 789 n28
Bruszt, L 314, 661
Bryce, J 319
Buchanan, J 8, 149 n13, 154, 321, 330 n1, 343, 360, 363, 454 n34, 454 n35, 455, 505, 527, 534, 613, 711, 780, 789 n28, 951, 981, 984 n2, 986 n5, 990 n7, 991, 997
Bucovetsky, S 511
Budge, I 137
Bueno de Mesquita, B 22, 695, 699, 831, 832–3, 836, 839, 841, 842, 844, 845, 846, 847, 848, 870, 871, 872, 873
Buetler, M 457
Bunce, V 664 n6
Burbank, S 281
Burgoon, B 825
Burke, Edmund 303
Burke, M 952
Burrow, J 313
Burt, R 940
Bush, George W 295, 302, 304

Caesar 307–8
Cain, B 32 n5
Cairncross, F 739
Caldeira, G A 211
Caldwell, B 539
Calhoun, John C 305, 307, 1045
Callaghy, T 658
Callander, S 929 n15
Calles, Plutarco Elias 703
Callon, M 939
Calmfors, L 644
Calro, E 363
Calvert, R L 9, 15 n15, 45, 71, 79–80, 321, 322, 553, 1034, 1035 n2, 1047
Camerer, C 922, 957
Cameron, C 51, 130, 203 n2, 204, 211, 244, 245, 247, 249, 282 n8
Cameron, D 605 n1, 648
Campa, J 594
Campaore, Blaise 698
Campbell, A 31 n3, 153, 238
Campbell, S H 840
Campos, N E 697
Canavan, C 592
Canes-Wrone, B 244, 250, 252, 269
Caporaso, J A 758 n2
Cardoso, F H 760 n5
Careaga, M 363, 465
Carey, J M 112, 142 n1, 612, 728
Cargill, T F 12 n10
Carlsen, F 558
Carneiro, R L 717 n4
Carothers, T 663, 664
Carroll, R 147, 148, 149, 155
Carrubba, C J 172 n25
Casas Pardo, J 332 n4
Case, A 730
Casella, A 779, 933
Caselli, F 862
Cassing, J H 762
Castles, F G 366–7, 613
Cave, Richard 762
Cederman, L-E 769, 865 n20
Centeno, M A 716
Central Intelligence Agency 530
Cetinyan, R 863
Chan, S 873
Chandra, K 323, 324 n20, 853 n1, 861, 862, 865 n19
Chang, E C C 550, 559, 728
Chang, K 204, 248
Chappell, H W 214 n7, 252 n13, 575 n18
Chaudry, K A 716
Checchi, D 634
Chehabi, H E 694, 698
Chen, Y 454, 1045, 1046
Chernick, H 452 n26
Chhibber, P 367
Chiang Kai-shek 701
Chiou, F-Y 183, 184, 238
Chiozza, G 836, 839, 872
Choi, J K 961
Choung, J L 315 n5

Chowdhury, A R 549
Christensen, T 834
Chrystal, K A 548
Chua, A 715
Chwe, M 890
Ciccone, A 793
Claeys, E R 342 n1
Clark, D H 872, 873
Clark, W R 546, 550, 552, 555, 560, 593, 607
Clarke, E 487 n17
Clausewitz, Carl von 770
Cleveland, Grover 295 n5
Coase, R H 989
Coate, S 15, 37, 41–2, 46, 52, 57, 81, 98, 132, 323, 362, 448 n16, 450, 456, 553, 607, 908, 1019
Cohen, A 531
Cohen, B J 590
Cohen, G 124 n4, 548 n2, 549, 556, 607, 644
Cohen, J E 250
Cohen, L 280
Coleman, J S 709
Coleman, W J 862
Collier, K E 924
Collier, P 716, 857–8, 865
Collini, S 313
Colomer, J 103, 659
Colson, E 708
Condorcet, Marquis de 103, 319
Congleton, R 452 n26, 455 n41
Conley, J 481 n7
Conley, P H 247 n6
Conlin, M 41–2
Conquest, R 699
Conway, John L 427
Cook, T E 152
Cooper, R N 759
Cooter, R D 454 n34
Coppedge, M 560
Corsetti, G 560, 594
Corwin, E S 243
Corzine, Jon 61
Coser, L 315, 863
Cotta, M 126
Coughlin, P 74 n8, 92 n14, 93 n14, 94 n18, 449 n18, 450, 454, 997 n2, 1018 n6
Cover, A 204, 211
Cowhey, P F 765
Cox, G W 6, 9–10, 15 n15, 36, 93 n14, 95, 96, 103 n2, 107, 111, 125, 132, 133, 144, 145, 146, 148, 149, 150, 151, 152, 153, 154, 155, 156, 157, 158, 183, 187, 209 n4, 217 n10, 228–9, 230–2, 234, 238, 612, 613, 726, 909 n12, 910, 997 n2
Crafts, N F R 747 n6
Crampton, E 340 n6
Crawford, S E S 1032 n1
Crawford, V 909 n13, 912
Cremer, H 502 n1
Crémer, J 184, 185–6, 365–6
Crepaz, M M L 613
Crescenzi, M J C 845
Crisp, B 281
Crombez, C 230 n7
Crouzet, F 718 n5

Cukierman, A 546
Cusack, T 550, 555 n6, 606, 617
Czelusta, J 705

Dagan, N 779
Dahl, R A 208, 299, 302, 681, 778 n2
Dahrendorf, R 663
Dalton, Russell 30 n1
Damasio, Antonio 962
Damgaard, E 153
Dasgupta, P 316
d'Aspremont, C 412, 414, 415, 417, 421, 494, 1028 n12
David, P A 749, 809, 812
Davis, D R 818, 820, 848, 873
Davis, K C 214
Davis, O 65 n1, 66, 900, 997, 998
Dawes, R M 958
de Figueiredo, Rui J P 46, 215 n8, 216 n9, 260–1, 264 n4, 359, 474, 782 n13, 863, 1038
de Haan, J 473
de Jasay, A 982 n1
de Palma, A 88
de Viti de Marco, A 984 n3
Deacon, R T 448
Deb, R 376, 386
Debreu, G 65, 1021 n7
Dehousse, R 808
Dekel, E 928
Dell, F 314 n4
DeLong, J B 530
Delors, Jacques 803, 804
DeMeyer, F 417
Denzau, A T 6, 225, 229, 997 n2
Derby, Lord 686
Derthick, M 201
Desch, M C 869
Deschamps, R 414, 420, 421
Deutsch, K W 859, 860
DeWitt, J R 261
Dexter, A 759
Di Mauro, F 741
Di Palma, G 659
Diamond, J 740
Diamond, L 657 n2
Dianga, J W 716
Díaz, Porfirio 702
Diaz-Cayeros, A 364, 367
Dickhaut, J 959
Diermeier, D 123, 124, 150, 157, 162 n2, 165, 168, 170 n16, 171 n21, 172, 173, 174, 175, 176, 181 n3, 189, 906, 909 n12, 922
DiMaggio, P 939, 940, 941, 945
Dingell, John 228
Dion, D 146, 149, 157
Dion, S 550, 560
Disraeli, Benjamin 687
Dixit, A 92, 93 n14, 94 n18, 95, 96–7, 362, 417, 450, 609–10
Domingo, P 281, 282
Donaldson, D 408, 413, 417, 418, 420, 422
Döring, H 145, 156, 157
Dorussen, H 450 n19

Downs, A 13, 29–30, 38, 64, 67, 70, 110, 304, 324, 449, 553, 566, 569, 575, 579 n32, 839, 900, 911, 951, 1011, 1013–14
Downs, G 832, 846, 1036, 1043 n9, 1045
Drazen, A 446 n12, 526, 546, 548, 550, 557, 559, 566 n1, 734
Drèze, J H 781 n7
Driffill, J 644
Druckman, J N 181 n3
Duby, G 717
Duggan, J 72, 74, 75, 77, 78, 80–1, 81–2, 170 n17
Duranton, G 745 n4
Dutta, B 376
Duvalier, François 698
Duvalier, Jean Claude 698
Duverger, M 103, 106, 108 n10, 110, 472, 732

Easley, D 99 n24
Easterbrook, Frank 974
Easterly, W 465, 631, 782 n14, 847, 859, 865
Easton, S T 165
Eavey, C 921
Eckstein, H 103
Economist 525, 530 n5
Edelman, P H 432
Edgeworth, F Y 442
Edley, C 278 n6
Edwards, G C 243
Ehlers, L 385
Eibl-Eibesfeldt, I 961
Eichenberger, R 780 n5
Eichengreen, B 466, 467, 524, 590, 592
Eisenhower, Dwight D 135, 576 n24
Ekiert, G 662
Elgie, R 134
Elkins, Z 763 n9
Ellickson, R C 332
Ellingsen, T 779
Ellis, C J 558
Elman, C 834
Elster, J 659
Eltis, D 683
Ely, J C 956
Enelow, J M 450 n19, 998, 1018 n6
Engels, Friedrich 625, 634, 635
Engerman, S L 624, 633, 747
Epstein, D 211, 214–15, 258–60, 262
Epstein, L 130, 282
Epstein, R A 342 n1, 345, 347, 351
Erard, B 952
Eraslan, H 170 n17, 171 n20, 175, 176, 181 n3, 909 n12
Erikson, R S 35 n7, 43, 575 n19, 926
Ertman, T 688
Eskelund, J S 465
Eskridge, W 274, 275, 276, 283 n9
Esping-Andersen, G 604, 608–9, 647, 648, 649
Esteban, J M 882 n1
Estevez-Abe, M 616, 651, 819
Ethier, W J 745
Evans, C L 152
Evans, E J 686
Evans, P 270, 708, 937
Even, S 427 n2

Eyerman, J 875
Eytan, Z 12

Fair, R 34, 548, 567–8
Faith, R L 789 n28
Fajnzylber, P 632
Faletto, E 760 n5
Falleti, T 363
Fan, K 65
Farrant, A 340 n6
Farrell, D 126 n5
Fasiani, M 984 n3
Fatas, A 466, 467
Fatton, R 658, 663
Faust, J 558
Faust, K 939
Fearon, J D 322, 324 n18, 719, 767, 771, 832, 836, 839, 841, 853, 854, 857, 858, 859, 861, 862, 863, 864, 865, 870, 874, 890
Feaver, P D 872
Feddersen, T 16 n16, 123, 150, 157, 170 n18, 912, 933
Feenstra, R C 452 n27
Fehr, E 957, 959
Feinman, G M 717
Feinstein, J S 779, 952
Feld, L P 465
Feld, S 997 n2
Feldman, S 579 n30
Fenno, R F 8
Ferejohn, J 6, 32 n5, 81, 85, 150, 157, 162, 168–70, 181, 187–8, 217–18, 247, 250 n8, 274, 275, 278, 281, 282, 362, 566 n3, 569, 570 n9, 900, 921, 922
Fernandez, R 1036
Fernandez-Arias, E 465, 467
Ferrie, J 636
Ferris, S J 452 n26
Fey, M 72, 80–1, 925, 929 n15
Figueiredo, A C 145
Filippov, M 359, 364
Filson, D 872, 875, 876
Findlay, R 779, 792 n34, 893
Finer, S 633, 681
Fiorina, M 32 n5, 35 n7, 134, 251, 569 n8, 570 n11, 579 n30, 900, 917, 918–19, 920, 929
Fish, M S 663, 865 n19
Fishburn, P 396, 397, 398, 404, 432
Fisher, L 202
Fishlow, A 709
Fisman, R 702
Fleurbaey, M 376
Fligstein, N 937, 942
Flood, R 533
Fogel, R W 683
Fong, C M 952
Ford, H J 243
Fordham, B O 873
Forsythe, R 925
Fox, R G 860
Franchino, F 263
Frank, Andre Gunder 760
Frank, R H 962
Frank, Thomas 524
Franklin, M 172 n22

Franzese, R J 547 n1, 548, 549, 550, 552, 555 n6, 556, 557 n9, 559, 560, 604, 607, 645
Fréchette, G R 172 n24, 922
Fredriksson, P G 452 n27
Frendreis, J P 165, 172 n22, 173
Frey, B S 559, 766 n13, 780 n5
Frickey, P 274
Frieden, J A 589, 592, 594, 605, 618, 762, 764, 806
Friedman, B 281
Friedman, D 18, 19 n22, 21 n25, 779, 792, 794, 961
Friedman, M 643
Friedman, Thomas 757, 770
Frye, T 659
Fudenberg, D 249 n7, 710, 905 n9, 955, 956
Fujita, M 739 n1, 746 n5, 784 n23
Fukuyama, F 539
Fuller, L 208
Furtado, C 760 n5

Gabel, M 807
Gaertner, W 376
Gagnon, V P 863
Gailmard, S 215 n8, 260, 266
Galasso, V 456
Gallagher, M 105, 122 n2, 552
Galor, O 629
Gamson, W A 172
Ganev, V I 662
Gardenfors, P 376
Garfinkel, M R 533, 558, 882 n1, 891, 892
Garman, C 364, 367
Garrard, J 687
Garrett, E 274
Garrett, G 603, 605, 615, 644, 645, 648, 765, 802, 805, 1017
Garry, J 138
Gärtner, M 566 n1
Gartner, S S 872, 873
Gartzke, E 833, 875
Gawande, K 452
Geddes, B 107, 108, 659, 694
Gellman, A 933
Gellner, E 856, 859, 860
Gelpi, C 872, 873
Gely, R 275
Gerard-Varet, L 494
Gerber, Alan 45, 46, 61 n14
Gerber, E 925
Gevers, L 412, 414, 415, 417, 420, 421, 1028 n12
Ghezzi, P 592, 594
Giacomi, L 716
Giannetti, D 138
Giavazzi, F 592
Gibbard, A 383, 403
Gibler, D 875
Gibson, E 363
Gilardi, F 264
Gilbert, F 718
Gillespie, W I 452 n29
Gilligan, T 10–11, 143, 529
Gilpin, R 759 n3, 760 n4, 761, 836
Gintis, H 19 n22, 952, 953, 956 n1, 960, 961, 963
Girardin, L 865 n20

Girshick, M 421
Gladstone, W E 687
Glaeser, E 604, 610–11, 630, 631, 632, 634, 636, 638, 792, 975
Glaser, C 832
Glazer, A 444 n6, 558
Gleditsch, K S 315 n5, 833, 875, 876
Gleiber, D W 165, 173
Gleich, H 473, 474
Glicksberg, I 65
Gluckman, M 709, 711
Goemans, H 833, 836, 839, 845, 870, 872
Goeree, J 929, 932
Goldberg, L S 594
Goldberg, P K 452
Goldberger, A 579
Golden, M 728
Golder, M 554 n5
Golder, S 554 n5
Goldin, C 626
Goldstein, J 760, 767 n16
Goldstein, M 467
Goldstone, J 715
Goldthorpe, J 604
Gomberg, A 699–700
Gómez, Juan Vicente 698, 701
Gonzalez, F M 885
Goodhart, L M 550, 559
Goodin, R 409
Goodman, R P 448
Gordon, S 446 n10
Gore, Al 295
Gottschalk, P 634
Gourevitch, Peter 762, 764
Gowa, J 759, 761, 834, 869
Goyal, S 779
Gramlich, E 360
Granato, J 325
Granovetter, Mark 938–9, 940
Green, A 142 n1
Green, Donald 39, 45
Green, J 375, 380, 385, 480 n2, 485 n14, 487 n17, 489 n21
Greene, J P 1006
Greif, A 711, 714 n3, 715, 894, 951
Grey, Earl 686
Grieco, J M 834, 873
Grier, K 214 n7
Griesdorf, M 872
Griffin, J 409
Griliches, Z 579
Grilli, V 734
Grisanti, A 466, 473
Grofman, B 103, 105 n6, 110, 111, 113 n23, 115, 449 n18, 606 n2, 997 n2
Groseclose, T 10, 133, 230 n7, 234, 244, 247, 926
Grossman, G M 12–13, 50–1, 85, 450, 762, 763, 781, 826
Grossman, H I 792 n34, 882 n1, 893
Groves, T 487 n17, 489 n22
Grumm, J G 103
Grzymala-Busse, A 661, 662, 663
Guarnaschelli, S 927, 928
Gugerty, M K 865

Gul, F 384
Gurr, T R 857 n8
Gustavus Adolphus 719–20
Güth, W 957, 958

Haake, C-J 428 n4
Haas, E 802
Haavelmo, T 882 n1
Haber, S 695, 698, 700, 701, 702, 704, 705
Hagevi, M 155
Haggard, S 364, 367, 657, 663 n4, 716, 760
Hall, P A 612 n12, 614, 645, 650, 709, 1032 n1
Hall, R E 527
Hallerberg, M 466, 469, 471, 472, 473, 474, 554 n5, 560, 652, 734
Hamilton, Alexander 281, 282, 283, 292, 358
Hamilton, J T 261, 574 n16
Hamilton, W 955
Hamlin, A 290, 331 n2, 336, 340 n6
Hammond, P 412, 421
Hammond, T H 187, 244 n3
Hampton, Jean 292 n2
Hanby, V J 104, 105
Hand, Learned 40
Hanratty, M 624, 627
Hansen, J M 41
Hanson, G 742 n3, 820 n9
Hanson, S 662
Hanssen, F A 269
Hansson, I 80, 81 n13
Harberger, Arnold 447–8
Harden, I 464, 465, 473, 614
Hardin, G 380
Hardin, R 291, 292, 294 n4, 298, 300, 302, 304, 306, 308, 321
Harding, S 952
Harding, W 638
Harrigan, J 741
Harris, C 742
Harrison, Benjamin 295 n5
Harsanyi, John 41, 422, 454 n33, 909 n13, 956
Hart, R A 875
Hassard, J 939
Havrilesky 214 n7
Hayek, F von 360, 539, 945, 1046
Hayes, Rutherford B 295 n5
Heckelman, J C 558–9
Hefeker, C 592
Hegre, H 715
Heller, W B 151, 152, 190
Helliwell, J 741
Hellman, J 663
Hellwig, T 578 n29
Helpman, E 12–13, 50–1, 85, 450, 735, 762, 763, 826
Helsley, R W 751 n9
Henderson, E A 872
Henderson, J V 745, 750
Henning, C H 156
Henrich, J 952
Herbst, J 664
Herodotus 319
Herreiner, D 432 n9
Herron, M C 252

Hertzendorf, M N 59 n13
Herzberg, R 920, 1045
Hettich, W 450, 452, 452 n26, 453, 454 n36, 455, 527 n3
Hibbing, J R 304, 579 n30
Hibbs, Douglas 535, 546, 548, 553–4, 567 n5, 570 n11, 575 n18, 576, 577, 578 n27, 581 n36, 583 n39, 606, 607 n5, 644
Hicks, A M 560, 606
Hicks, M 717
Hines, J R 1025, 1026
Hinich, M 66, 74, 75, 77 n10, 449 n18, 900, 999, 1018 n6
Hirschman, A O 512, 744
Hirshleifer, J 17, 770, 781, 882, 883 n2, 929, 962
Hiscox, Michael 764, 819, 824, 825, 826–7
Hitler, Adolf 20, 702
Hiwatari, N 826
Hix, S 137
Hobbes, Thomas 290, 293, 297, 298–9, 300, 305, 713
Hobsbawn, E 778 n2
Hochman, H M 446 n11
Hoeffler, A 857–8, 865
Hoffman, D 662
Hoffman, Philip 719 n6
Hoffmann, S 801
Holmberg, S 114 n26
Holmes, O W 344, 352–3, 1043–4
Holmes, S 660
Holmstrom, B 491 n28
Holt, C 929, 932
Holtz-Bacha, C 50 n1
Hopfensitz, A 961
Horn, M J 260
Horowitz, D 322, 853 n1, 856, 859, 860 n14, 862, 864, 865
Hortala-Vallve, R 933
Hotelling, H 64, 70, 88, 449, 553, 900, 1011, 1013
Hotte, L 452
Howard, R M 261, 269
Howell, W 218, 244, 250, 261 n1, 873
Huber, E 604, 606, 613, 649
Huber, John 123, 142 n1, 146, 149, 215–16, 260, 262, 263, 264, 267, 268, 269, 446 n10
Humboldt, Wilhelm von 306
Hume, David 291, 292, 297, 306, 307
Hummels, D J 742
Humphreys, M 323
Hung, A 928
Huntington, S 657, 658, 659, 664 n8, 694
Hurwicz, L 480, 489 n21
Hussein, Saddam 699, 700, 844
Hutchcroft, P D 698
Hutchison, M 12 n10
Huth, P K 873
Hyams, P 717

Ichino, A 634
Ikenberry, G J 762 n7
Imbeau, L 554
Ingberman, D 154
Inglehart, R 325
Ingram, P 939
Inman, R 154, 360, 362, 453, 780 n3

Intriligator, M 888
Ireland, M J 873
Irons, J 558
Isaac, R M 921
Isard, P 533
Ito, T 549
Iversen, T 605, 606, 607, 613, 616, 617, 645, 646, 647, 648, 649, 651, 733, 819, 826
Iyengar, Shanto 43, 45, 50

Jackman, R W 115 n28
Jackson, M 81, 384, 386, 1040, 1041
Jacobi, T 204, 211
Jacobs, J 745
Jacobs, L R 252
Jacobson, G 32 n5, 45, 46
Jaggers, K 633
James, Scott 768
James II 678
Jefferson, Thomas 292
Jepperson, R 945
Johansson, E 95, 96
Johnson, G E 770
Johnson, Lyndon B 576 n24
Johnson, S 629, 674 n1, 678, 679, 685, 688, 691, 740, 751
Jones, C 152 n14
Jones, M 364, 427 n1, 429 n5, 466, 473
Jones, R W 819 n8
Jones Luong, P 660, 663, 664
Jöreskog, K 579
Jowitt, K 658

Kadane, J 997 n2
Kadera, K M 845
Kagel, J H 172 n24, 922
Kahler, M 767 n16, 770
Kahn, L 627
Kahneman, D 959
Kaid, L L 50 n1
Kalandrakis, T 170 n18
Kalyvas, S 864
Kandori, M 956
Kang, D 708
Kaplan, T R 432 n9
Karl, T L 657, 704, 715
Katz, L 624, 627
Katz, R 113 n24, 126 n5
Katzenstein, P 604, 605 n1, 762 n7, 765
Kaufman, R R 657, 663 n4
Kaufmann, C 857, 876
Kautsky, K 638
Kayser, M A 124 n4
Keach, W R 252 n13
Keech, W R 214 n7
Keefer, P 693, 697, 1005
Keen, M 505, 517
Kehoe, P J 517
Keith, L C 841
Keller, W 741
Kelley, S 252 n15
Kelly, N J 606
Kennedy, S 466
Kenny, L W 452 n26

NAME INDEX 1057

Keohane, R 645, 708, 710, 759, 762, 767, 801, 832, 836
Kernell, S 250
Key, V O 43
Keynes, John Maynard 516, 539
Khagram, S 634
Khaldun, Ibn 885
Kiefer, N 99 n24
Kiewiet, D R 47 n14, 202, 215 n8, 244, 466, 579
Kihlstrom, R E 51 n4
Kilgour, D M 428 n4
Kilson, M 657
Kim, M 882 n1
Kim, W 831, 837
Kim Il Sung 699, 700
Kim Jong Il 699, 700
Kinder, D 47 n14, 579
Kindleberger, Charles 759, 761, 762
King, D R 432 n9
King, G 165, 835
King, R G 700
Kinsella, D 875
Kirchgässner, G 453 n32, 465, 571 n13
Kirchsteiger, G 959
Kitschelt, H 606, 660
Klamler, C 427 n1
Klare, M T 716
Klaus, B 385
Klein, M W 558, 594
Kliemt, Hartmut 335
Knack, S 693, 697, 1005
Knetsch, J L 959
Knight, J 282
Knott, J H 244 n3
Kohl, Helmut 540
Kollman, K 367
Konrad, K A 894
Kontopoulos, Y 465, 560, 733
Kopits, G 466
Kopstein, J 662
Koremenos, B 767 n16
Kormendi, R 571 n12, 920
Kornhauser, L A 322
Korpi, W 604
Kotsogiannis, C 505
Kramer, G 81, 90, 165, 548, 566–7, 575, 579, 582–3, 608, 997 n2, 1023
Krasner, S D 761, 762, 767, 808, 836
Krehbiel, K 6, 7, 10–11, 30 n2, 130, 133, 143, 151, 162 n2, 168, 170 n16, 182, 203 n2, 217 n10, 224, 227 n6, 228, 230 n7, 238, 244, 247, 252 n15, 529
Krippner, G 939
Krueger, A O 446 n9, 627
Krugman, P R 739 n1, 743, 745, 746 n5, 819 n8, 822 n14, 823
Kugler, J 832, 836
Kunicova, J 728
Kuran, Timur 1007
Kurland, P H 1040 n6, 1042 n8, 1043
Kurz, M 88, 89–90
Kurzer, P 645, 648
Kuznets, S 87, 626
Kwon, H Y 606

Kydd, A 863, 864
Kydland, F 516, 532

La Porta, R 782 n14
Laakso, M 106–7
Lacina, B 858
Ladha, K 928 n13
Laffont, J J 385, 487 n17, 489 n21
Lai, B 875, 876
Laitin, D 323 n17, 719, 853, 856, 857, 858, 859 n10, 860, 863, 864, 865
Lake, D A 693, 761, 762 n7, 763 n8, 768, 769, 770, 842, 873
Lalman, D 831, 832, 836
Lamari, M 554
Lambertini, L 557 n9
Lamounier, B 315
Lancaster, C 542
Landes, D S 530
Landes, W 281
Lang, S 686
Lange, P 605, 615, 644, 645, 805, 1017
Lao-Araya, K 473
Lardeyret, G 659
Larocca, R 252 n14
Laslier, J F 376
Lassen, D 729
Laussel, D 75
Laver, Michael 6, 122 n2, 126, 128, 129, 136, 138, 146 n7, 150, 151, 162, 164, 165 n7, 166–8, 172 n22, 174 n29, 552, 606, 616 n16
Lavergne, R P 762
Law, J 939
Lazarsfeld, Paul 40
Lazear, E P 253
Le Breton, M 21, 75, 779, 788
Leamer, E 742 n3
Leblang, D 325, 593, 594, 873
Lederman, D 632
Ledyard, J 39, 74, 489 n22, 492 n30, 493 n31, 494, 495, 496, 498, 910, 911, 932, 958
Lee, S J 686
Lee, W 452, 452 n28, 1016, 1026
Lee Kuan Yew 698
Leeds, B A 873, 874, 875
Leibfried, S 366–7, 613, 804
Leibowitz, S 809
Lemke, D 832, 836
Leonard, D K 683
Lerner, D 657
Lerner, R 1040 n6, 1042 n8
Leroux, J 386
Levi, Margaret 709 n1, 718, 873
Levine, D K 955, 956
Levine, D P 758 n2, 930
Levine, R 700, 782 n14, 865
Levitsky, S 664 n6
Levitt, S D 32 n5, 50 n1, 59, 60
Levy, G 132, 451
Levy, J 833
Lewis, D 244, 261 n1, 269–70
Lewis, P H 698, 703
Lewis-Beck, M 548, 566 n1, 578 n29, 579 n30

Lijphart, A 103, 107, 182, 183, 472, 732
Limongi, F 145, 315 n5, 657 n1
Lin, T-M 450 n19
Lindahl, Eric 442, 454 n35
Lindbeck, A 74, 92 n14, 93 n16, 94–5, 450 n19, 1018 n6
Lindert, P 455, 604, 605, 687
Linz, J 659, 663 n4, 679 n2, 694, 698
Lipset, S M 315, 316, 625, 634, 657, 685, 690
Lipson, C 767 n16
Litvack, J 465
Lizzeri, A 468, 731
Lloyd George, D 687
Lo, Andrew 999
Loayza, N 632
Lobell, S E 771
Locke, John 31, 293, 297, 306, 308 n15, 342
Lockwood, B 362
Lohmann, S 98, 528, 530, 533, 535, 541
Lomasky, L 331 n2, 984 n2
Lomborg, B 525
London, T R 873
Londregan, J B 92, 93 n14, 94 n18, 95, 96–7, 156, 362, 548, 551, 568 n6, 574, 609–10, 697
Long, S B 873
Loosemore, J 104, 105
Louch, H 940
Love, J 944
Loveman, B 1046, 1047
Lowi, T J 528, 609
Lowry, R 152
Lucas, R E 644, 749, 818
Luebbert, G M 657
Lupia, A 124, 173, 215 n8, 278, 304, 529
Luttmer, E 630, 952

Ma, J 385
McAfee, R P 481 n5
Macaulay, S 944
Macaulay, Thomas 313
McCabe, K 959
McCarty, N 188–90, 244, 245 n4, 247, 251, 260, 267, 268
McCloskey, R G 208
McCubbins, M D 6, 9–10, 15 n15, 93 n14, 95, 96, 125, 132, 133, 145, 146, 150, 151, 152, 153, 154, 155, 156, 157, 158, 183, 202, 203, 203 n3, 209 n4, 213, 214, 215 n8, 217 n10, 228–9, 230–2, 234, 238, 244, 257, 274, 277, 278, 279, 304, 997 n2
MacDonald, S E 33, 35
MacGaffey, J 716
McGann, A J 606 n3
McGillivray, Fiona 826
McGregor, R R 214 n7
McGuire, M 894
Machiavelli, N 982
MacIntyre, A 765
Mackay, R 225, 229, 997 n2
MacKay, R J 6
McKelvey, R 15 n15, 44, 88, 135, 149, 155, 156, 163, 186–7, 379, 448, 449 n18, 454, 489 n23, 832, 900, 904, 905 n8, 907, 918, 919, 920, 921 n9, 922, 923, 927, 928, 997 n2

McKenna, M 338
McKeown, T J 762
Mackey, S 698
Mackie, G 308
McKinnon, R I 645
Mackintosh, James 313
Mackuen, M 43, 575 n19
McLean, I 900
McLennan, A 99 n24
McNeil, W 718
McNollgast 275, 278, 279, 280 n7, 282, 283
McPhee, William 40
MacRay, D 617
McVickar 638
Maddison, A 685
Madison, James 31, 291, 307, 308, 309, 313, 357, 1040, 1043
Madsen, H 548
Magaloni, B 281, 694, 703
Magee, S P 762, 763–4
Maggi, G 452, 1036, 1043 n10
Mahdavy, H 716
Mahdi, N Q 952
Mair, P 122 n2, 552
Majone, G 808
Malath, G 496 n40
Maltzman, F 152, 204, 210
Mani, A 550
Manin, Bernard 304, 725
Mankiw, N G 571 n12
Mansfield, E 834, 872, 873
Mantzavinos, C 1032
Mao Tse-tung 699, 700
Maoz, Z 839, 840
Marceau, N 446 n12
March, J G 212
Marchand, M 517
Marcos, Ferdinand 698, 701
Marcus, J 717
Mares, I 604, 615, 617, 618, 647, 648 n3
Margo, R A 626
Margolis, S 809
Marier, P 469
Marini, R M 760 n5
Marion, N P 594
Marks, B A 6, 209, 210 n5, 217 n10, 275
Marlow, M 360
Marshall, A 744–5
Marshall, J 1044
Marshall, M 633
Marshall, W J 8–9, 143, 154, 362
Martin, J L 941
Martin, L L 710, 767, 804, 805
Martin, L W 155, 164 n5, 171 n21
Marx, Karl 3, 87, 313, 718 n5
Marx, L M 498
Masciandaro, D 734
Mas-Colell, A 375, 380, 480 n2, 485 n14
Maskin, E 381, 415, 421, 710, 955, 956
Massicotte, L 726
Massó, J 384
Mastanduno, M 762 n7
Masuyama, M 153

Matsusaka, J G 465
Matsushima, H 956
Matthews, S A 244, 246, 251, 498
Maurer, A 695, 698, 699, 700, 701, 702, 705
May, K O 904
Mayda, A M 815, 824
Mayer, T 536
Mayhew, D 8, 225
Means, G C 304, 305, 1014
Mearsheimer, J J 869
Meciar, Vladimir 662
Meek, C 872
Meernik, J 873
Meguire, P 571 n12
Mehlum, H 882 n1
Meirowitz, A 151, 238, 260, 266, 268, 933
Meissner, C M 589
Meltzer, A H 85, 86–7, 98, 313, 448, 546, 604, 631
Meltzer Commission 542
Mendoza, J 792 n34
Menger, C 945
Merlo, A 165 n6, 170 n17, 171, 171 n20, 172, 173, 174, 175, 176, 181 n3, 909 n12
Merrill, S 111, 277, 449 n18
Mershon, C 165 n7
Mesnard, A 716
Messner, M 1037
Meyer, J 945
Michelman, F I 351
Mieszkowski, P M 448 n15
Miguel, E 865, 865 n21
Mihov, I 467
Milesi-Ferretti, G M 468, 469, 630, 640, 731
Milgrom, P 51 n4, 385, 951, 956
Mill, J S 306, 315
Mill, James 313 n1
Millar, J 466
Miller, Arthur 304
Miller, G J 187, 244, 450, 921, 928 n13
Miller, N R 905 n8, 908, 997 n2
Miller, R A 873
Mills, C W 212
Milner, H 645, 762, 767, 826–7, 1042, 1043, 1045
Milnor, J 421
Milošević, Slobodan 662
Mirabeau 565
Miranda, C 698, 703
Mirrlees, J A 442 n1
Mitch, D 687
Mitra, M 385
Mizruchi, M 940
Mo, J 224 n3
Moav, O 629
Mobutu Sese Seko 698
Moe, T M 212, 213–14, 244, 257, 260, 446 n10
Moene, K O 604, 647, 882 n1, 951
Molander, P 473, 474
Molyneux, R 999
Money, J 122 n1, 145, 180 n1, 181, 182 n4
Mongin, P 422

Monnet, Jean 803, 804
Monroe, K 566 n1
Montesquieu, Charles Secondat de 307, 357, 358, 778–9
Moore 624
Moore, B 609, 657, 684, 952
Moore, C 694
Moore, J 386
Moran, M J 201, 213, 263
Moraski, B 204, 244, 248
Moravcsik, A 802, 805, 807
Morelli, M 171, 172, 922
Moreno, E 281
Morgan, T C 840
Morgenstern, O 900, 903
Morris, I L 214 n7
Morris, S 98
Morrow, J D 831, 833, 837
Morton, R 51, 922, 925, 928
Moselle, B 894
Moses, J 645
Motyl, A 658, 662, 663 n4
Moulin, H 377, 384, 385, 386, 425, 429 n6
Mueller, D 340 n6, 446 n9, 452 n30, 454 n33, 454 n34, 526, 566 n1, 578 n28
Mueller, J 857
Muench, T 481 n7
Mugabe, Robert 678, 698
Mukand, S 550
Mundell, R A 645, 764, 769
Munger, M 449 n18, 998
Murdoch, J C 781 n8
Murillo, M V 664 n6
Murphy, K 624, 627
Musgrave, R 359 n1, 441, 442 n2
Muthoo, A 157, 889
Myerson, R 92, 189, 480, 491 n28, 495, 729, 905 n9, 909 n12, 910, 911, 925
Myrdal, G 744

Nacif, B 224 n3
Nadeau, R 578 n29
Nakamura, K 380
Nalebuff, B J 978
Nannestad, P 566 n1
Napoleon I 20
Nash, J 65 n1, 903
Nee, V 939, 945, 946
Neme, A 384
Neto, O A 613
Neustadt, Richard 242, 243
New York Times 531, 818 n7
Niemi, R 578 n29
Niou, E 831, 834–5
Niskanen, W 212, 446 n10, 455 n40
Nitzan, S 74 n8, 449 n18, 450, 454
Nixon, D 163 n3, 261, 269
Nixon, Richard M 135, 576 n24, 759
Noh, S J 893
Nokken, T P 204
Noll, R 214, 257, 278
Nordhaus, William 534, 546, 547, 572
Norris, P 115

North, D C 20 n24, 22, 84, 611 n11, 614, 617, 678, 685, 697, 709, 719, 747, 748, 751, 946, 956, 1003 n1, 1005, 1032
Novak, W J 342 n1
Nugent, J B 697
Nurmi, H 391, 393, 404
Nye, J S 710, 759, 832
Nye, J V 768 n17

Oates, Wallace 359, 360, 502 n1, 781 n10
Oatley, T 646
Obara, I 956
Obinger, H 366–7, 613
O'Brien, P K 685
Obstfeld, M 819 n8, 822 n14
Ochs, J 762
O'Donnell, G 659, 663, 664 n6, 664 n8, 694
Offe, C 659
O'Gorman, F 686
Oh, S 533
O'Halloran, S 214–15, 258–60, 262
Ok, E 951
O'Loughlin, J 657
Olson, M 22, 39, 42, 85, 98, 263, 380, 446 n7, 528, 530, 532, 609, 697, 781 n8, 894, 975
Olszewski, W 386
O'Mahony, A 764, 769
Oneal, J 870, 873, 876
O'Neill, K 366
Oppenheimer, J 928 n13
Oppenheimer, S 740
Ordeshook, P 15 n15, 40, 41, 44, 66, 74, 77 n10, 359, 364, 613, 831, 834–5, 900, 911, 920, 921 n9, 923, 924, 997 n2, 998, 1045, 1046
Organski, A F K 832, 836
O'Rourke, K 818
Ortuño-Ortin, I 1015
Osborne, M 81, 132, 323, 450, 607, 908, 1019
Ostrom, E 447 n13, 952, 1032 n1
Ostroy, J M 385
Ottaway, M 694

Pacek, A 578 n29, 581 n36
Pachón, M 147, 148, 149, 155
Pagan, A 582 n38
Pagano, M 592
Page, B 30 n1, 43, 44
Page, T 278
Pahre, R 761
Paldam, M 554, 566 n1, 578 n28
Palfrey, T R 36, 184, 185–6, 365, 366, 492 n30, 493 n31, 494, 495, 496, 498, 900 n3, 910, 911, 925, 926, 927, 928, 929, 930, 932, 933
Palma, G 760
Palmer, G 841, 873, 875
Palmer, H 578 n29
Panizza, U 366, 792
Pantaleoni, M 441–2
Pápai, S 385
Park, J H 549
Parks, R 997 n2
Partell, P J 841, 875
Pattanaik, P K 376

Patty, J 77, 449 n18, 454
Pauly, M 780 n4
Paz, A 427 n2
Peacock, A 441
Pearce, D 956
Peceny, M 876
Pedersen, E F 558
Peltzman, S 212 n6, 570 n11, 730, 767
Perot, Ross 61
Perotti, R 465, 468, 560, 604, 630, 648, 731, 733, 734
Persico, N 468, 731
Persson, T 88, 115 n27, 154, 360, 362, 452, 464, 468, 469, 526, 607, 612, 613, 630, 631, 724, 725, 727, 729, 730, 731, 732, 733, 734, 735, 826, 909 n12, 1017
Pesendorfer, W 16 n16, 912
Pesenti, P 594
Peters, H 384
Peterson, E 427
Petny, F 554
Petron, A 405
Pettit, P 332 n4
Pevehouse, J 873, 876
Pfahler, M 215
Phillips, A W 644
Piccione, M 928, 956
Pickering, J 873
Pierson, P 609, 613, 617, 649, 804, 808, 809
Pigou, A C 442
Piketty, T 98, 99, 314 n4, 627, 640
Pikhurko, O 427
Pinckney, Charles 1040, 1043
Pincus, J J 762
Pinochet, Augusto 844
Pinto, P M 764
Plato 20, 778, 982
Platt, G 33
Plott, C 69, 417, 900, 904, 915–16, 917, 918–19, 920, 921, 925, 928
Poe, S C 841
Pol Pot 699
Polak, B 894
Polanyi, K 615 n13, 938, 940, 948
Polborn, M K 1037
Pollack, M A 811
Polsby, N W 1035
Pommerehne, W 465
Pomper, G M 552
Pontusson, J 605, 606, 615 n14
Pool, I de S 759
Poole, K 33, 136, 184 n6, 233 n14, 697, 997 n2
Pope, J 251
Popkin, S L 304
Porter, M E 744
Portes, R 741
Posner, D N 856, 860, 861, 865
Posner, R 281
Postlewaite, A 481 n4, 496 n40
Poterba, J 154, 467
Potoski, M 261, 262 n2
Potters, J 51, 54 n9
Potthof, R F 428 n4
Powell, B 607
Powell, G B 559, 578, 579, 582

Powell, R 763 n8, 781, 831, 834, 835, 837, 863 n16, 890
Powell, W 941, 945
Prat, A 15, 46, 51, 53, 54 n7, 56, 60
Prebisch, R 760 n5
Preeg, E H 759
Prescott, E 516, 532
Preuss, U K 659
Profeta, P 452 n26, 456
Prunier, G 860
Przeworski, A 312, 314–16, 319 n10, 319 n11, 320, 325, 326, 603, 611, 644, 657 n1, 658, 664 n8, 697, 698, 705, 725, 865 n19
Puga, D 745 n4, 748, 749 n7
Puppe, C 432 n9
Putin, Vladimir 662
Putnam, R H 684, 767, 832

Qian, Y 630
Quade, Q L 659
Quah, D T 748
Quinlivan, J T 876
Quirk, P J 201

Rabinowitz, G 33, 35
Rabushka, A 322, 527, 858, 865
Radcliff, B 578 n29, 581 n36
Rae, Douglas 103
Ragin, C 613
Raith, M G 428 n4
Rakove, J 1006 n3, 1038
Ramsey, F P 442
Ramseyer, J M 766
Rasch, B E 149
Rauch, J 270
Rawaswamy, R 646 n2
Rawls, John 290–1, 292, 294, 296, 301–2, 303, 306, 330, 434 n11, 1035–6
Ray, D 882 n1, 892
Razin, A 467
Razo, A 695, 698, 700, 701, 702, 705
Razzolini, L 376, 386
Reagan, Ronald 203–4, 280, 638
Redding, S 742
Reed, S R 115
Reed, W 872, 873
Regan, P M 873
Reid, J P 304, 1006
Reidl, A 959
Reilly, B 104
Reilly, D 662
Reiter, D 771 n18, 844, 871, 872, 873, 875, 876
Remington, T F 148
Remmer, K L 694
Reno, W 716
Reschovsky, A 452 n26
Rey, H 741
Reyaud, Hervé 973
Reynolds, A 104
Rich, B 542
Richard, S F 85, 86–7, 98, 313, 448, 604, 631
Richards, John 767
Richie, R 305 n12
Rietz, T 925

Riezman, R 933
Riker, William 40, 41, 89 n9, 130, 182, 359, 362–3, 363–4, 367, 368, 446 n8, 603, 610, 839, 860, 900, 907, 997 n2, 1010 n1, 1032, 1036, 1037, 1040, 1041
Ringer, F 687
Riordan, M H 51 n4
Rioux, J-S 872
Riquetti, Honoré Gabriel 565
Ritschl, A 801
Robbins, J 466
Robbins, L 988
Roberts, J 51 n4, 481, 491
Roberts, K 415, 417, 421
Robertson, J M 425, 427
Robinson, J 603, 617, 629, 674 n1, 678, 679, 685, 688, 690, 691, 705, 716, 740, 751, 839, 842
Rocke, D 701, 832, 839, 1036, 1043 n9, 1045
Rodden, J 362–3, 364, 465, 613
Rodriguez, D 274, 275, 276, 277, 278 n4, 280 n7
Rodrik, D 581 n36, 582, 604, 631, 639, 648, 765, 815, 824, 1017, 1036
Röell, A 724
Roemer, J 71, 72 n3, 80, 81, 85, 87, 376, 451, 452, 452 n28, 553, 610, 1014, 1015, 1016, 1018, 1019, 1020, 1023, 1024, 1026, 1028 n12
Rogers, B 929
Rogers, J 184, 192, 193, 446 n11
Rogoff, K 526–7, 533, 534, 546, 548 n3, 558, 572
Rogowski, R 617, 618, 764, 765, 771
Rohde, D W 157
Roland, G 22, 154, 365, 452, 464, 729, 732, 733, 734, 779, 790, 791, 909 n12
Romer, P 648
Romer, T 125, 155, 203 n3, 226 n4, 230 n7, 448, 604, 921, 1027
Roosevelt, Franklin D 273, 304
Root, H 839
Roozendaal, P van 171 n21
Rose, A 592, 807
Rose, G 831, 834–5
Rose, R 552
Rose Ackerman, S 728
Rosenbluth, F 154, 612, 613, 616 n15, 766
Rosenbluth, N 732
Rosenburg, G N 208
Rosendorff, B P 1042, 1043, 1045
Rosenstone, S 41
Rosenthal, H 33, 125, 136, 155, 184 n6, 203 n3, 226 n4, 230 n7, 233 n14, 548, 551, 556, 557, 568 n6, 574, 578 n27, 900 n3, 921, 930, 932, 997 n2
Rosenthal, J-L 718, 719 n6
Rosenthal, S S 749 n8
Ross, G 803
Ross, M 604, 683, 704, 715
Rostagno, M 468, 630, 731
Roth, A 385, 922, 957
Rothenberg, L 183, 184, 238, 444 n6
Rothschild, M 99 n24
Roubini, N 124 n4, 465, 548 n2, 549, 556, 557, 560, 594, 607, 644, 734
Rousseau, D L 873
Rousseau, Jean Jacques 357, 358
Rowan, B 945

NAME INDEX

Rowe, D M 771
Rowthorn, R 646 n2
Rubinfeld, D 360, 362, 453, 751 n9, 780 n3
Rubinstein, A 607 n6, 912, 921
Rudalevige, A 244
Rueben, K 467
Rueda, D 615 n14
Ruggie, J G 765
Russell, P 281, 282
Russett, B M 839, 840, 870, 873, 875, 876
Rustichini, A 316 n9, 634
Rutherford, T 452, 452 n30, 456
Rutten, A 1006 n3

Saari, D G 391, 392, 393, 396, 399, 400, 401, 402, 404, 405, 406, 900
Sacerdote, B 636, 975
Sachs, J D 465, 548 n2, 560, 716, 734, 740
Sadka, E 467
Saez, E 314 n4, 627
Sahlins, M D 711, 719
Saijo, T 386
Sait, E M 1032, 1033
Sala, B J 204
Salanié, B 444 n6
Sambanis, N 858
Samuels, D J 131 n7
Samuelson, P A 442, 480, 759, 764, 814, 819 n8, 900, 986
Sanchez-Pages, S 892
Sandler, T 766 n13, 882 n1
Sanguinetti, P 364, 466, 473
Sargent, T 644
Sarkees, M 875
Sato, M 457 n42
Satterthwaite, M 403, 480
Savage, L L 973
Savioz, M R 465
Scalia, Antonin 346
Scanlon, T M 293–4, 296
Scarf, H 385
Schattschneider, E E 759, 762
Scheinkman, J 632, 975
Scheve, K F 820 n9, 824
Scheve, T 556 n7
Schickler, E 224
Schlesinger, J 606
Schmidtchen, D 780 n3
Schmittberger, R 958
Schmitter, P 604, 657, 659, 664 n8
Schneider, F 559
Schofield, N 129, 135, 149, 162, 163 n3, 172 n22, 187, 448, 450, 450 n21, 489 n23, 606, 832, 900, 904, 918
Schotter, A 1034
Schram, A 930
Schroeder, C H 261
Schubert, G 211
Schuessler, A 41 n8, 331 n2
Schultz, C 52
Schultz, K A 832, 839, 841, 873, 874, 875
Schummer, J 384
Schumpeter, Joseph 304, 453, 771

Schwartz, T 213, 214, 279, 905 n8
Schwat, B 958
Schweizer, U 770
Schweller, R L 832
Scotchmer, S 780 n3
Scott, J C 952
Scruggs, L 606
Seabright, P 464
Searle, J R 312
Segal, J 204, 208, 210, 211, 281
Segura, G 872
Sekiguchi, T 956
Seldon, A 527
Selfridge, John L 427
Sellers, M N S 342 n1
Selten, R 171 n19
Selznick, P 212
Sen, A 316, 376, 405, 408, 409, 417, 418, 419, 532, 943
Sened, I 163 n3
Serizawa, S 384, 386
Shadbegian, R J 467
Shambayati, H 716
Shannon, M L 845
Shapiro, Ian 39
Shapiro, M 214, 280, 571 n12
Shapiro, R 30 n1, 43, 44, 252
Shapley, L 189, 385
Shariq, S 1032
Shaw, M 148
Sheffrin, S 558
Shenker, S 385, 386
Shepsle, K A 6, 7 n6, 8, 11, 126, 128, 129, 135, 136, 146 n7, 150, 151, 157, 162, 164, 165, 166–8, 174 n29, 225, 226 n4, 260, 322, 447 n13, 528, 616 n16, 858, 865, 997 n2, 998, 1018, 1032, 1033, 1037 n3, 1041, 1042, 1044, 1047
Shi, M 559
Shibata, H 455 n40
Shin, T 942
Shipan, C 6, 142 n1, 181, 204, 215–16, 217–18, 244, 247, 248, 250 n8, 260, 262, 263, 268, 269, 278, 446 n10
Shishido, H 427 n2
Shleifer, A 630, 632
Shotts, K W 252
Shoven, J B 448 n15
Shubik, M 189
Shugart, M 103, 107, 109 n15, 112, 131 n7, 142 n1, 281, 472, 612, 728, 732
Shugart, W 452 n26
Shvetsova, O 130, 282, 359, 364, 613
Siavelis, P 145
Sibert, A 526–7, 534, 546, 572
Sidney, Algernon 303, 306
Sigelman, L 152
Signorino, C 836
Silvestre, J 1026
Simmons, B 589, 592, 645, 710, 763 n9, 833
Simon, H 212, 961, 971
Simon, J 314
Simpser, A 694, 703
Singh, N 18, 19 n22, 961
Singh, S 711, 714 n3, 715, 894
Sinn, H W 647

Siverson, R M 839, 844, 872
Skach, C 659
Skaperdas, S 444 n5, 781, 882 n1, 883 n2, 885 n5, 886, 890, 891, 892, 893, 894
Skidmore, M 466
Skilling, D 469
Skocpol, T 718
Slantchev, B 871, 872
Slaughter, A-M 767 n16
Slaughter, M J 820 n9, 824
Slezkine, Y 854
Slivinski, A 81, 132, 323, 450, 607, 908, 1019
Sloof, R 51, 54 n9, 56
Slutsky, S 997 n2
Smart, M 446 n12
Smelser, N 938
Smith, A 12, 124 n4
Smith, Adam 3, 306, 549, 836, 839, 847, 870, 872, 876
Smith, Al 635
Smith, S 148
Smith, Vernon 915, 916, 919
Smithies, A 900
Snidal, D 761, 767 n16, 834
Sniderman, P 33, 35, 44
Snyder, J 10, 32 n5, 35 n7, 36, 38, 46, 90, 95, 132, 133, 190, 191, 234, 248, 252 n15, 608, 715, 771, 834, 872, 873, 876, 926, 1023
Snyder, S K 204, 205, 206, 214 n7, 244
Sobel, J 909 n13, 912
Sokoloff, K L 624, 633, 747
Solingen, E 771
Sombart, Werner 625, 634
Somogyvári, I 148
Somoza, Anastasio 698, 701–2
Sonbeyran, R 892
Sönmez, T 385
Sonnemans, J 930
Sorauf, F J 46 n13
Soskice, D 607, 613, 614, 615, 616, 617, 647, 650, 651, 652, 709, 733, 819, 826
Soto, H de 716
Sotomayor, M 385
Spaeth, H J 208, 281
Spector, L 393, 394
Spence, A M 909 n13, 912
Spence, D B 261
Spiller, P 210, 215 n8, 275, 278, 283 n9
Spitzer, M 280
Spolaore, E 21, 634, 769, 779, 780, 781, 782 n15, 784 n19, 786, 788 n27, 789 n28, 790 n30, 792, 793, 794, 795
Sprague, J 611
Spriggs, J F 210, 269
Sprumont, Y 377, 383, 384
Sraffa, P 88, 101
Staal, K 779
Stacchetti, E 384, 956
Staiger, Robert 766, 767
Stalin, J 699, 700
Stam, A 836, 844, 870, 871, 872, 873, 875, 876
Stark, D 661
Starr, H 657
Stearns, Maxwell 974

Stegmaier, M 566 n1
Stein, E 363, 465, 466, 467, 473, 592, 594
Stepan, A 659, 663 n4, 679 n2
Stephens, J D 604, 606, 613, 649
Stephenson, M 282 n8
Stern, J 952
Stevenson, J 686
Stevenson, R 124, 164 n5, 165, 173 n28, 175, 176
Stewart, C H 35 n7, 1046
Stewart, R 277
Stienlet, G 473
Stigler, G 212 n6, 455 n39, 512, 517–18, 575, 767, 985 n4
Stiglitz, J E 442 n1, 527, 750, 766
Stimson, James 43, 575 n19
Stinchcombe, A 945
Stock, J 571 n12
Stockman, David 203
Stokes, Donald 32, 35
Stokes, G 530 n5
Stokes, S C 315 n5, 607 n4, 725
Stolper, Wolfgang 759, 764, 814
Storcken, T 384
Story, Joseph 1040, 1043 n10
Strange, W C 749 n8
Stratmann, T 60, 452 n30
Strauch, R R 466, 467, 472, 473, 474
Strauss, D A 349
Strauss, S 683
Stroessner, Alfredo 703
Strom, K 123, 124, 128, 129, 162, 164, 165, 171, 173, 174, 175, 732
Strömberg, D 728, 731
Stromquist, W 426
Stuart, C 80, 81 n13
Sturm, J-E 473
Su, F E 427, 428 n4
Sugden, R 376
Suijs, J 385
Suleiman, R 932
Summerhill, W R 697, 747, 748
Sundaram, R 81
Sunkel, O 760 n5
Sunstein, C R 349
Suny, R G 854
Suppes, P 414
Suzuki, M 575 n18
Suzumura, K 376
Svenson, P 153
Svensson, J 559
Svensson, L 385
Swank, D H 560, 606
Swedberg, R 938, 948
Swenson, P 603, 604, 605, 617, 618, 648 n3
Syropoulos, C 885 n5, 886, 890, 893
Szakaly, K 466

Taagepera, R 103, 105, 106–7, 109 n15, 110, 472, 732
Tabarrok, A 393, 394, 397
Tabellini, G 88, 115 n27, 154, 360, 362, 452, 464, 468, 469, 526, 607, 612, 613, 630, 631, 724, 725, 727, 729, 730, 731, 732, 733, 734, 735, 826, 909 n12, 1017

Talvi, E 466, 473
Tammen, R 832, 836
Tarar, A 767
Tarrow, S 688
Tate, N 841
Tawney, R H 688
Taylor, A D 425, 426, 427, 429, 431
Taylor, M 711, 955
Taylor, R 612 n12, 1032 n1
Thaler, R 957, 959, 1025, 1026
Thatcher, Margaret 127, 129
Theiss-Morse, E 304
Thelen, K 617, 618
Thies, M 155, 181 n3, 612
Thisse, J 739 n1, 784 n23
Thoma, M A 558
Thomas, R P 685, 709, 719
Thompson, E P 688
Thompson, J A 152
Thompson, M R 698
Thomson, E A 794 n36
Thomson, W 377
Thucydides 831
Ticchi, D 733, 826
Tiebout, C 22, 360, 512, 780
Tietz, R 957
Tiller, E 210, 283 n9
Tillman, E 873
Ting, M 38, 132, 190, 191, 268
Tirole, J 249 n7, 905 n9, 1036, 1039
Tocqueville, Alexis de 302 n11, 634
Tollison, R 951
Toma, M 452 n26
Tommasi, M 364, 466, 473, 592
Tomz, M 556 n7
Torvik, R 705, 882 n1
Trebbi, F 469, 727, 729, 730, 1036
Treisman, D 359, 361
Triffin, Robert 759
Trivers, Robert 954–5
Trujillo, Rafael 698, 701
Truman, Harry S 576 n24
Tsebelis, G 122 n1, 145, 150, 152, 153, 180 n1, 181, 182 n4, 187, 559, 560, 734, 1036
Tufte, E R 105, 546, 548, 549, 553, 559, 642, 644, 652, 778 n2
Tullock, G 8, 22, 149 n13, 154, 321, 330 n1, 343, 446 n9, 448, 454 n34, 527, 694, 696, 699, 711, 781, 951, 991, 997
Turtis, R L 698

Uebelmesser, S 456
Urbiztondo, S 215 n8
USA Today 524 n1
Usher, D 450 n20, 451 n23

Vail, L 856
Välimäki, J 956
van Creveld, M L 718, 982 n1
van de Walle, N 657, 660, 663 n4
van der Stel, H 384
van Newenhizen, J 396
van Wincoop, E 741

van Winden, F 51, 54 n9
Vanberg, C 57 n10
Vanberg, G 155, 171 n21
Vanden Bergh, R G 216 n9
Vansina, J 717 n4
Varshney, A 951
Vasquez, J 834
Vatikiotis, M 698
Veall, M R 314 n4
Veitch, J M 678
Velasco, A 465, 734
Venables, A J 739 n1, 741, 742, 744, 745, 746 n5, 747 n6, 748, 749 n7, 750, 780 n6
Verba, S 325
Verdier, D 763 n9
Verdier, T 705, 842
Vermilyea, T 214 n7
Vickrey, W 487 n17
Victor, J N 211
Vindigni, A 733, 826
Viner, J 780 n6
Vinhas de Souza, L 554 n5
Vlaicu, R 170 n16
Vohra, R 892
Volden, C 172 n25, 182, 224, 228, 247, 252 n15, 261–2, 263, 267
Volgy, T 834
Volij, O 779
Vollarth, D 629
von Hagen, J 154, 464, 465, 466, 467, 471, 472, 473, 474, 614, 734
von Neumann, J 900, 903

Wacquant, L 941
Wacziarg, R 779, 781 n7, 793, 794
Wagner, R E 534
Wagner, R H 863 n16
Wahlbeck, P J 210–11
Wałęsa, Lech 659, 661
Walker, M 480, 489 n21
Wallace, N 644
Wallenstein, A W E von 719–20
Waller, C J 535
Wallerstein, I 751
Wallerstein, M 603, 604, 611, 615 n14, 644, 647, 951
Wallis, John 1003 n1
Walsh, C 533
Walter, B F 863, 864
Waltz, K 832, 833, 834, 835
Wantchekon, L 704
Warneryd, K 888
Warwick, P 123, 165, 171, 172 n24
Wasserman, S 939
Waterman, R W 263
Watson, M 571 n12
Wattenberg, M 113
Wawro, G J 224
Way, L 664 n7
Webb, W A 425, 427
Weber, E J 856, 860
Weber, Max 265, 628, 944, 948

Weber, R 925
Weber, S 21, 779, 788
Weibull, J 74, 92 n14, 93 n16, 94–5, 450 n19, 1018 n6
Weingast, B R 6, 7 n6, 8–9, 11, 89, 135, 143, 151, 154, 201, 204, 205, 206, 213, 214, 215 n8, 225, 226 n4, 244, 248, 257, 263, 274, 275, 276, 277, 280 n7, 299, 321, 324 n21, 359, 360, 362, 363, 447 n13, 465, 528, 613, 617, 630, 675, 678, 685, 697, 709, 747, 748, 782 n13, 863, 951, 956, 998, 1003 n1, 1006 n3, 1038, 1046
Weinstein, D E 818, 820
Welch, I 929
Werner, S 833, 848, 872, 873, 875, 876
Wessels, B 114 n26
Weymark, J 417, 418, 422
Whalley, J 448 n15, 766 n14
Whateley, Thomas 304
Whinston, M D 450, 480 n2, 485 n14, 912
Whinstone, A 375, 380
Whitford, A B 270
Whitten, G D 559, 578, 579, 582
Wibbels, E 361, 469, 614, 617
Wicksell, Knut 442, 453, 454, 989, 990–1
Widener, J 657, 658 n3
Wiessner, P 952
Wildasin, David 87, 502 n1, 516
Wildavsky, A 202, 474
Williams, K C 924, 928
Williamson, J G 515, 818
Williamson, O E 301, 614, 761
Willis, E 364, 367
Wilson, C 171, 172
Wilson, Harold 565
Wilson, J D 502 n1, 511
Wilson, J Q 201, 213
Wilson, Rick 920
Wilson, W 243
Winch, D 313
Winer, S L 448, 450, 452, 452 n26, 453, 454 n36, 455, 456, 527 n3
Winstanley, Gerrard 306
Winter, E 171 n19
Wintrobe, R 446 n10, 695

Wittman, D 10, 14 n14, 15, 16, 22, 36, 37, 71, 80, 110 n18, 158, 304, 455, 455 n40, 456, 529, 553, 606, 779, 781, 782, 787, 794, 795 n38, 863 n16, 882 n1, 951, 998
Woglom, G 467
Wolff, E R 711
Wolff, G 466
Wolfram, C D 32 n5
Wood, B D 262, 263
Wood, E J 952
Wood, G 181
Wood, G S 303, 304, 342 n1
Woods, N 261
Woodward, C V 630
Wooley, J 550
Woon, Jon 234 n16, 238
Wren, A 646, 647, 648, 649
Wright, G 35 n7, 705
Wright, J R 211, 261
Wright, Sewell 579 n31

Xu, Y 376

Yarbrough, Beth 761
Yarbrough, Robert 761
Yeltsin, Boris 662
Yläoutinen, S 473
Yoshinaka, A 578 n29
You, J 634
Young, C 856
Young, H P 425, 429 n6
Young, L 762
Young, P 952

Zakaria, F 715
Zax, J S 360
Zeckhauser, R 781 n8
Zellner, A 579
Zeng, D-Z 427 n2, 428 n4
Zeng, L 835
Zodrow, G 448 n15
Zorn, C J W 211
Zukin, S 938
Zwicker, W S 426, 427

Subject Index

accountability:
   and coalition governments 729
   and electoral systems 468, 724, 726–7
      direct effects of 727–8
      indirect effects of 729–30
   and income redistribution 85
   and representation 724–5
   and retrospective voting 468
actor-network-theory (ANT) 940
Administrative Procedure Act (USA, 1946) 214
   and implications of 278–80
administrative state 256–7
advertising, *see* political advertising
Africa, and democratization 664
African Financial Community 588
age, and international trade 825–6
agency discretion 214–16
agenda-setting:
   and centralized agenda powers 155–6
      omnibus bills 156–7
      policy direction 156
   and judiciary 211
   and legislative organization:
      agenda-setting offices 145
      evolution of agenda-setting powers 146–7
      types of agenda power 149–51
   and negative agenda power 149–50
      gridlock 151–2
      reactions to gridlock 152
      roll rates of veto players 153
   and parliamentary systems 125–6
   and positive agenda power 153–5
      counterbalancing of 154–5
      decentralization of 154
   and presidential veto power 245
   and procedural cartel theory 229, 230
agglomeration, *see* economic geography
alliances, and anarchy 892–3
Allnut vs Inglis (King's Bench, 1810) 350
ally principle, and delegation 260, 262–3, 264, 266, 267, 269
altruism:
   and cooperative behavior 953
   parental 18
   see also behavior; cooperation
American Association of Retired Persons (AARP) 538
American politics, new separation-of-powers approach to 199–202, 218–19

and the bureaucracy 212–16
   agency discretion 214–16
   control of 213–14
   development of new approach 212–13
and causality 201
and decision-making sequence 219
and degrees of freedom problem 201
and implications for empirical analysis 201
and institutional interactions 200, 216–17
   telecommunications policy 217–18
and judicial review 217–18
and judiciary 207–12
   agenda-setting 211
   appointments process 211
   interactions with other institutions 207–8
   judicial decision-making 208–10
   legislative override 209–10
   limits on policy-making capacity 210–11
and the presidency 202–7, 241–2
   appointments process 204–7
   interactions with other institutions 202
   spatial model of budget problem 202–4
   veto rights 202–4
and strategic interactions 200, 218–19
anarchy:
   and absence of higher authority 881, 882
   and alliance formation 892–3
   and commitment problems 890–2
   and contracts 881, 882
   and guns vs butter trade-off 882–3
      determination of power 884–6
      technologies of conflict 883–4
   and hierarchical governance 893–4
   and impact of norms and institutions 890
   and international relations 881
   and motives for negotiated settlement:
      complementarities in production/consumption 888
      destructiveness of war 886–7
      risk aversion 887
      uncertainty 887–8
   and role of the future 890–1
   and rules of division and level of arming 888–90
   and trade and security policy 893
anthropology, and the state 709
appeasement 837
appointments process:
   and American presidency 204–7, 247–9
   and judiciary 211
approval voting, and voting theory 396–7
   see also voting behavior; voting theory

Argentina 314
  and federalism 359
  and financial crisis 595
  and repression 681
Arrow's theorem, *see* impossibility theorem
audience costs:
  and international conflict 841
  and war 874–5
audience democracy 304
Australia, and constitution of 338
authoritarian government, *see* dictatorships and authoritarian government

balance of power, and conflict 831
  see also international conflict
Ballot Act (UK, 1872) 686
bargaining:
  and bicameralism 187–8
    concurrent majorities 188–9
    fiscal prudence 190–1
    malapportionment 191
    super-majorities 189
  and cabinet stability (Diermeier-Merlo model) 173–4
  and coalition formation:
    demand bargaining 170–1
    sequential bargaining (Baron-Ferejohn model) 168–70
  and committee decision-making 917–18, 921–2
  and international bargaining 766–8
  and partisanship 607
  and presidential veto power 245–7, 250–1
Baron-Ferejohn model, and coalition formation 168–70
Baumol's 'disease' 538
behavior:
  and cooperation 952, 953–4, 963–4, 978
    altruism 953
    evolution of strong reciprocity 960–1
    explanation of 953–4
    internal norms 961
    as means not end 954
    mutualistic cooperation 954–7
    pro-social emotions 962–3
    requirements for model of 955–6
    strong reciprocity 957–60
  and evolutionary models of 4–5
    co-evolution of memes/genes 18–20
    equilibrium 17
    evolution of strong reciprocity 960–1
    internal norms 961
    mutualistic cooperation 954–5
    other-regarding behavior 17–18
    parental altruism 18
    pro-social emotions 18–20, 962–3
    reciprocal altruism 954–5
    shirking 19
    survival 17
    vengeful behavior 18
  and game theory:
    cooperation 956–7
    strong reciprocity 957–60
  and mutualistic cooperation 953

and other-regarding preferences 17–18, 952
and rational behavior 1034
and self-regarding preferences 952
and shortcomings of standard models 951–2
and social preferences 952–3, 957
  evolution of 953
behavioralism 30
Belgium:
  and budget process 473
  and ethnicity 854
  and federalism 366
beliefs 1005–6
  and colonial America 1006–7
  and inequality 637–8
bicameralism 193–4
  and chamber preferences 184
  and coalition formation 175–6
  and definition 180 n1
  and information aggregation 192–3
  and multi-dimensional models 186–7
  and multilateral bargaining theory 187–8
    concurrent majorities 188–9
    fiscal prudence 190–1
    malapportionment 191
    super-majorities 189
  and origins of 180–1
  and rationale for:
    compromise effect 182–3
    minority protection 181
    preservation of federalism 181
    stability 182–3
  and role of political parties 183
  and spatial models of malapportionment 184–6
  and spatial models of policy-making 181–4
  and super-majority requirements 183
  see also legislatures
borders:
  and border regions 788
  and defense/security issues 794–6
  and determination of 792
  and economic impact of 741
  and state size 779–80
  see also state size
bounded rationality 977–8
bravery 19
Brazil 325
  and authoritarian government 702
  and federalism 359
  and financial crisis (1999) 524
Bretton Woods system 588, 590, 759
budget process:
  and American presidency 202–4
  and coalition governments 734–5
  and ex ante fiscal rules 466–7
  and public finance 470–4
    centralization 470–1
    contract approach 471–2
    delegation 471–2
    enforcement 472
    impact of centralization 473–4
    impact of electoral rules 472
    stages of 470–1

Bulgaria 314
bureaucracy:
  and administrative state 256–7
  and centrality of 256
  and delegation 214–16, 256
    administrative dominance 265–6
    agency design 261–2
    ally principle 260, 262–3, 264, 266, 267, 269
    assumptions underlying models of 257–8, 268–9
    bureaucratic capacity 267
    commitment problem 268–70
    empirical tests of 261–4
    information asymmetries 266–7
    instruments of 257
    judiciary 269
    modeling of delegation strategies 257–61
    multi-principals issue 267–8
    nature of legislation 262–3
    policy uncertainty 259–60, 262, 263, 266, 269
    political context 264–5, 269–70
    political control 265
    political oversight 257, 264
    political uncertainty 260–1, 263–4, 266
    substitution effect 260, 263, 266
  and legal control of 277–81
    Chevron decision 280–1
    implications of Administrative Procedure Act 278–80
  and new separation-of-powers approach to 201, 212–16
    agency discretion 214–16
    control of 213–14
    development of 212–13
Burma 681
Burundi 679

cabinet stability 165
  and non-cooperative bargaining 173–4
  and structure-induced equilibrium 166–7
California, and special interest gridlock 530
Cambodia, and terror 699
campaign financing 46, 61–2
  and expenditure function 59–60
  and interest groups 50, 52
  and micro-founded models of 51
  and political advertising
    directly informative 57–9
    indirectly informative 54–7
  and public funding 59, 60
  and regulation of 51
  and vote share 50–1, 59–60
Canada:
  and economic openness 827
  and ethnicity 855
  and ex ante fiscal rules 466
candidates:
  and electoral framework 66–7
  and laboratory experiments on elections 922
    asymmetric contests 926
    candidate convergence 923

    median voter theorem 923–4
    multicandidate elections 924–5
    retrospective voting 923–4
  and policy-positioning 64, 81–2
    deterministic voting 67–72
    probabilistic voting, stochastic partisanship model 72–7
    probabilistic voting, stochastic preference model 77–81
  and political advertising:
    directly informative 57–9
    indirectly informative 53–7
  see also elections
capital mobility:
  and fiscal competition 504–5, 508–9, 518–19
    dynamics 514–17
  and welfare implications of 505
capitalism:
  and democracy 23, 601
    class compromise 603
    coexistence with 601–2
    diversity of capitalist democracies 603–4
    role of political power 604–5
  and institutional diversity 602
  and varieties of capitalism approach 602–3, 614–17
    coordinated market economies 615
    institutional complementarity 615
    liberal market economies 615
    relationship of economic/political institutions 616
    role of economic institutions 614–15
    state's economic role 650–1
    welfare state 615–16
  and welfare state 601–2
cartels 767
censorship, and United States Supreme Court 346
central banks:
  as domestic and international non-issue 523–5
  and independence of 533, 536
centralization:
  and budget process 470–1, 473–4
  and policy outcomes 185
  and voter preferences 185–6
charity 446
Chicago School 455, 767
Chile 314, 325
China 679
  and economic development 531–2
  and economic openness 827
  and ethnicity 854
  and repression 681
  and terror 699
cities:
  and attraction of 749
  and economic geography 739
  and economic policy 750–1
  and equilibrium size 750
  and labor mobility 743
  and market size/access 743
  and transport costs 749–50
  see also economic geography

citizen duty, and voting behavior 40–1
citizen-candidate model 909
    and equilibrium analysis of public finance 450–1, 452
    and partisanship 607
    and political failure 456
Civil Rights Act (USA, 1964) 276
class:
    and class coalitions 609
    and democracy and capitalism 603, 604–5
    and electoral systems 613
clubs 780
clustering 742–3
    and cities:
        attractions of 749
        economic policy 750–1
        equilibrium size 750
        transport costs 749–50
    and firm linkages 744
    and industrialization in New World 747–8
    and Krugman-Venables trade/location model 745–6
    and labor mobility 743
    and market size/access 743
    and sequential growth 748–9
    and technological externalities 745
    and thick labor market 744–5
    see also economic geography
coalitions:
    and accountability 729
    and agenda power 150
    and budget deficits 734–5
    and cabinet stability 165
        non-cooperative bargaining 173–4
        structure-induced equilibrium 166–7
    and distributive politics 602, 608–11
        class coalitions 609
        public policy-making 609
        racial politics 610–11
        re-bundling of issues 610
    and electoral cycles 549, 550
    and formation of:
        bicameralism 175–6
        demand bargaining 170–1
        efficient negotiations 171–2
        ethnicity 860–2
        sequential bargaining 168–70
        structure-induced equilibrium 165–8
    and government spending 732–4
    and institutionalism 162–5
        cabinet stability 165
        minority governments 164–5
        reappraisal of existing theory 163–4
    and non-cooperative approach, consequences for research 175–6
    and parliamentary systems 163
    and veto rights 150
Coase theorem 529
coercion:
    and organization of 719–20
    and public sector economics 446
    and societies with states 712–15
    and stateless societies 710–11

cognition:
    and change 1005
    and paradoxes 971–2
collective action:
    and cooperative behavior 963–4
        altruism 953
        evolution of strong reciprocity 960–1
        explanation of 953–4
        internal norms 961
        as means not end 954
        mutualistic cooperation 953, 954–7
        pro-social emotions 18–20, 962–3
        strong reciprocity 957–60
    and de facto power 676
    and economic development 530
    and the individual 985
    and objects of 986–7
    and organic state model of 981
    and political parties 9–10
    and unanimity rule 990–1
    and unitary or multiple decision-makers 983–4
collective choice:
    and collective preference theory 902–5
        core emptiness 908–9
        large populations 907
        opportunities for trade 906–7
    and game theory 905–6
        core emptiness 910–12
    and individual choice processes 973
    and public sector 443–7, 457
collective preference theory 902–5
    and core emptiness 908–9
    and large populations 907
    and opportunities for trade 906–7
collectivities, and social choice 972–3
committee decision-making 916–17
    and bargaining in multidimensional policy spaces 917–18
    and committee bargaining 921–2
    and core clustering 919–21
    and Fiorina and Plott's experiments 918–19
    and information aggregation 927–9
commitment problem 268–70, 675, 677, 890–2
Common Agricultural Policy (CAP) 803
common-pool problem:
    and public finance 465, 473–4
        budget process 470–1
        electoral rules 468–9
    see also pork-barrel politics
comparative institutional analysis 223
    and pivot theories 238
        analysis of roll rates 230–2, 234–8
        endogenous status quo points 233–4
Comparative Manifestoes Project (CMP) 137–8
competitive federalism 360
compromise effect, and bicameralism 182–3
Condorcet criterion 103, 392, 403
conflict, and intergenerational conflict 536–8
    see also international conflict; war
constitutional political economy 991–2
    and constitutions as rules of the game 330–2

constitutionalism 289–91, 307–9
    and citizen motivation 290–1
    and constitutions:
        as consequentialist devices 290
        costs of changing 308
        diversity of 307–8
    and contemporary work on 289
    and contractarian theories 289, 291–7
        contractual obligations 293
        contractualist argument 293–6
        falsity of 320–1
        moral theory 293–4
        objections to 291–3
        rationalist agreement 294
        reasonableness 293–4, 295–7
    and conventions 295, 297–8, 308
    and coordination theories 289, 297–9, 307–8, 321
        acquiescence 297, 298
        dual-convention theory 297–8
        and Hobbes 298–9
        mutual advantage 298–9
    and establishing government 299
        coordination 299–301
        empowerment of 301
        and justice 301–2
    and liberal distrust 291
    and limitations of constitutions 302
    and limited government 289, 305–7
    and mutual advantage 291
    and political economy approach 290–1
    and representative democracy 303–5
        audience democracy 304
        corporate democracy 304–5
        virtual representation 303–4
    as two-stage problem 301
constitutions 336–8
    as consequentialist devices 290
    and constitution-level decision-making 330–1, 336
    and costs of changing 308
    and diversity of 307–8
    and economic policy 723–4
    as expressive documents 329, 333–5, 339–40
        constitutional relevance 336–8
    and in-period decision-making 330–1, 336
    and instrumental activity 329, 333, 334, 339–40
    as legal documents 329, 331, 339–40
        enforcement 331–2
        intended audience 332
        reform of 332
    and limitations of 302
    and popular ratification of 336
    and procedural change 1042–3
        admission of new members 1046
        amendment procedures 1040–1, 1043
        emergency powers 1046–7
        escape clauses/nullification 1044–5
        interpretative courts 1043–4
        secession 1045–6
        suspension of rules 1044
    as rules of the game 329, 330–2, 339–40
        distinction from constitutional document 331
        enforcement 331–2

    intended audience 332
    reform of 332
    and social choice 973
    and state intervention 342
    and survival of democracy 320–2
contractarian theories:
    and constitutionalism 291–7
        contractual obligations 293
        contractualist argument 293–6
        moral theory 293–4
        objections to 291–3
        rationalist agreement 294
        reasonableness 293–4, 295–7
    and falsity of 320–1
contracts:
    and anarchy 881–2
    and United States Supreme Court 347
        contracts affected with the public interest 350–1
        contracts clause 347–8
        economic liberties 348–50
        takings clause 351–4
conventions, and constitutionalism 295, 297–8, 308
cooperation 952, 953–4, 963–4, 978
    and altruism 953
    and explanation of 953–4
    and game theory 956–7
        strong reciprocity 957–60
    and internal norms 961
    as means not end 954
    and mutualistic cooperation 953, 954–7
    and pro-social emotions 18–20, 962–3
    and reciprocal altruism 954–5
    and requirements for model of 955–6
    and strong reciprocity 957–60
        evolution of 960–1
    see also behavior
coordinated market economies 615, 650–1
coordination:
    and citizens in authoritarian regimes 1007–8
    and constitutionalism 297–9, 307–8, 321
        acquiescence 297, 298
        dual-convention theory 297–8
        and Hobbes 298–9
        mutual advantage 298–9
    and establishing government 299–301
    and international monetary relations 589
    and political organizations 42
    and political parties 10
Copenhagen Consensus 525
core:
    and committee decision-making 919–21
    and core emptiness 908–9, 910–12
    and hypotheses of 834
corporate democracy 304–5
corporate governance 724
Corrupt and Illegal Practices Act (UK, 1883) 686
corruption:
    and ballot structure 725, 727–8
    and district magnitudes 729
    and electoral reform 730
    and electoral systems 469
    and inequality 633–4
    and intra/inter-party competition 728

and judiciary 632
and plurality voting 725
courts, *see* judiciary; United States Supreme Court
Cuba 702
culture, and survival of democracy 324–6
currency policy, *see* exchange rates
cut-points, and spatial theory of voting 33–4
Cyprus, and ethnicity 855
Czech Republic, and democratization 664
Czechoslovakia 314
  and repression 681

decentralization:
  and policy outcomes 185
  and voter preferences 185
decision-making:
  and Administrative Procedure Act (USA, 1946) 278
  and bicameralism 192–3
  and collective preference theory 902–5
    core emptiness 908–9
    large populations 907
    opportunities for trade 906–7
  and committees 916–17
    bargaining in multidimensional policy spaces 917–18
    committee bargaining 921–2
    core clustering 919–21
    Fiorina and Plott's experiments 918–19
    information aggregation 927–9
  and game theory 905–6
    core emptiness 910–12
  and judiciary 208–10
  and social choice 972
  and unanimity rule 990–1
deindustrialization 646
delegation:
  and agency discretion 214–16
  and budget process 471–2
  and bureaucracy 256
    administrative dominance 265–6
    agency design 261–2
    ally principle 260, 262–3, 264, 266, 267, 269
    assumptions underlying models of 257–8, 268–9
    bureaucratic capacity 267
    commitment problem 268–70
    empirical tests of 261–4
    information asymmetries 266–7
    instruments of 257
    judiciary 269
    modeling of delegation strategies 257–61
    multi-principals issue 267–8
    nature of legislation 262–3
    policy uncertainty 259–60, 262, 263, 266, 269
    political context 264–5, 269–70
    political control 265
    political oversight 257, 264
    political uncertainty 260–1, 263–4, 266
    substitution effect 260, 263, 266
demand bargaining, and coalition formation 170–1
demand management, and the state 643–6
  and impact of international liberalization 645–6

and impact of rational expectations 644–5
and institutional environment 644–5
see also economic policy
demand-revealing mechanisms, and allocation of public goods 487–9
democracy:
  and capitalism 23, 601
    class compromise 603
    coexistence with 601–2
    diversity of capitalist democracies 603–4
    role of political power 604–5
  and characteristics of 312
  and Coase theorem 529
  and democratic transitions 617
  and distributive politics 601
    coalitional politics 602, 608–11
    institutional design 602, 611–14
    median voter theorem 604
    partisanship 602, 605–8
    see also Downsian model
  and inequality 632–3
  and paradoxes of rationality 43, 333
    attempted resolutions of 40–2
    rational ignorance 39–40
    rational non-participation 38–40, 304
  and representative democracy 303–5
    audience democracy 304
    corporate democracy 304–5
    virtual representation 303–4
  and survival of 312
    constitutions 320–2
    culture 324–6
    economic crises 318–19
    electoral chances 320
    ethnic divisions 322–4
    income redistribution 315–18, 319–20
    institutional choice 320
    military power 319
    moderate government 321
    nineteenth-century doubts over 313
    per capita income 314–15, 684–5, 705
    in poor countries 319, 320
  and theory of 679–82
    allocation of political power 679–80
    concessions by elites 680
    democratic consolidation 680
    elite coups 680–1
    emergence of 683–4
    relative political equality 679
    repression by elites 681
    transitory nature of de factor power 679, 680
  and uninformed voters:
    information aggregation 15–17
    information revelation 11–15
  see also democratization
democratic peace:
  and international conflict/war 838
    audience costs 874–5
    institutional constraints 840–1
    institutional incentives 842–5
    normative explanation of 840
    public opinion constraints 871–3
    selectorate theory 842–5

democratization 656–7, 665
    as commitment mechanism 690
    and elections 664
    and elite agency 658–9
        institution formation 659
        role of regime crises 658–9
    and political costs of 715
    and post-communist experience 659–60
        elite competition 662–3
        elite use of structures 661–3
        role of informal institutions 664
        role of the states 663–4
        structural legacies 662
        structures enabling elites 660–1
    and redistribution 604
    and structural preconditions 657–8
        authoritarian legacies 658
        economic performance/reform 657–8
    and theory of 679–82
demography, and intergenerational conflict 525, 536–8
dependency theory 760–1
developing countries:
    and assumptions about 1003–4
    and comparative political economy 530
development, see economic development; political and economic development
dictatorships and authoritarian government 22, 704–5
    as benign despots/stationary bandits 697–8
    and citizen coordination 1007–8
    and democratic transitions 705
    and economic growth 693, 697
        under co-opting regime 702
        organizational proliferation 703
        under terror regime 700
    and economic literature 694–5
    and insecurity of 694–5
    and lack of understanding of 693–4
    and launching organizations:
        co-optation of 701–2
        need for 696
        organizational proliferation 702–4
        strategies for dealing with 696–7, 704
        terrorisation of 698–700
        threat from 696
    and natural resource exploitation 700, 704–5
    and organizational theory of 695–7
    and political sociology literature 694
    and predatory nature of 698
    and property rights 693, 694, 697
        benign despots 697–8
        under co-opting regime 701–2
        organizational proliferation 703–4
        under terror regime 699–700
    and selectorate theory 842–5
    and social choice 972
    and survival of democracy 315, 325, 326
    and threats to 695
    and typologies of 694
Diermeier-Merlo model, and cabinet stability 173–4
'Director's Law' 610

discretion:
    and bureaucracy 214–16, 258–9
    and judicial independence 282
    see also delegation
distance, and economic impact of 740–2
distributive justice:
    and microeconomic approach to 374–6
    and representative democracy 303
distributive politics:
    and bicameralism 187–8
        concurrent majorities 188–9
        fiscal prudence 190–1
        malapportionment 191
        super-majorities 189
    and cross-national variations 603–4
    and democracy 601
        coalitional politics 602, 608–11
        federalism 613–14
        impact of electoral rules 612–13
        institutional design 602, 611–14
        partisanship 602, 605–8
    and impact of electoral systems 731–2
    and international trade 823–4, 827
        age 825–6
        compensation mechanisms 826
        economies of scale model 822–3
        factor specificity 824–5
        gender 825
        Heckscher-Ohlin model 815–18
        neo-Ricardian model 820–2
        specific factors model 818–20
        surveying of attitudes/support 826–7
        types of trade 824
    and median voter theorem 313–14, 604
    and new structuralism 617–18
    and state size:
        income inequality 790–1
        prevention of secession 788–90
    and varieties of capitalism 614–17
        coordinated market economies 615
        institutional complementarity 615
        liberal market economies 615
        relationship of economic/political institutions 616
        role of economic institutions 614–15
        welfare state 615–16
    see also income redistribution; inequality
distrust, and constitutionalism 291
divided government (USA) 134–5, 224–5
    and judicial independence 282
dollarization, in Latin America 590–1
domestic politics:
    and international conflict 832, 838–9, 875–6
        audience costs 841
        foreign aid 845–6, 847–8
        institutional constraints 840–1
        institutional incentives 842–5
        leaders' motivations 838, 839, 870, 871–2
        nation-building following conflict 845–7
        role of opposition 841
        selectorate theory 842–5
        tax and spending constraints 839
        theories of influence of 839

SUBJECT INDEX 1073

and war 869, 875–6
  audience costs 874–5
  leaders' motivations 870
  political institutions 870
  public opinion constraints 870, 871–3
Dominican Republic 701
dual-convention theory, and constitutionalism 297–8
duty, and voting behavior 40–1

economic and financial crises:
  and budget process 473–4
  and exchange rates 595
  and political impact of 716
  and survival of democracy 318–19
Economic and Monetary Union (EMU) 590, 591
economic development:
  and collective action 530
  and development theory 760–1
  and electoral systems 735–6
  and inequality 626–7
  and public choice 532
  see also economic geography; political and economic development
economic geography:
  and agglomeration mechanisms 742–3
    firm linkages 744
    labor mobility 743
    market size/access 743
    technological externalities 745
    thick labor market 744–5
  and borders 741
  and cities:
    attractions of 749
    economic policy 750–1
    equilibrium size 750
    transport costs 749–50
  and costs of distance 740–2
    implications for remote economies 742
  and cumulative causation 751
  and definition of 739–40
  and externalities 751–2
  and patterns of development:
    'great divergence' 747
    industrialization in the New World 747–8
    Krugman-Venables trade/location model 745–6
    sequential economic growth 748–9
  and spatial disparities 751
  and spatial relationships 739, 740
economic growth, and authoritarian governments 693, 697
  under co-opting regime 702
  organizational proliferation 703
  under terror regime 700
economic liberties, and United States Supreme Court 347
  contracts affected with the public interest 350–1
  contracts clause 347–8
  economic liberties 348–50
  takings clause 351–4
economic methods in political science 912
  and Arrow's influence 900
  and collective preference theory 902–5
    core emptiness 908–9

large populations 907
opportunities for trade 906–7
and Downs's influence 900
and game theory 900–1, 905–6
  core of cooperative games 901–2
  non-cooperative game theory 902, 906
  Poisson games 910–12
and rational choice theory 899, 900–1
and Riker's influence 900–1
economic policy:
  and cities 750–1
  and constitutions 723–4
  and form of government 724
  and impact of electoral systems 723–4, 735, 765
    direct effects on accountability 727–8
    direct effects on government spending 730–2
    electoral policy cycles 729–30
    indirect effects on accountability 729–30
    indirect effects on budget deficits 734–5
    indirect effects on government spending 732–4
  and role of the state 642–3, 652–3
    macroeconomic demand management 643–6
    socio-economic institutional environment 649–52
    supply-side strategies 646–9
  see also political-economic cycles
economic sociology:
  and definition of 937
  and different approach required 937–8
  and economic-social action 948
  and embeddedness 938–40
    criticism of concept 939
    network theory 939–40
    uses of concept 938–9
  and the field 941–3
    definition of 941
    organizational field 941
    structure of society 941
    uses of concept 942–3
  and institutions:
    definition of 945–6
    interest-based concept of 945–7
  and interest 943–4
    social relations 944
  and perspectives of 938
  and reciprocity-redistribution-exchange 948
economic voting:
  and clarifying incumbent responsibility 578–82
  and electoral cycles 548
  and Fair's model 567–9
  and Kramer's model 566–7
  and prospective voting 569–71
    pure prospective voting 571
    as rational retrospection 572–5
  and research on:
    challenges facing 584
    development of 582–3
    origins of 565–6
  and retrospective voting 569–71
    principal-agent relationships 570
    pure retrospective voting 575–8
  see also electoral cycles; political-economic cycles; voting behavior; voting theory

1074 SUBJECT INDEX

economics, and foundations of 976
economies of scale model of international
    trade 822–3
education policy, and inequality 629, 638
efficiency, economic 974
efficient negotiations, and coalition formation
    171–2
El Salvador 681
electioneering, and political-economic cycles
    545
elections:
  and analysis of 64
  and democratization 664
  and deterministic voting 67–8
    office motivation 68–70
    policy motivation 70–2
  and forecasting of 34
  and framework for 66–7
  and laboratory experiments 917, 922
    asymmetric contests 926
    candidate convergence 923
    median voter theorem 923–4
    multicandidate elections 924–5
    retrospective voting 923–4
  and legislature/parliament distinction 121–2
  and median voter theorem 29, 31
  and position-taking by candidates 64
  and probabilistic voting, stochastic partisanship
    model 72–3
    vote motivation 73–5
    win motivation 75–7
  and probabilistic voting, stochastic preference
    model 77–8
    policy motivation 80–1
    vote motivation 78–9
    win motivation 79–80
  and public funding 59, 60
  and spatial theory of voting 29–30
    candidate divergence 35–8
    criticisms of 30–1
    cut-points 33–4
    paradoxes of rationality 38–42, 43
    valence issues 32–5
  and timing of 32, 549
    parliamentary systems 124–5
    voter behavior 12
  and turnout 929–32
  and voters' sources of information 43–6
  see also candidates; economic voting; electoral
    cycles; electoral systems; median voter
    theorem;
    political advertising; political competition, and
    theory of; political-economic cycles; voting
    behavior; voting theory
Electoral College (USA) 295, 298
  and impact on government spending 731
electoral cycles:
  and adaptive retrospective citizens 547–50
  and coalition governments 549, 550
  and context conditionality of 548–9, 550, 551,
    559–60
  and economic policy 729–30
  and economic voting 548

  and election timing 549
  and electoral challengers 551–2
  and evidence of 548–9
  and exchange rates 595
  and monetary policy:
    partisan variant 535
    rational expectations 534–5
  and policy manipulation 550
  and policy targeting 549
  and policy timing 549
  and post-election electioneering 552
  and rational expectations 550–1
  and rational prospective citizens 550–1
  see also economic voting
electoral equilibrium 81–2
  and deterministic voting 67–8
    office motivation 68–70
    policy motivation 70–2
  and probabilistic voting, stochastic partisanship
    model 72–3
    vote motivation 73–5
    win motivation 75–7
  and probabilistic voting, stochastic preference
    model 77–8
    policy motivation 80–1
    vote motivation 78–9
    win motivation 79–80
electoral systems:
  and accountability 468, 724, 726–7
    direct effects on 727–8
    indirect effects on 729–30
  and ballot structure 726
  and categorization of 726
  and class 613
  and corruption 725, 727–8, 730
  and cross-country correlations 726
  and distributive politics 612–13
  and district magnitudes 726
    impact on accountability 729
    impact on government spending 730–1
    impact on policy 765
  and Electoral College (USA) 295, 298
  and electoral formulas 726
    impact on budget deficits 734–5
    impact on government spending 730–4
  and electoral incentives 102–3
    district magnitude 109
    ideological spread 111–12
    party divergence 110–11
    party factionalism 114–15
    personal votes 112–13
  and electoral rules 102
    Condorcet criterion 103
  and future research on 115
  and government ideology 733–4
  and impact of:
    bias toward large parties 109–10
    ideological spread 111–12
    localism of representatives 112–13
    on number of parties 106–8
    party factionalism 114–15
    party ideological homogeneity 113–14
    party non-convergence 110–11

on proportionality of party
    representation 108–9
  voting outcomes 527
  and impact on economic development 735–6
  and impact on economic policy 723–4, 735
    direct effects of accountability 727–8
    direct effects on government spending 730–2
    electoral policy cycles 729–30
    indirect effects of accountability 729–30
    indirect effects on budget deficits 734–5
    indirect effects on government spending 732–4
  and income redistribution 87–8, 90–2
  and list proportional representation 104
  and modeling outcomes of 452–3
  and monetary policy manipulation 547–8
  and plurality voting 104
  and politicians' incentives:
    direct effects on 727–8
    indirect effects on 729–30
  and presidential systems 107–8
  and proportionality continuum 104–5
    measures of proportionality 105
    swing ratio 105
  and public finance 468–9, 472
  and responding to external shocks 765
  and single non-transferable vote 113, 114–15
  and single transferable vote 112
  and stability of 725
  and strategic voting 102, 110
  and threshold of exclusion 104–5, 106
    proportionality of party representation 108–9
elites:
  and democratization 658–9
    elite competition 662–3
    portable skills 660–1
    use of structures 661–3
  and European integration 803–4, 812
embeddedness 938–40
  and criticism of concept 939
  and network theory 939–40
  and uses of concept 938–9
emergency powers 1046–7
emotions, and evolutionary models of behavior 18–20
endogenous institutions 4
  and legislative organization:
    committee expertise 10–11
    committee system 8–9
    political parties 9–10
    preference-based approach 7–8
  see also legislatures
endstate justice 376–8
  and endstate cum procedural justice 381–3
  and endstate/procedural justice complementarity 379–81
equilibrium:
  analysis of, and public finance 447–9
  applications of 451–3
  citizen-candidate model 450–1, 452
  issues to be covered 448–9
  median voter theorem 448
  party coalition model 451, 452

  probabilistic spatial voting models 449–50, 451–2
  problems faced by models 452–3
  spatial voting model 452–3
and bargaining games 188
and coalition formation:
  cabinet stability (Diermeier-Merlo model) 173–4
  demand bargaining 170–1
  efficient negotiations 171–2
  sequential bargaining (Baron-Ferejohn model) 168–70
  structure-induced equilibrium (Laver-Shepsle model) 165–8
and evolutionary models of behavior 17
and income redistribution:
  restricted tax schemes 86–7
  targeting of heterogeneous groups 92–8
  unrestricted transfer schemes 88–92
and institutions as 1033–5
and pivot theories:
  pivotal politics theory 227
  procedural cartel theory 229
and political advertising 52
  directly informative advertising 57–9
  indirectly informative advertising 55–7
and political behavior 4
and statutory interpretation 275
and survival of democracy 312, 321–2, 323, 324–5
see also electoral equilibrium
equity flows, and impact of distance 741
essential states, and neo-realism 835
Estonia, and democratization 664
ethnicity 852
  and definition of ethnic group 852–3
  and ethnic violence 857–8
    cross-national variation 857–8
    definition of 857
    deliberate provocation of 863–4
    intraethnic politics 863
    unitary actor explanations 862–3
  and politicization of 853
    as basis for coalition-building 860–2
    conflicting ethnic preferences 858–9
    cross-national variation 854–5
    impact of economic modernization 859–60
    political boundaries 856
    pork-barrel politics 861–2
    post-colonial environments 860
    primordialist explanation of 858
    research on 864–5
    temporal variations 856
    see also common-pool problem
  and racism and redistribution 1026
  and social relevance of 853
    cross-national variation 854
  and survival of democracy 322–4
Eurobarometer surveys 807
European Central Bank 591, 799, 803, 804, 810–11
European Coal and Steel Community 799, 801–2
European Commission 802, 804
  and delegation 263
European Council of Ministers 804–5

European Court of Human Rights, and *Bowman vs UK* (1998) 51 n2
European Court of Justice 799, 802
European Economic Community 799
European Exchange Rate Mechanism 524
European integration:
  and attitudes towards, survey data on 807
  and Common Agricultural Policy (CAP) 803
  and constitutional convention 804, 810
  and coordination problems 801
  and Council of Ministers 804–5
  and decision-making processes 805–6
  and democratic deficit 804, 806
  and development of scholarship on 799–800
  and economic motives 805, 806–7
  and European Coal and Steel Community 801–2
  and European Payments Union 801, 803
  and exchange rates 803
  and foreign policy 809–10
  and historical-institutionalist accounts 812
  and institutional approach 800–1, 802, 808
    commitment issues 802
  and interest group politics 806, 807
  and intergovernmental approach 800–1
  and issue linkage 802
  and monetary union 803–4
    attitudes towards 806–7
  and national preferences 806
  and neo-functionalist view of 808
    spillover effects 802–3
  and normalization of studies of 805–8
  and path dependency 808–11
  and political integration 804
  and role of elites 803–4, 812
    principal-agent slack 804
  and security concerns 801–2
  and Single Market Program 803
  and synthetic view of 807–8
  and transnational bureaucracy 803
European monetary integration 589
European Monetary System 589, 590, 591
European Monetary Union 469
  and ex ante fiscal rules 466
European Parliament 799, 802, 804
  and policy positions of legislators 137
European Payments Union 799, 801, 803
European Single Market 799, 803
European Union:
  and delegation 263
  and federalism 359
evolutionary fitness 4
exchange:
  and economics 989–90
  and politics as 992–3
exchange rates 591
  and Bretton Woods system 588, 590
    end of 759
  and centrality of 588
  and dollarization 590–1
  and domestic political economy of:
    choice of regime 591–3
    competitiveness/purchasing power trade-off 593–4
    electoral cycles 595
    electoral politics 593, 595
    exchange rate level 593–4
    interest groups and regime choice 592
  and European integration 803, 806–7
  and fixed rate systems 588, 589, 590, 591–2
  and free floating systems 588, 589
  and gold standard 588, 589
  and interest groups:
    exchange rate level 595
    regime choice 592
  and internation political economy of 588–9
    cooperation 590–1
    coordination 589
    nation state 588–9
  and regional regimes 588, 590–1
  and research on:
    challenges facing 596
    integration of domestic/international factors 595–6
    policy substitutes 595
executive:
  and parliamentary systems 122
    control of legislative agenda 125–6
    elections 124
    election-timing 124–5
    executive coalitions 128
    investiture votes 123
    minority governments 128–9
    no-confidence votes 122–3
    opposition parties 130
    parliamentary support coalition 128
    role of political parties 126–7
    single-party majority governments 129–30
  and presidential systems:
    divided government/cohabitation 134–5
    executive/legislature dependence 130–1
    role of political parties 131–2
executive orders, and American presidency 249–50
exit, and fiscal competition 512–14
experiments, *see* laboratory experiments
expertise, and legislative committee system 10–11
expressive activity 329
  and political behavior 333–5
    constitutional relevance 336–8, 339–40
expressive voting 41, 333–5
expropriation:
  and authoritarian governments 699–700
  and inequality 633–4

factor mobility:
  and fiscal competition 504–5, 508–9, 512–14, 518–19
    dynamics of 514–17
  and international trade models:
    Heckscher-Ohlin model 815–18
    neo-Ricardian model 820–2
    specific factors model 818–20
  and state size 794
fair division 425, 435
  and endstate justice 377
  and indivisible goods 432–5
    assumptions made 432–3

Borda Count 435
  efficiency 432, 433
  envy-free division 432, 433, 434
  paradoxes 432, 433, 434
  Rawlsian maximin criterion 434
and procedural justice 378
and several divisible goods:
  adjusted winner 429–32
  efficiency 431
  equitability adjustments 430
  equity 431
and single heterogeneous good:
  assumptions made 426
  cut-and-choose 426–7
  envy-free division 426–9
  squeezing procedure 428–9
and social choice 373
see also resource allocation
Federal Reserve System 541
federalism:
  and bicameralism 181
  and centralization/decentralization tension 358–9
  and distributive politics 613–14
  and economic problems 361
  and economic theories 359–60
    competitive federalism 360
    'Leviathan' theory 360
    public finance theory 359
    welfare economics 359–60
  and endogenous institutions 364
    intergovernmental fiscal systems 365–7
    political parties 367
    representation 365
  and goal of 358
  and necessity of 359
  and normative tradition 357, 367
  and perspectives on 357, 367–8
  and positive political economy literature 357–8, 361, 368
    intergovernmental fiscal systems 363
    nature of representation 361–3
    political incentives 361
    political parties 363–4
field, and economic sociology 941–2
  and definition of 941
  and organizational field 941
  and structure of society 941
  and uses of concept 942–3
filibusters 143
  and pivotal politics theory 225, 226–7
financial crises, see economic and financial crises
fiscal competition 502–3
  and basic model of 505–9
    American local government 505–6
    capital investment 506–7
    capital mobility 508–9
    interpretations and applications of 509–12
    property taxes 505–9
  and capital mobility 504–5
  and exit and voice 512–14
  and implications of 505
  and institutional change 517–18
  and labor mobility 504

and models of 504–5
  tax competition 504–5
and nature of 503–4
and normative implications of 512
and perfect competition 503
and policy choice 502
and resource mobility 512–14, 518–19
  dynamics of 514–17
see also fiscal institutions; public finance
fiscal institutions 465, 474
  and budget process 470–4
    centralization 470–1
    common-pool problem 473–4
    contract approach 471–2
    delegation 471–2
    enforcement 472
    impact of centralization 473–4
    impact of electoral rules 472
    stages of 470–1
  and electoral rules 468–9
    common-pool problem 468–9
    evidence of impact of 469
    political competition 469
  and ex ante fiscal rules 466–7
    effectiveness of 466–7
see also fiscal competition; public finance
fiscal systems, and federalism 361–3, 365–7
flat taxes 527–8
flypaper effect 1025–6
folk theorem 710, 955
foreign aid policy 845–6, 847–8
foreign direct investment, and impact of distance 741
foreign policy:
  and audience costs 874–5
  and public opinion constraints 871–3
see also international conflict
free riding, and spatial theory of voting 39
free trade 758
  and state size 782, 793–4
see also international trade
freedom of speech, and United States Supreme Court 344–6

Gallagher Index 105
game theory:
  and application in political science 900–1, 905–6
  and bicameralism 187–8
    concurrent majorities 188–9
    fiscal prudence 190–1
    information acquisition 193
    malapportionment 191
    super-majorities 189
  and coalition formation:
    cabinet stability 173–4
    demand bargaining 170–1
    efficient negotiations 171–2
    sequential bargaining 168–70
    structure-induced equilibrium 165–8
  and committee decision-making:
    bargaining in multidimensional policy spaces 917–18
    committee bargaining 921–2
    core clustering 919–21

game theory: (cont.)
    Fiorina and Plott's experiments 918–19
    and cooperation 956–7
    and cooperative game theory 901
        core of the game 901–2
    and folk theorem 710
    and non-cooperative game theory 902, 906, 978
    and Poisson games 910–12
    and political economy 528
    and social choice:
        endstate cum procedural justice 381–3
        endstate vs procedural justice 376–8
        endstate/procedural complementarity 379–81
        microeconomic approach to 374–6
        strategy-proof mechanisms 383–6
    and strong reciprocity 957–60
Gamson's Law 172
gatekeeping authority, and legislatures 6
General Agreements on Tariffs and Trade (GATT) 759
genes, and evolutionary models of behavior 18–20
geographical economics, *see* economic geography
geography, and fundamental importance of 740
    see also economic geography
Germany:
    and bicameralism 181
    and budget process 473
    and constitution of 320
    and ex ante fiscal rules 466
    and federalism 366
    and special interest gridlock 530
Gibbard-Satterthwaite theorem 383–4, 403
Gini coefficient 625
globalization 757
    and demand management 645–6
    and development theory 760–1
    and global governance 769–70
    and international financial crises 524
    and nascent phase of 759
    and sequential development 748–9
    and supply-side economic policy 648–9
    see also international trade
gold standard 588, 589, 590
governance, and global governance 769–70
government:
    and distribution of income 84–5
    and fiscal competition 503–4
    and purpose of 342
    see also income redistribution
Great Britain:
    and American colonies 1006–7
    and colonial America 1038–9
    and ethnicity 854
    and political and economic development 673, 685
        concessions by elites 688–90
        education reform 687
        emergence of democracy 686–7
        interpretation of 688–90
        origins of economic supremacy 685
        political reform 685–7
        reform of economic institutions 687
gridlock:
    and legislative organization 151–2

    and pivot theories:
        pivotal politics theory 225, 228
        procedural cartel theory 229–30
group rule utilitarianism, and voting behavior 41–2
Guatemala 681

habitus 941
Haiti 690
    and political/economic development 673–4
Heckscher-Ohlin theory:
    and international trade
        migration and investment 816–18
        trade in products 815–16
    and Open Economy Politics (OEP) 762
hegemonic stability theory 761–2
herestethics 130
Hungary 320
    and democratization 659, 661–2, 664
    and repression 681
Hyde Park riots (1866) 686

identity, and constitutions as expressive documents 337–8
ideology:
    and electoral systems 733–4
    and party labels 44
    and voter behavior 32, 34
imperfect information, and income redistribution 98–9
impossibility theorem 373, 601, 972
    and economic outcomes 973–4
    and markets 974
    and political competition 1028–9
    and social evaluation 409, 419
    and voting theory 405–6
income, per capita, and democracy 314–18, 684–5, 705
income inequality, *see* inequality
income redistribution 84–5, 99–100, 313–14
    and cross-national variations 603–4
    and electoral systems 87–8, 90–2
    and ethnic heterogeneity 630
    and federalism 365–7
    and imperfect information 98–9
    and increased preference for 631–2
    and intergenerational conflict 536–8
    and political institutions 630–1
    and proportional representation 87–8, 635–6
    and restricted tax schemes 85–8
    and role of government 84–5
        accountability of 85
    and survival of democracy 319–20
    and targeting of heterogeneous groups 92–8
    and unrestricted transfer schemes 88–92
    and voluntary redistribution 446
    see also distributive politics; inequality
India:
    and economic development 531–2
    and economic openness 827
    and election timing 549
    and ethnicity 856
    and federalism 359
indoctrination, and beliefs about inequality 637–8

Indonesia 702
industrialization:
  and inequality 626-7
  and the New World 747-8
  and newly industrializing countries 760
inequality 624-5, 639
  and American exceptionalism 634-8
    beliefs about inequality 637-8
    economic explanations of 634
    ethnic heterogeneity 635
    failure of left-wing movements 636-7
    political institutions 635-7
  and causes of 625-31
    demand for skilled workers 627
    distribution of skills 627-8
    economic development 626-7
    education policy 629
    ethnic heterogeneity 628-9, 630
    political factors 627
    political institutions 630-1
    religion 628
    technology 627
    welfare spending 629-30
  and cross-national variations 627-8
  and measurement of 625
    Gini coefficient 625
    Kuznets curve 626
    share of national income 625
  and political impact of 631-4
    corruption 634
    democracy 632-3
    expropriation 633-4
    increased preference for redistribution 631-2
    institutional structure 632-4
    reduced redistribution 632-3
  and state size 790-1
inflation:
  and macro political economy 532-3
  and public opinion 524
  see also demand management, and the state
information 4
  and aggregation of:
    bicameralism 192-3
    in committees 917, 927-9
    voting behavior 15-17, 44-5, 46
  and income redistribution 98-9
  and social evaluation and information
      invariance 417-19
  and voting behavior:
    information aggregation 15-17, 44-5, 46
    information revelation 11-15
    sources of information 43-6
institutional analysis 223
Institutional Revolutionary Party (Mexico) 367
institutionalism, and coalitions 162-5
  cabinet stability 165
  minority governments 164-5
  reappraisal of existing theory 163-4
  structure-induced equilibrium 165-8
institutions:
  and approaches to study of 6
  and choice of 1035-7
    preference drift 1037

status quo bias 1036-7
uncertainty 1036-7
veil of ignorance 1035-6
and comparative analysis of 7
as constraint 1034
and definition of 945-6, 1032
and distributive politics 611-14
and dynamic nature of 1032
as equilibria 1033-5
as game forms 1032-3
and interest aggregation 764-6
and interest-based concept of 945-7
and maintenance of 1037-40
  incomplete awareness 1038-9
  self-confirming equilibrium 1038-9
  self-generating revision 1038, 1039-40
  self-stability 1041
and new structuralism 617-18
and origins of 617
and problems in studying 976
and procedural change 1042-3
  admission of new members 1046
  amendment procedures 1040-1, 1043
  emergency powers 1046-7
  escape clauses/nullification 1044-5
  interpretative courts 1043-4
  secession 1045-6
  suspension of rules 1044
and research process 4
and Riker Objection 1032, 1040-2, 1047-8
and strategic social interaction and choice 1033
and varieties of capitalism:
  coordinated market economies 615
  institutional complementarity 615
  liberal market economies 615
  relationship of economic/political
      institutions 616
  role of economic institutions 614-15
  welfare state 615-16
instrumental activity 329
  and constitutions 333, 334, 339-40
interdependence 759
interest groups:
  and campaign contributions 50, 52
  and economic practice 530-1
  and European integration 806, 807
  and exchange rates:
    level of 595
    regime choice 592
  and older people 537-8
  and political actors 528
  and political advertising:
    directly informative 57-9
    indirectly informative 53-7
  and political economy approach 528-9
  and special interest gridlock 530
interests:
  and interest-based concept of institutions 945-7
  and Open Economy Politics (OEP) 762-4
    institutional aggregation of interests 764-6
  and sociological concept of 943-4
    social relations 944
intergenerational conflict 525, 536-8

International Coffee Organization 767
international conflict 838
  and democratic peace 838
    institutional constraints 840–1
    normative explanation of 840
  and domestic politics 832, 838–9, 875–6
    audience costs 841, 874–5
    foreign aid 845–6, 847–8
    institutional constraints 840–1
    institutional incentives 842–5
    leaders' motivations 838, 839, 870, 871–2
    nation-building following conflict 845–7
    public opinion constraints 871–3
    role of opposition 841
    selectorate theory 842–5
    tax and spending constraints 839
    theories of influence of 839
  and international political economy 770–1
  and national interest 831–2
  and the state 710
  and state size 781, 794–6
  and structural theories 832, 833, 837–8
    neo-realism 833–6
    power transition theory 836–7
  and transformation of field of study 831
  see also anarchy; international relations
international economics 739
international institutions, and monetary policy 541–2
International Monetary Fund 532, 541, 542, 589, 759
international monetary relations:
  and cooperation 590–1
  and coordination 589–90
international political economy (IPE):
  and early approaches of:
    dependency theory 760–1
    domestic theories 762
    hegemonic stability theory 761–2
  and future research areas:
    conflict and war 770–1
    endogenous state formation 768–9
    global governance 769–70
  and globalization 757
  and growth of 771–2
  and Open Economy Politics (OEP) 757–8, 762–3
    characteristics of 772
    institutional aggregation of interests 764–6
    interests 762–4
    international bargaining 766–8
    success of 772
  and origins of 758–60
  and subject matter of 758
international relations, *see* anarchy; international conflict
international trade:
  and distributional consequences 814–15, 823–4, 827
    age 825–6
    compensation mechanisms 826
    factor specificity 824–5
    gender 825
    surveying of attitudes/support 826–7
    types of trade 824
  and economies of scale model of 822–3
  and Heckscher-Ohlin model of:
    migration and investment 816–18
    trade in products 815–16
  and impact of distance 741
  and neo-Ricardian model of 820–1
    migration and investment 821–2
    trade in products 821
  and specific factors model of:
    migration and investment 820
    trade in products 818–19
  and state size 782, 793–4
  see also international political economy (IPE)
interpersonal comparisons, and social evaluation 408
intuitionism 294
investiture votes, and parliamentary systems 123
investment, and international trade models
  Heckscher-Ohlin model 815–18
  neo-Ricardian model 821–2
  specific factors model 820
Iran, and ethnicity 855
Iraq:
  and ethnicity 855
  and terror 699
Ireland, Republic of, and constitution of 337
Italy:
  and corruption 728
  and electoral reform 469, 723
  and ex ante fiscal rules 466
  and federalism 366

Japan:
  and election timing 549
  and electoral reform 723
  and electoral system 113, 115
  and ethnicity 854
  and ex ante fiscal rules 466
  and political/economic development 674
judicial review:
  and approach to 344, 354–5
  and balancing private rights/government interest 343–4
  and constitutional interpretation 1044
  and intermediate scrutiny standard 343
  and policy-making 217–18
  and protection of contract and property:
    contracts affected with the public interest 350–1
    contracts clause 347–8
    economic liberties 348–50
    takings clause 351–4
  and rational basis standard 343
  and social and moral issues:
    equal protection of the laws 346–7
    freedom of speech 344–6
  and strict scrutiny standard 343
judiciary:
  and bureaucratic delegation 269
  and judicial independence 281–4
    strategic interactions 282–3
  and legal control of bureaucracy 277–81
    Chevron decision 280–1

implications of Administrative Procedure
  Act 278–80
and new separation-of-powers approach to 207–12
  agenda-setting 211
  appointments process 211
  interactions with other institutions 207–8
  judicial decision-making 208–10
  legislative override 209–10
  limits on policy-making capacity 210–11
and policy-making 273
  statutory interpretation 276–7
and positive political theory 273–4, 284
  control of bureaucracy 277–81
  judicial independence 281–4
  statutory interpretation 274–7
and strategic interactions 274
  judicial independence 282
  statutory interpretation 274–7
and subversion of 632
and traditional legal analysis 273
justice:
  and choice of institutions 1035–6
  and constitutionalism 301–2
  and distributive justice 303
    microeconomic approach to 374–6
  and endstate cum procedural justice 381–3
  and endstate justice 376–8
  and endstate/procedural justice
    complementarity 379–81
  and procedural justice 378

Kikuyu 856
kleptocracy 85
Korea:
  and ethnicity 854
  and terror 699
Kuznets curve 626

Laasko-Taagepera Index 106–7
labor market:
  and agglomeration 745
  and service sector 646–7
labor mobility:
  and agglomeration 743
  and fiscal competition 504
laboratory experiments:
  and committee decision-making 916–17
    bargaining in multidimensional policy
      spaces 917–18
    committee bargaining 921–2
    core clustering 919–21
    Fiorina and Plott's experiments 918–19
  and competitive elections 917, 922
    asymmetric contests 926
    candidate convergence 923
    median voter theorem 923–4
    multicandidate elections 924–5
    retrospective voting 923–4
  and future research areas 932–3
  and importance of institutions 916
  and information aggregation in committees 917,
    927–9
  and link with experimental economics 915–16

and requirements of 915
and voter turnout 917, 929–32
laissez-faire 84–5
Latin America:
  and democratization 664
  and ethnicity 855
Laver-Shepsle model, and coalition formation
  165–8
law, and statutory interpretation 274–7
leadership theory 761
learning 1005–6
Lebanon, and ethnicity 855
legislative committee systems (LCS):
  and acquisition of expertise 10–11
  and exchange postulate 9
  and legislative choice 8–9
  and political parties 10
legislatures 4
  and definition 121
  and distinction from parliaments 121–2
  and gatekeeping authority 6
  and legislative choice 6
  and measuring policy positions of legislators 136–8
  and organization of 157–8
    agenda-setting offices 145
    centralized agenda powers 155–7
    committee expertise 10–11
    committee system 8–9
    creation of inequality 144–5
    evolution of agenda-setting powers 146–7
    legislative state of nature 141, 143–4
    negative agenda power 149–50, 151–3
    plenary bottleneck 143–4
    plenary time 142
    political parties 9–10, 147–9
    positive agenda power 149–50, 153–5
    preference-based approach 7–8
    regulation of plenary time 141–2
    types of agenda power 149–51
  and parliamentary systems 122
    elections 124
    election-timing 124–5
    executive coalitions 128
    government control of agenda 125–6
    investiture votes 123
    minority governments 128–9
    no-confidence votes 122–3
    opposition parties 130
    parliamentary support coalition 128
    party discipline 126–7
    role of political parties 126–7
    single-party majority governments 129–30
  and presidential systems 130–1
    committee system 135–6
    divided government/cohabitation 134–5
    electoral incentives for party cohesion 132
    legislative incentives for party cohesion 132–3
    role of political parties 131–2
  and separation of powers 121
  see also bicameralism
'Leviathan' theory, and federalism 360
liberal market economies 615, 650
liberalism, and international relations 832, 833

liberalization:
    and demand management 645–6
    economic and political 531–2
    and supply-side economic policy 648–9
    see also globalization
limited government:
    and constitutionalism 289, 305–7
    and United States Constitution 343
list proportional representation 104
Lithuania, and democratization 661–2
local government:
    and basic model of fiscal competition 505–9
        exit and voice 512–14
        interpretations and applications of 509–12
    and ex ante fiscal rules 466–7
    and transfers from central government 465, 467
    and United States 505–6
localism, and electoral systems 112–13
logrolling, and legislative choice 8
Loosemore-Hanby Index of Distortion 105
Louisiana 308
Luxembourg Income Study 604

Maastricht Treaty 806
macro political economy:
    and Coase theorem 529
    and death of 525
    and depoliticization of monetary policy 536
    and extreme unforeseeable events 525, 539–40
        requirements of international institutions 541–2
    and independent central banks 533, 536
    and inflation 532–3
    and inflation/stabilization goals 533
    and intellectual background:
        comparative political economy 530
        liberalization 531–2
        political economy 528–30
        public choice theory 527–8, 532
        social choice 526–7
        special interest politics 530–1, 532
    and intergenerational conflict 525, 536–8
    and monetarist revolution 536
    and political business cycle 534
        partisan variant 535
        rational expectations 534–5
    and political vulnerability 533–4
    and rationalization obsession 534–6
    and research program of 526
    and voter rationality 534–5
    see also monetary policy
macroeconomic voting, see economic voting
majoritarian postulate:
    and exchange postulate 9
    and legislator preferences 7–8
majority rule:
    and allocation of public goods 485–7, 489–91
    and core in committee decision-making:
        committee bargaining 921–2
        core clustering 919–21
        Fiorina and Plott's experiments 918–19
        multidimensional policy bargaining 917–18
    as object of study 985
malapportionment, and bicameralism 184–6, 191

Malawi, and ethnicity 860–1
market access, and agglomeration 743
markets:
    and impossibility theorem 974
    and legislative interference with 342
    and perfect competition 503
    and public goods allocation 480–1
    and public sector economics, property rights 444
    and regulation 342–3
mechanism design 373
median voter theorem 65, 70, 71
    and bicameralism 184
    and candidate divergence 35
        candidate preferences 37
        political parties' platform choices 37–8
        third parties 36–7
        valence issues 36
    and criticisms of 31
    and equilibrium analysis of public finance 448
    and income redistribution 313–14, 604
    and inequality 631–2
    and laboratory experiments on 923–4
    and paradoxes of rationality 43
        attempted resolutions of 40–2
        rational ignorance 39–40
        rational non-participation 38–40
    and partisanship 606
    as pivot theory 224, 239
        analysis of roll rates 230–2, 234–8
    and spatial theory of voting 29–30
    and tax rates 86–7
    and voters' sources of information 43–6
memes, and evolutionary models of behavior 18–20
methodology, and political economy 3–4
    see also economic methods in political science; laboratory experiments
Mexico 367
    and authoritarian government 702, 703–4
    and economic openness 827
    and financial crisis (1994–5) 524, 595
migration:
    and agglomeration 743
    and international trade 823–4
        Heckscher-Ohlin model 815–18
        neo-Ricardian model 821–2
        specific factors model 820
        types of trade 824
military power, and survival of democracy 319
minority governments:
    and agenda power 150
    and cabinet stability 173–4
    and institutionalism 164–5
    and parliamentary systems 128–9
    and veto rights 150
moderate government, and survival of democracy 321
monetary policy:
    and depoliticization of 536
    as domestic and international non-issue 523–5
    and electoral cycles 547–8
    and extreme unforeseeable events 525, 539–40
        requirements of international institutions 541–2
    and improvement in 524

and independent central banks 533, 536
and inflation 532–3
and inflation/stabilization goals 533
and intergenerational conflict 525, 536–8
and international financial crises 524
and monetarist revolution 536
and political business cycle 534
    partisan variant 535
    rational expectations 534–5
and political vulnerability 533–4
and voter rationality 534–5
see also economic policy; exchange rates; macro political economy
money supply, and monetary policy 533–4
motivation, and expressive activity 333–5
multimember districts 104
mutual advantage, and constitutionalism 291, 298–9
mutualism, and cooperative behavior 953, 954–7

nation state, *see* state, the
national identity, and constitutions as expressive documents 337–8
national interest, and international conflict 831–2
National Labor Relations Board 206–7, 213–14
national policy, and political economy research 1000
National Reform Union (UK) 686
National Rifle Association 14
nationalism, and modernist theories of 859–60
nation-building, post-military intervention 845–7
natural resources:
    and authoritarian governments 700, 704–5
    and state failure 715–16
neo-liberal institutionalism 767
neo-realism:
    and international relations 832, 833–6
        assumptions about 833
        bipolarity/multipolarity 834
        core hypotheses of 834
        defection strategy 835–6
        essential states 835
        evidential weakness 836
        falsity of theorems 835
        as non-cooperative game 833–4
        resource allocation 835
        stability 834–5
    and the state 837
neo-Ricardian model of international trade 820–1
    and migration and investment 821–2
    and trade in products 821
network theory, and embeddedness 939–40
new institutionalism, *see* institutionalism
New International Economic Order 759
new structuralism 617–18
New World, and industrialization 747–8
New Zealand 319
    and economic openness 827
    and electoral reform 723
    and ex ante fiscal rules 466
Nicaragua 701–2
no-confidence votes 122–3
NOMINATE, and measuring policy positions of legislators 136–7

oil price shocks 524, 759
open access orders 1004
Open Economy Politics (OEP), *see* international political economy (IPE)
opinion polls, and election-timing 124–5
opposition parties, and parliamentary systems 130
order:
    and anthropological perspective 709
    and international relations perspective 710
    and societies with states 712–15
    and stateless societies 710–11
Organization of European Economic Cooperation 801
Organization of Petroleum Exporting Countries (OPEC) 759
other-regarding behavior 17–18, 952

paradoxes:
    and fair division 432, 433, 434
    and ranking paradoxes 398–9
    and reconciling 971–2
    and voting behavior 38–42, 304, 333, 971–2
Paraguay 703
Pareto indifference 409, 412
Pareto optimality 379, 988–9
parliamentary systems:
    and distinction from legislatures 121–2
    and election-timing 32
        impact on voter behavior 12
    and legislature:
        elections 124
        election-timing 124–5
        executive coalitions 128
        government control of agenda 125–6
        investiture votes 123
        minority governments 128–9
        no-confidence votes 122–3
        opposition parties 130
        parliamentary support coalition 128
        party discipline 126–7
        role of political parties 126–7
        single-party majority governments 129–30
    and policy choice 6
    see also coalitions
Partido Nacional Revolucionario (PNR) 703
Partido Revolucionario Institucional (PRI) 703–4
partisan cycles:
    and adaptive retrospective citizens 552–5
    and context conditionality of 555, 559–60
    and electoral surprises 555–6, 557
    and evidence of 554–5, 556–8
    and partisan divergence 553
    and rational partisan theory 555, 556–9
    and rational prospective citizens 555–8
    and unemployment/inflation aversion 553–4
partisaneering, and political-economic cycles 545–6
partisanship:
    and citizen-candidate models 607
    and commitment issues 606–7
    and cross-national variations 607
    and demand management 644
    and distributive politics 602, 605–8
    and median voter theorem 606

partisanship: (cont.)
    and party activists 606
    and political bargaining 607
    and probabilistic voting 606
    and voter/party preferences 608
party coalition model, and equilibrium analysis of public finance 451, 452
party identification 997
path dependency:
    and European integration 808–11
    and political/economic development 674
peer effects 975
pension reform, and democratic support for 456–7
perfect competition 503
performance, and politicians 304
personal votes 32, 34
    and localism of representatives 112–13
Philippines 701
Pivot mechanism 487–9
pivot theories 223–4, 238–9
    and endogenous status quo points 233–4
    and gridlock interval 223
    and median voter theorem 224, 239
    and pivot points 223
    and pivotal politics theory 224–8, 239
        analysis of roll rates 234–8
        criticisms of 228
        divided government 224–5
        equilibrium 227
        gridlock 225, 228
        status quo points 227–8
        super-majoritarianism 225–6
    and procedural cartel theory 228–30, 238–9
        gridlock 229–30
    and roll rates analysis:
        comparative analysis 230–2, 234–8
        endogenous status quo points 233–4
        median voter theorem 230–2
        procedural cartel theory 230–2
        status quo points 231–2
    and status quo points 223, 227–8, 231–2
        endogenous 233–4
    see also median voter theorem
pivotal legislators 182, 275–6
plenary time 142
    and bottlenecks 143–4
    and legislative state of nature 143–4
    and organization of 157–8
        agenda-setting offices 145
        centralized agenda powers 155–7
        creation of inequality 144–5
        evolution of agenda-setting powers 146–7
        negative agenda power 149–50, 151–3
        political parties 147–9
        positive agenda power 149–50, 153–5
        types of agenda power 149–51
    and regulation of 141–2
plurality elections 726
    and bias toward large parties 109–10
    and definition 104
    and electoral policy cycles 729
    and impact on budget deficits 734–5
    and impact on government spending 730–3
    and leverage effect of 725
    and party non-convergence 110–11
    and public finance 468
    and voting theory 392
    see also electoral systems
Poisson games 910–12
Poland:
    and constitution of 337–8
    and democratization 659, 661, 664
policy uncertainty, and delegation 259–60, 262, 263, 266, 269
policy-making:
    and bicameralism:
        multi-dimensional models 186–7
        spatial models of 181–4
        spatial models of apportionment 184–6
    and centralization 185–6
    and decentralization 185
    and electioneering 545
    and institutional arrangements 6–7
    and institutional interactions 217–18
    and judicial decision-making 210–11, 273
        statutory interpretation 276–7
    and legislative choice:
        committee expertise 10–11
        committee system 8–9
        preference-based approach 7–8
        role of political parties 9–10
    and partisaneering 545–6
    and public opinion 43–4
    see also political-economic cycles
political advertising 61–2
    and candidate quality 52
    and directly informative 52, 53–7
    and equilibrium behavior 52
        directly informative advertising 57–9
        indirectly informative advertising 55–7
    and expenditure function 59–60
    and indirectly informative 51, 53–7
    and public opinion 43
    and rational voters 51
    and role of 455–6
    and vote share 50–1
    and voter behavior 12–13, 45–6
political and economic development 690–1
    and democracy 679–82
        allocation of political power 679–80
        concessions by elites 680
        democratic consolidation 680
        elite coups 680–1
        emergence of 683–4
        relative political equality 679
        repression by elites 681, 689
        transitory nature of de factor power 679, 680
    and development of 'good' economic institutions 682–3
    and Great Britain 685
        concessions by elites 688–90
        education reform 687
        emergence of democracy 686–7
        interpretation of 688–90
        origins of economic supremacy 685

political reform 685–7
  reform of economic institutions 687
and human cognition 1005
and inadequate knowledge of 1003–4, 1008
and non-incremental change 1004–5
and path dependency 674
and role of political institutions 683
and role of the state 718–20
  anthropology 709
  creation of institutions 709
  equilibrium path 712–15
  international relations 710
  necessity of 708
  state failure 715–16
  state formation 716–18
  stateless societies 710–12
and theoretical framework:
  changes in political institutions 678–9
  commitment problem and power 675, 677
  conflicting interests 675, 677–8
  de facto political power 676
  de jure political power 675–6
  persistence of behavior 677
  political institutions 676–7
  potential for change 677
  power as determinant of economic institutions 675
  primacy of political power 677–8
  resource distribution 675, 677, 678
  role of economic institutions 674
and variations in 673–4
political behavior, *see* behavior
political business cycle, and monetary policy
  partisan variant 535
  rational expectations 534–5
political competition, and modeling of 1010–11
political competition, and theory of:
  and citizen-candidate equilibrium 1022–3
  and endogenous-party Wittman equilibrium 1015–17, 1027
  and impossibility theorem 1028–9
  and inadequacy of Hotelling-Downs model 1027
  and multidimensional generalizations 1017–23
  and party faction model 1019–20, 1027–8
  and party-unanimity Nash equilibrium (PUNE) 1020–2, 1027–8
    flypaper effect 1025–6
    progressive taxation 1023–4
    racism and redistribution 1026
    taxation and non-economic issues 1024–5
  and the political environment 1011–13
  and unidimensional competition 1013–17
political economy:
  and bounded rationality 977–8
  and constitutional political economy 991–2
  and diverse approaches of 3
  and ethical norms 982–3
  and extending exchange nexus 989–90
  and future research areas 977
  and the individual 985
  and mathematization of 978
  and meaning of 3–4
  and methodology of 3–4
  and micro-foundations of 982
  and national policy 1000
  and normative relevance 988–9
  and object of collective action 986–7
  and omissions from 1003
    beliefs and learning 1005–6
    knowledge of development 1003–4, 1008
    nature of cognition 1005
    non-incremental change 1004–5
    political and economic development 1004
  and operational science of politics 987–8
  and Pareto optimality 988–9
  and political motivation 987
  and politics as a process 985
  and politics as exchange 992–3
  and problems for future research 997–1000
    adherence to strict rationality 999
    lack of common knowledge 999
    multidimensional issues 998
    need for interdisciplinarity 997–8
    non-linearity of political/economic systems 999
    oversimplification of game theory 998
  and size of nations 20–2
  and spread of 5, 20
  and the state 981–2
  and unanimity benchmark 990–1
  and unitary or multiple decision-makers 983–4
  and utilitarianism 983, 988
political parties:
  and candidate divergence 37–8
  and electoral systems:
    bias toward large parties 109–10
    ideological spread 111–12
    impact on ideological homogeneity 113–14
    impact on party factionalism 114–15
    impact on party numbers 106–8, 732
    impact on proportionality of representation 108–9
    non-convergence of parties 110–11
  and federalism 361–3, 367
  and ideological identification 44
  and legislative choice 9–10
  and legislative organization:
    access to high office 147–8
    agenda-setting powers 149–51
    party-rule symbiosis 148–9
  and normative analysis of public finance 454–5
  and parliamentary systems 126–7
    minority governments 128–9
    party discipline 126–7
    single-party majority governments 129–30
  and partisan cycles 552–5
  and presidential systems 131–2
    divided government/cohabitation 134–5
    electoral incentives for party cohesion 132
    legislative incentives for party cohesion 132–3
  and procedural cartel theory 228–30
  and redistributive politics 92–8
  and roll rates (US Congress) 153
    endogenous status quo points 233–4
    pivot theories 230–2, 234–8
  and voter behavior 31
  see also political competition, and theory of

political-economic cycles 545–7
　and context conditionality of 546–7, 559–60
　and electioneering 545
　and electoral cycles:
　　adaptive retrospective citizens 547–50
　　coalition governments 549, 550
　　context-conditionality 548–9, 550, 551
　　economic voting 548
　　election timing 549
　　electoral challengers 551–2
　　evidence of 548–9
　　monetary policy manipulation 547–8
　　policy manipulation 550
　　policy targeting 549
　　policy timing 549
　　post-election electioneering 552
　　rational expectations 550–1
　　rational prospective citizens 550–1
　and evidence for 546
　and partisan cycles:
　　adaptive retrospective citizens 552–5
　　context-conditionality 555
　　electoral surprises 555–6, 557
　　evidence of 554–5, 556–8
　　partisan divergence 553
　　rational partisan theory 555, 556–9
　　rational prospective citizens 555–8
　　unemployment/inflation aversion 553–4
　and partisaneering 545–6
　see also economic voting
politicians:
　and bureaucratic delegation 256
　　administrative dominance 265–6
　　administrative state 256–7
　　agency design 261–2
　　ally principle 260, 262–3, 264, 266, 267, 269
　　assumptions underlying models of 257–8, 268–9
　　bureaucratic capacity 267
　　commitment problem 268–70
　　control of 265
　　empirical tests of 261–4
　　information asymmetries 266–7
　　modeling of delegation strategies 257–61
　　multi-principals issue 267–8
　　nature of legislation 262–3
　　oversight of 257, 264
　　policy uncertainty 259–60, 262, 263, 266, 269
　　political context 264–5, 269–70
　　political uncertainty 260–1, 263–4, 266
　　substitution effect 260, 263, 266
　and incentive effects of electoral system:
　　direct effects 727–8
　　indirect effects 729–30
　and legislature/parliament distinction 121–2
　and performance 304
　and public finance:
　　budget process 470
　　common-pool problem 465
　　ex ante fiscal rules 466–7
　　principal-agent relationship 464–5
pork-barrel politics 530–1
　see also common pool problem
　and ethnicity 861–2

　and presidential governance 251
positive political theory (PPT) 912
　and collective preference theory 902–5
　　core emptiness 908–9
　　large populations 907
　　opportunities for trade 906–7
　and game theory 905–6
　　Poisson games 910–12
　and judicial independence 281–4
　and judiciary 273–4, 284
　and legal control of bureaucracy 277–81
　　Chevron decision 280–1
　　implications of Administrative Procedure Act 278–80
　and statutory interpretation 274–7
poverty 23
power:
　and democracy and capitalism 604
　and political and economic development:
　　allocation of 679–80
　　commitment problem 675, 677
　　de facto political power 676
　　de jure political power 675–6
　　as determinant of economic institutions 675
　　emergence of democracy 683–4
　　primacy of 677–8
　　transitory nature of de factor power 679, 680
power transition theory:
　and international relations 832, 836–7
　and the state 837
preferences:
　and collective preference theory 902–5
　　core emptiness 908–9
　　large populations 907
　　opportunities for trade 906–7
　and legislative choice 7–8
　and peer effects 975
　and preference drift 1037
presidential systems:
　and budget process 472
　and legislature 130–1
　　committee system 135–6
　　divided government/cohabitation 134–5
　　electoral incentives for party cohesion 132
　　legislative incentives for party cohesion 132–3
　　role of political parties 131–2
　and political parties 107–8
　see also United States presidency
pressure groups, *see* interest groups
primordialism, and politicization of ethnicity 858
principal-agent relationship:
　and economic voting 570
　and principal-agent slack 804
　and public finance 464–5
probabilistic spatial voting models 606
　and equilibrium analysis of public finance 449–50, 451–2
procedural cartel theory 228–30, 238–9
　and analysis of roll rates 230–2, 234–8
procedural justice 378
　and endstate cum procedural justice 381–3
　and endstate/procedural justice complementarity 379–81

property, and United States Supreme Court 347
  contracts affected with the public interest 350–1
  contracts clause 347–8
  economic liberties 348–50
  takings clause 351–4
property rights:
  and authoritarian governments 693, 694, 697
    benign despots 697–8
    co-opting regime 701–2
    organizational proliferation 703–4
    under terror regime 699–700
  and public sector economics 444
property taxes, and basic model of fiscal competition 505–9
proportional representation 726
  and distributive politics 612–13
  and electoral policy cycles 730
  and ideological spread of parties 111–12
  and impact on budget deficits 734–5
  and impact on government spending 730–3
  and income redistribution 87–8, 635–6
  and list system 104
  and modeling outcomes of 452–3
  and party factionalism 114–15
  and proportionality continuum 104–5
    measures of proportionality 105
    swing ratio 105
  and proportionality of party representation 108–9
  and public finance 468
  and single transferable vote 112
  see also electoral systems
proposal rights/powers:
  and American presidency 242, 247–9
  and legislative organization 149–50
  and positive agenda power 153–5
    counterbalancing of 154–5
    decentralization of 154
prospective voting 569–71
  and pure prospective voting 571
  as rational retrospection 572–5
  see also economic voting; voting behavior; voting theory
protectionism 759–60
  and gender 825
  see also international trade
protest movements, and United States Supreme Court 344–5
proto-coalitions 163–4
psychology, and economics 976
public appeals, and American presidency 250, 251–2
public choice theory 989
  and economic development 532
  and macro political economy 527–8
  and political corruptibility 528
  and taxation 527
  and United States Constitution 343
public constraints, and war 871–3
public finance:
  and allocation of, majority rule 485–7
  and collective choice 443, 444, 446, 457
  and common-pool problem 465
  see also pork-barrel politics
  and electoral rules 468–9

and equilibrium analysis 447–9, 457–8
  applications of 451–3
  citizen-candidate model 450–1, 452
  issues to be covered 448–9
  median voter theorem 448
  party coalition model 451, 452
  probabilistic spatial voting models 449–50, 451–2
  problems faced by models 452–3
  spatial voting model 452–3
and federalism 359
and governing institutions 443
and maximization of social welfare 442
and normative analysis 453–4, 458
  citizen-candidate model 456
  creeping constraints 457
  democratic support for policies 456–7
  efficiency and political competition 454–5
  political advertising 455–6
  political equilibria 455
  political failure 455–6
and political economy approach 448–9
and principal-agent relationship 464–5
and public sector economics 443–7
  behavioral assumptions 444
  coercive action 446
  decision externalities 447
  decision mechanisms 444
  equilibrium outcomes 446–7
  policy choices 446
  political competition 446
  role of markets 443–4
  taxes and spending 444–6
  voluntary redistribution 446
and social planner model 442, 443, 457
and transfers from central government 467
and transfers to local government 465
see also fiscal competition; fiscal institutions
public goods 84, 479, 987
  and allocation of 479, 481–2, 499
    Bayesian approach 492–4
    best mechanism for 490–1
    consumer behavior 483
    demand-revealing mechanisms 487–9
    doubts over 'Voting Works' 497–8
    incentive compatibility 484–5
    majority rule 489–91
    market processes 480–1
    mechanism performance 483–4
    mechanisms 482–3
    multidimensional issues 498–9
    public good environment 482
    Vickrey-Clarke-Groves mechanisms 487–91
    virtual cost-benefit mechanisms 494–5
    voting in large Bayesian environments 495–6
    voting in large environments 497
  and clubs 780
  and state size 781, 782
public opinion:
  and constraints on war 871–3
  and monetary policy 523–4
  and non-economic issues 524
public opinion: (*cont.*)

and policy 43–4
and political advertising 45–6
public sector:
 and collective choice 443, 457
 and governing institutions 443
 and maximization of social welfare 442
 and social planner model 442, 443, 457
 see also public finance

quantal response equilibrium (QRE) 928–9
Quebec 21

race:
 and inequality 628–9, 630
  United States 630, 635
 and United States Supreme Court 346–7
 see also ethnicity
racial politics 610–11
racism, and redistribution 1026
rational choice theory, and application in political science 899, 900–1
rational expectations:
 and demand management 644–5
 and electoral cycles 556
 and expressive voting 333–4
 and monetary policy 534–5
 and political-economic cycles 546
 and rational partisan theory 555, 556–8
 and voting behavior 335, 550–1
  prospective voting 572–5
rational partisan theory, and partisan cycles 555, 556–9
rational retrospection, and voting behavior 572–5, 583
rationalist approach to war (RAW) 770–1
redistribution, *see* distributive politics; income redistribution
Redistribution Act (UK, 1885) 687
Reform Act (UK, 1832) 673, 686
Reform League (UK) 686
regional economics 739
regionalism, and growth of 799–800, 805
regulation, and markets 342–3
regulatory politics 609
religion, and inequality 628
representation:
 and accountability 724–5
 and federalism 361–3, 365
 and voter preferences 185–6
Representation of the People Act (UK, 1919) 673, 687
representation theorem 454
representative democracy 303–5
 and audience democracy 304
 and corporate democracy 304–5
 and virtual representation 303–4
repression 681, 689
resource allocation:
 and endstate cum procedural justice 381–3
 and endstate justice 376–8
 and endstate/procedural justice complementarity 379–81
 and modeling of 89, 374–6

and neo-realism 835
and procedural justice 378
and public goods 479, 481–2, 499
 Bayesian approach 492–4
 best mechanism for 490–1
 consumer behavior 483
 demand-revealing mechanisms 487–9
 doubts over 'Voting Works' 497–8
 incentive compatibility 484–5
 majority rule 485–7, 489–91
 market processes 480–1
 mechanism performance 483–4
 mechanisms 482–3
 multidimensional issues 498–9
 public good environment 482
 Vickrey-Clarke-Groves mechanisms 487–91
 virtual cost-benefit mechanisms 494–5
 voting in large Bayesian environments 495–6
 voting in large environments 497
and selectorate theory 842–4
and strategy-proof mechanisms 383–6
and strategy-proofness 382–3
see also fair division
retrospective voting:
 and accountability 468
 and economic voting 569–71
 and laboratory experiments 923–4
 and principal-agent relationship 570
 and pure retrospective voting 575–8
 see also economic voting; voting behavior; voting theory
Ricardo-Viner theory:
 and international trade:
  migration and investment 820
  trade in products 818–19
 and Open Economy Politics (OEP) 762
rights, and welfare 374, 376
Riker Objection 1032, 1040–2, 1047–8
Riot Act (Great Britain, 1714) 1046
risk-pooling, and labor market 744
roll calls:
 and analysis of 136–7
 and United States Congress 133
roll rates (US Congress), and analysis of 153, 230–2, 234–8
 endogenous status quo points 233–4
Russia:
 and democratization 662
 and federalism 359
 and financial crisis (1998) 524
 and political/economic development 674
Rwanda 300, 302

Samuelson-Jones specific factors model 819, 820
Schelling conjecture 767
Second Reform Act (UK, 1867) 687
selectorate theory, and international conflict/democratic peace 842–5
self-interest, and voting behavior 38–42, 304
separation of powers:
 and judicial independence 281
 and legislatures 121

see also American politics, new separation-of-powers approach to
sequential bargaining (Baron-Ferejohn model), and coalition formation 168–70
Serbia, and democratization 662
service sector, and employment in 646–7
shame, and pro-social emotions 962–3
shirking, and evolutionary models of behavior 19
single non-transferable vote 113, 114–15
single transferable vote 112
single-member districts 104
Slovakia, and democratization 662
Slovenia, and democratization 661–2, 664
social choice:
    and collective preference theory 902–5
        core emptiness 908–9
        large populations 907
        opportunities for trade 906–7
    and collectivities 972–3
    and constitutional design 973
    and decision-making 972
    as descriptive theory 974
    and dictatorships 972
    and distributive justice 374–6
    and endstate cum procedural justice 381–3
    and endstate justice 376–8
    and endstate/procedural justice complementarity 379–81
    and fair division 373
    and game theory 905–6
        core emptiness 910–12
    and impossibility theorem 373
    and macro political economy 526–7
    and mechanism design 373
    and origins of 373
    and procedural justice 378
    and resource allocation, modeling of 374–6
    and social welfare functions 526–7
    and strategy-proof allocation mechanisms 383–6
    and strategy-proofness 382–3
    see also social evaluation
social contract, see contractarian theories
social evaluation 421–2
    and alternatives 408–9
    and Arrow's theorem 409, 419
    and axioms 413–16
        anonymity 413–14
        continuity 414
        independence condition 415
        independence of irrelevant alternatives 409, 412
        minimal equity 414–15
        Pareto indifference 412
        unlimited domain 412
    and information invariance 417–19
    and interpersonal comparisons 408
    and Pareto indifference 409
    and social evaluation functionals 409, 411–12
    and social evaluation orderings:
        dictatorial 415–16
        leximin 416
        utilitarianism 416
    and theorem statements 419–21
    and utility functions 409, 410

and utility profiles 409, 411
and welfarism 409, 411–13, 421–2
and well-being 409–10
    interpersonal comparisons 409, 410–11
    measurability 409–10
social groups, and voting behavior 41–2
social planning, and public sector 442, 443
social relations, and interest 944
social welfare:
    and inequality 629–30
    and maximization of 442
    and social welfare functions 526–7
sociology, see economic sociology
South Africa 681
South-East Asian crisis (1997–8) 524
Soviet Union, and democratization 662
Spain:
    and ethnicity 854
    and federalism 366
spatial models of policy-making, and bicameralism 181–4
spatial relationships, see economic geography
spatial theory of voting 29–30, 65
    and candidate divergence 35
        candidate preferences 37
        political parties' platform choices 37–8
        third parties 36–7
        valence issues 36
    and criticisms of 30–1
    and cut-points 33–4
    and equilibrium analysis of public finance 452–3
        probabilistic spatial voting models 449–50, 451–2
    and median voter theorem 29, 31
    and paradoxes of rationality 43
        attempted resolutions of 40–2
        rational ignorance 39–40
        rational non-participation 38–40
    and valence issues 32–5
    and voters' sources of information 43–6
    see also voting behavior; voting theory
specific factors model, and international trade 818–20
speech, freedom of, and United States Supreme Court 344–6
stability:
    and bicameralism 182–3
    and neo-realism 834–5
state, the:
    and anthropology 709
    and formation of 716–18
    and international bargaining 766–8
    and international monetary relations 588–9
        cooperation 590–1
        coordination 589–90
    as object of study 981–2
    and organic conceptualization of 981
    and political competition 1010–11
    and role in development 718–20
        creation of institutions 709
        equilibrium path 712–15
        international relations 710
        necessity of 708

state, the: (*cont.*)
    state failure 715–16
    stateless societies 710–12
    see also state, economic role of; state size
state, economic role of 642–3, 652–3
    and demand management 643–6
        impact of globalization 645–6
        impact of rational expectations 644–5
        institutional environment 644–5
    and socio-economic institutional environment 649–52
        actors' policy preferences 651–2
        as constraint 652
        regime types 650
        resistance to changes in 651–2
        varieties of capitalism 650–1
    and supply-side policy
        impact of globalization 648–9
        institutional environment 647–8
        service sector 646–7
        structural continuity 649
        wage levels 647–8
        welfare state policies 647, 648
    see also economic policy
state intervention, and constitutions 342
state size 20–2, 768–9
    and analytical framework for understanding 783–8
        average utility 785–6, 787–8
        border determination 792
        break-ups 791
        compensation for the dissatisfied 788–90
        efficient borders 787
        government type 783
        income inequality 790–1
        inefficient break-ups 786
        'Leviathans' 792
        majority voting 786, 787
        preferred government type 783–4
        taxes per capita 784–5
    and benefits of large size 781–2
    and costs of large size 782
    and defense/security issues 794–6
    and factor mobility 794
    and historical concern with 778–9
    and international economic integration 793–4
    and literature on:
        clubs and local public goods 780
        conflict and appropriation 781
        national borders 779–80
        trade blocs 780–1
statutory interpretation 274–7
strategic pre-action, and American presidency 242, 249–51
strategic voting 102, 110, 403–4
strategy-proofness:
    and allocation mechanisms 383–6
    and social choice 382–3
strong reciprocity 957–60
    and evolution of 960–1
structure-induced equilibrium, and coalition formation 165–8
substitution effect, and bureaucratic delegation 260, 263, 266

suicide bombers 18
super-majorities, and pivotal politics theory 225–6
    filibuster pivots 226–7
supply-side economics, and role of the state 646–9
    and impact of globalization 648–9
    and institutional environment 647–8
    and service sector 646–7
    and structural continuity 649
    and wage levels 647–8
    and welfare state policies 647, 648
    see also economic policy
survival:
    and evolutionary models of behavior 17
    and political behavior 4
Sweden 308
    and budget process 473
swing ratio 105
Switzerland, and ex ante fiscal rules 466

Taiwan 701
takings clause, and United States Supreme Court 351–4
taxation:
    and basic model of fiscal competition 509–12
    and federalism 363, 365–7
    and flat taxes 527–8
    and flypaper effect 1025–6
    and income redistribution:
        restricted tax schemes 85–8
        targeting of heterogeneous groups 92–8
        unrestricted transfer schemes 88–92
    and non-economic issues 1024–5
    and progressive taxation 1023–4
    and public choice 527
    and public sector economics 444–6
    see also fiscal competition; fiscal institutions; public finance
technology, and inequality 627
terror, and authoritarian governments 698–700
terrorism 1008
third parties:
    and candidate divergence 36–7
    and plurality voting 109–10
Third Reform Act (UK, 1884) 687
Thirty Years War 719–20
trade blocs 780–1
trade unions 644
    and inequality 627
transfer spending 609–10
Transparency International 727
Trinidad and Tobago 319
trust 975
Turkey:
    and ethnicity 855
    and political/economic development 674
turnout, and laboratory experiments on 917, 929–32

ultimatum game 18
unanimity rule 990–1
uncertainty, and choice of institutions 1036–7
    see also policy uncertainty
underdevelopment, and development theory 760

United States:
  and bicameralism 181
  and campaign financing 51
  and colonial period 1006–7, 1038–9
  and ethnicity 854
  and ex ante fiscal rules 466–7
  and inequality 634–8
    beliefs about 637–8
    economic explanations of 634
    ethnic heterogeneity 630, 635
    failure of left-wing movements 636–7
    impact of technology 627
    political factors 627
    political institutions 635–7
  and local government 505–6
  and terrorism 1008
  see also American politics, new
    separation-of-powers approach to
United States Congress 4
  and divided government 134–5, 224–5
  and judiciary:
    judicial independence 282–3
    statutory interpretation 274–7
  and legislative organization:
    acquisition of expertise 10–11
    agenda-setting powers 149, 150, 154–5
    committee system 8–9, 135–6, 145
    preference-based approach 7–8
    role of political parties 9–10
  and measuring policy positions of legislators 136–7
  as 'model generator' 131
  and political parties 131–2
    divided government/cohabitation 134–5
    electoral incentives for party cohesion 132
    legislative incentives for party cohesion 132–3
  and presidential veto power 245–7, 250–1
  and roll calls 133
    analysis of 136–7
  and roll rates:
    analysis of 153, 230–2, 234–8
    endogenous status quo points 233–4
  and suspension of rules 1044
United States Constitution:
  and Constitutional Convention (1787) 1040
  and establishment of 299–300
  and judicial review:
    approach to 344
    balancing private rights/government
      interest 343–4
    intermediate scrutiny standard 343
    rational basis standard 343
    strict scrutiny standard 343
  and limited government 343
  and procedural change:
    amendment procedures 1040, 1043
    interpretative courts 1043–4
  and public choice theory 343
  and representative democracy 303–4
United States presidency:
  and constitutional foundation of 243
  and judiciary:
    judicial independence 282–3
    statutory interpretation 274–5

  and legislature:
    divided government/cohabitation 134–5
    role of political parties 131–2
  and new separation-of-powers approach to 202–7,
    241–2
    appointments process 204–7
    interactions with other institutions 202
    spatial model of budget problem 202–4
    veto powers 202–4
  and political economy approach 253
    appointments process 247–9
    executive orders 249–50
    features of 241–2
    going public 250
    intellectual roots of 244–5
    legislative program 249
    proposal powers 242, 247–9
    research opportunities 252–3
    strategic context 245
    strategic pre-action 242, 249–51
    veto powers 242, 245–7
    veto threats 250–1
  and presidential governance 243–4
    normative implications of 251–2
  and relative weakness of 131
United States Senate, and presidential
    appointments 204–5
United States Supreme Court:
  and *Abrams vs United States* (1919) 344
  and *Adair vs United States* (1908) 349
  and *Allgeyer vs Louisiana* (1897) 349
  and appointments process 248–9
  and *Baker vs Carr* 183
  and *Baldwin vs GAF Seelig, Inc* (1935) 351
  and *Brandenburg vs Ohio* (1969) 344
  and *Brown vs Board of Education* (1954) 346
  and *Buckley vs Valeo* (1976) 51 n2
  and *Carolene Products Co vs United States*
    (1938) 344
  and *Chevron vs Natural Resources Defense Council*
    (1984) 280–1
  and compliance problem 283–4
  and constitutional interpretation 1043–4
  and *Coppage vs Kansas* (1914) 349
  and *Corfeld vs Coryell* (1823) 348
  and *Duquesne Light Co vs Barasch* (1989) 350
  and *Eastern Enterprises vs Apfel* (1998) 348
  and *Euclid vs Ambler Realty* (1926) 353
  and *Grutter vs Bollinger* (2003) 346
  and *Hawaiian Housing Authority vs Midkiff*
    (1984) 352
  and *Home Building & Loan Association vs Blaisdell*
    (1934) 348
  and judicial independence 281
  and judicial review 354–5
  and *Lochner vs New York* (1905) 349–50
  and *Loretto vs Teleprompter* (1982) 351
  and *Loving vs Virginia* (1967) 346
  and *Lucas vs South Carolina Coastal Commission*
    (1992) 354
  and *Marbury vs Madison* (1803) 273
  and *McConnell vs Federal Electoral Commission*
    (2003) 345, 346

United States Supreme Court: (cont.)
   and *Minnesota vs Clover Leaf Creamery Co* (1981) 347
   and *Munn vs Illinois* 350
   and *Nebbia vs New York* (1934) 350
   and *New York Times vs Sullivan* (1964) 345
   and *Penn Central Transp Co vs New York* (1978) 353
   and *Penn Central vs New York* (1978) 353
   and *Pennsylvania Coal Co vs Mahon* (1923) 352–3
   and *Plessy vs Ferguson* (1896) 346
   and protection of contract and property 347
      contracts affected with the public interest 350–1
      contracts clause 347–8
      economic liberties 348–50
      takings clause 351–4
   and *Reed vs Reed* (1971) 347
   and *Slaughterhouse Cases* (1872) 348, 349
   and *Smyth vs Ames* (1898) 350
   and social and moral issues:
      equal protection of the laws 346–7
      freedom of speech 344–6
   and *Tahoe-Sierra Preservation Council, Inc vs Tahoe Regional Planning Agency* (2002) 354
   and *Truax vs Raich* (1915) 349
   and *United States vs Addyston Pipe & Steel Co* (1899) 349
   and *Usery vs Turner Elkhorn Mining Co* (1976) 348
   and *Virginia Board of Pharmacy vs Virginia Consumer Council* (1976) 346
   and *West Lynn Creamery vs Healy* (1994) 351
   and *Yee vs Escondido* (1992) 351
urban economics 739
utilitarianism 983, 988
utility maximization 4
   and voting behavior 38–9

valence issues:
   and candidate divergence 36, 926
   and spatial theory of voting 32–5
varieties of capitalism 614–17
   and coordinated market economies 615
   and institutional complementarity 615
   and liberal market economies 615
   and relationship of economic/political institutions 616
   and role of economic institutions 614–15
   and state's economic role 650–1
   and welfare state 615–16
veil of ignorance 1035–6
Venezuela 319, 701
vengeance 18
veto rights/powers:
   and American presidency
      new separation-of-powers approach 202–4
      political economy approach 242, 245–7, 250–1
   and negative agenda power 149–50
      gridlock 151–2
      reactions to gridlock 152
      roll rates of veto players 153
Vickrey-Clarke-Groves mechanisms 384–5
   and allocation of public goods 487–92
Virginia School 455
virtual representation 303–4

voice, and fiscal competition 512–14
vote motivation, and monetary policy 534–5
voting, and allocation of public goods
   in large Bayesian environments 495–6
   in large environments 497
   majority rule 485–7, 489–91
voting behavior:
   and citizen duty 40–1
   and consumption approach 42
   and deterministic voting 67–8
      office motivation 68–70
      policy motivation 70–2
   and economic voting 548
   and electoral framework 66–7
   and expressive activity 333–5
   and expressive voting 41
   and game theory 910–12
   and group rule utilitarianism 41–2
   and impact of electoral rules 527
   and information aggregation 15–17, 928–9
   and information revelation 11–15
      candidate quality 15
      election-timing 12
      pressure group finance 12–14
   and laboratory experiments on elections 922
      asymmetric contests 926
      candidate convergence 923
      median voter theorem 923–4
      multicandidate elections 924–5
      retrospective voting 923–4
   and median voter theorem 29, 31
   and paradoxes of rationality 43, 304, 333
      attempted resolutions of 40–2
      rational ignorance 39–40
      rational non-participation 38–40
   and party identification 997
   and political advertising 12–13, 45–6
      directly informative 57–9
      indirectly informative 53–7
      role of 455–6
   and political-economic cycles:
      electioneering 545
      partisaneering 545–6
   and probabilistic voting, stochastic partisanship model 72–3
      vote motivation 73–5
      win motivation 75–7
   and probabilistic voting, stochastic preference model 77–8
      policy motivation 80–1
      vote motivation 78–9
      win motivation 79–80
   and prospective voting 569–71, 572–5
   and rationality 333–4, 335, 550–1
   and retrospective voting 468, 569–71, 575–8, 923–4
   and sources of information 43–6
   and spatial theory of voting 29–30
      candidate divergence 35–8
      criticisms of 30–1
      cut-points 33–4
      valence issues 32–5
   and strategic voting 102, 110
   and turnout 929–32

see also economic voting; median voter theorem; voting theory
voting paradox 38–42, 304, 333, 971–2
voting theory 390–1
   and antiplurality voting 392
   and Arrow's theorems 405–6
   and axiomatic representations 397–400
      chaotic dynamics 399
      ranking consistency 399–400
      ranking paradoxes 398–9
      shortcomings of 398
   and Borda Count 392, 399–400, 403
   and determining 'will of the voters' 400–3
      configuration of preferences 400–1
      neutral Condorcet requirement 401–2
      neutral reversal requirement 401
   and plurality voting 392
   and representing profiles 391–3
      approval voting 396–7
      creating profiles/profile lines 394–6
      procedure lines 393–4
   and Sen's theorems 405
   and strategic voting 403–4
   see also voting behavior

wage levels, and government influence on 647–8
Wagner's Law 87
war:
   and democracies 840
      audience costs 841
      institutional constraints 840–1
      role of opposition 841
      selectorate theory 842–5
   and domestic politics 869, 875–6
      audience costs 874–5
      leaders' motivations 870, 871–2
      political institutions 870
      public opinion constraints 870, 871–3
   and ethnicity 857–8
   and power-transition theory 837
   and rationalist approach to war (RAW) 770–1
   and state size 781, 794–6
   see also anarchy; international conflict
Washington Consensus 766
welfare, and rights 374, 376
welfare economics:
   and federalism 359–60
   and First Fundamental Theorem of 480
welfare state:
   and capitalism 601–2
   and development of 647, 648
   and typology of 608, 647
   and varieties of capitalism 615–16
welfarism, and social evaluation 409, 411–13, 421–2
World Bank 532, 727, 759

Yoruba 856

Zambia, and ethnicity 856, 860–1
Zimbabwe 677, 678